THE
CAMBRIDGE
ECONOMIC HISTORY

GENERAL EDITORS: M. M. POSTAN, Professor of Economic History
in the University of Cambridge, and H. J. HABAKKUK, Chichele
Professor of Economic History in the University of Oxford

VOLUME I
Second edition

THE
CAMBRIDGE
ECONOMIC HISTORY
OF EUROPE

VOLUME I
THE AGRARIAN LIFE OF
THE MIDDLE AGES

SECOND EDITION

EDITED BY

M. M. POSTAN

*Professor of Economic History in the
University of Cambridge*

CAMBRIDGE
AT THE UNIVERSITY PRESS
1966

PUBLISHED BY

THE SYNDICS OF THE CAMBRIDGE UNIVERSITY PRESS

Bentley House, 200 Euston Road, London, N.W. 1
American Branch: 32 East 57th Street, New York, N.Y., 10022
West African Office: P.M.B.5181, Ibadan, Nigeria

THIS EDITION

CAMBRIDGE UNIVERSITY PRESS

1966

First edition (edited by J. H. Clapham	
and Eileen Power)	1941
Reprinted	1942
Reprinted (U.S.A.)	1944
Second edition	1966

Printed in Great Britain by
Spottiswoode, Ballantyne & Co. Ltd.
London and Colchester

Library of Congress Catalogue
Card Number: A41-3509

THE EDITOR'S PREFACE TO THE SECOND EDITION

A quarter of a century has passed since the first volume of the *Cambridge Economic History* was published. In the meantime much more knowledge has accumulated and new points of view have emerged. The Editor and the publishers have therefore agreed that what was now required was not merely a reprint, nor even a corrected version, of the 1941 volume, but a wholly new edition brought up to date by modernizing some chapters and substituting wholly new chapters for those considered impossible to modernize. The chapters dealing with agrarian history in Italy, Russia and England at the height of the Middle Ages, and the concluding chapter dealing with Europe as a whole in the later Middle Ages, fell into the latter category, and the Editor accordingly commissioned Dr Philip Jones to write a new chapter on Italy (VII, § 2), Dr R. E. F. Smith to write a new chapter on Russia (VII, § 6) and Professor Genicot to write a new chapter on the later Middle Ages (Chapter VIII), while the Editor himself undertook to produce a new chapter on England (VII, § 7).

A number of other chapters have been revised by their original authors. Professor Parain has recast his chapter on agricultural technique (III), and Mr C. E. Stevens has carried out a similar operation on his chapter on the later Roman Empire (II). Professor Verhulst, in collaboration with Professor Ganshof, has revised the latter's chapter on France, the Low Countries and Western Germany (VII, § 1), and Dr R. S. Smith has brought up to date his chapter on Spain (VIII, § 3). Two of the original chapters, Professor Ostrogorsky's on Byzantium (V) and Professor Aubin's on the lands east of the Elbe (VII, § 4) have, in accordance with the expressed wishes of the authors, been reproduced without much alteration. The Editor has also decided to reproduce without modification chapters by authors now deceased which have now established themselves in historical literature as classical studies of their subjects and as characteristic products of their famous authors. The chapters thus preserved in their original form are those of Richard Koebner on settlement and colonization (I), of Alfons Dopsch on the agrarian institutions of the Germanic Kingdoms (IV), of Marc Bloch on the rise of dependent cultivation and seignorial institutions (VI), of Jan Rutkowski on Poland, Lithuania and Hungary (VII, § 5) and of Sture Bolin on Scandinavia (VII, § 8).

The corresponding bibliographies, however, were recast and brought up to date, and the Editor wishes to thank Dr E. Schremmer (bibliography for Chapters I and IV), Madame E. Carpentier (the same for chapter VI), Professor A. Gieysztor (the same for Chapter VII, § 5), and Dr A. Peetre (the same for Chapter VII, § 8) for having undertaken and carried out this painstaking work of scholarship. Two other bibliographies attached to chapters by living authors—that of Professor Aubin's chapter (VII, § 4) on lands east of the Elbe. and that of Mr Stevens on the later Roman Empire (II)—were also revised by other scholars invited by the Editor. Professor E. Birke revised the bibliography for Professor Aubin's chapter (VII, § 4); and a team of scholars led by Dr J. Morris revised Mr Stevens' bibliography on the later Roman Empire (II).

This second edition has incurred its due share of delays and misfortunes. Professors Bolin and Koebner died while engaged in negotiations with the Editor on the revision of their chapters; Mr Stevens was for various personal reasons prevented from completing the revision of his bibliography; illness compelled at least one other contributor to interrupt his work on his chapter. As a result some of the chapters, more especially Professor Genicot's, had to be brought up to date twice over to allow not only for the interval since the first edition, but also for the interval since the first draft had been submitted. The hazards of composite volumes are great and unpredictable. Though he himself is their worst casualty, the Editor wishes to express to the contributors his regrets for the delay and his gratitude for their patience and forbearance.

M. M. P.

CAMBRIDGE
March 1965

CONTENTS

PREFACE *page* v

LIST OF ILLUSTRATIONS xv

CHAPTER I

The Settlement and Colonization of Europe

By RICHARD KOEBNER, late Professor in the Hebrew University of Jersualem;
formerly Professor in the University of Breslau

The problem stated: ways of approach to it	1
The selected starting-point—Roman and Teutonic settlement	8
Tacitus' *Germania*: problems arising from it	13
German land-hunger: German assaults on the Empire	19
Late imperial agrarian policy	23
Barbarian settlers and conquerors inside the Empire	26
Zones of agrarian settlement in Western Europe	34
The medieval peasantry: village and field types	39
Clearing and settlement: monastic and lay colonization: frontier colonization	43
England and Scandinavia; Celts and Slavs	52
Mediterranean lands: the Arabs in Spain	54
Saracen, Viking and Magyar raiding and settlement	55
The life of the Slavonic East	57
The fortified settlements of the West	62
Depopulation: colonization in Spain and Germany	65
Conditions in early Capetian France; colonization: *hostise* and *bourg*: *villes neuves*	69
The low Countries and the Flemish colonists	74

The Cistercians   *page* 76

Forest villages: clearing in France, England, and
Germany: German colonization eastward   77

The new villages and towns of the East   86

Town and country   90

CHAPTER II

Agriculture and Rural Life in the Later Roman Empire

By COURTENAY EDWARD STEVENS, Fellow of Magdalen College, Oxford

Climatic conditions and agriculture: 'dry farming'
and deep cultivation   92

The plough: the farmer's year and his crops: olive and
vine   98

What classical agriculture achieved   102

Geological and climatic conditions north of the Alps:
agriculture and settlement there   106

The *villa*: political and tenurial conditions: the burden
of taxes: the law of A.D. 332.   109

Tenures akin to serfdom   115

Late imperial distress and its consequences   119

CHAPTER III

The Evolution of Agricultural Technique

By CHARLES PARAIN, Professor in the Lycée Henri IV

I   Roman and medieval agriculture in the Mediterranean
    area   126

II Agricultural conditions in the temperate zone   136

III Agricultural work and implements   142

IV The plants cultivated   158

V   Domestic animals and breeding   170

CHAPTER IV

Agrarian Institutions of the Germanic Kingdoms from the fifth to the ninth century

By ALFONS DOPSCH, late Professor of History in the
University of Vienna

German penetration of the Empire before its 'fall'   *page* 180

Goths and Lombards, their institutions   181

Burgundians and Franks   186

Saxons and Anglo-Saxons   189

Thuringians, Alemanni, Bavarians   194

The Carolingian empire: the *capitulare de villis*: Crown
and Church estates   198

Lay lordship: peasant holdings: beginnings of trade   202

CHAPTER V

Agrarian conditions in the Byzantine Empire in the Middle Ages

By GEORG OSTROGORSKY, Professor in the University of Belgrade

I   East and West in the Roman Empire   205

II   The free peasant village in the middle Byzantine
     period   207

III The struggle to preserve the small landowner in the
     tenth century   216

IV   The great landowners and their dependants in the late
     Byzantine period   222

CHAPTER VI

The Rise of Dependent Cultivation and Seignorial Institutions

By MARC BLOCH, late Professor at the Sorbonne

I   The problem   235

II   Seignorial types of the early Middle Ages   238

III The decline of slavery   *page* 246

IV Government and the rise of the *seigneurie*: from the colonate to the immunity   255

V Protection and commendation   264

VI Chiefs and villages   272

VII A general sketch of the evolution   283

CHAPTER VII

Medieval Agrarian Society in its Prime

§1. *France, The Low Countries, and Western Germany*

By FRANÇOIS LOUIS GANSHOF, Professor emeritus in the University of Ghent and ADRIAAN VERHULST, Professor in the University of Ghent

I The general framework: A. The extent of land under cultivation; B. The cultivation of the soil; C. The distribution of landed wealth   290

II The decomposition of the classical estate: A. Distribution of the *villa* at the beginning of the eleventh century; B. The break-up of the *villa*; C. The transformation of the demesne; D. The decline of labour services; E. The disintegration of the holdings   305

III New forms of manorial organization: A. Attempts at reorganization; B. Leases for a term of years; C. The new structure of the estate; D. The estate as the basis of the *seigneurie*   319

IV Changes in rural society   334

§2. *Italy*

By PHILIP JONES, Fellow of Brasenose College, Oxford

I Geography and history: A. The natural background; B. The economic background   340

II The rural economy: A. The revival; B. Reclamation and land use; C. Agriculture; D. Agricultural trade; E. Forms of rural settlement   352

III Rural Society; A. The manor before 1050; B. The decline of the manor (1050–1300); C. The re-organization of estates (1200–1500); D. The peasantry at the close of the Middle Ages *page* 395

§3. *Spain*

By ROBERT S. SMITH, Professor in Duke University, North Carolina

I   Geographical conditions   432

II   Social conditions and tenures   433

III Agricultural and pastoral pursuits   438

IV   Conclusions   447

§4. *The lands east of the Elbe and German colonization eastwards*

By HERMANN AUBIN, Professor in the University of Breslau

Early Slavonic life and society   449

The German immigrant and his influence   452

Settlement and its organization: charters of 'location' 459

Village types   463

Settler and *locator*   466

Colonial towns: ecclesiastical and lay lords: the peasant-nobleman and his *Vorwerk*   472

Vorwerk and *Rittergut*   477

Agriculture in the colonial East   479

Effects of German colonization on Slavonic society and the life of the East   480

§5. *Poland, Lithuania and Hungary*

By JAN RUTKOWSKI, late Professor in the University of Poznan

I   Landownership   487

II   Economic organization of the great estates   491

III Burdens borne by the rural population   496

IV   Colonization under German law   500

§6. *Russia*

By ROBERT E. F. SMITH, University of Birmingham

I   Introductory: A. Sources; B. The physical environment   506

II Settlements: A. Terminology; B. The forest zone;
C. The forest steppe zone; D. The total size of settlement; E. The layout of settlements; F. Large estates   512

III Farming technique: A. Implements; B. Methods of
arable cultivation; C. Animal husbandry; D. Hunting
and fishing   522

IV Social Relations, dues, landownership: A. Pre-Mongol
period; B. The Mongol invasions and after; C.
The Moscow period; D. Property and ownership   530

§7. *England*

By M. M. POSTAN, Professor of Economic History in the
University of Cambridge

I   The land: A. Reclamations; B. Land hunger; C.
Deterioration of the land   549

II Population: A. Colonization; B. The lure of aggregates; C. The rising trend; D. The decline   560

III The manorial estate: A. Patterns of settlement; B.
Manorial types; C. The buoyant demesne; D.
Manorial retrenchments   577

IV The landlord: A. Magnates and gentry in the thirteenth
century; B. Magnates and gentry in the fifteenth
century   592

V   The villagers: A. Idiosyncrasies of peasant husbandry;
B. Freedom and servility; C. Status and land; D. The
middle layer; E. The village labourer; F. The village
rich; G. Stability and change   600

§8. *Scandinavia*

By STURE BOLIN, late Professor in the University of Lund

I   The Scandinavian states, their geography   633

II   Village and farm settlement   635

III Village forms   640

IV   The village community   642

V   Stock-raising and subsidiary branches of agriculture   648

VI   The agrarian classes and the ownership of land   652

CHAPTER VIII

Crisis: From the Middle Ages to Modern Times

By LÉOPOLD GENICOT, Professor in the University of Louvain

I   Introduction   660

II   The labour factor: demographic evolution; A. The
     phenomenon and its variations; B. Causes; births and
     deaths, famine, plague and war; C. Consequences:
     volume of production, wheat and commodity prices,
     wage levels, land values   661

III Capital: disorder and destruction   694

IV   The political and social background   700

V   The lot of the masters—difficulties, reactions, results;
     A. The difficulties; B. The reactions; C. The results   703

VI   The peasants: individuals and classes; troubles in the
     countryside; A. Economic and legal classes; B. The
     rural communities; C. Popular revolts   725

VII Conclusion: development and preparation   739

BIBLIOGRAPHIES

Editor's Note   743

Abbreviations   744

Chapter I, revised by Eckart Schremmer   745

Chapter II, revised by J. R. Morris   755

Chapter III, by Charles Parain   761

Chapter IV, revised by Eckart Schremmer   765

Chapter V, by Georg Ostrogorsky   774

Chapter VI, by Mme E. Carpentier   780

Chapter VII, § 1, by François Louis Ganshof and Adriaan
            Verhulst   790

     § 2, by Philip Jones   795

     § 3, by Robert S. Smith   807

     § 4, revised by Ernst Birke,   809

     § 5, by Aleksander Gieysztor   813

     § 6, by Robert E. F. Smith   818

     § 7, by M. M. Postan   823

     § 8, by Arthur Peetre   831

Chapter VIII, by Léopold Genicot   834

Index   847

ILLUSTRATIONS

Text-figures

		page
1	The *Gewanndorf* in Old Germany (Geismar near Göttingen)	20
	From Meitzen, *Siedelung . . . der Germanen, Atlas*	
2	A 'forest' village (*Waldhufendorf*), Effeltern in Franconia	47
	From Meitzen	
3	Irregular strip fields in a medieval clearing in Burgundy, Is-sur-Tille, Côte d'Or	79
	From Bloch, *Les caractères orginaux de l'histoire rurale française*	
4	The stamp of Rome on medieval and modern Italy: centuriated land with a *Villa nova*, near Padua	110
	From Meitzen	
5	Enclosed fields about a hamlet in Central France: St Sauvier, Allier	244
	From Bloch	
6	Open-field with irregular subdivisions in Languedoc: Montgaillard, near Toulouse	289
	From Bloch	
7	European Russia: climate and vegetation	511
8	Tilling with *sokha*, harrowing and sowing	523
	From *Litsevoi svod* (*Muzeiskoe sobranie* No. 358; reproduced in *Istoriko-arkheologischeskii sbornik*)	
9	Swedish open-field village (seventeenth century), Otterstorpaby, Vaestergoetland	641
	From Meitzen	
10	The extension of woodlands in certain regions of Germany in the late Middle Ages: an example in the valleys of the Weser and the Diemel	662
11	Military operations and numbers of households in Ouges, Burgundy	676
12	Price of the basic cereal, spelt, at Namur from 1392 to 1490	685
13	Prices of some farm products in England, 1300–1500	686

Plates

The plough   *between pages* 152 & 153

1   Late medieval wheelless plough, with coulter and mould-board
        From H. S. Bennett, *Life on the English Manor*

2   Modern English wheelless ('swing') plough
        From *The Farmer and Stockbreeder*

3   Romano-British *aratrum*
        British Museum

4   Twelfth-century wheeled plough, also with coulter and mould-board
        From A. S. F. Gow, 'The ancient plough', *J.H.S.* 1914

Harvesters and gleaners
        From the painting by Peter Breughel

Political Sketch Maps

(At the end of the volume)

The Roman frontier and the Teutonic Tribes in the first and fourth centuries A.D.

The Empire of Charles the Great

Germany in the thirteenth century

CHAPTER I

The Settlement and Colonization of Europe

THE evolution of settlement and colonization during the Middle Ages is of historical importance from many points of view. It is associated with three great phases of development—three essential chapters in the history of the nations of Europe.

Settlement on the land helped to bring about that mingling and stratification of the peoples from which the European nations sprang. To say that all peoples were once in restless motion and that their lines of conquest or migration have determined the division of the land among them is not enough. For not all these movements affected the foundations of agrarian society; although some conquests which merely introduced a new ruling class—like the Norman Conquest of England— yet left their mark deep in the national life of the conquered territory. The movements of the peoples from which the states of the European world arose were only in part movements which transferred the use of the land to new hands on a large scale. But such transfers must be kept in mind; as must others of a more peaceful sort—migrations and transplantations and resettlements of social groups. Governments showed themselves solicitous, now for a denser population in some given area, now for the raising of the general level of agricultural production. Where land was the main form of property its owners would seek to add to its utility by closer settlement. The rise of commercial and industrial centres would increase the demand for agricultural produce. As a result there might be extensions of existing population groups, or migrations of groups. And such developments might be just as important for the formation of the basic strata of European society as the direct seizures of territory by conquering hosts and the crowds who followed in their train.

If we survey these movements in their historical sequence we are led back into an age in which, occurring peacefully and promoted ultimately from a centre of universal dominion, they prepared the way for a grouping of population quite different from that which developed later under medieval conditions. The Roman Empire pushed its frontiers to Britain, the Rhine and the Danube and created a wide zone for the spread of Mediterranean agrarian life and for the tranquil and fruitful evolution of all forms of settlement. Of this age of settlement the Romanic peoples were the permanent product, not it is true over the whole zone, but over the whole land-mass of South-Western Europe. But already in the last centuries of the Western Empire new elements

I

from beyond the frontiers had been mingled with this people: powerful groups of Germans had settled among them. And then that conquering movement which we call the *Völkerwanderung* in the narrower sense vastly extended the area of German settlement in the Alpine lands and in Gaul—which thereby became France; broke right through Roman Britain and made it England; and even in Italy left numerous groups settled on the land. Furthermore, the rule of the Franks put an end to the shiftings of the Teutonic tribes in Germany itself. With that the internal development of the lands west of the Elbe begins.

The process of settlement which followed the Germanic *Völker-wanderung* was the first of a series of events each of which affected fundamentally the structure of agrarian economy, and at the same time made its contribution to the building up of the European society of nations. Eastward of the area of Germanic settlement stretched that of the Slavs. The inroads of the Arabs and their associated people's introduced fresh social strata into South-Western Europe. The Scandinavian inroads of the ninth and tenth centuries, which shook all Western Europe, left behind them especially in England new groups of settlers and a new division of the land. About the same time, on the skirts of the Eastern Alps, a German peasant population began to push out into Slavonic territory. And when this process was finished, in the twelfth century, fresh migrations began, which carried the boundaries of North German culture from the Elbe through the adjacent Wendish lands into those of the Poles and Czechs, occupied the land of the Prussians and founded permanent settlements even in Hungary. Unlike the earlier processes of settlement this was not in its entirety the outcome of conquest. An appreciable number of the foreign settlers were called in by East European rulers who aimed at a more intensive economic development of their territories.

And this eastward German colonization of the twelfth and thirteenth centuries fits into a second series of events in the history of settlement which everywhere accompanied the development of nationalities. That is the process which, all over Western and Central Europe, brought about a fuller economic utilization of the soil. The sharply marked frontier which, in the last era of ancient history, divided the lands of Roman-Hellenic civilization from those of the barbarians divided also, so to speak, two spheres of the estimation of the soil. The use which Roman rule and Roman or Romanized society made of the provinces implied colonization in the strict economic sense of the term.

Various forces were working in that era to ensure or to increase the yield of agriculture and with it the maintenance and extension of agricultural centres—the state, which had to provide for troops and officials; commerce, which had to balance the inequalities of production in the various provinces; and not least those varied elements in society which lived or sought to live as *rentiers*, from aristocrats of senatorial rank to time-expired soldiers, for all of whom landed property was the most desirable basis of existence. These motives worked right up to the imperial frontiers, but did not influence in any way the social standards of the peoples beyond them, because of their social structure. Generally speaking, their agricultural activity was not yet directed towards the conquest of a stubborn environment. Of this the *Völkerwanderung* itself is the most obvious consequence. But the *Völkerwanderung* inaugurated a new economic era. In many areas of old Roman civilization its storms completed that ruin which the internal discord and the external dangers of the late imperial age had already brought about. But when the barrier between the Roman and barbarian worlds broke down, the traditions of the classical agrarian civilization began to influence the new peoples who, at the same time, unable to wander any further, had to accustom themselves gradually to an economic utilization of whatever lands they now occupied. Settlement became more dense: they learnt how to economize the soil. Settlement extended: they learnt how to make waste land productive and to clear woods. The process was an affair of centuries; it was always being interrupted by the ravages of war and had always to be associated with making them good. Not till the twelfth century have we clear indications that, throughout all Western Europe, the land was being fully used; from this time settlements were established even where the elevation, the density of the forest, or the risks of flood had hitherto been insuperable obstacles. The eastward colonization by Germans was primarily a transference into a fresh area of this effort to make a full economic use of the land. Peoples already settled there were themselves drawn into this colonizing activity.

Decisive incidents in the social evolution of medieval society were intimately associated with these economic processes. Like other activities directed to the opening up of new economic resources and forms of production, the colonization of the land became the foundation of an improved social status for large groups of those who participated in it. The general conditions of the class system among colonizing groups determined the sections of society which were able to share in the movement and the social advantages that they derived from it. In the Roman Empire men of affairs and ex-officials were the chief beneficiaries: colonization helped them to acquire estates and country 'places' which put them on a level with the imperial aristocracy or the patricians of the towns. The peasant won nothing but his living from the labour that created or improved cultivable land; he did not acquire that honourable rank in society which, according to the universal outlook of the ancient world, was reserved for those aristocratic classes. Society in the Romano-Germanic succession states was, it is true, thoroughly adapted to that relationship of landlord and tenant on which the agrarian system of the Roman Empire had rested. But with the 'barbarizing' of imperial territory and the establishment of 'barbarian' rule, those cultural and political assumptions which, in the last years of the ancient world, had determined the social importance of landed property and led to its creation lost their strength. The aristocratic life of the villa shrivelled up and its homes decayed. The decline of money-economy prevented the growth of wealth that might be invested in land. And finally came the collapse of that salaried army and civil service, which in the former social order had both facilitated the accumulation of property and provided the—no doubt burdensome—defensive armour behind which lords and their dependants, isolated from public affairs and functions, had enjoyed or dragged out their private lives. Ways of living in the new societies were vastly simpler: they were also purely agrarian. Landed property acquired social functions very different from those which had characterized it under the Empire. Its functions now affected the great majority of the population, but were sharply graded in accordance with the social stratification.

Landownership, which took the form of landlordship and the disposal of the forces of a multitude of dependants, became the basis of personal political power. Such landlordship also secured the independent life and efficiency of the Church. But a type of landownership only considerable enough to guarantee the owner's economic independence had also its definite social value. On such ownership rested the common rights of those sections of the population who had no share in political power, but who could make their influence felt in the legal life of rural society and the economic life of local society. Lastly, a claim to a share in the land enabled an important section of those who were dependent— including many who were not even reckoned free—to maintain their households; and under various legal forms such a claim had, or was acquiring, a secured and heritable character.

All these varied relations to the land served as incentives in the task of medieval settlement. They operated both on a small scale, in the extension of existing settlements and their fission into new ones, and on a great, in the conduct of comprehensive schemes of colonization. The extension of the area of settlement was an instrument for the building up of the great lordships. It was also a way out of the difficulties which the division of inheritance created for the lesser freemen. Finally, for many in the lowest ranks of the peasantry and those in danger of sinking into those ranks, it was a refuge from grinding poverty and practical bondage. It might even help them to rise in society. In the course of centuries these various aspects of the work of settlement were unrolled in a sequence which corresponded step by step with the social development of the peoples of Western Europe. Although our sources tell us little about it, doubtless in most places, during the centuries which followed the end of the great movements of the peoples, small land-owners added to their inherited holdings. Later, as the pressure of feudal lordship reduced them in number and importance, the division of land within the feudal state set a limit to the activity of the class of small freemen. Members of this class who wished to protect their social status by establishing new settlements were now obliged, like those peasants who were struggling out of bondage, to adjust their craving for land to their lords' claims over it. But landlords, lay or ecclesiastical, were not equally ready at all times to spend themselves on colonization in order to increase their power. We can hardly generalize from the evidence of colonizing activity which exists for the years about A.D. 1100. In later years, as has been already noted, the tendency was rather to make the maximum agricultural use of whatever land the lords already possessed. It is in this same period that we are most conscious of the enterprise of the peasant strata below them. At two points, during the eleventh, twelfth and thirteenth centuries, it leads to regular migrations —in Northern France, and in the movement of West German peasants into Slavonic lands east of the Elbe. These movements are very closely related to the contemporary migrations of other countrymen into the towns, where free industry guaranteed them a living and burgess rights a social position. In both areas the movement of agrarian settlement kept touch with the urban development of law; and in the area of German colonization eastward agrarian settlement was associated with the founding of towns.

The privileges which the colonists enjoyed had generally a favourable influence on the legal position of the old established peasants among whom they had settled. This influence made itself felt far into those Polish lands where very few immigrants penetrated. On the land, precisely as in the towns of this period, the economic achievement of the labouring man served to promote his social advancement—and that through the colonizing process. If we view the whole development of European society, this appears as perhaps the most important pheno-menon connected with medieval settlement and colonization. But its influence was rigidly limited. On the spiritual life of the age the work of the settlement movement left no lasting traces. The peasant class remained in the long run the least valued section of society, even in those regions which had seen most colonization. The gains which the settlement movement had brought to that class were gradually nullified by fresh applications of governmental and seignorial pressure.

If we try to grasp in outline the most important medieval movements of settlement and their significance in the development of nations, of agriculture, and of society, we must not forget that the physical framework of rural life merits historical treatment for its own sake. The layout of the settlements, their distribution over the face of the country as homesteads, hamlets, villages; the layout of the individual farmstead and peasant home; and not least the ordering and division of the area devoted to agriculture—all these structural forms of rural society had their varied local and historic types. The movements of settlement lose their full historical life if we fail to picture the types of settlement which accompanied or sprang from them. But with the knowledge now available, we cannot do this for each age and area quite clearly. Even the dependence of forms of settlements and the patterns of the fields on the conditions of their geographical environment is neither simple nor inevitable. The variety of types as seen in the modern world is the result of varied historical and personal forces, of changing environments, of cultural forces radiating from very many points. To an appreciable degree this evolution of the forms of settlement is connected with the history of the extension of the settled area and of the migration movements. But this connexion is not universal. Forms of layout and construction spread without being carried from place to place by migration. Research in this field is being conducted today by exceedingly delicate methods, but is of necessity highly specialized and localized. For both reasons its results are still at important points fluid and provisional.

A variety of approach characterizes all modern researches into the history of settlement. The classic historical method, the co-ordination and analysis of narrative reports and documents, still provides us with the guiding clues. Only because we have such sources at our disposal can we correlate the course of settlement with that of political and social history. But there are recurrent gaps in the results of this traditional method. Medieval chronicles abound in negative information, how this settlement was wasted and that destroyed; but they rarely tell us how anything was built up. The documentary evidence too is very unequal. Generally it is incidental and indirect. The exploitation of the land was carried out by means of lords' arrangements or neighbours' agreements which required no written record. A change appears however, though not quite a general change, in connexion with the great colonizing enterprises of the twelfth and thirteenth centuries. The written contract acquires greater importance if, before the lord can create a settlement, he has to come to an agreement with competing authorities, or with colonists and intermediaries strange to the place or the country. But such necessities were not equally urgent everywhere, even in the areas where colonizing activity was most widespread. We have abundant settlement agreements from the lowlands of Silesia; from Upper Saxony, Brandenburg, Pomerania and Mecklenburg only a few. Moreover the grants and charters of agreement always give an imperfect and often a not quite trustworthy picture of the process. They concern only the reciprocal rights of the parties and do not tell us about the settlers and how they settled. And as they generally contain only a plan, we cannot tell from any given document how far the plan was really carried out.

There are other materials for the history of settlement more closely associated with its internal life—finds; place names; field names; family names; peculiarities of law, usage and speech; finally the layout of villages and fields, actually surviving or recorded in maps. The most intensive research is directed to these things today. Archaeology, philology and the geographical study of settlement unite with historical research: physical geography combined with the analysis of soils and vegetations helps to unveil the past of the sites where men have settled. This formidable division of labour does not tend to easy synthesis of the results. Each line of inquiry evolves its own critical method; and this does not always lead to a growing certainty in the historical and chrono-logical interpretation of the individual fact. The progress of knowledge often obliges the inquirer to realize that phenomena may be similar without being for that reason contemporary. The history of the settle-ment movements and that of the civilizations of the various settled regions begin to throw light on one another but gradually.[1] Yet historical research receives from all these branches of study a stimulus whose importance grows every day.

In the light of these studies, the boundary between the prehistoric and the historic has lost its importance, both in the history of settlement and in agrarian history generally. There is nothing strange now in following out the evolution of the use of the land and the distribution of settle-ment groups, as determined by geographical, ethnological and technical forces, into epochs for which no literary or documentary evidence exists. And this analysis of primitive times might help us to understand better than hitherto the situations of the different peoples as they were when the literary tradition begins. Here however we cannot go so far back. We can neither peer into the dark prehistoric ages of central and northern European regions nor study the contemporary agrarian development of the Mediterranean lands. Both for the purpose of our preliminary observations and for those of the rather fuller sketch to which we now turn, the best starting-point for

[1] The different ways of arriving at conclusions in the study of settlement by the use of place names may be seen by a comparison of the work of F. Steinbach with that of A. Helbok. (See Bibliography.)

discussion is that point in time at which the frontier between these two civilizations had been pushed farthest towards the heart of Europe.

That frontier was established by the policy and administration of Hadrian. He clung to the conquests of his immediate predecessors, the Flavians, and of Trajan. But he abstained from any forward policy and defined the boundaries of the Empire, so far as they did not coincide with the courses of rivers, by the protective works gradually built along the frontier roads and chains of forts of his *limites*. The boundary of the Empire was also the boundary of settlement. The settlement policy of the Empire and the colonizing enterprises of its subjects combined to fill the area within the boundary with uniform structures, whilst beyond the boundary, in the territory of tribes kept at peace by alliances with Rome, there was no colonizing expansion at all. The uniformity of social structure inside the Empire is most clearly shown by the fact that the dominant Mediterranean unit of settlement, the town, pushes farther and farther inland and is adopted by the conquered peoples. No doubt at the end of the second century urban centres were not spread uniformly everywhere. But those parts of Europe in which they are not found, or hardly found, are simply those which, for geographical or historical reasons, were backward—mountainous districts, except those whose mineral resources attracted enterprise and led to the setting up of towns, like the Alps of Noricum; or young frontier districts far from the Mediterranean, like the eastern parts of Upper Germany between the Rhine and the *limes*, the most northerly parts of Gaul and Lower Germany, and North Britain.[1] In Gaul one notes how the urban development of the North lags behind that of the South. We must always bear in mind that the Romanizing of Europe was still in progress when the catastrophes of the third century—military revolts, peasant rebellions and barbarian invasions—threw the Empire into a state of confusion, which was indeed followed by one of greater calm but hardly by one of economic recovery.

Urbanization was a fundamental principle of Roman policy. The self-government of the town territory was the pillar of imperial government. Internal order depended principally upon a uniform urban organization and civilization, and on the discipline of the imperial armies. The prosperous landowning class was led to settle in the towns and to take pride in their official service and their adornment. *Hortari privatim, adiuvare publice, ut templa, foros, domos extruerent*: this educational work in Britian, for which Agricola was praised, was carried

[1] It is not possible to include in this account the history of Africa and the East although, as Rostovtseff's great work has shown, the policies and tendencies of imperial settlement become clearer when viewed as wholes.

on with great energy by the rulers of the following century all over the Empire. They were helped materially by officials and merchants, and by provincial veterans who had been Romanized through military service and wanted to return home and live as prosperous landowners in the towns. The new way of living had also, as a rule, some of its roots in native habits of settlement. Greek and Phoenician civilization had influenced the coastal districts; the Illyrian, Iberian and Celtic hinterlands contained central tribal settlements, often fairly populous, in which the leading families had their place. The economic horizon of the individual town was naturally in most cases narrow. Only a few showed so intensive an industrial and commercial life as Aquileia, Lyon, Trier, Cologne and Augsburg, which profited by their favourable situation for trade and the proximity of important bodies of troops. The towns of Britain, for example, seem to have had a predominantly rural character: the ruins of the houses of Silchester lie scattered far apart 'like cottages in a village'.

The character of the town determined its influence on the surrounding country. In a few cases the consuming power of a great camp or of an industrial population working for export stimulated the production of foodstuffs in the neighbourhood. Elsewhere, as in the plantation districts of Southern Spain and the Adriatic coasts, the rural area itself produced the goods which the town exported. But everywhere the households of those landowners who formed the upper class of the towns absorbed, directly or indirectly, a very important share of what the countryside produced. To these households were attached the centres of economic life, the villas, established on the land. The buildings of such a villa stretched all round a square courtyard. Often a country house for the lord was associated with them. If possible it was in the Italian style and placed, as the classical writers on country life had advised, on a rise overlooking the fields of the estate. These villas scattered about the land were, like the towns, typical units of Roman civilization. They were often built earlier than the towns. Even in regions but sparsely urbanized, ruins of Roman villas have been found, as in Belgium. Like the towns they are monuments of a society profoundly interested in the maintenance of the yield of agriculture. Together with their standards of life, the Italian landowning class introduced into outer Europe the organization of the large estate. The lord's villa, which served as the economic headquarters, was adjacent to a village where the workers— usually slaves—lived together. Remote parts of the estate were let out to peasants, who might be free *peregrini*, clients of the lord, or freedmen, or slaves, as local circumstances determined. Proprietary rights were remodelled in various ways by the influence of Roman authority. Both for the setting apart of *ager publicus*, with its colonies of veterans, and for the fixing of boundaries to the *territoria* of towns, new surveys were required, in connexion with which in certain regions—demonstrably along the Danube—Roman centuriation was applied. We note that these surveys were made the occasion for preferential treatment of lords settled in towns as against country landholders. It is not, however, clear to what extent the dependence of the peasant population on the lords was increased by these proprietary regulations and by Roman rule in general. Even before Roman times a society based on a strong independent peasantry was not to be found among any of the conquered peoples.

So in all probability there was no marked difference between proprietary relations in provincial and those in Italian villages. In spite of the efforts of the emperors of the first century, the Italian peasants had become tenants of the Roman aristocracy. The spread of rural settlement, the increase of villages and arable land, was really the affair of the great proprietors. Of these the emperor was the greatest. His administration had worked at African colonization with the utmost energy in order to feed Rome. In the European provinces also more was required of agriculture than in pre-Roman times. Artisans, merchants and officials must be fed. The lord must make his estates pay for his more luxurious way of living and provide constant contributions for the city and the state. This all meant an extension of cultivated land and more peasant holdings. In Italy peasant farmers, *coloni*, had taken over lands which had once been slave-worked wine and oil plantations; for the slave economy was no longer profitable.

Yet the extension of peasant holdings in Italy was far behind its optimum. In A.D. 193 Pertinax issued an edict to encourage the utilization of land that had been neglected all over the Empire; Italy was particularly mentioned as in need of attention.[1] In the north-west of the Empire also there was a definite and significant limit to the extension of peasant settlement. It never seriously attacked the forests. In Gaul, in Germany east of the Rhine, and in Britain, traces of large-scale clearing in Roman times have been found only in those state forests from which the word *saltus* was transferred to state property in general. Smaller clearings were often undertaken to make room for villas which yet had to be near the woods. But beyond this it seems that private settlement was confined to the areas which had long been used for tillage and pasture.[2] In view of the growth of population, this points to an increased agricultural yield as a result of Roman influence. But it also suggests that this influence failed to stimulate initiative among any

[1] Rostovtseff, *Studien zur Gesch. des römischen Kolonats*, p. 391 n.
[2] Jullian, *Hist. de la Gaule*, v, 5, pp. 179 f.; H. Aubin, *H.Z.* v, 141, pp. 6 f.; Fox, *The Archæology of the Cambridge Region*, p. 224.

large section of the peasants. There can be little doubt that an extension of cultivated land at the expense of the forests would have been economically advantageous. Urban and rural labour would have been mutually stimulated. But the most powerful motive for an expansion of rural settlement is always the desire of the individual to profit from his own toil. The founding of new homes has at all times been the goal to win which peasant stocks have undertaken the heavy task of reclamation. Roman provincial society, with its preferential treatment of the towns, was not a favourable environment for this task. The turning of forest into arable, with long drawn out toil, for the benefit of a lord in a remote town, was not the most attractive way of making a living.

A direct colonizing influence of the state was felt in regions whose annexation had only been completed under Domitian and Trajan—the *agri decumates* and Dacia. With them must be classed the Danube bank of Pannonia, in which permanent Roman camps had only been set up since Vespasian's day. If Roman colonization has not left so many traces in Britain—apart from the South-East, which was closely associated with Gaul and accessible to every Roman influence—as along the boundaries of Upper Germany and Rhaetia, it must be remembered that in Britain it was spread over an appreciably greater area rather remote from most of the cultivated parts of the Empire. All these newly conquered regions had this in common—that in consequence of their more primitive agrarian conditions they were peopled thinly as compared with the older provinces. The wars of conquest had reduced their population still further, and many natives had fled before the Romans. On the other hand, these lands had to bear the heavy burden of maintaining the armies which were quartered in them and along their frontiers. As a result of all this, the state was obliged to play a specially active part in colonization. It had to increase the yield of the settled land, to extend its area, and at the same time to augment the number of settlers.

So far as possible an attempt was made to arouse the economic interest of the natives by the way in which the garrisons were located. In England, on the Neckar, on the Danube, we note how the Roman forts were placed close to old settlements, and how these grew under the stimulus from the garrisons, and sometimes developed into towns. But this stimulus alone was not enough. Small areas were assigned to the legions, which were cultivated by the natives under their supervision. In Pannonia they were called *prata legionum*: clearly we must attribute to them the maintenance of a strong peasant class there. The whole of the *agri decumates* were treated as domain and split up into *saltus*. And, at any rate in Upper Germany east of the Rhine, the extension of settlement into previously unoccupied districts is demonstrable. On the eastern

rim of the Black Forest, for example, and on the lower slopes of the
Swabian Jura there was a heavy clearing of woodland in Roman times.
But it was definitely limited. The crests of the hills were left, except
perhaps—as in the Allgau—to provide for road making. The
coniferous forests were untouched. Colonizing activity was generally
limited by the provincial authorities to what was essential for military
purposes. The same applies to the introduction of colonists from outside.
In Britain and Pannonia the natives appear to have met all requirements.
At the eastern end of the frontier chain, in Dacia, the situation was
reversed. The primitive Thracian population had been so thoroughly
exterminated in Trajan's wars that great stretches of territory had to be
assigned to newcomers. We can understand why these colonists were
brought not from Thracian lands in the Balkans but from Asia. Soldiers
and veterans were specially conspicuous among those who received
grants of land from the state on the Danubian frontier and in the region
of the Upper German and Rhaetian *limes*. But we must not picture
them as peasant settlers: they paid rent for small villas, employing on
these native and imported labour.

This labour from the beginning included Germans.[1] Ever since
Caesar's time groups of Germans had again and again sought settlement
on the lands of the Empire, and others—the Mattiaci and remnants of
those Marcomanni most of whom had wandered east—accepted
Roman rule easily when the *agri decumates* were occupied, just as the
Batavi and the Frisians had in the north. But it is of the Frisians that
Tacitus tells how once they declared themselves dissatisfied with Rome's
high-handed disposition of its public land and tried to reoccupy the
agros vacuos et militum usui repositos by force (*Ann.* XIII, c.54). This
situation was reproduced on the largest scale along the Danubian
frontier at the beginning of the reign of Marcus Aurelius. Germans
from across the river, Marcomanni and Quadi supported by Longobards who had pushed into their territory, made violent demands for
land in Pannonia. The governor refused his permission—and a stubborn
war of the Marcomanni and other frontier tribes against the Empire
was the result. What they sought was nothing less than that secular aim
of the Germans, eventually realized in a world of new states—a fresh
division of Roman provincial soil that would permit of their settling on
it as owners. So we turn to the antecedents of this sustained pressure,
the internal conditions of Germany.

Along almost the whole length of Rome's European frontiers
German tribes were her neighbours. Of the Celts, after Hadrian's wall
had been supplemented by the Antonine fortifications from the Forth
to the Clyde, only the pastoral clans of the Caledonian Highlands and

[1] For further discussion of this question, see p. 180, below.

those of Ireland remained outside the Empire; and along the eastern section of the Danubian frontier, from the plains of the Theiss to the steppe coast of the Black Sea, lay the territory of the Sarmatians—who seem to have been essentially nomads. Northwards to Scandinavia, eastwards until beyond the Vistula, stretched the German *Hinterland*. There was at that time at least as much perpetual motion in it as there was permanent settlement. Those Longobards who joined the Marcomanni and Quadi in the attack of A.D. 162 had their tribal seat on the lower Elbe. The Swabian tribes of central Germany were also on the move south; probably their pressure explains the advance of the Chatti towards the *limes* about the same time. The fresh grouping of the Swabian tribes, which turned them into 'Alemanni', must have begun shortly after this. 'Easily moved to migration' Strabo labels the peoples who occupied the two banks of the Elbe. In the second century also came the movement of Gothic tribes south-east from the lower Vistula which brought some of them to the Black Sea.

Over against these wanderings of the East Germans and the Elbe Germans, among the tribes nearer the Roman frontier we notice at first only such neighbourly friction as Tacitus described a few decades earlier. Settlement or movement of Germans—it should be added—affected only a very small part of the area named after them. We must think of some four-fifths of the land as covered with forest and swamp.[1] Settlement was confined, as it had been for thousands of years, to those localities which were both open and dry.

So German settlement was both unstable and limited—and yet already the pattern of its medieval development was indicated. To grasp it from within we must go back once more to that Roman who first studied it comprehensively. You cannot write about the Germans of Tacitus' *Germania* without discussing the book and the man. What seems partly over-simplified and partly ambiguous in his account acquires life and precision when we come to understand the ideas that lay behind his phraseology. Obviously he glances now and again from Germany to Rome. More important still, his account of the Germans is written from the standpoint of traditional Roman thought. He took it for granted that you could apply to German ways of living the same tests that you would use in estimating the position of a well-to-do Roman citizen. And he was always the cultivated man of letters speaking to men like himself. When he wanted to grasp German characteristics, he did not compare them with Roman realities, but with the characteristics of the Roman citizen of the literary tradition. The allusions to this tradition are mostly only passing references or bits of

---

[1] Cf. O. Schlüter's *Karte Germaniens zur Römerzeit* (*Reallex. d. german. Altertumskunde*, I, 424 f.), which however needs correction in detail. (Cf. Hömberg, pp. 22 f.)

quotations; that was part of the fine style of rhetorical writing, a style tainted with affectation.

The typical German of the *Germania* belongs to the substantial landowner class. He keeps open house. He stays long away from home to attend the Folk-moot. He is always ready to join a campaign (c. 21; 11; 14). It is taken for granted that he has slaves and lets out part of his land (c. 25). So far as Tacitus knows, he is the German counterpart of those Romans who are expected to perform their full duties as citizens and possess all the civic virtues. This fact is decisive in judging Tacitus' criticism of the domestic economy of the German *Paterfamilias*. The way these restless warriors wilfully neglect their households and their farming, their blending of energy with idleness, says he, is 'a remarkable contradiction in their character' (c. 15). For, as he assumes and his reader understands, the representative Roman will fulfil the duties of householder, citizen and warrior. Only so can he have a balanced character. It is not a weakness in the comparison that Tacitus reproaches the Germans with their unwillingness to handle the plough (c. 41). He does not mean that they were poor idle peasants; rather that they lacked energy as householders; for the typical Roman citizen householder, according to the good old paternal tradition, himself lent a hand in the farm work.

And when he wishes to indicate the legal and economic conditions of the German landowner's way of living, Tacitus makes use of literary references to a classic, to the book from which Roman landlords learnt the rules of rural economy, M. Porcius Cato's *De agricultura*. The much discussed statements in c. 26 of the *Germania* are made with constant reference to the preface and first chapter of this book. That is how we must read them if we would understand them.[1]

Cato begins by contrasting agriculture, the citizen's most honourable calling, with the most shameful—usurious profit-seeking, *fenerari*. Our fathers in their laws punished the usurer (*fenerator*) more harshly than the thief. But they called the *vir bonus* a *bonum agricolam bonumque colonum*. Cato then starts his advice to the Roman landlord with a disquisition on those qualities of the land and of its site which should be considered when an estate is to be acquired. Finally he enumerates the various ways of utilizing an estate and places them in order of merit—first vine growing; then irrigated gardening (*hortus inriguus*). Meadow land (*pratum*) comes fifth and arable (*campus frumentarius*) only sixth.

Compare this with what Tacitus' c. 26 tells us of the Germans. He

---

[1] The conflicting interpretations of Tacitus' concise phrases make up, as is well known, a long chapter in modern historical research. They are summarized in Kulischer, *Wirtschaftsgeschichte*, I, 12 ff. See too Steinbach, *Gewanndorf*, pp. 37 ff.; *Selbstverwaltung*, pp. 25 f., 40 ff.

too speaks of usury (*fenus*) before he comes to agriculture—but only
to say that among the Germans there can be no competition between
these two ways of making a living. 'Usury they do not know, and so
are better protected from it than if it were legally forbidden.'[1] Follows
Cato's second topic, the acquisition of landed property. Among the
Germans this is regulated strictly by communal occupation, the act of the
whole community, through which its members mutually guarantee
one another's possession.[2] The extent of land occupied always corresponds with the number of those who are to make use of it. Then it is
divided: shares of various value are dealt out according to the recognized claims of individuals (*secundum dignationem*). And the extensive
areas always occupied and used (*camporum spatia*) make division easy.
Throughout Tacitus is pointing to the contrast between the position of
the Roman citizen whom Cato advised and that of the German of
corresponding social status. The Roman acquires land as an individual:
he buys land already fully settled: the buyer must proceed rationally.
On the contrary, the acquisition of land in Germany consists simply in
the division of what was originally occupied. Not individual opportunities for acquisition are the determining factors but the standards of
the occupying group, which provides itself with land enough to satisfy
the graded claims of its members. From this description of the acquisition of land Tacitus turns finally, like Cato, to its use. He links
this to his remarks about the great size of the land assignments. 'They
change the arable yearly—and there is land to spare': each individual
has more than he need cultivate. That, Tacitus suggests, is all that the
Germans know of economy. 'For they take no pains to make the best
of the fertility and extent of the land. They plant no fruit trees; they
mark off no meadows; they irrigate no gardens (*ut . . . prata separent et
hortos rigent*); the land simply has to yield the corn crops.' In short,
Cato's advice about the graded types of cultivation has no meaning for
the Germans. Those types which he sets above arable farming they do
not know; they are corn growers and nothing else.

Tacitus wishes to make it clear that the Germans are not tempted to
any economic activity beyond the use of their land; but they do not
make a rational use of it. The conditions on which they hold it prevent
that. The abundance of land excludes all thought of economizing its
use; and they have not the technical knowledge of diversified uses.
Their economy is, from this point of view, primitive. These mainly

[1] The tacit reference to Cato makes Reeb's description of these words (*Commentary*,
p. 47) as 'painfully obvious' beside the point.
[2] *Agri pro numero cultorum ab universis invicem occupantur, quos mox inter se secundum
dignationem partiuntur*. The reading *invicem* is disputed: but there is no accepted
emendation. My interpretation of the passage substantially agrees with that of Dopsch,
who had also recognized that its point lay in the comparison with Roman conditions.

negative conclusions acquire their chief significance for us because they illuminate incidentally the fundamental principles of land division on which the settlement of the Germans was based. The land which is at the disposal of the individual free German is the share due to his recognized social position of what he and his fellow tribesmen had collectively 'occupied'. It is a *folcland*, a κλῆρος. The land settled by a tribe is what that tribe acquired collectively, what it acquired by conquest. For a time it might be held collectively, until the members of the tribe had come to an agreement about individual claims. The division once made was permanent: free trade in land was unknown. But Tacitus emphasized the fact that the act of division did really create individual property, which belonged to the holder and his heirs in perpetuity. And he does not fail to note that the shares are not equal: *secundum dignationem*, according to his social rank, is the way in which an individual's claims are weighed. Here Tacitus is making another literary point; he is correcting the most famous of writers about the Germans without mentioning him. Caesar had maintained that a German had no property in land: the land was redivided yearly among family groups with a view to avoiding inequality (*G.B.* VI, c. 22). Well, Divus Julius was mistaken,[1] Tacitus implies. Land was divided; that is agreed. But it was divided into greater and lesser shares, and not every year. Only the arable of the individual holding was shifted every year (*arva per annos mutant*).

That the individual family got a share of the tribal land was the first characteristic of German landownership. A second basic social principle of the German way of settlement seemed strange to Roman observers. The free German lived permanently and exclusively on the land that he had inherited. His home was never part of a larger settlement, least of all of a city. When Tacitus brings out this fact in c. 16 he is well aware that he is pointing to a remarkably crude divergence in German customary ways of living from those of all civilized peoples, not merely of the Romans. In the traditional literary view of the 'social contract' the fundamental institutions of a well-ordered life are the cities; *domicilia coniuncta quas urbes dicimus*, as Cicero once put it (*Pro Sestio*, 42, § 91). With conscious reference to this definition—and not missing the chance of rectifying it a little—Tacitus says that the German peoples do not inhabit *urbes*, not even *inter se junctas sedes*. They prefer to live scattered over the land, as only uncivilized races do elsewhere. *Colunt discreti ac diversi, ut fons, ut campus, ut nemus placuit.*

Yet this 'scattered settlement', as the very next sentence shows, is nevertheless a settlement in villages, in *vici*. These villages are loose

---

[1] This view is rendered the more probable because Tacitus had other controversies with Caesar. Cf. Norden, pp. 316 f.

structures however: 'they are not like ours; one house is not closely attached to the next; each has space about it'. As a rule, so Tacitus suggests, a few free German landowners form a village group. Their tenants settle near them in the village; so do their slaves, who are treated 'as coloni'. The slaves' children and the lord's children grow up together: *inter eadem pecora, in eadem humo* (c.20). The village lords, the free Germans, themselves live in rustic simplicity. Their houses are roughly built of timber and mud. For granaries and places of retreat in the cold of winter they enlarge caves and holes in the earth (c. 16). The lands of the village as a whole seem unusually wide, but the fields set aside for tillage relatively small (*superest ager*, c. 26). What the free Germans value most are great herds of cattle (*numero gaudent*, c. 5).

So much Tacitus tells us directly. His picture contains only the main lines, which can be filled in in various ways. It shows us the sort of village in which small groups of average Germans settled. But how are we to conceive of the settlements of the leading families, the *principes*, the *nobiles*? They need more land, cattle, labour power and houseroom. They have followers always at their table and the table must be generous (cc. 13, 14). No doubt they have their share in the land *secundum dignationem*. And we must assume that the German princelings and other leading men did not share a settlement with the common freemen, but had whole villages for themselves and their dependants.

We must next consider the influence of family ties on settlement. Caesar had long ago written of the sharing of land among groups of kindred (*B.G.* VI, c. 22); but the tribes to which he attributed this system cannot be assigned any permanent organization of property and were apparently not in a position to settle down finally. In the definite sharing out of the land, as described by Tacitus, it is not a group of kindred, a clan, but the individual tribesman who appears as proprietor, with the obligation to hand on his share to his descendants. And in fact it would appear that the village group was not as a rule the same as the group of blood relations. The law of the Salian Franks, at a later date, contemplated the case in which, for lack of heirs, mere neighbours would have a claim on the inheritance (*Edict. Chilperici*, c. 3); this indicates a distinction between blood relations and neighbours. In one way however the communal sharing out of the land no doubt favoured the settlement of blood relations as neighbours; the shares resulting from it must have been big enough to provide room in the near future for several families, if the arrangement was to have any permanence. In the case of the leading families, who settled down in isolation from the first, division among heirs must also have led to the growth of regular 'clan villages'. Such noble clan settlements are found in various countries after the *Völkerwanderung*.

We must not picture 'Tacitean' villages all over the map of Germany. Their organization implied regular arable farming, and that was not found everywhere. The Germans on the North Sea coast did not mind their cattle and catch their fish from village settlements, but lived in small groups on little hillocks rising from the marshy flats. These *Terpen* or *Warfen* were artificially heightened as a protection against stormy tides. And perhaps the eastern tribes, who began to move south-east about A.D. 200, still lived at that time in the unstable conditions of landownership and settlement which Caesar had assumed to be universal in Germany.

But in the heart of the West, and right up into Scandinavia, the system of land division and settlement indicated in Tacitus' account was clearly prevalent everywhere. It was from these regions that there started those campaigns of conquest of the *Völkerwanderung* times which led to the establishment of village settlements. And in the results of this establishment the traces of the system can still be seen.

The ritual practice of throwing a hammer, under fixed and difficult conditions, to determine the limits of a man's property in the village, is of old German origin.[1] So are those rules which regulated the use of the fields in the primitive village, and remained operative in the medieval village wherever German settlement was really dense. In laying out the village a division was made between the land assigned to the use of individual households and that which was available as common pasture for all the villagers, free and unfree. Both parts constituted interconnected complexes; the lands destined for the plough were grouped in special sections of the whole territory of the village. The grouping was essential in order to leave plenty of room for the herds, 'in whose numbers men rejoiced', and at the same time to keep the herds out of the corn. This is how we must account for the fact that wherever German influence affected settlement, a layout of the corn land which contributed to these ends was repeated—the familiar long strips.[2] To deal with these strips, the heavy wheeled plough drawn by several pairs of oxen was in use even in early German times.[3] But the

---

[1] For the meaning of this ritual, which has nothing whatever to do with the clearing of the waste, see Grimm, *Rechtsaltertümer*, I, 94 (66).

[2] The obvious tendency of German settlement to be associated with the long strips has usually been explained, since Meitzen's time, by the use of the heavy plough. Only a few scholars have connected it with the necessities of extensive cattle rearing (C. Ostermann, pp. 199 f.; F. Steinbach, *Selbstverwaltung*, pp. 49 f.). But for primitive times especially, this explanation seems the more illuminating.

[3] Such a plough is to be found at least as early among the Celts as among the Germans; see the well-known reference to its use among the Alpine Celts (Pliny, *Nat. Hist.* 18, c. 172). The claim that it had reached Britain in Celtic times (Collingwood and Myres, pp. 211, 442) has hardly been established. See below, p. 150, and R. V. Lennard in *Dopsch Festschrift* (1938), p. 70.

arable strips were not yet at that time interrupted by the division of the fields into sections meant to be dealt with as units at the same time— *Gewanne*, furlongs: the individual holdings were not yet cut up into bits lying in several such furlongs. These features of the 'open-field system' first developed in the medieval peasant village. The working of the furlongs implied a more careful handling of the yearly change of the land under cultivation, and a stricter communal discipline of agricultural practice, than we can connect with the careless village lords of the society that Tacitus describes. And the subdivision of holdings which made the furlong organization necessary only suits the conditions of a later time: it went hand in hand with the growth of the village population, through the repeated subdivisions of inheritances among a peasantry that was no longer mobile and had learnt how to extend the arable land by clearing operations.[1] The long drawn out furrows and strips were independent of the furlong system.[2] The primitive German strip system is best represented by those so-called *Esch*-fields, which have survived in Westphalia into modern times; their strips are quite extraordinarily long (300 to 600 metres) and are not interrupted by the boundaries of *Gewanne*.

The economic sense of the Germans was not yet sufficiently developed to wring a greater yield from the soil if settlement tended to exceed the supply of open and accessible land. When a German tribe secured for itself some district by conquest it set aside for division among its members only so much open land as was needed *pro numero cultorum*. Later, the reserve land which had not been used at first was cut up into shares for members of the community. When that point had been reached, the position of the Chauci as described by Tacitus was reached also: *tam immensum terrarum spatium non tenent tantum Chauci, sed et implent* (c.35). Both in the division of the land and in the formation of the settlements, the dominant motive was the craving to extend so far as possible the area which the single great household could exploit by its own efforts and with the aid of its *servi* settled on the land. Roman observers—Tacitus' authorities—saw this and were of opinion that the craving had scope enough in Germany; but the Germans did not share that opinion. They were always thinking that someone else had land that they wanted. Generally speaking, they had no notion of extending the settled area by clearing the mighty forests in which their islands of

---

[1] See the vivid illustrations in Steinbach (*Gewanndorf*, p. 54); Hömberg, pp. 27 ff.; T. A. M. Bishop (*Assarting*, pp. 29 ff.).

[2] Cf. for France, Bloch, *Caractères*, pp. 35 ff. Also pp. 50, 61; for Germany, Hömberg, pp. 35-40. Hömberg showed the valuable evidence of the layout of the *Esch-fluren* for the primitive field layout, after H. Rothert and R. Martiny had proved that this layout was older than that *Einzelhof* system of Westphalia, which Meitzen had assumed to be primitive.

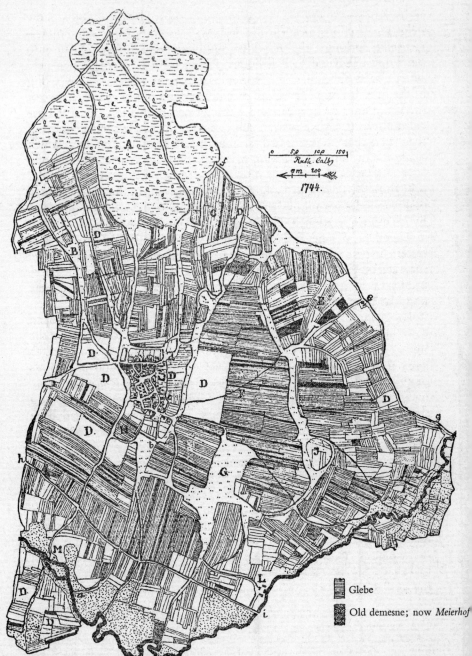

FIG. 1. The *Gewanndorf* in Old Germany (Geismar near Göttingen) in its developed form; eighteenth century. A, wood; B, G, J, scraps of common; D, a late created noble holding.

settlement were imbedded. Those thinner woodlands which were found on the outskirts of the virgin forest were, it is true, not an absolute obstacle to agriculture; and the Teutons of Jutland and Scandinavia seem actually to have preferred these stretches of country for their settlements.[1] In view of the lead given by the Romans' strategical or colonizing forest clearances in the frontier provinces, the absence of large-scale clearing cannot simply be explained by the technical incompetence of the Germans. They valued the primeval forest: it was impassable and untouchable. There were great frontier stretches of forest between the tribes. The heart of the forest was the seat of the Godhead; there it displayed its awe; there it claimed sacrifice and humble submission. This religious tradition is not merely mentioned by Tacitus and illustrated in the case of the Semnones; it lived on among the Saxons and in Scandinavia, and was transferred in Baltic lands to the peoples who there succeeded the Germans. Among the Alemanni, as late as the eighth century, Abbot Pirmin denounced those rites of prayer and magic which propitiated the secret powers of the forest depths and the forest soil. We cannot say that this numinous atmosphere absolutely forbade the pushing of settlement into the woods. But it was a hindrance, and is at least evidence that the Germans looked on the woodland in whose midst they dwelt as an unchangeable thing.

That was why individual acquisition of land did not evolve among them; why each free tribesman disposed of only so much land as the body of his associates had assigned to him at the conquest and division. And this rule, the basis for the settlement of the different tribes, again determined the only way in which their constantly reviving need for fresh soil could seek satisfaction. Whenever German freemen developed a craving for more plough-land, more cattle, more villages, there was no way for them but to join with people who shared their craving. They might accompany the whole tribe on an expedition of conquest, or they might risk an attack somewhere with a strong party of like-minded men.

So we understand the new phase of these movements which sets in with the Marcomannic wars. It was new in two aspects. For the first time German tribes sought to conquer on Roman soil that land for settlement, of which, constituted as they were, they never had enough. Then, in the course of the next century, the hordes of land-hungry German fighting men, who stormed against the *limes* and the Rhine frontier, formed fresh tribal associations which in the end completely absorbed many of the older tribes. They were not, however, compact political entities, but split up into independent groups, each with its own leader. From A.D. 213 the Romans had to fight masses of Germans on

[1] See the evidence of F. Mager, Sjöbeck and R. Sernander; and cf. K. Wührer, pp. 14 ff.

the *limes*. Suevi from the middle Elbe formed their core. They called themselves Alemanni. Their name meant the 'united' people, or so the Romans supposed. In the middle of the third century other groups which crossed the lower Rhine were already known as Franks. They themselves were being pressed upon by a movement from the lower Elbe. The Saxons from Holstein were pushing across the lower Weser and absorbing the tribes of those parts.

The Empire had only been able to hold this fierce movement in check by bringing fresh German lands under its rule and inducing their inhabitants, by force and by example, to adapt themselves to the settlement system of the Romans. Marcus Aurelius aimed at this: he would have created fresh provinces north of the middle Danube. Commodus his son, the spendthrift of a great inheritance, abandoned the ambition. He merely protected his frontier against the Marcomanni by a de-populated no-man's land. This short-sighted and half-hearted compromise was partly responsible for the Danube frontier becoming subsequently a gate of entry for destructive forces. But the catastrophe of Roman policy on the frontier only became inevitable because the Empire behind it had lost the strength to serve any longer as a civilizing power. The reign of a single emperor whom neither citizens nor soldiers could respect sufficed to reveal their profound antagonism to one another and destroy that alliance between them on which the state rested. Commodus' fall led on to the fight of the provincial armies for the crown. The military rule of the Severi rose over a terribly wasted Empire; it dissolved in a wild struggle of the armies and their leaders which lasted half a century. The Illyrian emperors, elevated from A.D. 249 by the armies of the Danube, were faced by a new German problem there. The wanderings of the East Germans were over, and along the whole line, from Noricum to the Black Sea, tribes of Gothic stock stormed against the frontier. Alemanni and Franks broke into the provinces of Germany and Gaul. It is hard to determine how far these campaigns had in view actual conquest, how far merely the weakening and wasting of the Empire. The permanence of the achievements against the Germans of emperors who realized their responsibilities— Gallienus, Claudius II, Aurelianus, Probus—was always weakened by the shortness of their reigns: most of them were murdered by rebellious troops. Diocletian was the first to be favoured both with less turbulent armies and a slackening of the German offensive. But meanwhile the German world had expanded and the Roman world had changed its social and economic organization.

Rome had been forced to abandon her outworks across the Rhine and the Danube—Dacia and the *agri decumates*. German tribes now ruled and occupied soil which for a century and a half had been subjected to

Roman colonization. In both regions the new rulers made short work of the legacy of Rome. But rule and occupation were managed differently by East and West Germans; so the two regions had not the same destiny.

Dacia was now the south-western wing of a huge area over which the Gothic tribal groups were scattered. After they had been forced to accept the Danube as their southern boundary, they lived for decades at war among themselves and with the Thracian and Sarmatian natives. When these wars died down, in the reign of Constantine the Great, the old province of Dacia was divided among the Gepidae, the Taifali and the Tervingi or Visigoths. The dominion of the last stretched to the Dniester; here it touched that of the Greutungi or Ostrogoths who occupied the steppes as far as the Don. On the steppes these Germans adopted the traditional economy of the steppes: they became nomads. The Dacian Goths led a more settled life; but on their earlier plundering campaigns on both sides of the Aegean they had not learnt to value the Roman provincial urban or rural civilization. Both went down before them. They let the mines of Transylvania, its greatest treasure in Roman eyes, go to ruin. They were incapable of living in peace with the colonizing landlords and of learning from them. Some of the old population had held out in Dacia when the Roman armies had practically evacuated it; but when in Aurelian's reign complete abandonment became certain, they migrated to fresh homes given them by the emperor south of the Danube. Evidently only servile cultivators were left behind: they transmitted the vocabulary which forms the basis of Roumanian. To this labour force were added enslaved prisoners of war, and also slaves of the conquerors' blood. But even so, the Goths, with good soil at their disposal, could not or would not organize an agriculture which might support them adequately. The most important material basis of their life was their relation with the Romans, who feared their fighting spirit and coveted their military aid. Presents and mercenaries' pay flowed into their territory and taught Roman merchants the way there. But the merchants' main task was the carrying of food into Dacia. If the import of corn across the Danube was checked, the Goths were in danger of famine.

It is well known that finally, in A.D. 378, the Visigoths sought shelter in the Empire and left to the Huns the land which a century before they had won from the Romans. During this same century, another German people had founded a settlement in the West, which was to endure, in an abandoned Roman province. The Alemanni had settled down in the *agri decumates*. They were hardly less warlike and restless than the Goths. The right bank of the Rhine, which had been in their hands since about A.D. 260, always served as the starting point for devastating raids into Gaul. But the very fact that they never established friendly relations with the Empire forced the Alemanni to become more self-sufficient economically than their Gothic contemporaries. They utilized almost the whole of the area in the *agri decumates* that had been settled under the Romans. In its northern parts at least—in the Wetterau—traces of Roman field divisions survived to modern times; here, it is obvious that the German agrarian economy succeeded the Roman directly. And it may be assumed that it was the same in many other places.

Yet one may not speak of a carrying-on of the Roman tradition of settlement. The Alemanni did not step into the economic system of Roman colonization; on to the soil that Rome had colonized they transplanted an economic system of German type. The urban life that had developed and had stimulated agriculture in the frontier provinces could not go on as before, if only because it had been conditioned—far more than in Dacia—by the needs of the local garrisons. And the new rulers took no interest in its revival. As Ammianus Marcellinus relates (XVI, 2, 12) they hated the Roman towns, 'those walled tombs', and let them fall to ruins. They seldom adopted the Roman manner of building and made no use of the villas and villages from which the Romans had fled, not even of their sites. They built their own rude settlements some little way off. And there are significant limits to their maintenance of the old cultivated areas. Forests often grew over land that had been tilled in Roman times. Such places were probably not spacious enough for large-scale pasturage, and so did not tempt the Alemanni to make use of parts of them as arable.

While the occupation of soil that had once been Roman was being completed in this primitive fashion, inside the Empire the government and the landowners had to face a change in all economic relations. Civil war and barbarian invasion had ruined town and country. For decades the emperors, partly to pacify the troops, partly to meet political opposition, had done nothing to hinder the plundering of the towns and the humbling, the very extirpation, of the higher strata of citizens. The urban centres of Gaul, Upper Italy and the Balkan peninsula had been the main objects of the Teutonic invasions. Losses of men and of wealth had brought their development to a halt. True, the imperial fiscal policy could not do without them. The personal responsibility of their magistrates, of curial family, was an important reserve guaranteeing the payment of the taxes. But the use of this guarantee meant a perpetual depression of urban economic life. So the towns lost their power to stimulate rural settlement. Meanwhile the evils which were reducing them to misery often affected the country also. When the decades of torment through troop movements and foreign invasions closed, there was plenty of vacant land in the Balkans for the refugees from Dacia, and in Gaul for barbarian prisoners of war. This shows how the country had been wasted. 'The fields were neglected; cultivated land became forest.' Lactantius who describes these terrible things lays the blame on Diocletian's military and civil reforms; their burden had reduced the peasants to despair. His statement indicates that the new compulsory social order which Diocletian introduced often added fresh evils to the old, without altogether curing them. Yet the statement is one-sided. Faced by the necessity of using up the resources of the Empire that they might maintain and put in order the machinery of state, Diocletian and his successors at least tried to give its rural economy a firm organization which would resist the progressive decay, render a revival possible, and secure a permanent if scanty existence for small peasant holdings.

The great proprietors, helping and competing, followed the same object. In this class new men predominated—products of the political and social revolution of the third century, officials and officers. The fall of the old provincial aristocracy allowed them to accumulate even greater possessions than their predecessors. Their estates were often scattered over various districts, with tenants great and small. As the towns lost their power to attract, the lords and their staffs preferred to live in the country. So the villa retained its importance; and a typical product of the age was the fortified villa. It was now often the centre of a public administrative area. For the owners of great scattered masses of landed property managed to withdraw them from the financial and judicial organization of the *civitates*, and to administer them like the crown lands as *saltus*. They even undertook to be responsible for their dependants' dues to the state.

Inside and outside these domains, agriculture served the state directly. Direct supply of the army and the administration by deliveries in kind and *corvées* had proved the safest sort of tax-paying during the chronic administrative and economic crises of the third century. In this and other ways Diocletian perpetuated the emergency measures of an age of crisis. To guarantee the steadiness of the supplies in kind, the bureaucracy henceforth took comprehensive and continuous control of agricultural settlement. The administrative foundation of this control was Diocletian's Cadastral Edict; periodically repeated returns fixed for every holding the extent of its cultivated area, with the *jugum* as unit, and the extent to which the labour of men and animals was employed on it, with the *caput* as unit. This survey was useful for the planning of the Empire's economy as well as for raising its taxes. The lord was compelled to cultivate his estate to the full extent recorded, and the peasant to keep up his recorded services. Constantine I applied on each side legal safeguards whose principles he borrowed from the Hellenistic tradition of the East.[1] To maintain the cultivated area the ἐπιβολή principle was applied: when land became waste, the neighbouring proprietors were responsible for its delivering again to the state its share of the assessed local yield. Aurelian had made the urban magistrates responsible on this principle; Constantine allowed the magistrates to share the responsibility with the landowners of the district. The permanent service of the peasant was secured by obliging the *colonus* and his progeny to reside and work for ever on the land where he now was. This 'binding to the soil' was not an act of extraordinary enslavement: it was only the application of another Hellenistic principle—the hereditary duty of service at one's prescribed native place (*idia*; *origo*)—which was applied also to urban magistracies and callings.

This stiff mechanical legislation was not the only means tried for encouraging rural settlement. The *emphyteusis* was taken over from the Hellenistic East. This form of contract was used especially for large farmers (*conductores*) who undertook to cultivate waste land or tumbled-down estates. The owner took no rent for two or three years; after that the farmer paid a fixed rent and acquired a heritable right to the land for the duration of the lease. The state favoured this colonizing tenure by reducing its claims, especially by easing the ἐπιβολή. It also undertook to find labour power for the land whose cultivation it required. Military success on the river frontiers, which continued for a time from Aurelian's reign, brought in many German and Sarmatian prisoners. These were mostly assigned to private estates, not as slaves but as *coloni*—as had often been done under the earlier Empire. Peasants of German blood soon became familiar on the estates of Gaul.[2] Both the army and the revival of agriculture depended on the recruitment of prisoners. There was an old device that served both these ends. The emperors had encouraged the settlement of the frontier troops in peasant colonies near their headquarters. Now, groups of prisoners were required to garrison prescribed places and cultivate prescribed estates. In Northern Gaul these barbarian settlers—usually described as *inquilini*—were called *laeti*. The word is probably of Teutonic origin; in name and fact the *laeti* corresponded to the Frankish *liten*, who were half-free farmers on lords' estates in Germany. This social class obviously sprang from the subjection of Germans by Germans in the wars that took place during the movements of peoples when the great tribal leagues were formed.

The legal and social position of the settlers was thus one which they already understood: it was now fixed and made hereditary. Compact

[1] Cf. the discussion in Ch. v, p. 206.
[2] Cf. p. 180, below.

settlements of such German and Sarmatian peasant-soldiers are found —under the name of *terrae laeticae*—on the imperial domains of Northern Gaul. The villages of *milites limitanei* in the Alpine Provinces are akin to them.

A trustworthy estimate of the economic results of this policy of settlement can hardly be formed. From Britain, from the Mosel land and from Southern Gaul we have evidence of a still active and comfortable country life until about the year 400. But this prosperity can hardly be traced to the compulsions and demands of government. Britain had suffered less than other provinces from the troubles of the third century, and on the Mosel the capital city of Trier stimulated its environment. But the compulsions of Diocletian and Constantine had at least this influence: they introduced into rural economy types of organization and tendencies in development which would become basic in the future organization of rural settlement, and would so remain when the imperial power which imposed them had collapsed.

The most important fact in this connexion is that farming tenure as a rule became hereditary. That was as true of the *emphyteusis* tenant as of the *colonus*. The *colonus*, as contemplated by lawmakers, was the head of a family bound permanently to a given peasant home and a given piece of land. In the eye of the law this hereditary relation was not loosened by the fact that it rested on an indirect and dependent form of property. That a given piece of land should be held for generations by the same family was no novelty of that age; but it is important that from this time forward such a perpetual link between the peasant and the soil seemed general and normal.

Probably the fixing of the size of peasant holdings and of the economic services due from them were affected in the same way. Here too the compulsory imperial order may have influenced the coining and the spreading of standard arrangements. The peasant's holding had a standard estimated yield both in the economy of the state and in that of his lord. Claims from both left him with hardly any margin of produce to be sold freely in the town. The inclination of *coloni* to wander away, against which Constantine's legislation was directed, may have been due to their previously depressed economic position, which left them the barest living for their families when these claims had been met. On the other hand, it was the task of the state to guarantee to the peasant family this limited livelihood. The regular returns of *capitatio-jugatio* gave not only an occasion for, but a stimulus to, a genuine policy of peasant protection.[1] That the imperial administration really cared for the weak among the rural population is most clearly seen in the appointment of a *defensor plebis* in A.D. 365—just before the Empire collapsed.

[1] For the situation in the Byzantine East, see Ch. v.

No doubt too the military holdings of the *laeti* and other frontier troops on state land constituted typical small agricultural units of the class that the administration wished to encourage. Finally, the desire of both the state and the great landlords to recover land that had gone out of cultivation established a very important economic tradition, which as a general thing was new.

In short: during the century that followed Diocletian's reign the Empire pursued a policy of standardizing the conditions of peasant proprietorship and maintaining and extending the area under cultivation, as a measure of self-preservation. These tendencies had permanent significance: when the Empire had finally collapsed they still persisted. But they were not able to save it. Effective as they may have been in particular regions, they failed to repopulate the devastated frontier provinces. That was not possible because—in the West at least—imperial victories only held back the invasions of the Germans for a time. The Emperor Julian threw the Alemanni back from the middle Rhine but had to assign to the Salian Franks a compact area for settlement in the northern part of the provinces of *Germania Inferior*, on the Meuse. The ease with which masses of aliens were received into the Empire suggests how much it had been depopulated. Twenty years later, the Visigoths, fleeing before the assault of the Huns, found room south of the lower Danube in that province of Moesia which had once before been opened to people from the northern bank. And this time, as is well known, the experimental admission of solid masses of aliens led to a fatal catastrophe. It was the first step in the continuous advance of German armies across the Empire—with its devastating raids, usurpations of authority, organized occupations of the land, and those large-scale migrations which form the watershed between ancient and medieval history.

This, the most catastrophic episode in the history of European settlement, made fundamental changes in the occupation of the various regions of Europe, from the beginning of the fifth until far into the seventh century. We can only deal here with those acts of occupation which were decisive in determining the ethnographical map of the Middle Ages.

The Huns set in motion first the Goths and then the tribes in the heart of old Germany. They flooded into the Empire—in a memorable winter's night of the year 406 Vandals and Suevi, mixed with Alans from the steppes, crossed the Rhine on the ice to enter frontier districts which had been stripped of their Roman garrisons. A continuous emptying of old settled areas in the heart of Europe began which tempted the Huns, and later the Slavs, and then fresh waves of Mongols, to press forward into them. At about the same time the Salian Franks were able to move westwards from Limburg towards the lower Scheldt, then southwards up the Lys as far as Artois; and so won the starting point for their later imperial expansion. But the accord established after 418 between the government of Honorius and the Visigoths in Gaul had more direct influence on the establishment of the new world of nations. For the first time, the soil of a Roman province was allotted to a German tribe as an independent military organization and a recognized stratum of aristocratic landholders. Half a century later, this tribal settlement became that Visigothic empire which controlled the Iberian peninsula. But before that its political influence had affected the history of settlement in the remotest parts of Western Europe. The Roman Empire finally lost control of its remote northwestern provinces in Britain: the island was left open to the entry of Germanic tribal elements from the lands between the North Sea and the Baltic—Angles, Saxons and Jutes. This 'Anglo-Saxon' occupation of Britain gradually came to include something like the same area that Rome had once effectively controlled. The Celtic population was not merely conquered or driven into the West and North. Enterprising British leaders from Devon and Cornwall had a hand in the 'barbarian' occupation of Gaul, when they led their followers into Brittany. Meanwhile the emptied northern homes of the Teutonic conquerors of Britain—Jutland and its islands—were occupied by Danes from southern Scandinavia.

The decisive epoch in the history of settlement for Central Europe—old Germany and the adjacent Roman provincial regions on the Rhine and upper Danube—came with the end of the years of crisis during which Attila's empire threatened the whole European West. The victory on the Catalaunian plains did not only free Western Europe once for all from the Hunnish peril: it did away with the last hindrance to the spread of Germans from Central Europe. The Alemanni extended their settlements in all directions—into what were to become the Palatinate, Alsace, Switzerland and Bavarian Swabia. In the North, Franks from the middle Rhine crossed the stream to dispute with the Alemanni a frontier in the valley of the Moselle. In the East the Alemannic push impinged on the associated Thuringian tribes, who also were spreading out on all sides, and then on groups of Marcomanni, who moving forward from the land of the Boii in Bohemia brought with them the name of Boioarii. They and the Alemanni occupied Vindelicia and Rhaetia. At one and the same time the Danube and the Rhine ceased to be political frontiers or frontiers of settlement. Through the old Roman provinces new masses of warriors from Eastern Germany moved on towards Italy. Eastern Germany and Bohemia were left vacant for Slavonic tribes, who pressed forward across the Oder from their old homes north of the Carpathians. It was the Eastern Germans who in 476 brought about the formal end of the Empire in the West.

Its end helped to determine the division of the West among the conquering tribes. The Visigoths crossed the Pyrenees and took nearly all Spain from their Teutonic forerunners. In Gaul, the Salian Franks reached the Seine; and when the Empire had collapsed at Rome, Clovis founded in Gaul and on the Rhine the greatest state which the *Völkerwanderung* produced. For a time Theodoric the Ostrogoth, from Italy, kept the Franks in check. His successors were unable to do so. Burgundy, Alemannia, Thuringia and eventually Bavaria also came under Frankish control. The conquerors could not settle all the land that they controlled. But they spread far beyond their original territory. Northern Gaul down to the Marne and the Seine manifestly had a closely reticulated Frankish settlement. Between the Seine and the Loire it was less close, yet still important. In Germany, the Alemanni had to withdraw before the Franks to a boundary running from the forest of Hagenau and the northern promontories of the Black Forest east of it to the point where the transition from the Swabian to the Frankish Jura marks it to this day. So on their extreme south-eastern front the Franks had both Bavarians and Slavs as their neighbours. This projecting block of Frankish occupation—which left their tribal name as its permanent witness: Franconia—finally reached the Thuringian forest on the north; for the defeated Thuringians had to content themselves with the land between the Thuringian ridge, the Harz and the Unstrut. West of that, between the Diemel and the Eder, the tribal and imperial bounds of the Franks again coincided. In the Rothaar mountains and the Rhenish-Westphalian hill country their rule gave way to that of the independent Saxon tribal group. In the early days of their Empire the Franks did not try to conquer the Saxons, but joined with them in that conquest of the Thuringians which gave the Saxons the land north of the Unstrut as far as a point west of the junction of the Saale with the Elbe.

The settlement of these West and Central European boundaries was followed, shortly after the middle of the sixth century, by a rearrangement of those of the South and South-East. Justinian overthrew the Goths in Italy and brought their settlement there to an end. He tried to restore imperial authority throughout the Mediterranean and brought North Africa, Italy and parts of Spain for a time under his control. But in so doing he used up his military resources and especially his Illyrian veterans. Italy was insufficiently guarded, and in the East the threat of Slavs and horsed Mongolian Bulgars and Avars replaced that of the Goths. The Avars at the same time pressed on the only Teutonic tribal group which still lay east of the Alps in Pannonia, the Lombards from the Baltic. The year 568 was decisive in many ways: Alboin led his Lombards, with Sarmatian and Bulgarian allies, into Italy just when Byzantium was busy in Asia with the Persians. Slavs, driven or dragged forward by Mongol nomads, were impelled to occupy the mountainous marginal lands of the Hungarian plain. Between the Dinaric Alps and the Save, and between Save and Drave, came the Croats. Other groups of Slavonic settlers, the 'Slovenes', spread north-west into the foot-hills and valleys of the Eastern Alps—right to the edges of the Vienna basin, which the Avars held. Yet other Slavs, who, it appears, were likewise dependent on the Avars, gradually established themselves in Bohemia and on the plains north of the Central European mountains; for the westward and southward movement of the Germans had left these lands free. The Franks withdrew their pickets from the right bank of the Saale; and in course of time the Saxons left to the Slavs all the land up to the rivers Aller and Ilmenau and northward to the lower Elbe so far as a line terminating in the Gulf of Kiel. And so by far the greater part of Old Germany fell gradually to the Slavs.

Within two centuries, in every part of Europe peoples had poured into one another's areas of settlement. There is hardly a region in which we have not to take account of intensive changes of ownership. Natur-ally the process of exchange was never complete: many Germans, for example, must have remained in their ancient seats. In Gaul and Spain Roman landlords acquired a legally recognized position, by means of formal acts of division of property, after the Visigothic and Burgundian occupations. In Frankish Gaul, Roman proprietors were pressed down in the social scale but not systematically dispossessed; and the tradi-tion which ascribes a policy of extirpation to the Lombards in Italy seems, as a generalization, exaggerated.[1] Naturally there were far more dependent peasants who stayed on the land, or came back to it after a temporary flight, than there were survivors of the old landowning stratum. Often their numbers were added to by forcible subjection, demonstrably in Italy, but also elsewhere. The same fate befell surviving Celts in England—'welsh' became a name for the unfree—and conquered Germans in Germany, like the Thuringian subjects of the Saxons. The same thing must have happened to the German remnants in the lands occupied by Slavs.

These are some general traits in the transfer of population brought about by the great movement of peoples. The numbers and density of the newly settled stratum of conquerors varied almost *ad infinitum*. The Slavs must have occupied their vast area of settlement very lightly

---

[1] Paul. Diac. *Hist. Lang.* II, 31, 32. Criticism in Schneider, *Burg und Landgemeinde*, p. 35; Lot, *Hospitalité*, p. 1005.

indeed. But the number of German lords in South and South-West Europe was also small in proportion to the territory occupied. An estimate of the total number of Vandals and Alans in the year 429 is 80,000, including all the families; and the number of the Visigoths at the same date is believed to have been no more than that. The Franks, the Alemanni and the Anglo-Saxons, however, must have been much more numerous; that is certain, though we have no basis for numerical estimates.

This unequal distribution of Germans over the various parts of the Empire must not be taken as a decisive indication of inequalities in the treatment of the Roman or Celtic native populations, either by different conquering groups or in different provinces. Only the mounted nomads of the East, the Alans for instance, remained destroyers and plunderers long after their initial incursions. Everywhere the German occupation, even that of those Germans who accompanied the Alans in the invasion of Spain, finally took the form of permanent and agricultural settlement. But this sedentary phase was preceded nearly everywhere by a phase in which existing settlements were destroyed and their occupants plundered or scattered. Alemanni, Franks, Bavarians, Anglo-Saxons, all took possession of old settled districts in the lands that they conquered—but they always chose new sites for their dwellings.[1] That is clear proof of a temporal gap between conquest and settlement; and short as that gap may have been, it was still a time of devastation. The same thing is found even in those regions where Visigoths and Burgundians conceded a formal division of the land. There is indisputable evidence—for example in the *Poema conjugis ad uxorem* attributed to Prosper Aquitanus—that the Roman proprietors went through a period of the greatest uncertainty and impoverishment. The Burgundian laws for the division of land—diverging from the Roman quartering system—gave the new German proprietor two-thirds of the land, but only a third of the *mancipia* of the Roman proprietor (*Lex Burgund.* c. 56). This division seems at first hard on both parties: one gets land with inadequate labour power, the other more labour than he can use or maintain. But we may assume that the arrangement was intended to meet the needs of both. The labouring population had been scattered during the phase of devastation. The Roman required a majority of the survivors if he was to make a minor part of his property productive again quickly. But the German was accustomed to extensive agriculture and could manage a greater area with less labour.[2]

[1] There is so much detailed evidence to this effect that the author cannot accept Dopsch's assumption of continuity between imperial and medieval settlements. [See Dopsch's treatment of the subject in Ch. IV, below. Ed.]

[2] Different interpretations of the passage in the *Lex Burgund.* have been given hitherto.

Thus, this regulation is proof of a decline in the number of slaves as a result of the loosening of social bonds. This decline also created new labour conditions which were to become permanent. Indeed, in the German kingdoms on imperial soil the institution of the villa with its dependent holdings survived. And the villa still housed some slaves who worked on the land which directly belonged to it. But such slaves no longer formed the majority of the labouring force. The lord's 'own' land was kept in cultivation mainly by the services of tenants from the rest of his estate. Such services were in fact the principal payment which the tenant made for the land he held; they were more important than the *census*. The tenant might be a freeman, an *aldio* or *lite*, or a slave. These differences of status might be reflected in the size of his holding or the weight of his services; but they were of secondary importance compared with the universal association, for all classes of tenants, of tenure with service. This organized linking up of the cultivation of the 'demesne' with that of the holdings was not altogether unknown in Roman provincial life; but it was not at all widespread under the later Empire. It only became of fundamental importance after the *Völkerwanderung*. Obviously it grew up at a time when the administration of the *villa* was short of labour, and the control of labour was not easy. The Germans were familiar with slaves, freedmen and *liten* who had their own *penates*, as Tacitus said; now the dependent tenant owing services became the main support of the lord's establishment. In the former Roman provinces, peasant economy and settlement became still more important for the landlords than they had been under the emperors.[1]

The storms of the *Völkerwanderung* had another destructive effect which influenced the whole social and economic fabric of European life. They put an end to the system by which landowners, especially those of the middle sort, regularly lived in towns. The Germans had not lost their dislike of town life. So those Roman *possessores* who were able to hold their own with them were obliged to live regularly in the country. They did not move all at once; the narratives of Gregory of Tours and the verse of Venantius Fortunatus are still full of scenes from the lives of Gallo-Roman town-dwelling rentiers. But by Carolingian times this society has vanished away. It has been forgotten that, according to the Salic Law, the Roman was a second-class freeman—with only half a Frank's wergeld.[2] Evidently, by going into the country and mingling with the free Franks they had got rid of this mark of social

---

[1] Cf. p. 246, below.

[2] The literally degrading character of this rule cannot be explained away on merely technical grounds, as e.g. by Stutz (*Abh. Preuss. Ak.* 1934, Nr. 2). H. Brunner (*Deut. Rechtsgesch.* II, 614) had inclined to this view, but abandoned it in the main later (*loc. cit.* I, 2nd ed., 335 f.).

inferiority. It was not they who initiated the subsequent revival of town life.[1] Long before that the towns must have lost all real importance as consumers of agricultural produce: European rural society in the main was now working to feed itself.

One can distinguish in Western Europe three zones of agrarian settlement in relation to rural society after the *Völkerwanderung*. In Spain and Southern Gaul, the Visigoths; in the Rhone country and the Western Alps, the Burgundians; and in Italy the Ostrogoths, and the Lombards after them, appeared in place of or beside the Roman landlords. This was the first zone. The association of Burgundian ownership with the old-time estates is remarkably illustrated by the persistence of Celto-Roman place names. Settlement by the lesser German proprietors in village groups could hardly result from the way the land was divided in South-Western Europe. It would have agreed neither with the habits of life to which these 'faring men'[2] had become accustomed in decades of migration, nor with the ratio between their numbers and the wide regions which their leaders now controlled. As the Franks pressed on the Burgundians and curtailed their territory, population naturally became denser on what the Burgundians retained. A law of King Godomar provided for fresh divisions of the land and stipulated for more consideration of the Roman *possessores*. But that did not imply any creation of villages; and the early dissolution of the Burgundian realm stopped all further evolution. Lastly, the Lombard conquest of Italy came at a time when the Germanic *Hinterland* had already calmed down. So it also led in the main to the creation of lordships. The Lombard warriors for the most part settled *in fara*. The individual campaigning group which took possession of some estate was a band of blood-relations with their dependants. There were, however, peasant settlements scattered about the conquered land for political and military reasons. Roman military colonies of *milites limitanei* provided the model for the peasant community of the *arimannia*, into which some Lombards and perhaps more members of associated tribes were collected—*arimanniae* were established particularly on the Alpine frontiers and near urban centres; their peasant members were to defend important strategic points.

For the whole of this South and South-West European zone the early Germanic traditions of settlement had no significance. The incorporation of Southern Gaul in the Frankish Empire seems to have made no difference; and Visigothic Spain kept its native structure until the Arabs

---

[1] In view of these facts Pirenne and Vercauteren's explanation of the decay of town life in late Frankish times mainly by the growing difficulty of Mediterranean trade seems to me artificial.

[2] 'Faramanni', *Lex. Burg.* tit. 54, 2. Cf. F. Beyerle, *Germanenrechte* (*Ak. für deut. Recht*), x, 190.

overran it in A.D. 711. But the conditions were quite different in the northern parts of the old Roman Empire—those which Franks, Alemanni, Bavarians and Anglo-Saxons occupied. In this, the second great zone of settlement, the Germans were more numerous from the beginning and were reinforced decade after decade. There was opportunity here for the establishment of villages of the primitive type; and besides them the Germanic nobility—old nobles of blood or new nobles of service—got control of greater and more diversified estates.

The *Pactus Legis Salicae*, the codification of the laws of the conquerors of Northern Gaul compiled under Clovis, in its *Titulus de migrantibus* (45) pictures a vivid scene from the times of the wandering in which the 'Tacitean' village spring to life. Some Franks have settled down together on the land of a former Roman villa. A newcomer wants to join in and the earlier settlers are not agreed about his admission. The law decides that the veto of a single proprietor shall decide against him, even if 'one or several' want to admit him. The wording makes it clear that we are not dealing with a big village community. Some three or four neighbours, it would appear, are not agreed about the admission of a fifth.[1] We found the free German proprietors scattered over the land in just such groups in Tacitus' time—though the princely families might own whole villages. The grouping was now reproduced by the Franks on Roman soil. But the old communal disposal of shares in the land by the tribal assembly no longer existed: it was the individual body of settlers who had to agree about the division. And in the very first decades of its rise, the royal authority decides that the rights of the first settlers are not to suffice to exclude newcomers; for another section of the Law (*Tit.* 14, § 4) declares that the *migrans* must have his wish, if he comes recommended by the king. And breach of this rule is far more heavily punished than is the violation of a neighbour's veto on entry. Evidently this last was a new law of Clovis. We recognize those migrants who, after he had established his rule, straggled in from the lower Rhine and the first Salian-Frankish settlements on the lower Scheldt to the new headquarters of the Empire in 'France'. In the Walloon country, North France and Lorraine the Frankish occupation led to much more transference of property than on the lower Moselle, where most of the place names are Celto-Roman. It was to the king's advantage to encourage settlement in Gaul, though without unduly cramping the population already established there.

Considerable remnants of the native population must also have been preserved, to serve the king—who took over the Roman imperial lands —and his nobles on their estates. The Frankish noblemen preferred to

---

[1] This question of numbers has not been properly appreciated in the extensive discussions of the *Tit. de mig.*

settle in neighbourhoods which the Gallo-Roman nobility had chosen
before them. Their graves are found near the Roman roads, the rivers, the
old urban centres. Deep into Gaul—in Picardy, about Laon and Soissons,
in Normandy—this is more marked than in the regions near the later
linguistic frontier in Belgium, where place names indicate specially
dense German ownership. It is true that place names composed of a
personal name and the common Germanic name endings -*ingen* and
-*heim* point to ownership by Frankish chieftains. But probably in
places so named there were often both chieftains' settlements and settlements of free villagers, a large owner and a few smaller ones sharing
the village land. This type of place name disappears between the Seine
and the Loire, though archaeological evidence indicates plenty of
aristocratic settlement. The Frankish nobles were no longer accompanied by Frankish settlers.

The areas of final settlement by Alemanni and Bavarians had not been
so thoroughly Romanized as those of the Franks in Gaul. So we do not
find the geographical gradations that can be traced in France. But we can
trace the three typical ways in which old German settlement tradition
was transferred to Roman soil: the great compact estates of the privileged
families, the small village settlements of free tribesmen, and lastly the
groupings of such tribesmen's settlements about those of the privileged
families. Finds in the old *agri decumates* reveal splendid burials of great
men surrounded by more modest graves of the lesser men. And evidently that clause in the Law of the Alemanni (*Tit.* 86) which refers to
boundary disputes between families has this aristocratic structure of
society in view. Two *genealogiae* quarrel about boundaries. The local
count must occupy the disputed area and have the case settled by ordeal
of battle. How could quarrels arise in which the division of property
was so uncertain that only the ordeal could decide, and the matter in
dispute so important as to make the ordeal necessary? We are not
dealing with village squabbles about a balk that cannot be traced or an
overgrown footpath. The controversy is between large owners whose
properties march with one another in open waste land. Evidently the
initial division of land among the Alemanni largely applied to families
with very wide claims. The land originally assigned to them often lay
with its bounds against neighbouring settlements still undetermined,
even after several generations and several divisions of inheritance. But,
beside these *primi Alamannorum*, the law knows *mediani* and *minofledi*,
small owners. We cannot be quite sure that this division goes back to
the times of the *Völkerwanderung*. But at any rate the 'row burials' date
from those times. Among these village cemeteries are some which contain
no heavily armed and richly adorned noble remains but only those of
modestly equipped tribesmen. And in Württemberg there is a very

ancient type of village in which the property of a comparatively large homestead—the later *Rittergut* or *Meierhof*—consists of compact fields and meadows side by side with the cut-up peasant *Gewanne* of the villagers. But the contraction of the territory of the Alemanni, under pressure from West and North by the Franks, forced the majority of them to content themselves with modest properties in some small village settlement.

In Britain, east of the Welsh border beyond which the natives retained their independence, the small political groups which emerged from the Anglo-Saxon conquest established frontiers against one another. In each of them, and in each of the *folk* or *provinces* into which they were divided, there were from the first leading families with large property and ordinary tribesmen who reproduced the small German villages. Places lying close together whose names are compounded with the same personal name indicate large properties of early date. Occasionally a compact stretch of property, which was only gradually filled with settlements in the course of the Middle Ages, points to a similar primitive assignment of land, of the sort that led to disputes among the *genealogiae* of the Alemanni. But on the other side stands the evidence of c. 42 of Ine's Wessex law—every *ceorl* who has a share in arable and meadow, and sends cattle to the common pasture, must lend a hand in fencing the corn and hay to keep the cattle out. It is a freeman's village with no lord.

Yet the mixed village containing freemen and a lord's hall was obviously important in early Anglo-Saxon times. Place names of the personal name plus -*ingas* type are thickly scattered over Eastern England from York to Sussex, that is to say over the area earliest occupied by the Anglo-Saxons. The structure of the names evidently suggests the way in which the occupation had been organized—by a leader surrounded by ordinary tribesmen. At a later date, pure peasant villages were often distinguished from such half peasant, half noble, villages by the name Ceorla-tun (Charlton, Carlton). Anglo-Saxons were wary of settling too close to the ever-restless Welsh border. Here, agriculture continued to be carried on by small Celtic peasants living in hamlets which were thinly scattered over great stretches of waste. Elsewhere such hamlets of the conquered rarely survived, and only in regions which the conquerors did not prize—hilly or marshy land. British names have survived in such regions in Lancashire; and on the downs of Southern England archaeologists can trace the bounds of Celtic cornfields— groups of rough rectangles quite unlike the long strips of the Anglo-Saxon open-field. In the lower country these strips predominate: it was there that the conquerors settled and worked.[1] To what extent they

[1] Though it is quite superfluous to assume that the Celts had occupied only the higher ground.

utilized remnants of the Roman villa organization and of the colonate, unhappily we cannot ascertain.

We pass to the third zone of German settlement—the zone in which there were no Roman traditions and into which the *Völkerwanderung* only brought fresh German tribes in place of those that had moved away or been conquered. This includes the Frankish territory on the right bank of the Rhine and the lands of Frisians, Saxons, Danes and Scandinavians. Here there was no break with the 'Tacitean' tradition of settlement. Friesland was dominated by a markedly egalitarian division of property. Elsewhere the migration of so many fellow tribesmen to Gaul and Britain necessarily gave elbow-room to those who remained behind. Evidently for a very long time the families of those possessed of full tribal right controlled large compact holdings. Among the Chamavic Franks of the lower Rhine the title *homo Francus* long remained a monopoly of the upper stratum of freemen. Such well born people regularly had their own family forest (*Lex Franc. Cham. Tit.* 42). Further South among the Ripuarian Franks settlement is concentrated in the main into great properties geographically distinct from one another. Among the Saxons, the position of the leading families had been strengthened constitutionally and economically. They are the *edelinge* as opposed to the *frilingen*, and to the dependent soil-bound *laten*, who doubtless sprang from the conquered population. The *edelinge* had the right to divide among themselves the use of the waste and woodland that lay between the settlements. In Denmark the distinct property of the lord, the *ornum*, in the middle of the peasant community, has all the features that we have described—it is bigger than the peasant holdings; it is not mixed up with them; and it has special forest privileges. Finally, the *Odal* estates are of fundamental importance in the story of Norwegian settlement. Legally, they were subject to very strict rules of inheritance by collaterals. Geographically, the scattering of *Odal* homesteads thinly over the country was always characteristic.

It is these separate properties of an upper social stratum that we must have in mind when, in various regions, we come across evidence of some connexion between the bond of neighbourhood and the blood tie. The leading families had often reserved to themselves great continuous stretches of land with the definite intention that their descendants should live together on them. That is, as we have seen, the explanation of the Alemannic *genealogiae*. The life of an Anglo-Saxon saint of the tenth century translates *provincia* by *maegth*. The district is held together by the unity of a leading family. Something similar is indicated, when, in the Latin version of a Northern saga, a king demands the cession of twelve *gentes*. In another saga the principle is laid down that 'we should regard and treat brothers' land as undivided'.[1]

The development of such group settlement by noble families was interrupted or checked whenever noble property was being increased by generous grants from the king. The evolution of a feudal society made land granted by the king the principal element in the landed property of the nobility; and such grants always had to remain in a single hand. Feudal society evolved on Frankish territory; that explains why there are fewer traces of ancient settlements of noble blood relations there than elsewhere. On the other hand, it was without doubt in the Merovingian Empire that those forces first gained strength which dominated the course of settlement in Western Europe during the whole of what we call the Middle Ages—the forces of the peasantry.

When the nations came to rest after their wanderings, the characteristic medieval peasantry came into existence—not as a single uniform social stratum but in two distinct primary divisions, which were however pressed closer and closer together in course of time. There were the tenants who owed services on some lord's estate, but acquired thereby secure holdings of their own. And there were the small freemen, members of a village community settled on the village fields. Originally they were both in rank, and as landholders and sharers in common rights, in a decidedly better position than their more servile fellows. But gradually their economic position was assimilated to that of the dependent peasants. Their numbers grew from generation to generation and there was no more land to maintain them. Once the settlement was completed, the descendants of the first settlers had not the mobility that their forefathers, the 'faring men' of the great wanderings, had enjoyed. Everywhere the existing division of the land was guaranteed by a powerful public authority: small freemen had no chance of improvising an occupation of 'foreign' land. So most of them became simply 'peasants'. At first the average Frank in Gaul, or Anglo-Saxon in Britain, may have lived much as his ancestors did among their German forests; if he were fortunate, as a small 'lord' who had been able to get a few slaves or freedmen as tenants, without ceasing to work on the land with his family. But as generations succeeded one another conditions worsened. The need for unceasing work determined the small owner's way of life. In the end he might not have enough land to live by, and might have to get some from a lord—either paying rent for it or doing work for it like a dependent holder. The diminishing reserves

---

[1] The often quoted phrase of a Bavarian formula, *in vico et genealogia*, seems less convincing. It may only refer to village names of the type 'personal name *-ingen*'. Possibly the *Kluften* of Dithmarschen and Frisia sprang from primitive family group settlement; but the date of their origin is uncertain.

of land only came into the hands of the common man through those of
the nobility and the church, to whom the kings made the initial grants.
Beside those districts in which archaeological evidence, or the prevalence of place names in *-ingen* and *-heim*, suggest an early occupation,
lie districts of North-East France—to about as far south as Orleans—
of place names in *-court*, *-ville* and *-villers*; in the Rhineland and South
Germany of places in *-weiler*, *-weil*, *-wyl*. These names indicate aristocratic settlement: the occurrence both west and east of the Rhineland
of the Roman *-villare* termination with a Teutonic personal name
points to the spread of the Frankish nobility over the whole empire.
Further it is noticeable that the places in question grew up on what had
once been royal land. The power of the crown rested on that of the
nobles and the clergy; and it had to leave local authority to them. For
that very reason the small freeman was obliged to seek their protection
more and more. His function as fighting man and member of the
tribal community dwindled into insignificance: his life became just a
part of that of his village.

Meanwhile there was need for more homesteads on the occupied
land. They might be established in one of two ways. The villages
might be allowed to grow; or dependent hamlets and homesteads
might be created. The second method was more in harmony with old
German tradition than the first. So we find it applied in the land of the
Alemanni; while in much of that settled by the Franks a tendency to
the creation of bigger villages is conspicuous. In the village of dependent
tenants under a lord the multiplication of households went further. On
the lord's domains in France, where the Roman administrative tradition
was still active, there grew up compact settlements whose arable in
Carolingian times contained many hundreds of hectares. The *terra
indominicata*, which as a rule lay apart from the 'tenancies', was near a
lord's 'court' and a big village. In external appearance the villages in
which traces of Roman provincial life survived differed from the new
ones that grew up on German soil. They were more compact, more
easily supervised: they were grouped about a central space, or laid out
in regular lanes; while the German and English village types have been
labelled by modern scholars 'thrown together' villages (*Haufendörfer*)
or 'nucleated', but not ordered, villages.[1]

We cannot follow the growth and remodelling of villages from
generation to generation. We only begin to get any documentary
picture of the results from the eighth century. They show us something
of the proprietary relationships and of the economic life of the village,
dominated by the system of standard units of peasant property, the

[1] But the primitive Anglo-Saxon village excavated at Sutton Courtenay had houses
in rows.

open-field system, and the regulated use of commons. From the seventh century at the latest, measurements of property and of obligations to a lord, or to the taxing authority, were made in units of *Hufen*, hides, *mansi* and so on. The underlying ideas are reflected in Bede's translation of the Anglo-Saxon hide as *terra unius familiae*, and in the Latin *mansus*, which originally implied not the land but the homestead. And this gives us both ends of the peasant scale. For no doubt the original hide was the respectable holding of a free peasant family; on the other hand the *mansus* was a unit in the organization of a seigniorial group; and *Hufe* is only directly applicable to rented land. All the family's claims to pasture, woodland and water are part of the standard unit. But the name of the unit is also applied to the normal extent of its landed property, and in particular to its arable.[1]

When land was first taken over at the time of the *Völkerwanderung* such uniform standards were hardly yet in use. The *Lex Salica* knows nothing about them. When the law *de migrantibus* leaves the decision about the entry of a new member into a rural group now to the group and now to the king, it shows clearly that there were as yet no normal units of agricultural property. Evidently the unit system had its roots in local custom; and the evolution of the village is reflected in it. The standardization of representative holdings, especially of the arable holdings, became necessary when the soil that served a given group of settlers had to feed more households. Such units were required in comparing the new holdings, which now became necessary, with those already in existence.

This reckoning by *Hufen* or hides is found closely associated later with the open-field system; the strips of a holding scattered over the furlongs form parts of hides, which are also so scattered. That association also goes back to this period of social and political consolidation—and the open-field system itself is a product of the development of the village. As households increased and more land was brought under the plough, whilst all lived together in the same village, it was not the natural thing to give one heir all his land near to the dwelling houses, and another all his in a remote and newly cultivated part of the fields; symmetrical results were achieved by giving each his share of old and new land. The resultant dismemberment of property made the peasants highly dependent on one another for any improvement or regulation of agriculture; and so grew up that familiar handling of village economy on a communal basis which was associated with the open-field system down to modern times.

That law of Ine of Wessex (*circa* A.D. 700) which strengthened the obligation of the villagers to assist in the fencing of corn and hay fields

[1] Cf. the discussion on p. 201.

points towards the beginnings of village growth and the development of the open-field. The growth of village population and the breaking up of the shares in property necessitated the regulation of common duties and their enforcement by fines. But it was unusual for a king to assist the village community in this way. That community had developed spontaneously and as a rule enforced its economic discipline itself. The fact of its being organized affected the whole area. It led to the fixing of the boundaries of the various communities. The different villages or groups of settlers were still divided from one another so far as possible by tracts of country that were useless, or nearly so—forest, thorn-brake, marsh. In these wastes boundaries were determined: the process can be traced in eighth- and ninth-century England and in descriptions of German marks. The villagers had always used land not required for the plough as pasture; and the forest round about the utilized land had supplied them with timber and pannage. These customs of user, with those of water, came under communal control, and the rights of the various proprietors were determined by the community. But by no means all waste land belonged to communes and was divided between them. From the beginning, privileged property had privileged claims on such areas. When we hear of 'members of a mark' who have shares in them, although the bounds are not properly determined, the rights in question are very often not those claimed by some commune, but are privileged rights of single great proprietors who live near the area in question and so are its 'mark men'. Moreover large forests and wastes were often reserved for the greatest proprietors, for the king above all. In the Frankish Empire the conception of 'forest' was based on this royal ownership of the woods.

For the whole evolutionary process here described, an economic change that affected the greatest and smallest establishments alike—an increased interest in the yield of the land, and above all in its yield of bread corn—was just as fundamental as the pressure towards immobility which political consolidation brought with it. The Germans of this period had Roman tradition to thank for the extension of meadows, gardens and vineyards. The increased importance of corn growing can certainly be traced to the same influence, although the Germans may already have been familiar with all the principal varieties of grain.[1] Arable farming came only slowly to full recognition as against cattle farming. The Merovingian kings preferred to levy tributes of cattle on conquered territory both in Gaul and Germany: they recall Tacitus' Germans who rejoiced in the numbers of their herds. It was not yet taken for granted that the Anglo-Saxon *Gesithcundman*, who received

[1] Cf. p. 159, below.

land from the king for service in the *comitatus*, would keep it so far as possible under the plough: King Ine had to protect himself carefully against such warriors deserting him and leaving half, or more, of the hides that he had entrusted to them untilled (c. 64). But very early records reveal the change of waste land into arable—by the clearing of forests. There is Burgundian and Visigothic legislation of the sixth century relating to *exarta*, 'assarts'. From that time, all through the history of medieval settlement and colonization, the progress of clearing, the growing contraction of forest in favour of tillage, is with us. It is the countryman's preliminary task, the task by which he makes fresh landed property.

Hitherto we have had little to say about clearing as a basic factor in the history of settlement. The Romans, and those provincials whom they educated, only rarely had occasion to curtail the woodlands; and the Germans never deliberately embarked on any such undertaking. We noted a greater interest in clearance in later imperial times, after the devastations of the third century and the first barbarian inroads. But there was not then any attack on ancient forests, only on the woods that had crept over neglected agricultural land. When we hear of clearing in the earliest medieval times, it is probably of this kind of clearing that we must think: brushwood had to be got rid of on neglected provincial soil. In Merovingian times monasteries were deliberately founded on such 'tumbled-down' land. There was also the leisurely clearing of the forest verges to get more pasture, which reduced the waste zones between the settlements. 'Brabant' was originally a name for such zones: in the Belgian province that bears the name, a province already settled in Roman times, hundreds of Frankish settlements appeared from the end of the sixth century. A third and higher stage then set in, what we call clearing in the special sense—the felling of great stretches of primeval forest and undergrowth in the thick woods. This stage was reached in Carolingian times; we must assume that it resulted from secular experience of the other, and easier, types of clearing. So the Germans had become fit for the task to which Joshua in the Bible urged the children of Joseph: 'if thou be a great people, then get thee up to the wood country, and cut down for thyself there' (Ch. 17, v. 15).

It was not only the need to make room for new settlements that encouraged clearing. There was another motive inciting peasants who were still clumsy and ignorant of how to make the best use of land to attack the forest—the unpleasant discovery that land already in use did not fulfil expectations, or the fear of such a discovery. The Bavarian law book of the eighth century deals at length with quarrels over the possession of *pratum vel agrum vel exartum*, in which both parties speak of the labour that they have expended on the land in dispute. One has just put it into cultivation. His opponent explains that he once inherited it, and cleared it and weeded it (*Tit.* 17; I, 12). Such disputes would not have been possible unless many pieces of land had once been under the plough and then long neglected.

Clearing is no doubt one of the processes that the Germans learnt in the conquered provinces from Roman neighbours and dependants. Churchmen stood high among their teachers. For, precisely in the transition period from the Roman Empire to the Teutonic domination, the Church was brought into close contact with agriculture. All she could now expect from the state was gifts of property and land to use. It was her task to see that what she got became productive. Survivors of the Roman aristocracy gladly accepted ecclesiastical office and added their own estates to those of the Church. They were living supporters of the Roman traditions of estate ownership and estate management. The poems of Venantius Fortunatus make clear in charming fashion how thoroughly at home an Italian felt in the houses of his ecclesiastical hosts in Gaul. One of them, Bishop Leontius of Bordeaux, he praises especially because he had turned a villa of his from a wolf-haunted waste into a place where men could dwell once more (*Carm.* I, 81).

The care of the bishops was supplemented by a special function of the monasteries. It would be a misconception of the monastic spirit to speak of colonizing monks in this era. Monks had to seek remote waste places in order that they might more completely shun all worldly things and convert the neglected souls to be found there. It was not their business to make the waste place habitable or to feed its lost sheep with agricultural knowledge. But to go into the wastes of Central Europe was a different thing from going into those of the Mediterranean lands from which monasticism came into the regions of Germanic settlement. There, waste meant forest and marsh which called for hard labour if they were to support even the simplest life. So it was fortunate that monastic teachers in the Roman Church had decided that monks had both a right and a duty to work on the land. St Augustine had maintained that such work was not a mere consequence of the curse on fallen man, but was part of his natural calling as a gardener in Eden; and that therefore it was in full accord with the holy life of the monk. And the rules of Benedict of Nursia required *opera manuum cotidiana* as a check upon *otiositas inimica animae*. In the West, the Irish monks under Columba first planted monasteries in waste places; but from the seventh century they were followed by Benedictine houses. Over and over again the monks established themselves in wooded and little settled regions, and so took an active part in the work of clearing.

But their indirect influence on settlement was more important than their direct influence. As they pushed into the woodlands and felled the trees they helped to dispel that religious awe which the Germans had to overcome before they would attack thick forest. The attraction of the Church's miraculous powers was transferred to the holy men in the woods, and brought the laity to settle near them. And lastly, the landowner who wished to acquire merit by a gift to the Church preferred and might even be obliged to give a piece of land that he had cleared for some ecclesiastical foundation. The two motives last referred to worked with special strength in the Frankish Empire from the time when a great access of relics to the monasteries began—about the middle of the eighth century. St Gallen, Lorsch, Fulda, and rather later Werden on the Ruhr, received gifts which soon made them rich proprietors. All of them got much cleared land. The first charters of Werden show vividly how the provident Abbot Liudger exhorted the laity to use the *comprehensio*, which belonged to them as fully qualified members of the mark, for clearings in the interest of his monastery.

By admitting peasant settlements to their neighbourhood, and especially by the struggle to increase their own lands, the monasteries—set up at first in 'the wilderness'—completely changed their environment and themselves. Their practice was assimilated to that of those centrally placed churches and monasteries which were the leading supports of seigniorial organization and agriculture in Carolingian times. The position in 'the wilderness' was often only a fiction—a legal description which monasteries accepted to make their property unassailable. The assimilation could not fail if the Church wanted to evangelize the masses. Winfrid (Boniface), the Anglo-Saxon who organized the rule of Christianity in the heart of Germany systematically, also gave a powerful stimulus to the foundation of settlements in association with the churches. And altogether apart from any alleged secularization of the Church, the churches had a sustained need for extensions of the land at their disposal. They had to balance losses of property to the feudal nobility. They had often to feed the king and his train, and always the poor and needy; and for this they must dispose of food supplies. Lastly, the network of parishes had to be enlarged. For all this, clearing had to supplement the tithe; and the more clearing the more tithe. So the needs of the Church harmonized admirably with the craving of small freemen and peasants for fresh property. In Carolingian times the *precaria* was utilized with special frequency in the case of forest or waste land handed over to laymen to be cleared.

The state as well as the Church wished to extend settled land and increase the number of settlements in the heart of Europe. From the eastern German frontier wars of conquest were waged; and for the first time in this region conquest carried with it the need to secure the conquered country and its *Hinterland* by regular colonization. The first princes who were active in this way were not the Frankish kings themselves but their independent sub-princes, the Bavarian Agilolfinger. They had pushed into Slovene land in the Alps and along the Danube and made use of the Church as a colonizing agent. That was the start of Passau and Salzburg. Duke Tassilo founded the monastery of Kremsmünster with the express object of administering and extending land newly won in the Danube valley.

In the North and just across the Frankish frontier, Charlemagne's conquest of the Saxons gave a fresh impetus to clearing and settlement. True, we do not hear of the king clearing conquered land to secure his position: for that end he used depopulation. And the establishment of the new north-east boundary against the Slavs was a military not a colonizing measure: across the Elbe and the Saale a chain of forts was created, some of them on Slavic soil. But behind the former Eastern frontier, on both sides of the middle and lower Rhine, in Hesse and along the Main, a pushing back of the forests set in at this time owing to the fact that the recent conquests made this region for the first time a part of the central imperial mass. The forest of the Ardennes lost its primeval character in the east, about Luxemburg. A capitulary of the year 813 from Aachen instructed the royal agents to select people competent to do clearing work. In view of the reluctance of the crown to undertake clearings on its 'French' estates, we may connect this encouragement with German territory, and especially with that along the lower Rhine. In the Hessian hill country the colonizing activity of the monastery of Fulda may certainly be connected with a desire to encourage closer settlement along this Frankish frontier in the heart of Germany. Here too we find a Saxon supporter of Charles and the Church organizing clearings and settlements. Further to the South-West, the mark survey of Heppenheim shows that just before A.D. 800 the Odenwald was not much cultivated; but shortly afterwards it contained many *Bifänge* (assarts). It was probably in this region that the so-called 'forest' village (*Waldhufendorf*) first developed in Germany.[1] Its layout differed fundamentally from that of the traditional nucleated village with its open fields. The houses were not crowded together: they stood in an orderly row along the street. The holdings were not scattered over the furlongs: their subdivision was avoided, and there was no thorough-going common use of the woodland. Behind each of the houses, its land stretched in a long continuous strip, reaching into and including part of the wood. Villages of this sort were most naturally

[1] The same type of village is found in France, and the place of absolute origin is unknown: there may have been more than one place.

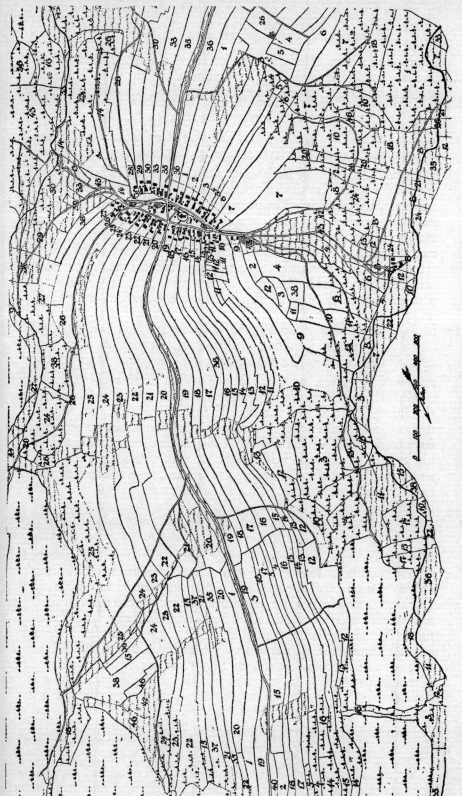

FIG. 2. A 'forest' village (*Waldhufendorf*), Effeltern in Franconia.

set up when settlers in hilly country wanted to acquire as much arable land as possible. The settlement was laid out along the valley bottom; and each landholder slowly acquired his arable by working up to the wooded heights.

Everywhere the Church had a share in the newly won land, and its intervention was of great advantage to the state. The surviving charters do not tell us how far seats and estates of the nobles were established by clearing. In any case the place names in -weiler, which in France were associated with the creation of noble property, are found in the cleared regions of Germany; and the names of fortified places are also often met with on old forest land. The increased military power which the Empire required in the East called for an increasing number of fighting men's residences.

So in the time of Charlemagne and his successors, in the German parts of the Empire, all the socially powerful elements were concerned with the extension of settled land on forest soil—peasants and small proprietors, spiritual and secular lords. But each section had its own interests; and the competition among them was shown in many significant ways as clearing went forward. The lords had to see to it that land of theirs which was suitable for clearing did not fall into the hands of peasant communities, but was cultivated under their own guidance and control. The words *Beunde*, *clausura*, *septum*, all of which—as sometimes also *Bifang*—refer to land marked out for cultivation outside village territory, reflect this policy of theirs. The crown meant to secure a share of the yield derived from the utilization of forest land which it had granted to men who made arable out of it. This *Medem*, usually a seventh of the yield, is often referred to in grants from late Carolingian times. The Church was obliged to deal with the tithe owed from cleared land, and to arrange for divisions of tithe between the older churches and the new parishes on it. As cultivation was everywhere making progress, the great spiritual and lay lords who wanted to get their forest land occupied found themselves obliged to offer specially favourable terms in order to attract colonists. About the middle of the ninth century we find that the standard peasant holding on land won by clearing was the bigger *Hufe*. It was first worked out on royal land, and so was called in later times the *Königshufe*. Charlemagne helped to augment the labour supply in Frankish territory by settling Saxon hostages there. That the labour supply had often to be reapportioned between old and new cultivated land is shown by an ordinance of Louis the Pious, which threatened the vassal who neglected his *beneficium* in the interest of his hereditary land with loss of the *beneficium*.

The vigorous expansion of the area under occupation which is reflected in all these episodes was not always thoroughly economic in this period either, as the last case quoted shows. No doubt the continuity of cultivation in the old village fields was increasingly secured. The two- and three-field rotation systems developed; and the scattered holdings of the open-field made it almost essential that the individual peasant should observe the regular times for working them. But land won by clearing was not immediately so much cut up as the old fields: here the settler was not under the control of his neighbours. So in the older cultivated countries it was not in the lord's interest to give peasants as great freedom to attack the woods as they had in the heart of Germany. Besides, the claims of the chase opposed any such freedom. This is how we must explain the cautious, even obstructive, treatment of forest clearing in the classical documents of royal and ecclesiastical estate management during Carolingian times. The documents deal primarily with the old settled regions: mainly with France. It was here that the strict forest law was developed which forbade any curtailment of the forests without the king's consent, even in districts which had already passed from the crown to the Church or the nobility. The *capitulare de villis* of Charlemagne's time, the clauses of which bearing on this point refer to all the western side of the Frankish Empire, definitely puts the protection of forests before clearing: there may be clearing in appropriate places, but the fields are not to grow at the expense of the woods (c. 36).[1] Abbot Irminon of St Germain-des-Prés, in those decades of his administration which are surveyed in his *Polyptychon*, had only undertaken clearing at two points in the widely scattered possessions of his monastery—and at two other points he had allowed new forests to grow up. So far as the lords could control the cultivation of the land, they seem to have extended it in open country, not on forest soil.

It was evidently such extensions that made room for a class of tenants who were to play a particularly important part in the later history of French settlement, the *hospites*. We meet them first on the estates of St Germain. Irminon vacillated between the word *hospes* and the statement that a *colonus*, a *colona*, or a *servus* had a *hospicium*. The *hospes* and the *hospicium* are allied. The primary meaning of *hospicium* is just 'house', or in a rural context 'peasant household'. But words—as their use indicates—involve the thought of *hospitare*, to settle or provide with a dwelling. In the vernacular *hospicium* and *hospitare* were translated by *herbergement* and *herberger*. So a *hospes* of St Germain is a man whom the monastery has furnished with a house on its estates. As a rule he will be an immigrant to those estates. Yet the term does not in itself imply that the settler is a 'guest' or 'foreigner'. And as first used it had no connexion with clearing. Of the two 'manors' of St Germain

[1] This interpretation has been disputed, but appears to be correct.

in which clearing had been carried out, one had only four *hospites* and the other none at all.

The position of the *hospes* on the estates of St Germain is marked by the fact that originally he had nothing but his *hospicium*, his dwelling; but no doubt this was his heritable property. Besides it, he regularly received an allotment of land, with which some obligation to work on the lord's land might be associated. The land was not necessarily heritable and its extent might be altered by the lord. No doubt the lord used this sort of tenure because he did not always want to commit himself to definite assignment of *mansi* and allotments when developing his estates. This meant that at first the *hospites* were by no means the best placed peasants in the seigniorial group: there were unfree as well as free men among them. But there was always a certain social advantage in the possession of the little homestead. In the rank and size of holding, the *hospes* might be compared with the cottar or border of Domesday Book. His holding need not be somewhere on the outskirts of the village land: sometimes on the lands of St Germain *hospites* were assigned to the parish church for its maintenance. But they seldom held a whole *mansus*. Indeed the *mansus* unit was in decay during Carolingian times in France. Terms such as *manselli* or *curtiles* indicate already the rise of smaller normal units for peasant holdings.

Charlemagne's later years presented new, and in part similar, problems of colonization both on the extreme French and the extreme German frontiers of his Empire. After the defeats of the Saracens and the Avars the Empire was faced with the problem of providing military defence and economic reconstruction in the wide regions which it had won from its enemies: they were now desolate. For their military and political administration the *Markgraf* was instituted. When Charlemagne died the Spanish Mark reached to the Ebro. It retained that boundary until the middle of the ninth century. The East Mark embraced the Danubian lands from the Enns to the extreme limit of the Eastern Alps, and on the Hungarian plains to the great bend of the Danube. The Danube valley had been settled only thinly under the rule of the Avars: Frankish ways of carrying on war had left it an utter waste. So was the Spanish Mark; and even the adjacent 'French' province of Septimania had suffered terribly.

Therefore resettlement had to be undertaken quickly and carried on for decades at both points. The methods were much the same in the Western and Eastern Marks. The conquering armies were no longer made up of landless warriors, as they had been when the Empire was founded. There was no question of mass settlement by small proprietors. Natives and neighbours of the two regions formed the bulk of the population; but they were to a large extent subjected to new lords. For the crown took advantage of the opportunity to claim the conquered territory for itself, as having no lord, and to make generous grants from it to the Church and the nobility. In order to quicken the pace of settlement, it authorized its grantees to occupy waste land in the neighbourhood of their estates. The Bavarian churches and monasteries were entrusted with this mission in the East Mark. On both sides of the Pyrenees new monasteries were founded and they threw off cells as centres of economic activity. The creation of lay property was closely associated, both in Septimania and Spain, with the military organization of the frontier. The owners—called *Hispani* even in the Septimanian zone of settlement—received their land under the legal form of *adprisio*, which gave them a heritable claim in exchange for the duty of personal military service. Their tenure was thus akin to feudal tenure; but beside the great noblemen, peasants were given land under this same form of *adprisio*. There were *minores* and *inferiores* mixed with the *milites* or *maiores*, though all were settled fighting men. The social position of the *minores* recalls the Lombard *arimanniae* and the Byzantine soldiers' holdings established by Heraclius.[1] In the East Mark there was no analogy with this linking of military organization to the establishment of small holdings. There the principal supply of labour came from the Slavic Alpine inhabitants, who willingly undertook the work of forest clearing. German colonists also are found settling among them. Evidently the land had the same attraction for settlers from adjacent Bavarian territory as the land about Lake Constance had for Alemannic settlers, at this time and earlier: there was space enough to build little hamlets in which each settler had a respectable holding. The settlers were welcome because they contributed to the security of the country, to its Christianization, and to the yield of the tithe, which the newly converted Slavs paid only grudgingly. The oldest surviving account of a settlement based on the big '*Königs*' *Hufen* refers to a little village in a clearing in an eastern gateway of the Alps which had been established on royal land and then given to the church of Salzburg: *ad Labenza ad Wisitindorf de terra exartata . . . mansos integros VIII, id est ad unamquamque coloniam jugera XC.*

The colonization of the Spanish Mark and of the East Mark went on in this fashion until the time of Charlemagne's grandsons. Meanwhile the Frankish Empire was breaking down. By 900 'France' and 'Germany' were beginning to form. At the same time the whole of the West, as the migrations of the fifth and sixth centuries had left it, was continuously and fearfully shaken by new movements of the peoples outside, on the north, on the south, on the east. It is time that we looked beyond the Frankish Empire.

[1] See below, Ch. v, p. 207.

In England, conditions were not favourable to so varied and vigorous an extension of settlement in forest and waste as in Germany at the time when it was completely dominated by the Franks. The little Anglo-Saxon kingdoms lacked the powerful organizing force of a strong state. Progress in clearing depended on peasant initiative. Perhaps only comparatively few peasants had the requisite enterprise; but here and there a good deal was accomplished. Place names in *-field* and *-wood* record the growth of new settlements in the 'marks' of the old villages before the Danish invasions. Sometimes the name records the man who did the work; and then we may think of one of those driving peasants who 'throve so that he had fully five hides of his own land, church and kitchen, bell-house and burhgate'; and so deserved the rank of thane.

The Teutonic North—the Danish Islands, Jutland, Sweden and Norway—was far more backward. The interior was in every case thickly wooded; and the people clung to their inherited religious awe of the woods. There is a Saga that tells of a king who ordered clearings in Wärmland. The Gods punished him with a failed harvest and his men killed him as a sin offering. Ancient villages not established in clearings are called, in the later Swedish law, 'villages of pagan times' in so many words. Peasant discipline was developed and extended in the open regions, in the *Wang*. The practice of *solskifte* had probably been evolved in those pagan times: it lays down that, when a field has become so large that it cannot be taken in at a glance, the plots shall be reassigned according to the 'points of the compass'.[1] It was made for growing villages—and the fact that the village grew meant that men had not room enough in the land. Starting from this simple discontent, the Northmen developed a power which opened to them immeasurable distances. They were a whole people of warriors. The spirit, on the religious side, was revealed in the worship of Odin, the God of those who fall in battle. On the social side, we see it shown in the high value set on warlike fellowship, and the unquestioned belief that the most honourable and manly way of acquiring wealth was by looting after victory. Moreover, unlike the West Europeans, the Northmen were not mere agriculturists; as wandering traders they had acquired great mobility at sea. Beyond the seas they could choose the point to raid, to conquer, perhaps to colonize. From the end of the eighth century they had become conscious of this superiority; and the Viking age had begun.

The eastern neighbours of the Germans and the western and northern neighbours of the Anglo-Saxons—Slavs and Celts—were in this era not nearly so close to the Teutonic peoples in social and economic organiza-

[1] Cp. p. 645, n. 2, below.

tion as they had been in the age before the great *Völkerwanderung*. Among both Slavs and Celts tribal organization was dominated by the blood relationship of the agnatic group. Among the Celts, and probably also among the Western Slavs, this blood relationship also dominated the way of settlement. In Wales, Scotland and Ireland the land was divided among clans and septs, each under the strict patriarchal rule of its chieftain. The groups of cousins into which they were subdivided (*gwelys*, i.e. beds) were also groups of settlement. The families of a group either shared great common dwellings, or lived close together in little hamlets, except when—as notably in the Scottish Highlands— they were scattered in separate homesteads over the whole territory of the clan. The land of each clan was in principle the common property of its members. So far as it was pasture, it was shared among the households of the clan according to their graded rights. The arable was similarly shared; but the division was not permanent, nor the shares heritable. According to the law of the Irish *tanistry*, a chief divided the land afresh when the membership of his group had changed. This variable assignment of arable to a household assumed that agriculture was entirely subordinate to pastoral activities. Neither the social nor the economic organization of the clan allowed a true peasant population to evolve. The clans were warlike territorial groups which readily fought one another. The upshot of the fighting often was that whole clans sought distant pastures. After the end of the sixth century such migrations were confined to the Celtic regions; Celts from Ireland often moved into Scotland.

We have only very uncertain and scrappy knowledge of social conditions among the Slavs before about A.D. 1000. But those *generationes*, which according to Cosmas of Prague formed the basic units of Czech society, were organized patriarchally like the Celtic clans, and must have been settlement groups. Probably we must assume something similar in neighbouring and kindred lands. Among all these peoples, agriculture was a subordinate activity. They did not learn from their German neighbours to use the heavy wheeled plough: they tilled all land, light and heavy, with a sort of wooden hook. Probably most free Slavs were accustomed to work for their living. Yet their economic energies were very undeveloped. The most prominent and best attested feature of their primitive state is their failure to make full use of what labour supplies they had. They sold them in bulk to strangers: the word slave, which is found in use among the Arabs of Spain as well as in all Teutonic and Romance languages, is the legacy of this export of men. And the economic carelessness which lay behind it is clearly shown by the fact that these slaves worked excellently for their alien masters in most varied conditions. As landworkers they were tested by Byzantine emperors in Asia Minor and Bavarian dukes on the Danube. Considering the vast spaces available for the Slavs, this export of men must have left settlement very thin. So there was no inclination to spread out beyond those spaces. The superficial use of the land is indicated by the instability of the individual settlements of the Slavs on the central European plain. Within the areas recognized as theirs, the little villages of wooden huts were often shifted about. Fortified central sites were more permanent. They were a regular and essential element in the organization of Slavonic settlement: we find the name Belgrad ('the white fort') in the Serbo-Croatian land, on the Pannonian plain, and on the Baltic. The sites preferred were those with natural protection—heights, river mouths, islands in swamps. And at least the more important forts were 'residential': privileged members of the tribe had quarters there.

So far we have been occupied with lands and peoples whose agrarian civilization must be rated lower than that of the least developed parts of the Frankish Empire. To these, the Mediterranean lands present the sharpest possible contrast: in them the classical agrarian civilization was able to survive all political and racial changes. True, in Lombard Italy at the time of its incorporation in the Empire of Charlemagne the urban element in the classical organization of settlement had not yet reacquired its old importance. Landowners still lived almost exclusively in the country. We have seen already how, side by side with the great proprietors, the free peasant communities of the *arimanniae* helped to maintain the area under cultivation. Besides, the classical form of lease for the utilization of neglected land, the emphyteutic lease, had not lost its importance. But it was no longer employed to establish big holdings. From the ninth century we find it used mainly for the planting and care of vineyards. The tenant gets very good terms. For a series of years (six, in the earliest instance) he pays no rent at all; later a reasonable yearly sum or share of the produce.

But the Western land in which a plantation system was most widely promoted during this era was Spain. Its Arab rulers took the greatest interest in fine and exacting crops. Artificial irrigation, already well known in Spain, was improved and extended by them on oriental models; its superintendence was the business of the state. On the east coast it was employed for rice and sugar-cane, elsewhere for orchards and gardens. The native labour supply was supplemented from Africa, by men of the race whose military qualities had made the conquest possible, the Berbers. Disappointed and refractory veterans, they gave their lords plenty of trouble; but after Abdar-Rahman I had established the Emirate of Cordova with a Berber army (755–6) they acquired an established and appropriate place in the settlement of the country. They were traditionally mountaineers, cattle tenders and olive planters. Mountainous country also gave them security in case of friction with their rulers. So they did not settle in the fertile Andalusian plain, but extensively in the highlands between it and the southern coast. There were colonies of Berbers also further north, wherever there was room for them in the mountains—and always they were herdsmen, or olive and fruit planters, who took no interest in tillage. The first generations of conquerors were continuously reinforced from Africa. And these migrations set in motion others, directed towards other European coasts. Following Arab leaders, Libyans and Fellahin crossed the seas to acquire land from these leaders by sharing in their victories. North Africa under the Aghlabides, who had broken away from the Caliphate of Bagdad about the year 800, became a new and vigorous centre of racial eruption outwards.

So as Charlemagne's Empire grew, and with the growth of its power broadened its agrarian basis, there came from the boundary seas of Western Europe, the Northern and the Southern, vicious attacks of Northmen and Saracens, both ready to fall upon the exposed stretches of the Romance, German and Celtic world with the primary intention of plunder, slaughter and destruction—but both also equipped for the establishment of new governments and new settlers in the lands that they had harried. It was because of political troubles in Norway that Viking bands first began to settle in conquered territory instead of coming home with their loot. About the year 820 their settlement began in Ireland. Near the same date Saracens began to settle in the most westerly possession of Byzantium, Sicily. After these first successes the Vikings attacked all along the coasts of the North Sea and the Channel, the Saracens along those of Italy and Southern France. Everywhere they penetrated far into the interior. Neither in England nor in the Carolingian lands did they find any system of fenced cities or well-manned forts to hold them up. That scattering of the population which had preceded the settlement of the first Teutonic conquerors now proved fatal. There is no need to tell again the story of how England all but succumbed to the Danes; how the Northmen again and again made the lands along the Rhine and the Seine unsafe; how Vikings invaded the Mediterranean; or how Saracens laid Rome waste, held out for long in South Italy against the arms of the Frankish king, and until far into the tenth century took tribute in Provence from their fort at Fraxinetum. Towards the end of the ninth century there came from the east another devastating attack, which for decades could not be resisted with effect—that of the mounted Magyars who occupied the Pannonian steppe. Within a few years they ruined the whole Carolingian work of government and settlement in the East Mark. They raided as far as

Tuscany and Southern France. It was only the consolidation of the German Empire, proved at the battle of the Lechfeld (955), that put an end to these Magyar invasions.

Both Magyars and Saracens raided far beyond the ultimate bounds of their settlement. For settlement the Saracens concentrated on Sicily. The island made a stout resistance: it was, as it always had been, a land of towns and strong villas, and it had to be conquered town by town. Palermo fell in 831, Taormina the last Greek city not till 902. Conquest and destruction left room for a new population. Berbers and other African fighting men were settled, some on old town lands, more in the country round about. Generally speaking, they and the many who followed them from their native lands were established in open country. Hundreds of new villages were scattered over Sicily.

The story of the Northmen's acquisitions of territory was quite different. It touched many lands, East and West. Besides Ireland, parts of Scotland and the Isle of Man were occupied. About 860–70 their power was at its height: they were raiding and conquering along Western coasts and up Western rivers, among Slavonic tribes between Lake Peipus and Lake Ladoga, and in England. Early in the tenth century their attacks on the Channel coast led to Rollo's acquisiton of the country about Rouen as vassal of the French King. He and his son then extended 'Normandy' far westward towards Brittany. But the Northmen could not have made their influence felt so widely had they aimed everywhere at agricultural settlement. In Ireland and Russia they did not expect their followers to settle on the land and become trust-worthy subjects: they made grants which enabled them to share in the work of government and profitable commerce. They founded states in the same spirit in which they had formerly set out on their raids. But elsewhere their conquest had results similar to those of the great *Völkerwanderung*. A few hundred Norwegian families left the track of the raiding voyages to settle in empty Iceland. There, with no warrior king and no looted wealth, scattered free and far apart over a hard land, they carried on their old life; and their descendants gave Teutonic tradition its mightiest written form. In France and England the North-men took control, so far as possible, of the existing rural economy. Rollo's first official act was to have the land surveyed and to make grants to his followers. But he immediately set himself to attract 'men of various origins' and 'filled the land with his own warriors and with these other immigrants (*advenis gentibus*) and so built it up after its prolonged harrying'. The account suggests that the Norman warriors were the lords, the other strangers their peasant colonists. But the lords formed an important class of landowners built up in accord with old Teutonic tradition. They were endowed with land *secundum digna-*

tionem. In Normandy, especially in the departments of Seine Inférieure and Manche, a type of place name is very widespread which is based on a Norman personal name, and originally ended with a Scandinavian syllable, usually *-tot* (= *-toft*). Sometimes the syllable survives; sometimes it has been replaced by *-ville.* Such place names suggest that round about the prominent Normans who gave their names to villages, there settled groups of small freemen who naturally called their settlements so-and-so's *-holm,* or *-gard,* or *-toft,* or *-bol. Bol* is the Scandinavian term for the arable part of a holding,[1] and retained that meaning in Norman dialect especially in connexion with small peasant holdings. True, the peasant element among the Normans soon lost its separate existence. Normandy adopted the French feudal organization of society, with its sharp cleavage between peasants and knights. Only the knights' way of life was respected. Descendants of the humbler Normans were grouped with their neighbours the native peasants, except where they were able to join with knights in the work of conquest in Apulia, Sicily or England.

In England, the settlement of Scandinavians in the southern parts of the Danelaw was extensive enough to leave a deep mark on place names, even after the English reconquest of those shires. But the deepest mark was in the region of the Five Boroughs and in Yorkshire. The *-thorps* and *-bys* are thickly scattered over Lincolnshire, the North Riding, and parts of the East Riding. Among them you may occasionally find an Ingleby, which shows that there the English were a minority, the Scandinavians the main stock. Danbys and Normanbys distinguish different groups of conquerors. From the families who occupied these settlements sprang a peasantry which was able to maintain its independence through the troubles of the eleventh century. The sokemen of the land of the Five Boroughs had such a free tenure that their descendants in the twelfth century could endow churches with land. Nowhere else had the old Teutonic tradition of settlement been better preserved.

Taken as a whole, the migrations of the ninth and tenth centuries changed the composition of the European peoples in only a few limited areas. But their influence on the European social structure was not confined to those areas. They gave the impetus to the emergence of new types of political and social organization; and from this time forward these types determined the form which settlement would take.

The Slavonic East and the Romance-Teutonic West, already so far apart in their development, were also affected in different ways by the storms of Scandinavian conquest. The Northmen did not succeed in establishing fully independent states in France or England; even where they supplanted the previously settled aristocracy or peasantry, in the end they were incorporated into the existing political order. In the

---

[1] Cf. p. 644, below.

East, on the other hand, the conquests of Northmen and Magyars preluded the foundation of new, extensive and powerful states. The dominion of the Varangians, the 'Ruotsi', with Kiev as its centre, extended into the regions of the Volga and the Vistula. Its Teutonic rulers adopted the speech and customs of the conquered Slavs, just as their cousins in Normandy were assimilated to their French environment. Among the Magyars of the Hungarian plains, dynastic quarrels, following on their expulsion from the German East Mark, led to the unitary autocratic kingdom of the house of Arpad. In this case the conquering class managed to impose their own language on many of the conquered Slavs, though they learnt from them the elements of a settled life. Meanwhile, west of the Russian and north-west and north of the Magyar dominions, two great states grew up out of the loose structure of the West Slavonic tribes. All Bohemia came gradually under the control of the Czech house of the Premyslids. About the middle of the tenth century, the German Empire under Otto the Great was making headway against the Slavs of the Mid-European plain: its outposts were stretched north and south between the Elbe and the Oder. But further east, on the lower Vistula and the Warthe, Misica (Mieszko), founder of the Piast dynasty, built up out of a number of tribes the nucleus of the Polish Empire. For a time, the course of political events made it seem likely—early in the eleventh century— that all West Slavonic territory would be united under the Poles. But in fact their dominion itself very nearly collapsed. When it had recovered, the territory that it controlled effectively extended from the lake-covered flats of Prussia and the rivers Netze and Warthe to the Carpathians in the south. On the west it reached only a short way beyond the Oder, where it receives the Warthe; but further south in Silesia to the Sudeten Mountains. On the Baltic, the Pomeranian lands between the estuaries of Oder and Vistula were loosely controlled by it. The Wendish lands, between Poland and the Elbe, had in the south become dependent on the German Empire—as the Margraviates of Meissen and Lausitz—but remained independent further north. Bohemia had extended its dominion over the Moravian tribes as far as the western edge of the Carpathians.

The dominions of the Bohemian, Polish and Hungarian princes were shut in by dense boundaries of forest, in which no clearing was permitted. The state, won by conquest, was to remain a single stronghold. Connected with this policy was that creation of great fortresses which soon became a fundamental feature of life on Slavonic soil. After conquering the various tribes and princely houses, the Premyslids, the Piasts, and also St Stephen of Hungary, divided the land into administrative districts each of which had a fortress as its centre. Whilst the districts were modelled on the counties of the Frankish-German Empire, the system of divisional fortresses was in sharp opposition to the system which, at this very time, in Germany and France, was undermining that of the county and robbing it of its utility to the central government. In their early days, Bohemia, Poland and Hungary knew no feudalism. There was a landowning nobility of professional soldiers who acquired a great deal of the prince's widespread lands. But the prince only alienated his land in moderation and was careful not to transfer judicial or fiscal authority to his men and their heirs. The constitution of the 'castellanies' preserved all royal powers and compensated the poorer nobility for the absence of regular feudal fiefs.

In Bohemia and Poland the fortress of the *Castellania* was an extensive camp, surrounded with defensive works, laid out with lanes like a town, and full of buildings—the greater for the court, the administration and the church, the lesser for the garrison of 'knights'. The whole of its buildings were normally of timber. The inhabitants of the villages in the district had many varying links with it. Freemen came to it for justice. Those of them who could claim to be *milites* were called up for service from it, and we may assume—though the evidence is not quite conclusive—that they did regular garrison duty. For there were still no other precise external qualifications for the rank of *miles*, like the Western oath of fealty and grant of a fief.[1] The fortresses of Boleslav Chrobry of Poland were held by crowds of his companions in battle and his 'courtiers', who were connected with the prince and with one another, as in the primitive German *comitatus*. (The *drushina* of the Northmen in Russia was the prototype.) Later these warrior-groups were dissolved. But the district fortress still served as the almost permanent residence of important groups of the nobility; both the high functionaries and no doubt also those poorer *milites*, '*militelli*', who held no more land than an average peasant. The peasantry of the district owed taxes and services; these obligations due to the prince were levied from the fortress and in part performed there. Among the personal services were fortress building labour and fortress garrison duty. The taxes were levied in kind on the cattle and cultivated land of the village. Besides, the Czech or Polish peasant owed his prince or the officials of the fortress service in hunting, in travel, and in the carriage of men and goods. And he was bound to assist in such military work outside the fortress as the building of bridges and the care of the frontier forests.

---

[1] According to the evidence assembled by Z. Wojciechowski the Polish *jus militare*, which assigned many privileges to 'knights', is of later date, developing in the thirteenth century, which was also the era of the dissolution of the castellanies. The text is based on this view.

In addition to these public obligations, the peasant had others arising from his dependence on a lord or from his personal bondage. The documents hardly suggest the existence of true peasant proprietors; freemen below the rank of *miles* had become tenants of the crown, the nobility or the Church. For the unfree, the administrators of the crown lands had worked out a highly differentiated system of dues and services. These were owed by unfree families from generation to generation. They included dues in kind (fish, honey, hides, grain); craftsman's work; and work at the lord's stable, his hunt, his kitchen or his dining-hall. In 1057 Duke Spitignev made over to the Collegiate Church of Leitmeritz 'from every craft (*de omni arte*), and from every fortress district (*ab omnibus suis civitatibus*) a servile couple with their children, to carry on the said craft'. Here it appears that the organization appropriate to the crown lands was also found in the castellanies. They served as centres of economic activity and control.

But they functioned in a very different way from the great landlords' establishments of the West. They were not the headquarters of great agricultural undertakings, but collecting places into which flowed the renders from many individual peasant holdings. Taxes, services owed to the state, rents and servile dues, with tolls and monopolistic profits of trade, formed the varied elements of a huge system of tribute that was administered from the fortresses. The system provided the material needs of the state. Its form was perfectly appropriate to the economic conditions existing when the power of the princes grew up. Arable farming was still relatively subordinate. The fortress had no special lord's demesne attached to it. Neither the tenants nor the servile peasants were, for the most part, required to work hard on the land; their numerous compulsory activities were of a very different sort. That agriculture was regarded as a normal part of peasant economy the Polish plough-tax (*poradlne*) shows. But the families whose special business it was to supply arable produce formed only one hereditary and professional group among the dependants of a princely landlord.[1] Bohemian, Polish and Silesian sources refer to *aratores* and *rustici* in this sense. Dues in grain appear also as typical obligations of those peasants who are called *hospites*; they actually were 'guests' or 'foreigners', that is to say immigrant farmers whom the lords settled on their lands with fixed conditions of rent and for set terms of years.

If this was the economic organization of the central princely fortresses we cannot assume anything very different in those of the greater and lesser nobility. Many noblemen were relieved of an appreciable part of their economic cares during spells of maintenance in the fortress of

---

[1] Cf. p. 492, below.

their prince. Nor was the Church interested in a more intensive agri-cultural life until far into the twelfth century. It was more concerned to provide itself with sources of income in tithe and castellany revenues than to acquire endowments of land.

All these facts must be taken into account if we are to understand the circumstances in which peasant settlement developed. The multifarious compulsory services required of the peasant obliged him to live a regulated economic life. But they did not oblige him to aim at a maximum production of cereals. And so the Slavonic economy was not stimulated to conquer fresh soil in order to extend arable farming. It was not at all likely that the peasants would of their own accord aim at an object that their betters neglected. They were not urged to extend the village fields as far as possible, or to find new land when extension of the old fields was impracticable. The lesser Teutonic freemen who occupied land in Western Europe had felt this urge, as the stabilization of political authority and the spread of the seigniorial system made settled peasants of them. They had learnt to prize regularly cared for fields and meadows as the normal foundations of a way of life with which the freeman's social respectability was bound up. The Slavonic peasant, controlled by the now strong political authority that emanated from the fortress, did not acquire this attitude of mind. For his social position was not based on free, and as a rule securely heritable, owner-ship. The sole question for him was how to make both ends meet, and how much land he must till in order—together with what the meadows, fisheries, and woodlands gave him—to guarantee his living and enable him to perform his obligations as a subject.

What we know of the Slavonic villages agrees with these considera-tions. Their field grew in course of time. Here too the generations brought intermixture of holdings. But the Slavonic 'chessboard' fields show no tendency to a regulated system of furlongs and *Hufen* or hides. Their plots made up a medley of irregular blocks. They retained the old hook-shared plough (*Hakenpflug*). The only form of clearing that they practised was by burning off the thickets—with a view rather to tem-porary cultivation than to a permanent acquisition of soil: you cleared the brushwood from one place and it grew again when you moved to another. The villages were often some distance from the fields: the huts stretched for choice along some water's edge, or lay in a rough circle about a green (*Rundlinge*). Most of the settlements remained small. If population grew a fresh one was laid out in the neighbourhood of the old one. Both lords and peasants often changed the sites of their dwellings. In Poland, not the village, but a wider group of settlements (*opole, vicinia*), was the legal unit of those who had joint interest in the fields of the district.

These conditions reflected the spirit of primitive Slavonic society, as did the domination of the land and its economy from the fortress. With slight modifications, similar conditions were to be found in countries adjacent to Poland and Bohemia in which the basis of the population was Slavonic, whether the ruling class remained Slavonic or whether it had been replaced by foreigners. In Hungary the peasants both owed heavy services to the fortress of the 'castellanies' and lived in small shifting settlements.[1] A Synod from King Koloman's time (1096–1114) ordained that church villages must not move too far away from the church itself. The Magyar nobility still retained something of the restless way of living of its ancient plundering days. Otto of Freising, on the second Crusade, observed with amazement the huts of the Hungarian *vici et oppida*, more often made of reeds than of wood. The noblemen built no manorial halls, and instead of living on their estates preferred to be in camps as much as possible: for months in summer they frequented the tented camp of the king. In the Wendish lands on the Baltic, the 'gentry' had permanent dwellings in the fortresses, some of which as in Poland were laid out like towns. Here they lived from the yields of the chase and from the renders of their peasants; and with these supplies they maintained a hospitality which deeply impressed the German missionaries of the twelfth century. The wretched tenurial condition of the Slavonic peasantry, which crippled energetic settlement, was revealed brutally later, when the princes called in German colonists and in places, for their benefit, forced the older inhabitants to seek new quarters.

In the tenth and eleventh centuries the German rulers of the lands of the Sorbs, east of the Elbe and Saale, took over the fortress system and its economic organization. The margrave's knights were concentrated in the fortress; the peasants of the castellany fed them. True, the knights gradually adopted a way of life more in accordance with that of their fellows in Old Germany. They began to live among Sorb villages, which had been given them as 'manors'. The native peasantry then owed service to these 'manors' direct. This change in their conditions of dependence led to a gradual introduction of German features into the villages and fields: the old small hamlets were often consolidated: the irregular blocks of the shares in the fields were divided into the furlongs of the three-field system; and long strip acres were added to them. But probably these innovations did not occur until, from about 1100, German colonists had been settled among the Sorbs.

The period of fresh migrations, which in the East led to the establishment of new states based on the fortress system, in Western Europe also gave the strongly fortified settlement an outstanding place in the

1 For Hungary at a later date, see pp. 494, 499, below.

organization of society. But the fortified places of the West soon
developed on lines totally different from those of the East; and many
various forms of settlement became associated with them. The emer-
gencies of Scandinavian, Saracenic and Hungarian raids led first of all
to the establishment of ample places of refuge with strong garrisons. In
Italy, France and Germany the chief of these were the episcopal residences; as seats of churches, officials and merchant colonies they were
already relatively important agglomerations. Elsewhere the fortified
camps of the Scandinavian invaders were imitated. In England and
Flanders social structures arose which recall the fortress districts of the
East; the territory won back from the Danes was divided into districts,
with central fortresses. In all such fortified places, as about the king's
person, groups of professional fighting men were stationed. (The
English knightly and the German ministerial class sprang from such
groups of retainers.) But in the history of settlement these creations
marked only transitional stages. The professional fighting man wished
to live as a noble man; and that implied not only service to his lord but
economic independence as a resident landowner. So the increase of the
knightly class led to its endowment with halls, dependent peasants'
holdings, rights of jurisdiction and claims to services previously owed
to the state. The number of 'noble' residences associated with village
settlements grew. In France, as early as the ninth century, they became
the fortresses of knights. Royal control over fortification weakened:
nobles built their own strong houses on the land—their *châteaux* and
firmités, at first mere block-houses. Dependent peasants were obliged
to group their homes about the lord's strong place, and the village was
often named after it—*firmitas castrum*; *La Ferté Vidame*. In Normandy,
it is true, strong dukes, though they gave hundreds of villages to single
noblemen, forbade them to build their own castles. Such building
was always the sign of a weak central government. In Italy, judging by
the country of Florence-Fiesole, the number of noble castles grew slowly
until about 1050; but very fast during the investiture struggles. So it
did at the same time in Germany; and in England during the anarchy
of Stephen's reign.

The princes, bishops, and great feudatories could not do without
knights to defend their principal fortresses. But sooner or later the
knights claimed some of their lord's land. This set limits to the size of
knightly garrisons; and it was in the interest of princes, lay or ecclesiastical, to further that movement of population which would leave the
defence of these central places to civilian inhabitants, to men who
came there not to do garrison duty but to get a living. The great fortified
place became a town; the burgesses became its permanent garrison.
Throughout Western Europe traders and craftsmen formed the main

element of the population in the market and 'lane' quarters of these towns. The increase of noble residence on the land was a chief cause of the growth and local concentration of this urban population; for it meant an increase of those households which made relatively frequent and heavy demands on the market. In the south however—Italy, Spain, Southern France—besides the merchants and craftsmen, the large and small landowning nobility contributed decisively to town growth at an early date, by building for themselves town houses. The course of this process is obscure. No doubt the needs of the age of invasions gave the first impetus. Later, the desire for social contracts and a share in urban commerce encouraged the process. In any case, the movement was spontaneous, not directed from above; the leaders in it became leaders in the struggle for communal independence.

Eventually, in these same countries, the desire for concentrated and protected dwellings spread to peasants who were not even full owners of their land. In North Italy, from the time of the Saracenic and Hungarian invasions, there grew up *castra* of peasants only. The first known to us date from about 900—near Verona and Lucca. Their foundation is provided for by a collective contract. The site is acquired from the count or ecclesiastical lord by a group of settlers in return for a modest rent. They build their own houses and undertake to maintain the fortifications. These are to protect not only themselves but also peasants from other villages of their lords. Originally directed against external enemies, this arrangement was kept alive by internal feuds. Tuscan peasants demanded formally that their lords should permit such fortification. It was to the lord's interest to let, not only the site for houses, but also adjacent fields and vineyards to the inhabitants on easy terms. The *borghi* were made extensive, and new settlers with new collective contracts were attracted to them, if there was land available for further use.

So the new arrangement contributed directly to the extension of cultivated land and a more intensive use of the land already occupied. A similar influence spread gradually from the towns. Around them there grew up agricultural zones of specially dense occupation and careful tillage. William Fitz Stephen's account of London shows how characteristic this was of a flourishing twelfth-century town. The security which an adjacent town gave and the demand of its markets worked together. Sooner or later the burgesses themselves became parties in this suburban agriculture. That was natural: they were always being recruited from the land. Their vegetable gardens and vineyards were to be found everywhere in suburban territory. What a great part the townspeople took in the harvest is shown by an eleventh-century story from Cologne: the town seemed empty in harvest time. There was also some genuine peasant element in the town populations, working its own or rented land; but in a rising commercial and industrial town it must have formed a dwindling minority. The fields which had always belonged to the place or to its lord were not available to immigrants. This situation is revealed very clearly for several English boroughs by the discrepancy between the number of the inhabitants and the small area of ploughland returned in Domesday Book.

But for centuries the towns grew too slowly to become dominant centres of agricultural expansion. Early in the thirteenth century the woods still lay thick about Paris on every side. A more decisive influence on the extension of settled land came of necessity, during the era of expanding feudalism, from the great lords with their judicial and administrative power. They could control the balance of cultivated and waste land in their sphere of authority. After the age of devastating invasions, they were faced with the necessity for reconstruction almost everywhere in Western Europe. In some cases great areas had to be formally repopulated. In England the immigration of Scandinavian peasants had been of assistance; but outside the Danelaw the losses of population were not made good for generations. William the Conqueror settled large bodies of peasants near Carlisle in districts which had lain waste since the Viking times. On the Continent, however, the history of organized colonization of unoccupied land on a broader basis than before had begun again with the measures of reconstruction of the tenth century. We have seen already how Rollo of Normandy brought settlers *de omnibus gentibus* into the land which his own men had wasted. They found surveyed territory at their disposal; they were promised security of tenure. Here, for the first time, the settlement of a region was based on the enlistment of colonists from a wide area. And the opportunity was taken to offer the settlers the necessary standard holdings and uniform conditions of settlement. The procedure was soon imitated in Anjou, where Count Fulk the Good, after the Norman wars, invited many countrymen from adjacent provinces to cultivate land which was very attractive to them, thanks to its long compulsory fallow. He promised them favourable terms. About the same time the Bavarian churches were equally systematic when they recovered their Austrian and Carinthian lands after the repulse of the Hungarians. They found the land, which had been 'deserted for years', without inhabitants and reverting to forest. Its cultivation could not be adequately restored by the predial services of the locally settled Slavs. So free colonists were sent from Bavaria. The typical conditions of their settlement are shown by charters in which the crown sometimes gave them extra land to settle, sometimes guaranteed their legal position. Land grants to lords were based on the big *Königshufe*; although such *Hufen* were

5

often subdivided when the lords made grants to peasants. The settlers claimed to be subject only to Church officials and free of the king's judicial or fiscal authority; and their claim was allowed.

Meanwhile, in the north of the Iberian Peninsula, the native population came together amid the wastes created by war, to form new states with their own national stamp. The hundred years during which the centre of Western Europe suffered from and overcame invasions from the circumference were also full of strife between the Arabs and the little princes of the former Spanish Mark, and of the Cantabrian Mountains. In the West, the Christians occupied what had been the waste glacis between them and the Arabs as far as the Upper Douro. But until about the year 1000, that is so long as the Caliphate of Cordova stood erect, a final decision was delayed: the occupied land was constantly fought over. The Carolingian method of *adprisio* by military colonies of lords and peasants was no longer applicable. In Spain, as all over Western and Central Europe, the peasant's military functions fell into the background: his business was to feed the knight. In Spain, as in other countries, fortresses dominated the life of the country: the provinces of Catalonia and Castile were named after them. And fortress building took the same turn as in Italy and Southern France. There were fortresses for knights only and fortresses whose occupants were mainly agriculturalists. Wifred of Barcelona (A.D. 874–98), the first Prince of Catalonia, founded Cardona as a centre for the settlement of landowners and peasants; a hundred years later its inhabitants had acquired property all about, 'both in Christian and heathen places, in waste as well as in settled land'. The charters which, from the time of the Fuero of Leon (1017–20), were granted to the larger towns show that the cultivation of fields and plantations, and indeed the working of small holdings, were a main source of the inhabitants' livelihood.

The settlement of these waste conquered lands had to be based on the recruitment of privileged colonists. True, they were people from very straitened circumstances. Some came from the northern mountains; some had been driven, or had fled, out of Arab territory. But the demand for them was greater than the supply. A peasant was a valuable property for whom lords quarrelled. Churches and knights had to acquire from the prince the *licentia populandi* for their estates. As early as the ninth century the legal security of the colonists was based on a principle which had a great European future. Wherever a group of them was settled, there they were given, together with the delimitation of their land, a series of legal guarantees which were to apply to all future members of the settlement. A local law was established: either the prince issued it, or he empowered the lord of the place to issue it.

The groups of settlers were small at first; the oldest written *fuero* (alleged to be of the year 824) applies to five families who had come *ad populandum ad villa Brania Ossaria*. But they were given room enough for growth. This was both in their own interest and in that of the lord and the prince. No one could tell whether newcomers would arrive in large or small groups, from near or from far; but it was necessary to look ahead and see to it that any immigrant family should feel sure of its future. This was secured by making the law of the first settlers and their descendants a law for the whole place. The desire to attract more and more immigrants, so that the place might grow, lay also at the back of later urban *fueros*, and was sometimes clearly expressed in them.

These eleventh-century town charters are the most striking evidence of how the progressive conquest of the Peninsula stimulated colonization. There was always fresh conquered and waste land; and what lay behind required more intensive working. Again and again we come across specialists in settlement, men who made a business of laying out settlements and recruiting colonists for them. Now a nobleman does this work for the king—*Senior Eximinio Garscia qui fuit populator*, for example; now a priest or a monk feels that he is serving God by bringing colonists to till His earth. After about 1050, however, the colonizing movement receives further impetus from beyond the Pyrenees: peasants seeking land follow the French crusaders of the *reconquista*.

Just as in Spain and Portugal, in the German East Mark along the Danube there was continuous and general colonization. Since the time of the Emperor Henry II the royal administration had been extending its influence on every side. The Mark was carried to the Bohemian-Moravian frontier, and south-eastward as far as the Leitha region. From the abundant supply of ownerless land the Crown could freely endow vassals; but colonists were needed to cultivate it. The royal administration itself began the work. The grantee found a village and village territory surveyed, and often houses with peasants in them. The Babenberg Margraves were very active in this connexion. The settlers came partly from Bavaria as before, partly from the East Mark itself; but many from much remoter districts. The Babenbergs sprang from Franconia: they sent there for knights and peasants. In the same way the Crown and the Church brought peasants from their Old German manors. There was no need for organized recruiting or for privileges to attract recruits: the lords brought colonists from places where they knew that there was surplus population. In these circumstances no general uniform colonists' law developed. There was the same grading of peasant status and property as in Old Germany. There were both serfs and free men; and among the free some had heritable though rent-paying tenures, some mere leases for years. But the economic and political needs of the land to be colonized made the peasants with better tenures, the *Hübner*, an important element in the population.

The river valleys of the Eastern Alps were colonized in much the same way. But in them, and further into the mountains, a settled Slavonic population survived. Some were free independent peasants; some as serfs worked on the royal domains or cleared adjacent forests. For safeguarding the frontiers, there was already a similar zone of mixed colonization in the foothills of the Bohemian and Thuringian Forests. Charles the Great had founded the Mark 'Nordgau' in a land settled by Slavs; and so Slav and German peasants were mingled. Immigration from Franconia increased from the time that Henry II founded the Bishopric of Bamberg, on the western edge of this region.

This progress of colonization along the German frontier reminds us that in the old settled districts also settlement in the forests was still progressing. The two movements were connected. Colonists of the Alps and the 'Nordgau', as evidence from about the middle of the eleventh century shows,[1] took the plan of the 'forest village' (*Waldhufendorf*) from the Odenwald in their native Franconia. Evidence of the steady growth of arable along the middle and lower Rhine comes from the continuous grants of tithe on *novalia* by the archbishops of Cologne to chapters and monasteries, from about the year 1050. The clearing activity which this reflects can hardly, however, be regarded as a new achievement of those decades; the grants indicate rather that the cathedral had all the income of this kind that it wanted and could grant away new tithes. Clearing in these regions did not only extend existing village territory: place-name terminations in *-scheid* and *-auel* (or *-ohl*), which first occur from the ninth century, point to settlements in old forest land. There is more evidence of peasant than of landlord activity in this clearing work. When Bishop Willigis of Mainz (975–1011) founded the monastery of Disibodenberg on a forest-clad hill, he found settlements all around in the Hochwald and Soonwald, but no provision of parish churches; the neighbouring peasants had not waited for the lord to act. In the age of the Salian emperors, two Westphalian bishops were reckoned model landlords, Meinwerk of Paderborn and Benno II of Osnabrück. But forest clearing is not mentioned by the biographers among their economic activities. How the work of clearing was divided between lords and peasants is perhaps best shown in two episodes from the Rhineland. His peasants pressed Archbishop Siegfried of Mainz to let them cultivate the waste hill country near Rüdesheim; but he insisted that it should all be turned into vineyard.

---

[1] *Mon. Germ., D.D. Conr. II*, nr. 229; *Hen. III*, nr. 321.

That this was not the peasants' original wish is shown by his freeing them from *corvée* and easing their tithe 'so that they would till the land more willingly'. The peasants of the villages round about a monastery near Trier had often encroached on its woods, and turned them into fields *propter diversas pauperum necessitates*. The Archbishop confirmed these encroachments retrospectively and relieved the woods, for the benefit of the monastery, of that *forestalis lex* which, if observed, would have stopped all clearing. Such instances show how eagerly, even violently, the peasant set about the acquisition of fresh land. The lords had no need to incite him; only to control him. They had to prevent any unsuitable or damaging use of the land, to protect the woods from devastation. The right to protect hunting areas, the 'forests' which were not all woodland, had often passed from the crown to the princes, who did not let it slip so easily out of their control: at about the same date as the cases just quoted the monastery of Brauweiler had to beg the Archbishop of Cologne for leave to clear no more than a single *Hufe* of its forest.

Lords as a class neither could nor would gratify their tenants by putting vacant land at their disposal regularly. The *Hofrecht* of Bishop Burkhard of Worms gives a vivid picture of an arrangement between the episcopal officials and a descendant of one of the bishop's men, who had left his native village because he saw no future there, but had failed to establish himself elsewhere, and had come back when he heard that his patrimony had fallen vacant.

But on the other hand it is remarkable that the decline of the peasantry with free status and proprietary rights, which in Germany and elsewhere accompanied the growth of feudal power, in no visible or demonstrable way checked their craving for fresh land. Very much the reverse in early Capetian France. The care in organizing the utilization of the land which many princes had shown during the age of recovery soon died away. Society was terribly dislocated. The breakdown of royal power was followed by complete feudal anarchy. The typical lord lived by and for constant fighting. The village huddled about his château reflects the resultant situation of the peasants. Villages with no château were often ruined, and wide stretches of land became waste. And this ruin of villages increased the risks of those that survived. Feudal lords knew how to take care of themselves; but there was not much safety for any-one else. The arbitrary handling of feudal burdens—tallage, services, fines—drove or kept the peasants away from many places fit for settle-ment. And the lords might administer their usurped forest rights with terrible severity. When the Count of Vendôme discovered irregular clearings in one of his woods he had the houses burnt down and the crops mowed off. 'That was fair', says the monk who tells the story:

even a churchman could not put in a word for a peasant's obvious needs as against a lord's rights. The Church showed far more comprehension of the peasant point of view than the nobility. But churchmen could not even protect their own estates completely against the encroachments of feudal superiors. Monasteries and peasants suffered together. The monasteries often were not able to get all their lands worked: parts were left to go waste. What they had lost is best seen in the era of recovery after 1050. It is remarkable how often at that time they induced their lay neighbours to give them, not land to get cultivated, but privileged sites on which peasant houses could be built. Evidently they were in less need of cultivable land than of reasonably safe homesteads for their tenants. The many acquisitions of land by the monastery of St Jean d'Angely in the Saintonge, for example, stress the possibility of providing *arbergement*. But the monks of the neighbouring priory of St Gemme rejected the request of the Duke of Aquitaine that they should settle a piece of land that he had given them with the bitter retort that they would have no settlers; the duke's bailiffs and foresters would give them no peace. We get a picture similar to these southern ones from Morigny, between the Loire and the Seine, and from the autobiography of Suger of St Denis, who made many *villas exhospitatas* into *villas rehospitatas*. Sometimes his colonists had to drive robbers away; sometimes a place was completely wasted by the oppression of neighbouring lords.

So in France the cultivated area contracted, whilst in Germany no limit could be seen to the opening up of forest land for cultivation. England's position was comparable with that of Germany. She had not only wide stretches of primeval forest, such as that of the Sussex Weald, but even near the most thickly settled regions there was abundance of woodland at the close of the Anglo-Saxon era. England evidently shared the tension between lords who wished to preserve forests for hunting and peasants who coveted forest land. The decline of the woods in East Anglia in the twenty years following the Norman Conquest, which is proved by the decline of pannage for swine recorded in Little Domesday, can hardly be ascribed to the new lords; rather to tenants who cannot have been very closely supervised in the early years of the new regime. But the Conquest which swept away the old lords also ruined many of their dependants and destroyed their homes. That large body of settlers which William brought to Carlisle in 1092 was not the product of surplus population. Domesday gives us the picture of a people who would need generations of quiet if they were to reoccupy fully all the partly or completely neglected land. In view of this relative abundance of land, William might feel doubly justified in imposing on England that severe forest law against settlement which he administered with uncommon harshness in Normandy. Whole counties were scheduled as 'forest'. Hundreds of families were evicted. A severe game law was enforced and penalties were imposed on assarting.

Thus in the old settled regions of Western Europe, from the close of the age of invasions until the twelfth century, progress was governed by the varying balance between a peasantry growing by natural increase and the restrictive policies of its feudal lords. But organizing ability that looked to the future was not lacking on either side. From above and from below, plans were prepared for collecting groups of settlers and concentrating them at particular points in the general interest. We have already noticed the continuous workings of such plans in Spain and on the German–Slav frontiers. From about the year 1050, an organized process of settlement began also in North France and adjacent regions in Flanders and Holland. But here there was no uniform development. In France places wasted by feudal wars, in the Low Countries coastlands, subject to inundation, were those first colonized. A third movement came with the spread of Cistercian houses in the twelfth century. It was certainly no accident that the population of the towns grew fast and the communal movement developed in these regions at the same time; and it was from them that the great adventurous eastward migration of the Crusades started. But there is more contrast than likeness between these movements and those of peasants seeking land. It looks as though the craving for land and for contented work on it became self-conscious and strong when weighed against the call of the town or the call to adventure in a holy war. This we cannot prove, only surmise. But we can get a clear enough picture of the special features of each of the three movements that we have mentioned.[1]

In France, amid the troubles of that feudal anarchy which was wasting the country, monastic houses were eager to get land cultivated and settled. They were not merely interested in increasing its yield. Sometimes only the settlers' homesteads were on monastic land, their fields on that of some lay lord. Besides the families of its own dependants, landless peasants from devastated places or in flight from tyrannous lords sought the assistance of the Church. The giving of help to such

---

[1] The account which follows of the *âge des grands défrichements* differs in some important points from other accounts: (i) it is assumed that the movement proceeded gradually from the recovery of wasted land to extensive clearing of forest land, (ii) the author can see no decisive evidence for the view that the age of great clearings was conditioned by an unusual growth of population, a *révolution démographique*, (iii) in dealing with the French *hospites* he holds that not enough stress has usually been laid on the distinction between the type of peasant farmers, classed as *hospites* since Carolingian times, and the groups of colonists so described from the eleventh century. If the word is translated 'guest' every *hospes* is assumed to have been a colonist: a different view is put forward here; cf. pp. 48–50 above.

petitioners accorded with the widespread desire in ascetic ecclesiastical circles to show sympathy with the masses. And the insecurity of life on the land could only be lessened by means of a denser settlement and the strongest possible units of settlement. But as newly established villages could not be exposed at once to the pressure of neighbouring lords, the Church had to treat with these lords. Sometimes they were easy to deal with; sometimes the Church had to make concessions to win a disclaimer of rights, or for a promise of protection against robbery that would not be the protection of a robber. So the way was prepared for the system of *pariage*, the division of seignorial rights between the Church and a secular lord. The feudal neighbour often gave the neglected land, and the right to receive dues from it, as an act of piety. In this way the Church frequently acquired the right to undertake clearings in old forest areas which could supply both land and materials for the new settlements.

The monasteries attached such new colonies to themselves in the south as well as in the north; but they were specially active in the north. There they soon developed standard conditions of settlement on uniform principles. The colonists were admitted as *hospites*. Each received his *hospitium*, his *hostise*, a piece of land with room enough for his house and yard and a scrap of arable—in one instance said to be usually reckoned at a quarter of an acre, and never substantially more. The grant of this *hospitium* set up a permanent relationship, for the grantee and his heirs, to the seignorial grantor; he paid a yearly rent of a few pence and gifts of hens, oats or bread. So far the institution was what it had been at the time of Irminon of St Germain. At both dates the mere position as *hospes* did not imply any precise economic conditions. Sometimes *hospites* were isolated individuals among villagers with a different custom, or were united in small groups of six to twelve households; in such cases they had often to work at forest clearing, though not always. But now *hospites* were also collected into strong groups in village colonies of thirty to eighty households. The object was to bring adjacent waste or forest land under cultivation: that was what the settlers offered to do. So the acceptance of the *hospitium* carried with it the lease of the land to be cleared, for which as a rule a fixed share of the yield (*champart*) was paid as rent, an arrangement appropriate to the conditions. These new colonies of *hospites* formed villages of small economically independent farmers. They might be connected with a central seignorial establishment and be bound to put their oxen at its disposal at stated times. But they were not units in a regular economic group: they had not been settled together to provide labour power for a demesne. The monastery would commission one of the brethren to organize and direct the colony. The many-sided activity of such a clerical administrator, by name Baudouin, is vividly described in the Morigny Chronicle.

The economic conditions of such a group of *hospites* were by no means easy or promising. But their legal position was attractive enough. The burdens and restrictions imposed on the *servi* were not for them. If they had been unfree, their lord's claims expired, if not asserted within a year and a day. Besides, they were protected against lords and lords' officials.[1] And such a settlement needed no lord as protector. Its legal security was enforced by the respectable capacity for self-defence of a big village of many small *hospites*.

Research is still needed into the geographical distribution of this type of settlement, its development and results. It seems to have originated in the region south and south-west of Paris. The provinces to the north and north-east of this—Île de France, Picardy, Champagne and others—were specially favourable to such colonization, for they had always been lands of big villages. Further west, in Maine, conditions were not so favourable. The rocky, broken nature of the country, with the absence of great plains and great forests, had always favoured settlement in scattered homesteads. But it is significant of the social need for denser settlement that the big village found its way into this region in the second half of the eleventh century. Such a planned village was called a *bourg*. The churches—above all St Vincent of Le Mans—associated the foundation of *bourgs* with the building of daughter churches: they acquired from the count and other lords the *licentia faciendi burgum*, which included judicial immunity. The *bourg* was not fortified, but was made as populous as might be, and to this end was given market rights. But the settlers (*hospites* or *burgenses*) were normally countrymen, and their rents were based on the extent of the bit of land that they had to make cultivable. Here too the lord who gave the privileges had often first given the land for the *bourg* to the Church. Inspired by the Church, he might start a *bourg* of his own side by side with the ecclesiastical *bourg*. That is a characteristic feature of the whole movement: the Church's colonies of *hospites* were imitated by the laity.

The very highest laymen were influenced: Louis VI (1108–37) helped ecclesiastical and lay lords in their colonizing work by grants of privileges. And he imitated them with his *villes neuves*—Torfou, Augerville, Lorris and the places endowed during his lifetime with the carefully worked out Charter of Lorris. The principles of the *hospites* settlement are applied with little change in these villages of colonists; but the king has more to give. The peasant's 'toft' is not a quarter of an acre but half an acre. He is expressly freed from *taille, tolte, aides* and military

---

[1] It is not possible to inquire here how it happened that his immunity became a permanent part of the law for *hospites*.

burdens. The king's judges must swear to observe the settler's privileges and renounce all arbitrary imposts. These comparatively few foundations of Louis VI can hardly, however, be treated as parts of a colonizing plan. They were obviously connected with his attempt to pacify the royal domain. Lorris in particular was to act as a centre of security in the Gâtinais, distracted by feudal strife; and its charter anticipated its development into a market town.

The Crown took an important step when it granted written privileges to the settlers. Clearly the Church's *hospites* had not received such charters. The new practice was based on the way in which the settlement came into existence. The royal administration did not do all the work itself. It preferred to leave arrangements to those already on the spot, or to the first colonists, giving them a charter to help organization and recruiting. The same motives had been dominant in connexion with the issue of the Spanish local *fueros*, the *cartas de poblacion*; in both cases local privileges sprang from the need to build up local settlements. Suger of St Denis, the king's fellow-worker and pupil, made masterly use of colonies of *hospites* and chartered *villes neuves*, when reorganizing his abbey's estates. He did not always use them when he found an estate in decay: he might repair the buildings and make stiff use of rights over servile tenants. But he was proud of the big villages of colonists that he had established, both because of the high regular receipts that the Church received from them, and because they were centres of peace.

It was under Louis VII, and Suger's influence, that the *villes neuves* finally did the work for which his father had only prepared the way. They were spread wide over the royal domain. Most of them received the Charter of Lorris, *ut villa cresceret in brevi*, as the charter of Villeneuve-le-Roi (Yonne) puts it. They helped to pacify the crown lands and to strengthen the links between the king and the masses. Churches and lay lords saw their people migrating to them, and complained to the king. Louis VII and Philip Augustus his son, who carried on his work, were obliged to promise certain lords not to receive their *serfs* and *hôtes* into royal *villes neuves*; and Philip even renounced the right to found more such places in one region on the borders of Champagne. But foundations of *hospites* settlements by great feudal lords, especially by the Church, increased; and the crown utilized their work. It often made its consent to foundations conditional on sharing in their control and revenues; and by this *pariage* it absorbed them into the system of *villes neuves*.

The region of the *hospites* colony extended as far north as Flanders, where it approached the region of coastal colonies. The coastlands repeatedly lost their agricultural value, especially their grazing value, through inroads of storm-driven tides. About the middle of the eleventh century, lords and peasants combined to avert these losses. There is evidence of dyke and canal building from the time of Count Baldwin V (1035-67). He was praised for making unprofitable land fruitful and a place for herds. Evidently he brought colonists from the interior into the threatened areas, where they developed the *polder* system. The same thing happened in Seeland and Holland. On the island of Walcheren, after the Danish invasions, settlement was concentrated about three 'Burgs' (of which Middelburg was the chief) and three parish churches. In the eleventh and twelfth centuries the island acquired church sites named after the lords of the villages. Evidently, the 'knights' of the 'Burgs' found it in their interest to equip the land with peasant holdings. The situation was however such that they did not try to create regular 'manors' with demesne and services: the peasants who settled on land along the coasts formed a class of economically independent farmers.

These peasants of the marshes were themselves men of enterprise. Whilst fields were being won from the sea in the Netherlands, some of them used the experience they had gained there to acquire fresh property in a similar but distant land. In 1106 six Hollanders—five laymen and a priest—joined with the Archbishop of Bremen in a scheme for cultivating bog land on the Lower Weser. They undertook to bring a number of their own people into the country: several hundred *Hufen* were to be created, several parish churches to be founded. The Hollanders undertook the whole burden of the work. They acquired the land as heritable property subject to quit-rent; and they accepted responsibility for its division; for the refunding of the sources of revenue pledged to acquire it (mainly tithe); and for the organization of courts and parishes. To protect the communities of colonists from the burdens of feudal jurisdiction, they agreed with the archbishop that he should abandon his rights in return for an annual payment from each *Hufe*. This stipulation recalls the protective measures taken by French monasteries when establishing their colonies of *hospites*, and may perhaps have been influenced by them. For the rest, the undertaking had little in common with the founding of such settlements. Both for the lord and the settlers, the end in view was not the creation of villages out of *hostises* but the sharing out of arable and pasture land.

For decades the settlement of Netherlanders in the marshes of the North Sea coast went on. But they did not confine themselves to the marshes; they went also into the Saxon forests. On the western slopes of the Harz, and further north between Hanover and Minden, great lords put land at their disposal for clearing; and there they established settlements resembling the *Waldhufen* villages. The sole documentary evidence of this immigration that we have—a pact between the Bishop of Hildesheim and four representatives of Flemish *advenae*—reflects very clearly their mobility and restlessness. They sell their property. They suddenly disappear and reappear. One of them lodges for a long time with another of his countrymen, with all his goods; and dies there. All this suggests the conditions of their life. Many of them established themselves in the land between the Weser and the Harz; place names ending in -*hagen* record their settlement. But they retained that habit of seeking fresh homes which led them subsequently further afield.

The outward influence of the colonizing enterprise of these peasants from the Netherlands was of small account at first compared with that of the contemporary colonization which Cistercian enthusiasm initiated. The original Cistercian reform had not aimed at great and widespread economic achievements; far from it. It sought spiritual things and solitudes remote from the world. Cistercians were not to live in comfort on rents, but in penury in the wilderness, by the labour of the brethren. Yet there was a conflict of ideals; for they also believed in the pure monastic system, the priestly consecration and complete spiritual training and discipline of the monk. A way of reconciliation had been prepared by other monastic orders, who had admitted their lay servants to the vow and the community as *conversi*. The *conversi* might be peasant labourers, and might do most of the necessary work. This solution had nearly been reached by the congregation of Hirschau, who employed *conversi* to establish monasteries in the waste, the monks co-operating as directors. Two foundations of theirs which helped to open up adjacent territory for colonization were made possible by this method—St Peter in the Black Forest (1093) and Pegau on the White Elster in the land of the Sorbs (1101). But the Cistercians alone adopted the principle that the labour of the *conversi* must provide the whole maintenance of the brethren. And this principle equipped them fully for colonizing work, when every side of their life had been stimulated by Bernard of Clairvaux, who joined the order in 1112. The foundation of daughter houses began at once in France; after ten years in Germany; after fifteen in England. Then the work spread over the whole Catholic world; and by 1152 there were 328 houses. All had been set up 'in the wilderness': each meant a conquest over forest and marsh. They spread to the very confines of the Western settled world at the same time (1131-2)—the Yorkshire moors, and Slavonic lands on the Saale. And everywhere peasants who would undertake the vows and labour of the *conversi* had to be recruited. So the spread of the Order involved peasant migration. True; the *conversi* lived as single men in communal dwellings like the monks, and worked only for the monastic 'grange'. They had to renounce the normal object of peasant settlement, the acquisition of a home and property. That the Order could always find men ready to work at land reclamation on these conditions shows the power of the ascetic ideal and of the desire for salvation. But it shows more clearly still the close association of the heavy tasks of clearing woods and draining marshes with the traditions of peasant life in all parts of Western Europe.

And so the Cistercian settlements achieved something very different from what they had aimed at. Giraldus Cambrensis, a thoughtful observer, was moved to make some very modern reflexions subsequently—while the Cistercians hungered for Christ and strove to eat their bread in the sweat of their brow, the spiritual virtue of *pietas* gave rise to the worldly virtue of economic *providentia*; by piety they had become rich, and they were now in danger of the sin of *avaritia*. Such psychological analysis was not common among his contemporaries. But everyone saw that the grants which great men had made to the monks out of respect for their piety taught important economic lessons. The Cistercians' success encouraged imitators. Lords began to realize that they had considerably more forest than they needed. They curtailed it bit by bit, out of deliberate economic policy, and no longer merely when a land-hungry applicant approached them. The Cistercian example was not the only incentive. The clearing process already begun went forward by its own weight. The oftener a lord yielded to particular needs and requests, the more ready he became to arrange for clearings to increase his income. Growth of markets and towns steadily improved the prospect of a secure cash yield from extended arable farming. Finally, it was not to be forgotten that the rivalry of political powers, from the middle of the twelfth century, necessitated a fresh strengthening of the knightly class; and that a knight must have land from which he can live.

Naturally, we cannot follow out the progress of forest clearing in Western Europe, in this its final decisive phase, with the geographical and chronological precision that we could wish. But every inquirer gets the definite impression that clearing and settlement went on actively, in Germany, North France and England, in the twelfth and thirteenth centuries. About new villages we can learn from charters and place names. But these do not measure the work done. Almost everywhere, place names dating from this period are few in comparison with those certainly or probably older. Casual references however point to a very general extension of the field areas of the old villages, or of those of settlements associated with them. Villages grew, or hamlets and scattered homesteads grew up near them. This peak era in the medieval utilization of the land was specially favourable to the spread of small isolated settlements.

Yet in France the progress of clearing is connected most obviously with the rise of settlements conceived of from the first as important places—the *bourgs*, colonies of *hospites*, and *villes neuves*. The charters seldom tell us how the scrub or the wood that had to be cleared away had grown—whether it had spread over land once cultivated or was primeval. In any case monastic houses, when establishing colonies, early acquired the right to extend clearing into ancient forest. This practice was greatly extended during the twelfth century. Lay lords were at first decidedly inclined to limit such assarts. Sometimes the king will only sanction permanent extensions of arable, when ancient forest is left untouched. But gradually more and more *villes neuves* grow up on forest land. The king now leads the way: some of Louis VII's foundations are named from the woods on which they encroach. Those village charters, such as the Charter of Beaumont, which in North-east France and the adjacent parts of the Empire imitated and improved the principles of the Charter of Lorris, had some significance in connexion with colonization. The Charter of Beaumont, it is true, was very seldom granted to newly founded villages; and its later wide extension was used, as a rule, to attach the old inhabitants to their village, rather than to attract settlers to new ground. But Beaumont acquired its significance as an important outlier of the ecclesiastical territory of Rheims by extending its fields in the hill country of the Argonne. We find the same association of the issue of a charter with assarting, at the foundation of villages by the same church in the forest of Ardennes. Thirteenth-century Normandy was one area of extensive clearing and big colonists' villages. Great inroads were made on the woods. Villages were laid with the *long boel*, single strip holdings behind the homesteads along the road—as in the German *Waldhufen* villages.

The *villes neuves* system was the most convenient for an assart colony on a large scale. It was not required when a couple of houses sprang up somewhere in the extended territory of an old village. Areas of 100, 240 and 300 arpents, such as Notre Dame de Paris let out to be cleared and cultivated in 1185, 1202 and 1219, must soon have been cut up into very small bits, if room was to be found on them for several peasant households. We can understand why the Church made the establishment of every *hospes* a case for separate approval. From the time when gradual clearing had won a definite place in seignorial economy, colonization was carried out even in the neighbourhood of the *villes neuves* principally by the creation of hamlets. This development tended also to bind the dependants to their lord; those who created and rented such fields and hamlets could have the hope held before them of a freedom that was now a recognized possibility—as when the monastery of Arrovaise in Artois undertook to treat its colonists *tamquam sartatores*. How profoundly opinion as to the relative values of forest and settled land had changed since the eleventh century is shown in the obituary of Albericus Cornu, who died Bishop of Chartres in 1243. As canon of Notre Dame de Paris, he had helped to get woods cleared and arable

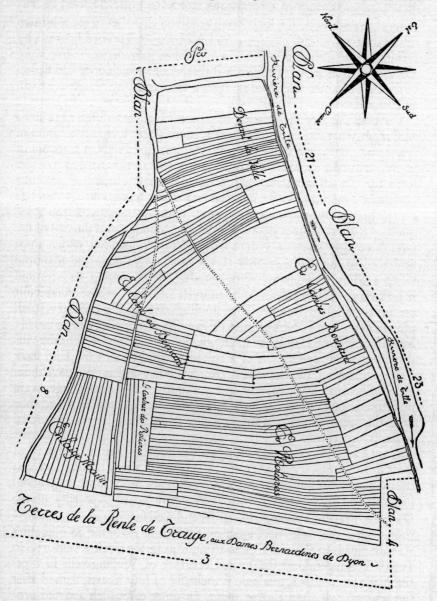

FIG. 3. Irregular strip fields in a medieval clearing in Burgundy, Is-sur-Tille, Côte d'Or.

created in three parishes; in two of them to get new storage barns (*grangiae*) built; and in the third a new village. He had created rent and tithe for the Church, and had got rid of the burdensome forest jurisdiction of the Count of Champagne and other lords. The woods, the chapter agreed, had 'for long been so useless that they were a burden rather than a source of income'. And Albericus was praised because, by turning them into arable land, *multa ornamenta ecclesiae nostrae dedit*. Another striking piece of evidence is that woods which once had names of their own, in the later Middle Ages were named by preference from an adjacent village.

The beginning of the clearing movement was very different in England from what it was in Northern France. There were no colonies of *hospites* or *villes neuves*; no systematic building up of new villages out of many small households. This suggests that, by all her internal troubles from the Conquest to the reign of Henry II, England had not, like Northern France, been so disorganized as to leave villages desolate everywhere and turn peasants vagrant. Yorkshire, wasted at the Conquest, was an exception. Here, evidence beginning from the end of the twelfth century shows a system of property widespread which must be traced to the recovery after the devastation. Beside the manorial villages whose inhabitants were mainly villeins, owing services and heriot, there are almost an equal number of others whose inhabitants are nearly all free farmers. The holdings are of the ordinary small peasant type (one or two bovates of 17 to 20 acres). The village usually has a lord, who lives in it but has no manor court. This 'lord of the vill' is evidently the descendant of a colonist who brought the land back under cultivation; then gradually attracted other settlers; and gave them some of his land, cultivated or still waste, to farm. These villages were therefore as free as those of French *hospites*; though, unlike them, they were the outcome not of administrative contrivance but of individual peasants' enterprise.

Only free peasants could show such enterprise. So the recovery of Yorkshire is a further proof of the established fact that, in England, this stratum of the population had survived to an appreciable degree and had not lost its craving for property. This is true especially of the Danelaw peasants descended from Scandinavian immigrants. Here— though also elsewhere—free independent tenants are found co-operating with the lords in the work of assarting during the twelfth century. In 1150 a knight endows the little monastery of Wallingwells in Nottingham: the arable is made up principally of four assarts, named after the peasants who had cleared them. In other cases such assarted properties form important parts of the estates on which barons establish their knights; and individual peasants endow the Church with their *sarta*, or parts of them, as small freemen did in the Carolingian era. And it must be remembered that, just as in Anglo-Saxon times, assarting helped many freeholders to rise, and even to become knights. No doubt those tenants' complaints about landlords' enclosures, which led to the Statute of Merton (1235), were directed against proceedings in which members of their own class were deeply involved.

Where freemen had independent control of village common land they often divided it up among themselves. But not all dividing or clearing favoured the extension of economically independent peasant holdings. Surveys of great manors often show assarted land either added to the demesne or let out in small scraps. The monasteries played a special part in the great land-reclamation activity of the age. The Cistercians developed sheep farming in the north—sometimes, as men grumbled, at the expense of existing villages. As a result of their activity in getting land cleared, the English monks were obviously infected with the lust for gain, which mastered the love of solitude. The Chronicle of Pipewell Abbey (Northamptonshire) complains bitterly of this. The first generation of monks (from 1143) had loved and tended the groves near the abbey, *sicut mater unicum amat filium*. But already in John's reign their zeal had cooled: four *bosci* were put under the plough. The exploitation of assarting and settling had much to do with the struggle over the forest laws which fills early Plantagenet times. The stiff administration of the law was aimed not only at the protection of the game, but at least as much at the making of profit out of the need of both lords and peasants for more cultivable land. If an assart was treated as a purpresture it had to be roundly paid for. It was against this exploitation that the barons protested in the Charter of the Forest of 1217—and won decisively. Acts of assarting were condoned, but the licence for assarting was retained. However, the retention lost much of its value when the king found himself obliged to concede that one forest after another should be disafforested. Though assarting is not generally mentioned as the object of the concession, there can be no doubt that it profited by it.

In Germany also evidence shows that lords were interested in the making of *novalia* from the middle of the twelfth century. Ecclesiastical lords count it a meritorious thing, and lay lords with extensive forest rights are no longer insistent on their full maintenance. In 1168 the Abbot of Ellwangen received from the emperor the forest district of Virngrund only on condition that he left the control of hunting and timber felling to the Duke of Swabia; but the duke is bound to the abbot not to undertake or approve any *devastatio* of the woods by clearings. There in Swabia, as also in West Germany, the areas newly won for tillage and settlement were principally on high ground. The

6

tendency in this direction was already noticeable in the eleventh century. In the Black Forest and the Alpine valleys men settled on elevated sites previously shunned. On the lower hills were *Waldhufen* villages and isolated homesteads; on the higher extensive cattle-alps with their chalets. These peasant holdings away from the settled territory had from the first great economic independence, as a result of favourable tenures or even absolute ownership. So the new phase of settlement suited those peasants for whom an adequate independent holding was a thing to aim at.

The occupation of the high ground shows that the wants of such men could not be met in the old settled areas. Newly won land might be divided up, but many land-hungry peasants could not get a share. And many a peasant was always unwilling to put much work into his old holding, if newly cleared land close by promised easy yields for the near future. The *bûman* who neglects a bit of land contemptuously because, for once, it gives him no yield, becomes a proverbial and symbolic figure.[1] All this explains why, in that age, the conflict between lords and peasants over forest land became, if anything, more acute. The peasants always wanted more than lords would willingly give: they encroached on it or took it by force. There are complaints of such things from Hesse, the Lower Rhine, from Liége and from Hainault. In Thuringia, the Landgraf issued a severe edict against the leaders of organized bands that occupied his woods. And the stewards of the abbey of Einsiedeln carried on a bloody war with the *lantluten von Swiz* who *den walt in dem daz gotzhus gelegen ist, minzeton oder mineton und bawton*.[2]

Thus conditions in Germany were ripe for large-scale colonization which would satisfy more of those peasants who desired economic independence. But, just as formerly in Spain and Austria, this was only possible with a reformed central political authority. That was not quite lacking in the old Empire; but it only developed there locally. On its western boundary, Hainault was dominated by policies familiar among the princes of Northern France. The chronicler Giselbert of Le Mons tells of the founding of villages annexed to forts early in the twelfth century. From the middle of the century, the count and his great men are active promoters of *villae novae* and of *pariage* contracts. Charters and place names (*Forest, Sart, -sart, -roeulx* and so on) indicate heavy inroads on the woods. Giselbert himself in 1210 undertook an important clearing operation for his Chapter. True, in Hainault colonizing activity had always to keep pace with the destruction of public and

---

[1] 'Spervogel', *Minnesangs Frühlling*, ed. Lachmann, p. 30.
[2] Which may be paraphrased: 'the peasants of Schwyz hacked down the forest surrounding the monastery and cultivated it'.

private war. In Swabia, the free peasants, with their free holdings on cleared land, helped to build up regions over which territorial princes had direct authority; but there were a great number of small competing lordships there. Wide areas in which the organization of the state and the organization of settlement could go forward together, looking to the future, were only to be found on the eastern boundaries of the Empire, and beyond them in Slavonic lands and in Hungary. And in fact in these lands German immigration did colonizing work of an intensity and comprehensiveness unequalled in medieval history.[1]

Settlement movements and ways of dividing and arranging settlements, first visible about 1150 on the middle and lower Elbe, were always spreading east and south-east until in the second half of the fourteenth century they reached Red Russia. The movements form a single whole. The process spread from one land to another. Each wave of migration produced a second; and similar legal and economic structures recurred far apart. The leaders of the whole movement were predominantly Germans. Their followers everywhere were mainly German peasants and townsmen. In many countries, German speech won its way in alliance with the German legal and economic tradition. All this one has in mind when calling the whole process the East German Colonization. But that term is inadequate on two sides. For the colonizing work in Austria and the Alps was virtually over when the other movement began. And secondly, wherever German immigration proceeded, the native population took an increasing part in the reformed way of settling on the land and using it.

Every motive that we have so far seen at work in the history of medieval colonization was operating in this great colonizing process. Often regions wasted by war and social unrest had to be restored. Often forest and swamp had to be made cultivable and high ground occupied that previously had been avoided. But the colonists also pressed into old-settled open country, and there initiated a more intensive use and denser settlement of the land. Everywhere considerable coherent villages were set up—some in compact form, about a central 'place', a street, or a village green and pond; some in the looser form of the strung-out *Waldhufen* village. All were planned. When possible, several neighbouring villages, or even several groups of villages, which could have relations with one another, were established at the same time. The planning was completed organically by coupling rural colonization with the foundation of towns.

This orderly procedure was made easier because the East German Colonization, where it was most effective, was associated with the

---

[1] With the following paragraphs compare the detailed discussion of eastern colonization in Ch. VII, Sec. 4, below.

urgent need to strengthen political supremacy and territorial administration. A change in the balance of political power explains the first phase of the movement, a change that took place in the dominions of the German East on both sides of the Elbe.

Until about the beginning of the Hohenstaufen era these regions lay beyond the horizon of that section of the peasantry which, in the west and the south, was fighting for its standard of property. The Marks between the Saale and the Elbe were only separated from the region of East Frankish colonization by the Thuringian Forest and Fichtel Mountains. Yet for a long time not many colonists reached them. From about 1100 attempts to bring the two regions together can be traced. Count Wiprecht of Groitzsch, who held land south of Leipzig, and encouraged ecclesiastical colonization there, had family connexions with Franconia, and from there brought peasants—mixed Germans and Slavs it would appear—to clear his forests. Every colonist was able to establish himself in a small hamlet of his own. Evidently Wiprecht was imitating the Frankish lords of the upper Main and of Austria. Near his lands and southward of them, the bishops of Naumburg combined clearing and village-making with missionary activity. But the country was insecure and immigrants few. When, in 1140, Bishop Odo rebuilt the twice-destroyed church in Reichenbach, he included seventeen places in its parish. The creation of settled districts out of many small occupied sites suggests, as in the case of Count Wiprecht, that abnormal offers of land had to be made to attract colonists to an unprofitable district. Even the Cistercians would not stay there at this time: they withdrew from Schmölln near Altenburg to Pforta in Thuringia. This nearest hinterland of the Sorbenland Marks itself needed settlers: the bishop called in men from Holland.

The situation was the same further north, where German and Slav provinces adjoined one another on the Elbe. Imperial frontier lands, like the Magdeburg country and the Old Mark of Brandenburg, were in great need of immigrants at a later date. The northern frontier wing, the boundary between Holstein and the Obotrites in Wagria and Mecklenburg, was the scene of bitter fighting. On the German side, the two fighting leaders, Provost Vicelin of Neumünster and Adolf of Schauenburg, Count of Holstein, were the first to combine conquest and missionary work with thorough colonizing activity. Vicelin colonized the Holstein marshes and woods. Adolf colonized densely the western part of the wasted land of Wagria which had fallen to him— the lake country between Lübeck and Kiel. His recruiting and settling work of 1143, described in the highly coloured Biblical language of the chronicler Helmold, has become a classic episode in the history of colonization. And in fact it was important; it showed for the first time how, in an area of some hundreds of square kilometres, parts could be covered with new villages at once and the rest reserved for future colonization. At the same time the merchant colony of Lübeck was established. Recruitment of colonists was based on uniform and significant principles. The Count's agents applied first to the coast dwellers, from Flanders to Friesland, who had emigrant traditions; next to Westphalians, from his native country. These groups were to stimulate the neighbouring Holsteiners to risk crossing the old Slavonic frontier. The different groups were not mixed: each had its separate area. But the enterprise was not a complete success. The Slavs attacked while the work was in progress and the colonists did not hold together. The Holsteiners were jealous of the 'foreigners' and diverted the anger of the Slavs against them.

Ten years after this doubtful start the whole face of things was changed. An immigration had begun which Helmold could describe in such phrases as: 'the Slavs gradually declined in Wagria'; 'Germans poured into the land of the Obotrites'; as far as Schwerin the land had 'become a Saxon colony'. This clearly happened because Henry the Lion of Saxony had mastered Mecklenburg. There was a similar forward movement all down the line of the Elbe. It corresponded with the gradual consolidation of German power along the frontiers. Albert the Bear had made good his title of Margrave of Brandenburg; his authority now stretched across the Havel, as did that of Archbishop Wichmann of Magdeburg further south; though the archbishop's territory was less consolidated. Their success strengthened the position of the Margrave of Meissen further south again, between the Saale and the Elbe. All this made the region attractive to immigrants; and particularly in the northern area, after decades of fighting, the devastation of the land made immigration essential. The need was the more pressing because in the regions which had come under German control—most of Mecklenburg remained under its native princes—the partial replacement of Slavs by Flemings and Germans was aimed at. The native population was better treated in Meissen; but there too wasted land and forest land that might be cleared attracted settlers. It is significant that the imperial administration, whose chief territorial interests were in South Germany, tried to establish a dominion of its own on the Pleisse. So right along the line of the Elbe, north of the Erzgebirge, at all points at once, arose the need for new or remodelled settlements and for immigrants to do the work. With it went the need for military control and ecclesiastical organization. But this time the Church and the lay lords could not easily themselves attract the peasant forces by whose work they might live. The task was too great. The knights of the frontier princes, mostly members of their households, seldom had close enough ties with estates to the west to be able to draw settlers from them direct. To get the settlers, and to plan and establish the settlements, a specially qualified type of economic official was wanted. Each village presented its own problem. The best arrangement was to set over the village a man who could be trusted to bring in settlers and divide up the land. Moreover these village 'undertakers' must work with one another. At the start, they must collaborate in fixing boundaries. And they could not expect successful recruitment if they competed recklessly in trying to attract people from a distance. They had to act together; first to secure immigrants, and then to distribute them over the available areas. By such co-operation we must in all probability explain the remarkable early success, and the continued success, of the recruitment. The confidence with which so many Western peasants migrated into Slavonic lands, hitherto quite unknown to them, was not due to the offer of a place in this village or that, but to the knowledge which the migrant acquired of the framework of the whole colonizing scheme. He knew from the start that he would not be left on some isolated site; and he could count on the chance of being able himself to select the final position of his homestead.

Of this side of the process, its controlled territorial organization, our sources tell us almost nothing. But the co-operation of the 'locators' as we may call them, adopting a later name for these organizers and local directors of the movement, is shown by the identity of their demands and functions. From the very beginning in any village that they founded they reserved to themselves the post of judge—*Schultheiss* or *Burmester*—with, as a rule, two-thirds of the profits of justice; and besides that a holding in the village, free of rent and tithe, which was usually at least twice the size of the normal peasant holding. Tithe arrangements obliged the lay lords to come to terms with the churches affected, before the immigration got under way. The arrangement about the office of *Schultheiss* was connected with the fact that—just as in the earlier Spanish colonization, in a *ville neuve*, or in a Flemish settlement in Western Germany—the individual village was the judicial and legal unit. This judicial independence helped to secure the colonist's position in East Germany; he could be quite sure that he would not come under some entirely strange territorial jurisdiction.

These outlines of the system of village creation were adopted from the Flemings and Hollanders who, in the first instance, must have provided as great a relative proportion of the locators as of the colonists. The systematic distribution of land to the local leaders entrusted with the settlement can be perceived in Western Mecklenburg, in the Bishopric of Ratzeburg. Both in old Slavonic villages which were to be reorganized and in the new ones, tithe-free *'settinke' Hufen* were set apart for them under Henry the Lion.[1] In the foothills of the Erzgebirge, the wave of immigration from the west met a strong current from Franconia, the chief southern source of emigrants: it was flowing at the same time towards Egerland and Bohemia. This current was obviously not directed by locators. Franconian colonists near Meissen were obliged to go to law with their lords over rights which in 'located' villages had been made clear in the original contract of settlement. In northern territory also, once the movement was well under way, many peasant colonists certainly arrived without the help of any intermediary. But in view of the size of the area to be settled, and the great distances from which settlers had to be brought, the locator was and remained indispensable. No doubt he was rarely a mere peasant. We cannot assume that every colonist who became a *Schultheiss* had previously taken part in the expensive and difficult work of recruiting for his community and creating the village—nor, on the other hand, that everyone who did take part in such work had no higher aim than to become a village *Schultheiss*. The locators of Wichmann of Magdeburg, whom we meet in the charters, know Latin. One is a vassal of the archbishop. Generally speaking, we may assign these men to the class which, in other places, directed the trade and self-government of the rising towns. Often this classification is demonstrable; and the work of 'location' called for the same personal capacities and material resources as were required in a prominent burgess. Locators had to co-operate on journeys into distant places; to deal with foreigners; have property to be risked in a venture; and some knowledge of law. For the burgess of those days it was more or less immaterial whether he employed these capacities and resources in agrarian enterprises or in trade and town government. Indeed, many people came to the new colonial towns with their eyes fixed from the start on the acquisition of landed property. The law which the Margrave of Meissen granted to the new town of Leipzig about 1160 regulated this very thing. And Archbishop Wichmann in his charter for Jüterbog (1174) explained that the foundation of the town was of importance *ad edificandam provinciam*. We cannot prove from the documents that Jüterbog burgesses were concerned with 'location', or that founders of villages sold their posts in them to establish themselves in the town with the proceeds; but both things are probable.

Flemings and Hollanders were the pioneers. They are mentioned in Mecklenburg and near Magdeburg. They push as far east as Flaeming by Jütcrbog, south towards Meissen, and up to the 'Bohemian forest mountains' (the Erzgebirge) as Helmold says. They were always specially entrusted with the cultivation of marshy land. That other,

[1] The term *settinke* is evidently connected with the 'settling' functions of the locators.

West German, groups soon followed and imitated them can be seen clearly in the charter references to 'Flemish law' and 'measured by the Flemish hide' (*Hufe*); but unhappily tradition does not tell us how the bands of emigrants came together. The new settlements were made both economically and legally attractive. Settlers received for moderate fixed rents holdings which were heritable and freely alienable. They could feel sure that—these obligations once met—there would be no pressure on them from above. What this hope and this legal security meant, a story from the Lower Rhine very clearly shows. It records the troubles of a land-holding peasant of the monastery of Siegburg whom the lord imprisoned because he would not comply with illegal claims. Such grasping and arbitrary treatment, we are told, *multos vendere patrimonium et ad peregrinas migrare terras compulit.*[1]

The strength of the migratory impetus is shown by the way in which the colonists, besides occupying formerly wasted or easily cultivable land, attacked the high woods from the start. This was a task for that ecclesiastical Order which had been specially interested in it in the West —the Cistercians. Their economic capacity was so highly prized that the margraves in Egerland and Meissen granted them far more land than they could make use of by their traditional method of cultivation by *conversi* for their granges. But they adapted themselves to the new conditions, and gave land to rent-paying peasants against their own rules. So they came into competition with the Orders of Canons Regular— Praemonstratensians and Augustinians of Arrovaise who had taken an important part in the clearing of the West, and had now acquired extensive grants in the colonial territory.

The Cistercians pressed further forward—into the Slavonic principalities: Bohemia, Mecklenburg, Pomerania and Silesia. There they acquired estates on which the establishment of colonists was expressly provided for. These colonists received the same legal position as those of the Elbe region: they were rent-paying peasants, whose dues were strictly regulated in the contract of settlement. Their privileges constituted the first modest beginnings of a comprehensive reconstruction of economic and national conditions in these principalities.

The princes and other great landowners of Slavonic Central Europe had remained uninfluenced by German rural economy so long as it was characterized by the manorial type of organization. The new economy of the Elbe colonies proved more worthy of imitation. There, the seigniorial income was being steadily increased by the rents derived from the labour of self-contained households of trained colonists. But such labour was generally unobtainable from the native

[1] *Miracula S. Annonis*, MS. fol. 58 *verso*. The MS. is in the Düsseldorf Library; the reference was kindly communicated by Prof. W. Levison of Bonn.

Slavonic peasants, except from those of Central Bohemia. Thus in Silesia, the *liber fundationis* of the monastery of Heinrichau shows how, even in the first half of the thirteenth century, local feuds, penal confiscations, and the economic helplessness both of knights and peasants were always tearing fresh gaps in the settlement of the land, which could not be closed. And one great problem, to which the latest developments in the West called special attention, could least as a rule be solved by the skill of the local peasantry—the felling and clearing of the vast forest areas which had been kept untouched for strategical reasons. King Geisa of Hungary († 1161) had already called in Flemings and Germans to fell the frontier forests of Transylvania.

Meanwhile forces were at work in the German colonial Marks which might be employed for more comprehensive development. The second generation of colonists were hungry for as much land as their fathers had. The economic achievement of the locators along the Elbe tempted enterprising men to imitate them further east, where more available land offered even better prospects. The bidding was keen; but the supply of land was so ample that neither locators nor settlers were in danger of getting in one another's way. Between about 1210 and 1230 German colonists entered parts of Mecklenburg, Pomerania, the extended Brandenburg Mark, Silesia, Moravia and Great Poland. The first colonization of Silesia was carried out by 'undertakers' and peasants from the Elbe–Saale region. Their land measures—the great 'Frankish' and the smaller 'Flemish' hide—are witnesses to it; so are their legal traditions, with Frankish, Flemish, Magdeburg and Halle laws. The Franconian settlers came from the foothills of the Erzgebirge; and in Silesia they showed a preference for hill country.

The course and character of East German colonization in these regions, and in the territory that the Teutonic Order conquered a little later in Kulmerland and Prussia, is dealt with elsewhere. Here we need only stress one aspect of the settlement organization which deserves special attention, in relation to the beginnings of the movement, but also with reference to the course of events in the west and south—the importance which towns and burgesses acquired for the task of rural colonization. Town life was a new factor in Eastern Central Europe. Before the era of colonization, the princes had controlled buying and selling in markets in a monopolistic fashion which arrested the development of a native merchant class. Now they relied entirely, for the promotion of trade, industry and mining, on those German burgess colonists to whom they conceded the erection of towns and the founding of communal institutions. But the German rural colonists were also deeply interested in town life. The Slavonic type of market, it is true, had given them opportunities for disposing of their produce. But a town, with its court of justice, assured to them something more. It increased legal security, as against both native rural Slavs and the lords of land and justice, whether Slav or German. This association of peasant and urban settlement was most firmly organized in Silesia. There, as early as 1220, the duke and the locators began to establish groups of colonists' villages, each of which had as its centre of trade and justice a colonial town. To these grouped settlements was transferred the term *Weichbild* which in North Germany meant the area of a town's jurisdiction. The Slavonic villages lying between the groups gradually adjusted their layout, their economic life, and their law to those of the Germans; and the *Weichbild* system became the basis for the administration of the whole country.

To burgesses in towns founded in a countryside still in course of development, the chance of acquiring landed property was always present. This fact had a growing influence on the organization of settlement. Town-making went on fast in the second and third quarters of the thirteenth century. Commercial prospects justified very little of it indeed. Burgesses in the more important towns would hardly have tolerated the rise of so many insignificant ones, had not the market radius of the small places remained as a rule exceedingly limited. The whole process was only possible when the burgesses, who had to defend and govern the towns, could be given the prospect of safe incomes from the ownership of land. The Teutonic Order—influenced perhaps by Mediterranean precedents—even tried deliberately to encourage a landlord class in its first colonial towns. The Law of Kulm assumes that the most substantial burgesses will hold forty *Hufen* and more. And in Silesia, Brandenburg, Mecklenburg and Pomerania, towns were founded, not only with villages about them, but even oftener with from 40 to 300 arable *Hufen* of their own. These endowments eased the town finances; and also gave burgesses opportunities for acquiring land, of which it is evident that they often took advantage. Besides, a burgess could always share in the 'location' of village colonies in the neighbourhood of the town, most easily under the Silesian *Weichbild* system. The burgesses of the little town of Löwenstein understood the business of founding villages well enough to be able to advise the Abbot of Heinrichau, when he had to buy out a rural locator. In some instances, it is true, we find only a few people sharing in the operations: the man who undertook to establish a town might, by himself or with a single colleague, act as locator and owner of the *Schultheiss* right for the villages of the district.

The relation of the townsmen to the land was not then quite uniform. Some townsmen were agriculturists, others drawers of agricultural rents. Both types are to be found in other regions in the same period.

The protection of the town walls and the possibilities of urban economic and social life were obviously attractive for landowners from among the upper peasantry. This was the dominant class in the many boroughs chartered at this time in England. In Westphalia, in order to protect their territory, ecclesiastical lords—the Archbishop of Cologne, the Bishop of Paderborn—encouraged the peasants of whole villages whose lands marched with one another to break their villages up and unite into small towns. After their experience of the wars of these princes, this 'sunoikisis' was readily accepted by the peasants. Reconstruction in Languedoc, after the fearful devastation of the Albigensian wars, took the form of *bastide* building; and the *bastides* seem to have invariably been inhabited by peasant-burgesses. An increase of urban population through the continuous immigration of rural rentiers is specially noticeable in Florence.

These phenomena must be taken into account in any attempt to understand why the expanson of rural settlement that went on everywhere, from Poland to Spain, between 1100 and 1300 did not make the peasants into an independent factor in the social and political life of the peoples. They were always losing to the towns their economically strongest elements. And so, in the later Middle Ages, the way in which population was settled and distributed in Western and Central Europe had a certain resemblance, in spite of cultural differences, to what it had been in that Roman Empire which Teutonic migration had brought to the ground.

CHAPTER II

Agriculture and Rural Life in the
Later Roman Empire

IN the third century A.D., St Cyprian, bishop of Carthage, found
common ground with his opponents in supposing that the world,
which ancient physical theory compared in its development to the
life of man, was now approaching senility. Morals, art, justice, were
decayed, population had diminished; and the woeful tale is headed
with a statement that the weather was not what it had been. A complaint of this type throws doubt incidentally upon the truth of what
follows it. There may, indeed, have been a slight worsening of climate,
at least in North-West Europe, with lower temperatures and heavier
rainfall; but it is doubtful whether it had occurred in time for St
Cyprian to observe it; and even so it is legitimate for an inquiry into
the agriculture of the Later Roman Empire to start with the postulate
that its climate was not significantly different from that of today.

Yet it is worth staying an instant with this pessimistic bishop, for the
words of his complaint indicate the problems which faced the Roman
farmer in his battle with nature, and will even help to remove certain
misconceptions of them. 'There are no longer', said St Cyprian, 'such
winter rains or such summer heat.' The words illustrate properties of
climate which are vital in determining the agricultural methods of the
Mediterranean region, the core, it might be said, of the Roman Empire.
In this area, the mean monthly rainfall of June, July, and August seldom
exceeds four inches except in the high altitudes, and over its greater
part varies between one and two inches. This zone of summer drought
comprises the area of the whole Roman Empire, if its northern pro-
longation into Gaul and Britain is excepted; indeed, to a geographer,
there is no more remarkable aspect of Julius Caesar's career than his
extension of the Roman Empire into a climatic area distinct from it.
For elsewhere the climate has homogeneity, and while the mass of
ancient agricultural doctrine is concerned with Greece and Italy,
modern observation reinforced by the hints of ancient authors allows
us to establish general principles valid throughout the Mediterranean
region. Whether there is also a homogeneity in time is another matter,
hard to decide and vital of decision, for almost all the agricultural
doctrine is extant in books written before our period commences.
Palladius and the few valuable facts of agrarian practice contained in
that untidy manual of country superstition, the *Geoponica*, are all that

we can call the primary authorities of this period; and the obvious fact that they repeat the maxims and often the words of their predecessors may be misleading. A military author of the fourth century tells his readers the organization of the Legion: research has proved that he deceives them; no such regiment had paraded for 200 years. Into the minds of those who read such antiquarianism it is hard to enter, but, given their existence, how can we know that Palladius really described the 'Farmer's Year' of a contemporary farmer? Yet it is probable that he did, and that his loans from earlier writers are loans that he had a right to make. The Arab of the Dark Ages and the visiting English 'improvers' of the eighteenth and nineteenth centuries describe a system in substance the same as that which emerges from the pages of Palladius and of his sources, too; and this they do because the conditions of climate impose it, so that today the science of the Industrial Revolution finds difficulty in making changes.

The nature of the cultivable soil plays a part in determining the system of agriculture, though its part is less important than the climate's. 'It is weather rather than soil', said Theophrastus, 'that determines the harvest'; and his remark at once illustrates this point and shows that though differences in cultivable soil exist, and were indeed classified by the ancients, the pedology of the Mediterranean region permits generalization no less than does its climate. It is a region of crystalline plateaux alternating with folded mountain chains, on which periodic elevation and subsidence have worked. These geological movements have smoothed the slope of the mountains and covered them with Tertiary deposits of limestone, sandstone, or marly clay. The mountain chains, high enough to catch the rain of sea-borne winds, suffer denudation with each rainy season, and the rivers become raging torrents, rolling their heavier, and carrying in suspension their lighter, particles of detritus. Thus were formed deltaic plains of recent alluvium, such as those of the Guadalquivir, the Po, and the Eurotas. Occasionally under plateau conditions the slow course of streams, seeking a descent, created similar alluvial deposits, such as are found in the upper waters of the Halys in Cappadocia. Geology, therefore, made a threefold division of Mediterranean soil, the alluvial plain, the Tertiary slopes, and the mountains; and to each ancient agronomists assign its share in agricultural production. The mountains, where still forested, sheltered the woodman, the tanner, and the charcoal-burner, pursuing their occupations in conditions which hardly differed from the prehistoric, and which attracted little notice in literature save from a romantically minded orator who might yearn for the simple life in a charcoal-burner's hut. Stripped of their timber, the highlands provided summer pasture for flocks and goats under the rough conditions that made the shepherd too easily a kidnapper and a brigand. The Tertiary soils were suited to crops, the thinner higher land to the planted, the lower to the sown; the alluvial lands nourished store beeves. Land of this last class was not, however, common in the Mediterranean region, and thus it is not one of extensive stock-raising; moreover, the attacks of the liver-fluke in days before remedy was possible must have reduced the population of sheep and even of cattle on lands which seem at first sight suitable to them. Large areas of lush meadow are comparatively rare; it is instructive indeed to note that in one of them, the upper Halys, around Caesarea, there were large imperial estates the maintenance of which from private encroachment is attempted by legislation of Justinian (A.D. 527–65): here, as we know, horses were bred in early times for the Great King of Persia, and it is not improbable that on these estates were stud farms for the cavalry that formed an ever more important arm of the Byzantine field force. We shall see that throughout this period imperial tended to give way to private ownership. Yet it is not uninstructive to note that imperial estates, maintained as such into the Byzantine period, are found in lush river valleys such as the Tembris, lands suitable for horse-breeding, where they have even survived occasionally as crown property into the Ottoman Empire.

The relative scarcity of stock-raising land had more than one effect upon ancient life. It affected, for instance, the diet; and it should be no accident that, while literary men (and the so-called 'Apicius' with his recipe book) could make play with famous vineyards, there seems no hint in Greek or Roman life of a famous cheese. And Caesar, campaigning in central Gaul, commended the discipline of his soldiers who accepted a diet of meat without a grumble. Moreover it has an indirect, though important, effect on the general pattern of farming. Summer droughts made it difficult to grow cruciferous root crops (turnips, etc.) without irrigation and hay was similarly in short supply. Thus there is nothing corresponding to the 'high farming' as developed by eighteenth-century English agronomists in ancient technical writers. Animal husbandry was based principally on what is called 'transhumance'. It was, as it still is, the practice to move beasts along regular tracks (once called *calles*, now *tratturi*, *drailles* and other words of obscure local derivation) at regular and indeed prescribed intervals from the summer grazings of the hills to the lowland pasturage. With the growth of unimpeded commodity movement in the period of general Roman domination there was a tendency for cereals on land not notably suitable for them to be grown merely for the local market, so that lowland pasturage seems not to have been in short supply. But with the loss of Egyptian and African resources to the Western Empire in its last centuries, it appears that even Southern Italy, where Seneca had once commented on the 'deserts of Apulia', was growing cereals as it had grown them long ago, so that there was competition for winter grazings. Herds under the ownership of the distant ruler, whether Roman emperor or Gothic king, always tended to suffer to the profit of powerful local magnates. But while they put difficulties in the way of Marcus Aurelius' shepherds as they travelled the *calles*, the Gothic king (his name is lost) found it hard to procure pasturage at all for his own herdsmen at the end of their travels. In these circumstances the temporary pasturage of a cereal farmer's fallows and the possibility of thinning down autumn sowings as they came through (both mentioned by the technicians) must be remembered, as they were perhaps remembered by the poet, Silius Italicus, who thought of a shepherd on Monte Gargaro looking down on burning stubbles in the plain and thinking of the benefits for pasturage in months to come. Nevertheless grazier and ploughman tended (the story of Cain and Abel embodies the notion) to dwell in worlds apart, so that it is likely that much of the cultivated land in the Mediterranean was by modern standards under-manured. It is true that the ideal amount of manure demanded by Columella was 1440 *modii* per *iugerum* (about 550 bushels to the acre) and that this figure—though, since neither the state nor the composition of the manure is given, comparison is dangerous—seems reasonably equivalent to modern practice. Nevertheless it would be quite impossible to determine how far this ideal was realized even in Spain and Italy, the native and adopted countries of Columella. It is surely significant that the farmer was urged to shifts of all kind in the quest for fertilizing agents. Pigeon and poultry dung were to be collected, weeds and scrub brought in from the fields and lees from the wine-vat added to the compost. Moreover there is some evidence to suggest at least that, even if flock-masters were competing for pasturage in Italy, in regions of the Eastern Mediterranean the stock population was hardly dense enough for competition. Thus the cadastral records of a portion of Mytilene shows as objects assessable for taxation one horse, 29 head of cattle, something more than 150 sheep and something more than 20 goats upon estates showing a sown area of about 870 English acres: on Thera island the proportions are three oxen, two asses, and fifteen sheep to 275 acres. It is possible that there are details in the booking of stock which escape us; a certain amount of animals grazing on one estate may have been booked as stalled in others for which we have no data. But even if this is admitted, the contrast with modern Greece (certainly not over-stocked) is striking. Evaluating the cattle, in accordance with modern census practice, as equivalent to five units of sheep and goats, we have an overall figure for modern Greece of about three 'head' per acre of cultivated land. Moreover a record of similar type and date from Lydia shows virtually no stock at all. It would obviously be unwise to press the evidence of these chance documents at all hard. Nevertheless they do correspond to what can be inferred from the social history of the period. There was a greater demand for meat now that more barbarians were entering the army, but the attitude of the army to neighbouring grazings is censured as arbitrary by emperors and can hardly be considered as scientific by us. And there were the depredations of invaders; there were the requisitions, regular and irregular, for the imperial post and other purposes against which villagers complained and favoured communities were privileged, all reducing the number of livestock. Indeed it is not at all surprising to find a law of Valens (A.D. 366–78) forbidding the slaughter of calves 'in the interests of agriculture'.

Thus it was especially necessary for the farmer to develop the techniques of cultivation if his land was to give a satisfactory yield; and it was evidently felt to be essential that the growing crop should not compete with weeds, so that all technicians insist on the necessity of repeated ploughing. It was normal to plough land three times, but Vergil advised four, and there was even land in Italy, according to Pliny, which was ploughed nine times over. The soil was cross-ploughed and then ploughed obliquely, so that in a well ploughed field it should be impossible to tell which way the plough had last gone. Work involving such an amount of labour-time, four days' work, according to Columella, per *iugerum* (about two-thirds of an English acre), assumes an ample supply of cheap labour, and this has been a primary condition of Mediterranean agriculture down to very modern times. But for good farming such methods could not be avoided. Weeds compete with the seedlings for essential nutrients and above all for water the conservation of which was no less controllable by such techniques. Moreover the rainfall of the Mediterranean lands is irregular and frequently violent; the soil must not only be clean but well pulverized to take it when it comes, or there is serious 'run-off'—devastating to the top-soil, especially in the basin of the Mediterranean, where so much cultivation must necessarily be on more or less of a slope. The periods of rainfall tend to coincide with a critical period in the growth of young plants, and in a waterlogged soil excessive moisture tends to prolong the winter cold and prevent the young seedlings warming up. It was sensible, therefore, for the ancient technicians to advise the most careful attention to field drainage during the winter months; they mention field ditches, tile drains and the once familiar 'bush' or 'bavin' drains. Moreover the practice of 'ridging', which it will be necessary to describe more fully, could play its part in the removal of surface water. Thus one problem was solved by draining, but the other presented by

St Cyprian's 'summer heat' taxed the farmer's ingenuity because it was opposed to that already solved. Whereas it was important for him to dispose of surface water from the 'winter rains', it was even more important to ensure that sufficient water remained in the ground to provide against a short-fall in the rain supply and to minimize the losses by transpiration and evaporation which must inevitably occur in the summer. He solved his problem by methods which, transported to America by Spanish conquerors, have there received both scientific attention and the name of 'dry farming'. Transpiration from a growing crop could not indeed be readily controlled, but transpiration from weeds could be averted by their elimination. Nevertheless for all his determination and skill a farmer was seldom permitted by his water resources to take more than a crop in alternate years; indeed to sow immediately on land which had borne a crop was a proverbial Greek metaphor to describe improvidently avaricious behaviour. In fact he required the carefully husbanded rainfall of two years to produce the crop of one. The fallow, of course, must be kept clean of weeds, as the technicians earnestly advise. Indeed American experiments have shown that soil in such condition may have as much as ten times the quantity of moisture as when left alone. The farmer, we are told, might risk ploughing it during the summer heat, so that weeds encouraged by the spring rains might be properly removed. And by virtually inviting the action of the summer sun on the soil he was, while losing the moisture of the immediate top layers, insulating its lower layers from evaporation.

After taking the crop it was normal to plough the stubbles in, often after burning them, thus giving the shepherd of Monte Gargaro his hopeful prospect, though, as we have seen, his hopes might be delusive. The purpose of burning was not so much to encourage the growth of edible grasses as to restore potash, phosphorus and other nutrients to the soil. In addition during the following year of fallow the stubble and residues of the crop could provide energy for 'specialized bacteria' in the soil to fix nitrogen from the air into forms suitable for the next crop.

The technicians, especially those from the eastern Mediterranean, where rainfall is less, complete their advice on stirring the soil with stress on the advantages of digging. The actual soils of the Mediterranean region are more often shallow than not. To break up the subsoil would at the same time extend the root-range and increase in depth the catchment area of water resources, while untapped reserves of phosphorus and other valuable nutrients were made available. It was, in effect, equivalent to subsoil ploughing, which is a normal concomitant in modern times for this type of farming. But if labour costs

7

or mere laziness prevented digging, the ancient farmer could argue, like his Castilian descendant, that he had better leave well alone. To blame, therefore, the ancient farmer for neglecting the 'over-turn' plough is to misinterpret his problem; to blame him, as modern agricultural historians have been ready to do, for wasting energy on repeated ploughing is even more seriously to misinterpret it.

Thus the plough, the main function of which was the removal of weeds (the Italian peasant in the days of old Cato had a special god to assist him), could be of simple construction consisting of share, share-beam, plough-beam and handle. It was further used for 'ridging', which would assist winter drainage if the seeds were sown on the ridges and protect the newly sown corn from the frequent and erratic winds of the area, if the seeds were sown in the furrows between them. Indeed not infrequently the Mediterranean farmer manages to avoid the choice in the hope, it seems, of getting the best of both worlds. For this a furrow was driven by the plough, to which was affixed, according to the heaviness of the soil, pegs or boards on one or both sides of the share-beam. These appliances, misleadingly named mould-boards by northern students, spread out the soil scuffed aside by share and share-beam, so as to form the ridges; and so common was the practice that the ordinary word for furrow—*sulcus*—comes in the latest agronomic writer, Palladius, to denote these ridges, earlier called *lirae* or *porci* (pigs or almost 'hogsbacks'). Harrowing to break up clods after ploughing was, Pliny implies, a confession of defeat, but the harrow was honourably used to smooth down the soil, if the seedlings were too deeply covered in 'ridging', and to assist in the maintenance of a clean fallow. Ancient agronomic authors describe toothed harrows, and hand rakes were also used for this purpose; a two-pointed prong was used for the digging, and in reading Vergil's graphic description of 'throwing' it at the soil, the gardener can almost feel himself at work.

It should now be possible to interpret the 'Farmer's Year' as it is described in ancient textbooks and even figured on mosaics. The land was ploughed in January and February and, if necessary, re-ploughed in March. During the summer months it lay fallow, cleaned occasionally by harrow, rake and hoe and by a single ploughing, until it was ready for the final ploughing that preceded the normal autumn sowing. This was usually accomplished in October; and 'ridging', with harrowing, where necessary, secured the right conditions for the young plants to make rapid growth in the spring. At this period it was especially necessary to conserve moisture and avoid the competition of weeds for it, so that the ancients correctly advised careful harrowing and hoeing at this time. They realized too, as does the American 'dry farmer', that over-sowed land might so exhaust the water resources that there was not enough to support the final ripening; and they advise that it might be necessary to thin the seedlings by grazing. Continual hoeing—for the elimination of weeds, as we can interpret the ancient doctrine—is advised as the summer heat approaches. Meanwhile it was in the farmer's interest to harvest his crop as early as he dared, in the eastern Mediterranean as early as mid-May, in Italy in June or early July. If he delayed it might be parched and deprived of nutritive value. The crop was reaped by hand-sickles and not infrequently only the ears were taken off, leaving 'headers' of straw normally to be burnt or ploughed in, as commented on above. The grain was thrashed by flails, by the tread of oxen, or by the *tribulum*, a heavy board studded with flints and driven over the floor by animal power. In towns with a large and reasonably certain demand, and perhaps in large villas, it was ground in mills turned by horses or donkeys, but in most parts of the Empire the women still ground at the hand-mill as in Biblical days. Archaeologists have indeed noticed during the course of Roman history some technical improvements in the machine used, the rotary hand-quern, but it is an interesting commentary upon the unmechanical character of ancient civilization that it made little use of the water-mill. A poet of the first century B.C. extols it as a labour-saving device, and a succession of small mills have recently come to light in Provence. One may expect that refined archaeological exploration may give other examples. Nevertheless the absence of reference to water-mills in the juridical texts compared with the frequent mention of litigation over weirs and water-rights in medieval documents, suggests that the Roman world was very different from the medieval with its picture of a mill on every manor that had a stream to turn it. And we are many centuries away from the windmill. Horse and donkey mills have been found, for instance in London and at Pompeii (where the buildings show little consideration for the animals), and it may be no accident that we can prove the water-mill for the great capitals of Rome and Constantinople, with their heavy demands for ground flour. A shortage of appropriate low-grade labour combined with the soldier's traditional dislike of menial toil may explain its appearance on Hadrian's Wall.

The technique of corn-growing was applied with the necessary variations to the production of a variety of vegetable and fodder crops, which after harvesting or cropping could be turned in as green manures; the sturdy lupin giving a canopy of closed vegetation being the most favoured. Many of these, as beans and peas, being ill-adapted to face the Mediterranean winter, were sown as spring crops, and it was recognized that cereals themselves could be so grown, though on the whole spring sowing was deprecated unless it was demanded by the nature of the plant and the climate or by a failure of the autumn crop.

The ancient farmer had accumulated in centuries of practice a large body of doctrine upon the relations of crop and soil; and perhaps because agricultural technique was the possession rather of the conservative and practically-minded peasant, than of the scientific thinker, the doctrine tended to develop on this line rather than in the direction of sacrificing the perfection of soil suitability to the advantages of a varying rotation. Ancient authors are unsystematic and casual in their treatment of it, and most of them seem to have regarded the change of crop on land as an exception justified either by the soil or the climate. On low-lying volcanic soil, well-watered and rich, liberties could be taken. In Campania, for instance, the land was cropped all the year round, with *Panicum*, with millet, and with a green crop. This looks dangerously like overworking the soil, and it may be no accident that this is a district which reveals evidence of derelict land in the fifth century. More commonly rotation was practised because fortunate climatic conditions permitted it; a wet summer, for instance, might allow a spring-sown green crop or even a spring wheat or barley to be slipped into the ordinary crop-fallow rotation, and it is significant that the authorities assign to the Alps and the Po valley—regions where more than the normal summer moisture is to be expected—the principal development of such a practice.

Careful application of 'dry farming' techniques enabled the ancients to grow not only sown crops but trees yielding fruit of economic significance: and of these the olive, the vine, and the fig were the principal. Early attempts at geographical restriction are not relevant to our period, in which the olive is known throughout the Mediterranean region outside the mountain areas, where it could not stand up to the cold. Its spear-shaped leaves lost little by transpiration in the summer, and its long widely spread roots could catch ground water over a wide distance; an over-rich soil, however, caused the tree to run to wood, so that the ancients preferred a hillside to the rich plain soil, where, moreover, hot summer winds might parch the fruit. Pruning, especially spring pruning, diverted the nutriment of the tree to fruitage and the cuttings of pruning might be used for grafting, which offered advantages over propagation by seedlings grown in nursery beds, in that the plants were less likely to revert to the wild state. Seedling culture, however, permitted the development by selection of varieties suitable to the land, and it is perhaps a proof of continuous arboricultural progress that while ten varieties were known to Columella in the first century, Macrobius in the fourth mentions sixteen.

Naturally even for a tree with such root advantages as the olive, water conservation was necessary, and the technique already mentioned of plough and hoe was employed. Indeed the necessity of cultivating the olive field induced the farmer to grow a crop on it, and the added circumstance of shading, so well appreciated by modern 'dry farming' exponents, could be utilized. On a field at Tabace in Africa it is reported that olives grew under palms, figs under olives, vines under figs and corn under vines. It is not clear what the economic objective of this agricultural *arboretum* may be—after all, the resources, especially the water resources, of the field cannot be utilized more than once over. We may perhaps think of general protection afforded by the larger to the smaller phytological units down the scale.

The cultivation of the vine itself illustrates the conditions of the Mediterranean climate, as well as the 'dry farming' technique devised to meet them. If occasional summer moisture was expected, indeed, if the conservation of water in the ground was thought to be adequate, vines were allowed to grow upwards, being propped, trellised or festooned between the trees of an orchard. This method secured sunlight for the grapes at the period of ripening and increased the yield; moreover, the ancients thought, not apparently incorrectly, that the finest juice was yielded from shoots that were allowed to climb as they would naturally do. Above all, the method protected the grapes against ground vermin, the menace of which is revealed in the legend of Apollo Smintheus, the mouse-killer, and in the fable of the fox and the grapes: the fox, used to grapes grown at ground level, was defeated by a trellised vine.

For there were many districts where vines had to be grown low in spite of mice and foxes; by this method they could escape the drying summer winds, while the sprawling leaves protected the ground itself from the action of the sun, and if they were deliberately covered with dust, the loss of water by transpiration was reduced. Moreover, the saving of working costs in props and trellises was considerable. The vinetender's problem was linked, in fact, with the amount of sunlight available: sunshine control, neither too much nor too little for grape and ground, was the key to his problem.

But, however solved, the principles of pedology which have been set out above were not the less applicable; and all writers insist on continual, thorough, and deep cultivation of the ground, that the precious water should not escape; so clean must the land be, that ideally no crop, save an occasional green manure, should share the vineyard.

Water conservation, then, proves to be the principle at work in the technique of cultivation, whether of sown or of planted crops. If in spite of the technique the water supply was inadequate, either because the climate was after all too arid, or the water demands of the plant too great, methods of irrigation were applied. The numerous decisions of the jurists upon water rights are eloquent testimony to its importance, and an inscription with plan of an aqueduct, probably the Aqua Crabra, near Tusculum, exists, on which is recorded the names of the properties, the number of pipes supplied and the hours when they could be opened. A similar document has been found near Lamasba in Numidia, from which we learn that the spring could even be utilized to irrigate lands in the hills; this argues the use of high-pressure pipes and some kind of ram, and quite primitive cultivators made use of the wheel and the Archimedean screw to raise water to their fields. Moreover, this inscription illustrates conditions which were the rule throughout North Africa. An inquiry conducted in Algeria for the benefit of French colonists elicited the information that in almost every commune there were vestiges of Roman hydraulic works. Streams had been dammed, water stored in reservoirs, ponds, and underground tanks, to be transferred to the land by aqueducts and canals. The mayor of a commune calculated that there would be a gain of more than 12,000 acres of cultivable land in it if the Roman works were put into repair.

With such methods of irrigation, the 'dry farming' technique could be supplemented, and plants successfully grown which under ordinary Mediterranean conditions yielded small and stunted fruits. Thus onions, cabbages, lettuces, and peas were grown in irrigated lands, as was the most estimated fodder crop, the 'Poa Medica', lucerne or alfalfa, introduced, as the name implies, from the East, probably about the fifth century B.C. A single sowing lasted ten years and four to five crops could be taken per year. It is instructive to notice that the plant is said almost to have disappeared in Europe during the Dark Ages. It is a question whether one should explain this by the under-stocking to which attention has been called, or by the decline of intensive irrigation, which may be expected in a period of storm and strife. Perhaps each cause reacted upon the other, for failure of irrigation, which may affect the disposal of water from the land as much as its introduction to it, certainly converted good pasture land into malarious swamps. The desolation of the Pontine Marshes seems to date from this period, and an inscription of Theodoric the Ostrogoth records a vain attempt to drain them.

There were areas in the ancient world in which irrigation was not a complement of 'dry farming', but a substitute for it, where the whole existence of the population depended on the watering of the land by overflowing rivers and the deposition of their suspended soil-particles as the water retired. As early as Herodotus, travellers in Egypt and Mesopotamia wondered at a way of life far removed from their own, and it is necessary to comment especially upon the agrarian conditions of Egypt, since the possibility of collecting large aggregates of the population in capital cities depended much upon the certainty of the Egyptian harvest. In the first century A.D. Egypt contributed twenty million *modii* of wheat per year (about five million bushels) to Rome, which represented about a third of the total supply, and in the reign of Justinian, eight million *artabae*, equivalent to about seven million bushels, were sent yearly to Constantinople.

The Nile rises annually with the melting of the snows and the periodic rains at its sources, and is in flood between August and October; during these months it is led away in canals from the river the bed of which, like the Mississippi, has been raised by continual soil deposition above the surrounding lands. The canals deposit the flood water in basins bounded by dykes. After the Nile has dropped sufficiently the water is returned to it lower down by outfall canals. The irrigation period under favourable conditions succeeded the harvest and preceded the cultivation and sowing of autumn crops. It was important, however, to control the water at other times than in the 'safety period' when the land was idle, lest the unharvested corn should be drowned on the one hand, or the sowing hindered on the other. Egyptian documents are full, therefore, of references to the maintenance of the canal system, so that irrigation could operate at all, and of the river banks and the dykes so that it should operate as desired. In a period of misgovernment or inefficiency dykes fell down and canals were choked, so that in A.D. 278 the Emperor Probus was forced to send detachments of the army to repair them. In normal years, however, the work was performed by the compulsory labour of the cultivators, for which they might or might not receive pay. In a papyrus of the sixth or seventh century A.D. a *solidus* (about 13 shillings) is paid for the movement of 150 cubits of dyke earth.

Where local conditions did not admit of regular flooding, such as in the Fayum, which had been largely brought into cultivation by private persons under beneficial leases, irrigation was practised under conditions similar to those of Africa and elsewhere; the water-table was high, so that wells could be dug and the water raised by hydraulic instruments. In the 129 days for which the items of expenditure on an Egyptian property of the first century A.D. are recorded, various irrigation machines were working on 92 of them.

Under Egyptian conditions, the land almost keeps itself in heart, as the irrigation continually deposits small quantities of new soil rich in nitrogen and ammonia: nevertheless, manuring was useful if not essential, and the very richness of the soil caused a rank growth of weeds, which needed the cultivator's attention.

It is convenient at this point to discuss the social consequences of the 'dry farming' and irrigatory methods of agriculture which are characteristic of such large portions of the Roman Empire. Here it must first be stated that the picture which the agronomists draw is of what the system should do, and Columella himself proclaims that this was far from what it did. We happen to know, for instance, that in spite of his insistence on repeated ploughing, the tenants of an African estate were required to perform no more task-work with the plough than with the harrow. Moreover large portions of the Mediterranean region were still on prehistoric cultural levels—in Strabo's time periodic redivisions of land were the rule in Dalmatia. A hint of the distinction between ideal and real is given by the statements of yield: the ancients were too preoccupied with the exceptional to be useful statisticians, so that alleged yields of 100- and 150-fold may be neglected if not distrusted. But there is the probability that the data for the tithed lands of Sicily are correct, and their moderation inspires confidence. Here, according to Cicero (first century B.C.), the yield varied between eightfold and tenfold, and this with an average seeding of $2\frac{1}{4}$ bushels per English acre represents a harvest of 20 or more bushels. The volcanic lands of Mount Etna were, however, exceptional, as was Etruria, which, as Varro states, produced ten- or fifteen-fold. Columella's general average for Italy is fourfold, which represents about 9 bushels per acre. It looks a small return, yet it is most instructive to note that observers of Italian agriculture in the days before the Industrial Revolution give figures which tally exactly with those of the ancients. Symonds corroborates Varro for the yield of Etruria; Balbo and Pictet report a four-fold average in Piedmont. And the negligence which these observers attribute to the agriculture of their own time, under-manuring, neglect of weeding, show how ideal is the picture of the ancient agronomists.

This is not surprising, for the agriculture both of 'dry farming' and of irrigation can be called intensive: it made heavy demands on the worker's energy and depended for its profitable character on a supply of cheap labour. And while its value was increased by the fact that on mixed farms the varieties of crops grown enabled the worker to be active throughout the year, the advantage gained on this side was, we may conjecture, largely offset under the servile or quasi-servile tenures by which most land was cultivated in the later Roman Empire. These tenures we must in due course discuss, but for the moment we can make the point that under them personal incentive was lowered in an agricultural system where it was all-important; and that its decay shows itself partly in downright strikes from work of which we have evidence, but still more, no doubt, in inefficiency. Moreover, with the growth of large estates, the 'master's eye', the value of which early writers well recognize, was less often seen. Particularly was the labourer's effort necessary on the irrigated land, for not only must the crops be watered and the pump-wheel turned, but the task of keeping channels and aqueducts clean was heavy; while the cost of repairs, if once negligence allowed them to choke, must often have been prohibitive. Extensive irrigatory systems demanded in the ancient world a strongly centralized administration, and we shall see that this was just what the government of the later Roman Empire failed to give. Civil war and disturbance increased the effects of mismanagement, and the results are seen in the state of the irrigated North African lands after the rebellions of Firmus and Gildo. Official inspectors reported in A.D. 442 that in the provinces of Africa Proconsularis and Byzacena out of 5,975,858 *iugera* (about 4,000,000 English acres) of land originally cultivable, 2,683,148 *iugera* (about 1,750,000 English acres) had become derelict. Under 'dry farming' conditions, such a diminution would be less expected and more reparable; nevertheless, the 'dry farming' technique had its own disadvantages. The tools were primitive, and with the rudimentary metallurgy of the ancient world remained so, while the effort of continual ploughing made the relation between labour time and production as unfavourable, if not more so, than on irrigated lands. Over-cropping, or neglect of the fallow year, to which a cultivator might be especially tempted by a menacing taxation-demand, would reduce the fertility of the already perhaps under-manured land, though to speak of actual soil exhaustion is dangerous. The famous Rothamsted experiment shows that on land continually cropped without manure, the average yield, after a quick initial decline, remains constant; and the constant Rothamsted yield, it may be noted, of 10 bushels per acre, exceeds the Italian average of Columella. Nevertheless, if over-cropping reduced rather than cancelled the yield, soil denudation was probably a potent factor. Increasing disafforestation has made Mediterranean rivers more torrential so that the risk of a violent 'run-off' removing the soil altogether was great on derelict or negligently managed land. The dry winds of the hot summer could have a similar effect; moreover, with the heavy seasonal rains negligent drainage might have bad effects on productivity.

A further point arises, not indeed from the farming technique itself, but from the attitude of the ancient world towards it. So often was the agricultural producer a slave or serf, that the thinking man, whose thinking life was passed in the towns with townsmen, accepted rather than understood what the peasant was doing, and though agronomists such as Varro advised experiment, the theory that crops were suited to soils inhibited rotation and over-stabilized agricultural activity. Moreover, there were other factors in this agricultural rigidity, which derive from the ways of ancient thought itself. In the ancient world of the city-state the man was confronted directly by the state; and his legal rights had often grown out of his relations with it. Furthermore, in the Roman Empire rights existed (or at least jurists proclaimed that they existed) on provincial soil because their recipients were precarious grantees of the Roman government. It is difficult not to believe that landowners respected the doctrines of state-authorized jurists, however much moderns may criticize their historical validity. The consequences are deep and important. Private accountancy modelled itself upon that of the state, and a system adequate for checking peculation was useless to suggest to a landowner how he could 'cost' his agriculture in terms of profit and loss. The supremacy of the state and the suspicions of the central government kept company law backward in the Roman world, so that no facilities existed for joint-stock agricultural enterprises or agricultural banks; and even the possibility of raising capital for farming improvements was trammelled by the ancient mortgage laws, which, devised for the security of state debts, were but slowly and inadequately applied to the relations of the private citizen. Much, therefore, contributed to make agriculture of the later Roman Empire stagnant, and, especially in so far as it depended on irrigation works, much to make it vulnerable.

Though some of these considerations affect the agriculture of the lands beyond the Alps, in the main their problems must be separately considered. Here, as the expectation of summer rainfall increases, we pass gradually from an area of 'dry' to one of 'humid' farming. Unfortunately, the ancient agronomists are almost silent upon the farming technique of lands outside their own. And though medieval practice in the northern lands, if it cannot be proved actually to derive from the ancients, must, as based on the same natural factors, resemble it, yet the degree of resemblance is so difficult to state with certainty that medieval practice is better left to the medievalist. Thus the ensuing sketch, if slight, will gain in security.

The agrarian differences between these northern lands and the Mediterranean region have their origin in geological no less than climatic distinctions. Here we have extended areas of flat or but slightly elevated plain-land, alternating with chains of chalk or oölite hills, with occasional intrusion of archaean and palaeozoic mountain ranges, as in the so-called 'Highland Zone' of Britain. These regions from a pedological point of view present, on the one hand, 'strong' lands bearing in a natural state more or less dense forest, the lowland loams and clays, and, on the other, light soils, the chalk and oölitic uplands, and the sands, gravels, and loess of the lowlands. The 'strong' soils were better agricultural land than most of the Mediterranean region, but they were, so to say, agricultural land *in posse* rather than *in esse*. Prehistoric man had sought the easier but less profitable soils, and archaeological evidence shows that there he remained, often throughout the period of the Roman Empire, living in timber or dry-stone hut-ments, little, if at all, different from those of his ancestors.

The possibilities, however, of northern agricultural progress lay mainly in the utilization of the heavier soil. Greatly encouraged by the growth of a market in the Roman armies of Gaul and Britain, the movement gathered strength: entrepreneurs attacked and won conquests in the loam terrains and upon the lighter clay. Throughout the early Empire, the conquest proceeded; but as the hope of profit necessarily diminished, its rate declined. In Gaul, indeed, the advance seems to have stopped before the third century, and ground was actually lost in the ensuing insecurity and turmoil when, as we shall see, the population decreased. In Britain, however, it proceeded well into the fourth century, though there was still much ground which might have been won. The incentive to such progress was also, to some extent, climatological. In contrast to the Mediterranean lands the regular and abundant rainfall of North-West Europe was adequate in itself for taking a crop each year. The fact that the common practice was to crop for only one or two years and follow with a period of fallow is explained by the need for a period for recuperation of fertility. In these areas the fallow was not the 'bare fallow' of the Mediterranean technicians' ideal but a fallow of weed, grazed by the cattle, the land receiving the benefit of their manure. And it was not only the arable fields themselves that provided it but the outlying browse areas. The ideal of northern ploughing was, as stated by Small in 1784, to 'cut a slice of soil, to move it to one side and to turn it over'—with the object of ploughing the weeds in. As we have seen, the normal Mediter-ranean plough had quite a different purpose; but a famous passage in Pliny, unfortunately corrupt, tells us that somewhere in the North, in Rhaetia or in Gaul, a wheeled plough with coulter and a spear-shaped share existed, which did just what Small advised. Pliny does not mention a mould-board for this implement, and his account rather implies that the share or share-beam turned the sod, but to attach one, as is normal in medieval northern ploughs, was not a difficult applica-tion of Mediterranean 'ridging' practice. It is interesting to note that the name given to the implement in the manuscripts of Pliny—*plaumoratum*—however it is to be emended, seems to contain some derivative of the root-form of the northern word 'plough'. Hints of the extension of such an implement in the North are not lacking. The name of the Northern French plough, *charrue* or *carruca*, derives from the Gallic word for a wheeled vehicle, and the distribution of heavy iron coulters, a necessary concomitant of this type of plough, is wide-spread over northern lands. The crop-rotation employed in the northern lands in ancient times is not recorded. As water conservation was not so essential, it was possible even in the negligent conditions of medieval cultivation to gain by the substitution of a three-course rotation for the alternation of crop and fallow. It has been suggested that we can infer it on an agricultural unit on Salisbury Plain (Fighel-dean Down), but the complete intermingling of 'two-field' and 'three-field' systems on a map of Common-field English agriculture as published by Gray suggests that the three-course rotation is unlikely to have been the dominant in ancient days. But it is difficult to say how ancient the substitution may be. Certainly, in Britain, a distribution map of these two systems ('two-' and 'three-field') shows them so intermixed as to suggest that the latter is merely a medieval improve-ment on the former. In parts of France, down to the eighteenth century, there were still parishes which had no definite field-system at all, where cultivation roamed, as it were, at will over the lands of the village, and no doubt such a primitive method was in early times more widely distributed: and this again hints that northern agriculture may have been richer in potentialities than in practice. The cereals grown were wheat, barley and oats, which in varying proportions had all been standard grain crops since the Bronze Age. Rye as a cultivated crop seems to be a Roman introduction. Of fruit-bearing trees, apple, plum, damson, and cherry are known; Clement Reid, analysing seeds from the refuse pits of Silchester, noted vine and fig as Roman importa-tions to the flora of Britain, and indeed remains of a vineyard have been found at the villa of Boxmoor (Herts); pear, peach, chestnut, and apricot he noted as absent. The northern lands have always been pre-eminent for stock-rearing, and, indeed, there is some evidence that in the later Empire certain corn lands of Britain were actually turned down to grass. Moreover the scythe and the technique of well-sinking, both gifts of the Roman conquerors to North-West Europe, were in their different ways beneficial. But the size of the animals was much smaller than in the present day. The Romano-British, for instance, and the modern Hampshire sheep differed by some 12 per cent in the length of their metatarsal bones.

From the soil itself we proceed naturally to the relation of the culti-vator to it as expressed in the mode of settlement and of the partition of holdings in the settled areas. Here the unevenness of the archaeological record makes generalization difficult; and the variations are manifold, deriving often from the very remote prehistoric past. In the barest summary two general types of land-settlement, the nucleated and the discontinuous—town or village and hamlet or farm—divided the

Roman Empire; and while topographical determinants, notably the incidence of water-resources, will go far to explain why we find one type dominant in an area and not the other, they do not take us the whole way. Nor is the sociological distinction altogether satisfactory. How, for instance, are we to class a group of half a dozen hutments on the Dorsetshire chalk or in the Vosges? Nevertheless the nucleated type tends to be the more normal in the Mediterranean area, while the discontinuous is dominant (during the Roman period) in North-West Europe. Similarly there are two types of land-holding: the common unenclosed field and the enclosed plot held in severalty; and all the combinations of the two types which we assert, both of land-settlement and of land-holding, can be found or inferred inside the Roman Empire. Naturally the archaeology of a common holding is always difficult and often impossible to establish. Nevertheless common-field agriculture had been practised at least here and there in times before the modern in virtually every European province of the Roman Empire, and it is difficult to believe in a huge (and undocumented) agricultural revolution in post-Roman times. There is a difference, however, in the shapes of holdings inside the common fields. In the south they tend to take the form of rectangular plots, in the north of long strips—a difference that corresponds to the distinction between types of plough and types of farming that have been studied above.

In general, however, we are probably right in seeing a gradual retreat of the common-field agriculture, for which we have the evidence of Homer, in favour of individual holdings, which are the norm, for instance, in classical Greece, and it is likely to have been assisted by the peculiarly Roman institution of 'centuriation'. Whatever were the facts for the original territory of Rome itself, allotments of land (whether corporate—to a *colony*, or to individuals in a settlement scheme—as of the Gracchi) were effected within the framework of blocked-out rectangular areas which eventually became standardized as squares of 200 Roman *iugera* (about 125 English acres): they were called 'centuries' (*centuriae*) as adding up to a hundred of the 2-*iugera* plots which had been traditionally allotted by Romulus. Allottees, like Greek colonists, received their individual plots; and the technical manual of the Surveyors' Corporation (*corpus agrimensorum*) speaks, as one could expect it to speak, of divisions inside the 'century' (*limites intercessivi*). In Italy itself 'centuriation' survives to perfection down to the present day, notably around Capua and over most of the Lombard plain. The export of Roman institutions of local government especially to Western Europe connoted the export of centuriation, which appeared—irregularly, the technicians claimed, in areas where the institutions themselves did not. It has been suspected, for instance, in

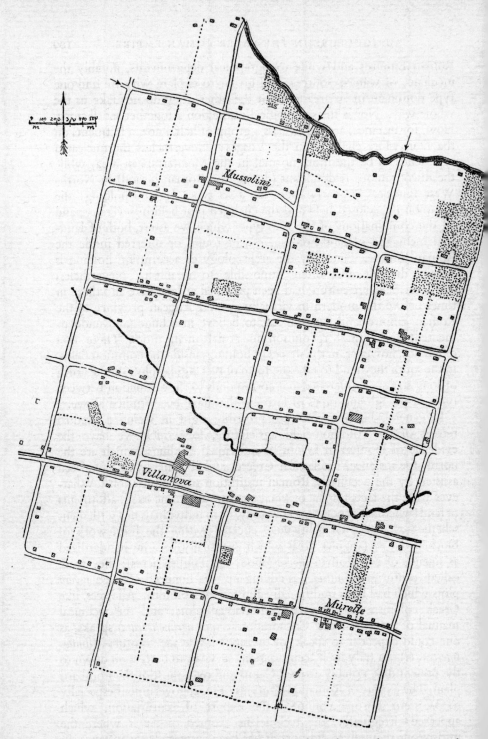

FIG. 4. The stamp of Rome on medieval and modern Italy: centuriated
land with a *Villa nova*, near Padua.

Britain near the colony of Colchester, where on their doctrines it would be in order, and to the north of Rochester, where it would not. Outside Italy it is principally at home in Africa, especially in the 'old' republican province corresponding to Tunisia and eastern Algeria. Here air-photography has shown that virtually all the cultivable land has been blocked out and has revealed the divisions inside the boundaries of the centuries of which the technicians speak. They are as good as always rectangular and there are more often than not a hundred of them inside the block. One would suspect that a cultivator might work more than one of these holdings; indeed a collection of conveyances of the Vandal period (*Tablettes Albertini*) (not actually, it seems, concerned with 'centuriated land') shows holdings very much intermingled, though there is no trace of common or even partnership owning except on a family basis.

Square plots of remarkably similar size associated with 'hamlets' of three or four hutments are found in Britain, notably on the Wessex chalk, on the South Downs and in the Fens; indeed the 'hamlets' themselves remind us of the family holdings of the *Tablettes Albertini*. But their background is quite different, being utterly native (they appear in the Iron Age of North-East Holland and Denmark) and perhaps deriving from the very primitive plots of digging-stick cultivation. The reason for their limited distribution can only at the moment be surmised. The primitive hutment is, moreover, the usual settlement type associated with this field system. Elsewhere in North-West Europe it may persist (defying all but the most dedicated and skilful excavator) through the Roman period. Normally its place is taken—occasionally we can prove that it was succeeded—by a specimen of the famous 'Roman villa', a farmhouse, always rectangular, usually consisting of half a dozen or more rooms and essential outbuildings.

The field system of these villas still remains mysterious. What should be more than merely their gardens and orchards have been occasionally noticed by air or ground survey, but they are normally found in areas of which the post-Roman cultivation system was the common field of strip holdings. We may be entitled to think of an agrarian revolution effected in England by Anglo-Saxon invaders, but political and tenurial history (as well as the data of archaeology) make it hard to think of Franks in France along these lines. Indeed in parts of the Vosges which have reverted to forest since the Roman times, long terraces clearly intended for cultivation can be observed associated with very simple 'hamlets', the field system suggesting at least the strips of the 'common field'. But the relation between strip ploughing, whether or not practised in a common field, and these individual farms is as yet altogether uncertain.

Below even a Wessex or a Vosges cultivator, at least in respect of standard of life, are the inhabitants of 'Mardelles', pits, averaging 50 feet across, roofed with tree trunks, which can now be seen as ponds on the heavy clays of Northern Lorraine and their British equivalents, the ditched enclosures of much the same area, which have been studied especially on the equally heavy clay of North-East Wilts (the so-called 'Highworth sites'). We can imagine swine-herds in the depths of the forest: at least they contribute to the variegated scene of 'Rural Life in the Later Roman Empire', though hardly recognizable indeed as part of it, save by the occasional potsherd for the excavator's spade. The picture is completed over all the Empire save in its most backward regions by the luxury establishments of the property owners, the *domini*. Already in the Higher Empire the Younger Pliny has a *genre* description of his great country mansion which is corroborated by remains throughout Italy; already the Emperor Claudius was fulminating against men who tore down houses in Italian towns, presumably to sell the materials for use in such mansions. In the provinces, even in Britain, imitations of them are known contemporary or little later; but the great age for luxury establishments is the fourth century. In Africa mosaics of this date picture the towered two-storied mansions of territorial magnates, and Pliny is consciously imitated in a description of a mansion similar to his by its Gallic owner, Sidonius Apollinaris. That the mosaics are accurate and the literature veracious is shown by the remains themselves. A villa at St Ulrich (Moselle), to take but one example, has 125 rooms and covers more than 100,000 square feet of ground. If such mansions are being erected at the expense of urban property in the first century of the Empire, their great extensions would seem to coincide with urban catastrophe. The connexion is still obscure, but we might wonder whether there had not been some sort of shift in moral attitude. Rich men were now spending not for the common good but for their own. It is appropriate that the poet Rutilius Namatianus in the fifth century affirms a tendency that we had deduced from the words of Claudius: in Etruria, says he, large villas have taken the place of small towns.

Such magnificent establishments invited the cupidity of barbarian and brigand: it is not surprising, therefore, that the fortification of villas, which leads to their transformation into the castles of the Middle Ages, was already proceeding. A law of A.D. 420 permits the fortification of houses in the eastern provinces; and the wall and gates built almost in the same year by the Gallic prefect Dardanus at Sisteron 'as a protection for all on the estate' are eloquent of similar conditions in the West. The villages of cultivators too were protecting themselves, the 'castles' where dwelt the tenants of African estates are known from inscriptions, and when Jerome translating the Vulgate met the Greek word for village, he normally rendered it as 'castle'. The small villas of farmers in Northern Gaul have been replaced for the most part by villages which still remain as a feature of the French landscape. When the transformation from villa to village occurred is still a mystery; but the cessation of coins in most of the villas before the end of the fourth century hints that it may have begun even in the later Empire.

Every cultivator during our period felt the reality of the Roman Empire with its taxes and the system behind them; but the unfortunate amalgam of rhetorical vagueness and legal precision which characterizes imperial enactments of this time has made the system as 'dark' to modern students as it was apt to be, according to a Law of Theodosius II (A.D. 405–50), for the taxpayer himself. In very truth the principle of it seems to have been comparatively simple and based on the two main taxes of the early Empire, the land-tax (*tributum soli*) and the poll-tax (*tributum capitis*). The general breakdown of the third century expressed itself at its most acute on the monetary side, so that taxes could not be usefully collected on traditional lines or servants of the state (especially its armed servants) adequately paid; extraordinary levies in kind were necessary. It seems to have been Diocletian who adapted the principles of the old land-tax to the fact of a mainly natural economy. A land survey for fiscal purposes had existed since the reign of Augustus and was presumably the basis for the creation of fiscal units known as *iuga* (yokes), which could vary in size according to the quality of the soil. In Syria, as we happen to know, twenty, forty and sixty *iugera* were named as respectively equivalent to the *iugum* according to their descending scale of productivity. And there were similar categories for other crops. There were two, for instance, for land growing olives, one for an area supporting up to 225, another from 226 to 450. The assessment was nominally revised every fifteen years— specifically, as we might expect, as a result of tax-payers' grumbles; and the budgetary period was normally five, though the payers were not spared extraordinary demands within it. Once the total number of *iuga* had been worked out and the prefecture (the standard geographical unit for assessment and collection) had calculated, let us say, how much barley the state machine needed in the prefecture, a division sum would quickly determine how much was liable on each fiscal unit and how much each property should be expected to contribute.

The poll-tax (*tributum capitis*) was maintained, also in the terms of reference of natural economy, and in Egypt, where there was relatively little difference in the fertility of cultivated soil, it persisted alongside and independent of the land-tax. But elsewhere it could be used, it seems, as a flexible instrument to correct the unfairness of a system by

8

which, for instance, a *iugum* of 226 olive trees was assessed equally with one of 450 but more heavily than one of 225. The more fertile the land of an estate, the greater its population of livestock might be expected to be. The poll-tax, the *capitatio*, as it was now called, included accordingly—and this seems to have been an innovation—everything on the property 'that breathed' (the lawyers express it this way): farmer, slaves, serfs (*coloni*) and all manner of livestock. The unit of 226 olive-trees, for instance, would be expected to involve less labour than that of 450, and so, while being assessed equally under the land-tax (*iugatio*) might be expected to involve the property in less liability under the poll-tax. The two imposts thus formed a comparatively equitable whole and could in many areas be practically treated as one tax. Greek could coin a word (ζυγοκεφαλι) for the notion of *iugatio* + *capitatio* which Latin could not do. The system was complicated but not impossibly complicated. Nevertheless it is clear that sudden crises might destroy the natural balance of 'breathing population' and cultivated acreage, needing a fresh approach which the government had no time to give. It was simpler to take the line of Valentinian I in Illyricum and Theorodius I in Thrace and abolish the poll-tax outright. There is a possibility that the land-tax was similarly abolished at one time in some part of the Gallic prefecture.

Polemical writers, Christian and pagan, fulminated against the financial stringency of pagan and Christian emperors, and a sober historian, Aurelius Victor of the mid-fourth century, confesses that taxation became harsher as time went on. But the absence of statistical information makes it difficult to say how harsh, honestly exacted, it really was. We learn that just before the Vandal invasion the *centuria* of cultivated land, the normal unit, as we have seen, of assessment in Africa, was charged, with the tax commuted to money, as liable to a tax-payment of $6\frac{2}{3}$ gold *solidi*, but the figure has little meaning unless its purchasing power at the same time and place can be estimated. The record of conveyances under the Vandal kingdom of Africa some forty years later—the *Tablettes Albertini* already noticed—are helpful here. With the prevailing price of gold (1963), the *solidus* would be worth about 35s. 9d. so that the tax charge per *iugerum* would be virtually 7d., which looks low enough until we realize that the sale price of an olive with its accompanying land was no more than $4\frac{1}{2}d$.— only a hundredth of the present Tunisian values. The position of our African cultivator seems very unfavourable, if we compare him with a person of the same approximate status in a backward part of Europe today. Immediately before the war, a Bulgarian peasant paid on an average the equivalent of 3s. 4d. per acre on his land. Moreover prices for the 'industrial' goods that our peasant might need were relatively high. A pair of shoes, for instance, were worth nine of his olive trees.

Moreover, imperial legislation shows with continual repetition that in practice the taxes were most inequitably collected. It is not surprising that a traveller might find men living in remote deserts 'to escape taxation'; their normal holdings would become derelict, but it might be long before the government accepted that they were. Procopius mentions the merciless treatment of Palestinian landowners under Justinian (A.D. 527–65), when taxes were exacted on land from which 100,000 persons, as he alleges, had disappeared in a religious insurrection. Two hundred years earlier Constantine (A.D. 306–37) had earned gratitude by striking off 7000 poll-tax payers from the registers of the Gallic Aedui.

Such a system of taxation which depended upon the most intimate connexion between the labourer and the land would hardly be practicable unless that connexion were stabilized. By A.D. 332 indeed a Law of Constantine presumes that the lessee of a landowner, the *colonus*, is tied to his plot, though precise enactments to this effect for individual provinces occur in the law books under later dates. Moreover we learn that the provisions of such legislation were eventually applied to all landworkers, whether settled on estates or farming on their own. Indeed so axiomatic did it appear, as time went on, that the labourer should be tied to his plot, that Justinian regards it as 'against human nature' (*inhumanum*) if he were not. Nevertheless, no government could have put through such legislation unless the social conditions of the time had favoured it. Certainly the difficulties of keeping the machinery of the Roman Empire turning had led the government to think in terms of compulsory stabilization: the trades of shipmaster and baker had been declared hereditary and unquittable some twenty years before the enactment of A.D. 332. The existence of small, independent cultivators up and down the Empire must not, indeed, be forgotten. A law of 342, for instance, to the East, notes that persons owning even less than 25 *iugera* of land may be liable to serve in municipal senates. And our African peasants, of the *Tablettes Albertini*, though living under the *dominium* of another (who was, in fact, continually building up his property at their expense), have, by a tenurial oddity surviving from centuries past, the *cultura Manciana*, the right to buy and sell property as they will. Nevertheless the Later Roman Empire is a world of large properties with their cultivators tied to them, and it will be worth while glancing briefly at the tenurial conditions of its most important areas to see how it became so.

In Italy, the process of Roman conquest had brought large portions of the lands of Italian communities into Roman hands and in Sicily Rome had taken over the similar confiscations of earlier conquerors such as Hiero of Syracuse. Much of this land was occupied by wealthy men with capital who treated it as their own and attracted the attention of land reformers, on the whole, as it seems, with little permanent effect. If there were, for instance, small properties created by Tiberius Gracchus in Apulia, archaeology shows that they had soon vanished, so that Seneca's 'deserts of Apulia' in the first century A.D. were also the Apulia where, as he said, men were able to hold properties 'as large as kingdoms', often as *Fundi excepti*, exempt from the jurisdiction and the fiscal demands of any neighbouring city. The *ager publicus* formed the foundation of the large properties, which were at once virtually the only use for wealth and its indication as a status symbol. Petronius' *parvenu* must offer his guests wine, 'of course from my own estates— Terracina or Tarentum, I don't know which!'. These *latifundia* (the ruin of Italy, Pliny the Elder called them) were usually worked originally by gangs of cheaply purchased slaves; but with the diminution of the slave supply they were subsequently broken up in whole or in part into the leasehold tenures of farmers (*coloni*), sometimes indeed manumitted slaves, to whom the master supplied the farm-buildings and tools and from whom he sometimes took a portion of the produce as rent. The contract was in origin perfectly free on both sides, and the lessees not infrequently very mobile. Nevertheless foreign competition and the rival attractions of city luxury both for himself and for his landlord's capital weakened the position of these tenants: they were chronically in debt; and the problems of 'tenants' arrears' occupy many pages in the writings of the jurists.

In areas, however, which had come more recently into the orbit of Hellenic or Roman civilization, and in Egypt, where agricultural necessity virtually prescribed in the conditions of the ancient world a despotic control, tenures, based not on free contract but on something like serfdom, were far commoner than in Italy and Greece. Often prehistoric invasion or religious sanction had imposed quasi-feudal relations between the cultivator and his lord, whether prince or priest. It was both Hellenistic and Roman policy to weaken the power of feudal and priestly overlords either by taking over the administration of their land and their serfs itself, or, where they were suffered to persist, subjecting them to control. The most convenient controller was an existing city administration. Thus grants of Asiatic land, which, it should be noticed, assume that the serfs are granted with it, prescribe normally that the grantee shall book his land in a city territory. Where such administrative control did not exist, it was often possible to create it by founding a city, and governments promoted their far-reaching schemes of urbanization not least because it permitted this control of private tenancies. Nevertheless, urbanization was not always practicable and certain landholders escaped it, their holdings becoming similar in type to the Italian *fundi excepti*. Thus Asia, in the earlier Empire, is divided into city territories, in which many types of tenure, not least of large estates, existed, and the non-urbanized land, the χώρα, in which there were blocks of imperial holdings and islands of private or temple properties. It is no accident that in the Late Empire episcopal list of Hierocles there are in the Greek-speaking East episcopal sees the names of which contain the Latin word 'saltus', commonly used in the West as a virtual synonym for *latifundia*. On both city-lands and χώρα, especially on the latter, the ancestors of the cultivating populations had been feudal serfs, and though Roman law did not recognize actual serf-dom, their own case was little different. In complaints to the emperors, they point out that they have been settled on the land 'since the days of their ancestors', and threaten to abscond in language which shows that this, though legally permissible, was in fact most unusual.

Egypt, where until the time of Severus there were, outside Alex-andria, virtually no cities at all, reproduces for that reason in some degree the tenurial history of the Asiatic χώρα. Most of the naturally irrigated land belonged first to the Ptolemaic king and later to his successor the Roman emperor, and though private property was grow-ing at the expense of imperial, the bulk of the land in the higher Empire belonged to the category of what was still called 'royal'. Such land was cultivated by rent-paying tenants, whose position of nominal freedom was little different from serfdom. They were reminded by edict that it was their duty to remain in their homes at work, and were liable to punishment or at least to recall if they ran away; they were often compelled to lease specified plots of land and to perform such work as the government thought necessary for maintaining the agriculture of the country; they were moved about arbitrarily from one village of the 'royal land' to another, and their rents were arbitrarily revised.

In Africa, the cultivator's position approached that of Egypt and the East, but the road was very different. Here the republican Roman government had humbled and almost extirpated a great exploiting community, Carthage. It was a land, like Egypt, which had virtually no town life at all, but where, unlike Egypt, much capital was needed, if the land, which promised large profits, could be made to yield them. Only men of wealth could, in the absence of extended state credits, make a success here; and it is no surprise, therefore, that republican legislation, as revealed in the famous law of 111 B.C., envisages the grants of land to large exploiters partly in the anomalous category of rent-paying private ownership (*ager publicus vectigalisque*), partly in that of tithe- or tax-paying tenancies of the *ager publicus*, where the position differed in practice little from private ownership. In Africa, in fact, the possibilities of profit for its individual members and the absence of an urban tradition tempted the government to connive at the type of tenure which governments, Hellenistic and Roman, had striven in Asia to avoid, the *agri excepti*. Often a single estate, we are told, was larger than a whole city territory, and its village population looked like that of an ordinary chartered town. Nero endeavoured to cut the knot by executing five men, 'who owned half Africa', and converting their land to imperial property; but what was to happen to it then? The government endeavoured to foster urbanization as best it could, but in the main it had nothing better than to lease the estates to men of wealth who sub-let to cultivators. These lessees became the virtual proprietors of their estates, and their heirs inherited their leases. The cultivators had no assistance from the forms of Roman law, and their relations were arranged by administrative enactments of the government. From specimens of these enactments we learn that they were liable to the imperial lessee for a proportion (normally a third or a quarter) of their produce, and for six, or sometimes more, days' work upon the portion of the estate which the lessee had in hand. Their only remedy against irregular exactions lay in petition to the Emperor: but the Emperor's administrators and the lessees were men of the same interests, and it was not theirs, so that their plight was often hard. 'Poor peasants', they called themselves, 'miserable servants and children of the imperial domains', and they were right.

For many provinces of the Empire the data of land-tenure are insufficient; but Northern Gaul and Britain demand a word, for while local conditions were very different, here again the results were much the same. Here, too, town life hardly existed, but there was neither a trained administrative staff to organize confiscated private property as in Asia Minor, nor were there, as in Africa, such opportunities for Italian investment in landed property. Towns were created as administrative centres while the land seems to have been regranted to the local chiefs. A type of place-name ending, according to Dark-Age and even Roman documents, in -*anum* (Montans) or -*anicum* (Sauxillanges = Celsinianicum) in the south and -*acum* (actually a Celtic suffix, thus Antony = Antoniacum or Floriac = Floriacum) dominate French toponymy and the occasional Celtic name—Berny = Brennacum—may justify the conjecture that the settlement doctrine goes back to the earliest days of the conquest. These estates corresponded roughly in size with a French parish, and on them the landlord lived surrounded by his tenants. Irish and Welsh analogies show that in Celtic countries the Celtic conquest had reduced earlier populations to serfdom, and they show too that agrarian debt was a potent factor in assimilating free-standing farmers to its level. Caesar's statement that 'the people of Gaul are little better than slaves' is illustrated by these analogies, which hint that, though the intervening stages are dark, in the West too it was no revolution to bind the cultivator to his plot. Thus bound, the class survived the fall of the Empire in the West, and their tenurial conditions are illustrated by post-Roman land-books. From these we learn that, as in Africa, the owner held portions of the estate (*fundus*) in hand, and that the subject tenants were liable to services upon it. In the villa of Neuillay (Indre), to take an example—church land, but originally the *fundus Noviliacus* of the Gallo-Roman Novilius—the land in hand contains about 125 acres of arable and there are in the estate about 360 acres of arable held by nine tenants. Thus it is doubtful whether in any province the measure of 332 did more than apply legal formality to what was already a practice, for in all provinces estates, whether imperial or private, existed, on which such a relation could easily develop. Of these the imperial estates themselves increased in number by confiscation and the escheatment of intestacies, so that imperial *agri excepti*, exempt from city dues and jurisdiction, were found even in city territories. But the tendency was even stronger towards the growth of private property at the expense both of small ownership and of imperial lands. It is instructive to glance at the way in which this occurred.

The Roman Empire grew rapidly, too rapidly, indeed, for new conquests to cover their costs, and by the second century these costs were heavy and there was no more hope that the continual warfare would pay for itself. It was essential, therefore, that production should expand, and quickly, in the new conquests. This need was met by the founding of towns, and though a too rapid urbanization often increased unduly the overhead charges, there is evidence that the productivity of the newly conquered lands was in fact increased. At the critical moment, however, in the reign of Marcus Aurelius, the Empire was smitten with a violent epidemic of plague and at the same time by invasion on every frontier; moreover, throughout the next century plague was endemic, and scarcely a province was spared from barbarian attacks. Thus the loss both in labour power and in capital equipment was tremendous, and could only be made up by additional burdens upon what survived; land was lost to cultivation, partly because its cultivators had perished, partly because they had taken to brigandage. We have some statistics to illustrate this—documents from Africa have already been quoted: in Italy we hear of no less than 35,000 acres of Campanian land reported as derelict in A.D. 395, and in the neighbourhood of Ephesus an inscription of the fourth century A.D. reports that out of 7499½ taxation units (*iuga*) 703 were uncultivated. In Egypt, indeed, where the obvious selfishness of taxation ever prompted the population to evade it, where natives prided themselves on the scars of the collector's whip, matters were worse; a papyrus of the fourth century A.D. from the Fayum village of Theadelphia, which tells us simply that the whole population has absconded, presents no unusual case.

There was a real danger that the Empire might fail to support the charges of keeping it in being; and with the multiplication of officials, the increase in the size of the army and the maintenance of a second capital, the charges had increased. The government saw the danger and grappled with it: conquered barbarians were settled in droves upon vacant land, where they formed so dangerous a mass that freedom of movement had, as it seems, been denied to them long before the law of 332, and anyone who was able was invited and even compelled to accept grants of waste land under obligation to secure their cultivation. Such lands, held, as juristic language expressed it, under a 'development' or 'emphyteutic' lease, paid a reduced rent or were even occasionally rent-free, and by such leases what had formerly been imperial property passed into virtually private possession. Moreover, as former imperial domain, it was exempt from the interference of authorities of a neighbouring city, and this may well be the model for general exemption of this type for the estates of all senators, for it was above all members of the senate who owned the great estates. A Gallic chronicler, indeed, can use 'senators' as a simple synonym for 'large proprietors'. In the climate of the Later Roman Empire it is not surprising that in A.D. 397 the discovery was made in its eastern part that 'in some provinces half of the regular taxes from senators were in arrears'. The responsibility for their collection was transferred to the local authorities, though in the West matters seem to have remained as before; and the general independence of these large proprietors in matters fiscal is illustrated by the fact that they were occasionally permitted to assess their own taxation. Moreover when the land-tax had been commuted to a money payment, it was necessary to obtain food-stuffs above all for troops by compulsory purchase (coemptio); the large landowner was often able to have the purchase price fixed so high that on balance he obtained much, if not all, of his taxation back by his profit on the deal. Governments fought against these devices for tax evasion, as they fought to encourage the small lessee. But in both efforts governments were the prisoner of their own constitution. As responsible for fiscal administration they understood the danger of large feudal holdings such as had been attacked centuries ago, but it was their very members who profited personally by them and were enabled to ensure that, if lands were compulsorily given on lease, they and their friends secured the more favourable and left to the poorer proprietors the obligation of the more burdensome and difficult.

Indeed the lot of the small independent proprietor was increasingly hard. The highest class of such, those qualified to sit in the municipal councils of cities, the *curiales*, were responsible for the tax assessments, and if less came in than was anticipated, their property was liable for the deficit. They were normally responsible for the collection too, an especially uninviting task when it was necessary to deal with a powerful senator. It is to be expected that they tried continually to have collection entrusted to imperial officials. In Gaul they seem to have been successful, but it was an unusual success. Moreover the city revenues which it was their duty to administer were sequestrated from time to time for imperial needs, so that their own property became increasingly liable for the needs of their city. Below them were the classes of owners who, like them, were responsible with their property for the duties imposed on them. The government was anxious that men like these should remain as property-owners, while they were as anxious to get rid of their property and its contingent responsibilities. Veritable strikes against landownership occurred in this time, above all in Egypt, and we see the strange phenomenon of legislation forbidding property-owners to alienate it. Attempts to check this were vain, for the advantages of a strong man's protection, especially if he dwelt on *ager exceptus*, were great, so that men risked punishment to transfer themselves to it, even though it involved the loss of their goods and placed them in a relation to the patron even worse than that of the bound serfs; a relation without security of tenure or rent, terminable or alterable at the will of the patron. Patronage of this type was exerted, indeed, not only for property-owners, but for tenant *coloni* themselves: smaller proprietors found themselves simply elbowed out by the more powerful, so that when they tried to collect their rents, they were met with showers of stones from their erstwhile tenants, encouraged by the new patron. Even imperial estates suffered in this way: as early as the third century, Lydian tenants had threatened to transfer themselves to private ownership for their better security, and in the sixth Justinian complains that private land-grabbing was so rife that in Cappadocia there was virtually no imperial property left. Above all, in Egypt patronage completely transformed the land-tenure between the fourth and the sixth centuries. Where once all had been either imperial ('royal') land or properties of various sizes securing the performance of state duties, it came about that almost every acre was owned by a few landowners who kept private armies of *bucellarii*, private prisons (which the law forbade), a private postal service, and who even coined private money.

Thus the Empire returned to the feudal conditions which it had attacked centuries before; the great estate was now the normal tenure, the owner of which paid himself the taxes for his *coloni*, and superintended, moreover, their spiritual needs, providing an estate church and an estate bishop, and even forcing them to conform to that version of Christianity which he favoured. Such an estate tended to develop an economic unity comparable to that of the Egyptian documents. Thus the large Belgian villa of Anthée was smelting its own iron and handling its own cloth, so that its excavated plan reminds us of a plantation establishment in the 'Old South' of the United States. Indeed the decline of the towns in the third century, the full causes of which are still obscure, may be both the cause and the consequence of estate 'autarchy'. Though trade was not extinct in local products of long-established repute—Menapian hams appeared on the eastern market often enough to gain mention in the price edict of Diocletian, and a description of the Mediterranean in the fourth century records certain commercial movements—yet commercial activity was much restricted, not least because the government in its struggle for survival made exorbitant demands upon it. Moreover, it was discouraged by the rigorous organization of workmen and transport agents into fixed, hereditary, guilds on whose services the government had the first call.

Thus the heavy agricultural round was now accomplished upon a simpler stage. Now very rich and very poor faced each other. There was a scarcity of labour on the land, so that schemes of capital development, irrigation, and drainage could not be undertaken except by governmental initiative, and as this was rarely forthcoming, the agriculture did not go forward. On the other hand, the cheapness of the labour enabled it to be profitable, at least for the landowner, provided that it was left reasonably undisturbed. The senatorial order, whose fictitious Roman domicile exempted their lands and themselves from local obligations, especially amassed large estates and large fortunes. The holy Melania, we learn, possessed properties in Gaul, Italy, Sicily, Africa and perhaps Britain, with an income of about £25,000 a year, computed according to present-day gold values. And among the greatest of these landlords was the Christian Church. Constantine's donations to Pope Sylvester alone are credited with an annual income, again assessed at gold prices, of £40,000, and comprised *Massae*, consolidated units of estates, in Italy, Sicily, Egypt, and the East. The wealth of private owners can be appreciated when it is realized that there were senators whose single incomes were more than a fortieth of the whole revenues of the Western Empire in the fifth century.

The cultivator saw little of these profits, yet in regions where his life was undisturbed by barbarians, there seems no doubt that he saw something. The men of the Thames-valley villages gained little from the Empire, yet it is the fact that in their dismal cabins they were getting in the later Empire more pottery and that of a better quality. The Romano-British peasant, if we may judge from his skeleton, was not an under-nourished man and did not suffer from rickets. His average height, it is true, was more than an inch lower than the modern average of his class, but his bones were strong and not liable to fracture. His diet may have been deficient in milk and the vitamins that protect from rheumatism. Yet after the demands of landlord and tax collector there was still coarse bread grain to wear down his teeth and he had, as it seems, good meals of pork and mutton. In the East, explorations in the Decapolis show the ordinary population dwelling in well-built houses of squared stone, and in Asia Minor, the monumental evidences of the later Roman Empire argue a standard of life higher at least than that of the modern Turkish village. Nor is this altogether surprising: with the decay of town life, the country cultivator had no longer to support the overhead charges of those expensive, unproductive buildings and charities which are attested by so many monuments and inscriptions. In fourth-century Constantinople there were 50,000 recipients of charity: from this we may guess the number of unproductive mouths that must have needed filling in centuries of high urbanization. Nevertheless, if disaster reduced his rent and tax-paying power, his owner, faced himself with the deficiency in the taxation account, obtained, as Salvian tells us, relief for himself which was not passed on to him; and in a society where absentee landlords were common, the arbitrary extortions of the owner's agents plagued his life. A sermon of St Chrysostom, though delivered certainly to point a moral, may be quoted, for it illustrates finely conditions which cannot have been uncommon:

Who could be more oppressive [he says] than landlords? If you look at the way in which they treat their miserable tenants, you will find them more savage than barbarians. They lay intolerable and continual imposts upon men who are weakened with hunger and toil throughout their lives and they put upon them the burden of oppressive services. They use their bodies like asses and mules, or rather like stones, hardly letting them breathe, and they strain them equally in good years and bad, never giving the slightest relief. They make them work all through the winter in cold and rain, they deprive them of sleep, and send them home with empty hands, indeed with debts still to pay. Moreover the tortures and beatings, the exactions and ruthless demands of services which such men suffer from agents are worse than hunger. Who could recount the ways in which these agents use them for profit and then cheat them? Their labour turns the agent's olive-press; but they receive not a scrap of the produce which they are compelled illegally to bottle for the agent, receiving only a tiny sum for this work. Moreover the agent extorts more oppressive interest than even pagan law allows, not twelve but fifty per cent from a man with a wife and children, who is filling the agent's barn and olive-store by his own labour.

What were the feelings of a cultivator towards a system that punished any attempt at self-improvement and set the luxury of his betters in such sharp contrast to his own? In an age when even bishops could not always sign their names, it is likely enough (in Britain it is nearly certain) that he could write no book to tell us, and frequently he spoke only the native patois of his country. It was hardly possible for him to obtain redress of grievance in a legal way. The sturdiest of his class escaped their burden by joining bands of brigands, who terrorized their countryside. In Gaul brigandage was endemic, military action had been necessary to suppress it in A.D. 285, and in the fifth century a chronicler baldly informs us that 'all the slaves of Gaul had joined the Bacaudae' (an indigenous word by which such brigands were known); these men held law-courts and parliaments, like Robin Hood, 'under the greenwood tree'. In Africa, *circumcelliones*, seeking vengeance at once against religious persecutions and social wrongs, smote property-owners with 'the Israelitish cudgel' 'for the Praise of God'. The government enacted that no shepherd in Italy should have a horse, for it was certain that he would become a brigand if he had one. The historian Zosimus mentions that the men of Pamphylia fought well against the Goths, because they had been well trained for war by continuous battles with brigands.

Such escape was for the bold; others showed only a dull resentment towards the Empire with its expensive and cumbrous machinery which did so little for them. But their resentment was not ineffective. When soldiers of the Empire were branded, like runaway slaves, it was obvious that men were no longer willing to fight for it: and in many provinces barbarian invaders found an eager welcome from the subject classes, for under a barbarian king, though their status was not improved, they had no longer to bear the expenses of Roman government. Thus the Empire was forced to depend upon highly subsidized barbarians for its defence; and when, with the loss of Africa, the West could no longer pay its defenders, they turned and broke it. Only in the East, where wealth and clever policy had held the barbarians at bay, until religion banded all in unity against the Moslem assailant, the Empire lived on.

CHAPTER III

The Evolution of Agricultural Technique

BETWEEN the great agricultural enterprises of antiquity based on slavery, which survived in a modified form as the great manorial estates of the Carolingian era, and the great capitalist estates of modern times, lie the small farming units characteristic of the feudal period. After the charges due to the lord had been paid, these small tenant farmers aimed first and foremost at providing subsistence for their families. But at the same time their energy and the productivity of their holdings were sufficient to sustain the great movement of reclamation which reached its peak in the twelfth century. The evolution of agricultural technique in the Middle Ages which made these changes possible can be divided into three main phases:

(1) From the fifth to the tenth centuries the introduction of a series of technical innovations, some large and some small, and the diffusion of others inherited from Roman antiquity, but not hitherto widely adopted, increased productivity on the small units to an extent which gave them an economic advantage over the larger estates worked by forced labour. Among such innovations were the wheeled plough, modern harness, the flail, the water-mill, improved ways of harrowing fields, made possible by the use of the horse as a draught animal, the extension of more easily grown crops such as rye and oats, the first attempts at a three-year rotation. Such simple tools as the hoe and the flail brought great advantages to those who used them; and acquired an immense economic significance because they came to be used in enormous numbers and because they could be used for long periods during the working year. Polish ethnographers have calculated that in their country the use of improved flails increased productivity by about 100 per cent.

(2) In the course of the eleventh century the growth of agriculture was accompanied by several changes which made the great capitalist estates possible. The yield of cereal crops increased greatly. Lack of documentation and the wide diversity of conditions in different regions, and even on different estates, obliges us to confine ourselves to approximate figures, but it appears that the yield of wheat in the Carolingian era was no more than 2 or 2·5 to 1, whereas in the two centuries between 1200 and 1400 the average yield on the lands of the Bishop of Winchester was as much as 4 to 1. The growing use of iron undoubtedly made agricultural tools both stronger and more efficient. As a secondary result of the clearing of the wastes large areas of newly reclaimed land on

the periphery of the more anciently cultivated lands came into the hands of single tenants. Finally, by his stubborn and patient labours the small farmer so transformed the countryside as to facilitate and to intensify cultivation. Clearing the fields of stones, making slopes more gradual and taming water courses, particularly by installing water-mills, are examples of such laborious but effective improvements. Excavation of the Roman baths of Les Fontaines Salées in the basin of the upper Seine has also revealed that the valley of the Cure was terraced at the end of the fourteenth century and that the spoil from levelling the contours and reducing the steep slopes of the hillsides provided earth for embankments. It is more than likely that these enormous movements of earth were organized, and the labour necessary to carry them out, imposed by the Abbot of Vézelay who ruled over the region.[1]

(3) In the early fourteenth century when sheep-farming on a large scale grew in response to the increasing demands of industry, a new type of large agricultural enterprise—one with a capitalist organization—emerged. One such undertaking was to be found on the Artois estates of Thierry d'Hireçon, Bishop of Arras, who died in March 1328. These estates produced largely for the market and were cultivated by direct agricultural labour with the sole object of drawing the greatest profit from their operations. The agricultural methods used were advanced for the period, and as a result yields were very high: as much as 8·7 to 1 for wheat at Roquetoire, and 12·8 to 1 at Gosnay.[2]

I. *Roman and medieval agriculture in the Mediter-ranean area*

Medieval agricultural technique is connected with that of the Roman Empire along two lines. What was specifically Mediterranean in the Roman technique survived in Southern Europe without serious modifi-cation right through the Middle Ages. Roman skill and organizing capacity had developed it so thoroughly that further progress was not easy. Geographical conditions, if anything, deteriorated: instead of progress we see at times a perceptible decline. Meanwhile this classical Mediterranean technique was serving as a model further north. At many points a close affiliation can be traced between it and the technique of North-Western Europe in the Middle Ages, in spite of the long up-heavals of the age of invasions. In fact, most of what had been learnt

[1] See R. Dauvergne, *Sources minérales, thermes gallo-romains et occupation du sol aux Fontaines Salées* (Paris, 1944.)

[2] See B. H. Slicher van Bath, *Accounts and Diaries of Farmers before 1800 as sources for Agricultural History*, A.A.G. Bijdragen 8 (Wageningen, 1962).

from Rome survived on the great imperial or ecclesiastical estates; and Roman technique was the basis of the later developments, in which however new needs and different geographical conditions played an essential part. Let us recall its principal features, confining ourselves to agriculture proper and to cattle rearing.

Prehistoric agriculture, and classical agriculture also, was practised mainly on light soils, easy to work, and not over moist. In Britain as in Gaul, in Roman times, the high grounds where such soils were found were preferred: sometimes they were abandoned later and invaded by the forest. But Italy, a transitional land between the Mediterranean area proper and the humid North, contains—as we have seen—both light and heavy cultivated soils, of whose different needs Roman agricultural writers were well aware. In the provinces also the heavier soils were beginning to be cleared and tilled under the Empire. No doubt the technical progress made under the Empire was connected with the need to utilize these heavier soils. Drainage had been understood even before the days of Roman domination: in the Pontine Marshes and at several points in Etruria a network of *cuniculi*, subterranean tunnels sometimes as much as 15 metres below the surface, carried away sub-soil water. Less elaborate systems were known and practised in later times.

The 'two-course' Mediterranean agriculture was based normally on autumn sowing—of wheat or winter barley (*Hordeum hexastichum*). Among the wheats, agricultural writers distinguish between *triticum*, which included winter wheat (*Tr. vulgare hibernum*) and rivett (*Tr. turgidum*), and *far* or *far adoreum*.[1] The description of the various sorts of *far* are not precise; but it is certain that the *farra* were husked wheats. Probably the main original sort was emmer (*Tr. dicoccum*), to which under the later Empire was added spelt (*Tr. spelta*).

Fallowing not only rested the soil after an exhausting crop but preserved its reserves of moisture in a dry climate. That is why the two-course rotation survived, with only local exceptions, as the normal Mediterranean rotation until modern times. For more complex reasons it survived also in France throughout a zone of varying width north and north-west of the Mediterranean region proper.

But, as we have seen, if moisture is to be preserved weeds must be kept under, and the surface soil must be kept thoroughly pulverized; hence those three or more workings of the fallow which imperial writers, improving on their republican or Greek predecessors, recommend.[2] They were not recommended for all soils, or at the same

[1] Spring wheat and spring barley (*Hordeum distichum*) were also known. But Columella (II, 9) explains that spring wheat will hardly succeed except in cold countries with moist summers.

[2] Pliny recommends five for heavy soils and mentions a maximum of nine in Tuscany.

times for all: wet, heavy soils were to be worked later than light soils; and poor soils were to be worked only once, just before sowing. Very probably the three workings were kept up in the Middle Ages, at least on the best organized estates. (They are found today in very conservative regions in the Western Mediterranean, such as Sardinia and Majorca: the first in January or February, the second between March and May, the third often after the first autumn rains; and a fourth is needed to cover the seed.) It is equally probable that on estates short of teams, or on poor soils, only two workings were given, or perhaps even only one. But in favourable conditions the normal three were exceeded. Olivier de Serres, at the end of the sixteenth century, notes that 'good farmers' of Provence, Languedoc and of the Comtat Venaissin worked their land five, six and seven times.

The wheelless *aratrum* was well suited to the often shallow Mediterranean soils. The team was usually of oxen; but cows and asses were used on the very light Campanian land. The fixing of 'ears' (*aures*) to the plough, for ridging and covering the seed, was a Roman improvement.[1] We hear also of the coulter (Pliny, XVIII, 171). Its names in modern European languages suggest its Roman origin—*coutre*, coulter, *Kulter* (also Sech for the Latin *secum*, *seca*). But whereas the 'ears' were widespread and are still in use in Mediterranean regions, even today a coulter is uncommon enough on an old-fashioned *araire*. It is probable that originally the coulter was mounted on a separate tool which went before the plough to break up the clods on deep soils. For deep ploughing Columella (II, 2) recommended the additional use of heavier ploughs fitted with larger shares. As for the wheeled plough, no doubt Vergil had learnt about it in his native province;[2] but it had come there from the North and was never widely utilized in Mediterranean lands.

For that deep hand-working of the soil which took the place of sub-soil ploughing a hoe was used, either plain or toothed. The spade was—and is—much rarer. With the *pastinum*, a kind of two-toothed hoe, deep soils were worked down to two or three feet. Columella only mentioned its use for vineyards; but it evidently spread, for Palladius advises it also for orchards and vegetable gardens. But he notes that it was not much used in remote provinces. There seems no doubt that the tradition of this manual work persisted through the Middle Ages; if it was very laborious, it considerably increased fertility. Olivier de Serres praises those Dauphiné farmers who worked their lands very deep every ten or twelve years: by his day they used,

---

[1] Cf. p. 151, above.
[2] As Servius says of him: *currus dixit propter morem provinciae suae, in qua aratra habent rotas, quibus juvantur.*

together with the mattock, a long narrow-bladed spade (*louchet*) which had come with its name from the north. In the south-west similar work is done today with a two-pronged fork: it is called *pelleversage*. But for the same work in Majorca, where it is done about every four years, they still cling to the hoe.

After the plough the toothed harrow is the most useful implement on a farm. Did the ancients effectively introduce it? No doubt Varro describes it and Festus' comment on him is explicit. But even today it is rare in South Italy, and only begins to be common north of the centre. In Southern France its use only became general in the nineteenth century. Is this a case of retrogression? Varro speaks only of a limited use: 'to pull out the weeds'. He covers his seed with a plough. But Pliny (xviii, 180) certainly seems to refer to the use of a toothed harrow for this last operation. However that may be, the ancient harrow was as a rule nothing but a wooden frame with wattles woven across it, merely an improvement on the primitive bundle of thorns dragged across the ploughed land to break up the clods.[1] This task (*occatio*) was also done by hand, with a toothed mattock (*rastrum*) or with a hoe (*ligo*) when the clods were hard. But on light soils the repeated workings sufficed to prepare the tilth, as an old Roman proverb emphasizes: *veteres Romani dixerunt male subactum agrum, qui, satis frugibus, occandus sit.*[2]

While the corn was growing the soil still had to be kept loose and free of weeds. Since Cato's time it had been usual to hoe it (*sarrire, sarculare*) twice, first in January–February, and then early in March. Lastly, early in May, it was weeded (*runcare*). In vineyards still more was done. Columella advised at least two hoeings for old vines, winter and spring, but monthly hoeings for young ones. All this attention, this repeated working, was the most original and progressive feature of Roman as opposed to oriental and even Greek agriculture, and one cannot emphasize too strongly the value of such a bequest to the Middle Ages. In Africa today the Kabyles who have preserved many Roman traditions are most particular about hoeing and weeding, whilst the Arabs, with their oriental habits, once they have sown the seed leave it until harvest.

Of all agricultural operations, harvesting varied most, from place to place, but also with the size of the holdings and the cost of labour, as Pliny remarked. Sometimes the stalks were pulled up by the roots—the most primitive method and the most exhausting for the land. More often sickles were used, the stalk being cut half way up—as it was near Rome—or at its foot, as in Umbria. But there was another method

---

[1] Cf. p. 98, above.
[2] Columella, ii, 4; Pliny, xviii, 179.

which almost entirely disappeared from Europe after classical times: the ears alone were pulled off from a bunch of stalks with a kind of comb. This method was only applicable where crops were thin. On the huge demesnes of Gaul, the Gallo-Romans had even made a regular machine out of the comb-like implement. A single ox pushed before it a big chest on two small wheels. There were teeth on the front of the chest. These tore off the ears, which fell back into the chest. So Pliny and Palladius explain. Now, are we to reckon the disappearance of this machine in the Middle Ages as an instance of technical retrogression? Surely not. It was very wasteful, especially of the straw. It simply replaced the primitive combing process because—as Roman writers correctly noted—labour was lacking or dear, and agriculture was of the extensive kind that produces thin crops.[1] As population grew, labour became abundant and an increased yield essential.

For threshing, the Mediterranean lands sometimes used the simple beating stick—no doubt for the smaller harvests. But they also early employed more effective methods, methods so effective that they remained unchanged till the nineteenth century. The oldest was the familiar treading out by oxen; but Columella already preferred horses. The horse or mare replaced the ox at varying speeds in different places— in some parts of Haute Provence not until the fourteenth century. This change suggests a general improvement in agrarian conditions; for instead of using the farm oxen, one had to hire a small herd of mares— twelve is the number we hear of at the close of the Middle Ages. (We must not however neglect the pressure of the lords, some of whom made the hiring of these mares an obligation, a *banalité*.) The way the corn was prepared for threshing deserves notice. When it had been cut low down, the ears were taken off subsequently and carried to the threshing floor. When it had been cut half way up the stalk, it was put in a heap to dry in the sun and then threshed out. This had the advantage of economizing one operation, the taking of the ears from the straw.

More advanced processes included the simple threshing stone, easy to make but giving only poor results, the *tribulum* and the *plaustellum*.[2] These had probably been devised to improve the yield from simple treading out by cattle. But their use spread wherever a shortage of cattle made rather elaborate and expensive implements necessary and even profitable: *si pauca juga sunt adjicere tribulum et traham possis*, Columella says. The *tribulum*, as already noted, was made of a wooden board studded with points of flint or iron: it was dragged by two oxen,

[1] Pliny notes (XVIII, 262) that, again to save labour, hay was cut with a bigger scythe on the *latifundia* of Gaul than in Italy: the big scythe went quicker but did not cut so close. The modern French scythe is probably just this Gaulish scythe, better handled and with a finer edge.
[2] Cf. p. 99, above.

and to add to its efficacy the driver weighted it heavily or stood on it. In the *plaustellum*—Varro adds the adjective *poenicum*—the points were replaced by cutting wheels. Both implements, which have the advantage of breaking up the straw ready for the cattle to eat, are still in use, especially in Tunisia and Spain.

To clean the grain, mixed as it was with straw and fragments of straw, fans were used; or it was all thrown up with shovels when the wind was blowing, and the grain fell while the straw was carried away.

A few words must be added on tree and fruit growing, which is rightly regarded as the distinctive feature of even the most highly developed Mediterranean agriculture. The vine and the olive, especially the vine, which need careful attention, hold an important place in Roman agricultural literature. But these branches of Roman cultivation, on their technical side, are interesting mainly to the scientific agri-culturalist. All one need say here is that such a high degree of technical maturity and adaptation to climatic conditions had been attained in Roman times that, in methods of planting and managing vines, during the Middle Ages and often even in our own day, classical tradition has generally been followed. In Spain there were already, as there are today, low vines—separated with no support but their own stock. Italy used many methods: in Etruria and the plain of the Po the vine grew up elms, maples, and other trees in regularly spaced rows. Again just as today, fruit trees and vines were often planted in the fields where cereals were grown.[1] Between the tenth and the twelfth centuries it became general in Emilia to dig a drainage ditch on two sides of such fields, which made it possible to extend vine growing to heavy damp soils.

Cattle-keeping, the main business of primitive times, had lost its importance with the development of corn-growing—and changed its character. Whereas in early days great and small cattle were kept mainly on natural pasture, the making of artificial meadows and the growth of fodder crops had allowed stall-feeding to develop and helped improvement by breeding. Artificial meadows were not very pro-ductive unless irrigated; but dry meadows were not without value, especially if manured. In them the cattle fed winter and summer. But they also yielded some hay which was stored for the winter. However, in spite of the efforts made to add to them as much as possible, the dry climate limited their use, and it was necessary to use leaves from the woods and hedges or else fodder crops. In winter, and even after June when fresh grass ran short, the cattle were fed on leaves of elm, poplar, oak, fig and ash. Pigs of course ate acorns in the woods. But besides all this, as early as Cato's time the growth of fodder crops was

[1] Cf. p. 101, above.

strongly recommended. Those which the Romans used were vetch, lucerne,[1] fenugreek, chick-pea (*cicercula*), and *farrago*, which was a blend of barley, vetches and other leguminous plants, eaten green.

It is uncertain whether in Cato's time transhumance was practised, that half-way house between nomadism and fixed cattle farming. The Mediterranean lands favour it because winter grazing grounds in the lowlands often lie close to ample mountain pastures. It is not expressly described before Varro; but then he deals with long-distance trans-humance. In the most uneven Mediterranean regions many village lands stretch from the mountain tops to the plain or the sea. Very probably in such places, where it was so easy, transhumance had been practised from the most remote times. But long-distance migration implies a strong central power to organize or enforce it. It was the development of *latifundia* under the later Republic and the Empire that favoured its extension. Medieval facts illuminate in a striking way the transformations in agriculture which a renewed predominance of cattle farming over arable farming entailed. In Southern Italy, the plain of Tavoliere was given up more and more in winter to migratory flocks of sheep. The system was encouraged and organized in the thirteenth century by Frederick II of Sicily. When passing the customs station at Foggia, the flocks paid a poll tax: the royal treasury thus got considerable sums without much trouble. The same thing occurred in the Papal States, where the profits went to the Pope, monasteries and great lay nobles. But the multiplying of migratory flocks ruined cultivation, not only because they devoured everything, but also because they made rough grazing lands almost useless for the settled cultivators, and so robbed them of any chance of raising the indispensable working cattle. Further, transhumance employed few hands: it left great stretches of plain land half desert, and so helped greatly the transformation of low-lying grounds with bad natural drainage into malarious swamp—the Agro Romano, the Tuscan Maremma, part of Apulia. The droveways themselves, often more than 100 yards wide and widened out further at intervals into 'riposi', still occupied some 37,000 acres in Southern Italy at the opening of the present century. In Spain the formation of vast estates after the wars of reconquest favoured similarly the development of transhumance in Castile. Alfonso IX, at the end of the twelfth century, allowed the inhabitants of Segovia to graze their sheep all over Castile—except in vineyards, gardens and sown fields. Alfonso X authorized the cattle-masters of Murcia to seek for pasture in the kingdom wherever they liked. In 1347 fresh privileges granted by Alfonso XI formed the first charter of the Mesta.[2] So in the thirteenth

---

[1] Cf. p. 102, above.
[2] Cp. p. 439, below.

and fourteenth centuries one can follow out the progress of trans-humance and the heavy price paid for it in agricultural decadence. In Southern France the same periods witnessed the same transformation. Thus in 1242 Henry III granted to the monks of Saint Mary of Ronce-vaux free pasture for ten years throughout the dioceses of Bayonne and Dax. A document of 1368 tells us that thirty-seven flocks came down in winter from Roncal and Sarasaz in Navarre to the *landes* of Bordeaux.

But in contrast to the course of events in Castile and Southern Italy, where transhumance continued its ravages right into the nineteenth century, the sedentary cultivators of Southern France resisted them, and in Provence rural communities joined battle successfully with the great proprietors of migratory flocks during the fourteenth century. The break up of vast domains even brought back a less extensive and less damaging type of cattle farming. In the mountains of Vercors in the Dauphiné the monks of Léoncel were in the habit of sending their flocks in winter into the plain of Valence where they owned extensive lands: it was a case of what is called 'inverse transhumance', descent from the mountains to the plains. But towards the middle of the fourteenth century, the division of the abbey estates between the monks who stayed in the mountains and an abbot *in commendam*, established on the plain of Valence, forced the monks of Léoncel to keep their flocks in the folds during winter and to begin a more intensive management of them.

One should not leave Roman agriculture without noting that it had already prepared the way for a decisive type of progress which is only met with much later, towards the end of the Middle Ages, and then only in limited areas: the progress which rests on the supply of enough fertilizers to the soil and the parallel suppression of fallowing.

But first let us underline the organizing, one might even say the rationalizing, spirit of the Roman agricultural writers. They are not satisfied with proving the utility of this or that method, with insisting in a general way on the blessings of regularity and order. They want to figure things out: they are always thinking of cost prices and their improvement: *summa spectanda, ne sumptus fructum superet*, Varro says. Cato works out the personnel and the head of working cattle required for two typical estates. Varro resumes and completes the calcu-lation and tells us how Saserna has got more use out of a plough and its teams. Columella is equally careful about agricultural costs. This frame of mind led to a perpetual search for higher yields and lower costs. Great proprietors, at least the most intelligent and active among them, applied the principles in daily life. The younger Pliny wanted to buy a neighbouring estate because he thought that by uniting the two he could economize appreciably in labour.

To return to fertilizers: *stercus quod plurimum prodest*, Varro asserts. Where there was stall-feeding as Cato describes it, the dung was carefully preserved. So was the dung of birds, especially pigeons, and was used—among other things—for the meadows. This special use of pigeon dung continued all through the Middle Ages and beyond the Mediterranean area. But the stable manure produced under these excellent conditions was inadequate. All sorts of supplementary devices were tried. Flocks were folded on the fields that were to be sown. Manure was made by scattering straw and stubble in the farmyards: the cattle trampled and fouled it, and so made a tolerable fertilizer. The practice became an established one; in the Middle Ages it was known in England; in all Southern France and in Spain village streets and the neighbourhood of farms were strewn with the unsavoury and unsightly litter until very recent times. When straw was not available, oak-leaves, bean-stalks and all kinds of plant refuse were used: right down to our own day the box clippings, collected in masses on the Mediterranean *garrigues* and buried in the soil green, have served as an excellent fertilizer.

From the earliest times the fertilizing value of wood ashes had no doubt been known: cultivation of burnt-over forest land is everywhere a primitive practice. Shepherds fired the dry pasture in summer and found more grass after the first autumn rains. There were however more disadvantages than advantages in this practice: it did much to ruin the Mediterranean forest vegetation. Sometimes also the stubble was burnt, not collected, after harvest. At the opening of the Middle Ages stubble burning was known to Isidore of Seville; and at the opening of modern times we have the evidence of Olivier de Serres: 'many people handle the stubble still better by burning it on the land: the fire prepares the soil to admit the coulter and rids it of an infinity of weeds, insects and harmful seeds.'

But Roman agriculture knew yet another substitute for farmyard manure, of first-rate importance for future agricultural progress— green manuring. Even Cato advises the burying of lupins, bean-stalks and vetches. Such leguminous plants, which absorb nitrogen direct from the air, exhaust soil far less than those which must draw nitrogen from it; when buried they enrich it infallibly.

Thus under the most favourable conditions, the Romans, who gave so much attention to the maintenance of fertility in the soil by manuring, and had recognized the peculiar value of the leguminous plants, were able to dispense with fallowing and cultivate some of their lands, the *restibles*, every year: *terra quae quotannis obsita est* (Varro, I, 44). Columella advised the following rotation for them: cereal, vetches; cereal, *farrago*. The advantage of growing crops that have to be hoed had even been observed. Columella, speaking of turnips or rape before a white crop, observes: *subactum solum pluribus iterationibus aratri vel rastri largoque stercore satiatum postulant. Nam id plurimum refert non solum quod melius ea proveniunt, sed quod etiam post fructum eorum sic tractatum solum segetes opimas facit.*

The problem then arises: since the Romans had worked out exactly, by practical experience, a thoroughly satisfactory method of dispensing with fallow and adding considerably to the yield of agriculture, why did they not generalize it, why did it only manage to survive the political ruin of the Empire with the utmost difficulty, whilst other agricultural methods came triumphantly through the centuries of decadence? Firstly, it would seem, because even in the greatest days of Roman agriculture the suppression of fallowing was never more than a happy exception, except no doubt on particularly fertile soils. Campania, with its rich volcanic soil, could carry several crops a year, according to Strabo. Then, climatic conditions were an obstacle to the general use of this most intelligently worked out system; and as time went on geographical conditions became more and more unfavourable in the Mediterranean areas proper. In these areas, fallowing is at least as necessary for maintaining the humidity of the soil as for resting it. Fallow could only be abolished where there was enough rain. Further, in the Mediterranean climate a three-course rotation is not possible: spring sowing does not succeed. So there are no cereal crops, such as spring oats, specially useful for feeding cattle and horses. Unirrigated meadows and fodder crops give only poor returns. Cato and Columella, it has been noted, praised these crops but could not do without leaves as cattle food. Now the Mediterranean forests, which lacked resisting power and were not automatically reconstituted, were already in a very poor state under the Empire, in the oldest populated regions, and got rapidly and continuously worse until recent times. Since forests were indispensable auxiliaries for cattle farming, even if fallowing were suppressed, and since the forests gave less and less help as time went on, one can understand how the balance was so easily upset, even in regions not too badly watered, and upset disastrously at the ordinary level of ancient and medieval agricultural technique. Not enough cattle, not enough manure. Not enough manure, no way of abolishing fallow or of raising heavy fodder crops. (Though these exhaust the soil less, they still have to get from it everything but the nitrogen.) With a shortage of fodder crops, no means of rearing enough beasts. There was no escape from the vicious circle. And where transhumance was extensively adopted to increase the flocks of sheep, the disturbance of the balance between cattle-rearing on the farm and arable cultivation was disastrous.

We see how it was that this very progressive system of a Mediterranean agriculture without fallow was destined to remain only a dim light during long medieval centuries. And where did the light dimly burn? Precisely where climatic conditions were most favourable, in North Italy. It was at Bologna and at the end of the thirteenth century that Pietro dei Crescenzi began a new propaganda for green manuring; it was at Venice in the sixteenth century that Torello in his *Ricordo d'agricoltura* systematically inculcated a rotation in which fodder crops should replace fallow.

II. *Agricultural conditions in the temperate zone*

The great agricultural novelty of the Middle Ages in Western Europe was the three-course rotation, which developed either from the Mediterranean two-course or from systems of temporary cropping. It was an innovation which must nonetheless be thought of as an ideal not always easy to apply because of the large number of factors which are present in any set of agricultural conditions. From these variables emerge a variety of different combinations which approach the model of the three-year rotation.

The two-course system had spread widely in Gaul and Britain, in the wake of the Roman legions, and perhaps even before their arrival. But in the poorer parts of these two countries, and in all Germany, much more primitive systems of temporary cropping—on forest land, moorland, and especially on open grassland over which the forest had not spread—were normal in the fifth century, and had not been altogether got rid of at the close of the Middle Ages. Forest land was sometimes regularly cleared, sometimes occupied for a time only, after the wood had been burnt to fertilize it. Clearing began on plains, in valleys, and on the great terraces of mountain slopes. But on steep slopes and in high places difficult of access, men were satisfied with the temporary cultivation of ground burnt over—as they still are in Corsica and in the forest of Ardenne. (As a rule only one crop was taken off it, originally oats; only from the eighteenth century also rye.)

This clearance by burning was still practised near Paris in the twelfth century, and was widespread in the Alps as late as the eighteenth. In 1447 the men of Diois in the Haut Dauphiné explained that they were forced to adopt it instead of regularly clearing parts of the forest because, as they were very short of meadow land and so of cattle, they had not enough manure for an extension of permanent cultivation. But the method had been forbidden in the Oisans from about 1350. The Oisans was then very short of forest: people burnt cow dung and heated ovens with straw. The barbarous method of clearance by burning could only endure where the forests seemed inexhaustible. It involved no application of fertilizers; but it squandered precious natural wealth, and often turned forest land into increasingly unproductive moorland.

Temporary cultivation of grassland (*Feldgraswirtschaft*) also assumed a scanty population and plenty of space, but its effects were less destructive. It had also the advantage over clearance by burning that, as it was carried on by groups of some size, it gave experience of organized working in common, and so prepared the way for the three-course rotation. Part of the land was tilled for a year or a few years; then it lay fallow for many, and was used for grazing. There could be no arboriculture. But fertilizers were not required and the manure, which was not however very abundant because the beasts spent most of the year in the open, was heaped in winter about those subterranean dwellings in which the Germans took refuge from a rigorous climate.

At the close of the Middle Ages this system survived intact in some isolated districts, no doubt where population was stable—such as Frisia and the Sarre. In a modified form and in association with other methods it was much more widespread. In the district of Antraigues in the Vivarais, in the fifteenth century, many meadows were tilled every twenty years. In Scotland temporary cultivation in the outfield was linked with the continuous cultivation of the infield without any fallow. In the fifteenth century we hear of *wüste velder, die man nennet auszvelder*, in the Rhenish Palatinate.

Continuous cultivation (*Einfeld*) on a small portion of ground in proximity to human habitation was still practised at the beginning of the nineteenth century in the west of the Low Countries and the north-west of Germany. The cereal crop grown was always rye. A certain minimum quantity of manure was essential, which explains why we find this system in regions where stock-raising predominated; but even there it was necessary to spread turves taken from the waste lands on the fields thus cultivated without interruption. This system was also practised in the forest regions of upper Hungary; in this way the periodic clearings of ground overwhelmed by scrub, which were necessary under systems of temporary cultivation, could be avoided.

How was the transition made to three-course husbandry with its winter corn, spring corn or other crop, and fallow? As it led to a considerable increase in the total yield of agriculture, the growth of population may often have been a determining factor. Besides, the three-course system has purely agricultural advantages of great value. Firstly, the risks of very bad harvests due to weather are greatly reduced, since they are spread over autumn- and spring-sown crops, with different conditions of growth and harvest. Secondly, agricultural work—ploughing, sowing, harvesting—is spread better over the year. In

Mediterranean lands, harvest is over early in the summer and, with fine autumns, winter sowing can be drawn out late. In temperate humid climates, what with harvests which were never over and the more sudden arrival of the inclement season, autumn ploughing and sowing had to be more hurried.

The Romans realized these advantages; but the impossibility of a systematic development of spring crops, because of the climate, prevented them from attaining a genuine three-course rotation. Columella, in determining the most complete use for a team of oxen, had even calculated the extra yield resulting from considerable spring sowings. Similar calculations no doubt played a part in the working out, and in the success, of the three-course husbandry. We find them in the English writers on agriculture of the thirteenth century, when they argue that a plough team that could work 160 acres on a two-course system would serve for 180 on the three-course. After subtracting eight weeks for holy days and other interruptions they took $\frac{7}{8}$ acre a day as a unit of cultivation, raising it to 1 acre for the second ploughing. They then demonstrated that in the 44 weeks left, at six working days a week, a plough team could carry out just as well the three ploughings needed on 80 acres under crops (two-course husbandry on 160 acres) as the three ploughings of 60 acres needed for the winter sowing, and the one ploughing which preceded the sowing of 60 acres in the spring (three-course on 180 acres). Even with only two ploughings for the winter crop, the advantages of the three-course system, though less, would still have been quite clear. Thus the English writers, with their calculating and rationalizing minds, proved themselves excellent successors to the Romans.

As for the disadvantage arising from the three-course rotation, that it reduced the stubble-grazing area and so the possibilities of rearing cattle, this was no doubt barely considered while there was still plenty of forest and common pasture. Another drawback also was only realized in course of time. The plots of any given owner were scattered about the various 'furlongs' into which the village fields were divided. At the outset, when each plot needed at least a day's work, the scattering was rather more advantageous than not. A single tenant's holding all on one kind of soil would often require to be worked quickly, when the soil was in the right condition, and harvested quickly. Plots with different soils are ready for working at different times. But when sub-division of plots increased, by partition among heirs, and a plot needed less than half a day's work, more and more time was wasted in moving from plot to plot. The multiplication of plots also multiplies quarrels among neighbours. Cases often went to the courts about encroachments of a furrow or two. No doubt great abbeys and great proprietors endeavoured to rearrange their lands at an early date; but it was a rather awkward process to carry through. Among the small holders things were always getting worse. In certain regions the inconvenience was felt so strongly that an effort was made to avoid its consequences by systematically re-allocating the arable among the members of a community. In an early Danish system, known as *fornskifte*, the allocation of the fields was indiscriminate. But in a later system (*bolskifte*), one unit of land in each quarter (*skifte*) was assigned to each *bol* or manse for its separately cultivated holdings, and the units thus allotted to each tenant were all arranged in the same order. However, the order of the larger units within the quarters did not follow a set pattern. In the *solskifte* system (or division according to the sun), probably established in the thirteenth century, the rules of allocation reached their ultimate limit. The unit of allocation was henceforth no longer the *bol*, but the individual strip. The place of each strip in the different quarters was arranged according to the position the holder occupied in the village, so that the latter always had the same neighbours and thus the likelihood of quarrels was reduced. A similarly methodical system of dividing the fields appears also to have existed in Germany.

It is possible that the use of the horse as a draught and farm animal may have contributed greatly to the use of a more and more strict three-course system, at least in lands like France where men seldom ate oats. Unlike oxen, horses need plenty of grain—and that was usually supplied by the spring oats. It looks as though there were a connexion on the one hand between districts of small holdings, the use of oxen, and the two-course system; and on the other between districts of average or large holdings, the use of horses, and the three-course. The lord had also to be supplied with oats for the horses he used in war or for travel.

With these general notions in mind, it becomes easier to picture the spread of the three-course system. Certainly the system cannot go much beyond the Carolingian era, in which, as all the evidence suggests, it began to be applied on the vast well-organized demesnes of the crown and the great abbeys of Northern Gaul. It spread gradually from these progressive centres; but even in them it did not necessarily attain all at once to its final regular form.

In the first place, we must not assume that even considerable spring sowings required it. As the English treatises show, you could have both spring and autumn sowings on a two-course basis: *de terris bipartitis bebent ad carrucam octies viginti acrae computari, ut medietas pro warecto habeatur et medietas alia in hieme et quadragesima seminetur* (Fleta, II, 72).

Then there were transitional forms between the Mediterranean two-course, and the strict three-course, in which fallow land, autumn-sown land, and spring-sown land are equal. We already sometimes meet the strict three-course in northern Carolingian France; but often there is much more winter than spring corn: *arat perticas VII ad unamquamque sationem: arant ad hibernaticum perticas III ad tramisum II: arant ad hibernaticum x, ad tramisum III*, and so on.[1] We must assume that some of the land was worked with two courses, while on some the three had been adopted; or that fallowing was elastic and that some land lay idle for two years or more. No doubt both things happened at once as we see much later in Poitou. At Naintré, near Châtellerault, in the eighteenth century the two systems are found in the same commune. Wheat lands were worked on the rotation—wheat, spring barley, fallow; rye lands almost all on that of fallow, rye. And in the sixteenth century there was found sometimes in the Haut Poitou a fourth section of the fields, which included arable land left in temporary fallow to give it a longer rest than the normal year. We must never forget that all the fallows could not be manured; but you could balance the lack of manure by mixing up, as it were, three-course with temporary agriculture. So in 1225 the foundation charter of the village of Bonlieu, in Beauce, prescribes that the rotation shall be the usual one, but that a peasant, *par pauvreté ou pour améliorer sa terre*, may leave it fallow for several years. *Par pauvreté?* He might, for instance, be short of draught animals.

In Germany and in the thirteenth century, there are constant inequalities between autumn and spring crops. The explanations of this lack of strict regularity are always the same. Either meadows were ploughed up from time to time to refresh them; or, outside the regulated *Gewanne*, there were others, made perhaps by clearing, and not subject to the strict routine. Besides, the three-course rotation had apparently never penetrated those north-western regions where cattle-raising predominated or where continuous cultivation (*Einfeld*) was carried on. At the beginning of the nineteenth century its northern-most limit ran from south of Bonn to Minden and Hanover.

In England, the distribution of two-course and three-course cultivation, within the open-field region, makes it clear that the spread of the latter has nothing to do with racial influences, but that it was a form of agricultural progress not applicable with equal ease everywhere. In the thirteenth century the two-course seems still to have been the more common: it was dominant especially on the chalky and not very fertile uplands of the South-West, whereas the richer soils were already in great part under the three-course. Obviously three-course cultivation takes more out of the soil. We have a few accounts of a passage from

[1] From Irminon's *Polyptyque.*

one system to the other, from the end of the thirteenth and the beginning of the fourteenth century. But it was especially after the sixteenth century that progressive tendencies would become marked in two-course regions—to lead however not to a three-course but to a four-course system (e.g. 1, wheat; 2, spring barley; 3, vetches or oats; 4, fallow). In France, two-course cultivation survived in the south-east for climatic reasons; but also in the south-west, the centre, and the west, for a variety of reasons, among which the poverty of the soil over wide areas was of fundamental importance.

There was a fresh and decisive stage to be reached after the adoption of the three courses: the suppression of the fallowing. But for that various conditions had to be fulfilled. First, technical conditions which would permit heavy manuring. Every holding had one corner which never rested—the garden. But there fertilizers of all sorts were applied to an extent which was impossible on the whole cultivated area. Roman writers had pointed to the ultimate solution—fodder crops; but that called for a finished technique and, as we shall see, cattle farming could still be carried on by more slovenly methods which kept down the supply of dung greatly. Second, juridical conditions: common rights of all sorts and especially 'common of shack', *vaine pâture*, were a difficult obstacle. Third, economic conditions: a rapid extension of production required a parallel extension of effective demand. In the Middle Ages these conditions were fulfilled only in a few favoured and advanced countries, especially in North Italy and Flanders. In North Italy the persistence of Roman traditions and the presence of many highly civilized cities allowed agriculture to be as elaborate, as meticulous, as gardening. In Flanders, thanks to the climate and also to the fertility of the polders, cattle farming flourished and there was abundance of manure; and, as in Italy, there were the greedy markets of rich and populous cities. Probably also the growth of population there helped to eliminate fallowing: it hastened the cultivation of old commons, woodlands and pastures—whereas in the Walloon country, where population was stable, the commons have survived to this day. The disappearance of wood and pasture limited the basis of cattle farming without destroying it, because the meadows were rich; and the loss of these extensive resources in cattle food promoted the use of the intensive, the fodder, crops. In Flanders, fallow was sometimes replaced by fodder crops or turnips by the end of the thirteenth century; and so the cattle farming rested on a new and increasingly firm basis. Another solution was to combine the three-course system with a grass course extending from three to six years (1, winter grain; 2, spring grain; 3, fallow; either 4 to 6 or 4 to 9, meadow).

But we must distinguish carefully the reasoned practice of Flanders from what elsewhere was a mere expedient—as in that Norman lease of 1275 where the lessee undertakes *terras eas laborare seu excolere et serere per sessonem ita quod in gascheriis pisa seu fabas facere poterimus si nobis viderimus expedire.* Any thorough suppression of fallow in similar conditions might be treated as an abuse and forbidden by agreement. Some of the North Swiss *Weistümer*, for example, impose definite restrictions on the cultivation of the fallows. It must be said that the hesitation to do away with the fallow was not wholly unjustified; the purpose of fallow was in fact not only to give the soil a rest, but also to clean it. The inconvenience resulting from the cultivation of artificial fodder crops like lucerne on the fallow fields was that it fouled the land and gradually declined in yield. The true solution was not found until the eighteenth century: the *Fruchtwechsel* of the German agronomes, and the Norfolk four-year course which brought in every four years a plant capable of cleaning the soil (1, turnips; 2, barley; 3, clover; 4, wheat).

III. *Agricultural work and implements*

Throughout classical times and during the early centuries of the Middle Ages, the plough was always drawn by oxen. On light soils and on poor men's land cows and asses might be used. But the ox was the indispensable worker until there came an innovation, long discussed and often successfully opposed—the use of the horse.

Early in the ninth century, in Irminon's *Polyptyque*, the ox always draws ploughs and carts, the horse carries men and their baggage. The mention of a plough horse in the Salic Law—*si quis caballum qui carrucam trahit, furaverit*—is exceptional, and is to be explained by the abundance of horses among the Franks. In the second half of the eleventh century, when Jean de Garlande enumerates the parts of the plough, he mentions *juga in quibus boves trahunt*. But he also mentions *epiphia equina*, and explains, *epiphia dicuntur collaria equorum*. Probably the horse was already being used on the land in the Paris region. In subsequent centuries its use there became general, and in texts of the late fifteenth century the ox is rarely mentioned as a draught animal. About 1450 Gilles le Bouvier contrasts regions where horses are used, such as Champagne, the Duchy of Orleans and the region of Chartres, with those which still use oxen, like Anjou, Maine and Brittany. In High Normandy, at the same date, the horse was common. But the west, centre and south of France, with some islands in the horse-zone like Alsace, still employed oxen. In most of the ox countries, the two-course rotation, often combined with poor land, did not produce enough grain for the upkeep of many horses. In the regions least favoured of all, cows and asses had to be used. In 1428 the *doléances générales* show that in the Oisans (Dauphiné Alps) cows were employed. But even in ox country, the prestige of the horse already stood high. In Alsace and some western regions were to be met at times odd teams in which several yoke of oxen were preceded by a horse or two. In Auvergne and the south-east, the mule often took the place of the ox. It is worth noting, as a document of 1741 from the Bas Quercy shows, that in this as in other matters great landowners might encourage progress: an owner lets a *borde* to a *métayer* and provides him with *duas equas cum una polina pro laborando predictam bordam.*

In southern Europe there is a distinction between Italy and Spain. Italy kept to the ox; and by the fifteenth century the buffalo had already been acclimatized in the country about Rome, where it was very useful on heavy land. But in Spain, probably as a result of French influence, the mule was already spreading—a fact of which agricultural writers of the seventeenth and eighteenth centuries complained. In Germany, the horse—introduced first of all on the great estates of the south and the Rhineland—had hardly come into general use until the very end of the Middle Ages. In Flanders it was used, but had not driven out the ox. In England oxen, often stoutly defended by agricultural writers, were employed as well as horses: their use depended on the district, and probably also on the size of the holding. There were eight-ox ploughs, and ploughs with four oxen and four horses, or even six oxen and four horses.

If North-East France was not actually the pioneer in replacing the ox by the horse, it had at least carried through the replacement most thoroughly. Why? The answer of agricultural writers is perfectly clear.

English writers of the thirteenth century discuss the question of costs just as they do in connexion with the crop rotations. The horse eats more oats. It has to be shod, the ox has not.[1] (Gilles le Bouvier was amazed to find oxen shod like horses in Lombardy.) So it costs three or four times as much to keep a horse as to keep an ox. Then the ox is more patient, and stronger; when he is old he can be sold for slaughter, while of the horse you can sell only the hide. They might have added that oxen are less liable to disease than horses and that the harness is cheaper. So they do not hesitate to prefer the ox, except on stony soils which hurt his feet. As for the argument that the horse moves faster, it fails to persuade them; for they are convinced that unscrupulous

[1] It does not seem as if the nailed horse-shoe appeared until the eleventh century, perhaps because of the use of the rigid shoulder yoke. The Romans knew only the 'hoof-boot' (*hipposandale*).

ploughmen will not let it do so: *La malice des charuers*, says the anonymous *Treatise of Rural Economy*, *ne souffre mie la charrue des chevaux aller
hors de leur pas plus que la charrue des bœufs*. All these opinions persisted;
they are found completely unchanged in Arthur Young.

The French writers of the sixteenth century, on the other hand, attach
most weight to the horse's greater speed. They reckon that a horse does
in a day as much work as three or even four oxen. In moist temperate
climates time is often an object. So farmers would rather incur *despense
et hasard que de faire trainer en longueur tout leur labourage, auquel consiste
tout l'espérance de leur négoce*—according to Olivier de Serres.

The reason why the horse only began to take the place of the ox, as a
general thing, after the tenth century is clear. A horse could not
profitably be harnessed to a plough until it had been given a modern
collar. We know now[1] that in ancient times horses had collars of soft
leather which came round their necks just where the trachean artery
comes under the skin. This interfered with their breathing so that they
could not do full work. No known representation of the stiff modern
collar which rests on the shoulders, and so is effective and natural, is
earlier than about the tenth century. It has been suggested with great
probability,[2] that modern harness, first with the breast strap, then with
the stiff collar, came from North-East Asia between the fifth and eighth
centuries A.D.

There were improvements also in the harnessing of oxen. Though
less important and not so clearly advantageous they nevertheless have
economic interest; and they help us to trace certain currents of civilization. In antiquity the yoke usually rested on the ox's withers and was
kept in place by a strap under the neck. But Columella says that in
some provinces the yoke was tied to the horns. He only mentions this
practice to denounce it, as he says nearly all experts did. If we are to
trust Olivier de Serres, so did most oxherds in the sixteenth century.
But those who used their oxen both for ploughing and for drawing
carts preferred the horn attachment: it held the cart back better on
downhill gradients. A little earlier, the German Heresbach, although he
shared Columella's opinion personally, was not able to claim for it such
general support. This was because, in spite of the experts, the horn
attachment had gained ground. A decree of the Count of Brienne of
1056 exempts an ox with broken horn from cartage duty. In the
Hortus deliciarum of Herrad of Landsberg (1170), that is in Alsace, oxen
are harnessed to a plough by the horns. Most later pictures, it is true,
show the yoke on the withers, though a wooden frame often takes the
place of the strap. But gradually horn-yoking came into favour, at

[1] Thanks to the researches of Commandant Lefebvre des Noëttes.
[2] By M. A. Haudricourt.

least in France, and from there—at some time or other—it spread over nearly all Spain. In isolated backward parts of Spain today survivals of withers-yoking show that horn-yoking has superseded the older practice. Italy on the other hand has adhered to the withers yoke. We ought to note also that in a sculpture at Chartres an ox is shown with a stiff horse-collar. In a Norman lease of 1447 six collars are referred to *c'est assavoir 4 pour bœufs et 2 pour chevaux*. But this method of harnessing had no great future; since one reason for using oxen was that a yoke was far cheaper than two collars.

For both agricultural and commercial transport—because there were no roads or only bad ones—the backs of men and animals were utilized. Farm inventories regularly included hand-barrows. Towards the thirteenth century the wheelbarrow—called *chivière roulleresse* in 1445 in High Normandy—was introduced, and was very useful in flat countries. For heavy transport, when the state of the roads permitted it, there were various two- and four-wheeled vehicles. In discussing transport on the bad medieval roads, writers are apt to overlook the invaluable sledge. In Old Breughel's well-known 'Haymaking' there are baskets of mixed vegetables on a sledge. So late as the early nineteenth century in French Flanders, farmers used this primitive vehicle in times of thaw or very heavy rain. In parts of Wales at the same date, it was common; and in steep stony places in South-Eastern France it is in use still.

As the flocks and herds fed mostly in the open—in woods, in meadows, pastures and fallows—their droppings were lost, or only fertilized the fields slightly, unless the beasts were folded on them. Town manure was not easily transported: in 1447–8 the manure from the stables of the Archbishop of Rouen was thrown into the Seine. So there was less manure available for agriculture than the increased head of cattle could have provided.

Great proprietors might buy manure or take it as a due; as in England they did by the *jus faldae*. So far as they did either, the small man's land suffered still more.

As all fallow land could not be manured, leases often prescribed which fields should have the preference, and forbade the sale of stubble, straw or hay. The English writers were specially interested in fertilizers. They explain in detail how manure should be prepared on the farm and how used on different sorts of land. They advise the collecting of no more stubble than is needed to repair thatch, and the ploughing in of the rest.

But the great innovation in the temperate regions after Roman times was marling. Pliny says that Gauls and Britons discovered it; in Britain, he says, they sank pits which might be 100 feet deep to get

10

'a kind of chalk'. Seeing how old this practice was one might expect it to have spread gradually over all Western Europe. Nothing of the kind; and that because, as Fitzherbert says in his *Surveyenge* in the sixteenth century—'marle mendeth all manner of grounde, but it is costly'. Either because marling had never been general in Gaul, or because it had gone out of use in many places during early medieval times, the *Edictum Pistense* of 864 had to force reluctant *coloni* to cart marl. At the close of the sixteenth century de Serres says that marling was very well known in the Île de France, Beauce, Picardy, Normandy and Brittany. In the fourteenth century it is often mentioned in leases of the abbeys of Mareuil and St Vaast in Artois. In Normandy agreements were frequently made about it: you marled every fifteen or eighteen years. It is noticeable that all these provinces except Brittany had a progressive agriculture. Equally significant is the silence of sixteenth-century documents from Poitou. Yet Pliny mentions that the Pictones, with the Aedui, had made their land very fertile with the help of lime. In the Montmorillonais the arable soil often lies directly above a bed of marl, and then yields abundantly. So the method might have been re-invented—but it had not.

As to paring and burning—was that already widespread in the Middle Ages? We cannot be sure. The process is to cut off the top layer with its vegetation; dry the turves; heap them into smothered fires; burn them, and spread the burnt earth and ash. Today the process is considered barbarous, because it gradually destroys the humus and impoverishes the soil. But for a time it gives fine yields—hence its former success in Brittany, in the Massif Central and in the Causses, in Provence, in Languedoc and in Northern Spain. In seventeenth-century England it was called 'Devonshiring'; so it may well have been a medieval practice, in the south-west at least. When Isidore of Seville distinguishes between *incensio stipularum* and *cinis*, with the explanation: *cinis est incendium per quod ager inutilem humorem exundat*, he may refer to paring and burning, which in that case must have been known in Spain in the sixth century. But for France, Bernard Palissy, in the sixteenth, speaks of it as an unusual process employed as a rule every sixteen years, to fertilize the soil, by farmers in the Ardennes. A little later de Serres, who praises it, says it has come *des bois essartés et brulés sur les lieux*, a statement which fits that of Palissy and might suggest a rather recent origin. Not so very long ago *essartage* in the Ardennes was carried on in two ways—either by burning branches and dried vegetation freely on the soil, or by smothered fires, that is exactly as in the paring and burning process.

The Arabs are credited with a great development of irrigation in Southern Europe. We have to inquire what they brought on the

technical side. The Romans used irrigation canals and ditches especially
for meadows. They knew also how to construct various 'engines' for
raising water—the beam water-lifter always known by its Arab name
shadouf; the Archimedean screw; the pump of Ctesibius; the lifting
wheel with a hollow rim, worked either by hand or by water; the
lifting wheel with a string of pots round it, which was apparently
always worked by hand. All were used mainly in gardens, and the
simple *shadouf* was the one that spread farthest. Spanish gardeners used
it in the sixth century and gave it the nickname of *ciconia*, a word which
has passed into the Romance languages. We do not know when it reached
Belgium, where Old Breughel so often drew it, or Germany where it
had certainly arrived before the beginning of the fourteenth century,
when it is shown in the Dresden MS. of the *Sachsenspiegel*. There were
big lifting wheels at Toledo in Mohammedan times. Do those of
Languedoc and the Comtat Venaissin go back to so early a date? Again,
we are not sure.

It is the spread of the *noria* apparently which was due in particular to
the Arabs.[1] We do not know whether the Romans had geared their
wheel with its string of pots so that an animal could be harnessed to it.
At any rate, although the Arabs may have spread this improvement,
they did not invent it: in the West they sometimes used for it the
Persian word *doulab*, sometimes a word which means sprinkler, *saniya*.
The word *noria* is derived, through Spanish, from the Arab *naôra* which
was applied in Morocco to lifting wheels driven by water. The *noria*
spread much more slowly than the *shadouf*, which suggests a later
appearance. About Albi it appeared beside the *shadouf* only after 1830.

The principal debt of the West to the Arabs was the great extension
that they gave to irrigation by more or less complicated systems of
branch canals, with perhaps a perfection of the collective control of the
distribution of the water. They introduced those tropical crops which
require regular irrigation over wide areas—cotton, sugar-cane, above
all rice. Rice was known to the Romans, but as in imported article.
The Arabs spread its cultivation in Spain and Sicily. Its importance in
Sicily is revealed in the report of the Arab Governor Al Mulei on the
export of foodstuffs in 1253. The cultivation of rice only got to North
Italy in the fifteenth century: we hear of it on the Pisan plain in 1468
and in Lombardy in 1475. Lastly, there was the orange. The bitter
orange appears to have been grown in Sicily from the year 1002; but
the sweet orange was apparently not introduced into Spain and Italy
before the fourteenth century.

The example set by the Arabs was followed after they had been
driven out. In the thirteenth century, for example, the villages of

[1] Cf. p. 440, below.

Fustiñana and Cabanillas in the Ebro valley dammed the river and made a small irrigation canal from it. Spanish *huertas* served as models for small irrigated areas in the French South: on the lower Durance the oldest canals—used both for irrigation and to work mills—appear to date from the twelfth to thirteenth centuries. In Italy the first important irrigation works began in Lombardy in the twelfth century; in Emilia later. At the beginning of the fourteenth century, the irrigated meadows of the Milanese, the famous *marcite*, were already most productive. Further north, pastures were improved by irrigation. Not much imagination or technical skill is needed to draw little water channels from a stream crossing a pasture; and this kind of irrigation is found as far north as Germany. But the most ambitious irrigation schemes, in which streams were tapped at considerable distances, are found from the fourteenth century in the mountains of the High Dauphiné—at the outermost edge of Arab influence, as it were. Neighbouring communities agreed to allow canals to cross one another's territories. That of St Laurent du Cros, in the Champsaur, was obliged to rent the alp of Bayard from that of Gap. In 1442 it was authorized to dig a *béal* to tap the river Drac far upstream, because the land to be irrigated was above the valley bottom.

Many small peasants had not enough land for a plough. In Western France they sometimes formed groups to keep a common plough. But more often they were forced to cultivate by hand: we often hear of the 'hand husbandman' in France. We must also keep in mind the many rather inaccessible or very steep fields—often abandoned in modern times—and that conservatism which on hilly and stony ground thought that the plough was out of place. In the Vivarais the men of Pourchères complained in 1464 that, in their stony land cut up by ravines, any harvest meant much toil with hoe and spade. In the Oisans (Dauphiné Alps) nearly all cultivation was with mattock and hoe; the village of St Christophe explained in 1428 and 1458 that the *araire* could not be used on its steep stony fields—but it is used there today.

In southern regions hoes were used almost exclusively. For a long time their heads were square or triangular; though the Romans had known, and extensively used, the hoe with a two-pronged head. Further north, the square- or triangular-headed hoe was much used in vineyards. It is suitable for stony soils, a fact which explains its geographical distribution. Pronged hoes were still rather rare at the close of the Middle Ages, though we hear of a *houe fourchée* in 1460 in Normandy. There are Mediterranean regions where they were still not in use at the opening of the nineteenth century.

In compact, homogeneous soils the spade gives better results than the hoe. It had the further great advantage that it could be more cheaply made, either all of wood, or of wood edged with iron—the *pala ferrata, pelle ferrée*.

As with the hoe, the pronged spade, or fork, is an improvement, which was already known by the Romans, on the ordinary spade. A three-pronged fork is shown in the Dresden MS. of the *Sachsenspiegel*. Its use is connected with metallurgical progress and a greater production of iron. By the close of the Middle Ages it was widely used in Germany and Belgium. A partial replacement of wood by iron, for straw and dung forks, is found at about the same date: such things are recorded in High Normandy in the fifteenth century.

In connexion with the plough, there are two great problems—the origin and adoption of the wheeled plough; the origin and adoption of the mould-board. We must be careful not to assume that either spread rapidly or uniformly over Western temperate Europe. Our sole authority for the place of origin of the wheeled plough is a famous and corrupt passage in Pliny; from which we may locate it in the country south of the upper Danube.[1] Pliny's Gallia apparently means Cisalpine Gaul. On the one hand, favourable conditions for the appearance of the wheeled plough seem to have existed to the north of the Alps on the eve of our period; they were, in particular, heavy soils, a temperate and damp climate, the use of the two-handled *araire* and the association of the four-wheeled cart with agricultural work. On the other hand linguistic evidence shows that the plough was already in common use in Central Europe in the sixth century.

But in the first century of the Christian era was the wheeled plough much known outside Rhaetia and Cisalpine Gaul? Assuredly its use spread very slowly. From Britain, through all Gaul, to the right bank of the Rhine there was a great extension of corn growing in Roman times. But all over this region it was the Mediterranean *araire* which came in first, and long survived. The wheeled plough can only have been introduced directly, on land not previously worked by the *araire*, in non-Romanized parts of Germany, where cereal growing played only a limited part in systems of temporary agriculture. It may even have been specially appreciated there because of the frequent shiftings of settlement and the need of a heavy plough to clear long neglected land. For what are its advantages over the *araire*? First, you can put more pressure on the share because the wheels give a *point d'appui*; and second there is no drawback—in fact, the reverse—to making the share heavier and bigger and so more powerful, whilst the *araire* that

---

[1] The argument is based on G. Baist's emendation of Pliny, *H. N.* XVIII, 172, which makes it run *non pridem inventum in Gallia duas addere rotulas, quod genus vocant ploum Raeti*. And cf. p. 18 and p. 107 above.

has to be moved about on a beast's back or in a cart must be kept light.

Assuming that the wheeled plough was spread from non-Romanized Germany, when may it have been adopted in North-Eastern France? Relying on linguistic evidence, Frings postpones the adoption until after the break-up of the Empire, and credits it to the Franks. In fact the word *Karch*, from *carruca*, with the meaning 'vehicle', survives in what was in Roman times a frontier zone, from the middle Rhine and the Main to Swabia and the upper Rhine. The change of meaning from 'vehicle' to 'plough' for the word *carruca* did not therefore take place while Latin was still spoken in that frontier zone, in which German subsequently replaced Latin and in which the Frankish word *ploeg* came in with the wheeled implement. In North Gaul, the German word not having been adopted, the Gallo-Romans made use of the old word *carruca*, because of its meaning. This is Frings' argument.

In England the existence of wheeled ploughs during the Roman era has been inferred from the discovery of Roman coulters; but the coulter, which was a Roman invention, had been applied first to the *araire*.[1]

However this may be, the wheeled plough came only slowly into Northern France and England. In the second half of the eleventh century, Jean de Garlande's Parisian dictionary mentions no wheels as parts of the plough. In England, as in Northern France, the *araire* is pictured in MSS up to the thirteenth and fourteenth centuries; and until the end of the fifteenth in Flanders (Hours of Turin). In the Walloon country the existence today of a considerable area in which the plough is called *errère* (*errère à pe= araire; errère à rolette= charrue*) seems to witness the long survival of the antique *araire* in this conservative region. The old Scots plough, so 'beyond description bad' that an expert of 1793 refused to describe it, never had wheels at all. It was no light *araire* however, but a heavy thing drawn by long teams of oxen. And the heavy wheelless 'swing' plough is still used on English clays.

Why did the *araire*, at first sight so inferior, survive at all? Partly for reasons of expense. Small holdings had to retain it when larger ones could afford a *charrue*. 'The plowes that goo with wheles', Fitzherbert wrote in the sixteenth century, 'me semeth they be far more costly than the other plowes.' He was not very warmly in favour of them, and in fact they were not superior for all purposes. Early in the nineteenth century, in a part of Buckinghamshire, two ploughs were in

---

[1] For a discussion of the coulters found in England see R. V. Lennard, in the *Dopsch Festschrift* (1938), p. 70. Lennard proves conclusively that 'a large coulter does not necessarily imply a wheeled plough'.

concurrent use—one of wood and without wheels, the other more modern, of iron, with wheels. In winter and early spring the soil was too soft for wheels, and the first was used. In other regions also the *araire* was long retained for light tasks. In Artois a sort of *araire* with a long-drawn-out share, and neither coulter nor wheels, was used to clean and lighten the soil.

It is difficult to be sure of the exact moment when the mould-board made its appearance and at what point it was regularly associated with wheels. Iconographic evidence is too uncertain for us to rely on it. It is recognizable on the Dresden MS. of the *Sachsenspiegel*. We can prove its existence in Northern France towards the middle of the fifteenth century; in England in the fourteenth or fifteenth century. It was perhaps more rapidly diffused in Flanders. To begin with, it was merely a flat wooden plank, serviceable only on strong stoneless land such as the Flemish clay. Flanders had become an active centre of agricultural improvement: we find there at the end of the thirteenth century a wooden support for the reins, on the fore-carriage of the plough, which spread to North France and the Middle Rhine. But, no doubt because of its imperfect development, the mould-board was only in partial use at the close of the Middle Ages. In one and the same German MS. of about 1480[1] can be seen a plough with 'ears' and one with a mould-board. A few years later Heresbach is found explaining when a mould-board is used: *ubi humus solidior, ala ad dextram vomeris partem additur quae cespites proscissos versat: haec ala est amovibilis, ut reverso aratro in alteram partem transferri possit, si libeat.*

Technical improvements in the plough made its work more efficient. There was also improvement due to more frequent working of the soil. This came in two stages: the first when, between the eleventh and the thirteenth century, three workings for winter grain superseded two; the second in the fifteenth century, when the winter grain sometimes got four and the spring grain two, and when there was also a tendency to begin work earlier. In this as in other matters, it is certain that there was no automatic spread of the improvements on the best managed land to land in general; not even a low one. Big enterprises had plenty of teams and plenty of labour. Better organization would produce these results. On small holdings, where land was perhaps not very fertile, two workings remained the usual thing, whilst the great ones, or small ones on very good land, were given their three and then four.

Gregory of Tours, praising the fertility of the plain of Dijon, notes that it needed only a single working: *arvis semel scissis vomere semina jaciantur et magna fructuum opulentia subsequatur.* Perhaps this was land

---

[1] The *Mittelalterliches Handbuch* of Prince Waldburg-Wolfegg.

lately cleared. But we must suppose that elsewhere poor peasants could often only work their land once, to the detriment of the yield.

In the ninth century and subsequently the first ploughing of the year was for the spring sowing. It was usually in March; according to Vandelbert, a monk of Prüm in the Eifel of the ninth century, it might be in February for barley; but on the Prüm demesnes it might also go on into April. Then in May the fallow got its first working. In Eastern France and Western Germany this was regularly left till June, perhaps for climatic reasons, perhaps to leave the fallow longer for grazing. The second working seems to have come only just before the autumn sowing. From Lorsch, in the diocese of Worms, we have very precise dates: *arare debet in mense junio atque iterum in nativitate S. Marie* [8 Sept.] *ut sit seminatum in missa S. Remigii* (1 Oct.). But for the end of sowing there is a great range of dates, due may be to differences of climates, soils and crops. St Martin's (11 Nov.) is given for the Abbey of St Vincent at Metz, no doubt as a *terminus ad quem*. Some French sources refer to a third working; but this may as well be a harrowing as a regular ploughing to cover the seed according to the old Mediterranean technique.

Indications of a third working before the autumn sowing seem to appear early, but only sporadically, from the end of the Carolingian era in Western Germany, where, as in later centuries, there was some- times a double autumn working: *mansionarius arat nobis 1 die in vere, in Junio, in autumno 2 dies*. But it is possible that this should be interpreted only as the ploughing to cover the seed.

It is the English writers of the thirteenth century who set out the three workings as a doctrine, and one must suppose that their teaching, no doubt based on a previous wide practice, was followed more and more on large demesnes. In them the extra ploughing is not a doubled autumn one, but a spring one, for choice in April and so before the traditional first 'labour'. They advise that it should not be too deep. The second (*binalia*) is put off to St John's day; nor should it be too deep, but it has the merit of killing thistles and other weeds. The third (*tercialia*) is the old second: it should be two fingers deeper than the second and the furrows should be close together, to secure a more regular distribution of the seed.

As to a fourth 'labour', Norman leases of the fifteenth century often mention the obligation to sow wheat on four *areures* and oats on two. This obligation usually applies, however, only to part of the sown area: it requires an extra effort that was not possible for the whole with the available teams and labour. In 1362 at Sainte Geneviève-en-la-Forêt- de-Blais (arrondissement des Andelys) we have still the two or three

God spede þe plou3 & sende vs korne I now

The plough (*for descriptions see over*).

1. Late medieval wheelless plough, with coulter and mould-board.
2. Modern English wheelless ('swing') plough.
3. Romano-British aratrum.
4. Twelfth-century wheeled plough, also with coulters and mould-board.

Harvesters and gleaners (from the painting by Peter Breughel).

'labours'. But already in 1401 at Braquetuit (arrondissement de Dieppe) we have four *areures* for wheat and two or one for oats. In 1407 at Villiers-en-Vexin half the wheat area has its four *areures*, the other half three.

This multiplication of workings in High Normandy was ahead of the general practice of the time. In the sixteenth century, in his *Maison rustique*, Estienne only advises three for autumn-sown crops, though he adds *il faut tant de fois labourer et relabourer que la terre soit toute en poudre s'il est possible*. The first he puts early in the winter, *aussitôt que le fumier est épandu, pour assouplir la terre* (for manure spreading he advises St Martin's); the second about mid-June, on heavy damp soils, but about mid-September if they are poor and dry; the third shortly after. Sowing comes in mid-October. It is significant that the first 'labour' is pushed earlier than ever, following the tendency already apparent in the thirteenth-century English writers, and in opposition to the traditional servitude of 'common of shack'—*vaine pâture*. It is still more significant that Estienne advises the sowing of spring oats and barley after two 'labours'.

With de Serres comes the final statement of the doctrine of early 'labours': the first as soon as possible after harvest, to clean the land of weeds as early as may be and open it to winter frost and rain; the second before Christmas; the third towards March. In spring and summer the soil must be turned up as often as is necessary to keep it clean, except in July and August, when it should only be worked after rain. These repeated workings, it must always be remembered, have also the object of making good their lack of depth: *es provinces où l'on met 4, 5, ou 6 bêtes à la charrue à roues, faisant de profondes raies en labourant, semblables à de petites fosses, on se contente de donner aux terres 2 ou 3 œuvres avant l'ensemencement.*

The seed was covered by either a plough or a harrow. We have seen that the Romans knew the modern harrow, but that they made limited use of it, mainly to tear out and remove weeds. Ibn al Awam of Seville, who wrote a very complete *Book of Agriculture* in the twelfth century, speaks of the harrow on the authority of a certain Cassius, who knew only this very use for it, with that of levelling ploughed land. It is clear too that it was then unknown in Mohammedan Spain, because this Arab writer takes trouble to give a most exact account of how it is made.

The modern harrow then was only used fully and widely in West temperate Europe and after the beginning of the Middle Ages. Nor did its use spread very rapidly even them. Many poor peasants who could not get this rather costly implement went on dragging thorn faggots over their fields and, if necessary, breaking the clods with wooden mallets. Olivier de Serres, who thought highly of it because it covers the seed far faster and distributes it more evenly than a plough, regrets that in many places prejudice is an obstacle to its use, though he allows that it does not suit stony ground such as is often found in the Mediterranean region. But it began to spread from the early Middle Ages. The harrow, for breaking which the Alemannic laws imposed a fine as high as that for breaking the fore-carriage of a plough, must have been a modern type. And it appears both on the Bayeux tapestry and in many later illustrated MSS.

Developed from a wooden frame into which thorn branches were woven, it was originally square. The triangular kind was certainly an improvement, because it was more handy. It is referred to already in a terrier of Cambrai cathedral of 1275; but elsewhere it is hardly found before the sixteenth century. The Grimani Breviary, early in that century, shows a square one still in use in Flanders. The trapezoid seems to be a transitional shape, which appears at least from the fifteenth century. Finally, and it is a curious fact, the Middle Ages were acquainted with a rolling harrow, an ancestor of the modern Norwegian type. Both Ibn al Awam and de Serres describe it and both compare its cylinder to a weaver's beam, as if they were quoting a common source. In Ibn al Awam it is a cylinder of oak with teeth, used to break clods and level difficult ground. In de Serres it is made of two cylinders or rollers covered with strong iron spikes, *lesquelles par le mouvement des rouleaux montent sur les mottes et les brisent entièrement.*

Usually the harrow was drawn by a horse, sometimes by two, even where the ox was the normal draught animal. As a harrow must move rather quickly, if its work of breaking the clods is to be done with effect, the horse was more appropriate to it. It would seem that this connexion between horse traction and effective working contributed to the success of the harrow in temperate regions. (Ibn al Awam's harrow was drawn by two oxen, in the old Mediterranean way.) On the other hand the harrow probably encouraged the use of the horse on the land, in districts which previously had used the ox.

In modern agriculture the roller completes the clod-breaking and levelling work of the harrow. The Romans had only advised its use for levelling the threshing floor. It does not seem to have been widespread in the Middle Ages. No example of a roller drawn by animals has been found in medieval Normandy, only a hand roller with a long handle like that shown in the Luttrell Psalter. But already towards the middle of the sixteenth century it was recommended in France by Estienne—*pour esmotter ce qui surmonte*—and a little later in Germany by Heresbach. We do not know where it was first used as a complement to the harrow. But as a Picard dialect word for it—*ploutroir*—is found about the year 1550, it must have been fairly well established by that time. At the end of his section on harrowing, Fitzherbert adds (in 1534) that farmers 'about Ryppon ... use to role theyr barley grounde after a showre of rayne, to make the grounde even to mowe'.

The weeding of corn crops, so prominent in Roman agriculture, was a regular practice in England, Artois, Normandy, the Rhineland and no doubt many other places: thistles were the chief enemy. The work seems to have been done more thoroughly and ingeniously in England than elsewhere. English illustrated calendars of the twelfth and thirteenth centuries insert it under July, with a scene not found in other countries. The weeder has in one hand a long wooden fork which holds the thistles in place while, with the other hand, he cuts them with a little sickle on a long handle. Agricultural writers of this period forbid weeding before St John's day: for if you cut thistles too early each root throws up three or four. Yet fourteenth-century English calendars put the scene back to June. Why? Perhaps two successive weedings had been introduced, as the Romans had advised, and as Estienne was to advise later.

In harvesting, the Middle Ages, as compared with classical times, were marked, first of all, by the disappearance of the harvesting comb and the machine based on it. *Faucille*, *Sichel*, sickle, all come from the Latin. Did Gaul and Britain get the name with the thing, or did the Latin names spread with an improved sickle? Certainly sickles had been known before the conquest; but their use can only have been generalized with the agricultural progress that Roman domination brought.

The ordinary medieval sickle was toothed. Descriptions and pictures show that the stalk was usually cut halfway up. The lower straw was either eaten off by cattle; taken away for thatch, for litter and for stall feeding; or used to heat ovens in districts short of wood, like Beauce and the South of Brie. Sometimes it was ploughed in. But as the Middle Ages wore on new methods began to appear—either the long scythe, previously used only for hay, was used for corn: or new implements were devised, the short scythe (*sape*) and perhaps the great sickle (*volant*). The long scythe was first used on the long stubble. But natural as its use for the harvest seems to us, the transition to it from the sickle had serious difficulties to surmount all the way from the Middle Ages to the nineteenth century. First, there was a juridical one; where stubble was common property, the scythe which reduced its length was forbidden. Then, even in level countries, it was not always easy to adapt the scythe to its new use and to acquire new working motions. Above all, as it was probably necessary to plough in furrows, it was also necessary to smooth the surface before using the scythe.

Ploughing for winter-sown cereals had of course to be ridged so as to drain the ground. Thus, the general use of the scythe required, at least on damp and heavy soils, an improvement in technique which was easier to realize in the first place for the spring-sown cereals. So at first the scythe was only used for harvest within limits and in progressive countries where labour costs had to be considered. It was no doubt used first for oats, then for barley, last of all for wheat. At the end of the fifteenth century oats were sometimes scythed near Paris; but apparently the scythe was used earlier for oats, barley, and even wheat in Normandy and England. Did they use an ordinary or an 'armed' scythe? In Flanders, about 1500, there was a scythe in use with a small half circle fixed close to the blade, which helped in the cutting of cereals. It is to be seen in Old Breughel's 'Harvest' and in the Grimani Breviary.

The short scythe (sape), called in old days a pique, is used particularly in Flanders and adjacent districts. It is held to do the work quicker than the sickle and even than the long scythe. It was probably first used in the neighbourhood of Alost before the fourteenth century. The Turin Hours (1450–1500) show a harvester using a sort of short-handled scythe but without the hook which is normally used with it. But short scythe and hook, in their modern forms, are clearly seen in the Da Costa Hours and the Grimani Breviary soon after 1500. In Artois, where the sape remained a characteristic implement in Arthur Young's time,[1] in the first half of the fourteenth century blé soiet (cut with the toothed sickle) is distinguished from blé piquiet (? cut with a pique).

We know from Heresbach that in the sixteenth century scythe and sape were both used in Western Germany, as a result probably of influence from progressive Flanders. His exact descriptions of implements and of the conditions under which each was used are most valuable. The toothed sickle was used in Juliacensibus, ubi laetioribus campis frumenta densius et in majorem proceritatem excrescunt. Evidently the sickle remained the implement best understood. The sape was appropriate for wheat and rye: his account of its use is almost word for word the same as Arthur Young's. His long scythe, used for light crops, was even better 'armed' than the Flemish implement: alii falce majuscula verriculata, longo manubrio, et ligneis quasi cratibus denticulatis affixis utraque manu segetem abradunt.

Finally it is possible that the volant, that great sickle with a smooth edge, was known to medieval France. It has even been assigned a Gaulish origin. It does better work than the toothed sickle. But as it

[1] Young's account (Travels, 1794 ed., II, 131) is worth quoting for English readers: 'the short handle of the pique is made to rest against the elbow; he holds it with the right hand only, or rather hand and arm; and in his left he has a stick, with a hook at the end of it, with which he draws or holds the corn in the right position to receive the stroke'.

completed its conquest of southern and western France only in the nineteenth century, a very ancient origin and use are unlikely. Perhaps it may be identified in the fifteenth century, in the *très riches heures* of the Duc de Berry, where a big sickle appears to be used with a swinging stroke. In any case, when trying to solve the problem, it must be borne in mind that in the fifteenth century the normal meaning of *volant* was a bill with a wooden handle. This was also called a *goiart*. It was used, as it is today, for tasks like hedging; but also for cutting grass. According to Estienne and de Serres similar implements were employed to remove the stubble after harvest.

In threshing also the Middle Ages were inventive. Here the novelty was the flail. What is believed to be the oldest reference to it is in St Jerome (*Com. in Isaiam*): *virga excutiuntur et baculo quae vulgo flagella dicuntur*. The flail then, an improvement on the beating stick, would date from the fourth century at latest.[1] Probably it was devised in Gaul; for both *Flegel* and 'flail' come from *flagellum*.

It soon replaced the beating stick in all Western temperate Europe where the method of joining the two parts together was gradually perfected: it appears regularly in medieval calendars. It was cheap and easily made at home. But it did not win its way everywhere: fairly compact islands where the beating stick was used survived recently, especially on the skirts of Mediterranean France. It is unlikely that in the temperate regions the flail had been generally preceded by treading out the corn with cattle. The climate is too uncertain for that; and to do it under cover requires great buildings such as only rich men can afford. Probably it was only introduced, as it only survived, here and there. In a contract of the Carthusians of Bonvante of 1370 there is a reference to the season *quo blada dictorum religiosorum flagellabuntur cum equabus suis*. True, Bonvante is not far from the Mediterranean zone; but the word *flagellare* suggests that the flail was in ordinary use there also. Yet we hear of treading out corn by horses in barns so far north, and so late, as Norfolk and the eighteenth century, where it was associated with another custom familiar in Mediterranean lands—the separation of the grain from the straw by throwing it with a shovel from side to side of the threshing floor.

If threshing was done with the flail, when was it done and where? The two questions are linked. If one threshed in the open, the work had to be finished early in the autumn at the latest. If one threshed under cover, the work could be spread over the slack season when nothing was being done on the land. But threshing under cover called for spacious barns which small men could seldom possess. In fact, according to the calendars of the fourteenth and fifteenth centuries,

---

[1] Cf. p. 99, above.

threshing was very often done in August; but unfortunately we cannot always tell whether or not it was done in the open. It is the more remarkable that an eleventh-century English calendar shows two men threshing with the flail in December, while others winnow. The English writers of the thirteenth century mention threshing in barns; and indeed, according to Strabo, this practice was established in England long before the Middle Ages. For France, Germany and Belgium there is evidence, but mainly from the end of the Middle Ages, that threshing in barns went on far into the winter. Probably the practice became more and more general, except in the South and West of France. Estienne, in the sixteenth century, recommends threshing three months after harvest at the earliest: for even when the corn is harvested ripe it improves, so he says, in the barn.

To complete this survey of agricultural work, something must be said of fencing. Cornfields, meadows and vineyards had to be protected against men and beasts—domesticated animals grazing on the fallows and wild animals that swarmed in the woods and were reserved for the lord's hunting. Fencing was by ditch, wooden fence or quickset hedge.

The last raises the problem of enclosure, which can only be touched on here incidentally; for it extends far beyond the field of agricultural technique. Cato already advised the planting of elms or poplars on the outskirts of the fields: they would furnish wood and also leaves to feed the flocks. But the practice was debatable. Varro had his doubts about it, though he allowed that the Sabines employed it and that it hindered quarrels between neighbours, by defining the bounds of properties. But he feared the harm which live hedges might do to the crops: they were only useful beyond question when on the north side of a field. This little controversy, unsettled from Cato to Varro, provides the essential technical arguments for and against enclosure, and helps us to understand the conflicting decisions which—after many hesitations we may suppose—would contribute so much to diversify the rural scenery of Western Europe.

Besides hedges of trees, Varro mentions various sorts of fencing, all of which the Middle Ages would use, their choice being determined much more by the destined use of the enclosed land than by regional custom—thorn hedges, wooden fences, ditches and banks, stone walls. The Franks and other barbarians protected crops, sometimes by ditches, sometimes by fences which—according to the Bavarian law—had to be as high as the breast of a middle-sized man. Carolingian practice was much the same: the *Polyptyque* of Irminon distinguishes *tuninus* fencing—the palisades of stakes and poles, or the heavy trellises, with which courts and farmyards were surrounded; fences (*sepes*) made of posts with three horizontal bars and used for corn and meadows; and fences of split logs (*paxilli fissi*) round vines and also corn. The pictures in later MSS. very often show fences of hurdles. All these types of fence might be used for private fields. But as a rule it was doubtless enough to protect the outer circumference of a whole 'furlong', or of some smaller block of plots bounded by roads. Whether the right of *vaine pâture* led to a compulsory annual destruction of the fencing, or merely to the opening of gaps in it, we can only guess.

Hedges of trees seem, very often at least, to have replaced fences surrounding not whole 'furlongs' but the fields of individuals: they saved the great expenditure of time on periodical renewings or re-pairings of the fences. The Turin Hours shows us a Flemish field, at the end of the fifteenth century, surrounded both by a wooden fence and by trees planted some distance apart—a transition stage, as it would seem, between the dead and the quick type of fence.

Systematic enclosure must have been established and generalized at various dates in different regions. In ancient Ireland, where land was owned tribally, it was impossible: the annals suggest that hedges began to be planted about the end of the sixth century. In Normandy and Maine, enclosed today, corn and other crops were fenced in the Middle Ages: enclosure, as a system, was still incomplete. The completion of enclosure often required the efforts of several generations, parti-cularly in districts where live hedges were associated with ditches. In Poitou and the Limousin, sixteenth-century leases begin—or more probably carry on—the practice of requiring the lessee to enclose this garden, that field, to dig so and so many yards of new ditches, the spoil from which is to be set with bushes or even fruit trees. Ditchers were sometimes brought into Poitou from so far afield as Brittany, to enclose meadows, woods or vineyards. Two almost contemporary docu-ments from High Normandy show clearly that, in the same country and for the same types of land, fences and hedges of trees might coexist— the latter being the ideal towards which progress was necessarily slow. In 1462 the lord of Bec-Crespin paid a man seventy sous for cutting and carting thirteen or fourteen loads of poles and posts to enclose a plantation of graftings. In 1478, at the manor of Frêne-l'Archevêgne a new apple orchard was surrounded with 100 oaks to protect the young trees. Among the advantages of the live hedge, this protection of crops against cold winds and storms was important.

IV. *The plants cultivated*

Among the cereals a first group includes millet, wheat and barley, all known since the earliest times. A second group contains spelt, rye, oats and buckwheat, the cultivation of which only developed fully—or even was only begun—during the Middle Ages.

From neolithic times there appear in the Swiss lake dwellings several varieties of *Triticum vulgare* (ordinary soft wheat, winter or spring) which came from South-West Asia; *dicoccum* (French *amidonnier*, German and English, emmer), cultivated in ancient times in Egypt; and *monococcum* (*engrain*, *Einkorn*), which grows wild freely in Asia Minor and the Balkans, and which came into the West by way of the Danube. Two other important varieties of *Triticum* were added later: in the bronze age in the Alpine region *Tr. spelta* (*épeautre*, *spelz*, spelt) and later still *Tr. durum* (hard wheat), which can only be grown in the Mediterranean area of Western Europe. It is generally supposed to have been brought by the Arab invaders into North Africa, Sicily and Spain; but it may also be supposed that it was also cultivated by the Berbers in Roman times, although the Romans themselves grew only soft wheat.

It is often difficult to distinguish the varieties when referred to in documents or in agricultural writings. For instance the French word *épeautre* seems not to have been applied only to *Tr. spelta*. In fact one might expect to find the same simplification in practice as is found in the Roman treatises. The huskless wheats, whose grain is uncovered, *Tr. vulgare* and *Tr. turgidum*, were distinguished from the husked wheats, in which the husk clings closely to the grain and is only removed with difficulty, *dicoccum*, *spelta* and *monococcum*. The Romans ground the huskless wheats in a quern, the husked were crushed with a pestle— a practice which survived into the Middle Ages, but for what sorts of wheat at that time we do not know; until recently in a few isolated localities in Southern Italy wheat in husk, i.e. spelt (called *farro*) was crushed with a pestle. In French *monococcum* was usually called *petit épeautre*, which shows that the distinction was based mainly on the size of the grain. The Anglo-Saxon *spelt*, it is said, could mean either *dicoccum* or *monococcum*. *Tr. spelta* seems to have gradually superseded the other husked wheats; but we can hardly expect ever to be able to determine when and how.

Nevertheless archaeological finds give us a general idea of the history of wheat in Western Europe. Ordinary soft wheat makes the best bread flour. (But it is also the most subject to disease, at least the im- proved varieties with high yields are.) That is why this wheat, which was comparatively little grown in early medieval times, came into use more and more as agriculture improved. Sometimes it was grown in gardens! But the demands of the well-to-do and the high prices that it fetched led to a large-scale cultivation. In 806 the *modius* of wheat cost 6*d*. against 4*d*. for rye and 3*d*. for barley or spelt. It is probable also that lords often intervened directly to require in leases greater and greater proportions of *Tr. vulgare*. In Hesse an ecclesiastical estate was let in 1281 for twelve years: the contract was that it should carry 18 per cent of wheat on the winter field for the first six years, but 25 per cent in the second. *Tr. turgidum* was much grown in the west, centre and south of France, and only gave way gradually before *Tr. vulgare*. It is in fact coarser and more productive than soft wheat and yields more regularly. But its bread is not so good. Yet it was valued while bread was still baked at home because, like rye bread, the bread made from it does not dry up and keeps fairly well.

The evolution of the husked wheats was faster. *Tr. monococcum*, with a poor yield, but extremely rank growing and that in the worst soils, was spread over all Central Europe in neolithic times, from Troy to Denmark. It vanishes from the North in the Bronze and Iron Ages. Today it is grown only in limited areas, particularly in Spain and South Germany. It gave way as much to rye as to spelt.

Tr. dicoccum also had got to Denmark in neolithic times; but it again vanished from the North, before rye mainly. It seems to have persisted in the Rhineland throughout the Middle Ages, but in France it was generally replaced by *Tr. spelta*, which yielded fine flour. Quoted already in Diocletian's edict, *spelta* spread—but only for a time—to Southern France and Spain. In the *Breviarium* of Charlemagne it is given as the most widely grown grain. In Irminon's *Polyptyque* dues paid in *spelta* are prominent. According to the rules of Adalard, 400 monks at Corbie ate bread made from it. It was also fed to horses. But in the later medieval centuries it was losing ground and now is confined to Swabia, Switzerland, and less important patches in Belgium and Spain. For though better than *dicoccum* and *monococcum*, while still a strong growing plant resistant to cold and damp, its character puts it below *vulgare*, which in the end dominated all temperate Europe. Further south, hard wheat, well suited to the climate, remained as an immigrant from Africa, where little else was grown between the Arab invasion and the nineteenth century.

Of all cereals, barley is the most tolerant of climatic changes: it can resist drought in desert climates, and its early maturity saves it in cold climates. In Scandinavia it will grow even further north than rye. Known since neolithic times, it was used in the Middle Ages for porridge or for bread; fermented, it made beer; horses ate it instead of oats, especially in the South; pigs were fattened on it. It was grown either as winter grain (*Hordeum hexastichum*) or more frequently as spring grain (*H. distichum*). The Merovingian kings took their principal tribute from Germany in barley, and it held a leading place among the cereals in Carolingian times. But a few centuries later its importance began to decline, except in Mediterranean lands, and the decline has been continuous. In fact it needs a fertile and well-tilled soil, and probably it has often been replaced by the less exacting rye.

Millet, indigenous in the extreme East, was brought west by the nomads of the steppes who found it admirably suited to their temporary agriculture: some varieties mature in three months and can stand great heat. And its cultivation, which had spread in Europe from neolithic times, is well suited to soils too light for wheat, provided they are naturally rich or have been heavily dunged. Two varieties were chiefly known in antiquity and the Middle Ages: *Panicum miliaceum*, spread all over Europe, and *Panicum italicum*, confined to southern and Alpine regions. In Roman times it was an important human food in Britain and Gaul (especially in Aquitaine, where it has survived best), on the plain of the Po and in the Campania. Medieval man still used it in North Italy, the Pyrenees, and south-western and western France, where peasants often lived on it, while selling their wheat or handing it over in dues to their lord. But a similar but more prolific grain began to compete with it in southern regions after the Arab invasions: sorghum. Pliny had mentioned a large-grained millet brought from India: it may have been sorghum. If it was, it did not succeed in his day. Diocletian's edict does not mention it, and it is fairly certain that the Arabs reintroduced it. It had reached North Italy by the twelfth century at latest, and often supplied the poor man's bread. But millet held its own until the arrival of maize, a more formidable rival than sorghum.

We come to the cereals which gave medieval agriculture its novel aspect—oats, mainly grown as the spring crop, and rye, almost always sown in autumn. In Germany the land under winter corn was sometimes called the *Roggenfeld* and that under spring corn the *Haberfeld*.

Oats came into Europe mixed with *Tr. dicoccum* as a weed. In certain northerly climatic conditions, it proved the more resisting of the two: then patient human effort improved it and made an independent cereal out of it. It has been found in lake dwellings of the bronze age; but it was a weed to Vergil, and though Columella ranked it incidentally as a fodder crop, Pliny wrote *primum omnium frumenti vitium avena est*. But he noted that Germans made porridge of it, and that the men of the Oönes isles in the Baltic lived on birds' eggs and oats. As porridge it held a great place in medieval dietaries in the north—Germany, Artois, Scotland. It was used like barley for beer. But above all, and increasingly, it was fed to horses, and its cultivation spread where horses replaced oxen as draught animals. In Irminon's *Polyptyque* annual dues of oats come to only 77 *modii*, against 1057 *modii* 10 *sextarii* of spelt and 97½ *modii* of wheat. But subsequently, in the Paris area, dues of oats became as important as those of wheat or of the mixed corn (*méteil*; English, maslin) which had replaced the spelt.

Rye too was at first a weed mixed with the common wheat, which it supplanted in cold continental Europe because it grew more freely and resisted low temperatures better: only barley, as we have seen, will grow further north. The origin of rye explains that of maslin, which became so important in the Middle Ages, south of the rye region: it was not an artificial, but a natural and primitive mixture of rye and wheat. Pliny is the first to mention rye, among the Taurini. His reference suggests that in the Alpine region the wild plant had not yet been much improved. But already in Diocletian's edict (as *centenum sive secale*) it comes third, after wheat and barley. For the same period, archaeology has traced it in Switzerland, Hungary and Transylvania. No doubt it was about that time that it began to spread in Gaul, where in the end it became the chief grain on poor mountainous or flinty soils, especially in the centre of France and the north of Belgium. Its great expansion in the centre and north of Germany, where it became dominant, took place only after the fall of Rome and probably under Slavonic influence: during the early Middle Ages it is specially common in the then Slavonic districts of Holstein, Mecklenburg, Brandenburg, Saxony and Silesia. The Anglo-Saxons must have known it before their migration; for it had an important place in medieval English agriculture, especially on small holdings, though it seems to have lost ground towards the close. In Italy the barbarian invasions certainly helped much to extend its use: it spread even to the South where, among other names, it was sometimes called significantly *germanum*.

Buckwheat (*sarrasin*) did not come till the fifteenth century, brought by Mongols from the Far East. The first mention of it is in Mecklenburg in 1436. Afterwards it spread rapidly to the extreme West: it is known in Normandy in 1460, and in Brittany towards 1500. There it was singularly successful and became an important human foodstuff. In fact it did very well in cleared moor and heath and on dried-up swamps and burnt-over turbaries. By 1536 the naturalist De la Ruelle could assert that, although only come of late years from Asia, it was already widely cultivated in France.

There is not much evidence of attempts to improve the various cereals. English writers advised a change of seed each year and the use of seed grown elsewhere. But, in France at any rate, this advice was not followed.

Besides the cereals, certain plants were grown in the fields to feed men or beasts and to supply industrial needs.

The growth of supplementary foodstuffs developed mainly during the last medieval centuries. In Artois, about 1310, on the estate of Roquetoire the spring sowing was composed of 25 to 30 per cent of oats, 50 to 60 per cent of vetches, 15 per cent of peas and five per cent of beans. At Westerham, in South-East England the proportion of leguminous crops in the spring crops rose between 1300 and 1350 from 0.6 per cent to 10 per cent. But these crops had been important since Merovingian times: there are turnips, beans, peas and lentils in the Salic Law. With vetches added, the list of the crops which recur constantly in medieval documents would be complete. Beans, which went sometimes into bread, peas, of which there were several sorts, and vetch, which was fed to beasts green or as grain, were more widespread than lentils, which need a moist soil. Turnips (*Brassica napus*) and, above all, rape (*Brassica rapa*) were important, but mainly it appears in defined areas such as the French Centre or German South. Already in the first century A.D. Pliny put rape immediately after the cereals and wine as an important crop in Italia Transpadana.

But vetches were not the only fodder crop. At least as early as the thirteenth century we hear of *dragée*, which is no other than the Latin *farrago*, a mixture of leguminous plants and barley, sometimes also of oats or rye, grown to be eaten green. The same word was used for a mixture of cereals—barley and oats, oats and wheat, oats and rye—which was harvested for the grain (the English 'drage' or 'dredge corn'). Finally, it is probably from the close of the Middle Ages that the first artificial meadows must be dated, with the appearance of clover in Flanders. In the South, chickling (*lathyrus*: the common cultivated vetch) which was known in Quercy in the fifteenth century would reach Poitou in the sixteenth under the name of *jarousse*.

For oil, temperate Europe could not look to the olive. The walnut, which grows fairly far north, gives excellent oil; but it was not enough, and its yield is uncertain when there is any risk of late frosts. Besides wild grains and fruits, such as beech-mast, in the later Middle Ages rape seed (*Brassica rapa oleifera*) was used, and then cole-seed (*Brassica napus oleifera*), which is recorded at Bousbecque, near Lille, in the fifteenth century. And no doubt poppy-seed oil was known. Dues paid in poppy seed were not necessarily meant for oil; but the oil is mentioned in Artois and Normandy in the fourteenth century.

Of textile plants, flax had been known from remote antiquity; hemp had come from Asia much later. But probably it was widespread in all western Europe before the destruction of the Roman Empire. More easily grown than flax, it had its place in most family economies. It was grown on moist rich ground by the water-courses. The cultivation of plants for dye wares—dyers' weed, woad, madder, saffron, and that of teazels—developed side by side with the textile industries.

Hops, first mentioned in 768, spread only very slowly with the use of beer. In the fifteenth century Dieppe imported them from Holland and England; and they were extensively grown in Germany.

Medieval horticulture has a markedly archaic aspect; it was only in the sixteenth century that the New World brought the potato, the haricot, the tomato. Moreover horticulture remained very dependent on the Mediterranean, where the art was remarkably vigorous. Perhaps only water-cress is of Nordic stock. The French word *cresson* comes from the Frankish *Kresso*. It is therefore probable that the Gauls learnt from the Franks to gather wild cress, which was then improved and grown in regular water-cress beds, first mentioned towards the end of the thirteenth century.

Until about that date, horticulture had lived on the direct heritage of antiquity, as we find it in the *Capitulare de Villis* and Anthimus' *De observatione ciborum*, written shortly after A.D. 500. First the leguminous plants—peas, beans, lentils—and the roots—rapes, turnips—which were also grown in the fields. Then radishes, carrots, parsnips. These last two were confused with one another till the sixteenth century, a confusion which survives in several dialects of South-East France. The existence of an old Teutonic word *Möhre* for the carrot does not imply a German origin, nor a very ancient German use of it; since at first *Möhre* most probably stood for any edible root. Besides the roots, there were the familiar cabbage, leek, onion, shallot and garlic. Then plants eaten as salad or cooked—lettuce, chicory, mountain spinach, beet, blite, garden cress, rocket; probably too purslain, which Pliny mentions. The lists in the *Capitulare de Villis* and in Anthimus include also plants which, outside the Mediterranean area, were only acclimatized at a later date— asparagus, melon, probably also the cucumber, and the *courge*, a word which before the introduction of pumpkins from the New World was probably applied to the gourd. To the true vegetables must be added many aromatic and seasoning plants. Medieval, like classical, cookery aimed at complicated systems of seasoning: simplicity in the cuisine seems to have been first introduced in France—but not before Louis XIII. Anthimus' treatise on foods, written for Clovis' son Thierry, shows how carefully the barbarian chieftains kept up the tradition of ancient cookery: *apium, coriandrum et anetum vel porriones in omni ciborum coctura miscentur*, he explains. Exotic spices, being too costly, were replaced by such plants as parsley, chervil, mustard, 'britlae' (perhaps chives), sage, savory, coriander, anise, fennel, dill. As the true cummin will not grow in the temperate zone, meadow cummin was used in its place. Although not given in the *Capitulare de Villis*, hyssop, sweet marjoram and basil had probably spread at an early date. Saffron was grown both as a condiment and as a dye in parts of Southern France, of Austria, and of Styria; and most extensively about Aquila in the Abruzzi. Thyme, on the other hand, as a garden plant appears not to be mentioned before Estienne's *Maison rustique*.

A list of seeds bought in 1360 for King John's household when he was a prisoner in England gives an idea of the essentials in a garden of the fourteenth century—cabbage; onion; 'porète', in all probability leeks; lettuce; mountain spinach; beet; parsley; hyssop; borage; purslain; garden cress and several other plants of secondary importance. Borage is a newcomer to such a list: it probably dates from the thirteenth century. This innovation is a prelude to the great development of gardening that came in the fourteenth and fifteenth centuries, when new varieties of old vegetables or completely new ones arrived in temperate Europe—mainly from Italy. But Italy was often a transmitter of Arab influence. Ibn al Awam, writing in the thirteenth century and in Southern Spain, knew spinach, sorrel, and various varieties of lettuce, cabbage and onion. This reveals the activity, patience and resource of Arab horticulture at that time. Henceforward we hear of such things as branching peas, early peas, Roman cabbage, white cabbage, red cabbage. De Serres says that the seed of the white cabbage (*choux blanc cabus*) was brought from Spain and Italy; and the word *cabus* is apparently borrowed from the Italian. The red cabbage is still more interesting. It is very resistant to cold and probably came from Flanders, a fact which anticipates the place that Flanders was to take in the improvement of vegetables, after she had already been a pioneer in crop rotations and in the improvement of agricultural implements.

In the sixteenth century the *Maison rustique* speaks of white Roman lettuces. But at the end of the fourteenth century the *Menagier de Paris* comments on the superiority of the lettuces of Avignon, which were also white. He says that Monseigneur de la Rivière, who made several journeys into Papal Avignon about the year 1389, introduced this variety into the North—a notice deserving quotation, for we seldom know the exact stages, and the method, of the diffusion of a new variety.

We must count among the new vegetables sorrel, spinach and melon (originally called *pompon* in French), which came north in the thirteenth and fourteenth centuries, and perhaps celery. About the same time strawberries appear in gardens. Spinach gradually drove out its less tasty predecessors, the chief of which was mountain spinach. The Italian wars brought more additions to the garden crops. It is said that that best of all melons, the cantaloup, which came from Armenia, was first grown in Italy at the Papal villa of Cantalupi, and that Charles VIII brought it into France. Charles had also brought a Neapolitan gardener, Don Pacello, whom Louis XII set over the royal gardens. It was then that artichokes and asparagus came into France. So by 1517 Antonio de Beatis could say of the gardens of the château of Blois: *vi sono quasi di tucti fructi che sono in terra de Lavoro* (Campania). Before reaching Paris, artichokes and asparagus halted some time in the kindlier climate of the Loire valley: when Francis I was at Meudon he had them sent from Blois.

These additions to garden vegetables coincided with a rapid development of market gardening near the towns, itself connected with the growth of urban populations. Drained marshes were often used, as so many vegetables are greedy of moisture; so from *marais* came the word *maraîcher* to describe the grower of vegetables on a large scale. At Vizille, near Grenoble, in the middle of the fifteenth century, the inhabitants lived mainly by growing garlic and onions. From the close of the Middle Ages Brittany sent vegetables to England. At Frankfurt-am-Main, in 1440, there were 42 master gardeners and 24 journeyman gardeners; and from 1454 a boat was regularly employed to bring in vegetables from Bingen and Mainz. The curiosity and luxurious tastes of lay or ecclesiastical lords, or even of rich bourgeois, who sometimes got good seed from great distances, helped this development of horticulture. A regular seed trade was one result. According to a vote of the town council of Poitiers, in May 1453, the inhabitants had to get their seeds for salads from a local merchant who brought them from Milan. In 1510 the Abbey of Ilsenburg in the Harz bought at Magdeburg seed of onion, parsley, carrot or parsnip, white cabbage and anise.

In the fifth century A.D. those temperate regions which the Romans had occupied already knew our most important fruit trees—apple, pear, walnut, chestnut, plum, peach, cherry, quince, medlar, service, cornelian cherry, hazel-nut. We know from Pliny how quickly the cherry had spread over the Roman world since Lucullus brought it from Asia Minor in 74 B.C. The fig had been pushed as far North as possible: the Emperor Julian tells how the Lutetians used straw to protect fig trees from frost. Just as in the Middle Ages, curiosity and the difficulties of transport led to resolute attempts to acclimatize Mediterranean plants. Estienne says that he had seen in Paris pistachio-nut trees, which are as delicate as olives. Almonds were extensively grown in High Poitou in the sixteenth century: they have now almost disappeared. The introduction of the tree into France from Egypt has been credited to Jean de Villages, an agent of Jacques Cœur; but Gilles le Bouvier, about 1452, says that abundance of almonds were grown in Languedoc and Provence. The apricot is believed to have come into Provence during the Crusades. The white mulberry was only known in Tuscany from about 1340: before that the black variety was grown. The white was brought into France about 1440—but with no great success—by some gentlemen of Dauphiné and Provence who had followed René of Anjou on his Italian expedition. It only began to spread at all widely under Charles IX.

It is more important to record that the walnut—for its oil—and the chestnut—for its flour—were grown as much as possible, especially in the French Centre. About Paris their crops were most uncertain; and since the Middle Ages their number has declined. At Sigy, not far from Provins, in 1660, there were walnuts along the roads and round the fields. Today they are nearly all gone: the yields were not worth the trouble. And in forests the chestnut has lost ground.

However, even the most common fruit trees were grown with care and on a large scale only late in the Middle Ages. For generations, wild fruits gathered in the forest were the mainstay of consumption. Not all were wild in the sense of self-grown. On the edges and even in the heart of the woods rough fruit trees bearing small fruit were planted: they interfered with no one's habits. Nearly a dozen sorts— apples, pears, medlars, quinces and others—grew in the Norman woods. When the woods were felled the fruit trees were carefully preserved. Their growth on a large scale was interfered with, not only by the survival here and there of systems of temporary cultivation and period- ical redivision, but more generally by the existence of common rights, which threw the fields open to grazing before most kinds of fruit were ripe, and by the damage which the cattle did to young trees. The oldest texts of the Salic Law mention neither gardens nor orchards; the later mention *pomaria* and *peraria*, probably in enclosures near the houses. When such enclosures and the gardens became inadequate, light-leaved trees like cherries and peaches were planted among the vines.

We do not usually find clauses in Parisian or Poitevin leases obliging metayers to plant so many fruit trees a year before the sixteenth century: these plantations then went on so steadily that we may assume that the thing was new. In Normandy however the movement began rather earlier; it was already well under way in the second half of the fifteenth century.

Not merely was planting pushed on: efforts had been made to improve the quality of the fruit even before the extension of the gardens and orchards was taken in hand. Improvement of quality thus encouraged extension, we may assume. New varieties, especially of apples and pears, began to appear. As in the case of the vegetables, they were spread by way of trade or by exchanges between religious houses. The specially prized trees were elaborately manured, dug about, pruned and protected. In Normandy in 1254 a lessee agrees to cultivate an acre of garden on an island, to plant within two years grafted apple and pear trees, and to fence the garden well. In Artois in 1320 the Countess Mahaut has brought grafted trees from Burgundy: she buys also about Beauvais. And she makes money out of her gardens by selling fruit in good years. In 1365 two men of Oissel in Normandy sell 104 grafted apples, 10 grafted pears and 104 vine-stocks. In 1511 the monks of St Germain fetch 300 plum-trees from Reims for their estate at Cachan near Paris.

The cider apple deserves special attention. Cider and perry are mentioned in the *Capitulare de Villis*. But the cider must have been made mainly from wild or coarse apples; and one can understand why beer was preferred. However, from the twelfth century cider-making is fairly often mentioned in Normandy; in the thirteenth it crosses to England, perhaps under the influence of Norman abbeys. But it was only in the fourteenth century that cider began to rival beer in Normandy: it is not quite clear why. No doubt in years of bad harvest cereals were not allowed to be used for brewing. But this cannot have been decisive, or the decision would have come much earlier. It was probably the arrival and spread of good varieties of cider apples which led to increased production of cider which the well-to-do would drink: the poor would drink anything and, in fact, continued to drink an inferior perry. All varieties of cider apples now grown in Normandy differ from the wild forest apple: some came from the Basque country, where the use of cider is very old. (Basque grafted apples were used at least as early as the sixteenth century.) Gradually cider made from the cultivated apple drove out that made from the wild. In 1486 the Archbishop of Rouen still had 70 bushels of apples gathered in his woods at Déville to make verjuice. But the same year 70 grafted trees were planted in his orchard. More were added next year: in 1499 and 1500 five dozen trees were planted and others were grafted.

The vine, as everyone knows, was cultivated in the Middle Ages far beyond its present zone—in Flanders and England and in high Pyrenean valleys, for example. Every effort was made, where there was the least chance of success, to produce on the spot wine for the sacrament and wine for the consumption of the well-to-do. The methods employed for making wine help to explain why it could be made so amazingly far north. Grapes that did not ripen, and green grapes, were made into verjuice. Verjuice was made even where conditions for ripening were very good—in Quercy and the Bordelais, where the work was done at the end of July. Moreover, following a classical habit, honey was added to the wine—and cinnamon, coriander, or sage, which assuredly changed its flavour but concealed its thinness and roughness. And besides that *vin cuit* was prepared.

In the typical instance of the Rhineland, the Romans had acclimatized the vine; and the Moselle vineyards began to be famous in the second century. The barbarians only ruined viticulture partially: soon they became keenly interested in it. With Carolingian times its extension proceeded again vigorously on royal and ecclesiastical demesnes. By the ninth century it is spread in all the provinces of Worms and Speyer. It extends gradually in the Rheingau; then further afield into comparatively unfavourable regions such as Swabia, Franconia and Thuringia. After that, it is less a case of penetration into fresh districts than of the multiplication of vineyards and the adoption of better sorts of vines in those where the industry was already acclimatized with some success. From the valleys, the vine was carried up the slopes. In the Rheingau, the men of Eibingen and Rüdesheim secured from Archbishop Barbo (1031–51) a grant of wooded slopes above the villages to make vineyards of them. Towards 1200 the monks of Eberbach planted the Steinberg, which became famous. However, these new plantations only yielded prized vintages after long and patient toil: in the Middle Ages they were not so famous as the vineyards of Bacharach.

And what of progress in viticulture? All that happened was that the Mediterranean technique was adapted to less favourable climates. The vines were regularly propped up on poles to get more sun. In the eleventh century the foundation charter of the Abbey of Muri, southwest of Zürich, lays down a programme of work which recurs with minor variations throughout the Middle Ages—you manured; pruned; hoed over once before Easter; tied up the shoots; hoed again before Midsummer; layered some of the shoots; and to help the grapes to ripen you removed any leaves that covered the clusters. The calendars show pruning in February or March. Two workings are, so to speak, standard; but no doubt there was a tendency to do more in the best cared for vineyards, such as those of the Bordelais. Another operation, well known to the Roman writers, is mentioned in Provence and Poitou—*déchaussage*, clearing the foot of the vine-stock of surrounding earth: this was done before pruning.

As in antiquity, willow plantations often went with vineyards. They supplied the withes for tying-up and the barrel-hoops. In the Rhineland the monastery of Eberbach, when letting meadows, always retained the willows.

V. *Domestic animals and breeding*

At the beginning of the Iron Age climatic changes gave the north-western parts of Europe near the seaboard a unique appearance which they have preserved up to our own time. The climate became damper and cooler in summer, and thus more favourable to animal husbandry. Winter temperatures were probably not markedly lower, but, except in the extreme west, snow made it necessary to over-winter the cattle in stables. Thus, a new type of habitation (*Hallenhaus*), in which large numbers of animals could live under the same enormous roof as human beings, came into use in the regions between the east of the Low Countries and Denmark. This kind of dwelling, typical of the *éleveurs-polyculteurs*, i.e. men engaged mainly in various types of animal husbandry, contrasted with the habitations with transverse divisions (*Querhaus*) of the *cultivateurs-éleveurs*, i.e. of mixed farmers engaged in both animal husbandry and arable farming, which were common in inland areas.

Long after the opening of the Middle Ages, cattle, which had dominated the life of primitive Celts and Germans, remained the essential element of personal property among the people least affected by Roman civilization. The conquered Saxons paid an annual tribute of 500 cows to Clotaire I; and much later paid 300 horses to Pepin the Short. Their cattle rearing at that time rested on the use of the natural resources of forest, marsh, moor and open grassland. There were no cultivated meadows: cereals were grown on a small scale in a system of temporary cultivation which involved an unsettled life.

In the extreme west, Ireland and Scotland, where Rome had never ruled, remained in a still more primitive condition. According to Dio Cassius the Caledonians, at the beginning of the third century, dwelt in tents and had neither towns nor fields. They lived on milk, game and wild fruits. They had great herds of cattle and sheep, and small swift horses which they reared in their wild mountains and marshy meadows. Similar conditions survived well into the Middle Ages in Wales and especially Ireland. The Welsh ate little bread, living mainly on milk, butter and cheese; and English surveyors of the fourteenth century noted that there was no regular individual property in land, but that groups of families shared common grazing rights over great stretches of country. There were summer shielings with their huts, and winter pasture in valleys where the principal dwellings were. Fifteenth-century Ireland remained, in great part, a country of wandering pastoralists— more so than Wales because its climate gave rich grazing at all seasons. Its people did not mow the grass for hay, and built no stalls for their cattle, but moved themselves and their huts as the beasts used up the grass.

This picture was certainly no longer true for England and Gaul— except perhaps Belgium—when the Western Empire fell. Their agriculture had developed greatly under Roman rule and the people were finally settled in towns, villages and hamlets. But it helps us to understand both the considerable, often predominant, role, and the usually extensive character, of cattle farming in temperate Europe throughout the Middle Ages, especially on the moist oceanic coasts of Brittany and Norway. (According to Gilles le Bouvier Norway raised quantities of horses and cattle: the beef was salted down in barrels and shipped as far as Flanders.) Nevertheless, in the romanized countries a new thing was beginning to appear which was preparing the way for ultimate progress—care for the improvement of the breeds of animals. The Gauls valued good breeding, at least in horses, much more than the Germans, according to Caesar. The Romans had introduced more method and continuity into their selections and crossings of breeds: in Spain they had paid special attention to sheep, and obscure as their work is they seem at least to have prepared the way for those selections and crossings which, at a later date, with the introduction of the merino, gave such exceedingly important results.[1]

The utilization, generally the common and often almost the exclusive utilization, of natural grazing grounds and of woods, at no more cost and no more expenditure of time than was involved in the guarding of the flocks and herds, gave the men of the medieval countryside an extended but a temporary advantage. Up to a point, this advantage counterbalanced their inferior agricultural technique and their great social inequalities; and so the elementary needs of the great majority were met. It must never be forgotten that, for a period that varied in length with the place, the agriculture of temperate Europe, just because it developed in regions absolutely virgin or relatively new, remained in a privileged position; during the same period this privileged position was already far away in the past for most Mediterranean lands.

Use was made not only of natural grazing and of stubbles, and of fallows before their first ploughing, but also of marshes—a surprising fact but one that the sturdiness of the breeds of domestic animals explains. They were taken into the marshes in summer. The marsh also furnished reeds for litter and grasses which made a poor hay—but in winter the cattle were not fastidious. As for the forests, they were the peasant's providence. They fed his horses, unless there was some local rule against it, his cattle, his sheep, his goats, with their leaves—eaten green in summer and gathered dry for winter—and the grass of their open glades. His pigs ate the acorns and beech-mast. The Laws of the Alemanni refer to *buricae*, *puriae*, which were either huts of some kind or enclosures for the beasts in the forests; and in the thirteenth century herds of unbroken horses (*equi silvestres*, *indomiti*) were kept in the forests of the Moselle Valley. But apart from such extreme cases—

[1] Cf. p. 439, below.

which can be paralleled from sixteenth-century Normandy and else-where—the forest provided a part, but often a great part, of the feed of every kind of domestic animal.

Forests were variously handled according to their various uses. The high woods of oak and beech gave timber for the carpenter and pannage for swine. The copse woods, with a greater variety of trees regularly cut over, provided firewood; and in their low thickets the beasts fed easily on leaves. In Normandy the rule of the forests was this: goats were kept out usually though not always; beasts were not allowed in the inner forests in May, or from mid-May to mid-June, but might graze on the outskirts; from about mid-August they were again ex-cluded, for it was the time for gathering wild fruits. In the forest of Évreux grazing began for most kinds of animals on St Andrew's Eve (29 Nov.) at noon and ended—after the May interruption—at mid-August. In the forest of Ardenne the horses and horned cattle ran free winter and summer: they might have to seek their food beneath the snow. And so there developed a local type of forest horse, small, quiet, and very sturdy. There were special rules for the pannage of swine. In Normandy it began late in September or early in November and went on, for periods varying from nine days to several months, until Lent. In the forest of Ardenne it began at St Rémi (1 Oct.) or St Denis (9 Oct.) and ended at the end of December, at Candlemas, or even later when acorns were specially abundant.

But as these facilities for cattle keeping encouraged the growth of population and that made more clearing necessary, the facilities were always being limited and the pressure on them increased. In the Oisans (Alps of Dauphiné) complaints are made in the fifteenth century of the lack of hay: cultivation had covered all the lower land, and hay had to be sought in high and almost inaccessible places. And since grazing beasts were apt to ruin young copses, forest resources were likely to be reduced automatically, apart from any deliberate clearing. This led to their abuse, especially towards the close of the Middle Ages, when cattle rearing for large-scale marketing had developed here and there. In the Diois (High Dauphiné) the forest of Saou in the fifteenth century fed many horses, besides sheep, oxen and pigs. One big horse breeder put in 40 horses, two others 160 between them. Probably they used them in summer for treading out the corn in Provence. But the small men suffered. The horses were put in before the sheep, and the sheep found little to eat. A petition to the lord reminds him of a decision of 1340 that no one should put into the forest more than eight mares and eight colts. No doubt the forest itself suffered as much as the small users from the inroads of such large herds.

Great proprietors tried to stop the threatened destruction of their forests. In France, Louis IX and his successors often bought up the commoners' rights, ceding to them part of the forest in absolute ownership; and lords followed the example. Elsewhere the rights of user were restricted. In Ardenne, from the thirteenth century the period for which copses might not be cut over was extended. Sheep were early excluded from the forests, although goats—excluded as a rule—were still allowed into copses more than seven years old in the Liège country in 1551. But useful as such measures might prove in the long run, they could upset the small man's way of life when brutally applied. Hence the loud protests of communes and the interminable lawsuits which delayed forest protection. In 1308 the Abbey of St Germain-des-Prés had allowed the men of Antony and Châtenay, near Paris, to put cows, oxen and calves into the wood of Antony *après la cinquième feuille*— for a consideration. From 1427 the monks vainly tried to go back on this concession. In 1523 they were explaining to the master of woods and forests that the woods were being ruined by the cows and would have no value in the future. Evidently the ravages of the cattle kept down the brushwood; and the more it was reduced the more it was ravaged. But how could you rob the villagers of an essential means of livelihood? The master of woods and forests compromised by forbidding access to copses less than seven or eight years old.

So the close of the Middle Ages saw the first difficult beginnings of a decisive transformation in the methods of cattle rearing—its prerequisite becoming not the forest but the cultivated meadow. In time this would change forest scenery. Except in some districts such as the south-west of France, the forest would cease to be a vast grazing ground and become more and more a place for rationalized timber production: in the end its very trees would change. For pasturage deciduous trees are essential. But conifers produce timber quicker. It has been estimated that, whereas in the Middle Ages the German forests were two-thirds deciduous, now the same forests are two-thirds coniferous.

Cultivated meadows, sometimes manured (especially with pigeon dung) and irrigated (even as far north as Germany), had existed since antiquity in romanized countries, and in Germany since the Carolingian era, when *Feldgraswirtschaft* declined fast. But these meadows were comparatively rare and often monopolized by the lords, who thus alone acquired the reserves of hay needed for improved cattle rearing. Common rights which threw the meadows open to the herds of the commune after the first, or sometimes after the second crop, reduced, but did not abolish, the drawbacks of such a monopoly, a monopoly which increased the technical superiority of the large over the small holding.

However in several regions, such as Normandy, Flanders and parts of England, where agriculture was most advanced and most prosperous, meadows were greatly extended, especially as a result of the improvement of marshes. There is no sign of any large-scale project of draining in the English Fenland during the Middle Ages; but there was continuous piecemeal encroachment upon the edges of the fens. The first result was meadowland, though with good fortune the meadow might later become arable. A comparison of Domesday statistics with those of early fourteenth-century subsidy rolls brings out a remarkable change in the prosperity of the Fenland as compared with the surrounding upland, most marked in the silt area near the sea, but noticeable also on the peat soil further south.[1]

But it was in Flanders especially that the winning of land from the sea, followed by drainage work, furthered both the increase and the improvement of cattle. Stages in this progress can be distinguished, coinciding with those in the drainage. The land acquired was first used for sheep—especially from the eleventh century. Sheep were driven on to the *schorres*, seaside meadows, while these were still exposed to periodical tidal flooding. When their drainage was complete, the *schorres* were either ploughed or used as meadows for horses and cows. According to the charter of the Franchise of Bruges (1515) the inhabitants of the country lived by fattening cows which they bought lean in neighbouring regions. Thanks to the lush nourishing grass and the care given to the cattle, Flanders evolved strong and heavy breeds.

The rabbit, whose domestication was slow, was the only addition to the domestic animals made in the Middle Ages. All that happened was that the importance of the various species varied with changes in demand—for oxen, or plough horses, or sheep for their wool. On the huge demesnes of the Teutonic Order sheep suddenly become much more important about 1400: oxen and pigs change little. At Brandenburg sheep increased from 1645 to 4440 between 1380 and 1392, and at Christburg from 1900 to 3200. In breeding, it is hard to say what precisely can be attributed to the Middle Ages. There was certainly no systematic and controlled breeding. But the purchases of foreign sires which are fairly often recorded show that the first crossings from which existing breeds have sprung are often very distant. Because of its military value, the horse was bred with special care on great estates, as appears already in the *Capitulare de Villis*. It was fed on fresh grass, hay, straw, oats (when oats had gradually replaced barley and spelt) and vetches—peas and beans too. Certain countries were early famous for

[1] English writers of the thirteenth century calculated that two cows or twenty sheep fed *de marisco salso* gave as much milk as three cows or thirty sheep fed on leaves, ordinary grass, or stubble.

their horses: Normandy was one of these. We have the accounts for King Philip VI's considerable stables at Domfront in 1338. There were 2 stallions, 28 brood mares, 28 colts and a working mare. They were considered appropriate presents for people in high places: 20 mares and 16 colts were given *aux demoiselles de Me. la Reine et de Me. la Duchesse et à Philippe de Praelles pannetier du roi.*

As saddle horses the anglo-arabs are today unrivalled. In France the area from which they spread extends north of the Pyrenees, to beyond Toulouse on the east and to the boundaries of Poitou and Berry on the north. This is roughly the area occupied for a time by the Saracens, and it seems evident that the breeding of horses with an Eastern strain goes back there to the early Middle Ages. Horses from the Limousin were much prized. In 1153 the Bishop of Soissons gave five serfs for one; in 1312 Philippe le Bel paid 500 livres for two. Spanish jennets were bought for high prices: the Andalusian variety, hardly distinguishable from the Arab, was long the favourite saddle horse in France. But northern breeds were also appreciated. About 1312 Philippe le Bel was buying palfreys in Germany, Frisia and Denmark. In 1370 horses for Normandy were bought at Bruges. In the fifteenth century there was a considerable import of English horses through Dieppe, encouraged no doubt at first by the presence of English troops in Normandy; but a revival of the import in 1478 and 1480 must have been due to fashion.

Mules in some districts worked in the fields: they were also used as saddle and pack animals. Already in the eleventh century noble ladies are riding mules in the Bas Limousin. The mule was an important pack animal in the Cevenol part of the Vivarais and on the plateau of the upper Loire in the fifteenth century: we hear of muleteers and merchants with anything up to ten mules. The ass was the poor peasant's beast in many places; but in the plough its work was as poor as its typical master.

Of cattle there is little to be said. The fattening of oxen for the table was still only casual. Even in a progressive country like Artois, on the demesne of Roquetoire, there were often one or two oxen being fattened —they got vetches and oats then—but never more. At Bonnières, from All Saints 1327 to Trinity Sunday 1328, three oxen were fattened—and eaten at the feast of the Bishop of Arras. It seems that those Cotentin oxen which Froissart thought the finest in the world were plough animals. However the growth of towns probably encouraged the raising of oxen for slaughter. That was being done on the land of the Celestines at Porchefontaine near Paris in 1507.

We are specially well informed about sheep breeding in the fourteenth century, thanks to John de Brie, who wrote for Charles V in 1379 a treatise which we know from a sixteenth-century summary. Sheep fed in the open all the year round—in June where there were plenty of thistles, *car la pâture des chardons leur est bonne,* and from August on the stubble. In winter, in time of thaw or rain, they were given bean haulm, not pea haulm. In Artois they were given vetch, with some oats for ewes with lamb at foot, or for sheep being fattened. From the spring to the end of autumn they were folded on the arable at night. There was always danger of wolves, and John de Brie recommends as sheep-dogs big mastiffs with heavy heads and spiked iron collars round their necks. The spread of sheep-farming produced a characteristic improvement in the shepherd's crook which almost certainly originated in Flanders at the end of the fourteenth century. Before that time this crook was merely fitted with a hook at the tip, the original of the bishop's crozier, with which the shepherd caught the sheep's leg as it tried to elude capture. In place of this simple crook appeared a more elaborate version which was fitted with a little shovel with which earth could be thrown to frighten the sheep on the run.

Probably the great migrations of the early Middle Ages helped to diversify the breeds of sheep in Western Europe by bringing, directly or indirectly, breeds from the Eurasian steppe. The Arab invasions acted in a similiar way in North Africa. Before the Arabs came there were Berber sheep of great antiquity and *barbarins* of the Syrian big-tailed stock. The *barbarins* were confined to Tunis and the East of the present department of Constantine, which suggest that the Phoenicians may have brought them. The Arabs brought their own small-tailed sheep; a breed very superior to the others and much the most widespread in Algeria today.

Further, in temperate Europe purchases of sheep from a distance—like the purchases of horses—prepared the way for methodical modern breeding. Spanish sheep and goats are bought for Maine and Normandy in the fourteenth century. And the reputation of English sheep seems to have followed English armies on to the Continent. The 96 which were landed at once at Dieppe in 1425 may have been for the commissariat. But the Cotswold rams licensed for Spain in 1464 were for crossing with the merino.

The little domestic industry of butter and cheese making deserves a few words. The Greeks had learnt about butter from the Scythians, though they and the Romans hardly used it except for anointing. But Pliny says that among the barbarians its use differentiated the rich from the poor. In the Middle Ages it spread everywhere but remained something of a luxury, beef-fat and lard being more widely used. Nearly all the inventories from the end of the fifteenth century drawn up in the neighbourhood of Paris contain butter pots and churns; but it is significant to note in one of them 80 lb. of lard against 13 of butter. Holland and Flanders were famous for their butter. Gilles le Bouvier tells us that Brittany made and exported a great deal; and butter was one of the commodities which paid 'lastage' when 'carried out of England to parts beyond seas' in 1303.

Several countries were also great exporters of cheese—England, Holland, Normandy, Auvergne, Brie. Philip Augustus provisioned his castle of Falaise with English cheese; and it was still coming into France in the fifteenth century, by way of Dieppe and Calais. The reputation of Brie was by that time well established. No doubt, as at so many points in agricultural technique, the monks' love of good living and interest in organization often gave the first impetus to development. Early in the sixteenth century, the farmer of the Celestines of Porchefontaine owed them 30 dozen of cheeses a year *de la forme et patron qui lui ont été montrés par lesdits Célestins sans être ébeurrés*. Sour milk and sour milk cheese, which with butter had been a staple food of the nomads of the steppes and the barbarians generally, seem to have disappeared fairly soon from the dietary at least of the well-to-do; but some curious survivals have been noted in Normandy. Cheese making was also carried on in alpine regions with the opening up of the summer pastures on high mountain slopes. Nevertheless before the twelfth century in Bavaria there is no mention in charters of the pastoral way of life even though by the thirteenth century thousands of cheeses were owed on all manors. Landlords granted tenants specialized leases (*swaiga*) of six cows for which a rent of 300 cheeses was usually fixed.

About the swine, most essential facts have been given already in connexion with their pannage. They were fed besides on barley, wheat and beans. From the first century A.D. Belgian pigs were well known even in Italy. They ran wild and were remarkably strong and speedy. Swine breeding was also an important business among the Franks; and at the very close of the Middle Ages German lords kept immense herds, up to as many as 500 head.

Last come the bees and the poultry. The Church's demand for wax and the use, in some countries, of beverages made with honey ensured attention for the beehives. One can hardly speak of specialization, but in some appropriate places bee-keeping was highly esteemed. On the sunny slopes of the Cevennes, in the southern Vivarais, the *Estimes* of 1464 record a number of apiaries with 40 hives, and one with 90. Wild honey was also collected in the woods; in the barbarian laws even the property in wild swarms had been regulated.

Hens and geese were the principal farmyard birds. The right of keeping pigeons was often a privilege of the lord. (From two small manors in the village of Grantchester, King's College, Cambridge, their lord, got 2–3000 pigeons a year for the College table in the fifteenth century.) Ducks and the peacocks and swans eaten at feasts were less important. Rabbits still were mainly wild, running with other game in the lord's warrens. In the first century B.C. the wild rabbit, a native of Spain, was a novelty in Italy. It is doubtful whether there was an Anglo-Saxon name for it (there certainly was for the hare) and it is not mentioned in the *Capitulare de Villis*. But it spread as fast as it always does and became a danger to the crops. Late in the Middle Ages, and in a few places, it was domesticated and reared in hutches (*clapiers*). But the tame rabbit was always considered much inferior to the warren rabbit.

To summarize: during the long and confused centuries between the fall of the Western Empire and the dawn of modern times agriculture developed widely and powerfully in temperate Europe, especially in the area which includes Eastern England, Northern France, Flanders and the Rhineland. It was based on processes and implements inherited from the ancient world. The creative activity of the Mediterranean area was, so to speak, exhausted after it had achieved almost all that was possible—exhausted except in the domain of horticulture in which, with the help of Mussulman Spain reacting on Italy, it continued to lead the way. On this basis, and sometimes also on independent foundations, was built a series of original structures linked together in a coherent and well-balanced whole. Cereal growing was to a great extent remade. But the new system had its weak points of which, as has been seen, the method of rearing animals was the weakest. Relying too much on the irrational use of natural resources which were not inexhaustible, the rearing of animals would have to face increasing difficulties, which would react dangerously on the whole agricultural system. The three-course rotation of crops, which was the great medieval innovation, could not function properly unless, side by side with the arable fields subject to this rotation, the farmer also had at his disposal sufficient feeding stuffs to sustain the plough animals and those other animals which provided manure; such fodder came from woods, pasture and meadowland. But from the end of the Middle Ages onwards these resources shrank dangerously, because of the increasingly strict forest laws and continued clearance of the waste, while the deductions of grain, straw and fodder which were necessary to pay tithes and feudal rents were an additional drain on available supplies. Then, in the coming centuries, the need for a new agricultural revolution would slowly become apparent.

CHAPTER IV

Agrarian Institutions of the Germanic Kingdoms from the fifth to the ninth century

THOSE Germanic states which were set up on the soil of the Western Empire after its dissolution were of decisive importance in the economic development of medieval Europe. Modern scholarship gives us a conception of the conditions under which they were established appreciably different from that which so long prevailed. A flourishing Roman civilization was not swept away by wild hordes of barbarians. The new Germanic states were not the swift consequence of a mighty clash of arms, in which the Romans lost land and liberty, followed by the further spreading of the primitive civilization of their Teutonic conquerors. 'The West Roman Empire passed away without commotion', as a recent student of the problem has put it.[1]

Long before dissolution came at the end of the fifth century peaceful penetration by the Germans had been going on; and that penetration was not simply military. Primarily it was economic. So early as the end of the fourth century the Bishop of Cyrene in Africa had the impression that there was hardly a family left without a Goth or Scythian as waiter or butler, cook or bailiff. Germans had not only risen to the highest ranks as soldiers or officials; great masses of them had found economic employment. Naturally there were crowds of German prisoners, reduced to slavery, scattered over all the Empire. But among the veterans, who were settled in the frontier provinces and furnished with land, there were just as many Germans. The emperors themselves, as early as the middle of the second century, had settled tens of thousands of subject barbarians in thinly populated parts of the Empire, to provide the land with new cultivators and the army with a vigorous stock. Particularly after the Marcomannic war great crowds of German warriors, with their wives and children, were assigned to important landowners and settled on their great estates, on condition that they were employed only in agriculture and were bound to the soil,[2] unless indeed they volunteered as soldiers. The removal of Britons from England and their settlement in the *agri decumates*, on the Main, in the Odenwald and along the Neckar, were the outcome of a system that was known under Trajan

[1] Sundwall.
[2] The *inquilini*.

and greatly extended under Marcus Aurelius. Under Probus, in A.D. 277, some of the conquered Germans were sent to colonize the outer provinces, such as Britain and Northern France. Those composite Romano-Germanic states which arose in the fifth century in Italy, Gaul, Spain and Africa are only the completion of the great movement which had in fact begun long before Caesar's day. It starts with a peasantry of *coloni* and the entry of many Germans as inferior household servants; then it spreads to the rank and file of the army as constituted by Alexander Severus; next it grips the officers and officials; and ends with the setting up of regular barbarian states in the midst of the Roman population. The Germans by no means came into contact with the Romans only as enemies, perhaps on a threatened frontier, or only as traders who exchanged goods with them on the Limes where German and Roman were neighbours. They do not appear simply as soldiers in the army or as veterans settled along the boundaries of the Empire. Not only did they find their way into the imperial administration; they pressed through endless little channels into domestic and agricultural life, in which they were employed in the ordinary everyday jobs.

So the economic 'fall' of the West Roman Empire was completed with no great shock. This is especially conspicuous in Italy itself. There also barbarians had been settled repeatedly in the past—Marcomanni by Marcus, then Alemanni and Taifali in the years 370–7. The mercenaries, to deal with whom there already existed a *fiscus barbaricus* in the middle of the fifth century, now demanded regular grants of land, as they often had before in other places; and they were only using well-worn precedents when they called their leader Odoacer to be king. Following out the Roman quartering system, he assigned a third of the Romans' land to his men as their permanent property. (He had been treating the Romans quite considerately, and had ordered provincials from Noricum to be brought over the Alps into safety, when he could no longer hold the province.) The actual areas of land thus ceded by the *possessores* to their *hospites* were not uniform, for according to the Roman quartering system account had to be taken of each 'guest's' rank.

When in A.D. 491 the Ostrogoths under Theodoric conquered Italy a greater proportion of Roman land was no doubt taken. The lands which Odoacer had given his men (*sortes Herulorum*) passed to the new conquerors. But these did not suffice the far greater crowd of Goths; so new sharings-out had to be made. A prominent Roman, Liberius, who had made himself useful under Odoacer, was given the task. The assignments of land were made in writing (*pittacia*) with great consideration for the Roman proprietors. Often Goths and Romans lived side by side as common owners (*praediorum communio*): the Goth was the Roman's co-proprietor (*consors*). The Roman proprietors remained completely free. Gothic settlement was most dense in upper Italy and the East (Samnium, Picenum). Thinner in the West (Campania, the neighbourhood of Rome, Tuscany), there was little of it in South Italy and Sicily. It was not a settlement of whole districts by compact masses of newcomers: it was more like the spreading of a wide-meshed net. The decline in the Italian population as a result of previous wars, and the partial falling of the land out of cultivation, eased the re-division. By the acquisition of the imperial *patrimonium*, and by confiscations for treason, the king got property enough to provide for his military following. A fair proportion of the land now again brought under cultivation appears as let out to *coloni*. Gothic names are found among them. Marked inequalities in the distribution of landed property are conspicuous. Besides the nobles serving the king appear large landlords (*potentiores*); the freemen are divided into *honestiores* and *humiliores*. The late Roman agrarian system was still producing its wretched social consequences. First Theodoric and after him especially Totila (A.D. 541–52) found it necessary to support the peasants against the landlords' tyranny. Theodoric instructed his officials to keep down corn and wine prices and, besides that, he had 20,000 modii of corn distributed yearly among the people. He also forbade the alienation of ecclesiastical lands in A.D. 507.

After the breakdown of the Ostrogothic dominion there came a revival of the great landowners' economic power under the Byzantines (A.D. 553–68).[1] By Justinian's pragmatic sanction of A.D. 554 King Totila's land grants were annulled and the property restored to the Romans. So the old Roman system once more acquired powerful support.

The Lombards conquered Italy in A.D. 568. How they occupied the land is not clear, for there are no sources of information in the early years. Yet in spite of the military conquest there can be no question of any general enslaving of the Romans and appropriation of their land. The emergence of the *aldiones* (half-free folk) has misled people. With their personal freedom many Romans may also have retained their land —only burdened with dues and services. They became *tributarii*. It is significant that many Romans, not only servile but also free, fled away to the Lombards to escape the tyranny of their Roman lords; for among the Lombards freedom would be respected.

Devastation during the conquest and the years of warfare no doubt left much land lying waste, and provided the chieftains with an easy way of endowing their war bands (*gesindi*). The Lombard freemen did not become mere landlords, enjoying without toil rent from the dues of their dependants, and themselves doing no agricultural work. A good

[1] See below, p. 206.

many of the smaller proprietors cultivated part of their land (their *sa a* or *sundrio*) themselves; and on the greater estates direct cultivation is found side by side with leasing and payment for land by *tributarii*. From the first occupation there were great inequalities in property. Beside the poor stand richer folk. The kinship groups (*farae*) may still have had great importance as the place names in *fara* suggest; but the persistence of war and the mingling of races must soon have broken them down. Nowhere can we trace any remnants of common property. Where communal life is found, as in the numerous house communities, it exists because of its economic advantages. There was plenty of artificial kinship—*adfratatio*: it was used to ease the burden of dues and services and prevent the land from falling in to the lord for lack of heirs. The true waste land—forest, rough grazing, waters—remained undivided for common use, shared in proportion to the size of the arable holdings.

With the rise of Authari the era of the chieftains (dukes) came to an end (A.D. 574-84). They handed over half their property to the king, and at the same time an adjustment was arranged with the Romans. There was some sort of land-sharing between them and their Lombard *hospites*; but we do not know what form it took. In the years of peace that followed romanization made great strides, which could hardly have happened if at the very outset of Lombard rule there had been a complete dispossession and enslavement of the Romans. Probably the Roman population was superior to the Lombard not only in civilization but also in numbers.

Transfers of property must have been greatly facilitated by King Rothar's recognition in A.D. 641 of the right to make dispositions by will for the salvation of one's soul. Besides that, freemen who had no sons might dispose of property by gift. The laws of Liutprand (A.D. 713-35) recognize the equality of Roman with Lombard law in the relations of daily life. Marriage of Romans with Lombard women is permissible, and this must have led to increasing racial fusion.

The persistence of late Roman economic institutions is revealed both in estate organization and in the various forms of contract for the hire of land. The Lombards did not live together in compact groups. In Tuscany the ancient place names have survived pretty uniformly right up into the mountains. Church dedications show a similar distribution of pre-Lombard saints' names. On the other hand in places which existed in antiquity names of specifically Lombard saints are common, not infrequently side by side with the sanctuaries of the subject Romans. Along the frontiers, for purposes of defence and on the Byzantine model, the Lombards established freemen (*arimanni*) on public land, for which they had to pay rent. Their holdings, like the Byzantine soldiers' holdings, were entered in official lists, to protect the state against losses through their sale. In this way some free rural communities grew up, and long retained their independence, on the lands of the Lombard state.

In Spain and the South of France, just as in Italy, the Germans found Roman institutions intact and strongly rooted. The Visigothic settlement in Southern Gaul under King Walia took place early in the fifth century. In the mid-century Theodoric began the conquest of Spain which Euric (A.D. 466–85) practically completed. The copious legislation of the Visigothic kings enables us to follow the evolution of economic relations tolerably well. According to Euric's law, two-thirds of the old Roman *fundi* were assigned to Goths, the Romans retaining only a third. But the Visigoths like the Ostrogoths appear as *hospites* who spared many of the Romans' rights of property. King Athaulf left various Roman estates near Bordeaux quite free of any Gothic *hospites*. Where the boundaries of the old *fundi* were not clear, decision lay with a mixed commission to which both Goths and Romans sent elected representatives. Euric's law employs the usual terminology of the Roman *agrimensores*. Romans were protected against arbitrary encroachments. There was no assignment of land by lot: the term *sortes* simply means shares, and is used of divisions among the Goths themselves.

As estates varied greatly in size, the Visigoths did not live entirely on the dues of their dependants but were concerned directly with agriculture from the beginning—especially the smaller men among them. Everywhere there is individual landed property, freely utilizable and not subject to any claims of the family group (*Sippe*) or the remoter kindred. The way in which the land had been shared up obliged Goth and Roman to live side by side: in some places they made joint use of the undivided woodlands and pastures. Obviously, when the sharing was arranged, the Gothic *hospes* would acquire rights of user over these. If one of the associates (*consortes*) made a forest clearing, the other had to be compensated by the assignment to him of an equivalent area of forest, or if there were no more forest left by a share of the cleared land. This passage in the *Lex Visigotorum* (x, 1. 9) shows that we need not here assume a German *Markgenossenschaft*; the Roman *compascua* of the *agrimensores* is a sufficient explanation. The shares of the Goths varied, as we have said. The king could make grants from his ample royal lands. Since alienations, purchases and exchanges, as well as testamentary dispositions, were allowed, property became mobile and unequal and, even when it had not originally been so, scattered. Further, that old Germanic pledge of immobility, the heir's absolute claim (*Warterecht*), was set aside as early as Euric's reign.

At first the marriage of Goths and Romans was forbidden. But

Leovigild (A.D. 568–86) abolished the prohibition and gave sons and daughters equal rights of inheritance. Racial amalgamation went on apace, especially after Recared I (A.D. 586–601) became a Catholic and declared Catholicism the religion of the state. With the growing power of the Church came a fresh stimulus to the break-up of the old proprietary arrangements, through the steady growth of gifts and bequests to it. And as many Romans lived among the Goths, and some actually —as Salvian of Marseilles testifies for Southern France and Orosius for Spain—went over to the Goths to avoid the tyranny of their Roman lords, there must have been a gradual Roman penetration even into whatever compact Gothic settlements may have originally existed.

The typical Visigothic form of settlement was by no means that detached homestead which according to Meitzen's theory they took over from the Celts. There were certainly village-settlements. According to the *Lex Visigotorum* they must be assumed normal. They are not later creations. Moreover Celtic elements survive in the village names of Auvergne.

North of the Visigoths stretched the kingdom of the Burgundians, who had settled in Savoy at the beginning of the fifth century. Thence they spread southwards in the region of the upper Rhone and Saône toward Lyon and north-eastwards over the Jura. Sometimes they had been called in by the provincials themselves, and as *hospites* were given two-thirds of the corn land; of the homesteads, orchards, woods and pastures a half; of the servile dependants a third. Probably there was plenty of untilled arable and little labour power to work it. But the land was not shared in compact areas, the Burgundian hunters and wanderers preponderating in the hilly forest-clad Jura, for example, the Romans keeping to the fertile plains. It is clear from the *Lex Burgundiorum* that Romans and Burgundians lived side by side in the same place. Here also the detached farmstead was not the rule: the greater part of Burgundy and a part of Franche Comté is a land of villages. The sharing was a sharing of property. Burgundians acquired land, not merely some special kind of usufruct. Private property in meadows and vineyards is there also. Where joint property in arable still exists, according to the *Lex Burgundiorum* the co-proprietors can at any time demand a division. But common waste, especially in the form of woodland, persisted. The *Lex Romana Burgundiorum* contains a provision that woods, alps and pastures shall be common to all, and to each in proportion to his property. We find house communities of *consortes*; but we must not assume that the *consortes* were usually mixed Romans and Burgundians, for the *Lex Burgundiorum* prescribes that the houses of the two races are to be kept apart even in the same settlement. The Burgundians were interested in the exploitation of their own lands, for the *Lex Burgundiorum* lays down that the clearing of the common woods shall not be so conducted as to give unfair advantage to any single co-proprietor.

Burgundian like other kings drew on their abundant royal estates to endow their followers. But every man so endowed might not claim the usual third of the dependants and two-thirds of the corn land in the place where he was settled as a *hospes*, but must be content with less.

The private law of the Burgundians favoured the further sub-division of the land. It was usual for the father to share it with his sons even in his lifetime. He had free disposition of what remained his. The son was in the same position with regard to his share. But this did not apply to a share acquired from the Romans. Already about A.D. 500 there seems to have been plenty of alienation. The king decrees that only those may sell their land who have a share or property somewhere else. If such a Burgundian is obliged to sell, no *extraneus* shall be preferred to the Roman *hospes* as buyer—the 'foreigner' is excluded. Laws were also directed against too numerous gifts and bequests. Those which were not made in writing and witnessed, were to be invalid: five or seven witnesses were required. Further an age, fifteen years, was fixed below which no one might execute a sale or a gift or an emancipation.

Among the Burgundians also property was very unevenly divided. Beside the *optimates*, who are equated with the Roman *nobiles*, appear *mediores* and *inferiores personae*, the former described as *ingenui*. Once there is mention of *majores personae* in opposition to freemen—evidently larger proprietors, but doubtless holders in the village territory. These rules and indications taken together suggest a scattering and mobilization of landed property.

The Franks seem to have proceeded in a totally different fashion from those Germanic tribes so far discussed. In their oldest law, the *Lex Salica*, nothing is heard of the sharing of land with Romans. It used to be believed that, in keeping with the old conceptions of German 'barbarism', the Franks took the land by force and enslaved the Romans, or even extirpated them as Christians. Archaeological finds have given us a new basis from which to judge these things. Holwerda, making use of them, has maintained that the Frankish Empire was not the result of an offensive war. The course of development was linked with that of the later Empire and there is no violent discontinuity. We hear in the earliest centuries of our era of the settlement of Frankish tribes on Roman soil. Apart from the Batavians who with the Frisians had accepted Roman domination and become highly prized auxiliaries, Sigambrians were settled by Titus on the left bank of the Rhine in A.D. 80. There must have been an unusually important settlement of Franks in Gaul towards the end of the third century. In A.D. 286

Maximian made a friendly agreement for Frankish settlement in the lands of the Nervii and Treveri, as well as in Brabant and on the Moselle. Rather later, Frisians, Chamavi and Chattuarii, having broken into Batavian land and been defeated there by Constantius Chlorus, were settled on the Somme and the Oise, and even as far afield as Troyes, Langres, Dijon and Autun. In the fourth century Franks are named among the tribes who were settled in Gaul as military colonists (*laeti*). In Julian's time Salians had crossed the Rhine into Roman Toxandria and had been confirmed in their new possessions by the emperor. Apparently the Chattuarii migrated into the land of the Cugerni on the left bank of the Rhine some time before A.D. 392. As a result of all these movements, Northern Gaul must have been half German before Frankish kingdoms were set up in the fifth century. Already in the fourth Franks had great influence at the Roman court and attained high military and official rank there. Early in the fifth the *Notitia Dignitatum* records Frankish *laeti* in Brittany. Roman generals like Stilicho, Aelius and Egidius both fought with Franks and received them on Roman soil. In A.D. 451 Franks fought on the Roman side against the Huns.

Thus sections of the Franks had long since acquired land in Gaul, settled among the Romans, and come to know their civilization. In the fourth century German colonists (*laeti*) had appropriated land without imperial sanction, and in A.D. 399 Honorius was obliged to take action against this abuse. His ordinance begins with the significant statement that people from various tribes have resorted to Roman territory because of the profit to be got from holding land there as *laeti*. Evidently the blending of Romans and Franks was an old story. The original text of the *Lex Salica* has not been preserved. What we have is a later compilation with alterations and insertions, not earlier than the time when Clovis ruled alone (508–11). It was compiled after the establishment of the unitary Frankish state when, the Alemanni and the Visigoths having been conquered, the old tribal kingdom of the Franks had long since acquired a universal character. If we had a record from the days of the tribal kingdom, like those of the other German stocks, we could ascertain the character of the original settlement from it. When this *Lex Salica* was compiled there was no occasion to tell of the antiquated situation at the time of the first settlements, even had the early sixth-century compiler known about it. Possibly the Franks also had taken shares of Roman lands, for they had given the Romans military service and protection. At all events their settlement had been peaceful. They allowed a great deal of the old order to endure and they left the freemen their property.

Their king took over both the imperial land and the Church land, with all estates that had lost their lord. From these he could make grants to his military servants, the more easily because the Germans had been in the habit of thinking of such grants as temporary—for so long as the service was rendered, or for so long as the king who had made them lived.

Clovis, who had dispossessed the local kings with a high hand, took up a conservative attitude towards the old Roman order. How conservative is best shown by his adoption of Catholicism. That he did not adopt Arianism like so many other German kings was certainly due to the consideration that a great part of the population of his kingdom was Roman and Catholic. The *Lex Salica* tells us plainly that his Roman and Frankish subjects were regarded as equals. Roman landownership was preserved: we have the *Romanus possessor*, the *Romanus tributarius*. There was no oppression, no enslavement. Frankish civilization grew from the soil in conjunction with the late provincial Roman civilization. We must not think of the names ending in -*heim* as those of Frankish 'manors', over against which we can set family-settlements ending in -*ingen*.[1] Nor is the village system specifically German, nor the system of scattered homesteads specifically Celtic. The suffix -*ing* or -*ingen* may imply any kind of connexion, by no means only that of the blood. A place name ending in -*ing* may also indicate a family-settlement or the settlement of a landlord or fighting chieftain with his people. Place-name study shows that the Franks took over at the outset old cultivated ground and settled on Roman and Pre-Roman sites. We have seen that the wealth of the Frankish kings was made up of Roman imperial estates. Nearly all the old Frankish palaces rose on soil which had been occupied in Roman times. The administrative organization of the Franks was directly linked with the Roman organization that preceded it. The district (*Gau*) names show this. They are constantly compounded with the names of the chief places in Roman *pagi*, and names of towns and forts—Köln-gau, Bonn-, Deutz-, Metz-, Worms-, Speyer-, Lobden-, Nidagau and many more.[2]

That so-called 'neighbours' right of inheritance' which has been regarded as an old Frankish agrarian institution and was abolished by an edict of Chilperic (561–84), as well as the village community's right of protest against the settling of strangers among them (*Lex Salica*),[3] can both be traced in the Graeco-Roman law of the ancient world. Simple economic considerations amply explain them—the natural interests of the villagers over against their lord, to whom fixed dues are owed. Also the untilled land which forms part of the 'village' (*terra subseciva* = *Mark*) had to pay its tax: the so-called 'supplement'—ἐπιβολή, Latin *junctio*—persists in the Germanic mark, and finds here its counterpart.

[1] See above, p. 36.
[2] For a different point of view see above, p. 24.
[3] See above, p. 35.

In the oldest Frankish formularies of Angers and Tours (seventh and eighth centuries) it is significant to find still in the enumeration of the appurtenances of an estate the words *junctis et subjunctis*, a clear indication of the great influence of late Roman on early Frankish agrarian institutions.

Private property in arable land must be assumed to have been the rule when Frankish kingdoms were first established. No certain trace of communal agriculture or communal ownership can be found. He who by his own labour cleared the waste and made it cultivable became its owner. There was no communal agriculture carried on by free village communities. Where communal agriculture is found, it is a later manorial creation. The name Frank, which used erroneously to be taken to mean free, cannot be used to uphold the sociological theory that all the tribesmen were free and equal. It comes from *frak* and means audacious, thrusting. Actually there was no equality among the Franks. The nobility had not disappeared in the years of migration and war. It was always being formed anew by warlike prowess. The body of freemen was not economically uniform. Inequality of property is there from the very start. Our sources tell of richer and poorer. The *Hufe* (*mansus*) is not a normal freeman's holding, but a measuring unit for property composed of a house, arable land, and rights in the waste (*Mark*). We meet also the old Roman terms (*sortes, acceptae*) which like *Hufe* (which comes from *haben*) mean simply a unit of property. So we understand why the *Bifangsrecht*, the right to carry out a clearing of the waste, is not uniform for all, but is proportionate to the size of the holding. Now since people of position, clerical and lay, had shares in the village mark, and the king, the greatest of them all, could always and everywhere give even 'foreigners' the privilege of settling in village territory, the villages and their marks soon acquired a very variegated aspect, and so-called 'mixed marks' became the rule.

Circumstances very different from those examined so far were decisive in the growth of the Saxon tribal state. It did not spring up on Roman soil: it had hardly any contact with the Romans. It was founded by conquerors from Holstein who crossed the Elbe, led by a highly privileged class, the *Edelinge*, who took a ruling place in the state—they were the lords; the *Laten*, who included the conquered inhabitants, were settled on their land. Classes among the Saxons were more sharply and deeply divided than among the other tribes, for racial differences came into play. Freemen (*liberi*) formed the second class. The *Frilinge*, small peasants, were the lower class. Some of them were freedmen (*libertini*) and, as 'less free', were regarded as not much better than the *Laten*. These last were really servile, bound to the soil, though they had more rights than the Frankish *Liten*; they bore arms, paid fines for breach of the peace or the law and were present at the assemblies of the people.[1]

The forms of settlement fit these social relationships. For it had become evident that the peasants' homesteads of the eighteenth century were not, as Justus Möser held, survivals of the oldest form of settlement. Nor is Meitzen's view tenable that the scattered Westphalian homesteads are of Celtic origin and that the villages were formed later by their agglomeration. Subsequent research, especially into place names and prehistoric sites, has shown that villages existed in the remotest times. In old Westphalia, village-settlement and homestead-settlement were not in general sharply distinguished: extensive areas show a mingling of the two. And the place names point to a widespread settlement by groups with a lord; for very many ending in -dorf contain a personal name as prefix. Excavation shows that before the Franks came there were not only fortified camps of refuge for the tribes but also halls belonging to the nobility. These became the main centres of resistance against Frankish conquest. Some of the fortified halls of old Saxony were turned by the Franks into 'palaces' after the Carolingian annexation. The finds of Roman coins, some of which go back to the fourth century, reveal the treasuries of Saxon chieftains. And it is significant that these finds have been made in places where chieftains' fortified halls certainly existed, or on old routes that ran by them. No certain proof can be found of settlement by landowning clans or free communities. The patronymic place names ending in -ing are commonest among the names of homesteads.[2]

It has often been thought that a direct survival of old German clan settlement could be recognized in Schleswig-Holstein, especially in Dithmarschen. There the free peasants (*Bonden*) were supposed to have survived from primitive times and maintained their free institutions, with communal control of the mark. According to this theory the oldest settlements were villages of kinsmen, founded by the '*Slachten*' (*Geschlechtern*) and their subdivisions, the so-called '*Kluften*'. But later inquiries have shown that the '*Slachten*' are in part at least artificial creations which included strangers. As Dithmarschen and Holstein were the original home of the Saxons, what we have learnt of Saxon social arrangements imposes the greatest caution. The widespread occurrence of lords and their dependants may well have prevailed in old Saxon times, and the whole tribal structures may have been continuous. The facts about the Frisians merit careful attention. Even in Roman times

---

[1] Against this view (that of Lintzel) doubts have recently been expressed, the federal union of the tribes being emphasized (Brandi) and the theory of a conquest called in question (L. Schmiedl).

[2] This is not true of England. Our -ings, -inghams and -ingtons, if ever they were mere homesteads, very early became villages, as Domesday shows [Ed.].

they held some of the land which they hold today. They have spread from their oldest home by the Zuyderzee right to the Ems. As early as A.D. 12 Drusus brought them under Roman control. In the fourth and fifth centuries they were spreading eastwards and in the middle of the sixth they became dependants of the Franks. Their home was the inaccessible marsh which is cut off by moor and swamp from the high *Geest* (sandy soil) of the interior. Settlement may well have been made from the sea, and then pushed upwards from the marsh to the *Geest*. As far back as we can go we find regular open-field villages in Drenthe and Ostfriesland. The need for dyke-building involves the co-operation of many settlers. The oldest surveys contain place names in *-thorpe* and *-wick*.

Gifts to the Church, with sales and exchanges, early led to dispersion of property. As the grazing land was naturally extensive, gifts are defined as land of so many beasts or oxen. The existence of *Hufen* cannot however be denied. *Sortes* and *mansi* are mentioned in the oldest sources. The words *hove* and *uurde* may have a similar meaning. The layout of the fields in blocks rather than strips may be due to later consolidations. As the soil of the *Geest* varies in quality, scattered strips would be required if equality of holdings were to be established among the settlers. Division of the marshes, used for grazing, would not have been worth while. The need for economic co-operation against a common natural danger explains the form of the settlements, even if we reject the notion that the marshes were settled by free communities. At any rate lordship had great importance in early times. The gifts of lay lords to the Church prove it, and so do the place names, which often contain the genitives of a personal name—Edulfesuurd or Vuilbandasuuic.

Moreover Friesland lacks just those forms of property which have been regarded as indications of settlement by free communities—the marks. Meitzen's contention that common enjoyment or communal control of marks would not fit in with the geographical conditions is invalid. Common land (*mêne, mente*) is found both in the marsh and on the *Geest*. But it is not the common property of free 'markers', but infertile and unprofitable land left undivided for the general use of the inhabitants, in proportion to the size of their holdings. Pasturage there is watched by common herdsmen to prevent individual villagers from getting an unfair share. The term *hamrik* or *hemrik* does not mean a common mark, but merely the whole territory of the village community.

The union of several family groups to make up a village community can be illustrated only from very late sources—so late as the seventeenth century. We now know that the general freedom of the Frisian peasantry was also a late product, and that in older Friesland there was a

very considerable number of unfree peasant families. Various considerations unite to make probable the assumption that the formation of
common property came late. Nor is it true that the Frisians in early
times did not practise agriculture, but were primitively pastoral. Tacitus
tells of those Frisians who had pushed down to the lower Rhine in
Nero's time, that they promptly settled in permanent homes and tilled
the ground (*Annals* XIII, 54). What he adds—*utque patrium solum exerce-
bant*—shows clearly that this had been their regular practice in their
original home.

Property was very unequally divided. The *Lex Frisiorum* shows
nobles on one side of the free men, half-free *Liten* and serfs on the other.
The specialized horse breeding which extensive pasturage facilitated is
still found in Carolingian sources, where we meet with *caballarii*.

The records of the founding of the Anglo-Saxon kingdoms tell us but
little. As a result it has been possible to hold diametrically opposite
views about it. Seebohm's school postulated the persistence of Roman
institutions and treated the manor as an offspring of the Roman villa.
Other scholars have assumed that the old Roman and Celtic settlements
were destroyed and the surviving population enslaved by the conquerors. Something can certainly be said for either view. Probably
conditions varied. I am inclined to maintain that in England also there
was not a conquest and re-founding of economic life completed once
for all. The Angle and Saxon seafarers had trade relations with Britain
before the final conquest and had made settlements there. Before the
conquest also they had established themselves on the lower Rhine and
there come into direct contact with Roman civilization. They had been
strongly influenced by it, as the Anglo-Saxon words borrowed from the
Latin show. It was there in Northern Gaul that they became acquainted
with Christianity and learnt something of house- and road-building, of
fruit-growing and agriculture. No doubt there was in England as elsewhere much plundering and destruction in the wars which followed the
fall of the Roman Empire in the fifth and sixth centuries. The firing of
Roman towns and villas which the spade reveals is sufficient proof of
that. But it is doubtful whether, on this account, we are warranted in
assuming the complete destruction of all Roman settlements.

Anglo-Saxon settlement did not take place according to a uniform
pattern—whole districts being assigned by lot to family or kindred
groups. Later terms like *folcland* and *terra unius familiae* certainly do not
prove that sort of settlement; the less so as in the interval great changes
had come about, especially through the development of royal supremacy. As long ago as 1848 Kemble himself explained that place names
in -*ing*, even when patronymics, may describe the followers of a chieftain, or the dependants of a lord. So they may well apply to settlements

of 'manorial' type. All that we know of the conquest, and especially of the origin of Angles and Saxons in Schleswig-Holstein, points to a military organization. The tie of military loyalty and service must no doubt already have prevailed over the older ties of blood.

The English open-field system is not a sure sign of an agriculture once really communal. The scattered strips and their persistence through centuries are no proof of the absence of private property, or of communal principles directed towards the maintenance of equality. In fact the way of dividing the fields tells in favour of the view that, just as on the continent, these fields were the private property of the villagers; or that in villages of dependent cultivators, which assuredly existed beside the freer villages, the dependants enjoyed fixed tenurial rights which could not be arbitrarily changed.

In the oldest Wessex laws, those of Ine (drawn up in the last years of the seventh century), we can recognize private property in land. The fact that the term *gyrde landes* occurs (§ 67), applied to the holding of an individual, implies its separation from the property of the community, just as the grant of *bocland* by royal charter implied private property. The same law of Ine contains also evidence against the existence of communal agriculture; for the case is anticipated of a peasant holding land from another for a term of years and paying rent. There is no sort of proof of the supposition that the various tilled 'lands' reverted after the harvest into a really common open field. Assignment by lot occurred only on ground controlled by a lord, not on that of free peasants; and even so it applied only to meadow and waste, not to the arable. And where it occurred, rational considerations account for it.

Both in the oldest charters and in Ine's and Alfred's laws we meet with a division and intermixture of the property of various owners inside the same area of settlement. And these scattered holdings are not found only in compact 'manorial' villages; we find them also in the villages of small free peasants. Ine's laws show that such people had rented land from the lords for their own use. And then we find Celto-Romans too among the free proprietors. The terms *tributarius*, *manens* and *casatus* do not always mean unfree dependants: already in this early age they may describe free settlers. Welshmen were granted free land by the king, for which they paid him rent. The open-field system cannot have been a rigid compulsory organization imposed by the lords of -*tons* and -*hams*.

Eastward and southward of the continental Saxons the Thuringians had settled. Among them it was once generally supposed that those primitive German conditions which Tacitus sketched had survived untouched. For the Romans never got there: marsh and forest covered the land. Now modern prehistoric research has shown that Thuringia was well occupied in prehistoric times. At the beginning of our era the

Hermunduri were settled in the country south of the Harz and Finne and east of the Werra as far as the Erzgebirge. Pushing south, they came into active commercial contact with the Romans. After them other German stocks, in particular Angles and Varini, as is reflected in the title of their common law, *Lex Angliorum et Werinorum*, wandered in from the north. Angles settled along the Unstrut where a district (Engilin) was named after them. The Varini settled down between the Saale and the Mulde (Werensfeld near Bernburg)—just when is not certain. Some would date their immigration in the third and fourth centuries. In any case, in the fifth there was an independent Thuringian kingdom, which presumably resulted from an amalgamation of these tribes.

The dominant form of settlement was the nucleated village (*Haufendorf*), whose very character and field-system presuppose long settled conditions. The *Waldhufen* or 'row' villages of the Thüringerwald are probably later creations that were not established by the Saxons who came in from the north. After the first settlements were made the land, still densely wooded, was cleared in a great colonizing movement into which men of other stocks were drawn—North Swabians, Frisians, Hessians (Schwabengau; Friesenfeld; Hassegau). When Sigebert the Merovingian was beaten by the Avars on the Elbe in A.D. 562, Avars and Slavs pressed into the land between the Elbe and the Saale. In the seventh century there was great fighting with the Slavs: Dagobert in A.D. 632 had to make a campaign from Mainz into Thuringia. He had Saxon support. So about A.D. 700 the Thuringian territory of the North Swabians, Frisians and Hessians came under Saxon control. It was not reconquered by the Franks till Pippin's day (A.D. 748).

According to the *Lex Angliorum et Werinorum*—which however only exists in a Carolingian copy of about 802–3—there were considerable class distinctions. A noble's *wergild* was three times that of an ordinary freeman, and six times that of the half-free. Since a freeman could transfer his inherited possessions to whomsoever he would, a subdivision of landed property was inevitable. It appears in the field divisions of the typical German open-field village—with its 'furlongs' (*Gewanne*) and scattered strips. That 'lordship' was widespread, the class distinctions and the existence of freedmen plainly show. The oldest endowment charters and surveys of the richly endowed monasteries of Fulda, Lorsch and Hersfeld reveal property scattered over a wide area.

The Alemanni, like the Franks, had entered into relations with the Romans as early as the beginning of the third century. In the fourth century at latest they had attained permanent settlements on Roman soil. From the Main, they spread south over the *limes* to the Lake of Constance, eastwards to the Lech, westwards to the Rhine, which they had crossed by the middle of the fifth century: they occupied a great part of the Palatinate, Alsace and Switzerland. With their conquest by the Franks (496) they began to be driven out of their northerly territory. But Frankish influence in these pre-Carolingian times must not be exaggerated, for the old separate and distinct tribal life stands out markedly.

The Alemanni were an especially warlike race and undoubtedly did much damage when they broke across the *limes*. Yet on many Roman sites old Alemannic settlements have been traced. Names ending in -*weiler* cannot, it is true, any longer be conceived of as indications of a direct transfer of Roman civilization. Their founders were Germans. The foundation was carried on from the seventh to the tenth century. It began in the west and ended in the east of the South-West German 'weiler area'. It is to be noted nevertheless that names ending in -*villare*, with a German personal name and a linking vowel, in Württemberg, Baden, Switzerland and Alsace-Lorraine, are found everywhere in the narrow compass of the area which has yielded Roman finds.

We have been taught by the spade that the oldest settlements were not clan ones, as places with names ending in -*ingen* were once supposed to be. The clan did not settle in a compact body, but by families spread in separate groups of homesteads or hamlets (*weiler*), each of which had its own burial ground. There can be no question whatever of communal agriculture by the clan when the land was first occupied. Nor can such settlements have included important groups of non-Germans. What had been Roman state property passed into German hands.

Graves and their contents give proof of social differentiation.[1] A few graves are distinguished by their wealth of funeral gifts: we assume specially rich and socially prominent personages. There must have been some servile folk. Indeed there may well have been a high proportion of the 'less free' in those hamlets. No doubt there were already lords and dependants. The termination -*ing*, -*ingen* indicates not merely attachment by blood (the *Sippe*) but any kind of attachment: attachment to one's lord, or to one's war chieftain.

Like the other laws, those of the Alemanni (from early in the eighth century) reveal no certain evidence of joint ownership of the mark by the Hundred or the Community. On the contrary, a fully developed 'manorialism' appears and a pronounced social stratification, with *meliores* and *minofledi*.

It was long held that the Bavarians settled originally in groups of blood relations, because so many place names in -*ing* and -*ingen* occur in the older records. This theory can now be counted obsolete. Assuredly

---

[1] See above, p. 36.

the Bavarians did not enslave and deprive of their land all the inhabitants of the conquered territory any more than the Alemanni did. The -*ingen* place names are often found along the old Roman roads, and it has been pointed out that the former Roman forts and more important Roman sites appear as royal property of the Agilolfing dukes in early Bavarian times. The romance place names of the Salzburg country and the Inn valley also point to this transfer from Roman to Bavarian governmental hands. There were -*ingen* places where the duke had overlordship from the time of the immigration, or where he himself was the lord. The oldest sources show no difference in the economic organization of -*ing* places and other places.

The widespread supposition that the Bavarians at their first settlement preferred to occupy scattered homesteads is certainly not accurate as a generalization. The lie of the land no doubt had its influence. In the mountains it might encourage this type of settlement; though very many of the scattered homesteads of today are the result of colonization from the tenth to the twelfth centuries. As its technical terms show, the economy of the alps was already developed in Roman times. The scattered homesteads in the area of Bavarian settlement are no more a racial peculiarity than they are Celtic in their origin. Most certainly lordship existed when Bavaria was occupied. The Bavarians were an amalgam of Germanic tribes known to the Romans as particularly warlike—Marcomanni, Quadi, Naristi, Suevi from the Danube. Their military organization showed itself in the way the conquered land was occupied. The war-leaders and local chieftains won plenty of land for themselves and shared some of it out among their fighting men and their civil subordinates ennobled by office. In the Bavarian Law of the eighth century lordship appears as an institution of old standing—we have the lord's hall (*casa dominica*) and the services of the *coloni*. The great noble families, which are mentioned in it, had certainly extensive landed property, as had the Church; for the Bavarians were early converted. The hypothesis that, at the time of the Law, the freemen also were lords, in the sense that they did not till their own land but had it tilled for them by half-free and servile dependants, cannot be accepted in that form. Probably a fair number of them were lord and peasant in one, working part of their land themselves and letting off the rest.

The Franks soon took the first place among the German tribal kingdoms. The rest were steadily brought under their rule—the Alemanni in 496; the Thuringians in 531; Bavaria soon after under Theudebert (534–48) and the Frisians by the middle of the sixth century. Only the Saxons were able to maintain their political independence until the day of Charles the Great. But this Merovingian Empire was moving to its fall, as could be seen already by the end of the seventh century. Pirenne has argued that in the economic sphere itself there is a deep cleavage between the Merovingian and the Carolingian Empires. Whereas under the first, the old Mediterranean-based economic map still survived, this was ripped up by the irruption of the Arabs. In Carolingian times the economic centre of gravity was shifted to the North. The old classical course of trade, which had kept the Merovingian Empire a Mediterranean state, came to an end. The land of the Franks, cut off from the sea, became an inland state dominated by agriculture, a peasant state with no distant views. Things were made for use, not for exchange, and the ninth century became the golden age of the self-sufficing household (*geschlossene Hauswirtschaft*). For, Pirenne argues, trade and commerce in Carolingian times had only local importance, playing a subordinate part in the whole economy of the Empire. According to this theory, the German conquest of Gaul brought no revival of the decadent ancient world but merely accentuated its decadence. The Merovingian age was a time not of lusty youth but of degeneration. What the German barbarian invaders had not achieved, that the rise of Islam secured—a complete change in the face of the world, above all in its economic features. So the argument runs.

But modern research, paying special attention to the results of the study of German antiquities, has shown that the closed economy of the Mediterranean basin had been loosened and broken through long before, even before the Merovingians. Moreover the North did not first acquire economic importance through the roping off of the Mediterranean. Its importance was no new thing; for the Baltic landbridge carried a considerable traffic from the Black Sea and the South-East to the North, and the long distance oriental trade from Asia and Egypt had its most important emporium in Greece.

The Frankish Empire had very successfully welded together German and Roman civilization on the old Gallic soil, and to do it had won the help of the Catholic Church, whilst other German tribal states, remaining Arian, remained also markedly backward as a result of the religious differences. The Carolingian Empire built on Merovingian foundations; but its northward extension—the final absorption of the Saxons—was no more decisive than that alliance with Italy and the Papacy which at the close of the Merovingian era had been utterly lost.

The initiative came from the pope. Already under Charles Martel he turned to the Frankish mayor of the palace for help against his Lombard oppressors. It was refused. But Charles' son and successor Pippin, when he dethroned the Merovingian king, made an alliance with the pope to secure sanction for his *coup d'état*. So in the new great Frankish Empire the two strong youthful powers, Roman Papacy and Frankish Kingship, stood side by side. The Frankish king was the protector (*patricius*) of the Church and, after the fall of the Lombard power (A.D. 774), with its help he rebuilt the Roman Empire of the West (A.D. 800). Southern Gaul was made safe against the Arabs and the Spanish Mark was established as a glacis beyond the rampart of the Pyrenees. The overthrow of the Saxons, brutally as it was carried out, had yet materially strengthened the German element in the new empire. The safeguarding of the East, and the putting into order of the hitherto more or less independent duchy of Bavaria, had given the Empire—with its equally German Ostmark—a new eastward orientation. This was no inland state. North and South it touched the sea, and the great trade routes of the world ran together in its spacious territory. Charles the Great's plan to join the Rhine to the Danube by a canal was in some sort the natural consequence of the ripe growth of his dominions. With new seafaring provinces on its northern and southern frontiers—Frisia and Saxony; Spain and Italy—the mighty area between acquired new outlets. Moreover a great internal colonizing movement now again began, followed by the eastward spread of Christianity, with new bishoprics—Würzburg, Salzburg—as its centres.

At one time scholarship was unduly obsessed by the *Capitulare de Villis*, which was regarded as an ambitious economic programme of the new emperor. Model economic institutions, it was supposed, were to be set up on the royal domains, which were to be imitated uniformly on the other great estates, ecclesiastical and lay. Charles placed the centre of gravity of the whole economy on the domains, and created an economic autarky, finding sustenance for himself and his court by residence first at one then at another of his palaces. Today our gaze is no longer concentrated on the *Capitulare de Villis*. More intensive study of other sources, of charters and surveys as well as of many other capitularies, enables us to draw a more complete and more lifelike picture of Carolingian economy. The *Capitulare de Villis* has lost its critical importance, because we know that it was aimed not so much at a planned economy as against abuses which had broken out in the south of the Empire especially, while Charles' son Louis was in charge there (A.D. 794). It applies only to those royal estates which supplied the king and his court, not to all his lands. Only a part of these were cultivated direct. Probably the greater part was let out for rent and services on various tenures, among which we can already recognize 'hereditary rent' (*Erbzins*) and metayage. Further, there was yet a third group of estates, those which the king had granted as fiefs in return for military or administrative services. A separate record of these was kept, because of the specially great danger that they might be lost to the crown.

The administration of the royal domains was apparently by no means a model when the *Capitulare de Villis* was issued. The regulation that there should be adequate accounts and entering up of the various receipts had in fact not been observed by the officials, and had to be insisted on anew. Far more model conditions were to be found on Church estates. Gregory I (A.D. 590–604) had long since created a well-planned administration for the *Patrimonium Petri*. The development of the different forms of land tenure may probably be traced to the Church, which at an early date both disposed of a great deal of land and had developed the method of the *precaria*, to bind up its economic interests ingeniously with those of donors. Metayage is found already in the seventh-century formularies of Angers, and probably goes back to Roman times.

Direct cultivation for the king was practised where his estates lay thickest. It is found especially on the patrimonial lands of the Carolingians which lay between Rhine, Meuse and Moselle, and in the Ardennes. Here the Frankish kings very often dwelt before Charles fixed his residence permanently in Aachen. But generally speaking royal property was widely scattered; for even the first Carolingians by their rich endowment of the Church and of their vassals broke up their compact estates. We discern not strict centralization but a far-reaching independence of the various domains (*fisci*), an independence which distance and the lack of appropriate means of transport made inevitable. Royal property and Church property lay often side by side and mixed up in the same village, together with that of great lay lords and of small free cultivators. The royal palaces themselves had no central importance in the economy of the land. They were not the points at which markets or towns developed later. Even the better known palaces never became towns. Not Ingelheim but Mainz, not Aachen but Cologne, showed a town economy at that time. Nor did Tribur or Bodman on the lake near Constance. So too in Bavaria the palaces of Osterhofen, Oetting, Ranshofen, Mattighofen, remained unimportant places; just as in the North-West did Attigny, Kiersy, Thionville, Gondreville, Verberie, Samoussy, Ver and Herstal.

The sizes of the individual *fisci* varied greatly. There were extensive compact domains covering several square miles, and smaller ones which covered much less. Estimates have been put forward varying from 1000 acres with 3000 acres of forest (Baist) to 13,750–27,500 acres (Lamprecht). However they are quite uncertain! It is not easy to ascertain whether or not there was strict subordination of the administration of the domains to the central administration of the court. A royal *provisor villarum* is once mentioned, but it is doubtful whether this was a distinct and permanent office. The man referred to was also a *missus regius*. And the *missi dominici* were in general under the control of the government. In any case the superintendents of the individual royal domains (*judices*)

had a very free hand in their administration. Their subordinates
(*juniores*) were *villici* or *Meier* (*maiores*). The *Capitulare de Villis* decreed
that the *maiores* should not be chosen from among the more important
folk (*de potentioribus*). Some of these *Meier* were themselves directors
of a domainal administration, perhaps in places where the domain was
of no great size. The economic organization was many-sided and
various. There was no general uniform rigid scheme. Crown land did
not fall altogether outside the bounds of a count's authority. He had
jurisdiction in cases affecting the *fisci* as well as over complaints of
outsiders against those who dwelt in a *fiscus*.

The estates which were intended to supply the court, the so-called
Tafelgüter, had to make provision (*servitium*) for fixed periods in turn.
When they were free from this obligation their produce could be sold
locally. The economy of the royal domains was by no means that of a
self-sufficing household, in which all the produce raised is consumed;
it was an economy that marketed goods in hope of gain. The royal
capitularies instructed the *villicus* to strive to improve the income. In
the *capitulare* of Aachen (801–13) Charles the Great gave general
instructions to the *villici* to arrange fellings of timber so as to improve
the *servitium*. In the *Capitulare de Villis* too, various passages reflect the
desire for increased yields and fresh sources of income whenever possible. The king wished to get a conspectus of the content and size of the
yields of his domains by ordering adequate accounting for the individual
items. There is a streak of rationalization in all this, which appears also in
the reports of the reform of the *Tafelgüter* in Aquitaine by Louis the Pious.

The Church also carried out a deliberate economic policy, as its
regulations for the *precaria* show. Numerous donations of real property
were made to the Church by private individuals for the good of their
souls. The donors frequently received the land back to enjoy its use
during their life time. The pious desire to make such gifts to the Church
was further stimulated by returning to the donor, by means of the so-
called *precaria remuneratoria*, more usufruct than he had actually given.
The state found itself obliged to interfere. The *precaria* it must be
allowed had great social importance: they secured provision for the
donors in case of sickness, old age or invalidity. Again, in cases of
military service and journeys to Rome or on pilgrimage, provision was
made by means of *precaria* contracts for the wives and children of the
absentees or of those who fell in battle. Ecclesiastical estates under a
natural economy thus fulfilled in various directions those economic
functions which today, in a time of fully developed money economy,
are performed by the great insurance and banking companies. Small
landless freemen also had opened to them the possibility of winning a
livelihood, with some prospects of profit, by means of the grant of land

in return for a rent (*precaria data*). But there can be no doubt that such contracts occasionally brought with them injury to the ecclesiastical landlords, the *precaria* involving the alienation of a part of their property. For this reason the king repeatedly ordained that these leasing contracts should be recorded by charter, and that the charters should be periodically renewed.

There were constant exchanges of land between ecclesiastical lords. Very often the object was merely the rounding off of their estates. (In many chapters, as for instance at Freising, these charters of exchange were entered in a special book, the *Codex commutationum*.) Not infrequently however the method of exchange may have been adopted in order to acquire in kind what could not have been otherwise acquired because of the canonical prohibition of the sale or alienation of ecclesiastical property. There is an uncommon multiplication of these exchange operations from the middle of the ninth century. To a great extent they served the same ends as the *precaria*.

The ownership of whole villages by ecclesiastical lords was by no means a general thing. Their property was scattered—as is to be expected from the way in which it was acquired—by a great number of gifts of single *Hufen* or fragments of property often lying in different places. The extension of the demesne which they cultivated themselves, like the carrying out of clearing in the woods, was not to any great extent the result of well thought out planning: it came about by donation and exchange of clearings (*Bifängen*; *comprehensiones*); and colonization was encouraged by the *precaria* system. By the extensive use of these leases of land, the ecclesiastical lords attracted plenty of free labour: the land was let with the obligation to improve it (*amelioratio*). So at the same time landed property was increased and progress in the utilization of the land secured. This acquisition of property by labour (*conlaboratus*, *adquisitio*) was expressly emphasized in connexion with the *precaria*. Clearly the striving after gain, the chance of increasing the amount of productive land, lay behind it all. Sometimes the *accolae* or 'landsettlers', who carried out clearings and so completed an acquisition from the waste, appear as dependants of the manor. They formed as it were the outer circle of the manorial landholders, and their tenure was in some cases by limited revocable lease only. Share-tendency, especially that of metayers (*medietarii*), was already widespread; and free cultivators here and there had land assigned to them which had been kept hitherto in the lord's hands, on condition that they handed over half the produce. In Carolingian times even, we can descry the *Meiergut*: certain manors are assigned, that is leased, to their *Meier*, their *villici*, in return for fixed rents. Clerks were forbidden to show avarice by becoming *villici* or farmers of land.

Lay lordship often grew at the expense of royal or ecclesiastical lordship; through gifts of land to the king's followers and assignments of it as fiefs to his officials; or through fiefs which officials acquired from the Church in their capacity as *Vögte (advocati)*[1] or otherwise. Though much was really 'loan land', the royal capitularies show clearly that it was often claimed as the property of the holder. The service of the king now played a much more important part than in the earlier period. More and more counts and other royal officers acquired extensive landed property; and although it was only 'loan land', in fact it was frequently bequeathed.

Lay lordship was graded. Taxation to meet famines was assessed on *comites fortiores* and *comites mediores*; and with these latter were grouped for this purpose those *vassi dominici* who possessed 200 homesteads. Those who had less than 30 however were not obliged to pay the tax. Every vassal who had twelve *Hufen* must have a coat of mail. Normally, four *Hufen* was the minimum holding for the full freeman; one of two or three *Hufen* was reckoned to be small.

The *Hufe*:[2] very different meanings have been assigned to it—the normal holding of a freeman at the original settlement; the holding of a servile dependant which was capable of maintaining a family. Either meaning agrees better with a particular economico-political theory than with what is found in the sources. We have just seen that for a free man a holding of four *Hufen* was not large; on the other hand several unfree men might occupy a single *Hufe*. *Hufe* is generally a neutral term like the German words *Hof* or *Gut* or *Landlos*. It was a unit of account which actually had no single meaning. In different districts it represented varying numbers of 'acres' or 'yokes'; often 30 of these went to the *Hufe*. The lord's *Hufen* too (*mansi dominicales*) were not always compact properties or well-defined manorial homesteads; their parts might lie in different places. The *Königshufen* are the result of clearings made on royal property, and because of the less entensive cultivation of such newly cleared land they are big—60 yoke and more.[3] Besides the *Königshufen* there were private *Hufen* of this sort, of from 60 to 120. The land that made up a *Hufe* was spread over the various furlongs (*Gewanne*) of the village fields. Sometimes a half *Hufe* is simply called a *Hufe*. But we cannot always, when parts of *Hufen* are mentioned, conclude that whole *Hufen* had been broken up. Just because the *Hufe* was a general term, parts of *Hufen* may be primitive; they may for example have arisen from clearings. The *Hufen* of free proprietors were

---

[1] The *Vogt, avoué, advocatus*, was the lay representative and agent of an ecclesiastical lord. As such he was entitled to certain land and other rights which he was always tempted to stretch and if possible make hereditary.

[2] See above, p. 41 and below, p. 227.

[3] See above, p. 48.

divisible; those under manorial control were not. The lords' economic interest in the stability of their rents made them hostile to division. To each *Hufe* belonged, beside the homestead (*area*) and the arable, a share in the common mark. This was made up of the uncultivated land— wood, pasture, waters and alps—which was left undivided for the use of all. Access to the mark was a very important economic asset for the villager; it gave him building wood and firewood, pasture for his cattle and horses, and pannage for his pigs in the oak woods.

There were various types of mark—lords' marks, mixed marks, and marks of free tribesmen. By Carolingian times the last must have been already very rare; for as a result of the many royal land grants and the donations of private people, both ecclesiastical and civil lordship had spread widely and had got a firm footing in the villages side by side with free tenure. There were constant conflicts between lords and villagers about the use of the mark. So we find formal sharings (*divisiones*) by which one part was reserved for the lord, made part of the demesne, the other left for the use of the villagers. Naturally, there were also quarrels among lords, for lay magnates—counts for example—often infringed ecclesiastical rights of user. Boundary settlements were arrived at by a decision of the neighbours (*vicini*), who declared on oath what they knew of the development of relevant customary rights. The Council of Ver (A.D. 844) felt bound to make a stand against the encroachments of the laity on the lands of the Church, and paid special attention to harmful *divisiones* which often amounted to secularizations of ecclesiastical property.

In coming to an opinion about agriculture and social conditions on the land it is important to bear in mind that even in these early centuries —from the fifth to the ninth—the various German tribes were already familar with towns and markets, in which industry and trade developed.[1] The produce of rural districts was not all consumed on the spot in self-sufficing households. In part at least it was brought to market and carried into the towns, to be sold there. This meant new possibilities of agrarian development. Agricultural produce could be more advantageously disposed of, to meet consumers' needs and the shifting of demand; for a price system was already established.

Further, the way was opened for social change as peasants' younger sons found fresh chances of work in the towns. They could serve as hired labourers (*mercenarii*). The great attraction of the cities and market towns even for the dependent tenants on great estates is distinctly attested in the *Capitulare de Villis*. The numerous manumissions of servile folk, to which the great number of still surviving manumission formularies testifies, must certainly in part have been

[1] See Vol. II.

a consequence of their migration to the towns: and we know from the legal cases about freedom that such people also deserted their lords irregularly, and sometimes were received by the townsmen. According to some of the tribal laws (the Burgundian for instance) freedom could be bought. That would open possibilities of social and economic betterment to wide circles of the rural population. Then again, the peasantry did not only pay their debts in kind; they were very familiar with the use of money. And this greatly eased and encouraged the economic intercourse between country and town.

The price edicts for agricultural produce (grain, wine, cattle) which Charles the Great was impelled to issue (in the years 794 and 806) show that there was 'profiteering' in such things, and that the great lords themselves took part in it to the hurt of their peasant tenants. The edict on just weights and measures and the laws against false and light monies were also meant to help the peasant. So too the legal rules against the selling by night of animals and all articles liable to have secret defects. The care for their people which the Germanic kings, from Theodoric and Totila onwards, manifested again and again in the attitude that they took up towards inordinate profit and the injury of the humbler country-folk was a strong barrier against those social and economic dangers which everywhere and uniformly accompanied the growing economic ascendancy of the great landlords. The lawgiving of the Germanic kings enables us to understand why peasants should transfer themselves from Roman to German lords—there were better conditions, both economic and social, in the Germanic kingdoms. The very aim of the governmental control through *missi dominici* was to seek out the grievances of the oppressed and redress them.

CHAPTER V

Agrarian conditions in the Byzantine Empire in the Middle Ages

I. *East and West in the Roman Empire*

THE eastern half of the Roman Empire was economically stronger and more thickly populated than the western half, and it survived the crisis in which the latter perished, though only after the most exhausting and difficult external and internal struggles. For even the sounder eastern half of the Roman polity had the same troubles as the western half, and in spite of all their differences the political, as well as the economic, and particularly the agrarian, conditions were in many ways similar. The decline in the population did not make itself felt so severely in the East as in the West, while in the former with its overabundance of cities the growth of *latifundia* was accomplished more slowly. But here, too, for centuries development was affected by the marked shortage of labour and by the increase in private estates. And here, also, there were the same results—the widespread absorption of the state lands and of the small landowner, and the binding of the peasant to the soil. This process was vigorously opposed by the more highly centralized government of the East, but such opposition was limited by the financial needs of the state; and to the very end it remained unsuccessful.

These financial needs of the state were at all times responsible for the moulding of agrarian conditions in Byzantium. The taxation of Diocletian had imposed the hereditary ground tax on the peasant, and the so-called *capitatio-iugatio* which he created continued throughout the early Byzantine period, linking together the head and ground taxes. Regarded from different points of view *caput* and *iugum* denote the same taxable value: the *iugum* is the piece of land that can feed a *caput*, and the *caput* stands for the human labour expended on a *iugum*. And so the *capitatio*, just like the *iugatio*, is related to the actual soil, and a *caput* cannot represent either townsfolk or the landless. In the same way, a *iugum*, in order to be taxable, must have its corresponding *caput*. The efforts of the government were therefore of necessity directed towards keeping a balance between *iuga* and *capita*, by finding a *caput* for every available *iugum*. Owing to the scarcity of labour this was no light task, and it was for this reason that the exchequer made every effort to bind the *caput* when it was found to the corresponding *iugum.* And so ever-increasing masses of the rural population were tied to the soil. This is a particular instance of the widespread compulsory fastening of the population to their occupation which scarcity of labour forced the later Roman Empire to pursue systematically. During the course of the fourth century the fettering of the *coloni*, even in the eyes of the law, appeared throughout the Empire; for financial considerations compelled the government increasingly to deprive the *coloni* everywhere of their freedom of movement.

Above all, the overburdening of the rural population with taxes hastened the *patrocinium* movement. In order to mitigate the pressing demands of the state the small landholder put himself under the protection (*patrocinium*) of a powerful lord, and in return placed himself and his land at the service of his patron. The Roman and Byzantine emperors vigorously opposed this development and fought it for many centuries, often with very severe measures. Yet it was the government itself, driven by financial and military needs, which had handed over the peasants to the landowners. To ensure the tax returns, it had entrusted the collection of taxes from the *coloni* to the landowners, and for the army's sake had made them responsible for recruiting the *coloni*. The dependence of the *coloni* was the inevitable result of the landowners' responsibility for their tax returns and their military service. The *coloni*, legally free, lost their freedom of movement and became the serfs of the large landowners (*glebae adscriptitii*, ἐναπόγραφοι).

Even in Egypt, relatively the most densely populated part of the Empire, both small freehold peasant property and the once enormous crown and state domains were systematically absorbed by large private landowners. The land of the imperial domain could not find the necessary labour, and the crown resorted more and more to compulsory leasing of its deserted estates. In Egypt the system of the so-called ἐπιβολή (*adiectio sterilium*) had been established from the earliest times. Under it the inferior state land was assigned compulsorily to private landowners (*proximi possessores*) to work, and they were forced to undertake the responsibility for the return of the tax levied upon the property allotted to them. From the close of the third century this system was employed throughout the Empire, and it was soon used, not only for state land, but also for deserted and dilapidated estates of private owners who were unable to answer for their taxes. But such a method could only succeed if those to whom the land was allotted had the necessary economic resources, and so this system, too, ended by contributing towards the increase of large estates. All along the line it was the large landowner who won, and who not only economically checkmated the crown but gradually monopolized important functions of the state.

The struggle against large landed property which the central authority had prosecuted with great vigour, even in Justinian's time, was unable to bring about any fundamental change in conditions. The predominating feature of rural economy in the early Byzantine period was the great private estate. Great landowners and their dependent *coloni* were the typical figures of the age.

II. *The free peasant village in the middle Byzantine period*

From the seventh century onwards the Empire entered upon a completely new phase of development. Economic and social, as well as political and cultural, conditions showed an entirely different aspect. The period of the later Roman Empire comes to a close, and the history of the medieval Byzantine Empire begins. The Byzantine polity which had survived the collapse of Justinian's work of restoration and the invasions, first of the Persians and then of the Arabs, underwent an internal regeneration. Byzantium had suffered greatly in territory; for Roman Mesopotamia, Syria, Palestine, and the granary of Egypt, were lost to the Arabs. But the very limitations imposed by the new frontiers gave the Byzantine Empire greater stability and internal unity; it had new and much firmer foundations on which to build. The system of government and the administrative divisions of the provinces, the financial arrangements and the organization of the army—all this was new. Socially the character of the Empire changed, and henceforth its economy stood upon a new basis.

It was the great Emperor Heraclius (610–41) who breathed fresh life into the ageing Roman Empire and restored it by his decisive reforms. His institution of themes not only created a new system of administration and a new military organization, but it turned the course of Byzantine agrarian development into fresh channels. Just as the binding of the peasant to the soil in the earlier period was due primarily to financial and military needs, so in the middle Byzantine period was his freedom of movement markedly encouraged by the new organization of the army and the alterations in the system of taxation. Heraclius's institution of themes introduced a strong military element into the imperial administration. The Empire was divided into large military districts—the themes—and each was placed under a governor (*strategus*) who controlled both the military and the civil government of his province. But most important of all were the military settlements within the newly created themes; the so-called 'military estates' (στρατιωτικὰ κτήματα) came into existence and were granted out in return for military service. While the army of the early Byzantine period was largely composed of troops of foreign, and mostly Teutonic, origin, Byzantium now gradually recruited its soldiers from within the Empire. A peasant militia drew from its own soil both the means of livelihood and the resources for waging war.

This creation of military estates shows that it was in Asia Minor, then the backbone of the Empire, that enough unoccupied land was to be found. This is not surprising after the devastating invasions of the Persians and Arabs, which must have swept away so many large land-owners. Heraclius's successors continued his work, and in order to colonize the military holdings in Asia Minor they brought into the Empire many elements of foreign, and especially Slavonic, origin. For several centuries to come this institution of military estates by Heraclius and his successors was the very foundation of Byzantine military power. It was a system that afforded great relief to the budget and solved the terrible problem that had arisen after the great barbarian migrations, when the Empire found that the sources from which its army had formerly been recruited were no longer available. It had the further advantage of establishing an important body of free peasants in the Byzantine provinces; for, while the eldest son of a soldier (*stratiotes*) succeeded to his father's duty of military service, the rest of his offspring swelled the free peasant forces which could be occupied in the clearing of untilled ground. Thus a free peasantry developed side by side with the soldiers settled on the land, and, as the latter were the mainstay of the military, so the former, in their capacity of taxpayers, were the backbone of the economic and financial power of the Byzantine Empire. There was neither economic nor social difference between the tax-paying free peasants and the soldier peasants owing military service, who had moreover to pay certain taxes. Economically the military holdings were exactly like the peasant holdings, and socially the soldiers and the free peasants belonged to one and the same class. They were frequently placed in the same administrative and fiscal grouping and were treated by the imperial legislation as a single category.

Although Byzantium certainly had uncultivated land in the Middle Ages, it did not then suffer from so serious a scarcity of labour as it had in the earlier period. This indeed is largely due to the extent to which foreign elements had settled within the Empire and given it new vigour. It was moreover this fact which made possible a fundamental alteration in the system of taxation. In the place of the interdependence of the *capitatio* and the *iugatio* there was a separate levy of head and ground taxes, from the seventh century onwards. The head tax, which appeared in the form of a personal tax levied on the family (really a hearth tax: καπνικόν), fell on all taxpayers without exception. It was no longer levied on the assumption that it was related to the occupation of a definite unit of land, and the exchequer was therefore no longer concerned to the same extent as formerly with the binding of the taxpayer to the soil. And so from this time onwards there is an abatement in the restrictions placed upon the rural population.

The appearance of a solid stratum of free and free-moving peasants is most clearly revealed in the famous Byzantine Peasants' Law (νόμος γεωργικός) that was drawn up, certainly at the end of the seventh century, and in all probability under Justinian II (685–95).[1] The Law is assuredly not to be regarded as an act intended to do away with the peasants' obligation to the soil. There was no question of any general repeal of this by means of legislation; on the contrary, the strengthening of the free and free-moving peasantry in this central period, as explained above, was the result of a complicated development conditioned by many different factors. The Peasants' Law has a more modest object: it sets out a number of regulations for the protection of both mobile and immobile peasants' property. But it undoubtedly takes account of a free and mobile peasantry, and hence its special historical value, for it supplies the evidence for the existence at the time when it was drawn up of a large population of such independent cultivators within the Byzantine Empire. The mobile peasantry who had as good as disappeared in the early Byzantine era had now become so important that it was necessary to draft a law particularly relating to them. It is true that there were always serfs in Byzantium, just as there were always powerful secular and ecclesiastical landowners; but, while in the early period it is the great landowner and his soil-bound *coloni* who completely dominate the picture, the Byzantine provinces are now increasingly characterized by small free-peasant holdings.

If we combine the evidence of our sources we get the following picture of the free Byzantine peasant in this central period. As in the West, so in Byzantium we find two main types of peasant settlements: the nucleated village (τὸ χωρίον) and the separate farmstead (ἡ κτῆσις). In the case of the isolated farmstead the peasants' property was not in scattered plots and the arable land lay immediately round the farm buildings. It was a self-contained farming unit, a kind of hamlet, comparable to the later Russian *chutor*. But the far more common type of settlement was the nucleated village. In the middle of its land stood

[1] Scholars still disagree on the question whether the mention of Justinian in the title of the Peasants' Law is to be regarded as an erroneous allusion to Justinian I, or, rather, as Vernadskij, *Byzantion*, II (1925), 169 f., suggests, as a reference to Justinian II. In the solution of this disputed point the decisive factor seems to us to be that the majority, and certainly the oldest, manuscripts give the Law as an extract ἐκ τοῦ Ἰουστινιανοῦ βιβλίου (singular), whereas if Justinian I had been meant one would certainly expect to find βιβλίων (plural).

the little group of peasants' houses lying close to one another, with their farmyards and vegetable gardens. This was the centre round which the peasants' property was grouped, the arable land, the vineyards, and so on. Their land (στάσις) was usually divided up into several little fragments (μερίδες, κατατομαί) which lay scattered in different places. Like the orchards and vegetable gardens, the vineyards were as a rule fenced. The arable land usually did without any fencing, but there is no doubt that it was in every way the hereditary property of the individual peasants. According to the older theories, the village community in Byzantium was characterized by communal ownership and periodical sharing out of all the village land, the individuals to whom it was allotted being allowed only a limited use of it for a stated period. It is necessary therefore to lay special emphasis on the fact that, as in the Roman, so in the Byzantine Empire, property and land were always hereditary and individual possessions. The holder, even if he were merely a peasant living in a village, had complete and unlimited legal right of disposal over his land. The Byzantine sources show quite clearly that peasant land was handed down from generation to generation by inheritance and that it could be freely alienated by the possessor just as he chose—by sale, by gift, or limited lease.

Besides the arable land and the vineyards which were the personal property of individual peasants, there was the unallotted land. It was usually pasture land and woods which remained unallotted, but sometimes there was other land which seemed less suitable for cultivation or was for the moment superfluous. If necessary this could also be parcelled out to individuals to be absorbed into separate economic units and to become their private and irrevocable property. When our sources speak of dividing the land, it is not, as we used to suppose, a question of periodically apportioning all the village lands, but of a subsequent parcelling of the land originally left over because it was not needed. These allotments had the effect of assisting the ordinary process of bringing the land gradually under cultivation. As we have already emphasized, in the early medieval period the Byzantine Empire had an increasing amount of cultivable land that was not in use. The problem of how to satisfy the desire for land had not yet arisen. It was only a question whether the capital and the equipment necessary for bringing fresh land under cultivation were available.

The tilling of his fields was the chief occupation of the Byzantine peasant and the chief support of his existence; but the vineyards were also of great importance. Most peasants seem to have possessed vegetable gardens, and beekeeping was very general. Cattle breeding played a prominent part. It was the possession of cattle more than anything else that was the measure of a man's wealth. As the pasture land mostly remained undivided, the cattle of all the inhabitants of the village grazed together, under the care of the village herdsman, who was paid by individuals in proportion to the number of their cattle. And then there were the village mills—both windmills and water-mills—which generally belonged to the whole village community. Craftsmen, who very often played such an important part in the villages of the neighbouring Slavonic towns of the Balkans, are practically never to be found in the Byzantine villages. This is accounted for, not so much by the fact that the Byzantine peasants supplied their necessary domestic equipment, their tools, their clothes and so on, from within their household (for to a great extent the Slavonic and the West European peasants did the same), but rather by the fact that Byzantium was much richer in cities, and the village therefore stood in closer relation to the town where the peasant could satisfy his needs. Moreover, markets were held periodically in the country districts, and these facilitated exchange between village and town and probably held a significant place in agricultural life. The privilege of holding a market gave the district thus favoured a considerable advantage, and there seems to have been not a little dissension over the fixing of the sites for country markets.[1]

There was naturally a great deal of difference in the amount of property held by individual peasants. There were the big peasants, who had fine holdings, cultivated valuable crops, possessed large herds of cattle and even slaves, bought land or took it on lease. Then there were very poor peasants who could not work their land and who tried to lease it. In such cases it was usually a question of a short-period lease arranged on the metayer system ($\dot{\eta}\mu\dot{\iota}\sigma\epsilon\iota\alpha$), whereby half the yield went to the tenant and the other half to the owner of the land. In the case of a long lease for the more valuable kinds of cultivation ($\mu o \rho \tau \dot{\eta}$) the tenant ($\mu o \rho \tau \dot{\iota} \tau \eta s$) kept nine-tenths of the produce. At least that is according to the provisions of the Law. But the facts that questions arising from this kind of arrangement must have become specially acute, and that the Peasants' Law expresses the regulations relating to it in biblical phrases, indicate that this principle was not always adhered to. In any case there are frequent instances of the payment of the tithe by the lease-holder, but to all appearances the arrangements varied appreciably, according to the respective economic and social positions of the tenant and the owner. With the development of a money economy rent was increasingly, and in later times almost exclusively, paid in money, which meant that the terms varied very much and were arranged to suit individual needs. When state land was leased the rent ($\pi \dot{\alpha} \kappa \tau o \nu$) was simply treated as a tax, and there was practically no difference between the government tax and the rent.

[1] Cf. Basil II's novel of 996 (Zepos, *Jus*, I, 271 ff.).

The superfluous energies of the richer peasants were employed in bringing under cultivation additional land outside the village boundaries. If a peasant had the necessary capital and equipment it was not unusual for him to leave the village and settle down outside its territory, building himself a house and transferring thither his activities. So there arose on the outskirts of the village individual properties with their own buildings, very like the hamlets of the separate farm settlements which we have already mentioned. Sometimes these were fairly small peasant holdings (ἀγρίδια) worked by the owner, but sometimes there were also large estates (προάστεια) run with slaves or small lease-holders. These new settlements and the formation of individual properties of this kind were frequently caused by the division of inheritances; some of the heirs would retain the old farm in the village, while the rest would found for themselves separate new farmsteads outside the village boundaries. If, however, economic resources did not run to this, and provided that none of the heirs went into the city as day-labourers, or to other men's farms as farmhands, if, in fact, all the heirs stayed in the village, then they either worked the family land jointly, or undertook to divide it. This last arrangement naturally led to further splitting up of peasant property, and in time this subdivision and scattering seems to have reached extraordinary proportions. To remedy this evil a procedure somewhat like the present-day 'cleaning-up of the fields'[1] was adopted. This was used particularly in cases where a peasant's property lay in two different villages, when, at the peasant's request, the government official would transfer it, so far as possible, to one place.

This complicated village formation, with the compact central settlement, the confused patchwork of peasant-owned plots lying around it, the unallotted commons and fallow land, and the individual estates on the outskirts, all went to make up a commune. This commune (κοινότης, ἀνακοίνωσις, ὁμάς, μετουσία) represented, however, not so much an economic, as an administrative and fiscal unit. It possessed economic functions only in so far as the inhabitants of a village were naturally united by economic interests and joined together to protect them. Moreover, the self-governing rights of the Byzantine village community were of a very limited nature, for nothing took place in a Byzantine village without government supervision and even the most trivial matters of daily life were controlled by the government officials. The tax inspector (ἐπόπτης) visited the village for regular and periodically recurring inspections as well as for extraordinary ones made necessary by special circumstances. He undertook the measuring and valuation of the land, and not only levied the general tax on the village

---

[1] *Feldbereinigung*: the technical German term for that rearrangement of holdings which in England accompanied the enclosure of open fields.

district, but also assessed the taxes of the separate members of the commune. He was naturally also responsible for deciding all remissions and reductions in taxation, for defining their extent and the time allowed for payment, all of which involved a thorough examination of the circumstances of the taxpayers. He also ratified the transfer of property in cases of inheritance and division among heirs, or of purchase and gift, in order to transfer the taxes to the new owner or to allocate them among the heirs.

The financial factor was of primary importance in deciding the character of the Byzantine commune. The Byzantine village community was a fiscal unit. The village formed a fiscal district ($\dot{v}\pi o \tau a \gamma \dot{\eta}$ $\chi \omega \rho i o \upsilon$) and a general tax ($\dot{\rho} i \zeta a \ \chi \omega \rho i o \upsilon$) was laid upon it, which was then distributed among the individual properties. All property which shared in the payment of this general tax was part of the commune; moreover, the owners of individual estates, who had cut themselves off from the village and carried on a separate economic existence, were members of the village community, in that they had a share in the fiscal burden of the mother-village. On the other hand property exempt from the tax was separated from the commune, even though it lay within the boundaries of the village; and further, if property lying among the peasant-owned plots was taken possession of after the valuation and taxing of the village and then subsequently burdened with a special additional tax ($\pi \rho o \sigma \theta \dot{\eta} \kappa \eta$) and separately inscribed in the tax books, it did not belong to the commune, but was considered as a separate 'independent' property ($\dot{\iota} \delta \iota \acute{o} \sigma \tau a \tau o \nu$). This was a characteristically Byzantine feature. It is true that in actual fact the 'independent' properties were mostly large estates. But that was not the deciding factor, for this 'independence' was a purely technical one for fiscal purposes. In connexion with this classification, the ownership of the property, its size, the position of the plots, their condition or economic resources—all that was immaterial. One thing only was important: it had to form a special fiscal unit, whether by reason of carrying a special tax and being inscribed in the tax book under a special heading, or by being exempt from taxation and—in the case of complete exemption for an indefinite period—removed from the registers.

The members of the commune were responsible as a body ($\dot{a} \lambda \lambda \eta \lambda \epsilon \gamma$-$\gamma \acute{v} \omega s$) for the payment of the taxes. If a peasant lapsed into poverty or abandoned his property, then another, generally his neighbour, had to pay his taxes for him and thus acquired the right of usufruct on the land in question. But if the absent man paid his taxes regularly his property remained inviolable. He who paid the taxes was the possessor. This typically Byzantine principle became fully developed in this period in the so-called *allelengyon* system, which represented a continuation, and at the same time a variation, of the late Roman system of the *epibole*. For, if in the late Roman period, as a result of the serious scarcity of labour, the forced transfer of fallow land was the primary consideration and the imposition of the burden of taxation only a consequence, in medieval Byzantium it is the additional tax which is the decisive factor and the transfer of property the inevitable and logical result.

The *allelengyon* system of payment imposed excessively heavy charges on the peasantry, and this sufficiently explains why membership of a village community was considered burdensome, and why a peasant usually preferred to own a detached property.[1] The taxes were extraordinarily heavy, quite apart from the *allelengyon*, and the additional liability, not only for one's own taxes, but also for those of others, frequently ruined the people upon whom it fell. When the government levied the *allelengyon* on abandoned property, this more often than not had the effect of forcing the decision to emigrate upon those who had so far remained behind, simply because they could not face this extra burden. To prevent the withdrawal of even more taxpayers and greater depopulation than ever, the government found itself forced to give up taxing abandoned property and to remit any such payments, that is, to annul the *allelengyon*. If the absent owners did not return within thirty years this remission of taxes was transformed into a final exemption, and so there appeared the exempt property (κλάσματα, later known as ἐξαλειμμένα), which was thus cut off from the village community. This phenomenon was already known as early as the seventh century, and after the tenth it seems to have become particularly widespread. The appearance of exempt property actually meant the gradual break-up of the system of paying extra taxes, and, although this was still legally and theoretically valid, yet it usually proved unworkable in practice. The rights of ownership over exempt land fell to the state, which could sell, lease, or grant it. Such property was usually lost to the peasant village, for it can scarcely be supposed that the peasant who himself, or whose ancestors, had been unable to take over property merely because of the liability for payment of taxes would, thirty years later, have been in the position to purchase it or even to take it on a lease. This was only possible in exceptional circumstances, and generally the exempt property, when it did not remain in the possession of the state, fell into the hands of the great landowners; and this is one of the factors which contributed to the disintegration of the peasant village communities and the absorption of peasant-owned land into the great estates.

When an important landowner had obtained a plot of ground lying

[1] In this connexion cf. the interesting remarks in the novel of Constantine VII Zepos, *Jus*, I, 216).

in the middle of a village it was only natural that he should attempt gradually to buy up the land round about and that the neighbouring small owners should become first economically and then legally dependent on him. Another factor which accelerated this same process was the direct alienation of different parts of the village to secular or ecclesiastical landowners, either by sale or long-term lease or as a gift. Men who took monastic vows usually made over their property to the monastery, and very often the devout Byzantine before death bequeathed his personal and real estate to a monastery. Thus the great landowners penetrated into the village, the secular lord above all through purchase, the ecclesiastical through purchase but also very often through bequest.

III. *The struggle to preserve the small landowner in the tenth century*

At the beginning of the Middle Ages when the Byzantine Empire had emerged from the turmoil of the invasions of both the barbarians and the Arabs it showed a lack of economic and social differentiation. But this marked a period of transition. Gradually once more a definite class system and, at the same time, the development of great landed estates became noticeable. As early as the end of the eighth century we see the rise of various powerful families, but by the end of the ninth and the beginning of the tenth centuries the aristocracy had so much power, and had succeeded in being recognized as a privileged class to such an extent, that it claimed to fill the higher positions in the army, and was able, by the repealing of older laws, to secure for itself important economic privileges.[1] The marked capacity of this class for economic expansion found its real outlet in agriculture. In Byzantine cities commerce was so strictly controlled that there was little scope for private initiative; trade and industry were regulated down to the smallest detail, and jealously supervised by the government. The only outlet for the development of private enterprise on a large scale or for the use of superfluous capital was in the acquisition of rural estates. The 'powerful' men (δυνατοί), as the more important and economically stronger elements of Byzantine society were called, greedily consumed the property of the 'poor' (πτωχοί, πένητες). They bought up the holdings of peasants and soldiers, and made their owners dependent upon them.

This was very dangerous for the Byzantine state, for both its financial

---

[1] *Tactica Leonis*, ed. Vari, II, § 25. Cf. also II, § 17 ff.; IV, § 3; *Nov. Leonis*, 84, 114, ed. Zepos, *Jus*, I, 152, 186.

and its military strength depended on the existence of the small freehold peasant property. The reduction in the number of peasant holdings meant that the state lost its best taxpayers, the decline of the military holdings that it was deprived of its soldiers. The system created by Heraclius, which was responsible for the strength of the medieval Byzantine state, began to be undermined, and the danger of the feudalization of the Empire was in sight. The Byzantine emperors were very well aware of what was at stake. They strenuously attempted to protect the small peasant-owner and they vigorously opposed the forces of feudalism. And so there began a bitter struggle between the rising owners of great estates and the central authority, a struggle which lies at the heart of the whole development of internal politics in the Byzantine Empire of the tenth century. It is both the most important and the most dramatic phase of Byzantine agrarian history, and it determines not only the later evolution of agrarian conditions, but also the fate of the Byzantine Empire.

The imposing legislation of the Byzantine emperors for the protection of the small landowner began with the novel of Romanus I Lecapenus (919–44). This law of April 922 first of all restored the old pre-emption right of the neighbours (προτίμησις) which Leo VI (886–912) had restricted in the interests of the landed nobility, and it formulated this institution in a new and significant way. In cases of the sale of peasant land five categories were to enjoy the right of pre-emption in this order of preference: (1) relatives who were joint owners; (2) other joint owners; (3) owners of plots mixed up with the property to be sold; (4) owners of adjoining plots who were jointly responsible with the seller for taxes; (5) other owners of adjoining plots. It was only when all these declined to purchase that the land might be sold to outsiders. This system was intended to protect the small landowner from being bought out by the 'powerful' and at the same time to prevent further subdivision. The 'powerful' were to have no right whatsoever to obtain further possession of peasant land, except in cases where they owned property in the villages concerned (which might, as we have seen, easily be the case as a result of the purchase of an exempted property, thus giving the 'powerful' a pretext for the further buying up of peasant land). Moreover, they might not accept gifts and legacies from 'poor' men, unless they were related to them. He who was convicted of breaking these regulations was to restore the purchased property without being compensated and in addition to pay a fine to the state treasury, provided he was not protected by a ten-year, or in the case of a military holding even a thirty-year, prescription.

This act, in spite of its severity, did not have the desired effect. As a result of the long and severe winter of 927–8 the empire was afflicted with an extremely bad harvest and there were outbursts of terrible famine and devastating plague. The 'powerful' profited from this time of distress, for they bought up the land from the starving populace at ruinously low prices or took it in return for providing food. This led to Romanus I's novel of September 934, when the emperor denounced with the utmost severity and bitterness the selfish greed of the 'powerful', who had 'shown themselves to be more merciless than famine and plague'. Yet he did not insist on a general restitution of all purchased property, as one would have expected from the strict prohibitions of the law of 922. It is true that all gifts, legacies, and similar transfers were declared invalid, and in addition all property had to be restored without compensation, if it had been bought for a sum less than half its fair price. But if it were a question of legal sale, then the return of the property was conditional on the repayment of the purchase price within three years. As far as the future was concerned, Romanus renewed the prohibition of any acquisition of peasant land by the 'powerful', while he insisted that land already acquired should be returned freely to the former owner and a fine paid to the state treasury. This, however, was for the future, and it is clear from the novel of 934 that, in spite of the stern tone, the government measures could not be applied with the severity anticipated. It may be safely assumed that a great deal of the peasant property acquired during the famine remained in the hands of the 'powerful', for it may certainly be doubted whether a peasant who had been forced by distress to sell his land would be able in three years to get together the amount necessary for the repayment of the purchase price. Even in the case of illegal purchase which, according to the requirements of the law, should have been followed by gratuitous restoration of the acquired property, it is doubtful whether the peasant was always, or even generally, given back the rights over his property, for it must be realized that the men who were open to conviction for illegal purchase would usually be the local officials placed over him, or their relatives and friends.

In fact not only did the 'powerful' retain their position, but the buying-up of peasant property continued, and the successors of Romanus I had to issue new laws and to take even stricter measures for the preservation of the small landowner. Constantine VII (944–59), after he alone was in control of the government, in his law of March 947 forbade once more the purchase of peasant land, and insisted on the free restitution of illegally acquired property. Then when land was sold by the 'powerful', other things being equal, peasants were to enjoy the right of pre-emption. Yet for previous purchases the rule which provided for repayment of the purchase price in cases of restitution still held good; though it is, however, true that the law of 947 freed the poorer

sellers whose resources were less than 50 gold pieces from this obligation.[1] But later, as we learn from a novel of his son, the 'powerful'
exerted pressure to compel Constantine VII to revoke these prescriptions and to content himself with prolonging the period for the repayment of the purchase price from three to five years.

The Byzantine central authority was naturally most eager to protect
the military holdings. These were in the same position as the peasant
holdings, and came, on the whole, under similar regulations. A law
of this same Constantine VII emphasized the inalienability of the lands
from which the soldiers derived their livelihood and means of equipment. And indeed the holdings of both the mounted soldiers and the
marine troops of the themes were said to have been worth at least four
pounds of gold, and those of the paid sailors of the imperial fleet two
pounds each (according to other statements from five to three pounds).
The regulations by which illegally acquired military holdings might be
taken from the purchasers without compensation were to be strictly
observed, and, moreover, it was not only the former owner who might
claim the restitution of the military holding, but also, according to
claims of priority, the relatives up to the sixth degree, then those who
were jointly responsible for the labour or military services, as well as
the poorer soldiers who paid their taxes jointly and, finally, the peasants
who belonged to the same fiscal district. The period of uncontested
possession necessary for land that had formerly been a military holding
was lengthened to forty years.

But it was useless. Just as Constantine VII had had to repeat the
provisions of his father-in-law, Romanus I, so his son, Romanus II, had
to introduce new laws to prohibit this buying-up of peasant and
military holdings which had so often been forbidden. If imperial
legislation shows an ever-increasing severity, the great landowner's urge
to expand seems even more overwhelming. The central government
could only slow down the absorption of the small landowner, it could
not suppress it. Against the united front of all the 'powerful' even the
might of the autocratic Byzantine Empire was of no avail. The great
landowners and the officials formed, so to speak, a caste. The more
important officials and officers naturally sought to obtain an estate in
the provinces; as we have seen, they could scarcely invest their money
in any other way; while the richer landowners strove, for their part, to
rise into the official class and to secure for themselves, by taking over
an official post or buying an official title, the social standing and connexions which they lacked. Usually the 'powerful' man was a great

---

[1] The Byzantine gold-piece (νόμισμα) contained 4·48 grammes of gold, thus
representing metal to the value of about 15 gold francs; 72 *nomismata* gave one pound
of gold (about 1096 gold francs).

landowner and an official at one and the same time. These facts are significant enough to explain why the government measures, in spite of their severity, could have no success. It was in the interests of those responsible for the execution of these measures to let them drop. It was the most powerful economic, the most eminent social, elements in the Empire whose will was diametrically opposed to that of the central administration. But most important of all, perhaps, was the fact that often the will of the peasant ran counter to the intention of the government. The excessive burden of taxation produced a new wave of the *patrocinium* movement. The poorer peasants renounced their burdensome freedom and placed themselves under the patronage of a powerful master, thus gaining relief from the pressure of duties and services. This explains how it was that the peasants not only sold their holdings to the 'powerful' but often gave them away, which simply meant that they voluntarily became the serfs of the landlord in order to escape from misery and insecurity and to find protection against the excessive state taxation, and, above all, the extortions of the tax-collectors. So the government which was attempting to protect the small freehold landowners usually had to contend, not only with the opposition of the great landowner, but also with that of the peasant himself.

The aristocracy was always strengthening both its economic and its political position. In the person of Nicephorus Phocas (963-9), a representative of one of the largest and richest families of magnates in Asia Minor, ascended the throne. The Byzantine government had hitherto opposed the great landowners' tendency to expand. Now the 'powerful' had their revenge. It was sufficient for Nicephorus Phocas to put an end to the preferential treatment given to the small landowner; his law of 967 deprived the peasants of the prior purchase rights in cases of the sale of property by the 'powerful', and in the name of justice it restored equality of treatment between the 'powerful' and the 'poor'. Conditions were such that this formal equality meant in practice the handing over of the small peasant proprietary to the 'powerful'. On the other hand, as a great military emperor, Nicephorus sought to strengthen and increase the property of the soldiers, but this in fact was to lose the character of peasant property. In future the value of the inalienable minimum of a military holding was to be not four, but twelve pounds of gold, and the emperor justified this by pointing to the new and more effective military equipment. This change must certainly have meant that the Byzantine army would henceforth be composed of a different social class. The heavily armed soldiers of Nicephorus, for whom he attempted to guarantee a holding worth twelve pounds of gold, could no longer be the old peasant militia. They could in all likelihood only be recruited from the rising class of the lesser nobility.

But while Nicephorus tried to foster the increasing strength of both greater and lesser secular nobility, he opposed the growth of ecclesiastical possessions. Since Gibbon's day it has been generally assumed to be an axiom that the increase of church and monastic lands was detrimental to the interests of the Byzantine Empire. But this is by no means obvious. As long as there was a surplus of unused land capable of cultivation, the growth of ecclesiastical property was an asset rather than otherwise, particularly as church and monastic estates in Byzantium were in principle liable to taxation. But as soon as any scarcity of land became noticeable, the further growth of ecclesiastical property at the expense of more productive forms of ownership, especially of peasant ownership, must have caused the state great anxiety. For the public utility of the ecclesiastical lands was naturally less than that of other landowners; and besides the principle of the liability of churches and monasteries to pay taxes was often broken, and their property frequently exempted from the burden of taxes, through the granting of privileges. The law of Nicephorus Phocas forbade all transfer of land to churches and monasteries and also prohibited new foundations, pointing out that earthly riches were prejudicial to the true monastic life, and that there were numerous old foundations in a state of economic decay which men should assist with grants of money instead of making unproductive transfers of land and founding new houses. This bold law of Nicephorus Phocas was repealed by his immediate successor, John Tzimisces (969–76), who, however, being himself a member of a great family, seems otherwise to have continued Nicephorus Phocas's agrarian policy.

The last to fight against the rise of the great landowners was Basil II (976–1025), the greatest of the Macedonian house. He acted with unparalleled energy and proved to be the strongest and bitterest enemy of the landowning aristocracy. He had already broken the political ambitions of the Byzantine magnates in a terrible civil war, and now he set out to curb their economic ambitions. He resumed the anti-aristocratic policy inaugurated by Romanus I Lecapenus, and not only continued it with unwavering consistency, but made it considerably more severe. By his law of 996 Basil II repealed the legislation legalizing the purchase of land by the 'powerful' after a definite period of delay. His radical policy was such that he did not fear to confiscate, even when there was no legal justification for this. But the most potent measure which he took in his struggle against the great landowners was the decree that the 'powerful' should pay the *allelengyon* for the poor, i.e. should be responsible for the peasants' tax arrears. Thus the burden of the *allelengyon* system which had, up to then, been borne by the neighbours of the insolvent taxpayer—according to the principle of the general liability of the whole village community for the payment of taxation—was transferred to the great landowners alone, without their being granted the right of usufruct on the property concerned. This measure had a two-fold effect: it gave the treasury greater certainty of securing the *allelengyon* money the payment of which, as we have seen, was often beyond the resources of the peasants; and it dealt the 'powerful' another heavy blow.

The opposition was crushed, but the moment that Basil II died it rose again. The death of Basil II was the turning-point in both the political and the economic development of the Byzantine Empire. His ineffective successors were not in a position to continue the struggle. Only a few years after his death the 'powerful' succeeded in getting the *allelengyon* payment abolished, and with it went, for ever, the whole system of additional taxes, which had been a fundamental element of the Byzantine method of taxation. The peasant could no longer pay the additional taxation, the 'powerful' would not. And the immediate interest of the treasury in the retention of this system grew less because, as the central administration became weaker from the eleventh century onwards, the system of farming out the taxes arose. This meant that, in the provinces where that method was employed, the tax-farmer took over the general responsibility for the payment of the taxes. It is true that the laws protecting the small landowner were not officially repealed, but after the death of Basil II the long series of these laws came to an end, which amounted to the same thing. For, as even the government regulations of the tenth century, in spite of their extreme severity, had been unable entirely to suppress the buying-up of peasant and military lands, now the passively benevolent attitude of the government meant that the great landowners' capacity for expansion could develop to the full. The destruction of the small freehold properties continued unrestricted; the great landowners absorbed the land of the peasants and soldiers and made the owners their serfs.

The 'powerful' had won. The central authority was forced to capitulate to them in the end. It had to give rein to a development which it could no longer check, and to leave the field open for the vigorously advancing class which had achieved both economic and social predominance. Thus the economic and social foundations on which Byzantium had previously rested had collapsed. The state relaxed its strict centralization and the feudalization of the Byzantine Empire began, the small freehold landowner being sacrificed in the process. Certainly there were free peasants in the late Byzantine period; but, whereas in the middle Byzantine period, from the seventh to the beginning of the eleventh century, the free and freely moving peasantry is the chief factor in agrarian development and the backbone of Byzantine agriculture, from the eleventh century onward, just as in the early period, the great landlord dominates the scene. The agrarian history of the late Byzantine period is that of great landowners and their dependants.

IV. *The great landowners and their dependants in the late Byzantine period*

The decay of the peasant and military holdings implied a considerable fall in the state revenues and a fatal decrease in military resources. From the military point of view the Byzantine state was so impoverished and so weak that, from the second half of the eleventh century onwards, its very existence was imperilled. If the Comnenian dynasty succeeded in restoring Byzantine supremacy and creating a new army, it was only at the cost of extraordinary sacrifices on the part of the people. They were burdened more heavily than ever by the excessive taxation and the numerous public services required of them; and still the taxes were relentlessly increased. It was considered by no means unusual for the tax-farmers, when they undertook to levy taxes in a certain province, to make themselves responsible for collecting twice the nominal amount; this was regarded as a normal matter and scarcely worth mentioning.[1] Besides the actual tax assessment, the tax-farmer had to secure an additional sum for himself, for this was, after all, the point of his bargain. The high-handed extortions of the tax-officials and the tax-farmers were the subject of continual complaint from the Byzantine taxpayers. The population felt the oppression of their misdeeds even more than the actual burden of the taxes and the raising of the sums required.

Besides the land and head taxes, which went to make up the actual state tax (δημόσιον, δημόσιος κανών, and also simply τέλος), the rural population had to pay a whole series of regular and extraordinary dues, and to furnish various perquisites to the tax-collector. In addition there were the payments in kind and the labour services, the number and range of which were particularly oppressive in the late Byzantine period. Since the financial strength of the state had decreased at a time when its military needs were more varied than ever, and since the far-reaching decline of the native military resources compelled the government to recruit large numbers of foreign mercenaries, the population was for the most part engaged in providing for the defence of the country and in supplying the needs of the army. It had to find material and labour for the construction of ships, forts, bridges, and highroads. Above all, it had the crushing duty of giving the imperial officials and

---

[1] Cf. Zepos, *Jus*, I, 334.

the army food and lodging (μιτᾶτον, ἄπληκτον), of doing transport work (ἀγγαθεία), and of supplying troops passing through with every kind of provision either free or at a very low price.

In principle the whole population of the Empire was liable for these duties; but whereas the small landowner was completely at the mercy of the high-handed officials and military officers, the great landlord was able to protect himself from them to a far greater extent, and even to obtain an imperial order forbidding officials and officers from setting foot on his land. Such privileges had originally been granted by imperial chrysobull to churches and monasteries as a sign of the emperor's special favour. From the eleventh century onwards such grants increased in number and were frequently made to secular land-owners as well. The imperial chrysobull granted exemptions (ἐξκουσεία) from part, or the whole, of the taxes and public burdens. Often only a partial remission was granted at first and a number of payments would be expressly excluded from the exemption, above all the land tax, the pasture tax, and the obligation of constructing fortifications, which in the last centuries of the Byzantine Empire had generally been replaced by a cash payment. The landowner could, however, make a further request and obtain a new chrysobull granting him full economic and financial immunity. The Byzantine state observed great caution in granting legal immunity, yet the exercise of lesser jurisdiction by the landowners, of which there are isolated instances as early as the eleventh century, seems to have been by no means unusual after the fourteenth century. Legally the great landowners were not favoured and they were subject to regular taxation; but through the granting of privileges more and more exceptions were made, mostly in favour of them and of the more influential monasteries.

There were three kinds of great landed property in Byzantium: the crown land, the estates of the nobles, and ecclesiastical and monastic land. The crown land (θεῖοι or εὐαγεῖς οἶκοι, also ἐπισκέψεις) consisted of the private property of the imperial family and the actual state domain. In principle, and technically for administrative purposes, the state land was distinct from the imperial private property, but in actual fact the emperor had control over the state land, just as he had un-restricted control over all the state resources. The state land seems to have been scattered throughout the Empire, now in large massed estates, now in small parcels having their origin in the taking over of exempt property. It certainly had no fixed extent. Out of the great reserve of state and imperial domain, lands were continually being given and lent to persons who had rendered services to the state or had been able to win the emperor's favour, and above all to churches and monasteries. On the other hand the state was continually receiving new

land, not so much from exempt land, which counted for little by reason
of its small extent, but rather from the very frequent confiscation of
estates, which was the punishment of those imperial officials who had
been convicted of hostility towards the government or who had fallen
into disfavour.

But if state property fluctuated in amount, ecclesiastical property was
in a condition of continuous growth. For it was continuously fed by
the endowments of the devout of every class, from the emperor down
to the humblest peasant. The alienation of land once dedicated to an
ecclesiastical institution was, on the other hand, forbidden by ecclesiastical and secular law, and therefore only possible in exceptional cases and
under special circumstances. The most influential churches had very
considerable possessions, especially St Sophia at Constantinople. Sometimes the estates of the individual prelates, metropolitans, archbishops,
and other churchmen, grew to important size. Closely related to the
church were the charitable institutions, extraordinarily numerous in
Byzantium: orphanages, homes for the aged, free hostels for travellers,
hospitals, and so on. They enjoyed the most munificent support of the
devout Byzantine emperors, and were likewise richly endowed with
landed property.

But the most important part of the church's property consisted of
the monastic estates. By reason of the reverence with which monastic
life was regarded in Byzantium, most of the gifts of land naturally went
to the monasteries, and came from such sources as pious foundations for
a particular purpose, grants of land from those entering a monastery, or
bequests. It was, therefore, above all to gifts that the gigantic and ever-
increasing estates of the monasteries scattered over the whole Empire
owed their origin, and it was but rarely that their growth met with
even temporary opposition from the government. On the contrary,
the monasteries enjoyed the most generous imperial privileges and
received rich gifts of land from the emperors. Many Byzantine
monasteries, whose records we are studying today, give the impression
of a flourishing economic life and reveal an unlimited capacity for
territorial expansion. But the economic conditions of individual
monasteries were very varied. Those which enjoyed no privileges were
often far from prosperous; they had taxes to pay and all the public
duties to fulfil; they also had to supply recruits and were exposed to the
violence of the civil and military officials. Land that was subject to
taxes and public duties could in certain circumstances become a burden.
But the prohibition of the alienation of church land hindered any
normal economic regulation and the attainment of a right proportion
between the supply of land and the resources necessary for working it.
The monasteries which prospered were those which controlled sufficient

capital and the necessary labour, and which had been able to obtain from the emperor immunity from the state taxation; and it is just these monasteries whose records have come down to us. But it would seem that side by side with these there existed many poor monasteries and derelict monastic estates. While the former, which were economically flourishing, strove to increase their property, the latter, whose activity had diminished and who lacked capital and labour, attempted to get rid of land that had become unremunerative. This is the key to the understanding of the institution of the *charisticarioi*, which provided an outlet for the monastic economic activities that had been checked by the principle of inalienability. It is true that the leasing of monastic land offered a certain compensation for the veto on alienation; but even leasing beyond a certain period was usually forbidden to churches and monasteries. Moreover, there was not merely a problem of monastic lands; there were also impoverished monasteries which were in need of economic assistance. Such monasteries, together with the lands belonging to them, were given over to the so-called *charisticarioi*, who were influential laymen with great capital resources, and whose function was to administer the monastic lands in question and to attempt to restore their economic health. This institution, which was known from the fifth century onwards, spread enormously after the late tenth century, and reached its climax in the eleventh century. Again and again it met with strong opposition from the Church; and so, as at the Council of Chalcedon as early as 451, it was sternly and repeatedly condemned by later synods. For instead of looking after the financial well-being of the monasteries, the lay administrators regarded them as financial concerns for their own profit; and they cared even less for the moral and religious obligations of monastic life than for the economic interests of the monasteries. But this system nevertheless continued to exist and was expressly defended by several influential prelates, the reason being that, in spite of its many disadvantages, it must have fulfilled a vital need of monastic economy. From the period of the Comneni onwards the system of the *charisticarioi* began a new phase in its development. The emperors took into their own hands the granting of the *charisticaria*, in order to confer monastic estates—and certainly not the worst—as benefices. Henceforth the system served the interests of the state, not those of the monasteries and churches, while the abuses connected with it only increased in number. This stage marks the degeneration of the institution and apparently the beginning of its collapse.

In every period it was the property of the great lay landowners that expanded most conspicuously. It was their hunger for land which devoured the property of peasants and soldiers; it was they who, as *charisticarioi*, seized for themselves inalienable church land. The nature and extent of the secular nobles' property were very varied. Both the greatest magnates and highest dignitaries, as well as the lesser officials and officers, belonged to the class of the 'powerful'. However sharply the distinction between 'powerful' and 'poor' stands out, yet the boundaries were never rigidly fixed: status was determined, not by origin, but by the way of life, and so ultimately by the financial circumstances of the individual at any given moment. Peasants who had become rich and managed to amass considerable property and no longer needed to earn their living with their own hands—these were counted among the 'powerful' without further question.

But, besides the landowners who had recently risen from the ranks and the holders of the less important official posts owning relatively modest estates, there were the possessors of the great *latifundia*, owning enormous groups of estates with hosts of serfs and herds of thousands of cattle. Often they had their seats in the capital, where they occupied important posts and drew the revenues of their property. For them the acquisition of land was a safe way of investing their wealth. From the eleventh century onwards, the landowning nobility, having carried the day and defeated the imperial power on both economic and political issues, thus making the state the defender of its interests, was generally able, like the churches and monasteries, to secure far-reaching privileges by means of imperial chrysobulls. But the most striking phenomenon in the life of the late Byzantine provinces, and the most characteristic accompaniment of Byzantine feudalization, was the *pronoia* system which appeared after the middle of the eleventh century. As a reward for services rendered or as a basis for the discharge of definite official obligations, the Byzantine magnates received lands to administer (εἰς πρόνοιαν), and with the land were handed over the peasants living on it who became the *paroikoi* of the *pronoetes*. A grant of *pronoia* differed from an imperial gift of land in that it was given—at least to begin with—for a definite period, generally for the lifetime of the recipient, and could therefore neither be alienated nor inherited. In return the *pronoetes* received far-reaching privileges and rights of immunity. From the time of the Comneni the *pronoia* system was given a military character, in order to provide a certain compensation for the widespread disappearance of military holdings. The *pronoetes* had to perform military service and to supply a certain number of soldiers according to the resources of the property granted him. The term *stratiotes* is now frequently applied, not to the old peasant soldier, who, it is true, is still occasionally met with, but who now plays a quite subordinate part, but rather to the *pronoetes*, whose levies, together with the foreign mercenaries, form the basis of the Byzantine military strength in the late period. The process of evolution had now produced a situation in which the great landowner became the chief support of the Byzantine Empire and, through the *pronoia* system, the chief source of its military power. Thus the *pronoia* system became more and more important and widespread, and even found its way beyond the Byzantine frontiers into Serbia and the territory of the Venetian republic. Lands of varying size, sometimes smaller estates, sometimes larger ones, as also fishing rights, salt works, and so on, were granted out to *pronoia*. In the area allotted to him the *pronoetes* himself raised the taxes, part of which he paid to the treasury, part of which he kept for himself. Hence the more important *pronoetai* must have had their own administrative machinery. The *pronoia* lands were more or less autonomous and were as a rule outside the central administrative system, a fact which tremendously accelerated the process of feudalization. When in A.D. 1204 the Western powers set up the Latin Empire in Constantinople, and the Western barons created a number of principalities for themselves in Greek territory, they found that they were completely familiar with existing conditions, which they could take over without much alteration. They used the significant terms *fief* and *feudum* as adequate equivalents of the Byzantine *pronoia*. The Frankish rule in Greek lands furthered the process of feudalization, and produced conditions typical of a highly developed Western feudalism, with a complicated hierarchical system of relations between vassal and lord such as Byzantium had never known. But even on purely Byzantine soil in Asia Minor, as far back as the middle of the thirteenth century, there is an instance of a *pronoetes* who calls himself 'imperial vassal and knight' (λίξιος καὶ καβαλλάριος).[1]

The last stage was the conversion of the conditional and temporary possession of the *pronoia* estates into hereditary and unrestricted ownership. The distinction between *pronoia* estates and the hereditary estates vanished so completely that the very term *pronoia* gradually lost its real meaning and was applied to the most varied kinds of property. In the same way in Muscovite Russia the distinction between 'pomestya' and 'votcheny', i.e. estates held temporarily on condition of discharging military service and hereditary estates, disappeared, even though the development in the two cases differed here and there in detail, and at many points was quite different. The assimilation of the *pronoia* estates to other Byzantine property was made easier by the fact that, on the one hand, in the late Byzantine period great landed property of all kinds, except in so far as it was protected by privileges, was liable for the supply of recruits, and that, on the other hand, with the growing power of the *pronoetai* and their ever-increasing assertion of their independence of the central administration, the actual military services of the *pronoia*

[1] Miklosich-Müller, IV, 81 (of the year 1251) and *passim*.

estates diminished faster and faster as time went on, until at last they were scarcely different from the modest liabilities of the hereditary estates. The tottering power of the state could no longer oppose the efforts of the Byzantine magnates, and from the fourteenth century onwards estates originally granted κατὰ λόγον προνοίας were more and more frequently, as a result of pressure from the *pronoetai*, handed over κατὰ λόγον γονικότητος, or κατὰ λόγον δεσποτείας,[1] i.e. they became the hereditary property of the *pronoetai* and were lost to the state. The circle was complete: the hereditary landowners had obtained far-reaching privileges such as applied originally only to the conditionally granted fiefs of the *pronoetai*, while the *pronoia* estates enjoyed all the advantages of private and hereditary property.

However varied and diverse the different kinds of Byzantine estates were, the principles on which they were worked were on the whole the same. On state and imperial domains, on ecclesiastical and monastic estates, on the hereditary and the conditionally granted property of the nobles, there were always the two means of economic development— tenancy and serf labour. On the other hand, as the ancient world falls more and more into the background, slaves become less important, and in the last centuries of Byzantium disappear completely. The most usual form of lease was the *emphyteusis*, well known as far back as the late Roman period, that is, the hereditary lease with liability for the improvement of the land leased. With the so-called perpetual *emphyteusis* (διηνεκής ἐμφύτευσις) the contract was valid for three generations; the short-term *emphyteusis* (ἐμπερίγραφος ἐμφύτευσις) was usually for 25 or 29 years, this being accounted for by the fact that residence on the landlord's ground for 30 years made the tenant his lord's *colonus*. Such considerations must have had less and less weight as time went on, and although the lease for a stated period is found existing side by side with the 'perpetual' lease, it was chiefly used on ecclesiastical and monastic estates; for church land was in principle inalienable, and could only be leased for an indefinite period on the estates of certain churches. But it seems that with every kind of tenancy it was possible to renew the lease, in which case the tenant usually had to pay a fine, or entrance fee, equal to twice the annual rent. In matters of detail conditions of tenancy were very varied and were settled according to the relations existing between the contracting parties. If it was a question of clearing untilled land for the cultivation of valuable crops, then it was agreed that the payment of rent should not begin until several years after the contract.[2] In the eleventh century the normal rate of annual rent for a lease seems to have been 1 *nomisma* for 10 *modioi* of arable land (1 *modios*

---

[1] Cf. Sathas, Μεσαιωνικὴ Βιβλιοθήκη, I, 39 ff.
[2] Miklosich-Müller, III, 237 f.

is about $\frac{1}{12}$ hectare).[1] In the fourteenth century the rent for a lease was somewhat lower, for then, in an age when the Byzantine gold coin was about two-fifths of its original value, one paid 1 *nomisma* (*hyrepyron*) for 25 *modioi* of good land or for 50 *modioi* of inferior land.[2] The rent of vineyards was about ten times as high as that of arable land of average quality.[3]   Seeing that with the ever-widening extension of money economy the actual price level did, on the whole, rise very appreciably in the last centuries of the Byzantine Empire, these data imply a relative fall in rents. The explanation of this can undoubtedly be found in the devastation of the large estates in consequence of foreign invasions and the generally chaotic conditions in the decline of the later Empire. In the division of the produce in kind between the owner of the land and the tenant, the former seems to have claimed no longer the tenth, but only the half of the tenth.[4] All points to the fact that the economic decline in the age of the Palaeologi brought misfortune to the land-owners, in spite of the powerful position which they had secured for themselves.

The lands of the dependent *paroikoi* were the most economically productive part of the landed estates. One could scarcely say that there was any fundamental difference between the *paroikoi* of the state (δημοσιακοὶ πάροικοι) and the *paroikoi* of private landlords. The state *paroikoi* could always be transferred to the *pronoia* of either a secular or an ecclesiastical lord. A transference of this kind could mean either the deterioration or amelioration of the condition of the *paroikoi* according to the general situation of the landlord, whose land might or might not have to bear many public services. For the rest the position of the *paroikoi* of one and the same landlord could be very different in individual cases, as we shall see. From the legal point of view the *paroikoi* were completely distinct from the free peasants, in so far as they had only a *dominium utile* over their land, while the land of the free peasants was under their *dominium directum*. But there was no economic or social gulf between them; economically the comparison did not usually tell in favour of the free peasant. It often happened that members of the same family were under a neighbouring landowner, some as free peasants and some as *paroikoi*. Priests and other clerics often had the status of *paroikoi*, and they could, indeed, be the *paroikoi* of *pronoetai*.[5] The land of the *paroikoi* was their heritable possession. The landlord could not evict them, and indeed he had a vital interest in keeping his *paroikoi*. The relation of the *paroikoi* to the lord was so defined that they paid him a

[1] *Id.* IV, 15 (of the year 1073).
[2] *Vizant. Vremennik*, XVII, Prilozh, Nr. 92 (of the year 1323).
[3] Uspensky, *Materialy*, XXX, 1 ff., 21 (*Practicon* of the monastery of Chilandariou).
[4] *Vizant. Vremennik*, XVII, Prilozh. Nr. 30.
[5] Miklosich-Müller, IV, 71, 81.

rent and as a rule had to perform prescribed services on the lord's demesne. But they kept their personal freedom. One might say that the *paroikoi* were bound to the soil of 'the manor', not personally, but financially and economically. They could not leave their lord in so far as they had economic and financial obligations towards him; if they did, the lord could demand, and in some circumstances compel, their return. It was not unusual to find the *paroikoi* leasing land from another lord with the permission of their own lord. There are instances of their settling in the nearest town—presumably as craftsmen—and if they made their due payments their lord had no cause for complaint.[1] This makes it clear that there were *paroikoi* who owed the landlord rent alone and had to perform no direct services. Indeed the owners of large lordships did not need to demand labour services from all their *paroikoi*. So far as possible, the services were valued in money and commuted, in the same way that the state often took money payments in lieu of obligatory labour services. But the *paroikoi* were normally employed on the estate in definite manual and team works. Then there were also agricultural labourers who had no property of their own, but who lived on the estate as farm hands. They took the place of the slave labour by means of which Byzantine estates in the early Middle Ages were still largely worked. It is significant that they were called δουλοπάροικοι or πάροικοι δουλευταί, which shows clearly how like they were to slaves.

The *paroikoi* who had their own land mostly lived in villages as the free peasants did; the arable land was grouped round the peasant homesteads which, with the orchards and vegetable gardens, formed the centre of the village. Usually the peasant families were very large; married sons often remained on their father's farm, so that family communities grew up, although these never reached the size of a Serbian *zadruga*. The main concern of the Byzantine peasantry, the free as well as the servile, was always the arable land and the vineyard, and, after these, cattle breeding; in certain districts the cultivation of the olive was also very important. As in the late Roman period, so in medieval Byzantium and also in the contemporary Muscovite kingdom, it was possible to distinguish between three grades of land according to their value. In the thirteenth century one paid almost 1 *nomisma* (which was then worth three-quarters of its nominal value) for 1 *modios* of good, 2–3 *modioi* of medium, and 5–10 *modioi* of inferior land; for vineyards one paid then on an average about 6 *nomismata* for 1 *modios*; an olive tree with the land belonging to it cost about 1 *nomisma*, without the land about ⅓ *nomisma*. Usually the property of the *paroikoi*, like that of the free peasants, was divided into several small strips of land. There is an instance of a *paroikos* who had 75 *modioi* of land altogether (i.e. about

[1] Cf. Miklosich-Müller, IV, 2 f.

6 hectares) and possessed not less than thirteen separate parcels: one also finds minute parcels which were only 1 *modios* in size.[1] One of the monasteries on Athos was given by the emperor 748 *modioi* of the best land on the island of Lemnos, and this was divided into 22 separate plots of land of which some were only 3 *modioi* in size.[2] There were no doubt larger properties, but as a rule the lands owned by the state and the lands of the monasteries, mostly acquired by bequest, were widely scattered in fragments. Hence the great variety of conditions of possession; all kinds of landownership lay intermingled and intersected. There is a case of a single village that belonged partly to a monastery, partly to a private landowner, and partly to the state.[3]

It would be wrong to conclude from this that there was any real land shortage, for Byzantium never lacked idle land. The greater part of an average estate remained, as a rule, uncultivated, used at best as grazing ground, a great deal was leased out, for the holdings of the *paroikoi* certainly formed the most productive, but also the smallest, part of the landed estates. The difficulty in making proper use of the larger estates was partly due to the primitive conditions of economic technique; for in this respect the Byzantine Empire, so far ahead in culture, was in many ways far behind the West. Thus Byzantium to the end of its days continued to employ an extremely uneconomic and antiquated harness for draught animals, while by the tenth century the West had evolved a greatly improved method of harnessing, which from the thirteenth century onwards was also found in Serbia. True, as we have already said, in medieval Byzantium the superfluity of uncultivated land was not so great, the need of workmen not so pressing, as in the early Byzantine period; and in times of economic activity the classes which were then strongest showed a marked desire for land. But it must be remembered that this desire was only for the best kinds of land. It is an open question whether, for the big landowner who seized the property of the peasants, it was not in the first instance really a matter of acquiring labour by reducing the free peasant to the position of a serf rather than of acquiring land. Monastic documents often give the impression that the monasteries, as recipients of imperial bounty, laid the greatest stress, not on the gift of the actual land, but on that of the *paroikoi* allotted to them.

Paroikoi were distinguished according to their possessions and their economic potentiality. In estimating this, the conception of the ζευγάριον was used, which meant primarily a yoke of oxen; but in a derivative sense, like the Roman *iugum*, it meant an economic and fiscal unit, in which the peasants' wealth and tax-paying capacity was measured.

[1] *Vizant. Vremennik*, XVII, Prilozh. Nr. 40.
[2] *Akty Russago na svyatom Afone monastyrya*, Nr. 25 (of the year 1407).
[3] Miklosich-Müller, V, 192 (of the year 1350).

A property was said to consist of so many ζευγάρια, and peasants are described, according to the value of their possessions, as ζευγαράτοι, or βοϊδάτοι, or also as ἀκτήμονες. The *zeugaratoi* were those *paroikoi* who had a yoke of oxen and a plot of land of a given size and quality, that is, land that could be managed with the help of a yoke of oxen. The actual area varied with the quality of the land and with local conditions from less than 100 to even more than 200 *modioi* of arable. This was the normal size of an adequate peasant holding. Besides the *zeugaratoi* there are occasionally found *duozeugaratoi*, who had a double share of land and two pairs of oxen. Those *paroikoi* who were known as *boidatoi*, on the other hand, had only a single ox and half the normal unit of land. Lastly, there were the *aktemones* who had no land, and no draught animals, except perhaps a donkey. The payment owed varied with the holding. On one estate in the seventies of the eleventh century the *zeugaratoi* paid a ground tax (συνωνή) and a hearth tax (καπνικόν) of 1 *nomisma*, the *boidatoi* paid ½ *nomisma*, while the *aktemones*, being landless, contributed no ground tax, but only had to pay the hearth tax (½ *nomisma* if they had a donkey, ¼ *nomisma* if they had no draught animal). Domestic animals were subject to a special tax, the grazing tax (ἐννόμιον); for the bigger cattle 1 *milesarion* (a silver coin worth $\frac{1}{12}$ of a *nomisma*) per head, for sheep 1 *nomisma* per 100 beasts.[1] The landless folk were mainly occupied about the flocks and herds. Nevertheless, the boundaries between the various categories were not rigid. The landless folk might be provided with land and the corresponding equipment and promoted to the class of the *zeugaratoi*.[2] Since there was no lack of land, landlessness was usually only a transitional stage.

The status of προσκαθήμενοι, which often appears in the sources, was also an intermediate one. Usually peasants who had settled on the land of an estate only a short time back were so described. After a definite time they became *paroikoi* and could be inscribed as such at the next official inspection, whether as *zeugaratoi* or as *boidatoi*, according to the possessions which they had meanwhile acquired.[3] In the late Byzantine period there is plenty of binding to the soil; but among a large part of the population there is also plenty of wandering. The later the period and the more uncertain the conditions in the declining Empire, the more often we find this floating class of 'foreigners', the 'free' (from the point of view of taxation), the 'unknown to the treasury' (ξένοι, ἐλεύθεροι, τῷ δημοσίῳ ἀνεπίγνωστοι). Some of these were probably inhabitants of the districts devastated by hostile invasions, some people who had once been free peasants, or *paroikoi* who had fled from im-

---

[1] Miklosich-Müller, vi, 15 (of the year 1073).
[2] *Izvestiya Russ. Archeol. Inst. v. Constantinopole*, vi, 36.
[3] Cf. Miklosich-Müller, iv, 182.

poverished estates. Sooner or later they settled down on the property of bigger and richer landowners to become their *paroikoi*. This colonization was doubtless to the interest of the landowners, who thus gained new workers. So we see how big landowners—so far as our sources tell us they are nearly all rich monasteries—protect themselves by securing beforehand a chrysobull giving the imperial assent to the settlement of such people. But the landlords concerned do not merely wait for the appearance of new settlers: they know how to entice them by various devices. Here we meet a phenomenon that is of great general significance in economic development: the smaller and poorer estates lost their workers, who flocked to the bigger, the richer, and—what is perhaps most important of all—the privileged, estates.

Impossible as it is to make any generalization as to whether the condition of *paroikoi* was better on imperial or private property, on the estates of the Church, or on those of the secular nobles, it is, however, a clear and unmistakable fact that the *paroikoi* on the bigger and more privileged estates were in a considerably more favourable position than those on the smaller and unprivileged. The less land an owner possessed, the greater the demesne from which he lived in proportion to the whole estate and so the smaller the number of his *paroikoi*, the more must he burden each *paroikos* with demesne services. On the other hand the *paroikoi* on the bigger estates which had more workers could give their chief attention to the cultivation of their own plots, since their work would be less necessary on their lord's land. The difference between the privileged and unprivileged estates affected the position of the *paroikoi* even more strongly. If, by reason of an imperial privilege, an estate enjoyed exemption from taxes and from public services, this was a great advantage, not only for the owners, but also for the *paroikoi*. No doubt, the claims of the state were transferred to the owner, but part of the burden fell away, above all the particularly onerous duty of entertaining officials and quartering soldiers. To this extent the position of the *paroikoi* whose lords possessed immunities was doubtless more favourable than that of the free peasants—a circumstance that explains much in Byzantine development. The *paroikoi* who had to meet the full force of the demands of both private landowners and the state were in a very different position. It is clear that they were tempted to migrate to the privileged estates; and in any case they were so terribly overburdened that their powers of production were affected, which inevitably reacted on the economic prosperity of their lords.

This explains why the small estates everywhere fell into ruins, and also why the unprivileged big estates grew increasingly poorer, while only the very large estates which were endowed with rights of immunity flourished. These separated themselves from the enfeebled state, entered into competition with it as autonomous powers, and cut into its economic and political foundations. The course taken by Byzantine agrarian history provides at every stage the key to the understanding of the whole historical evolution of Byzantium. Just as the power and the internal stability of the Byzantine Empire in its best days were based on sound agrarian conditions, so its downfall was in great measure determined by the less happy course of its subsequent agrarian history.

CHAPTER VI

The Rise of Dependent Cultivation and Seignorial Institutions

I. *The problem*

Our object being to inquire into the origins of the rural *seigneurie* in Western and Central Europe, our first task must necessarily be to form as clear an idea as possible of what it was like when fully developed. You cannot study embryology if you do not understand the grown animal.

The seignorial system, or to use the name under which it is known in England, the manorial system, was not based on slavery in the true sense of that word. Whatever their legal status may have been, even if it went by the name of serfdom, the peasants who composed a *seigneurie* were in no sense human livestock, fed by their master and owing the whole of their labour to him. They lived on the produce of fields that they cultivated on their own account, which were usually handed down from father to son; and if the opportunity occurred they could sell or exchange the produce in order to procure other necessaries of life. They usually formed little rural communities with a strong esprit de corps; exercising common rights over waste land where their flocks could graze and they could gather food; able to regulate the arable land itself in the common interest with a jealous insistence. But they did not work only for themselves, or for Church and ruler: a great part of their toil went towards the maintenance of one who stood immediately above them.

To this lord, as they called him, the cultivators of the soil owed, first, a more or less important part of their time; days of agricultural labour devoted to the cultivation of the fields, meadows, or vineyards of his demesne; carting and carrying services; and sometimes service as builders or craftsmen. Further, they were obliged to divert to his use a considerable part of their own harvests, sometimes in the form of rents in kind and sometimes by means of taxes in money, the preliminary exchange of produce for money being in this case their affair. The very fields that they cultivated were not held to be theirs in full ownership, nor was their community—at least in most cases—the full owner of those lands over which common rights were exercised. Both were said to be 'held' of the lord, which meant that as landowner he had a superior right over them, recognized by dues owed to him, and capable in certain circumstances of overriding the concurrent rights of the individual cultivators and of the community.

Finally, the lord did not merely draw from his peasants valuable revenues and an equally valuable labour force. Not only was he a *rentier* of the soil and a beneficiary of the services; he was also a judge, often—if he did his duty—a protector, and always a chief, whom, apart from any more binding and more personal tie, those who 'held' their land from him or lived on his land were bound, by a very general but very real obligation, to help and to obey. Thus the *seigneurie* was not simply an economic enterprise by which profits accumulated in a strong man's hands. It was also a unit of authority, in the widest sense of the word; for the powers of the chief were not confined, as in principle they are in our capitalist enterprises, to work done on his 'business premises', but affected a man's whole life and acted concurrently with, or even in place of, the power of the state and the family. Like all highly organized social cells the *seigneurie* had its own law, as a rule customary, which determined the relations of the subject with the lord and defined precisely the limits of the little group on which these traditional rules were binding.

For more than a thousand years the *seigneurie* as thus defined was one of the dominant institutions of Western civilization. Firmly established already in many lands at the dawn of the Middle Ages, its reign over the European countryside came to an end only in times which historians, accustomed to reckon in centuries, would describe without hesitation as recent. Although it was overthrown, while still in full working order, by the French Revolution in 1789 and 1792, it finally came to an end in Central Europe only as a result of the democratic movement of 1848. England, with still greater respect for the past, waited until 1 January 1926 before removing the last 'manorial incidents' from her law; though it is true that for very many years they had been little more than empty legal survivals. In the course of such a long existence the institution of the *seigneurie*, which had always differed in character from place to place, inevitably underwent many and often very profound transformations. One feature might disappear while another became more accentuated. From the close of the Middle Ages, for example, services may be seen giving way almost completely to dues in money or in kind throughout Western Europe and Italy; while in Eastern Germany the demesne swallows up most of the dependent peasant holdings, and their tenants are brutally depressed to the level of a wretched rural proletariat. In England the governmental aspect of the manor gradually loses a great part of its legal force, henceforth being only enshrined in social habits or merged in the political domination of a class; the squire-archy, in short, emerges slowly out of manorial lordship. But in what science has the presence of variations or varieties ever interfered with the recognition of a genus? The fundamental features here recalled define accurately a clear and distinct type of social structure, which had great resisting force and by which through the centuries man's destiny has been so powerfully influenced that even today, in every country on which it left its mark, the divisions of property, the distribution of rural dwellings, the countryman's habits of mind, can only be explained by reference to its ancient and now abolished authority.

It must be admitted that the genesis of this institution which has held so great a place in European history remains singularly obscure, because the documents are few and for the most part late, also because they are terribly scattered, in time and still more in place. In Gaul, Italy, the Rhineland, they scarcely allow us to form any distinct picture of the *seigneurie* earlier than the ninth century—and then it was unquestionably very old. For England we must come down almost to the Norman Conquest. Before the great descriptions to be found in the Carolingian surveys or in that of William the Conqueror, we must do as best we can with a few most fragmentary scraps of evidence, or the indirect witness of archaeology, place-name study, or the study of the meanings of words. It is needless to say how little we know of German society before the great invasions. Perhaps we are not always fully aware of our desperate ignorance of the fundamental structure of whole sections of the Roman world, and in particular of Eastern Europe, in imperial times. No doubt we have the fine inscriptions from African estates; and further east, preserved by the fortunate drought of a desert climate, the invaluable archives of so many great Egyptian estates, from the time of the Ptolemies downwards. But is it possible to believe that a few centuries of a common political domination can have sufficed to obliterate the diversities between societies so different in their conditions of life and historical traditions as those of the Nile Valley, Berber Africa, and Gaul? And the picture that might be composed by lines taken in turn from a village of the Fayyum under the Lagides, from an imperial *saltus* on the high plateaux of Algeria, and lastly from a monastic *fisc* of Charlemagne's Île de France—would there be any real chance that this would express a genuine continuity? No doubt Egyptian and African evidence can throw precious light on the origins of the Western *seigneurie*. But only if we ask of them what they can legitimately supply. That is information, not about the actual thing that we are studying, but about analogous things. In short, we must treat them as documents of comparative history.

And it is on comparative methods that we must mainly rely. On comparisons of the European development with parallel developments that may be studied outside Europe? No doubt. But also, and perhaps mainly, on systematically conducted comparisons of the various regional developments within European civilization itself. For the establishment of the seignorial system was not carried through in all of them at the same date nor with the same rhythm; nor was it everywhere equally complete. These divergences and these imperfections are of the nature of experiments, to which special attention should be given in causal analysis. Unhappily, inquiry in this direction has not hitherto been so persistent as could be wished. Confined to their special provinces, scholars have not as a rule posed their questions widely enough to bring the diversities clearly into the light. So true is this that, in this capital matter, we are dealing not with settled conclusions but with an inquiry that is still proceeding.

These considerations determine at once the limits to our ambitions and the method of the inquiry. To state the main problems with all possible precision; to suggest cautiously some working hypotheses—modest as these achievements may seem, the historian of seignorial origins today should not aim at anything more striking. Moreover he cannot follow strict chronological order. He might as well try to follow a track by night. He must start from what is least imperfectly known, collecting one by one various indications which may help him to understand a more remote and more obscure past. Such a method of exposition must necessarily be rather slow, and very unlike that appropriate to questions that have been more completely answered. At least it will follow faithfully the actual lines of research; and perhaps, after all, one may interest a reader best by describing to him how one groped for truth in the laboratory.

II. *Seignorial types of the early Middle Ages*

We are still far from the possibility of constructing a map of the 'seignorialization' of Europe; but we may at least try to distinguish roughly the principal areas which such a map, could it be completed, would mark out with a precision that today is out of the question. First, we discern a vast area throughout which the *seigneurie* was firmly established in the ninth century, and no doubt had been long before that; where for many centuries it influenced the whole of social life profoundly—most of Italy; North-Eastern and South-Eastern Gaul, with its Catalan and Rhenish promontories; and even beyond the Rhine great regions of Southern and Central Germany. Secondly, a region of late but marked 'seignorialization'. England is its chief constituent area, but probably we ought to add, though with a still later start and a much less vigorous growth, Denmark. Then come the regions of incomplete 'seignorialization'—South-West Gaul, the Saxon plain.

Last, the lands that have no *seigneurie*—Friesland, Dithmarschen, Norway, perhaps Sweden. It will be simplest to begin our search in the first area and, more particularly in Gaul, because of the greater abundance of sources. And naturally we shall go back as far as we can with any confidence, that is, as we have already said, to early Carolingian times.

It must not be forgotten that even for Carolingian Gaul our knowledge is very fragmentary. We know much about only one class of *seigneuries*. They are found in the region of big villages north of the Loire, and are themselves unusually big. Those that can most easily be described belonged to monasteries. But we know enough of the royal estates to be able to say that, in their main lines, they hardly differed from the ecclesiastical; and as these last had come to the Church by gifts, sometimes made only a few years before the documents provide us with a detailed account of what had been given, we are entitled to hold that the general lines of the picture apply equally to the estates of the great lay aristocracy at that time and place. This is the type from which our inquiry must necessarily start: later we may extend it to other types.

Seigneuries of this type were distinguished by the union, and that extremely close, of a very great area cultivated directly by the lord—the demesne, or as it was usually called, the *mansus indominicatus*—with little dependent peasant holdings which, following a rather later usage, we shall call the 'tenancies' (*tenures*).

The management of the demesne radiates from a group of buildings—dwellings, barns, cattle sheds, workshops—sometimes fortified, and known as the court, *curtis*, that is—the enclosure. Around it lie gardens, ploughlands, vineyards, meadows. As a rule the *mansus indominicatus* also includes forest land, often very extensive, and grazing lands. But since they are generally subject to rights of user by the community, these stretches of woodland and waste are not so completely at the lord's disposal as the other parts of the demesne; for the moment let us leave them on one side. Even when limited to its cultivated fields and meadows, the *manse domanial* remains very great. Its area will regularly be one-third, one-half, or sometimes almost even the equivalent, of that of the similar lands held by the body of peasants. So two very grave problems faced the lord. A 'marketing' problem: how to make the best use of the produce of this extensive agricultural enterprise. A 'labour' problem: how to find hands enough to keep it going. Turn for the moment to the second.

Wage labour proper was not of much account. It was not unknown; but it was only called in now and then, for those great seasonal operations in which men volunteered to work for hire. On the other hand, on most demesnes there still lived some slaves who, being fed by their master, worked always under his orders; they were called his *proven-diers*, because they got their *provende* (*praebenda*) from him. The surveys (*censiers*), whose main object was to determine the relation of the lord with his tenants, as a rule pay very little attention to this servile personnel of the court; the description of the estates of Saint Germain-des-Prés mentions them only once and then quite incidentally.[1] But we have nevertheless enough textual references to justify us in counting the slaves as a normal element of nearly every *seigneurie*. What we should most like to know would be their numbers. Unfortunately we seldom can. But everything suggests that they were small, at least in relation to the size of the huge fields of the demesne. There were excep-tions no doubt. But the exceptions were not due so much to a great abundance of slaves as to the existence here and there of small demesnes. Thus in A.D. 862, on the 'royal manor' of Ingolstadt, the 22 slaves of both sexes attached to the court might themselves have done nearly all the work needed to cultivate fields then limited to about 110 acres.[2] The case—it has no parallel in Gaul—is worth quotation, because it illustrates excellently the extreme variety of seignorial types, due in great part to the survival of ancient arrangements. It was without doubt an exceedingly rare case, especially among royal estates. On the majority of *seigneuries* in Carolingian Gaul the situation must have been much more like that on those Italian *seigneuries* which happen to have left to us rather more precise information, and where we see, for example, in the ninth century, on a Farfa estate, a group of only 93 fed slaves against one of more than 1400 tenants. Early in the tenth century, on the immense estates of Santa Giulia of Brescia, we find, it is true, an appreciably higher proportion; but still only 741 against nearly 4000. And the reckoning includes the relatively large group of strictly domes-tic slaves. The very modest gangs of agricultural workers which slavery thus provided, though useful because they were always at hand on their master's farm, were obviously incapable of meeting the needs of those great employers, the aristocracy, the king and the Church. These had to look in a very different direction for their principal labour supply.

The 'tenancies' furnished it, in the form of the compulsory services of their holders. Each tenant, as a rule, had assigned to him some of his master's fields, to be tilled for the master. But this ingenious form of piece-work could be applied only to a relatively small fraction of the demesne. The rest was cultivated by means of labour services, applied either to carting or to the numerous and varied daily jobs of any agri-cultural undertaking. Periodically the peasants were called together,

---

[1] xxv. 8: fimina de fisco dominico.
[2] *Mon. Germ. Diplomata regum e stirpe Karolinorum*, vol. I, *Ludowici Germanici Dipl.* no. 30.

often bringing their teams, by the directors of the *seigneurie*, and despatched to do whatever was required at the moment. These services, usually occupying several days in the week, were immensely burdensome to the peasant, much more so, as things then were, than the various dues supplementary to them; but without them the central undertaking could not have flourished, nor even carried on. Had the little peasant holdings been vacated, the lord's barns would have emptied and his fields lain fallow.

The first striking fact about the organization of these *tenures* is its regularity. The greater part of the soil held from the lord was split up into units, in theory indivisible, called *manses*. These in turn are arranged into groups, and each member of each group bears approximately the same burden. Postponing the problem of the *manse*, let us consider the principles which determined the classification of these master-cells of the seignorial organism.

There were two main groups of *manses*, those called servile and those called free. They were not necessarily found side by side on every *seigneurie*. But most *seigneuries*, especially the greater ones, contained both sorts. Three marked characteristics distinguished the two groups. Usually less numerous on any given *seigneurie* than the free *manses*, all told the servile *manses* were certainly much fewer; on the lands of Saint Germain-des-Prés, as known to us from the early ninth-century survey, there were only 191 servile against 1430 free; on those of the Bishop of Augsburg, at about the same date, there were 421 against 1004. The servile *manses* are also regularly smaller than the free *manses* of the same *seigneurie*. Lastly, they have different burdens, heavier and—when services—more indefinite. More subject to the master's arbitrary power, in this and many other features such as exemption from military requisitions—that honourable obligation of free men—they recall the lowly status of slavery. So do the names of the two groups. In the beginning, the servile *manse* had been the holding of a slave—but of a slave settled on the soil, turned into a farmer, and consequently far removed in his daily way of life from his colleague the fed slave (*provendier*); the free *manse* had been the holding of a free man.

However, by the ninth century, this antithesis no longer agreed strictly with the facts. No doubt the burdens originally laid on the soil remained. Besides, the doctrine, if not always very precisely the practice, of personal law still distinguished—according to the old standards—the slave landholder from the free, who was generally called a *colonus*. But it did not follow that the soil and the man were always in the same class. Plenty of *coloni* held servile *manses*. Still more peculiar—for these free holders of land once stigmatized as servile may well be freedmen, or their descendants—free *manses* might be held by slaves. This anomaly struck and worried contemporaries just as it does us. That is why some surveys, while still keeping the two traditional categories apart, chose terms to describe them which, neglecting all legal standards, were based simply on differences of obligations. By a significant vacillation, the compiler of the '*polyptyque*' of Saint Maur-des-Fossés sometimes wrote 'servile *manses*' and 'free *manses*', sometimes—and even when referring to the very same holdings—'*manses* which owe manual services' and '*manses* which owe team services'. Later, the distinction was to disappear altogether from the vocabulary of surveys.

It is then perfectly clear that the antithesis of these two sorts of tenure originated at an appreciably earlier stage of social evolution, although for lack of sources we can only trace it in an era of decline. It opposed to one another two elements in the seigniorial structure, which in fact were being steadily welded together—two sedimentary strata of which no one could state *a priori* that they had been laid down at the same stage of development, or under the influence of similar conditions. Here is a formidable problem for research; but before tackling it it will be well to complete our bird's eye view of the field of early 'seigniorialization'.

Although a legal entity and, as such, incapable of division, the *manse*—in regions of nucleated villages—was only very seldom in fact a single undivided stretch of land. It was usually made up of many strips scattered over a much divided soil. The demesne itself was made up as a rule of various fragments, usually bigger than those of the peasants, but more or less mixed up with them. The tenants' houses were in the village, round about the court; so that the rural scene itself reflected the interdependence of the constituent parts of the *seigneurie*, and greatly facilitated the working of the system, by placing the man who owed services near the place where they were needed. But we must make no mistake: there was no exact correspondence between village territory and *seigneurie*, though sometimes they did correspond. Even neglecting for the moment any completely independent peasant holdings that might survive among those that were dependent on some lord, many a village had several lords; and even in regions where settlement was highly concentrated a *seigneurie* might include *manses* scattered over the fields of several villages, sometimes relatively remote from the centre; so much so that, as is seen in the Montierender survey, some of the lord's men made a longish journey before reaching the demesne on which they had to work. Elsewhere, it became necessary to abandon the services due from *tenures* which were too remote.

And there existed already, in the Gaul of those days as in contemporary France, vast regions where men lived not in villages but scattered in smaller groups. There the *manse* was a single block of land, or nearly that. About the house of the *masoyer* (*mansuarius*) were grouped his lands, generally very extensive, for—since we are here dealing with regions of poor soil—they were only tilled intermittently, harvests alternating rather capriciously with fallow on the same plot. So constituted, and inhabited as a rule by one or two good-sized families of the patriarchal type, the *manse* lay sometimes quite by itself. Elsewhere, with a few others, it formed a tiny hamlet. Obviously such a scattering of the rural population was inimical to collaboration between demesne and tenancies. It presented awkward practical problems, of which various sections of the survey of Saint Germain-des-Prés relating to the woodlands of the West give us a clear notion. There being no big village to serve as the unit of administration, each 'estate' included a large area covered with a loose network of dependent *manses*. Although it existed, the demesne strikes us as uncommonly small when compared with other geographical regions: only 10 per cent of the cultivated area at Boissy-en-Drouais; 11·5 per cent at Villemeult; whereas about Paris it touched more than 32 per cent at Villeneuve-Saint-Georges and more than 35 per cent at Palaiseau. If a *mansus indominicatus* in the woodland country was given to monks, they might be obliged to turn it into tenancies, because they could not conveniently make direct use of it.

But it must be clearly borne in mind that these difficulties were mainly those of the great *seigneuries*, themselves integral parts of landed properties both huge and widespread. Always difficult for the administration, because it was necessary to divide the produce into two parts— one to be disposed of on the spot without too much loss, the other to be dispatched to a single and often rather distant point of consumption, the monastery—properties of this class became still more awkward to manage, when to the distance between the various units of administration was added, within those units, too great distances between each tenancy or each field of the demesne. These conditions were much less unfavourable to little lords who lived on the spot. Consider the *seigneurie* of Ebbon and Eremberge, right in the woodlands of the Corbonnais, which they gave to the monks of Saint Germain-des-Prés, to receive it back from them, by the way, perceptibly increased, as a *precarium*, that is, in return for a rent in money. It is of no great size— about 120 acres of arable and 48 of meadow; whereas monastic *seigneuries* usually reckoned several hundreds, even thousands, of acres. But it is made up of a *mansus indominicatus* and nine tenancies, so divided that the demesne covered rather more than 34 per cent of the arable and about 57 per cent of the meadowland, which naturally meant heavy services for the tenants, services which in this case were at the lord's discretion. So it reproduces at every point, only on a much smaller scale, the structure of that classical *seigneurie* of which a *fisc* of the Church or of the king provides the giant type. People so modest as Ebbon and Eremberge were not able to compile fine surveys. That is why our sources do not tell us much about these little rustic lordships. But they emerge here and there, through some lucky documentary reference, made up, according to the nature of local settlement, now of a fraction

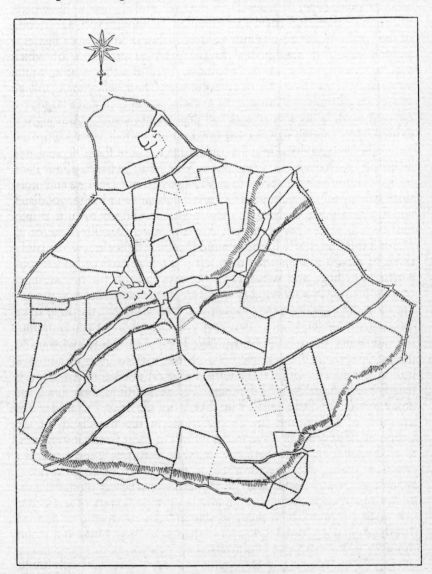

Fig. 5. Enclosed fields about a hamlet in Central France: St Sauvier, Allier.

of a village, now of a hamlet or even of some scattered *manses*. Perhaps, all things considered, they were the most numerous kind of *seigneurie* to be found on western soil. Their internal constitution does not seem to have differed much from that of their bigger sisters; and they could adjust themselves easily enough to any type of settlement.

In its essential features, which are all that matter here, the picture of the *seigneurie* just sketched for Carolingian Gaul would be correct, almost line by line, for Southern and Central Germany and for Italy, about the same date. But for Italy there is a weighty reservation.

North of the Alps, contractual relations between individuals played an insignificant part in the inner life of a *seigneurie*. In spite of their looseness, which itself indicates a legal habit of mind very different from ours, the texts give a very clear impression that the relations between the master and the little cultivators were determined more often than not by custom alone, a custom the same for all the group, or at least for all *manses* of the same class. Exceptions there doubtless were. The agreements for protection, of which we shall speak later, usually went with a grant of land. Often enough the generosity of the lord was, in truth, only apparent; he was merely giving back some property which his client had previously surrendered to him, now burdened with fresh obligations; and the game of surrender and regrant simply transformed a holding formerly autonomous into one under authority. But the question whether the grant was real or nominal did not change its profound significance; in either event it ended by creating a tenure which we may say was rooted in contract—with this limitation however, that although it was the product of two acts of will, the agreement had no sense save as part of a vast system of custom. Agreements of this type are as a rule singularly vague; they do not determine exactly either the liabilities of the land or, what is still more curious, for how long the recipient is to hold it. That is because they tacitly assume the local custom; and the customary rule as to the second point was almost invariably that of heredity. There can really be no doubt that, whether by tradition or by sufferance, tenancy normally went from father to son. True, some *manses*—regularly described as *censiles*—were actually let for terms of years. But they are very rarely found.

As for the *precarium* contract, also a kind of letting for a limited period, its range under the Carolingians was confined almost exclusively to persons in rather high places and to estates very far removed from those of peasants; though at an earlier date it may have been wider. It was in regular use between the religious houses and the lay aristocracy, whose members found in this legal procedure an easy way of snatching *seigneuries* or parts of *seigneuries* from the Church, while nominally only renting them. It is very rarely met with in the relations between the lords and their men. Custom, on which they were based, gave its own perpetuity to the rights over land of the majority of these dependent folk.

Now Italian conditions contrast with these in two marked ways. Not only did a great number of Italian peasants hold lands burdened with dues and services to a lord by a regular contract (the *livello*). This contract, further, gave them a tenure limited in time, either to one or more lives, or—and more usually—to 29 years, so as to avoid the prescriptive rights which went with a 30-year tenure. It is in fact highly probable that more often than not the lease was renewed at the expiry of the fixed period. Some deeds even anticipate this renewal and fix the price that is to be paid for it. The practical reasons which everywhere favoured heredity were at work in Italy as in other countries: labour was so rare that what a lord most feared was its loss. Yet such a tenure was none the less by definition temporary, and rested on a contract explicitly formulated at each renewal. The contrast so revealed between the societies north and south of the Alps is a structural difference which must always be borne in mind.

III. *The decline of slavery*

In the description just attempted, one fact above all claims attention. It is not enough to say of the ninth-century *seigneurie* that it contained only a few slaves housed and fed on the demesne. The institution itself, its fundamental principles, assumed a society in which really servile labour played only an unimportant part. If there had been plenty of slaves for sale, and their work had covered their cost, why exact so many services from your tenants? And as the burden of dues was necessarily in inverse relation to that of services, would not good sense suggest taking from the *manses* more of the crops and fewer days' work? But that is not all. Itself the antithesis of a slave system, the *seigneurie* had grown up precisely when such a system was on the decline. On this falling curve of slavery the ninth century marks only a point, but a point in fact very near the end.

No doubt we must not exaggerate, even for the Roman world, the position held by vast *latifundia*, tilled by gangs of slaves, sometimes in irons. The existence of a numerous free peasantry—who might all the same be under the domination of magnates or chieftains—is proved by indisputable records; and, as we shall see, it was on this basis that the *seigneurie* itself was in great measure built up. Yet it is nevertheless true that round about A.D. 1 slavery was very widespread in the Empire; that the rich in particular had at their disposal great troops of slave labourers whom they employed, not only in domestic work and handicrafts but also in agricultural work; that especially on great estates, apart from some paid labourers hired in times of pressure or for specialized tasks, the work was done almost exclusively by slaves. Even in Germany, slaves, though no doubt many fewer, were found in all comfortable homes; at the time of the invasions the chieftains brought slaves of their own race into *Romania*; in raiding there they got plenty more. At the start of the Merovingian era, Gregory of Tours and the contemporary lives of the Saints, with the letters of Gregory the Great for Italy, give us a quite clear impression of a society in which the slave is still a very familiar type; in which you sell in the markets of the Frankish Kingdom captives from Italy; at Naples captives got by raids from Gaul; in which women slaves grind at the mill in the lord's court and slave shepherds tend the flocks. Two or three centuries after the age of the great Carolingian surveys, in which already the importance of slavery had dwindled so much, it played only an insignificant role in the greater part of the West, and a role exclusively domestic.

The decline of slavery is incontestably one of the most notable facts in our western history. Like all great facts, it is hard to explain. Broadly one may say that three groups of causes, converging, brought it about—the military, the religious, and the economic.

Servile labour, as the men of the ancient world were well aware, almost always gives a wretched return; many hands to finish off few jobs, that is apparently its motto. The slave is a form of capital with modest yield, the more modest because you must deduct from his output the cost of his keep. He is, besides, a fragile form. If he is sick he has no output, but the costs of his keep run on. If he dies—and his life was often short, especially if he were enrolled in the great teams of the *latifundia*, where living conditions were necessarily very harsh—or if he runs away, so does the capital invested in him. Was it not Varro who, for this reason, advised employers to prefer, in unhealthy posts, free wage-earners whose death would cost them nothing? All this has little importance so long as the slave can be replaced cheaply. If he cannot, losses may swallow up profits. Now the birthrate on a slave estate is hardly ever high enough for the regular maintenance of a herd of slaves. Experience has proved it: of all forms of breeding, that of human cattle is one of the hardest. If slavery is to pay when applied to large-scale enterprises, there must be plenty of cheap human flesh on the market. You can only get it by war or slave-raiding. So a society can hardly base much of its economy on domesticated human beings unless it has at hand feebler societies to defeat or to raid. That was the position of the white men of the West Indies towards black Africa from the sixteenth to the nineteenth century; of Abyssinia yesterday, surrounded by primitive and ill-armed tribes; of old Rome in her days of conquest. The legions had supplied huge labour battalions, who toiled in the field or on the public works under the lash or the threat of the *ergastulum*. The relative peace of the first two centuries of our era appears to have made their recruitment appreciably harder. New methods then began to appear in the administration of the *latifundia*; to which we shall refer shortly. Evidently the return to an almost chronic state of war, with the repeated attacks of Persians and barbarians, produced subsequently some revival of the slave trade, in spite of Rome's military decadence. The great invasions at the end of the fourth and the beginning of the fifth century led to a further revival. And it was not only the invaders who made money by slave dealing: anyone rich enough could seize the opportunity. The records show that when the Germans had ravaged a country they sold their prisoners readily in *Romania* itself. But all this meant only a temporary rise in the general downward movement of the curve of slavery.

At first sight it may seem astonishing that the very warlike Middle Ages had so few slaves. Here religious considerations intervened. Not that Christianity proscribed slavery as such. At least the prevalent form of Christian doctrine that soon became official did not. As between those extremists who were not afraid to teach the slave to despise his master and even run away from him and the Council of Gangra which excommunicated them in A.D. 324, the future lay with the Fathers of the Council. Like the great philosophies of antiquity, Christian ethics as ordinarily received made it the master's duty to treat his slaves well, because they were his brothers in Christ; but according to St Paul it was also the slave's duty to obey his master. A deliberate supporter of the established order of society, the Church was profoundly indifferent to all plans for reforming this world below, so negligible in its eyes compared with the City of God: 'Christ', Primasius of Hadrumetum writes, 'came to change men's hearts, not their conditions of life.' A structure of ideas, in which it is not difficult to recognize the use of some devised by pagan wisdom, helped to support the conclusion. Slavery was no doubt opposed to the Law of God (the philosophers had said, to the Law of Nature). So, for that matter, was property. But both institutions sprang from the Law of Nations, to which, ever since the Fall, mankind ought to submit as to a necessary evil and a well-deserved punishment. No doubt the freeing of slaves was an act of piety; and it is not impossible that the desire to win salvation may have had something to do with the numerous manumissions during the first centuries of the Middle Ages. But we shall see that other, and much more earthly, causes contributed at least as effectively to the great momentum of emancipation. It was never a sin to have slaves, even to have Christian slaves. When a slave born in paganism was baptized the

Church rejoiced. She never required the new convert to be set free; rather she hoped that, by faithful service, much better than that of his comrades who remained in sin, he would show to his master the loveliness of true religion.

On the other hand, the Church refused resolutely to sanction the enslavement of Christians, true Christians, that is, Catholics. By so doing she merely extended, but so widely as to alter its whole character, a rule that had come down from the most remote past of pre-Christian civilizations. The slave had always been, before all else, a captive: beyond the little territory of the tribe or the city stretched a vast region peopled with men who had no rights at all. You could seize them as and when you wished. Now the new religion had replaced the tiny pagan city by the immense city of the spirit, to which all Christians belonged. Outside this *societas christiana* you might still treat men as cattle and, if you took them prisoners, keep them as slaves. But if a Christian captured another Christian he was obliged to respect his free status. Perhaps one of the finest triumphs of Christian ethics was the enforcement of respect for this maxim, slowly to be sure, for it is still being recalled in England early in the eleventh century, but in the long run most effectively. So it came about that the perpetual wars among Catholics left numberless dead; prisoners who sometimes sighed their lives out in dungeons—it was William the Conqueror's principle that they should; but, after the age of the great invasions, hardly any slaves. Yet you could hunt for slaves in the countries round about; Celtic Christians of the far West, generally treated as heretics; Islam; Slavonic, Baltic or Finnish 'paganries'; and even, from the eleventh century, Greek Christians who by that time were all but cut off from the Catholic world. But these were all distant lands, or lands difficult of approach. They could supply warriors or traders with a few slaves; they could not maintain a great servile economy.

Still that does not explain everything. In the Roman world itself, the division of *latifundia* into small farms can be clearly traced from the second and third centuries; eras, no doubt, in which human merchandise was becoming more rare, but in which the supply was far from exhausted. Later, during the early Middle Ages, the tenurial system managed to establish itself, although in fact the existing servile population, if it had been employed in the old fashion, might have been exceedingly useful, and although the slave trade itself was far from extinct in the West. Setting out from the frontiers of the Slavs, or from Britain, slave caravans guided by slave-traders still traversed Germany and France in the tenth and eleventh centuries; but it was to reach ports from which the goods could be shipped to Byzantium or, more often, to Mohammedan Spain. The captives kidnapped beyond the Elbe, when they were

not in this way disposed of outside Western Christendom, were used—
even in Germany—much oftener as tenants for the waste spaces of a
seigneurie than as domestic slaves in the lord's court. Even the revival of
seaborne trade, from the twelfth century, which put on to the Mediterranean markets a much greater supply of wretched creatures, kidnapped
in North Africa, the Levant, or on the shores of the Black Sea, though it
filled rich establishments with domestics and concubines, and added a
few slave farm hands, did little more—except perhaps in the Balearic
Islands and in Sicily. Obviously the working of great estates by slave
labour was no longer considered possible or desirable. The grouping
about a central establishment of dependent holdings, saddled with dues
and services, was preferred. That was because the control of a great
rural establishment based on slavery raises very delicate problems of
administration, which can only be solved with success in a particular
economic and mental environment. The maintenance of great masses of
human beings must be provided for without using up all the produce
of the soil on their keep—or any of the most profitable produce. With
part of the income—but never at any time the whole—men must be
bought continuously to maintain the stock of labour. In short, an
economy must be kept going—on a large scale and with intelligence—
based on exchange and profit, an economy which the conditions of life
and the growing scarcity of ready money ever since the later years of
the Empire made it a less and less simple matter to organize. It is easy
to follow, in the letters of Gregory the Great, the parallel progress of a
sort of economic debility—revealed at one time by grave difficulties in
the commissariat, at another by the abandonment of great cattle-
breeding enterprises—and of the replacement of troops of slaves by
tenants. Slave labour requires close oversight: long ago Columella had
recommended the system of small farms on parts of the estate too
remote for frequent visits by the *pater familias*. Now an aristocracy of
men who were primarily soldiers was singularly ill fitted for that kind of
oversight. And its retainers, fighting men and little else, could not give
much help. As for the monks, they ought to be spared every kind of
work which would distract them from prayer, liturgy, and the practice
of asceticism. Lastly, estate management requires careful account
keeping; a thing which became more and more difficult for average
administrators, in the ignorance and disorder which the great distress
of the opening Middle Ages brought with it. The repeated, and almost
puerile, instructions which abound in the estate ordinances of the ninth
century—in Charlemagne's *Capitulare de Villis* or the statutes of Abbot
Alard of Corbie—show us how hard it was for the great men to make
their subordinates apply the most elementary rules of book-keeping.
To adopt tenancy as a solution was the line of least resistance. Labour

kept itself; the families, each settled on its scrap of land, grew in the natural way. It was merely necessary to take care that the days of work on the demesne were duly given—and that was mostly done for you by custom. As soon as slaves, at the places of sale, were no longer a commodity attractive because abundant, and therefore cheap, the new tone of social life and the new habits of mind were all against any effort to maintain the old, and far too complicated, methods.

The evolution which had affected the slaves in this way would be reproduced, rather later, almost feature by feature, under the operation of the same causes, in the case of the vassals. They had originally been a fighting *comitatus* and they had fed in their chieftain's hall. Gradually it was thought more convenient to give each of them an estate on which he and his family could live. It was assumed that he would still perform his old duty, just as the slave—now liable to render services—went on working on the demesne. But the vassals' duties were of quite a different sort—instead of humble agricultural labour, military service, attendance at the lord's court, 'counsel'. Moreover the fief which owed them was not a peasant holding; it was as a rule itself a *seigneurie*, large or small. There are weighty differences; they led to absolutely opposite social classifications. But viewed from the economic angle, the positions of the two classes are fundamentally similar. Under the early Norman kings, many an English abbey, after having tried to keep armed knights about the place and feed them at its own expense, had to make up its mind to assign fiefs to them, cut out of the monastic lands. Whether you liked it or not, the social environment, from top to bottom of the social scale, was against the 'prebend', the system of maintenance on the premises.

In fact, the troops of slaves who had once lived on the great estates dwindled away from year to year mainly because their masters were always turning them into tenants, 'hutting' them, as the phrase was: giving each his own hut (*casa*), of course with the necessary fields. Evidently this reduced the land which the lord had formerly cultivated himself. Huge as they seem to us, the *mansi indominicati* of the ninth century must have been appreciably smaller than the *latifundia* which had preceded them. Sometimes the slave, now turned into a farmer, was freed at the same time. But often he remained legally in slavery. There had always been some grants of land to slaves. But in the time of Varro, Cicero's contemporary, they were not usually given regular holdings—just scraps of land big enough to carry a few cattle, as rewards for good service. In the first century Tacitus found, or thought he found, slaves with their own *penates* in Germany; and he marked the contrast with Roman usage. (Perhaps what he really found were not true slaves, but that superior grade of dependants, conquered folk or freed men, whom the Germans called *laet*: *lidi*.) Clearly, the practice spread shortly after his time. Jurists writing about A.D. 200 treat it as normal. It went on spreading in the following period. Imperial policy helped to strengthen it. As we shall see, the government, anxious both to keep up the yield of the land and to facilitate tax-collecting, had decided under Constantine that the freeborn farmers, the *coloni*, ought to remain on their farms from generation to generation: the lessors might not evict them. If its plan was not to miscarry, government could not overlook the now important group of *servi casati*. Already in 367–75 a law, which refers expressly to the policy previously adopted towards the *coloni*, absolutely forbade the sale of 'rural slaves, whose names were on the tax-rolls', without their land. That, it is true, only prevented the master from making easy money out of his slaves by selling them apart from the soil to which they were henceforward bound. Inside the servile group, thus tied to a given area, he could do as he liked. But apparently he was deprived later of a right which, it might have been thought, was of the essence of property in slaves—that of diverting the personnel of the 'tenancies' to other tasks. We have lost the relevant evidence: we do not even know whether this principle was established by imperial law or simply applied by the lawyers. But its existence is beyond doubt; because after the fall of the Western Empire Theodoric abolished it in Italy by his edict. Once a farmer always a farmer: the rule applied alike to freeman and slave. In other words, whether the *latifundia* had been cut up to make holdings for slaves or for humble freeborn men, it was legally impossible to go back to the system of slave-gang tillage. True, we do not know how far this legislation was applied. Issued near the end of the Empire, its life was in any case short, and no doubt economic forces worked more powerfully than any law. For there is every reason to think that the transformation of slaves into tenants went on after the invasions during the first centuries of the barbarian kingdoms.

Let us make the best picture we can of the position of the 'hutted' slave. In strict law he remains a slave, unless formally freed; as a slave subject to his master's arbitrary authority; generally speaking excluded from the courts of law; unable—in a barbarian state—to sit in an assembly of freemen; unfit for Holy Orders. Originally, the land that he tilled was in no sense his: it was only a detached bit of his master's, and his master could take it back at will. Carolingian surveys still go on saying of these men 'that they must serve whenever they are told to do so'. Their holdings, according to the primitive classifications servile *manses*, had their defined duties, often very humble indeed; even should they by chance hold free *manses*, their wives might owe weaving labour, owe it perhaps in the lord's workshops, a thing that could not be demanded of any free woman. But, in practice, the master has 'hutted' men whom he used to keep because it pays him to do so. There is no reason why he should not let the arrangement become hereditary. And as the whole object was to make a man responsible for his own maintenance, and as he paid rent both in dues and services, he must be left time enough to till his land; failing that, he can neither live nor pay. So he and his fellows will only be employed within limits on the demesne. As he has the status of a cultivator he must be allowed some initiative. The Lombard law, which forbids him to sell land without permission, allows him to sell cattle, if it will be good for his 'hut'—and that is a dangerously elastic provision. Finally, since he has his own hearth, is head of a little household, perhaps even has some other slaves as farm labourers, he is inevitably freed from the more direct pressure of his master's power. In short, at once slave and tenant, in the end he is likely to become much more tenant than slave. His obligations tend to be regulated more and more by customary rules which, though not quite the same as those affecting freemen, form a sort of appendix to them. And as all medieval society was dominated by the idea that what was customary was also right, breach of these customs—which are set out in the surveys—soon becomes a wicked thing; and after that, a crime. Speaking of the royal slaves, clearly distinguished from the *coloni*, the free tenants, the bishops assembled in 858 at the synod of Quierzy address Louis the German thus: 'Let your officers be careful not to require of them more than they rendered in your father's day.' In 905 a royal *missus* forbade the Abbot of St Ambrose at Milan to impose on his slaves at Limonta heavier burdens than they had owed when they belonged to the king. From the ninth and early tenth centuries the various grades of dependent cultivators are in process of assimilation into a single class, although originally they and their holdings had been in classes far apart. The process was far from completed. Most of the surveys still refused to mix up free and servile *manses*. Official terminology, legal rules, with their strict lawyerly style, maintain as best they can the line between the free and the servile tenant. Habit and common speech had already nearly erased it.

It is curious that this fusion—accomplished in that great creative epoch of the tenth and eleventh centuries, an age whose terrible shortage of documents has hidden from us the details—did not lead to the disappearance of the word *servus* (become *serf* in Romance speech) nor yet to the wiping out of the idea of servitude. We are not here concerned with the actual history of medieval serfdom. But the survival for almost a millennium of words which seem to recall slavery may bring—has in fact often brought—such errors in its train, that a sketch of the main lines of evolution is called for. Among the members of *seigneuries*, in the twelfth and thirteenth centuries, many—far more than the Carolingian slaves, 'hutted' or not—are held to lack that legal quality called freedom. Yet neither the French or Italian *serfs*, nor the German *Eigene*, nor the English *bondmen* are slaves; not even as a rule descendants of slaves. Not slaves in the legal sense, because they do not belong in body and goods to a master; their relations with their lords are fixed by custom; they have their own possessions; and no one regards them as human beings devoid of rights. Still less slaves in the economic sense: they do not live on the demesne; they have their fields for which they pay dues and services; in short, they are tenants. Even the 'every day' serfs in Germany (*Tageschalken*; *servi cotidiani*), unknown elsewhere in the West except in Sardinia, though they owe daily services as their name implies, are much more like labourers than slaves: they have their own cottages and scraps of land. What really has changed is the very content of the notions of 'free' and 'unfree'. Henceforward the 'free' man is the man who can choose his own lord—as a vassal does, whose homage must be renewed as lord succeeds lord, under pain of losing his fief no doubt, but in theory of his own free will; as the peasant also does who is only bound to his lord by holding some *tenure*, or living on some particular spot. That is the position of the French *libre vilain*, the German *Landsasse*, the English *socman*. The 'unfree' man, on the other hand, is the man bound to a lord by a tie that is personal and hereditary, a tie which in some fashion attaches to his body from birth, and is in consequence rather degrading and socially incapacitating. These new forms of very ancient juridical conceptions, appearing— as it strikes us—rather late in time, had occurred inside *seigneuries* already formed, *seigneuries* with no slaves. We may even say that they assume the absence of slaves. For such changes of meaning were only possible because the notion of slavery had lost its ancient content, almost spontaneously.

Instructive as these facts are, it must not be forgotten that they bear only on one aspect of the *seigneurie*, and that perhaps not the most important aspect. Using the terminology of the Caroliongian surveys, the rise of servile *manses* is perfectly explained by the decline of slavery and slave gangs. This decline may therefore suffice to account for the formation of that very rare type of *seigneurie* which contained servile *manses* only, like Drancy, held in the ninth century by Saint Maur-des-Fossés. But it will not explain the formation of any other type. No doubt some free *manses* had a similar origin: there must have been among them a fair number of farms of ex-slaves who had been freed at the same time that they got their land. The freedman almost always remained bound to his old master, now his patron, and because his tenant, if he was not that already. We could not understand the multiplication of manumissions, during the first centuries of the Middle Ages, if these relations of tenurial and personal subordination had not persisted. Manumission did not imply the loss of all rights over a man; it only modified the nature of his subordination. In a word, the movement towards 'freedom' was at that time, in many ways, merely an episode in the decay of the *latifundium*, which was being gradually replaced by a regime of dependent tenure. It is also likely that the great proprietors when splitting up their demesnes were sometimes led to 'hut' a few landless or evicted freemen on some of the new-made holdings. That would lead to the creation of more free *manses*. But can we really suppose that all, or even the majority, of the little holdings which, although dependent, were labelled 'free', can have arisen in either of these two ways? Apart from the fact that our texts, in some cases, clearly tell a different story, mere probability is against any such hypothesis. Can we picture, across the ages, these societies of ours as built up exclusively from crowds of slaves, here and there a few day labourers, with above them all a handful of masters? We have then to explain how innumerable peasants, by ancestral status free—in the primitive sense; not slaves—had got entangled in the meshes of the *seigneurie*. That is really the crucial problem.

IV. *Government and the rise of the* 'seigneurie': *from the colonate to the immunity*

Only a few centuries were needed for the transformation of most of the slaves into tenants. A much longer time elapsed before the peasantry as a class was so transformed. Even in those areas earliest 'seignorialized', the existence of completed *seigneuries* of the classic type from Carolingian times by no means excludes other kinds of rural organization. The best comparison available for the condition of the Italian or Frankish countryside during the early Middle Ages is undoubtedly to be found in Latin America of the nineteenth century. The *haciendas* of Mexico or Chile, with their villages of *peons* in strict subjection, never formed a network so close as to leave no room for small independent landowners. In some French provinces, such as Burgundy, for which the documentary evidence is particularly abundant, we can clearly watch a long drawn out conquest by the *seigneurie*, resulting in uncertain and shifting relations with the conquered soil, right down to the thirteenth century. This is even clearer in England; and over wide areas conquest would never be complete. This very slow motion gives the historian opportunities for ascertaining and measuring the flow at many points. But it greatly complicated the movement, which passed across a series of very different social systems; so that care must be taken not to transpose automatically into a remote and misty past facts established for a later, and better documented, age. The simplest method will be to examine in turn the various agents whose working we can discern.

Older historians paid special attention to the action of the state, no doubt because the relative abundance of surviving governmental regulations made that action more easily traceable. But in this matter two great periods must be kept carefully apart—the last centuries of the Roman Empire; the age of the barbarian kingdoms, of the Carolingian Empire, and of its decline.

From our present point of view, the fundamental institution of the Later Empire is obviously the colonate. But the term must be used precisely; scholarship has suffered too much already from its vague use. The word *colonus* originally meant simply a cultivator. It was used early to describe, more particularly, one who cultivated for someone else, a farmer, a tenant. We may therefore, quite properly, describe as a movement towards the colonate that increase of small independent holdings so characteristic of the Roman world from about the second century. But it is probably wise to give the term that stricter legal meaning to be found in the legislation of the fourth and fifth centuries. Since Constantine's day, or perhaps rather earlier, there had been a great change in the situation of those cultivators who were not also proprietors: the law bound them from father to son to the land that they held—at least when they had held it for a certain period, which came gradually to be fixed at thirty years. So the *colonus* is no longer just a man who tills the land of another man. That he always is; but as this fact henceforward entails serious legal consequences, he is something more—a man who cannot quit his land and whom no one can detach from it. Personally, he remains free, in the sense that he is no one's slave, and so escapes the open brand of slavery. Imperial law never confused him altogether with the 'hutted' slave. But a sturdy fiction made him slave of a thing—his own fields, the clods to which he sticks, as they say, so closely that he cannot be pulled from them 'even for an instant'. In short, in the colonate so understood we are not dealing with an economic practice, in itself almost universal, but varying in extent from time to time. We are dealing with a legal institution, well defined and highly significant of a particular phase of history. Its possibly Hellenistic precedents do not here concern us. Its being and strength came not from the past but from the environment. It was introduced, like one of the wheels of a well-designed mechanism, into a vast scheme of social order conceived by a government on the defensive. In this Empire that resembled a besieged city safety seemed to lie in strict discipline, methodically organized food supplies, a regular yield of the taxes. To gain these ends, the emperors or their staff saw no better way than that of attaching almost every man, by hereditary and unbreakable ties, both to his mobilization centre and to his tax quota; the decurion to his municipal office (here the laws themselves draw the parallel with the colonate in so many words); the soldier to the army; the artisan to his trade *collegium*; lastly, the farmer to his fields.

These compulsions had not been devised in the interest of the great landowners. They bore on them also, and for that matter galled them. It was no longer possible, without breaking the law, to recover a bit of land in order to increase the demesne; to replace a tenant by a better man; to make provision in vacant parts of the *villa* for peasants who had run away from another lord. However, the new legislation cannot have seemed altogether unfavourable to the great landlords; for they had in some sort anticipated it by the simple exercise of the pressure of the strong upon the weak—so much so that one might perhaps even call the laws class legislation. A constitution of 244 shows us, in effect, that at this early date proprietors were trying, quite illegally, to retain tenants or their heirs after the expiry of their leases; and even that it had 'often' been necessary already to declare this practice illegal. It was because the labour problem had become acute in an empire where population was declining and influx of slaves slackening. If you had a man you did not lightly let him go. Imagine a system of control today under which an employer might not dismiss his men, nor the men leave the factory. No doubt it would be incompatible with economic liberalism, inimical to business expansion except by the buying up of rival concerns—yet it would most certainly transform each business into a disciplined group, exceedingly stable, in which the employer's authority over men who could only get a living on his premises would be greatly increased. Especially if the law made no mention of wage-rates. Now the imperial rescripts about the colonate never breathed a word about the tenants' burdens, except to refer to the custom; and as we shall see custom could be changed without too great difficulty. The comparison does not run quite on all fours, because it neglects differences of social environment. Yet it may help to suggest the way in which the binding of the *colonus* to the soil reinforced most effect-ively the dependence of small landholders on their lord. The institution so created ended in making perpetual relationships which apparently had often been thought of as temporary or revocable: it changed obligations of private contract into rules of public law, to the enforce-ment of which the state directed its still considerable powers.

More than that. Working along another line, policy towards the colonate ended by making the yoke of the aristocracy on the peasant

17

heavier. Not that emperors ever adopted the principle of governing through a caste of lords with quasi-legal powers. On the contrary, they always showed themselves properly suspicious of any interference between the sovereign and his subjects by local patrons or chiefs. But officials were too few, the administrative machinery too difficult to handle, for direct and permanent access to the masses; whether they would or not, emperors had often to make use of the higher ranks. It is very characteristic that—apart from some rules peculiar to the Hellenistic East, and based on its special traditions—not all peasants, which would have been logical, but only farmers were attached by the law to the soil. That was because the matter could be left to an existing authority and, if the law was not obeyed, a conspicuous individual, the great proprietor, could be called to account. Men were raised for the army from among the *coloni* by this same individual. More serious still, if we bear in mind how tragic the tax burden was for taxpayers and the financial problem for the government, was the fact that this *dominus fundi* was responsible for collecting the taxes of his tenants. After all, only inscription on the tax rolls made the system work; a rescript of 399, the more interesting for us because it applies to the West—it is addressed to the Pretorian Prefect of the Gauls—states that the *coloni* are 'the plebeians assigned by inscription to an estate'. And as the old word *colonus* might be considered ambiguous, because as we have seen it meant simply a man who cultivates the land of another, technical language referring to these fiscal arrangements tended more and more to describe the farmer bound to land that he had held for 30 years by the more exact term of *colonus adscriptitius*, even just *adscriptitius*. This recourse to the collaboration of the great men involved such dangers for the central power and was so closely associated with all the principles of the colonate that when, at a later date and in the East, emperors from the time of the Heraclian dynasty were trying to improve the machinery of the state, they believed that they could only do it by an entirely different agrarian policy which should foster communities of self-governing peasants. In the West, the Empire never had time to reverse the engine.

No doubt the law of the colonate had certain advantages for the cultivator. If he was not absolutely sure of keeping the same farm for ever—for being attached to the whole *fundus*, not to any particular part of it, he could always be moved legally from one to another—at least he was safe from actual eviction. He no longer ran the risk of becoming that most wretched of beings, a landless man. But his inability to move as he liked was so suggestive of servility, his dependence on a great man had such humiliating aspects, that these characteristics of his tenure soon brought with them a string of other restrictions; and the whole body of them became the criteria of a new social class placed at the very bottom of the ladder, in spite of its theoretical 'freedom'. By a significant change of language, where the old lawbooks talked about the *patronus* of the *coloni*—a classical name for a man who could give orders to a still free dependant—the later just used the word master (*dominus*), as you would for a slave. Already, in one of the earliest documents dealing with the institution, Constantine threatened with chains *coloni* suspected of planning desertion. That was the regular punishment of runaway slaves. Two and a half centuries later Justinian could write that it is not certain which is the worse, the condition of the slave or that of the *adscriptitius*.

Such were the laws. One would like to know how far they were carried out; especially those regulating that attachment to the soil which, to be effective, needed such elaborate police supervision. No doubt there were soon abuses enough, and more as the Empire declined. Society was not adapted to the strait-waistcoat that it was told to wear. In the fifth century Majorian complained of 'the dodges of those who will not stay in that state of life to which they were born'; and one chance bit of evidence tells us that *coloni* managed to slip from their native soil even into the imperial bureaucracy.[1] Yet this legislation of social defence must have contributed greatly to strengthen the tenurial system.

But quite evidently it did not create it. The laws never said that little independent peasants should submit to the authority of stronger men. They merely laid it down that a man who holds his land from another may not quit; and so will remain, with his descendants, perpetually bound to a subjection towards this patron, or this lord, which assuredly goes far beyond the ordinary economic relation of tenant and landlord. There would be no sense in such a policy unless it affected a numerous class, and it could hardly have worked—probably the very notion of it could not have arisen—unless it had been based on social customs which had long favoured the dependence of the weak. Even heredity and continuity of tenure were well known in practice long before they were prescribed by law, and before labour shortage forced the great land-owners to adopt them. The Antonines were ruling over an empire that had no need to contemplate laws of Constantine's sort when the farmers on an African domain described themselves as 'children born and brought up on the soil of the estate'.[2] The system of the colonate is only intelligible if we suppose that there existed before it a sort of embryo *seigneurie*.

Although an imperial law had proposed, in so many words, to fix the *colonus* to the soil 'for eternity', the legislation whose principles were

[1] *Nov. Valentin.* III, XXVII, I.
[2] *C. J. G.* VIII, 10570, ll. 28, 29.

laid down by Constantine was really only influential for a very short time, at least in the West—just as long as the Empire survived, or as long as it retained its vigour; no longer. This alone warns us not to exaggerate the influence of imperial policy. No doubt, in the barbarian kingdoms, *coloni* remained bound to their old masters, and the more securely as the personal nature of the tie became stronger, in a society which understood much more easily the notion of subjection to a person than the subtle fiction of 'servitude' to a piece of land. But the rule of bondage to the soil was not applicable if the state was not strong enough to track down runaways and, if necessary, impose its will on those who gained by welcoming them. The principle is of universal application. You cannot have a peasantry effectively bound to the soil without a strong central police authority; as in the Roman Empire; in Tsarist Russia; to some extent in Plantagenet England, in contrast to twelfth- or early thirteenth-century France. What police authority had the Merovingians? Or the Lombard kings? In fact, neither the barbarian laws nor the Carolingian capitularies contain a line that forbids tenants to desert their land, or the master to tear them from it. It is the lord's business to keep his tenants, legally or illegally. As the hallmark of a class, the legal principle of *adscription* fell into neglect. A new public law was to intervene in another way.

The difficulty which the later Empire, strong as it was, had found in direct government could not fail to be more acutely felt in the states which sprang up among the debris of *Romania*. The barbarian kingdoms could not handle the mechanism of administration that they had inherited. As for the old Germanic system of freemen's assemblies, it functioned with difficulty amid grave social transformations, and was ill suited to huge kingdoms, whose needs and whose size were utterly different from those of the little tribes and tribal leagues of yesterday. Finally, the decline of trade and the growing scarcity of money made the extension, or even the maintenance, of a large salaried officialdom more and more difficult; whilst every kind of obstacle to communications hindered the action of the central power. It seems that the Visigothic monarchy had already appreciated the possible means of making good this lack of direct control. The point was recognized quite clearly when the Carolingian dynasty, under Pepin and Charlemagne, made its ambitious—and in the long run vain—attempt to utilize the relation of dependence, which already held men together, for the maintenance of public order. 'Let every lord put pressure on his dependants, that they may better and better obey and accept imperial orders and instruction': that phrase from a capitulary of 810 summarizes with trenchant brevity a thoroughly deliberate policy.[1] But already almost

---

[1] *Capitul.* I, no. 64, c. 17.

everywhere practices had grown up, through sheer necessity, which the Carolingians, for their part, could do no more than systematize, though they tried to do this with characteristic energy.

Quite in harmony with Roman tradition, the barbarian kingdoms had as a rule trusted the lords to bring their free followers to the host; to levy from them, and subsequently transmit, supplies in kind for the army; and to handle the taxes in the same fashion, so far as any taxes survived. The sacrifice of the tax revenue itself ordinarily found in Frankish 'immunities', to which reference will be made shortly, together with that of all the public services made in special—but very rare—grants, marked however a step forward and a most decisive one. But the innovation, in principle at least, affected primarily the judicial field.

The judicial history of the barbarian states presents many very complex and often obscure problems. What makes them especially troublesome is the difficulty of drawing the essential yet infinitely delicate distinction between what the law prescribed and what really happened. A full discussion is out of the question here. Yet the broadest lines can easily be made clear. By a series of privileges, in the Frankish state called immunities, which have parallels under other names almost everywhere and especially in Anglo-Saxon Britain, the kings grant to certain lords rights of jurisdiction over their lands and the men who lived on them, even when free. As a matter of fact, the Frankish immunity, in its strict sense, seems to have been granted almost exclusively to churches. Whether it was ever extended to laymen is disputed; if it ever was, the thing happened very rarely; for the formularies ignore it. But a similar result was reached by the working of the donations which were so freely made by the king to his followers sometimes in the form of benefices, sometimes as out and out gifts. The royal domains too, controlled by their own administrators, were largely withdrawn from the authority of the king's regular agents; and their position was in fact that on which the immunities for religious houses had originally been modelled. Now when a royal domain was granted to a private person it was regularly given 'the whole immunity' which it had previously enjoyed, as the texts put it. Probably the larger part of great men's estates came to them in this way from princely generosity; and no doubt they had early been able to extend the advantages enjoyed on that part to their hereditary lands, either by express grant or by simple usurpation. The princes were influenced in making the grants, or tolerating the usurpations, by various motives—piety or, if that is preferred, anxiety about their own salvation, in the case of ecclesiastical *seigneuries*; the pressure of the aristocracy, eager to increase its own authority and, above all, to keep the detested officials of the crown from intruding on its lands (their exclusion was the essence of the Frankish immunity); finally, the fact already noted, that no prince was able to act effectively in such matters, either in person or through trustworthy agents. The royal concessions, it should be added, were not absolutely comprehensive. In certain cases and for certain crimes they reserved the rights of the king's courts, the sole business of the grantee, in such circumstances, being to insure the appearance in court of his subordinates; and no doubt the kings, when acting in this way, thought that they were sacrificing what they were very likely to lose in any event in order to keep what might be saved. Only, as it happened, since the state got weaker and weaker—on the Continent, after the collapse of the Carolingian Empire; in England at the time of the Danish invasions—the lords kept those judicial powers that had been given them and usurped all or part of the rest, though the extent of these usurpations varied greatly from country to country.

Now in this way the *seigneurie* acquired a powerful instrument of consolidation and expansion—not merely through the bare right of judicial decision, but also and perhaps mainly through the confusion of this right with the right to issue orders and punish those who disobeyed; in Frankish terminology, the *ban*. This valuable right had originally been reserved to the king and his representatives. Even so, it had been in danger of falling into private hands. For the high officials, exercising it as agents of the king, often monopolized it for their own advantage. The capitularies reveal clearly the way in which counts, or their subordinates, were apt to treat as their own dependants those whom the state had entrusted to them. They went so far as to force the unhappy and almost defenceless freemen to work like 'corvéable' dependants in their fields and vineyards and meadows. Many a group of men was annexed to a *seigneurie* in this lawless fashion, there can be no doubt. But the working of the immunities had far wider and far more durable results than this. Among those who lived on immune land, or those who though living outside it had commended themselves to its lord, a great many had at the outset been very loosely bound to the lord and owed but little to him. The *ban* allowed him to stiffen up both the relationship and its practical burdens. It is significant that, on the Continent, many of the largely novel rights which lords are claiming from the tenth century onwards—especially the monopoly of mill, oven, and winepress—are ordinarily called *banal* rights. It is not less significant that in England, where in many ways the course of events was so different, the typical tenure of a free man came to be called socage, from soke, the exercise of judicial power.

But, here again, we evidently have to do with a development which, though capital, is still secondary. Let there be no mistake: immunities and the like gave legal force to an existing movement, and canalized it; strictly speaking, they created nothing. Indeed it was not before Justinian's day that the law, for the first time, did expressly permit the *dominus fundi*, in one particular case, to chastise his *coloni* 'moderately'; and of Western countries, only Italy obeyed Justinian. However, there had always been one exception: ever since *coloni* were first bound to the soil, the law had made it a lord's duty to keep them there by force. But for the state to require great proprietors to hand over malefactors found on their lands, as it did, was already a partial delegation of public authority. Moreover is not every huge enterprise almost necessarily led to provide its own internal policing, indeed its own courts? In our case, this necessity was the more strongly felt because the enterprise formed a close group, isolated in the country, and often a very long way from any centre of government. The sort of thing that we can see, almost under our eyes, on a Latin American *hacienda* can help us to imagine the play of forces on an average Roman *fundus*. In fact, our sources show clearly that, from the end of the Empire in the West and in the first centuries of the barbarian kingdoms, the 'powerful', who naturally exercised the traditional right of punishing even their 'hutted' slaves, and maintained discipline when slaves quarrelled among themselves, stretched these powers so as to include all their dependants. So much so that the emperors felt obliged to prohibit private prisons in 388—for freemen of course; the slaves' *ergastulum* had always been there. Rather more than a century later the biographer of St Cesarius of Arles, boasting of his clemency, tells us how very few strokes of the rod the good bishop inflicted on his 'free' dependants or on his slaves. On the legal side, this private justice, in so far as it was not considered simply as an abuse, was not easily distinguished from ordinary domestic discipline or settling of disputes. In fact it was already a rudimentary seignorial justice; for the 'immunity' could not have worked with success if its recipient had not long been used to play the part assigned to him in his grant.

Beyond doubt the story of seignorial origins is closely bound up with that of the states. These, as a matter of fact, made history less through their legislation than by their sheer debility. The *seigneurie* grew at their expense. In this connexion nothing is more significant than the history of one single word: the word written *angaria* in the Latin sources. It came from the term which, in Achaemenian Persia, was applied to the messengers of the Great King. Borrowed, by way of Hellenistic civilization, from that old Iranian monarchy which served as a model of empire for the Mediterranean world, the Romans used it, first of all, to describe levies made for the postal service; then to any services owed to the state. The Middle Ages applied it to services (*corvées*) owed to the *seigneur*: there were in fact hardly any compulsory services but those. It would appear that requisitions for the king's army, still often referred to in Carolingian surveys, were subsequently swallowed up into the dues demanded from the tenant by his master. Each line of inquiry leads to the same conclusion; these effects of vicissitudes in the strength of the state; the particular character of its decadence; perhaps in some degree that decadence itself; none of these things could be explained without the underlying system of a dependent peasantry, on which the forces from above played. It is the nature of that substratum that we must now try to examine.

V. *Protection and commendation*

It is well known that the later years of the Roman Empire witnessed, not the birth of a system of personal patronage, for the institution had remote precedents in all constituent parts of *Romania*, but at least its immense expansion. The best, because the simplest and most comprehensive, formula describing what the weak man expected of his strong protector—the client of his patron—is that of St Augustine. 'To any one who threatens him a great man's client replies: So long as my lord here is safe and sound you can do nothing against me.' We must remember that the adversary so addressed need not be a private enemy or a rich oppressor. He may just as well be a recruiting sergeant, a judge, or—most likely of all—a tax-gatherer. The state, which expected a great deal from weak men and did not quite know how to protect them against the worrying of its own servants, had difficulty in bending the strong to its will. To avoid its pressure, there was no surer means than to hide in the shadow of some high-placed or rich individual. It was not always willingly that a man acquired a master in this way. To increase his authority, his prestige, his fortune, every fairly high-placed personage wanted to surround himself with as many dependants as he could: they owed him help, service and sometimes actual dues. The great man could thus exert every kind of pressure—and no doubt his seizure of control, whether abrupt or gradual, was at least as common as the spontaneous search for his protection.

Many of these clients were peasants: *clientela rusticorum* is a contemporary and semi-official term. Among the many kinds of agreements for protection, one of the most stringent, but probably not least common, was that by which the small cultivator transferred his land to his patron. He was not as a rule actually dispossessed. He gave it to get it back again; but henceforward as a *colonus*. So the great *fundi*, with their massed dependent tenures, extended their nets further and further. And individual acts of submission were not the only sort.

Whole rural communities sometimes accepted a protector. Thus arose that *patrocinia vicorum* so often denounced in the laws. For the establishment of these 'one-man' villages, villages from which that man could so easily exclude royal judges or tax-gatherers, rightly appeared a very grave evil. The emperors fought against it, but without much success. Forbidding it for the future in 415, they were obliged to condone all the past. It is true that this collective subjection seems to have been mostly found in the East. But it is hard to believe that the West was quite free of it. It did not create *seigneuries* in the medieval sense. The protector of a village, there can be little doubt, received presents or dues from his clients, by way of recompense; but being a stranger and having usually no demesne there, he did not claim services; and the land was not at law 'held' from him. Even when the villagers were *coloni*, they sometimes chose a patron whom they thought would be a better protector than their *dominus fundi*. He was usually a soldier. In this case patron and landlord were not blended. But, as we learn from a discourse of Libanius, the patron tended to supplant the lord. It was not yet strictly a seignorial system. That assumes the union of power over men with power over land. But it was clearing the way for it. Already the shadow of the soldier-lord is being thrown across the countryside.

After the invasions this drift towards order and obedience was naturally accentuated. It spread to Germanic societies which—apart always from Scandinavia—found themselves for the first time closely associated with the Roman world in the same political organizations and, as time went on, in a common civilization. The movement drew fresh strength from the collapse of state authority combined with the last attempts made by rulers to exercise powers which, weak as they were, they had not resigned themselves to lose. We have several records of peasants who surrendered themselves and their lands to a master in order to avoid military service. There was another motive force at work: the weakening of the principle of consanguinity—in clans, tribes, or similar groups; groups which, in Germany and perhaps even in *Romania*, had long been thought of as a man's adequate shelter against the arrogance of the strong. Friesland furnishes a most illuminating instance: a land where there was neither lord nor vassal, it was also one of the lands in which the bonds of blood proved most durable. Relations between lord and dependant naturally borrowed some fresh colouring from the influence of Germanic tradition; *chivage*, which became a characteristic test of complete subjection, is no doubt connected with the poll taxes of freedmen (*lites* or *Lazzen*) in Germanic law. The habits of the German *comitatus* left their mark on the relationship of lord and vassal. At length, as all know, there blossomed out what we generally call the feudal system—defining it by criteria drawn both from the rules which bound the higher ranks and from the scheme of political organizations. No doubt it would be more exact to call it the system of vassalage and of the fief. A very simple and striking test proves that there was some relationship between feudal institutions and the essentials of the seignorial system. Most societies which had no *seigneuries*—such as Friesland, Dithmarschen, Norway—also had no vassalage and no fiefs. No doubt there is at least one exception: Sardinia, with no vassalage and no feudal tenures, nevertheless had rural *seigneuries*. Still, there remains this general coincidence. And there is a fact perhaps more significant still: regions imperfectly 'seignorialized' were also imperfectly feudalized. Here the test is the number of allodial holdings. An *alleu* (*allod*) was a holding absolutely free, over which no superior had rights, which owed dues or services to no one, the possession of which involved no loyalty or obedience to any individual. The little rustic holding that had remained outside the seignorial net was an *alleu*. So might a *seigneurie* be in spite of its basic stratum of dependent tenants, provided the lord owed homage for it to no one. Now, wherever we find a comparatively large number of allodial *seigneuries*, we note that far more peasant *alleux* than are to be found elsewhere have also survived, for a long time, or even permanently: in Saxony, for example, or in South-Western France. Again, England before the Conquest, where relations of vassalage were most imperfect, had also a very loose system of dependent peasant tenures. These coincidences cannot be the result of chance; and in fact the relation between these two sides of the social structure are tolerably clear. Both reflected the same needs, though at different stages of the social hierarchy; and in both the needs expressed themselves in customs which were in many ways similar.

In the upper social classes, the bond of protection and subjection was embodied in two legal acts, often simultaneous. The personal act: homage, with its symbolic rite and usually its oath. The real act: the owner of an *alleu*, in this case normally a *seigneurie*, yields it to his lord, to receive it back from him henceforward as a fief involving military and other services, and the obligation of fidelity. Turning to what we may call the peasant classes—using the term to cover actual cultivators of very varied grades—we notice a most striking parallel between the base and the summit of the social hierarchy: we find that these humble folk also deliver up to the lord both man and land.

Defective as our sources are, from Carolingian times to the twelfth century two sorts of characters or references exist in really impressive numbers. At one time we see the peasant, just like the humble folk of the later Empire, yielding his land to a lord, then resuming it, but burdened with dues and services. 'There are here', the survey of Santa

Giulia of Brescia records from about the year 900, 'fourteen free men who have handed over their property to the hall (*curtis*), the condition being that each shall do one day's work a week.' At another time it is the man himself who seeks the protection, the *mundium* of a lord, 'commends himself' to him in the phrase which is specially common in England. Few things are more instructive than this word *commandise*: it was also applied for a long time to the homage of a vassal, and by this double use shows clearly the original relationship of these two degrees of personal subordination. But there was a capital difference between them. The high-born man submits himself and his life alone: the little man almost always gives away his posterity; and that was why obligations of this sort, which robbed the descendants of any power of choice, seemed opposed to freedom and came in the long run, as we have seen, to be described as servile, in that new sense which the word gradually acquired.

Perhaps because the personal bond was in this way so strict, the two sorts of submission were less necessarily associated among the lower than among the upper classes. The high-placed owner of an *alleu* who accepts it as a fief must take his vassal's oath. The peasant owner can quite easily change his coat for that of a tenant without changing in any way his personal status. In tenth- and eleventh-century Burgundy tenures of this kind were often expressly called *franchises*: even the dues which they owed were also often called *franchises*. The tenant was in this way labelled a freeman. But we must take care in our interpretation: the *franc tenancier*—the *Landsasse* of German surveys—it is true was attached to his lord by bonds far less galling than those of serfdom: they did not rob him of the social privileges of 'freedom'; and, above all, they did not bind the 'bodies' of his descendants. All the same, he became one of a disciplined group: he owed help and obedience to the lord of his land, and might expect from him some measure of protection. It can never be too often repeated: in the Middle Ages to be free was not to be masterless; it was to be attached to one's master in what was felt to be an honourable, and was not an hereditary, fashion. The protection offered by the lord in case of danger was moreover—as our sources show—the already discounted payment for the new burdens accepted by his small holders.

When we turn to the acts of personal surrender, which are apparently at least the more numerous, we note with some surprise that as a rule they make no reference to the land. The only dues usually stipulated for are those laid on the man himself or his descendants: most often they take the form of a poll-tax. But who would suppose that the protecting lord expected to get only these very modest sums? Everything indicates that—except in the obviously rare cases in which he was dealing with indigent landless men—he used the disciplinary powers which were recognized as his to bring the property of his client under control and burden it with dues and services—either by tacit agreement, or even by a breach of the original contract. So that when by chance the land already owed a quit-rent to someone else, there was risk of such a dispute as that which broke out at the opening of the tenth century between the Abbey of St Gall and the church of Constance, between the old lord of the soil and the new lord of the man. From the eleventh century, the *mundiales* of the monasteries of Lorraine, whose name clearly refers to the protection, the *mundium*, of these humble folk, owed quite heavy agricultural services.

We must not be misled by the mere form of these contracts. We must deal with them as cautiously as with the 'patronates' of the later empire. The medieval contracts of subjection regularly purport to be inspired by the free will of the new subject and especially, when the lord is a church, by piety. But in social life is there any more elusive notion than the free will of a small man? Competition between large and small farming found in other ages, which made the small man's position difficult, is not in question here. Apart from its demesne, the *seigneurie* was nothing but an agglomeration of small dependent holdings: a peasant *alleu*, once handed over, simply took its place in the mosaic without any change in its cultivation. But there were many other forces at work to make the small man pliable; from hunger—sometimes a declared cause, but generally in the case of landless labourers—to the wish to share in those common rights which a lord reserved for his dependants; up to that sheer oppression, about which the written contracts are of course chastely silent, but which many other sources disclose.

Consider, for instance, the charter of the monastery of St Mihiel which records the tribulations of a widow in a village of Lorraine. She was a well-born woman—the document says 'noble'—and her land, classed as an *alleu*, was by tradition exempt from all burdens. Nevertheless the officials of a neighbouring lord claimed a quit-rent from this little estate. All that the lady could do to escape their persecution was to accept the protection of the monks. But for this way of escape, can we doubt that the *alleu* would soon have become a *tenure* of the village tyrant?[1] Elsewhere, if violence did not create ties, it strengthened them remarkably. The chronicle of the Swiss monastery of Muri has made famous the adventures of the peasants of Wolen, about the middle of the eleventh century. Free allodial holders, they had seen fit to seek as protector a powerful man called Guntramm; they surrendered their lands and got them back for quit-rents. This was all that they had agreed to.

[1] A. Lesort, *Chronique et chartes . . . de Saint-Mihiel*, no. 33.

Their position was thus more favourable than that of the older tenants who owed heavy services. But Guntramm soon tried to bring them down to the same level. He demanded plenty of work on his demesne. He claimed payment for their traditional use of the forest. Relying on their rights, the peasants decided to make a protest. They went to Solothurn where the king was staying. But among all the great barons this handful of rustics, with their coarse patois, could not get a hearing. When their village passed subsequently to the monastery, the services had been sanctioned by long usage: the monks continued to exact them. In this troubled society, whose central authority could not get into effective touch with the masses, violence helped to transform social conditions the more effectively because, through the play of custom, an abuse might always by mutation become a precedent, a precedent a right.

It cannot be doubted that many new *seigneuries* were created in this way—probably far more than we shall ever know. For our sources have the grave defect of telling us almost exclusively about the great *seigneuries*, which also were usually the oldest. The seignorial system was far from losing its powers of growth by the end of the first feudal age. Any possessor of a fair-sized rural estate—a peasant grown rich, a manorial official grown important in his master's service, a lucky man-at-arms—had only to stop tilling it all himself, cut two or three holdings out of it, or attach some other peasant's holdings to it; and soon this parvenu would become a lord in a small way. For in those days it was hard to think that one man could hold land of another, especially if it was held from father to son, without being, by that very fact, in some way under his landlord's authority. Feudal society did not understand purely economic relationships. Justice itself was so close to the business of carrying out judicial decisions, that the right to levy dues on land carried with it, almost automatically, the right of deciding cases that arose out of the levy: we actually know of a *vilain* in the Île de France, as late as the twelfth century, who although a tenant had a sub-tenant below him, and who managed to establish his claim to judge his sub-tenant if he did not pay his quit-rent.[1] The distinction between a lord and a mere lessor, between a subject and mere lessee, would only be established very slowly, and by the action of a jurisprudence more refined than that of the early feudal centuries.

But we must admit that most cases clearly known to us reveal not so much the absolute beginnings of seignorial power as the extension of powers already existing. Here and there—in Germany particularly down to a rather late date—we see whole villages submitting themselves to some great man who, however, owns other villages. Elsewhere,

---

[1] *Cartulaire du prieuré de N.D. de Longpont*, no. 35.

fairly important groups submit by common consent. But usually, like the fourteen freemen of Brescia or the villagers of Wolen, they submit, whether they like it or not, to some ancient *seigneurie*. And most of the acts of submission are those of single families. As only a master already strong could protect a man effectually; as only a prominent personage of this kind could put decisive pressure on a man (we must always consider heads and tails!)—the protector of lands or body was generally an individual, or religious institution, already protecting other dependants in the same fashion. So a *seigneurie*, once only a modest nucleus, threw out long tentacles on every side. This dispersion through growth raised serious problems of administration. It certainly did make the working of the system of labour services and the upkeep of vast demesnes appreciably more difficult. But no essential change had been made in the nature of the institution. Even when the lord was a new man in every sense of the word, his relations with his tenants were likely to be modelled on a traditional plan. The very silence of so many documents as to the precise meaning of the tenant's burdens, a silence which can only be explained by an implied custom, is in itself exceedingly instructive.

But one country provides us with a still more significant experiment. Consider the structure of English society during the century before the Norman Conquest. The great men have vast demesnes cultivated largely by slaves—for slaves remained much more numerous at this time in England than on the Continent—but also with the help of tenants' services. Other slaves are established on the land. Side by side with these servile tenures are quantities of little dependent holdings, whose holders are still counted freemen. They are for the most part regularly protected by someone. Anglo-Saxon society is exceedingly disturbed, like the continental societies, and the independence of the weak is gravely endangered. Like the Carolingian state, the Anglo-Saxon state wishes humble men to have superiors who can vouch for them; it is extremely suspicious of lordless folk. (It also makes use at the same time of methods of collective responsibility unknown in Frankish Gaul.) Yet there still survives a very dense network of peasants whose land is held from no lord—held allodially, as they would say elsewhere. Everything has its parallel across the Channel. And yet it is hard to speak of an English seignorial system. At most there is only the first sketch of such a system. All the institutions are so loose, so shifting, so ill adjusted, that they cannot produce well articulated and disciplined groups fit to conduct economic enterprises that will function properly. The holdings are often scattered far and wide, not conveniently arranged about a central demesne. Some of the dependants seem only to have commended their persons. But many have 'come to the lord with their land'. Among these, some can break their tie with him at will: 'they can go with their land to whatever other lord they wish.' Sometimes jurisdiction is with one lord while service is owed to another; or jurisdiction over a man is with a lord to whom he is not commended. And as the role of judicial assemblies of free men, on the German model, remains considerable, it complicates matters; for the king may have handed over one of these 'hundred courts' to some great man, his perpetual delegate, who will thus become one more personage on the list of those upon whom the peasant is, in some sense, dependent.

It is not our business to try to explain how, out of all these diverse elements, the conquering aristocracy, with brutal vigour, managed to build up the manor. But the value of one significant word should be stressed—the classic word 'manor' itself. In the Norman French of the conquerors, it had nothing to do with jurisdiction. It meant a good substantial house, such as a Norman lord usually occupied. But when they had to find a label for the complex whole of dependent farms and subject people which henceforward was grouped about the fields of the demesne, one name came naturally to their lips—the name of the headquarters from which orders were issued, and to which were brought both the lord's harvests and the pennies or the produce that tenants owed. In just the same way in Eastern France *cour*; in Italy *corte*; in Germany *Hof*—that is, in each case, the lord's own dwelling enclosure— often served to describe the whole *seigneurie*, including the *tenures*. In England, in the early days, hall was readily used as the equivalent of the foreign word. The house of the local magnate was the necessary centre of every genuine *seigneurie*.

The lesson to be drawn from England is clear. Castile enforces it, if anything with greater emphasis; because in Castile no conquest, imposing by violence arrangements favourable to the interests of the conquerors and agreeable to their habits, had come to disturb the natural course of evolution. Castile too had known a system of peasant commendations which, under the name of *behetrías*, often embraced whole villages;[1] but it only led very late and very rarely to the establishment of *seigneuries* properly so called, on the French, German or Italian model. Relationships of commendation, of the sort that we find in the feudal era and that immediately preceding it, were able to give to an existing seignorial system immense expansive force; but by themselves were powerless to create such a system, and to make of it a clearly defined social type, juridically and economically dominant. In those countries that were 'seignorialized' profoundly and spontaneously, seignorial origins go back to social arrangements older and unhappily much more obscure than feudalism or the patronate of the later Empire.

[1] Cf. p. 435, below.

VI. *Chiefs and villages*

The surest index that we have of the existence of rural chiefdoms in primitive Europe comes from the study of place names. Everywhere, masses of the most ancient villages bear the names of men, generally followed by a proprietary suffix which varies with the language. In *Romania*, Germanic personal names in combinations of this kind usually indicate that the place was only named after the invasions, and so do not take us very far back. But the map swarms with Roman names. In France for example there can be no doubt that the vast majority of the Antonii of Antony or Antoigné, or the Flavii of Flaviac or Flavy (to quote a couple of examples from among thousands) lived under the emperors. Here and there older ages of Gaul are revealed: Brennus, of the legendary capture of Rome by the Gauls, survives in the Brenats and the Bernys. Roman or Romanized Italy has its Corneglianos and Savignanos. Germanic countries show native personal names with various suffixes, of which the oldest are in *-ing* and in *-heim*. (The old view that the *-ing* suffix implied tribes or clans has given way to the view that it merely implies any sort of dependence; the Heuchlingen may be Huchil's men or his relatives, perhaps both.) But it is not enough to establish that names of this sort exist almost everywhere; we ought to be able to measure their density, which obviously varies from region to region. Unfortunately place-names study has not yet reached the statistical stage. It does, however, seem that the density is particularly high in Gaul.

Naturally, names of this sort had no guarantee of immortality. A revolution in village life might always lead to a change of name. But for that, names with a Celtic element would obviously be far commoner in France than they are; moreover we know about medieval rebaptisings of villages. Yet such changes occurred only sporadically and at long intervals. (We shall see shortly why they were probably most frequent at the opening of the Roman era.) As a rule, the settlement and its territory retained, through the ages, the name of some long forgotten person; as if a half religious reverence clung to the memory of the ancestor whose aura still floated over the soil. What precisely had this eponymous hero been when alive? A great proprietor who assigned land to his slaves? All that we know of old Celtic, Italiot or German society—in which slaves were beyond a doubt infinitely fewer than free men—or, indeed of the society of the Roman era, in which there was never anything like a complete system of rural slavery, absolutely excludes this as a general explanation. Was he a lord? In the medieval sense of the word it would be an anachronism so to describe him. Yet whatever juridical word would fit him best—and in this connexion we must recall, with Antoine Meillet, the extraordinary mobility in Indo-European languages, of substantive expressive of the authority to command—how can we fail to suppose that this man whose name the village took was some sort of a chief or, in the phrase that French documents of the *ancien régime* still applied to the seigneur, 'le premier habitant'?

Scanty as narrative sources are for these remote times, they still yield a little valuable information. Caesar pictures Gaulish society before the Roman conquest as dominated by an aristocracy of 'knights' who owe their strength to their 'clients'. This latter Roman term could give only an approximately accurate notion of the Celtic reality. To Caesar's mind it implied men free but dependent. Themselves probably of very varied rank and condition, they would be attached to the chief by all kinds of ties of subordination and interest, including—as so often, under our eyes, with the Chilean *peon* and his *haciendado*—that of debtor and creditor. Although some may have lived in the master's house, there were certainly far too many of them for that to be the rule: how could he have fed them? And as they cannot have been concentrated in the towns, which were few and unimportant, they must have been, for the most part, countrymen. Besides, the great men who were surrounded by these vast clientèles were also rich men. Most of their wealth must have come from the land. But how? Likely enough slaves cultivated some land for them directly—some modest embryonic *mansi dominicati*. We cannot imagine that they had vast slave gangs working on *latifundia*. There is no suggestion that crowds of slaves surrounded them. Can we doubt that they drew largely on requisitions or gifts from peasant clients? And that there were whole dependent villages is not merely a matter of conjecture. Caesar tells us that Lucterius the Cadurcian had the fortified 'town' of Uxellodunum dependent on him. It is highly probable that this was not an exceptional arrangement.

Turn to a related society at a parallel stage of evolution, first-century Germany. Tacitus calls the hereditary chiefs of little local groups *principes*. In the same language, familiar to Latin writers, Livy had pictured the 'princes' of the eagles' nests among the mountaineers of Northern Italy: *principes castellorum*. And this is how Tacitus describes the revenues of these odd little potentates, or at least that part of their resources which did not come simply from their own land cultivated by a few slaves or freedmen whom they sometimes set up as farmers. 'It is the custom', he says, 'that each tribesman shall give the chief presents either of cattle or of part of his harvest. These free gifts are marks of respect, but they also supply the needs of those who receive them.' This description is most instructive. The gift, Tacitus insists, is free. But it is also customary. In a society ruled by respect for the past, a traditional gift is very near indeed to an obligation. After all—gift and custom—we may say without exaggeration that these linked notions dominated the beginnings of seignorial dues and services. In the Middle Ages dues were usually called simply 'customs'; as if, when you thought of any due, you had in mind immediately its sole juridical basis. And page after page could be filled with the deliveries in kind, in money, or in service which—throughout the whole evolution of the *seigneurie*—were described as gifts, prayers, *demandes*, *bede* (that is, in modern German, *bitte*), boon-work, *bienfait* (*beneficium*, in the *polyptyque* of Montierender), *requête*, *eulogies*. Simple terms of courtesy, for the most part, no doubt, or even hypocritical disguises of harsh compulsions; when a man was angry or perfectly frank he might talk about 'exactions'. Yet the terms had often some correspondence with ancient fact. First you made a request, doubtless accompanied by gentle but firm pressure; later you made a demand, arguing from precedent. Those 'oblations' of capons, of pigs, of loaves and even of money which, as late as the twelfth century, some Lotharingian tenants had to bring to their lord in person, when they paid him solemn visits on certain great occasions, differed very little from the gifts reported by Tacitus. Like them they were marks of respect; like them they symbolized submission in its most concrete form; like them, in the end, they were made obligatory by an iron tradition.

There is no great difficulty in finding other relevant evidence. The most useful comes from societies which were absorbed into western civilization rather later than those referred to so far. The *machtierns*— that is to say chiefs who stood surety for their men—referred to in some Armorican sources of the ninth to the eleventh century, have been much discussed. There can however be no great doubt about the main features of the institution. Some Latin ecclesiastical writers who relish both the pun and the hit at a lay power call these *machtierns* the parish tyrants: they 'own' the parish (*plebs*: Breton, *plou*): they 'reign' over it by hereditary title. They witness grants of land in the parish. Perhaps they sometimes levy a fine when land changes hands by sale, as the medieval seigneur did later. In fact we know that they became vassals at an early date. Some of them are even found among the vassals of the Frankish Empire; some founded knightly families.[1] We can hardly fail to recognize them as ancestors, part ancestors at least, of that Breton seignorial class which later documents reveal. In a kindred society, that of Wales, though at a still later date and no doubt under the influence of neighbouring English institutions, the 'kings' of the *cantrefs* or hundreds became lords of the ordinary sort. This last instance

[1] A. de Courson, *Cartulaire de l'abbaye de Redon*, nos. CXCVI, CCCLX.

shows us clearly how an embryo manor, and under favourable circumstances a real one, could develop itself around the nucleus of a small demesne the cultivation of which had been mainly entrusted to slaves, by subjecting different categories of dependants to food-rents, to the duties of forced hospitality, and to some services. In this case the dependants would include *taeogs*, probably for the most part men of a conquered race, and free tribesmen who had to obey the chief in spite of their hereditary 'liberty'.

Analogies can be drawn, hints can be taken, from more remote civilizations. The history of the Comans, established on Hungarian land in 1243, starts indeed quite differently from anything Western. They were in fact pastoral nomads who had taken abruptly to a sedentary life. Western peasantries had only passed from a collecting and hunting to an agricultural civilization very slowly, and in remote ages. But much can be learnt from the way in which, among these former shepherds, a nomad chief was gradually transformed into a landed proprietor. In the Maghreb today a great man—often a marabout—may succeed, by an equally significant transformation, in securing control over a rural community and making it tributary to him. Even among the Thai of Indo-China there are distinct traces of a similar process. The chiefdoms of black Africa, when we get to know them better, will no doubt also furnish examples.

Coming back to the European *seigneurie* we can unearth in it various survivals from a very remote past. We have all heard of those practices which old French feudal lawyers called *droits ridicules*, a term which shows how much the practices surprised them. They are such things as games, dances, various rites (a compulsory bath for example) which the inhabitants of certain villages, or some of them, and particularly the young folk, had to perform before their lord. Belated attempts were made to find rational explanations of these things; but really they had none. Take the famous duty of flogging the moats of the château on certain nights, in order, so they said, to prevent frogs from disturbing the lord's rest. Would the sound of beaten water be really more conducive to sleep than the sound of croaking frogs? Why only on certain nights? Was the lord to lie awake the rest of the year? Let the folklorist explain these customs if he can. What concerns us is that in them the seigneur acts the probably very ancient part of a kind of president over ritual practices which have come down, there can hardly be any doubt, from an immense antiquity. And if the *jus primae noctis* sometimes did exist (and there are a few ugly suggestions to that effect, especially in documents from the Pyrenees) we most certainly have not to interpret it as the product of a petty tyrant's lust. We must look rather to some very old rite by which the chief deflowered virgins; and for this parallels could be found for us by anthropologists.

But the inquiry must not be conducted solely from the side of the lord. We can get just as important evidence from the study of peasant society itself. The master of a slave gang has no organized group with which to deal. The authority of a chief, on the contrary, is super-imposed on such a group but does not abolish it. It is therefore of the utmost importance to observe that in the countries with which we are concerned the *seigneurie* had by no means killed the village community. As far back as we can go, we find the two institutions living side by side. However dependent the rustic might be on his master, he was still always under the authority of the village group of which he was a part. That group never lost its own collective life, often very intense. No doubt its cohesive force varied with regional traditions and forms of settlement. But let us consider, for example in France, the districts where it was most fully developed. We shall find them unquestionably north of the Loire and on the Burgundian plain. In this land of big villages, open fields and long strips, regularly grouped in 'furlongs', the face of the country with its distinctive design suggests irresistibly that the original occupation of the soil was planned. Collective grazing rights over the stubble, and the compulsory rotation which forbade the cultivator to choose his own crops, were binding on all, often even on the seigneur and his demesne lands. Now this was also the classical area of the *seigneurie*, the one in which it was oldest and most solidly estab-lished. So it would be a grave error to assume any necessary opposition between the bonds of the village community and those of the *seigneurie*. Although custom was mainly responsible for the maintenance of the collective rights over the fields and the grazing arrangements, there was necessarily occasional intervention by some regulating authority with the sanction of some court in reserve. Under medieval conditions the lord's was the only court—and its members were often peasants. At law, the lord alone could issue orders, through his right of *ban*. In practice however he often left a fairly wide field for the action of the community itself, especially in the election or nomination of the village officials who saw that the rules were kept. Methods varied indefinitely, not only from region to region, but also from place to place in the same province. Yet it is never to be forgotten that even when the lord had the most complete monopoly of the issue of agrarian orders, he was always supposed to act in the interests of the community and as the interpreter of its tradition.

But two chief classes of evidence above all enable us to establish the survival of very ancient village institutions underlying the *seigneurie*. They also make clear the fluctuations in the progress of seignorial power. They come from the history of peasant agriculture and from that of common rights.

The *manse* we have already met. There is no more mysterious institution in all agrarian history. Nor is there any whose interpretation, if ever we can be quite certain about it, will throw more light on the remote pages of that history. A complete and certain interpretation is not yet possible; but some facts about the *manse* are already sure.[1]

First, that it is found almost all over Europe, under all sorts of names; *mansus* most often in Romance lands, but in Western Gaul under that of *factus*, a desperately obscure old word; *Hufe* in Germany; *hide* in England; *bol* in Denmark; possibly *ran* in Armorica. Contemporaries already recognized that these words all meant much the same thing; and the facts behind them were markedly similar. Because of the nature of our sources, the functions of *manse*, or *hide*, or *Hufe* (omit for a moment the *bol*) appear most clearly to us as part of the seignorial organization. It would obviously be a mistake to assume *a priori* that this aspect of the institution was primitive. But, as it is the aspect most easily examined, we may well begin with it.

In the medieval *seigneurie* a *manse*—for convenience we will keep to that word—was the customary unit of tenure. But all holdings were not *manses*. The *manse* often had as its neighbours, and on the same *seigneurie*, dependent holdings otherwise described. Their names varied: in Gaul the commonest was *hôtises* (*hospicia*); also *apendariae, laisines*, later *bordes* or *chevannes*; in Germany *Schupposen*. Just like the *manse*, the *hôtise* served as a unit for surveying purposes. In this period, we never hear of renders in money or kind or services as due from separate pieces of land. Apart from the strictly personal obligations, it was the entire holding, whatever it might be, that owed. Whether one tenant held it all or not was of no great importance. Although scattered all over the fields, its parts, from the seignorial point of view, made up a single taxable unit. But often the liabilities varied, in an oddly capricious way, from one *hôtise* to another. The *manses*, on the contrary, as we already know, were divided into well-defined juridical classes: *serviles*, *ingénuiles*, occasionally *lidiles* (from the Germanic *laet*, latinized as *lidus*, a freedman or sometimes the member of a conquered population). Within each category, and on the same *seigneurie*, the obligations were in theory uniform; so much so, that if you knew what was owed by the first on the list, you knew about all the rest. It is true that, now and then, there were subsections with different obligations within the same category. These anomalies, which in fact did not make things much more complicated, were found almost exclusively on the great

[1] Cf. p. 41 and p. 202 above.

seigneuries. Probably they reflect their history, each subsection corresponding to a fresh accession to their vast complexes of lands and rights, which had been built up stage by stage. Thus the rules for a *hôtise* were the result of the circumstances of each individual case; the rules for a *manse* were a matter of group custom. If we bear in mind further that there were always far fewer *hôtises* than *manses*; that they were on the average considerably smaller; and that, finally, among their very miscellaneous occupants are often found men expressly described as newcomers (*advenae*), we can hardly fail to see in them little holdings created late, on land hitherto unoccupied, by squatters, some of whom came from a distance while some were perhaps just younger sons of needy local families. The very words *borde, chevanne, Schuppose*—which literally mean 'cabin'—are significant. This practice of extending the description of the dwelling to the land dependent on it was common enough: the word *manse* (*meix* in Middle French, *mas* in Provençal) also, strictly speaking, meant the cultivator's dwelling. But the man who had a *manse* had a real house; he who held a *hôtise* seems to have had nothing but such a hovel as the custom of many villages—and not so long ago—allowed paupers and immigrants to build for themselves on the fringes of the commons, provided the materials were shabby enough. Documents later than the Carolingian surveys suggest that holders of *manses* were the only people who had a full share in the rights of common. In fact a *hôtise* was frequently a tenure *in posse*; when it had reached a certain size—probably by bringing fresh land under cultivation—the lord might decide to assimilate it henceforward to a *manse* or half *manse*; as if a well managed *seigneurie* ought, in contemporary language, to be all *amansée*. In short, the *manse* was the representative, and certainly the primitive, cell of the 'seignorialized' village.

But a still more important feature differentiated it from the *hôtise*: its permanence. No doubt during the era in which we can first clearly grasp the methods of seignorial administration, that is the ninth century, its indivisibility seems no longer absolute. Often two or more tenant householders live side by side on the same *manse*; a thing almost unknown on the *hôtises*, because as these had no standard size, if one of them was cut up, you simply said that there were now two or more. But the *manse* remained a fiscal and administrative unit, even if split among several holders. The surveys very seldom show the least interest in the way in which the land and its burdens were divided up among the heads of the holding families. The burdens, the only thing that mattered, were those of the *manse* as a whole; the coparceners owed them in common and, no doubt, jointly and severally. But it can hardly be supposed that the subdivision of the *manse* was a primitive thing. It would appear to be only the first stage in that disintegration, which was to lead—at amazingly different dates in different regions—to the disappearance of the *manse* itself. A unit of survey which, once it no longer coincided with the working facts, appeared only as a fictitious entry in the books of seignorial administration, could only be preserved by a great effort, an effort that was almost bound to fail in the long run. We notice that the survey of Saint German-des-Prés is already forced, whether it likes it or not, to find room in its statistics, indeed sometimes in connexion with the levying of dues, for the hearth as a unit. Other documents of the same date prefer to reckon by households, or by *coulonges* (*coloniae*), each containing a single ménage of tenants, rather than by *manses*. The way in which the documents have survived enables us only to observe the system, which was no doubt very old, at a time when—at least in the big villages of northern Gaul—it was already in a state of decay. Everything suggests that the original rule had been everywhere: one *manse*, one family. It was Bede who translated the English word *hide* by *terra unius familiae*.

The energy which the seignorial authorities expended in trying to maintain the system is sufficient proof that, by its regularity and stability, it greatly helped the levying and guaranteed the yield of the dues. But there is more direct evidence to the same effect. In 864 Charles the Bald is trying to check the threatening break-up of the *manse*. His expressed aim is to preserve the *seigneuries* from 'confusion', indeed from 'destruction'. In fact when, at a later date, the break-up was complete it became necessary to assess the dues on each parcel of land or on every house; and to require services from each head of a household in person. This was a great and troublesome complication which helped to hasten the remodelling of the *seigneurie* itself. Following the matter further, we can be sure that some of these *manses*, so useful to the lord financially, had been made by him in his own interest and all of a piece. These were the servile *manses*, cut out of the demesne for the use of the 'hutted' slaves. So too, no doubt, were those formed here and there, in conditions probably parallel, to establish freedmen (*manses lidiles*). But can we believe that the whole system was made by the lords? That the *manses ingénuiles* in particular, or most of them, were so made? This would imply that they functioned only inside *seigneuries*. But there were *manses* or *Hufen* in the Frankish state, and in England *hides*, in the hands of freemen who were subject to no one, either in person or for their lands, and who themselves cultivated holdings so described, as the Carolingian military capitularies, among other documents, testify. As for the Danish *bol*, it was to be found all over a country which at that time was in no way 'seignorialized'.

The history of public finance provides further valuable evidence.

Taxing authorities in great states made use of the *manse* or its equivalent; perhaps from as far back as the Roman Empire, if it is true—as it may well be—that the taxable units originally corresponded with agrarian cells of this type. The unit was officially called a *caput* or *iugum*, but in the provinces we know that there were a great variety of equivalents for these terms. We know too that Franks and Anglo-Saxons used the *manse* or the *hide* as the unit, when they made their levies to buy off or to fight Scandinavian pirates. This fiscal use reacted in the end on terminology: in Frankland the demesne which the lord himself culti-vated was also called *mansus* or *Hufe* (but with a distinctive prefix: *indominicatus, Salhufe*). If in England, on the contrary, the demesne was never called a hide, the reason seems to be that this was because it was not taxed, whereas among the Franks it was. However, no one would fancy that peasant *manses*, whether *tenures* or *alleux*, were simply invented and put on the map by bureaucrats who lacked a proper survey. Apart from anything else, their date and their regional dis-tribution are all against such a notion. We hear of *manse* and *Hufe* and *hide* well before the Scandinavian invasions; and the tax system of the later Empire, which one might perhaps be tempted to accept as the creator of the Roman *mansus*, could obviously not have created the *Hufe* beyond the Rhine, or the *hide*; still less the Danish *bol*. Evidently, governments or their experts did no more than utilize a system of land division already existing and widespread in ancient European rural society, and the lords did the same, for their own ends.

Terra unius familiae: Bede's words give us in all probability the key to the institution in its primitive form. But we are not to think of the little matrimonial family of our later ages. Ill informed as we are about the history of blood relationships in the dawn of our civilization, there is every reason to think that the group, whose original shell was the *manse*, was a patriarchal family of several generations and several collateral households living around a common hearth. Subsequently, the progressive distintegration of these large groups of blood relations, accompanied no doubt by a growth of population, led to the break-up of the *manse* itself; and the indivisibility that the lords were striving to maintain, from the ninth century onwards, was perhaps only a survival of old communal rules of inheritance which they had adjusted to their own interests. In the same way the Turks, as supreme landlords in Yugoslavia, preserved the integrity of the peasant *zadruga* until very recent times. It is certain that subdivision among many heirs, entailing a perpetual rearrangement of the tenancies, could not be viewed favourably by authorities anxious to maintain a regular levy of rents and services. In fact, they only acquiesced in it under pressure of changes in the surrounding legal atmosphere; or when the fines that they could exact at the deaths of tenants yielded more than the annual dues, and so made an increase in the number of occasions on which a fine could be secured advantageous to them. This only began to happen when the seignorial system was nearing its decline.

So we have every reason to suppose that the primitive occupation of the soil was carried out by patriarchal groups. Sometimes they lived apart from one another; in that case, protected by their isolation in regions of scattered settlement, they usually manifested remarkable power of resisting subdivision. Elsewhere they formed parts of larger, nucleated, village communities. Their shares were not equal. Tacitus had observed this inequality in the German villages long ago. And in the ninth-century surveys, although their descriptions are not so detailed as might be wished, nothing is more striking than the immense differences in area among *manses* of the same class within the same *seigneurie*. The exceptions to this that we find are probably to be explained by a secondary settlement in which the plan was made artificially regular. This lack of uniformity in the size of the typical *tenure* is, at first sight, the more surprising as it contrasts with the almost absolute uniformity of burdens. At Villeneuve-Saint-Georges, for instance, the smallest free *manse* has exactly the same burdens as the largest which, besides having 40 per cent more meadow and 60 per cent more vines, contains rather more than fifteen times as much arable land; and each was worked by a single household. It is perfectly clear that these ancient peasant societies had nothing democratic about them, quite apart from any lord's power. On the other hand, it is of the greatest interest to observe, in connexion with the origins of that power, how the burdens laid on a whole category of different-sized *manses*—sometimes up to nearly a hundred in great *seigneuries* and big villages—were strictly equalized. The patriarchal family being the primitive cell of rural society, each owed the chief the same weight of dues—or, if you like, of presents—and the same amount of work.

No complete account of the lord's relations with the village community can be derived from study of the cultivated land alone. For however great its contribution to livelihood, agriculture had by no means altogether displaced the very ancient practices of pastoral life, hunting, and food collecting. By his fields alone the peasant literally could not have lived. All about the area more or less permanently cultivated and, when under crops, held in strict individual or family possession, he required access to immense stretches of common waste left in its natural condition. These moors and marshes and forests did not merely furnish necessary food for his cattle. His own nourishment depended on them; for wild vegetables and fruits were even more important in his dietary than wild game. Nearly all his implements were of wood. His fire was of wood or turf. His beasts were littered on heather or dry leaves. Even his arable needed the waste; for generally it got no fertilizer except sods of turf or piles of reeds spread on the land before the seed was sown. In villages where there was no lord, or where the lord's power was a late growth, the village community sometimes retained absolute control of these common lands; it owned them, in feudal phrase, *en alleux*. It is noticeable moreover that where common rights were specially important to the peasant—as in the largely pastoral life of the Alps and Pyrenees—there the lord's hand always lay less heavy than on the neighbouring plains. So too on the shores of the North Sea, in Friesland or Dithmarschen, the need for collective effort to drain marshes or keep out the tides probably acted as an obstacle to the progress of the lord's power. For anything that made a community more coherent favoured its independence. But throughout the greater part of Europe, where common was essential but still only a sort of annexe to the arable, the lord almost always extended his power over commons as well as over fields.

If we were to trust formal language, we might even think that this power had wiped out that of the peasants at a very early date. The ninth-century surveys generally treat forests and grazing land as part of the demesne. But that was the result of a simplification—heavy with consequences, as it proved. A turn of phrase common in the Frankish documents describes the realities better. When a charter of sale or gift enumerates the elements that make up a *seigneurie*, it usually inserts, side by side with the fields, meadows or vines of the demesne, and its profits from the *tenures*, the *communia*; thus indicating that the land subject to collective use was also placed under the master, and yet that he remained compulsorily obedient to 'common' usages over it. Such overlapping rights are repugnant to the relative precision of our more developed juridical thought. But we must not boast of our clarity: how would our immediate ancestors, trained on the strict Roman law, have described the so-called property of the humblest shareholder of a great company in its goods? In any case these entanglements were in no way strange to men who saw a whole hierarchy of rights, one above another, resting on nearly every scrap of land. It is no doubt vain to look for the true medieval 'owner' of the commons. But who 'owned' the *tenure*? The cultivator? His lord? Or, with the establishment of the feudal system, one of the various personages of whom the lord held in fief, or in sub-fief? The truth is that the peasants' rights of user over the commons, and the lords' superior rights, were regarded as equally worthy of respect. The latter were recognized—as in the case of the *tenures*—at one time by certain levies from the individual peasants; at another, and apparently a later, time by a quit-rent on the common land, paid by the village community as a whole. And of course the demesne had its share of all common rights.

That this system, with its many dangerous uncertainties, led to frequent disputes and abuses of power the documents give eloquent witness. The earliest struggles between lord and community about woods or wastes—or at least the earliest certainly known—date from the ninth century. They became specially bitter after the great clearances of the eleventh, twelfth, and thirteenth centuries had considerably reduced the area of surplus land; at a time when the revival of Roman Law had given the lord a formidable new weapon. Too often it was a case of earthenware pot versus iron pot. But there was no weakening about the principle of divided rights. 'Flowing water and springs, meadows, grazing grounds, forests, *garrigues* and rocks', the Customs of Barcelona record, about 1070, 'belong to barons not to be held *en alleu*' (that is, in disregard of any rights but their own) 'or as part of their demesne, but in order that their people may enjoy them at all times.' The lord was not merely the chief of individual men, and as such endowed with authority over what property each man held; he was also the chief of a group, and consequently the supreme master of lands subject to group use. So that the *seigneurie*, so far from being in opposition to the village community, was dependent on its existence for a particularly important aspect of its own powers and revenues.

VII. *A general sketch of the evolution*

After this search down converging roads, we must now try to describe that whole evolution which ended in the appearance of the classical seignorial system; or rather, those evolutions. For we are bound to take regional peculiarities into account. These we have stressed from the first. In the various curves, many sections must show the dotted lines of hypothesis—and others must remain blank.

In the beginning, we catch glimpses of peasant communities under their chiefs, to whom the various families (in the wide sense) that made up the group owed ritual gifts, and no doubt also assistance in a general way, which would be sure to take the form of certain services. The existence of these village chiefdoms is clearly attested in Gaul before Caesar and in Germany before the invasions; it may be traced in the society of Armorica; it appears more distinctly in that of Wales. We may assume something of the sort in ancient Europe more or less everywhere. Evidently we are here in touch with one of the oldest lines of cleavage in our civilization. Medieval and modern nobilities grew up much later and in a very different environment. The medieval nobility, as defined by the custom and law of the twelfth and thirteenth centuries, was distinguished by its hereditary calling to knighthood. The noble man was normally also a military vassal; and it was from the customs of vassalage that the noble class, once it had been consolidated, borrowed its way of life, its class cohesion, and the fundamental rules of its law. These are all relatively late institutions. But, viewed on his economic side, the noble man is also a man who lives by the land without working on it. He is at once master and exploiter of those who do the work. In short, the typical noble fortune is a seignorial fortune; so that we can hardly fail to recognize in the distinction between nobles and common folk the direct outcome of that ancient cleavage which had occurred in the dawn of history between 'client' peasants and the local chief who was fed in part by what they gave him; between the people of Brennacum and that Brennos who gave his name to the village. And it is hard not to believe that, in spite of repeated re-modellings, of social rise and fall and the luck of all sorts of adventurers, the old core of the noble class was formed by the descendants of these rustic chieftains, among whom were recruited—for they had to be recruited somewhere—most of the vassals and most of the knights. The stories already told of that Breton *machtiern* who became an emperor's vassal, and of that other one who founded a knightly family, are no doubt symptomatic.

But the word 'chief' is beyond dispute much too vague. From what sources did these people draw their power or prestige? It is particularly tempting to link primitive village organization with that of the clan or the tribe, and to imagine behind the figure of the lord-to-be the old man of a group of kindred, or someone who claimed his place; the group, of course, being bigger even than that of a patriarchal family. This may sometimes have been the actual course of events. A Bavarian formula of the Carolingian era seems to identify *vicus* and *genealogia*. We know from our sources and from place names that the Lombards and Burgundians, and from place names that the Franks, sometimes settled on the land of *Romania* in *farae*, groups bound by blood relationship. But a point already noted, to which reference must again be made, suggests that the facts were rarely so simple.

As early as we can study the *seigneurie* we find that it by no means always corresponds with the village territory. On the contrary, the territory is frequently divided among several seignorial allegiances. Many scholars, in many countries, have noticed this, almost always with the same surprise; for the notion that there must be an exact correspondence seems innate. In fact, as comparison of special studies proves, what each historian inclines to treat as an exception in his region was really, if not exactly normal, at least exceedingly wide-spread. No doubt in many instances we are dealing with a secondary subdivision. In particular, as the habit developed of 'housing' vassals who had previously fed at their master's board, great lay lords and ecclesiastical communities were obliged to cut fiefs out of their lands, on which these armed followers might live. These grants were often made up of fragments cut from much greater *seigneuries*, indeed even out of *manses* taken here and there from different *seigneuries*. The vassal would be more faithful if his scattered fee made autonomy on his part difficult. In this way the break-up of villages between many masters increased perceptibly. The working of donations, and indeed of sales, to the Church had similar effects: if you had a whole village you did not always give or sell the whole of it. Add to these divisions those due to inheritance. And yet it is evident that we cannot always, or even ordinarily, explain the presence of several seignorial authorities, side by side on the same ground, by a supervening disintegration. Often enough we can see a directly opposite evolution—towards integration. Look at the hamlet of Mons Acbodi, in the wooded land of western Gaul, early in the ninth century. Besides the little *seigneurie* of Ebbon and Eremberge already described, there were four *manses*. One after another they were given to Saint Germain-des-Prés, by individuals whom we are fully entitled to regard not as cultivators but as overlords of the soil drawing dues from it. The monks joined them to the *seigneurie* of the married couple; and the whole, by an agreement with Eremberge who was probably by that time a widow, became a single seignorial estate, held from the Abbey as a *precarium*. It would not be difficult to point out traces of a similar concentration elsewhere, in Domesday Book for instance.

If we are to form a just notion of the odd juridical medley that might exist on some estates, we must take into account, besides the holdings dependent on different lords, those that had no lord at all. The survival of these independent islands, their fields mixed up with those of adjacent tenancies, was apparently in no way opposed to the existence of a very ancient system of rural chiefdoms as attested by place names. It was certainly not without good reason that, at some point in Gallo-Roman history, the inhabitants or the neighbours of the village of Florac in the Bordelais had got into the habit of calling it the village, the land, the estate of Florus. Yet at the very end of the Middle Ages peasant *alleux* were still to be found there. And this instance is quoted at random from among a crowd of others.

In order to try to understand what may have happened in such cases, the best way without doubt is to examine one of the rare countries in Europe where we can watch, at a date which makes it visible, the birth of a central village authority. Friesland, we know, was for centuries a land without lords. However, from the fourteenth century, we can see rising above free communities the authority of chiefs, *Häuptlinge*. They were strong enough, especially in the east of the country, to force peasants, who were called their subjects (*Undersaten*) and whom in return they undertook to protect, to work for them, to fight for them, and to obey the rulings of their courts. But these new dynasties did not, in general, manage to create true *seigneuries*; at most, as their latest historian puts it, only 'amorphous' ones. Neither the economic nor the political conditions were favourable to the strengthening of such local authorities from that time forward. But we have here evidently, at least in embryo, an institution which, under more favourable conditions, might have grown from chiefdom into *seigneurie* proper. Now two points deserve to be especially borne in mind. Most of these potential *seigneurs* appear to have been simply peasants richer than the rest, and—more important still—men who had managed to surround themselves with armed followers, living with them in fortified manor houses. Secondly, their most appropriate name, and that which in fact contemporaries usually gave them, was not so much chief of a village as chief in a village. For in many places several families of their type had sprung up, and it was only in course of time that occasionally—but not always—the most powerful stock managed to get rid of its rivals. We may well suppose that many genuine *seigneuries*, far back in time, had no other source than some such differentiation of wealth and strength, in short a lordship *de facto* which by gradual mutation became a lordship *de jure*. And as it was simply a member of a group who, rising above the crowd, received first one man's submission and then that of another, you might have in a single community several such chiefs, with independent families surviving beside them. No doubt that was not the story of all seignorial villages. There were mass submissions too; but neither were they the only sort. When we read in the *Fors* de Bigorre, about 1110, that the right to control the use of the village boar should belong to the 'best knight' of the place—that is the one whose family was strongest, richest, or most respected—we can hardly fail to recall Friesland with its little communities divided by tradition among their several rustic potentates.

Whatever their origins, and the more we knew about them, the more varied we should probably find them, these village chiefdoms of early days were still far enough from the genuine *seigneurie*. It is in Romance countries that they can most clearly be seen acquiring the true seignorial character, but only very gradually.

Roman domination, in its early years, would seem to have worked in two ways. The abundance of servile labour that conquest supplied, and the confiscations of land, helped rich men to build up directly cultivated demesnes on a much larger scale than before. The slaves formed a much greater part of the rural population, and great *latifundia* were sprinkled among the peasant holdings. As for the groups dependent on village chiefs—in their case it seems we must distinguish rather sharply between the position in Italy and that in the rest of *Romania*. In spite of the vast areas cultivated by slave gangs, there was no lack of farmer or tenant groups on Italian soil. But everything suggests that they were less widespread there than elsewhere. The slow and harsh conquests, the Social Wars, the work of colonization, the rearrangements of property, must have destroyed the power of many a little local Italian dynasty. However that may be, it is certain, in any case, that the numerous small independent cultivators, whose existence in Italy imperial sources prove, appear still more clearly in early medieval records—the records of that very general practice of the temporary lease of land, the *livello*, which, as has been seen, was essentially different from the hereditary tenure which prevailed beyond the Alps. In the Provinces, on the other hand, the establishment of a scientific tax system—a thing Italy, as is well known, had long lacked—helped to stiffen relationships hitherto no doubt rather lax. Subordinate tenancies were not entered in the tax books under headings: they were all included under one *fundus*, the complex estate of the local magnate. It was probably at this time that so many old Gaulish villages, entered under the Roman or Romanized name of the magnate of the day, were rebaptized for ever. Every system of land taxation aims at simplicity, and in almost every civilization, when a new authority has introduced such a system, the effect has been to make more rigorous any half-developed relationships of peasant subjection that may have existed already; in British India, for example, early in the nineteenth century, and in Iraq in our own day. Later, the colonate tightened the peasants' bonds again: the simple dependant, whose land, far from being a fragment detached from a greater estate, had been known within the memory of man to belong to the patrimony of his family, was easily confused with the farmer who held his by a recent grant. The magnates who appear in the funeral bas-reliefs of Igelou or Neumagen receiving offerings and dues from their tenants had already the air of *seigneurs*.

But the great fact that, from about the second century, would give the *seigneurie* very nearly its final form was the decline of slavery. Its action would be felt beyond the Roman era; and then it would be operative even outside the Romanized world. The decline would not have been so important had there not previously been formed the great demesnes cultivated directly by their owners. We have seen how these *latifundia* were partially cut up into servile holdings; but only partially. Even if complete cutting up had been desired, there would not have been slaves enough to occupy the whole of such vast areas. Unless the land was to tumble down into waste, new sources of labour supply had to be found. They were found in the services of dependent peasants. Services had not been unknown in the old colonate. But they had been a much less serious burden than the dues in money or in kind. As the inscriptions of the African *saltus* show, they were hardly used except at the peak points of the agricultural year—ploughing, weeding, harvest—and, being thus cut down to a few days a year, their main use was to limit that of hired labour at these critical moments, although some such labour was occasionally needed. It is significant that classical jurists when discussing the letting of land never mention services. It is probable that under the later Empire many more began to be demanded, sometimes quite illegally. In one of his homilies, St John Chrysostom appears to refer to such demands;[1] and one cannot but suspect—the sources do not justify any certainty—that they may have been in part responsible for the terrible *jacqueries* of this period. The lord's demands certainly continued and became more urgent after the invasions. The laws of the Alemanni and the Bavarians have preserved for us the main part of a law from the first half of the seventh century which regulated the obligations of ecclesiastical *coloni*. Comparing this law with the information that we get from the Carolingian surveys of two centuries later, we see clearly a heavy increase in the labour services demanded from free *manses*. Near Paris, the *polyptyque* of Saint Maur-des-Fossés, compiled in the ninth century, seems to contain a memory of the introduction into one of its villages of services previously unknown there.[2] Such an increase of burdens was, beyond question, incompatible with the custom which, since the Roman era, regulated strictly—as both codes and inscriptions prove—the relation of landlord and tenant, within each *fundus*, *praedium* or κτῆμα. These customs were certainly maintained and respected by the courts of the barbarian kings. But there were many ways of getting round them. Sometimes the public powers interpreted them very loosely: in spite of the protests of royal and ecclesiastical *coloni*, a capitulary of Charles the Bald did not hesitate to include some entirely new tasks—one of them at least, marling, clearly presented as a recent technical innovation—under the heading of legitimate obligations. Simple abuses of power, leading to the establishment of precedents, were probably even more important. And pressure on the weak was freely disguised, as usual, under pious phrases about 'prayer'. The lord's *corvée* itself, in Romance countries, gets its name from this disguise (*corrogata*: the service 'collectively craved'). That did not make it less harsh; and no doubt when kings denounced the oppression of the poor, as they so often did, they had in mind,

---

[1] *Hom. in Math.*, 61, 3 (Migne, *P.G.* vol. LVIII, col. 5911).
[2] Guérard, *Polyptyqye*, II, 287, c. 16.

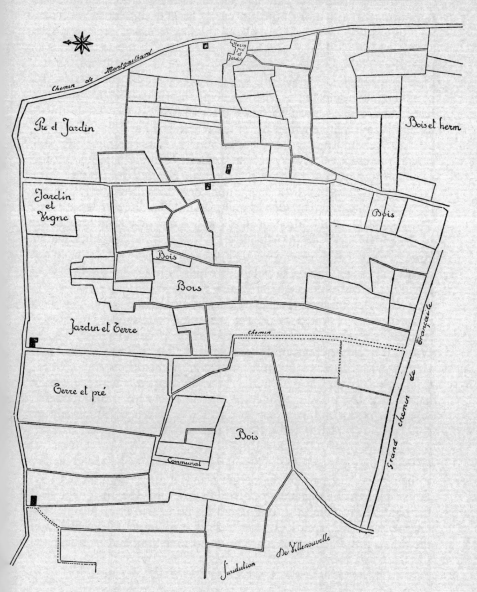

FIG. 6. Open-field with irregular subdivisions in Languedoc: Mont-gaillard, near Toulouse.

among other things, these burdens that were being imposed without any kind of justification in ancient custom.

Yet from that time forward new factors in the situation favoured the imposition of still more burdens. As a natural consequence of that widespread insecurity which replaced the *Pax Romana*, in many places a concentration of homesteads can be noticed during the early medieval centuries. This obviously encouraged seignorial control and the use of labour services. Above all, the general establishment of personal commendation and the usurpation of public rights—mainly those of justice and of *ban*—strengthened the lord's grip, and enabled him to extend it to holdings which had hitherto escaped him.

Thus behind the classic *seigneurie* our inquiry reveals long and obscure beginnings. A very ancient structure of rural chiefdoms was the essential nucleus, and about it the centuries deposited their successive layers one by one. Then the economic conditions of the early Roman era created the great demesnes facing the family holdings of dependants. The conditions of the late Roman era and of the early Middle Ages led to the coexistence, and subsequently the fusion, of *manses* cultivated by 'free' tenants with the new servile holdings, and, above all, linked the demesne to the holdings, of whatever type, by heavy bonds of service. Finally, the institutions of the feudal age gave the *seigneurie*, always aggressive, its finishing touches as a disciplined group whose members were harshly exploited. And yet the rural community had always retained a great measure of collective action under its chiefs. To the system thus slowly built up by one deposit after another Western and Central Europe owed some of the most significant aspects of its civilization, especially during the Middle Ages. In societies where there were hardly any slaves, and in which the only property that really mattered was property in land, nothing but this system of dependent agriculture could have kept alive the military and clerical aristocracies, or even monasticism itself. The Blessed Raimon Lûll, in his *Book of the Order of Chivalry*, once expressed with brutal frankness what appeared in his day to be a necessary part of the divine plan: 'it is seemly that the men should plough and dig and work hard in order that the earth may yield the fruits from which the knight and his horse will live; and that the knight, who rides and does a lord's work, should get his wealth from the things on which his men are to spend much toil and fatigue.'[1]

[1] Raimon Lûll, *Libro de la orden de Caballeria*, ed. J. R. de Luanco, I, 9.

CHAPTER VII

Medieval Agrarian Society in its Prime

§ I. France, The Low Countries, and Western Germany[1]

I. *The general framework*

THE regime of the great estate in Western Europe underwent, between the eleventh and fourteenth centuries, a transformation which cannot properly be understood without some preliminary examination, in the same geographical and chronological framework, of three phenomena. These are the modifications which took place respectively in the extent of land under cultivation, in the management of the soil and in the character and distribution of landed property.

A. *The extent of land under cultivation*

One of the most essential features of the period under consideration is that it was a time of land reclamation on a large scale. This became extremely active from the second half of the eleventh century onwards, and was evidently associated with the growth of population which seems to have occurred at this time. The problem has been discussed in an earlier chapter but some recapitulation and expansion will be in place here.[2]

In France, the movement appeared earlier in some regions than in others; land was being reclaimed from the sea in Flanders from the beginning of the eleventh and perhaps as early as the tenth century; the attack on the forests on the clay soils of the banks of the Saône and on the Beaujolais hills began in the second half of the tenth century; the first serious attacks on the forests of Normandy and Maine seem to date from the same time, while the attempts to bring the plain of Roussillon, ruined by the Arab invasions, under cultivation were perhaps earlier still. Nevertheless in the kingdom as a whole and in neighbouring regions like the Dauphiné, although the clearances sometimes began in the eleventh century, the twelfth and thirteenth centuries were the real age of reclamation. This is true alike of long-civilized districts like that between the Seine and the Loire and of the Alpine forest zone. Progress was not indeed uniform everywhere. Thus in Normandy the summit of

---

[1] The main part of the chapter is Prof. Ganshof's text, as it was published in the original edition. Many additions and corrections, some of them very important, have been made by Dr Verhulst. Prof. Ganshof has gone through these and approved them.

[2] Cf. p. 71 above *et seq.*

the curve does not appear to have been attained until rather a late date
about 1260, under St Louis; and it should be noted that while the
clearances ended almost everywhere round about 1300, they were still
going on long afterwards in the South-West.

With the exception of Western Lotharingia, where conditions resembled those in Northern France, the state of affairs in Germany was
somewhat different. There, the twelfth century was the great age of the
Urbarmachung. West of the Elbe, the clearances seem to have ceased after
the first half of the thirteenth century; the colonization of the Slav
districts east of the river was absorbing all available energies. Almost
alone the Bavarian Alps were still the scene of attempts at reclamation,
though often with merely ephemeral results.

This great effort all over Western Europe to bring ever wider
stretches of land into the service of mankind was the result of a series of
initiatives. Although the following statement is due to the present
state of our documentation and may therefore not always correspond
to the reality, we still think that first among those who took the lead
were the religious houses. The older Benedictine monasteries attacked
the wastes in the north of Flanders, the forests and wastes of Roussillon,
the marshes of Saintonge, the forests of Maine, Île de France, and
Bavaria, and the uncultivated lands in the high valleys of the Vosges
and the Alps of Switzerland or the Dauphiné. A still more important
role was undoubtedly played by the new monastic orders which appeared in the twelfth century, the Premonstratensians and above all the
Cistercians; there is something at once more resolute and more systematic about their methods. In the solitary places in which for preference they founded their abbeys, they undertook the assarting of
waste lands. Dutch place names that end in *-rode* and French ones
in *-sart*, which in present-day central Belgium (Eastern Flanders,
Brabant, and Hainault) signify reclaimed woodland areas, may often be
traced to the work of the 'white monks' or the followers of Saint
Norbert, and the work of the Cistercians in clearing the forests of
Normandy seems to have been no less important. But it was Germany
between the Rhine and Elbe (we are not here concerned with the
colonial East) which benefited more than any other country from their
efforts. A whole series of daughter-abbeys sprung from the Rhineland
monasteries of Altenkamp and Altenburg made a powerful contribution
towards transforming the woodlands and heaths of Saxony, Thuringia,
and Lusatia into arable and pasture; similar work was done in Bavaria
by other houses of the same order.

A certain number of ecclesiastical princes likewise played a decisive
part in the clearances. One has only to call to mind those large-scale
operations of repopulation and reclamation, real *poblaciones*, which

were undertaken by the bishops of Grenoble in the Graisivaudan, so cruelly ravaged by the Saracens. In Germany it was Archbishop Frederick of Bremen, in 1106, who first called upon colonists from Holland to reclaim the low-lying boggy region to the north-east of his see, and his example was followed by his successors. Recent studies, however, tend more and more to attribute the earliest attempts at assarting to the laity, to territorial princes and to seignorial agents. The systematic nature of their efforts, especially the creation of the *villes neuves*, of which more later, must be emphasized. In this connexion, the case of the counts of Flanders is significant. In the twelfth century the counts lavished grants upon the abbeys and chapters recently founded in maritime Flanders or in the Ypres region behind it; sometimes they received 'new lands' (*terrae novae*) still exposed to the inundations of the sea, sometimes waste lands (*wastinae*), sometimes sheep-pastures (*bergeries*, *bercariae*) and meadows designed for vast goose-greens, which had but recently been reclaimed from the waters. The object appears to have been to bring into use two waste regions in the interior of the county, the marshy coastal zone and the zone of woodland and heath stretching from Ypres to Bruges. The religious houses were thus the agents of a deliberate policy of drainage and clearance on the part of the counts. Alongside these efforts by territorial princes, which will serve as a few examples out of many, may be placed those of the king of France himself, in the interior of the royal domain. More than one assart between the Seine and the Loire was undertaken under his auspices in the twelfth century. His motives, however, like those of other lay lords, were political rather than economic, for his concern was mainly to destroy the haunts of brigands who menaced the communications between Paris and Orleans, and to make the roads safer by multiplying new settlements in the district.

The fund of labour at the disposal of those who set on foot these clearances was not the same everywhere. The Cistercians to a very great extent set their own hands to the plough and a large part of the credit for the Order's achievement must go to the lay brothers or *conversi*, working under the supervision of the monks. But in the main the conquest of the soil of Western Europe, from the end of the eleventh to the beginning of the fourteenth century, was the work of peasant labour. The tenants of cathedral or collegiate churches, of monasteries, and of lay lords, cleared the unproductive parts of the estates to which they belonged, and from marsh and heath, woodland and coppice, carved out new fields to lie alongside those long under cultivation. Such are the *Rotures* referred to in the fields of the ancient village of Spoy in Burgundy, and such too the *Paelvelt*, the *Dummelvoer* or the *Boeckxdonck* which came to be added to the three original fields of the

Brabantine village of Grimbergen. Likewise in Périgord where all the communal lands of our own day were added progressively in successive rings around ancient Romano-Gallic estates which provided the sites of the corresponding medieval villages. It would be easy to multiply such instances almost indefinitely. It was with the labour of their own people, too, that some lords undertook clearances on a larger scale and at times remote from the centre of their estate administration. Thus the reclamation of the upper valleys of the Vosges was carried out by the Lorraine abbeys of Remiremont and Saint-Dié, by means of the labour services of the *mundiliones*, or men under their protection.

In many cases, however, 'foreign' labour was used; colonists, in the true sense of the word, were called in. As a result of the growth of population in the eleventh century and the impossibility of an indefinite subdivision of holdings on the older estates, a considerable and growing reserve of surplus peasant labour had come into existence. The legal status of the men of which it was composed inevitably varied enormously, but this mattered little to the landowner in need of 'hands', and, barring unhappy accidents, it was likely to remain unknown in the new home of these colonists, or *hospites*, as the contemporary documents frequently call them. Lords anxious to clear their woodlands, or to substitute field and meadow for waste and heath, would offer their 'guests' particularly favourable conditions as to tenure, personal status, and seignorial rights. These conditions varied from place to place, but their common characteristic was that they established a privileged class. This is true of the *hospites* whom Suger settled on the land of the abbey of Saint-Denis, when he was reforming and tightening up its administration (c. 1125); or those whom he set to cutting down the forests of new estates such as Vaucresson. It is true of the *hôtes* to whom the monks of Saint-Vincent of Le Mans, in the eleventh and twelfth centuries, would grant some uncultivated piece of land on condition of bringing it under cultivation, or whom they would invite to establish themselves in some new settlement or *bourg (burgus)* destined to be the starting point for clearances on a larger scale. It is true of the *hospites* whom the chapters, abbeys, and lay lords of Hainault employed in the twelfth and thirteenth centuries to lay down new meadows or ploughlands. It is true, also, of those Dutchmen and Flemings who in the twelfth and early thirteenth centuries betook themselves in ever greater numbers to the lower Weser and Elbe, and by building dykes and establishing a system of drainage won the land to a fertility never known before.

For the *hospites* often came from afar. The Flemings and the Dutch established in the extreme north and shortly afterwards in the east of Germany were no exceptions. Large numbers of Rhinelanders and probably of Westphalians too followed their example. In France it has been observed that in the twelfth and thirteenth centuries Limousins and Bretons helped in the deforestation of the left bank of the lower Creuse, and men of Saintonge took part in the peopling of the district at the mouth of the Garonne (Entre-deux-Mers). Considerable effort was needed to recruit new settlers, to remove their households, to provide them with indispensable tools and to feed them throughout the first months. In such cases the lord often hesitated to undertake alone the necessary organization, publicity, provision of capital and parcelling out of land. He sought associates and entered into written contracts with them. This was almost always the case with the reclamations carried out in North Germany by colonists from the Low Countries or from the Rhineland and Westphalia. The landlord would employ a *locator*, who frequently belonged to a knightly family; the *locator* would divide the land among the immigrants and for some time at least would direct operations. Recent researches have brought similar cases to light in France; such is the case of a knight named Eudes to whom the monks of Saint-Avit of Orleans gave the task of populating and putting into cultivation their lands of Cercottes in 1207; in Brie in the thirteenth century a good deal of the recovery of land from the forests was directed by clerical persons who undertook the business of clearance wholesale and dealt in their turn with sub-contractors. Often also the lord of a 'wilderness' went into partnership with another lord by means of one of those contracts known in France as *pariages*. Thereby each party undertook to contribute his share. One provided the land and the rights, the other the powers and the connexions required to find the men and the money with which to settle them.

In the present stage of our knowledge it is impossible to give even approximate figures for the area brought under cultivation during the eleventh, twelfth and thirteenth centuries. We can do no more than state the bare fact that the increase was considerable and point to the retreat of forest, heath, marsh, and bog, even, in the coastal districts, of the sea itself, as the counterpart of this extension.

We have already had occasion to remark that a necessary consequence of the clearances was the creation of new settlements, some nucleated and some dispersed. Sometimes the type of settlement established was determined by the nature of the soil or by the general lie of the land. The isolated farmsteads of the Flanders seaboard were built on ancient silted-up watercourses cut off one from another by meadows, by low-lying peaty ground and by marshes. The villages they formed were properly speaking street-villages, but they were so loosely grouped as to dislocate the links that bound habitations into village communities. In the country west of Paris, where for the most part the villages are few and relatively large, one nevertheless comes across a considerable number of small scattered hamlets; this is because huge stretches of forest often prevented the pioneers of the thirteenth century from grouping themselves into villages at the centre of large areas of cultivation. Other factors of a completely different order may have led to the same consequences; for example it has been rightly pointed out that the Cistercian rule, by ordaining that monks should live apart from laymen, caused the 'granges', or centres of cultivation, of the Order to be established far from villages, even in those regions where grouped settlements were the rule.

It appears, nevertheless, that the deliberate choice of isolated habitations by most of the pioneers who established themselves in uninhabited regions became common in the thirteenth century. In France we can observe this phenomenon in Brie, the Massif Central and in Bresse; it can also be seen in the Low Countries in Northern Flanders and in Brabant around 's Hertogenbosch, as well as in Germany on the Bavarian plateau. This new method of occupying the soil had its effect on the landscape which was now dominated by permanent enclosures.

However, the essential factor to grasp in discussing the effect of the assarts is the appearance of numerous new settlements. Some were created by lords, as were the *villes neuves* of Flanders, Hainault, Northern France, Normandy, the Île de France and Burgundy, the *bastides* of the South, and the *bourgs* of the West, all of which served to accommodate the *hospites* who came to clear the wastes. The colonial villages in North Germany and the *Waldhufendörfer* hewn from the forests of South Germany have an analogous origin. Others were spontaneous formations. In most cases these belonged to the period of dispersed colonization of the thirteenth century which seems to have succeeded the period characterized by the foundation of the *villes neuves*.

B. *The cultivation of the soil*

The period envisaged here saw no considerable progress in the manner the soil was cultivated and certainly no general progress in agricultural technique. As far as the cycle of cultivation was concerned, it can be said that the triennial rotation, with a strict limitation of the fallow year to a third of the arable area, was in use in regions where the lands of the great abbeys had been intensively exploited since the Carolingian period, especially on the loamy soils of the *Parisian basin* and in certain parts of Northern France and the Southern Low Countries. Here and there, for instance in the southern parts of France, this triennial system had been introduced only from the ninth century on. In other places, however, especially on the less homogeneous soils, the rhythm of arable cultivation remained much less regular and each year vast portions of the arable soil remained unsown. But it was not until the end of the thirteenth century that, in certain economically advanced regions and where clearances had stopped earlier, we can discern a tendency to reduce the fallow, for instance in Normandy where the first application of a four-year rotation appeared.

It can safely be said, however, that a greater activity prevailed, and that more effort was made to get a better yield from the land. Where it is possible to compare the average yields of seed with those of the Carolingian times the superiority of the thirteenth century is obvious. This rise in agricultural yields was probably already under way in the twelfth century, especially on the better-managed estates like those of the abbey of Cluny. The chief cause was the greater effort put into working the land made possible by the great reduction of labour services, with which we shall deal later. This meant that the peasants were able to devote all their attention to the cultivation of their own holdings, and thus to bring about a marked increase in their returns. The improvement of the peasant's tools added to the efficiency of his work, especially because of the more general use of iron. There was an improvement in haulage in the eleventh century, and more efficient methods of harnessing draught animals were adopted, while about the year 1200 the horse replaced the ox in ploughing on the plains of the Paris basin, Picardy, Flanders and Lorraine.

It is of some interest to observe that while the type of agrarian economy does not seem to have changed, and while, for instance, over the greater part of France arable farming and stock-raising were associated, there were often changes in the use to which the soil was put. In Flanders the lands reclaimed from the sea generally served at first for the feeding of flocks; a considerable number of these sheep-runs and goose-greens were transformed into arable fields during the twelfth and thirteenth centuries. The same thing happened to many meadowlands in other districts. In certain corn-growing regions the need for increasing production was so great as to bring under the plough marginal lands which subsequently had to be allowed to revert to pasture; in Germany this was notably the case in the mountainous parts of Bavaria. In France, a considerable development of vine growing can be observed during the tenth and eleventh centuries. Newly cleared lands were often planted with vines where soil and aspect permitted; moreover, large landowners would occasionally convert arable lands of low yield into vineyards, particularly in the West.

It must further be noted that in certain regions colonization by dispersed dwellings and even by enclosures, which was discussed above, modified profoundly their agrarian economy. The use of common lands and the periodic erection and demolition of temporary enclosures enabled the old collective economy to use arable lands alternately for individual cultivation and communal stock-raising. This collective economy was now replaced by a system of agrarian individualism with stock-raising on natural pastures as the chief resource. This basic change in the system of cultivation, particularly noticeable in Flanders during the thirteenth century, was without doubt stimulated by a more active trade in meat, wool and leather, mainly in the neighbourhood of the great cities.

This relative intensification of cultivation doubtless had more than one cause, but it seems clear that the essential factor was an increase in demand. While in the preceding period a part of the produce of the estate had certainly been sold outside it, production had not been organized with that end in view. In the twelfth and above all in the thirteenth century, on the other hand, the towns were providing an increasingly important outlet for agricultural produce, so much so that it was becoming more and more essential to organize production with a view to urban markets. In this respect the Cistercian abbeys were often in the van and at an early date were organizing their estates with a definite view to the victualling of towns.

c. *The distribution of landed wealth*

It is impossible here to give a detailed account of the distribution of landed wealth in France, Western Germany, and the neighbouring countries between the eleventh and fourteenth centuries. It will at most be possible to indicate certain tendencies or certain variations.

To begin with the royal possessions, there certainly seems to have been a progressive increase in the landed wealth of the Capetian kings of France. The graph is indeed far from being regular; considerable losses took place, notably under Robert II and Philip I, as a result of donations or restitutions to religious houses, and also through the usurpations of many vassals and sub-vassals in the interior of what is usually known as the royal domain. But from Louis VI onwards these began to be recovered, and under the rule of his successors, especially Philip Augustus, the considerable extensions of the royal domain brought about a corresponding increase in the king's wealth, through the acquisition of the whole or part of the property of dispossessed territorial princes. The annexation of Normandy in 1204 is particularly deserving of attention in this respect in view of the exceptional number of estates, lands, and franchises which it brought into the patrimony of the dynasty. The annexation in 1271 of the southern territories belonging to Alphonse of Poitiers—Poitou, Toulousain and their appurtenances—brought no less an increase in wealth. On the other hand, the grant of portions to the princes of the royal house necessarily produced a diminution in the extent of the king's landed possessions.

In Germany the situation was very different. As in France, the great *fisci* of the Carolingian period, comprising several *villae*, were broken up; and neither in extent nor in structure was there henceforth any essential difference between royal and ecclesiastical estates, even when the name of *fiscus* continued to be attached to these now autonomous domains. But despite large gifts to religious houses, the landed wealth of the German monarchy remained very considerable in the eleventh and twelfth centuries, consisting as it did not only of entire domains, but also of other elements, such as the enormous game reserves constituted by the 'forests'. It was distributed over the whole of Germany. Usurpations were not unknown, particularly in troubled periods like the reign of Otto III and the minority of Henry IV, but they were followed, notably in Saxony under the latter king, by efforts at recovery and at the extension of the royal domain. The results of these efforts were wiped out in the intestine strife following upon the Investiture Quarrel, and from this time onwards there was a pronounced decline in the territorial wealth of the royal house. The policy of the first Hohenstaufen, aiming at the formation in South-West Germany, especially in Alsace and Swabia, of a considerable collection of estates (*Hausgüter*), had only ephemeral results, and the decadence of the German monarchy in the thirteenth century definitely precluded any possibility of a reaction capable of stopping the rot.

The great majority of our sources, original charters, cartularies, documents concerning estate administration and chronicles are of ecclesiastical origin. Hence the vicissitudes of the property of religious houses are relatively well known. The patrimony of the Church was enriched by many new acquisitions during the period under discussion. To this end various factors contributed. First, the phenomenon treated in an earlier chapter, the absorption of small properties belonging to free men who had placed themselves under the protection of religious houses, continued throughout the eleventh century, and is still to be encountered in some regions of Germany and also in France at the beginning of the twelfth century. Rich churches with accumulated revenues at their disposal would round off their estates by lending money on 'mortgage', i.e. by arranging a loan secured by a piece of property of which the income went to the lender without reducing the principal. As pursued by the abbeys of Normandy, Flanders, and Lotharingia, this practice has been the subject of detailed study, but it is also to be met with elsewhere. In the eleventh and twelfth centuries it led to the incorporation of a not inconsiderable number of domains, isolated pieces of land, and revenues derived from land, such as tithes, into the patrimony of the creditor churches; for borrowers often found themselves unable to redeem properties given as security for loans. In

certain countries, for instance in Flanders and the Lotharingian principalities, this activity of the monasteries as credit institutions persisted
right to the end of the thirteenth century. But two reservations must
be made for this later period: the use of mortgages was almost entirely
confined to the new foundations, as distinct from the older Benedictine
abbeys; and the new riches which they acquired by this means consisted
no longer of land but almost exclusively of tithes.

There must also be taken into consideration the successful recovery
by many religious houses of lands previously usurped from them.
Recoveries of this sort were especially frequent from the second quarter
of the twelfth century onwards, under the influence of the victorious
Gregorian ideals. It should be noted however that the amount of land
so recovered never or hardly ever equalled the mass of property which
had been seized from the Church in the late ninth, the tenth, and the
eleventh centuries. The restitutions which were made under the
influence of the ideals of the Reform movement were of the nature of
bargains in which both parties abandoned some of their rights and claims.

The new acquisitions of religious houses from the eleventh to the
thirteenth centuries were principally the result of donations. There was
a considerable flow of these until towards the end of the latter century
though they diminished progressively in volume. The decline in royal
gifts is particularly striking; in Germany even more so than in France,
where royal liberality had never been comparable with that of the
Saxon and Franconian kings and emperors. After the turn of the
eleventh and twelfth centuries, when the Investiture struggle was at its
height, the gifts of the German sovereigns to the Church became less
frequent. They grew rarer and rarer during the twelfth century, and
came to an almost complete stop in the thirteenth. It seems hardly
possible to trace a common graph for the donations made by territorial
princes and nobles; their amount would depend on the wealth of each
individual, on his attitude towards the Church, and on changes in his
power and policy. It may, however, be safely affirmed that by the
thirteenth century, in some districts by the middle of the twelfth
century, this group of benefactors was no longer making donations to
religious houses in any number or of any size. The additions to ecclesiastical estates resulting from the generosity of kings, princes, or nobles
were subject to the same rule which we have already noticed in the case
of acquisitions of land and land-revenues by means of mortgages. The
older Benedictine abbeys were the recipients of very few gifts during
the thirteenth century or for that matter during the greater part of the
twelfth; the principal beneficiaries were monasteries and chapters
belonging to more recent orders, Cistercians, Premonstratensians, and
Austin Canons. On this point detailed studies devoted to Flanders,

Brabant, and the Lotharingian county of Namur all lead to the same conclusion. For instance, take the case of two Cistercian abbeys founded during the course of the twelfth century, De Duinen in Flanders, Villers in Brabant; by the end of the thirteenth century each of them found itself, thanks to the generosity of the faithful, in possession of an estate of about ten thousand hectares. A sampling of the sources relating to other regions indicates that this phenomenon is not peculiar to the three principalities mentioned.

We must also inquire whether there were any changes in the character of the grants during our period, and if so what those changes were. To this it may be answered that in all the diverse regions of France, Germany, and the surrounding countries, if local variations of secondary interest be excluded, a similar process is everywhere apparent. In the first place, grants of a whole *villa*, of a domain in its entirety, such as more than one church used still to receive in the tenth century and (at any rate in Germany and by royal grant) in the eleventh century, were now quite exceptional. The lands given to religious houses during the eleventh and twelfth centuries were normally fractions of estates, frequently termed *allodium* or *praedium* or stated to correspond to one-half, one-third, one-quarter of a *villa*. Often enough the monastery would attempt to gather the *villa* together again either by obtaining fresh grants, or by purchase. Sometimes the grant would be specified as a seigniorial demesne (*mansus indominicatus*), a fraction of a demesne, or so many *Hufen* or *manses*; when the latter were at all numerous they would often be extremely scattered. Consider, for example, the elements which went to make up the endowment of Saint-Pierre of Lille by Baldwin V, Marquis of Flanders, in 1066; the chapter received 95 *manses*, which, with the manse averaging about twelve hectares, is a good deal; but these *manses* were scattered over 23 different localities, in none of which it obtained more than fifteen. Frequently a grant would consist of a few *bonniers*, or roods or acres, or a field, a meadow, a sheep-pasture (*bergerie*), crofts (*courtils*), a wood, or the like.

But side by side with land, other kinds of wealth appear with increasing frequency in the grants; tithes, fractions of tithes (often the *bodium*, corresponding to two-thirds of the tithe of a place), quit- and other rents, rectories (*altaria*) with their endowment and their regular and occasional revenues, rights of user, among which fishing rights merit particular attention, and *novales*, or tithes of 'new lands' in newly cleared or newly drained districts. When the grant brought not the whole, but only a part of an *altare* or a right derived from land within the patrimony of a church, the beneficiary would often try (particularly in the case of tithes) to obtain the remainder just as they tried to reconstitute estates of which they were given fragments.

In the thirteenth century *altaria* and revenues derived from land, of which tithes were by far the most important, occupied a far more important place than land itself in donations to religious houses. Grants of land were now becoming smaller and smaller in area, and donors frequently burdened them with life charges.

We shall not venture to express a categorical opinion on the question whether as a whole the rural property of the Church increased or diminished between the eleventh and the fourteenth centuries. If the *terminus a quo* be placed towards the end of the third quarter of the ninth century, there can be no doubt that there was a decrease, and indeed a very marked decrease. And even within the chronological limits covered by the present chapter, it is not unreasonable to assume that, taking the whole of Western Europe from the Pyrenees to the Elbe, there was a diminution.

For although these centuries were marked by recoveries and by numerous grants, and indeed by grants which in certain countries and at certain times had an almost wholesale character, the losses were none the less considerable. Usurpations committed by kings, territorial princes, *avoués* and other lords, and likewise by the estate officials, had all robbed the religious houses of large parts of their estates; we shall return to this matter in detail when discussing the decomposition of the estate. Other parts had been lost, in fact if not in law, through enfeoffment; in these the religious houses retained only a *dominium directum* which was progressively being stripped of most of the attributes of a property-right in favour of the *dominium utile* of the vassal. Often, too, large portions of the ecclesiastical patrimony were granted by contract of 'precaria', that is to say, for an annual quit-rent (*cens*) which was both minimal and symbolic, to great families whose protection and favours the Church wished to obtain or to preserve.

The property of the older Benedictine abbeys had been harder hit than that of any others. This was chiefly because the tenth and also the eleventh and early twelfth centuries were the heyday of the usurpations, and at that time the rich Benedictine monasteries were alone in offering a prey to lay attempts at seizure. Not quite alone, indeed, for several episcopal sees and collegiate churches suffered in the same way; but these on the whole had defended themselves or had been defended more successfully. Furthermore, as we have seen, the older Benedictine abbeys did not reap fresh benefits from the grants made to religious houses during our period. This is a suitable place to refer to the marked growth of the possessions of a few Benedictine abbeys in the second half of the twelfth and the first half of the thirteenth century achieved by purchase. These purchases, which were more often than not acts of deliberate policy, are indicative of economic prosperity, or perhaps rather of considerable optimism. Purchases of this sort have been studied for two Flemish monasteries, the abbeys of Saint-Amand and Sint-Bavo. The latter acquired within the space of a few years hundreds of hectares of woods, heathlands, and marshes in Northern Flanders, from which it hoped to draw large revenues after reclamation. The enterprise was, nevertheless, a failure. It has been shown that at Saint-Amand this policy of large-scale land purchases was far too ambitious and caused serious financial difficulties in the third quarter of the thirteenth century which did but increase with the fourteenth century. And there is no reason to suppose that the situation was any different at Sint-Bavo. This is one of the reasons why many of the older Benedictine abbeys became impoverished and were sometimes even ruined by the end of the thirteenth and in the fourteenth centuries; they fell into debt and had to alienate part of such property as remained to them. The example of Saint-Germain-des-Prés is noteworthy. The 22 domains listed in the *Polyptyque* of Abbot Irminon comprised in all about 32,748 hectares at the beginning of the ninth century; and this was certainly only a part of the landed property of that famous house. A rental of 1384 gives the whole property of the abbey as about 2434 hectares, enfeoffed lands being naturally omitted. We are, indeed, compelled to compare the position at dates well outside our period, and it must be remembered that the second half of the fourteenth century in France was a time of particularly acute crisis; doubtless not all Benedictine abbeys underwent such catastrophic changes of fortune as Saint-Germain-des-Prés. But it is safe to say that the wealth of these abbeys was, without exception, in decline everywhere up to the end of the thirteenth century. In thirteenth- and fourteenth-century Germany great Benedictine abbeys do not seem to have enjoyed effective possession of more than 300 *Hufen* (of about 30 *Morgen*), or, allowing about 10 hectares to the *Hufe*, 3000 hectares. For comparison let it be recalled that under Charlemagne an official statement inserted in the *Brevium exempla ad describendas res ecclesiasticas et fiscales* attributed 1507 *manses* or *Hufen* to the church of Augsburg alone.

Much less is known about the landed property of laymen; the sources are rarer and less explicit. Those territorial princes who had succeeded in maintaining or extending their power had certainly not seen their property diminish, and in many cases it could not but increase. Such was the case with the majority of the princes in what was to become the Low Countries, the Count of Flanders, and the Lotharingian dukes and counts. It was also true of Germany, though in the thirteenth and fourteenth centuries the extent of the princely estates seems to have been greater in the interior of that country than on the Rhine, where princes were more numerous. The amount of princely landed property grew in

Germany at the expense of the monarchy and the Church, especially during the twelfth and thirteenth centuries. In France, on the other hand, the growth in the royal power resulted in a great reduction of the number of territorial princes, particularly in the thirteenth century; and the sum total of their landed property followed a course opposite to that described for Germany.

In the present state of knowledge it would be both difficult and dangerous to say what changes took place in the amount of land held by lay lords other than territorial princes. Here local differences are too considerable, and we shall confine ourselves to remarks of a very general nature. During the first centuries of our period, the eleventh and twelfth, the property of the nobles must have increased materially as a result of usurpations, enfeoffments, and appointments to the position of *avoué*; though this increase would be less in districts where a strong power like that of the counts of Flanders, the dukes of Normandy, and certain German prince-bishops could curb these activities. Over the greater part of Germany the increase in the landed wealth of the nobility, particularly the estates of medium size, continued throughout the thirteenth century; but this does not seem to have been the case in France, where the growing power of the central government was now better able to prevent the acts of violence which until then had served the interests of the barons. Moreover, as will be seen further on, the economic and political crises of the fourteenth century, which in France even more than in Germany had a serious effect upon all landed property, fell particularly heavily on the property of the nobility.

Peasant proprietorship no longer occupied a place of real importance during the period here dealt with, though it never disappeared entirely. It remained very important in Frisia; and although in North Germany, Saxony, and Thuringia (where it had originally been particularly vigorous) it was very much reduced during the eleventh century to the advantage of the king, the Church and the nobles, it was far from being eliminated. It survived also in other parts of Germany, and is to be met with in several parts of France, including Brittany, the South-West, Burgundy, and also beyond the frontiers of the kingdom, in Provence. Moreover, side by side with older peasant proprietorship, on the whole in retreat, there were growing up during our period, if not a new peasant proprietorship, at any rate peasant holdings possessed of most of the attributes of legal ownership. We shall have occasion to return to this matter in studying the effects of changes in estate administration.

In concluding this outline, a word remains to be said about the landed wealth of the bourgeoisie. As soon as trade began to enrich the burgesses of the towns to an extent which allowed them to withdraw from their business a part of their wealth and use it as a foundation for a more stable fortune, they began to buy lands in the country. This normally happened at a fairly early date in those districts where towns first developed a vigorous growth; it is visible in Flanders as early as the twelfth century. But its chief period is the thirteenth and fourteenth centuries. It should, however, be observed that from the beginning the rural properties of the bourgeoisie were in the nature of investments pure and simple. Except in very small, semi-agricultural towns the burgesses neither tilled the soil themselves nor organized its cultivation; they were content merely to collect its revenues.

II. *The decomposition of the classical estate*

The dominant fact in the history of estate institutions from the eleventh to the thirteenth centuries is the decomposition of the *villa*, or of what we may call the 'classical' estate. Its structure and economy have been analysed in an earlier chapter, and indeed it was in the Carolingian period that it was most widely distributed and was in the most perfect state of equilibrium, even though this equilibrium was often delicately balanced and easily upset.

A. *Distribution of the* 'villa' *at the beginning of the eleventh century*

The 'classical' *villa* was far from being the general rule even at the beginning of our period; indeed, as we have seen, it was far from being so even in the preceding period. It must further be noted that the *villa* was not always a great estate, even when it presented all the features described in the *polyptycha* of the ninth century.

In Northern and Eastern France it would often be about the size of a large village—sometimes even of several villages; and there were many estates of this type further south too, between the latitude of Paris and the river Loire. In Brittany the estate was much smaller. In those parts of the West where it existed, such as Normandy and Anjou, it was generally of medium size; so too in the Midi, and often in Burgundy also. Large, sometimes very large, *villae* predominated in the basins of the Seine, the Oise, and the Somme, and were widespread to the north of the frontier of present-day France, in the south of modern Belgium, around Tournai, in Hainault, in Brabant south of Brussels, in the districts around Namur and Liège, and also in the Ardennes. In Dutch-speaking Flanders and Northern Brabant, in Holland, in the prince-bishopric of Utrecht (the *Sticht*), and in Guelderland, the classical estate was less common, and where it did occur often seems to have been rather small. In Maine, in the West, the *villa* was almost unknown. There the larger landed properties were made up of a number of holdings or *bordages* (*bordagium*) constituting quite autonomous farms and frequently of one or more of the *bourgs* whose origin has already been explained. The latter sometimes served as centres of collection for the rents due from the tenants who cultivated their lands solely on their account and were exempt from all labour services. The same holdings, sometimes called *borderies* and most often formed into groups, are to be met with in other regions of the West, such as Brittany, Normandy, Poitou, Saintonge, and Anjou.

In Germany, the estate, or *Villikation*, was nowhere unknown. But it was extremely rare in Frisia, and in its classical form infrequent both in Saxony and in Thuringia. It was far more widespread in the West (the Rhineland, Lorraine, Alsace), in the centre (Franconia) and in the South (Swabia and Bavaria). The abbey of Werden on the Ruhr provides us with a characteristic illustration of this statement. It owned truly classical estates on the Rhine, in Friemersheim and the district round, and also in Eastern Saxony, round Helmstedt. But it also had in Saxony a very large number of *manses*—between 450 and 900; these were extremely scattered, constituted separate unities, and were only grouped into *ministeria* to facilitate the collection of dues, whence the German name of *Hebeamtbezirke* given to these groups.

Finally it should be observed that the *villa* or *Villikation* occurred on the estates of lay lords as well as on those of churches or kings. The estates of lay lords, however, usually seem to have been smaller in area and subject in their extent and structure to a greater mobility.

The above rapid survey suggests that the 'classical' estate may at any rate be considered the typical form of land management at the beginning of the period under consideration. It is therefore appropriate to make the changes which took place in its structure the central point of our narrative.

B. *The break-up of the* 'villa'

In discussing the distribution of landed wealth, allusion was made to the losses, both of whole estates and parts of estates, which were suffered by ecclesiastical estates as a result of usurpations and enfeoffments. At this point it is the loss of parts of estates which calls for particular consideration, for it was one of the most important factors in that disintegration of the *villa* which was so characteristic a feature of our period.

In point of fact, it was no new phenomenon; it had occurred to many religious houses as early as the tenth century. For instance, it has been possible by comparing inventories at the beginning and end of that century to trace the evolution of the estates belonging to the abbey of Marmoutier, in Alsace. It is clear that the majority of them had greatly diminished in extent because large portions had been enfeoffed, willy nilly, to *avoués*, *sous-avoués*, or vassals of the Bishop of Metz. Such a situation had certainly been of common occurrence, in France as well as in Germany.

The process went on in the eleventh and twelfth centuries and was accompanied, as it had been in the preceding century, by usurpations pure and simple which were not even veiled by the juridical pretext of enfeoffment. This is observable everywhere where the history of the estates of a monastery has been studied: it took place in those of Reichenau, in Swabia, and of Werden on the Ruhr, in the Rhineland; in the estates of Lobbes in the region of Sambre-et-Meuse and in those of Saint-Bertin, Sint-Bavo and of Liessies, in Artois, Flanders, and Hainault; in those of Saint-Denis in 'France' and of the abbey of Saintes, in the South-West. A strong impulse was given to the process by the obligation laid on the German abbeys in the eleventh and again in the twelfth century to maintain numerous vassals and *ministeriales* for the royal service. In general, on the monastic estates, the estates forming part of the *mensa abbatialis* seem to have suffered worse from enfeoffments, and hence to have undergone greater losses, than those of the *mensa conventualis*. The abbey of Saint-Amand, which has been recently studied, provides an example of this.

Besides the above-mentioned factors in the breaking-up of estates, in which we have been mainly concerned with ecclesiastical and especially with monastic estates, there was another which was peculiar to lay estates, to wit, the division of lands among co-heirs. To this must be added pious gifts to the Church, the majority of which, from the eleventh century onwards, consisted, as we saw, of fractions of estates. In certain districts, such as Hainault and the Namur region, where a study has been made of lay estates in the eleventh and twelfth centuries, the conclusion has been reached that there were no longer any entire *villae* remaining in the lords' hands.

The partition of estates led to their multiplication, and, thus inevitably, to new groupings. On the one hand it became necessary to attach to some centre of administration the scattered fragments of estates whose unity had been destroyed by enfeoffments or usurpations; and sometimes new acquisitions due to the generosity of the faithful were similarly attached to it. On the other hand it was sometimes found advantageous to break up a seignorial demesne which had become too large in proportion to a reduced number of tributary *manses*. Whatever factors may have been at work—and account must always be taken of those which were accidental or local—there is no doubt that such multiplication and grouping took place. One of the best examples is that of Friemersheim, a *fiscus* belonging to the abbey of Werden on the Ruhr, on the left bank of the Lower Rhine. This immense estate, which carried a single unit at the end of the ninth century and during the tenth century, was divided in the eleventh and twelfth centuries into a series of separate estates, Burg, Friemersheim and Asterlagen, the first two forming part of the *mensa abbatialis*, while the third belonged to the *mensa conventualis* and as such was administered by the provost.

This fragmentation was only one aspect of the decomposition of the classical estate. We must now turn to some processes of even greater importance: the changes that affected the demesne, the decline of labour services and the disintegration of the holdings.

c. *The transformation of the demesne*

The majority of *villae* in the early eleventh century still seem to have retained a demesne, even though it might be already diminished as a result of enfeoffments, usurpations, or other factors. In the opinion of the writer it is impossible for this period to give any estimate of the average ratio borne by the extent of the demesne to that of the holdings. The nearly equal totals (16,020 hectares and 16,728 hectares respectively) of the demesnes and manses on the 22 estates of Saint-Germain-des-Prés which are listed in the *Polyptyque* of Irminon at the beginning of the ninth century are unlikely to have remained the same at the beginning of the eleventh century. It may be surmised that the first total would have diminished more than the second. Nor is it probable that the generally accepted figure of between one-quarter and one-half, for the ratio between the cultivated lands of the demesne and those of the holdings on the great estates of what is now France between the eighth and tenth centuries, holds good for the beginning of the eleventh century, though the diminution in the demesne is impossible to estimate. For Germany, it has been calculated that in the eleventh century demesnes covered rather more than 13 per cent of the estates of the abbey of Lorsch, and about 20 per cent of those of St Emmeram of Regensburg. But these figures are given with reserve, as a mere indication of an order of magnitude.

One of the most important contributory factors in the diminution of the demesne in the eleventh and twelfth centuries is to be found in the usurpations carried on by the estate officials, chiefly by the stewards or bailiffs (*maires, meier, maiores, villici*) but in a lesser degree by other agents (provosts, foresters, and so on) and, on ecclesiastical estates, often by the *avoués*. Those of the stewards or bailiffs, which may be singled out for particular notice, took a great variety of forms. They would appropriate for themselves a large part of the revenues which they were entrusted with collecting on behalf of the lord. They would add lands belonging to the demesne, sometimes the demesne farm itself, to their own *ex-officio* holdings. This conglomeration of lands they would claim to hold as a fief and naturally as an hereditary fief, for they usually succeeded in making their functions hereditary. The process is clearly illustrated in the case of the steward of the *villa* of Halen, belonging to the abbey of Sint-Truiden and situated in the present-day Belgian province of Brabant. The conduct of Jan the steward, by origin a serf, was such that he was rightly termed *reddituum villae ipsius plus quam dici potest vorago...et calamitas*. He took advantage of the anarchy at the end of the eleventh century to get possession of part of the abbey property which rightly belonged to the demesne, and to raise himself to a higher status. He was succeeded by his son Macarius, who continued his depredations, and went so far as to convert his house into a stronghold. In 1146 the abbot was obliged to conclude an agreement with him which had the effect of legalizing the usurpations of father and son. It was no longer merely a question of lands appropriated by the *maire* and held as if they were his own. The *curtis* was openly in his hands; he no longer had to answer for the rights he exercised as steward; the poll-tax due from the members of the *familia*, the rents of the *mansionarii*, i.e. the tenants holding lands in the *terra mansionaria*, the bridge tolls, and a whole series of other productive rights were in his possession. To the abbot he owed but two quit-rents a year of fifteen *solidi*, and lodging for a day and a night (but without free supply of bread, wine, or forage) on the occasion of the general courts held three times a year. It was further agreed that he should hold in fief the neighbouring land of Meldert, which his father had seized.

Our example is taken from a section of the Low Countries—Lower Lotharingia—which at that time was part of Germany. But it is only one instance of a general phenomenon. The same sort of thing is to be found upon almost all the estates of German churches and abbeys which have been studied; at Reichenau and Saint Gall, in Swabia, and at Paderborn in Westphalia, to cite but a few examples. In Germany it was complicated by the fact that there the stewards and other estate officials like the cellarers (*cellerarii, Kellerer*) had become members of that aristocracy of the unfree, that knighthood of servile origin, the *ministeriales*, and so could count on their fellow *ministeriales* to support their pretensions. But even though this addition to the difficulties of the lords did not arise in France, the usurpations of stewards, provosts and foresters followed the same course there as elsewhere. For a proof of this, one has only to read the little treatise which Abbot Suger wrote on his reorganization of the property of Saint-Denis, and it would be easy enough to support these examples by cases drawn from other parts of the French kingdom as distant, and as different from one another as Flanders, the Chartres district, Burgundy, and Saintonge.

In many cases the lords were obliged to cut their losses and to recognize the stewards' usurpations. An important part of the demesne lands, often including the former *casa indominicata*, or *Fronhof* of the German estates, would be abandoned to the steward, who would cultivate it for himself and collect a part of the rents of the holdings, also for himself. He would owe to the lord only *redevances forfaitaires*, quit-rents (*cens*) up to a fixed amount, and generally also strictly limited hospitality rights. Examples abound, extending from the mid-eleventh century to the thirteenth century; they are met with in Western Germany, in Lotharingia, in Flanders, in Northern France, to quote only the regions where 'soundings' have been taken. Most date from the twelfth century. The case of the estate of the abbey of Sint-Truiden, at Halen, quoted above, is a typical example.

Thus in many cases a great part, sometimes the greater part, of the demesne had become a distinct estate, to which there were likewise attached rights and sometimes lands among the holdings of the original *villa*. The steward, thus turned lord, often had an agent to run his farm for him. This was certainly the case on the *villicatio* of Burg and Friemersheim, held of the abbey of Werden on the Ruhr about 1230 by one *Wilhelmus de Vrimershem, miles*. The same was true of the *maire* of Douchy, an estate of the abbey of Sint-Pieter of Ghent, in Hainault; a charter of 1220 mentions a *villicus* nominated by the *maire* to exercise his powers on the spot. These will suffice as examples.

Yet on other ecclesiastical estates we can discern in the second half of the twelfth and the first half of the thirteenth centuries successful attempts to eliminate the *maire*, either by buying out his office, or by legal process. Of this certain estates of the abbey of Saint-Amand in the North of France provide examples. At Papegem, one of the abbey of Sint-Bavo's estates east of Ghent, the abbey, after having attempted in vain to recover the free disposal of the demesne so as to restore direct exploitation, nevertheless succeeded in imposing on the *maire* a system which enabled it to be closely associated with the management of the demesne. In this case, as on many other estates, the steward remained charged with the collection at the *Fronhof* of those estate revenues which had not been abandoned to him, and was answerable to the lord for them.

These few instances show that, even though the usurpations of estate officials were indeed widespread and affected to a considerable degree the integrity and direct cultivation of the demesne on many estates, it would nevertheless be wrong to believe that the great landowners deliberately diminished the area of the demesne or abandoned its direct management. We must therefore examine the cases where the demesne was parcelled out among the tenants: cases easily found in documents of the period.

In the first place there were certain demesne strips which used to be cultivated not by means of the 'week-work' due from the tenants (the *curvada* of the Carolingian *polyptycha*) but by means of what has been called piece-work or *corvée aux pièces* (the *riga* of the same documents), whereby a certain piece of land had to be tilled by the occupant of a certain holding. These fractions of *culturae* were called *ansanges* (*ancingae*) in the Lorraine district, and *petitorii iornales* along the lower Rhine; but they are also found elsewhere. They generally ended by being converted in the eleventh or twelfth century into holdings at a quit-rent (*cens*), greatly to the advantage of the tenants upon whom the burden of their cultivation had originally rested. If the lords thus resigned themselves to give up these portions of the demesne to their tenants this may well have been due to the half-hearted way in which the tenants performed the labour services assigned to them with the land. In this case again we can hardly speak of a deliberate policy on the part of the lords.

Other lands were removed from 'direct' cultivation by the creation in the eleventh and twelfth centuries of holdings for the serfs attached to the demesne farm, who had originally been supported on it. This was of widespread occurrence; it is to be found both in France and Germany. These creations were usually small holdings, clearly distinguished from the *manses*, and sometimes had a special name like *curtes*, or *dominicales curtes* on the estates of the abbey of Sint-Truiden. In many German-speaking regions they were designated by the words *kot* or *Haus*; hence the various names applied to their occupants, *kossaten* or *Kötner* in Brabant, the Rhineland and Saxony, *Häusler* in Swabia. Probably the *serfs cottiers* in France had the same origin. In these instances, as has been shown for the estate of Zingem between the rivers Schelt and Leie to the south of Ghent belonging to the abbey of Sint-Bavo, the motive appears often to have been to preserve and attract the labour necessary to cultivate the demesne by creating tenancies so small as to oblige the occupants to hire themselves out to the lord.

These instances of the diminution of the demesne could be multiplied but they all show that this phenomenon was not the result of a deliberate policy of the lords. Mostly the abandonment or the parcelling up of the demesne was accidental and something which the lords could not have resisted. Even when they made up their minds to divide some of the demesne among the tenants one suspects them of having been forced to do so by labour difficulties. In general, the lords even in the twelfth century were reluctant to sever permanently their connexion with the demesne lands.

What has just been said about the diminution of the demesne does not apply in the same way to the wastes and less fertile parts of the demesne—the *Beunde* of the German documents—and the poor or water-logged grasslands. Efforts were made to bring them under cultivation, or to improve them, by what we have termed 'local' clearances. The division of land, at any rate in France, present-day Belgium and on the left bank of the Rhine, was carried out by means of grants not *à cens* but *à champart* (*campipars*, *agrarium*) or *terrage* (*terragium*), that is to say, in return for a share in the produce. As it was almost exclusively arable land which was being handled in this way, the rent would be fixed in sheaves; very frequently the tenant had to pay the twelfth sheaf, though heavier rates, e.g. the tenth, sixth, fifth, or fourth sheaves are to be met with. It would appear that in certain parts of France, for instance in the district round Paris, grants *à champart* were not originally hereditary, but became so before the thirteenth century. This, however, is exceptional; nothing similar has been found in those parts of modern Belgium, like Hainault and the Namur district, where *champart* and *terrage* have been studied.

Attention has been drawn to the fact that in the region of the Middle Rhine and Moselle during the second half of the twelfth century grants of the *Beunde*, or of large portions of it and even of other parts of the demesne, were being made not to individuals but to groups of tenants. This has been misinterpreted to support an erroneous belief in a primitive communism. It is perhaps to grants of this nature that we must look for the beginnings of some of the 'marks' to be found in many parts of Germany and in the east of what is now the Netherlands at the end of the Middle Ages and in modern times, which in appearance were collective estates belonging to peasant communities.

The creation of secondary centres of cultivation to which peasant holdings were sometimes attached can in certain cases be explained by the clearing of parts of the demesne. Often these secondary centres would cease to be directly dependent on the lord, and would be granted at quit-rents, sometimes after they had been appropriated by estate officials. Thus upon the estate immediately surrounding the abbey of Sint-Truiden there were in the twelfth century two secondary *curtes* besides the *curtis indominicata* of the abbey. Of these, that of Melveren was cultivated directly, but that of Metsteren was held at a quit-rent by *forestarii*. Parallel cases seem to have occurred on the estates of Saint-Denis in France and on the Rhineland estates of Werden on the Ruhr, at the same period.

While, as has been said, meadowlands were generally retained in demesne longer than arable lands, they also were sometimes granted to tenants. To cite only one example, out of the eight demesne meadows on the estate immediately surrounding the abbey of Sint-Truiden, three were held at quit-rents, or in other words had become or had been divided into tenancies, in the twelfth century.

It may perhaps also be mentioned that during the twelfth and thirteenth centuries the tenants' efforts to consolidate and increase to their own advantage the rights of usage which they enjoyed in the demesne meadows, woodlands and wastes (*warechaix, terres vagues*) often amounted in practice to the complete expropriation of the lord. It is difficult to get a clear idea of this process because it has left no traces in the documents except here and there where there was a struggle in which some lord succeeded in preserving a part of his rights. Such was the controversy which arose between the abbot of Saint-Bertin and the tenants of his estate of Arques, over a *mariscus* the use of which they had entirely usurped and which they were proceeding to treat as their own possession; in 1232 the abbot managed to enforce regulations limiting the rights of the tenant community. A similar solution was adopted in many other places: when a lord, were he proprietor or tenant in fief, saw his right of usage and even his ownership of part of his lands disputed and threatened by the tenants enjoying the use of them, the situation was ended by coming to an agreement. Usually this meant a partition of the land in dispute, and over the part whose use had been abandoned to them the tenant community did in fact exercise most of the attributes of legal ownership. This was the origin of many 'commons' in Belgium and Northern France.

But even if the lords appeared ready to give up some uncultivated and less fertile parts of the demesne, it must not pass unnoticed that the clearing of these could often lead to an extension of the arable lands of the demesne which would compensate for its reduction in size. Only certain landlords took part in such clearing undertakings; they were smaller landlords and abbeys belonging to orders of recent foundation, such as Cîteaux or Prémontré, of which more will be said later. Many examples can be found in Flanders, the Namurois, the North of France, Burgundy and elsewhere, and they reflect the vital attachment of the proprietors to the direct cultivation of their own lands.

What appearance did the demesne present after all these transformations had taken place? In some places it disappeared altogether, but as a general rule it survived, though in a greatly diminished form. In the estate of Thiais, on the Seine, belonging to the abbey of Saint-Germain-des-Prés, the demesne had an area of 257 hectares at the beginning of the ninth century, and only a little over 91 hectares in 1384. A sampling of the sources relating to districts so distant and so different from each other as the districts round Paris and Hainault suggests that this was the general trend, at any rate from the point of view of the sort of change in size which took place. Naturally the extent of the demesne varied from district to district, so that no general rule can be laid down.

Neither must it be forgotten that the descriptions in the Carolingian *polyptycha* frequently referred to exceptionally large demesnes. So far as the ideal size of a lord's estate goes, we have, for the twelfth century, an unimpeachable witness in Suger, the celebrated abbot of Saint-Denis, who in the account he wrote on his own administration (*liber de rebus in administratione sua gestis*), gives us his opinion as to the extent of a demesne. Suger believed that a demesne was necessary, but he wished it to be reduced in size; he thought it should consist of a house which would serve as a residence for the monks charged with running the manor and as a lodging when the abbot was on his travels, a garden and a number of fields just sufficient to provide for the needs of the ecclesiastical personnel living in the manor house, barns to store the product of tithes and revenues in kind delivered by the tenants; sheep pastures, and if necessary a fishpond and some vines; in all a medium-sized farm which could be run by a few servants, and which could make use of the additional assistance of men subject to labour services in times of heavy agricultural work.

We shall now consider the history of these labour services.

D. *The decline of labour services*

In estimating the importance of this phenomenon it must be remembered that labour services, at least in the areas north of the Loire, were the principal dues owed by tenants of the *villa* to the lord, being far more important than quit-rents (*cens*) and that both industrial and agricultural *corvées* were extremely heavy. Labour services were gradually reduced to insignificance during the period under study. Their decline can be detected as far back as the end of the Carolingian period and it became progressively more marked.

One of the principal reasons for this can be traced to the breach which the enfeoffments and usurpations had caused in the relations between demesne and holdings charged with services. The movement, as has been said, certainly began before our period, at any rate in France, the kingdom of Burgundy, and the westernmost parts of Germany. Other factors also came into play. One of them—and it was of capital importance—was certainly the resistance of the tenants, who hated sacrificing the cultivation of their holdings to work on the lord's fields. The struggle, carried on as it was by a sort of passive resistance, has left little trace in the documents, but that it took place appears to be beyond dispute. The fragmentation first in fact and later in law of the unit of tenure, the *manse* or *Hufe*, with which we shall deal later on, played into the hands of the resisters and made the task of the lord who tried to exact regular labour services very difficult. Account must also be taken of factors of a less fundamental and less general character. Since the twelfth century, perhaps since the second half of the eleventh century in areas of early town development, the attraction exercised on tenants by the towns and later by the privileged *bourgs* may have led lords to reduce their demands for labour services in order to dissuade tenants from deserting their estates. Moreover, during and after the eleventh and twelfth centuries lords, and especially ecclesiastical lords, not infrequently wanted above all else to have fixed revenues at their disposal, and themselves encouraged the commutation of labour services for rents in kind or in money. It was the period when the growth of exchange put more money at the disposal of tenants while at the same time it made it easier for the lords to engage wage-labour. In the end, the labour provided by those who owed such service became superfluous, or 'useless' to repeat the expression in a document of the abbey of Marmoutier in Alsace of 1117, to which we shall refer again. The improvement of agricultural tools, new methods of harnessing animals and the use of horses obviated the need of the lord to assemble large teams of workers, while labour services of another type were still being created by the use of the *bannum*.

The reduction and sometimes complete suppression of labour services did not take place everywhere at the same time or in the same fashion. In France, in the neighbouring parts of the kingdom of Burgundy and in Germany west of the Rhine, it occurred fairly early. But there were some local differences. Industrial services, which had disappeared almost completely over the greater part of France, at all events in the district round Paris, by the first few years of the twelfth century at latest, did not disappear until the beginning of the next century in the county of Namur. Agricultural services, where they did survive, were no longer of very great importance; instead of three days a week, a burden current in the Carolingian period, they would now amount to a few days—two, three, six, ten, occasionally but rarely more than ten—a year. These figures have been observed in the villages around Paris, as for instance in the old estate of Thiais, belonging to the abbey of Saint-Germain-des-Prés; Flanders and Hainault show similar results. Sometimes agricultural labour services disappeared altogether. This seems to have been the case as early as the eleventh century on the estates of the abbey of Saint-Bertin, while out of 120 villages in which the other great Flemish abbey of Saint-Vaast of Arras had tenants agricultural services survived in ten only in the twelfth century, and in six of these ten the maximum was three days a year. On the estates of the Benedictine abbey of Affligem, founded towards the end of the eleventh century on the borders of Flanders and Brabant, no trace has been found of agricultural services. On the lands of the abbey of Marmoutier in Alsace, the *servitium triduanum*, or three-days-a-week corvée, was still being exacted in the tenth and the first years of the eleventh century. But it became obviously more difficult to impose as the latter century proceeded, and in 1117 it was abolished and replaced by a money rent. Labour services on the demesne meadows—fencing, mowing and haymaking corvées—in general survived longer, and the same is true of carrying services.

In Germany beyond the Rhine, the movement was slower and less general. Whereas on the left bank of the river, on the estates of the abbey of Werden on the Ruhr, at Burg and at Friemersheim, building and labour services had been all replaced by rents in wheat, oats or in money by the end of the twelfth century, a three-days-a-week corvée, applying to numerous tenants, is still to be met with on some estates in Saxony at the same time. On the other hand, on other estates in Saxony and Franconia about which it has been possible to gather information the field corvées had been very much reduced, although these were sometimes still as much as one day a week. As was the case west of the Rhine, work in demesne meadows and carrying services generally lasted longer than the others.

The diminution or disappearance of labour services necessarily had the effect of breaking the close connexion which had existed in Carolingian times between the demesne and the holdings. Henceforth tenants had greater freedom in disposing of their productive efforts. They could grow more on their own lands and sell the surplus on the market in order to obtain the pennies that were demanded of them. So far as the demesne was concerned an important and indeed inevitable change took place in the method of running it. The *servi proprii* or *quotidiani*, the *hagastaldi*, the *solivagi*, the *provendarii*, that is to say the domestic serfs who were the descendants or successors of the slaves formerly attached to the demesne farm, were too few in numbers to work unaided the *culturae* of the *terra indominicata*. Hired labour indeed now played a far more important part than it had done in the eighth, ninth, and tenth centuries. On the estates of the abbey of Sint-Truiden, at the end of the eleventh century and the beginning of the twelfth, the monks had recourse largely to hired labour not only for the tillage of their fields, but also for mowing and haymaking in their meadows; and this is far from being an isolated instance. But, speaking generally, hired labour could not be more than complementary to that drawn from other sources. In spite of the increase in population of which we have already spoken, the available supply of hired labour was insufficient to enable demesnes of the Carolingian type to be cultivated entirely by its means.

E. *The disintegration of the holdings*

To understand the process of the disintegration of the holdings we must begin with the unit of tenure of the *terra mansionaria*, generally called *mansus*[1] or sometimes *masura* in the Romance districts and the Germanic borderlands, and *Hufe*, *hoeve* (most often in the latinized form *hoba*) in the Germanic districts proper. Sometimes the terms *colonia, colonica*, or in Southern Gaul *condoma, casalis*, have the same meaning. The *hostisia* (when this word does not mean the holding of a *hospes*) common between the Rhine and the Loire, the *accola* and *borda* (F. *borde*) found in the West and in Roussillon, and the *apendaria* to be met with in Languedoc, are smaller holdings.

The size of the unit of tenure naturally varied considerably; it was a function of the productivity of the soil and of other factors too. However, we shall not go far wrong in reckoning the average size of the *manse* or *Hufe* at something over 10 hectares; say from eleven to sixteen. Such an estimate would appear to be justified by a sampling of evidence relating to the Parisian district, the Midi, Brabant, Flanders, Lorraine, the Moselle country, Franconia, and Bavaria. It must however be borne in mind that some *manses* were much smaller and others much larger than the average.

During our period the number of *manses* upon the older estates often diminished considerably. This was usually due, as in the case of the demesne, to usurpations and enfeoffments. The evidence of the sources, even when those are discounted which express the exaggerated complaints of such and such a bishop or such and such an abbot, is irrefutable. To quote only a few examples, the seven estates of Marmoutier in Alsace not immediately surrounding the abbey contained 173 *manses* at the end of the tenth century and only 113½ at the beginning of the eleventh century. In the early twelfth century more than 30 *manses* were lost to the Halen estate of the abbey of Sint-Truiden, thanks to the activities of the *avoué* and of a neighbouring lord. At Friemersheim and Burg, Rhineland estates belonging to the abbey of Werden on the Ruhr, the 54 *manses* in existence in the mid-eleventh century had been reduced to 38 by the end of the twelfth century. Sometimes, however, such losses might be partially repaired, when the *terra mansionaria* of one estate was increased by adding to it lands which had originally belonged to another and from which they had become separated as a result of inheritance or subdivision or of the alienation of single *manses* or groups of *manses*.

As early as the end of the tenth century, and to an even greater extent during the eleventh and twelfth centuries, certain *manses* were tending

[1] See above, p. 277.

to become detached from the rest by reason of the special duties laid upon their holders. This phenomenon was by no means new; compare for example the tenures of the *caballarii* of Saint-Bertin in the middle of the ninth century, or those of the *scararii* of Prüm at the end of it. But it now became both more common and more widespread, at any rate in Germany, including the westernmost parts of that realm. *Manses, que cum caballis serviunt*, thus singled out of the mass of ancient free *manses* in several of the Alsatian estates of Marmoutier, appear during the first half of the eleventh century, but are not yet distinguished in the documents of the tenth century. The *equiarii mansus* to be met with on the estates of Werden on the Ruhr in the twelfth century probably had the same origin. In the opinion of the writer these *manses* did not always constitute the *fiefs de service*, or *Dienstlehen*, of *ministeriales*. But they clearly enjoyed a privileged status so far as the dues of their holders were concerned, and they did not play the normal role of *manses* in the life of the estate.

But the most important feature in the process of disintegration of the *terra mansionaria* was the decomposition of the *manse* itself. This is a fact common to all the countries here discussed, and it had been long on the way. In the ninth century it was by no means uncommon for two or even three households to be settled on the same *manse*. At a very early date it is observable that the dwelling-house and close do not share the lot of the farmland making up the holding; in the eleventh century, and sometimes earlier, the former under the name of *mansus* (*meix*, *mès*, *mas*) or *curtile* (*courtil*) is clearly distinguished from the *territorium*, *sors*, or *terra*. While the *curtile* generally remained entire, the other lands were divided. This had already happened throughout most of France by the twelfth century. In Lotharingia conditions were the same as in Northern or Eastern France; by the end of the twelfth century the *manse* was almost gone as a unit of tenure, even as a divided holding, in Brabant, Hainault, and the districts round Namur and Liège. It survived only as a land measure, the equivalent of a certain number of *bonniers*. Moreover, in Lorraine and around Namur it had given way to a smaller unit, the *quartier*, which in its turn was often subdivided in the thirteenth century. In all these districts and throughout the greater part of France the *manse* had ceased to be even a rent-collecting unit. It seems, however, to have preserved this attribute longer in enclosed districts, notably in the Limousin, where the lands were grouped around the dwelling houses, and also in certain open-field districts, for instance in Flanders, on the estates of the abbey of Sint-Bavo in the region of Aalst, where the survival of a strong manorial system and a less advanced social structure right on into the thirteenth century (which we shall have to refer to again) help to explain this phenomenon. In

Germany, including the Rhine and Moselle districts, the *Hufe* was also divided in the twelfth century and especially in the thirteenth into fractions of one-half, one-quarter and even one-eighth (*Halbehufe*, *Viertelhufe*, etc.). But this division, while putting an end to the *Hufe* as a unit of cultivation, generally allowed it to survive as a unit of collection.

In places where the break-up of the *manse* was both early and complete, it resulted in a regrouping of holdings. As a result of divisions among heirs, or alienations, a *curtile* or *mansus* might be joined to lands derived from another *manse*, from the break-up of the demesne, or from clearances. In this way there were formed the entirely new holdings which in thirteenth-century Flanders, Hainault, and Northern France were frequently called *hereditas* (Fr. *héritage*; Dutch *erve*), and which now preserved only the feeblest connexion, if any, with the older *manse*. The *hereditas* might, indeed, consist of a farmhouse (*curtile*) alone or land alone, but usually it comprised both.

III. *New forms of manorial organization*

The break-up of the *villa* was but one aspect of the changes in manorial organization which began in the tenth century, were in full swing in the eleventh and twelfth centuries, and were completed in the thirteenth. Besides the negative aspect which we have been dealing with hitherto, we have to discuss the positive aspect of this change. While the connexion between demesnes and holdings was broken, while labour services were declining and holdings disintegrating the lords had been seeking to adapt themselves to the new circumstances; and from their efforts at adaptation were born new forms of manorial organization. Before describing these, something must be said about the efforts at reorganization and in particular about one of the methods of which use was made.

A. *Attempts at reorganization*

The only attempts at reorganization known to us during the period under discussion were those on the ecclesiastical estates. These efforts were numerous, and some of them appear to have been in the nature of a continuous process. Allusion has already been made to the attempts made by many religious houses both in France and Germany to build up by gift or purchase the complete *villae* of which they had already been granted parts. To judge by the situation revealed in documents of the thirteenth and early fourteenth centuries, this policy met with success only in a very limited number of cases. The same is true of the efforts made by many religious houses to recover estates or parts of estates usurped by kings, princes, nobles, and even bishops; there were, as has been said, some restitutions of this sort, but altogether they represented but a small proportion of what had been seized.

Besides these continuous efforts, there were those undertaken from time to time on particular estates. The history of many abbeys and of a few cathedral or collegiate churches preserves the memory of some abbot or prelate who, in the twelfth or thirteenth century, employed his gifts as an administrator in an effort to bring order out of the chaos which threatened the property of his house. A famous instance is that of Suger, who reorganized the estates of Saint-Denis during the second quarter of the twelfth century. His reorganization, of which he himself has left an account in his *Liber de rebus in administratione sua gestis*, remained the foundation of the economic life of the abbey until the eve of the Hundred Years' War. No less remarkable, though in fields more modest than that illustrious and wealthy house, were the achievements of Meinhard (1132–46) at Marmoutier in Alsace, about the same time; of Abbots Henry and Baudouin of the abbey of Sint-Bavo of Ghent in the first half of the thirteenth century; and, in the mid-thirteenth century, of Hugues-Varin at the abbey of Liessies in Hainault, and of Willem van Rijckel at the monastery of Sint-Truiden at some distance to the North-west of Liège.

The striking feature about these attempts is their lack of any general guiding principle. Such men worked in a hurry, they made the best of what they had, they simplified, they were opportunist in their methods. Yet, as we have already had occasion to observe, the preservation of the direct management of the demesne was often one of their major preoccupations. This did not necessarily imply a return to past conditions, as was the case with Meinhard, who wanted each estate to have its *terra indominicata* and *terra mansionaria*; but even so it is chiefly dominated by the desire to simplify administration by making the types of holdings more uniform. On the other hand Suger probably represented best the general tendency. He was concerned to maintain or to create within each manorial unit a demesne generally of small extent, although the measures he took were most directly inspired by local conditions. The *curia* of Saint-Lucien, close by Saint-Denis, was cultivated by *servientes* who paid an insufficient *cens* to the abbey; he settled eighty *hospites* on the land there, constructed a new *curia* (La Courneuve) and it produced twenty pounds more a year. At Le Tremblay, Suger bought back the *exactiones* of the Countess of Dammartin, and built a new *curia* with a grange to receive the produce of the *champart*; these and other measures considerably increased the income from the estate. The situation at Beaune-la-Rolande, in Gâtinais, was improved by the recovery of usurped pieces of land, the lightening of royal *exactiones*, the introduction of *hospites*, and the encouragement of vine-growing. At Guillerval, near Étampes, in the same district, the abbey revenues were increased by the creation of a *curia* to replace the one usurped by the steward, and the substitution of a produce-rent for a quit-rent.

One of the features which may be distinguished as common to the various attempts at reorganization is the creation of a larger number of property-groups, in order to assure a more regular collection of revenues, especially from isolated properties. During the rule of Abbot Meinhard at Marmoutier, the original number of four *curtes* on the remoter abbey estates in Alsace was increased by thirteen new foundations; and this is typical. Parallel examples could easily be multiplied in France and Germany. Another common feature was the compilation of inventories; that made and kept up to date by Abbot Willem van Rijckel of Sint-Truiden between 1249 and 1272 served as the basis of his reorganization. Yet another feature was the special attention paid to the careful collection of all revenues, quit-rents, produce-rents, and tithes, and to their revaluation when circumstances permitted. Finally, in certain instances new methods were adopted, as we shall see later on.

The few documents which are preserved concerning the manorial administration of princes and nobles at the end of the twelfth and in the thirteenth centuries show that the attempts made by many of them to secure better management and bigger revenues from their estates were marked by the same main features. These—inventories, regrouping of properties, a rigorous control of revenues—were all to be found on the estates of the Count of Flanders in the early twelfth, perhaps as early as the late eleventh, century; but it is impossible to generalize from facts concerning so exceptionally rich and powerful a personage.

One observation concerning these attempts at reorganization remains to be added to those already made. In the course of the twelfth century and to an even greater extent of the thirteenth religious houses were generally alienating the remoter properties from which they drew some particular commodity. This is not to say that they gave up the practice of using certain estates for specialized forms of production. In the thirteenth century Saint-Denis drew its corn supply mainly from the estate of Cergy on the Lower Oise, and in the second half of the twelfth century the abbot of Werden on the Ruhr got all his breeches from his Saxon estates in and around Lüdinghausen. But really remote properties, far from the centre of administration, like those which religious houses in the Low Countries held in the distant vine-growing districts of the Rhine, Moselle, Champagne, and Paris, which were difficult to run and to defend against usurpations, were most often sold or exchanged. For the development of trade was now making it easy to buy wine or other commodities not produced on the spot.

B. *Leases for a term of years*

Among the measures undertaken to reorganize the estate was the adoption of a new method of granting land, letting it out on lease for a fixed term. This is so important, both in itself and in its consequences, that it must be discussed in some detail.

The first grants for a fixed term appear to have been expedients dictated by special circumstances, as when in the first half of the twelfth century the abbey of Saint-Denis leased the estate of Beaune-la-Rolande, in Gâtinais, to the *servientes* who managed it, for the sum of 30 pounds per annum, renewable annually. There were cases of this kind elsewhere, for example the leasing in 1126 of a mill on the estate of Harnes in South Flanders, by the abbey of Sint-Pieter of Ghent, and six cases of lease for a term of years known in Normandy during the twelfth century, the first two dated 1110 and 1113.

But apart from such rather isolated instances, we must wait until the second half or end of the twelfth century, or even as late as the thirteenth century, before leases became a very common way of cultivating an estate. In France there are examples dating from 1183 and 1200 in Maine; they are encountered in Burgundy in 1227, perhaps 1216, and in 1219 in Roussillon. In the Low Countries, they were quite usual in Hainault and around Namur by the end of the twelfth century; but the first known documents relating to Flanders, Brabant, and the Liège district in which they occur are not earlier than the second quarter of the thirteenth century. In Holland leases appear to have been a novelty at the end of that century. In Germany beyond the Rhine, the earliest evidence for the region where they were to develop most widely, Lower Saxony, dates from 1176. These commencing dates are given only by way of indication; exhaustive study would perhaps enable them to be pushed further back. Moreover, the majority of leases must have been made verbally, so that no trace is left of them.

It appears that the use of fixed-term leases first spread more or less widely on the estates of great lords like princes or bishops, that is, the lords who were most remote from their lands. In Namurois, for instance, about the year 1200 only the lands of the count himself and the chapters were farmed out; the abbeys in this region, which were usually modest in size, did not follow suit freely until the middle of the thirteenth century.

The success of the farm lease became both evident and widespread during the second half of the thirteenth century. Its success appears to have been made certain by the financial crises through which many abbeys and landed proprietors were passing at that moment, when leasing of demesne lands was often undertaken as part of a deliberate policy. It was systematically utilized by abbot Willem van Rijckel who, in tackling the financial problems of the abbey of Sint-Truiden in the middle of the thirteenth century, had to reorganize radically the management of the abbey estates. In consequence of the parlous state of their finances, between the middle of the thirteenth century and the year 1281, the abbey of Sint-Pieter of Ghent not only leased all its *curtes* and the lands appertaining to them, but also a large number of separate parcels of land, especially in polders reclaimed from the sea, and certain tithes. A *Liber inventarius* drawn up in 1281 on the occasion of a reform in the estate organization shows that out of a total revenue of £228.17s. belonging to the office of the *custodia*, £196 came from leases and only £32.1s. from quit-rents; similar proportions occur in other offices of the house, notably in that of the provost of Brabant. At the end of the thirteenth century even lands owing quit-rents were leased; in other words the right of collecting rents due from land was farmed out. The same policy can be seen on the estates of the abbey of Saint-Martin of Tournai in 1275, and on those of the abbey of Sint-Bavo of Ghent in 1300. These examples could be easily multiplied. It was nevertheless still too early for the spread of these new practices in different regions to be plotted on a map.

The practice of granting fixed-terms leases seem to have been applied in the first place to demesne farms, which were very often leased in this way throughout the thirteenth and fourteenth centuries. The older *curtes* of the estates were often so dealt with, and still more the *curtes* of recent creation, over which the estate officials had not yet been able to acquire rights prejudicial to the lord. In some parts of Germany the lords made systematic efforts to get such rights abolished and to impose leases upon stewards; for example in Lower Saxony, where the name *Meiergut* was first given to *curtes* leased to *Meier*.

But fixed-term leases were not confined to demesne farms and to the lands belonging to them. A large part, sometimes even the whole of the land still in demesne, was often divided up and let to farmers for a fixed term. This applies mainly to the *culturae* (*coutures*), or arable fields and to the wastes (the *Beunden* of the German documents), but we also meet with leases of meadows and even of woods. Thus in 1280 twelve peasants shared in unequal portions the 24 *bonniers* of tillage which previously the canons of Saint-Lambert of Liège had themselves cultivated in one village. Elsewhere, on the frontiers of Flanders and Hainault, according to the rent book of the lords of Pamele-Oudenaarde, about 1275 an ancient demesne was farmed out every year *bonnier* by *bonnier*. It may also have been so in part of Normandy, for the thirteenth-century rental of Mont-Saint-Michel lists more than 200 leases in Verson and Bretteville alone. But this piecemeal leasing does not seem to have been widespread in the thirteenth century. It was rare for customary holdings previously granted in perpetuity at quit-rents (*cens*) to be subsequently let out on lease by the lord, even when chance caused the *dominium utile* to revert to him. Examples are to be met with on the estates of the abbey of Sint-Truiden in the thirteenth century, but these appear to be isolated. There was, however, one region where this observation certainly does not apply, viz. North-Western Germany and in particular Lower Saxony. The lords there were usually enfranchising their semi-free tenants during the thirteenth and fourteenth centuries; their method was to buy up the reversion of their holdings, and to let them out again, usually after regrouping them into larger units, under the name of *Lathufen*, but this time for a fixed term *an Meiersstatt*, i.e. on the model of the *Meiergüter*, or *curtes* let on lease. Similar leases in Hessen went by the name of *Landsiedelleihe*.

Leases for a fixed term were applied not only to land, but also to rights and dues. In the thirteenth and still more frequently in the fourteenth century, tithes, rectories, various rights of user, and miscellaneous revenues were all let on lease. This happened everywhere; there was even one district of France, Auvergne, where rights and dues appear to have been leased before the same system was applied to rural properties.

Fixed-term leases took two different forms: leases in return for a share of the harvest (*bail à part de fruits*) and leases for a fixed rent (*bail à ferme*).

The former was a lease by which the landlord was paid a rent corresponding to a certain proportion of the crop and sometimes also of the natural increase of the livestock (*bail à cheptel*). This proportion was not always the same; sometimes it would be one-third, or one-quarter, but most often it would be one-half, whence the names *medietaria*, *métayage*, *Halbpacht*, and in Dutch *helftwinning*, often applied to the contract. There were other more general terms, e.g. the German *Teilbau*, and the Dutch *deelpacht*; in Hainault a produce-rent in which the lord's share was one-third was called *tierce part*. The lessee was called *medietarius*, *métayer*, *Halfmann* or *Halfen*, *halfwinner*. *Métayage* is to be met with in all the districts where leases for a term were in use; it appeared at the same time as the lease for a fixed rent, to be dealt with later, and functioned alongside it as a recognized form of tenure during the thirteenth and fourteenth centuries. In some regions, however, it soon fell into disuse, notably in parts of Northern France, Flanders, Hainault, the Namur and Liège districts, and in Western Germany. On the other hand, it became firmly established in Artois and over a great part of Western and Southern France, notably Anjou, Maine, Limousin, Poitou, Roussillon, Quercy, and Provence; it was also popular in Burgundy. In most of these districts it seems to have been an adaptation of local custom; the *medietaria* occurs there in the eleventh and twelfth centuries, in the form of a customary holding in perpetuity with a rent equal to half the produce, apparently a variety of the *champart*. Temporary leases *en métayage* probably arose out of attempts to give greater flexibility to this form of tenure.

In a *bail à ferme* the landlord's rent consisted of a quantity of goods or a sum of money which was fixed for the duration of the lease, or varied only in accordance with provisions made at the time the contract was concluded. Thus the return from such leases was not proportional to the yield of the soil. Except in the regions already mentioned where *métayage* continued to expand, the fixed rent superseded it. It went by various names: *firma* (*ferme*, or in Normandy *ferme muable*) was widespread in France and part of modern Belgium; *amodiatio* in certain parts of France. The terms *commissio*, *pensio* were used in Germany, and *pactum*, *pactus* (Dutch *pacht*) in Dutch- or Low-German-speaking countries.

The duration of *métayages* or fixed rents varied very much. Some were made for the life of the lessee, as was still frequently the case in thirteenth-century grants of *curtes*, both by ecclesiastics and laymen. In the same century leases for life became less common. The duration of the concession shrank little by little, as the movement of prices and output was more clearly understood in the world of manorial management. The duration also differed according to the region concerned. In some parts long leases were the rule, as for instance in the Chartres district in the thirteenth century, where few leases were for a shorter period than twenty years. In Normandy the term varied from one to fifteen years. In Hainault, *curtes* (commonly called *censes* in French or Picard documents) were most often let for a term of from three to eighteen years. In Lower Saxony the term was from three to twelve years. It is noticeable that in general the term was most often for three or a multiple of three years, which is explained by the practice of a triennial rotation on the field. Indeed, in the leases *à ferme* or *à métayage* concluded by Willem van Rijckel, Abbot of Sint-Truiden, it was generally stipulated that the land was let for six years of four harvests. This was to prevent the employment of a method of cultivation which might exhaust the soil—the *Raubkultur* of German economists.

The grant of a lease was frequently accompanied by special provisions. It was not uncommon for the lessor to supply at least a part of the stock and implements; sometimes clauses in the lease would insist that respect be paid to rules or usages relating to cultivation, e.g. to the manuring of fields. Sometimes the lessee would have to give sureties or pledges for the payment of the rent and the performance of other conditions.

The profound difference between grants of land for a term of years and the grant of permanent holdings was not grasped immediately by contemporaries everywhere. Opinion on this point varied from place to place. In Burgundy and Auvergne, for instance, until the fourteenth century and even later, a lease of land was treated as if it were really a sale, though of temporary effect; and the lessee was held to have a real property-right in the land. This right was also allowed to the lessee over the greater part of Germany. On the other hand, in the future Netherlands, the lease early developed as a vigorous and distinct institution; in the mid-thirteenth century on the estates of the abbey of Sint-Truiden, near Liège, leases were regularly revoked when lessees defaulted on the rent. More remarkable still, as early as 1201 the court of the Count of Hainault rejected all attempts to assimilate leases *à métayage* to grants *à champart*, holding that only those who held *sub censu vel reditu aliquo seu in feodo* had a customary tenement with a real right in the land (*tenuram vel jus*); a *métayer* could not enjoy the status of a *tenancier*, or any real property-right, but must be content with a mere personal and non-hereditary right.

What was the cause of the adoption of leasehold from the end of the twelfth century onwards? The decline and partial disappearance of labour services is only an ultimate cause. The employment of those subject to labour services had indeed often been replaced by that of hired labourers. It is, of course, very likely that the financial difficulties in which many landed proprietors, and especially abbeys, found themselves in the middle of the thirteenth century arose from the growing disequilibrium between the profits of direct cultivation of the demesne and the cost of the agricultural wages required to run it. This is probably what forced several abbeys to give up direct management and to adopt the leasehold system. The difficulty here and there of finding agricultural workers could also have had the same effect. It is also probable that the desire of the lords to share in the increased productivity of the soil had a great influence in the spread of leases. Leases permitted the adjustment of rents at relatively short intervals and thus allowed for the movement of prices. They had also the advantage of allowing the lord to choose a 'farmer' or a *métayer* for his personal qualifications, because *quem bonum terrarum cultorem noverat*, to quote a Hainault charter of 1201; and to get rid without difficulty of men who did not carry out their obligations. The lord gained more freedom in the disposal of his lands, and was assured of a more substantial profit from them. But when all is said we cannot but ask ourselves whether the adoption of the *bail à ferme* was not really due to the lords' desire to defend themselves against a continual decline in the value of money, carrying with it a depreciation in fixed money rents (*cens*). This explanation may hold good for the end of the Middle Ages and for the sixteenth century, but it seems to be of doubtful validity for the period under discussion. It is improbable that contemporaries in France and Germany were clearly aware of the decline in the value and purchasing power of money, a subject for that matter little studied up to our own time. The administrators of the royal estates in the *bailliage* of Rouen in the thirteenth and even in the fourteenth century, in letting out land for rent, appear to have made little difference between customary holdings for fixed quit-rents and leases for a term of years, charging virtually the same amount in both cases. This attitude may be explained by their mistaken belief in the stability of the currency and also by the fact that to them letting on customary tenure for rent (i.e. in perpetuity) had the advantage of greater ease of administration and relative freedom from the risk of losses through vacancy. But while the appearance and spread of leases for a term of years was of great importance, they did not become so general during our period as to oust altogether the system of customary tenures, save in certain parts of Germany such as Lower Saxony, and to a lesser extent Westphalia, Northern Hesse, Bavaria, and the high Swabian plateaux. In France most peasants continued to hold their lands by tenures of inheritance, and the same seems to be true of South-Western Germany, Hainault, and the Namur region. In the last two districts, the properties let out on lease were mainly largish farms (50 hectares and upwards around Namur) which had been carved out of the dismembered demesnes. In Flanders, judging from the few facts at our disposal, the *bail à ferme* was from the end of the thirteenth century the normal method of exploiting the large farms and also, in the polder regions along the North Sea and the Western Schelt, of a number, perhaps even most, of the parcels of land which had been won from the sea since the end of the twelfth century.

It must be emphasized that this question has been the subject of but few monographs or preliminary studies, and that any conclusions must therefore be imperfect and provisional in the extreme.

c. *The new structure of the estate*

It is now time to describe the new forms assumed by estate organization during the course of the twelfth and thirteenth centuries. Speaking very roughly, two types of estate can be distinguished: those which retained, at any rate in its general outline, the classical *villa* structure, and those in which there was no trace of this structure, either because it had disappeared, or because it had never existed. Both types might easily occur among the estates of a single lord.

To begin with the former type of estate: it must be emphasized at the outset that it hardly ever corresponds to a present-day village or to what under the *ancien régime* was a rural parish, still less to a group of villages or parishes. Most villages were divided among several estates, and many estates had lands in several villages; this was a consequence of the disintegration of the *villa*, which has already been discussed.

The demesne or home farm did not present everywhere the same aspect. We have seen that a very large, often the largest, part of it had frequently been usurped by the steward along with the original *curtis*, and had thus become a separate estate, completely distinct from the rest of the *villa*. When this happened, the remainder of the demesne, with a new *curtis*, would be put under the authority of a new official, often himself termed *maior* or *villicus*, who would act as the lord's agent. He would direct the cultivation of the demesne and it would often be devoted to relatively specialized crops such as vines, hops, and pulses, or sometimes to stock-raising. The labour services which survived would be used to work a few *culturae* or a few meadows and to ensure the transport of crops or beasts to market. However small the demesne, the labour services were never enough to cultivate it, and more frequent recourse had now to be made to hired labour. Moreover, with the thirteenth century there was a great increase in the partial or total commutation of labour services, though this was perhaps less marked on the smaller lay estates than on the great estates of the Church and the princes. The agent who managed the farm would also collect the rents of lands leased for fixed rents or to *métayers*.

If there had not been on any given occasion a definite separation between the lands abandoned to the steward and the part of the demesne remaining in the lord's hands, there would generally not be a new *curtis*, or a new agent. The successor of the former steward would continue to direct the cultivation of what remained of the demesne on the lines indicated above, but often he would run it, at least partly, for his own profit, most frequently paying the lord only a *redevance forfaitaire*, or in the case of a lease a fixed money-rent or a share of the harvest.

Whatever the origin or the composition of the peasant holdings, they now had one common characteristic: they paid dues in money or in kind, to which labour services had become purely accessory. It is hardly possible to generalize as to the relative importance of rents in kind and rents in money. It has been calculated that of 1131 holdings out of the 1330 belonging to the abbey of Saint-Vaast of Arras between 1170 and 1192, a quarter paid a money rent, another quarter a rent in money and cereals, and the remaining half a rent in money and capons, together with an occasional loaf of bread. But generalizations are impossible, and account must be taken of local conditions; thus while in Roussillon in the twelfth and thirteenth centuries rents were almost always in kind, they were usually mixed on the estates held by the abbey of Werden on the Ruhr, in Saxony and on the lower Rhine. In certain districts there was a tendency to replace quit-rents by *champart* or *terrage* when occasion offered; we find this for instance in the Namur district, in the twelfth and thirteenth centuries. More remarkable is the fact that throughout a great part of France during the second half of the twelfth and in the thirteenth centuries, around Orleans, in Normandy, in Languedoc, in Roussillon, in Poitou, and in Burgundy, produce-rents and rents in kind were frequently converted into money-rents. That the tenants gained by this is obvious. But what of the lords? Their chief object seems to have been a greater ease of administration and a more regular revenue. They detached themselves little by little from their rural background and adopted a less rustic behaviour. In acting like this they were perhaps under the delusion that the value and purchasing power of money would remain fixed. This delusion was to persist in the fourteenth century, and was so strongly held that both in France and in Germany a certain number of temporary leases were converted into permanent and hereditary ones, i.e. into something identical with customary tenures paying a fixed *cens*.

During the twelfth and especially the thirteenth centuries more and more of the customary holdings were moving in the direction of a form of tenure which owed a simple quit-rent and no labour services, the *freie Erbleihe* of German writers. Some holdings had enjoyed this status from time immemorial; others acquired it through being at some time attached to an estate too remote for labour services to be practicable; others again were privileged through having been created as a result of reclamations (such as the *sartes* or *sarts* of the Namur region) and yet others had been freed of labour services by commutation or otherwise.

We have described how the changes in the estate during the later twelfth and thirteenth centuries rendered the holdings more and more independent of the lord. The change was clearly to the advantage of the tenant, as is shown by the history of the *complant*, that is to say, the contract which was the original basis of many holdings in France and the neighbouring countries where the vine or the olive was cultivated. This contract, common in Burgundy, Dauphiné, Auvergne, over the whole South, including Provence, and over the whole West including Southern Brittany, provided for the grant of a piece of land by the lord to the *complanteur*, who at the end of five years would return one-half of it, planted, to the demesne, retaining the other half in tenure at a quit-rent or produce-rent. Such was the general rule in the eleventh and twelfth centuries; in the thirteenth century the clause providing for the return of one-half of the land to the demesne disappeared almost completely.

It remains only to consider the other elements making up an estate. We have already described how the commons had been the subject of conflicts between the lord and the tenants; conflicts which were generally ended by a settlement and often by partition. During the thirteenth and fourteenth centuries the lords made new efforts to defend and sometimes to extend rights of this sort. Then there were mills, and in some districts salt-pans, and such rights as the entry fine when a holding changed hands, and so on.

The attention which we have just devoted to quit-rents and manorial rents amongst the other income-producing elements on the estate must not allow us to forget that these, during the first half of the thirteenth century, represented no more than a contribution to the revenue of the lord whose greatest profit came from the cultivation of the demesne itself. Thanks to rent rolls (*censiers*), we possess knowledge of the lords' income from rents which is vividly at variance with what little we know of the revenues coming from the cultivation of the demesne, and this could easily distort our judgment. It has been shown above, of course, that the demesne retained a very real vigour and importance, at least until the middle of the thirteenth century. It was only towards the end of the thirteenth and in the course of the fourteenth centuries that the estate very often became a mere rent-paying institution. This characteristic appeared earlier and more strongly in those conglomerations of land in which the *villa* structure had disappeared, or had never existed. In such 'pseudo-estates' the only bond of union was geographical; they consisted of *curtes* leased or granted at quit-rents, single holdings or groups of adjacent holdings, parcels of land let on lease, and various dues such as tithes, the revenues of rectories (*altaria*), and so forth. All organic connexion between these elements was lacking. The group existed simply as a unit of administration, chiefly for the collection of revenue by a seignorial representative who played the part and often had the title of receiver.

Mention has been made of tithes and *altaria*, and the growing importance of these elements in ecclesiastical estates must be insisted on. Tithes, which had been usurped on a large scale by laymen during the tenth and eleventh centuries, were very largely recovered by the Church during the twelfth and thirteenth centuries. But they had now become the property of abbeys and chapters instead of parish churches, and from about 1150 to 1250 were the principal source of wealth of many a religious house. The fact that they had usually remained proportionate to the yield of the soil made them particularly valuable as a source of revenue. Rectories were also a source of a variety of revenues, and thanks to the glebe (*dos*) and casual receipts (*oblationes*, etc.) they played at this time an important part in the income of religious houses. To take only one example, which it would be easy to multiply for both France and Germany, about 1150 tithes and *altaria* played a much greater part in and produced a far greater share of the income of the great abbey of Echternach, in Luxemburg, than did landed property.

Tithes and *altaria* were principally to be found among the properties of the Church. On the other hand, in the thirteenth century many estates, even those of laymen, included rents levied on lands in which the lord had no other property-right. Abbeys and cathedral or collegiate churches often acquired these by donation, and both they and laymen frequently bought them for cash.

Some space must be given to the estates of the new monastic orders, Austin canons, Praemonstratensian canons, and Cistercians, which were particularly prosperous during the twelfth and thirteenth centuries. Little need be said of the Austin canons beyond the fact that the wealth of their houses seldom consisted in landed property on any scale. Their lands were mostly scattered peasant holdings, attached for administrative purposes to some *curtis* which acted merely as a centre for the collection of rents. By far the greater part of their patrimony consisted in tithes and *altaria*, if we may judge by the example of the numerous abbeys of this order which flourished in Southern Flanders and around Namur during the twelfth and thirteenth centuries. The organization of the estates of the Praemonstratensians or Norbertines, was somewhat different. Tithes, which they were at pains to acquire or to collect together again where they had been divided, and appropriated churches certainly played an important part in their economy, but so also did land. Like all estates built up relatively late in the Middle Ages, these possessions were usually very scattered, but were grouped as far as possible round *curiae* created for the purpose. The canons farmed a good deal of their land themselves, undertaking both cultivation and the reclamation of wastes. The *curia* would then become the centre of an estate, which in Flanders and Brabant might be as much as 50–100 hectares. A *magister curiae*, himself a regular canon, would direct the work, which was carried out by lay brothers, assisted by lay servants or *famuli*. The average number of lay brothers on each of the fifteen *curiae* of the abbey of Ninove, in South-East Flanders, was seven or eight. But all this did not preclude the granting of pieces of land as peasant holdings.

The organization of the Norbertines was mixed in type; that of the Cistercians was homogeneous, at least in the golden age of the order in the twelfth century. The *Instituta generalis capituli apud Cistercium* confirmed by the Pope in 1152 were formal on this point: *Ecclesias, altaria, sepulturas, decimas alieni laboris seu nutrimenti, villas, villanos, terrarum census, furnorum seu molendinorum redditus et cetera hiis similia monastice puritati adversantia nostri et nominis et ordinis excludit institutio.* All the essentials of manors and manorial groups, lay and ecclesiastical, were excluded, save only the bare earth. On it the 'white monks' worked, clearing wastes (mention has already been made of their leading share in this movement), raising crops, and pasturing their cattle. *Grangiae* or *curiae* served as centres of administration for their lands, wastes, pastures, and ploughlands. As gifts of new land came to a Cistercian abbey, new granges would be established; the abbey of Villers in Brabant, founded in 1146, had created fifteen of them by the end of the twelfth century. Reclamation, tillage, and the care of flocks were undertaken exclusively by lay brothers (*conversi*) assisted by a few *famuli*; the *grangiarius* who directed operations was himself a *conversus*.

The methods of estate management characteristic of the Praemonstratensians and the Cistercians were not maintained in their entirety. In the Norbertine abbeys, direct cultivation gave way before rent collection; by 1300 most of them had given up cultivation by lay brothers and those of the *curiae* which had not already been granted in return for quit-rents were let on lease. As for the Cistercians, as early as the twelfth century they had begun to be less strict in the observance of their rule. Through accepting donations as they stood, the abbeys were acquiring holdings held by quit-rent or produce-rent, and also tithes. In the thirteenth century it is not uncommon for a single *grangia* to have attached to it lands under direct cultivation, lands granted in return for a *cens*, and even also lands let on lease. In the fourteenth century the system of the *conversi* was to encounter a grave crisis and to disappear almost completely as an economic institution, and this meant the end of the method of direct cultivation. Like the other ecclesiastical lords, the Cistercian monasteries were to become first and foremost landlords, *rentiers* of the soil.

D. *The estate as the basis of the* 'seigneurie'

During the period from the tenth to the thirteenth centuries, side by side with the great transformation which was changing the Carolingian *villa* into the loosely organized forms of estate which we have been describing, another process was at work: the estate was becoming a *seigneurie*. Of course, the Carolingian estate was already a *seigneurie* in a very considerable degree; the lord, *potens vir*, or church, exercised a jurisdiction which, though certainly very limited, was all the more real because it dealt with what were later to be called cases of *basse justice*, that is, in effect, those which occurred most often. He had at his disposal the legal sanctions essential for maintaining order on the estate and assuring its cultivation. Churches, benefiting by the privilege of immunity, contrived to consolidate and extend these powers. In the

Carolingian period we meet the first signs of a custom which was to become widespread: the use of the word *bannum*, to describe this right to judge, to command and to punish, whereas the term properly signified the right to judge, to command and to punish wielded by the king and his representatives. The decay of central authority, especially in France, and the grants to ecclesiastical magnates, to bishops and even to abbots, of powers normally appertaining to the public authority, especially in Germany, were the principal factors making for a new increase in the power of the lords between the tenth and twelfth centuries. Nor must it be forgotten, at any rate so far as the increase in the power of lay lords is concerned, that many of them, through their position as *avoués* of ecclesiastical estates, had acquired an authority beyond the limits of their own lands, or had abused their positions to acquire or to extend such an authority.

It is difficult to grasp this process in detail; but the evidence which has been assembled regarding West and South-West Germany, Alsace, Lorraine, Hainault, Burgundy, and the district round Paris, would, in so far as it is permissible to generalize from it, appear to lead to the following conclusions. On the one hand, the lord was extending his authority beyond the territorial limits of the estate, strictly so called; he extended it to lands held by 'precarial' tenure, to lands not in themselves belonging to him, but inhabited by persons under his protection (*homines sancti, censuales,* etc.) and to adjacent lands which had no connexion, even personal, with him, but which he had brought under his authority, or which had been placed under his control by royal decree. On the other hand, within the estate itself, he was extending his power to control all who happened to live on it whether or not they were his 'men' or his tenants. Finally, by use of his *bannum*, he imposed on all alike a number of dues, the justification for which was no longer any property-right in the land, or any authority over persons by reason of their legal status, but simply the fact that by legal or illegal means he had got into his hands a part of the dismembered authority of the state.

In this way there was being constituted, principally from the eleventh century onwards, a new kind of *seigneurie* typified by its very name; for it was called *bannus* (*Bann*) throughout the greater part of Germany, including Lorraine, and *potestas* (*poesté*) in most of France. To the rights he exercised as lord of an estate, the *seigneur* would add a number of others, varying very much from place to place and often provoking disputes between neighbouring *seigneuries*. During the eleventh, twelfth, and thirteenth centuries more and more importance came to be attached to these rights of seignorial origin (*exactiones*, as they are often called in the documents) in proportion as the rights of estate origin weakened and diminished in number and yield. Thus it was sometimes possible, in the twelfth and thirteenth centuries, to obviate the results of the decay of the older corvées by the creation of new corvées imposed on all the inhabitants of the *seigneurie*: maintenance, industrial, carrying, mowing, ploughing and other corvées which, however, were much less numerous and less heavy than the estate labour services at their zenith. The right to lodging was extended in the same way and occasionally also the military service due from villeins. The seignorial monopolies or *banalités*, which developed considerably between the eleventh and fourteenth centuries (monopolies of mill, oven, winepress, of the sale of certain products like wine, and so on), had the same origin.

Finally there was a tax which belonged to the same group of seig-norial *exactiones*: the tallage or aid (French *taille, aide*; Latin *tallia, auxilium, precaria*; German and Dutch *Bede*), which became an essential part of the life of the *seigneurie* during this period. In the eleventh century it was neither fixed nor regular, but was levied whenever the lord needed material assistance and upon all his dependants. It was called the arbitrary tallage, or the tallage at will. The interests of the lord and those of the persons subject to tallage led to a change which was not carried through without violent collisions, and which took very varied forms. The important point is that sometimes as early as the twelfth century, and as a rule (though there were exceptions) in the thirteenth, the character of the tallage levied on the inhabitants of a rural *seigneurie* altered. First it became periodical, usually annual; that was in the interests of the lord. Secondly, its amount became fixed; this was in the interests of the tallaged. This fixed tax was called in France the *taille abonnée*. The sum due would be assessed among the inhabitants of the *seigneurie* on the basis of their possessions; extent of land held, number of horses, and so forth. Sometimes 'extraordinary aids' would persist in addition to the tallage.

The aspect of the *bannum* which most helped forward the development of seignorial exactions was certainly the right of jurisdiction. By pro-viding for the punishment of those refusing to obey, it made possible the organization, often in the face of lively resistance, of a system of burdens which at least in part were new. Proof of its importance may be found in the fact that over a great part of thirteenth-century Germany the surviving corvées, chiefly transport and building corvées, were owed to jurisdictional lords and to *avoués*, and that in France both the *banalités* and to a certain extent the *taille* were linked with rights of jurisdiction.

IV. *Changes in rural society*

We are dealing here not with changes in the legal status of the rural population, but with changes in its social condition. The problem has two main aspects: on the one hand the degree to which the rural population was dependent upon the lords, and on the other hand the extent of its prosperity. Obviously facts relating to personal status are essential to a discussion of these matters, just as conceptions of private and public law are inseparable from any account of the estate and the *seigneurie*.

A survey of Germany at the beginning of the period under discussion, i.e. in the eleventh century, would show that except for a still quite large number of small and middling free proprietors, mainly in Frisia, Saxony, and Thuringia, the greater part of countryfolk were in a state of definite dependence upon the lords of estates or estate-groups. Their dependence was both real, resulting from their tenure of land, and (except for wholly free tenants) also personal, by reason of the more or less extensive restrictions on liberty which characterized their status, whether they were serfs (*Leibeigenen*) or whether they belonged to one of the numerous categories of 'protected' persons (*Hörigen*). The same is true of the westernmost parts of Germany, i.e. Lotharingia, and also of the most northerly part of the kingdom of France, especially Flanders and the neighbouring regions.

In Central and Northern France the lords' dependants were usually divided into two distinct groups: the serfs (*servi*), mostly descendants of the serfs of the Carolingian period, and the non-serfs, called by various names (*villani, hospites, manentes,* etc.). The former found themselves in a strictly dependent relationship to their lord; the latter were reputed free, though the restrictions placed for the lord's benefit on the free disposal of their persons and goods make it doubtful whether they should be recognized as such. For a long time, at least till the twelfth century in certain regions, the villeins and the serfs, although living side by side on the territory of the same *seigneurie*, remained quite distinct. But a common way of life, frequent intermarriage, and the growth of a knightly class which widened the gap between freemen-become-knights and villeins remaining in a state of dependence on the lord, help to explain how eventually villeins and serfs became fused into one class. Some districts were exceptional, e.g. part of Languedoc where serfdom seems to have been much less widespread than in the districts of the Seine and Loire, and possibly Provence, beyond the borders of the French kingdom, was too.

The ultimate fate of the rural masses was not the same everywhere. In France, as the disintegration of the classical estate proceeded, the autonomy of the 'dependent' population increased. The formation of new communities of inhabitants in the towns and even in the country districts, often through the creation of rural communes which were sometimes of revolutionary origin, encouraged villeins and serfs to seek enfranchisement. From the beginning of the twelfth century there were developments in various regions which ended either in the total disappearance of the class of serfs or in their numerical increase. This was the result of two main factors, which in practice were frequently complementary, intermingled, or confused. There was, on the one hand, the creation, to which reference was made in discussing the clearances, of new settlements whose inhabitants enjoyed a privileged status. Such were the *villes neuves* founded in such large numbers in Northern and Central France during the twelfth and thirteenth centuries, and the *bastides* (some of which were never more than villages) founded in the South, especially during the thirteenth and fourteenth centuries. On the other hand, there was the grant of charters of enfranchisement, 'customs' agreed to by the lord at the request of the inhabitants of the *seigneurie*. Such was the 'charter' of Lorris in Gâtinais, granted by King Louis VI in the first half of the twelfth century, which served as a model in Gâtinais, Sénonais, Orléanais, Auvergne, and Berry; and the 'law' of the *ville neuve* of Beaumont, in Argonne, granted by Guillaume aux Blanches Mains, archbishop of Rheims, in 1182, which was similarly a model in the County of Rethel, in Champagne, and beyond France also, in Luxemburg, the County of Chiny, Barrois, and Lorraine. The promulgation during the twelfth and thirteenth centuries of these charters of enfranchisement, of which but two examples out of many have been quoted, was generally brought about through a revolt of the inhabitants of a *seigneurie* against abuses in the lord's administration, often backed up by revolutionary action on the part of a sworn commune. Often the lord would exact payment for the grant.

The essential feature of the constitutions granted to the *villes neuves* and of the provisions of the charters of enfranchisement was the limitation of the arbitrary will of the lord and the reduction of the dues burdening the inhabitants. They applied, that is to say, as much if not more to free villeins, as to serfs. They had the effect of suppressing the traditional signs of personal subjection (*chevage, mainmorte* and *formariage*) for a group of men in the same rural *seigneurie*.

In Normandy, where only a minority of tenants were serfs, no serfs were found after the first years of the twelfth century. In certain regions like the district round Paris and the Beauce, individual or collective acts of enfranchisement, usually in return for a money payment, brought about the disappearance of serfdom before the second quarter of the fourteenth century.

But in other regions like Champagne, the Franche-Comté and Vermandois, exactly the opposite happened. In these regions *chevage*, *mainmorte* and *formariage* came eventually to be considered as truly servile charges and those subjected to these charges were thought of as serfs. This assimilation of the characteristics of serfdom in the regions mentioned was pushed to such lengths that people came to attribute a state of servitude to the whole rural population.

Thus the movement of enfranchisement had not only the effect of widening the social gulf between those serfs who remained and the rest of the population; it also developed a new conception of serfdom, as a state in which the burdens imposed on individuals were completely arbitrary. The trend of opinion in the thirteenth and fourteenth centuries was towards the view that serfs, by reason of their inherently inferior status, were subject to the arbitrary will of their lord; on them alone there now rested all the burdens and restrictions which had formerly been common to all 'dependent' cultivators of limited freedom. In the twelfth century it had been common for lords to take measures to prevent their tenants leaving the estate. By the late thirteenth and fourteenth centuries this restriction had become the distinctive mark of the serf, and the Roman lawyers, who had hesitated between assimilating his status to that of the slave of antiquity (was not the serf also called *servus*?) or to that of the *colonus* of the later Roman Empire, found in imperial decrees on the colonate provisions justifying the novel claim that 'the serf is bound to the soil'. Contemporary with the enfranchisement of the mass of the French rural population was a similar movement in the districts which, at the end of the Middle Ages, were to unite to form the Netherlands. We shall not enter into details here. In Flanders enfranchisement appears to have been completed in the thirteenth century, at any rate over the greater part of the County. Perhaps the special privileges given to the *hospites*, who reclaimed, drained, and brought under cultivation the Flanders seaboard, contributed towards the early granting of the status of freemen to the inhabitants of that region. Over the whole country, but especially in the North, where as we have seen the domanial regime was weaker, the enfranchisement of serfs and semi-free dependent cultivators must have started as early as the twelfth, or even in part in the eleventh century, perhaps without the need for definite measures. When the Count, in 1232, suppressed the *melius catallum*—a mild form of *mainmorte*—for those under the jurisdiction of the *scabini* in the castellany of Bruges, the decision obviously applied to a population which could not, or could no longer, be held to be servile. Serfdom survived longer in certain parts of Flanders, for instance the Aalst district. In Hainault, where the question has been more closely studied than elsewhere, a situation has been found very similar to that of Northern France; speaking generally, the enfranchisement of the rural population took place there in the second half of the twelfth century and in the thirteenth. The means by which it was brought about were the creation of *villes neuves* and the grant of *chartes-lois*; to

22

which must be added, since in Hainault the lay patronage (*avouerie*) of ecclesiastical estates was very flourishing, the restraints imposed by numerous religious houses on their *avoués*. As in France, the result of these measures was essentially a limitation of the arbitrary power of the lord and a restriction of personal burdens. The *chartes-lois* of Hainault did not bring about the disappearance of serfdom; some of them, indeed, do not seem to have applied to serfs.

Passing from Hainault, which as a Lotharingian county formed part of Germany, to Germany proper, it is equally plain that there too from the eleventh century to the thirteenth the rural population was acquiring a greater and greater degree of personal freedom. Here the process was not due to measures of enfranchisement, but to the changes already mentioned in the organization of the estate. While serfdom properly so-called (*Leibeigenschaft*) was on the decline, the various groups of semi-free 'dependent' or 'protected' cultivators (*Hörigen*) remained important, and among them were to be found the descendants of many servile tenants. In the North, however, in the region of the *Marschen* there were numerous colonists of Flemish, Dutch, or Rhenish origin, who were acknowledged to be personally free and enjoyed a privileged status (sometimes called *flämisches Recht*) so far as their tenure was concerned.

Charters of enfranchisement designed to limit the arbitrary power of the lord are not met with in Germany. The records of the rights and duties of the inhabitants of a *seigneurie*, sometimes quoted in this connexion, are either collections of customs established by the lords themselves (*Hofrechte*) or 'statements of rights' (*Weistümer*) drawn up on the basis of an inquisition among the inhabitants by lords, usually ecclesiastics, as a protection against the pretensions of their *avoués*. They generally contain no innovations, at any rate not before the fourteenth century. They were in common use all over Germany, including Lorraine.

A greater freedom in relation to the lords did not however necessarily imply an improvement in the condition of the rural population; it might bring with it serious disadvantages. Thus in the thirteenth, and fourteenth centuries the *Laten* of Lower Saxony, who had been freed by their lords from all labour services and numerous other obligations and had become leaseholders instead of 'customary tenants', were yet in a position far more unstable and precarious than the *Laten* of Westphalia, who had remained 'customary tenants' personally subject to their lords, who were making a strong effort during the fourteenth century to bind them to the soil. This latter attitude of lords towards their *Hörigen* was tending to become general in Germany at that time.

A word must also be said concerning the special position of peasant populations settled in mountainous districts such as Switzerland and the

Dauphiné. There, vigorous communities of freemen, independent of all domanial bonds, were to be found in the thirteenth century. Their existence must be attributed at least in part to the settlement in this region of free colonists or *hospites* come to reclaim the wastes. Nevertheless the very growth of such communities and the search for new lands to which it led brought them into conflict with the lay or ecclesiastical lords who claimed to exercise rights of one sort or another over the land, while on other occasions conflicts of this kind would be started by the lords themselves, desirous of increasing their authority and their revenues. Usually the struggles, which were at times very violent, were brought to an end by agreement in the fourteenth or fifteenth century. Agreements thus reached generally favoured the freedom of the members of the community as against the lords.

In conclusion it may be useful to summarize the evidence which we have been able to assemble concerning changes in rural society between the eleventh century and the beginning of the fourteenth. In the first place, as a result of the dissolution of the classical *villa* and the progressive loss of force of the *dominium directum* over the rural tenancies, the tenants tended more and more to become in practice small or middling peasant proprietors. They were still, indeed, subject to real or seigniorial burdens of a personal kind, but these burdens were becoming steadily more limited and less heavy. Moreover, it was the tenants who chiefly benefited by the rise in the value of agricultural produce. This is illustrated by the fact that it was in the districts where urban markets most easily absorbed the produce of the countryside, such as the region around Paris and Beauce, that the enfranchisement of the rural population by purchase was earliest and most widespread. The implication is that the sale of country produce had really enriched the peasantry and enabled them to accumulate liquid capital reserves.

Yet there existed above and below this prosperous middle rank of the peasantry two groups, one poorer and the other getting richer, both of whom tended to remain apart from the village community. The growing disparity of wealth could indeed be considered as the most marked change in the structure of peasant society during the period of agrarian expansion in its final phase in the thirteenth century. Set in motion by the growth of the rural economy, this differentiation in the social categories of the peasantry was to begin with favourable to the lords who turned it to good account. In doing so, they accentuated the movement further. But then in its turn, it became one of the most active factors in the adaptations to which the seigniorial economy was subjected at the end of the thirteenth century. New dangers menaced the wealth of the lords which they were, at any rate for the time being, in no condition to withstand.

Medieval Agrarian Society in its Prime

§ 2. Italy

I. *Geography and history*

A. *The natural background*

In his commentary on Dante's *Divine Comedy*, the fourteenth-century humanist, Benvenuto da Imola, describes Italy as 'a house of many mansions'. Starting from Rome, the *arx sive caput*, he proceeds to show how each region has been assigned its place in a naturally ordered household. Thus Tuscany is the bedchamber 'because it is the fairest province', and Lombardy is the banqueting hall, 'because Lombards are given to feasting and large appetites'; Romagna is the fruit garden because it is 'fertile in every part' and the March of Ancona is the *cellarium*, 'because it has the sweetest wines, oil, and figs'; Apulia finally is the stable, 'because there are found the noblest horses, copious forage and wide, level fields' and the March of Treviso is the pleasure garden 'because of its lofty woods'. Composed barely twenty years after the Black Death, the purpose of this pedestrian rhetoric, as of most past writing on Italy, was to praise not to instruct. Instructive it is, nevertheless, that of all things in Italy Benvenuto should have chosen to emphasize the regional diversity; for in the history of Italy, and especially rural Italy, the first and most conspicuous fact is the inexhaustible variety of local development. Even today past and present are found incongruously mixed, while whole centuries divide the North, where the Agricultural Revolution made some of its earliest conquests, from the South and islands, which have yet to be subdued. In Sicily land continues to be tilled with a 'pre-Adamite' *Hakenpflug* (*aratro chiodo*), in Sardinia ox-carts of Roman name and design are still in common use, and in parts of the mainland archeologists may study 'Vergilian' ploughs and Roman types of oil press still at work. In Central Italy medieval forms of tenancy have been uneasily adapted to the needs of mechanized farming, while in Southern Italy the problem of *latifundia* has defied solution from the Roman to the Italian Republic.

It has been a matter of long debate how far such regional differences are the product of physical environment. For Italy, despite its natural frontier of Alp and sea, is not and never has been 'a geographical expression', but a land on which climate and geology have combined to impose sharp natural divisions. In a country, more than two-thirds of which may be classed as hill or mountain, there is little place for the broad distinctions of 'highland zone' and 'lowland zone', 'champion'

and 'woodland'; in Lombardy alone there are wider variations of elevation and climate, soil and vegetation, than in the whole of Germany.
The mountainous relief has determined particularly the distribution of
cultivable soils, the best of which are concentrated almost wholly in
the lowlands; the soils of the uplands, which, outside the western Alps,
Calabria and Sardinia, are mainly soft formations, limestones, sands and
clays, are frequently unstable or of poor fertility, less suited to sown than
to planted crops, or, on the higher slopes, to pasture, scrub and forest.
But the lowlands are not all equally productive, nor are they equally
spread. The only expanse of fertile plain is the valley of the Po, and
even here there are tracts of leached or peaty soil; in peninsular Italy,
and especially the South, lowland areas are few and limited, while some,
like the Roman Campagna or the Tavoliere of Apulia, are resistant to
intensive cultivation.

This natural inequality of North and South, created by land formation,
is deepened further by differences of climate. Though both regions belong
to a common climatic system of seasonal summer drought, in upper
Italy this is offset by a well-distributed rainfall, which permits continuous
plant growth through most months of the year; sown crops flourish
and, on the Northern Plain, yields are exceptionally high. In lower
Italy, by contrast, from the Tuscan Maremma south, rainfall is concentrated in the short, mild winter, plant growth ceases with the spring,
and the sudden onset of summer heat (*stretta di caldo*) is a constant threat
to harvests; grain yields tend to be low, but tree crops prosper, especially
the drought-resistant olive, almond and fig. The climatic frontier,
however, is not sharply drawn. 'Winter killing' on undrained land is a
danger in the South; the 'stretta di caldo' visits the Northern Plain; and
the northern lakes shelter Mediterranean crops of olives and citrus fruits.
Central Italy forms a transitional zone. The east is colder and drier than
the west, the highlands colder and wetter than the plain. One familiar
effect of altitude is the seasonal alternation of lowland pasture in winter,
when the hills are under snow, and highland pasture in summer, when
the lowlands are parched.

Of even greater importance in creating regional differences is the
influence of the mountains on the plains. In most areas the highland
snows melt early, moisture drains rapidly away during the rainy season,
and the rivers, often dry in summer, become raging torrents. So flood,
accompanied by hillside erosion, and lowland sedimentation, is as
common a problem for Italian farmers as drought. But in certain
favoured districts the mountains benefit the plain. In parts of the
South, where rain falls on limestone and other permeable slopes,
moisture is filtered underground to emerge as spring and ground water,
and fertilize the lowlands. These are the Southern 'garden areas',

famous since antiquity, of Campania, Sulmona and coastal Sicily. Again, in Upper Italy, on the north side of the Po, the snows and rains of the high Alps, where rain falls most in summer, keep the rivers of the plain perennially supplied, while along the margin of the lowlands, from Piedmont to Venetia, gravel terraces throw out water in thousands of springs and *fontanili*. This is the region described by Tacitus as 'the most flourishing side of Italy' and by medieval writers as the 'paradise of Italy'.

It was specially fertile districts like these which for long gave Italy itself the name of an earthly paradise. The provincial contrasts of North and South, of arid and irrigated areas, were either ignored by writers or blamed on social conditions; and when at last in the nineteenth century the contradiction emerged between literary tradition and statistical fact, it was thought that Italy must have physically changed at some time since antiquity. But inquiry shows that this facile theory rests on a misreading of history. Deterioration there has certainly been, especially in the South. With the passage of centuries the hills have become more denuded, the rivers more torrential, and the lowlands encumbered with more alluvial marsh; in places the period of summer drought may also have increased. But these disorders were already well advanced in Roman times, when the coastal plains of Southern Italy, Latium and Etruria were invaded by malarial swamp; and their cause has been, not the growing inclemency of nature, but the persistent mismanagement of land, in defiance of climatic conditions, which have suffered no demonstrable change, in the Middle Ages or later. Medieval records, like Roman records, say little directly about climate; but like Roman records, they disclose many familiar effects and contrasts of Italian climate and topography, and, more important, describe a technique and routine of farming, determined by conditions of climate, which has not significantly changed from antiquity to the present day. Climatic fluctuations there may have been, but their sequence is uncertain, and their effect concealed by the operation of economic influences. They did not disturb the traditional processes of farming, still less determine developments in medieval rural life. These had their own chronology, independent of physical conditions, and were governed by cycles, not of climatic but of economic change.

B. *The economic background*

That Italy, in common with the rest of Europe, progressed through a cycle of economic change in the course of the Middle Ages, is now an established commonplace. It is also clear that the phases of successive stagnation, growth and decline, through which the economy passed, however indefinite in detail, fail to conform to the conventional divisions of 'ancient', 'medieval' and 'renaissance' history.

The discrepancy is most emphatic, perhaps, in the earliest period, from the fifth to the tenth century, when forms of social and economic life came to prevail, which had developed already in the later Roman Empire. The period began in conditions of unparalleled waste and depopulation, from which recurrent invasion, war and disorder for long prevented recovery. Production declined to a miserable level and wealth was confined to few hands; trade was feeble, money in small demand and supply, and exchange was largely by barter. These facts are naturally impossible to illustrate with figures. At its lowest point, about 700, the population is said to have fallen to less than 5,000,000 or possibly 4,000,000 souls; but this is mere conjecture. Similarly, for *agri deserti* there are no statistics after the fifth century. It is only certain that vast areas reverted to forest and scrub; and although in places declining cultivation may have slowed the rate of erosion, neglect of ancient drainage works and embankments also intensified damage caused by flood. With the spread of waste, pastoral farming may have gained over tillage, at least in Lombard Italy; and although Latin manuals of husbandry were copied in monastic *scriptoria*, their teaching was probably never so removed from practice. For the intensive methods of Roman agriculture there was no longer any demand. The overseas market for Italian produce had declined in the early Roman Empire; now inter-regional and local markets also contracted. Of the shrunken population the great majority laboured on the land; and land, an instrument of political as much as economic power, was almost the sole source of subsistence, revenue and wealth. Though the Roman cities, with few exceptions, escaped total destruction, most were even more decayed than the countryside. The dense perimeter of vineyards, orchards and gardens, which had once enclosed the Roman city, now dwindled and withdrew inside the walls; even the largest towns were invaded by cultivated fields, pasture and waste, and many places, which custom continued to denominate *urbes* and *civitates*, retained only a doubtful title to the name. They survived primarily as centres of provincial and diocesan government, and their society was largely composed of landlords, clerks and officials, possessed of estates *tam in civitate quam extra civitate* for provision of their basic needs. Nor did *possessores* congregate only in the towns; many preferred to live outside in villages or manors (*curtes*), or the fortified 'boroughs' (*castella*), which during this period emerged increasingly as rival centres of public and seigneurial administration, disrupting the ancient unity of town and *territorium*.

Between town and country the traditional division of function was gradually weakened. In the town citizens raised food from fields and common pastures; in the country peasants manufactured goods and implements, and lords kept servile staffs or servile craftsmen and levied products of domestic industry as rent. In these conditions there was little incentive to agricultural improvement or specialization; rather did landowners seek to diversify their holdings and the produce of their estates. Not since Rome united Italy had the need or the practice of self-sufficiency been so widespread and compelling.

No doubt the regression to habits of 'natural economy' was less pronounced in Italy than in other parts of Europe. Organized commerce persisted and by the eighth century was clearly beginning to expand; and there was sufficient trade, even regional trade, in agricultural commodities to induce great landlords to organize the transport and marketing of produce. But it does not appear that this activity had any effect on farming or estate management. In farming technique, it is true, Roman methods were not entirely abandoned. In a few places Roman canals and irrigation works are known to have survived and, in many lowland areas, the Roman system of centuriated fields.

From the seventh century onward there is evidence also of land reclamation and improvement. Indeed not only was improvement (*melioratio*) a condition of most land leases of the period; by the late eighth century, in parts of Central Italy, a special form of grant had evolved which offered beneficial terms to tenants developing land with planted crops (*ad plantandum, ad pastinandum*). Few leases, however, involved any capital outlay by the owner. The scarce resources of the time were not attracted into tillage, and what planning there was, on the larger estates, was planning for consumption, not for sale. It is likely too that progress in reclamation was severely checked by the renewal of war and devastation in the late Carolingian Empire. Only toward the end of the period do signs at last appear of continuous development. Then, throughout the economy, the process of growth became suddenly rapid, intense and sustained. A new phase of revival had begun.

Of this economic renaissance (the true Italian renaissance) the main facts are too familiar for emphasis. Between the tenth and fourteenth centuries the population of Italy rose approximately twofold, reaching a total variously assessed at 7,000,000 to 9,000,000 inhabitants. The rise was accompanied by an even larger growth in the volume of production and exchange, which raised *per capita* income at home, and abroad gave Italy unprecedented primacy in European trade and industry. Most spectacular was the increase, unparalleled elsewhere, in the size of urban population which, although in no place ever so dense as that of ancient Rome, in many towns rose rapidly from a mere 5,000 or 6,000 souls to 30,000 or more, and in some to over 50,000 (Bologna, Palermo),

90,000 (Florence), and even 100,000 (Milan, Venice, and possibly Genoa). This urban growth was not the effect of simple natural increase, still less of colonization; few towns of medieval Italy were newly planned foundations, and of these the most conspicuous, Alessandria and Aquila, were the product more of strategic than of economic policy.

The principal cause, as onomastic and other evidence shows, was a vast spontaneous movement of rural emigration, partly to form new centres, like the Tuscan market towns of Greve and Figline, but mainly to form new quarters, like the Florentine suburb of Oltrarno, in existing *civitates* and *castella*. One characteristic effect, therefore, of economic advance, was a radical redistribution of population between country and town, the measure of which may be partly gathered from contemporary statistics. Thus in the territory of Bologna (*c.* 1300 square miles) it is estimated that, by the middle of the thirteenth century, there were some 12,000 'hearths' in the city, against 17,000 in the *contado*, which, if urban and rural households are assumed to have been of equal average size, would give a demographic ratio of roughly five to seven. Comparably high ratios are attested, between the late thirteenth and early fourteenth centuries, at Padua (territory 980 sq. miles, ratio 2:5), and Perugia (480 sq. miles, 5:8), while at S. Gimignano and Prato, small towns with small territories, the proportions rose to as much as 3:2 and 13:10 respectively. In the kingdom of Naples and Sicily, finally, Beloch's calculations suggest that, of a total population approaching 2,500,000 in the later thirteenth century, 50,000 resided in Palermo, 30,000 in Naples, 25,000 or so in Messina, 10,000 in Catania and so on. Such was the rate of *inurbamento* that in the neighbourhood of certain towns, like Pistoia, Chieri and Moncalieri, it was the cause of some depopulation; while at others, notably Siena and Bologna, it had to be restrained by law, in the course of the thirteenth century, to protect the interests of tillage and the urban food supply.

By that time, under the mounting influence of urban trade and policy, to produce food and raw materials had become the primary function of the country population. The larger and richer the towns became, the more they shed of their Dark Age, rural character: fields gave way to buildings, common lands were broken up, and a growing proportion of townspeople engaged in trade and industry. Urban markets and, wherever possible, urban governments also, extended increasing control over the countryside, and the ancient Roman economy, based on exchange between territory and town, was steadily re-established. On great estates domestic workshops decayed or disappeared and 'industrial' rents were abandoned. Rural manufacture was limited or regulated and even the peasantry began to acquire the cruder products (*panni romagnoli*, etc.) of urban industry.

To what extent the greater cities depended on rural markets is difficult to determine, but trade certainly expanded into the most secluded districts; and if much local exchange was still transacted by long-term credit or barter, the reason now was as often failing supplies of money as inadequate demand. In fifteenth-century Genoa, where coin was chronically short and of constantly changing value and variety, peasants made payments by cheque. A new society, urban, rich and mercantile had come into existence.

The transformation was permanent and affected the whole fabric of Italian society and civilization. But if progress was secure, it was not uninterrupted nor everywhere the same. In the last two centuries of the Middle Ages, and notably between 1350 and 1450, the trends prevailing in the previous age were radically if temporarily reversed. The population, struck by a series of famine and plagues, fell precipitously. The extent and chronology of decline are not precisely measurable; but although the population never seems to have sunk as low as its Dark Age level, and by the later fifteenth century was beginning rapidly to recover, it was still, probably, in 1500 below the pre-plague maximum. Even more prolonged, it is suggested, was the fall in production and exchange which, although general to Western Europe, was aggravated in Italy by adverse changes in the pattern of international trade.

Symptomatic, once again, of the general economic movement was the situation of the towns, many of which were almost halved in size and never recovered their earlier numbers during the Middle Ages. No longer now was immigration subject to legal restriction; rather was legislation passed, especially after the Black Death, to encourage *inurbamento*. Even so it is possible that the demographic relationship between town and country was changed. Mortality may have been higher in the town, recovery quicker in the country. At least it would appear from rough calculation that the ratio of urban to rural population had dropped, by the later fourteenth century, to about 1:1 at Prato, 1:2 at Bologna and 2:7 at Padua, and in the mid-sixteenth century to 1:4 at Padua and 1:3 at Perugia.

These summary facts and figures, however, hardly define the complex conditions of late medieval Italy. Though much remains obscure and interpretations vary, it is generally agreed that, however severe the depression, the Italian economy reacted to it with energy and resource. If Italians lost the monopoly, they retained the supremacy in trade; if certain markets contracted, others were enlarged; if established industries declined, others took their place; and if urban development was generally arrested, in a few places it was vigorous and sharp. By the later fifteenth century Venice, Milan and possibly Genoa had all recovered a population of 100,000 souls, and now they were joined by

Naples. This growth was no doubt partly due to political development, which drew settlers from subject towns to the capital cities of new territorial states. But migration from the land also continued, and not merely after plague; and in the early sixteenth century there were still a number of territories where a third or more of the population was concentrated in the towns: at Crema, for example, and Parma, Cremona and Verona. In Southern Italy the proportion of urban to total population even began to rise. Development was not the same in all regions.

Regional variations were nothing new in the late Middle Ages. In Italy, throughout the medieval period, they were almost as pronounced as the secular variations in general economic growth. Of all local differences the most conspicuous was that of North and South. In summary terms it may be said that in the North the effects of growth were greater, in the South the effects of decline. The contrast is illustrated by the greater relative increase of the Northern population which, during the thirteenth century, in parts of Tuscany and the Lombard Plain reached a density exceeding 200 persons per sq. mile, as against a Southern average of 100 per sq. mile in the Kingdom of Naples, 60 or so in Sicily and even less in Sardinia; and this discrepancy may have been sharpened in the later Middle Ages. Urban population figures disclose a deeper division. They show that of the 26 major towns which by the end of the thirteenth century may be said or supposed to have possessed a population of over 20,000, only three lay south of Rome, while of the remaining 22, five were in Tuscany and twelve on the Northern Plain.

These figures contain a statistical summary of Italian medieval history; urban history in the North, provincial history in the South. In the North the growth of towns was revolutionary. Here urban government passed to communes and conquered the countryside; here urban immigration was most intense and drew upon all classes, from noblemen to serfs; and here, finally, the urban economy changed and towns emerged of a type unknown in ancient Italy, commercial towns like Genoa and Venice, industrial towns like Florence, where trade was the dominant activity and the principal source of wealth. Very different were conditions prevailing south of the Tuscan Maremma.

Here urban immigration was feebler and in places constrained, as at Aquila and Chieti. Few large cities were mercantile and none industrial; the precocious trade of the maritime towns was checked in the thirteenth century, when control of Southern overseas commerce passed to northern 'Yankees'. There were no urban communes, merely universitates, with a few rights of government and powers in the country around. The ruling class was feudal and lived near the land, and land was the principal source of wealth. Medieval Italy, therefore, witnessed a regional development, forecast but never complete in Roman times: the economic supremacy of North over South. Beside the local difference of country and town, a wider distinction emerged, between a densely populated urban and 'industrial' Italy and a sparsely populated 'feudal' and 'agrarian' Italy, the second of which was slowly reduced, as a source of food and raw materials, to 'colonial' dependence on the first. For a time, in fact, Sardinia and Corsica were colonies of Genoa and Pisa.

The 'two Italies' were not in perfect contrast. If the South was mainly feudal, so was most of Piedmont, Friuli and the Tyrol; if the South was mainly agrarian, so were the Ferrarese, Romagna and the March of Ancona. It is easy to identify the North with its metropolitan cities and define its economic development solely in terms of the Commercial Revolution. But beneath the regional differences medieval Italy, like Roman Italy, remained a predominantly agricultural country, and even in the most industrialized areas, the majority of people continued to work on the land or draw on land for subsistence. Even the towns, for all their growth in size and economic complexity, retained the character, in varying degrees, of communities of landowners. The urban communes and *universitates*, founded in the eleventh and twelfth centuries, were the creation not of merchants but of landlords; many urban immigrants were or became landholders; and landownership was the first ambition of all urban classes. So one result of urban growth in Italy was a great increase in the number of landowning townsmen. Property remained a qualification for urban office or citizenship and land the primary basis of direct urban taxation. It is the early urban tax records which show particularly what a high proportion of townsmen held land: nearly two-thirds at Macerata in 1268, and roughly the same number at Chieri (1253), Moncalieri (1268–85), Perugia (1282–5) and Orvieto (1292). The properties were extremely subdivided, and at Moncalieri less than half were sufficient to support a family. Yet it does not seem that the balance was redressed by activity in trade or industry. In every case, the trading population was relatively small and undistinguished. At Orvieto only 8 per cent of assessed heads of households were registered as tradesmen, and these were not merchants or entrepreneurs, but artisans and retailers.

Haphazard though these figures are, they represent the nature of most Italian towns. They were agricultural towns, mixed societies of noblemen and rentiers (*milites*), of shopkeepers, artisans, notaries and peasants (*pedites*). In size they varied greatly, from several hundred to several thousand households, but common to them all was their indeterminate urbanity. Their urban function was established by the meeting of regular markets and the presence of professional traders, often organized in craft or merchant guilds; but their trade was mainly local, and their manufactures, even of cloth, rarely attained the scale of industry. Their urban status was also proved by the condition of their inhabitants, who were *cives* or *burgenses*, legally distinct from rustics, and commonly self-governing. They had town halls and palaces, public squares and frequently a cathedral. But farm animals roamed their streets by day and were stabled in their walls at night; the business transacted in their *parlamenta* was largely concerned with the management of commons, the election of agrarian officials and the publication of statutes regulating agricultural routine; and their self-styled *cives*, who in Southern Italy particularly were often mere peasants, were in the habit of withdrawing at harvest time, when the courts of law closed down, *pro faciendis eorum recoltis*. In Italy no line divides urban from rural history.

The forms of urban settlement perplexed even contemporaries. By tradition the towns of higher dignity were the 'cities' or *civitates*, but many of these were very small and, in Lower Italy especially, were what Benvenuto da Imola called *parvule civitatuncule*. Of greater importance, frenquently, were the towns described as *terrae* which, down to the thirteenth century, in parts of Italy at least, were commonly known as *borghi*, unwalled centres of trade. Next in conventional order came the large class of *castra* or *castella*, sometimes still called *oppida*, which were walled settlements often found in combination with *borghi*. Of these a certain number, like Prato or Crema, were large and flourishing towns, endowed with territory and jurisdiction. More often they were market towns, like Castelfiorentino or Castell'Arquata, centres of local government, defence and exchange. But a great many were simply fortified villages, insignificant *castelletta* of 30 or 40 households.

In these smaller places town and country met, and the difference between them economically was too fine to formulate. For if towns and *castella* were often imperfectly urban, many *villae* and *villaggi* were also imperfectly rural. Not only were certain industries, like cloth-fulling or mining, of necessity located in the country. As trade of all kinds increased, so did the number of village artisans, smiths, carpenters and masons, millers, bakers, cobblers and *merciai*, though a place still remained for the pedlar. The increase may have been slow. Thus, in the *contado* of Pistoia, toward the middle of the thirteenth century, barely 5 per cent of the rural population was recorded as practising a trade, and this has been quoted to support the theory that during the Middle Ages artisans were concentrated increasingly in the towns. But what the evidence indicates is rather the contrary movement, and the steady diffusion of rural tradesmen in even the most sequestered places, from the hinterland of Sicily to the Emilian Appenines.

The demographic ratios of town and territory, therefore, give only the roughest guide to the effective distribution of agricultural and commercial population. Inscribed on the books of the great urban guilds were hundreds of artisans who lived, not in the city, but in the villages, *castra* and semi-rural boroughs of the subject *contado*; while inside the walls of even the largest towns there were *laboratores terrarum* and also, especially after the Black Death, land in plenty for them to cultivate. The distinction of town and country was nowhere absolute.

Even less precise was the distinction of trade and agriculture. Not only was most trade connected with agricultural products; the two activities were often closely associated. Even at the humblest level of society many peasants, as we shall see, were part-time artisans or industrial workers, while most village tradesmen also held some land, though they did not always cultivate it themselves; the fifteenth-century account-books of a blacksmith at Stia (Casentino) suggest it was common practice for rural artisans to levy payment partly in the form of labour services (instead of cash or kind). Similarly in the towns, though most of the landless population were probably employed in trades, many artisans were part-time peasants, while the wealthier minor guildsmen were often possessed of sizeable estates. But it is among the merchant classes that the combination of land and trade is most conspicuous. Landowning *negotiatores* are almost as old in Italy as the oldest surviving records, and in precocious towns like Venice already occupied a prominent place in the early Middle Ages. By the thirteenth century in nearly all the larger cities, great merchant dynasties appear, like the Bardi and Frescobaldi, who were also owners of great estates, with villas in the country and palaces in the town. The early history of these estates is permanently lost to view. To some extent, undoubtedly, they comprised hereditary holdings located in the place of family origins; but the larger part was certainly acquired. 'To buy land', says Guicciardini, 'is one of the objects for which merchants are accustomed to labour'; and nowhere is this instinct better displayed than in medieval Italy. Land conferred power and status; it could also be rendered profitable; above all, it offered security at a time when safe investments were few, company liability unlimited, and bankruptcy an ever-present threat.

So landholding, though less diffused, was no less common in commercial than in agricultural towns. At San Gimignano in 1314, 61·8 per cent of all property owners, holding 84 per cent of all land, were resident townsmen. Here and in other cities which were notable centres of trade, there were legal holidays at harvest time (although not for commercial courts), and owners spent the summer months in *villeggiatura*.

And when, in the thirteenth century, conflict developed between *nobiles* and *pedites*, *magnati* and *popolani*, the cause was not, as sometimes said, antagonism between landed and mercantile interests. The 'magnates' were often merchants, the *popolani* landlords. No doubt this blending of classes was peculiar to certain cities. In most Italian towns a fairly sharp division persisted between the landed nobility and the rest, especially perhaps in Southern Italy where, after the Norman Conquest, noblemen are generally said to have disdained contact with trade. Not so in the larger cities of the North. Here from a date well before the commune, an alliance developed, in politics and commerce, between landowning nobles, who invested in trade, and traders who invested in land. Social divisions were loosened, wealth became the test of 'nobility', and although the distinction was jealously upheld between *gentiluomini* and *mercatanti*, it served mainly to differentiate one generation of *gente nuova* from another. New families and old families met in a common business class, with capital in land and trade; the only question of importance is not their name or origin but the distribution at different times of their investments.

From the tenth to the early fourteenth century, it is generally assumed that the prevailing movement of capital was from land into trade; business profits were high and if much merchant capital was put into land, landed capital was also mobilized for trade. With the late medieval 'recession', however, the trend is said to have changed. Whereas, in the thirteenth century the return from commercial investments rose to 50 per cent or more, in the later fourteenth and fifteenth centuries the average was nearer 15–20 per cent, as compared with a return of 4–6 per cent from land and livestock, rising to 30 per cent or more in favourable conditions, and a return of up to 12, 16 and even 60 per cent from State loans. Capital therefore began to desert business and a new type of magnate emerged, sedentary, lavish, pleasure-seeking, who spent his wealth increasingly on land and country houses and the patronage of arts and letters. The argument is plausible but difficult to prove. No reliable means exists of measuring statistically the tendency of late medieval investments and what remains is bound to be inconclusive. From as early as the thirteenth century we find great merchant families, like the Sienese Salimbeni, withdrawing from trade, and by the fourteenth century there is evidence of a growing class of rentiers who lived entirely from land (and government stock). But beside these *scioperati*, and often within the same family, many instances still recur of men whose wealth lay primarily in trade. In fifteenth-century Genoa land and business capital seem even to have been divorced, an aristocracy of money confronting an aristocracy of land. In Florence also there were still many *gente nuova*, while in Venice, according to Machiavelli, the ruling *gentiluomini* continued to draw their principal wealth from trade. If change there was, it was clearly not the work of one generation or century.

Nor was 'the return to the land' a return to the country. No doubt many urban statutes of the later Middle Ages refer to 'rural' citizens who lived on the land, but *cives selvatici* were nothing new. Already by the thirteenth century some communes had begun to relax the duty of urban residence in favour of *cives veteri*; and throughout the communal period there persisted a class of rustic nobles (*nobiles rurales, nobili del contado*) who refused to desert the country. But there is no sign of a late medieval secession from the towns. Botero in the sixteenth century, like Salimbene in the thirteenth, still contrasts the town-dwelling nobles of Italy with the country-dwelling nobles of France; and it was only at the end of the Middle Ages that the provincial aristocracy of Latium and Southern Italy moved into the cities. Nor does the evidence regarding the other orders of society suggest that the changing relation of town and country population in the later Middle Ages had profound economic effects. At Florence, according to the *matricule* of the lesser trade guilds, one half or more of all registered smiths, butchers, tailors and other minor tradesmen still lived in the city, while most of the remainder, numerous though they were, resided in the market towns and *castra*. The non-agricultural population was distributed much as before. A Pisan tax list of 1407 records no peasant cultivators or labourers in the town. A Ligurian survey of the early sixteenth century mentions only a handful of rural artisans round Genoa. Here and in other Northern towns, by all contemporary testimony, the main business in 1500 was still acknowledged to be business. In Lombardy the fifteenth century was a time of industrial expansion. In Lower Italy, by contrast, the late medieval increase in urban population was accompanied by no corresponding economic growth. It was here most conspicuously that the Italian towns 'tended to become again what they had been in late antiquity: hungry parasites feeding on the tribute of half-starved peasants' (Lopez).

So throughout the Middle Ages the regional contrast remained between the 'industrial' Italy of the North and the 'agricultural' Italy of the South. It was in industrial Italy that the greatest changes occurred in rural life.

II. *The rural economy*

A. *The revival*

That rural Italy in the Middle Ages experienced radical change has been recognized since the early days of the Agricultural Revolution, but writers have not been all agreed about its causes or chronology. In the judgment of political economists, like Sismondi and Cattaneo, medieval Italy gave perfect proof of the doctrine, ascribed to Arthur Young, that agricultural development depended on towns and trade. To Young himself, however, the facts were not so clear: 'if trade and commerce did much for Italy, which cannot be doubted, you must look for their effects', he said, 'not in the country, but in towns'; though progress occurred in husbandry it began before the communes, and owed little or nothing to their subsequent expansion. Young's opinions now have only antiquarian interest; but the problem of priority, casually raised by him, still occupies historians of medieval economic growth. Whether revival began in agriculture or trade, and whether rising population was the cause or consequence of rising productivity, or both simply the result of improved political conditions, Italian records of the tenth and following centuries do not show. What they emphasize rather is the close interrelation of urban and rural development. The same sources which indicate a growth in population, towns and trade, also reveal increasing demand for land and agricultural produce.

One measure of this is a rapid rise in prices, too sharp to be accounted for by inflationary changes in coinage or the supply of precious metals. At the very beginning of the period, from the tenth to the eleventh century, land values rose in parts of Tuscany and Lombardy by as much as four- or fivefold in the space of a few decades; in the Milanese, specifically, they doubled between the early eleventh and mid-twelfth centuries, and again between the mid-twelfth and mid-thirteenth. It was much the same at Lucca. The rise affected all classes of land, arable, waste and wood, and despite government regulation, especially of grain, seems also to have affected, in much the same degree, all types of produce, from food and stock to raw materials. In Lombardy and Tuscany a further symptom of development was a substantial increase in the standard measures of weight and capacity: the *staio* (bushel) and the pound. The effect on agriculture of increased demand was simple and predictable: old land was improved, new land reclaimed, and farming became a field for enterprise and investment. Most immediate and most profound were the changes in the use and exploitation of the land.

B. *Reclamation and land use*

One of the earliest signs, in fact, of economic revival is evidence, beginning in the tenth century, of unaccustomed pressure on the use and occupation of land. In the language of contemporaries 'hearths' were being 'multiplied' (*foce multiplicate*). The increase of households took partly the form of the simple subdivision of holdings. Such,

23

according to Peter Damiani, was the 'practice of the day' (*moderna consuetudo*) that land assigned to a few tenements, *ex antiquo more*, should be allocated to many (*in plurimum divisa*). Surviving charters fully bear this out. In particular they reveal, in the frequency of contracts touching small parcels of land, that holdings were extremely loose and fragile units, subject to constant rearrangement by transfer and partition. From the number of such transactions, in tenth-century records, it has been concluded that the fragmentation of holdings had reached the point of causing a crisis of overpopulation and underemployment on the land, which was only relieved, in the eleventh century, by the action of enterprising landlords in consolidating estates and driving redundant rural labour to settle in the towns or on new land. In this respect agrarian revolution preceded urban revolution. The morcellization of property, however, and the custom of partition continued without interruption, so that in the late twelfth and thirteenth centuries a number of towns in Upper Italy even enacted laws to encourage consolidation (*ingrossatio*). Rural population also continued to rise, in spite of urban growth; while, most important of all, the settlement of new land began at a very early date, suggesting that any tendency to rural congestion was quickly corrected by expansion in the country itself. From the late ninth century onward there is evidence of growing activity to extend cultivation, which under the combined pressure of rural and urban demand rapidly assumed the dimensions of a general movememt to increase agricultural production. To a great extent, as will be seen, this effort was put into raising output from existing farm land; and there was doubtless a good deal of unrecorded investment in the reconstruction and improvement of farm buildings, mills and other installations. But the most spectacular change was in the acreage of land in productive use.

The movement was most intense in Upper Italy, especially the Lombard Plain, where population growth was most rapid, capital most abundant, government most active, and natural conditions most favourable to agricultural development. Here, as in Northern Europe, between the tenth and early fourteenth centuries, vast areas of pasture, wood and fen were reclaimed for cultivation. Old settlements expanded, new settlements formed, and the whole agrarian landscape was permanently changed. The record of this transformation, still largely unconsulted, is preserved partly in the topography and toponymy of post-medieval Italy, but mainly in contemporary sources. Of these the most specific are leases of waste land and charters of colonization, but numerous though these are, they far from exhaust the textual evidence of reclamation. More copious are the casual references to newly cleared land (*essarta, runci*, etc.) or tithes on newly cleared land (*novalia*), to canals, dykes, and irrigation works, previously unmentioned, and most of all to place names which originate in acts of unrecorded colonization (Ronco, Selva, Cortenuova, etc.). It is during this period also that documents relating to the Church—charters, canons, and in the thirteenth century *rationes decimarum*—record the disintegration of the old parochial system, based on the large territorial unit of the *plebs* or collegiate minster, and the organization of smaller parish districts to meet the needs of increasing population, of new churches and chapels, and of newly created *villae*. From the later twelfth century the charter material is joined by the codes of village and urban statute, most of which have something to say about the use and development of land. A number explicitly mention works of reclamation or the growth of new villages, while a few incorporate privileges designed to attract settlers *ad runcandum et laborandum* and encourage colonization.

This wealth of evidence permits no doubt of the magnitude of growth. The degree and rate of development, however, are not so easily assessed. Progress was certainly greatest, as land values show, in the lowland and suburban areas; but by the twelfth and thirteenth centuries, the mountain valleys and highlands also were beginning to feel the pressure of land-hungry population. In the Apuan Alps and Ligurian Apennines, the Garfagnana, Casentino and the mountainous parts of the Valpolicella, new settlements appeared, while on the upper slopes of the Alpine valleys, formerly abandoned to pasture, land was reclaimed or colonized, though not exclusively by local people. It was during the age of medieval *défrichement*, between the twelfth and fourteenth centuries, that German-speaking colonists invaded the Val d'Aosta, Valsesia and the Tyrol and Venetian hinterland.

Even more indefinite than the limits of land settlement are its phases and chronology. In time it may be possible to show that in Italy, as elsewhere, colonization was most energetic between the late eleventh and earlier thirteenth centuries; but proof is made difficult by the imprecision of the sources and their very unequal distribution in period and place. Because of this it is even a matter of debate how far Italian settlement is a product of medieval or ancient influence. Many places which first appear in medieval records may be of older origin and many of the sites of Roman Italy now unidentifiable may survive, renamed, in medieval villages. Archeological and toponomastic study may eventually solve these problems, but archeology and its allied sciences have so far been exploited only by ancient historians, and place-name study is still undeveloped. More use has been made of iconographic evidence, but before the fourteenth century and the re-emergence of 'landscape into art' this reveals little about the aspect of the countryside.

Much medieval reclamation was probably of a nature to pass

unrecorded, the product of piecemeal clearance in the woodland verge of
established farms and villages. How far this process had advanced by the
thirteenth century appears from the outbreak of litigation about village
woods and boundaries and the introduction of seignorial and statutory
restrictions on the use of land and livestock. One form of control, most
severe in the neighbourhood of towns, was the limitation on keeping
animals (excepting only by butchers), sometimes all kinds of stock, but
usually *bestie minute*: pigs, sheep and especially goats, which in most
suburban territories were prohibited outright, and even in mountain
districts were commonly restricted, partly in defence of pasture but also
of vines and crops. Outside the areas of densest settlement, particularly
in the highlands, statutes were rather directed against the misuse of wood
and pasture: against the overcharging of commons and the pasturing
of 'foreign' beasts, against unregulated grazing or felling of wood and
export of timber, and finally against indiscriminate assarting and clearance. Occasionally, in feudal provinces like Piedmont and the Tyrol,
these laws were intended partly to uphold the forest rights of lords; but
the overriding purpose was to safeguard threatened resources of waste
and common land.

Behind this legislation lay generations of unobtrusive, and often,
perhaps, unauthorized, encroachment. Characteristic are the changes
on the estate of S. Ambrogio at Origgio near Milan, where, despite the
enactment in 1228 of limits on deforestation, the amount of wood on
peasant holdings declined from 45·3 per cent in 1241 to 15·9 per cent in
1320. As in the earlier Middle Ages the conventional instrument of
improvement was the individual lease of land, by private lords or
communes, *ad meliorandum* or for clearance. Recorded grants of the
latter class are relatively few, but they were common enough to justify
inclusion, with other specimen contracts, in the first notarial formularies
compiled in the thirteenth century.

It was particularly by individual leases that, between the eleventh and
thirteenth centuries, many places came into existence, in Piedmont, the
Veronese and elsewhere, bearing the names of original settlers (*casale
Roberti*, etc.), or that settlements like Frigido in the Lunigiana grew by
slow accretion into villages, *borghi* and *castella*. In this period, however,
unlike the earlier Middle Ages, reclamation was often too urgent to
wait on piecemeal enterprise; and so, from as early as the tenth century,
when land laid waste by invasion was systematically re-colonized and
numerous *castra* collectively built for defence, examples multiply of
organized development by peasants, lords and governments. Waste
land was transferred in block to village communities or groups of settlers
for subdivision into standard arable lots. Typical of this procedure was the
agreement reached in 1118 between the bishop of Asti and the villagers

of Vico for the partition of woodland into *sortes* to be held for corn-rents, or the grant in 1272 by the bishop of Ivrea to the inhabitants of Alice of the whole Val di Chy to disafforest and plant to vines. On the great ecclesiastical estates of the Tyrol and Trentino professional 'undertakers' were used, during the thirteenth century, of the kind employed in East German colonization; but this was largely a local practice. More characteristic of Italy was the part played in reclamation by communes. An early example of this is the grant, in 1141, by the commune of Genoa to the commune of Porto Venere of a large tract of waste for conversion to orchards and vineyards. A more impressive case is the policy of planned development launched at the end of the twelfth century by the commune of Verona. One result of this was the creation, in 1185, of the colony of Villafranca, a free peasant community of 180 households established near the Mantuan border on some 800 acres of unsettled land, most of which was parcelled out in 4-acre holdings (*masi*), the remainder being reserved for wood and pasture. In the thirteenth century many other communes, especially in Piedmont and Tuscany, established *borghi franchi*; but of these the greater number seem, like the new towns, to have owed their origin to strategic rather than economic policy. Often they were placed on existing sites and some were formed by depopulating nearby villages. Even Villafranca was founded partly for defence.

The principal evidence of collective action lies in a different field, in the organization of flood control, drainage and irrigation, which, owing to climate and physical structure, have always been indispensable conditions of land improvement in Italy. It is characteristic that, in the agrarian vocabulary of medieval as of modern Italy, the technical term for reclamation—*bonum facere* or *bonificare* (first attested in the twelfth century)—was applied pre-eminently to this kind of work; and it was work which, by its very nature, demanded collaboration. Organized *bonifiche* were begun at an early stage, by partnerships of landholders or by landlords and tenants and then passed increasingly under the super-vision of urban communes, most of which, by the late twelfth or early thirteenth century, had published legislation, and even established magistracies, to regulate the maintenance and use of waterways. In hill country the dominant purpose of water control was to obviate soil erosion by various systems of field formation and drainage (*sistemazioni*). What progress in this was made before 1300 is difficult to estimate in the absence of visual records. Of the later systems of permanent hillside drainage (*cavalcapoggio*, *girapoggio*), no evidence has so far been found; but, in Umbria, Tuscany and especially Liguria, the ancient practice was certainly revived of re-modelling slopes, with more or less complexity, by the construction of *lunette*, embankments (*gradoni*), and terraces, of earth (*ciglioni*) or stone. The greatest development, however, was not in the hills but in the lowlands. The need here was not so much to conserve soil as to defend and reclaim it from flood. Unregulated streams, frequently changing course, threatened vast areas of land with seasonal devastation. One remedy for this was the simple, if unneighbourly, device of diverting rivers; but the main resource was dyking and embankment. The region worst affected was the lower Po valley, and here, already in the mid-eleventh century, documents of the Modenese abbey of Nonantola show that peasant communities were charged with the duty of maintaining river banks. Then, in the next two centuries, the work was increasingly taken up by towns: Padua, Mantua and the communes of Emilia; and by the later thirteenth century nearly all the major rivers, from the Mincio and Brenta to the Secchia and Panaro, had been extensively dyked and wide tracts of fertile territory recovered for reclamation.

To some extent lowland reclamation was the effect of natural agencies: of erosion in the hills, sedimentation in the plains. Thus, in the territory of Mantua, before embanking began, land was uncovered for cultivation by the action of Apennine streams in pushing north the Po. Similarly in the course of the Middle Ages the steady eastern drift of the Emilian and Romagnol rivers slowly filled with alluvial deposits the ancient swamp of Padusia. For the colonization of such newly emerged land, much of it covered with wood, we find, from the late eleventh century, collective leases *ad meliorandum* being granted by owners of great estates like the margraves of Mantua and the archbishops of Ravenna. From one series of leases by the bishop of Bologna and abbot of Nonantola an entire colony of villages arose (Cento, S. Agata, etc.), in the twelfth and thirteenth centuries, on land filled up (*colmata*) by the Panaro and Reno. From settlement on natural *colmatae* it was a short step to the process of controlled alluviation (also called *colmata*), whereby river-borne silt was channelled artificially on to marshy ground. Of this practice there is evidence, from the mid-twelfth century, in lower Venetia and also Tuscany, where the early statutes of Pisa (1162) provide that, in time of spate, the banks of the Arno should be broken, partly to protect the city, but also to raise the surrounding plain by progressive sedimentation.

For the maintenance of *colmate*, however, and for all sustained improvement in most lowland areas, systematic drainage was essential. From the tenth and eleventh centuries, therefore, on the Lombard plain particularly the records reveal increasing activity in the construction of ditches (*fosse*), drains (*dugali*) and, finally, canals and comprehensive systems of drainage. Not all this effort, certainly, represented reclamation. Canals, mostly the work of communes, were largely built for

navigation, water-mills or machinery, and drainage was often simply
addressed to improving old land or regulating marsh; but some canals
were clearly constructed for drainage, and some drainage was extended
to unreclaimed land. In North and Central Tuscany and the lower Po
valley, collaboration in fenland drainage by village communities, *consorterie* and great ecclesiastical landowners is sporadically attested from
the late tenth century. Then, in the twelfth century, the communes
intervened. In 1199 the commune of Verona assigned 500 acres of
marshy land to a group of 400 persons, bound in association to maintain
drainage works. In the thirteenth century, canals were cut by the
commune of Padua, for drainage to the Venetian lagoon, and by the
commune of Cremona for drainage into the Mincio. In Tuscany,
by the same period, lowland reclamation is thought to have progressed
so far as to permit a general movement of the road system from the hills
into the valleys; but a similar change is traceable in the Ligurian Apennines and may have been rather due to a growing replacement of pack
animals by carts.

To drainage, which controlled seasonal flood, the natural complement was irrigation to control seasonal drought; and in this also great
advances were made. Often, indeed, in medieval records, no clear
distinction is indicated between irrigation systems and drainage; the
two techniques were related and, where possible, combined. Not
everywhere, however, were conditions equally favourable. In the
hills and highlands particularly, and in the drier peninsular provinces
of Upper Italy, irrigation was restricted, as it still is today, to certain
privileged areas where easy access to markets encouraged some limited
seasonal irrigation of market-gardens and orchards. In this form we find
it, by the thirteenth and fourteenth centuries, near several Tuscan towns,
and on the slopes of coastal Liguria and the upper Adige valley. In the
arid Val d'Aosta there may also have been some irrigation of corn.

Profoundly different was the development on the lowlands of
Northern Italy. Here, during the Middle Ages, it is possible to observe
the evolution of a new agricultural landscape of irrigated grass and
arable fields, which was destined to become, before 1500, the admiration
of Europe. The process began early, and already in the late eleventh
century there are references, in Piedmont, to partnerships for the maintenance of irrigation works. Shortly after, in 1138, the first record
appears in Italy of permanent water-meadows or *marcite*, on the estates
of the Cistercian abbey of Chiaravalle near Milan. From that time on,
progress became intense. From rivers and streams, canals and *fontanilia*,
irrigation ditches or *rogie* were derived in increasing number. For
purposes of irrigation two canals were built, between 1177 and 1229,
by the commune of Milan: the Naviglio Grande and the Muzza, which

are still among the largest of their kind. Private law and legislation kept
pace with the development, to control and also promote it. In particular
the ancient Roman right of compulsory *aqueductus* was revived and
amplified. By the middle of the thirteenth century, irrigation works
had spread to all districts, north of the Po, from Western Piedmont to
Cremona. South of the Po, in Emilia, where water supply was dependent on irregular Apennine streams, irrigation was rather more limited
and subject to state control. But here too, by 1300, in the territory of
Parma, Modena and Bologna, it had begun to encroach on farm and
meadow land. By irrigation and drainage, dykes, canals, and ditches,
medieval farmers and engineers were preparing changes in Northern
Italy far exceeding anything achieved in Etruscan or Roman antiquity.

It was otherwise in the parts of Italy most exploited in antiquity: in
Lazio, the South and the islands. In these regions medieval development
was much less ambitious, and even the simplest forms of growth are
relatively inconspicuous. Surviving records are fewer here, but they
also contain less evidence of progress in colonization, clearance and the
management of land.

Early in the period, widespread colonization (or re-colonization) has
certainly been attributed to the Arab settlers in Sicily, but of this very
little is known. Unambiguous records of organized settlement (or resettlement) are found on the southern mainland, after the Saracen
invasions of the tenth century, and in Sicily after the Norman invasion
of the eleventh. In the thirteenth century a few colonies were also
founded by the Hohenstaufen and Angevin kings. These disconnected
projects, however, were mostly on a small scale, and sometimes unsuccessful. More important are the traces of unsystematic clearance and
expansion. Thus, in parts of Apulia and Campania, the Marittima and
Campagna, a notable increase seems to have occurred, from the tenth
century or earlier, in the number of small centres of settlement called
casalia. In the twelfth and thirteenth centuries familiar signs also appear,
in the South as in the North, of competing claims for uncultivated land
and the subdivision of woodland into assarts (*cese*). In the thirteenth
century finally, in the South as in the North, papal *Rationes* disclose the
existence of new villages and churches.

Compared with the North, however, such places are few and locally
limited in number. Moreover, compared with the North, Southern
town and village statutes seem much less generally concerned to protect
pasture and wood and limit or ban livestock. This was partly because
most waste land was owned by the crown or magnates who kept large
areas 'in defence' (*difese*) for hunting and grazing rights. But it would
seem to indicate also a less intense development in land utilization.

For the hesitant progress of Lower Italy, the blame has sometimes been laid on social conditions: on the absence of a wealthy middle class, on the predominance of papal or feudal monarchy and territorial lordship. There was no lead from the state, and, failing the state, no social class with initiative or capital for effective reclamation. In practice, however, it does not appear that in Latium or Southern Italy feudal rights were more obstructive or government policy more indifferent to the needs of land improvement than in other feudal areas of Italy or Europe, where greater changes took place. Even in this backward region some development was promoted by landlords and rulers, and if their efforts were limited or rewarded with little success, the reason partly must be sought in the formidable difficulties facing improvement in the South. To generally harsh conditions of climate, soil and relief, had been added, since antiquity, the problem of reclaiming large areas of denuded uplands, eroded slopes, and lowland marsh and malaria, which, under the prevailing climatic system, cannot be supposed to have got much better in the early medieval centuries of receding settlement and declining population. Malaria, the principal enemy, was as much the effect as the cause of depopulation, and its incidence, though far from clear, does not seem to have varied between Roman and medieval times. It is judged that, in the Middle Ages, the infection dominated most areas below 600–900 feet; and this was a fatal check to all schemes of reclamation.

Apart from woodland clearance, therefore, mostly in the hills, development in Lower Italy was confined to certain favoured districts, with near-by ports or markets, and to certain types of enterprise. Thus, at various times between the tenth and thirteenth centuries, irrigation farming, mainly for fruit or 'monsoon' crops, was established or extended in parts of Apulia and Campania, the Abruzzi, Sardinia and coastal Sicily (where it was probably introduced by the Arabs). In Sicily, Campania and the Beneventano there was evidently some progress in hillside terracing, for the cultivation of tree-crops; and in most districts, on the slopes and drier ground, there was a good deal of piecemeal plantation. But of systematic *bonifiche* there is scarcely any sign. In the hills some modest work was done by local communities for the regulation of streams; but in the malarial lowlands attempts at reclamation were few and mostly futile. Here, and in the arid hinterland, it was, and remained for centuries, both simpler and more profitable to leave land undeveloped.

In the later Middle Ages the contrast of North and South was sharpened by conditions of economic recession and population decline. On the reasons for the decline Italian records have so far thrown little light. In the Roman Campagna and parts of the South there is mention already of deserted villages as early as the thirteenth century: but the cause of depopulation was partly war. All that can be said with confidence is that, by about 1300, the pace of previous growth had begun to slacken, and that in certain places, for example Moncalieri, the limits of profitable reclamation seem to have been reached if not exceeded. This would support the recent hypothesis that overpopulation or over expansion on to marginal land prepared the way for the devastating dearths and epidemics that followed in the fourteenth century. In Italy, however, the demographic trend in the late Middle Ages was not uniform throughout the country. Whereas in most regions the rural population seems to have fallen fairly constantly from the mid-fourteenth to the earlier fifteenth century and then begun to recover, in a number of mountain areas like the Tyrol and Trentino, the Alps of Bergamo, Como and Piedmont, and the Ligurian Apennines, the tendency was rather the reverse, leading in the course of the fifteenth century to overpopulation, increasing emigration and, in the Bergamasco at least, to the total abandonment of certain valleys.

This highland emigration may help to explain the contrasted effects of plague and depopulation in the North and South of Italy. Nearly everywhere, it may be said, there was some contraction of settlement and cultivation, accompanied, presumably, by a fall in the value of land and, after 1380, in agricultural prices. In upper Italy, however, the disturbance to rural life seems to have been only temporary. Here, according to Matteo Villani, one result of the Black Death was that peasant cultivators 'wanted to farm only the better lands and abandon all the rest'. The response to this of the public authorities was to impose immediate restraints on the movement of rural labour. Between 1348 and 1387 a series of laws was published by the communes of Florence and Perugia tying tenants to their holdings and threatening heavy penalties for the neglect of cultivated land. Similar decrees were enacted by Florence and Treviso to compel wage labourers to take up farms. During roughly the same period, from 1364 to 1428, to temper force with persuasion, a number of governments in Tuscany, Umbria, the Marche and Emilia tried to attract immigrant, or bring back emigrant, peasants, by offering tax immunities and other concessions. The effect of these various measures is difficult to assess. In the territory of S. Gimignano there is evidence that after the Black Death, notwithstanding legislation, rural settlement became concentrated on the better farmland. In other parts of Florentine territory, the tax survey (catasto) of 1427 reveals cases of recent migration from less prosperous districts, like the Valdambra and upper Arno valley, to the neighbourhood of the city; and it was no doubt due in part to internal movements like this that the population of

Arezzo and *contado* fell by half between 1390 and 1480 and that during the fifteenth century episcopal visitation records show considerable decay and depression in the countryside of Pisa and the Casentino. This was the equivalent in Tuscany of highland emigration in the North.

In parts of Upper Italy, therefore, shortage of labour, following plague, caused some dereliction of land, but it was mainly marginal land in mainly marginal areas. Of widespread *Wüstungen* on other lands there is scarcely any sign. What is much more notable in this region is the rapid resumption of reclamation and improvement. Indeed in many areas, Lombardy especially, it is hard to detect any moment when such activity ceased. Well before the end of the fourteenth century there is evidence of reconstruction, partly no doubt on old lands but also on new. By the end of the fifteenth century land values were rising again, even in backward districts like the Montagna Bolognese; and restrictions on clearance and enclosure, which in places may have been relaxed, were being universally reinforced. As before, there was progress in drainage and *sistemazioni*, which were now improved by methods previously unknown or unrecorded in Italy. On hill-slopes, in Tuscany, Liguria and Venetia, terracing and embankment were extended, and the first steps were taken in *sistemazioni a cavalcapoggio* and 'girapoggio'. On the lowlands, in Emilia, Venetia and Lombardy, improved systems of permanent drainage began to be developed, with fields divided by rectilinear ditches, waterways and tracks (*cavedagne*) and ploughed into wide cambered ridges (*colle*, etc.). At the same time, all over Upper Italy, we find evidence of work proceeding, by private and public initiative, in the reclamation of marsh and irrigation, sometimes under the direction of distinguished artists and engineers, like Francesco di Giorgio Martini and Leonardo da Vinci. The only difference from the past was that public initiative was now passing from communes to despots, but this political change was without economic consequences. Most of the new dynasties of the fourteenth and fifteenth centuries were responsible for large-scale schemes of *bonifica* or canalization. Particularly energetic were the Visconti and Sforza, who, between 1359 and 1471 constructed a whole series of canals in the Basso Milanese (the Binasco Pavese, the Bereguardo, the Martesana, etc.), all of which were extensively used for irrigation.

This and the neighbouring regions, from Piedmont to Ferrara, now became the chosen land of irrigated fields and water-meadows. When the French invaders crossed Lombardy in 1495 they found it 'tout fossoié comme est Flandre'. To them the whole territory appeared one of the best cultivated and most densely settled in the world. By the early sixteenth century, Spanish fiscal records show that in the lower Lombard plain, from Pavia to Cremona, 85 per cent of all land was in cultivation, in the non-irrigated upper plain about 75 per cent, in the hill zone of Como, Bergamo and Brescia over 50 per cent, and in the mountains more than 30 per cent. Well might Guicciardini say that Italy was a country 'cultivated not less in the most mountainous and barren parts, than in the plainest and most fertile'.

His words did not refer to Southern Italy. Here, and in the Maremma, from Tuscany south, the devastation of the late Middle Ages was widespread and prolonged. Large areas reverted to waste and pasture, and innumerable settlements decayed or died right out. In the Kingdom of Naples no less than a third, and in Sardinia no less than a half, of all centres of population became uninhabited in the fourteenth and fifteenth centuries; and although comparable figures are lacking for Sicily, the proportion there was almost certainly the same. Further north, in the Marittima, Roman Campagna and Tuscan Patrimony, large numbers of *castra* and *casalia* tumbled down to ruin, and conditions were scarcely better in the Sienese Maremma where the population fell by 80 per cent in the later fourteenth century, inflicting a loss from which the region never recovered. To relieve the story of desolation contemporary sources have little to say about attempts at re-colonization or *bonifica*. Some deserted villages were slowly re-occupied, some schemes were launched, for example by Siena, to repopulate wasted areas, and some efforts were organized to drain marshy land; but success in almost every case was limited. By the later fifteenth century there is evidence of reviving pressure on common wood and pasture, but as much in the interest of grazing as of tillage. The decline seemed irreversible. From this time on the South became the backward area of Italy, and the Maremma and Campagna the dreary wilderness described by generations of travellers to Rome.

So radical a change was not simply the effect of declining population. As will be seen, political and possibly economic causes played a contributory part, but also, it seems likely, some deterioration in conditions of the land itself. It is notable that depopulation was most severe in the lowlands, and if one reason for this was growing insecurity, especially on the coasts, another was growing danger from *corruptio aeris et aquae*. Because of this a number of lowland villages and towns, between the thirteenth and fifteenth centuries, are known to have been abandoned or partially deserted in Apulia, the Abruzzi, the Campagna Romana and the Maremma; and it was mainly because of this that, during the fifteenth century, attempts at re-colonization in the Maremma and elsewhere had to be given up. But the spread of malaria was simply a sign of much more serious disorders which were rendering lowland areas more unwholesome or intractable. Everywhere, from the shores of Sicily to the Tiber delta and the Maremma coast, there is evidence of increasing sedimentation, of ports and harbours silting up, and of encroachment by littoral marsh, indicating changes in the river regime, the rate of alluviation, and the limits of flood. Nor were these disturbances confined entirely to the South or Central coastlands.

In Upper Italy also, by the later Middle Ages, the problems of lowland regulation were clearly becoming more acute. Hydrographic research in Emilia has shown that rivers were becoming more impetuous and irregular, increasing the difficulty of flood control in winter and of navigation and water-supply in summer. The effects were plain and widespread. In the Valdichiana and the lower Po valley, on the Tyrrhenian coast from Pisa to the Valle di Diano, and all along the Adriatic from Eraclea to Loreto, we read of obstructed ports and lagunes, of invasion by swamp, and of fields and settlements abandoned to fenland pasture. More often than is stated the purpose of late medieval *bonifiche* may have been to recover land already once reclaimed. With marsh came also malaria, previously unknown (or unrecorded) in the North. Established already by 1300 in the Valdichiana and the coastal parts of the Marche, it had spread by 1500 to the Versilia and the northern shores of Liguria, and to a number of places on the Adriatic seaboard from Romagna to as far as Istria.

To some extent, no doubt, the growth of these conditions was the fault of incapacity or neglect. In the territory of Pisa, for example, the re-formation of marsh in the fifteenth century was blamed on negligent owners, who were letting well-drained land revert to pasture for cattle raising. Prolonged depopulation must also have weakened efficiency. Rimini, with a population of 5500 in 1524, was declared incapable of reclaiming a harbour which, in the fourteenth century, with a population of over double the size, it had managed to maintain with ease. Certain it is that, even in Upper Italy, both in Tuscany and on the Lombard Plain, many schemes of reclamation, drainage and irrigation were proved ineffective or left untried in the later Middle Ages. Sometimes this was due to opposition from vested interests, more often to the lack of coordinated enterprise in a politically divided country, but perhaps the commonest reason was sheer inadequacy of capital and technical resources. More ambitious than scientific, even public undertakings failed to check the progress of marsh land or control the course of rivers, so that some discouraged observers, like the sixteenth-century agronomist, Agostino Gallo, were driven to the conclusion that all such work was futile.

It is possible that, in places, agencies were at work which it was beyond the power of any government to control: secular movements of the coast-level, the steady process of natural alluviation. But, in the widespread deterioration of the Italian lowlands, it is difficult not to recognize also the familiar symptoms, under Mediterranean conditions, of long-continued land abuse, of overcropping, overgrazing, and especially disafforestation, leading to increased soil erosion and flood. That abuses occurred is not mere speculation. Already in the early fourteenth century laws were being enacted in Western Piedmont (and Savoy) to meet the complaint that destruction of wood was causing erosion and *diluvia*. By the sixteenth century it had become a commonplace in legislation and literature to blame the disorders of the lowlands on deforestation in the hills. In practice lowland deforestation may also have had harmful effects; at least it is thought that some of the worst lowland soils, like the leached *terra rossa* of the Lombard Plain, may be the product of woodland clearance during the Middle Ages. The extent of medieval clearance can no doubt be exaggerated. The worst excesses of deforestation came later, during the 'Enlightenment', when medieval forest laws were indiscriminately repealed. But even in the Middle Ages laws were often ineffectual or tardy. To expanding demand for land they had to adjust an expanding demand for timber, for industry and shipping as well as building and household purposes; and in a country naturally poor in forest the result was often disastrous. For domestic needs alone, the city of Milan, in the later thirteenth century, consumed 150,000 loads of firewood every year. To supply the needs of shipbuilding, Pisa is said to have stripped the woods of the Florentine Mugello, and Genoa the forests of Liguria; in consequence, by the thirteenth century Pisa was importing timber from Naples, and Genoa, in the fifteenth, from the Alps and overseas. By contrast, in Venetian territory, at Savona and in the kingdom of Naples, laws had to be issued during the fifteenth century to protect forest for shipping; while in Tuscany and Emilia similar legislation was published to preserve wood for domestic use and building. All this would seem to indicate a growing shortage of timber, but of re-afforestation, the only effective remedy, there is little evidence in medieval Italy. By the end of the Middle Ages, there were certain regions, such as Sicily, which had once exported timber, but were now having to get it from outside. Despite all legislation, the destruction of wood continued, and with it the degradation of land.

The effects of disafforestation were aggravated by inefficient management of land. However great the achievement of medieval technique, progress in reclamation was not accompanied by equal progress in soil regulation or drainage. Over the greater part of Italy field drainage, when practised at all, remained rudimentary, and was most deficient where most needed, in the hills and broken country. Most of the permanent drainage systems, perfected in the Middle Ages, were limited to favoured areas near the towns and major highways, or to certain types of land and cultivation. On arable land in particular their advance was checked by the common practice (to be mentioned later) of grazing stock on stubble fields, a custom peculiarly widespread in the South and islands, where physical conditions made *sistemazioni* especially urgent.

It was therefore mainly on planted land that hill drainage was developed. Even there permanent drainage was limited to surface drainage; covered drains are only mentioned, before the sixteenth century, in the works of agricultural writers drawing on Roman sources. It was possibly also from Roman authorities that fourteenth-century and later agronomists derived the idea of contour ploughing as a check on soil erosion; but contour ploughing, like contour drainage, was evidently slow to spread. Long after the Middle Ages the complaint continues to be heard that cultivators prefer the lazier system of vertical ploughing (*rittochino*) which, although acknowledged to be the most effective on certain clay soils, on most land is a cause of persistent denudation. By such malpractices the hill farmer added to the difficulties of the lowland farmer. But the prevailing system of lowland drainage also had its defects. This was the custom of ploughing land into temporary ridges or *porche* (*a magolato*) before the autumn sowing. Though fairly effective on sloping ground, it was later condemned for exposing crops dangerously to summer drought, and because, when badly managed, it reduced fields to a concave shape (*a scodella*), preventing effective drainage. Even the improved Northern system, with wider *porche* and permanent ditches, suffered from this weakness.

The history of land utilization in medieval Italy, therefore, cannot be reduced to the simple formula of progress in the North and retrogression in the South. Even in the North gains were balanced by losses. According to Luther the losses outweighed the gains; and this was a judgement of God. An alternative view is that the judgment was of Nature. Like the South during antiquity, the North in the later Middle Ages was paying the price of overexpansion in a period of intense growth. But in Northern Italy, which was not so physically vulnerable as the South, land abuse was more resolutely resisted, the disorders were much less extensive and their effects were largely redeemed by development elsewhere, not least in agricultural production and technique.

c. *Agriculture*

It is perhaps in the agriculture of medieval Italy that the regional, as distinct from the chronological, variations in economic growth are most conspicuous. As in trade, so in farming, leadership passed during this period from Lower to Upper Italy. Upper Italy now produced the principal writers on agriculture: the Bolognese Pietro dei Crescenzi († 1321) and Paganino Bonafede (fl. 1360), the Florentine Michelangelo

Tanaglia († 1512) and, later, the Brescian Agostino Gallo († 1570). And Upper Italy also made the greatest progress in agricultural technique.

In agricultural technique it is generally supposed that medieval Italy, unlike Northern Europe, witnessed no revolutionary change: all that conditions permitted was a return to Roman farming. This opinion is unexceptionable, if by Roman farming is understood the system described by the Latin agronomists: a model system of intensive cultivation, practically free from collective restraints, except in part on waste land held or used in common. Roman records, however, do not reveal how widely this was practised. Medieval records do. In particular, they disclose the existence of much more primitive systems, of extensive cultivation, accompanied by communal rights and communal regulation.

To begin with, during the Middle Ages, there is almost universal evidence of common wood and pasture, owned or used collectively and collectively administered; and this, we shall see, was an integral part of the agricultural system. Hardly distinguishable from common waste, in many regions of Italy, was land assigned as meadow. In the Alps and parts of the Northern Plain, and all over the peninsula and islands, meadow was often nothing more than common grassland, seasonally 'defended' and divided up for hay; while much of the rest, though held in severalty, was subject to common pasturage, after a period of common 'enclosure'. With communal control of waste and meadow was combined, in many districts, the duty to pasture beasts together under common village herdsmen; while everywhere the enforcement of controls was entrusted to common officials, *saltari* or *campari*. Common rights, however, and the jurisdiction of *campari*, were not confined to wood and grass, but over large areas were also extended to cultivated land. In the pastoral highlands especially, and the arid cornlands of the Maremma, Campagna and the hinterland of Southern Italy, Sicily and Sardinia, various forms of common-field agriculture prevailed. In the Alps and Northern Italy, the intermingled strips or plots seem to have been held in perpetuity; but in parts of the Roman Campagna, the South and islands, they were merely seasonal holdings, which shifted with the course of cultivation. In either case the land was almost always unenclosed, being simply 'banned' or put 'in defence' during the growing season; and whether closed or open, arable holdings everywhere were subject to common rotation (*Flurzwang*), common pasture (*vaine pâture*) and often common gleaning. Permanent enclosure was normally confined to plots of planted land (gardens, vineyards, etc.) near the villages or towns; but even these were often open, especially in the South, to the rights of common pasture and of gathering leaves for forage. In a few areas also, both sown and planted fields were subject to a common right to reclaim neglected land or to cultivate for subsistence (*ius serendi*). In Sardinia the arable itself was largely common land, redistributed every year among the village community. Elsewhere in Italy there is little evidence of such collective ownership, except of holdings let by communes or temporary intakes from waste. These last, however, were numerous, and although often appropriated to full private possession, they may explain the traces of common arable, regularly re-assigned, found centuries later in parts of the Alps and peninsular Italy.

These communal practices often present an appearance of great antiquity; and, although ignored by Roman records, it may not be accidental that they are found most widely established in places where Roman traditions had suffered least barbarian influence. It is possible, all the same, that during the early Middle Ages, open-field husbandry gained ground generally in Italy. If so, then one effect of reviving population and economic growth, was a widespread revolution in the agricultural system, accomplished by land enclosure. Already by the period of the earliest urban statutes (about the year 1200) all trace of a common-field system had disappeared from certain precocious areas, like the lowlands of Milan. Elsewhere on the Lombard Plain, and in Liguria and Tuscany, it is possible to study, in the thirteenth century, the progressive restriction or abolition of common of shack and gleaning; and by the later Middle Ages these rights had practically gone in most of the hill and lowland areas of North and Central Italy, except where common pasture was retained (or re-imposed) by public statute in the form of compulsory agistment of transhumant stock. Increasingly the right was recognized of every owner to 'defend' his land and appoint his own *camparo*; and although much land in severalty was still left unenclosed, the custom also gradually spread of hedging fields and properties, especially when the arable was planted with trees. The decline of common rights was not confined to the North. In Latium also, and Southern Italy, particularly Campania, there is evidence of a general tendency to limit *vaine pâture*, especially on planted land, and protect individual *difese* on stubble fields; while even in Sardinia, though communalism still prevailed, the custom of re-dividing arable had begun to decay in places by the end of the Middle Ages.

Nor was it only on arable land that common rights were reduced. Most of the waste reclaimed for tillage was originally common land; and of the unreclaimed remainder a growing proportion was appropriated, by grant or usurpation, to individual use. Private wood and meadow, rare in the early Middle Ages, steadily increased, and with it developed the right to exclude common pasture. Round the cities of Upper Italy the commons were quickly consumed, and in Lombardy, by the sixteenth century, had practically disappeared; everywhere else they survived, but their history during the Middle Ages is a record of increasing conflict about their limits and exploitation.

Two agrarian systems, therefore, the customary and the individualistic, came to dispute the soil of medieval Italy; and to each corresponded different methods, extensive and intensive, of agricultural production. Of the two systems, medieval writers, like Roman writers, expounded only the second; and for this they were generally content to rely on their Latin predecessors. Their doctrine was, in Tanaglia's words, *usar Palladio spesso e Columella*. But they were no slavish copyists of Roman authorities. They also had new things to say, and if in certain matters, for example the management of olives, their teaching was sometimes inferior, in general the farming described by them (and in other contemporary sources) not only equalled but in places surpassed the best of Roman practice.

Among the novelties discussed were a number of new crops, unknown or undeveloped in ancient Italy. They came mostly from the Levant and, with few exceptions, they were first established, by Greeks or Arabs, in the South of Italy and Sicily. The most important were the 'monsoon' crops: rice, sugar-cane and cotton; the mulberry for silkworm culture; and the citrus fruits, the lemon and the bitter orange. From the thirteenth century onwards these crops began to be introduced into Upper Italy also, though whether from the South or from overseas is not always certain. Thus the citrus fruits (joined in time by the sweet orange) were established in Liguria and on Lake Garda, and as luxury crops in Tuscany and the Marche. In Tuscany abortive attempts were also made at growing rice and sugar but rice cultivation was successfully promoted in Lombardy by the Sforza, and soon began to spread to neighbouring districts. About the same time, mulberry growing was systematically begun in various northern provinces, though at first in limited districts. Of greater prominence in Northern Italy than most of these specialized crops were certain new types of bread corn: sorghum (*meliga*), first mentioned in the ninth century, and then widely adopted, and buckwheat (*grano saraceno*), which entered Italy some time in the fifteenth century. Maize (often confused with *meliga*) was an American exotic.

If some crops were new, others were raised for new purposes or on a new, unprecedented scale. Most notable of these were dye plants: woad, saffron and madder, which spread with the demand of urban manufacture to a growing number of districts from the early thirteenth century. Urban demand also stimulated fruit growing and horticulture, in which, by the sixteenth century, Italy had acquired a European reputation. But the main development, inevitably, was an intensified production of the basic, traditional crops: grain, olives and vines. Of these three, agricultural authors gave most attention to the vine; and, indeed, throughout the Middle Ages, when much more wine was consumed than today, no commoner form of improvement is found than the planting of land to vines. The ancients also had made special study of viticulture, perfecting the seasonal works of dressing and the methods of propagating vines: and in medieval Italy this traditional lore was faithfully reproduced and, as leases show, applied. But revival was accompanied by improvement, partly in technique, but particularly in diversity of production. By the Middle Ages most of the Latin varieties of vine had all but disappeared and, as Andrea Baccio pointed out in his learned treatise on wines (1596), what are described in medieval sources were entirely new varieties, developed by selection or import, which not only differed from the old in name, type and locality, but far exceeded them in number. Best known, apart from the muscatels which were grown nearly everywhere, were the *trebbiano* of Tuscany and the Marche, the *vernaccia* of Liguria, the *schiava* of the Po valley, and the 'Greek' and 'Latin' wines of the South, all of which were established and rapidly spreading before the end of the thirteenth century. By the sixteenth century over 50 noble vintages are named.

A comparable achievement often claimed for medieval agriculture was a general revival in the cultivation of wheat, which is thought to have been largely superseded in the early Middle Ages by inferior but more hardy and easily cultivated grains, such as oats, barley and rye, sorghum and the millets (common millet and Italian millet, called *panicum*). For this development, however, the evidence is much less conclusive. That urban demand may have caused some increase of wheat production is likely; except in periods of scarcity, the bread of townsmen (even gaol-birds) seems to have been mostly wheaten in the thirteenth and later centuries. But for the peasantry and poorer classes, who formed the bulk of the population, bread did not become the primary food, nor wheat the primary grain. According to locality, their common diet consisted of soups, porridges (*polenta*) or 'rustic loaves' (*pane rustico*), prepared from various mixtures (*mesture*) of the poorer grains (including spelt) and pulses, collectively known as 'corn' (*biade*) and generally raised for beasts as much as men (*porcis et rusticis*, as one source says of *meliga*). In mountain districts chestnut flour and acorns were also common food. Only of the South, particularly Sicily, do some authorities state (and then in the sixteenth century) that wheat was the normal bread corn. The reasons for this, however, were not social but climatic. In the Mediterranean region, owing to summer drought, only those grains can be generally grown (without irrigation) for which winter and early spring temperatures are sufficiently high. In

Italy this meant that many 'rustic' grains (millet, *panicum*, sorghum) could only be raised extensively as summer crops in the moister parts of Upper Italy and Campania. The other grains (wheat, barley, rye and even oats) were mostly winter-sown, except in highland districts; but of these rye (and possibly oats and, later, buckwheat) was restricted mainly to areas of winter cold and acid soil, like the Tuscan Apennines, Piedmont and the Alps, where it formed the principal grain. The result was that in the 'summer arid' regions, wheat, combined with barley and beans, was the dominant corn crop, whereas elsewhere its place in cultivation was often still subsidiary.

The distribution of grains, therefore, was largely climatic, and, except for a certain increase in the cultivation of rye, it does not seem to have changed significantly, despite economic fluctuations, from classical to barbarian or medieval times. Similarly, in the types of wheat chosen for cultivation, climate played as strong a part as economic influences. Of the husked wheats, while spelt was widely grown in Upper Italy, in the South there is greater evidence of the more drought-resistant emmer (*farre*). Again, among the naked wheats (which were much more common than the husked), though the soft varieties, best for bread, were cultivated everywhere, hard wheat, (*Tr. durum*), which is most adapted to Mediterranean soil and climate, retained a prominent place in the agriculture of the South. More difficult to grind than the soft wheats, it may have been used principally for unleavened cakes or *pasta* (a type of food unrecorded in Roman Italy, but in the peninsular parts of medieval Italy already known, by the early fourteenth century, in all its familiar forms: *vermicelli, maccheroni, lasagne*, etc.).

Climatic influence may also be traced in the development of other crops. Flax and hemp, for example, though grown in most districts, were particularly products of the North. Fruit farming flourished especially on the northern lakes and in Liguria, Romagna, the Marche, and the 'garden' areas of the South. Olive growing, on the other hand, though again widely diffused, was concentrated in the Southern provinces, notably Apulia: while certain crops, such as cotton, sugar and *sulla* (another Arab import) were exclusive to the 'deep South'. Regional differences also appear in the cultivation of the vine, but they relate more to the methods than the extent of viticulture. As in Roman Italy, wherever moisture was sufficient, vines were raised on stakes, trees or trellises (*pergole*), to increase yields by exposing the fruit to sunlight; but in drier districts, especially of the South, they were grown unsupported as *arbuscelli* or left to trail on the ground. This partly explains why in Southern Italy, outside Campania, vines and other planted crops (excepting sometimes olives) were normally grown apart, leaving the vast open cornfields bare of cultivated trees. In the rest of Italy, by contrast, the ancient custom spread of raising sown and planted crops promiscuously in *campi arborati* or *piantate*, though vines, in accordance with the best opinion, were still commonly grown together in vineyards or *pancate* (adjacent rows). But behind these differences of landscape lay deep natural differences in the whole practice of farming.

Except on irrigated land, both sown and planted crops continued to be grown, as in Roman times, by techniques of cultivation which forecast the practice, without the theory, of modern dry-farming (*aridocoltura*). On arable land indeed, according to some authorities, increased production was mainly achieved by a return to the Roman two-course system of dry-farming husbandry, which is believed to have been neglected by the Dark Ages for more rudimentary systems of *Feldgraswirtschaft* and temporary cropping. In the nature of things such theories are hard to prove. It can only be said that, by the communal period, in most parts of Italy, land was rarely left uncropped for more than one season. In certain regions, however, the custom persisted, long after the Middle Ages, of sowing land only once in several years. In the Alps and other highland districts, sporadic 'slash and burn farming' (*Brandwirtschaft*) (*debbio*) remained a common practice; while in the dry areas of the Tuscan Maremma, Lazio and the South, the normal course of cultivation consisted of one or two years' pasture followed by one year's fallow and one or two years of grain (*terzeria, quarteria*). Whatever the dominant system, however, land was worked almost everywhere on principles appropriate to dry-farming conditions of cultivation. Both crop land and fallow (*maggese*) were subjected to repeated cultivation, the first by the hoe, the second by the plough, to pulverize the topsoil and produce a surface mulch. According to locality (and the requirements of local statute) the fallow was ploughed and cross-ploughed from three to six or seven times (Pliny's figure of nine is not recorded); and often the hoe was also used, and in Northern Italy the harrow, to weed and work the land, cover seed and break up clods at sowing.

Being functionally little different from the hoe, the plough commonly remained a simply constructed *aratro*, of share-beam and share, ploughbeam and handle, to which were added, for the purpose of ridging and covering seed, two 'ears' (*ale, tavolette*) of unequal size. On small plots and in hilly districts ploughs were often not used at all, but only hoes and spades. For deep cultivation, so important in modern dryfarming, the spade was the recognized implement, and in Tuscany some urban statutes made systematic digging (*vangatura*) a regular part of the arable routine. The spade indeed gave better returns than the plough, a fact which Arthur Young later mistook as proof of bad husbandry; but the plough could not work so deeply (Crescenzi) or pulverize so well (Gallo). So frequent cultivation, if prescribed by technique (as modern historians insist), was also demanded by the type of plough (as later Italian agronomists complained).

However, the relative influence of technology and technique varied markedly from place to place. In practice neither plough types nor plough teams were everywhere the same. On the open fields of Sicily, for example, the usual plough was a pre-Roman *aratro chiodo*, and the usual draught animals were mules. Everywhere else oxen were the normal plough beasts, yoked in teams of two or four on light soils, on heavier soils in teams of six or eight. In most districts beasts were yoked abreast, but in northern Italy, by the fifteenth century, there is evidence of composite teams of horses and oxen, harnessed in file. In North and Central Italy, moreover, we find that the ploughs to which large teams in particular were attached were not all traditional *aratri*. Other ploughs, with mouldboards, coulters, and occasionally, wheels, were also in common use, of which the principal were the *perticarium* and the *ploum*. The *perticarium*, a light, wheelless plough, is first attested in Central Italy during the twelfth century; but the *ploum*, a true asymmetrical plough employed in the late Middle Ages on the clay soils of the lower Lombard Plain, would seem to claim descent from the implement of similar name mentioned in the Lombard laws and even earlier by Pliny. Whatever its origin, in Italy the heavy plough was an instrument of individualistic farming: the common-field plough was the ard.

Even with these improved implements, the main purpose of ploughing was pulverization. But the presence of better ploughs, with better methods of traction, helps to account for the progress made in field drainage. It would also explain Crescenzi's statement that in Lombardy and Romagna much longer furrows were ploughed in his day than in Roman times. Since the Roman furrow was the basis of ancient land measurement, it has been considered the more remarkable that, despite this departure from Roman practice, so much should have survived of the traditional Roman field system. The fact is not in doubt. As the modern landscape testifies, all over the Northern Plain, and in many other lowland areas, medieval farmers continued to cultivate their land within the undisturbed limits of ancient *centuriae*, which contrasted in their symmetry, as they still do today, with the irregular plots (*campi a pigola*) of the hills and open-field areas, where centuriation had never been imposed. However, as both Roman and medieval records prove, centuriated fields were divided up, like other fields, into parcels of different size and shape, which presumably took the form of long strips where long furrows prevailed, and of square plots where cross-ploughing was used. In either case, it was later objected, the impression was of 'disagreeable uniformity' (Symonds), and this effect, in many areas, was further increased by the habit of ploughing the 'broad lands' (*vannegie*) into smaller strips or 'stitches' (*quaderni, aiole*).

By subdividing plots medieval farmers were able to produce, by the same techniques as for grain, a large variety of other crops, from spring corn to dye plants and especially 'hoeing crops' (*sarchiate*) or pulses. In what relation these crops were grown is often impossible to determine, but there can be no doubt that from an early date they were raised increasingly in rotation. Under the pressure of expanding demand the need was felt to increase the yield as well as the extent of cultivated land. In open-field areas particularly, this was partly attempted by the self-defeating practice, denounced in many laws, of sowing grain in two successive years (*ringrano, ristoppio*). A more rational alternative, of which there is evidence from the thirteenth century, in various parts of Italy from Sicily to Piedmont, was to introduce a three-course system of cultivation, with spring grain or legumes (*colture marzenghe*). From this it was often a simple step to more complex rotations; and Crescenzi speaks of land fallowed only once in five, six or seven years. But beside land infrequently fallowed, of which he had partly learned from books, Crescenzi also refers to land not fallowed at all; and that here he was quoting from experience, and not simply from ancient authors, is demonstrated clearly by contemporary records. In Lombardy from as early as the twelfth century, and in Tuscany from the thirteenth, the practice is distinctly attested of sowing the fallow with one or more spring and summer crops. The system commonly adopted was that of 'bean husbandry', a simple course of alternate pulse and wheat; but by the later Middle Ages all kinds of rotations are indicated, especially in the North: of beans and flax, hemp and grain, millet and grain, and so on, with every possible combination of quickly ripening catch crops. Only on irrigated land was the fallow suppressed outright in favour of rotation meadow. Elsewhere the effect was rather to limit the fallow period to a few intermittent weeks or months of intensive ploughing and digging. In the Valdarno *vangatura* was considered alternative to fallowing, and laws and leases came to insist that all land should be dug over in the course of each rotation. But not everywhere were such strict rules enforced. Admiring foreigners, like Commynes, were quick to note the absence of fallowing in Italy; but local observers tended to be more critical. Too often rotations were abusive and irrational; and by the sixteenth century some North Italian agronomists were beginning to talk of soil exhaustion and the evils of overcropping, and to praise the conservative South, where land was regularly rested.

For the abuse of overcropping and the demand for increased output which produced it, the agricultural system itself may have been partly responsible. At its most advanced, medieval farming, like Roman farming, was 'labour' not 'capital-intensive', relying little on the aid of mechanical invention, and intensive labour could mean more mouths to feed. The capital lavished on land investment seems to have produced few technological advances, and of these the most important were related more to the processing than the cultivation of crops.

Characteristic were the developments, common to Italy and Europe, in the methods of corn milling, marked first by growing use, from the early Middle Ages, of the water-mill, with its North Italian variations of the floating mill and the tidal mill, and then, in the thirteenth century, by the introduction to parts of Upper Italy of the new-fashioned wind-mill. A specifically Italian novelty was a weight-driven grain-mill, recorded at Milan in 1341. Horse-mills and donkey-mills remained in common use, especially in peninsular Italy where summer drought often caused water-mills to fail; but of the primitive mortar and hand-quern, so common in Roman Italy, medieval records say nothing. Similarly in the process of wine and oil production, though rudimentary methods persisted and the Roman models of press and mill left little room for improvement, some slight technical advance is attested, by the late Middle Ages, in the use of water power to drive oil-mills.

On the other hand, in the operations of tillage, apart from changes in the plough, there is no sign of technological development, even on the large lowland farms of Northern Italy, where it might have been expected. The metal parts of implements may have been improved in quality, though not according to Gallo, but of labour-saving innovations no evidence has yet been found. Grain was still reaped with the hand-sickle (*falce dentata*), threshed by flails or the tread of draught animals, and winnowed with the shovel. Not before the seventeenth century did Italians invent (and fail to exploit) the first mechanical seed drill.

What returns could be expected from the prevailing techniques of husbandry medieval writers do not say. That productivity as much as production increased in the Middle Ages has been plausibly inferred from the movement of population to the towns and from the spread, to be noted later, of commercial forms of tenancy, particularly *mezzadria*. But it does not always appear that returns were best where farming was more intensive. Contrasting conditions in North and South, the six-teenth-century writer, Guiseppe Falcone, observes that in Sicily, Apulia and the Terra di Lavoro, land produced so copiously that farmers had difficulty in storing their grain, whereas in Lombardy the fields were cropped so mercilessly that land refused to produce at all. Of Sicily, where farming was more primitive, it is in fact reported, about

1550, that the grain yield in a normal year was ten-fold, in a poor year eight-fold, and in a good year twelve-fold; but these statistics (which hardly differ from those given by Cicero sixteen hundred years before) may be matched by records of similar returns in the Valdarno and Polesine during the fifteenth century.

It is more relevant to notice that these were all regions famous for fertility. Figures from other districts, which show a normal yield of three- to six-fold, would rather confirm the conclusion of historians that the return from land in both North and South did not vary significantly from the four-fold average of Columella's Italy. No doubt these calculations ignore the greater variety of production and the rich returns from planted crops. But they suggest that medieval enterprise may have been more successful in increasing the area than the productivity of cultivated land. Traditional methods produced traditional results. For low yields and uncertain harvests Gallo placed the blame on defective techniques of sowing. Climate also may have played a part. But the main reason, now as in the past, was a radical weakness in the system of farming itself: inadequate fertilization of soil arising from a general failure to integrate arable and livestock husbandry and so produce a sufficiency of feed, stock and natural manure.

To this defect are traceable most characteristic features of medieval Italian agriculture. More even than the exigencies of dry-farming technique, it explains the practice of fallowing and repeated cultivation, for according to contemporary doctrine there was no better means to restoring land than a scrupulously clean fallow (*maggese nudo*). Similarly, the preference for bean husbandry, where fallow land was cropped, was based on the knowledge, inherited from antiquity, that leguminous crops enrich the soil, especially when ploughed under. They were therefore sown, as the records state, *ad impinguendum agrum* (Lombardy), or *ad bonam caloriam* (Tuscany), to be turned in after cropping as green manure (*sovescio*). Not all rotations, however, were so beneficial. In some places, for example the Tyrol, even *sovesci* were forbidden; while all authorities were careful to insist that, if land was sown with cover crops, it must be regularly manured. 'After vetches and lupins', says the poet Alemanni, 'other crops may be grown, but only if the farmer assists the seed by gathering ash and refuse, spreading dung, or setting fire in season to the stubbles.'

The alternative to fallowing was fertilization, but the variety of means described for this reveal it to have been a problem. Stubble-burning, an ancient custom, was common all over Italy, especially the South and Centre. Grassland too was regularly fired, particularly in the highlands, where burn-beating (*debbio*) was part of the traditional system of cultivation. Wood ash, mentioned by Alemanni, was another favoured fertilizer which the highlands were specially fitted to provide; in the Bolognese Apennines wood was burned systematically to produce ash for sale. A local refinement on wood ash, indicated by Gallo, was a mixture of vegetable ashes which had been boiled to make lye. By spreading fields with this, or better still with lime, inferior land in upper Lombardy had been rendered highly fertile. Gallo therefore favoured extending the practice, but most significant is his argument for doing so: it would help supply the frequent deficiency of animal manure.

So explicit a statement is not the less instructive for standing almost alone. From the observations of most writers, Crescenzi among them, it might be inferred that the most valued of all fertilizers was also the most abundant. Repeating faithfully their Roman authorities on the properties of natural manure, they advise farmers to collect and preserve the dung of all animals and birds and describe in detail the proper methods of treatment and application; and certainly there are records enough to show that practice corresponded to theory on farms in the most progressive parts of Italy. Yet precisely here, in Tuscany, Emilia and the North, we find that, even on large farms, the use and disposal of litter and manure were often strictly regulated, while small farms were commonly compelled to buy it. The demand was such that by the thirteenth century in many areas of Upper Italy a regular trade had begun to develop in agricultural manure; but supplies were evidently limited, to judge from the laws passed to check profiteering, and the lands which profited most were suburban farms and market gardens which could draw on the copious refuse of the towns and major highways.

Of conditions prevailing generally, outside such privileged districts, a better idea is given by the widespread practice of grazing stock on stubble fields and fallows (*stabbiatura*). Commended by agronomists as a method of manuring land, it is found all over Italy, no less in regions of 'enclosure' than of open-field husbandry; and it was probably the copious dunging of land in the periods of fallow and pasture that contributed to the high yields reported in certain parts of the South. But even the benefits of *stabbiatura* were limited, for the grazing of stock was restricted to certain seasons; while its good effects were largely incidental to the purpose of meeting the ultimate problem of all in medieval farming: the provision of animal feed.

In Italy this problem was especially acute. Owing to climate much of the land was deficient in meadow and forage, especially winter forage. The lack was sufficiently serious for Crescenzi, writing for model farmers, to advocate the autumn culling of stock; while others advised buying beasts in March, when their lean condition would reveal all defects. The first deficiency was hay. Cultivated meadow was scarce and, without irrigation, normally allowed only one, or at most two, cuttings a year. Yet, despite the practice of crop rotation, in few places was the defect made up by increased production of fodder. It is true that most crops other than wheat were partly sown for fodder, while some, like oats, lupins and turnips, were grown for nothing else. But, in face of the demands of rising population, human needs came first. In Tuscany urban statutes restricted the sowing of fodder crops in the interests of wheat; in Emilia, Venetia and the unirrigated parts of Lombardy, the typical rotations, with summer grain and industrial plants, left little place for forage. So under normal conditions fodder crops and hay had to be fed sparingly, and on many farms were supplemented with measures of straw, leaves (*frasche*), mast, chaff and grape skins (*vinaccia*). Straw was often the only winter feed. It was therefore the custom to reap grain at the top or half-way up, the stubble being partly cut, partly left for grazing. In the same way, the use of leaves for forage encouraged the practice of supporting vines on trees and intermixing sown and planted crops.

In these conditions farmers generally were compelled to keep their sedentary stock to a minimum. Only draught animals were commonly stall-fed, and not in every region. In peninsular Italy, especially the South, a more characteristic practice was to 'defend' particular parcels of land (*mezzane*) for the pasture of plough oxen, and sometimes other beasts. No doubt on all but the smallest holdings, outside suburban areas, it was customary to breed a stock of pigs, sheep or goats, with sometimes an ass or two; so much is suggested by the Florentine tax lists of 1427. But nearly all such *bestie minute* needed pasture for part of the year, if not for all the year. For raising stock in numbers, farmers in most districts, even of intensive agriculture, were forced to rely on open grazing in arable fields, meadow and waste; while in regions of extensive agriculture, it was mainly the needs of pastoral farming which perpetuated the practice of *Feldgraswirtschaft*, *vaine pâture*, and the agrarian organization that went with them. On arable land the period of open grazing varied with local conditions, but, except where the crop–fallow rotation was interrupted by a year of pasture, it was commonly limited to winter. In some places standing crops were also grazed for a period. Then, with spring, the fields were put in defence. Except in parts of Sicily, where grass was closed in winter, the open season on meadow land was generally much the same. During enclosure beasts were strictly controlled and wherever possible were put to pasture on rough grazings and woodland. Every estate, according to Falcone, should possess a piece of wood; but in many densely populated areas reclamation had largely consumed the waste. On the Florentine plain, for example, and in the neighbourhood of Verona the only grazings, apart from the fields, by the later Middle Ages, were along the open wayside.

In any case, in most of Italy, pasture land, even where abundant, was normally only seasonal. Animals therefore had to be moved to winter or summer grazing. Indeed, in many places, statute made it compulsory, in the season of enclosure, to remove all kinds of stock, with the exception of plough oxen, which always had grazing privileges, sick beasts and a few goats or cows for milk. As a result livestock farming in medieval Italy remained an activity largely unrelated and even hostile to arable farming, since it depended on seasonal migration and could only be practised on a massive scale where natural wood and pasture were extensive: in the Alps and other mountain districts and in the open-field regions of the peninsula and islands.

Of transhumant grazing agricultural writers have virtually nothing to say. Yet in the rural life of medieval Italy no custom was more widespread or familiar. In some form it existed in almost every region. Sometimes the movement of livestock was limited and local, as in the Marchesato of Calabria and many Alpine valleys where lowland and highland grazing lay conveniently together, or in northern Tuscany and Emilia where lowland farmers let out beasts or rented pasture in near-by Apennine villages which in turn sent stock to winter in the plain. But far more characteristic than these small-scale migrations was the long-distance movement of large composite flocks and herds, mustered together from wide areas and from many different owners, landlords and tenants, townsmen and villagers. Every autumn, from the western Alps to Sicily, multitudes of animals were driven from the hills to the plains, to return the following spring, partly depleted by losses and sales, partly enriched with new stock. The most frequented trails (*tratturi*) were those which ran from Piedmont to the Dauphiné, from the Alps to the lowlands of Lombardy, Venetia and northern Emilia, from the Tuscan Apennines to Romagna and the Maremma, and from the Abruzzi to the coastlands of Latium and Apulia. The numbers of beasts were often very considerable, especially in peninsular Italy. In 1257 nearly 22,000 sheep are recorded as passing through Sienese territory between the Garfagnana and Maremma. In 1462-3, according to Pius II, more than 100,000 Aquilan sheep wintered in the Roman Campagna. Five years later, in the Tuscan Patrimony alone, papal officials registered the entry of 66,251 pigs, 110,120 sheep, and some oxen and other *bestie grosse*. In Apulia during the fifteenth century the number of migrant sheep rose to over half a million.

Inevitably such massive movements required elaborate organization, not only to manage the beasts in transit, but even more to secure the grazing right on stubble fields and commons, and inevitably there was conflict—between graziers and sedentary farmers, in the lowlands and along the *tratturi*, between flockmasters and landlords who wanted their grazings for themselves, and, most of all perhaps, between contending interests in the pastoral highland villages over licence to admit *foreign beasts*, including animals held on lease from townsmen and other rich outsiders. But the conflict was unequal, at least in the later Middle Ages, when most Italian governments found reason to favour the trans-humant graziers. Thus Venice, to promote the wool industry, enforced the rights of migrant shepherds to claim compulsory agistment (*pensionatico*) on farms in the lowlands of Padua, Vicenza and Treviso. Similarly Florence, in the later fifteenth century, reaffirmed the right of landlords (who included the Medici) to pasture cattle, horses and pigs on all classes of land in the Pisano. But state intervention was most emphatic in Central and Southern Italy. Here, in the fifteenth century, on the vast winter grazing grounds of the Maremma, Lazio and Apulia, government monopolies of pasture rights on demesne, private and common land were established (or reorganized) and vested in special 'Customs offices' or *dogane*: the *Dogana dei Paschi of Siena* (1419?), the *Dogana Pecudum* of Rome (1402?) and, most ambitious of all, the *Dohana Menae Pecudum* of the crown of Naples (1443). In return for lucrative rents (*herbatica*) and transit dues (*fide, tratte*), these institutions controlled and protected the movement of all livestock, allotted all winter pasturage and, in the Tavoliere of Apulia at least, even regulated the cropping of land by imposing a strict rotation of herbage with corn. In 1549 two-fifths of all land in Apulia subject to transhumant grazing was arable. At least it was well manured.

Whether arable or waste, most grazing land in Italy was not merely seasonal. Often it was also inferior. By far the greater number of animals raised, whether migrant or sedentary, were therefore *bestie minute*: sheep, goats and swine. Open-range cattle raising, frequently transhumant, was certainly practised in places: in Apulia, for example, and some other southern areas, on the wetter lands of the Roman Campagna and lower Po and Arno valleys, and most obviously in the Alps (though even here, unlike today, sheep preponderated). In mainly marshy districts again, there was some breeding of mules and horses in Apulia, Campania and Sicily, and of buffaloes in Tuscany, the Campagna and the South. But these were local activities, over-shadowed everywhere by migratory sheep-farming.

In most areas cattle were few, and in many insufficient, and they were bred mainly for work. The dominant breeds have still to be studied, but the commonest seems to have been a type of red or dark brown cattle, of the kind commended by Roman authors as providing the best draught oxen. Though sturdy of frame, by later standards they were small and underweight, and their milk yield was scanty. Cows in fact were generally used as plough beasts and were called, like oxen, *buoi*. Dairy and beef cattle were not yet raised in numbers, even near the towns. There were none on the farms round Florence in 1427. A demand for beef, as for dairy produce, had certainly developed, especially among the rich and urban classes; but it was not always easy to satisfy. When the city of Venice in 1529 tried to extract from its subject territory a yearly quota of 15,000 store-beeves, it was forced to reduce its demands by nearly half, and later by half again, in face of energetic complaints about lack of feed, the harm threatened to tillage, and the sacrifice by local towns of their limited supplies of meat, milk and cheese. In the Veronese more than half the villages were declared unable to produce beef-cattle at all. Conditions were hardly better in most other parts of Italy. Oxen sold for killing were mostly *bestie inutiles*; and the meat generally eaten (and many went without) was not beef but mutton, especially wether mutton (*castrato*), or pig meat: pork, bacon, *salami*.

Only pigs were raised wholly for slaughter, partly for flesh, partly for lard, the commonest fat in use. Sheep were bred rather for wool and milk than meat. Sheep's milk and cheese, according to Crescenzi, were better than those of cattle, and the bulk of the cheese consumed in Italy was probably *pecorino*. But the prime product of sheep-farming was wool, and in order to raise the grade of wool some care was spent in the Middle Ages on the nurture and selection of sheep. Most Italian sheep were coarse-woolled breeds, often clipped twice and even three times a year; but beside these were certain other 'gentler' breeds (*gentili*), which were clipped only once and were reared for fleeces alone. They are found particularly in late medieval Apulia which, together with Venetia (Veronese) and possibly the Maremma, continued to produce, as in Roman times, the finest quality fleeces; and it was to improve the Apulian breed of sheep that Charles of Anjou, in the thirteenth century, imported new stock from Africa, and Alfonso of Naples, in the fifteenth century, introduced the merino from Spain. But in Italy pastures were often too tough for select and sensitive breeds. When Ludovico Sforza brought prize sheep from Languedoc to Vigevano their fleeces soon coarsened 'because of different air and pasture'. And even where grazings were good, improvements in sheepfarming, as in stock husbandry generally, was retarded by the custom of herding beasts in common.

It is not to be wondered that medieval agronomists pay little attention to stockfarming and even assign it less space than smaller matters like horticulture. And yet, even in animal husbandry, there were certain parts of Italy where intensive methods of production were successfully applied, especially in cattle breeding. They lay principally in the Po valley, from Piedmont to Emilia. No doubt over most of this area climate and physical conditions particularly favoured stock-breeding, but not everywhere, nor without assistance from agricultural technique. In the Bolognese, a dry district, it was not the climate, but the technique of crop rotation with increased output of forage, that enabled farmers in the thirteenth century to dress their fields with double the amount of animal manure prescribed by Roman text books (in Tuscany they used less) (Crescenzi), and by the sixteenth century to breed especially heavy plough-oxen (Gallo). Similarly on the wetter soils of lowland Lombardy and Piedmont, where permanent grassland yielded feed for sufficient stock to permit the manuring of meadow, the production of hay and fodder was enormously increased by irriga-tion, which not only fertilized the land but also encouraged the cultiva-tion of regular rotation meadow. From irrigated meadow, with the help of manure, three to five crops could be taken; from the *marcite* of Milan as many as seven or eight.

In these irrigated areas, therefore, from as early as the thirteenth century the typical forms of medieval husbandry began to be dis-carded. Corn and hay (joined in the sixteenth century by clover and lucerne) took the place of corn and wine, dominant elsewhere in Lombardy; cattle-rearing steadily ousted sheep-farming, and beasts were raised, not only for work, but increasingly for milk and beef. By the late Middle Ages new varieties of cattle were being bred round Parma and Ferrara, and throughout the region the products of intensive stock husbandry were supplying an export market. Already in the fourteenth century the 'Parmesan' cheese of Lodi, Piacenza and Parma was in wide demand abroad. In the fifteenth century Lombard butter was being sent to Rome. And in the sixteenth century neighbouring areas, like the Veronese, were importing cows from Pavia, beef cattle (*manzi*) from Parma, Cremona and Reggio, and also large numbers of swine from Reggio, Parma and Modena. And for all this there were no precedents in antiquity. The Po valley livestock industry was a medieval creation.

D. *Agricultural trade*

Lombard livestock was not the only commercial product of Italian farming. One motive implicit in the whole development of medieval agriculture was the desire to produce more for trade. No doubt the trade was mainly local, at least in the urbanized North, and the growth of production determined first by local demand. Not only landless townsmen but many peasants and landlords had to supply part of their needs from outside; and if this they often did by direct dealings among themselves, their main resource inevitably was purchase in local markets. But in no place were local markets at all times sufficient. The very nature of the country and its climate compelled some regional specialization and exchange, between highlands and lowlands, wet areas and dry; and this natural interdependence was deepened further by disparities of economic and demographic growth. All areas were vulnerable to periodic dearth, but whereas the agricultural provinces, especially the poor and sparsely-populated South, normally produced a surplus of food, the rich and populous industrial provinces were frequently unable to grow enough. Thus Florence, in the early fourteenth century, was reported to draw only five months' food from its territory each year; Genoa, with an estimated wheat consumption of 22,000 tons a year in the middle of the fifteenth century, received no corn from its hinterland at all; while Venice, with even larger demands, failed to achieve self-sufficiency, despite extensive mainland conquests in the later Middle Ages.

The result was intense inter-regional trade, in which 'industrial' Italy tried to balance its imports of primary products from 'agricultural' Italy by selling manufactures. The policy was not always successful. Apulia had little market for Venetian merchandise or the Maremma for that of Genoa. In other ways too the rule of regional reciprocity broke down. Thus the industrial Milanese could sometimes export corn, while the pastoral Alps and Apennines had to fetch it from outside. Nor was it only by regional trade that the varying needs of provinces were met. From modest beginnings in the Dark Ages, survivals perhaps from antiquity, Italy became increasingly involved in a world-wide trade in food and materials, which created a parallel relationship between home and overseas market. The industrial districts imported produce, the agricultural mainly exported it, but this division once again was not rigid. As Italian commerce expanded, so the market grew for the products of Italian farming generally, and agriculture everywhere began to respond to changes in international trade.

The relative claims of local, regional and overseas markets appear most distinctly in the grain trade. The principal corn-producing regions remained, as in Roman times, various parts of the Po valley with Romagna and the Marche, the Maremma, and a number of Southern provinces, especially Apulia and the islands. But of these the great majority served local and regional markets and only Apulia and Sicily seem to have commanded resources enough for regular export abroad. In Sicily, conventionally famed as the 'granary of Italy', the surplus of corn (wheat, barley, beans) is said to have reached in favourable years as much as one-third of the crop; in Apulia the maximum has been estimated, for the early fourteenth century, at some 86,000 quarters of wheat, 'perhaps enough to feed 100,000 men' (Mickwitz). Much, possibly most, of this corn was marketed in Upper Italy; but large quantities were also shipped to other parts of the Mediterranean, if not further afield, while the Northern cities, especially Genoa and Venice, in turn imported grain from overseas, as well as from nearer home.

Not very different was the pattern of trade in most other products. Of wine a substantial amount was imported, at least of quality wines from Crete and occasionally France. By the later Middle Ages, however, an increasing number of Italian wines, both select and ordinary vintages, were also being exported regionally and abroad: from the northern frontier districts to Germany and Switzerland, from Liguria to Spain, Flanders and England, and from the Marche via Venice to the Levant. But once again it was southern products which bulked largest in trade: the *vino greco* and *vino latino* of Campania and neighbouring districts. The wine of other districts, Liguria in particular, was mainly absorbed by local urban markets. The same was true even more of oil and fruit. In Upper Italy Como, Liguria and the Marche all exported oil, but mostly to near-by areas; the main centres of production were Gaeta and the Apulian towns, pre-eminently Bari, and from these places most surplus oil seems to have gone overseas, especially to the Levant. Fruit also was exported from various parts of Italy, in particular Liguria, Romagna and the Marche; but in foreign trade the handbooks of Pegolotti and later merchants clearly imply that the principal products were the fruits, nuts and almonds of Campania, Apulia and Sicily. To emphasize further the regional inequality, there were certain food exports exclusive to the South: Sicilian and Campanian *pasta*, exported at least to Rome; Sicilian rice, imported by the Genoese; and above all sugar, especially Sicilian sugar, which was distributed in the fifteenth century all over North and Central Europe.

In the products of livestock husbandry trade was much more limited to regional exchange inside Italy itself. But again the primary exporters were the provinces of the South; and even in the North it was not intensive stock-breeding, but transhumant and open-range grazing which produced most for export. The cheese of the Brescian highlands commanded a better market than the 'Parmesan' of the plains; and the livestock fairs, frequented by foreign buyers, which are mentioned in the fifteenth century, were located not in the lowlands but in the Apennines and close to the Alpine valleys. Here sheep, cattle and horses were all offered for sale. Lombard sheep are recorded in Genoese and Pisan commercial documents of the fifteenth century, while Lombard horses had a European market already in the twelfth century.

But trade in Lombard cattle was probably confined to the North, where demand was more than sufficient; indeed a number of districts (Bresciano, Veronese, etc.) had partly to import stock from Switzerland and Hungary. By contrast the South and islands exported all kinds of livestock, mostly to Upper Italy, as well as large quantities of salt meat, *salami* and cheese, ox hides, lamb fells and wool. Though generally too coarse for luxury textiles, which were woven from foreign fleeces, Italian wool was the only material available for ordinary cloth. It was therefore taken not only for local industry and homespun, but also by great towns like Florence; and for these the main source of supply was the transhumant sheep industry of the Abruzzi, Apulia, Sicily and Sardinia.

The only agricultural exports in which the North surpassed the South were industrial crops, textile plants and dye plants, in which medieval Italy seems to have been largely self-supporting. Flax and hemp, it is true, were exported by a number of southern districts, sometimes to foreign ports like Marseilles; the South too was the only exporter of cotton and, for most of the period, silk; while the greatest single centre of trade in saffron, in the later Middle Ages, was the southern province of Aquila, which at the end of the fifteenth century was supplying markets in Germany as well as Italy. But the bulk of commercial hemp and flax was grown in northern provinces: Piedmont, Lombardy, the Bolognese and Romagna; the southern silk and cotton crop was too small for use in Northern industry; while the cultivation of saffron was most diffused in the North and Centre, particularly Tuscany, from which as early as the thirteenth century it was imported into England, France and the Levant. Of the other principal dye plants, madder and woad, the main centres of production lay all in Upper Italy. Madder was grown for export in Romagna and for a time also in Lombardy, until in the fourteenth century its place was taken by woad. The first region to develop woad was Tuscany which exported it in the thirteenth century to Northern Italy and possibly Northern Europe. Then, in the fourteenth century, two rival industries arose, one in the Bolognese, the other, more important, in Lombardy. Over a vast area extending from Tortona to Casteggio, where woad had never been grown before, its cultivation was systematically developed. By the fifteenth century Tuscany itself was importing 'Lombard' woad, and so, in massive quantities, were Spain, England and the Low Countries, and even, on a smaller scale, Southern Italy.

The long-distance movement of agricultural products was inevitably handled by great merchant companies, for the most part Venetian, Genoese and Florentine. Largely for this reason more is known of the international food-trade than of local trade or the dealings of growers with buyers. What information there is, is also late. In the fifteenth century Genoese merchants in Sicily travelled inland to make bulk purchases of grain, partly at least from producers. At the same period woad merchants in Lombardy and saffron buyers in the Abruzzi employed local agents to go round buying up the crop from growers. But it was just as common a practice for merchants to buy in local markets and fairs. To an unsuspected extent, the custom was observed in late medieval Italy of holding annual fairs, often livestock fairs, some of which drew traders from a wide area, like the great concourse of horse dealers which met at Chieti (Abruzzo) in 1485. Here and in the periodic markets, merchants and agents must often have encountered the large and elusive class of small tradesmen and dealers, the *mercatores bladarum, victualium et bestiarum*, whose business lay in the urban and local food trade. All the large towns had daily food markets and often weekly stock markets as well; but in addition to these, and closely related to them, were numerous rural markets, meeting on different days of the week from Mondays to Saturdays, in the dependent *castella* and *borghi*. To maintain relations between rural and urban markets was one function assumed by local *mercatores*. In the suburban districts of a number of towns the purchase of products by middlemen was restricted or forbidden. It was therefore in the *contado* that professional dealers principally operated, going the round of the markets, and also, it is likely, the farms, purchasing commodities from peasants, bailiffs and landlords. The late medieval estate accounts of Florentine merchant-landlords are full of records of crop sales to dealers of all kinds. Peasants commonly disposed of their crops in a single sale-contract, often for future delivery. Landlords, on the other hand, could more easily afford to calculate, and in accord with the advice of the Florentine Paolo da Certaldo, spread their sales evenly over the year: grain in October, January, March and May, oil in Lent and autumn, wine from Lent to August.

Landowners, however, did more than regulate sales; they also engaged in trade itself, even long-distance trade. In fifteenth-century Lombardy, the Bottigelli family of Pavia were both growers and exporters of woad. In fourteenth-century Tuscany, landowning merchants like the Peruzzi maintained shops in town (the Frescobaldi still do) for the sale of wine and produce from their lands. Many also kept taverns, wayside *alberghi*, for the purpose. Peasants too, it must be said, sometimes retailed produce, especially suburban farmers; a number, indeed, may have been professional dealers. But the scope of their activity was small and often, we shall see, deliberately restricted by their lords. In the South and Sicily the great baronial landlords engrossed the marketable surplus of peasants and small proprietors and speculated in the export of grain and oil. In Sicily particularly, during the fifteenth century, the magnates virtually monopolized the grain trade; in Naples, at the same period, members of the nobility are known to have kept ships; and even the kings of Naples did not disdain to share in the hire of trading vessels for selling corn abroad. Similarly, in Upper Italy, we find the Malatesta of Rimini and other lords of Romagna exporting the grain from their estates and even forming companies for trading in corn.

For those well placed to exploit it, farming was clearly a source of substantial gain. From the proceeds of their vineyards alone the Frescobaldi in the fourteenth century are said to have built a villa. To capture a share in the profits was one reason why townsmen invested in land. And not only land was the object of investment. By the thirteenth century it was clearly a widespread practice, at least in Upper Italy, for people of all but the poorest classes to speculate by advancing money to peasants, against future delivery of crops, and by buying up livestock to let out to farmers. Usually the quantity of stock was small, a plough beast or two, but sometimes it was large. One merchant of Florence in 1419 had 600 sheep pasturing in the Casentino; a merchant of Aquila in 1335 had a flock of 9000. And stock-leasing, we shall see, was only one part of a general movement to commercialize agrarian contracts. As markets grew, farming became increasingly a branch of business. From the later thirteenth century, in Tuscany and the North, business methods of accountancy, culminating in the fifteenth century in double-entry forms of book-keeping, began to be applied also to the management of estates; and what the estate accounts reveal, in a large number of cases, is a system of production adjusted as far as possible to the varying demand of markets. Production for sale, indeed, was so much the custom that an Italian visitor to England, at the end of the fifteenth century, was moved to comment with surprise that 'agriculture is not practised in this island beyond what is required for the consumption of the people'.

No doubt the anonymous observer was mistaken. Not only did he misjudge English farming but also, by implication, that of Italy. For nowhere, even in Italy, did commercialized farming predominate; and such refinements of commercial agriculture as single-crop tillage are difficult to find. Exclusively cash crops, such as woad, were grown in rotation with corn or on separate parcels of land as a lucrative sideline. Specialization, where practised at all, was most developed near the larger towns and seaports. On estates about Venice, by as early as 1100, vineyards and orchards had taken the place of all former arable land; and so round every city there grew up horticultural suburbs, which in the neighbourhood of maritime towns like Genoa and Naples, Bari and Palermo, steadily expanded to supply markets abroad. But even in these privileged areas mixed cultivation was probably the rule. Everywhere else the first concern of producers, particularly peasants, was to provide for household subsistence. So crops like hemp and flax were grown for use on farms all over Italy, promiscuous cultivation prevailed where since it has disappeared, and sheep-farming was widespread even on the Lombard Plain. Many monastic and capitular communities seem almost as self-contained in the late as in the early Middle Ages; and also on lay estates, owners generally followed the ancient rule, first formulated by Cato in a comparable period of agrarian development, to sell as much but buy as little as possible. Their ideal, at least as defined in tracts for *padri di famiglia*, was not a capitalist but a self-sufficient estate, which would furnish the landlord's table with *dapibus inemptis* (Tasso). Poggio Bracciolini even condemned English nobles for trafficking in wool and grain. His Italian contemporaries, we have seen, were guilty of the same offence; but the produce which they marketed was normally nothing more than the natural surplus arising on great estates of the basic crops, particularly grain. Grain was the principal product of the Medici estates in Mugello during the fifteenth century; grain in quantities to feed the whole of Florence for several days formed part of the wealth of Palla Strozzi, richest Florentine citizen in 1427; and grain from patrician estates supplied six-sevenths of the bread corn entering Bologna in 1496.

There was no national market to encourage specialization. Neither politically nor economically was Italy one community; and the physical structure of the country, which made for variety and intercourse, also created difficulties of internal communication more formidable than most in medieval Europe. Despite notable improvements in all forms of communication, sea and water transport remained incomparably cheaper than transport overland; and the commodities most affected by the difference were precisely the low-priced but bulky products of farming, especially grain and wine, for which transport charges occasionally rose to 160 per cent of cost price. In a mountainous country poor in navigable streams, this meant that many inland districts were thrown upon their own resources while frontier and coastal areas were turned as naturally to foreign as to domestic markets: the Tyrol toward Germany, Sicily toward North Africa, the maritime towns to countries overseas. Thus for Genoa it was cheaper to ship grain from abroad than bring it overland from Piedmont or Lombardy; indeed, by building vessels of large tonnage and combining them in convoy, the Genoese in the later Middle Ages were able to cut the freightage of corn to 10–25 per cent of sale price.

More difficult to circumvent were the obstacles arising from public policy in a disunited country: tolls, duties and export licences, variations of coinage, weights and measures, and most of all government restrictions on trade, to all of which the regional unification of Italy in the fourteenth and fifteenth centuries made much less radical difference than is sometimes supposed. Trade restrictions indeed were as much the effect as the cause of impediments to commerce. Foodstuffs, significantly, were once again the goods principally affected; for of all activities food supply was the business which states could least afford to abandon to the costs and hazards of uncontrolled trade. To avoid the dangers of shortage, to which low yields and bad harvests exposed every region, and in the larger cities to keep down the cost of living and consequently wages, all governments in Italy, especially the towns, tried to secure 'an abundance' of cheap food, as far as possible by local self-sufficiency. The effects of the policy are evident in all sides of rural life, from colonization to land tenure. It was to provide 'abundance of corn' (copia blavorum) that the government of Verona undertook bonifiche in 1199. To the same end numerous towns and villages made the cultivation of specific crops compulsory by statute, often, as later critics complained, in defiance of natural conditions and the rational use of land. In the duchy of Milan the natural spread of stock and dairy farming was threatened in 1482-3 by a law to reconvert meadowland to arable, in the interest of 'abundance'. In Piedmont farmers were obliged to grow olives and almonds, typically southern crops, and strove to raise corn at inclement altitudes. The practice of overcropping must also be largely blamed on urban food policy. Nor were controls limited to the use of land. To prevent losses the date of vintage and sometimes of other farming operations was fixed by law, and even the relations of lords and tenants were closely supervised, as the statutes of Assisi explain (1469), to ensure all land was cultivated. On the same grounds the movement abroad of wage-labourers was restricted. But even more than the production of food was distribution controlled. For this purpose, in all the greater communes, the ancient institution was revived of the civic annona (though without frumentationes) and entrusted to officials variously known as commissioners of Annona, Grascia and Abbondanza. First claims on all produce, including often the stock and produce of transhumant graziers, were assigned to local needs. Harvests were registered and the export, even the local movement, of crops and animals restricted. To cheapen supplies to the urban consumer, landlords and peasants were encouraged or compelled to deliver all surplus produce direct to the urban market. Prices, when need arose, were fixed. And a mass of laws was enacted in restraint of hoarding, forestalling and re-grating, and all kinds of dealings, like the advance purchase of crops, outside the appointed market places. When these various measures failed, as commonly they did, to prevent the threat of dearth, imports were anxiously sought and subsidized. In towns like Genoa, permanently dependent on foreign supplies, the organization of imports, with bounties and commissions, was a regular part of government activity.

Beside this activity in favour of consumers there is little enough to see of laws to protect producers. Only in a few towns (Arezzo, Molfetta, Lecce) do we find the import of wine forbidden in the interest of local growers. Yet before concluding with nineteenth-century writers that the food policy of medieval states was the ruin of farmers and farming, it may be asked what importance should be given to laws, so many of which stand in open contradiction with practices known to have been habitual. That food laws were no dead letter, there are court records enough to show; but that they were also a serious check to commercial farming is much less certain. Many restrictions, no doubt, were purely emergency measures, while others were limited to certain areas or to certain types of produce. Most comprehensive were the corn laws, but even these were not always strict or effective. Corn prices fluctuated sharply, though less perhaps in maritime towns like Genoa than inland towns like Florence, and the profits resulting, often large, went to the merchants and producers; the losses, also often large, were borne by the government. Governments were not impersonal but, even in commercial towns, were composed largely of men with interests in the land. Despite legislation, therefore, the food market could often be manipulated and it was understood that landowners would wait to sell when prices rose, though churchmen were sometimes warned against this. And there is plenty of plaintive evidence, in chronicles and elsewhere, that opportunity remained for profiteering as well as profit, not only in the corn-exporting regions of the Centre and the South, where barons controlled the grain-trade and even rulers sometimes exported produce to the neglect of local needs, but also in the towns of Tuscany and the North, especially in the late Middle Ages, when landowning oligarchs and despots increasingly dominated the government. In Romagna it has been suggested that one ambition of aspirant *signori* was to free themselves from statutory restrictions on food export.

In practice it was impossible to isolate farm production, even corn-growing, from the wider influence of regional and international trade. Some Italian products indeed may have been more dependent on foreign than domestic markets: Sicilian sugar, for example, or the oil of Apulia and the quality wines of Campania. For some of these crops demand remained fairly constant throughout the Middle Ages. Wine in particular seems to have preserved its reputation as the most profitable cash crop for markets of all kinds. Other crops were not so fortunate. Thus, in the late fifteenth and sixteenth centuries, Sicilian sugar, Lombard woad and Italian saffron all lost their foreign markets. The principal reason seems to have been competition from rival products, partly grown in Europe itself, partly in places opened up by geographical discovery. It is tempting, however, to see in these developments some evidence of the general movement detected by certain historians in European farming as a whole, according to which, in the period of late medieval recession a greater fall in the price of grain relative to other prices caused farmers everywhere to go over to commercial crops and livestock husbandry, until at the end of the Middle Ages the trend was reversed with reviving population and a widespread return to grain. In Italy it was certainly during the fourteenth and fifteenth centuries that dye plants and sugar were most extensively grown. And during the same period there was no less certainly a considerable increase in grazing.

An advance of grazing, particularly sheep farming, is attested all over Italy, but most of all in the Tuscan Maremma, Lazio and the South. The evidence is largely indirect but nonetheless conclusive: increasing legislation to check the overcharging of commons, especially with migrant stock; abusive 'enclosure' of commons for pasture by Southern lords; the foundation of public grazing monopolies; the introduction of the merino sheep. So serious was the retreat of corn-growing in the region round Rome that Sixtus IV (1471–84) and later popes tried to protect and extend it, but without apparent success. In Apulia also, by 1500, as population rose, there is evidence of sharpening competition for land between graziers and farmers; nevertheless between 1463 and 1536 the number of migrant sheep increased from 600,000 to 1,048,000. Various reasons have been suggested for the growth of grazing over tillage: in Sicily, the displacement of Tuscan by English cloth in the fifteenth century, which reduced Tuscan imports of grain; on the southern mainland the restriction of English wool exports to Italy; in the Campagna and the Sienese Maremma, the grain policy of the state which killed the corn trade and discouraged arable farming. That is to say it was conditions of trade which controlled the actions of landlords. In the Roman Campagna, however, the records rather imply that grazing spread simply because the local *latifondisti*, like their predecessors in antiquity, found it the cheapest way of exploiting their domains. Notable also is the fact that almost all the areas affected suffered depopulation. It is therefore necessary to inquire, further, how far the increase of grazing was the cause or result of changes in rural settlement.

E. *Forms of rural settlement*

In the history of Italian rural settlement, as far as it has been studied, the custom has been to emphasize political rather than economic influences. Thus, of the two contrasted forms of settlement, nucleated and dispersed, which ever since remote antiquity have divided the soil of Italy, it is commonplace that, during the reign of the *pax romana*, an increasing part of the population tended to dispersed habitation, in grouped or isolated farms (*fundi cum casis, villae*). Then, it is said, in the following centuries of disorder and devastation, the inhabitants of the open country tended to concentrate again in villages, hilltop *castra* and towns, though many continued to live in undefended hamlets (*fundi casales, casalia*), *mansi* or farms, and merely withdrew to *castella* for protection. The building of *castella* was most intense from the tenth to the twelfth century, in the period succeeding the Arab and Magyar invasions, but the activity continued throughout the Middle Ages. In 1292 the *contado* of Orvieto was divided for administration among 17 *castra*, 20 *pleberia* and 56 ville. The *contado* of Florence in 1376 is described in an official survey (admittedly selective) as having as many *castra* as villages. And the Monferrato is represented by Benvenuto da Imola as a region *habens infinita castella in collibus fertilibus*. Between villages and *castra* it would probably be true to say that the typical unit of habitation in fifteenth-century Italy was still the nucleated settlement. But the reasons for this were not merely or mainly military. As geographers have shown, forms of settlement, like the hilltop villages of the Monferrato, which seem to owe their origin to needs of defence, may be kept alive even to the present day by the no less powerful influences of social habit, the distribution of holdings, and, most of all, the nature of the land and its agricultural system. Medieval records fully bear this out.

They show, for example, that in the regions of extensive farming, especially the South and islands, the habit continued to prevail of settlement in villages (*casali*) or large agricultural centres (*borghi, terre,* or what German geographers later called *Bauernstädte*), because on the open fields and pastures, which, under the system of *Feldgraswirtschaft*, covered most of the land, labour was merely seasonal and holdings merely temporary. Fixed holdings, continuously cultivated, were limited to plots (vineyards, etc.) in the precincts of the villages. In these regions it would even appear that in the later Middle Ages the concentration of settlement increased, and that the *Wüstungen* and decay of villages were partly the effect of emigration from smaller to larger centres. Growing political disorder has been normally blamed for this and in many cases clearly was responsible. Indeed, already in the fifteenth century, the French traveller, Gilles de Bouviers, describes Apulia as uninhabited because of wars, and observes of the Roman Campagna: *En ce païs a grant foison cités et villes, et n'y a nulz villaiges pour les guerres*. But Calabria, no less disturbed, he says, was full of *villaiges*. It may therefore be more than coincidence that many deserted villages declined into stock farms. The feudal classes, who were generally the cause of disorders, were also the chief promoters of grazing and 'enclosure'; and although nothing is said of sheep-eating men, it is possible that sheep-farming contributed to depopulation.

It was certainly under economic influences that the pattern of settlement changed in the areas devoted to intensive husbandry. But here the opposite tendency is evident. In defiance of wars and mercenary companies, the population began to descend from the hills to the lowland and disperse into hamlets, farms and villas (though the farms were often towered and the villas fortified). This medieval revival of the Roman landscape has still be be properly studied; but the movement of descent was already proceeding by the mid-twelfth century, when the Tuscan community of Figline migrated into the lowlands, drawing settlers from near-by castles, some of which, including old Figline itself, subsequently declined into farms. Later, in the fifteenth century, the Florentine *catasti* reveal many semi-deserted *castra*, from which the inhabitants had moved to the open country, though sometimes retaining a *casetta* 'for use in wartime'. By 1500 a number of castles, like Castiglion Fatalbecco, had entirely disappeared, and today their name and site are both unknown. The concurrent process of dispersal is even more difficult to glimpse; but again, in the twelfth century, a tax-roll of Pavia already shows two systems of settlement established: a *Dorfsystem* in the Lomellina, a *Hofsystem* in the country between Pavia and Milan. Thereafter the evidence increases, especially near the towns of Upper Italy, of isolated farms and villas, often with *case da lavoratore* attached, though how many of these were new farms on new sites only careful research will show.

By the early fourteenth century the transformation was far enough advanced to enable Pier de'Crescenzi, in his treatise on farming, to follow his Roman authorities and begin by describing a model *villa* (with *case da lavoratore*) set amidst compact fields in the open country. Compact properties, however, as Crescenzi's own experience testified, were not to be found ready made. They had to be constructed. In association, therefore, with the dispersal of settlement, we find a parallel movement of consolidation of holdings into farms (*appoderamento*): large stock farms (*cascine*) in Lombardy, small or medium mixed farms (*poderi*) in Emilia, Tuscany and Umbria. The process was slow and unobtrusive. In late medieval Tuscany, Florentine records show that the component parts of *poderi* were often not contiguous. Nor, at this stage, did every farm possess its own buildings; some tenants continued to live in near-by villages or towns. Even so, all the signs suggest that a re-arrangement of land was steadily proceeding and, with it, of the rural population. In the territory of Lodi, in the fourteenth and fifteenth centuries, there is evidence of ancient settlements, villages and *castella*, being progressively depopulated by conversion into large, unified dairy farms or *cascinali*; the displaced inhabitants removed to neighbouring *borghi*. Much the same is hinted in contemporary Tuscany and, later on, in the Lower Milanese.

In the areas of intensive agriculture a new landscape seems to be emerging, of compact, isolated farms, rationally arranged and adapted to the productive needs of the time; and this was largely the result of a quiet but no less revolutionary change in the distribution and management of land. Inseparable from the history of settlement is the history of landholding and agrarian society.

III. *Rural Society*

A. *The manor before* 1050

In no sphere of Italian agrarian life is the local variety of medieval development so remarkable as in land tenure and social organization. In the history of Europe generally it is traditional and convenient to describe rural society in terms of the *villa* or manorial system, of its rise in the early Middle Ages and its subsequent supersession by the system of putting estates to farm or working them with wage-labour. The same formula has been applied to Italy. It is increasingly recognized, however, that manorialism and peasant unfreedom were very unevenly distributed, and nowhere is this more apparent than in Italy.

In the early Middle Ages it is true that in Italy, as everywhere else, an increasing amount of land was absorbed by great estates. From various motives—piety, poverty, fear of outrage—the humble proprietors, *minores* and *minimi*, were induced in growing numbers to surrender their land and independence for the status of tenants or *commendati* of the Church or lay nobility. The Church in particular profited, and by the eighth century is thought to have occupied one-third of all land in Italy. At the same time it is evident that in Italy, as north of the Alps, the custom prevailed of dividing estates, even small estates, into demesne and tenant land, and that, whatever the practice in later Roman times, the demesne was now commonly exploited with the labour of tenants as well as household slaves; on the archbishop of Ravenna's estates in the territory of Padua labour services, in the form of week-work, are recorded already in the mid-sixth century, earlier than anywhere in Europe. To save costs, landlords preferred to settle their slaves on holdings in return for rent and work. On the 59 manors (*curtes*) described in a rental of S. Giulia of Brescia about the year 900, the number of household slaves was still roughly 700; but the bulk of the labour on the monastic demesne was performed by tenant families, some 800 in all, owing 60,000 services a year.

This change, begun in the Roman Empire, from a system based on the labour of landless slaves to a system based on the rent and services of tenants, produced corresponding changes in the status of peasant cultivators. Under the new regime, status mattered less to lords than tenure, with the result that tenure increasingly influenced and even determined status. Slaves who became tenants ceased to be wholly rightless and were often partially freed; freemen who became tenants ceased to be wholly independent and were often bound, by force or interest, to their holdings and their lords. This levelling effect of tenure is probably enough to explain the formation, by the eighth and ninth centuries, in Italy as in Northern Europe, of a large class of dependant peasants, variously known as *massarii* or *coloni, manentes, villani* and so on, who, although not normally *servi*, could only change their condition by formal act of enfranchisement, were liable to manorial justice (*districtus*) and were subject to restraints on movement, alienation, inheritance and sometimes marriage. But, as in Northern Europe, the process was powerfully advanced, especially after the Frankish conquest, by the feudalization of public powers, which brought hitherto independent men under the control of lordship and guaranteed all kinds of exactions by the new tie of fealty. Not only rights of private justice and taxation arose in this way, or in due course *banalités*; to the same source may be traced many later 'rents' and services, including agricultural services, as well as seasonal offerings and hospitality (*albergaria*), controls over marriage and inheritance and other 'unaccustomed' charges (*soprusus, abusus*). The obligations were of composite origin which twelfth-century manorial documents curtly define as 'all that a villein owes his lord'.

Enough has been said to indicate the common agrarian development of early medieval Italy and Europe. A closer view of conditions, however, at once reveals regional differences. Thus, the concentration of landownership was probably greatest in the latifundial South, where the prevailing agricultural system hardly tolerated small-scale enterprise. Manorialization, on the other hand, was most advanced in the North. In central Italy there were provinces, notably the Campagna and Marittima, where the manor seems never to have been known;

while over much of the South the pre-manorial system long persisted of cultivation by slave-labour. In some ill-documented districts, including the whole of Sicily, labour rents are not attested before the Norman conquest. Slaves perhaps were more plentiful in the South, or demesne farming more active in the North. But even in the North there were some estates still worked by slaves in the late ninth century, and others, especially in the highlands, where manorialism was very precariously established; while in all parts of Italy, as has often been pointed out, systematic demesne farming was hindered by the frequent fragmentation of properties. The typical estates of early Italian records, even the *latifundia*, were not compact units, coincident with villages, but agglomerations of holdings disposed about a central manor or simple manor farm. On lay properties one cause of this was the custom of partible inheritance; on church lands, the promiscuous flow of small scattered donations, which frustrated orderly development.

The general effect of fragmentation was to encourage the practice of putting property to farm. Down to the ninth century, in Byzantine Italy at least, the late Roman custom persisted of letting estates to rent-collecting bailiffs (*conductores*) by short-term contract. But beside this continued, on church property in particular, the ancient abuse of leasing land to magnates by long-term grants of *emphyteusis*, *precaria* or *libellus*, for nominal rents, mostly in money. As a result a great deal of property in early medieval Italy is removed from observation and the system by which it was managed can only be conjectured. At the same time such grants strengthen the impression that, even in the Lombard and Carolingian periods when manorialism was at its height, the prevailing tendency on Italian estates was towards indirect methods of exploitation. It is sufficient to note that in Italy the typical manorial record is not the survey but the lease, and the typical manorial charge, in both surveys and leases, not labour but rent.

By rent must be understood a variety of payments, part cash, part kind, including seasonal offerings (*exenia*) of livestock and produce. Most rustic rents were probably foodrents and many were partiary rents, which in the case of wine, oil and fruit often rose to as much as half the crop. Grain rents were generally lower, ranging from a third to a tenth or less, and were only assessed at a half when the owner advanced some seed-corn or stock. But contracts of this kind, fore-runners of *mezzadria*, were rare in manorial Italy. Normally tenants provided the working capital for their farms, and also probably for labour on the demesne.

Largely for this reason rents were generally moderate by later standards. In the cultivation of holdings landlords as yet took little interest; they simply fixed the time of corn harvest and vintage, which they sent round agents to supervise. They were also content to leave most tenants undisturbed in their holdings. At least, by the ninth century, most grants to peasants were in form or effect hereditary, though often subject to periodic renewal. In substance, if not in name, they resembled the *libellus*, the type of lease prevailing in Italy north of Rome. This contract, normally of 29 years, required tenants to reside and improve their holdings, limited or forbade alienation, and commonly involved forfeiture for non-payment of rent or neglect. In the papal states and Southern Italy fines for entry or renewal were normally charged as well; but in return *libellarii* everywhere enjoyed fixity of rent and tenure. By the late Carolingian period this was probably true of peasant tenancies generally: duties were balanced by rights. But only an indeterminate number of holdings were yet based on written contracts like the *libellus*; though cartularies give only a very imperfect view of the peasantry, they confirm the evidence of the few surviving rentals that a large class of tenants held only by custom. Even in written contracts, obligations were sometimes summarily defined as 'the custom in that place' (*consuetudo in ipso loco*).

By custom, as by lordship, differences between tenants tended to be obscured. But neither by custom nor by lordship were peasants, even villeins, reduced to a uniform condition of dependence. If manorialization varied from place to place, so within each manor did the economic, tenurial and legal status of cultivators. Even in the Lombard period there were 'rich' and 'poor' *coloni*, *coloni* who had slaves and livestock, or land, slaves and *coloni* of their own, and *coloni* who were forced to combine their meagre resources (*substantiuncula*) by compacts of *adfratatio* in order to pay their rents. There are hints too of a general distinction between tenants who owned plough-oxen and rendered *opera boum*, and others who had no stock and simply owed manual works. Restraints on alienation were not so strict or uniform as to forbid re-arrangement of holdings or differences of wealth. The differences of wealth, however, continued to be influenced by inherited distinctions of judicial status, which both tenants and lords, from opposite motives, contended to uphold or amend. The distinctions were partly legal, partly, by contamination of tenure and status, tenurial. Servile tenants (or holders of *case servule*) tended to be burdened with heavier works than other dependent tenants (or holders of *case massaricie*), and perhaps had smaller holdings; free *libellarii*, by contrast, commonly owed more rent than labour services, while the class of *comendati* were often charged with merely token dues.

Even more variable than manorial burdens was the incidence of lordship and private jurisdiction. No formula, indeed, could express the confusion of rights, part patrimonial, part seignorial, which by the end of the Carolingian period landlords all over Italy had come to exercise in differing degrees over tenants, 'vassals', *homines* and *fideles*. Jurists were later to compound the confusion with terms from Roman law, but they were never able to define peasant 'servitude' or clarify forms of subordination which ranged from slavery and serfdom to mere dependence on feudal or franchisal jurisdiction. Rural society remained obstinately heterogeneous. Not all peasants became dependent, not all were even tenants. In the North particularly, freeholders and small proprietors survived in substantial numbers—many were both—and there were even free (unmediatized) communities. Despite the efforts of lords, *Grundherrschaft* and *Gerichtsherrschaft* refused to coincide.

The claims of lordship and manor in fact were of largely independent origin, the first the product of political, the second of economic, conditions. This explains why, in the tenth century, when the political system remained weak but the economic system began to revive, feudal lordship continued to develop, while the manor showed signs of breaking down.

The motives behind the breakdown are not expressed, and it is simply a presumption that, under the influence of economic recovery and rising population, lords and tenants found a common interest in change. All the records show is the growing failure of landlords to maintain the manorial system of labour by household slaves and tenants. Household slaves, continually reduced in number by manumission or investiture with holdings, were now becoming more costly to replace, because of failing supplies on the market; of those recorded in the tenth century most were *ministeriales*, too valuable and often to exalted for labour on the land, and even these were so scarce in places that landlords had to share them. At the same time tenant labour was becoming more difficult to exact, partly perhaps because holdings were being divided, but also because tenants were becoming less willing to serve. Tenants by lease were increasingly exempted from labour dues; customary tenants, near the towns at least, were getting their works commuted; servile tenants, *libertatem anhelantes*, were contesting their liability to services, or seeking release in flight and migration to the towns. On many estates, moreover, the number of labour-free tenancies was greatly increased by grants of land, single or collective, for improvement or colonization. Most of these grants were *libelli* or similar long-term contracts which, in return for a moderate food-rent, conferred on tenants, whatever their original status, very ample rights of seisin, with fixity of rent, freedom of movement, and commonly freedom of sale. Of similar nature were many of the numerous contracts concluded between villagers and lords in the tenth and eleventh centuries for the construction of *castella*, which brought into existence all over Italy a new class of tenants, part peasants, part knights, the *castellani* or 'burgesses', whose tenancies were normally perpetual and often alienable, and whose obligations, apart from guard or military service and subjection to seignorial justice, were again predominantly rents.

By the eleventh century, in some precocious areas like the Genovese and Lucchesia, the manorial system had practically disappeared, while in others, such as Campania, new methods of exploiting estates, by wage-labour or competitive lease, were coming into use. For the present, however, such novelties were rare. For most lords the natural alternative to traditional forms of demesne farming were traditional forms of lease; and in fact, from the late ninth century, Italian records are increasingly filled with instruments of emphyteusis, *precaria* and *libellus*. Not all of these, however, were grants of demesne land, and only a small proportion were leases to peasant cultivators. By far the greater number were concessions to people of rank and substance—knights, lawyers, merchants, as well as other lords—who let their holdings to others; the properties transferred were not mere pieces of land but often entire manors, lordships or *castella* as well as churches and tithes; and the terms of tenure were often purely nominal. Properly defined such contracts, as the *Libri Feudorum* observe, were not true leases at all, but a device for fraudulent alienation (*fraudulenta alienatio*); and indeed, on church estates particularly, we often find them cast in the form of collusive grants in pledge for a 'loan', on payment of a 'fine', or in 'remuneration' for a token gift of property or cash.

What these transactions denote, therefore, is something more than a change in estate management. They indicate, with other evidence, a revolution in property. By feudal grant or usurpation, by deeds of sale or exchange, but most of all, it seems, by perpetual leases, the great estates of crown, Church and nobility were being broken up and redistributed among a new middle-class of landholders, *gente nuova* of obscure origin, who found in the renting of land a convenient means of building up property and exploiting the opportunities of agricultural development. The process was not unopposed. To protect the integrity of lay estates, noble families, from the late tenth century, began to enforce rules of joint ownership by kin or *consorteria*; while on church estates, from the late ninth century, laws and charters were repeatedly issued to forbid all long-term grants, whether by lease or enfeoffment, except to peasants 'more colonico ad fruges annuatim persolvendas'. The measures were not ineffectual, and in the eleventh and early twelfth centuries a certain amount of church property was recovered by surrender, gift or sale; but at no time was the class of mesne tenants seriously disturbed. Rather were their claims consolidated, on both lay and ecclesiastical estates, when the emperor Conrad II, in his *Constitutio de feudis* of 1037, granted all *milites* succession to their fiefs and protection for their holdings by *libellus* and *precaria*.

At all levels of society new forces were arising, free peasants, *castellani*, middle-class landowners, variously engaged in agriculture, crafts and trade. And it was among these aspiring classes, created by new economic conditions, that during the tenth and eleventh centuries, in Upper Italy especially, common interests resulted in common action against the whole established order, feudal and manorial, culminating in the organization of communes, in villages, towns and *castra*. Neither in towns nor villages was collective activity new. In rural society it was ancient and traditional, maintained through all revolutions of economic and political regime by the common necessities of farming, of policing fields and boundaries and administering common land (*vicinalia*, etc.), and by the common demands of State, Church and landlord. Long before the tenth century there are casual but revealing references to village and manorial custom (*consuetudo loci*), to the habit of village assembly (*conventus ante ecclesiam, fabula inter vicinos*), and to villagers acting and contracting together to defend common land, build churches, elect priests, and administer parish glebe. Of ancient origin also was the right later attested in many conservative areas of Italy of keeping land within the village group by *ius prelationis*. But of organized self-government, except perhaps in parts of the Alps, nothing seems to have survived in manorial Italy. This came only with the liberating influence of economic and social revival, of reclamation, colonization, markets and trade. The way was prepared by collective agreements for founding new settlements and *castra*, which made the relations of tenants with lords corporate and communal. And it was particularly in the *castra* and larger villages, with their enterprising élite of knights, tradesmen and freeholders, that the earliest cases occur of collective franchise. Such was the grant in 983 by the emperor Otto II of fishing rights and tolls to a select group of *homines* in the castle of Lazise (Verona); the diploma of Henry III in 1055(?) freeing the *homines* and *arimanni* of Piove di Sacco from impositions (*iniusta servitus*) by the bishop of Padua; and the charter by Montecassino in 1061 to the men of the castle of Trajetto, restricting rents and charges, and acknowledging freedom of movement, alienation, and marriage. And when, just after 1050, the first rural *communia* appear, in the territory of Lucca, they are not associations of insurgent villeins but rather exclusive groups of *castellani* and knights.

Similarly in the towns it was to members of the gentry, *arimanni* and tenants of *res libellarias et precarias* that the earliest charters of

26

privilege were addressed (at Genoa, 958; Mantua, 1014; Ferrara, 1055, etc.), and it was the same class which led the way in founding the urban communes. Rural and urban communes matured together in response to similar conditions, and their primitive constitution had much in common.

B. *The decline of the manor* (1050–1300)

Their aristocratic origin explains why the Italian communes had less revolutionary effects on agrarian society than might at first be expected. Certainly, the period of communal expansion, from the eleventh to the thirteenth centuries, witnessed the final dissolution of the manorial system in Italy. In some parts of Western Europe the manor was successfully adapted to conditions of economic growth; in Italy, where manorialism was feebler and commercialism stronger, the common reaction of both lords and tenants was to rebel against its rigid restraints.

That dependent tenants of all classes, faced with new possibilities of betterment and freedom, became increasingly intolerant of traditional claims on their labour, persons and goods, hardly needs documentary demonstration. For many peasants, land reclamation by beneficial lease, a movement now at its height, offered one easy way to improvement. To an even larger number, burdened with modest customary rents in money or kind, rising prices and land values must have brought unexpected gains and the means to emancipation. More often than before legal status and social condition failed to coincide, and by the thirteenth century there must have been many like the peasant of Arquà from whom, it is reported in 1196, his lord borrowed money, boasting he had the best *vilanus* in the place. Behind the stereotyped formulas of manorial vocabulary was concealed an increasing diversity of wealth and occupation. In a series of formal contracts of 1254 the Tuscan *castrum* of Empoli is represented as a community of undifferentiated *fideles, homines* and *coloni*, all rendering small, uniform payments to their lords of grain, money, and pepper; 20 years later the first notarial records of Empoli reveal a complex society of peasants, craftsmen and traders. But Empoli was only a minor commune; for tenants anxious to quit the land and better their condition, the widest opportunities lay in the towns. What proportion of urban immigrants were dependent cultivators it is impossible to calculate. Many, we know, were free proprietors, *libellarii* or rustic vassals, who often retained possession of their land and even some connexion with their lords; among the inhabitants of fourteenth-century Florence there were still *homines* of the Albizzi and other local magnates. But a large number were certainly serfs; on no other supposition is it possible to explain the size and composition of the great urban communes, with their massive working class. Whether the migrants were serfs or simply *fideles*, many landlords inevitably took the course of resisting their migration. Yet, with rapidly rising population, it was no longer the paramount interest of lords to detain peasants on their holdings, still less to perpetuate forms of tenure and dominion which yielded diminishing returns of economic rent and revenue. Between lords and tenants, therefore, there was often room for accommodation. If tenants desired to free their persons, many lords desired to free their land and introduce more remunerative methods of exploitation. According to their situation, both sides contended for change; and in the process the old system decayed and, especially as townsmen acquired land, a new one took its place.

In all this the influence of towns is plainly evident; but urban influence must not be mistaken for urban policy. Italian townsmen were never 'free soilers'; too many were themselves serf-owners, as long as serf-dom lasted; and even when, in the thirteenth century, the middle class (*popolo*) came to power in many communes, their attitude to serfdom remained, by northern standards, conservative and illiberal. *Stadtluft* in Italy, both North and South, often took up to ten years to free serfs, while property qualifications excluded them from citizenship and in many places also from the *popolo*. Pisa in the twelfth century refused citizenship to *rustici*. A number of other towns withheld emancipation from the serfs of citizens or friendly lords, while encouraging serfs of hostile lords to immigrate. Others again concluded treaties for the extradition of fugitive *servi*. Even where, as in the Marche, peasant immigration brought communes and feudatories into constant conflict, a settlement was usually arranged whereby lords recovered part of the tenants' holdings or some other compensation for the threatened loss of revenue and land. Urban policy varied with expediency and interest. Thus, during the thirteenth century, Bologna and other towns proceeded, as we have seen, to prohibit immigration by *vilani* and other peasants, in order to protect the cultivation of estates and the taxable capacity of the countryside. At the same time, Bologna and certain other towns adopted the seemingly opposite policy of peasant emancipation. But similar motives prevailed. Serfs were not amenable to communal authority. Accordingly, in 1256–7, Bologna decreed the manumission of some 6000 *servi* in its territory; they were to resume the 'perfect and perpetual liberty' granted man in paradise, and then register for taxation by the commune. All future ties of dependence were forbidden. Between 1200 and 1350 similar laws were enacted by Assisi, Vercelli, Florence and various other communes, and the dominant purpose in every case was the same: to suppress seignorial authority, break the *vinculum fidelitatis* (Florence), with all the rights over *manentes* and dependent villages it sanctioned, and clear the way for the *honera civitatis* (Vercelli), *ut jurisdictio comunis amplietur* (Florence).

If rustics were to be taxed or judged, summoned to war, or compelled to till the land and perform services with carts and oxen, it should be by the commune alone. This was the ultimate object of all urban policy: not peasant emancipation but power. They pursued the policy by every means, sometimes by war, but more often by peaceful purchase, surrender, or agreement. The *borghi franchi* established by some northern towns were probably peopled by peasants already independent; the main freedom granted was some immunity from taxes and *corvées*, and the purpose administrative or strategic. In practice the campaign against private lordship and dependent tenure was tempered, like the laws on immigration, by respect for the rights of friendly feudatories, and there was often compromise. The property rights of lords were generally safeguarded and some indemnity obtained for their loss of seignorial powers. At Bologna they were paid compensation and recovered the *peculia* and moveables of the enfranchised *servi*. In other cases peasants surrendered part of their holdings or redeemed them, together with their freedom, from the commune which had expropriated their lord.

The main effect of urban policy, therefore, was to separate after centuries landlordship and lordship. Often its action was only indirect: intransigent lords, like the bishop of Volterra, ran up debts in conflict with the towns and were forced to sell concessions to their own dependants. Often too the success of communal policy was limited; in most urban territories there remained some areas subject to feudal control. But in urban and feudal areas alike the agrarian system changed, the only difference being that, whereas in town territory the break with the past was often absolute, in predominantly feudal regions it was limited by seignorial authority and interest. In southern Italy the Norman conquest may have brought some enlargement of seignorial power, with new charges and *banalités*, and even a temporary increase of labour services. But everywhere, sooner or later, the old regime was modified; and the principal instruments of change were not urban statutes but, as in other countries, charters of village franchise, acts of manumission and commutation, unobtrusive leases of demesne and waste land.

Charters of franchise, defining or abrogating seignorial rights, were granted with increasing frequency to an increasingly wide class of subjects and tenants, from the eleventh to the thirteenth century, and by 1300 few villages in Italy can have received no privileges, however partial or limited. They were characteristic of the feudal order, and where feudalism persisted, continued throughout the Middle Ages, developing into codes of village law. Many lords, especially in Northern Italy, agreed not only to limit their rights and rents, but to commute, lease, sell or give them, wholly or in part, to the village or *castellum*. Whatever form the transactions took, all types of rent and right were affected. Most conspicuous were rights of mainly public origin, authorized by *honor* or *districtus*: tallage, *fodrum*, *albergaria*, carrying-services, monopolies, castle-guard, judicial powers and so on. In Upper Italy particularly, villagers were often admitted as well to a share in administration, and so converted from community to commune.

By itself the regulation of rights like these, however important for rural life, did not necessarily influence agrarian economy or affect only peasants. In some regions, such as Piedmont and Western Venetia, rents and services were generally ignored by charters. Peasant status might equally remain untouched. In 1170 the lords of Vimodrone (Milan) sold their rights to the community, but reserved them over their tenants, creating as it were two villages (*tanquam due ville essent*). Some lords even removed their tenants elsewhere. But there was no uniformity. In 1229 the lords of Pasano (Liguria) declared the inhabitants *liberi homines*, with rights of government and freedom from jurisdiction, 'nisi tanquam vassalli domino', and all claims 'colonarie conditionis'. In 1274 the men of Alpignano (Piedmont) were freed 'ab omni specie servitutis', namely tallages, *fodrum*, *mariagia*, and charges on sale and inheritance. A distinction is suggested between grants to tenants and to feudal subjects, 'manorial' and village franchises, but it is often fragile, especially where rights of all kinds were indiscriminately removed, or where lords retained their patrimonial and seignorial rights undifferentiated and entire. Then there were rights, particularly limiting inheritance and alienation, which touched subjects and tenants equally. Grants therefore occur all over Italy, which also fixed or reduced rents and labour services, abolished or limited restraints on marriage, inheritance and sale, controlled distraint, and conferred freedom of movement.

What collective grants did not achieve was quietly effected by deeds of individual manumission or commutation. These have left fewer traces behind but must have been fairly common. They appear regularly in North Italian law-books of the twelfth and thirteenth centuries, and are in fact recorded in most districts outside the South and Lazio. Both *servi* and *manentes* were freed, the first by traditional Roman formula, the second by clumsy terms of absolution from all services, dependence (*obsequia*) and incapacities, especially restraint of movement. Of much the same effect were the various forms of commutation, converting seignorial dues to rents in kind or money.

Acts of this kind, completed by simple usurpation, did more than any urban policy to transform rural society. By 1300 the class of rustic *servi* had practically disappeared, and in the greater part of Upper Italy all other forms of bondage, personal and praedial, had either become vestigial or been altogether suppressed. *Vilano*, once a term of status, was now a term of abuse. In much of the South also, restraints on peasant freedom had been relaxed, and *servi* were mostly domestic slaves (*sclavi*); but here serfdom was slower to decline. As late as the fifteenth century, southern records refer to *angararii*, personally bound to their lords and forbidden by royal ordinance to leave their land; and similar survivals are found in other feudal districts. In the Tuscan and Emilian Apennines, despite repressive legislation by Bologna and neighbouring towns, forms of rustic vassalage persisted, akin to servitude, which bound tenants by ties of fealty to *angaria* and *perangaria*, military service, and private jurisdiction. In Friuli and the Tyrol a dwindling class of *Leibeigene* and *servi de masnada* survived to the fifteenth century. And in Piedmont there were still, in the sixteenth century, peasants subject to *servitude nommée taillabileté et mainmorte*. But nowhere did serfdom retain economic importance. Even where peasant emancipation remained incomplete, nothing survived of the classical forms of manorial organization. The manor, like its name (*curtis*), had gone out of use.

The decay of the manor in Italy is rarely described in detail. The appropriate sources are lacking. The process has to be inferred from direct or indirect records of the leasing of demesne, and from declining evidence of labour services. Even charters of franchise and manumission mark only isolated moments of transition. But the general tendencies are hardly to be mistaken. By the twelfth century, on many estates, demesne farming had ceased, and the word *donnicatum*, when used at all, referred to land not let to mesne tenants. Clearer still is the trend in labour rents. At the village of Cicognara, about the year 900, the abbey of S. Giulia owned a manor comprising 19 slaves (*praebendarii*), 23 *manentes*, and a large demesne worked by 3588 annual labour services. Four centuries later, in 1275, a commune had grown up in the village, governed by statutes which still reveal some ploughing and other *opere*, but of a purely seignorial kind. By 1347 S. Giulia was drawing no revenue at all from Cicognara, and the only works even formally due were carrying services. This decay of services, though not always so vividly shown, was universal in Italy, precocious in regions like the Milanese, where they had vanished by the thirteenth century, more slow in the feudal areas, where they lingered until after the Middle Ages. Grants of franchise did much to reduce them, and also manumission, since *servi* and *manentes* were the classes burdened most

with works; but acts of commutation, often combined with manumission and franchises, probably did more. What labour dues continued
to be levied in the later Middle Ages were either seasonal works,
limited in number, or carrying services and seignorial *corvées* unconnected with tillage.

By the end of the thirteenth century all that survived, in most areas,
of the old agrarian order was the traditional system of tenures and
rents. In origin more ancient than the manor, they also long outlived
it. They continued all over Italy, and even where nothing else remained
of lordship or manor, customary rents, often combined with fealty,
persisted in great numbers, especially on church estates. Fealty in such
cases was a formal incident of tenure, without implications of service
or subordination; between the rustic 'fief' and other perpetual holdings,
livelli and the like, there was no observable difference, and in fact by
the thirteenth century they were all coming to be classed together
in law.

Common to them all was a right of possession, protected not only
by custom or contract but often now by franchise, which in its mature
form conferred on tenants an alienable *dominium* over land, scarcely
different from that of an owner burdened with a permanent rent-
charge. No doubt most perpetual tenancies had been originally
inalienable, but during the twelfth and following centuries, especially
in urban territory, lords were forced by degrees to grant what they
were often powerless to check, and recognize freedom of sale.

Apart from rent, it must also be said, perpetual tenants were commonly charged with the duty of improvement (*melioramentum*), and
undoubtedly throughout the medieval period many hereditary holdings were in fact, or in origin, the creation of beneficial grants for
reclamation; but by the thirteenth and following centuries, the greater
number were simply customary holdings, on which the obligation to
improve had become purely nominal. Rents, too, in many cases, were
merely nominal payments, relics of ancient acts of surrender and
commendation; while a large proportion of the remainder, at least
where fixed in money, were of steadily diminishing value. From the
assized rents of 'ancient holdings' (*poderia antiqua*), the Tuscan monastery of Camaldoli was drawing no more than a few shillings on many
of its estates in the later thirteenth century. To the extent that owners
were dependent for income on such inconspicuous *censi*, they must
have been all the readier to sell concessions to their tenants. Nor were
customary rents enlarged by the partition and re-arrangement of
holdings, which we find proceeding, as stated above, from as early as
the tenth century; normally the undivided tenement remained, as a

unit of account, the basis of assessment. From the twelfth century, it is true, both inheritance and alienation had become generally subject to the levy of entry-fines and charges for renewal; accordingly, hereditary leases came to be described as 'sales for rent' (*venditiones ad fictum*). Most urban statutes also forbade unlicensed alienation, and by the thirteenth century it was usual for lords to reserve a right of first refusal, often at a beneficial price. Finally, both laws and contracts empowered owners to evict *livellari* without compensation for arrears of rent after two years or more, and even in case of neglect or failure to improve. But entry-fines did not always suffice to raise the value of rents; they varied notably, from 2 or 5 per cent up to 25 or even 33⅓ per cent of purchase price or capital value, but generally they were moderate. Nor, in practice, were lords always free to exercise controls on alienation or their right to evict. The power of custom was strong, but even stronger was the power of many perpetual tenants. For not all were simple cultivators. As in the past, a large number, on church estates particularly, were magnates, merchants or townsmen, who by inheritance or purchase were possessed of hereditary holdings. And, as in the past, ecclesiastical authorities in the twelfth and thirteenth centuries tried to recover land from mesne tenants and avoid new grants by 'fief' or *libellus* to anyone but peasants. They also introduced restrictive clauses into leases to prevent the alienation of holdings to other owners or their *servi*; and some, more specifically, forbade sales to townsmen, or opposed tenants becoming citizens themselves. But all to little purpose. Great estates remained encumbered with a large hereditary class of mesne tenants. Prominent among the earliest urban statutes were laws to protect this class. And it was doubtless for the benefit of this class also that a number of towns, in the late twelfth and thirteenth centuries, took the logical step of promoting the allo-dialization of perpetual tenures.

It is natural, therefore, to inquire how far the dissolution of the manor represented the decline of old estates and a redistribution of property. In feudal Italy the question hardly arises: noble families doubtless changed, though whether as rapidly as in contemporary France only research will show; and church estates, here as elsewhere, were partially dismembered by mesne tenancies. But the structure of landownership remained essentially the same, and in the Campagna and South particularly, outside the 'garden' areas, the established *latifundia* continued to prevail. In Upper Italy, by contrast, traffic in land was intense; and, by the later thirteenth century, private deeds and, still more, public tax-surveys reveal a pulverization of landholding which can only be explained on the assumption that many ancient properties had been progressively broken up. To some extent this must have been due to reclamation from waste, of which the great domains of the early Middle Ages had been largely composed. Something must also be allowed for usurpation, of which ecclesiastical records particularly preserve many traces. But more than anything it is usual to emphasize the subversive effect on landownership of commercial revolution. Overtaken by a money economy, the older estates were condemned, it is said, to irretrievable debt and destruction. And indeed, in the twelfth and thirteenth centuries, commonplace themes of all sources are the financial distress of lay and clerical lords, the decay of noble houses, the rise of merchant landlords and *gente nuova*. In Tuscany, by 1200, many churches were afflicted with heavy debt, and because of debt, in certain cases, were obliged to sell their freedom to dependent cultivators. Most acts of manumission, in fact, and many charters of franchise, were in some measure contracts of sale and exchange, which could easily be read as evidence of a general crisis of fortunes on ecclesiastical and feudal domains.

Yet, even in the commercial North, it would be wrong to speak of the ruin of old estates, still more of a wholesale transfer of land from 'feudal' to 'merchant' families. Some transfer there was, but the evidence of Florentine account-books, few though they are before 1300, would suggest that merchants acquired their lands piecemeal from persons of every condition (including other merchants). Land-traffic seems to have been most lively among the middle class of landholders, the gentry and *livellari*. On the estates of the bishop of Mantua, nearly all fiefs changed hands in the short period between 1230 and 1260, but not those of the greater tenants and nobility. Similarly, the taxation lists of Orvieto and other towns indicate, beside the subdivided holdings of the small and medium proprietors, the obstinate survival of large domains. Helped no doubt by the principle of family solidarity, many aristocratic *consorterie* managed to keep hold of their estates; and if some members were poor and fell into debt, others had means to lend money and buy additional property. The movement of land was not all in one direction. The dissolution of some domains was the benefit of others. Precisely in the thirteenth century feudal families like the Este, Visconti, and Malatesta of Rimini, destined to become *signori*, were building up their territorial power by purchase and emphyteutic grants from churches. The loss of the Church was the gain of the nobility. Yet, many ecclesiastical bodies also prospered in this period. Not only the new religious orders, but also old foundations multiplied their holdings, despite the enactment of mortmain laws by communes in the thirteenth century. Quite often, indeed, their debts were incurred in the acquisition of land. Debt was not the sign of destitution.

Churches, it is true, had spiritual income, and secular lords the chance to improve their fortunes by business investment or marriage. But it was not due to help from outside if old estates persisted, nor only to failing revenue within if many of them declined. Folgore da Sangimignano († 1332?) describes Tuscan nobles who mortgaged castles to meet the cost of chivalrous display. Nor does it always appear that lords gained less than their dependants from charters of manumission, commutation, or franchise. By manumission they often recovered holdings, by other grants they obtained new rents or the means to buy new land. To secure a calculable income, the bishop of Luni in 1230 sold to the people of Gragnana his claims to *opere*, *collecte*, and other impositions in return for a fixed rent of wheat and wine. About the same time the cathedral chapter of Verona was selling for large sums to the local community the perpetual lease of its rights in several villages, in one case using the money to buy up land and acquire, instead of scattered and disputed jurisdiction, a concentrated property in one place.

In many instances, no doubt, the result of such transactions was simply to increase the number of customary rents. But customary rents, when numerous enough, could still produce sufficient revenue and, in feudal Italy especially, though enlarged by the profits of lordship, continued to form a substantial part of seignorial income and yield enormous surpluses for sale. Perpetual rents could also be amended. In the twelfth and thirteenth centuries there is evidence of a definite policy on great estates in Tuscany, Lombardy and the Tyrol to replace surviving money rents by rents in kind, in defence against devaluation. But, most important of all, traditional rents could be suppressed outright and, by slow degrees, the whole manorial legacy discarded in favour of more productive methods of managing estates. And this, in fact, was the procedure increasingly adopted, from the twelfth century on, by all classes of landlords, on church estates and lay estates, old properties and new. The greatest medieval change was in the management, not the ownership, of land.

c. *The re-organization of estates* (1200–1500)

As elsewhere in Europe, the new methods of management were applied to both demesne and tenant farming. Demesne farming did not invariably cease with labour services. On the contrary, to the end of the Middle Ages many owners of all classes continued to work some land *ad manus suas*, and for this they came to rely on wage-labour, hired by the year, the season, or the day. The use of wage-labour was clearly common already by the end of the twelfth century, when demesne is mentioned on a number of estates without labour services; by the fourteenth century it had come to prevail even on estates, such as those of Camaldoli, which retained labour services. Not very different was the system of cultivation by *conversi*, adopted by the Cistercians and other monastic orders; by the late Middle Ages, at any rate, no sharp distinction is observable between *conversi* and ordinary labourers. The practical effect of the change of method was not always great. Farm hands had to be maintained much as demesne *servi*. Casual labourers were often paid in kind, just as previously, it would seem, dependent cultivators had often received meals at the lord's expense and sometimes even wages. In a few cases we find labour rents being commuted to pay for the hire of *operarii*.

Demesne farming in the later Middle Ages was most vigorous in the open-field areas of Lazio and the South, where large-scale enterprise was in some form unavoidable. On the cornlands of Sicily indeed, and possibly also Apulia, the modern system of farming, mainly by wage-labour, may already have been well developed as early as the fourteenth century. But all over southern Italy the Crown and greater landlords (or their lessees) continued to raise demesne crops and livestock, especially migrant sheep, though these were often also let out and were largely reared on common arable and waste. Similarly, on the *latifondi* of the Marittima and Campagna stock-raising, and also probably corn-growing, were practised extensively by great families like the Gaetani and Orsini. In Upper Italy, by contrast, demesne arable is rarely mentioned, and most direct working, even by magnates like the Este and Malatesta, was normally restricted to vineyards, orchards and other closes, accompanied in pastoral areas by some stock-farming. There were certainly exceptions. At Camaldoli, in the late fourteenth century, demesne farms continued to supply up to half the grain revenue from the monastic estates in the Casentino. But generally demesne farming seems to have been a marginal activity, partly, it seems, because it did not always pay. Already before 1300 labour costs had obliged the abbey of Chiaravalle to put its granges to farm; *conversi* were becoming hard to recruit, and by 1350 most other Cistercian houses seem to have done the same. For similar reasons the count of Savoy divided and let his demesne vineyards at Rivoli in 1330. Later in the fourteenth century we find the Modenese abbey of S. Caterina getting into debt to pay farm wages.

Whether from this or from other causes, demesne farming in Italy continued to decline. In Lombardy, by the fourteenth century, it had been almost everywhere abandoned: on the estates of the bishop of Pavia the *pars dominica* was now the share of crops taken by the lord as rent. By the fifteenth century little remained elsewhere outside the South, and even here landlords were beginning to change to a rental system. The leasing of demesne, therefore, proceeded steadily throughout the Middle Ages; and if owners sometimes resumed farms for a

period, as did the monks of Camaldoli after 1350, there is no evidence
of widespread variations in the trend. Demesne was leased in various
ways, sometimes to village communities, more often to single peasants
or farmers. Often it was let piecemeal, especially where property was
scattered or composed mainly of vineyards, *oliveta* and other intensively cultivated land. Wherever possible, however, *curie* and granges
were let entire as farms; and, as the terms of tenancy show, this was
something more than a mere measure of convenience. To let property
was not necessarily to neglect it. Behind the farming of demesne may
be discerned the influence of a new policy with regard to the leasing of
land. Down to about 1200 most demesne, as other land, was let by
long-term contracts of traditional type. Then a radical change appeared.
New forms of commercial lease began to be widely adopted: short-
term grants for heavy rents of both land and livestock, in which the
owner often came to assume the part of entrepreneur. Tenant-farming,
in short, was being developed as a substitute, not an alternative, of
demesne farming. The result was a reform in the management of
property more far-reaching than any other in medieval Italy.

Commercial leases are first attested in Campania during the tenth
century and Apulia during the eleventh. Then, from about 1150, they
begin to be recorded in all other parts of Italy. By the thirteenth
century they are regularly represented in the lawbooks, juxtaposed
with the conventional contracts of perpetual tenure, vassalage, and
serfdom. They spread more rapidly in some districts than others:
sooner in the lower Valdarno than the Casentino or Lunigiana, and
sooner probably in the Milanese and Lodigiano than round Mantua,
Brescia and Bergamo. In Paduan territory they appear before 1200,
but hardly earlier than 1400 in backward Friuli; and while they progressed quickly on the rich Emilian plain, customary tenures held their
own in the hill-villages behind. It was the same in Latium and the
South, where competitive leases were most diffused in the regions of
garden culture. But in the corn-growing districts also types of short-
term contract were introduced. In the Campagna and other areas of
transhumant grazing terminal leases were adopted for the grant of
winter pasture. And all over Italy speculative leases of plough beasts
and other stock came into general use. By the later Middle Ages commercial tenancies are found on properties of all kinds, from peasant
holdings to *latifundia*, from the lands of Camaldolese eremites to those
of merchant-bankers. It is generally assumed that commercial leases
were the work of commercial landlords, of town-dwelling capitalists
resolved to make farming pay. If so, the older landowners were quick
to follow their example. In the thirteenth century and later the Church
repeatedly forbade grants of more than three to five years. Frederick II

extended a similar limit to leases of crown land. And although such laws were probably directed most against mesne tenancies, they must also have influenced the general principles of leasehold. It may not be merely an accident of record that the earliest memorials of the terminal lease are almost all ecclesiastical.

In developing short-term contracts, it was plainly the purpose of Italian landlords to exploit the profits of agriculture by every means short of direct farming. Between direct and indirect farming, however, the difference was not always sharp. In practice the new forms of lease evolved in medieval Italy were often barely distinguishable from wage-contracts. The resemblance is most evident in the type of agreement adopted in the areas of extensive farming, where holdings were impermanent. In late medieval Sicily short-term contracts came to take the form of seasonal grants of arable to tenants called *paraspolari*, who merely sowed and cropped the land with seed and capital lent by the lord in return for a share of the harvest. In the twelfth century *parasporo* was a term for labour rent; the change of meaning betrays the change of system. Similar contracts or *societates* are found in Latium, Sardinia and the Marche: men were hired to work (*locati a lavorare*) as rent-paying labourers.

More characteristic of Italy as a whole than these work-contracts (forerunners of modern *metateria* and *compartecipazione*) were the true commercial leases, developed first in areas of intensive farming, which were grants for a period of years, and not simply of land but also of integral farms, livestock and buildings. Like perpetual grants, these leases were basically of two kinds: those for fixed rents (*afitto*), usually food rents, especially grain, and those for share-cropping. Share-cropping was traditional and over much of Italy was not radically changed by the short lease: a half was normally taken only of wine and tree-fruits, of grain a lower proportion or a fixed amount. Where land was fertile, however, and developed by active investment to the medieval limit of productivity, the custom developed of taking half or even more of all the crops and frequently more than half the wine.

This was *mezzadria* in its various forms, first recorded in the ninth and tenth centuries, but outside Campania only in a few long leases. From the twelfth century it spread rapidly in parts of Tuscany, Umbria, the Marche and the Northern Plain. It prospered, therefore, in regions of commercial wealth, but not in all or only there. Moreover, as Florentine account-books show, if business families preferred *mezzadria*, they also let *afitto*; often in fact farms were let indifferently, *amezo* and *afitto*. Grants *afitto* tended to be longer than grants to share-croppers, which were sometimes limited to one or two harvests, but the two contracts had much in common. In both the conditions of tenure were strict and the terms increasingly specific. The ancient obligation of tenants to reside and cultivate responsibly was elaborated in detail. They could not sell or sub-let or leave without giving notice. Landlords also had to give notice, but could evict for breach of contract or neglect. Tenants were forbidden to work off the farm, while their work on the farm was closely controlled. Rotations and ploughings and the use of manure, the increase of vines and olives, and the dates of sowing and harvest, which the owner or bailiff were to attend or supervise, were all precisely laid down. In addition it was forbidden to cut vines or trees or cart away hay, straw or dung. Much of this regulation applied especially to share-croppers, in particular *mezzadri*. Exclusive to *mezzadri* were further clauses controlling the division of crops, stock and expenses, including farm wages, and protecting or limiting livestock in the interest of the lord.

Once again these conditions attest the nature of terminal leases, and especially *mezzadria*, as increasingly a means of hiring labour. In later times the *mezzadro*'s share of crops was often called his wage. Not that *mezzadria* ever became a purely wage contract. In the Middle Ages it was defined a *societas*, and in practice it was a form of partnership, a contract *ad laborandum*, in which lord and tenant collaborated to cultivate a holding instead of a demesne. The *mezzadro* shared the costs of production. In thirteenth-century Tuscany he was often induced to pay them all (a further sign, perhaps, of land scarcity and rural congestion), but this was not the rule. To get more rent, the owner also had to share expenses. In 1212 the bishop of Luni commuted the works of his tenants at Sarzana to a grain rent and leased them the demesne: in return he demanded half the crops, if he supplied the oxen, but otherwise a third. Similarly by a ten-year lease of 1183 the Venetian monastery of S. Maria della Carità demanded half the grain, if it supplied half the seed corn, otherwise a third. From the ninth century onwards this was the normal principle in grants for half-shares, and as *mezzadria* was extended in the later Middle Ages to less productive farms, owners had to advance more working capital. The tenant's duties grew proportionately and a 'debate' began, which continued till very recently between the two sides. Practice varied considerably, but generally the lessor provided, in addition to the land, a farmhouse and buildings, which it was his part to repair or improve, with vats, wine presses, and other installations; he also gave some seed-corn, vine props and manure. Usually he owned the livestock, especially plough-oxen, which he advanced the tenant on various terms, and sometimes he shared the cost of wage-labour.

Beside terminal leases of land, and often combined with them, similar forms of contract, for fixed or partiary rents, were adopted for the lease of livestock. Of these by far the commonest, and also the most ancient, was another type of partnership, the grant of beasts 'at halves' or *a soccida* (=*societas*). In late medieval Tuscany *mezzadri* were usually charged with half the value of the oxen, which they then held 'for half profit and loss' with the owner; commonly other animals were shared as well. Short-term stock leases, however, were not used only by landlords and tenants. It was principally by *soccida* that townsmen, in the thirteenth and later centuries, let out beasts to farmers, sometimes making profits of 30 per cent or more; and all over Italy, by people of all conditions, grants at halves were employed in stock-raising and dairy-farming, often on a large scale. At Venice the government encouraged *soccida* to help the urban meat supply, and in many Italian cities butchers habitually raised stock in this way.

The rapid progress of commercial leases inevitably raises the question, by what methods they were introduced. But no development in Italian agrarian history is more obscure than the transition from old tenures to new. Too often records simply show the new system in working order. It is clear at least that the leases were employed almost wholly on developed land, from which owners desired to draw the benefits of previous improvements; on unimproved and waste land perpetual grants remained the rule. No less clear is the tendency, especially in grants by *mezzadria*, for the properties let to be not mere scattered parcels of land but increasingly farms with farmsteads, often larger than customary holdings. On old estates, of the Church particularly, Tuscan records prove that many of these farms were former demesnes, let, from the thirteenth century on, undivided or in blocks. Others again may have been peasant holdings, recovered by manumission or escheat, and leased on amended terms. But something more than these unobtrusive changes is needed to explain the rapid transformation visible on many Italian estates of the later Middle Ages. At Vallombrosa, for example, between the late thirteenth and later fourteenth centuries, we find a large domain of traditional type, comprising customary tenures and vestiges of feudal lordship, converted in the space of a hundred years to a property composed almost wholly of compact farms (*poderi*) let by competitive lease. How the change was accomplished appears in part from a number of contemporary deeds, which show the monks systematically buying up lands, largely from tenants and *fideles*, with the purpose presumably of throwing them together into larger tenements for leasing. Similar activity, if not so intense, is found on other monastic estates; and there are hints enough in the records that what monks could do, laymen had probably long been doing better. One object indeed of the urban 'ingrossation' laws must have been to promote such a re-arrangement of property.

The propagation of commercial leases, therefore, was accompanied by the consolidation of holdings, in the course of which, it may be supposed, large numbers of customary tenants lost or vacated their land. Several times in the fifteenth century the Venetian government acted to prevent the eviction of *livellari*, in one case reminding the owners, who were nuns, that 'the merciful are blessed', in another condemning as 'unjust and inhuman' the expulsion of peasants who 'in the sweat of their brow and at great expense' had developed the land for farming. And there were generations of strife behind the peasant protest of 1518 against a parliamentary law in Friuli forbidding all further *livelli*. But whatever the means employed, by the later Middle Ages, in many parts of Central and Northern Italy, a new agrarian landscape was clearly being created, of commercial tenancies in the open country, customary tenancies in the villages and *castra*, the first let to cultivators, the second largely held by artisans and cotters.

The revolution was not confined to tenure. With the consolidation of holdings went also, from the later thirteenth century on, a re-concentration of land in great estates, particularly in Tuscany and the North. The two movements, indeed, were closely related, and there is reason to suspect that the 'ingrossation' laws, whatever their professed purpose, were often invoked to justify the expropriation of small holders by large. Large holdings, however, grew in various ways, not only by outright purchase but also by feudal and emphyteutic grant, and the beneficiaries were owners of all classes. Some were established landlords who added to existing estates: monastic houses like S. Ambrogio, Camaldoli or S. Giustina of Padua, feudal families like the Mirandola or Malaspina, or wealthy despotic dynasties like the Carraresi, who are said to have owned a quarter of Paduan territory by the end of the fourteenth century. Many others were merchant families of the great commercial towns, such as the Florentine Guicciardini, whose fourteenth-century account-books show them steadily engrossing property in the upper Valdelsa, or the Medici, who assembled a vast domain in the Mugello and extensive grazing lands in the Pisano. Property continued to pass into the hands of urban owners, but the richer townsmen took the greater share. It was mainly by transfer to the *popolo grasso* that, in the territory of Corinaldo (Umbria) between 1460 and 1480, the proportion of land in smaller holdings was reduced from 40 to 25 per cent. At Bologna in 1496, 63 per cent of the population possessed no land at all, 19 per cent had only minor holdings, and most property was engrossed by the urban patriciate. At Modena in 1546, 88 per cent of all land was held by the duke, nobility and clergy.

The rise of the new system, therefore, like the decline of the old, was accompanied by a redistribution of property. But neither in the organization nor the ownership of land was the rate of change uniform. Property, even large property, remained much divided, particularly in the poorer districts; everywhere vestiges of the old system survived beside the old; and at the end of the Middle Ages Italian estates were even more diversely administered than at the beginning. Their only common feature was the prevalence of indirect over direct exploitation. Not only was most land let to peasant cultivators, or much land, on older properties, still let on perpetual mesne tenancies; in the later Middle Ages, to carry the tendency further, the practice began to spread of letting out entire estates by short-term leases to capitalist entrepreneurs, variously known as *fittabili* in Lombardy and Emilia, *mercanti di campagna* in Lazio, and *massari*, *affittuari* and *gabellotti* in the South and Sicily. In Lombardy, on Church lands, this farming of estates has been identified as an abuse arising from failing revenue, especially money revenue, aggravated by debt and dilapidation. All over Italy, in the later Middle Ages, the Church exhibited symptoms of moral and material decay, and among the most disturbing signs was a fresh wave of lay encroachment on ecclesiastical property. As in the pre-Hildebrandine period, the main instrument of depredation remained the long-term lease, and much of the reclamation undertaken by families like the Gonzaga was carried out on church land occupied in this way. But in Lombardy churchmen made increasing use of short-term leases *afitto*, which they sold or granted for nominal rents to speculators, creditors or kinsmen, who then sub-let on commercial terms to peasants; in practice the grants often became perpetual, with the result that, by the sixteenth century, numerous churches had been dispossessed of much of their land or revenue.

The case of Lombardy, however, may be exceptional. Not everywhere was the dissipation of church land so widespread or prolonged; as always in the history of mortmain, if some domains declined, others revived or prospered. Still less was the practice of farming estates everywhere the consequence of financial weakness. Even in Lombardy what the records rather indicate is a growing tendency, from as early as the thirteenth century, for great landowners of all kinds, monks, clergy, and magnates like the Visconti, to delegate the care and improvement of property to short-term lessees; but the terms of tenure were normally strict, the rents fairly high (£1770, fl. 6400 etc.), and sometimes the landlord even shared expenses. In Tuscany, where bailiff farming remained the rule, the few cases of large-scale terminal leases amount to little more than the transfer, for substantial rents in kind, of the revenues and responsibilities of inconveniently situated estates.

Similarly, on the *latifundia* of Latium and the South most contracts of the kind were commercial and competitive, and were sometimes indistinguishable from the lease of a bailiwick (*bajulia*). In a series of grants of fiefs and manors by the Sicilian baron of Convicino, between 1491 and 1504, precise conditions were laid on the farmers regarding subleases to peasants, the sale of *herbagia* on pasture and stubble, the use of wood, the type and quantity of rent-free livestock, the amount of crop and fallow.

Of greater general significance, however, than the terms on which estates were let, was the fact that they were let at all. If a 'return to the land' was in progress in late medieval Italy, it cannot be taken to indicate a universal concern by owners for enlightened management or agriculture. On many properties innovation in farm practice, the arrangement of holdings and the forms of peasant tenure, was the work not of landlords but of enterprising middlemen on the make. Even where estates were kept in hand it was a matter of common complaint that the wealth lavished on landed property was spent more often on display than rational improvement. In Tuscany the taste for building country houses was denounced as a vain extravagance from as early as Dante's day, but still the fashion spread. Of the Florentines, the Venetian ambassador observed in 1527 that 'they have this weakness, that they go about the world to make a fortune of 20,000 ducats and then spend 10,000 on a palace outside the city'. But habits were no different in the North. In Venetian territory itself, of some 1400 villas, classed today as of artistic interest, 15 were built in the fourteenth century, 84 in the fifteenth century, and over 250 in the sixteenth century. Of the villas built in the late Middle Ages a certain number, it is true, like the famous Villa Sforzesca at Vigevano, were model farms administered by the owner. It was also for villa-building families, and partly by villa-owning landlords, that a growing number of books was published, from the middle of the fifteenth century, on estate management, farming and country life. But the interest they served was more Arcadian than practical. Most Italian villas were 'pleasure domes', 'domus jocunditatis', like the Bentivoglio palace at Ponte Poledrano, which by critical observers were simply regarded as wasting good farm land; while the bulk of bucolic literature was dilettante or worse, conceived in the spirit of Petrarch, who dabbled with plants and called himself a 'farmer' (*agricultor*). For the practical business of farming, as for all forms of industry, a new spirit of disdain was beginning to spread, by 1500, among the upper classes of Italy. More and more the care of land was abandoned to managers or farmers, denounced by one sixteenth-century writer as 'gente rustica et idioti'. In protestation serious authors like Gallo condemned absentee landlords and preached the principle of direct farming as essential to good husbandry. One prince, Federigo Gonzaga, even promised tax-reliefs in 1530 to owners working land themselves; but to no evident purpose. Not even *fittabili* seem to have engaged in high farming. The dominant concern of lords and lessees was not with cultivation but with the maximum production of rent; and for this the later medieval system of peasant farming by commercial lease provided an adequate instrument. Only later, in the eighteenth century, when agricultural development became of urgent interest, did criticism begin to take effect, and then the complaint was not only against the defects of peasant farming but also against the abuses of a system which put rack-renting before improvement, discouraged tenant enterprise, and placed oppressive burdens on the peasantry.

D. *The peasantry at the close of the Middle Ages*

For the peasantry, therefore, as for farming, the late medieval return to the land, if a return there was, would be no unqualified blessing. And hardly more to their benefit was the corresponding cult of country life. Addressed to a predominantly urban audience of land-owning patricians, almost all agronomic and pastoral writings, from Crescenzi's treatise on, respected urban prejudices or reproduced urban attitudes to rural society. What these attitudes were is expressed with impressive unanimity by Italian urban statutes. According to them, peasants were the basest order in society (Stat. Bologna, 1454), natural-born 'inferiors' (Ancona, 1478), inspired in their dealings with the rest of mankind by 'malice', 'malignity', and 'insolence' (Pistoia, 1296, Arezzo, 1327, Parma, 1494, etc.); only in exceptional circumstances, therefore, could it be publicly acknowledged that, in common with the rest of mankind, they were *generati a deo* (Siena, 1306). Consistently with these opinions, citizenship in urban law, like *nobilitas* in feudal law, was sharply distinguished from *rusticitas*, and could only be acquired on abstaining from all 'mechanic' and 'rustic' employments. In regarding peasants as a class apart, degraded by nature and function, literature agreed with the law. In Italy, as in Europe generally, the peasant was transformed in the Middle Ages from a subject of admiration into an object of contempt and mistrust. Humanist writers half-heartedly revived the classical ideal of rustic simplicity, but for Petrarch (who confessed to harshness with his tenants) and for a number of Vergilian poetasters it was clearly hard to comprehend. The noble shepherd they were willing to accept, but not the honest husbandman. In most writing, where noticed at all, the peasant remained the figure of medieval satire, a creature more animal than human, dirty and deceitful, ill-housed, worse fed, dressed in 'hempen homespun' (*canevazo crudo*); and on the few occasions when the rustic speaks for himself, it is in the same character of down-trodden brute, the product of whose labour is so much devoured by others that his only wine is water, his only bread *un puo' de sorgo*, and his only dwelling a wattle hut unfit to shelter his cattle.

As a commentary on rural conditions, there was clearly far more truth in the medieval than the classical literary convention. But, however close to reality, it was still only a convention. Between the peasant of fiction and the peasant of fact there were many different degrees of affinity, and even in the humblest details there were very wide variations. If many peasants were housed in hovels, it is also a commonplace of iconographic and written records, that all over Upper Italy, even in mountain areas, buildings of wattle, timber and thatch were being steadily replaced, from at least the thirteenth century, by houses with wood, stone or terracotta tiles, or by sturdy stone-built farmsteads of a kind still met with today. Again, if rustics were dressed in homespun and even simply skins, household inventories and other documents show that a number were owners of manufactured woollens, coloured stuffs, fustians and sometimes silks, And if there is no need to question that peasants were miserably fed, there is evidence enough that many were of a condition to feed their families well. Wherever sources exist, like the Florentine *catasti*, to give an extended view of the peasant population, the first fact to emerge is the sharp inequality prevailing, even in small communities; beside the destitute, who have nothing to declare for taxation, are the well-to-do, who can spare several hundred pounds to dower a daughter. Greater still were the contrasts, if not in wealth at least in occupation, between the peasants of different regions, between hillfarmers, plainsmen, and suburban market-gardeners, between transhumant sheepfarmers and sedentary share-croppers. Not all rustics, in terms of occupation, can be classed purely as peasants. Many divided their time between husbandry and other trades. For highlanders especially, in the poorer parts of the Alps and northern Apennines, it was a regular custom to work abroad for a season or longer, as carriers or muleteers, dockers (in Genoa), porters (in Venice), seamen and, even more, soldiers; for balancing the economy of mountain communities, war, it has been said, was an essential industry. Mixed occupations were also common in maritime districts like the Genoese and the Terra di Lavoro, and round all the larger cities. Of many smallholders in villages near to fifteenth-century Florence it is impossible to tell what their main employment was. Even tenant-farmers took jobs in urban industry, though the Florentine Badia forbade this. And what peasants themselves were unable to earn, their womenfolk often did. Most yarn for the Italian wool and cotton industries was country-spun.

It is natural to ask how far the contrasts of rural society, disclosed in the later Middle Ages by the greater abundance of records, were the product of late medieval conditions, and what general changes may lie behind them in the status of the peasantry. In Europe as a whole it has been observed that the dissolution of the manor 'was accompanied by a marked improvement in the position of the peasantry', but that 'this advance of the rural classes was not everywhere maintained in the later Middle Ages' (Eileen Power). In Italy also, during the Middle Ages, the peasantry are commonly said to have passed from personal to economic servitude. In the first phase of the transition, from the tenth to the thirteenth centuries, it is generally agreed that the material condition of cultivators improved. Not only was most reclamation and development accomplished with peasant capital; as seen above, the decline of personal servitude itself was largely the result of greater prosperity, arising under the traditional system of fixed rents and tenures. Many tenants became the owners or effective owners of their holdings, and of the small properties abounding in thirteenth-century records a large proportion were certainly held by peasants. Even in Latium and the South there is evidence of numerous smallholdings (*burgensatica*, etc.) in the areas of intensive cultivation round the villages and towns.

A further sign of economic improvement, in rural as in urban society, was a rapid development in the same period of collective rights among the peasantry. By the same charters of liberty, which guaranteed the personal and possessory rights of peasants, corporate privileges also were increasingly granted: powers of local government, the control or ownership of commons, and a great variety of other practical rights. And so, by the thirteenth century, there had risen all over Italy a multiplicity of rural communes and *universitates*, endowed with a village constitution of councils and elected officials, exercising varying powers of legislation, jurisdiction and even taxation. Established first by the upper classes of village society, it was not always a democratic constitution. Often the rural gentry demanded separate powers when they did not proceed to form a separate commune; while the unfree and the indigent were represented in the early commune only through their landlords. But although these disparities long persisted, especially in feudal territories, a large part of the peasant population was progressively admitted to an unprecedented power of deciding their own affairs. Their common rights and duties are recorded in thousands of codes of village statute, regulating all phases of rural life. In most statutes, apart from rules of ordinary criminal and civil justice, agrarian laws naturally predominate: police measures for the protection of fields and property by crop-watchers and *campari*; ordinances requiring the cultivation of specified crops; and, in open-field areas particularly, a mass of rules determining agricultural routine, enclosure and rights of common. Rights of common, by the time of the statutes, were often rights of property. As a means of adjusting the rival claims of villagers and lords, much pasture and wood, in the North especially, was transferred in the twelfth and thirteenth centuries to the management of villages by lease, gift, sale or partition. *Terra comunis* or common land became *terra Comunis* or land of the commune, to be disposed of by common consent; and gradually this communal patrimony was extended to include all kinds of other property, not only land but also corn-mills and ovens, wine and olive presses, fulling mills and brick-kilns, many of which were administered as village *banalités*. Even tithe was sometimes leased by village communities; and many communes continued to own their churches, manage parish glebe, and exercise rights of advowson. But property rights were not the only concern of rural statutes. There were also laws to regulate village trades and tradesmen: assizes of measures, bread, wine and meat, and distrustful restraints on millers and *tabernarii*. There were sanitary measures for keeping streams, wells, and highways free of filth, and precautions against fire, including laws to abolish thatch roofs. And there was a good deal of conventionally puritan legislation against tavern-haunting, gaming, blasphemy and Sunday work. A common duty was attendance at village funerals.

The rural communes continued to function throughout the Middle Ages; most of their statutes, indeed, survive in editions of fourteenth-century or later date. But they never achieved autonomy, remaining subject almost everywhere to feudal or urban domination. Still less were they able to achieve independence of economic and social pressures from outside. From an early date, in fact, the progress of commercial farming and the reclamation of waste, the intrusion of capitalist landlords and the encroachment of leasehold on 'copyhold', and finally the consolidation of holdings and dispersal of rural settlement, all combined to weaken the customary relations on which village organization reposed and peasant prosperity depended. In the rural statutes of the late Middle Ages it is notable that village communes appear much stronger and village society more compact in the areas of pastoral and co-operative farming. Here, particularly in the Alpine valleys, Lazio and the South, the laws are conceived in an exclusive spirit to keep out 'foreigners': to monopolize local wood and pasture, restrict all sales of property to neighbours by *ius prelationis*, and, in the Alps at least, confine all common rights and privileges to old-established families (*originarii*).

But even in these conservative regions there is evidence of bitter conflict between landlords and peasants and different classes of peasants
over the use and lease of village land. The truth is that the dissolution
of the manor, which emancipated the peasantry, was simply part of a
wider revolution, which eventually worked to their loss. To custom
succeeded competition, to status contract, and already before the
thirteenth century the disturbing effects on rural society were beginning
to appear. In particular peasants began to lose hold of their land, and
in the process economic differences, already present on the undissolved
manor, became sharper and more extreme. In Italy the 'agrarian
problem' is far older than the sixteenth century.

A number of peasants throve in the new conditions, acquiring wealth
as tenants, proprietors, or both, renting several farms together or even,
in the fifteenth century, farming entire estates as *fittabili* and *gabellotti*,
and lending money and letting stock at interest to neighbours. Such
contadini grassi are a common theme of literary satire, and in the Florentine tax lists of 1427 a few of their kind are found established in most
parishes surveyed. But for every peasant who prospered there were
others who went to the wall, smallholders and *livellari*, who fell victim
to engrossing landlords and capitalist farmers. From as early as the
thirteenth century, in Lombardy and Tuscany, we read of independent
peasants having to sell their holdings and assume the condition of
labourers or leaseholders or quit the land for good; and although their
numbers are impossible to calculate, there can be little doubt that in the
re-consolidation of property which marked the later Middle Ages
a large proportion of the dispossessed were simple cultivators.

The change was admittedly slow, and not everywhere did it act
with equal force. In many areas, of the South particularly, smallholders
had never become a numerous class; in others they survived unmolested
by the movement of expropriation. They survived particularly in the
highlands and in suburban and other districts of predominantly garden
culture. So in Sicily there remained a class of alodiaries or emphyteutic
tenants, the *borgesi*, from whose ranks were recruited many of the
gabellotti. The concentration of landownership was most rapid and
revolutionary in the fertile parts of Tuscany and the Northern Plain.
Even here smallholders obstinately persisted (though not all were
merely cultivators), but more and more they were pushed aside from
the more profitable land. By the fifteenth century there were villages
in the territory of Florence and Siena from which they had almost
disappeared. By the sixteenth century, in Paduan territory, only one-
twelfth of all property was left in the hands of villagers. Round Parma
and Piacenza smallholdings and hereditary tenures persisted only in
the hills; in the plain large farms prevailed, leased commercially to

peasants or *fittabili*. The same tenurial geography was emerging all over the North.

Among the reasons suggested for the decline of peasant ownership was the subdivision of holdings, both customary and freehold. In this connexion it is relevant to note that over much of Northern Italy, from the tenth to the thirteenth century, it was common to regard peasant holdings as constituting fixed units, or *mansi*, of uniform size (usually 12 *iugera*, *c.* 25 acres); and in fact on newly settled land such standard tenements often were established. But few retained their original integrity. Most were broken up. And it is possibly a sign of increasing inequality that, after 1300, little more is heard of the *mansus*, except as a fiscal unit, on old land or new. Only in certain Alpine districts, notably the Tyrol, do we commonly find undivided *mansi*, held together by patriarchal households (*casate*). Not that subdivision was a universal principle. The family group was the normal unit of agricultural production, and among peasants, as among lords, joint-ownership or tenancy remained a widespread custom. In the ownership of capital equipment, such as corn-mills and oil presses, not only kinsmen but also neighbours are sometimes found combined. But wherever peasant property is described in detail, the land is generally much partitioned, the families often limited to three or four *bocche*, and many of the holdings plainly too small for subsistence. At Casale (S. Gimignano) in 1315 there were 15 farms (*poderi*), 7 fields (*culture*), and 155 parcels of land shared among 156 owners and tenants. At Carpi (Modena) in 1448 the land was divided into 11,000 pieces among 1300 people. Nor, outside the highlands, where the peasant's wealth was often in his flocks, was deficiency of land much compensated by ownership of stock. On the contrary, it was just where the nature of the land or of market conditions made investment in stock, buildings and equipment least attractive or necessary that smallholdings proved most tenacious. They held their own least where land demanded or markets encouraged the formation of big farms, with more labour, large plough-teams or abundant stock and equipment. On estates round Florence, in the fifteenth century, there were farms of up to 300 *staiora* and tenant families of twenty persons or more. Parallel cases must have been commoner still on the lower Lombard Plain. There was no place for *mansi* once holdings began to vary with needs of production.

If anything, the distribution of livestock was even more unequal than the distribution of land. Most animals were the property of landlords and, in Upper Italy, townsmen; while of the stock in peasant ownership the greater part, even in pastoral districts, was concentrated in the hands of a prosperous minority. In this lay the origin of most disputes arising over common land. Inequality was sharpest in the ownership of cattle, particularly plough oxen. The price of cattle was high. In the Bolognese Apennines, during the fourteenth century, a yoke of oxen could cost almost as much as a farm. More perhaps than technique of tillage this explains the absence of plough beasts on many small farms, especially in the highlands: cattle were too few and expensive. It also explains the bewildering complexity of arrangements by which Italian peasants, in the thirteenth century and later, secured the use of oxen for their farms. Sometimes, as at Montalboddo in the Marche, they concluded *societates plovi* for co-operative ploughing. But by far the commonest practice was to hire cattle on various terms, by the day, for a season or a period of years, by *soccida* or some other type of contract. A good deal of other stock was rented in this way; and not only stock was rented. If animals were costly, so it seems were implements. Accordingly we find, for example in the statutes of Fano (1507), rules for the renting of mattocks and spades. The material conditions of the late medieval peasantry has to be assessed in terms not only of land tenure but of a multiplicity of contracts between tenants and lords, rustics and townsmen, poor peasants and rich peasants, relating to capital and stock.

It was by reference to working capital, specifically oxen, that medieval lords and governments commonly chose to classify peasant society. In particular they developed the distinction between peasants who disposed of plough beasts (*bubulci*, etc.) and farmed full holdings (*mansi*, etc.), and mere 'hand husbandmen' (*manuales*, etc.) who occupied simply messuages (*sedimina*, etc.) and worked land with the hoe. It was not a new distinction, but in post-manorial Italy, uncomplicated by legal differences of bond and free, it acquired a new importance. Employed already in the twelfth century for assessments to taxation, the classification in its final form may be quoted from the late medieval statutes of Emilia which divide the peasantry into cultivators (*bubulci*), labourers (*bracentes*), and farmhands (*familiares apactoati*). It was a classification that cut across differences of landownership and tenure to what appeared, through all the variety of peasant condition, the fundamental division in rural society. Economically the mass of peasants seemed to fall into two principal classes, of labourers and farmers—the classes later distinguished in France as *manoevres* and *laboureurs, manants* and *bourgeois* (cf. Sicilian *borgesi*). In the fiscal records of Florence the peasant population of many lowland parishes is divided, in the fifteenth century, almost wholly into labourers on the one hand, and tenant-farmers or *mezzadri* on the other.

Wage-labourers are first casually mentioned in the tenth century and are then recorded in growing numbers from the twelfth. They became most numerous on the cornlands of the South and Sicily, where, it is said, by the fourteenth century the great majority of villeins had been converted into hired or tenant-labourers. But all over Italy records refer to wage-working ploughmen and reapers, gleaners, threshers, wine-harvesters and others, as well as farm servants (*garzoni*, etc.). Of these the great majority were paid by the day for seasonal work, and many were migratory. In the Marche and Abruzzi itinerant ploughmen and threshers toured farms with oxen and horses. In Central and Southern Italy gangs of peasants travelled each year to harvest corn in Lucania, Apulia, and the Roman Campagna, Elba, Corsica and Sardinia. Of these and similar migrants in Tuscany and the North a large proportion were hill-farmers who worked in the plain before their own crops ripened. Wage-labourers, therefore, were not entirely landless. Many were smallholders, some were members of tenant-farming families, and a good number were simple cottagers. For this reason it is hard to treat wage-labourers as a class or describe their general condition. Most distinct were the farmhands, whose terms of employment seem often to have been quite generous. Casual labourers were commonly paid in kind, but scattered records of money wages in Tuscany and Emilia suggest that, in the late fourteenth and early fifteenth centuries, rates of pay were good. In Italy, as elsewhere, their condition may have improved after the Black Death. But, as seen already, labour legislation was promptly passed to discipline their claims; and in general governments saw to it that their wages, terms of hire, and freedom of movement were severely regulated. Employers were even forbidden to compete by providing them with meals; and some towns, such as Mantua and Bologna, where labourers were known expressively as *malnutriti*, conscripted *opererii* to ease the labour market.

Even more subject to statutory control was the class of tenant-farmers, particularly *mezzadri*. These have sometimes been described as forming a peasant aristocracy, but the opinion is hardly confirmed by what is known of the attitude of peasants to commerical leases or the conditions on which they held. Normally they had no land of their own and most of their livestock was rented or shared with the owner; in many places *mezzadri* at least were legally bound to hold all stock of the lord. Their rents also, whether partiary or fixed, were often burdensome, and of any marketable surplus remaining to themselves their lords had the refusal. As between fixed rents and share-cropping, their preference is rarely expressed. On Florentine estates we find tenants sometimes avoiding grants *a fitto*; but at Bologna and certain near-by towns in the later fourteenth century *fitti* were regarded as so exposed to peasant 'deceits' that they were suppressed outright in favour of *mezzadria*. Conditions obviously varied; but by the end of the Middle Ages, when *mezzadria* had spread to include poorer tenants on poorer land, it must often have been oppressive. In Tuscany most tenants owed *prestanze*, credits advanced by the lord of money, seed, food, and sometimes even clothing; and although such loans formed an integral part of sharecropping, to be cleared off by seasonal payments or at the termination of the contract, they could easily accumulate into a permanent bond of debt. In practice, no doubt, landlords were often glad to let both debts and tenants go. Florentine records reveal frequent changes of tenancy. But according to urban statute, tenants with undischarged debts could not change their holdings, and by this restriction, as was pointed out by eighteenth-century observers, *mezzadri* could be tied as firmly to the land as any of their villein ancestors.

Equally reminiscent of seignorialism were the ample powers granted landlords to imprison and distrain, which, unlike public officials and other outsiders, they were free to exercise against the peasant's stock and wainage. The generous statutory right to evict was also freely used; and although it was not uncommon for tenants to renew their leases, it was also not unknown for them to be ejected on reaching old age. Such cases may not typify the relations of lords and tenants; but it cannot pass unnoticed that literature and law alike, and even sometimes the phraseology of leases, treat as natural a relationship of suspicion and resentment. One critical moment came just after the Black Death when share-croppers, like labourers, tried to improve their position by demanding a larger capital contribution from landlords. But once again the law was ranged against them. Under Italian urban statute tenant right was emphatically landlord wrong.

The interests of landlords, however, determined much more than the law regarding tenure. They influenced the whole of urban policy in the countryside. To advance the rights of landowners laws were passed, from the thirteenth century on, suppressing village customs which excluded foreigners from local land or the use of local commons, and extending the ancient responsibility of village communities for anonymous crime and damage to include a new obligation to protect and cultivate the property of townsmen. Village bye-laws were subjected to regular inspection and were gradually standardized in accordance with urban statute, especially in matters touching the safeguard of land. Increasingly, rural communes became the instrument of urban policy, particularly fiscal policy, and from this too urban landlords were able to draw advantage. With the conquest of the *contado* the peasant classes became collectively subject, through their communes, to numerous impositions: *corvées* (*factiones*), purveyance, and above all payments in men and money, especially money. Townsmen by comparison were less heavily burdened. In particular they and their farm stock were exempt from *onera personalia et rusticalia*, and so some-times were their tenants, especially, after the rise of despotism, the tenants of *signori* and their favourites. One result of this was conflict in the distribution of local charges: peasants tried to pass themselves off as citizens, villagers tried to check emigration to the towns and the encroachment of urban owners. But much the most critical effect of urban fiscal policy was to involve the rural classes in ruinous debts, particularly debts to townsmen.

In medieval Italy the countryside was by no means the least attractive field of enterprise for the money-lender. The peasant's lack of capital was the opportunity of the speculator, and nothing in rural records is more conspicuous than rural debt. Debts were of all kinds, and money loans are often impossible to distinguish from the mere extension of credit on goods and other types of current obligation, by which agrarian society was largely held together. Rural money-lenders, moreover, were not normally professionals, though Jews are found practising in quite small places. More often they were prosperous peasants or local tradesmen, and in some parts of the Florentine *contado* in 1427 men of this type seem to have had claims against almost all the surrounding population. But many were also landlords and townsmen, and more often than appears on the surface the commercial dealings of townsmen and peasants were in fact loan-contracts. This was true especially of advance purchases of crops, in which the concealed interest rates were high and the risk for peasants severe. Already in the early thirteenth century we find townsmen at S. Gimignano seizing the land of small-holders for the non-delivery of quite trifling amounts of produce (as the urban law of their creation entitled them to do). Of similar effect, if not intention, were many contracts of *soccida*, which despite papal prohibition often took the usurious form of grants *ad capitale salvum*. By reason of such transactions smallholders were frequently more seriously burdened than tenant farmers; and the commonest cause recorded for the sale of peasant property is debt.

That debt was merely or mainly due to urban taxation is obviously not implied. In the uncertain world of the peasant loans were 'in the nature of things' (Tawney), and the only source of supply was private credit; grain-banks had barely made an appearance, before 1500, at Spoleto and Macerata. But in Italian records of the later Middle Ages no single cause of rural distress is so insistently mentioned as debt to the state or to private individuals arising from taxation. Because of this, numerous peasants in Tuscany, from as early as the thirteenth century, were compelled to sell their holdings or commend themselves as *livellari* or *conversi* to lay and ecclesiastical lords. In 1339 the commune of Florence had even to reduce the rural tax assessment because so many peasants were surrendering land to townsmen and others and moving into the city. From the same cause many villages in Upper Italy were forced to levy rates for the use of commons, or lease or sell their land outright, often to urban capitalists who, contrary to law, advanced them money for taxes and obtained usurious control of their affairs. So indirectly urban policy increased the land and rents of urban owners, and both increased peasant poverty and debt.

It is not to be wondered that, in the late fourteenth and fifteenth centuries, under despotic or foreign rule, villages often sought independence of the towns. Yet there is little to show their position was improved, still less to confirm the common opinion that the rural classes were better off under despots than under communes. How little forms of government mattered in agrarian development is shown by the conditions of the peasantry in the feudal parts of Italy, particularly the South. Here the trend was much the same, and it would almost be possible to speak of a 'seignorial reaction' in the later Middle Ages. In the South, it is true, peasants near the larger towns suffered from urban privilege in the distribution of taxes; but the main burdens were the heavy exactions of the Crown and, even more, an almost uninterrupted growth, in the Angevin and Aragonese periods, of feudal powers and abuses. An increasing number of towns and villages fell under baronial control, and the dominant tendency, outside the royal demesne, was to create a uniform class of 'vassals' who, independently of tenure or status, were subject not only to seignorial justice, monopolies, and restrictions on the sale of produce, but also in places to agricultural services and illegal restraints on freedom of movement, marriage, and entry into a craft. Already distinguished in the fourteenth century from *liberi homines*, by the sixteenth century such baronial *vassi* were coming to be described as *vere servi*. In late medieval Lazio also feudal lordship grew stronger, though without limitations on peasant freedom; while from the feudal Tyrol, where serfdom continued its slow decline, there come murmurs in 1313 against the re-imposition of labour dues and the oppression of free peasants by nobles and officials. By the close of the Middle Ages there are even reports of seignorial abuses in the great urban territories of the North, where the *signori*, securely installed as princes, were in process of re-creating feudal lordship. At Parma, by the mid-fifteenth century, three-quarters of the *contado* was back in feudal hands.

Neither in feudal nor urban territory did the peasantry submit without protest to the post-manorial regime. In Italy, as in Europe, the later Middle Ages were marked by recurrent peasant unrest and insurrection. Sporadic revolts there had always been and occasional acts of murder; and from as early as the twelfth century there is legislation in northern towns to protect landlords from threats, assault, and organized boycott by villagers and tenants. Organized resistance was naturally not the rule. For peasants driven desperate by debt or oppression the instinctive decision was to try their luck elsewhere; and all over Italy, in the later fourteenth and fifteenth centuries, we read of such miserable migrants, regulated, as was seen above, by a confusion of contradictory laws to punish them as fugitive debtors and attract them as settlers to vacant land. But at times the rural classes acted together. In the South they took to brigandage, a habit that became endemic; in parts of the North they occasionally went on strike; and in various places they broke out in revolt. Risings occurred at Parma in 1385 and Piacenza in 1462, at Pistoia in 1455 and 1473, in Southern Italy during the reign of King Ferrante, and in the Tyrol, Trentino and Friuli at various times from the early fourteenth century down to 1525. The main grievance, however, was almost always taxation and misgovernment; deeper dissatisfactions are rarely expressed. At Pistoia, it is true, there were undertones of resentment against abuses of eviction and distraint, and in Friuli one cause of revolt was conflict with lords over terms of tenure and rights of common pasture; but here, and in the Trentino, political faction and discontent played a powerful part, and in the Trentino the influence of foreign example. In Italy itself there is no sound of general protest against the social order, no egalitarian doctrine, no Jacquerie. The tax register was the target of peasant hatred, and even armed risings were mostly short and bloodless. They produced no contagious upheaval. Normally the peasant classes applied for peaceful remedies, presenting petitions to the government or, in feudal territory, supplicating franchises. In the Tyrol, by a rare exception, they had access to parliament.

Typical of peasant discontents in late medieval Italy is the tax complaint submitted by the rural district of Verona in 1475. The basic grievance was simple: countrymen were moving to Verona, becoming rich, and getting their lands assessed with the town; townsmen were buying peasant property and committing the same offence; in consequence the town grew rich and the country poor; it was therefore requested that town and country receive a common assessment. More interesting is the reply. It was stated first that only 72 peasants in 35 years had become citizens of Verona; on the other hand peasant properties had multiplied in places and cottages been rebuilt in stone. Then follow some general remarks. It was not true that townsmen were better off than peasants. Peasants got their food and fuel, goods and stock for nothing; townsmen had to pay gate duties, though with tax allowances to compensate. This was why only countrymen rendered *corvées*, and not only the rich but the poor; to make the urban poor pay taxes would depopulate the city. But most important of all was the fact that townsmen had to bear the cost of urban life, of culture and 'civilization' (*vivere civilmente*).

In Tuscany there was a proverb: 'The country is for producing animals, the town for producing men.'

Medieval Agrarian Society in its Prime

§ 3. Spain

I. *Geographical conditions*

A glance at the topographical and meteorological characteristics of the Iberian Peninsula is the first prerequisite of the study of Spanish economic history. The contrasts of terrain, climate, soil, and other physical features for a country occupying less than 200,000 square miles are uncommonly sharp. From the lofty Pyrenees, which fall a little short of preventing land communication with France, to the Sierra Nevada in the south, high altitudes prevail, the mean elevation of Spain exceeding that of any European country except Switzerland. Most of the interior forms a high, rugged plateau (*meseta*) broken by numerous mountain chains. Access to the Biscayan coast is blocked by the Cantabrian cordillera extending from the Pyrenees to the westernmost coast of Galicia. Similarly, the highlands of Aragon impede communication between Castile and the Mediterranean, except through the valley of the Ebro.

Between the mountain ranges, which generally run from east to west, lie the valleys of the five principal rivers. The Guadalquivir has always been navigable as far as Seville, and the Ebro carried some commerce in the Middle Ages; as a rule, however, the river currents are too swift and the rainfall too uncertain for the development of inland waterways. Leaving the arid *meseta*, one may descend easily to the fertile Andalusian plain where fairly abundant moisture is counterbalanced by intense summer heat. Rainfall in the north and west is abundant, Santiago's mean annual precipitation of over 64 inches being the maximum for Spain; on the other hand, parts of the south-east have an annual rainfall of less than 8 inches. Generally, the Mediterranean regions enjoy an equable climate, but the Castilian *meseta* and the uplands of Aragon are very cold in winter and extremely hot in summer.

Geographic variety, producing diverse modes of agricultural and pastoral life, and the isolation resulting from the natural barriers to interregional intercourse, largely account for the exaggerated separatism of Iberian peoples. The history of Spain, like that of Germany down to the nineteenth century, 'may be summed up in the one word *Particularismus*'.[1] The pronounced differentiation of social and economic phenomena arising from isolation and separatism, accentuated by the varied and shifting patterns of political control, present serious obstacles to a comprehensive survey of agrarian conditions. To discuss *Spanish*

[1] R. B. Merriman, *The Rise of the Spanish Empire*, I, 35.

agrarian conditions in the Middle Ages requires the introduction of qualifications and exceptions at every turn. No problem better illustrates the pitfalls of generalization than the thorny question of feudalism.

II. *Social conditions and tenures*

Older writers, undertaking works of synthesis upon a meagre basis of fact, reached diametrically opposite conclusions as to the existence of a Spanish feudal system. In recent times, a few scholars have produced material from the archives supporting the thesis that full-fledged feudal regimes flourished in Roussillon and Catalonia—regions essentially Frankish during the era of reconquest. As for the rest of the peninsula, particularly Castile, the safest conclusion seems to be that it possessed 'much feudalism but no feudal system'. The study of feudalism is important for economic history insofar as it throws light on the conditions of the rural population. Unfortunately, the study of the character, efficiency, and well-being of agricultural workers has interested few investigators. Information on these topics appears as by-products of work primarily concerned with medieval property rights, land tenure, and legal institutions.

The various arrangements for appropriating land were in large part products of Spain's unique role in making Europe safe for Christianity. Iberia, except for the mountainous enclave of Asturias, was overrun by Moslem invaders during the eighth century. The Reconquest, which by the end of the thirteenth century restored nine-tenths of the peninsula to Christian rule, created the necessity of repopulating and defending a vast area and reorganizing land and labour for production. Although a significant portion of this territory remained under royal jurisdiction, much of the conquered territory came under the direct control of those on whom the king depended for the military and financial means of waging war. Only two classes, the nobility (in part a creature of the Reconquest) and the clergy, were in a position to benefit permanently from these circumstances. Thus, an oligarchy of noblemen, military orders, and the Church acquired titles and rights of one sort or another over most of the medieval countryside. These were the ultimate landlords, and in some regions the immensity of their holdings gave birth to the perdurable problems associated with latifundia, entail, and mortmain.[1]

---

[1] J. Vicens Vives (*Historia social y económica de España y América*, II, 8–46) furnishes the best summary of the results of resettlement (*repoblación*) in the different regions of peninsular Spain and the Balearics. Apparently, the extreme concentration of land-holdings in modern Extremadura, for instance, may be traced to thirteenth-century grants of 300,000 hectares to each of three military orders. In Andalusia the Archbishop of Toledo received, in the thirteenth century, a grant of 2000 square kilometres.

Slaves, serfs, tenant farmers, and wage-earners formed the backbone of agricultural labour. While it is impossible to ascertain what proportion of the rural population was genuinely enslaved, it is clear that the Reconquest added to the ranks of Moorish slaves in Christian Spain and of Christian slaves in Moslem territory. An active slave market existed in Catalonia, where early in the fifteenth century the provincial government, alleging a serious shortage of labour, undertook to insure slave owners against loss from the desertion of their human chattels. Slaves worked the estates of some monasteries, and the ownership of a slave or two was a frequent luxury in the higher clerical ranks; but the Church often lauded manumission, forbade the sale of Christian slaves, and inveighed against the cruel treatment of bondsmen, perhaps achieving in some degree the amelioration of their condition. In any case, it seems likely that slaves were more important as personal servants than as field workers. The great mass of the rural population enjoyed an economic, social, and legal position somewhat better than that of slaves, considerably worse, no doubt, than that of a free landed peasantry. On the latter point information is scanty, although it seems clear that nuclei of unencumbered farms operated by peasant-owners flourished continuously, particularly in Valencia and Mallorca.

In its early stages the Reconquest created a class of cultivators who owned the land they tilled. The frontier between Christian and Moslem Spain was a broad expanse of sparsely settled or uninhabited territory which could be colonized only by offering land on advantageous terms. In this area the free peasant farmer, owner of a small acreage, was the typical settler during the ninth and tenth centuries. Subsequently, the status of the Castilian peasant-owner changed for the worse. Because of actual need, during long decades of dynastic and baronial warfare, or as a result of the violence and intimidation of the upper classes, many peasant-proprietors faced the necessity of buying 'protection' from a prince or count, an abbot or a bishop. The price of this service was the loss of the peasant's freehold, the payment of annuities, or some other economic obligation in token of his acceptance of the lord's patronage. Thus arose, especially in the thirteenth century, the *behetrías*, *solariegos*, *abadengos*, and similar tenure systems in Asturias, Castile, León and Aragon. All implied some measure of personal and economic subordination, although the degree of subservience varied from century to century and from region to region.

The fourteenth-century *Becerro*, or 'Celebrated Book of the *Behetrías* of Castile', catalogues over 600 villages whose residents had individually or collectively accepted a lord's patronage and records in detail the seignorial dues required of each peasant. Most of the evidence supports the conclusion that an increasing burden of dues, perhaps reaching its apogee in the fourteenth century, had the effect of absorbing the full economic rent of the peasant's land. Except for security of tenure and limited rights of inheritance, ownership amounted to little more than a legal fiction. Thus, it is difficult to distinguish between seignorial or feudal types of tenure and simple tenantry. Tenants on crown lands (*realengas*) were in a sense privileged, since 'the king was somewhat less oppressive than the lord'.[1]

The variety of contractual and customary obligations assumed by peasant cultivators was almost infinite. The serfs (*payeses de remensa*) of Catalonia paid as ground rent either a fixed canon (*census*) in kind or a certain percentage of the crop. Payments of the latter type ranged from one-eleventh to one-half of the principal products, shares of one-quarter and one-fifth having been common for vineyards and olive groves. In twelfth-century Aragon vineyards commonly rented for one-third of the wine produced; in Aragon and Navarre the *exáricos* (non-Christian farmers in Christian Spain) continued the Moorish practice of paying quit-rents of one-tenth to one-fifth of the crop. Wheat, barley, and wine were by far the most common produce rents on the estates listed in the *Becerro*; but money dues, usually nominal in amount, are also stipulated in this fourteenth-century record. On the monastic estates (*abadengos*) of Sahagún the peasants paid rents of one-half the produce and bore one-third the expense of raising it. Since custom was strong and the bargaining power of the farmer generally weak, the observed variations in rents and dues may not be explained wholly by differences in the physical condition of the land. Furthermore, low rents may have been combined with a long list of complementary labour services.

In fact, it was the rigid and oftentimes arbitrary structure of the dues and personal services demanded of the peasant which contributed most to his servile condition. Customary labour services were depended upon for exploiting the demesne farm. Catalonian serfs generally devoted not more than six days a year to working the lord's land; a day a month appears to have been the maximum. But tenants of the monastery of San Pedro de Cardeña (Burgos) worked the monks' farm twice a month, furnishing their own oxen; and once a year they hauled wine to the wine cellars and supplied the monastery with firewood. Boons of one or two days a month prevailed on the *behetrías* of Castile. More important, perhaps, in Spain as elsewhere, than the absolute amount of labour required was the fact that it was demanded when the peasant needed to attend to his own crops.

Other requirements besides boon work prevented the peasant from taking care of his own fields to the best advantage. A typical town

[1] J. Vicens Vives, *op. cit.*, II, p. 246.

charter granted to Soria in 1256 established penalties for picking grapes before a certain day of the year; and farmers in Peñafiel could not begin to cut their grain until the church bell gave the signal for tax gatherers to occupy the fields and collect the tithes. Finally, when the farmer had harvested his crop, he was often restrained by 'bans', such as those which forced him to grind his grain at the lord's mill or press his grapes in a monopolized wine press. On the *abadengo* of Sahagún the monks forbade their tenants to have ovens in their cottages, lest they neglect to use those of the monastery. When the friars wanted to sell their wine, no one else could offer wine for sale in the same market; when they wanted to buy supplies, other potential buyers were excluded from the market.

A characteristic of much non-slave labour in agriculture was the prohibition or severe limitation of its migration. Both the Catalonian *payeses de remensa* and the peasants on the Castilian *solariegos* were generally regarded as perpetual tenants, bound to the soil (*adscritos a la tierra*) like the *coloni* of Roman times; and their personal status was hereditary. Similarly, the Moorish farmers in Christian Spain were bound to the land they formerly owned. A serf's lord changed with the alienation of the land; unlike slaves, however, such tenants could not be dispossessed or disposed of independently of the land. Custom and law required the apprehension of those who abandoned their rural homes and sanctioned the confiscation of personal property for 'desertion'. Doubtless the narrow margin between subsistence needs and current production tended to impel the landlord to demand, and the peasant to accept, relative immobility. In the early centuries of the Middle Ages, 'the proprietor of the land has an interest in attaching the cultivator to it, and the latter, as long as he is not aroused by the prospect of a better opportunity, accepts a condition which with the passing of time and changing economic conditions must have seemed intolerable to him'.[1]

Much more difficult of explanation are the so-called 'evil customs' (*malos usos*) to which Catalonian serfs and some other classes of peasants were subjected. In substance, the *malos usos* were contingent property rights executed by the lord upon the possessions of the tenant in the event, for instance, of intestacy.[2] Chief of the 'evil customs', *remensa personal* signified the obligation of the serf to purchase personal redemp-

---

[1] E. de Hinojosa, *El régimen señorial y la cüestión agraria en Cataluña*, p. 221.

[2] There were at least six *malos usos*: *remensa personal* (payment for redemption), *intestia* (the lord's right to take one-third to one-half of the peasant property if he died intestate), *exorquia* (the lord's right to a son's share if the peasant died without issue), *cugucia* (a penalty for the peasant's wife's adultery), *arsina* (compensation for fire losses but not restricted to arson), and *firma de spoli* (dues payable in connexion with a wife's dowry).

tion as a condition of leaving the land. Although sometimes the price of redemption was small (e.g. 2s. 8d. for a daughter leaving to get married), in most cases the cost, in money or goods, was too heavy for the peasant to 'redeem' himself in a lifetime of work. Furthermore, under a royal decree of 1202 lay lords in Catalonia could invoke the *ius maletractandi*, which empowered them to resort to force and confiscation of property to prevent peasants from abandoning the fields.

Humane and economic considerations played a part in the movement for abolition of the evil customs. Where the former prevailed, the customs were removed gratuitously; in other cases they were done away with in exchange for fixed annual dues. Thus, in 1231 a peasant contracted to pay one-ninth of the grain and vegetables he produced in return for complete exemption from the *malos usos*. Whereas, at the peak, probably less than half of the rural population was subject to the evil customs, by 1395 not over 20,000 Catalan families (chiefly tenants of ecclesiastical estates) were so restricted. All of the *malos usos* were abolished by the *Sentencia Arbitral de Guadalupe* (1486), which 'did little more than crown and consummate a work of which the greater part had already been accomplished'.[1]

The disappearance of the 'evil customs' and other improvements in the peasants' status were fundamentally responses to economic changes that extended beyond the countryside. By far the most important was the rise of towns and the growth of industry and trade. The urban demand for labour, the right of asylum usually enforced in the cities,[2] and the increasing disposition of the rulers to favour the rising mercantile class at the expense of the landed gentry created opportunities which encouraged the peasant to risk abandoning his farm and feudal lord. Cognisant of the better lot of workers elsewhere, the rural population grew restive. Toward the close of the fourteenth century abortive uprisings in Catalonia and Majorca presaged the fifteenth-century peasant revolts, which ended with the intervention of the Crown.

The increasing use of money made it less difficult for the serf, if he were one of the Catalonian *payeses de remensa*, to acquire the price of 'redemption' or to commute labour services and other feudal dues. Money payments were not necessarily less onerous than payments in kind; but, as they appear to have been preferred, particularly in periods of rising prices, commutation may be recognized as a concession to the peasant-cultivator. The Black Death accelerated commutation, although other forces had inaugurated the practice before the

[1] R. B. Merriman, *op. cit.*, I, p. 480.

[2] As late as 1350, in the Cortes of Perpignan, the king granted the petition of the military *brazo* that the year-and-a-day privilege in force in Barcelona and other towns be abrogated; but there is reasonable doubt that the right of asylum was often denied to peasants seeking the 'free air' of urban centres (J. Vicens Vives, *op. cit.*, II, p. 250).

fourteenth century. An urban monied class invested in lands for the sake of profit, and landlords of this type were more concerned with efficient production than with the preservation of ancient customs. Finally, opportunities arose for the serf or tenant farmer to exchange his lot for that of a hired hand, although 'freedom' might be purchased at the expense of seasonal unemployment.

Farm hands (*peones* and *obreros*) are mentioned in the *Becerro*, and unattached farm labourers working for board, clothing, and shelter (if not for money wages) are encountered in all periods. Some, of course, were artisans rather than field hands. The élite among the free farm labourers were the Castilian *quinteros*, so called because the remuneration for their labour with a yoke of oxen consisted of one-fifth of the crop. Equally well paid were the shepherds and teamsters employed by the owners of the migratory sheep.

A growing wage-earning class required a wider use of money than obtained during the early period of the Reconquest. No satisfactory wage data have been found for periods prior to the last half of the fourteenth century; but in Aragon hoe hands, wine pressers, vine planters, pruners, and grape pickers worked for wages on the estates of the Saragossa and Huesca cathedrals, and in Navarre the royal vineyards and orchards employed much the same categories of free labour. Data are insufficient to construct an index of agricultural wages: in all probability farm workers benefited from the increase of real wages which, so far as can be determined, was pronounced during the last half of the fourteenth and the early fifteenth centuries. The Castilian Cortes of 1351 approved a statute of labourers, fixing maximum wages for several classes of agricultural workers, in response to the allegations that 'those who went to work in the fields demanded such high wages that the owners of the farms could not comply'.[1] The same Parliament, probably sanctioning a practice from which few departures had been permitted, decreed that the working day should begin at sunrise and end at sunset. The Cortes of 1369 re-enacted this legislation which, unlike modern labour laws, set a 'ceiling' to wages and a 'floor' to the hours of work.

III. *Agricultural and pastoral pursuits*

An important chapter in Spanish agrarian history is the relation between agriculture and grazing. The merino sheep, 'Spain's great contribution to international trade and to the pastoral industry of the

---

[1] 'Ordenamientos de menestrales y posturas', in *Cortes de los antiguos reinos de León y de Castilla*, II, pp. 75–124.

world',[1] were probably introduced from Africa in the twelfth century.[2] Important differences separated the sedentary from the migratory branches of the industry. Climate and topography especially favoured migrations. Travelling hundreds of miles over a network of sheep-walks (cañadas), the sheep found summer pasturage in the northern highlands and wintered in the frost-free valleys of the south-west. The progress of Christian arms forced the Moors to abandon migratory grazing, but the relentless crusade against the infidels opened up the Andalusian and Extremaduran grasslands to Spanish-owned flocks.

With the organization of the Aragonese Casa de Ganaderos in the twelfth century and the chartering of the Mesta in 1273, the owners of migratory sheep (whose number grew to over 2·5 million in 1447) were united in powerful guilds. Some small-scale graziers belonged to the Mesta, but the most influential members were the military orders and ecclesiastical bodies. Among other objectives, the guilds strove to enforce Visigothic laws which allowed the trashumantes unrestricted access to unenclosed or waste land; but with the rise of towns in the twelfth and thirteenth centuries many municipal charters reserved the commons and enclosed pasture for non-migratory sheep and forbade the intrusion of migratory flocks. It was not until the fifteenth century that the Mesta attained sufficient political and economic power to dominate the pastoral industry and so impede the agricultural enclosure movement. Meanwhile, wool was furnishing Spain the principal commodity in its export trade.

Although medieval agriculture was hampered by grazing less than is commonly supposed, 'the Castilian forest suffered severely from the regular visits of the millions of migratory sheep'.[3] From the Visogothic Fuero Juzgo to the Mesta charter of 1273, grazing privileges permitted shepherds to cut branches for corrals, fences, and fuel, and to burn trees in the autumn for the sake of better spring pasturage. Conservation measures adopted in the thirteenth century may have helped to postpone the nation's most serious problem of deforestation to the fifteenth and sixteenth centuries. Hunting, though undertaken for the most part to satisfy food requirements, was often detrimental to agriculture. Until the Siete Partidas, legislation took the form of game conservation, and the farmer was frequently at the mercy of hunters who had the same regard for property lines, vineyards, and growing crops as an animal at bay.

[1] J. Klein, The Mesta, p. 6.
[2] Cf. p. 172 above, and R. S. Lopez, 'The Origin of the Merino Sheep', Jewish Social Studies: Joshua Starr Memorial Volume, v (1953).
[3] J. Klein, op. cit. p. 307.

In many regions improvement in agriculture waited upon the development of irrigation. The Visigoths preserved their inheritance of irrigation projects built by the Romans.[1] The Moors, it is generally agreed, were not innovators in hydraulic science; but the improvement and extension of irrigation was undoubtedly one of their most valuable contributions to Spanish agriculture. By the twelfth century the Moors, 'who knew how to drain rivers with precision and to distribute water economically',[2] had irrigated an estimated 25,000 acres around Saragossa, and other important systems antedating the Reconquest were found in the Genil valley in Andalusia, in the Segura basin in Murcia, and in the valley of the Segre in Catalonia. One of the great prizes of the victorious Christians under James the Conqueror was the magnificently irrigated *vega* of Valencia. Before his death in 1276, James added the *Acequia Real* to the existing seven canals which drew water from the Guadalaviar River and confirmed rights to use the water 'according to the manner established and customarily employed in the time of the Saracens'.[3] Disputes over the distribution of water were settled in the *Tribunal de las Aguas*, an informal court of 'practical' landowners and cultivators which has functioned successfully from the tenth century to the present.[4] The Moors, as has been seen,[5] also introduced the noria, an animal-powered, bucket-and-chain apparatus still used in Spain for raising irrigation water from wells.

In many other ways, while Christian soldiers were demonstrating the superiority of the cross to the crescent, agriculture owed permanent improvements to the long sojourn of the Moors. Colmeiro exclaimed enthusiastically: 'The irrigation works, the names of trees, plants, flowers, and fruits—everything, in fact, testifies to an Arab origin or bears witness to the profound revolution of these people who broke with the tradition of Roman agriculture.'[6] Unfortunately, the data supporting Colmeiro's sweeping assertions are not all worthy of acceptance; no one knows just how many things were really lost in the darkness of the sixth, seventh, and eighth centuries. In many instances the Moors may receive credit for innovating because of their success in reviving agricultural arts, including the cultivation of certain crops,

---

[1] Thus, the *Fuero Juzgo* (lib. viii, tit. v, ley 31) established penalties for the theft of water from irrigation canals.

[2] I. de Asso, *Historia de la economía política de Aragón*, p. 97. It should be noted that irrigation was well developed in Roussillon, where the Moorish influence was transitory (J.-A. Brutails, *Étude sur la condition des populations rurales du Roussillon au moyen-âge*, p. 6), and cf. p. 147 above.

[3] R. Gayano Lluch, *Els Furs de Valencia* (Valencia, 1930), pp. 206–7.

[4] Gayano Lluch (*op. cit.* p. 202) refers to authors who credit Al Haquem II (962–6) with the founding of the 'Water Court'.

[5] P. 47 above.

[6] M. Colmeiro, *Historia de la economía política en España*, II, pp. 178–9.

which somehow survived the period of Visigothic domination. Likewise, not unimportant contributions were made by the Mozarabs, or Christians in Moslem territory, who were generally welcomed as exceptionally productive members of the community until the advent of the fanatical Almoravides and Almohades. It has been said that 'the material civilization of the Hispano-Arab states is certainly due as much to the Christian element, conquered and submissive, as to the triumphant Berber, Arab, and Syrian elements'.[1]

In spite of the hyperbole, the statement that 'agriculture deserved the name of a science in Arab Spain at a time when it was only manual labour elsewhere'[2] is a well-earned tribute. Ibn Khaldun produced a book on agricultural economics which 'far excels any similar treatise of Christian Europe for centuries';[3] Ibn Loyon composed a didactic poem on the management of fields and gardens; and the twelfth-century botanist, Aben Albaithar, described some 200 species of vegetables and edible plants. Worthy of special note is the twelfth-century *Book of Agriculture* from the pen of Abu Zacaria. Extracting copiously from ancient writers, notably Columella, and from the works of Arab contemporaries, Abu Zacaria surveyed virtually every phase of agronomy, horticulture, irrigation, meteorology, entomology, and veterinary science. The treatise is surprisingly uncritical in part,[4] but its practical value was deemed sufficient to justify its translation into Spanish in 1802.

The predominance of fruits and vegetables in the Moorish diet encouraged the maintenance of fine market gardens and orchards, the best of which were found near Cordova, Granada, and Valencia. Abdar-Rahman I (756–8) is said to have sent emissaries to Syria, India, and Arabia for the seeds of exotic fruits and flowers, which were acclimatized in Cordova prior to their propagation in other parts of the Khalifate. At the risk of conveying a false impression of the variety in the medieval diet, one may call attention to the principal fruits and vegetables produced in Spain, at least by the twelfth or thirteenth century. Apples, dates, figs, pears, plums, and quince were known to Imperial Rome as Spanish products. Cherries, citrus fruits, peaches, and strawberries were probably first brought to Spain by the Moors. A list of common vegetables in Moorish Spain, at the time Abu

---

[1] P. Boissonnade, 'Les études relatives à l'histoire économique de l'Espagne', *Revue de synthèse historique*, XXII (Paris, 1911), p. 216.

[2] J. W. Thompson, *An Economic and Social History of the Middle Ages*, p. 547.

[3] *Ibid.* p. 548.

[4] Zacaria gave the following formula for fattening pigs: wash the animal with human urine and then anoint the tail with the juice of orach leaves mixed with olive oil and wine! He warned against setting out olive trees in the presence of a menstruating woman, a man with a 'legal impurity', a bachelor, or an adulterer, lest the fruit be small.

Zacaria wrote, includes several varieties of beans and peas, cabbage, carrots, cucumbers, egg-plant, endives, garlic, leek, lentils, melons, parsnips, peppers, squash, spinach, radishes, and turnips. Almonds and filberts were grown in many places; other nuts, including chestnuts and walnuts, were cultivated or gathered wild. As the nineteenth-century translator of the *Book of Agriculture* admitted considerable difficulty in finding modern equivalents for twelfth-century Arabic names of plants, fruits, and trees, allowance should be made for differences between medieval products and those bearing similar names today. On the whole, that part of the peninsula in Moorish hands was more abundantly supplied with produce than Christian Spain, and the reward of a more varied diet must have been one source of inspiration for the Reconquest.

Wine and olive oil, which was Spain's most important export in Roman times, have always stood high in the list of essential food and drink. Providentially, the Moors are believed to have supplied the country with new olive trees from Africa after the native trees were decimated by drought in the ninth century. As in the Roman period, exports of oil from the Mediterranean provinces bulked large in the overseas trade which Catalonia developed so vigorously in the thirteenth and fourteenth centuries. Not all Moors were as temperate as the Prophet exhorted them to be. Wine was one of the objects of their extensive viticulture; furthermore, from rice, figs, and dates the followers of Mohammed made beverages of 'extraordinary potency'.[1] In Christian Spain, where the humblest yokel abhorred water, the cultivation of vines was almost as common as the production of grain.

In all probability, the Moors introduced both sugar and cotton to Spain. Tenth-century chronicles mention the cultivation of sugar cane, and Abu Zacaria spoke of cane as a common crop in twelfth-century Granada and Seville. The cotton plant came in from Arabia or Armenia at an uncertain date. A limited amount of fibre was produced in Valencia, perhaps as early as the tenth century; on a larger scale its production was carried on in Granada and Andalusia, although Vicens Vives reports that cotton and sugar production languished after the Moors left Southern Spain.

Flax and hemp, together with dyestuffs such a cochineal and kermes, were Spanish exports in ancient times, and their production was continued or taken up anew in the Middle Ages. No one knows when

---

[1] A. Ballesteros, *Historia de España*, II, p. 88. Occasionally a ruler arose to smite the curse of liquor. The Khalif Ozman in the tenth century prohibited the use of wine in Valencia and ordered the destruction of two-thirds of the vines, leaving one-third to produce raisins and grapes (Gayano Lluch, *op. cit.* p. 203).

the silkworm arrived on the shores of Andalusia, but it is certain that a great increase in the production of silk resulted from the successful propagation of several varieties of mulberry trees in Moorish Granada, Murcia and Valencia.[1] Southern Italy and Eastern Spain 'wrested from the East its monopoly in the cultivation of mulberries and the raising of silkworms'[2] and stimulated the silk textile industry in Western Europe.

Rice production, probably another contribution of the Moors, was practically confined to the kingdom of Valencia, where then as now adequate irrigation made it possible to flood the fields. The rapid expansion of rice growing in the thirteenth century caused alarm because of the supposed danger of contagion and epidemic from stagnant water, and in the following century the raising of this crop was occasionally prohibited. Saffron, widely demanded for culinary, medicinal, and industrial purposes, was an export crop of considerable value, certainly by the thirteenth century. Chief centres for the cultivation of this plant were Aragon, Catalonia, Granada, Toledo, and Valencia.

Of course, the production of many of these commodities was localized, while restricted demand and limited facilities for interregional trade prevented the marketing of goods over a wide area. An exception may be made for the cereal grains. Bread was everywhere the staff of life, and the raising of grain the primary consideration in the disposition of arable land. The commonest grains were wheat, barley, millet, oats, and rye, of which the first two were export crops during the time Spain helped to feed Rome. Wheat and barley are also the most frequent grain dues found in the *Becerro*; on the whole, the evidence of this record suggests that fourteenth-century Castile produced approximately equal quantities of the two grains. The species and the quality of grain raised in different regions is a matter of speculation, but all of them, in one form or another, were basic foodstuffs for man and beast.

Medieval Spain both exported and imported grain. Although Asso waxed eloquent over the ability of Aragon to supply wheat to far-off Syria, no available data prove that for the peninsula as a whole exports normally exceeded imports. Grain frequently passed down the Ebro in foreign bottoms at the same time that other parts of Spain were importing wheat from abroad. In the fifteenth century, and probably earlier, even Saragossa resorted to the practice of stopping grain ships on the river and forcing them to unload a portion of the cargo to

[1] Asso (*op. cit.* pp. 121–2) asserted that the Moors brought the mulberry tree as far north as Saragossa.
[2] P. Boissonnade, *Life and Work in Medieval Europe*, p. 236.

satisfy the needs of the city. After the thirteenth century, Barcelona and Valencia regularly subsidized imports of grain;[1] and, to replenish public granaries in time of scarcity, some towns obtained royal licences to stop grain ships at sea and compel the owners to sell the grain to Spaniards.

Town charters of the eleventh and twelfth centuries frequently authorized municipalities to establish 'just' prices for provisions sold within their jurisdictions, thus paving the way for a flood of price-fixing ordinances in the next three centuries. Perpignan fixed maximum prices for seven kinds of meat in 1303; and between 1300 and 1332 Barcelona established legal retail prices for capons, kids, hens, eggs, partridge, pigeons, rabbit, pork, beef, mutton, and fish. On a national scale, Alfonso the Wise (1252–84) made at least one experiment with the price-fixing panacea for short harvests and rising demand. In the wake of a calamitous epidemic the Castilian Cortes of 1351 set maximum prices for barley, rye, wheat, and wine; again in 1369 and 1373 (and certainly other years) parliamentary price-fixing was invoked.

The extent to which price-fixing, adopted ostensibly for the benefit of the urban population, and ubiquitous sales taxes worked to the disadvantage of the agricultural producer varied widely, since all producers were not equally dependent upon markets. The growth of towns, the rise of fairs, and itinerant merchants quickened their interest in market phenomena; on the other hand, the idea that there was a strictly 'closed' agrarian economy in any country during the Middle Ages is gradually being dispelled.

Price history provides one measure of the increasing importance of markets in which agricultural commodities were exchanged for money. An exhaustive search for data from which to compile price indexes has uncovered only discontinuous quotations for Aragon and Navarre in the last half of the thirteenth century; adequate statistics do not appear before the second half of the fourteenth century. The data, which are restricted as closely as possible to competitive market prices, represent the purchases of hospitals, cathedrals, and the royal household. Barley, cheese, chick-peas, lambs, lard, hens, hogs, oats, olive oil, rye, saffron, wheat, and wine are among the products quoted discontinuously in 1275–1325; prices for a longer list of agricultural commodities were found for 1351–1500.

Agricultural prices in Navarre ranged from a minimum of 21·7

---

[1] Thus, in August, 1347, the city government of Barcelona authorized contracts with merchants who agreed to import grain during December of this year. The importers were to receive a bounty of 8*d.* per quarter (*cortera*) of wheat, 4*d.* for a quarter of barley. Bounties were actually paid on nearly 100,000 quarters of grain (*Rubriques de Bruniquer*, IV [Barcelona, 1915], p. 164).

(1421–30= 100) in 1351 to a maximum of 96·8 in 1390; the trend was irregularly upward for almost 50 years. The indexes for Aragon, Navarre, and Valencia in the fifteenth century depict violent year-to-year fluctuations resulting from erratic crops, shifts in demand, war, and political interference with production and trade. In 1451–1500 the trend was sharply downward in Valencia; in Aragon the downward pressure on prices was offset to a significant degree by increasing the tariff of gold coins.[1]

Sheep, chiefly valued for their wool, and other domestic animals provided medieval Spain with meat, hides for the leather-goods industry, and 'horse' power. Cattle pastured with sheep on their semi-annual migrations, and many estates owned cattle, goats, horses, asses, and mules in numbers sufficient to dispel the idea that only the sheep were allowed to graze. The will of a Count of Barcelona (993) left 147 cows and 47 mares to be distributed among fifteen monasteries. Although cheese appears early as an article of food, beef cattle were far more important than milch-cows. Swine roamed the wooded areas everywhere, but, especially in the north-east, feeding on acorns; and the consumption of pork was relatively high because it 'removed suspicion of Judaism'. The ubiquitous hen was conspicuous among rents in kind; ordinarily, only one hen a year was required.

Besides oxen, which were used almost universally for ploughing and draught, the Moors encouraged the use of mules, asses, and, to a lesser extent, horses for farm work, presumably because of the greater efficiency of these animals.[2] Yet, in a memorial read before the Economic Society of Madrid in 1795, Miguel Antonio de Texada insisted that the displacement of oxen by mules was one of the causes of agricultural decadence in the late Middle Ages. Thanks to the Moors, the native Spanish horse was improved by cross-breeding; but this animal may have continued to be of greater importance to the *caballero* than to the rustic. Military necessity also explains the fourteenth-century Castilian law which prohibited the ownership of more than two mules, except when one possessed a proportionately larger number of horses.

Little is known, except by inference and analogy, of the implements and methods of cultivation and harvesting. The following seem to have been all the tools of a Catalonian farm described in an eleventh-century will: a plough and ploughshare, a hoe, a 'large' hoe, an adze, an axe, a pruning-hook, a sickle, and a shovel. The crudeness of the tools often necessitated the repetition of the work, and time was lost from the breaking of implements mostly made of wood. Abu

---

[1] E. J. Hamilton, *Money, Prices, and Wages in Valencia, Aragon, and Navarre, 1351–1500* (Cambridge, Mass., 1936), pp. 107–8.
[2] Cf. the discussion on p. 143 above.

Zacaria's *Book of Agriculture* contains a diagram of a twelfth-century harrow, with large wooden teeth, probably a superior type of tool for the time.

Surface areas were frequently reckoned in labour-time units or as the space requiring designated amounts of seed. The *aranzada* (or *pariliata*), which was the area a man and a yoke of oxen could plough in a day, was about an acre in thirteenth-century Castile.

In spite of their frequent depredations on farming land, the roving sheep were welcome at certain seasons because of their contribution to the productive powers of the soil. Leases sometimes specified that tenants should keep vineyards and olive groves well manured, an exceedingly difficult task where the land was poor and barnyards relatively scarce. Zacaria wrote extensively on the selection of fertilizer (dung, urine, human excrement, ashes, and decayed vegetable matter) appropriate to different soils and crops, but his precepts were entirely empirical. The Spaniards were pruning their orchards and olive groves at least as early as the twelfth century. Zacaria displayed an unusually complete knowledge of grafting; he probably had first-hand knowledge of methods employed in grafting fig, olive, citrus, and other trees. Underground silos for the storage of grain were in use, possibly continuously from Roman times. The use of horses for tramping grain in the open, so that the wind would blow away the chaff, made progress—there are parts of Spain in which this method has not varied in the last 600 years—but threshing with the flail persisted in many rural regions.

Of crop rotation, we have little precise knowledge. In Spain as elsewhere bare fallowing was universal, sometimes after one crop, sometimes after two or more. The three-course rotation was certainly known; but it is likely that—for climatic reasons—over a great part of the peninsula the two-course was predominant, as it seems to have been in the fertile province of Roussillon. There has been no adequate study of the Spanish field systems. No study of manorial organization suggests the probable lay-out of fields and pastures and woodlands in relation to the village, the lord's castle, or the monastery. Fallow fields were thrown together for common pasture; co-operative labour in ploughing, cultivating, and harvesting was not infrequent; and the drawing of lots for the available strips of arable land was practised in some places; but the extent to which 'collectivism' in the broader sense of the word prevailed is a moot point. Commons belonging to the crown and to the towns comprised many thousands of acres— much of which was wooded and never broken to the plough. But the 'communal' use of woodlands, springs, pastures, and other natural resources usually entailed collective, if not personal, responsibility for the payment of taxes and dues and carried with it restrictions as to the number of cattle that might be grazed or the amount of firewood that could be cut. Deprived of Marxian inspiration, one would find it hard to agree that in the Middle Ages, as in 'every period of Spanish history', we find 'communal holdings on a collectivist or even Communist basis'.[1]

IV. *Conclusions*

Burdened with the brunt of the Reconquest, it was Spain's lot to pay most of the cost of 'saving' all Europe. Centuries of intermittent warfare took their toll in neglected fields, while the 'devastation caused by the interminable incursions of hostile troops rendered the naturally infertile *meseta* more barren still, and discouraged men from any attempt to till the soil'.[2] Standing armies, though not so large as often reported, not only withdrew men from productive occupations but also encouraged vagabondage and mendicancy, especially in Castile where the *ley de vagos* has an unbroken history from the Middle Ages to the twentieth century. During lulls in hostilities professional soldiers, accustomed to plunder, were loath to return to peaceful employments; and idleness came to vie with military and ecclesiastical services as a most honourable occupation.

Artificial barriers to trade seriously curtailed the division of labour, as did the defects of the means of transport, the dearth of sound money, the confusion of weights and measures, sumptuary legislation, and the lack of adequate marketing facilities in general. Embargoes, internal tariffs, and other political impediments to commerce created the perdurable force of regionalism, separating Christian provinces and towns from each other as effectively as Catholic regions were shut off from territory in the hands of infidels. The Reconquest did not eradicate economic isolation within the peninsula. The *Corona de Aragón* was always a loose confederation of semi-independent kingdoms whose economic 'nationalism' persisted almost unaltered after the union of Castile and Aragon in 1479. Throughout the sixteenth century, the Aragonese enjoyed only the same rights as foreigners in the Castilian overseas possessions.

In 1955 approximately two-fifths of Spain's 50,000,000 hectares were under cultivation; forests and grazing land comprised one-half the total area; and waste land amounted to about 10 per cent. Comparable figures for land utilization in the Middle Ages do not exist, but it is

---

[1] J. H. Retinger, *Tierra Mexicana* (London, 1929), p. 12.
[2] R. B. Merriman, *op. cit.*, I, p. 86.

safe to say that more land was idle and fewer acres cultivated by the medieval Spaniards. Unfortunately, the lack of reliable data left room for the illusion of extraordinary prosperity in the Middle Ages. As Spain's New World adventures became unprofitable, her political economists conjured up a picture of a wealthy and populous country in medieval times, in contrast to the poverty and depopulation of the seventeenth century.[1] In general, the positive limitations to the productive capacity of the agricultural economy deserve more emphasis. Christian and Moorish Spain alike experienced frequent droughts, floods, plagues of locusts, and harvest failures. Epidemics, recurrent for centuries before the Black Death, followed in the wake of famine and hunger. In modern times, still predominantly an agricultural country, Spain supports with difficulty some 30 million inhabitants. This is surely three times, and probably four times, the population of peninsular Spain at any time prior to 1500. At best the fields and orchards and pastures and vineyards of medieval Spain provided not too generous rations for seven or eight million Christians, Jews, and Moors. Yet, in view of the resources Spain was able to muster for the conquest of the New World, one may err on the low side in appraising the nation's material progress in the late Middle Ages.

[1] See, for instance, Juan de Valverde Arrieta, *Despertador, que trata de la gran fertilidad, riquezas, baratos, armas y caballos que España solía tener, y la causa de los daños y falta, con el remedio suficiente* (Madrid, 1578).

Medieval Agrarian Society in its Prime

§ 4. The lands east of the Elbe and German colonization eastwards

When the Western Slavs, from their home between the Dnieper, the Carpathians, the Bug and the Pripet marshes, percolated slowly as far as the Eastern Alps, the Saale, the Elbe and the Gulf of Kiel, into lands that Germans had abandoned, their very modest economic life corresponded with their youth as a people and the simplicity of their political and social organization. The latter had not developed beyond the stage of the patriarchal family and clan. It seems likely that such groups were also the units of economic life. For the Western Slavs this is not proved. But the legal position of these groups, and the place of the kindred in matters of inheritance among freemen at a later date, suggest their primitive economic significance.[1] Life was still to a great degree based on the collecting economy—fishing, the gathering of wild honey, and trapping; but the Slavs brought animals with them into their new territories, at first mainly swine. They were, however, acquainted with agriculture; and its practice was encouraged by their occupation of lands which Germans had formerly tilled. But they were not numerous enough to occupy them all at once; and there must have been some reversion to woodland. They may have learnt something about the arts of daily life from the few Germans who remained behind; but no marked influence of this kind can be traced.

Our sources tell us little about Slavonic life before the tenth century; and even then what we learn is more political and social than economic. We find the Wends, between the Elbe and the Oder, at the time of the German conquest still in a state of almost tribal organization, with chieftains and under-chieftains. But Moravia, and later Bohemia and Poland, became strong principalities, with officials and professional fighting men—and at the same time with an influential clergy. Increasing political activity and the maintenance of these dominant groups had to be provided for. Grants of land and services legally imposed were the solution. The princes acquired vast estates. Endowed from these, officials, members of the *druzyna* (the 'followers') and 'knights' swelled such nobility as had survived from among the chieftains of primitive times. The Church also was splendidly endowed. About the supply of labour one thing is clear—the persistence of a class of slaves, much diminished as it was by the export slave trade.[2] They were called Smurden

---

[1] Cf. p. 52, above.   [2] Cf. p. 53, above.

by the Sorbs, Smarden by the Poles; that is, the Dirty Folk. Less clear is
the way in which the bulk of the people, originally free, was subjected
to services. The process must have been slow and not uniform; but
it is evident that this class could not hold its own against those above it,
and suffered from the growing power of the princes. Its legal fall into
a state of dependence began with the imposition of an endless series of
obligations to the state, some of which—such as 'carriages', and hospitality for the prince and his officials—had direct economic value. And
as claims to dues and services were transferred from the prince to the
nobility and the Church, the freeman became dependent on a lord.
Some freemen commended themselves to lords, to safeguard their
inheritance or to acquire land. In short the class of true freemen
dwindled away. At best, there were some survivors personally free but
settled on a lord's land.

Social conditions developed in the same way, from the tenth to the
twelfth century, among the Wends who lived along the Elbe, as they
came under German rulers. A fully developed state and Church had to
be maintained. Conquest gave a complete royal prerogative over land.
Thanks to this, margraves and knights, bishops and monasteries were
gorged with it—and the peasants who lived on it.

So, and for similar reasons, the situation was reproduced that had
developed in the German peasant world after the creation of the Frankish
Empire and the establishment of the Church—a society with a sovereign
prince; beneath him upper-class lords of the soil in their various grades;
and over against these a lower, mostly soil-bound, or completely unfree
population of the true economic producers; though no doubt there
were intermediate types—warriors who worked for their own maintenance, like the *Withasen*[1] among the Sorbs, or the noblemen impoverished by divisions of inheritance among the Poles.

If in this way a class division by vocation superseded a division by
blood and birth, it was operative only in the agricultural sphere.
Industrial and agricultural activity were closely associated; long-distance
trade was in foreign hands, those of Jews, Moslems, Vikings and Germans. Native economic life was concentrated in the villages. These
were very small and were still often moved about. The frail unsightly
huts of the common people were easily knocked down and rebuilt.
Agriculture had increased; millet had become prominent, beside the
other usual types of grain. As open or easily cleared land was brought
into use, the arable consisted of irregular blocks, often scattered over
the woods and heaths. Cultivation was unsystematic and extensive, and

---

[1] These were mounted men owing military service, of the tribes between the Elbe
and the Oder. At a later date under German rule, they mostly held no more than a
single *Hufe*. They often served as local headmen.

its sites were constantly changed. The plough was the so-called 'hook' (*uncus*) drawn by two oxen or one or two horses. It only scratched the ground; but it is not true that the Slavs cultivated only light sandy soils. Where they found heavier soils clear of forest they worked them also. As there were no field-ways to individual peasant's fields in the blocks of land, and as the cultivated area was shifted from time to time, there must have been, technically, what might be called communal agriculture. Agricultural dues were therefore based not on areal units but on the number of ploughs employed. The original way of levying tithe in the Slavonic Church points in the same direction. Normally every tenth sheaf should have been taken from the fields. Instead of this, we find in various places—on the Wendish frontiers, in Pomerania and Poland—a frequent, though not universal, fixed charge in kind, or even in money, imposed on those liable to tithe. So also many dues were levied by the head-man (*starosta*) or the lord's agent (*centurio*), not on individual holdings (which hardly existed) but on groups of neighbours who yet were not a legal commune, or on greater units such as the Polish *opole* (*vicinia*).[1] Among these dues, for instance, was the *narzaz* in cattle, perhaps a pasture due. Although agriculture made progress, cattle and horse keeping and collecting still played a great part in the Slavonic economy: the swine were now relatively less important.

The lords used their land in part as a source of dues and services as already explained; but they cultivated part of it themselves. We have no clear picture of the extent of their *curiae, allodia, predia*, as they are called. Later evidence suggests that they contained at least enough arable for several plough teams. Labour conditions are also obscure. Servile ploughmen and herdsmen there certainly were: there might also be services of various kinds from the dependent tenants. How the two types of labour were interconnected is not clear. The most striking trait of this old Slavonic lordship is the existence of groups of men owing personal services, often living side by side. We meet cultivators (*aratores*), herders of mares, swineherds; constantly fishermen and honey collectors; in places beaver trappers, hunters of many kinds, stablemen, cooks and various handicraftsmen. All had land by which they lived. We can trace a progressive differentiation of functions, but one that is determined primarily by the interests of the lords as consumers. It goes furthest in connexion with the hunting that they loved, and in their domestic establishments. Yet it supplies distinct incentives to the evolution of Slavonic economic life in this period. Based on this organization, which required a fair amount of economic guidance, the lords built up their self-sufficing natural economies. Only a few goods —slaves, furs, wax—went in bulk to those distant markets which

[1] Cf. p. 61, above.

foreign traders opened up. Characteristically, they are products of the very earliest type of collecting and fighting economy; not of the later more intensive developments. The whole organization is very much looser than that which Germans introduced under similar conditions; for the Germans had inherited traditions from the Roman villa.

The new institution of *hospites* helped to build up these service-owing groups. At first the *hospites* were no doubt immigrant freemen who were able to enter into contractual relations. But the class, as found in Bohemia and Poland in the twelfth century, contains many servile individuals who had been granted fixed contractual conditions of tenure and service. The tenure was always uncertain. But the legal limitation of the burdens reveals a rise of the lower classes, no doubt secured by the need for better qualified labour. Early in the thirteenth century we find craftsmen in particular established as *hospites* in Silesia and Poland; but the tenure was also used to attract agricultural colonists. Growing population led to some gradual extension of the cultivated area. It was usually a case of crude 'assart' by burning on the margins of the forest, which did not always mean a permanent addition to that area. Traces of this earliest native clearing epoch are found in the place names in -*ujezd* (Czech), or -*ujazd* (Polish), which implies the demarcation of an area by riding round it. Such names are found in lowland Bohemia and Moravia, in the Lusatias, Silesia and—less frequently—in parts of Poland. There was as yet no attack on the great primeval forests, which required heavy and systematic felling.

Among the Baltic peoples, from the original Prussians up to the Esths, conditions resembled those of the second phase of Slavonic evolution: a population as a whole still uniform; a collecting and agrarian economy in which herds were important; incipient differentiations of property; and a modest nobility sprung from the leaders of patriarchal family groups.

During the later Middle Ages, from the twelfth century onwards, this rural economy of Central and North-eastern Europe was transformed, mainly as a result of German immigration. Existing developments were caught up and absorbed into the transformation. But the East German rural colonizing process, which gave direction, form and power to it, was only part of the wider so-called German East Movement. For centuries, in medieval and modern times, that movement has taken most varied forms: frontier defence and conquest; the foundation of monasteries; mercenary service or commercial penetration; every kind of cultural influence and especially migration and the founding of town and villages. We must know something at least of the main lines of this migration and settlement if we are to understand the transformation of rural life.

Germans were already moving east in Charlemagne's time, across the southern part of the ethnographic frontier, as it then was, crossing the Pustertal and running along the Enns. Between 800 and 1100 an area about corresponding to the Austria of 1919, in which the Slavonic population had been very thin, was Germanized. Agrarian institutions of the old South German type were introduced, as has been seen.[1]

Meanwhile in Old Germany forest clearing, embanking, and draining went forward. Towards 1100 progress was being made across the densely forested frontier along the Saale and the Elbe. Further east, Marks of the Empire were created—Meissen, the Lusatias—in which imperial officials backed by German knights ruled a native Slavonic population. In the twelfth century similar Marks were established lower down the Elbe, from Brandenburg to East Holstein. Mecklenburg and Pomerania were brought into vassalage to Germany, as Bohemia, Moravia and Poland already had been.

Christian missions went hand in hand with German rule, Praemonstratensians and Cistercians being specially active.

The German margraves and bishops, and later the Teutonic Knights in Prussia, had to make their rule secure. The settlement of Germans allied in faith and blood was an obvious means. From that an increase of military, financial and economic resources might be expected. The spiritual and lay lords who were called in from Germany and endowed with land, and the surviving native noblemen, imitated the policy in their own interest. Old Germany was ready to supply what the Marks demanded. There were men enough willing to go; for population was growing and peasants were becoming more conscious of the economic drawbacks of feudal obligations. Some were uprooted by the inundations on the North Sea coast and by the frequent local famines. And there was merit in fighting unbelievers. The internal colonization of Germany had furnished varying, but well-tested, types of field, of village and of law. They had already been tried out in the Danube valley and the Eastern Alps. And urban life had gradually developed to a point at which the main lines of town layout and town law were established and could be imitated on fresh sites. Of all these things the German lords of the eastern front made increasingly zealous and systematic use from the beginning of the twelfth century.

The Slavonic princes of the East soon learned to imitate them. The eastward pressure of the Empire, and the struggle with the stronger and better equipped German territories, forced them to aim at a swift and comprehensive strengthening of their states. As things stood, this could not be expected to spring from native sources. Anything that these could yield in the way of greater political and predial freedom, or

[1] Cf. p. 51 above.

technical economic development, was far inferior to what might be attained through the import of Germans and German methods. The nobles and the Church imitated the princes for their own economic advantage. Their many charters show what great things they hoped from colonization by Germans or in the German style. A thirteenth-century Polish chronicler tells how the Bishop of Gnesn, by laying out villages, raised the money yield of a certain district from 1 to 800 marks.

So the two sides competed with one another in the work of German colonization. A colonizing fever broke out. Princes set great enterprises on foot—the Margrave of Meissen, before 1162, settled at his own expense 800 contiguous *Hufen* in the frontier forests of the Erzgebirge —or they urged monasteries and immigrant German noblemen to do so. The native lords everywhere sought to get yields from lands which had hitherto given no yield. Monasteries and knights acquired woods and wastes by purchase, to settle them with Germans and often to sell them when settled. A regular body of entrepreneurs developed who organized colonization to profit by it. The Church, in its own interest or under pressure from the princes, came to terms with the German settlers over the regulation of tithe.

Whether the lord was a German or a Slav, colonization went on in much the same way. German wars of conquest or conversion neither exterminated the heathen natives nor even drove them out. In the twelfth century, speaking generally, they affected only the immediately adjacent frontier strips of Brandenburg, East Holstein and Mecklenburg; and again in the thirteenth, and more severely, East Prussia. True, German lords sometimes forcibly transplanted Wendish peasants, heathen generally. But with that the Slavs were quite familiar. And the wars of the eastern peoples among themselves were at times very destructive. But apart from these occasional devastations, and although native cultivation had made some progress, there was cultivable land enough and to spare in the East. Even open and naturally accessible areas were still utterly unexploited, judged by German agricultural standards. But above all there were vast reserves of potential arable in some of the forests, and in marshlands that the natives did not know how to dyke and drain. This is true especially of those immense strategic frontier forests which the Slavs had left untouched and which were in the hands of the princes.[1]

It was under these conditions that Germans migrated eastward from Austria towards Southern Moravia and Hungary, even before 1100; and in the twelfth century crossed the Saale-Elbe line everywhere up to the Baltic. They moved forward on a broad but irregular front. The

[1] Cf. p. 57, above.

southern wing was far ahead, and had reached remote Transylvania and the foot of the Tatra in the second half of the twelfth century. The northern front, down to 1200, lay about the line—West Bohemia, the Lusatias, the Middle Mark of Brandenburg, Central Mecklenburg. There were commercial outposts as far away as Riga. Early in the thirteenth century, the migrants crossed Pomerania, Eastern Brandenburg, Silesia, and Northern Moravia. They then broke into the New Mark, Great and Little Poland and Eastern Bohemia. By the 'thirties they were across the new territory of the Teutonic Knights on the Lower Vistula, by Kulm and Thorn. Effective settlement in Prussia, it is true, only got under way from 1280, after great rebellions had been crushed; but then it moved swiftly and reached its peak between 1300 and 1350. On the northern and southern edges of the Carpathians German colonization had reached the Dunajec before 1300; by about 1350 it had crossed the San and entered Red Russia, whilst it filled wide mountain regions in upper Hungary. This extension coincided with more intensive development in older colonized regions—but not in all of them. Parts of Mecklenburg and Pomerania were not much affected; the interior of the Lusatias and of Pomerelia, with the Slavonic cores of Bohemia and Moravia, hardly at all. The farther east it went, the more broken up the movement was. It had passed its peak by 1350, having already slackened to the west. At some isolated points on the extreme east— Red Russia, East Prussia—it continued, and even into modern times. It was about 1350 that the last group of German forest villages was built in the Egerland. At that time, in a section of mid-Silesia, where most of the arable had been won from the forest by German settlers, further felling for settlement was checked. In Poland, the first royal orders for forest conservation come from about 1450. By the close of the Middle Ages the outer limits of the region that was more or less permeated with German colonists stretched from Transylvania to Estonia.

The migrants came from all the German stocks—High Germans for the South-east; Middle Germans for forest work in the centre: Flemings, Seelanders and Hollanders for dyking and draining. The great extension of the movement is only explained by the fact that colonists bred colonists; for all over the world new settlers have big families. Migration from Old Germany in many cases slackened early. Conditions of tenure in the colonized areas also encouraged this colonization by colonists' families. Law or custom favoured the undivided inheritance of peasant holdings; so there were many younger sons without land.

Not only all German stocks but all classes participated—clergy, knights, traders and craftsmen, peasants. Miners also came into the metalliferous Sudeten and Carpathian ranges and their outliers, and into the salt-bearing country about Cracow. Not all these classes, however, were represented everywhere. Only knights and a few townsmen were found in the Eastern Baltic lands. In Eastern Poland, in Central Bohemia, Moravia and Hungary, there were again few but townsmen, with knights and ecclesiastics.

And all those classes took a hand in the remodelling of agrarian institutions. It was not merely that the various social and economic groups had to be adjusted to one another; not merely that every non-agricultural migrant or group of migrants increased the demand for agricultural produce—besides all that, each class had its own contribution to make, its special influence to exert. The clergy and the nobility, higher and lower, responsible as landlords and as lords of the natives' bodies for new settlement and the shifting of settlements, often took the initiative or the actual leadership in agrarian reform, and in connexion with it laid out demesnes of their own. The knightly class also provided some organizers of settlements.[1] That was even truer of the burgess class. But the peasants were by far the most influential element in the whole movement. There was continuous peasant colonization all the way from the Elbe–Saale line to that of the Bober and the Oder; and a great deal east of that, from Pomerania, through the New Mark of Brandenburg, to Silesia and Northern Moravia. Eastward again stretched two long tongues of colonization—one across the Vistula to Prussia, only checked by the collapse of the Teutonic Order in the fifteenth century; the other across Little Poland into Red Russia, and by the sixteenth century in places even east of Lemberg. Between them the line curved far back: the flats of Great Poland were hardly touched. In the heart of Bohemia and Moravia were only islands, though often important islands, or scattered fragments of colonization. Two streams of colonists—one from Silesia and one from the Danube—united to play on the mining districts of Upper Hungary, where the prevalence of place names in -hau indicates active clearing by Germans from the thirteenth to the fifteenth centuries. In Western Hungary a strip broader than the modern Burgenland was Germanized; but the heart of the Hungarian plain was untouched. Beyond it, in Transylvania, three great blocks of German civilization rose on peasant foundations.

This area of peasant occupation was only the core of the area affected by the whole German East Movement. Outside it lay the Baltic settlements of the Knights and widespread German urban settlement. This last reached beyond, and often served to hold together, the very patchy settlement by peasants.

But for this peasant occupation, however, that agrarian transformation of the East which we are now to describe would have been unthinkable. In its beginning, only Germans could transmit those

[1] See p. 461, below.

forms of law, economy, and settlement which they had developed; handle them with complete success; or extend and adjust them to a colonial environment. For a long time Slavonic and Baltic peoples could at best only imitate the externals of German life. So we shall expect to find least real transformation where there was only a German lord, or an imitator of one, with indigenous workers. At first that was the situation in the Marks: from the tenth to the twelfth century immigrant monasteries and knights were given by the princes villages of servile Wends. As German colonization set in, these were assimilated more or less to German standards. Often things went so far as a complete adoption of German law and a complete new layout of the fields in the German style. This so-called 'economic Germanization' was frequently followed by the linguistic. Even east of the Marks, for example in Silesia and Great Poland, such developments were common on old settled land. Several of the small Slavonic hamlets might be thrown together, or the village and its fields might be extended. Often the native population was taken into the new German village community. Here and there in the colonized territory, natives—or in Pomerania and Mecklenburg Danes—filled out the ranks of the Germans. This occurred both in the early years, when German immigrants were rare, and towards the end of the medieval colonizing era, when the supply was failing more and more. At first the Teutonic Knights seldom put Prussians into new villages, and usually kept the races apart, whilst their neighbour the Bishop of Ermland did the reverse—mixing the races even in individual villages. But towards the end of the fourteenth century the Order itself was obliged to make more use of Prussians and other non-Germans, because the flow from Old Germany had long since dried up and the descendants of the settled German colonists were not numerous enough for the work. Settled under Germans, in villages with a German field system, the natives tended to be Germanized in working habits, in culture, and in speech.

In Courland, Livonia and Estonia all the labour was native, since already the Knights and the ecclesiastics were generally organizing demesnes of their own. So here any agrarian reform had to come exclusively from above.

As time went on the German agrarian system began to spread at other points also beyond the limits of German colonization. It appears, for example, though often in modified form, on the northern and eastern edges of Silesia and especially in Poland, under Polish lords and among settlers who were predominantly Poles. This was the so-called colonization 'under German law'.[1] It spread far beyond the German colonization. In Poland some 1500 villages are to be found—mainly in the

[1] Cf. p. 500, below.

west and south—with the name *Wola*, that is 'Freeton'—usually combined with a personal name or an adjective: evidently they had at some time been legally privileged. Although many of these, especially in the east, are products of modern enterprise, it is certain that the phenomenon can be traced to the gradual influence of medieval German settlement on the Poles. From the spread of the *Waldhufendorf* [1] we may infer that all Southern Poland, especially the Carpathians and their foot-hills as far as Lemberg, and northward to the Upper Wieprz and the Bistrica nearly to Lublin, was newly settled or reorganized on German lines between the thirteenth and the fifteenth century. The same is probably true, though the type of village differs, of great parts of low-land Moravia.

But we cannot now clearly separate areas of German colonization from those of colonization 'under German law'. Pure German agrarian organization, introduced by pure or nearly pure German settlers, is most probably traceable where absolutely new land was won—especially in marshes and bogs, as on the Lower Elbe, in the Harz lowlands between the Ocker and the Bode, and on the delta of the Vistula about Danzig. For work of this kind only German immigrants were properly qualified. They were specially qualified also for the work of forest clearing; and though not all of it can be ascribed to them, they were primarily responsible for the clearing of the great continuous forests. They carried the new way of settlement eastward along the Sudetens and Carpathians as we have seen; and no doubt they were mainly responsible for the clearing of East Prussia. But on old-settled land the native and the German ways of settlement interacted, and the native way was to some extent immediately transformed. For the Middle Ages we cannot say precisely how the races were divided, since in later centuries non-Germans have been Germanized extensively, and *vice versa*. What we can ascertain is the diffusion of German or non-German land-measurements or dues, as shown in the documents; of village and field types still surviving or shown on old maps; or of concessions of German agrarian law, which we can often trace in a variety of ways even when no charter survives. Place names are not decisive evidence even when we have the medieval form. A place with a German name was probably founded by Germans. But immigrants often retained native names of villages, fields, and regions.

All that we can say with confidence is that, sometimes intermixed with areas of German settlement and sometimes stretching well beyond them, important areas remodelled their native agrarian organization on the German plan, without experiencing any extensive immigration of German peasants. Exact modern research has however revealed very

---

[1] Cf. p. 46, above and p. 465, below.

weighty evidence for medieval forest settlement by pure Germans in what are now Polish-speaking districts of Southern Poland. So one is inclined to assume that the introduction of the new agrarian organization did not occur over a very wide area entirely apart from German immigration. The regions affected by the immigration here assumed were, so far as we know, parts of Great and Little Poland and Central Moravia. Central Bohemia as a whole seems to have been very little changed as a result of the medieval German East movement; and Central Hungary not at all.

The arrangements that the Germans established sprang from those of Old Germany, but were not identical with them. The earliest colonists introduced some changes, and further change came as colonization moved eastward. One dominant fact is to be noted—the evolution of definitely marked types of organization, which show uniformity at least over considerable areas. For this there are various causes: most German colonization was on the *tabula rasa* of virgin soil, or at least on occupied land that could be legally treated as virgin: when innumerable new or remodelled settlements were made in a short time, the same procedure tended to be reproduced: each settler owed much the same obligations to his prince or lord; and princely or seignorial power was usually strong enough to stamp uniformity on the whole process. This last consideration is specially true of Prussia, where the Master of the Teutonic Knights directed most of the work himself, and settlement was on a planned system. On the other hand the special conditions in eastern regions led to a fresh combination of the traditional elements of German life, so that a distinct colonial agricultural organization came into existence.

The natural environment in the eastern regions—climate, surface features, the character and fertility of the soil—were not so different from those of Old Germany as to require any thorough alterations of method. What differences can be traced at first were due mainly to the influence of native political or economic traditions. Subsequently, the natural environment influenced agrarian organization and brought about greater changes. The modern transition to large units of agricultural production in the East is not unconnected with its natural fitness for large-scale corn growing and corn export.

There are so many and such important features common to the new colonial agricultural organization over the whole area now under discussion, that compared with them the by no means negligible modifications due to varying local conditions, the peculiarities of native law and economy, and the extent to which these were transformed, fall into the background. And since this whole East German and East European

agrarian transformation was brought about through and by actual
settlement, the processes of settlement must now be examined.

Settlements were made in every case on the land of some lord.
Nowhere do we find the absolute peasant property (*Allod*) that had
once existed widely in Old Germany, and was still to be found there.
The *Allod* mentioned in the so-called Kulmer Handfeste of 1233—a
primary law for the lands of the Teutonic Order—is not a true property
but a derivative right of tenure by hereditary quit-rent (*Erbzinsrecht*).
Nor has *Allod* its full meaning when applied to the type of demesne
called later a *Vorwerk*.[1] Originally most of the land had belonged to the
princes, whether natives or conquerors, who had vast areas at their
disposal, especially of uncultivated waste and forest—the very places to
which colonists went. The Teutonic Knights claimed complete royal
prerogative over land, and there were also native lords for colonists to
deal with; even in the Marks, in Brandenburg for example, Slavonic
Supans had survived; and naturally, wherever there were surviving
native princes, there was also a native aristocracy. Even the Knights left
the free upper-class Prussians in possession, provided they were loyal;
and so did the Church in Prussia. New immigrant lords, monastic or
knightly, acquired gifts of land or fiefs from the princes and native lords
—very largely with a view to colonization. It was the princes especially
who wished to exploit their waste land and make it yield knights' service
and peasants' dues.

The grants were often very extensive and the ecclesiastical orders
were the chief beneficiaries, especially the Cistercians and the Praemonstratensians, whose great days coincided with the beginning of colonization in the twelfth and thirteenth centuries. But since the unit of
ecclesiastical ownership was a single monastery, the centralized knightly
orders became greater owners. Particularly in the thirteenth century,
the three great orders of knights acquired very extensive property in
the most various eastern regions. Much of their land was suitable for
settlement. Not only did the Teutonic Knights acquire from the Duke
of Masovia that territory east of the lower Vistula which they were able
to make into a regular state; but even before that they had acquired
great estates elsewhere, in Moravia for instance, and for a time in
Transylvania. Similarly the preceptories of the Templars and the
Knights of St John were scattered more or less over all the eastern lands.
The Cistercian Abbey of Leubus in Silesia illustrates the amount of land
that a single house could have entrusted to it for settlement: partly in
association with daughter houses, it received from the Duke of Silesia
500 *Hufen* in the Bober-Katzbachgebirge in 1216–18; 400 more in 1225
in the see of Lebus on the Oder; in the same year from the Duke of

[1] See p. 476, below.

Great Poland 2000 *Hufen* on the Netze, and 3000 more in 1233 lower down the stream. In this region of the Warthe and the Netze, the Duke had already granted the Teutonic Order 500 *Hufen* in 1224, and a large estate to the Templars, who also acquired 1000 *Hufen* about Küstrin in 1232 and 3000 about Utsch in 1233. The figures can be used to trace the growth of colonization.

Individuals were similarly endowed, and undertook settlement on a large scale. The Teutonic Knights in the early days of their rule in Prussia, and again round about 1300, made grants to knightly or burgess capitalists of from 100 *Hufen* (over 4000 acres) up to 1440 *Hufen* (more than 93 square miles). Among the grantees was a man of knightly family from Meissen who was also carrying on large-scale colonizing operations in North Moravia. And this is not an isolated case of a colonizing undertaker who moved eastward step by step. The endowment by the Margraves of Brandenburg of the so-called 'castle-owning nobility' (*Schlossgesessener Adel*), to protect the frontier against the Poles, was on a particularly extensive scale. Among them the von Wedels had no less than 59 villages in 1337; and in 1374 they got 5000 *Hufen* more as a fief. There were similar developments in Bohemia. German settlement along the upper Moldau was due to the famous family of the Witigonen in competition with the Cistercian houses of Goldenkron and Hohenfurth. Where endowments were so great, the work of settlement was certainly not completed at a stroke. Moreover those who had most land of their own, that is to say the princes and bishops, would only set up a village now here and now there. Actually the two processes approximated to one another; and did not differ in essentials from the single 'locations' carried out on smaller estates. *Locatio* in the charters means the laying-out of a new or the remodelling of an existing settlement. The Low German equivalent is *settinge* or *besettinge*. The Sachsenspiegel renders *locare* by *beseten*.[1]

Every *locatio* required a great deal of management: the site of the village, the way it was to be laid out, and the division of the fields, must be chosen with due consideration to all relevant factors. Topographical considerations bearing on access to water or risk of flooding must be taken into account; also in early days considerations of security; and always considerations of economy. The measurement of fields and their subdivisions called for skill in surveying. The procuring of German settlers was a special problem. Often they came from great distances. In early days, near the first frontiers, they came of their own accord, especially the Flemings; or a colonizing lord drew on his own people in Old Germany. In the first recorded case of a German settlement on virgin soil east of the Saale, in 1104, Wirpecht of Groitsch brought

---

[1] Cf. the XII *hida gesettes landes* in Ine's Law, § 64.

peasants from his mother's estate near the Main. We may suspect that the orders, especially the knightly orders who did so much colonization, drew settlers for the East from their network of estates widespread over Germany. But where such links with Old Germany were lacking, the attraction of colonists presented greater and greater difficulties as settlement went forward, especially for non-German lords. The demand was for a long time greater than the supply. We may infer this from the very attractive conditions offered to colonists at the start. We have sufficient evidence from the first half of the twelfth century that it was necessary to send agents to recruit emigrants in the various German regions.

Lastly, every colonizing enterprise required heavy capital expenditure: on the costs of the eastward trek; on the maintenance of the settlers until the first harvest or longer; on house-building and the timber for it; on church-building; and on the provision of mills, mill-streams and mill-dams, of inns and butchers' stalls. Hardly any details have survived, but we know something of the total costs, and we can infer them from the earnings of those who did the work. Middlemen often undertook or shared in the raising of the funds. To fulfil all those functions, for which the lord lacked the necessary experience or connexions or cash, the so-called locator had slipped in between him and the settlers. He undertook a single 'location' *en bloc* at his own risk, and saw to all the technical work. We meet locators on the middle and lower Elbe from about 1150, and from that time forward almost invariably in connexion with the village and town foundations over the whole North-eastern colonial area. Their work is much less conspicuous in the South-east. In Upper Lusatia and Great Poland the family name of Siedelmann implies the locator. In Pomerania the charters call him *possessor*, which suggests a German '*Besetzer*'. The terms *magister indaginis* and *hagemeister* also occur locally.

These men sprang from the most various classes. We meet both knights and peasants. Where the stream of colonists flowed rather feebly, as in Upper Silesia, we find native locators as early as 1250, in the great days of colonization. But so far as we can trace their origin, most locators were burgesses. The burgess class was the one most disposed to put acquired capital into land. As colonization went forward greater demands were made on the locator's capital. Out-and-out purchase of the land by him is found occasionally in early days on the Elbe: it became the rule in Silesia from about 1250. Even when he could re-sell to the settlers, in whole or in part, he had to stand out of his money for some time.

We learn about the 'location' system from the charters, especially from the contracts between locator and lord. The survival of these has been curiously patchy. The most abundant are from Silesia and the Prussian Ordensland. We have hardly any rural contracts from Mecklenburg, Brandenburg or Meissen; only a few from Bohemia or Moravia. But for the whole period they give us a very distinctive picture of the locator—a typical entrepreneur with technical knowledge of agriculture. We meet powerful families of the class, active in various lands, and always ready to employ their knowledge and great capitals in new directions as colonization developed. Then there are town locators who conduct one foundation after another and hand on the work from father to son. And we can assume that in rural areas, of which we know less, the professional locator who went from one successful job to another did at least part of the work.

Their earnings show the high value that was placed on their work, and how indispensable it became. For determining these, a system developed early which, although it varied in detail with the district, with the size of the operation, and with the date, remained uniform in principle even beyond the Middle Ages in the North-east. In the South-east the locator type, where it exists, is less developed. In Southern Bohemia it appears not to exist. Even in the North, a lord who was capable of acting as locator need not employ one. But even then we may conclude from the uniformity of the results that the system of village creation worked out by the locators had been followed in the main. We must examine this system in detail before returning to the question of the locator's earnings.

Medieval rural colonies always took the form of compact villages, and that was no doubt one reason for their success. Scattered homesteads in colonized territory are to be regarded as later developments— with perhaps a few exceptions. In Meissen, for example, a few hamlets were laid out in early times. But villages soon became the regular type, and their size tended to increase. Near Ratzeburg on the western Baltic coast, in the twelfth century 12 *Hufen* was an average size; so it was for long in Mecklenburg. In Western Brandenburg that would have been small. In Central Brandenburg villages of 30–60 *Hufen* seem already customary; and further east the big village was dominant. Early in the thirteenth century, in Silesia and adjacent regions where there was plenty of forest land to settle, 50 *Hufen* was the standard size. But villages varied greatly in the number of their *Hufen* and the size of their fields, and the *Hufe* as we know was a variable unit. In Brandenburg we find villages of German colonists often with 60–80 *Hufen*, and even more. The Teutonic Knights, whose colonies were the most uniform of all, usually favoured 60. But there were exceptions everywhere.

As to form, we must discuss the village and its field system separately. We do however find definite types of village associated customarily with definite types of fields. Of village forms, the so-called *Rundling* occurs in the strip of country nearest to Old Germany. The homesteads are laid out about a green—often with its pond—so that their out-buildings form a fairly continuous wall enclosing the village. This used to be considered a typically Slavonic form; but that is uncertain. It is not found deep in Slavonic territory and is found in places where Slavs never settled. Certainly it was planned with a view to defence; and that may explain its prevalence in the districts most fought over as the Germans advanced east.

A second type is also enclosed but more extended. There is the 'street village', made up of two rows of homesteads close together, facing one another; and the 'place' or 'plot' village (*Angerdorf*) in which the street, otherwise similar, widens out into an oblong or lancet-shaped 'place', where the church and oven and so forth are, and often the village pond. There are local variants of these forms, but as a rule in each district one is predominant. Thus the lowlands of Silesia have very uniform 'street villages' and 'plot villages' ; the Prussian *Ordensland*, a type transitional between the 'street' and the 'plot' village.

The third main type, as opposed to all these, has a loose ground plan. Homesteads along the street or by the stream do not stand shoulder to shoulder but 100 to 200 yards apart. The essential character of this type of village only becomes clear from its association with a particular way of dividing the fields, shortly to be described. But we can already note a gradual falling into the background of defensive considerations, and a greater prominence of the more economic.

The village types described are the genuine types of the colonizing era. This their emergence in bulk shows. But older Slavonic or other native types survived, mostly developed from the original, very irregular, hamlets.

Planned, systematic, field types were brought by the German colonists everywhere into the East; and the native types were more or less remodelled after them. Both for survey and the assignment of liabilities, the *Hufe* or *Lehen* was the foundation of the German land system. As in Old Germany, the *Hufe* included all the essentials of peasant economy—homestead, garden, orchard, arable land; in certain instances also forest and an appropriate share in the common property of the village and in common rights over wood, water, and pasture. But there was more than one kind of *Hufe*. From among the varieties brought from Old Germany, two in particular gradually became prominent—the small, or Flemish, of about 42 acres; the large, or Frankish, of more than 60. Beside them, on the Baltic coast there was the so-called *Hagenhufe*. The Flemish was mostly used on cultivated land, the Frankish on land cleared from forest: but the Teutonic Knights reckoned by the Flemish on both.

The *Hufe* could be laid out in various ways. There was the traditional

Gewanndorf, with its from three to more than 20 *Gewanne* (furlongs) in the fields of the dominant three-field system. Every *Hufe* had its strips in each *Gewann*. There were no field ways to the strips, only to the *Gewanne*. These could not be made geometrically accurate; but in this respect the colonial open-field was an improvement on the Old German. The *Gewanne* were fewer and more uniform, the strips more regularly laid out.

The tendency to some rational consolidation of each cultivator's shares in the fields, which appears here as a reaction against the often exaggerated subdivision and intermixture of the fields in Old Germany, continued to operate as colonization proceeded. In the forests of the Upper Main had sprung up the so-called *Gelänge* fields in which a considerable consolidation of individual holdings was already attained. The villages attached to them also show attempts to connect the homestead as much as possible with its land. Ultimately the development resulted in a new type of village and field, in which each *Hufe* was a single continuous area of plain regular form; and on it the homestead stood. This type was to become extraordinarily widespread in and beyond the German colonial area. The *Hufen* stretch side by side in long narrow strips, usually terminating on the village street or the brook. Each contains everything needed in farming—meadow by the brook; arable; grazing land; forest. The homestead stands at the foot, separated by a *Hufe*'s breadth from the next. The homesteads go to make up the long village with loose ground plan already mentioned, which from its regular association with the strip *Hufe* has been called the *Waldhufen* or *Hagen-* or *Marschhune* village—for this lay-out was chiefly adopted on forest land or in connexion with dyking.

In laying out open fields with *Gewanne*, a fixed and immediately practicable plan was needed from the first. Whole *Gewanne* could only be added as time went on by co-operative effort. But a single-strip *Hufe* could be added to a *Waldhufen* village at will, if land was available. In such villages the locator was usually assigned a fixed number of *Hufen*. Now and then he had the luck to get more, when the site was favourable and the fields could be extended. Even where the village and its fields were restricted to the original plan and size, several such standard villages might be established one after another.

As a result of these considerations, *Gewann* fields were found mainly on old cultivated land; but also on land cleared of forest, if it was level. Except where native types of fields survived, more or less modified by German influence, the true *Gewanndorf* dominated the wide plains of Germany beyond the Elbe. It is found also within the Sudeten ranges and so far afield as Hungary. Villages with *Gelange* fields are found at points of transition from old cultivated to cleared land, all the way

30

from Thuringia to Moravia, Great Poland, East Prussia, and the Burgenland, the type becoming clearer as you go east. Lastly the *Waldhufendorf* is characteristic of cleared land in the mountains and the approaches to them. It is continuous from the Erzgebirge along the Sudeten mountains to the Carpathians, and spreads far north and south of them, as we have seen. Often an unbroken chain of such villages stretches for miles up a valley. At the valley head—only reached late in the Middle Ages—the *Hufen* are often dwarfed into short narrow strips. But we find the *Waldhufe* also widespread in the plains—of Lusatia, Silesia and South Poland. As the *Hagenhufe*, it is found in the Baltic hinterland from Mecklenburg to Pomerania; and as the *Marschhufe* in the dyked land about Danzig.

Rural colonization in the East was based predominantly on holdings of 'full lands' by peasants. Their size varied with the quality of the soil, local custom and the varying *Hufe*. Moreover the immigrants must have had some say in the matter. We are not even sure that average holding and *Hufe* coincided. It is thought that in Brandenburg and East Prussia two *Hufen* per settler was normal. If so, the normal village in the Ordensland of 60 *Hufen* would have only twenty full holdings.[1] We hear of men who hold half or two-thirds of a *Hufe*; seldom of those who hold more than two; never of those who hold more than four. The land register of Sorau in Lower Lusatia, made in 1381 when colonization was finished, contains a majority of holdings of less than one *Hufe*.

Property in land subject to material burdens was seldom transferred or created by purchase. A derivative right of occupation under some lord was universally prevalent. But the consequences were exclusively material. That precious personal freedom which the German immigrant had acquired when he left his home—if not earlier—was not affected by his new tenure. Where the rulers were not Germans, the colonists were privileged in the matter of obligations to the state, which amounted to an easing of their economic burdens. The varied, often uncertain, and possibly very oppressive burdens in the way of dues and services to which the native populations were liable were regulated in their interest. The arrival of Germans facilitated a change to a more developed system of public liabilities. And the German was guaranteed his own penal and property law, and his own courts.

The tenure was heritable, with a quit-rent (*Erbzinsleihe, Erbpacht*). The lord was ultimate owner: he inherited in default of heirs. But the colonist's position was excellent: his female descendants and collateral relatives could inherit. He could sell, provided he gave his lord the first refusal. In fourteenth-century Bohemia the lords established their claim

---

[1] The rest being lord's, *Schultze*'s, or church land, with some scraps for 'gardeners'.

to approve the alienation of *Hufen*; but this did not become part of the law of the land. As a free man the peasant could leave his land at will. In one recorded case only (in Silesia, in 1206) had a German settler to find an adequate substitute before leaving. This looks like an effect of Polish influence; for in Casimir the Great's Great Polish Statute of 1347 it is made applicable to all peasant settlers under German law. Perhaps the Statute only gave legal recognition to a customary practice.

Holdings by *Erbzins* were burdened with dues to the lord. But these were fixed and moderate. There was the yearly quit-rent in money or in kind—grain primarily, or rather grains: rye, wheat, barley and oats; or any two or three of them grown locally. Peas occasionally and hens are mentioned. Replacement of payments in kind by payments in money made progress with the years. It occurs in the earliest colonizing times. A late-settled district such as Pomerania usually employs money from the start; an old-settled district like East Holstein will have payments in kind, which are commuted occasionally in the thirteenth, but more generally not before the fourteenth, century.

Many factors must be taken into account in interpreting the bare figures of the burdens imposed on each *Hufe*. In early days there was often only a small payment *pro recognitione terre*, especially on Church land: for the Church looked to the coming tithe from virgin soil. Gradually, however, the dues grew into a substantial rent in kind. In the centuries now under discussion the purchasing power of money was declining sharply. We must not consider any of the rents apart from the tithe, or the payments in money apart from those in kind. Nor must we forget the varying sizes of *Hufen*. The results are confused and uncertain; but we can extract standard figures at least for certain precise dates and places. For the second half of the twelfth century a money payment of 2s. per *Hufe* is normal. Over wide areas in the thirteenth, Silesia and Great Poland for example, it is a quarter-mark (*Vierdung*); towards the end of the century, and in the fourteenth, a half-mark. This last was the average payment in the Ordensland of Prussia. But for late foundations and on exceptionally good land, like that about Danzig, it might rise to 2, 4, 6 or even 10 marks.

In spite of all variations and complicated interrelations of payment in money and in kind, one can establish for many districts something like a normal burden on the settler's *Hufe*. The Sorau register of 1381 mentions, from the big *Hufe*, nine groschen at Midsummer and nine at Michaelmas, and three bushels each of wheat, rye, and oats; from the 'Flemish' *Hufe* only six groschen, one bushel each of barley, rye and oats, with one bushel of tithe-oats. Charters from Great Poland for the decades from 1243–1333 give almost uniformly twelve measures of corn (usually mixed corn of three kinds) and a quarter-mark. The Teutonic

Knights regularly prescribed money-rents, to which was added 'plough-corn', the secularized tithe.

Tithe was handled in many ways, yet there are definite tenden-cies in their development. For German settlers, the general rule was to fix it clearly and once for all. Sometimes a payment in threshed corn, the same for every year, was fixed; so the cultivator could freely choose the day of delivery, and any possible interferences by the tithe-owner were excluded. Or tithe might be fixed straight away in money; often in the form of 'the Bishop's *Vierdung*'. We should like to form some conception of what the aggregate of these burdens meant to the peasant. But general estimates are not permissible, because the value of money, and its relation to the dues in kind, varied far too much. We can only say that the burden in itself was tolerable; and as the dues were fixed from the first the peasant gained by any improved yield of his land. Finally, the progressive depreciation of money during the era of coloni-zation made his cash payments easier.

The first colonists under German law had no work to do for their lord, as peasants once had in Old Germany and Slavonic peasants still had; and that remained the rule. Perhaps it was Polish influence which led a lord in North Silesia, so early as 1283, when laying out a village under German law, to stipulate for three days' ploughing from every *Hufe*. The same thing is often found in Upper Silesia, and in Bohemia, in the fourteenth century. But the village of Kremnitz near Landshut, between the Vistula and the San, which was actually German, not merely 'under German law', knew nothing of 'manorial' services in the fifteenth century. Under the Teutonic Knights in Prussia, services were regularly demanded from German peasants from about 1350. In Ermland in 1390 the local custom was described as six days' mowing for hay, and the carriage of wood, oats and fish. But even in Prussia, so late as 1427, there were no arable services. So, apart from these special and late develop-ments, the normal colonist had nothing to do with the cultivation of his lord's land. He was neither part of a 'manor', in the old Western style, nor of a *Gutsbetrieb* such as developed later in the East. His holding was his own: for his lord it was simply a source of rent. What services he owed not as tenant of a lord but as subject of a prince will be described later.

His inclusion in a village community did set certain bounds to the peasant's economic freedom. The village community was one of the most valuable things which the Germans had brought east with them. But the form that it gradually took there was less developed than that of the West. In early days in the East we still hear of the free election by the community of its head-man—called usually the *Schulze*; also the *Bauermeister, Hagemeister, Richter* or *Vogt*, from which comes the Polish *wójt*. Later, such a thing is a rare exception, though we meet it in a few

MEDIEVAL AGRARIAN SOCIETY IN ITS PRIME 469

German villages in Prussia. Either the lord nominated the *Schulze*, or, more usually, the office became the heritable property of the locator. So far then the village was put under authority. This gave opportunities for the depression of the peasantry in later times. Yet the two or three 'justices' (*Schöffen*) who sat with the *Schulze* were in their way organs of village self-government. But the Eastern village community differed fundamentally from the Western in having, as a rule, no appreciable area of common land, no *Allmende*, of its own, because it was established on seignorial ground. There were only the greens and the roadside margins; some scraps of brushwood, bog, heath or moor, for pasture and the collection of firing; seldom a real wood. The intercommoning of several villages in a mark, often with very extensive forest rights, was unknown. So the individual cultivator was conscious of communal pressure, or communal support, only when the village fields were intermixed—with their rights of transit across neighbours' lands; their compulsory crop rotations, and fixed dates for ploughing and sowing and reaping; with their 'common of shack' on stubble and fallow, often the only available form of pasture. In the *Waldhufen* type of village there was none of all this. The peasant was perfectly free to farm his own long strip of land, unless there was common stubble grazing, as there might be. But even if unimportant for agricultural technique, the village community was very important for the healthy social life of the peasantry. Although in its Eastern form it lacked many things and its organs were less developed than in the West, it was greatly strengthened from the start by the fact that nearly every village of German settlers was both a minor judicial area and a separate parish.

The relation to the state of colonists under German law deserves notice because of its direct and indirect effects on economic life. There were very great local differences between the Marks and the native principalities. But nevertheless a uniform line of development can be traced throughout. The settlers came directly under the prince, even when established on private land. The number of prince's villages was high everywhere, in the Prussian Ordensland absolutely predominant. And in other villages the lord never crept in as an intermediate political authority between settler and prince. Moreover German settlers in non-German states were free of the services and burdens which natives owed their country, as we have seen. The duties required of them were few and well defined. They were connected chiefly with defence. But the settlers were fully involved in that new tax system which developed during, and in consequence of, the German colonization, and which utilized the possibilities of money economy that the colonization had brought with it, after the antiquated Slavonic system of services and dues had broken down. In fact they themselves brought the new system.[1]

Ecclesiastical relations needed to be regulated as much as political; and the regulating movements ran parallel. Normally each new village built its church and became a parish. To endow the church, a *Widmut* or *Widem* of one or two *Hufen* was set aside from the first. Besides that, each *Hufe* or each house often gave a small yearly offering to the parson. All this was easily arranged; but tithe was not. Where lords were ecclesiastics, tithe was often a greater incentive to colonization than rent. But there were all sorts of difficulties about it. The claims of the bishops clashed with those of the princes, who sometimes claimed the tithes from land newly brought under the plough: they did this in East Holstein, Mecklenburg and parts of Silesia, for instance. Settlers bargained over the method of levy, as we have seen. Germans who came under the jurisdiction of the Polish Church were surprised to meet the claim for Peter's pence. Many of them managed to reject it. Others resisted it for years—especially in Silesia, already completely separated from Poland—because they counted it a part of Polish law and so a symbol of unfreedom.

To facilitate their establishment on virgin soil, immigrants were given certain years during which they were free of all liabilities. Many more free years were often given in early times than later. We meet ten to twelve, even eighteen to twenty; but usually less. There is as a rule a marked difference between the allowance made on old cultivated land to be laid out on German lines, or on easily cleared and quickly productive land, and on that which required laborious clearing. Sometimes provision is made for a gradually mounting rent.

We do not know certainly how far the lord or the locator helped the settlers on their trek and in the work of settlement. Where forests to be cleared did not provide the necessary timber, we can infer from the practice in the new towns that it was given them free. But we know very little about the date, the extent, or the price of land purchases by peasants. As early as *circa* 1150 we hear of fees paid to lords for recognitions and admissions; and once, near Leipzig, of a price—4 'talents' for 14 *Hufen*. In Bohemia we often meet a substantial entry fine (*arrha, laudemium*). But we have no agreements between settlers and locators to tell us what settlers paid for their *Erbzinsrecht*. We must assume that they did pay in the later colonizing period; for then the locators bought the land at stiff prices, as a rule 6–12 marks per *Hufe*, but often

---

[1] It was only from the fourteenth century that a new movement, opposed to the spirit of the age of colonization, led to frequent transfers of sovereign rights from princes to various sorts of landlords, and created a starting point for claims to economic services which contributed greatly to the later development of the *Rittergut*.

much higher, and once so high as 48 marks (in 1294), as adequate evidence from Silesian charters shows. In an isolated instance, when the Council of Elbing in Prussia had two villages laid out in 1332, we learn that settlers paid 6 marks 'advance rent' (*Vormiete*) per *Hufe*. We learn about this because it was paid direct to the lords, although a locator was at work. The sum is four times the yearly rent, itself three times the usual Prussian rent of half a mark, because the land was near a town.

As for the locator's earnings, these—in spite of all local variations—soon came to be fixed on certain definite principles, so far as they depended on grants from the lord. The size of the village of course affected them; so did the changing circumstances of eastern colonization as time went on. In the early stages the lords might grant their locators money, or corn, or help in building mills: of this there are cases from Silesia in 1228 and 1237; from Ermland in 1254 and even so late as 1359. But the success of colonization reversed the position, as we have seen. Locators did so well that they were ready to pay for land to be settled. But we must freely admit that their business was risky. Many settlements hung fire and had to be primed again; many failed completely.

Their earnings evidently contained most various elements. Always a part of the village land was one element; either so many *Hufen*, or a given proportion of the total number of *Hufen*. In early days this was often one in three. It sank later to one in six, or to the one in ten that was common in Prussia. The locator got his *Hufen* free of rent and often free of tithe. Sometimes he himself received the rent from a group of *Hufen*.

A second element came from the right to build inns and mills. This was often very important. Before Germans brought in water-mills or horse-mills, the East had used hand-mills. Nearly every fair-sized village got a mill of the new sort. It was generally rented; so the colonization produced a class of rent-paying millers. Sometimes there were other rights enjoyed by the locator—over fisheries; ground game; bakers' and butchers' stalls, when the village was allowed them; over the smithy or the bath-house; the right to keep a big flock of sheep; a monopoly of brewing or hop-growing, even one of bee-keeping.

Thirdly, his position as judge and overseer of the village (*Schulze*, or what not) brought him a share in the profits of justice in his court of first instance; usually a third of the fines. Occasionally—though very generally in the Ordensland—he had also a share in the profits of higher justice.

Because he became the *Schulze*, his whole complex of property and rights was called the *Scholtisei* or the *Richterei*; and because it was all hereditary, the *Erbscholtisei* or *Erbrichterei*. It was often, though by no means always, granted to him as a fief. Why this or some other form was chosen we do not know. Its value was appreciable: a *Scholtisei* might be sold for 50 or 70 marks.

As the locator became the *Erbschulze*, every village got a man who stood above the peasants in wealth and in official and social position. From about 1300, in Silesia for instance or in Pomerania, he was given greater military duties. He must be mounted. Nevertheless he did not stand too far above the peasants socially: he and his class were their natural leaders. However, the business-like, capitalistic spirit of the location contract worked the other way. It allowed a locator to sell his *Scholtisei* freely; and the hereditary character of the office only made it a better security—it in no way guaranteed his permanent connexion with 'his' village.

One difficulty that the German migrants eastward had to face was a lack of those facilities for the division of labour and access to various markets to which they had been accustomed. Early settlements were often isolated from any market at all. That explains why in particular the immigrants from progressive Flanders stipulated in the early years for at least some limited measure of those commercial privileges which were usually reserved for places with markets, and for boroughs. The Flemings who were settled by the Bishop of Meissen in Kühren (between Leipzig and Dresden) in 1154 were expressly given permission to sell bread, beer and meat among themselves—but not to strangers. Archbishop Wichmann of Magdeburg, a great colonizer, went further and in 1159 gave the Flemish settlers of Wusterwitz an annual privileged fair. A similar blending of the economic functions of settlements which were usually kept distinct appears rather later in the East. It occurred to the abbess of Trebnitz in Silesia in 1234 that her new village of Thomaskirch might require butchers' stalls. In the same year the duke of Great Poland gave market rights to the village of Powidz, when he began to call in Germans. In fact, in this period, the founding of villages with markets, *villae forenses*, is common in these two provinces. In Pomerania in 1262 a village near Stettin gets brewing, baking and slaughtering rights—but, and this is characteristic, only for its ten 'free years'.

Meanwhile a deliberate extension of the tried processes of settlement had provided far more generously for the marketing needs of immigrant German peasants, and had satisfied many other requirements also. The further colonization moved from its base in Old Germany and from the first new advanced trading towns, the more peasants demanded some market to which they could sell their produce and in which they could buy essential manufactures and articles of commerce. The system of dues, taxes and tithe in money shows clearly enough both that they understood a money economy and that their lords expected them to understand it. On the other hand the towns, whose foundation these same lords encouraged, wanted a German countryside to live by —so far as they did not live by long-distance trade. Wichmann of Magdeburg himself conceived of the region (*provincia*) of Jüterbock in what is now Brandenburg as a unity when, *ad edificandam provinciam*, he laid out the town of Jüterbock as *exordium et caput provinciae*. He had already begun to settle Germans in the country, especially 'Flemings'. About the year 1200, as colonization neared Upper Lusatia, a method was devised for uniting rural and urban settlement very closely. Duke Henry I transferred it to Silesia with great and rapid success. Each form of settlement helped the other. Prosperous burgesses often took over neighbouring villages from the duke, acquired property in them, and brought in settlers. Bishop Laurence I of Breslau carried the system before 1220 to the episcopal lands on the Neisse, and from there into Upper Silesia, east of the Oder. Already in 1210 the duke of Great Poland had experimented with it in the valleys of the Warthe and Netze. In Eastern Kurmark it developed naturally, as the foundation of towns after 1230 got abreast of the earlier village settlement. Beyond Silesia, Northern Moravia shows the same close association of central market towns with a group of villages round about; and from there the system passed into East Bohemia. We are often ignorant of the exact process; but it is well reflected in the law. Although the villages are not always associated with a town founded at the same time, to be their legal centre, but are sometimes linked to such a town subsequently, the object is the same, to break down the isolation of the German village in a strange rough land. Contemporaries recognized and deliberately planned the association of villages with both an urban higher court and an urban market. A Great Polish charter of the early fourteenth century says—*ville supranominate ad forum et ad judicium debeant pertinere*. The inclusion of their village as a subordinate judicial unit in an urban *Weichbild* was always of economic value to the peasants. For it completed the exclusion of the immigrant German from native law. The town of Posen illustrates the wide sweep of this system of town and country planning. Its locator in 1253 was given seventeen adjacent Polish places which the grand duke of Great Poland wished to have colonized by Germans. In the lands of the Teutonic knights, experience in older colonized regions led to the adoption of a uniform system in which this association of town and country was the rule. The system was the main force in the opening-up of Prussia.

It favoured a separation of social and economic functions which in the early days of colonization had sometimes been blended. Town and village were sharply distinguished. It is certainly no accident that it was precisely in colonized regions that the conception of the *Bannmeile*, the zone to protect urban handicraft, was specially emphasized. This was in keeping with the rationalism of a young country. The towns were exceedingly active in seeking recognition of their claims to an industrial monopoly; and usually their success was complete. Only a few essential rural handicrafts were excepted—especially smiths, wheelwrights, bakers and butchers; and attempts were made to confine the first two groups to repair work. Regular handicrafts were concentrated in the towns. The towns were specially jealous of their profitable monopoly of brewing—acquired from the prince—and strict in enforcing it. The lack of a strong class of Slavonic rural handicraftsmen, and the absorption of the immigrant German villagers in their colonists' work of clearing and building, favoured the aims of the towns. Town policy also ruined the old Slavonic settlements of specialists. This restriction of the eastern village to purely agricultural activity must be regarded as one of the facts which help to explain its later subjection to the *Gutsherrschaft*.

Although so far the fact has been emphasized that the colonizing process was based on the peasant holding, it must not be forgotten that other types of estates of all sizes were also called into existence. To the greater some reference has already been made—the demesnes of churchmen and knights, and the complex estates of the *Schulzen*.

Among churchmen only the Cistercians had a special type of rural economy. The insistence on *labora* in the Benedictine rule, and the institution of lay brethren, led the followers of St Bernard to create those important establishments, the *grangiae* or *curiae*, which they worked themselves with the help of the lay brethren. The wide experience which they brought from the West, and the strict discipline of their half-monkish labour, made these establishments models for the peoples of the East in the twelfth and early thirteenth centuries. The Cistercians also did clearing work. But beyond the Elbe they secured the services of native villagers from the very first, and adopted the system of letting out land for rent—at first naturally to Germans—much earlier than their Ordinance of 1208 permitted. The so-called foundation charter of the monastery of Leubus in Silesia (of 1175) already assumes such German settlement. So the grange, as the only form of Cistercian economy, fell into the background in the East; as the system of lay brethren declined, it soon lost its advantageous labour system. Many granges were let to peasants for rent, the rest were assimilated to the demesnes of other ecclesiastical lords, which differed in no important way from those of princes or noblemen, either before or after the age of colonization.

When the German East Movement began, it did not much affect the 'demesnes' of Slavonic lords. New villages of peasants could spring up near the old *allodia* or *curiae*. It was only when those native villages from which the lords had drawn manual or team services began to be transformed that the organization of labour was affected. The resultant decline in servile labour power was met in part by a reduction of the 'demesne'. That happened also where productive land from the 'demesne' was used for peasant settlement. This was certainly a common occurrence. The widespread break-up of great estates which the lords had kept in their own hands has been called a characteristic of this period of agrarian history in Bohemia. This is more or less true of other regions in the East. But it must always be remembered that a very considerable part of these 'demesnes' had been utilized most superficially or not at all; and that parts of them remained in the lord's hands. In old settled districts a radical transformation on German lines was not always undertaken. Often there was only a partial change of native tenurial conditions and burdens. Lords retained their right to extend their own 'demesnes' with the help of the tenants' services. Even when a lord decided to undertake genuine colonization, he was not obliged to abandon all his claims to services. In the Mark of Brandenburg, next to rent-paying German villages are often found villages with the same name but full of Wends who render services. At the very close of the Middle Ages, in the bishopric of Breslau, there may be even in villages under German law isolated holdings under Polish law, and liable no doubt to the old Polish services. Finally, the instances already quoted of arable services assigned to villages under German law, when first laid out, are best explained as being connected with 'demesnes' on which such services had always been performed under Polish law. In that way, but varying with the region, many 'demesnes' survived from precolonial times. Silesia's wealth of charters gives some idea of their extent. We meet with *allodia* of from four to six ploughs which have survived the colonizing process.

But the process also created new ones. Often they were set aside for the lord when a village was founded, or especially allocated to particular uses. The princes wished to increase their military resources at least as much as to strengthen their financial and economic power through peasant settlement. They wanted more knights. So they encouraged service on horseback by men most of whom were heavily armed. Though far fewer than the peasant holdings, those that owed knight service were a not less important element in the whole process of eastern reorganization. A knight might be given one or more villages to lay out. He could employ a locator or not; could give him the manor-house, or keep it for himself, He became lord of the village, or part of it. According to the *Handfeste* of Kulm of 1233, for every 40 *Hufen* which anyone bought from the Order, service with one armoured horse and at least two others was due; a smaller number of *Hufen* owed a horse and light arms. In other cases, holdings owing knight service were created at the same time as the village but without such a close connexion with it. Any such holding, even when given by the princes or the higher nobility or ecclesiastical foundations under feudal law, was invariably called an *Allod* (in Latin, *predium, curia, villa*, or *dominicale*). In the fourteenth century the German word *Vorwerk* appears. It was applied at that time to the chief manor itself, not as today in East Germany to a subsidiary establishment. The following figures give some idea of the number of such knightly estates at the close of the colonizing era: in the various districts of Brandenburg there were 1375; that is in the Old Mark, 72; in the Ucker Mark, 169; in the Middle Mark, 207; in the New Mark, 187. About 1350, in the principality of Breslau in the heart of Silesia, there were more than 200 *allodia*, very many of them ecclesiastical. This was a land that had always been thickly settled.

The size of the lords' *allodia* was not considerable. For the land between the Saale and the middle Elbe it is put at 3–6 *Hufen*; the land-book of Sorau gives an average for that part of Lusatia of 2–4; though in the very fertile country near Breslau, in the middle of the fourteenth century the size of the *Vorwerk* certainly varies from 5–7 up to 10–11 *Hufen*. The Old Mark of Brandenburg in 1375 gives an average of only $3\frac{3}{4}$; in the Ucker Mark at the same date it rises to $6\frac{1}{4}$ (about 250 acres); in the Middle Mark to $7\frac{1}{2}$; whilst in the New Mark it was $8\frac{1}{2}$ (or about 360 acres) as early as 1337. Some of these *Vorwerke* had their roots in pre-colonial times. The fourteenth-century figures already include some peasant land, absorbed into knights' land since the colonization. Varying qualities of soil help to explain the great differences of size. In the Prussian Ordensland a normal size was 5–12 *Hufen*; but on the edge of the 'wilderness' near the eastern frontier they rise to 20–50, obviously including much waste, especially forest. As a whole, then, *Vorwerke* varied from the size of a big peasants' holding up to twice or four times the size of such a 'full land'. In estimating their social and economc value, it must be remembered that their yield might be supplemented by rents from dependent villages. So one can say of them in general that on the average they provided an independent livelihood on a scale sufficient for the then rather modest needs of the class who owed knight service. Their holders were peasant-noblemen, whose way of life and experience fitted them well to carry on further colonization. It has been seen that there was also a higher nobility. But its existence did not affect the normal methods of upper-class economy. Its estates were like those just described, and they are included in the figures quoted.

An exception is provided by the *Vorwerke* established by the Teutonic knights and Cathedral Chapters on the knights' territory, and that not only in Prussia but also in East Baltic lands. (During the era of colonization lay knights did not work demesnes of their own, but lived from the services and dues from native villages assigned to them by the Order or the bishops.) Many of these princely *Vorwerke* were very extensive, and often not merely because of appendant waste. Records of sowing on knights' demesnes in Prussia from about the end of the fourteenth century actually imply arable areas of from 425 up to even 3500 acres; that is from something above the maximum in Brandenburg up to about ten times that maximum.

Whether the land of a *Vorwerk* lay intermixed with that of the peasants or apart from it varied greatly from district to district. In Meissen, in districts with old Slavonic 'block' fields, it seems always to have lain apart; in the new German villages sometimes apart, sometimes intermixed. Intermixture predominated in East Holstein, separation in Mecklenburg, where only the *Settingehufen*, not the *Hofhufen*, were mixed with the peasants' acres. In the New Mark both systems are again found. In East Prussia separation prevailed generally. In *Wald-hufen* districts the problem did not arise, because there was no true intermixture even of peasant land.

If one compares all this with the familiar modern *Rittergut* of the East, the contrast due to the state of things created directly by coloniza-tion becomes very clear. Although there was landlordship from the first, there was not the close association of 'manorial' and peasant economy that developed later, especially in the organization of labour. Very many villages had no *Vorwerk*. The Brandenburg register from the fourteenth century already quoted shows, for example, that only 39 out of 318 villages of the Old Mark had a *Vorwerk* at all. The Breslau land-book of about 1350 gives similar results. Villages without a *Vorwerk* served merely as sources of rents for their lord. But even when a village had a *Vorwerk*—or several, a very common thing—the peasant holding was usually nothing more than that. An exception from this conclusion is provided by those 'manors' of pre-colonial origin whose dependent native villages had not been thoroughly reformed on the German model, as well as by new creations or remodelled villages in which, as has been seen, the example of native habits of service had been influential. In both these types indications of the subsequent labour-system of the *Rittergut* are found, which might lead straight to it. A complete comparison of the two periods of East German and eastern agrarian history could not overlook the fact that in the *Vorwerke* there existed points from which the great agricultural enterprises of the classes might expand; and that their landlordship had brought with it, for the owners of *Vorwerke*, a position in the villages which the charters describe as that of 'village lords'. This, in conjunction with the transfers of sovereign rights already mentioned, brings us to the beginnings of the so-called 'hereditary lordship' of the knight over the village. To distinguish late medieval conditions sharply from modern conditions, G. F. Knapp coined the formula—'the medieval knight was the peasant's neighbour'.[1] This formula can only be accepted if the limitations just mentioned are kept in mind; and even then only for German villages, or for those fully organized on the German plan and under German law.

To complete this sketch of the holdings which over-topped those of the peasants, the *Scholtiseien* may be recalled. As the figures show, their size came very near that of the *Vorwerke*, although on the average it was somewhat less.

The working of lords' 'manors' and of the estates of *Schulzen*, in spite of their different origins, was uniform to this extent: they were managed directly by the owner or, where he had more than one, by his official representatives. But their different origin was shown in their labour systems. *Allodia* from pre-colonial days everywhere preserved at least remains of the older system—servile domestics and perhaps also the services of dependent peasants. Team services were what lords chiefly demanded, for general transport purposes or for work on the land. A third group of dependants, standing between the first two, was made up of people who had no peasant holding but had got a scrap of land from the lord—technically a 'garden'—for which they did service. No doubt the class of 'gardeners' was composed mainly of humble natives; for in the Marks the Slavonic name of *Kossäten* was often applied to them. The general nature of their services, in detail very varied, is shown by the term used somewhat later in Meissen—*Handfröner*, 'hand-servers'. The considerable amount of work done by this class supplemented the daily work of the servile domestics and the seasonal team work of the dependent peasants.

But none of these permanent legally-bound labour supplies were to be found at the outset in the pure rent-paying villages created by colonization, or were available for the *Schulzen*. It was necessary to fall back in part on hired labour. We often hear of ploughmen on the estates of the Teutonic knights. But hired labour alone could not meet their needs. So they settled 'gardeners' systematically even in rent-paying villages. They are numerous late in the thirteenth century; in the fourteenth they are found everywhere. They appear in Prussian records from 1305. When a village was laid out each got about three 'acres' (*Morgen*). To supplement this they received a wage for their work. The amount of work and its remuneration varied greatly from place to place. A Silesian document of 1387 gives the following full account of a 'gardener's' rights and duties on an ecclesiastical manor; he reaps (and

[1] G. F. Knapp, *Die Bauernbefreiung und der Ursprung der Landarbeiter in den ältesten Teilen Preussens*, Bd. 1 (1887), s. 31.

gets one sheaf in twelve); threshes (and gets a twentieth of the grain); mows the aftermath (and gets one cock in three). He heckles hemp, cuts grass and brings it in, tends horses, spreads manure, and washes and shears sheep. For all that he is given his keep and already some money. Besides, he gets his bit of arable ploughed and his oil-seed crushed for him. This man was what was called a 'threshing gardener' (*Dreschgärtner*). The same type is found in Meissen. In Silesia however it occurs mainly on the splendid black earth soils of the centre, and on the loess of the upper province. Its occurrence reveals intensive arable farming.

The equipment of a *Vorwerk* was still very simple. Even in the fifteenth century, on Saxon territory, one or two plough teams and four to at most eight horses was the rule. The archives of the Teutonic knights confirm this impression. For the same period, two or three plough teams was the rule, even on *Vorwerke* ranging up to 1700 acres. In such cases the lord's ploughs cannot have done much of the cultivation. Only here and there were from five to fifteen ploughs kept up. The maximum comes from Marienburg, which also had the maximum acreage of 3500 already quoted.

These facts form the link between the agrarian organization and the agriculture itself. The small amount of arable on the *Vorwerke* is explained in part by the fact that the peasants paid so much of their rent in corn, towards the production of which the whole business of colonization was mainly directed. The yield was increased not only by extending the cultivated area but by improving methods and implements. Wherever conditions permitted, the Germans brought in their customary three-course rotation. That was decidedly more productive than the former unregulated *Feldgraswirtschaft*.[1] It is hard to estimate the effect of the immigrants' whole temper and stage of development, but it must have been considerable. They were accustomed to work hard and look to the future. Independence and responsibility were powerful incentives, hardly to be found in the older native rural society. Also the immigrants brought better implements; especially the heavy felling axe, and the iron turn-furrow plough with its wheels and mouldboard. The deep cultivation which this plough brought about was a decided improvement. Many heavy soils, especially the boulder clay, were first broken up by it. Buildings were greatly improved: the German farmhouse and out-buildings were solid. The crops grown have been mentioned in connexion with the corn dues. From them it appears that millet, a favourite grain of the Western Slavs, had been driven right out. Some special crops had been introduced in places before German

[1] Cf. p. 137 above.

immigration reached full flood. Non-Germans had had a hand in this, Romance-speaking people brought in by immigrant ecclesiastical lords. In Silesia and Little Poland we occasionally find Romance vine growers shortly after 1200. But Germans were mainly responsible for the great extension of vineyards across the Elbe. No doubt it was the liturgical use of wine which led to these extensions far beyond the appropriate climatic zone—even into Pomerania. The vineyards along the Elbe about Meissen and Melnik in Bohemia, like those of Grüneberg on the middle Oder, are today only the modest remnants of this medieval viticulture. Whether hops first became known in the East in the same way is uncertain. Documentary evidence of the settlement of Germans as hop growers in Silesia shows that they were specialists in the work. And naturally the German peasant brought his better fruit trees with him. In consequence of the establishment by Germans of woollen weaving and dyeing as regular crafts, woad growing was introduced from Thuringia into mid-Silesia.

In the whole picture, cattle farming stands far behind arable farming. The reverse is perhaps true of the *Vorwerke*. Some peasant country-sides were also devoted to cattle keeping—the Elbe flats of Priegnitz were. But as a rule it was only found on a large scale on lords' territory. It had been the favourite activity of the eastern peoples. It needed less labour than arable farming. The lords' enjoyment of grazing-rights over the village fields encouraged it. Breeding for the butcher could spread everywhere, as soon as towns provided markets. Appropriate regions, such as Mecklenburg, could try to imitate the breeding industry of their neighbours in Schleswig and Holstein.

The many sorts of horses, from the knights' charger to the farm-cart nag, were in great demand; but the better sorts were bred almost exclusively on the *Vorwerke*. Swine needed acorns or beech mast, not to be found everywhere. What most tended to break down a one-sided devotion to corn growing was the growth of a cloth industry that made sheep pay. Even before 1300 sheep were reared on a large scale in Meissen: it already had an export of cloth. The great contemporary sheepfold of a Cistercian house in Silesia may have been for its own use. But there also the rising importance of wool growing for market is shown, when *Schulzen* secure separate pasture for from 100 to 300 sheep, and when—about 1350—such separate pastures come to light as appurtenances of *Vorwerke* and free *Hufen*.

So far, the agrarian changes which what are now North-east Germany and the neighbouring countries experienced from the twelfth century have been examined from the point of view of those innovations which German immigration brought directly. The fact has, however, been emphasized, and illustrated from various regions, that these innovations were not confined to the German-settled area, but affected native conditions in varying degrees. It remains to explain more precisely the working of the agrarian movement started by German influence on the older populations of the eastern lands and their economic relations. Some repetition is inevitable, but much remains to be said; and the progressive influence on the indigenous agrarian development of tendencies already noted can be followed out.

The object is not to determine the indirect effects of German colonization on agriculture through the revolution that it brought in all other branches of the economy of East Central Europe, and through the increased absorption of that region into the complex economic conditions of the West. Of these effects it may be said in brief that the introduction of town life by the Germans first gave the East a complete, permanent, market-controlled economy, with division of labour. Here however we are concerned primarily with agrarian questions.

The older population was drawn most completely into the new movement when its members took part as settlers in the foundation of villages 'under German law', side by side with Germans. By so doing they shook off all bonds of former dependence and became members of German village communities. If they were actually mixed with Germans in the same village, not merely settled in their own villages among Germans, they naturally mastered the new constitutional and technical methods more quickly. But, as has been seen,[1] it is exceedingly hard to separate zones of pure German, mixed, and pure native settlement.

Equally radical changes came about when an area already cultivated was assigned to Germans or subjected to German law. In that case a bit of the old agrarian system of equal size simply disappeared. This occurred to some extent in the Marks; on a large scale on the rich lands of Middle and Upper Silesia; and was found also along the Baltic coast.

Often however, colonization had only a dilute effect on the native population and their agrarian life. Where conquering German lords imposed themselves on the Wends, in order to supply their own needs through a regular system of dues, they began to adjust both the position of the population and agrarian institutions more or less to German custom, partly for lack of German settlers and partly in imitation of them. There, in the Marks, native lords imitated the Germans, and the example spread to lands with native princes. The results varied greatly, but a common tendency can be discerned everywhere. It is towards a fixing and limitation of burdens, which had important consequences for their bearers—whether holdings or men. The limitation and fixing

[1] See p. 458, above.

of dues had occurred inside purely Slavonic society, with the institution of *hospites*. Now the German example led to more of it, and also to greater uniformity of groups of holdings. For, to secure equal dues, holdings of unequal size which had to yield them were standardized. All the way from East Holstein to Prussia, one now meets the 'hook', that is a land measure named after the Slavonic and Baltic plough, copied from the German *Hufe*, and treated similarly as a normal unit for normal burdens—services, rent, tithe. And far into the East it is very often called a *Hufe*, but with the prefix 'Wendish' or 'Polish'; or it is called a *Smurdenhufe*. It was generally half of the big 'Frankish' *Hufe*. The standardization of holdings must often have been associated with a reorganization of the field divisions. These were made more regular, somewhat after the German style. We may connect with this adjustment of Wendish habits to the new era those fields in 'blocks', but remodelled with strips, which are to be found in North-east Germany, frequently for example between Leipzig and Dresden. Far to the East, in Masovia, we come across ordinary intermixed open-fields from the fifteenth century, which indicate the further penetration of at least one element in the German agrarian system. In Lithuania, the Crown introduced the German system of *Hufen* after 1550. But behind any regulation of the fields stands the definite supersession of the old principle of communal economy and communal sharing of burdens, so far as these things still survived. Everywhere there now prevailed that individual ownership and responsibility which had been established among the Germans.

That was one way in which the processes here described affected men. Another was the rise of an appreciable proportion of rural workers to a better legal position. This was most true of the humblest of them, the *Smurden*, 'the dirty folk'. No doubt the lords went on taking servile manorial workers from this class. But some of its members acquired a certain amount of land; from among whom one group can be distinguished—called *Gärtner*, *Kossäten*, *Kötner*, and so on —who had to supplement the yield of their bits of land by wage-work; and a higher group who could live as full peasants, as the emergence of *Smurdenhufen* shows. In association with the regulation of their holdings, and the limitation of the rents and services, there went an improvement in native tenures. Long after all heathen, idle, or superfluous Wends had been summarily got rid of, things had already gone so far in Mecklenburg by 1285 that a free renunciation in court of a Wendish tenant's rights was required before land occupied by him could be transferred to a purchaser. The burdens are now attached to a determinate piece of land: the native peasants are personally free. So their former unfreedom fades away, at least in regions where German influence is strong. The old cultivated land of the Meissen Mark is a case in point: there this transformation of Sorbish conditions was widespread. But even there the natives never generally acquired the good German heritable tenure (*Erbleihrecht*). To a great extent a more insecure tenure prevailed. So, for example, the region in Lower Silesia famous for its peasant 'property' (strictly a heritable leasehold) was surrounded to the north and east by districts with these insecure tenures; and as you went east, such tenures were more and more associated with personal serfdom.

Conditions proved most stable where the population was given over to the typically Slavonic occupations of fishing and bee-keeping. Here the dues were regulated so as to bear on individuals, not on groups; but there was no change in the nature of the due—in fish or honey—or in the unfreedom of the payer. Such conditions were widespread in the Lusatias and in the Mark of Brandenburg. There were other specially Wendish dues, which suggest extensive cattle and poultry keeping.

The conditions in Prussia, in the end conquered entirely by the sword, were peculiar to it. Apart from a few freemen, the Prussians were either subjected with their holdings to a lord, under a system of mild serfdom, or torn from their holdings and assigned to another lord who might give them land or use them as landless labourers. Generally speaking, the Prussian natives were left in much the same position as their Slavonic neighbours.

Whilst in this way, in the regions north of the Sudeten Mountains, agrarian conditions were being adjusted to the needs of a progressive age under the obvious influence of German institutions, the heart of the Sudeten area, inhabited by Czechs and Moravians, proved the greater resisting power of its Slavonic population by extending the area of cultivation with its own unaided forces. In Bohemia there are more than 300 places called *Lhota*, sometimes with suffixes. There are 80 more in Moravia. The word first occurs in charters in 1199: most of the names date from the thirteenth and fourteenth centuries, though for many a later date can be proved. *Lhota* means approximately 'freedom' or 'freeing', and is used—among other uses—to describe an exemption from rent or tax for a period of years, granted when settlements were laid out on waste land. It is provable that some places got their names in consequence of such exemption. The distribution of the *Lhota* place names in the interior basin of Bohemia, in particular between the Moldau and the Sasawa, and in Moravia in the land below the mountains that divide it from Bohemia and Hungary, as well as the prevailing Slavonic character of the present populations, allow of the conclusion that to a considerable degree these names are witnesses to a process of Slavonic settlement that proceeded with a certain uniformity. What glimpses the charters provide show locators with their free *Hufen*, and the guarantee of 'free years' for each little settlement. Apparently German influence was at work. But an improved durable tenure, like the German heritable lease, did not develop.

This type of name passes into Silesia in the first half of the thirteenth century: the word *Lgota*, Germanized as *Ellguth*, occurs more than 60 times. In East Poland, as *Ligota*, it occurs more then 30 times; and in Slovakia, as *Lêhota*, more than 40. But in these regions it is not only rarer: some at least of the places named by it can be proved to have been laid out under German law. In Slovakia, the age of clearing indicated by the *Lêhota* places agrees exactly with that extension of colonizing German settlement which also occurred there rather late—in the fourteenth and fifteenth centuries. In Poland the *Ellguth* settlements along the line from Cracow to Kalisch verged on those places in *Wola* that have been referred to already.[1] Their connexion with colonization under German law can also be proved. So Bohemia and Moravia, with their internal colonization proceeding under Slavonic law, are exceptions among these eastern territories.

Surveying the course of events in the agrarian history of the lands east of the Elbe from the twelfth to the fourteenth century, and attempting to summarize the results, what first strikes one is the extraordinary extension of the cultivated area. Although in later centuries a few modifications were made here and there, a little more land was won for agriculture; yet by the end of the medieval German colonization eastwards the limits of land acquisition on forest soil in North-eastern Germany and the interior of Bohemia were already reached. There was never again peasant colonization in the forests; with that the whole area was satiated. In Upper Hungary the same point was reached in the fifteenth century at latest. But in Poland there was still room for the process to continue. So a native Polish movement, in unbroken continuity with that here described, went on during the fifteenth century; and was enlarged in the sixteenth by a revival of German peasant migration eastwards which persisted even into the twentieth. For land made utilizable by dyking and draining the story is different. The medieval movement stopped after the flats of the lower Elbe valley and the delta of the Vistula and the Nogat had been dealt with. It did not extend from the Elbe valley to the mere-land of the Havel and the Spree; it did not deal with the great inundations on the lower Oder, the Warthe and the Netze; and it did not spread upstream from the Vistula delta. The gigantic plans for settlement in these areas drawn up early in the thirteenth century were not carried out. Only in modern times did any change come.

[1] Above, p. 458.

The extension of the cultivated area was accompanied by a growth of population. The stabilization of political conditions through the rise of large states brought with it a steady rise in the native population. The immigration from Germany, and then from old into newly colonized areas, was even more important. No certain statistics can be given. But some notion of the extraordinary growth in numbers that the colonizing process brought may be inferred from the fact that in Silesia alone, between 1200 and 1350, about 1200 villages were founded. It has been reckoned that in East Prussia the knights and the bishops established about 1400 rent-paying villages, with a round 60,000 peasants' *Hufen*. These would require a peasant population of at least 150,000.

Thirdly, economic activity became more intensive, thanks to new human material, a new social order, and technical progress. In 1495 the bishop of Breslau said that, *gemeiniclich das polnische Volk zu verfolgunge der narungen und peud nicht goedert ist*.[1] The social structure of agrarian life in the East had been changed decisively by the insertion of a genuine, economically sound, and free peasant class. Of this class immigrants formed the majority. But they carried an appreciable part of the indigenous population with them—either to a position of complete equality, or to one at least better than that of earlier times. The entry of this peasant class into society finally did away with any surviving communal agrarian economy directed from above. It eased or even abolished unfreedom; it helped the break-up of great estates into free rent-paying peasant holdings, while allowing reduced 'demesnes' to survive; it led to individual peasant economy supported by a village community. Among items in technical progress need only be recalled the new layout of the fields, the three-field rotation, the better implements and the water-mills.

This all led to a great increase in production, especially of grain. The grain fed the fast-growing population of the colonized lands—urban as well as rural—and soon provided a surplus for export on a large scale. This export was helped by the opening-up of the eastern countries by river and sea transport. The shipping of corn from Brandenburg to Flanders and England is demonstrable from about 1250. In 1287 we have the first documentary mention of corn from the *Oesterlande* on the Flemish market. After that its export remained a regular thing, of first-rate importance both for the Baltic lands and for the consuming centres, far beyond the Middle Ages. Cattle and sheep farming also made considerable progress. On the whole they met the increased local requirements of butchers' meat, and supplied enough raw material for

---

[1] Which may be paraphrased: 'the Polish population as a rule is not fitted to manage domestic affairs or keep buildings in good order'.

the new cloth industry. But they created no important export values, except hides. It is very significant that those areas which competed in exporting the cattle, demanded from the fourteenth century onwards by Central Europe—the Hungarian Puszta, Podolia, Volhnyia, Lithuania— were precisely the areas that medieval peasant colonization had not reached. They still displayed the economic structure which characterized the Western Slavonic regions before they underwent that thorough agrarian reconstruction with which this narrative has dealt.

Medieval Agrarian Society in its Prime

§5. Poland, Lithuania and Hungary

After the conclusion of the Union with Poland in 1386, Lithuania was constantly under Polish influence, which made itself felt particularly in the conditions under which the large landed estates were held, and in the whole agrarian structure. The relations between Poland and Hungary on the other hand were much looser. There were only two short periods in the fourteenth century and another in the fifteenth when these two states were under a common ruler. Neither country directly influenced the other, and yet they have many features in common both in their political and in their economic structure. It is accordingly permissible to present the agrarian history of all three countries in the Middle Ages in a single chapter.

I. *Landownership*

The earliest documents throwing any light on the agrarian structure of Poland date from the beginning of the twelfth century. The land was at that time in the possession of the monarch, of the Church, or of the rural population who had inhabited the country for several centuries and are called by the sources sometimes *contribules*, 'fellow-tribesmen', but more frequently *haeredes*, 'heirs'. The growth of state organization led to a distinction between the general mass of the people and the knightly class, who later became the nobility and gentry and held the greater part of the land right down to the time when Poland lost its independence. There were both larger and smaller landowners among this class; but in the twelfth and early thirteenth centuries there was not yet that wide difference between the farms of the peasants and the estates of the gentry that there was in later times.

The monarch regarded himself as the owner of unoccupied areas, which accordingly could only be occupied with his permission. This principle, however, was not always respected in the thirteenth century. The monarch further extended his claim to all the land which was exploited by the peasantry. These territories were in course of time more or less freely reorganized in accordance with the economic requirements of the country and of the monarch; but there must have been considerable areas in later times owned by the knights which were never included within the possessions of the monarch.

In the eleventh century gifts from the monarch and from private individuals laid the foundations of the property of the Church. Almost all the dioceses received whole castellanies, embracing villages which had belonged to the monarch or to the knightage or both.[1] The bishop was granted the right of levying imposts and the powers attaching to the monarch, with certain limitations. Monasteries obtained their lands mainly by private benefactions, and afterwards rounded off their scattered villages by purchase or exchange into compact estates.

In the later Middle Ages the amount of land owned by the gentry was greater than that possessed by the monarch and the Church together. How this came about is not quite clear. Perhaps some of the knights had been holding their lands even before the rise of the Piast state. After that date the more important *haeredes* were incorporated among the large landowners. The richer ones were called to the military service of the state, and having in consequence obtained prisoners of war to work their land, themselves lost the habit of working on the soil or even of administering their country estates.

The process was hastened by grants of land by the monarch to *haeredes* in hereditary possession; and similar grants were made also to members of the monarch's *comitatus*, frequently in the thirteenth century, less frequently in the fourteenth.

The source material which has been preserved gives us but meagre information as to the size of the large estates. There can be little doubt that certain of them were scarcely distinguishable from the estates held on the same terms by the petty gentry. The upper limit of size is more difficult to determine, and accounts of individuals owning fifteen or twenty villages, some hundred *mansias* of plough land, or estates inhabited by tens or even hundreds of peasant families afford insufficient evidence on which to base conclusions.

Opinions are divided as to the proportion of the large estates to the whole area of the country at this period, some believing that the possessions of the monarch, the bishops and the larger private landowners were so extensive as to give the country a prevailingly latifundial character, while others are of the opinion that even at the beginning of the thirteenth century most estates were small, and that it was only during this century that the area occupied by the larger ones increased to a marked extent.

Only a few of the former *haeredes* entered the ranks of the great landowners, the majority, perhaps, becoming tenants, and ultimately peasants depending on the latter. Of these, the greater number passed under the supremacy of the monarch. Their hereditary rights protected them against every one but him, but he was able to absorb their fields in his own broad acres, and even to dispossess them entirely if it suited

---

[1] For the castellanies see p. 59 above.

his purpose. As the proprietary rights of the official and knightly classes were recognized and the economic organization of their estates was consolidated, the monarch's rights were extended to the lands of all who did not belong to these classes. The peasants thus lost their title to own land.

Not all the small estates were swallowed up, however. There were some knights who had but little land and cultivated it like peasants; and thus there existed a petty knightage, completely independent of the larger knightly landowners and economically distinguishable from the peasantry only by the fact that they were thus independent and paid no dues save to the State and to the Church. With the creation of the nobility some of these knights passed into it without changing their economic position, and notwithstanding the small extent of their estates they held them legally on almost exactly the same terms as their brethren who were large owners, all through the Middle Ages and down to modern times.

In Lithuania, particularly in the area inhabited by the Lithuanians, which was not organized as a State until the middle of the thirteenth century, large estates grew up a few centuries later than in Poland. The rise of the Lithuanian state was here a factor of great significance. As it extended eastward over territory inhabited by a White Russian population with an older tradition, the young Lithuanian state was brought into contact with a more highly organized system of landownership. The grand duke claimed possession of all uncultivated and uninhabited lands, which for the most part were covered with forest. As his power increased he extended his claims to areas which were economically productive. Very probably he was not uninfluenced by the example of the Teutonic Order. It was principally the small holdings of the common people which he regarded as the property of the State. After the Union with Poland grants of parcels of land in the wilderness are accompanied with increasing frequency by grants of land inhabited by peasants. As the State was built up, more than one of the larger landowners was deprived of his possessions. Particularly during the fourteenth century the grand-ducal estates increased in extent at the cost of the knightly estates.

Probably, even before the rise of the Lithuanian State, tribal or village leaders (*seniores, potentiores*) began to stand out from the mass of the common people, as well as leaders of territorial organizations (*reguli, duces*). As the power of the State increased some of them, or their descendants, obtained high official positions and in course of time became great landed proprietors. After the rise of the State there appeared an ever-growing number of warriors (*homines militares*), who also in course of time became great landowners. Apparently only the richer ones entered this higher class, for the others could not afford to go on distant expeditions. But whoever did improved his material and economic position by the booty, and especially the prisoners of war, that he brought home.

Thus the gulf continually widened between them and the peasantry from whom they sprang. Not only were their lands much more extensive than the peasants' farms, but, being occupied continually with war and the chase, they took ever less interest in the other branches of rural economy. Yet there were still at the end of the fourteenth century a number of boyars economically indistinguishable from peasants, who even in pagan times had had perhaps small, but hereditary, estates.

Private ownership of land on a large scale was promoted by the grants made by monarchs in the fifteenth century. The possessions of the boyars rapidly increased and numerous wealthy landed proprietors arose. Moreover, the privileges granted by the monarchs in 1387, 1413 and 1447, after the Union with Poland, likewise promoted the tendency; for Polish law recognized the Lithuanian boyars as having equal rights to the land with the Polish gentry.

The development of agrarian conditions in Hungary was greatly influenced by the circumstances that the founders of the Hungarian State were incomers from another district, between the Don and the Dnieper, where property distinctions existed which led to the later division into landed proprietors and dependent peasantry. Their tribal and family organization influenced the distribution of land in their new country, particular persons having special rights and the free transfer of land being subject to restriction.

All land not occupied by the Hungarian incomers was regarded by the king as his own property, and even in the eleventh century it constituted the greater part of the territory. The border districts were on a military footing, and even in the twelfth century were part of the royal domain. As the military organization of the country was perfected, lands were distributed in the second half of the tenth century among the royal servants and the knights (*servientes regis, milites, iobaggiones regis*), whether they were Hungarian or foreign, to be held direct from the king and free from the restrictions of tribal tenure. This land-distribution increased in scale during the wars of succession.

Until the end of the twelfth century the large estates, apart from the royal possessions, were scattered and comparatively unimportant. In the early years of the thirteenth century the king began to distribute lands on a large scale, and this practice ultimately led to the complete breakdown of the system of castellanies. In the thirteenth century the growth of the large estates was very rapid. For example, the endowments of the Benedictine abbey at Pannonholm in the days of St Stephen comprised ten manors, but in 1083 thirty, in 1216 forty-seven, and in 1240 eighty-eight. The efforts of Bela IV to regain the crown estates which had been distributed were unsuccessful. Later again there was a fresh increase among the large estates in the reigns of Lewis the Great and Sigismund in the second half of the fourteenth century.

The majority of large, compact estates were built up in the border districts. The thirteenth century saw the development of the nobility and of the landed property in their hands, which indeed by the year 1300 had become the dominating factor in the agrarian structure. The differences in wealth between various grades of knights, or later nobles and gentry, which at first sight were slight, were now continually accentuated, until the richer nobility (*barones, magnates*) came to be legally recognized as a privileged class.

In contrast to this higher nobility stood the gentry, possessing manors with at most thirty-two undivided farms. Some of them had no tenants at all, and cultivated the soil themselves like any peasant. Their number was always large and increased still more in the fourteenth century, when the petty castellans who had managed to maintain themselves so long received patents of nobility.

II. *Economic organization of the great estates*

In Poland the large farms of the *haeredes*, or later knights, seem to have been the germ out of which the separate large estates afterwards developed. They became gradually transformed into manors or seignories whose owners did not themselves do the work, but confined themselves to organizing and directing the activities of others. Similar manor farms were founded on the lands granted to the Church and laymen. The amount of arable land comprised in these manors varied considerably; some were no bigger than large peasant farms, while others may have extended to some hundreds of acres. In the twelfth and thirteenth centuries there were numerous manors devoted chiefly to stock raising. These are not to be considered as relics of pre-agricultural pastoralism, but exemplify the considered use of terrain for the purposes to which it was best suited, and a wise division of economic tasks. The lords' herds were entrusted to the care of particular villages, whose inhabitants had their own farms, and fulfilled their duties to their lords by looking after the herds. This organization was at the height of its development in the twelfth century, but in the thirteenth it disappeared.

By the twelfth and thirteenth centuries the social organization of these manors was complex. The work on them was done in part by a permanent body of servants, very frequently bondmen, who were employed not only as personal attendants of the lords' family, or in kitchen, garden or cattle-shed, but also in the fields, meadows and forests, and as artisans. There were agricultural labourers who had their own households and were perhaps allowed a certain freedom in looking for work outside the boundaries of the manor, and for whom paid work was of considerable significance; there were *hortulani*, who held small plots of land, or *inquilini*, who had no land. There was also the institution whereby peasant farmers performed forced work in various branches of manorial economy. On the estates belonging to the Cistercian monasteries, particularly in their early days, much of the work was done by the monks themselves, and especially by the lay brothers.

Apart from these few exceptions the most important factor in the economic structure of the great landed estates was the peasant villages which they included. Some of these had existed prior to their absorption in the larger unit and others had come into being later, partly by spontaneous colonization from the former. Such colonization might be taken under control by the landowner and directed according to his interests, as we find happening at the beginning of the twelfth century.

It is likely that most of these peasant farms were devoted to the tillage of the soil. In extent they were unequal, some being unable to maintain their own yoke of oxen and having to hire their neighbours' beasts. In such cases the occupiers might make their living by working for wages on other farms, or by stock-raising, forestry or some handicraft. The extent of the larger farms is sometimes described by specifying the number of teams required for their cultivation, some having two oxen (which were regarded as equivalent to one horse), others four oxen (or two oxen and one horse), and others again six oxen.

Besides agriculture the rural population practised fishing, hunting and various other pursuits. A certain specialization was probably the rule even before the rise of the large estates, and it was encouraged by the gathering of numerous workmen under uniform direction. Indeed increasing specialization was one of the most important changes introduced into village life by the great estates. We have no detailed information as to the various kinds of manorial employees, but we may suppose that they were mainly peasants living on their own farms. In certain cases their specialized duties did not interfere with their own work on their farms: they might be *sanctuarii* serving the more important churches, or *camerarii* at the manor house, taking messages with news or orders. Or they might be cooks in the lord's kitchen, or very possibly bakers or butchers to the manor. In all probability the same thing is true of the men employed to tend the horses, cattle and sheep or goats, while the lord's hunstmen, kennelmen and falconers, his beaver- and fox-hunters, might be drawn from the villagers who engaged in these pursuits in addition to working their fields, or who lived entirely by the chase. So it would be also for the most part with the lord's bee-keepers and fishermen and men engaged in rural handicrafts. After the growth of town life in the thirteenth century these rural craftsmen and artisans began to lose their economic importance.

In Lithuania the economic organization of the great estates is found to be in the main similar to that which prevailed in Poland, only that in the former country the characteristic forms appeared a few centuries later. Manors frequently grew out of large peasant farms, whose owners succeeded in entering the boyar class. It was only later that they increased to a size many times greater than that of the average peasant holding. The work of these seignories was performed mainly by bondslaves, descended partly from prisoners of war and partly from insolvent debtors, but employment was also given to freemen who were unable to maintain themselves on their own farms. In course of time, and especially in the fifteenth century, the practice increased of exacting forced labour for the cultivation of the lord's fields. Similar manors existed in the estates of the monarch and of the Church.

By far the greater part of the cultivated area was occupied by peasant farms, which were originally independent, but were later absorbed into the great estates after the rise of the Lithuanian State. The extent of these farms is not accurately known, for in medieval Lithuania not even arable land was measured. From later data and contemporary accounts relating to the neighbouring countries it would appear that the normal area was about 42 acres of arable land.

In the fifteenth century a marked differentiation was observable in the occupations followed by the peasantry on the great estates. This was partly due to differentiation in the structure of actual farms and villages, leading to differentiation of duties to the landlord, but in part it was merely differentiation of duties. In some cases there might be particular kinds of economic units side by side with other kinds in one and the same village; whereas in others there might be whole villages devoted to special pursuits or fulfilling special functions in certain branches of manorial economy. The differentiation might be manifested in the raising of stock—horses, sheep, or pigs—or in bee-keeping. Or again it might be observable in fishing, or more particularly in hunting, which required special foresters and gamekeepers, kennelmen, falconers and bowmen, and trappers of beaver and marten. In the fifteenth century the rural population became markedly differentiated, according as they followed this or that craft or pursuit. The towns as yet being little developed, there was a very considerable number of craftsmen of different kinds in the villages. The conditions in Lithuania at this time show a strong resemblance to conditions in Poland in the twelfth and thirteenth centuries.

As the peasant farms were absorbed into the great estates the legal position of the rural population became steadily worse, both as regards their right to hold land and their personal freedom. In the fifteenth century the liberty of the peasants to dispose of their soil was restricted, although for the most part they retained their hereditary rights. At the end of the fourteenth century the great majority of the rural population had still been personally free, and there was only a comparatively small number of bondmen. Even in the first half of the fifteenth century a grand-ducal peasant who passed to a third person in consequence of a grant of land might move away if he were unwilling to perform the duties laid upon him by his new lord. In this respect, however, his position was rendered notably worse by the grand-duke's promise, embodied in his charters of 1447, not to receive on his estates peasants who had left estates belonging to the nobility or gentry.

In Hungary economic work on the estates which have been mentioned above was organized with the help of various elements, of which one was the population inhabiting the country before the arrival of the Hungarians, another a part of the incoming Hungarians themselves. The number of these latter increased after the conversion of the Hungarians to Christianity and the cessation of their constant inroads into neighbouring countries, for some of them thereby lost their means of existence and were forced to take service under the king or the great landlords. They were given small portions of land on the latter's estates, where they retained their personal freedom, but lived in very modest economic conditions. A large number of them still followed the profession of arms, and some entered the ranks of the gentry. Those who remained at the beginning of the twelfth century were burdened with taxes; and since in course of time the principle became established that only the nobility and gentry might own land freehold, they were all finally absorbed into the great estates. They became a part of the monarch's domain, and when his lands were distributed they passed increasingly under the authority of private persons. In somewhat later times these two elements were reinforced by a third, consisting of foreigners who settled within the borders of the Hungarian state, Rumanians, Germans, and, in northern Hungary, Slavs.

In the early days of manorial organization the economic position of the rural population depended to a high degree on its legal position. With the rise of the Hungarian State the class of freemen came to comprise, besides the Hungarian conquerors, probably also the leaders of the local population, incomers (*hospites*) and freedmen. At the period of the invasion there were slaves, in the Roman sense, throughout the

territory occupied by the Hungarians, and their number increased with
the Hungarians' military raids. In so far as they were settled on the land,
they became transformed in course of time into dependants bound to
the soil, from which they were not taken away. The class of slaves
became gradually smaller, and vanished completely in the fourteenth
century.

As these elements became ever more closely included within a
uniform manorial organization, the legal position of the two groups
was regularized. The thirteenth century saw the creation of a legally
uniform class of rustics enjoying personal freedom, guaranteed by
statute in 1298 and 1351, and possessing their own movable property,
but settled on the lands of others and bound to the performance of
certain duties. Thus legally the slaves might be made equal with the
freemen, but economically the process was in the other direction, the
free being levelled down to the position of serfs.

After the regularization of the legal position of the rural population,
the main body of which was composed of *iobaggiones*, the basis of social
distinction became the amount of land which each family had for its
portion. The unit of calculation was the *sessio iobaggionalis*, but this
varied in extent not only in various parts of the country, but even in
neighbouring localities, between 12 and 25 acres, the most common ·
limits being 15–20. A *sessio* was originally a single farm unit, but
in course of time it was divided into two, four, or even eight
holdings.

Besides the *iobaggiones*, who were the most numerous part of the
rural population, we find a poorer class, the *inquilini*, who possessed
cottages and sometimes small plots of ground. Still worse off were the
sub-inquilini, who had no houses of their own and had to live and work
on other people's farms. In the fifteenth century the farms of the
peasants were greatly sub-divided, and the number of *inquilini* likewise increased.

The country people were further distinguished by their occupations.
Besides shepherds, horse-breeders, fishermen, and numerous kinds of
craftsmen, there were often also *vintiores*, specially occupied with
viticulture.

In addition to the peasant farms there were also manorial farms
(*allodia*). In the thirteenth century they were few in number, owing to
the undeveloped state of the towns and their prevailingly agricultural
character. As in Poland, these manorial farms only became more
widespread in the fifteenth century, as a result of the prosperity of
the towns and their consequent growing demand for agricultural
products. The already existing *allodia* were then extended and new ones
founded.

III. *Burdens borne by the rural population*

In Poland the burdening of the rural population with imposts and duties was the most important change in the social structure brought about by the rise of large estates. Two kinds of burdens are here to be distinguished: manorial services exacted by the great landed proprietors, and state burdens imposed by ducal law. In actual practice these two categories are not only in close mutual dependence, but are frequently so interwoven that they can no longer be properly distinguished. This was especially the case on the monarch's domains. There was, it is true, a twofold organization corresponding to the double character of the burdens laid on the people. As a rule compact estates comprising a number of villages and called *claves* ('keys') were administered from the manor-house (*curia*), which was also the residence of particular officials (*procuratores, villici*). Here the peasants brought their produce in payment of manorial imposts, and here they performed work in fulfilment of manorial exactions. These manor houses were stopping-places for the monarch on his constant journeys through the country.

All the 'keys' within the confines of a castellany had an important administrative centre in the castle (*castrum*). The administration of public services due under ducal law was the main bond uniting the villages of a castellany: not merely the villages lying on the monarch's *claves*, but all the other villages as well. Relics of this organization still existing in the sixteenth century permit us to suppose that even in the twelfth and thirteenth there was no clear and absolute division between the two categories of imposts. Before the granting of immunity from monarchal taxation the distinction was strictly observed on the estates of the Church and the knightage, but the extension of immunity caused the two categories to be confounded even here, since some of the burdens exacted under ducal law were not abolished but combined with the manorial exactions. It was only on the petty estates, particularly of the knights, where there were no manorial dues, that the burdens exacted under ducal law were kept entirely distinct.

In contrast to these last, concerning which we have much information in the charters of immunity, the manorial dues exacted in the villages under Polish law have left but few traces in documents between the twelfth and the fourteenth centuries. It seems likely that these dues were in fact more extensive and more varied than would appear from contemporary sources. Pecuniary rent, though sometimes mentioned, played but a small part in comparision with payments in kind. Of these the most important were payments of grain, which were made by the majority of the tenants on a number of estates whose records have been examined. They usually consisted of rye, wheat and oats, sometimes in the sheaf, but usually threshed. Sometimes payments were made in malt, while minor manorial dues might be discharged in fowls, cheeses, eggs, or flax. We often here of dues paid in honey, not only by bee keepers who made their living out of their hives, but also by agricultural workers and craftsmen; and often also of payments in fish. Among the productions of handicrafts which were brought in discharge of obligations were wheels, by the wheelwrights, wooden mugs and dishes by the turners, and tubs, bottles, mugs and pots by the potters. The amount of these payments was dependent on the extent of the farm from which they were exacted.

Obligations were also discharged in terms of labour: in the various operations connected with the production of grain, in the kitchen garden, in the meadows and the forest, at fishing and hunting. Among the craftsmen, the potters had to repair old earthenware vessels, the cobblers to repair boots, and the builders although possessing their own farms had to give their work when required. This labour was sometimes measured by the quantity of work done: at harvest, by the number of shocks mown; at haymaking, by the number of cart-loads of hay; in the forests, by the number of wagon-loads of timber which the peasants had to transport, or by the number of trunks which they had to saw up. Sometimes, again, it was measured by the number of days, which varied as a rule between five or six and fifteen or sixteen in the year. And sometimes neither its quality nor its quantity was predetermined. At the time of which we are speaking the rural population was regularly burdened with the obligations under ducal law sometimes indistinguishably combined with the manorial exactions. They were borne principally by the peasantry, since the knights who had peasants on their estates performed no duties themselves except military service, and the petty knightage possessing but small pieces of land enjoyed considerable relief from them.

Some burdens were directly connected with the various functions of the state; above all in the fields of communications, administration and military preparation. Thus the peasants were obliged to furnish men, horses and carts for the transport of the impedimenta of the monarch, or of his officials, or of foreign envoys. There was the obligation to receive and entertain the monarch, officials and envoys, with their huntsmen and other servants, and also to provide for their horses and dogs. The peasantry on these occasions had to give grain, honey, cows, pigs and wax. Further, there was the obligation to build and maintain fortified castles, and to furnish a guard or look-out for them. A minor duty was to apprehend transgressors.

There were also permanent imposts, the oldest being apparently the payment in livestock, originally pigs, but afterwards chiefly sheep and cows. Added to these were various monarchal monopolies, which affected alike the estates of the Church and the knights, such as the royal right to the income from mines, fairs, inns and mills.

In the twelfth century, and more particularly in the thirteenth, monarchs granted charters of immunity to certain ecclesiastical and knightly estates, exempting them wholly or partly from this or that obligation under ducal law. The earliest recipients of such charters were monasteries, but afterwards dioceses also obtained them. The range of economic immunity conferred varied greatly. Each charter had its own individual character, although particular provisions were repeated in various cases. The result was that only relics of the old burdens under ducal law were preserved until the fourteenth century. As far as the knights' estates were concerned they were all abolished by the general charter of 1374, which left only a land tax of two groats on each *manse*; while the estates of the Church were similarly exempted by the charter of 1381, fixing the same tax for peasants on episcopal estates, and four groats a *manse* together with certain payments in grain for the peasants on monastic estates.[1]

In Lithuania in the fourteenth century manorial dues were comparatively rare, but they became widespread and various in the century following, when they comprised various payments in kind: in grain (principally oats and rye), hops, hay, timber, sheep, cattle, pigs, domestic fowls, eggs, beavers and martens. The fifteenth century saw an increase of payments in money, hitherto almost unknown. The basis of taxation was not the amount of land cultivated, but the number of yoke oxen, the number of ploughs, the household economy (*fumus*), and further such sources of income as hunting reserves, nests of beavers, bee forests, and lakes. Forced labour was comparatively rare before the end of the fourteenth century, but in the fifteenth it became more common. In these two centuries peasants burdened with obligations to the monarch, the Church and the boyars formed the great majority of the rural population of Lithuania. Besides manorial dues they all paid dues to the Church, and the peasants subject to the boyars and the Church were burdened also with separate obligations to the state. The grand duke and the dukes were entitled to certain payments and services from the inhabitants of the boyars' domains, mainly in connexion with the defence of the country, the construction of fortifications and the maintenance of the armed forces. The duty of providing transport for the monarch and his officials, and 'stations' where they might find rest

[1] The Polish sources from the thirteenth century onwards regularly use the term *mansus*, much as it was used in earlier centuries in the West. Cf. p. 241, above.

and refreshment on their journeys, lay partly in the field of defence and partly in that of ordinary administration.

After the Union with Poland the estates of the Church and of the boyars were exempted from these state obligations, and the manorial imposts could consequently be increased. The first to obtain this economic immunity were the estates of the Church, and when grants of land were made to the Church at the end of the fourteenth and the beginning of the fifteenth century this exemption was incorporated in the title-deeds. In 1387 the boyars were exempted from certain personal services, and a royal edict of 1434 exempted the subjects on their domains from payments in kind for the benefit of the monarch. In 1447 the monarch resigned his claim to permanent money payments and labour from private-estate peasants in carrying stones and timber for the construction of castles, calcining lime, or cutting hay. This charter had the same significance for Lithuania as that of 1374 for Poland.

In Hungary the deciding factor in the imposition of duties was the division of the population into bond and free. The duties of the latter were very varied, and were frequently fixed for each farm separately. Sometimes they were purely symbolic. Besides the manorial dues the rural population on private estates was burdened with certain obligations on the state, in connexion mainly with its defence and the administrative system of castellanies. The distribution of estates in the thirteenth century led to the breakdown of this organization, the population of the lands distributed being excluded from the legal and administrative jurisdiction of the royal officials. In the thirteenth century the Golden Bull and later ordinances led to the exemption of the peasants on private estates from the burdens imposed on them by the castellany system.

The growth of large private estates was followed by changes very unfavourable to the rural population. The growth of trade and towns and the consequent prevalence of pecuniary standards, and the rise in the standard of life of the higher classes, led to the raising and regularizing of the dues exacted from the peasants. Payments in kind were required of peasants who had hitherto been exempt. Tithes were required of those who already gave forced labour. Fishermen were required to give agricultural products as well as fish. The institution of forced labour was extended: *sacriferi* were now used also as messengers, and those who had hitherto performed forced labour only in the fields were now required to transport wine, even beyond the borders of the country, and to maintain their horses on the way; a burden formerly shouldered by the lord. Work with the teams was exacted even of artisans and of *officiales*, the highest grade in the hierarchy of estate employees. Pecuniary rent was increasingly demanded in addition to the former payments in kind.

The worst effects of the growth of private landed property were, however, felt by those who before had been most favourably situated, the *iobaggiones castri* who had had for the most part only military duties to perform. They did not, it is true, lose their freedom to change their place of abode and still claim protection of the king, but their new lords could demand what duties they liked of them if they stayed. For these freemen absorption into the organization of a private estate was a great misfortune bringing a complete revolution in their position.

The dues, exacted from the *iobaggiones* thus newly incorporated in the great estates, were fixed in relation to the amount of land which they held. For each unit of land (*sessio*) mentioned above, a rent of at least 20 *denarii* was paid. Most frequently it was 40–60 *denarii*, and at the end of the Middle Ages was 100, or one florin. Manorial payments in kind were regularized by Lewis the Great in 1351. After the subtraction of the tithe for the Church a second tithe was to be paid to the landlord, which, being one-ninth of the produce that was left, was called *nona*. Owing, however, to the resistance of the peasants, this impost was exacted only in some parts of the country. Throughout the greater part of the country the peasants paid a fixed amount of grain (wheat and oats) independently of the quantity harvested, and even when they did not cultivate either of these crops. This payment was called *aconalia*, being assessed in tubsful (Hungarian *akó*). In the pastoral settlements of Roumanians in Transylvania a payment of stock was exacted, called *quinquagesima*. As late as the fifteenth century forced labour was rare. There were no fixed days as yet for work on the lord's land, but certain tasks were required from the inhabitants of single villages. At that period forced labour was no heavy burden, seldom exceeding a few days in the year. On the other hand the *inquilini* with little or no land were obliged for the most part to give labour, and paid very small money-rents. They made no payments in kind. There were also manorial monopolies, which have not as yet been investigated in detail. Only those who held land paid state taxes, which were not paid by *inquilini* or *sub-inquilini*.

IV. *Colonization under German law*

In Poland the system described above and known as the system of villages under Polish law gave way in the thirteenth and fourteenth centuries to colonization under German law. The history of the beginning of this movement in the last years of the twelfth century is doubtful. The main condition of the new type of settlement was the exemption of the village in question from Polish law, i.e. from the jurisdiction of the monarchal officials and the obligations under ducal law. Without the attainment of this immunity from the monarch, colonization under German law could not take place; and this colonization became an important factor leading to the extension of the economic immunity referred to above.

This colonizing movement was initiated and directed by some of the great landowners, as well as by the Church and the monarch. The Cistercians, who maintained active relations with the West, were particularly active in this field. As early as the twelfth century the landed proprietors showed an inclination to colonize their forest areas and to regulate the obligations of their peasants in pecuniary terms. In the thirteenth century the political situation no longer offered opportunities for settling colonies of prisoners of war, as had been done in the first half of the twelfth century, and consequently incomers from other countries were welcomed. And when it proved impossible to attract them in sufficient numbers recourse was had to local elements, more especially to the representatives of that half-nomad class who in the previous period had cleared forest land and transformed it into arable —an activity which was becoming less and less common. There were marked differences in the destiny of the population in various districts, some being greatly in need of fresh settlers, while others were not; but such inequalities could be neutralized by migration within the country itself.

When a colony was to be planted the services of a special agent, locator, were used, who then as a rule became headman (*scultetus, iudex*) in the village he had founded. Sometimes he might be the leader of a party of settlers and their spokesman in negotiations with the lord, but more frequently he was the latter's agent who looked for fresh settlers and arranged the terms of their coming. They were drawn from various social classes. Many were townsfolk, others servants from manor houses or administrators of estates, others again peasants. When a village was founded and the headman's farm was of considerable size we find increasingly frequent examples of a noble resigning his own lands, which were probably smaller in extent, and settling as the headman of a colony.[1]

The introduction of settlers from outside in days when communications were not developed required considerable financial resources. These were provided by the headmen, who in return for their trouble and expense received grants of land which frequently were of very considerable value. Colonization undertakings might in favourable circumstances be so profitable that a headman might pay larger or smaller sums for the right to 'locate' a party of settlers. Some headmen were so wealthy that they located and became headmen of several such

[1] Compare the discussions on p. 86 and p. 462, above.

parties; while others, less well off, clubbed together to carry out a location. In other cases, again, a large landowner had himself to bear at least a part of the expense and pay a headman for carrying out a contract. Colonization on a large scale in the more extensive forest areas was risky and could only be undertaken by institutions possessing capital, such as the Cistercian order or that of the Knights Templar.

In the early days of the movement an important part was played by Flemish and German settlers. These incomers from other countries, and also such as came from other parts of the same country, were in a better position than the local population in relation to their lord, for they had been able to make their own conditions beforehand, and the landowners realized that it was not to their interest to hamper the economic development of the newcomers by imposing the traditional burdens upon them. The village organization was therefore not decided by the sole will of the landowner, but by an agreement between the two interested parties. It is true that the location contracts defining the mutual relations of village and lord are drawn up in the form of one-sided charters, but in reality they are the result of an agreement between the lord and the agent who undertook to introduce the colonists.

These location contracts embody a definite programme of change in agricultural conditions and a legal framework within which this programme might be realized. Their most characteristic feature is the regularization of an important type of rural economic unit, namely the independent farm large enough not only properly to maintain the farmer's family, but also to furnish a satisfactory proportion of income for the landowner. The holders of such farms, known as *cmethones*, became the most numerous section of the rural population. Most frequently each family received a *manse* of arable land, or sometimes two, but in later times the amount was smaller, sometimes only half a *manse*. The amount of meadow was proportional to that of arable, but differed in different villages. The village as a whole received half or a whole *manse*, or even several *manses*, as common pasture land. The possession of such a farm carried with it various rights of fishing, hunting, grazing and cutting wood in the forests.

Provision was made not only for the *cmethones* but also, particularly in later location contracts, for *hortulani* with but little land, and also for a certain number of craftsmen; millers, inn-keepers, bakers, cobblers and smiths.

The income from the headmen's farms was considerably greater than that from the farms of the peasants. They comprised in the first place arable land, the extent of which is most variously described in the documents. Sometimes the number of *manses* is given, and may be five or six, or as many as twelve, or may be in proportion to the total number assigned to the village, say three for every ten; or it is simply stated that the headman takes all the *manses* over the number allotted to the *cmethones*. There may be a formal acknowledgement of his right to take for himself the best land, which in any case was implicit in his function of assigning each settler his portion. In addition to his *manses* of arable the headman had a large or smaller amount of pasture, maybe what was left after the peasants had received their share, together with something extra. The headman might either put tenants of his own on his land, or he might farm it, on a scale resembling that rather of a great landowner than of a peasant settler. He also had the right to settle a specified number (1–8) of *hortulani* to work for him, or one in every three cottages might belong to him. He possessed the right of laying down fish-ponds, catching fish in the rivers and lakes, and hunting or trapping hares, foxes and birds, and sometimes bigger game, and might also set up tree-hives in the forests. He might bring in craftsmen to work for him, and establish inns and mills. A sixth of the peasants' rent and payments in kind went to the headman, and a third of the general revenue of the village. Sometimes the inhabitants had to make him small payments in kind, or even to perform some compulsory labour for his benefit, though this is mentioned only in documents of late date.

The importance or otherwise of all these privileges depended on the degree of success attending the colonization project. In favourable circumstances the headmen might create for themselves farms rivalling those of the gentry in extent and economic level; whereas if fortune was against them they might remain merely rich peasants. There were also great differences in the prices for which they bought their offices.

A similar economic position attached to the dignity of parson, although it was more modestly endowed than was that of headman, usually with not more than one or two *manses* of arable, sometimes with the right of establishing a mill, or more rarely an inn.

In these villages under German law the duties and obligations of the *cmethones* were in strict proportion to the *manses* of land they held, and there were less differences between the assessments of particular villages than there were under Polish law. The main obligation resting on the peasant was the payment of rent, which was occasionally lower than usual if payments in kind were added. Fourteenth-century location charters show that rent was raised as money declined in value. As a rule each settler paid separate rent for his farm, collective rents paid by whole settlements being rare.

Further, almost all the location charters mention payments in grain, generally rye, wheat and oats, rarely also in barley, most frequently to the amount of 12 bushels. These two payments, in money and kind, covered both manorial and ecclesiastical dues, the proportion assigned to each depending on agreement between the landowner and the Church. It appears that usually the lord retained the money and surrendered the grain to the Church. Where payment was not made in threshed grain tithe was exacted in sheaves, or a special equivalent rent was paid.

Apart from these portions of grain only insignificant dues were exacted in kind. Particular farms were required to send eggs, chickens, capons and cheeses, and occasionally honey or other products. Special fees were sometimes charged for permission to hunt or fish or cut wood in the forest. There were also collective 'gifts', called *honores*, of cows, heifers, rams, pigs, hams, sirloins, or their money equivalent, made once or twice a year by a whole village on the occasion of specially solemn festivals. Further, a whole village would be obliged to receive the lord or his representative twice a year when he went on circuit to hold courts, and to give provisions, or money in lieu of them, for his *prandia*.

Labour exactions are mentioned seldom in thirteenth-century documents, more frequently, but still not often, in the fourteenth. It was usually a question of some few days' (two to six) work in the fields or at hay-cutting, transporting timber from the forest, furnishing the lord with conveyances for his journeys, and so on. Similar but much lighter obligations were imposed on the cottagers.

The headmen's farms were free from obligations to the lord, with the exception that one dinner had to be provided, or an equivalent money payment made, if he came to the village. Sometimes *honores* also were required, like those brought by the peasants. Headmen were obliged to present themselves with arms in their hands for military service.

All these dues, it is to be noticed, became operative, not immediately upon the founding of a colony, but after a period of years, which might be short or long, varying indeed from one to twenty-five, according as the settlers were farming land which was already fit for agriculture, or had to clear the forest before they could work it.

Manorial farms owned by the lords of villages under German law were of no great significance in the system. In the majority of cases there were none, and where they did exist they were of modest extent, not exceeding two to four *manses*, seldom more. Frequently such a farm was subdivided when a colony was founded.

Not all the plans outlined in location charters were realized. In some cases no village was actually founded at all, and the extent of those which were came usually short of what had been originally projected. The number of *manses* provided for was as a rule between 20 and 50, and occasionally was more than 100, whereas the commonest size attained was ten or fifteen farms of a *manse* each or even less. These small villages were unable to maintain the number of craftsmen it had been proposed to settle in them. The cottages with gardens where these craftsmen (therefore classed as *hortulani*) were to live proved insufficient for their livelihood, which they were accordingly compelled to seek by working for the richer *cmethones*.

The new system, nevertheless, proved so profitable to the landlords that they began to introduce it into long-existent Polish villages, which were 'made over', as was said, into villages under German law; immunity from state burdens was obtained for them, a headman was appointed, and the dues required of the inhabitants were modified. This might be done as an accompaniment to the introduction of a certain number of fresh settlers from outside, or it might be without this. At the end of the Middle Ages we find, besides this complete assimilation to the new system, cases of partial assimilation, the dues being made the same as in villages under German law, while other conditions, and particularly the legal system in force, were left unchanged. Nevertheless, the process did not go far enough, either by the end of the fourteenth century or later, to revolutionize the agrarian system completely. Even after the Middle Ages there remained villages, single or in groups, unaffected either directly or indirectly by the example of German law, and retaining manorial dues and other customs unchanged from the pre-colonization period. They were particularly to be found in the eastern parts of Poland.

In Lithuania the process of colonization under German law began considerably later than in Poland: not till the first half of the sixteenth century. Then, however, the new villages were organized on exactly the same lines as in Poland in the Middle Ages. They were to be found mainly in the western border districts of the country, particularly in Podlachia; but generally speaking they had no great influence on the economic structure of Lithuania.

In Hungary German colonization began earlier than in Poland. There were settlements of peasants in the twelfth century, but in the thirteenth the intensity of colonization increased after the devastations caused by the Mongol invasion. At the beginning of the fifteenth century it reached its culminating point, the greatest concentrations being in Transylvania to the east and in Zips to the north, though there were German colonies in other parts of the country also.

In Hungary as in Poland villages planted under German law were excluded from the jurisdiction of the royal officials and by virtue of special charters might follow their own laws and customs. Their inhabitants were also exempted from the ordinary obligations to the castellany, and had the right to move from the settlement if they desired.

After the lapse of some five, ten, or twenty years exempt from all obligations, the settlers had to discharge certain permanent annual duties. The manorial dues consisted mainly of money rent, and it was very common to fix a collective rent for a whole commune, or even district, though we hear also of rent paid by individuals in proportion to their holdings of land. The payments in kind, and above all the tithe of grain and wine, were usually assigned to the Church. There were also petty manorial payments, called *munera* or *honores*, and an obligation to provide night quarters and maintenance for the lord and his attendants, or his officials, when they passed on journeys. On the other hand the institution of compulsory labour is quite the exception. German law was applied not only to colonists of German nationality but also to fresh settlements of Slavs in Northern Hungary.

Medieval Agrarian Society in its Prime

§ 6. Russia

I. *Introductory*

A. *Sources*

Study of the medieval agrarian history of Russia is beset with many difficulties. The first difficulty is that the written sources, especially prior to the fourteenth century, are extremely limited. Russian chronicles are relatively abundant and varied, but they are not primarily concerned with matters of interest to the economic, still less the agrarian, historian. They refer, however, to famines, peasant disturbances and similar matters, and even quote from deeds, such as contracts, usually made between the princes ruling different parts of the territory. From the twelfth century, though, we have only two original deeds, the earlier of which is a grant with immunities, dated about 1130. The other, which at least one scholar does not accept as genuine, is a deed of gift from the late twelfth century or possibly early thirteenth century. There are a few other similar deeds of gift and sale which have come down to us, allegedly from a period prior to the Mongol invasions of the thirteenth century. None are original documents and some are certainly forgeries of later date.

The collection of legal material known as *Russkaya Pravda* is also an important source, the earliest parts of which were probably recorded in the first half of the eleventh century; it throws more light, however, on social relations than on economic matters. There are also later law codes drawn up in the centralized state, Muscovy, dating from the end of the fifteenth century. These are helpful supplements to the many hundreds of deeds, mostly from the fifteenth and sixteenth centuries, which have come down to us. There is, however, no equivalent even in these centuries to the abundant estate records available for the thirteenth and fourteenth centuries in England.

The lack of documentary evidence for economic history is not entirely due to lack of literacy. The formal adoption of Christianity in 988 or 989 and the gradual extension of the new faith throughout the area was accompanied by the spread of literacy at least among the clergy. It has also been argued that there was writing in the first half of the tenth century. It increased with the advent of Christianity, being used in both church services and chronicle writing, and it seems altogether unlikely that writing was restricted to these purposes alone. The discovery of documents inscribed on birch bark indicates that a writing material was readily available over the greater part of the Russian territory. Almost all such finds are from Novgorod, but isolated ones have also come from Smolensk, Vitebsk, Pskov and Chernigov: some of these documents are from the eleventh and twelfth centuries. Being perishable, such documents only survive in particularly favourable circumstances. Presumably many documents were lost in the numerous fires, some accidental, but more frequently due to the wars between princes or the invasions from the West or from the East. When documents became less rare in the fourteenth and fifteenth centuries they were still exposed to the same danger. When Tokhtamysh khan sacked Moscow in 1382 the churches in the Kremlin were said to be stacked to the vaulting with books gathered in for safety 'from the whole town and from the outlying places and the villages'; all were destroyed.

Our second difficulty is that the size of the area with which we are concerned is very large, but we can make only crude calculations of its actual extent. By about A.D. 1000 it probably covered more than 420,000 square miles. By the early thirteenth century, the area, including the enormous territories in the north at least nominally subject to Novgorod, had more than doubled in size, and amounted to well over 900,000 square miles, despite the constant threat to the south-eastern borders from nomadic steppe peoples. Subsequently, with the expansion of the Lithuania and occupation by Poles, Hungarians and the Teutonic Order, the southern and western territories were lost, and by the fifteenth century the area was reduced to perhaps 750,000 square miles. By 1505, when Ivan III died, Moscow had established her hegemony and the Russian State was about to start regaining the lost territories. This point has been taken as the chronological limit of this paper. At this time the territory amounted to about 850,000 square miles. Subsequently the eastward advance towards the central Urals gained momentum with the fall of Kazan' in 1552. The steady advance of the fortified defence lines in the south and south-east, as the Russians first held and then pushed back or absorbed the steppe dwellers, also took place in the sixteenth century.

Yet even when the territory was most restricted, in the mid-fifteenth century, it included areas of near tundra type, coniferous forest, mixed woods, and also forest steppe areas. The soils varied from acid bogs and leached loamy or sandy podzols to black earths (chernozems) rich in humus. Moreover, the peoples inhabiting the territory included not only Slavs, but also various Finnish peoples, in great part already assimilated, and other ethnic groups.

The very abundance of land itself posed problems. It meant that there was usually the chance of moving on and finding almost as good land available for cultivation elsewhere. Thus, small groups could hive off established communities and colonize new areas. It was never easy to win new farmland from the forest. This is shown by the value attached to old worked land and the lengthy periods of relaxation of taxation granted to peasants undertaking to clear forest land; but it was almost always possible, and was frequently preferred to the alternative of revolt. The dissatisfied could try to escape their troubles beyond the local border; this was easier in areas of open frontier, as in the southeast, than in the central areas where control was more effective. These borders, moreover, were often vague; documents indicating estate boundaries only infrequently refer to the limits imposed by neighbouring holdings. The result was that landlords were much concerned to retain and attract peasants to their abundant lands.

The size of the area, and the varieties of physical and ethnic environment it contained, have made the limitations of the documentary evidence more keenly felt. In Russia itself research into the country's past was dominated in the nineteenth century by the question of serfdom, especially after the formal liberation of the serfs in 1861. The history of the peasantry was frequently equated with the history of serfdom. The result was that the peasants themselves almost ceased to be the subject of discussion; the relationships with their masters had become the central topic. These were naturally discussed in terms coloured by gentry experience which did not always make adequate allowances for the all but unrecorded views of peasants, serf or free. It was partly for lack of sources, partly because of general interest in the historical development of Western Europe, that some scholars, such as Petrushevsky and Vinogradoff, turned to that area as a field of study. But the nineteenth-century preoccupation with documentary evidence, native or foreign, necessarily focused attention largely on the part played by the state; and in attempting to account for the origins of serfdom, and of the Russian State itself, historians of the school then dominant formulated the problems almost entirely in legal and institutional terms. The imposition of serfdom on the peasantry was conceived largely as if it resulted from free contractual agreements. Such views still survive, fossilized in some of our own standard histories. The reality of the situation, however, seems to have been that men became serfs both by commendation and through indebtedness incurred through loans, often in the form of implements or livestock. Moreover, as this process took place on lands over which the lords claimed jurisdiction, sometimes backed by grants of immunity, contracts were likely to favour them, rather than their peasants.

In the twentieth century, and especially since the 1920s, the situation has been much modified mainly because much more attention has been given to this subject in historical research than was ever done in the past. Scholars such as S. B. Veselovskii have made available new material, while others, such as B. D. Grekov, have put forward new syntheses. Moreover, the auxiliary historical disciplines, such as archaeology, have been developed and made use of with considerable success, despite inherent limitations, in illuminating periods which may be regarded as proto-historic. The opportunities for abstract speculation and schemes, afforded largely by the lack of documentary evidence, and fully indulged by many nineteenth-century historians, have not always been avoided in more recent work. At times archaeological analysis and interpretation has had to conform to the trend of the moment. Nevertheless, the mass of new material which has been collected, together with new interpretations, help to supplement the documentary sources and to avoid an over-institutional approach to the medieval agrarian history of Russia.

B. *The physical environment*

The physical environment of the lands occupied by the East Slavs in the tenth century varied considerably within the vast uniformity of the East European plain. In the north, south of the lichens and dwarf birch of the tundra, coniferous forest extended roughly to a line from south of Ladoga to Kazan'. This line indicates approximately the northern limits of Slav settlement at this time; but this open frontier was soon pushed forward to north and east by the colonization which extended the lands of Novgorod and of Rostov-Suzdal'. The coniferous forest, the northern *taiga*, consists mainly of spruce fir, larch, silver fir and cedar, but deciduous trees such as birch, aspen and alder are also found. As one moves south through the coniferous zone the areas of sphagnum bog become less frequent. The soils are podzols together with peat and marsh. The land, once scoured by glaciers, abounds with lakes and stagnant water and is strewn with boulders and glacial debris.

The lake region also extends to cover the north-western part of the next vegetational zone, the great triangle of mixed woods the south-east boundary of which approximates to a line joining Kazan' to Kiev. This zone consists mainly of deciduous forests, but also of some conifers. This triangle, composed mainly of poor podzol soils with extensive marshes north of the Western Dvina and of the Oka, as well as along the Pripet, contained all that was to be the core of medieval Russia. The open area of Opol'e, north-west of Vladimir, is noteworthy as an oasis of fertile grey earth; it was the basis for an exceptional local development and a source of grain for other areas. Moscow itself is in a large plain which remained well wooded till the late seventeenth century.

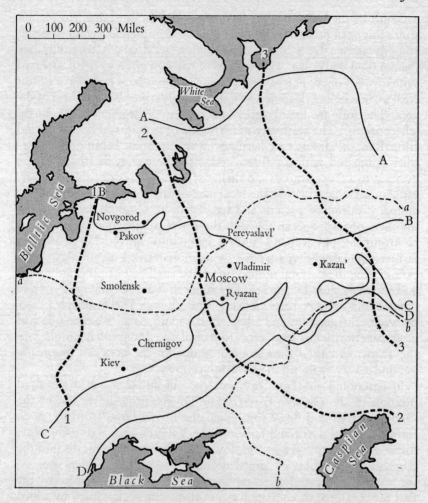

FIG. 7. European Russia: climate and vegetation.

Vegetation: A, northern limit of rye cultivation; B, southern limit of coniferous forest; C, southern limit of mixed and deciduous forest; D, southern limit of forest steppe.

Moisture: a, southern limit of surplus moisture; b, northern limit of area liable to moisture deficiency.

Winters	mean temperature in coldest month
east of 1 moderately mild	− 5°C to −10°C
2 moderately cold	−10°C to −15°C
3 cold	−15°C to −20°C

South of the zone of mixed woods is the forest steppe. In former times this extended much further south than at present, its limits being roughly shown by a line from Kishinev in Moldavia to Kuibyshev (Samara) on the Volga. Here blocks of oak and birch were interspersed with areas of open, grass-covered steppe. The zone is nowadays almost treeless, but, before clearance, woods probably covered 50 per cent of the area. The soils are mainly grey and dark grey degraded black earths (chernozems). The relatively narrow belt of grey earths which extend from Ryazan' almost to Chernigov was important because of its fertility compared with the forest podzols. Moreover, the forest steppe even up to a few centuries ago sheltered many more animals than now. Human activities, mainly the clearance of the forest, has changed the animal distribution pattern and has led to an absolute decline in the numbers of most species. Within the forest steppe zone two types of environment, physical and cultural, came into contact. The woodland farmers were doubtless attracted by its more fertile soils and its grazing possibilities; the pastoral nomads were attracted by its timber and water and abundant near-by pasture. As a result, this area became the zone of contact and conflict between Slav, Finnish and Turkic peoples, later between Christendom and Islam, Europe and Asia. Neither side had clear superiority for two centuries until the Mongols triumphed in the 1240s; extensive Russian colonization of the area did not really get under way again till the sixteenth century.

In describing the East Slav area the chronicler ascribed a central position to the Okovsk Forest. 'The Dnepr, now, flows out of the Okovsk Forest and flows south, and the Dvina flows from the same forest and goes north and falls into the Varyang Sea. From the same forest the Volga flows east and flows through seventy mouths into the Khvalinsk Sea.' Solov'ev said that Russia was a land of river sources; the mouths of these great rivers were outside the area occupied by the East Slavs. To the three river systems of the chronicler Solov'ev added the lake region of Novgorod; again, the mouth of the river system, the Neva, was not securely in Russian hands till the eighteenth century.

The importance of the river systems was thought to lie in their serving as routes of colonization and arteries of trade. The part played by agriculture and its relationship to colonization has till recently not been studied concretely and sometimes has been altogether ignored.

II. Settlements

A. Terminology

Most rural settlements were hamlets. The name which was probably used to signify a hamlet, *ves'*, was common to the Slavonic languages, but it is now found among the East Slavs only in Belorussia and the area west and south-west of Novgorod. The term for a hamlet now current (*derevnya*) only occurs in the sources from the fourteenth century on. In the Smolensk area, the Novgorod lands and in the north-west generally another term used was *pogost*. This meant both a hamlet (distinguished in modern Russian as *pogost-mesto*) and also the village centre of a relatively small area (*pogost-tsentr*), perhaps with a substantial part of its population engaged in handicrafts or trade and so approximating to a small town. Finally, *pogost* may refer to the area itself (*pogost-okrug*). But while in its original usage *pogost* indicates a settlement not on the estate of a landowner, *selo* seems, from the tenth century when it first occurs, to indicate a village on such an estate, or to be used in place of the later term *derevnya*; from the fourteenth century in the north the terms *selo* and *drevnya* seem to be almost interchangeable. As Christianity slowly spread after its formal adoption late in the tenth century, *selo* came, from the sixteenth century, to mean a village with a church. The next higher unit was the town (*gorod*), the term being used to indicate the area dependent on the town in at least an administrative sense. A larger administrative unit was a principality known as *volost'* or *oblast'*; each was usually headed by a member of the Rurik dynasty.

Two further terms need to be mentioned. The early Russian law, known as the Law of Yaroslav (*Pravda Yaroslava*) which is dated not later than the mid-eleventh century, refers to the peasant commune as *mir*. In the comparable clause of the Expanded Version of this law, dated to the twelfth or early thirteenth century, the term *mir* is replaced by *gorod*. More common in these early laws, however, is the term *verv'* which also seems to indicate a commune.

B. *The forest zone*

In many cases the precise location of isolated farmsteads and small hamlets is no longer known. Many of the 20,000 barrow burials recorded occur in groups near no recognized settlement. The distribution of these burial grounds suggests that there were near-by settlements, but that in the northern areas they were for the most part small. For instance, there is a cluster of barrow burials in the Volga region south of Kostroma, but each is small in numbers, usually not more than fifteen to twenty burials in each group; the barrow burial grounds of the central Dnepr region contain larger numbers of burials. North of the Volga, barrow burials are widely scattered in small groups, except for some very extensive clusters west and north-west of Novgorod along the upper reaches of the Luga and between the middle

Luga and the coast of the Gulf of Finland. Moreover, even where small hamlet sites are known, little material has been published about them.

Excavations at town sites such as Staraya Ladoga, Dmitrov and Novgorod in the forested north show that there were surface-built log huts from the ninth century at the latest. The dimensions of such huts were largely determined by the size of the available timbers; these rarely exceeded 25 feet in length, and were usually about 18 feet long. Many of the log huts found in the north, both at town sites and at the sites of rural settlements of various types, were about 15 feet long and nearly square. This is the approximate size of houses in Staraya Ladoga, Novgorod (where there were also many larger timber houses), Staraya Ryazan' and at a number of small sites in the central Smolensk area. Roofs were usually of straw thatch and were pitched in two directions. The stoves found in such houses were usually built of stones, often situated in a corner or against one of the hut walls and without a chimney; sometimes, however, there was no stove, only an open hearth. The expressive Russian phrase to describe this is 'to heat blackly' (topit' po chernomu) and recalls the phrase of Daniil Zatochnik (twelfth century) that 'unless you suffer the woes of smoke, you will not see the heat'.

Unfortunately, hardly anything seems to be known about changes in the size of peasant dwellings over time, although it is sometimes claimed that the complex type of peasant house containing a room with a stove (izba), an unheated room (klet') used as a summer bedroom and for stores, and a hall (seni) between the two, appeared some time in the tenth to thirteenth centuries. There does not appear to be any archaeological confirmation that houses of this type were common before the Mongol invasions. Owing to lack of evidence we do not know whether simple huts, together with their outbuildings, often of lean-to type, and storage pits, sometimes surrounded by a wooden palisade, were also typical of the smaller rural settlements. We know that isolated farmsteads and small hamlets of up to four houses existed at a later date, for they are recorded in many fifteenth- to sixteenth-century cadasters for the northern forest area. In the Moscow and Yaroslavl' areas, for instance, hamlets of up to three houses predominated, in the Rostov area those of up to two, and in the Kostroma area those with between two and four houses. The more fertile Opol'e area, however, had settlements of larger size, many with 20 to 40 houses.

Until recently the lack of documentary evidence led to the belief that the Russian village was not formed until the sixteenth century. This belief fitted in with the assumption of a high degree of peasant mobility, amounting it would seem almost to nomadism. Evidence which has accumulated in the last thirty years about the nature of the farming techniques used in these areas, as well as more recent archaeological evidence on settlement size, though still inadequate to generalize for all areas, suggest a need to modify this view substantially.

Evidence for the areas covered by the basins of Lakes Ladoga and Il'men, the upper reaches of the Western Dvina, Dnepr and Volga, and the Oka basin suggests that the most frequent size of rural settlement in the tenth to twelfth centuries was from four to six houses. The overwhelming majority of the settled population lived in settlements with more than five houses. This calculation is based on the assumption, confirmed at many investigated sites, that the distance between peasant dwellings was of the order of 60 to 80 feet. Many more excavations of complete sites are required, however, in order to confirm this assumption, which may underestimate the number of dwellings.

For the central Smolensk area we are fortunate in having an analysis of rural settlements for the period from the eighth to the fifteenth centuries. In the first phase, from the eighth to the tenth centuries, settlements seem to have been of medium size and unfortified, varying in area from about $1\frac{3}{4}$ to about 10 acres. The number of houses most frequently occurring was perhaps in the range five to eight, though the number of settlements investigated is too small to be at all sure of this. In the period from the eleventh to early fourteenth centuries settlements were more numerous and the majority were from 1 to $3\frac{3}{4}$ acres in area, though settlements of less than $\frac{3}{4}$ acre appear for the first time and some very large settlements are also found; frequently there were from seven to ten houses in each settlement. The third period, from the first half of the fourteenth to the fifteenth century, shows a decline both in the number of rural settlements and in their average area. The majority of settlements were now of from $\frac{1}{2}$ to 3 acres; the largest single group of those investigated had only one or two houses, though those with seven or eight houses also amounted to about a quarter of the total. These findings thus indicate a decline in the size of most villages up to the fifteenth century in this area, and possibly, though this is less certain, a sharp decline in the total village population of the area from the first half of the fourteenth century.

Information on the area south of the Pripet is extremely limited. A few clusters of fortified sites are known, ranging in area from about $\frac{1}{4}$ to $3\frac{3}{4}$ acres and dated to the tenth century. These seem to have been fairly densely settled and the smallest may possibly have contained six houses. A larger number of small unfortified settlements are also known, but no details have been published. In this area the houses, unlike the surface-built huts characteristic of the north, were partly sunk into the ground.

c. The forest steppe zone

More, though still insufficient, information is available for the forest steppe zone. Evidence of the eighth to tenth centuries from the fortified settlements of Monastyrishche in the Sula basin, near Romny, and Borshevo on the Don has given rise to some generalizations about the last stages of clan life and the emergence of monogamous units within the extended family. On the first site a group of eighth- to ninth-century huts, each of 20–24 sq. yds. and sunk about 28 inches into the ground, were found. Wooden beams supported the roof and there were cupola-shaped clay stoves. Some archaeologists subsequently interpreted the huts as having been linked by covered ways. However, the more recent excavation of a complete site of the Romny-Borshevo culture, the settlement of Novotroitse on the Psel, has called in question the alleged links between houses; it now seems likely that these fortified settlements consisted of separate dwellings, occasionally linked with a store-house or forge, for example, but with no covered ways between the dwelling houses. The houses themselves were small, 14–24 sq. yds. Of greater importance, however, is the fact that the settlements in the forest steppe at this period appear to be more compact than those known from the areas where surface dwellings were common. Novotroitse, for example, had more than 50 dwellings in an area of just under an acre, as well as over a hundred other structures such as store pits, outbuildings, etc. The length of time for which such sites were occupied, however, has also to be taken into account.

Dwellings in the forest steppe of the tenth to thirteenth centuries were most frequently of dugout type, but surface-built log huts are also known in the Kiev and Ryazan' regions. More than one house type evidently existed at this time in this comparatively densely settled area. However, the evidence available seems too fragmentary to allow one to follow at all easily the subsequent development of rural settlements in this zone.

d. The total size of settlement

The archaeological evidence from rural settlements thus seems to indicate medium- or large-sized open settlements, or, towards the steppe frontier, more densely settled fortified settlements which acted as places of refuge. This seems to have been the situation prior to the Mongol invasions of the thirteenth century. Subsequently, a decline in settlement size is implied by the information of many of the fifteenth- and sixteenth-century cadasters, which relate to the Moscow and Novgorod territories. Because many of these settlements were dispersed in forested country the numbers of dwellings in each settlement were small;

consequently, 'medium sized' here means, say, four to six dwellings, and 'large' means more than eight. However, archaeological evidence is, in the nature of things, lacking for single homesteads and very small hamlets, although numerous groups of barrow burials of the pre-Mongol period might be thought to imply such settlement, even when none has been found. If unrecorded, but suspected, settlements were added to the settlement map, we might find that the forested north was not as sparsely populated, compared with the wooded steppe, as might otherwise be supposed. The same point would seem to be relevant to the fourteenth- to fifteenth-century decline in total number of settlements for the central Smolensk area.

It is very risky to attempt estimates of population for early Russian history, but we are perhaps beginning to accumulate enough material from a variety of sources to allow some speculation, though for the moment it can be no better than that. Estimates for the total population of Kiev Rus' at around A.D. 1000 vary from I. D. Belyaev's 1·5 mill on to A. I. Yakovlev's 7·5–7·9 million. Urlanis arrives at a figure of 4·5 million, midway between these extremes; this figure fits well with what evidence there is and will be used for the purposes of this calculation. Since the available evidence seems to indicate that most settlements at this time had four to eight dwellings, if we assume 4 to 5 persons to each dwelling, the number of settlements may have been of the order of 110,000–275,000. This very crude calculation probably tends to underestimate the number of settlements for the total population assumed, because of the difficulty of observing the smallest ones. On the other hand, of course, if the number of persons in each dwelling were higher than assumed here, the number of settlements would be reduced. However, this calculation stresses the very small proportion of the probable total number of settlements on which our conclusions about the form of Russian medieval villages are based.

E. *The layout of settlements*

In most areas rural settlements were on rivers, since dense forest was colonized by river routes. These were important as lines of communication and for water supply. Few early settlements in Russia seem to have had wells. In the lake region of the north-west, as well as in other areas of marsh, bog and stagnant waters, settlements were often sited on the higher ground; but in most parts the hamlet or village usually stretched in a single or double line of buildings facing the water. It is possible, however, that prior to the tenth century a substantial proportion of settlements were fortified or had the concentrated, haphazard layout usual at fortified sites.

The alluvial soils of the river valleys were also in many cases well suited to farming; but while the numerous settlements of medium size imply adequate food supplies which came predominantly from cultivation and livestock husbandry, very little evidence is available about the fields on which these communities got their livelihood. The standard holding may have been of 22–27 acres. The Short Pravda (eleventh century) refers to the ploughing over and to the recutting of boundaries. This and other evidence shows that the cultivated fields, or the strips in them, might be separated either by unploughed balks or ditches, or by trees or wooden boundary posts bearing the incised emblem of the owner. Moreover, since the penalty for such an infringement of property rights was the quite high amount of 12 *grivny* (the value of a slave in this law, about 1½ lb. of silver), it seems probable that the land which the law was intended primarily to protect was not that of the ordinary villager but of the lord. The context suggests also that his holding might be contiguous or intermingled with those of the villagers. The Expanded Pravda also refers to the holding of the debt serf (*zakup*); the term used (*otaritsa*) is somewhat obscure, but evidently may refer either to a plot of land or to livestock.

There are, however, a few deeds of the first half of the twelfth century which refer to arable fields, with reference to estate boundaries. The grant of Izyaslav Mstislavich to the Novgorod Panteleimon monastery, for instance, lays down that 'the bounds of that land are from George's arable by the straight road up and from the road near Ushkov's arable along the upper side and to the right into the dell ...'. Evidently by this period the frontiers of worked fields were sufficiently well-defined and stable to be accepted as boundary lines; but information on their patterns seems to be entirely lacking. The very abundance of new land which might be brought into cultivation provided little incentive to intensify production beyond a certain level, and afforded means of escape to those who wished to avoid demands they considered too exacting. Areas under cultivation could escape the notice not merely of historians today, but at times even of contemporaries, if we take some sources at face value. In the fifteenth century, for example, in the central forest area a peasant could evidently till for eleven years an area subsequently claimed by a monastery to be its third field.

The communes mentioned in the early Russian laws are very difficult to identify on the ground. A large unfortified rural settlement of the eighth to eleventh centuries might be the only village in a commune, which would include the settlement, the arable fields, together with meadows, pastures and areas of forest, as well as stretches of water. On the other hand the Smolensk area on the Dnepr may have been colonized by the Slavs in groups of perhaps a dozen small families.

These, too, whether related by blood or by their common interest, might comprise a commune. Occasionally, due to the fortunate isolation of a group of settlements and their close approximation in dates, it seems possible to trace the process of colonization in detail for a limited area and to surmise the general limits of a commune. But, again, we do not know whether a district area (*pogost* or *okrug*) was made up of one or several communes. A charter of Rostislav Mstisla-vich, prince of Smolensk in the mid-twelfth century, mentions a volost with nine pogosts in it. Documents from the fourteenth and fifteenth centuries, however, suggest that terminological usage had changed and that volost and commune were sometimes equated at that period in the north-east.

A specific, though perhaps not typical, picture of a village is provided in a number of additional articles in some variants of the Extended Pravda. These, dating from the thirteenth and fourteenth centuries, calculate returns over a number of years on a holding with 22 sheep, 22 goats, 6 pigs (three of which were over-wintered), 2 mares, a 2-year heifer and 2 hives of bees. Two ploughlands in the village were sown with 16 *kadi* of rye (perhaps about 90 acres with 3½ tons). This gave each year 100 stooks (*kopny*), the size of which is not known for this period. But this interesting calculation is entirely concerned with incomings. The increase in livestock numbers, without any losses, is calculated over twelve years and the progeny are priced; the value of wool, cheese and butter, threshed grain and hay is worked out.

F. *Large estates*

The first direct reference to large estates occurs in the chronicle accounts of the regularizing activities of Princess Olga about the mid-tenth century. According to the chronicles '. . . her hunting grounds are throughout the whole land and her signs, and so are her places and villages . . . and along the Dnepr and the Desna are her fowling runs, and there is her village Ol'zhichi even now'. Vyshgorod was also Olga's. Ninth-century evidence hints at the private ownership of land, but it is not explicit.

It is sometimes argued that the development of large landed estates in the tenth century was due to the ideas brought by the Varyang (Viking) princes. The time lag of about a century between Rurik and Olga is accounted for by supposing that the princes needed it to establish their political hegemony before they could regard themselves as permanent and so develop their estates. An alternative argument is that the concept of large landed estates came from Byzantium. Olga was a Christian as well as a member of the house of Rurik. The extension of landholding among the great nobles, the boyars, and members of the princely retinues in the eleventh century might have resulted from the spread of Christianity through the courts of the princes and the twenty monasteries which then existed. Even if some such stimulus from Scandinavia or Byzantium played a part, internal development within the area had apparently reached a stage at which such concepts coincided sufficiently closely with economic and social possibilities for their acceptance and dissemination to take place rapidly. The ninth and tenth centuries saw rapid developments, especially in the forest steppe zone. There is evidence of tributary relationships in the ninth century and of large estates over which owners claimed some jurisdiction in the tenth century. Moreover, the appearance of writing sometime in the tenth century and the attempt to reorganize paganism prior to the adoption of Christianity are further signs of internal development.

In the late eleventh and early twelfth centuries a number of small fortified sites, which were castles, arose in the southern and central areas, although, as was frequently noted by West European travellers in subsequent centuries, they continued to be built entirely of timber. Usually such sites were about $\frac{1}{4}$ acre in area. They differ from the small rural settlements of this period not only by having fortifications, but by the variety of arms and ornaments, especially glass bracelets, found in them. On the other hand, they differ from towns in being closely linked with agriculture and having only a weak or narrowly specialized handicraft production. The emergence of these castles in the countryside is surely to be linked with the development of estates, as Olga's 'halting places' had been a century earlier. In the same period a series of town risings took place (in 1068, 1071 and 1113), and separate princely apanages were developing on the basis of landed estates. This proceeded so far that at the Lyubech congress in 1097 the princes, recognizing the need to face the nomads together, agreed 'Let each one hold his own patrimony'. The hegemony of Kiev was at an end. Wealth was concentrated in local centres and we must no doubt see the castle as the fortified residence of the lord of the estate as well as an element contributing to his military resources.

By the thirteenth century, then, the rulers were trying to treat the apanage principalities as their private estates. These estates seem often to have had a castle or other manorial centre, usually with its own farming activities, as a nucleus, but the overwhelming bulk of the estate's land was occupied by the peasant communes with their fields, villages and hamlets. By the late eleventh century the church had acquired large estates and ecclesiastical property was much extended by the more than 50 monasteries which had been founded by the twelfth century.

The most important aspect of this formation of estates was the extension of landlord's authority over the communes. How far this process was a major factor contributing to the formation of smaller settlements than in the earlier period is not clear, though it seems likely that the obligations laid on the communes by the landlords would sometimes act as an incentive to flight and might result in a new settlement, possibly consisting of only one house.

The acquisition of land by estate owners proceeded at such a rate that by the fifteenth century probably two-thirds of all agricultural land was held by the apanage princes, great nobles (boyare), servitors and the church. The residence of the lord or the monastery was now the centre of extensive land holdings, sometimes scattered and intermingled with holdings of other lords over a very wide area; it was also the hub of much economic activity and dealt with large quantities of produce of all kinds. As the centralized Russian state was emerging in the course of the fifteenth century these residences of the nobles on their estates were usually unfortified, but even at the start of the sixteenth century fortified boyar settlements were still occasionally being created in the north-east.

The size of the estates can sometimes be judged by the number of peasant holdings within it. An average peasant tax unit (vyt') of old plough land in the fifteenth century was 40 acres (5 desyatinas in each of three fields) or more. The area sown was perhaps comparable with the possible holding of Kievan times, but the very fragmentary data available indicate a considerable range on either side of this figure. Large estates must have contained many such holdings. The princes of Moscow became the greatest estate holders. Ivan Kalita's will of 1327 mentions over 50 villages, Vasilii Vasil'evich's of 1461 or 1462 more than 125, most of which were evidently the administrative centres of groups of villages. Allowing for the hamlets and other settlements attached to the villages, one might estimate a minimum of six houses for each village mentioned. Even if we assume that each house had a full tax unit of land, this would give Ivan Kalita's estate a minimum of about 12,000 acres of arable in peasant hands and Vasilii's about 30,000. This estimate, however, may well be very much too low because settlement size in some parts of the central area was considerably larger than is assumed here. The estates of apanage princes at this period also sometimes had 30–50 villages, and so might compare in scale with Ivan Kalita's estate. The normal late fifteenth-century allocation of land for a service tenure (pomest'e) was from 270 to 800 acres of arable, varying according to the status of the tenant. Such estates probably had two to ten hamlets on their land and perhaps ten to thirty households of peasants.

III. *Farming technique*

A. *Implements*

The main tillage implements were the ard (*ralo*), *sokha*, and the plough. The ard was a simple scratch plough with a single share-beam. This was often set at a steep angle to the ground; sometimes the share-beam was almost vertical. Forms with a sole are also found. *Sokha* (pl. *sokhi*) is a term which essentially means something branched or forked; it is used for implements with two or more share-beams; and this, as well as loose usage of the term, tends to cause a certain amount of confusion. It is necessary to distinguish implements with two share-beams, or a double share-beam, from those with three or more. The former are functionally between ards and ploughs; they crumble the soil, but by being tilted to one side, the normal position in use, they clear a furrow. The latter are functionally closer to harrows. Moreover, *sokhi* in the narrow sense of two share-beam implements are of two main types: those (*tsapuga, tsapul'ka*) with nearly vertically placed share-beams which are often rather widely set apart from one another, and those with share-beams placed at an angle and often curved so that the point or share enters the ground almost horizontally. The latter have share-beams close to one another and sometimes a spade-like board (*politsa*) is set between them with its lower edge jammed against one of the shares; this helps to crumble the soil or turn it aside.

Two problems at least concerning *sokhi* remain unsolved. First, the typological derivation of these implements is obscure. The view that they were derived from ards by increasing the number of share-beams was rejected in the 1930s in favour of the reverse process, the reduction of the number of sharpened branches on a fir-top used as a harrow. It seems that both lines of development may have taken place, but the use of the term *sokha* to indicate functionally distinct implements has not always been made clear enough to avoid confusion. The second problem is the apparent conflict of evidence between manuscript drawings of *sokhi*, all of which so far available show simple types with vertical share-beams and no board, and finds of shares characteristic of low-angle types in association with boards.

Ards and *sokhi* of all types might have iron points fitted to their share-beams and most of the evidence for the distribution of such implements in space and time is derived from finds of these iron parts. It is, of course, hard to be sure in every instance of classifying the objects found correctly, but the documentary evidence is both too meagre and too indefinite to be relied on alone. The chronicle entries under the years 964 and 981 referring to tribute being collected 'per ard' and 'per plough' are not to be taken as reliable evidence for the use of the particular implement mentioned; both were in use at this time. These references are indications of regular tillage and the existence of tax units of recognizable size. Similarly, the formula 'where the plough (or *sokha*), axe and scythe has gone', found in hundreds of fourteenth- and fifteenth-century documents, indicates in general terms the limits of arable land, woodland and meadows; whether the implement mentioned is a plough or *sokha* seems to be of no real significance. The

FIG. 8. Tilling with *sokha*, harrowing and sowing.

plough which was used was somewhat similar to the soled ards, but had a larger and more massive iron share. It is not certain that in all cases it had a mouldboard to push the soil aside or turn the slice.

Within the forest and forest steppe zones the distribution of finds of irons from these implements shows reasonable regularity, and this is so even though many of the reports could with advantage be fuller. There are a certain number of finds dating from the eighth century of both ard points (*naral'niki*) and shares, though these are small and likely to be from ards with soles rather than from ploughs. These finds are from the forest steppe zone. Finds dating from the tenth century onwards are more numerous; they show *sokha* irons in parts of the forest zone, and ard points, shares, some at least from ploughs, and coulters in the forest steppe. The area centred on Bolgar, near the Kama-Volga confluence, was particularly rich in types and had *sokha*-irons, ard points, shares and coulters. It has been suggested that this area may have contributed to the changes in tillage implement types, indicated by the presence of *sokha*-irons, which seem to have followed the Slav expansion into the northern areas with their new environmental problems. *Sokha* also occurs in two thirteenth-century sources as a tax unit. It seems that by the start of the fifteenth century the developed *sokha* with irons entering the ground at a low angle, and perhaps with a board, existed in the Novgorod area.

Within the forest zone the only finds dated to before the tenth century which may come from a plough-like implement are two small shares and a small coulter from a site in the Pripet area. Later finds occur in the open oasis of Opol'e with its relatively fertile degraded grey earths, and there is some documentary evidence which hints at the plough being used in the thirteenth to fifteenth centuries on church lands and in the Pereyaslavl', Yaroslavl', Galich and Novy Torzhok areas. In fact, it probably might be found in many northern forest areas where sandy soil provided adequate drainage. In the forest steppe zone, where the grass-covered black earths required the cutting of a slice, the plough had probably been in use from the ninth century.

Kosulya indicates a lop-sided implement, i.e., one which pushes the soil or turns the slice to one side only. The term normally meant a developed *sokha* fitted with a coulter and a fixed mould board. It also meant an ard without a sole, similarly equipped. At one time the theory was put forward that this implement was widespread in Northeast Russia in the fourteenth and fifteenth centuries and was to be associated with an advance in agricultural technique which contributed much to the emergence of the centralized Russian state. Recently, however, this theory, which has no evidence to support it, has been refuted.

B. *Methods of arable cultivation*

The implements which have been mentioned were used in various systems of farming, but there is no simple, direct correlation between implements and systems. Ard and *sokha* may be used in the slash and burn system of farming; the same implements, but especially the soled ards and *sokhi* with low-angle share beams capable of turning a slice, may be used in the shifting system, the fallowing system, where a bare fallow regularly entered the scheme of rotation (ranging from the two- or three-year fallow to long fallows of up to fifteen years), and the various forms of field farming (two-field, three-field) with regular courses of rotation. The plough in its developed form as a heavy implement may be used in the fallowing system and particularly in field farming. However, the systems themselves are not to be thought of as always being sharply differentiated from one another, nor as existing in chronological sequence.

Slash and burn farming, for instance, was probably the earliest system of farming practised in the forests of what is now European Russia; it continued as an exception till modern times, even for two or three years in collective farms in the mid 1930s in parts of Novgorod oblast. In the course of the millennia during which slash and burn was practised it was used for a variety of purposes: as a system of farming in the full sense, a work cycle ensuring the continuance of the desired ecology; as a method of clearing forested land in order to extend the arable area; as a subsidiary method to obtain high yields on limited areas within the framework of some other system. Yields in these cases were exceptionally high, 20- to 40-fold for grains being not unusual, compared with three-, five- or sometimes six-fold on normal, manured fields. So even though the areas cultivated were quite small, apparently not usually more than about 3 to 5 acres, the returns were comparable with or even slightly higher than those from the larger areas of the average peasant holding of regular ploughland.

The burnt areas, however, were not always used for grain growing. They were especially suitable for root crops and particularly the turnip which, in the north, was an important item of peasant diet. However, a high labour input was required; from this it has been argued that the method could be used only by the numerous hands of the extended family or a commune. More recently it has been shown that the labour inputs are not excessive in areas of poor podzols if account is taken of the relatively heavy manuring required on the fields of a regular rotation. In fact, it seems possible that lack of sufficient livestock in peasant hands, and the consequent shortage of manure and haulage power, was a major factor contributing to the continuance of forms of slash and burn associated with 'the clearances and patches beyond the fields (zapolitsy), and the turnip patches and hunting grounds'.

The difference between these uses of slash and burn and slash and burn used as a regular system can be illustrated by the difference in the timetable of work between ancient and modern practice. The brushwood and small trees, such as alder and birch, which seem always to have been the vegetation preferred, were cut down in ancient times in January or February, the old Slav month called sechen' (cf. sech', 'to chop, cut'); the dead wood was then burnt in March or April, the month called berezozol' (cf. bereza, 'birch tree'; zola, 'ash'). This period of three months or so would probably be sufficient, even in very small settlements, for the necessary work to be completed in time. In the nineteenth and twentieth centuries, however, cutting took place in late May or June, and the wood was left at least until early spring of the following year, if spring grains were to be sown, or till even later in the year. This change was dictated by the need to slash and burn, within the system of a three- or more course rotation in the period between spring cultivation and sowing, on the one hand, and harvest, on the other; slash and burn had to fit in with the timetable set by the rotation system and thus became modified.

In the Kievan period there is some, but not much, direct evidence for slash and burn farming. This is hardly surprising since fallowing (up to fifteen years) was probably the predominant system in the tenth to thirteenth centuries. Moreover, what little documentary evidence there is comes from richer and more advanced estates on which, if used, fire was simply a means of assarting. The documentary evidence for the fourteenth and fifteenth centuries suggests that burning was used to clear new areas in the forest. The burnt areas were not usually abandoned entirely after their initial use for a main crop, as in the slash and burn system, but were retained as meadows or sometimes subsequently entirely cleared and incorporated into the regular fields. Judging from the numerous references to new clearances in the forests in late fourteenth- to sixteenth-century documents, this was a period of fairly intensive and widespread agricultural colonization and expansion after the disasters of the Mongol invasions. It seems probable that if slash and burn as a system was not practised, fire was at least frequently used to clear the forest.

The cultivation of remote, isolated fields is also shown in fifteenth-century documents relating to the areas of Kolomna, Maloyaroslavl', Moscow, Novgorod and Pereyaslavl'. For instance, 'the Trinity peasants [i.e. those on the estate of the Trinity monastery], they say, till those wastes and go there to mow (*naezdom kosyat*) and on those wastes, they say, there is no house nor fence'. These forest lands, as they were sometimes called, might be areas formerly cultivated by slash and burn and then used for hayfields or temporarily abandoned, though for long periods. It seems more probable, however, that by this period these clearings were treated as outfield, supplementing the three-course or other system nearer the settlements. Nevertheless, there were instances when such remote fields seem to have been cultivated unobserved. There was a strong incentive for the peasants to conceal the total of their cultivated area, and small settlements scattered over vast forested areas would doubtless offer many opportunities.

The more extensive and irregular fallowing systems, with or without any regular rotation, seem to have been superseded by the three-course system at different periods in different areas. The presence of winter rye, probably the commonest grain in pre-Mongol times, is almost certainly evidence of fallowing, but is not in itself sufficient to say precisely what fallowing rotation was followed. It seems probable, however, that in the eleventh and twelfth centuries the three-course system was established, and perhaps predominant, in the Novgorod area. This may have been due to the incentive provided by a relatively high concentration of population (Tikhomirov estimates Novgorod's population as ten to fifteen thousand in the early eleventh century) in an area of poor soils and severe climate. The three-course system probably also existed in the Kiev area at this period. Whether there was three-course in other areas before the Mongol invasions is not known.

Documentary references to three fields do not occur until the fifteenth century, but the three-field layout may have existed earlier. References to the fallow system, for instance, do not occur till even later. At the end of the fifteenth century the cadastral surveys for both the Moscow and Novgorod areas assume the three-field layout and measure the land in one field only, sometimes adding 'and in two at the same rate'.

The evidence for the developed *sokha* in the Novgorod area by the start of the fifteenth century is not connected with the appearance of three-course rotation in the area; this had already taken place. But such implements, cutting and turning a slice, are best suited for the cultivation of fields unencumbered with roots and other obstacles. Their use may, therefore, have encouraged the grubbing out of roots, the formation of cleared fields and, in this way, the spread of conditions well suited to a system of regular rotation. An additional factor which may have tended towards an intensification of farming at this period was the increasing pressure of population on the cultivated area as numbers increased in the late fourteenth century after the catastrophic losses and disturbances due to the Mongol invasions and the attacks from the West.

Information on rates of sowing is extremely limited, but implies that the usual rate for rye in Moscow and Novgorod territories in the fifteenth century was 7 puds a *desyatina*, nearly a hundredweight an acre. One source adds that the rate for spring grains was twice this. Presumably this information refers to a three-course rotation. As regards other systems there seems to be no information. The seed was broadcast probably from a birch-bark basket, and then worked in with ard, *sokha* with steeply inclined share-beams or a harrow. Harrows varied from a fir-top drag (*vershalina*), or an implement consisting of a number of fir planks with the branches left on to project downwards (*sukovatka, smyk*), to various forms of multi-toothed *sokhi*.

It is likely that, as in more recent times, the slash and burn areas were surrounded by fences or palisades to keep out the larger forest animals. Similar protection may sometimes have been given to remote and isolated fields. In fifteenth-century documents fencing and wattle of this sort are mentioned in connexion with the regular fields and damage caused by livestock.

From Kievan times onwards grains, mainly rye, wheat and oats, but also barley, millet and buckwheat, were harvested with the sickle. Hay was scythed. Finds of scythes from the ninth century on in burials occur only in male graves, while sickles are mainly in female ones. The size of the heaps and ricks (*kopna, skird, stog*) of grains is undetermined, although it seems probable that they were sometimes used as units of measure. A seventeenth-century source defines *kopna* as being about 16 feet up and across and 21 feet around. Occasionally the sheaves were dried artificially and stored in barns and buildings adjoining the threshing floor. The grain was threshed with flails, apparently by an even number of persons, and winnowed in the wind with wooden spades.

Grain was commonly ground by rotary querns, many of which have been found from the Kievan and later periods. The mill, presumably water-driven, is mentioned in a document of 1270, and was evidently regarded as common on church estates; more numerous references occur in fourteenth- and fifteenth-century documents, but there is no mention of windmills in the forest zone in this period, presumably because the trees greatly reduced surface wind speeds. There were no horse-driven mills until the early seventeenth century. The flour produced was used for various sorts of leavened and unleavened bread and for thickening.

Apart from the grains, flax as well as hemp were grown in many northern areas; the Pskov area in particular exported both flax fibre and seed. Vegetable crops are known from numerous finds throughout the area; cabbage and turnip patches are mentioned in fifteenth-century documents for the forest zone. Pulses and onions also seem to have been widespread. There is some evidence for carrots, cucumbers and beetroot.

c. *Animal husbandry*

Animal husbandry played an important part in the tenth to fifteenth centuries. Livestock supplied food and a number of raw materials, as well as draught and riding animals. The horse was important for farming and transport, and also for war. It was the animal normally used for tillage. In the fifteenth century the people of Novgorod regarded the basic tax unit (*obzha*) as 'one man ploughing with one horse', a picture familiar from Kievan times. The ox was also used for ploughing in some areas, sometimes three abreast, but this was not very widespread. The horse, moreover, seems to have continued, despite the disapproval of the church, to be a regular item of food; it amounted to about 10 per cent of individual animals found. It is impossible to be sure whether this figure, obtained from town sites, also applies to rural settlements. In the great estates of the princes, of course, herds of horses for special purposes were kept by the fifteenth century and some grooms had become minor landholders.

If the horse is excluded, cattle were probably the main source of meat; although pigs were more numerous, carcass for carcass, they weighed less. Cattle account for about one-third of individual animals found, pigs for about 40 per cent, at most Russian town sites between the tenth and fifteenth centuries. Sheep, and many fewer goats, amount to about 20 per cent. Both pigs and sheep seem to have been killed off in autumn or winter, largely owing to the difficulties of providing adequate winter feed. Evidence from different towns, however, shows considerable variations in the composition of the herd, while that from the countryside is still too meagre to show any pattern. Animals were pastured in herds most of the year and, especially in areas of deep and continuing snow, stalled for the winter.

D. *Hunting and fishing*

Hunting, throughout the medieval period, also provided both food and raw materials such as pelts, hides, sinews and castor, part of which was traded. It is, however, very hard to give any general picture of the importance of hunting; the proportion of wild species attested varies from less than 1 per cent in Moscow and 2 per cent in Novgorod to 50 to 60 per cent at rural settlements in the wooded steppe and at Grodno—a forested area abundant in wild life. Animals hunted included elk, various deer, bison, steppe antelope, wild boar, bear, lynx, wild cat, wolf, fox, marten, otter, polecat and various rodents, the beaver being the most valued. For the nobles, of course, hunting, coursing and hawking were great pastimes and by the fifteenth century princes had officers and villages concerned with particular aspects of such activities; the local peasants supplied beaters and other services.

Fishing, too, was widespread and important. Sturgeon, pike-perch, bream, wild and pond carp, herring, pike, sheatfish, zope and 'small fish' are mentioned in the sources; place names refer to ruffe, crucian carp and perch. Fisheries were jealously protected, and the weirs in the form of palisades (*ez, ezh, kol*) that were frequently used in the relatively shallow waters were such valued possessions that in the mid-fifteenth century half a night's use of one was bought for one-and-a-half rubles, the price paid for a hamlet and its lands at this period. Another source implies that a night's catch might be 8 sturgeon, 240 sterlet, 400 pike-perch and 400 bream. Doubtless much of this was consumed by the owner's household, but part was sold on the market. Nets were commonly used, but hooks appear to have been somewhat infrequently found.

Throughout the forest zone, but especially where oaks were found, bees were important. It is possible that hives made from hollow tree stumps were known even in Kievan times; but much commoner was the practice of marking in the forest a tree where bees had nested (*bort'*) or where they were encouraged by forming hollows in the trees or placing hives there. The honey collected by climbing the trees with the help of crampons was used for sweetening food and for making mead, while the wax was used in candles and for caulking boats. Quantities collected seem to have been very large, and honey and wax were important items of trade. In the twelfth century, for instance, one prince had about 80 tons of honey in his cellars. It has been calculated that in Novgorod in a single year in the twelfth century about 380 tons of wax were weighed.

These amounts suggest that gathering honey and wax was probably very widespread since individual contributions seem to have been small. In the early sixteenth century, for instance, twelve bee-men had to deliver 180 lb. of honey. In the Moscow principality the prince's bee-men were organized by the beginning of the fourteenth century into a guild (*Vasil'tsevo sto*); in general, it seems that on the smaller estates the bee-men had been slaves, but by the fifteenth century they had become peasants living on the prince's land. By this time, too, the former process of collection from the localities and mead-making in them had been superseded by a greater degree of concentration in the estate centres.

These gathering activities, hunting, fowling, fishing and collecting honey and wax, as well as berries, nuts, fungi and other materials from the forests, varied in importance both between the households of the nobility and the peasantry and, within the peasantry, between different farming systems. For the peasantry miscellaneous gathering was essential: it supplemented the food supply; hunting and trapping may well have been an integral part of slash and burn, though somewhat less important in normal years in a three-course system; it provided pelts and hides for winter clothing and footwear. For the lords, too, it provided some food and clothing for their numerous retainers; but it also provided many of the luxurious dishes and furs which demonstrated the wealth of the court and went as gifts to foreigners or were traded. The peasant used trap, snare and net to supplement his cabbage soup and gruel; the noble hunted for sport.

IV. *Social relations, dues, landownership*

A. *Pre-Mongol period*

It is not possible to estimate the amount of peasant rents and services in the pre-Mongol period, nor to say what proportion were in kind and what in labour. Tribute (*dan'*) was evidently most important at the level of the principality, and remained so throughout the medieval period. In 945 Igor, 'wanting more wealth' to equip his retinue more richly, was killed when he went to exact a second tribute from the Drevlyane. In the following year his widow, Olga, whose name, as has already been mentioned, was associated with the emergence of large estates, 'imposed a heavy tribute on them; two parts of the tribute went to Kiev and a third to Vyshgorod, to Olga, for Vyshgorod was Olga's town. And Olga and her son and retinue went about the land of the Drevlyane establishing statutes and dues.' This tribute seems usually to have been in kind: furs, wax and honey, and slaves. In addition, the overlord and retinue on their progress through the tribal territory had to be supplied with food and accommodation, and also with some services, such as men to help on the 'hunting grounds' and 'fowling runs'.

In 964 when Svyatoslav asked the Vyatichi, near the Oka-Volga confluence, 'To whom do you give tribute? . . .', they answered, 'We give it to the Khazars, a shilling (*shchelyag*) an ard'. Possibly these early money payments could be made because the Vyatichi were near the Volga route to the markets, and silver mines, of Central Asia. Tribute, in any event, was evidently assessed by the amount of tilled land normally associated with an implement. This was so even though Svyatoslav spent much time on distant raids in the south, from the Danubian lands to Northern Persia. Tribute was, thus, becoming a regular exaction rather than merely irregular booty.

The first part of the Short Pravda, known as Yaroslav's Pravda, probably dates from the early eleventh century. It depicts a world where the blood vengeance mentioned in the tenth-century treaties with the Greeks had been modified by the possibility of payment when no avenger was available. The wergelds to be paid for the death of a man are all of 40 grivnas. The man (*muzh*) protected by this wergeld was probably simply any free man, a member of a peasant commune; but the same term was also used of men of high social position, so it may have related to members of the princes' retinues and councils.

Free men, of whatever status, were, of course, differentiated from slaves; two terms are used for the latter. The first (*chelyadin*) meant originally a slave in a patriarchal household, a prisoner of war; such slaves were traded abroad. Both articles in which they are mentioned in this law refer to their running away. Subsequently, in the late eleventh and twelfth centuries, a collective noun (*chelyad'*) derived from this term indicated the dependants as a group and gave no precise indication of status, though the latter was certainly a lowly one. The second term (*kholop*) is also known from a tenth-century chronicle entry. In the Pravda it occurs in an article which lays down that if a slave strikes a free man and flees to a house and the master does not give him up, then the master must pay 12 grivnas (the bloodwite for a *kholop* in the later section of the Short Pravda was 5 grivnas). Moreover, if the offended party subsequently encountered the *kholop*, he had the right to kill or, in another interpretation, to beat him. It seems probable that the term *kholop* became more important in the eleventh century in connexion with the development of landed estates and the settlement of slaves on the land. From the law, then, we learn something of social relations in the early eleventh century; for agrarian relations the implication of changes in the nature of the labour force associated with territorialization is the most significant feature.

From articles of the Pravda of Yaroslav's sons, which probably may be dated to the latter half of the eleventh century, we can form a general picture of a prince's manor with its officials and labour force, chattels and land protected by penalties. The senior officials, the steward (*ognishchanin*), tax-collector (*pod"ezdnoi*), prince's servant (*knyazh tivun*) and senior groom (*konyukh stary*), were valued at 80 *grivny* if murdered; the village reeve (*sel'skii starosta*), arable overseer (*ratainy starosta*), slave tutor (*rab kormilets*) and nurse (*kormilitas*) at 12. Those valued at 5 *grivny* were the contract man (*ryadovich*), dependent peasant (*smerd*) and ordinary slave (*kholop*). The mention of the arable overseer indicates that some of the dependants, serfs, peasants or slaves worked the land. Labour rent, thus, existed at this time on the lands supplying the castle which arose in this century.

The double payment, compared with the earlier section of the Pravda, points to the development of the manorial administration, as does the list of officials and the emergence of an intermediate category valued at 12 grivnas. The reeve and the overseer may, perhaps, have been responsible for dependent peasants (*smerdy*) and slaves (*kholopy*) respectively; a twelfth-century source mentions that dependent peasants live in villages; the overseer was more probably responsible for slaves working the demesne.

At the same time, of course, the majority of the population probably lived outside such estates. They were referred to as people, folk (*lyudi*) and were distinct from the various categories so far mentioned. Usually they were organized in communes (*mir* in the earliest Pravda, *verv'* in the later part of the Short Pravda), either rural or urban. Members of these communes were jointly responsible for murder within their limits. This was a heavy burden not merely because of the increased bloodwite now demanded, but also because of the need to feed the official concerned, his horses and men.

The Short Pravda gave in detail the amount of food to which the official collecting bloodwite (*vira*) was entitled, but payment in money, though not necessarily coin, was also possible: '7 buckets of malt for the week also a sheep, or a side of meat, or two *nogaty*; and on Wednesday a *rezana* or cheeses, and on Friday the same; and corn and millet as much as they can eat; and two chickens a day; 4 horses may be stabled and they are to be given as much as they can eat; and the official is to be paid 60 (8 ?) *grivny*, 10 *rezany* and 12 *veveritsy*; and a *grivna* on arrival; if there is need of fish during a fast, 7 *rezany* should be taken for fish; then the total money is 15 *kuny* a week; and food as much as they can eat; the officials collect the bloodwite before Sunday'. In this context 1 *grivna* = 20 *nogaty* = 25 *kuny* = 50 *rezany* = 150 *veveritsy*.

Such exactions were not only a heavy burden; they were also part of the process by which the authority of princes and other great men was extended over the peasants. The administration of justice thus provided income for the prince, maintenance for his officials and the possibility of extending his authority to new areas. The marvellous chronicle account, under 1071, of a rising on the upper Volga illustrates several aspects of this general process. The prince's man who was collecting tribute in the area received no help against the non-Christian wizards, leaders of the rising. He claimed they were peasants (*smerdy*) subject to his prince; but it was only when he threatened the local people he would not go away for a whole year that they immediately handed over the wizards.

In the twelfth century the continuing development of a society in which lords were extending their authority over the countryside is shown by the law known as the Expanded Pravda. The labour force now included a new category of dependants called *zakupy*. These were debt-serfs who had taken a loan (*kupa*) and were obliged to work for their creditors. From the point of view of law and jurisdiction these debt-serfs bore some similarity to slaves; for instance, they could only testify in petty cases. Similarly, terms used of such a man elsewhere include *kholop*, and *chelyadin-naimit*, both of which stress lowly status. It seems likely, moreover, that in many cases debt-serfs were able to work off only the interest on their loans; it was difficult to clear the capital debt; and flight, if unsuccessful, meant reduction to the status of a complete slave. At the same period, however, the complete slaves themselves become differentiated. It seems that, with the development of landed estates, the situation of the slave on the land came to approximate to that of other categories of dependants such as the debt-serfs. Moreover, following the rising of 1113, one of a series about this time, the law was modified somewhat in favour of the lowest categories of dependants. In these circumstances, a new term was introduced for a slave in the full sense (*obelnyi kholop*). The debt-serf and ordinary slave (*kholop*) had thus become somewhat similar in status and were clearly of higher standing than the full slave.

This law lists three sources of slavery in the full sense: if a man sells himself for 'up to' (it is not clear whether this means 'more than' or 'less than') half a grivna; if a man marries a slave without an agreement with her lord; if a man becomes a servant (*tiun*) or steward without an agreement. That servants were sometimes of servile status is also seen from the provision that allowed boyars' servants, but no others, to testify. An agreement (*ryad*) could be made on other terms. The old term for the man on a contract (*ryadovich*) seems now largely to have been replaced by *zakup*.

The dependant peasant's inheritance passed to the prince, if no sons survived, but there was an obligation to provide something for any unmarried daughters still at home. Boyar estates, however, did not escheat to the prince; they might pass to daughters. The home always passed undivided to the youngest son, the seniors presumably being expected to establish new farms for themselves. The wife's property was treated separately: she did not necessarily inherit the bulk of the estate and, judging from Church statutes, it seems improbable that monogamy was universal.

There is no certain information on the size of estates or the amount of the main obligation, tribute, per unit, nor even of what the unit amounted to in acreage, nor how often tribute was exacted. This is why it is impossible to decide in what proportions payments to landlords, such as boyars and abbots, and to the prince or state were made in kind and in labour. The general development of Kievan Rus' with the granting, as is known from the earliest genuine deed, dated about 1130, of villages 'with tribute, bloodwite and fines' seems to imply that considerable quantities of produce from farming and gathering activities were accumulated, both from produce rent and from labour on the landlord's demesne. It must be assumed that this local economic development was the basis for the emergence of apanage principalities which yet remained linked by race, language, religion, and by having rulers of the Rurik dynasty. In 1146 the 'fine house' which a prince, Igor, had built himself in his village was plundered during one of the numerous fights between the princes. '. . . There were plenty of provisions there in the store-room and the cellars, wine and honey, and every sort of heavy goods, even iron and copper . . .', and the church, next to its threshing floor, had 900 stooks (*stogi*) in it. 'And they divided Svyatoslav's place into four parts, both the treasury, and the store-rooms, and the goods which could not be moved, and there were 500 *berkovtsy* (about 80 tons) of honey in the cellars and 80 amphorae of wine ... and they left nothing of the prince's but divided it all and the 700 of the household.'

In the pre-Mongol period, then, estates were worked by a variety of dependants, some of servile status whose situation seems to have improved somewhat in the twelfth century and to have approximated to that of serfs. The peasants in the countryside outside the estates were increasingly brought within the influence of the princes, the great nobles and other landlords, including the Church. This was achieved both by means of claims to tribute, the administration of justice, the claim to rights over land (not only arable, but also forest, pasture and water), and because on occasions these lords lent equipment, seed and such like, so contributing to the development of a category of debt-serfs.

B. *The Mongol invasions and after*

By the time of the Mongol invasions in the thirteenth century the area occupied by the East Slavs was divided into a dozen or more lands, almost all of which were principalities. The political centre had shifted from Kiev north-eastwards to Rostov-Suzdal' where the fertile unforested area, Opol'e, had been colonized by Slavs for several generations. The princes contributed to the development of the region and engaged in town building with the help of servitors, noble and other, as well as artisans and traders. By the end of the twelfth century Vladimir, the capital, had given its name to the Grand Principality which had come about when Andrei Bogolyubskii chose not to reign in Rostov or Suzdal', the two senior towns with their own assemblies, but took up residence in Bogolyubovo, outside the hitherto subordinate Vladimir. He greatly developed Vladimir and filled it with merchants and artisans of all sorts. He attempted to rely on his squires and members of the junior retinue, rather than on his boyars; but a conspiracy by his servitors resulted in his murder. Nevertheless the princes were for the most part powerful enough to hold their servitors and great nobles in check. The agricultural wealth of the area, and the possibilities it afforded for trade contacts and town life, afforded a basis for these developments.

In the north the great city of Novgorod had acquired an empire extending to the river Ob' through boyar appropriations and monastic colonization. The boyars with the rich (*zhit'i lyudi*) and the Church dignitaries, effectively dominated the town assembly which nominally was the supreme authority. Princes were appointed, dismissed and their powers limited by treaties. They and their nobles were forbidden to acquire land in the Novgorod territory and to accept men on commendation. The large estates of the Novgorod nobles supplied materials for the artisan activities of the town and contributed to the important foreign trade with Gotland and the north German towns.

In the west, Smolensk was able to take advantage of its situation on the Dnepr which enabled it to participate in trade to north and south, and also between the Baltic area and the east. For this reason the town and its assembly was economically and politically important, but the princes, relying on their great landlords, remained dominant, unlike the princes in Novgorod.

In the south-west in the principality of Galicia-Volhynia the local boyars seem to have been relatively more important as great landlords than the prince; moreover, although there were a number of towns they were not really powerful centres and made little impact. The town assemblies provided no possibility for a political counterbalance to the boyars. In the late thirteenth century Galicia-Volhynia split into its two parts and these ultimately were incorporated into Poland and Lithuania respectively.

The Mongol invasions towards the mid-thirteenth century caused great losses in men and material. But it is reasonable to suppose that the towns bore the brunt of these losses, both because of the initial destruction of such centres and also because the nomads were anxious to acquire metal and handicraft workers who were mostly concentrated in the towns. Moreover, the overwhelming mass of the population, being in the countryside, in well-wooded areas not densely settled, had better opportunities for concealment and survival. With the establishment of Mongol rule new impositions came into existence. These included a general tax or tribute (*dan'*) and various other payments or provision of services such as maintenance of the Mongol post-horse system (*tatarskii yam*) and of Mongol officials. These demands, ultimately borne by the peasantry, would offset any improvement in the peasants' conditions likely to have come from any local scarcity resulting from peasants being killed or taken off as slaves.

There were, of course, regional variations in the incidence of destruction caused by the invasions. The central areas of Vladimir-Suzdal' and the southern regions more open to the steppe suffered most; but even in such areas destruction was not universal. Settlements might be razed to the ground, while others only a few miles away would be spared either by accident, or, in some cases, apparently with the intention of providing supplies for the invaders. Such regional variations, as well as the more important economic developments which has already led to the emergence of the various lands of the East Slavs, led to certain modifications in social relations; nevertheless, the social situation throughout the area had many common elements. Moreover, the immediate destruction wrought by the invaders was less important, in the long run, than the exactions they imposed during the centuries of their domination. The many hundreds of deeds which have survived from the fourteenth and fifteenth centuries enable us to perceive something of social and economic developments in a way which is impossible for earlier periods.

The peasants on landlords' estates in the period after the Mongol invasions owed a wide variety of obligations to their lords. About 200 terms are known which refer to obligations, but of the twenty or so which seem most widespread by no means all were regularly imposed on every peasant. Variations were due to the nature of the obligations, whether the landlord was lay or cleric, whether or not the lord had been granted an immunity, local differences and even personal whim, and also, no doubt, the nature of our sources.

The most important and widespread obligation was the general tax or tribute (*dan'*, sometimes called *poral'e* in the Novgorod territories), which was not always included when immunities were granted. There is some evidence that in the fifteenth century tribute was collected twice a year, in spring and autumn. This, in common with some other obligations such as keep (*korm*) for local officials, various payments for legal declarations and transport dues (*yam* and, in part, *podvoda*), was an obligation owed to the state. It was, thus, additional to any obligations of the peasants to the estate, and was also borne by those who were not peasants; only the slaves (*kholopy*) were not subject to state taxation. Tribute seems to have been paid in money from the fourteenth century onwards, but keep for local officials was at first in kind. The same applies to the transport dues. The term *yam* seems to have indicated a number of services connected with maintaining post-horse stations; these services were replaced by payment in the early fifteenth century. *Podvoda* was the supply of draught teams, apparently without the vehicle. Keep for Tatar officials and their retainers was also a heavy burden. A late fifteenth-century document mentions that 'people did not stay on that land because of brigandage. And also the Tatar emissaries passed by that road'.

Estate dues included the above, unless the immunist failed to collect the state's tribute for himself. There were also many others, such as those mentioned in the account of the monastic estate quoted elsewhere.[1] These obligations, again, were sometimes in money and increasingly so from the fifteenth century, but many were often in kind or labour. They included a variety of building and repair works, keep for estate officials and for horses, and domestic production of textiles and gear such as nets. In addition, there were demands for peasant labour for both field work and gathering. This covered the whole cycle of

[1] See page 539–40.

agricultural work on the demesne, but sometimes took the form of an allotment of an additional amount of land to be cultivated for the benefit of the lord; in the fifteenth century this seems sometimes to have been a sixth of the area held. Labour was also demanded for honey and wax gathering (*podlaznoe*), for fishing and hunting. The peasants also contributed to the lords' petty income, customary gifts bestowed on him or his officials on certain occasions or dates.

The nature of the estate modified the range of dues. Peasants on church lands paid tithe and certain other dues peculiar to the church as an institution. The demands on lay estates varied according to the area in which the particular settlement was situated and the interests of the lord. In some cases, produce was beginning to be sold off the estates and this might lead to increased concern by the lord for the demesne or for the exaction of trade imposts. Peasants, too, traded in agricultural produce, certainly from the fourteenth century onwards. This was mostly restricted to local markets, but was important as a means of acquiring the money they needed for tax payments. Numerous references to various forms of impost on trading and passage in the fourteenth and fifteenth centuries (*torg, tamga, yavka, pyatno, osminchee, veschee, myt, kostki*) illustrate the gradual but continuing extension of trade which was taking place.

A description of a rich boyar estate of this period is given by a deed of gift of about 1430 transferring to a monastery near Tver' sixteen hamlets. 'And 50 and 4 Novgorod rubles of head silver. And the livestock is 22 large mules and large horses, also 20 work horses. And of horned cattle, oxen and cows and small calves 65; goats and sheep 130. And to the monastery all the grain standing in the field and in the earth; and in the granary there are 77 tons (700 *korob'ya*) of rye, 220 tons (2000 *korob'ya*) of oats, $5\frac{1}{2}$ tons (50 *korob'ya*) of wheat, $5\frac{1}{2}$ tons of grain (barley (?), *zhito*), barley meal (*ovydnitsa*) $5\frac{1}{2}$ tons, buckwheat and peas and hemp $4\frac{1}{2}$ tons (40 *korob'ya*), and with all that which is drawn from that village.' Later evidence suggests this village had about 1200 acres.

Similar accounts of estates held by apanage princes may be found, but the largest landlord was the grand prince who had hundreds of villages, each of which might present a similar picture to that on the estates of apanage princes or boyars. It is, however, hard to distinguish the various ways in which he held land; the family domain was not sharply differentiated from the 'black' land, the 'land of the grand prince', that state land left when all that held by lords or institutions was excluded. Crown land was distributed to servitors, both free and slave; in some cases they worked land themselves as peasants, in others they were petty lords. Often these tenures were conditional on service. State land, insofar as it was occupied, was held by peasant communes for the most part, but sometimes by individuals in, for example, the Novgorod territories. The land deals and court cases recorded in the documents show that peasants in communes usually acted not as individuals, but through their own commune officers or, at least, in company with certain comrades (*tovarishchi*). This commune system also existed in the family domain and on the estates held by some of the greatest nobles, the wife of the grand prince, the metropolitan and the apanage princes.

As Crown land and State land were not sharply differentiated grand princes and the peasants living on their lands were apt to differ in the interpretation of their rights. Such peasants referred to the land as 'our volost ... black, taxed by the state from of old', 'the land of the Grand Prince'. The terms volost land, or stan land, indicated that the land was organized in these administrative units under the prince's local official; black land meant that it did not belong to lords, but was peasant land. Conflicts occurred because the peasants regarded the Grand Prince as responsible for their defence; he regarded the land, with the peasants, as his alienable property. The actual disposition of the land was to the peasants their own affair, based on their right to the land they or their ancestors had won from the forest by their labour. The formula 'where the plough (or *sokha*), axe and scythe has gone', already referred to as indicating the limits of arable land, woodland and meadows, in part reflects this concept; in part also, as Cherepnin has suggested, it was sometimes used by lords as one means of claiming land through their rights over those on that land. From the lord's viewpoint overlordship meant the peasant had no right to dispose of land he had won; that right rested with the lord, just as much as did his right to exact dues from his dependants.

A commonly held view, perhaps best known from Grekov's work, is that rent in kind was dominant in the period after the Mongol invasions and that labour rent was less important. The fourteenth-century evidence does not seem to support such a view. A very full picture of peasant obligations to their monastic landlord is given by a former abbot of a Vladimir monastery in 1391.

'. . . The big people from the villages of the monastery had to put the church in order, to fence in the monastery and its courtyard, to put up buildings, compulsorily (*vzgonom*) to till the whole of the abbot's demesne arable; to sow, to reap, and to carry; to mow hay by desyatinas and bring it into the yard; to make weirs in both spring and winter; to fence the orchards with wattle; to man the seine nets, to make ponds, to hunt beaver in autumn, to block up the springs; and at Easter and St Peter's they come to the abbot each with something in his hands; and the horseless peasants from the village thresh rye for the feast day and bake bread, grind malt, brew beer, thresh rye for seed; and the abbot gives flax to the villages and they weave nets (*sezhe*) and arrange the parts of the seines; and all the people from the villages on the feastday give a heifer, but once they besought me, lord, but not according to custom, with three sheep, and I excused them the heifer as I had no need of the heifer, but according to the old custom there is always a heifer on the feastday; and if the abbot rides into any village for a celebration feast, the hopper men give each a basket of oats to the abbot's horses.'

The big people are here evidently those with draught animals able to till the land and to cart and carry; the horseless peasants are responsible for processing the produce. Both are, however, liable to labour rent; it is therefore uncertain what were the causes and the economic consequences of the economic differences. From the viewpoint of the monastery both were dependant peasants. In fact, it was at this time, at the end of the fourteenth century, that the Russian term for peasant (*krest'yanin*) first occurs in the documents. This introduction of a general term which indicated workers on the land is sometimes taken as evidence of the emergence of a less differentiated labour force, on estates in the first place; subsequently the term came to include state peasants, those not on the estates of other lords or institutions. Unlike the nobles, who 'serve', the peasants are subject to taxation by the state (*tyaglo*) and in this respect they 'drag' or 'are drawn' (*tyanut'*), that is are subject to a specific administrative centre. Some authorities have made something of a mystery of *tyaglo*, but the sixteenth-century merchants of the Russia company understood it clearly enough as 'a yeerely rent or imposition'. Those subject to it were distinct, on the one hand, from nobles who served and, on the other, from slaves who were owned by their lords, and certain other similar categories, and on whom the state had no direct call.

The peasants, however, were far from being a homogeneous mass, and the terms used for them help in following something of social development in the fourteenth and fifteenth centuries. The lowest in status were the slaves (*kholopy*). These were often domestics, but there were also those who worked the land (*stradnye lyudi*) or were estate officials (*prikaznye*), servants, stewards, overseers and so on. The estate officials themselves held land and by the late fifteenth century some held immunities. The completeness of the slave's servitude is indicated by terms for the deeds relating to their status (*polnyi, dernovatyi*), by their being bought, sold, given away and inherited, and by limitations on their rights in law. If the lord killed a slave it was considered no crime, but a sin, and no bloodwite was to be paid. Slaves could not sue their lord without guarantors. It has been suggested that the testamentary manumissions of their slaves by the grand princes which occur from the mid-fourteenth century may have been a legal fiction which introduced servitude for the period of the lord's life. There is no doubt that such servitude limited to the life of the lord or by some other term existed on other estates in the fifteenth century. Nevertheless, complete slavery also continued to exist as the law code of 1497 indicates. The probable reasons for the change in the situation of the slaves are to be sought in the development of estates, the pressure for labour and the consequent need for lords to be able to reorganize their labour force from time to time. These changes, together with certain restrictions on peasant rights, led to the emergence of a new category of endebted men (*kabal'nye lyudi*) late in the fifteenth century. These were not slaves in law, but in reality their position approximated to that of the limited servitude of certain slaves. The obligation (*kabala*) recorded the debt incurred and the man had to pay interest on the amount through service.

It was in the second half of the fifteenth century, too, that 'silver' (*serebro*) became of greater importance. The 'silver-men' (*serebreniki*) have been regarded as those paying money rents; but the reassessment of the part played by labour rent in the post-Kievan period has led to modified views. Such terms, it is now held, sometimes refer to money rents, but may also indicate income from sales of produce or from peasants who have taken a loan (this may be the interpretation of the 'head silver' on the boyar estate mentioned in the deed quoted above, another possibility is that this term indicated the price of a slave). It thus seems that in some cases these terms may indicate men in debt whose standing differed but little from that of a slave.

The crop-sharers were in a somewhat similar situation. There is not much evidence relating to them in the central areas, but they are known from the fourteenth century in Novgorod territory. The 'halvers' (*polovniki*) were peasants who had for some reason transferred their land to a lord to whom they then became subject, paying half their harvest as rent. They may also have been created by the freeing of slaves; such men would not always be able to establish their own holding without help from a lord. Halvers, however, were distinguished from slaves; they were not subject to the taxes on the commune, but some paid at half rates to the Grand Prince, others paid tribute, one of the main items in state taxation. In Pskov *izorniki* were an equivalent of the Novgorod halvers. Essentially all the categories of debtors, debt-slaves and crop-sharers formed an intermediate group between slaves and dependent peasants, having similarity with both; in particular, the slaves (*kholopy*) came to hold land. They were also an intermediate group in time, leading on to the tied peasants enserfed by the centralized state.

The ordinary peasants were called people (*lyudi*). Princes wrote of 'my people', 'volost' or 'stan' people, 'people subject to state taxation'. The basic term for the peasants was frequently used with adjectives which indicated their origin, their overlord or their social position.

Another term was 'orphans' (*siroty*), but this may have been used of peasants not on their own land. The process of peasant resettlement and colonization in the period immediately following the Mongol invasions is difficult to trace for lack of sources. But a general picture of forest colonization may be drawn from deeds a century after the main invasion. For instance, a deed granted to a monastery in 1435 illustrates this. 'Whatever people the abbot summons to him to those Churovka wastes (*pustoshi*) and to the forest, to settle by the weir, from another principality, and not from our estate, from the Grand Principality; whoever settles in those wastes, those people are not liable to my tribute for twenty years; and whoever settles, in the forest, those people are not liable to my tribute for thirty years. . . .' Similar grants, offering relaxation of obligations for various terms, occur issued by other landowners and by officials on State land. The lengthy period of relaxation for those colonizing forest land reflects how laborious this process could be. The shorter period for resettling wastes stresses the difference between the two cases. The latter were areas already brought into cultivation at some time and then abandoned, either due to some calamity or possibly for fallowing in something like an out-field rotation. Such wastes were often granted by great landowners for a life or longer term to servitors who, in their turn, settled peasants on them. The peasants brought them back into cultivation and these 'live' lands with their new stock and improvements were to be returned to the owner at the expiry of the term. This was not merely a means of reclaiming lands abandoned to the forest; it was also a way of increasing the number of dependants on the estate. Mostly such peasants paid quit rent in kind after the expiry of the term of relaxation, probably because, at least to begin with, the wastes were at a distance from the settlements and their fields.

There are numerous references to forest clearance in the fourteenth and fifteenth centuries. This was achieved by both peasant initiative and landlords' policy. Peasant villages and even hamlets undertook clearances (*pochinki*) in the forest beyond their fields and these sometimes became the lot of elder sons who did not inherit the farm. Lords, for their part, tried to attract peasants by concessions or to settle their own dependants on the land.

Throughout the fifteenth century the documents reflect the continuing search for labour. A major problem was that each prince, as in the deed quoted above, was concerned to prevent losses from his own territory; every one was supposed to recruit from other lands. The only sources of manpower within any territory were peasants who held no arable land (*bezvytnye*) or domestics who could be settled on it; both were likely to be freed slaves. Those who had moved away and could be persuaded or compelled to return provided additional numbers, as might prisoners of war, some of whom were sold as slaves. The wars between the princes in the second quarter of the fifteenth century not only provided prisoners, but also created conditions favouring an increase in the various types of debt serfdom. The termination of these wars, however, curtailed these powers of apanage princes. Moreover, by the end of the century, too, the granting of conditional service tenure was becoming a developed system integrated into the centralized state headed by Moscow.

The main peasant category on whom these developments ultimately rested in the central areas were the 'old dwellers' (*starozhil'tsy*). These were settled peasants on landlords' estates or on state lands. Similar categories existed in Novgorod land known as 'ancient' (*davnii*) or 'old' (*staryi*) people. Like 'locals' (*tutoshnye*) or 'customary people' (*poshlye lyudi*) the 'old dwellers' were distinguished from 'arrivals' (*prishlye*) who might be excused their obligations for a term of years. The latter for the most part were peasants who had been attracted 'from another principality'; some were apparently peasants who had formerly been established in the locality, then gone away and subsequently returned; these were distinguished as *prishlye starozhil'tsy*. Grekov considered that 'old dwellers' were established as a category in order to distinguish them from increasing numbers of newcomers. More recently Cherepnin has argued that it was the declining possibility of attracting peasants 'from another principality' as the centralized state grew that led to the emergence of 'old dwellers'. There clearly was some mobility among dependants in the fifteenth century; slaves fled from their masters, peasants left to settle elsewhere; grants were made to landowners to enable them to set up 'freedoms' (*slobody*), i.e. settlements, often near frontiers, where the new inhabitants attracted from other areas were free of obligations for a period. Contrary tendencies were thus at work, evidently due to a shortage of labour. It is not possible to give an estimate of the scale of these movements, but Cherepnin is surely right to argue that the 'old dwellers' are to be regarded as a step leading towards peasant enserfment.

Such variations, however, do not seriously modify the general fourteenth- to fifteenth-century picture of a largely servile peasantry fulfilling obligations to lord and grand prince in labour, kind, and to a less extent in money. Nor was the situation of the 'black' peasants, those living on state land, essentially different by the end of the fifteenth century. They, too, had become subject to the basic range of state obligations and were, in any event, being increasingly incorporated into landlords' estates against their will, especially as the use of money spread and compelled them to conform to new standards, occasionally even to sell commune land to an acquisitive lord. This happened whenever the land was granted to a lord, cleric or layman, outright or in service tenure.

Much more important was the element of change introduced by the development of a centralized state and the growth of the Moscow principality. There is evidence that in the twelfth century landlords were sometimes being granted lands with rights to 'tribute, bloodwites and fines'. In the period after the Mongol invasions grants of immunities became commonplace, especially from the fifteenth century onwards. The nature of these deeds changed, however; while the earliest ones had been phrased in positive terms, those from the fourteenth century onwards are in negative terms: 'they have no need to pay any tribute . . .', etc. Such grants gave landlords public as well as private rights over the peasants living on the estate, but the nature and extent of these rights varied and, containing a very large element of custom, were liable to much dispute. As the centralized state became more powerful immunities granted to lords were restricted; certain categories of crime were withdrawn from their jurisdiction. Immunities were granted to landlords, while the peasants were granted relaxation of taxation as a means of attracting them to settle.

Such methods contributed to the process of largely internal colonization and to the recuperation from the Mongol disaster. As the grand princes came to have more state land at their disposal following the confiscation of Novgorod land after 1478 and from the Tatars after 1480, a system of service tenure gradually grew up. The term by which service tenure came to be known, *pomest'e*, only occurs from the late fifteenth century and the system of standard service tenure with obligatory military service only came into being in the mid-sixteenth century. This system came in at a time when the early method of the granting of rewards by giving a post from which the recipient might extract what he could from the subject population (*kormlenie*) had fallen into decay. At the same time, the process which had existed in Kievan times of making outright land grants to some court servitors, such as stewards, grooms and so on, was superseded by conditional grants in the fifteenth century. The grants of holdings to a wide range of lesser servitors, however, continued for much of this time.

The gradual extension and concentration of state power, together with the changing situation of servitors as the service tenure system continued to develop, led to restrictions on peasant movement. In

Novgorod the movement of debt-serfs and share-croppers was being controlled even by about 1300. In the central and southern areas the princes' treaties with one another in the fifteenth century forbade the acceptance of commendations other than in each prince's own territory. In the 1460's censuses were apparently introduced on the Grand Prince's estates, and the people recorded in them (*pis'mennye* or *danskie tyaglye*) were not to be moved. In about the same period there began to occur deeds limiting the peasant right of departure (*otkaz*). Several specify that the 'silver men' and share croppers may only leave at St George's day (26 November, Old Style). In the law code of 1497 the fortnight centred on this date was laid down as the only period when peasants in general, not only the debt-serfs and share-croppers, had the right to move. Each household had to make a clearance payment, the amount for forest farms being half that for those in long-cleared areas. The full amount was due only if the peasant had been there four years.

Peasant reactions to the changes in the fifteenth century were not limited to movement from one lord to another. In the central areas, where settlement was relatively dense and estate boundaries often contiguous, flight was difficult, but continual, and movement would frequently simply mean undertaking new obligations elsewhere. Resistance to landowners occurred, particularly to monastic colonization; the arrival of some monk seeking a retreat was enough to arouse fears and hostility, as many hagiographers record, from peasants who knew what the establishment of monastic lands would mean. There were also attacks on individual lords, and these seem to have been more frequent in the disturbed period of warfare prior to the mid-fifteenth century and again towards the end of the century. The law code of 1497 laid down the death penalty for anyone killing his master.

The emergence of a centralized state in Russia was hastened by the urgent need for the defence of a people, united by race, language and religion, against the Mongol domination and to regain losses to enemies in the West. It was made possible by the economic recovery and expansion after the disasters of the thirteenth-century Mongol invasions. As the power of the Moscow princes grew, the immunities granted to landlords were gradually restricted and demands for service in various forms from both landlord and peasant became greater, backed by the claim to dominion over the whole area. The two cases differed in that the landlord was granted lands in order to fulfil his obligations to the state, but the peasant had little more than his former resources with which to meet the new demands.

c. *The Moscow period*

By the time of the death of Ivan III, in 1505, that part of the area of

Kiev Rus' which had not been lost to the western invaders had recovered from the Mongol impact and had developed sufficiently to defeat the eastern enemy. The core of the new state, Muscovy, in the European forest zone, had been colonized by the Russians and 3-course rotation was predominant. At the same time the 'black' lands, the peasant communes formerly on state land, had almost all been brought under some immediate landlord. Agricultural produce was being sold in numerous local markets. Finally, a centralized state had come into existence.

This created a new set of circumstances. Within 50 years, in 1552, Muscovy was to be strong enough to defeat the Kazan' Khanate, the last major obstacle to Russia's eastward expansion. The state now drew its military and economic strength largely from the organization of much of its lands into service tenures, the tenants running their estates with the help of serf labour. In 1497 the Law Code (*Sudebnik*) had recognized the peasant's right of departure, but had limited it to the week before and the week after St George's day. This first generalized step by the centralized state towards regulating relations between lords and their peasants led to others which were eventually to result in the legal binding of the peasants to their lords. The year of legalized serfdom, 1649, was also the year of the founding of Okhotsk on the Pacific coast.

D. *Property and ownership*

The question of the nature of property in Russia is extremely complicated and cannot be dealt with here. Throughout the medieval period the relative abundance of all but the most suitable land, and the fact that agricultural implements could easily be made, combined to make peasant flight at least a possibility. When pressure from state and landlords became too great the choice for the peasant was revolt or flight. This ever-present threat to the landlords' interests inclined them to pay more attention to ensuring an adequate supply of the scarce factor of production, labour. The focus of interest was at least as much the labour market as the land market. Moreover, the function of property seems to have differed for the two groups. Peasants could and did sell their land, though often sales and similar deals were registered with or handled by the peasant commune or its officials. But such deals, and in such largely non-literate communities there were surely many not recorded anywhere, seem to aim primarily at raising the consumption level of the peasants. The land deals of the lords, on the other hand, seem in the main not aimed at directly raising the consumption level of the lord, but at raising vicarious consumption to increase his status and power.

Land had been claimed, held and, by the twelfth century, sometimes sold by individuals. But the tributary relationships between princes and peasants during the period of the early Rurik dynasty seem almost from the tenth century, certainly from the twelfth century, to have been backed by a claim to dominion over the whole area of the principality. This is implied by evidence in the chronicles. The statute of Vladimir Monomakh of the early twelfth century, moreover, included articles on the reversion to the prince of lands for which there was no male heir to succeed. In pre-Mongol times, however, even though the taking of tribute from the cultivators soon gave way to a more regularized running of estates, there seems to have been no single term for landed property. In the fifteenth century the term *votchina*, meaning a heritable estate, came into use.

Much is sometimes made of the contrast between the heritable estate (*votchina*) and the service tenure (*pomest'e*). Landlords of the former type of estate were not vassals and had the right of free departure, retaining their lands if they chose allegiance to some other overlord. While this is true in theory, in practice it is doubtful whether it had a great deal of meaning. The real situation depended partly on custom and largely on where the balance of power lay in each case. Moreover, heritable estates seem on occasion to have led to a decline in the power of their owners because of fragmentation through partible inheritance. The essential difference was not between heritable and service tenure but between landlord and peasant tenure.

Medieval Agrarian Society in its Prime

§ 7. England

I. *The land*

A. *Reclamations*

The course of English agriculture in the Middle Ages was dominated by the history of the land itself—its productivity, its relative abundance or scarcity, its use and distribution. This history is not yet ready to be written, but what has already emerged from its study is sufficient to enable us to map out its course and to place its main signposts.

Of the signposts the most important is the one which historians have placed at the beginning of the road, i.e. on the morrow of the Norman Conquest. This post is commonly taken to mark the birth of the English Middle Ages proper; but paradoxically enough what makes it so significant for historians of English land is that it stands a long way past the true starting point in English land settlement. To use the expression popularized by Mr Lennard, rural England of 1066 was already an old country. An historian of internal colonization must now accept that by 1066 the occupation of England by the English had gone far enough to have brought into cultivation and covered with agricultural settlement most of the area known to have been occupied in later centuries of English history. Most of the place names which were to form the grid of English parishes in subsequent centuries were in existence and recorded as settlements in the Domesday Book. Except in some regions, such as the eastern fens reclaimed in the seventeenth century or parts of Yorkshire devastated by the Conqueror or Welsh marches in the West and the Scottish borderlands in the North, the parish names of pre-eighteenth-century England already appear in 1066.

Equally revealing is the Domesday evidence of ploughs and ploughlands. If the numbers and geographical distribution of Domesday ploughs means anything at all, it would appear that in almost all the regions which were to grow grain in later centuries (with the possible exception of the period of Napoleonic wars) grain was already grown in 1066. The eleventh century tillage may have extended even further than that. The distribution of Domesday entries of ploughteams, as well as 'ploughlands' (*terre carrucae*), suggest that arable husbandry spread wider in the eleventh century than would at first sight seem credible. Much doubt still attaches to the area of land served by one Domesday ploughteam or to the real significance of the Domesday 'ploughlands', but the balance of probabilities appears to be that the area corresponding to a plough was most frequently equivalent to 120 acres and that 'ploughlands' as a rule designated land in arable use, and, taking England as a whole, were roughly as numerous as ploughteams. If these assumptions are right the totals of Domesday ploughteams and ploughlands in most midland and southern counties would correspond to an acreage under plough larger, sometimes much larger, than it was to be at the highest point of English arable husbandry in the second half of the nineteenth century.

Maitland, who was the first to hit upon this conclusion, offered it with that air of whimsical incredulity which he frequently assumed when playing with bold hypotheses. But had he known what historical geographers have recently told us about the underlying topography and soil geology he might have stood by his figures more firmly. For it appears from the soil maps that both the Domesday ploughlands and the Domesday ploughs were thick on the face of the land not only in regions and on soils best adapted to arable husbandry, i.e. on the fertile loams or the more open and better drained types of clayland, but also on soils which the farmers of later centuries were to regard as unsuitable for corn-growing—such as the cold, heavy and ill-drained clays of south-eastern Leicestershire, western Northamptonshire, the London Clay regions of southern Essex, the Weald, the Vale of the White Horse or the south-eastern parts of the Plain of Worcester. These were obviously lands of second or third order brought in by husbandmen of the eleventh century simply because the better lands had already been taken up.

These Domesday facts clearly denote dense, and hence ancient, settlement, the product of at least six centuries of internal colonization. They also compel us to moderate somewhat our claims for the colonizing achievement of the two centuries which were to follow the Norman conquest—the twelfth and the thirteenth. In so far as historians have occupied themselves at all with land reclamations they have been inclined to assume that it was in the two or three centuries of Norman and Angevin rule that the main work of reclamation was done. This assumption must now be revised. That this era in fact witnessed a great deal of internal colonization and reclamation goes without saying. The documents of that period abound with references to recent 'assarts' and 'purprestures', 'brecks' and 'conquests' and other names by which recently reclaimed lands went in the contemporary records. The colonizing activity was obviously widespread and important. But coming, as it did, at the end of six centuries of internal colonization, and conducted, as it had to be conducted, at a time when the best lands were in most parts of England already occupied, it bore every mark of a 'run-down'—the concluding state of a movement long past its climacteric.

One of its latter-day characteristics was its unequal incidence. There were great stretches of the country in which the whole of the cultivated soil appears to have been fully occupied and where no room was any longer left for further 'conquests'. Such were for instance the lands of the federated manors of Taunton in the Vale of Taunton—a highly fertile and densely settled region where in the thirteenth century reclamations could be only very small and sporadic. Similar conditions prevailed on many other manors of the anciently settled Huntingdonshire villages of the abbots of Ramsey or the manors of the abbots of Glastonbury on the 'dry lands' of West Somerset, to quote only two further examples.

Such large-scale reclamation as was still possible in the thirteenth century was mostly to be found on the peripheries of Anglo-Saxon England or else on those stretches of difficult and inferior land which, for various reasons, had been by-passed in the earlier and easier phases of internal colonization. Widespread reclamations were still going on in the south-west country, and it is indeed possible that most of Devonshire's combes and valleys and much of Cornwall's interior were not fully occupied until the thirteenth century. It also appears that in the twelfth and thirteenth centuries the colonizing abbots of Glastonbury and their tenants first began to draw heavily upon Sedgmoor marshes; that grain, mostly oats, began to be grown on a large scale on the land pastures of the easternmost Cotswolds belonging to the bishop of Winchester and that large-scale reclamations were undertaken in and around the salt marshes of the West Midlands and the western borders of the Cotswolds by the bishops of Worcester and in North-West Staffordshire by the de Lacys. Above all, on the outer perimeters of the eastern fens, villagers and some of the landlords made continuous inroads during the twelfth and the thirteenth centuries into lands which could be won from the marsh with the technical methods available to medieval men, more especially on the silt lands separating the sea-tides from the freshwater fens, or along the western rim of the great marshes, or on accessible fringes of the main fen islands. With these few land reclamations it is perhaps permissible to include the colonization of Denge and Walland marshlands to the west of the anciently occupied Romney marshes of Kent and on the Isle of Thanet, which appear to have been reclaimed for intensive pasture and arable in the same period.

Outside this peripheral belt of colonizable territory the only large areas not yet occupied in the twelfth century and still open to large-scale reclamation were in the so-called 'forests', most of them tracts of woodland or moorland reserved for the chase, where agricultural use was impeded by special forest laws designed to protect the game and tree cover. Most of the 'forests' were royal, and their area in the twelfth and the thirteenth centuries expanded and contracted as the successive kings 'afforested' and 'de-forested' different stretches of the country. The royal afforestations met with the persistent opposition of feudal landowners, and the conflicts over forests fill the annals of constitutional history of the thirteenth century. But what prompted the royal attempts to extend the afforested areas and provoked feudal resistance was not the renascent taste for venison or resurgent love of sport, but the rising value of forest land as one of the few remaining reserves of reclaimable territory.

By the end of the twelfth century, however, a large proportion of erstwhile forest had already been invaded by the colonizing villages and villagers, and kings as well as private landowners had begun to draw considerable profits from colonizers and squatters of every type. Historians are most familiar with reclamations in the forests of North Essex and East Hertfordshire illustrated in the documents of the canons of St Paul's, but the forest documents in the Exchequer as well as various manorial sources bear witness to continuous, and at times extensive, assarts in other royal and private forests, such as those of Rockingham in Northamptonshire, Chippenham in Wiltshire, Sherwood in Nottinghamshire, Needwood in Staffordshire or Charnwood in Leicestershire.

It is therefore not surprising that so many of the acres newly won in the twelfth and thirteenth centuries should have been marginal not only in location but also in quality. Their commonest local source—the village wastes and pastures—were usually to be found on soils or in positions which in more spacious times would not have been considered suitable for the plough. Fields, such as those which villagers of the twelfth and the thirteenth centuries carved out of the chalky uplands of South Wiltshire and Hampshire and which have left permanent scars on the downland landscape, did not make good cornlands. Little better were the oatfields which the villagers of Witney on the lower Windrush occupied on the Cotswolds plateau above them, or the new assarts which villagers of Oxfordshire were making in the Woodstock forest, or the assarts which the villagers wrested out of the thin and rocky soil of the outskirts of Sherwood forest in Nottinghamshire or out of the heaviest and most undrainable clays of the Weald of Sussex, or in the valley of the White Horse in Berkshire.

Indeed an historian on the look-out for signs of twelfth- and thirteenth-century colonization will sometimes find them in most unlikely places —on the thin and hungry heathlands of Norfolk breckland or in Suffolk 'Fielding' where no or almost no grain was to be grown in any other period of English history bar our own, or on the southern slopes of Dartmoor, well above the 1000 foot level, or on the skin-deep overlays of Longbarrow Warren above Winchester, which nearly five centuries later struck Cobbett as one of the most barren stretches of country he had ever encountered. These are not lands on which a society would draw for cultivation except in times of real land hunger.

B. *Land hunger*

Land hunger is indeed the verdict which the student of land use and utilization will have to pass on rural England in the thirteenth century—a land hunger which must have worsened as the thirteenth century was drawing to its close. The evidence of the gathering scarcity of land is not confined to what we know of the low quality of the lands available to the reclaimers. The scarcity of land manifested itself in a variety of other ways; and of these ways the rising values were perhaps best exemplified in our sources.

Land was dear and getting dearer. The movements of medieval land values are not, of course, easy to observe, still less to measure, since real values of most lands were wrapped in layer upon layer of legal fiction. The prices at which freehold land unburdened with obligation of service was sold could be genuine enough, but such sales, though not infrequent, have not left sufficient marks in our records to support statistical summaries and comparisons. The same applies to true economic rents received under contracts for free leases for terms of years. These were also common in the thirteenth century, but their terms were not disclosed often enough or recorded fully enough to leave behind any testimony of statistical import. Most of our evidence of rents comes from what we know about the customary rents of the main body of villagers, the tenants of villein or soke land; and these rents were not a full measure of land values. For full measure we must look to the whole complex of payments levied by the lords, or to what the Marxists call the entire 'feudal rent'.

Of the many and various payments exacted by landlords, the one which in theory was supposed to represent the *quid pro quo* for the land and was described as such was *redditus*, the customary rent proper, but its size was as a rule fixed by ancient custom (assized) and thus at first sight unchanged and unchangeable. However, in this as in many other cases the first sight is deceptive. The lords frequently found ways round the barriers of custom and contrived a variety of devices for bringing the actual payments for land nearer to its mounting economic value. One such device was the 'tallage'—the supplementary tax which the lords originally levied on their tenants in times of special need, but which on some estates, e.g. those of Crowland Abbey or of

St Swithin's Priory, Winchester, eventually became an annual tax rising in its incidence as the thirteenth century drew to its end. But the commonest and the most direct method of compensating the landlord for artificially stable rents were entry fines—a device similar in character and operation to the premium payments or 'key-money' which modern landlords adopt in similar circumstances. Sometimes entry fines, i.e. lump sum payments from incoming tenants, were themselves conventionalized and very stable, as on most estates on which the landlord found other means of raising the payment for land. But on many estates entry fines appear to bear a close relation to economic reality, i.e. to the quality of land, the size of holding, the anticipated length of tenancy. And where they were thus related to the economic worth of the land, they appeared to rise towards the end of the thirteenth century almost without a break.

Our best example of rising fines comes from the great estates of the bishops of Winchester and the abbots of Glastonbury, where the fines were still reasonably low in the first half of the century, and may have been lower still in the twelfth century, for which we unfortunately possess very little evidence. In the second half of the thirteenth century, however, they mounted at an ever greater speed until by the turn of the thirteenth and fourteenth centuries they reached exceptional heights. In the densely settled villages of the Vale of Taunton entry fines per virgate (admittedly a large virgate of 40 acres and more) could at times be as great as £40 and more; on the newly reclaimed Sedgemoor pastures of Brent and Zowy the entry fines per virgate were sometimes as high as £60.

The average fine was of course lower than this; the topmost fines obviously came from the best holdings and the longest lettings. Yet what these payments meant even in these cases is easily computed. On land as rich as that of the Taunton manors (with an average yield, less tithes and seed, at 8 to 10 bushels of mixed grains per acre), and even for virgates as large as 40 acres, the payment of an entry fine of £40 spread over a tenancy of say 20 years' duration might well represent in capital payment alone (i.e. not counting interest) as much as a third of the aggregate value of the crops during that period. The annual outgoings on rent and other payments were of course additional.

Of the other symptoms of land hunger the most significant was perhaps the shortage of pasture and of animals. The continuous invasion of marginal lands by the plough must have greatly reduced the available grasslands. In regions of mixed farming, i.e. in most of England in the Middle Ages, the frontier between corn and grass was always on the move. Owing to the publicity which the enclosures of the late fifteenth and sixteenth centuries have received at the hands of historians, we are well acquainted with periods when the frontier moved in favour of grass, but the movement most characteristic of the Middle Ages was in the opposite direction, i.e. cornwards.

By the beginning of the thirteenth century the movement had gone far enough to create a dearth of pasture in most areas of mixed-farming husbandry and to put a heavy premium on such pasture as remained. Meadow lands were of course especially rare and expensive and frequently fetched prices and commanded rents many times those of the best arable. Manorial surveys which put the annual value of arable between 2d. and 6d. an acre, would as a rule value the meadows at two, three or four shillings per acre. Pasture newly enclosed from waste was worth almost as much as good meadowland; while sometimes even unenclosed pasture was valued more highly than arable land.[1]

What is more, the recorded acreage of both meadowland and improved pasture on most of the demesnes in arable parts of England was very much lower than modern farmers would have maintained in the same areas at most other periods of English history. But what the evidence brings out most clearly and most persistently is that the villagers, even more than their lords, must have been underprovided with pasture. On nearly every manor for which we possess court rolls and for nearly every year for which they have survived we find innumerable fines imposed on villagers for sheep and cattle straying on to the lord's land. So regular were the fines for trespasses and so numerous were the villagers thus fined that historians may be forgiven for concluding that the fines were sometimes little more than supplementary pasture rents disguised as punishments.

Where pasture was so scarce and so dear the numbers of animals kept in the villages must also have been small. We do not possess much direct evidence of village flocks and no ways for measuring them for the country as a whole. But for some areas the assessments for royal taxes on moveables include animal livestock and are sufficiently detailed and reliable to justify approximate estimates of the animal population. These estimates are invariably lower, sometimes much lower, than the returns of animal population in the same regions during those years in the nineteenth century in which arable farming was at its highest and animal husbandry at its lowest. Thus on the double hundred of Blackburne in Suffolk—a region which had throughout English history specialized in sheep-farming—the total animal population in 1283 was barely one-half of the numbers returned for the same area in 1867 when the Ministry of Agriculture statistics of livestock begin.

[1] E.g. on Gilbert of Clare's Essex and Hertfordshire manors (*Inquisitions Post Mortem*, 47 Hen. II 27 (5)), or on those of Hugh de Vere, William Cantelow or Roger de Huntingfield (*idem* 48 Hen. III 31 (1), 38 Hen. III 16 (13), 41 Hen. III (20), 9, etc.).

These totals find their collaboration in other features of the villagers' animal husbandry in the late thirteenth century, above all in the unequal distribution of stock. The bulk of the villagers, even those whose animals were taxed, possessed on the average very few animals; a considerable number of villagers, even in the localities best suited to sheep farming and cattle grazing, possessed no animals at all. For if we are to believe the evidence of heriots—manorial death duties imposed upon the deceased tenants' animals—a large proportion of the villagers were exempt from the tax and were made to pay small money fines mainly because they had no animals on which the tax could be levied. Their numbers were always large enough, but they appear to have grown in the course of the thirteenth century. On some manors of the bishop of Winchester they were at one time as large as 47 per cent of the total numbers of tenants. On such estates as those of Glaston-bury Abbey or of the abbeys of Bury St Edmunds and Ramsey the numbers of men without animals were probably lower (the evidence does not permit anything in the nature of a reliable statistical estimate), but even on these estates tenants without animals occur with sufficient frequency to suggest that a scarcity of animals was at that time a common feature of mixed farming regions.

This restriction of our findings to the region of mixed farming must not be misunderstood. There were some parts of the country in which animal husbandry may have been the main or even the sole occupation of their inhabitants or where it must have played a predominating role in the local variant of mixed farming. These were, needless to say, areas in which pasture abounded and where average holding of pasture and average ownership of animals could be expected to be much higher than elsewhere. Our knowledge of these regions is largely confined to the manorial herds and flocks—we read about the great vaccaries of the de Lacys and other northern lords in the Pennines and in the Derbyshire Peak or on the moorlands and woodlands of North-West Staffordshire. There were manorial vaccaries and horse studs on the western estates of the Duchy of Cornwall, and large cattle ranches on the estates of the marcher lords on the Welsh border as well as in the interior of Wales. There were also numerous manorial vaccaries on the estates bordering on the great fens, such as those of the abbots of Ramsey, as well as great manorial sheep flocks on such predominantly pastoral manors as the Christ Church Priory estates on Romney Marsh or the Countess of Albemarle's estates on the Lincolnshire wolds. We must, therefore, be permitted to assume (the absence of evidence would not allow us to say more than this) that where the manorial demesnes devoted themselves so exclusively to sheep and cattle, the villagers—if villagers there were—did likewise.

The extent and importance of these pastoral areas must not, however, be allowed to colour our view of England as a whole. The predominantly pastoral estates were almost entirely confined to the highland and marshland zones unsuited to close occupation and incapable of sustaining arable communities. Except for these fringe areas, lands on which pastoral husbandry predominated were very few and getting fewer. The medieval Englishman's propensity to concentrate on corn-growing at the expense of sheep-farming or cattle-grazing is one of the hallmarks of the economic geography of the thirteenth century. In such 'natural' sheep farming areas as the downlands of South Wiltshire, the heathlands of North-West Suffolk or the uplands of the East Cotswolds only landlords and rich villagers appeared to graze substantial flocks of sheep. The average villager of modest substance could not afford to keep more than a cow or two, or a few, say, one to five, sheep. In this respect the supposedly sheep-farming regions of the south Wiltshire downs or the West Suffolk heaths differed little from the regions we should now consider as pre-eminently suited to arable husbandry. In both the typical small man was not a sheep-farmer but a cottager with 'three acres and a cow'.

This image of thirteenth-century England, densely occupied and therefore also predominantly corn-growing and deficient in pasture and animals, may not accord well with the bucolic versions of medieval life, which like all bucolic traditions is apt to high-light Damon the Shepherd rather than Piers the Plowman. But it will not surprise the student of the densely populated and under-developed countries of the modern world, and least of all the students of twelfth- and thirteenth-century agriculture in other European countries. In western Germany, the gradual spread of arable farming to pasture land, their *Vergetreidung*, gradually reduced the part which animals were able to play in the village husbandry, until a time came in the thirteenth century when their numbers fell to the irreducible minimum required to work the land. In the words of contemporary commentators they had by then become no more than a 'necessary evil'.[1]

c. *Deterioration of the land*

In thirteenth-century England as in West Germany the irreducible minimum was set by the immediate needs of arable farming—those of ploughteams—not by the more enduring but less immediate needs of manure which in his day-to-day decisions the medieval husbandman could presumably disregard or at least postpone. We might therefore expect that at times and in regions in which the animal population was

[1] W. Abel in *Zeitschrift für Tierzüchtung*, 76 (1961).

reduced to the barest minimum the land was bound to suffer. Apparently it suffered in many parts of medieval England.

Deterioration of the land, or, to give this phenomenon its older and less reputable name, the 'exhaustion of the soil', is not a hypothesis an economic historian can nowadays propound without drawing upon himself all the opprobrium which the older wholesale theories of soil exhaustion had deservedly drawn upon themselves. This traditional opprobrium perhaps accounts for the consistency with which historians have of recent years disregarded the indications of declining productivity of the land. The only recent studies of the subject—those of Beveridge and Bennet—purport to show that yields per acre, and certainly those per bushel of seed, were fairly stable throughout our period and therefore would not support the hypothesis of declining fertility. These statistics, so generally accepted, are not only technically imperfect, but also demonstrate the danger of extracting from medieval sources figures detached from their background. They all come from grange returns of the bishop of Winchester's demesnes. The bishops were, however, powerful and progressive landlords, who may always have held the best land in their villages and possessed more pasture than their tenants and also enjoyed the privileges of the fold, i.e. preferential claims to the manure of the village flocks. But the most important circumstance neglected by the statisticians is that during the later part of the period covered by the statistics the bishops were busily reducing the acreage of their arable demesnes, i.e. letting out the worst lands and concentrating their operations on the best, the more fertile, most conveniently situated fields. So if even in these circumstances their yields did not rise but remained stationary, this would denote not a stable but a declining fertility of the soils in the countryside at large. In actual fact, *pace* the published statistics, the bishop's actual yields also declined, and this makes it all the more probable that yields were falling even more on lands of other and less privileged cultivators.[1]

Our sources also contain other indications of declining productivity of land. One such indication is the frequent inversion of the relative values of old and new land. On many manors engaged in active reclamation in the thirteenth century, assarts were valued more than the fields anciently occupied and cultivated, and new assarts were often valued more highly than old assarts. And yet, if the order in which land was broken up and colonized obeyed any rational principle, the older lands should have ranked as better lands—more fertile, easier to work or more accessible. The fact that after the passage of time their values fell below those of later conquests suggests that their quality must

---

[1] This will be shown by a fuller and more critical study of the yields on Winchester Manors soon to be published by Mr J. Z. Titow.

have deteriorated and that the stored-up and still unexhausted fertility of newer lands accounted for their higher valuation.

Another indication will be found in the contraction of certain sown furlongs. Manorial accounts which happen to record the names and acreages of individual furlongs—such as those of the manors of St Swithin's Priory, Winchester, or the abbot of Glastonbury—often enable us to watch the acreages of certain furlongs declining to the point at which entire furlongs appear to go out of cultivation altogether. On these and other estates manorial accounts also report the letting out to villagers of some of the acres thus withdrawn from the lord's sowing, and the land is then frequently described as inferior (*terra debilis, terre avenae*).

The inferior acres thus let out will not always account for all the lapsed acreage since some of the old and tired land was presumably withdrawn from cultivation altogether. Where the withdrawal was so wholesale as to comprise whole fields and furlongs, the land could presumably revert to pasture, thus compensating somewhat for the pasture converted into arable. But where the demise was gradual and piecemeal, and where, moreover, fields were cultivated in common, land could not revert to permanent pasture without disrupting the routine of unenclosed open field cultivation. It might then be lost to cultivation altogether, except for autumn pasture on stubble.

This lapsing of the lords' acres and the sagging trend of yields need not be wholly blamed on the insufficient provision of manure. Agricultural historians and economists are nowadays apt to discount the penalties of manureless cultivation, and in doing so they usually cite the lessons of the so-called Rothamstead experiment, where the same plot of land has been cultivated without manure for nearly a century, without reducing the yield below a certain, admittedly low, level. The Rothamstead experiment, however, is not so relevant to medieval experience as it is sometimes assumed to be. Loams or clays retentive of mineral nutrients and yet sufficiently open and sufficiently well drained not to suffer irreparable damage to their physical composition could perhaps remain under plough with but little manuring. But, except on these lands, yields could not be stabilized except at a very low level; and given medieval implements, seeds and drainage, the low levels thus stabilized would very likely be much below the yields recorded in modern times at Rothamstead; indeed so low as to produce no return to the cultivator. Students of medieval cropping plans could cite numerous instances of fields which frequently yielded very little more than the equivalent of the seed sown.

Nevertheless it is true that shortage of manure need not always have been the operative cause of dwindling yields and lapsing acres. The conditions under which new lands were being taken into cultivation could in the end bring about the same results. Some of the lands, thin and hungry, could be worth cultivating only for short periods. Before long the stored fertility of the soil would be mined out, and the land would lie exhausted. This may well have been the natural history of the East Anglian Brecklands or the Hampshire and Wiltshire chalklands and some of the Cotswold uplands. At the other extreme of the soil chart, the newly colonized gaults and heavy clays, such as the lands in South-Eastern Leicestershire—cold, heavy and undrainable —would be so frequently water-logged in the winter as to break the heart, as well as the implements, of the ploughman. They would also be difficult to turn into fine enough tilth in the spring and thus waste much of the seed. Both types of land were also those most likely to suffer from insufficient manuring, and both presumably predominated among the lands abandoned by the plough.

This abandonment could go so far as eventually to catch up with the process of reclamation. When this happened the total area under cultivation would decline, and land would thus begin to be 'de-colonized'. This moment of de-colonization was in any case bound to arrive sooner or later as reclamation itself slowed down and petered out.

The petering out of colonization could be observed all over England as the last land reserves were being exhausted. Needless to say the point arrived at different times in different parts of the country. We have seen that in the anciently and thickly settled Vale of Taunton colonization had ceased long before the middle of the thirteenth century; on the bishop of Winchester's Cotswold manor of Witney or in the Chiltern manors of Wycombe or Ivinghoe new fields were still being carved out until the very end of the century. In the proximity of the Northamptonshire forests assarts continued to be made until the very middle of the fourteenth century, while in the weald of Sussex or some parts of Devonshire and possibly in parts of the western Pennines small piecemeal intakes continued until the end of the Middle Ages. But in general, and taking England as a whole, reclamation of the waste had slowed down and was on the point of stopping altogether somewhere at the turn of the thirteenth and fourteenth centuries. At that time the marks of retreating cultivation appear all over the map of rural England. By the end of the fourteenth century and throughout the greater part of the fifteenth century the English countryside, like that across the channel, had come to be dotted all over with abandoned sites, once arable but now relapsed into waste.

II. *Population*

A. *Colonization*

It is generally assumed that in the Middle Ages, as in most other epochs, internal colonization went in step with the contemporary population trends: as population increased or declined, so settlement expanded and contracted. This link appears to have been so close that historians have agreed to rely on land occupation and settlement for evidence of underlying population trends; and as this argument from colonization to population is well grounded in both sense and fact; that it will on the whole be accepted here. On the whole but not wholly. At certain times and in certain places the progress of reclamations seemed to possess a momentum of its own and to reflect more faithfully the condition of the land than the numbers of men on it. It is thus probable that if internal colonization was petering out towards the end of the thirteenth century this was not only because the pressure of population may have eased but also because all the colonizable reserves had been exhausted. Conversely it appears probable that at times when internal colonization was at its most active it may have outpaced the growth of population for the simple reason that new land was required not only to provide for additional mouths or to occupy additional hands but in order to compensate for superannuated acres. For if it is true that medieval husbandmen could not prevent some of their acres from deteriorating or even from going out of cultivation altogether, it must follow that they always needed some new land to redress the balance of the old. This is why so often, e.g. on some of the manors of Peterborough Abbey, or St Swithin's Priory, Winchester, or on some Sussex manors of the Pelham family, or on several of the bishop of Winchester's estates in the second half of the thirteenth century, we find piecemeal reclamations for the demesne continuing while the total acreage under plough remained constant or even declined.

For the same reason on a number of manors in the early fourteenth century and later, in places where colonization had long come to a standstill, the area under cultivation appeared to contract to a much greater extent than a slight decline in population might have justified. In these conditions the area under cultivation would be contracting twice over—both because the demand for land had slackened and also because land continued to age and to lapse. That this is not a purely theoretical possibility is shown by scattered yet widespread instances of contracting areas under cultivation in the late fifteenth century when population either ceased to decline or else had again resumed its upward ascent.

The concordance of settlement and population must therefore be qualified; but once properly qualified and cautiously used it can be of great help for the study of medieval population. For if population ebbed and flowed as area under cultivation expanded and contracted, the chronological landmarks of the colonization movements should also be the landmarks of the population trend. Both were on the up-grade until soon after the end of the thirteenth century and then slumped until some time in the fifteenth century. The same population trends are, however, also revealed by such independent demographic evidence as there is.

B. *The lure of aggregates*

Our evidence enables us to study the population trends though not perhaps to form estimates on the absolute numbers of population at any points of time. All such estimates are much more questionable than they might at first sight appear. The existence of such nation-wide surveys as the Domesday Book or such comprehensive taxation returns as those of the Poll Taxes of the seventies of the fourteenth century, have led countless antiquarians and historians to attempt statistical enumerations of the total of English population in 1086 and in the later centuries of the Middle Ages. But so uncertain is the data that the estimates inevitably incur the risk of errors on a truly heroic scale. If all unknown and uncertain variables in the Domesday Book and Poll Tax returns were given their least possible values, the estimate of English population both in 1086 and at the height of medieval population growth would come to not more than two-thirds, or possibly as little as a half, of the estimates formed by assigning maximum values to the same variables. Thus, if we assume, as Professor Russell does in his pioneering study of medieval population, that the Domesday record of tenancies comprised all the tenanted holdings, and that furthermore each Domesday tenancy represented one and only one household, and that each household contained no more than 3·6 persons, we shall arrive at the estimate of population in 1086 at just under 1¾ millions. Similarly, if we follow Professor Russell in assuming that the bulk of taxable English population were in fact netted in by the Poll Tax of 1377; that the under-enumeration was not greater than 2·5 per cent, i.e. about one half of the evasion of the English income tax of our own day as assumed by the national income accountants; that the proportion of children in the population was so small that the untaxed boys and girls under fourteen formed rather less than 35 per cent of the total population, we shall arrive at Russell's estimate of population in 1377 of just under

36

2·235 millions. If we then proceed to assume that the population had reached its maximum at the very eve of the Black Death and that the aggregate mortality directly attributable to the Black Death and the great epidemics of the '60s and '70s was no more than 40 per cent, we shall then arrive at the figure of 3·7 millions for the medieval population at peak.

On the other hand historians might argue that villein holdings in Domesday were mere tenurial units and may have been occupied by several households and that, furthermore, some holdings (i.e. those of the villein's sub-tenants) remained unrecorded. They might also prefer to follow the demographic indications of later sources and put the average size of a Domesday household not at 3·6 but at just under 5. Their final figure would then be very much higher than Professor Russell's 1¾ millions, perhaps 50 or even 75 per cent higher.

The disparity would be even greater for the estimates of population at peak. If we assume for the Poll Tax of 1377 an evasion of say 25 per cent (comparisons made between some 1377 returns and the relevant manorial sources suggest a degree of evasion much greater than this); if furthermore we assume a proportion of untaxed under-fourteens consistent with a family of 4·5 persons, i.e. some 40–45 per cent of the total population, the estimate for 1377 population will also turn out to be nearly 50 per cent above the minimum estimate, i.e. nearly 3 millions. If we then proceed to assume that the mortality attributable to the Black Death alone was about a third of the population (this is the generally accepted estimate) and that the combined mortality from other fourteenth-century epidemics was at least half that of 1348–9, the aggregate casualties of all epidemics would approach 50 per cent. It is furthermore possible that in many parts of England the population had begun to decline a whole generation before the Black Death, and certainly after the great famines of 1317–19. In that case the estimate of population at peak, i.e. at the turn of the thirteenth and fourteenth centuries, would appear higher still, and may turn out to be much more than twice that of Russell's, or nearer 7 millions than his 3·7.

Where the statistical possibilities can vary so widely and the margin of error be so great, no historian or statistician should commit himself to a firm estimate of population. To historians abreast of most recent researches the higher estimates may well appear to be more consistent with the economic and social conditions of rural England at the end of the thirteenth century than the lower ones, but this sense of consistency cannot and must not be expressed in global figures. Historians in search of demographic enlightenment may, however, console themselves with the thought that very little social and economic meaning can be read into total figures of population unaccompanied by the assessment of other relevant factors such as capital equipment or the state of technique. What is much more significant is the dynamics of population, its trend, i.e. how far it moved towards or away from a point at which the symptoms of relative over-population would become apparent. And on this question our evidence can give us somewhat less ambiguous answers.

c. *The rising trend*

The evidence of the rising population trend in the centuries between the eleventh and fourteenth has been on the whole accepted by historians without demur, even though most of it is indirect. We have agreed that the remarkable expansion of settlement and reclamation during that period can be taken as a sign of continually increasing population. Certain striking manifestations of expanding settlement, such as the numerous filial hamlets and villages budding off the older settlements—and we find them all over England—provide the most obvious topographical evidence. Equally obvious is the meaning of urban growth at the same period, for this was the time when immigrants from the countryside swelled the population of older towns to their maximum size and formed brand new urban centres.

Yet another sign is the proliferation and sub-division of holdings in the villages. In many places this proliferation is obscured from view by the artificial nature of so many of the manorial surveys, which list the lord's direct tenants and not the men who actually occupied and tilled the soil. But where the circumstances allow us to pierce the artificial screen of tenurial fictions, the proliferation of smallholdings is unmistakable.

However, more direct evidence is not altogether lacking. For a few places, such as the bishop of Winchester's manors of Taunton, we possess local records, such as those of 'hundredpenny', enabling us to reconstruct the movements of population over long periods. There the increase continued almost uninterrupted from 1209 to 1348, and the compound annual rate of growth was above 0·85 per cent; a low rate compared with, say, modern Ceylon, but higher than in Russia in the eighteenth and the early nineteenth centuries and high enough to have raised Taunton's population nearly two-and-a-half times between 1209 and 1311.[1]

But the most striking demonstration of this trend will be found in land hunger of which the signs began to accumulate quite early in the thirteenth century. Some of the signs—the exhorbitant entry fines and the high tallages—have already been mentioned. What has not yet been mentioned is the growing numbers of wholly landless men

[1] A.G.Rashin, *Naselenie Rossii za 100 liet*. Moscow, 1950.

revealed by our documents. There were many villages in the great estates of the abbots of Glastonbury and Bury St Edmunds, bishops of Winchester, priors of Christ Church, Canterbury, or abbots of Ramsey, where the numbers of cottagers with diminutive holdings and of all-but-landless men accounted for a third of the population and even more, and where the average holding per family was two acres and less.

Where men were so plentiful and land so scarce the normal advancement of men by succession to holdings was denied to many—perhaps most—of the young people. In many places the queues of men awaiting their chance of acquiring land became so long that the entire traditional routine of succession from father to son was disrupted. So valuable was the land and so high were the prices it commanded that men were tempted to sell long before they were due to retire. Purchase thus became a common method of acquiring land. On the Glastonbury estates in the second half of the century more than a third of the sitting tenants had acquired their holdings by various forms of open or disguised purchase and sometimes over the heads of the legal heirs whose claims they usually bought out. Numbers of men acquired land by marrying women with dowries and even more often by marrying widows with land. What made widows specially attractive is that they were, as a rule, allowed to keep the whole of the deceased husbands' customary holdings. On some manors, e.g. Taunton, the second husbands could retain the land on their wives' death, and were thus able to contract second marriages destined to produce later a further crop of marriageable widows.

With so much land changing hands by purchase and by marriage, large and growing numbers of young men and more especially of women unprovided with dowries or widows' portions were bound to descend to the position of landless or smallholding cottagers or unmarried spinsters. Hence the large accumulation of poor at the bottom of the social scale.

It is therefore no wonder that most other familiar signs of over-population made their appearance. A population whose land hunger was so acute and whose proportions of petty holders were so large, must have been moving ever nearer to the very margin of subsistence. Hence the high death rates which most invariably followed bad harvests. In years of bad harvest manorial accounts on more than one estate contained bailiffs' notes explaining the failure to carry out this or that operation or justifying its high cost by the *caristia operariorum*—the year was in other words so bad that labourers died off and were scarce. The same susceptibility to bad harvest is shown by the record of 'recognitions' of young men leaving villages to seek employment elsewhere. On the abbot of Glastonbury's manors, where the data of 'recognitions' happens to be most abundant, the numbers almost invariably fall in the years following bad harvests and famine. Finally there is the evidence of heroits—payments of death duties—which fluctuate sharply and frequently with harvests and prices. On estates, like those of the bishops of Winchester, which distinguish the heriots of poorer villagers from those of the richer ones, it is possible to observe how sensitive the village poor were to the variations of harvest, and how greatly the death rates among them rose in times when harvests were bad and food was scarce.

Is there any need to explain why in these conditions the demographic increases were destined to come to a halt sooner or later? With the proportions of smallholders increasing, with the death rates of poorer men high and rising, with large numbers of property-less women remaining unmarried, the population was sooner or later bound to lose its ability for growth.

To this we must add the possibility that as the colonizable lands were passing away and some older lands continued to deteriorate, bad harvests—and with them high mortality—could be expected to come to the villages with greater frequency and with increasing severity. The turn of the twelfth and thirteenth centuries certainly witnessed for brief periods a succession of unprecedented harvest failures and famines —those of 1272, 1277, 1283, 1292, 1311, 1332, and more especially those of 1317–19. Each of these visitations was undoubtedly due to natural causes. Above all, the years of 1317–19 were years of unparalleled downpours and inundations. Yet the unprecedentedly heavy toll which these harvest failures took, like the toll which similar calamities have taken in certain countries in modern times, could not have been due to natural causes alone, but to the calamity-sensitive constitution of society, and, above all, to the precarious balance between men's needs and the productivity of their holdings characteristic of an over-populated country and an over-extended agriculture.

D. The decline

These indirect reflexions of expanding population fade out of our records in the opening decades of the fourteenth century and eventually give place to the manifestations of an altogether contrary movement— that of demographic decline. By the beginning of the century the reclamation of lands slows down or ceases altogether even in places like the Sedgmoor vills of Glastonbury Abbey or the Derbyshire and Staffordshire manors of the Duchy of Lancaster, still abounding with lands no worse than those colonized a generation or two earlier. In a few regions such as the Weald of Sussex or the uplands of the West

Riding and North Lancashire it is still possible to observe a trickle of assarts and reclamations throughout the late fourteenth and fifteenth centuries, but elsewhere the process of internal colonization not only ceases but is succeeded by what appears to be a general retreat from the older margins of settlement. Rents, especially free rents, cease to rise and even begin to decline; on some estates entry fines fall, and become as purely nominal as they had been before the thirteenth century land hunger. In short, the demand for land is now slack, its supply is now abundant.

With the ratio of men to land altered, the areas of land under plough contract. The contraction is most conspicuous on the demesne where it is linked with the general reorganization of the demesne economy. In most parts of England the landlords, anxious to retain their tenants and to let out their vacant lands, proceeded to lighten the burdens of payments and to cancel altogether the remaining labour dues. In other words, the feudal rent fell and lost much of its oppressive power. Nevertheless numbers of peasant holdings stayed vacant for long periods of time; villages on the further frontiers of cultivation—such as the smaller hamlets at the heads of Yorkshire dales, or on poorer chalklands of the Hampshire and Wiltshire downland—dwindled to the very brink of total demise. A proportion, though not the majority, of deserted villages, which nowadays lie hidden under overgrown mounds and trenches, dates to this period, i.e. the late fourteenth and fifteenth centuries, bearing witness to the changing ratios of men to land and thereby also to the decline in population at the close of the Middle Ages.

Another suggestive indication of the turning demographic trend will be found in the behaviour of wages. In spite of the conventional valuations and expectations built into medieval wages (as indeed into all medieval prices) they were on the whole quite responsive to the changes in supply of labour or demand for it. We have seen that in the years following bad harvests and high mortality manorial bailiffs could be found complaining of the *caristia* of labourers, and in this context *caristia* meant both scarcity and high price. Taking the thirteenth century as a whole, money wages of agricultural workers were remarkably stable, but in view of the rising prices of agricultural produce, the stable money wages masked a fall in real wages. In real terms agricultural wages on the estates for which we have sufficient evidence, e.g., those of the bishop of Winchester, the abbot of Westminster or the abbot of Glastonbury, must have fallen at least by 25 per cent between 1208 and 1225 and by at least another 25 per cent between 1225 and 1348. The fall will appear all the more significant if it is remembered that on most manorial estates during the period the employment of wage labour greatly expanded just as the proportion of compulsory labour declined.

In all probability real wages were being kept down by the growing population and increasing supplies of labour. If this probability is admitted, the rise of agricultural wages in the fourteenth and fifteenth centuries must also be accepted as clear evidence of a corresponding reversal in the demographic trend. The trend of wages in the Winchester and Westminster manors turns upwards in the twenties of the fourteenth century and continues its upward course for another 120 or 150 years. Money wages for agricultural labour reached the highest point some time before 1450 and stayed at approximately that level, or very little higher, until about at least 1470; real wages, i.e. wages expressed in units of the amount of food they were able to buy, probably continued to rise until the last quarter of the century. The money wages of skilled and semi-skilled rural workmen—the thatchers, the tilers, the smiths, the carpenters—continued to rise even after the wages of agricultural labourers had reached their topmost level.

The rising trend of wages could of course be also explained in other ways. In theory wages could rise as a result of increased investment and of general expansion of production, more especially of labour-intensive arable farming. It is also possible to argue that agricultural wages rose because industrial employment, such as building and above all cloth manufacture, stimulated the demand for manpower. To the present writer neither hypothesis appears plausible. The hypothesis of increased demand for agricultural labour in agriculture itself is difficult to reconcile with what we know of the declining employment on the demesne and with the reduced area under arable cultivation. The possibility that the employment of labour by peasant tenants could have expanded sufficiently to provide substitute employment for men no longer wanted on the lord's demesne seems equally unlikely. It is the nature of peasant households of small and middling size to rely as much as possible on the labour of the members of the family itself. It was also in the nature of medieval village families, as in that of most peasant families, to be under-employed and thus possess reserves of labour force sufficient to deal with considerable additions to holdings. But even if we allowed for the possibility that the richer peasants employed larger numbers of labourers in the late fourteenth and fifteenth centuries than they had employed in the thirteenth, and assume for argument sake that peasant landholders employed as much hired labour per acre as the lord's demesne, we should still have to make allowances for the smaller aggregate area under plough, If so, additional employment in villages, however great, would be most unlikely to compensate for reduced employment on the lords' lands.

Even more implausible appears the hypothesis of industry compensating for the decline in the demand for labour in agriculture. The growth of the cloth industry in the fourteenth century was certainly very considerable. We must, therefore, presume that while the industry grew it set up an additional demand for labour capable of influencing the labour market. These influences, however, must not be exaggerated. The cloth industry is known to have grown in the fourteenth and perhaps also in the early fifteenth centuries; the belief that it continued to grow throughout the fifteenth century is based entirely on what historians happen to believe, but cannot possibly know, about the conditions in the domestic market for cloth. The only thing they know for certain is that the exports of English cloth, which had grown very fast in the fourteenth century, grew hardly at all between, say, 1420 and 1470, and that a number of towns, old and new, which had benefited from the great expansion of cloth exports in the fourteenth and early fifteenth centuries, such as York, Colchester or Norwich, declined or ceased to grow thereafter.[1]

What is more, even while it grew and even at its peak, medieval cloth industry could not have employed sufficient numbers of workers to make much difference to the price of labour in the country as a whole. We shall see presently that in the thirteenth century perhaps as much as a third of the total rural population was available for whole or part-time employment as wage labour. Their numbers then must on conservative estimates have exceeded a million or may even have approached two millions. Set against these numbers, the total additional employment—and it is only additional employment that matters —in the growing cloth industry of the fourteenth century could not possibly have been very significant, and could not have formed a proportion of the total labour force available for employment large enough to make a great difference to the aggregate demand for labour.

Contracting population must therefore be assumed to be the principal factor behind rising wages, and this is what contemporaries appeared to assume. When in the second half of the fourteenth century the Statutes of Labourers were under discussion, the evil of high wages was invariably blamed on the declined or declining population. Indeed so frequent are these imputations in fourteenth-century sources that it is sometimes difficult to understand why modern writers should be at all tempted to disbelieve them. Had sufficient attention been paid to the sentiments

---

[1] The decline in some of these towns after 1420 (as in the case of Norwich after 1350) is fully reflected in the charts published by Mr. Bridbury in *Economic Growth*, pp. 65 *seq*. The trend would have stood out even more clearly had moving averages been used to eliminate annual fluctuations, such as those of 1444, 1445 or 1446.

expressed in parliamentary petitions, e.g. the famous petition of 1368, the true causes of the rise in wages would have been better understood. It was obviously due not to the attractions of alternative industrial employment, but to causes blamed or implied in the petition, i.e. the competition of the rural employers and the eagerness of land owners to receive erstwhile labourers as tenants of their untenanted lands.

Compared to the causes of the demographic decline, its chronology may at first sight appear very simple, for until recently its main turning point did not appear to be in doubt. So deeply did the Black Death imprint itself on the imagination of the contemporaries and on the memory of their descendants that historians may perhaps be forgiven for their persistence in dating the beginning of the demographic decline with the great pestilence of 1348–9 and for explaining it accordingly. We have, however, seen that the ascending movement of population had come to a stop a whole generation, in some places a whole half-century, before 1348. This alone should be sufficient to warn us against ascribing the downturn of the trend to the mortality of the Black Death and that mortality alone.

The mortality was of course very great. Most students of the evidence agree that the pestilence must have carried off at least a third of the total population. Moreover it not only lowered, sharply and immediately, the numbers alive but also affected the numbers to be born in subsequent generations, since it appeared to strike hardest the infants, i.e. the would-be parents of generations to come. Yet it is doubtful whether by itself the mortality of the Black Death would have been sufficient to keep the population back for a period as long as a whole century and more. Even a simple arithmetical manipulation of birth rates and marriage rates appropriate to populations like that of medieval England would be sufficient to show that the relayed effects of the Black Death on the numbers of men and women in the child-begetting and child-bearing age groups should have largely spent themselves sometimes before 1400, i.e. 50 or even 80 years before the clear signs of resumed population growth became manifest.

Obviously the Black Death could not have been the sole cause of the demographic decline. To begin with, it was not the only pestilence recorded in our sources. In the 'sixties most parts of England suffered at least two other heavy attacks of the plague—those of 1361–2 and 1369—of a severity which might well have earned the whole decade the appellation 'black' had men's memories not been dominated by the apocalyptic events of 1348–9. The death rates in these plagues varied even more from place to place than in the Black Death but, if the evidence of Glastonbury records is to be believed, mortality in a number of places may have approached 20 per cent. According to chronicles and manorial documents, a whole series of outbreaks both national and local occurred all over England in the course of the last quarter of the fourteenth century and during the fifteenth century. These later outbreaks were very much milder and more local than those of the fourteenth century, but their aggregate effect must have been very considerable. It does not require much sophisticated demography to realize that a population whose net reproduction rate, even in periods unaffected by plagues, was very low could easily be prevented from recovering by a series of local epidemics which visited most places at least once and many places several times in the course of the 50 or 75 years before 1470.

The recovery might also have been delayed by economic conditions. In theory output per acre or per bushel of seed should have risen now that the poor and exhausted areas were withdrawn from cultivation. But this would not by itself have made it any easier to support increasing numbers of people on land. Moreover, it is quite possible that the process of de-colonization had not yet come to an end during the first half of the fifteenth century; that lands impoverished and abandoned in the previous generations were slow to recover or to return to cultivation. In that case despite the great decline in population the ratio of men to cultivable land may have changed too little to make it possible for men to marry and to set up house as often and as early in life as they could be expected to do in times when land was abundant.

The *histoire raisonnée* of the demographic decline in the later Middle Ages thus covers a longer period and is beset with more problems than is sometimes realized. The decline may go back to the beginning of the fourteenth century or even earlier; it may have been prepared by the economic conditions of the late thirteenth century, ushered in by the high mortalities during the bad harvests of 1317–19, drastically accelerated during the plagues of mid-fourteenth century, and further sustained by the recurrent plagues of the late fourteenth and fifteenth centuries, and perhaps also by the continued effects of agrarian crisis.

It was not until the second half of the fifteenth century that indications of demographic recovery begin to appear in our documents, but in some places the indications did not manifest themselves until the closing decades of the fifteenth and the opening decades of the sixteenth century. Even then population remained for a long time below the level it had reached at the end of the thirteenth century. It is even doubtful whether English rural population came up to its thirteenth-century peak until the very eve of the industrial revolution of the eighteenth century.

III. *The manorial estate*

A. *Patterns of settlement*

It is even more dangerous to generalize about the organization of medieval agriculture than about its physical and demographic background. The rules and institutions which regulated medieval agriculture and ordered rural society differed in almost every particular from place to place and from generation to generation. So great were the variations that no student of medieval agriculture would nowadays dare to assemble all the medieval agrarian institutions into a portmanteau model capable of accommodating the whole of England during the whole of the Middle Ages.

Needless to say, local differences appear sharpest at points at which local topography, soil and climate bore directly on agriculture and rural life. One such point was the physical layout of settlement and land occupation. The broad geographical distinction between the plains of South Midlands, East Midlands and southern counties on the one hand, and the downland, mountains and moorlands surrounding and traversing the midland plains on the other hand, was matched by corresponding differences in the size and type of rural settlement. The settlement typical of the arable plain was the larger village grouped either round a green or well-head, or else strung out along a roadway or a waterway. On the other hand, on marginal and recently reclaimed lands, in hilly landscapes and amidst high pastures, though not in the newly reclaimed fenlands, the typical settlement was the isolated farm or the small hamlet.

Superimposed on these differences in the layout of settlement, but by no means identical with them, were the differences in field systems. About these differences all historians were, until recently, fully in agreement. In their view holdings held in severalty and cultivated individually prevailed in hilly and mainly pastoral regions or on recently reclaimed land. But elsewhere, especially on the more anciently and densely occupied lands in arable plans, open fields were the rule. Within the open-field areas historians distinguished regions of two-field rotation and those of three-field rotation; and, following Professor H. L. Gray's precept, they would regard the thirteenth century as a period in the course of which a number of villages and manors tried to reduce their fallow and thus to intensify their husbandry by going over from a two-field to a three-field course.

Of recent years, however, these views of medieval field systems have drawn upon themselves a certain amount of criticism. Their very origin and antiquity have been questioned. Following recent German hypotheses, some historians in this country and in France have offered very much later dates for the open fields. What distinguished open-field systems from other land usages—so the argument runs—was the pasturing of village animals on post-harvest stubble, and this use of the stubble was a late innovation, made necessary by the plough-ing up of pastures in village wastelands in later stages of medieval colon-ization. The fully-fledged open-field system must therefore be regarded as a late-medieval device, not earlier, and in most places later, than the second half of the thirteenth century.

This theory agrees well with some features of our evidence. The surviving maps of common-field systems are invariably later than the thirteenth century, and some are post-medieval. The field arrange-ments they illustrate, with their symmetrical division into two or three equal fields comprising the entire village arable and with strips regu-larly distributed among the common fields, are perhaps too orderly to have spontaneously grown up in the course of centuries. They bear every sign of a relatively late tidying-up by landlords or village com-munities. We should look in vain for other evidence of field systems equally perfect in the earlier centuries of the Middle Ages.

Yet by itself this argument cannot do away with medieval open fields. Why should common-field cultivation be indissolubly linked with common pasture on the stubble? Is it not possible to imagine an obligatory sequence of courses and collective co-aration resulting solely from what the Germans call the *Streulage*, i.e. holdings composed of strips too numerous, too small and too dispersed to be cultivated and fenced in separately? Some such less perfect variants of common-field cultivation could be found in many documents of the twelfth and the thirteenth centuries. Early surveys and charters frequently describe holdings as lying in *utroque campo*, or declare certain pieces of land to be worth nothing every second or third year when the fields in which they were situated lay fallow.

Fields divided and managed in this manner must be assumed to have been cultivated in common even when they were not subject to the obligation of common pasture on the stubble. Moreover that obli-gation must not be linked too closely with the growing shortage of permanent pasture. To begin with, the object of stubble pasture was not only to feed the animals, but also to manure the land. It would be to the villagers' advantage to fold their animals on the arable however abundant their grasslands. And even if it were true that pasture on the stubble was becoming more indispensable as grasslands were con-tracting, why should the villages have waited till the later Middle Ages before adopting it? It is now generally agreed that wastes were being broken up and permanent pastures were contracting in the earlier Middle Ages, i.e. before the middle of the thirteenth century.

On the other hand in the later Middle Ages marginal arable was reverting to grass and permanent pastures were becoming again more abundant.

The entire historical problem of common fields, their origin and history has been unnecessarily complicated by defining the common-field system in too perfect and uniform a manner. It was possible for some villages to practise collective co-aration without common pasture on the stubble. It was also possible for some villages to have different sequences of crops on different parts of the village arable; to have a three-course rotation on some lands, two-field rotation or no recognizable rotation at all on others; to vary the size and composition of their spring-sown and winter-sown areas from year to year; and to dovetail arable with pasture and one system of rotation with another to suit the lay of the land and its physical properties, the vagaries of seasons, the changing qualities of old land and the progress of reclamation.

In other words, the variations in field systems considered in detail were far more numerous than the conventional distribution of two- and three-field systems would indicate. Whatever the local variant, some form of obligatory rotation would be found on most anciently occupied fields in the arable plains, but would probably be rare in regions mainly pastoral or recently colonized.

A combination of arable nuclei with large pastoral peripheries most appropriate to areas of sparse settlement would be that of infield-outfield—a system which a modern farmer would probably describe as one of convertible husbandry. It was to be found in areas as widely separated as the Breckland of Norfolk, the combes of Devonshire and the Scottish border; and it was bound to differ in detail from region to region. In general, under that system part of the land would be regularly manured and intensively cultivated while the rest would form the outfield from which portions could be periodically taken in, i.e. sown and cropped for a spell of years and then allowed to revert to waste or pasture. In some places the outfield would be drawn upon spasmodically and irregularly and the 'intakes' themselves would be small, so that the whole system would resemble one or the other of the primitive forms of intermittent husbandry. In others, the outfield would be taken in so frequently and so regularly as to resemble very closely the rhythm of a conventional common-field rota. It is indeed possible that some of the examples of a precocious four- or five-fold rotation in the thirteenth and fourteenth centuries, cited by some historians, were in fact nothing else than accelerated variants of infield-outfield cultivation.

With different forms of settlement and field system went a concomitant pattern of communal regulation. Most of the open-field systems called for combined operations. Collective payments had to be made from time to time to the lord of the manor or to the king; payments themselves had to be communally borne and apportioned. Some villages must therefore have provided themselves with the semblance of a community chest and of a local tax. And where there were communal duties and communal funds there were also bound to be communal officials. Their existence has left few direct reflexions in our documents, but in a number of places their activities are betrayed by oblique hints. Now and again, as in the Glastonbury manor of Ottery, the 'social guild' of the local parish church is revealed as the administrative focus of the village. Occasionally the lords blamed the communal actions they did not like on groups of obstinate 'ringleaders'. In other places we find the manorial officers themselves—the reeve, the haywards or the tithingmen—functioning as the representative officials of the community.

We can perhaps assume that communal organizations would be elaborate and, so to speak, tight in places where the manorial machinery was lax. Historians have frequently suggested that the role of the village community was most important in the eastern counties where manors were weak and vills were sufficiently large to comprise several manorial units. This however must not be taken to mean that communal organization was of little importance in the highly manorialized regions of Midland and southern England, in which the authority of a lord could frequently extend over all the lands and the inhabitants of an entire village. For in villages thus situated the daily needs of the manor itself, with its constant demands for services and payments and for collective undertakings of every kind, imposed upon the villagers the necessity of acting in concert, of attending village gatherings and of appointing officials. Indeed so strong is the collectivizing compulsion of the typical manor that historians, especially continental historians, have some- times been tempted to derive most of the communal arrangements, and even the common-field system itself, from the needs of the manor and the initiative of the landlord.

The two patterns of rural organization, the communal and the manorial, were thus combined all over medieval England. The com- bination could be very loose in regions like East Anglia, Danelaw or Kent or in the counties of erstwhile Northumbria, where the vill and not the manor made and enforced most of the collective regulations; or else it could be very close, as in Hampshire, Wiltshire, Somerset, Northamptonshire, or Huntingdonshire, where the authority of manorial lords was all-embracing and where the village administration was intertwined with the lord's own machinery. But no matter how the two systems combined, both were all but ubiquitous—the manorial no less than the communal.

B. *Manorial types*

The insistence on the ubiquity of the manor may strike a reader familiar with recent literature as somewhat retrograde. The tendency in recent writings on manorial history has been to disparage the ancient notions of the ever-present and all-important manor. For a number of years, especially since Stenton's study of North Danelaw, one regional historian after another has drawn our attention to parts of England upon which the manorial pattern imprinted itself but very faintly. North Danelaw, East Anglia, Kent, parts of West Midlands, the northernmost counties of England and the Welsh marches, have all been revealed to us as non-manorialized areas. Still more recently Kosminsky, in his study of the Hundred Rolls of 1279, has demonstrated that even within the inner core of manorialized England there were to be found whole stretches of country, e.g. entire hundreds in Oxfordshire and Warwickshire, in which the authority of the manorial lord, especially that of the smaller lay lords, over their tenantry and over the village lands was slight. In this way Maitland's famous dictum of 'manors, manors everywhere' has now been relegated to the repository of ancient formulas reserved for annual demolition by undergraduate examinees.

The relegation has been too drastic. Some manors did not dominate the countryside as much as others, had fewer functions or a more rudimentary organization and exercised a more remote control over the lives and the lands of the tenants, but manors they nevertheless were. The result of recent researches has been not to banish the manor from the so-called non-manorialized areas, but to bring out the great variety of ways in which manors diverged from their idealized image.

The most important divergences—important because they concerned the very essence of manorial economy—were to be found in the relative roles of demesne and dependent tenants. What these roles were in a typical manor is nowadays well known. The 'ideal' manor was bilateral; the lands composing it and the income it yielded were made up of two distinct parts. One part of the land comprised in the manor would be directly cultivated by the lord as his demesne, while the other would be in the hands of the lord's tenants and be cultivated by them. In an 'ideal' manor the land in tenancy and the number of tenants would be sufficient to provide the demesne with all the seasonal labour it required—the assumption being that even the ideal manor would employ permanent *famuli* for tasks requiring regular service throughout the year. The revenue which the landlords derived from their estates would therefore also be two-fold—the direct yield of the demesne and the rents which he received from his tenants over and above their labour dues.

In actual practice the relative importance of the demesne as a source of revenue, the extent to which it was cultivated by the labour of tenants and the degree to which the services of the tenants were geared to the demesne, differed from manor to manor. In this respect most manors in thirteenth-century England departed from the ideal type more or less. It would in fact be possible to arrange them in a continuous series, with manors wholly composed of lands in tenancy and yielding nothing else but rents (Germans call such estates *Grundherrschaften*) at one extreme; and manors all made up of demesne land and yielding all their revenue in the form of profits of cultivation (Germans would describe such manors as *Gutsherrschaften*) at the other extreme. The proportions and the manner in which these two elements combined varied from place to place and from period to period.

In considering the varying combinations of *Grundherrschaft* with *Gutsherrschaft*, the differences from place to place would be the ones to strike the attention of a student most forcibly. Some of these differences were deeply embedded in the very foundations of English regional history and, like these foundations themselves, may have reached to the hoary pre-English past of the tribes which composed the invading Germanic hosts. Professor Stenton has taught us to derive the regional pecularities of the Danelaw from the social structure and customs of the Danish settlers; Mr Jolliffe has similarly tried to account for the peculiarities of Kent and Northumbria by the still more ancient social pattern imported into these regions by the Jutes and the Northumbrian Saxons. More recently still Professor Homans has argued that a similar correlation existed between the medieval field systems and social arrangements in Suffolk and Norfolk and the tribal customs of the Frisians.

However, these regional differences with their tribal implications, even if they were accepted as established, would provide us with only one of the designs making up the palimpsest of English medieval society and of its manorial system. Geographers never tire of drawing our attention to the purely physical factors behind some regional differences in the shape of villages and types of manor. Most of them would contend that a typical manor with its large demesne and numerous tenancy would as a rule go together with a nucleated village and be most appropriate to the predominantly arable plains of central and southern England. By the same reckoning the hilly uplands with their small hamlets and pastoral husbandry would be unfavourable to the formation of typical manors with large arable demesnes and a numerous servile tenantry. It is indeed arguable that some of the regional differences in social structure in Northumbria and eastern England reflected the necessities of local husbandry as conditioned by topography, soil and climate.

Many, perhaps most, of the differences in manorial types form part of yet another design: that composed by the variations in landowner-ship itself. For landlords differed very greatly in their wealth and power, their function in society, their requirements as consumers. Some of these differences, especially among lay landlords, were frequently personal and accidental; lords could be efficient or inefficient, careful or pro-fligate, resident or absent, saddled with large or small households. But taking the landowning class as a whole it is possible to discern within it certain clearly defined groups, each distinguished by a different and a characteristic mode of exploiting land.

One such group most frequently singled out by historians is that of ecclesiastical landlords. We shall see presently that ecclesiastical land-lords themselves varied too much to be lumped into a single category, but this grouping can be useful as long as the term ecclesiastical is con-fined to the estates of the great Benedictine houses. As it turns out, we know more about these estates than about any other, and it is on these estates that manors closest to the ideal type will most frequently be found in the thirteenth century.

This predominance of typical manors on Benedictine estates is partly a matter of situation. The Benedictine houses were among the most ancient monastic foundations, and their endowments were as a rule sited in the most anciently settled areas and comprised some of the most anciently established villages in the country. But the main reason why on these estates the conventional manorial structure was so persistently preserved will be found in the character of the Benedictine communities and their material needs. They were resident communities, i.e. large collective households with high and rising standards of sustenance. Their direct requirements of food and fodder were great and growing and could best be safeguarded by direct liveries from their manor. Hence their tendency to maintain functioning demesnes on as many estates as were necessary *ad victum monachorum*. On the other hand the great Benedictine abbeys also needed ready money. The monks and their abbots did not live by bread alone but were regular buyers of cloth, condiments, books, vestments and other merchandise; they had to pay heavy taxes to the popes and the kings and they regularly indulged in costly building. These needs of cash could frequently be met by the sale of agricultural surpluses, especially on their outlying manors, but the chief source of money was rents and other rent-like payments of tenants. It is therefore not surprising that while most Benedictine houses in the late twelfth and thirteenth centuries maintained and at times enlarged their demesnes, they also looked well after their rent rolls and seldom provided themselves with manors wholly or mainly made up of demesne. The other features of Benedictine manors, such as strict enforcement of labour services and of feudal rights over villeins, stemmed party from the conservatism natural to institutional owners but mainly from the needs of active demesne farming.

Different again were the attitudes and practices of some other ecclesiastical landlords and above all the Cistercians. The Cistercian rule drove the monks to settle in places undefiled by daily contact with mundane humanity. They either established themselves in virgin wildernesses beyond the anciently settled regions of medieval England, or else created wildernesses by expelling the lay population in their vicinity. These predilections would in any case have made it impossible for the Cistercians to maintain villein tenants on their estates and to depend on the labour of tenants for the cultivation of their demesnes. The typical Cistercian estate was therefore a *Gutsherrschaft*, a 'grange', a property wholly made up and run as a demesne and cultivated by *conversi*, i.e. lay brethren of the order.

At the other pole of ecclesiastical land ownership, diverging from the ideal type at least as widely as the Cistercian estates, were the estates of the Templars and the Hospitallers. These estates were very large and wealthy, but they were run mostly for money incomes and were composed very largely of tenancies, often detached and dispersed, held wholly for rent. In the course of the thirteenth century the Templars reclaimed and colonized vast areas of land round Temple Brewer and Temple Newsam, in Lincolnshire and Yorkshire, as well as elsewhere. But the large and compact estates thus created were also conducted mainly for the sake of the money incomes they yielded.

Finally there were the episcopal estates which differed little from the lay estates of the same size. An episcopal estate resembled the great baronial estates. In most respects, i.e. the needs of the lord's household, its requirements of provisions and still greater needs of money, and its consequent inclination to run its manors partly as sources of provisions but mainly as sources of money income.

On their part lay estates differed from one another almost as much as the ecclesiastical ones. The differences between them were in fact more profound than those which marked them off, taken together, from ecclesiastical estates. At one extreme were to be found the possessions of smaller lay landowners and wealthier freeholders of non-military rank: most of them men whom the chronicles might describe as *agrarii milites*, i.e. knights who worked their lands and lived off them. Our sources do not tell us much about them, but such indirect evidence as we possess, coupled with what we can glean from the Domesday Book and the Hundred Rolls of 1279, suggests that on these properties, home farms or demesnes serving the needs of the owners' households played a relatively greater part than on most larger estates. The evidence of the Hundred Rolls and of Inquisitions Post Mortem also makes it clear that many of the small estates were under-provided with tenants and not greatly dependent on revenues from rents.

Needless to say the smaller estates themselves varied according to their size, the predilections of their owners and their geographical location. A larger knightly estate, like that of the Pelham family in Sussex, still comprised home farms as late as the fifteenth century, but being fairly large also possessed considerable rent-yielding properties. Somewhat similarly made up were the properties of the Fitz Hammes in Buckinghamshire or of the Beauchamps in the South Midlands. On the other hand small properties like that of James Grim of Leightonstone—with, if we are to trust the Hundred Rolls, very little rent—must have been typical of the multitude of petty estates in the thirteenth century which in the words of the 1368 Petition *vivent par geynerie de lour Terres . . . e que nont seigneurie ne villeins par eix servir.*

At the other extreme were the great honorial complexes which in some cases, such as that of the de Lacys and the dukes of Lancaster, contained hundreds of manors in all parts of the country. Although on all these estates functioning demesnes could be found until quite late in the thirteenth century and even later, a very considerable share (on the earl of Cornwall's estates the bulk) of the revenues, even in the thirteenth century, came from rents and feudal rights.

Another characteristic which distinguished these estates from those of humbler laymen was the managerial continuity and efficiency conferred upon them by conciliar administration. By the middle of the thirteenth century, and possibly earlier, most of the great honorial estates had come to be administered by officials of baronial councils and thereby acquired most of the features of institutionalized landownership commonly associated with monastic and episcopal properties. Not only were they resistant to sudden changes in economic conditions, but they were also insulated from the vagaries of private landlordship, such as absentee ownership or vacancies or confiscations, and even from those of division and assignment of incomes to heirs or widows. As we shall see later these estates were among the earliest to adjust themselves to the changed economic climate of the later Middle Ages by transforming the bulk of their income into rents. This they were able to do not only because conciliar administration was rational and efficient, but also because the lords' needs of food and fodder played a subordinate part in their economy.

Finally, manors varied according to their age. Most of the typical manors were as a rule the old ones: anciently established and therefore bearing the marks of their Anglo-Saxon and early medieval past. It is because the patrimony of the Benedictine abbeys and of the great baronial estates was largely made up of ancient and mature vills that typical manors are so often found among them. For the same reason estates carved out from the waste or assembled from smallholdings in later periods were less likely to conform to the manorial type. Thus the great Templars' estate had been assembled in purchases and donation, mostly small, all over the country in the generation or two proceeding the great survey of their possessions in 1185, and this may be why at that date they appeared to be made up of a vast miscellany of disparate rent-paying holdings. Similarly, estates carved out of recently colonized waste, like the abbot of Peterborough's manors of Belasize or Novum Locum, were not as a rule sufficiently provided with dependent tenants to be run as conventional manors. They were, therefore, either managed as 'granges', i.e. all-demesnes cultivated by labourers hired or drafted from outside, or else let out in rent-paying tenements. It is even possible to argue that one of the reasons why the manorial system in the Dane-law was so loose is that the Danish settlement was several centuries later than the Anglo-Saxon settlement elsewhere and thereby skipped the early stages in the development of serfdom and of the feudal estate.

These imprints of age on the physiognomy of individual manors should perhaps be considered in a somewhat different connexion: as illustrations of more purely historical (a Marxist might call them dialectical) variations through time. The differences I have so far reviewed were essentially morphological and contemporaneous. They were differences which a thirteenth-century Arthur Young might have noted as he passed from region to region and through village to village in the same region. But in addition there were differences which only an historian could observe: the changes in the organization of estates from period to period irrespective of their location or ownership.

The bias of these changes was away from the manor of *Gutsherr-schaft* type, i.e. away from demesnes cultivated by their landlords. A number of causes, not all economic, combined to set up a general drift in this direction. To begin with, there was the cumulative effect of occasional relaxations. Now and again an individual villein might be manumitted or his holding might be enfranchised by purchase or an act of grace; from time to time small portions of demesne might be alienated. But villein services, once relaxed, and the demesne acres, once granted away, would soon begin to grow a protective crust of village custom; and thus encrusted the relaxations could not be revoked even by the most acquisitive of landlords. In this way the manorial structure on many estates would wither away by the irreversible action of piecemeal change.

However, the most important factor behind the drift was an organic disability of a kind which would nowadays be described as 'managerial'. Where the demesne happened to be close to the lord's residence or to his regional headquarters, the lord or his deputies could exercise the day-to-day control without much difficulty. He could also in this case draw his supplies without the expense and risk of transport over long distances. But a large number, perhaps most, of the manorial estates were not so situated and had to be left in the charge of local bailiffs intermittently supervised by annual audits or by occasional visitations of the lord himself and his officials. Control as remote and spasmodic as this exposed the landlord to the inefficiency and dishonesty of his agents; and thus exposed, landlords from time to time sought to relieve themselves of their managerial risks by farming out the demesnes as going concerns, or else by dissolving them altogether into peasant tenancies.

c. *The buoyant demesne*

This shedding of the demesne—in itself a cumulative process—could quicken wherever and whenever conditions worsened: when prices and costs moved so as to reduce the profits of exploitation or when law and order so deteriorated as to impede the exercise of the lord's authority over his agents and tenants. On the other hand the movement could slow down or even come to a halt in periods when circumstances were favourable to demesne husbandry and to seigniorial control. A long period of stabilized or even expanding demesne cultivation would then interrupt the secular drift towards the *Grundherrschaft*, i.e. towards 'rent-roll' type of estate.

In most parts of England the manorial estates which had still kept their demesnes by the beginning of the thirteenth century went through some such period of revival at one time or another in the thirteenth century. In spite of recurrent political upheavals, such as the Baronial Wars in Henry III's reign or the interlude of weak and unsettled government in Edward II's time, the period between, say, 1175 and 1325 was one of relative peace and order. The organization of government and justice appeared to continue the progress begun under Henry II. It may well be that even in this period border raids and the passage of armies in the northern counties and on the Welsh marshes were ruinous to both landlords and peasants, but elsewhere life was relatively secure, traffic on the roads unmolested and the king's law enforced. There was thus little in the politics and governance of the time to interfere with the lord's control over his estates or with his disposal of his produce.

The economic conditions were also auspicious. As population continued to increase supplies of labour were getting more abundant, money wages remained stable and real wages were falling. They were falling because prices of agricultural produce were rising—rapidly until the second and third decades of the century and gently thereafter.

By a fortunate accident, or perhaps in response to new opportunities, gifted manorial administrators appeared on most great estates during the period. Among them were well publicized manorial administrators like Abbot Samson of Bury St Edmunds or Henry of Eastry of Christ Church Priory, Canterbury, as well as numerous lesser known but equally effective managers of monastic estates, like Abbots Michael Ambresbury and Roger Ford of Glastonbury, Abbot Thomas Marlborough of Evesham, Abbot Roger of St Albans, or that string of Peterborough abbots—Robert and Walter at the beginning of the century and Richard of London, William of Woodford and Godfrey at the end of the century—who built up the great agricultural wealth of their abbeys. We know much less about administration of the great lay estates, but it might not be altogether an accident that the two makers of what was to become the great complex of Duchy of Lancaster estates—Henry de Lacy and Edmund of Lancaster—should have been active during this period.

It is certainly not an accident that in this period manorial lords should have made the most important advances in rationalizing the technique of their management. The most important of these advances was, of course, the introduction of accounts. The manorial account in the form historians know it is a late twelfth- or thirteenth-century innovation—the earliest full-fledged account known to us being that of the bishops of Winchester of 1208/9. In the course of the subsequent 30 to 40 years the formalized bailiffs' accounts came to be adopted on most estates of any size. In spite of many local variations, the surviving accounts follow the same general pattern. They not only contain the same information grouped under the same headings, but conform to the same doctrine of accountancy, i.e. that of charge and discharge, These accounts charge the bailiff with the revenues due under the latest extent and record the payments he made as 'discharges' of his liabilities. Before long some lords, e.g. the Cathedral Priory of Norwich or the bishops of Worcester, began to derive from their accounts estimates of their profits or losses, but this modern function of account was not allowed to interfere with its original composition as a record of the bailiff's current liabilities. In this, as in most details, manorial accounts are all alike, and this uniformity of accounting procedure shows how anxious were the manorial administrators to learn from one another, and how speedily did administrative lessons spread from lordship to lordship.

The lessons came from certain much-used sources. One such source was the formularies designed to teach the manorial administrators the art of manorial accounting. But historians have always known that accounting was not the only art which improving landlords could now learn from books. Treatises on agricultural management, such as those of Walter of Henley, the *Senechaucy* and *Fleta* were all composed during this period. In addition manorial documents of some abbots, e.g. those of St Peter's Gloucester or Christ Church Priory, Canterbury, contain local sets of rules for efficient management, or excerpts from well-known treatises on farm management. The age was one of 'improving landlords' obviously interested in the rational exploitation of their demesnes. And it is permissible to conclude that the interest they evinced was prompted by the opportunities they now possessed.

Manorial accounts reveal the many different ways in which these opportunities were exploited. One was investment, another was technical innovation, yet another was a more rational employment of demesne acres. Although the lord's agricultural investments are difficult to separate from his other expenses and even more difficult to compare with investments in other periods, it appears that on most estates productive investment was very low by modern standards; but probably more was now being spent on buildings, mills, equipment, and, above all, on reclamations, than in any other period in the Middle Ages. And there were also numerous innovations.

Investment in livestock may have risen little, if at all, since shortage of pasture would have made it difficult to add to the manorial flocks and herds. On most of the great sheep-farming estates, e.g. those of the bishops of Winchester or the abbots of Glastonbury, there appeared to be an upper limit to the sheep flocks, it was repeatedly reached but seldom exceeded during the century. On the other hand investment in arable farming was undoubtedly accompanied by measures to increase output. W find landlords rationalizing their cropping systems, substituting three-field course for two-field, experimenting with different sowing ratios or with different proportions of crops. As a result of this experimentation, rye all but disappeared from demesne fields in most parts of arable England and was replaced by wheat. Drage, i.e. mixed barley and oats, also replaced pure oats on a number of estates. Leguminous crops began to play an ever increasing part. For, contrary to what we are sometimes told, leguminous crops were not a discovery of the later Middle Ages—the largest areas under beans so far found by historians is on Sedgmoor estates in the thirteenth century. Where legumes were introduced anew they often replaced oats as a spring crop.

In general oats were the crop to be reduced most in the later thirteenth century. The statistics of manorial oats must not, however, be misunderstood. Though the acreage under oats declined in most places, the decline was sometimes due not to the introduction of alternative crops, but to the letting out of oatfields. As I have already suggested, the poorer lands (and lands permanently given over to oats could rank as poorer lands) were sometimes let out or abandoned altogether merely because their yields descended below the level at which the lords considered them worth cultivating. But some manorial fields were probably let out not because yields were falling but because rents were rising.

It is possible to imagine situations—we certainly find them in our records—when the area of the demesne contracted even though its cultivation remained profitable. In general landlords who still possessed functioning demesnes at the beginning of the thirteenth century tried to maintain or even to extend the area under cultivation at one time or another in the thirteenth century. Broadly viewed, the period was, therefore, one of stabilized or expanding demesnes. Yet a rational and profit-conscious manager of a manor would repeatedly be confronted with the choice between rents and sales of produce. In considering the best use of a field, a furlong or a small plot, he might decide to let merely because at that particular time that particular piece of land promised more in rents than in sales of produce. In the second half of the century the dilemma must have presented itself more often than ever merely because land values and rents were at that time rising at a rate higher than grain prices.

It is very largely for this reason that so many of the prosperous and well-run demesnes, while maintaining and even increasing their profits, were reducing their acreages somewhat in the second half of the century. Most of the manorial demesnes of the bishops of Winchester which were stable and even grew in the first half of the century will be found shedding the less profitable fields, and yet increasing their incomes from sale of produce, in the second half of the century. The same appears to have happened on some Ramsey estates as well as on a number of Glastonbury manors, and elsewhere.

This partial retrenchment of the demesne areas at the time of the late-thirteenth century prosperity must not be confused with the retrenchment which took place in times of manorial crises before and after the thirteenth-century boom. The symptoms in both cases appeared to be the same, but the underlying condition was wholly different.

D. *Manorial retrenchments*

One such period of retrenchment preceded the thirteenth-century revival. In view of what we now know of the general drift away from direct cultivation it is not perhaps surprising to find manorial surveys of the late twelfth and early thirteenth centuries recording numbers of peasant holdings recently carved out of the demesne. But on most estates, perhaps on as many as eight or nine out of the fifteen or sixteen great estates of which twelfth-century surveys are available, the inroads into the demesne were too widespread or on a scale too large to be wholly explained as by-products of the slow and secular movement towards rents. Something must have happened in the twelfth century to accelerate the drift away from the demesne.

There was, in fact, every reason why the period between, say, 1130 and 1175 should have been specially unfavourable to the direct management of the demesne. These were years of civil war between Stephen and the Empress Matilda, of the disruption of central government and near-anarchy in the countryside. Both sides recruited their parties by wholesale subinfeudation of local followers and thereby let loose upon the country a swarm of strong men capable of wreaking their wills upon their neighbours. The outlying manors of many great estates, both monastic and lay, were at the mercy of local chieftains, traffic was insecure and tenurial obligations often unenforceable. The economic conditions were to match. We do not know for certain what happened to the general level of prices, but such evidence as we have (mostly that of royal purchases recorded on the Pipe Rolls of the Exchequer) suggests that differences in prices from region to region were greater than in the late twelfth or thirteenth centuries. This in its turn reflects the imperfections of inter-regional traffic—imperfections which must have grown because the king's highways were insecure and the peace of the market cross was in constant jeopardy.

This being the climate of the age, it is not surprising that the lords should have been more anxious than ever to rid themselves of direct managerial responsibility. The twelfth century, and perhaps also the eleventh, is the period of wholesale 'farming' of manors—an arrangement whereby lords let their demesnes and sometimes their entire manors to middlemen for a fixed rental of money and food, or money alone.

'Farming' was not of course the invention of the twelfth century. The practice may have always prevailed on royal estates; it left some traces in the earliest English agrarian records, and could be detected in the various tenurial contracts of late Anglo-Saxon era. Vinogradov and Lennard have also shown that 'farms' were widespread on royal lands as well as on lands of other landlords at the time of the Domesday survey. It is also probable that since the very earliest times manors, especially monastic ones, which appeared to be directly managed by the lords' agents, usually by individual monks acting as their abbeys' representatives, the managers, were in fact required to deliver to the lords' households fixed amounts of food and money and were thus to all intents and purposes 'farmers'. There is, however, little doubt that farming contracts were more general in the twelfth century than either earlier or later. They were now to be found on most manors on nearly all the estates for which mid-twelfth-century evidence is available. Moreover the documents frequently refer to them in a manner which clearly suggests that they had been instituted at some previous point of time. In at least one case, that of the bishop of Ely's estates, tradition has preserved the date, in the first quarter of the eleventh century, when the manors were first put out to farm. But even where records happen to be silent on this point the early history of the manors, their creation and stocking, as far as it can be reconstructed, would be unintelligible except on the assumption that some of the landlords who farmed out their demesnes in the twelfth century had at one time managed them directly. There is even less doubt about the period following the twelfth century, since our documents make it quite clear that a large number of demesnes and entire estates farmed in the twelfth century came under direct management in the thirteenth.

Whether farmed out or not—sometimes because they were farmed out—twelfth-century manors often suffered losses in stock and equipment. The depredations of farmers like Simon of Felstead, who farmed the Suffolk manors of the Trinity of Caen, or of Richard Ruffus, who farmed wards' manors in Soham and Kimbolton, do not stand out as exceptional.[1] Is there any wonder that on estates like those of Glastonbury or Ramsey, for which we possess surveys for both the first and the second halves of the century, the documents should record the impoverishment of the demesne and the diminution of its stock and recall "the time of Henry I" as the golden age of the estate's prosperity?

The loss was the lords', not necessarily his tenants'. In the twelfth-century estates which were not farmed as a whole, some of the demesne lands passed on into the hands of the villagers. Here and there the entire demesne might be let out to villagers, as on the Glastonbury manor of Grittleton, and would in that case be divided among them. But this was not the only way in which the lord's tenants benefited from his discomfiture. Numerous servile holdings were commuted

[1] *The Cartulary of Trinity of Caen*, Bib. Nat. *MSS. Latin* 5650; *Rotuli de Domanibus*, pp. 46, 49, 50, etc.

to money rent, and the commutations were often brought about by the tenants themselves. More will however be said about this presently.

However, this slump in the fortunes of the demesne did not last much longer than the underlying political and economic crisis. Peace and order came back after Henry II; prices began to rise concurrently. Most monastic landlords re-established their authority over their estates though they may not always have succeeded in regaining full possession of all the manors seized from them in the time of disorders. With prices climbing and wages stable the cultivation of the demesne was becoming more profitable. From royal records, especially from the *Rotuli de Domanibus,* a document concerned with the royal administration of the estates of widows of tenants-in-chief, we can gather that much was now being done to restock the demesnes and otherwise to repair the damages of earlier mal-administration. Most of the monastic landlords and apparently some of the lay ones, though not perhaps the king himself, were abandoning the system of farming and resuming the direct management of their manors. Here and there parcels of demesne land continued to be let out to tenants, but on most estates the acreages lost to the demesne by letting were more than compensated by new conquests of the waste and sometimes by acquisitions through purchase. In this way long before the end of the twelfth century the decline in the demesne economy appeared to be fully arrested and even reversed.

More final and irreversible proved to be the second phase of declining demesne fortunes—that following the thirteenth-century boom. The demesne economy was becoming less buoyant and the general prosperity of manorial landownership characteristic of the thirteenth century began to slacken on most estates as the century neared its end, and indeed alsmost everywhere after the disastrous seasons of 1317–19. The landlords' response to the changed circumstances was the same as in the twelfth century. They resumed the practice of 'farming' so that by the second half of the fourteenth century most of the largest estates began to be affected by it. By the middle of the fifteenth century very few demesnes—mostly home farms or Benedictine abbeys—still functioned under the direct management of their lords.

Some demesnes had by that time ceased to function at all. We have seen that on a number of manors piecemeal and sporadic letting-out of unwanted lands never ceased. We have also seen that on these and other manors the tendency to let was stimulated by high rents prevailing in the second half of the thirteenth century. In the late fourteenth century the movement gathered speed, even though the rents were no longer rising. Whereas in the earlier period the landlords' dilemma—to let or to cultivate—was how to choose between alternative roads to still higher profits, the same dilemma in the fourteenth and fifteenth centuries was how best to escape from threatening losses. The letting-out of the demesne in parcels had now become one of the ways of arresting the decline of profits.

What we know of the economic conditions of the time makes it easy to understand why demesne profits should now have been on the decline. Political events were on the whole unfavourable, though the damage they inflicted on the landlords and their husbandry is difficult to gauge. Even in the worst years of the War of the Roses the ruin of government could not have gone as far as in the mid-twelfth century. On the other hand the preceding 120 years of war with France must have hurt the landowners in a variety of ways. Edward III's war taxes and purveyances and his levies on wool harmed the landowners, especially the monastic ones. It is also possible to argue that the final establishment of the Wool Staple in Calais was to the disadvantage of domestic wool growers.

But if there may be some doubt about the political conditions, there can be none about the economic ones. In the first place there was the rise in costs caused by higher wages, which was in its turn caused by the fall in population. Having begun to rise in the first quarter of the fourteenth century wages continued on the ascent until some time in the second quarter of the fifteenth century, and stayed thereafter upon their high plateau until the end of the century. On the other hand current agricultural prices remained stationary, or perhaps even sagged somewhat. And as the bullion-content of the currency was reduced in 1343 and 1344, and again in 1351, 1412 and 1465, prices expressed in weights of silver were clearly on the decline throughout the period.

It is therefore not surprising that, with profit margins narrowing all the time, the lords should have tried to stabilize their incomes, as they had done in an earlier period, by letting out their demesnes to farm. This they sometimes succeeded in doing—at least for a time. Demesnes let out at farm in the years of temporary recovery from the Black Death yielded stable incomes as long as the original farming contracts were in force. Those landlords who in addition retained in their hands the manorial pastures and flocks were also able to profit from the buoyant demand for wool in the last third of the fourteenth century. The estates of the bishops of Winchester provide a good example of successful resistance to fourteenth-century adversities. At certain times in the second half of the century the bishops were able to build up their flocks to heights even greater than their thirteenth-century ceilings. Under William of Wykeham's ruthless management the other sources of manorial revenue also remained remarkably (though also pre-cariously) high.

Few estates, however, were equally able to benefit from the late-fourteenth-century flutter in wool prices, and very few indeed had a William of Wykeham to manage them. Those which had success-fully defended themselves in the closing decades of the fourteenth century saw their defences crumble in the fifteenth. Farming contracts could not insulate them for ever from rising costs of cultivation, since on a number of estates the values of the farms themselves fell. On the very large estates such as those of the Duchy of Lancaster, with pos-sessions in almost every part of England, the farms of demesnes ap-parently stabilized in the late fourteenth century declined at every subsequent re-letting and stood in the last quarter of the fifteenth century at a level seldom higher and often much lower than two-thirds of that at the beginning of the century.

The other farms, e.g. those of mills, followed suit, and so did the villagers' rents. Where land was let at commercial rent the downward movement left clear marks on our records and is easy to follow. 'Assized' rents, or the annual money components of customary rents, remained relatively stable, but we know that the full customary rents contained other components as well, including entry fines, tallages and, above all, labour dues; and most of these components frequently went down, more especially entry fines and tallages.

The adjustment of rents to the lower land values most familiar to historians is the release of labour services. Before long, most manors appeared to scrap the structure of customary rents and to convert entire customary holdings to leases, mostly life leases, for rent with light labour services. More about these leases will be said later; but it is important to note here that the conversion to life leases was in the main part of the general movement away from the old regime of labour services. Yet even with the service released, some of the customary lands remained difficult to let, and vacant holdings were hawked round unwilling takers, and had eventually to be re-let, if re-let they were, for lower money rents.

Needless to say, in speaking of the fifteenth-century manors and their demesnes we must guard ourselves from describing their condition as one of complete and irretrievable bankruptcy. A few full-fledged demesnes could still be found on some monastic and collegiate estates, e.g. on the manor of Grantchester belonging to King's College, Cam-bridge, or even on the estates of lay landlords such as the Pelhams in Sussex, or the Hungerfords in Wiltshire. But as a rule these demesnes were no longer representative of the agrarian system as a whole and were often restricted to lands directly serving the lords' kitchens. Elsewhere a number of lords still retained in their hands demesne pastures, so that by the sixteenth century landowners in sheep-farming counties like Northamptonshire and South Wiltshire could still be found deriving their income from flocks and herds as well as from rents. And even where the arable demesnes were finally given up in the fifteenth century the landlords had, before giving them up, sometimes tried to retrieve the fortunes of their estates by technical and economic innovations. In the midst of the late-fourteenth-century depression, and while the acreage of demesne was contracting, we find some manorial managers, i.e. those of the bishops of Winchester, or the abbots of Ramsey or the earls of Stafford, trying to remodel their field systems, enclosing and emparking disjointed fields, and continuing to introduce new crops, mostly legumes in the fallow course, and to experiment with different seeding ratios. Whether these innovations and experiments were more widespread or were on a larger scale than the 'improving' activities of thirteenth-century landlords is difficult to say. Most probably they were not. But it is equally probable that here and there they may have succeeded in relieving for a time the effects of the agricultural depression.

To historians new to the discussion of economic fluctuations, these instances of continuing activity of the manorial demesnes in time of depression may appear to disprove the fact of the depression itself. Some continental historians of medieval commerce have similarly quoted the evidence of continued commercial activity in fifteenth-century towns as proof that urban trade did not decline. But is there any need to argue that a decline in economic activity does not signify its cessation, or that even at the lowest depth of an agricultural depression agriculture never ceased and that at all times there were to be found acquisitively-minded landlords able to wring from their lands the highest possible revenues?

In spite of their endeavours the downward trend of manorial revenues was not to be arrested. For on most fifteenth-century estates not only were the profits of cultivation and the rents of occupied land declining, but in addition the area of occupied land was itself contracting. In the manorial accounts and surveys the references to vacant holdings *in manu domini* became a standing and often a growing item. The largest crop of land vacancies occurred immediately after the Black Death. Their number fell somewhat in the subsequent decade or two, but over the period as a whole the backlog of unlet lands and vacant holdings always stayed high. The land-utilization map for fifteenth-century England, had we been able to draw it, would not have been unlike the economic map of contemporary France and Germany—all pockmarked with *Wüstungen* and *terres vastes*.

The vacancies did not always denote the total abandonment of land by man. Many a holding listed as unoccupied in one part of a manorial account may be found again in another part, recorded as re-let at lower rent, frequently as pasture. In other words, what many of the vacancies signify is not the total abandonment of holdings but their descent down the scale of land-use and, frequently, their reversion to what they had been before they were broken up by the plough, i.e. pasture, even if only a tumbled-down one.

These reversions might be taken to justify the hypothesis commonly adopted by historians that throughout this period sheep-farming was expanding and thereby compensating for the decline of arable husbandry. This hypothesis may be true but cannot be accepted as proven. On estates which kept their demesne pastures while reducing their arable, such as those of the bishops of Winchester or the abbots of Glastonbury, we can find some evidence of increases in the numbers of sheep in the fourteenth or early fifteenth centuries, but almost none later. The limits to their flocks and herds which the landlords found difficult to exceed in the thirteenth century were very seldom exceeded in the fifteenth. On some manors, e.g. those in the northern and north-eastern groups of the Duchy of Lancaster estates, vaccaries and studs were greatly reduced and even altogether liquidated in the fifteenth century. The same need not be true of peasant herds and flocks, but in the absence of any reliable evidence about peasant husbandry, our pronouncements about peasant sheep and cattle in the later Middle Ages must remain no more than inspired guesses.

What we know is that, whatever may have been compensations for the decline in the demesne husbandry, they were far from sufficient to bring back the rural economy as a whole to the level which it had reached in the thirteenth century. The failure is most obvious at the most sensitive spots of agrarian economy—the marginal acres in most villages or the entire villages on the outer periphery of settlement and cultivation. These peripheral villages, no matter where we find them, in the upper reaches of the Yorkshire Dales, in the folds of the South Downs, amidst the heaths and sands of north-western Suffolk, shrank to mere shadows of their thirteenth-century selves, and, thus shrunk, lingered on until they were, on Professor Beresford's showing, finally snuffed out during the enclosures at the turn of the fifteenth and sixteenth centuries.

IV. *The landlord*

A. *Magnates and gentry in the thirteenth century*

So much for the change in fortunes of the lord's estates. What about the lords themselves? The problem, neglected for generations, has of late been rousing more interest, and some recent controversies about the landowning classes in the seventeenth century have shown that it can be debated pertinently, even if sometimes intemperately. In this controversy some historians tried to distinguish two separate layers within the landowning classes, the magnates and the gentry, reacting differently to economic circumstances, prospering or declining at different times and sometimes at each other's expense. Other historians, however, have argued that relative positions of the greater and the smaller landowners, considered as groups, remained roughly the same through history. Individual fortunes rose and fell but the balance of economic power as between the great families and the smaller ones was not thereby altered.

The same clash of hypotheses is also possible in the study of medieval landownership. Were the changes in the landowning classes between the eleventh century and the fifteenth merely metabolic, i.e., confined to the replacement of some great families by others, or were they also morphological, i.e. capable of altering the relative wealth and economic power of the class as a whole or of entire groups within it?

As most of the discussion of medieval landownership has so far been conducted by constitutional and political historians, and as constitutional historians have not until recently been inclined to question their sociological presuppositions, this conflict of hypotheses has, as far as medieval history is concerned, remained concealed from casual viewers and perhaps from the disputants themselves. But it is not necessary to delve deeply under the surface to discover that the history of landownership during the revolutionary decades of the Norman conquest has been treated as a purely metabolic process and told as a story of how Anglo-Saxon thegns and earls were replaced by William's followers. The subsequent history of the landowning classes has been told in the same manner, which happens to be the one best suited to the piecemeal reconstructions of manorial descents and to the study of twelfth-century charters by the methods of Horace Round. Yet on *a priori* grounds it appears highly improbable that major economic shifts, such as those which English agriculture and rural society underwent during the Middle Ages should not have affected the fortunes of the landowning classes; or affected in the same way and to the same extent landlordships of different sizes and types.

Thus in considering the agricultural expansion of the late twelfth and thirteenth centuries we must presume that the owners of land must have benefited from expanding settlement and from rising land values, and must have appropriated a great and growing share of the national product. It is equally obvious that the agricultural boom, with its rising aggregate production and prices accompanied by stable costs, was bound to benefit the agricultural entrepreneurs producing for the market. But from this it does not follow that all landlords should have benefited alike from both the rising land values and the increasing profits of cultivation. We know now that the two sources of landlords' income combined differently in different lordships, and that whereas some landlords depended mainly on rents, others involved themselves deeply with direct cultivation and with production of crops for sale. Smaller lay estates possessed limited opportunities for exploiting the rising land market; the smaller monastic houses of Benedictine type and small lay landowners, who themselves consumed the greater part of their demesnes' output, were also impeded from reaping the full benefits of a buoyant market for agricultural produce. The economic climate should therefore have been more favourable to magnates, less favourable to smaller estates and especially to the estates of smaller monasteries, petty knights and *francolani*.

This, however, is not the conclusion a diligent reader would derive from historical literature. The possibility that different strata of the land-owning class fared differently in the thirteenth century has never been brought into the open, but it has frequently been hinted at by writers concerned with the political conflicts of the time. They could not fail to note that the Baronial Wars of the thirteenth century and the constitutional changes, which accompanied and followed them, were somehow involved with social changes and economic history. Historians have as a rule taken the obvious view that the summoning of the knights of the shire to parliament and the various acts of legislation in the second half of the thirteenth century were prepared, and perhaps even necessitated, by changes in the position of the smaller landlords. These changes historians usually define in political or constitutional terms, though now and again they have tried to link them with social facts. Stubbs himself went as far as to admit that, considered 'as a political estate', the smaller landowners 'had class interests and affinities', and that 'the growth of these in contrast with the interests of the baronial class might form for the investigator of social history an interesting, if somewhat perplexing subject'.[1] Yet in spite of all temptations to turn social investigator Stubbs was wise enough to confine himself to the

[1] *Constitutional History*, II, 194, *seq.* Cf. Treharne in *Bull. Inst. Hist. Res.* XXI (1946–8).

story of how the knights had been drawn into the machinery of government, especially into inquests and commissions, and had become an indispensable element in country administration. Had he succumbed to his own sociological urges he might have been led to assume, as some of his followers have done, that the reason why the smaller landlords were able to play an increasing role in local government is that their wealth and their hold over land were also on the increase. The historians who have advanced this argument have had no difficulty in showing that the professional soldiers in William the Conqueror's host gained in wealth and status as kings and magnates of the twelfth century settled them on land and converted them into holders of knights' fees. Yet, however justifiable this argument may be for the late eleventh or early twelfth centuries, it does not permit us to conclude that knightly landowners continued to grow in wealth as a class all through the twelfth and thirteenth centuries.

Any such conclusion would be in conflict not only with what we have now learned about the economic changes of the time but also with what we can glean from the surviving records of land transactions.

These records bear witness to the accretions to the estates of lay magnates and of nearly all the great abbeys at the expense of smaller landowners.[1] It is these accretions that Stubbs must have had in mind when he wrote about the times 'when the greed for territorial acquisition is strong in the higher class' and when the smaller man is 'liable to be bought out by the baron'. The smaller man Stubbs refers to is the substantial freeholder, but he could well have said the same of numerous squires and knights. For it is precisely in this manner that families of gentry were losing their lands and coming near to extinction in some parts of the country. Numerous small landowners in the vicinity of Glastonbury manors were ceding lands to the abbots intent upon rounding off their possessions. In those eastern counties in which the abbots of Peterborough were interested, and especially in the Soke of Peterborough itself, the catalogue of families selling land to the abbot or to his villeins—the Gimiges, the Peverells, the Tots, the Gargates, the Southorps, the Solomons, the Thorolds—comprise a large proportion of local gentry and yeomanry. Some of them, e.g. Geoffrey of Southorp and Robert Paston of Castor, appear to have parted with large parts of their property in the Soke.

So if evidence of land sales is to be trusted, it would appear that the smaller landowners were losing their hold over land and with it, presumably, their economic importance in the countries. True enough, genealogists and students of manorial descents could quote instances of

---

[1] For Richard de Clare's purchases see *Inquisitions Post Mortem* 47 Hen. III 27 (5), Nos. 24 & 25 (Claret and Standon).

smaller landowners in the thirteenth century thriving into higher ranks of nobility by marriage, inheritance or royal favour; and here and there smaller private cartularies, like those of the Brays, tell the story of small knightly estates formed anew or enlarged. Yet set against the stream of land sales, this counter-flow of aggrandisements appears as a mere trickle. Our working hypothesis in that case must be not one of rising power and prosperity of smaller land-owners but one of a gathering threat to their position. If Simon de Montfort and Edward I's policy was designed—as we are told it was—to win the support of the knights, it was more likely to succeed not by bowing to their strength but by exploiting their grievances.

Thus viewed, the summoning of knights or *minores* to the successive parliaments between 1254 and 1294, ending with the final establishment of the practice in 1295, must be considered together with a whole series of enactments in the second half of the century, beginning with the clause in the Provisions of Westminster of 1259, which protected free-holders from the abuse of power by barons, and ending with the statute of *Quia Emptores* of 1290, which put an end to the continued formation of mesne tenancies. These enactments also link up with the expulsion of the Jews in 1290, if only because the smaller landowners were the chief clients and the chief victims of Jewish finance. The chron-icler may or may not have been right in alleging that the influence of the magnates was on the side of the Jews because the latter in their dealings operated with magnates' money. But there is little doubt that many of the estates pledged to the Jews eventually found their way into the hands of the magnates. According to a submission to the Oxford Parliament of 1258, *Judaei aliquando debita sua, et terras eis invadiatas, tradunt magnatibus et potentioribus regni, qui terras minorum ingrediuntur ea occasione.* The surviving evidence of Jewish obligations (*starrs*) fully supports the contention that the Jewish mortgages pro-vided the mechanism whereby great men were getting hold of the smaller men's land. The story how Robert and Henry Braybrokes and Queen Eleanor pursued their policy of taking over lands pledged to the Jews has been told several times; numerous abbatial acquisitions of lay lands are now also known to have involved lands of Jews' debtors; and there is every probability that further researches will uncover many more similar instances.

B. *Magnates and gentry in the fifteenth century*

Arguing on the same lines it might be possible to formulate a work-ing hypothesis concerning the relative fortunes of the greater and smaller landowners in a subsequent phase of English agrarian history, that of agricultural crisis of the fourteenth and fifteenth centuries. This was a time of falling land values, declining rents, vacant holdings and dwindling profits of demesne cultivation. We may therefore presume that the class whose income from land took the form of rents or farms must have suffered from the new dispensation: indeed must have been its main casualty. By the same token the smaller landowners may have suffered less, since most of them consumed a large proportion of their produce and presumably farmed away little, if any, of their land. Those of them who specialized in sheep and cattle must have suffered least of all, since pastures were now abundant and labour costs of sheep-farming were low. Their position would be comparable to that of the more substantial villagers who may have been hit by the rising costs of production but favoured by the falling prices of land and by new opportunities for increasing and rounding off their possessions.

These men would also be favoured by other, not all of them economic, features of the fifteenth-century scene. The rapid spread of demesne farms was largely to their advantage, for it was from among them that demesne farmers were frequently chosen. They were the chief beneficiaries of Mr MacFarlane's 'bastard' feudalism of the fifteenth century, for it was they who supplied the baronial chiefs with henchmen and retainers. Their ranks were also swollen by the richer villagers and merchants whose opportunities for rising into the landowning classes were now enhanced by the relative cheapness of land. The entire stratum of smaller landowners must thus have grown in size and extended its hold over gainfully employed land.

It is indeed much easier to diagnose the good health of the late-medieval gentry than to demonstrate the ailings of the magnates. The latter were too few to be treated to statistical averages and be presented as a group. Though profits of landownership in general were falling, some very great landowners, above all the Lancastrian princes, could add to their economic power by accumulating ever large numbers of earldoms and baronies. In general the number of separately held earldoms declined after 1340, since hardly any new earldoms were created under Edward III, and their members remained low in the fifteenth century. The topmost ranks were further thinned out in the dynastic struggles of the War of the Roses. There were thus fewer great men sharing the landed wealth in its baronial ranges. So while the aggregate profits of landownership declined, the individual shares of some exalted few might have grown sufficiently to raise their wealth above its previous levels.

Some landowners may have continued to do well even without adding much to their share of baronial properties. A landowner well provided with investable resources and able to concentrate on sheep farming could do well even in the midst of a profound agricultural depression. The Hungerfords, who rose in wealth and throve to baron-age in the service of the Lancaster family, derived much of their income in the second half of the fifteenth century from their pastures in Wiltshire, and altogether managed their estates so well that their profits suffered much less than those of most other landlords. Sir John Fastolf, as multifarious a profiteer as there ever was, found himself in a position to indulge in some purposeful agricultural investment and also to exploit the prosperity of cloth-working villagers on his land. And one wonders how much the comparative resilience of the bishop of Winchester's agricultural profits in the fifteenth century was due to the fact that for the greater part of the time the bishop was none other than the grasping Cardinal Beaufort himself.

However, the opportunities for moving against the economic tide were not available to most landlords. The estates of the Benedictine abbeys which happened to retain their grain-growing demesnes to the last possible moment suffered from high wages and sagging prices more than most other landowners. The Hospitallers and other landlords, like the dukes of Lancaster, the Percys or the earls of Stafford, who depended on rents and on manorial farms for the bulk of their agri-cultural income, were badly hit by the falling land values. In general, most of the greater estates will be found among the losers. They were hit by declining rents and farms, and they were either too deficient in capital or insufficiently provided with good grazing land or too badly equipped for aggressive estate management, to stem the move-ment of economic depression and to keep their heads above water.

The metaphor of 'heads above water' may perhaps give an exagger-ated view of the distress of landowners, even of the landowners who suffered most from the depression. The fall in agricultural revenues, great as it was, need not by itself have brought ruin to a great landlord's family. Its agricultural profits might, as in the case of the Staffords' revenues from their Gloucestershire estate, fall by nearly a half and yet leave an income large enough to suffice for a life of luxury and ostentation. Moreover it can with some justice be contended that what the landowning classes lost in agricultural revenues they could make good from other sources. Feudal landowners were, after all, a political and a military class and were at all times sustained by miscel-laneous seignorial revenues, fruits of office and profits of war.

On the whole, however, it is doubtful whether the majority of the fifteenth-century magnates who suffered from the agricultural depres-sion would be in a position to make up for the depression by additional feudal revenues. In most baronial budgets incomes from feudal rights played a smaller, often much smaller, part than the incomes from land; moreover feudal revenues and fruits of office, such as they were, did not become more profitable in the fifteenth century than they had been in earlier times.

The only non-agricultural revenue of the fourteenth and fifteenth centuries which, in theory, could be higher than non-agricultural revenues of earlier centuries was that of war, for the Hundred Years War was a 'bigger and better' war than any other medieval conflict. It is indeed arguable that the profits of the Hundred Years War from ransom, booty and offices and fiefs abroad were so high that, in spite of all that was happening to landowners' estates, the English landowning class, and especially its upper crust, emerged from the war richer than it had been 120 years earlier.

This argument has never been subjected to a proper statistical analysis, and, until it has been, it must be judged by a simple test of historical probability. Will it pass it? No doubt some men, of whom Fastolf was one, prospered in the War, but to view the whole of the landowning class with the eyes of a war profiteer is no less distorting than to view the working classes of our own day through the screen of pool-winners' lists. Medieval wars were lotteries in which all noblemen and gentlemen were eager to participate, but only a few could be certain to succeed. And of all the medieval wars the Hundred Years War, with its victorious phases alternating and ending with phases of defeat and retreat, would be the least likely to set the profits of war always flowing in the same direction.

Ransoms are a good example of profits flowing both ways. More prisoners were taken by the English than by the French, but until their names have been listed and paired off, we shall not know how much more numerous or profitable were the French prisoners than the English ones. Before the pairing is even attempted and the balance of loss and profit is struck, it is necessary to allow for the possibility that in the business of ransoms both parties might lose and that the English war leaders and captains in the aggregate might not emerge with net gains unless the promises of ransoms they wrung from French prisoners were many times greater than the promises they themselves had to make to French captors. Ransoms as a rule passed through many hands, were subject to deductions in favour of superiors and of the king, were frequently discounted with merchants, and bore heavy charges for collection and interest. In general the sums promised were larger than the sums actually paid, and the sums paid were larger than the sums actually cashed in by the captors. If we therefore assume (and the assumption fits such evidence as we have) that the captors received no more than, say, one-third or one-quarter of the amounts promised by the prisoners and their families, the total value of ransoms claimed by the English captors would have to be at least three times as great as the amounts claimed by the French, before the English gains from this source could even begin to equal the English losses.

Or let us take the profits of booty. Booty would be most remunerative on the occasions when it came from collective tributes from towns and fortresses and when, in addition, the king did not appropriate the lion's share of the proceeds. Such occasions did not, however, present themselves every day: they were certainly less frequent than occasions for miscellaneous soldiery pillage. But the fruits of the latter were apt to stick to the fingers of the lesser men. The leaders probably benefited from them more the lower they stood in the chain of command and the nearer they happened to be to the actual business of house-to-house or church-to-church pillage. In spite of the lurid accounts of pillaging exploits of a Hawkwood, or a Dagworth, or the Black Prince himself, the men in high command stood to benefit least from these most seamy benefits of warfare.

Offices and fiefs in occupied regions were a different matter. Some fiefs and offices were undoubtedly a source of profit while they lasted. We must not however assume that all offices, at home or abroad, were invariably profitable; it is equally uncertain whether the income of foreign fiefs always flowed, and flowed abundantly, into the magnates' pockets. We know surprisingly little how the foreign fiefs were administered or how they were apportioned between great men and smaller grantees, or how their proceeds were disposed of, or how they were affected by military campaigns and disorders or by the rules of residence imposed on English grantees. Above all these profits ceased the moment the occupied regions were abandoned, as they were between 1445 and 1453. By 1453 English rule also ended in Gascony—a province whence some English subjects of the king had drawn incomes for generations before the Hundred Years War. By the middle of the fifteenth century the net gain from this source must therefore have become very uncertain. If to this uncertain residue of gains we add the all-too-certain tally of costs—equipment and wages of soldiers unrepaid by the king, liveries of attendants, personal armaments and accoutrements of captains, and perhaps also penalties of absentee landownership—the final balance of the war as a whole for the baronial class in its entirety may well turn out to have been in the red.

Apart from the soldiers of fortune who 'struck it lucky' the men likely to come out of the war better off than they had been when they came in were the miscellaneous profiteers who took part in the war without sharing in any of its military operations—the clerks in charge of war chests and war supplies, the merchants and contractors who provisioned the troops and financed the payments and transfers of funds. Most of these men, like the successful soldiers and captains, eventually invested their gains in land, and thereby stimulated the land market and the changeover of properties. In this way new men were recruited to the upper ranks and, above all, the numbers of landowners of lower and middle rank were augmented. But the smaller landlords would in any case have gained, and in fact did gain, in both numbers and strength, from the social and economic trends of the period. To quote an earlier essay on this subject, we must not, in assessing the effects of the Hundred Years War, credit to the war what was due to the hundred years. The war was at most a makeweight, not the mainspring, of economic and social change.

V. *The villagers*

A. *Idiosyncrasies of peasant husbandry*

We know very much less about the economic conditions of the villagers than we do about the organization and evolution of the manor and its demesne. Our ignorance, however, is not a sufficient justification for assuming that all we have learnt about the lord's husbandry must also apply to that of his tenants. What little we can gather about the villagers from our records is sufficient to show that they did not always exploit their land in the same manner as the lord and did not all benefit or suffer in the same way as he did from changing economic conditions.

To begin with, the distribution of crops in villagers' fields was frequently different from that on the demesne. Allowing for the inevitable regional variations, it appears that on peasant holdings inferior grains, i.e. oats and barley, played a more important part and wheat a less important part than they did on the demesne. Various evidence, such as liveries of food to manorial servants or agreements about corrodies of retired parents, but especially the evidence of multure (millers' deductions from grain milled by them), suggest that barley and oats, or various mixtures of oats with barley, wheat and rye, formed a larger proportion of villagers' diet and of their crops than of the diet and crops of the manorial lords. On the other hand wheat was undoubtedly grown by villagers in most parts of England capable of growing it, since assessors to royal taxes of moveables often found wheat in peasant houses.

This apparent conflict of evidence—the greater importance of lower grains in peasant multures and the presence of wheat amongst peasants' taxable goods—is, however, somewhat unreal, since the two classes of evidence relate to two different problems. The evidence of multure is most relevant to the problem of diet, whereas the evidence of taxable goods is relevant to the problem of output; and the two are by no means identical. The villagers did not eat all the grain they grew and did not grow all their grain for food. Allowing again for regional and local differences it appears that wheat was to a large extent a cash crop to provide for the money outgoings of villein households, while other grains were grown largely for food and fodder. This division between crops to be eaten and crops to be sold will be found in most peasant communities burdened with money payments. The most recent and the best known instance of this is Ireland before 1848 where peasants grew grain for rent and potatoes for food.

This earmarking of wheat for special purposes was not a matter of choice but one of necessity. In many parts of the country the villagers had to earmark their wheat because their ability to grow it was small, certainly smaller than the lord's; and it was smaller because, compared with the lord, the villagers were apt to be underprovided with better land. This underprovision may go far back into the earliest history of land-use. It is quite possible, though not of course demonstrable, that a division of land between the demesne and the tenants in the earliest days of settlement favoured the lords. Feudal law conferred upon the lord the superior title to all the land in the village except that of freeholders; feudal order conferred upon him the power over the villeins' persons and properties. And even though custom and contract did much to limit the lord's monopoly of landownership and his exercise of power over men, they did not wholly deprive him of his various preferential claims. And it is difficult to imagine that his preferential claims did not extend to such good land as there was to be had.

This argument may be purely speculative—difficult to prove or disprove by available evidence. There is, however, a great deal of evidence to show that whichever may have been the division of land between the landlord and his tenants in the *Urgeschichte*, the dim beginnings of manorial history, it was bound to evolve to the disadvantage of the tenants in later centuries. To begin with, with his rights of fold and with his superior command over pastures the lord was better able to keep his lands in good heart. Then there is also the effect of demesne leases. We do not know what principle guided the lord in his choice of bits and pieces of demesne to be let out to tenants in the eleventh and twelfth centuries; but when the process is resumed in the late thirteenth century we very frequently find that the lands the lords get rid of first are the poorer ones, often lands described as *terra debilis* or *terra avenae*. When portions of demesne are let out to be broken up for the plough they are frequently (e.g. on the estates of the bishops of Worcester) described as 'overlands', or in other words as the uncultivated margins and fringes, the left-overs of the demesne fields. And this alone would in the fullness of time have raised the villagers' share of inferior lands and compelled them to grow higher proportions of inferior grains.

This however is not what historians have commonly taken for granted when dealing with medieval yields. In discussing here the evidence for declining productivity I have expressed some doubts about the current assumption that the yields of the lord's demesnes, especially those of the bishops of Winchester, were a proper measure for the productivity of medieval agriculture as a whole. The bishops' yields may perhaps be a sufficient guide to the yields of demesne lands of other lords. Some demesnes of the abbots of Tavistock or Crowland, or Westminster may have yielded more, while others like those of the downland manors of the Prior of St Swithin's or the salt marsh manors of the bishops of Worcester may have yielded less; but on the whole the Winchester yields were probably not far removed from the average (median) yields of demesnes so far studied by historians. Yet even if true, this would not be a sufficient reason for accepting them as typical of the villagers' yields as well.

In view of what we already know about the shortage of village pastures and livestock and of what we can guess about the lower quality of their land, we could not expect their output per acre to equal that of a well-managed demesne in the same locality. On the few thirteenth-century demesnes still ploughed and sown by compulsory labour services the work may have been perfunctorily organized and grudgingly performed; and the lord's yields may have suffered accordingly. On some manors demesne fields lay interspersed with the tenants' strips and were cultivated by tenants' ploughs and even sown with tenants' seeds: their yield must also have been as low as that of peasant acres. But on most demesnes in the thirteenth century fields were ploughed and sown by paid manorial servants; and demesne fields in the main lay apart from the villagers' holdings and were cultivated separately from them. On these demesnes the higher quality of the lord's land, his superior command over capital, equipment, pastures and folds were bound to tell, and his yields were bound to be higher. If on the bishop of Winchester's demesnes the average return for all his crops was about four times the seed at the beginning of the thirteenth century and three to four times at the end of the century, the output on his tenants' lands must have been lower than that: lower than three to four times the seed towards the end of our period.

These lower yields and lower overall output had to support fixed outlays much higher than the burden of charges on gentlemen's property. This particular difference between the peasants' and the gentlemen's households may not at first sight appear to be very wide.

Would not both of them draw from their land the food they ate and would not both depend upon the sale of their produce for their money income? Yet behind this apparent similarity lay a fundamental contrast. For the money charges incumbent upon customary, i.e. villein, holdings were heavy beyond all comparison with the charges borne by a manorial estate or even with those of substantial peasant freeholders. What they were is well known to historians though their aggregate weight has seldom been properly appreciated. So at the cost of appearing unduly repetitive I propose to recapitulate the catalogue of payments borne by villeins.

To begin with, nearly all customary holdings in the thirteenth century were burdened with money rent, supplemented by other rent-like charges like church-scot or various 'pennies' representing some very ancient commutations of still more ancient labour services. Then there were various 'farms' for additional pieces of land, payments of pannage of pigs, the agistment of animals and the use of lord's pastures. These were from time to time augmented by various 'once-for-all', or 'capital' payments, such as heriots from deceased men's property or entry fines from new tenants. There were also personal payments characteristic of a villein status such as 'chevages' or 'recognitions' levied on various pretexts, as well as marriage fines and, above all, amercements imposed in manorial courts for transgressions of every kind. The latter were punitive in theory, but were in fact so regular and apparently unavoidable as to constitute a regular imposition. On many estates, however, the miscellaneous fines were overshadowed by tallage which was frequently a heavy annual tax, almost as heavy as the rent itself.

Finally there were money equivalents of labour services. In places and at times in which labour services were commuted this equivalent would be directly paid to the landlord and might be eventually consolidated with the rent. But even where the services were exacted in kind they still frequently involved the villein in money outlays. There is much evidence to show that the holder of a tenement as large as a virgate or even half-a-virgate would often be unable to discharge his full quota of labour services without hiring a man to deputize for him at the demesne or to replace him at home.

To all these manorial payments we must also add the tithes to the church and occasional royal taxes. But even without these extra-manorial obligations the money dues of a villein tenant would absorb a very large proportion of his gross output. The proportions varied a great deal, but the average was very frequently near or above the 50 per cent mark. That this had come to be regarded as the landlord's normal 'rake-off' is shown by the terms of certain free leases. For when land was held freely on crop-sharing terms (*ad campi partem*) the lord's share was frequently one-half of the profits, as in continental *métayage*. Similarly on thirteenth-century manors on which customary tenants had recently come to hold their land free of most services other than rent, rents could easily rise to the *métayer*'s level: as on Thomas de Havile's Lincolnshire manor of Hacunby where bovates of 16 acres carried the rent of £1 each.[1]

The weight of the various money obligations was thus very great. But what differentiated peasant husbandry from the economy of the demesne was not only the weight of the payments but their obligatory nature. They were as a rule fixed; they were nearly all inescapable; and they had to be treated as prior charges. They could not be reduced to suit the harvest or the tenant's personal circumstances or to reflect his preferences for higher or lower consumption. In fact the tenant's need of food and fodder had to be covered by what was left after the obligatory charges had been met.

The height and the prior nature of these obligatory charges and the residuary character of all other claims on his produce not only determined the peasant's standard of life, the amount of his food, or his ability to invest, but could also affect the way in which he responded to economic changes. His responses would be frequently at variance, and often directly contrary, to those of manorial landlords. The situations which favoured the manorial estate and boosted its profits might depress and impoverish its tenants, and *vice versa*. Falling yields or sagging prices might induce the landlord to curtail the cultivation of his demesne but might compel the villein to increase his sowings and his sales; similarly rising prices or good yields would stimulate the activities of profit-conscious owners of demesnes but relieve the villein of the pressure to sell and hence also of the pressure to grow more.

These reactions, however, could not be uniform. They were bound to vary not only from place to place—this goes without saying—but also from one group of villagers to another in the same village. To be properly understood these responses must be related to the social and economic differences among the peasants. To these differences we shall now pass.

B. *Freedom and servility*

Differences in village society arranged themselves into two sets or —to use a more fashionable term—two patterns: one formed by the variations to the personal status of individuals, the degree of their freedom or servility; the other formed by variations more purely economic, i.e. those of income and possessions. As we shall see presently

[1] *Inquisitions Post Mortem* 30 Edw. I 106 (8).

the two patterns overlapped at some points but were by no means identical. If historians have been inclined to treat them as identical this is mainly because of the predominantly juristic origins of their studies. The pioneers of medieval economic history were lawyers, moreover German lawyers, who lived and worked in the early nineteenth century and drew their practical inspiration from the struggle for the emancipation of peasants. The founders of the subject in England—Maitland, Vinogradov, and to smaller extent Seebohm—were true disciples of the German masters from whom they took over the whole of their traditional assortment of topics. In this way the history of the English peasantry in the Middle Ages became that of freedom lost and regained, of the rise of serfdom in the earlier centuries, its dissolution in the later ones.

This story is consequently very familiar and requires little retelling. It is now generally accepted that, at the time of the Norman Conquest, villeinage, i.e. servile land tenure, was near its peak and that in the twelfth century the legal theory of villeinage was clarified and hardened by legal writers and royal courts, and villeinage became the characteristic condition of men and the commonest form of peasant tenure. It is now also accepted that the servile disabilities of villeinage gradually weakened in the subsequent century and almost wholly disappeared during the late fourteenth and fifteenth centuries. By the beginning of the sixteenth century little was left of medieval serfdom beyond certain legal and tenurial incidences of copyhold tenure.

This conventional theory has of recent years been trimmed on all sides. The same regional studies which have brought out the wide variations in manorial types have also revealed the corresponding variations in the personal status of villagers. Above all they have drawn our attention to the milder forms of dependent cultivation—those of sokemen, molmen and *censuarii*—which prevailed at the height of the Middle Ages in many parts of England and more especially in Danelaw and East Anglia. These studies have still more recently been supplemented by those of Kosminsky and others which have shown how substantial was, all over England, the minority of free villagers or of villeins unburdened with labour services.

Studies now under way threaten yet further inroads into classical doctrine of freedom and unfreedom. It has recently been argued that even if the theory of villeinage became more rigid and comprehensive in the twelfth century, the manorial practice in the same period was becoming laxer and the servile constraints looser. At some time during that century large numbers of villein tenures were converted into tenancies held wholly or mainly for money rent. This conversion of villein tenancies was apparently taking place at the same time as the various changes in the demesne—its curtailment or its 'farming'. It is therefore difficult to avoid the conclusion that labour services were being released either because the demesne was contracting or because the prevailing unrest and lawlessness were not only making it difficult to manage the demesne, but also making it impossible to enforce the obligations of villeins.

That some of the rent-paying tenancies resulted from one-sided action of 'disobedient' tenants is suggested by the very terminology of the documents. The term frequently used in the twelfth century to designate holdings recently converted to rent is 'molland', and the holders themselves are frequently described as 'molmen'. The presumption is that the terms derived either from *mala* meaning agreement or *mala* meaning lawless or arbitrary act. Nevertheless large numbers of villein holdings must have been transferred to rent by the landlords themselves. In fact many of the surveys of the twelfth and the early thirteenth centuries, such as those of the canons of St Paul's of the abbey of Evesham or the bishops of Worcester, frequently record the names of administrators at whose command this or that holding had been converted to rent.

Many of these conversions were outright commutations of all labour services into rent, but many, while converting into money the heavy labour dues, such as week-work, still retained certain seasonal or light services such as ploughing services or harvest boonworks. The conversions in these cases were not as drastic and clear-cut as in the case of molland; all that happened was that holdings previously held for very light money payments and heavy labour dues were now held for high money rent and light services.

It is because so much of twelfth-century commutation was of this kind and failed to wipe out all labour services altogether that some historians have failed to realize how far the change had gone by the beginning of the thirteenth century. It is still commonly believed that the bulk of the villein population in the heavily manorialized parts of thirteenth-century England continued to be subject to villein dues. The statistics which Kosminsky extracted from the Hundred Rolls of 1279 may have modified this view somewhat but have not done away with it altogether. It may nevertheless turn out to be wrong.

Even a cursory reading of thirteenth-century surveys would show that much, perhaps even most, villein land in that century was held on 'alternative terms'—*ad opus* or *ad censum*—at the lord's choice. When *ad censum*, the holdings were charged with high rent and very light services; when *ad opus*, they were liable to very light money payments and full labour services, including week-work. As the choice between the option was said to be the lord's, it would still be possible to regard all these tenancies as uncommuted villein holdings. Yet closer attention to figures and sums in the surveys and a careful comparison with manorial accounts will show how fictitious the so-called 'labour' options frequently were and how firmly had the rent alternative been established. The proof of this is that when the compilers of surveys, such as those of the bishops of Worcester at the end of the thirteenth century, came to aggregate the total values of rents and services they almost invariably used for the purpose the values at the rent option. The same is true of many of the manorial accounts. The rent charge for which the bailiffs of Crowland Abbey or those of the bishops of Winchester were charged were the rents payable on the *ad censum* option. When, now and again, on both these estates some of the villeins had to be recruited for seasonal labour they were 'allowed', i.e. excused their rents, and the allowances were recorded as deductions from the rent with which the bailiff charged in the account. In this way, by the beginning of the thirteenth century many manors and tenancies, which even Kosminsky has counted as uncommuted, had in fact been largely transferred from labour services to money rents. If so, the English village society as a whole must have moved further away from pure and full villeinage than is frequently realized.

However, for a time in the thirteenth century this process of commutation was arrested on some estates and even reversed on others. The same reasons for which the lord was now better able to exercise his control over the management of his demesnes may also have enabled him to resist better the pressure of his tenants. At the same time, the economic conditions provided him with both the incentive and the means for maintaining his claims where the claims were still worth maintaining. On the manors on which demesne husbandry was buoyant the landlord might wish to exact the labour services due to him mainly, because he needed more labour for tasks requiring the collective services of his tenants, such as ditching, dyking, building, carting and, above all, harvesting. But even where the supply of labour was more than sufficient for the needs of the demesne and a proportion of services was regularly relaxed ('sold') on an annual basis, it might still be in the lord's interest to preserve his claims to labour dues. They were, after all, a valuable part of his rent.

Indeed we sometimes find landlords using their claims for labour services as an indirect means of raising rents. Labour services were so ill-defined in earlier surveys that by re-defining them the lord could lay claim to heavier labour dues or at least raise their worth in money. These attempts to raise the burden of labour services by re-definition could be detected on a large number of estates such as those of the bishops of Worcester and Ely, those of the abbots of Peterborough, and others. Now and again the lords even tried to reimpose services on the men who had succeeded at an earlier epoch in converting their holdings into mollands.

The reason why landlords were now not only desirous to increase the weight of labour dues but also 'got away with it' are not difficult to guess. With the growing scarcity of land and with the lengthening queues of men waiting for it, the economic powers of a landowner over his tenants were more difficult to resist. This does not, of course, mean that the lord's encroachments were not in fact resisted. Judicial records of the thirteenth century abound with references to proceedings initiated by villagers in defence of what they considered their ancient right of holding for rent or for lighter services. In most of these cases the law sided with the landlords; and this attitude of the law may of course be nothing more than a manifestation of the feudal influences at courts or of the class bias of the judges. But there is little doubt that in most of these cases the letter of the law was on the landlord's side; that most of the rebellious tenants were in fact villeins who had obtained their release from labour services without a formal charter of enfranchisement or manumission. And this is of course further evidence of the 'illegal' origin of some twelfth-century relaxations as well as of the difference in economic and political climate of the twelfth and the thirteenth centuries.

This thirteenth-century reaction did not, however, endure for very long or spread to every estate. On some estates commutations of labour dues continued in a steady trickle; and on nearly all estates towards the end of the thirteenth century the surplus of labour services 'sold' from year to year grew as the demesne contracted. But it was of course in the fourteenth and fifteenth centuries that commutations again became as general and as frequent as they had been in the twelfth. During these closing centuries of the Middle Ages labour services finally disappeared, and so did nearly all the personal disabilities of villein status.

The final break up of medieval serfdom may or may not have provoked some reaction from the landlords. Older writers frequently depicted the generation following the Black Death as a period of social unrest generated by the lords' endeavours to put the clock back, to reimpose labour services and to keep wages down. The Peasant Revolt in 1381 was accordingly interpreted as a violent *riposte* of the worker to the manorial reaction and as an attempt by peasants to prevent the re-introduction of servile dues. This version of the fourteenth century's history and of its conflicts accords ill with facts. Employers of labour put up a resistance to the soaring rise of wages after the Black Death, and of this resistance the Statue of Labourers with their maximum rates was the result. The probability is that the main pressure behind the legislation came not from feudal landowners, who by now derived the bulk of their revenues from rents, but from the smaller men still cultivating their home farms. This at any rate is how the clash of interests is presented in the only contemporary discussion of the issues available to us—that in the Parliamentary Petition of 1368. But whether the demand for wage curbs did or did not come from feudal landlords, the curbs themselves proved ineffective. As we know now, the laws of supply and demand proved stronger than the employers' pressure and the legislation it produced; and wages continued to rise until some time in the fifteenth century.

Apart from the abortive agitation against the wage rise, the four-teenth-century attempts to restore labour services or to exact them in full, or otherwise to undo the commutations and the relaxations of the previous epoch, were very few and far between and were nearly all confined to the immediate post-Black-Death years. Even then they left fewer marks in our records and were presumably less frequent than the earlier, the thirteenth-century, attempts of the landlords to restore in full or to increase the labour services of the villeins. Somewhat more widespread may have been the attempts of some landlords to compel their villeins to take up vacant holdings, but on the whole these were also relatively few. Flight, competition between landlords anxious to attract settlers, and downright refusal of villeins to obey, defeated both the compulsory regulation of wages and the compulsory re-settlement of vacant lands. In the end economic forces asserted them-selves, and the lords and employers found that the most effective way of retaining labour was to pay higher wages, just as the most effective way of retaining tenants was to lower rents and release servile obligations.

Why, then, the Peasant Revolt? Why indeed! The revolt of 1381 possessed a number of features difficult to fit into the conventional pic-ture of villeins rising against oppression. In the first place it was not purely rural: some of its most famous incidents, i.e., the risings at St Albans, Norwich, Yarmouth, Bury St Edmund's, Ipswich, Winchester, Scarborough, Beverley and York, did not involve rustics, or at least rustics alone, and were not primarily concerned with labour services. Secondly, the hot-beds of rebellion included Kent, East Essex and Suffolk and Norfolk, where free tenure predominated and where vil-leins were in a minority and were less bound by manorial ties than in most other parts of England. The rebellion largely by-passed regions where villeinage was most widespread and oppressive, such as Somerset. True enough the rebels are reported to have attacked and ransacked manorial muniments and to have burnt court rolls. This does not however signify that manorial records were now unusually oppressive, or that they were now cited against villeins more frequently and unjustly than for centuries before.

An economic historian concerned with the Peasant Revolt can therefore do little more than warn other historians against too naïve or too economic a sociology of rebellion—a sociology which considers every rebellion as a direct reaction to intensified oppression or deepening poverty. A more sophisticated view of the Peasant Revolt would present it not as a reaction to poverty returned or to serfdom revived but as a demonstration that men were now so far advanced on their road to freedom as to resent more than ever the surviving vestiges of old oppressions. An even greater degree of sophistication would be to plead against an undue emphasis on economic causes, whatever they were. Were John Ball and the other seditious preachers mere weather-vanes of discontents they did nothing to generate, or were they and their ideas in themselves a source of unsettlement and unrest for which the manorial records, the machinations of lawyers and the manorial reaction were little more than convenient pretexts?

However, irrespective of their preferred interpretations of the Peasant Revolt, historians are now in general agreement that it was a passing episode in the social history of the late Middle Ages, and that it did very little to speed up and nothing to arrest the general movement towards commutation of labour services and the emancipation of serfs. This movement was not wholly completed by 1348 or even by 1399, but it was finally wound up in the last century of the English Middle Ages.

c. *Status and land*

The changes in legal status of villagers during the Middle Ages are thus known and understood as well as any movement in English social history. What may still cause doubt is the importance to be attached to them. To what extent was the condition or the social grading of this or that individual or this or that section of village population determined by legal status? How far were the changes in the legal status of villagers by themselves sufficient to raise or to lower their standard of life or their collective power in society?

The answer to these questions is not as obvious as it appeared to liberal historians in the nineteenth century. That free status was valued for its own sake, and that freedom was something to be treasured and looked up to, goes without saying. It also goes without saying that disabilities of villeinage were oppressive and that the medieval peasants were bound to resent them. According to the legal theory of the twelfth- and thirteenth-century lawyers, the villein's land and his live-stock belonged to his lord and could not be alienated without his consent. A villein could not change his place of residence or give away his daughter in marriage without the lord's permission. He was not permitted to sue his lord in king's courts; his right to enter into agreements concerning his goods and property, to bequeath or inherit land and livestock, to sit on juries and to serve on inquests, were in various ways limited by the lord's rights over his person and his property. Above all the services he owed to the lord were in theory uncertain, i.e. could be increased or changed at the lord's will.

In practice, however, these disabilities were much less oppressive than they appear in legal theory. Titles to villein holdings were protected by manorial custom so that villein tenants were hardly ever deprived of their land by the arbitrary action of their lords. They were also allowed to buy free land without let or hindrance and, in fact, bought and sold land—both villein and free—with and without the lord's permission. They also bought, sold, pledged and hired livestock; acquired and parted at will with moveable goods. The lord's permission to marry, to move away, or to enter into agreements was purchasable by fine, and hardly an instance of the lord's refusing to accept the fine has so far come to light. Labour services were also fixed by custom; and although we have seen that some lords in the thirteenth century were able to re-define the custom governing labour services to their own advantage, their ability to do so was probably rooted not in the purely legal disabilities of villein status but in economic conditions of the day.

Indeed the main weight of the villein disabilities was economic. The customary ('assized') rent of villeins was as a rule considerably higher than that of freeholders. And although the licences for marriages, migrations, sales and contracts, were all purchasable, purchased they had to be. Similarly, labour services were often discharged by hired substitutes or 'sold' or remitted for a consideration, from year to year. But both the hire and the annual sale of services required an outlay of money on the villein's part and added to his economic burdens.

So great in fact was the purely economic burden of villein status that in comparing the economic worth of a villein with that of a free peasant we must assume that, in order to maintain the same standard of life, the villein required a larger, sometimes a much larger, holding than a freeholder in the same village.

This does not, however, mean that free tenants considered in the aggregate were necessarily better off than customary tenants similarly considered. There were perhaps more freemen than villeins in the topmost layer of village society, i.e. among the few villagers with holdings of two or more virgates. Even in such predominantly villein society as that represented by the tenants of Glastonbury and Ramsey abbeys, most of the men holding more than two virgates were free-men. In the villages and manors surveyed in the Hundred Rolls of 1279, about 8 per cent of the freeholders but only 2 per cent of the villeins held more than one virgate each. On the other hand, small-holders were also relatively more numerous among the freemen, especially in counties and hundreds in which free tenures were wide-spread. In the Hundred Rolls free tenants holding quarter virgates and less formed 59 per cent of freeholding tenantry, whereas among villeins smallholders similarly defined formed only 27 per cent. Even if, in counting free smallholders, we make full allowances for their relatively light payments and so redefine the smallholding category as to exclude its upper layer, i.e. freeholders of quarter virgates, and confine our computations to men with truly diminutive holdings, i.e. five, or even three, acres and less, we shall still find that the freeholders with five acres and less formed 47 per cent, and men with three acres and less 37 per cent, of the total free tenantry. They were in fact a higher proportion of the free tenantry than the entire smallholding group (including the holders of quarter virgates) were among the villeins. Large as were the numbers of smallholders in the four or five fully manorialized counties represented in the surviving portions of the Hundred Rolls, they were higher still in regions, such as the Danelaw or East Anglia, where freeholders or near-free sokemen formed the bulk of the village population. Thus in the parts of Lincolnshire studied by Mr Hallam, e.g. in Sutton, Spalding and Pinchbeck, holdings under five acres accounted for 70 to 75 per cent of the total. The population on some Suffolk manors, e.g. the abbey of Bury St Edmund's, was little different.

It may be that the recorded numbers of smallholdings among free-holders and sokemen are greater than the numbers of villein small-holders simply because manorial documents happen to be more communicative about the former than about the latter. Petty free-holders, being freeholders, could acquire and hold land by charter and fee simple and thus have their titles recorded in surviving manorial and legal documents, whereas small tenants of bond land (especially if they happened to be sub-tenants of other villeins) sometimes held by informal titles and were unlikely to be recorded in the lord's surveys. But even when full allowances are made for this particular bias in our documents, the numbers of free smallholders will still appear large enough to require an explanation.

The explanation generally given is that free land underwent con-tinuous fragmentation partly because it was fully exposed to the solvent action of the land market but mainly because it was subject to partible inheritance. Rules of inheritance were of course intensely local, and varied from place to place more than almost any other feature of rural society. But overlaying these local variations was the broad distinction between the impartible inheritance of bond land and the partible inheritance of much of free land. Even in such 'free' regions as Kent or the Danelaw, 'villein' land was quite frequently transmitted to single heirs, the eldest or the youngest sons, though sometimes, in the absence of sons, it could be divided among daughters. On the other hand, free land of peasants and most sokeland could be transmitted to all the surviving children and be held by them in joint tenancy or—a much more widespread practice—be divided among them in equal portions. When and where the shortage of land was very acute, e.g. on the estates of the bishops of Winchester or the abbots of Glastonbury in the middle of the thirteenth century, the rules of succession to villein holdings may have become somewhat irrelevant, since, in times and places like these, the great majority of villeins—perhaps as many as 75 per cent—succeeded to land either by purchase or by marriage to heiresses and widows. Yet even in these cases the holdings were handed down whole or—as in the case of widows—nearly whole. By contrast, free appendages to villein holdings or entire free holdings would often be subjected to different rules of succession and could be divided among heirs. It is for this reason that free land was more fragmented than villein land and that the 'free' societies of Danelaw or East Anglia or Kent contained relatively larger numbers of small holders than the fully manorialized counties of the Midlands or the Thames valley.

Our conclusion thus must be that, judged by the size of their holdings, freemen were not necessarily the best-found group of village society. Their holdings were more disparate, i.e. more unequally distributed; but if averaged out they would not be much larger than those of the villeins. The true economic difference between the free and the unfree was not in the average numbers of acres they held but in the greater command over the income which their acres yielded. The unfree had to part in favour of the lord with a far greater proportion of their output than the freemen. To repeat—such was the burden of villein payments that even if, in the aggregate or on the average, freeholders and free sokemen were no better provided with acres than villeins, an individual villein would be poorer, perhaps much poorer, than an individual freeholder with a holding of the same size.

In theory, therefore, a villein could improve his economic condition by obtaining a charter of manumission releasing him of the various disabilities and payments of unfree status. Nevertheless, purchases of freedom were by no means frequent. Grants of manumission occurred more often on some estates than on others and were probably more numerous in the documents of the bishops of Winchester than in the documents of the abbots of Peterborough or Glastonbury. Yet, except for five or six years in which the total number of manumissions was ten or more (these were as a rule years in which free burgate status was conferred on inhabitants of towns newly created on the bishops' domains), the average annual number of manumissions on Winchester estates taken together was little more than five, and it is doubtful whether their cumulative total over 150 years since 1209 was much higher than 250. In any one year at the end of our period, in the 1340's, the total number of bishop's free tenants who had obtained their freedom by manumission or descended from manumitted villeins was smaller still, probably no greater than 70 or 80, or about 2 per cent of the bishop's entire tenantry.

Why so few? Lords did not of course grant charters of manumission easily or gratuitously, but historians have not yet brought to light a single instance of a manorial lord refusing to grant a charter for a price. And, high as the price sometimes was, it was seldom so high as to be beyond the means of the more substantial villeins, and certainly not higher than the prices they frequently paid for additional holdings of land.[1]

The solution of the puzzle may lie in the current valuations of land and status. The acquisition of full personal freedom, desirable as it was, may not have ranked as highly in the villagers' estimation as the additional land obtainable for comparable outlay. These preferences reflected the prevailing attitudes to land, and are often revealed in other ways as well. We find freemen marrying villein women for the sake of their land; we can even find men accepting villein status as a *quid pro quo* of a substantial holding. These preferences must have reflected the prevailing scales of values: in medieval villages, as in most peasant societies in all ages, differences based on land overshadowed other special distributions.

The distinctions based on land might themselves have been largely legal and tenurial. Land could be held freely or in socage or in villeinage; it could be held as a customary hereditament in perpetuity, or as a leasehold for life or for a term of years. Enough has already been said here about freeholds and bond lands, and about the heavier burdens of payments incumbent on the latter, to make it clear that freeholds and other near-free titles brought to their owners economic advantages as well as a social prestige denied to the villeins. Can the

---

[1] The £10 *legalis monete Anglie*, or even the 'eight marks of silver' instanced by H. S. Bennett as characteristic payments for charters of manumission, are very much on the high side. A large proportion of payments recorded on the bishop of Winchester's or abbot of Glastonbury's account are smaller than that. Cf. Bennett, *Life on the English Manor*, pp. 282-3.

same be said about the difference between customary tenures in perpetuity and the various types of leases?

What makes a plain answer to this question difficult is that customary tenures differed a great deal, and leases differed almost as much. The advantages of bond land held on ancient uncommuted tenures were obviously smaller than those of customary holdings held for rent, especially if the rent happened to have been anciently fixed. As for leases, it is important to distinguish the two main classes of manorial leases—the purely commercial lettings (farms), usually for short periods, and the life leases. The former were mostly to be found on demesne lands let out to villagers, or on some newly reclaimed wastes, or on surplus pastures. These 'farms', like the inter-peasant leases, played a very important part in that they relieved some of the effects of land shortage, helped to scramble the artificial uniformity of the virgated pattern and thereby made it possible for energetic or prolific peasant families to increase the scale of their operations and for some landless men to get hold of a little land. But as their rents were truly economic, i.e. fully measured the worth of the holdings, they could not make a very great difference to the well-being of the villagers in the aggregate or to the enduring economic differences among them.

Even more superficial must have been the effects of life leases at the lord's will; and yet we have seen that such leases become widespread at the end of the thirteenth and the first half of the fourteenth century. This rapid spread of life leases is bound to raise a number of questions. Why should they have become so popular at that particular time? Whose interests did they serve and what effect could they have had on the economic condition of the villagers? None of these questions can be resolved with any assurance, but the probability is that the spread of manorial leases for life played a smaller part in the economic and social evolution of the medieval village than its prominence in our records might lead us to believe.

The wholesale introduction of life leases was obviously associated with the commutation of labour services since the new leases almost invariably came in as replacements for the old customary holdings burdened with labour dues. Yet in itself the commutation of labour services did not require a change in the land title as radical as this. The great wave of twelfth-century commutations had not been accompanied by any wholesale transformation in the legal conditions of holdings. The titles by which the *censuarii* and the molmen of the twelfth century held their land were still those of villein tenure; and the thirteenth-century judges took every pain to make this clear to villagers who claimed free titles for their mollands. Similarly, during the commutations of the late thirteenth and fourteenth centuries holdings could also be commuted without any changes in legal titles. All that need have happened in these cases was for the money worth of labour services to be added to or merged with the customary rent. Why then should the commutation of labour services at certain times and in certain places have led to a wholesale changeover to life leases?

My tentative answer to this conundrum is that the tenures were thus transformed on the lord's initiative; and that their object was to preserve for the lord a chance of going back on the commutations at a future date. The emphasis in the leases is on their short span—as a rule one life only—and on the lord's will as the sole authority behind it. It therefore looks as if the lords were determined not to sign away their old rights in perpetuity.

However, we know now that the concessions embodied in life leases never came to be revoked. In the end the tenures they established became as permanent as the customary holdings of old and were frequently assimilated with the copyholds of the late fifteenth and sixteenth centuries. Thus viewed, the leases turned out to make very little difference to the condition of the peasant or even to the terms under which he held his land. The underlying process of commutation was of course of primary importance, but while it may have called forth the vast crop of life leases it was not by itself either initiated or even helped by them.

We are thus driven to the conclusion that the difference between the land titles, like the differences in personal status, though important, did not greatly influence the economic evolution of the village or create enduring distinctions of economic and social status in village society. These distinctions depended much more on the actual sizes of holdings and on the quality of the land and the use to which it could be put.

Needless to say, not all differences, not even all economic differences, were thus determined. Men's poverty or prosperity was not entirely or always a matter of acres. Human condition, or what in everyday speech is sometimes referred to as family circumstances, could at times be equally important. A family consisting of healthy and industrious parents and well-supplied with employable sons and daughters would fare much better than a childless couple, especially if they happened to be old or lazy or decrepit. Our records contain instances of tenants of large holdings, whole virgates, who had to be forgiven court fines on account of their poverty. When in 1296, Alexander Pope, a tenant of the prior of St Swithin's, Winchester, was forgiven the payment of heriot *quia pauper est*, his poverty was obviously real; yet he held an entire virgate. On the other hand we find in the documents men who at one time possessed in customary tenure nothing more than smallholdings but whose diligence, vigour and presumably family labour, enabled them to lease and otherwise acquire additional land. Individual villagers could by these means rise or fall all along the economic scale in the span of a single life. Men who in the prime of their lives were reckoned as substantial husbandmen could be found in later records treated or referred to as paupers. A few years before the outbreak of the Black Death, one Robert Stephen, a tenant of the abbot of Glastonbury, had to be forgiven the tax of two shillings because he had no goods on which it could be levied; yet some time reviously he was able to pay a price of over £30 for his holding. Other men on the other hand, could rise in the world equally fast. We possess numerous genealogies of wealthy village families whose wealth was founded by poor but industrious and acquisitive progenitors.

Yet in considering medieval rural society as a whole and its transformation through centuries we need not assign too great a role to variations and accidents of age, health or family, since they were wholly random and unstable. Enduring differences in the wealth of individuals and the more permanent demarcations between the different layers of society were nearly always reduceable to those of land, i.e. the sizes of family holdings.

What, then, was the distribution of land among villagers? In trying to answer this question it will be best to start with the thirteenth century, for which our evidence is most abundant. In most villages of that period holdings were distributed over the widest possible range, from cottages with hardly any land to peasant holdings large enough to function as small sub-manors. This distribution of land may not be the one suggested by superficial reading of manorial surveys. In a typical manorial survey of the thirteenth century most of the customary holdings and some free holdings are as a rule listed in regular and uniform units of virgates, half virgates and quarter virgates, or bovates and half bovates. These units are commonly and rightly regarded by historians as standardized shares in the common field of the village related to individual's contributions to the collective plough: the bovate or half virgate corresponding to one ox or horse in the plough team. Not only was land thus apportioned but the payments and obligations due from the land were similarly allotted—per virgate or per bovate. But does this necessarily mean that all actual peasant holdings fitted into this regular grid of virgated units?

Our first impulse might be to answer this question in the affirmative, for we know—or at least we are told—that the lords were interested in preserving the integrity of the virgated unit as standard for computing and levying manorial dues. But we also know now that the lords were unable to resist the action of the village land market, or the accretions to holdings by piecemeal reclamations, or the sub-divisions through inheritance, marriage and forfeiture. As a result most villagers in most villages either owned irregular portions of vigrates or added odd pieces of land to their virgated holdings, or, as we suspect, let out or leased from time to time entire customary holdings or portions of them. So even if at some distant past the bulk of the villagers had in fact been holders of virgates or symmetrical portions of virgates, in the twelfth and more especially in the thirteenth centuries they most frequently possessed or cultivated holdings which were both more unequal and more irregular than the virgated lists of tenements might suggest.

Where the sizes of holdings ranged widely and irregularly, all lines of demarcations between them are bound to be arbitrary. If, in the discussion to follow, such demarcations are nevertheless made, and the villagers of middling substance are distinguished from the rich and the poor, it is not because these distinctions are actually drawn in our sources or because no other distinctions are possible, but simply because this tripartite division may prove to be most serviceable for the under-standing of the true economic differences in medieval village society.

D. *The middle layer*

What makes the tripartite division serviceable here is that it enables us to isolate for study the middling group in thirteenth-century villages: the men in possession of customary holdings larger than those of substantial cottagers holding quarter virgates but smaller than those of full-fledged villeins with entire virgates and more. The bulk of such holdings—their statistical mode—would as a rule be found somewhere near a half virgate or a bovate, or the equivalent of say twelve to fifteen acres of arable land of average quality situated in one of the mixed farming areas of England.

In the thirteenth century the holders of tenancies of that size were the representative villagers of the time: representative by virtue of the existences they led rather than by the virtue of their numbers. Villages where customary holdings of this size predominated could of course be found in most arable regions, but in the large majority of thirteenth-century villages known to historians these holdings constituted no more than a large minority. In his classification of villein holdings in the four counties covered by the surviving portions of the Hundred Rolls, Kosminsky allots to the holders of half virgates 36 per cent of the total. Kosminsky's demarcations are somewhat different from ours, while his sample as a whole is somewhat distorted by the predominance of Oxfordshire (a third of the total) with its untypically low numbers of smallholders. Nevertheless his figures are not far removed from those to be found in manorial documents. The table below shows that on the predominantly arable estates of the bishops of Winchester and Worcester, or the abbeys of Glastonbury, St. Peter's of Gloucester, and the Canons of St Paul's, as well as on the southern and East Anglian estates of the earls of Lancaster or the fully manorialized possessions of the earls of Cornwall, the numbers of customary tenants holding little more than a quarter virgate but less than a full virgate, i.e. approximately more than eight and under thirty acres, was somewhat below the 30 per cent mark, seldom falling below 20 per cent but seldom rising above a third at the total. But whether they were or were not in the majority, their mode of existence, their standards of life, indeed their entire social condition, approached nearest the characteristic type of medieval peasant.

Table 1. *Distribution of holdings**

Estates†	Manors	Date	'Top rank' tenants	'Middle rank' tenants	Smallholders
Shaftesbury Abbey	17	late twelfth century	285	209	242
Canons of St Paul's	14	early thirteenth century	175	366	501
Bishops of Winchester	15	mid-thirteenth century	268	645	713
St Peter's, Gloucester	17	,,	264	158	363
Glastonbury Abbey	32	,,	359	593	1094
St Swithin's Priory, Winchester	4	,,	14	104	65
Bishops of Worcester	7	end of thirteenth century	132	188	120
Berkeley Estates	2	,,	16	17	43
	104		1503 (22%)	2280 (33%)	3141 (45%)

* Shaftesbury Abbey, B.M. MSS. Harl. 61; St Paul's, Domesday of St Paul's, Camden Society, 1857; Bishops of Winchester, MSS. *Pipe Rolls*; St Peter's, Gloucester, Rolls Series 33, 1863-7; Glastonbury Abbey, *Rentalia et Custumaria*, etc., Somerset Record

[footnote continued on page 620]

This type is of course a much idealized notion, a sociological abstraction. It has not yet been, and perhaps never will be, formulated with any precision, and least of all in historical works; but if the current uses of the term village and villagers, husbandmen and rustics in historical writings have any recognizable content, it is that implied in the current sociological notions of peasantry. These may themselves vary from writer to writer, but most of them agree upon certain common denominators. They all assume the 'peasant' to be an occupying owner or a tenant of a holding capable, but only just capable, of providing his family with a 'subsistence income.' Subsistence income, in its turn, is commonly understood to denote an income large enough to make it unnecessary for the family to depend on regular employment for wages, yet not so large as to permit the family to live wholly on the proceeds of rents or to enable it to work its holding entirely or mainly by hired labour.

What had to be the size of a holding capable of providing in the thirteenth century an income of this magnitude? This question does not admit of a precise answer, but answered it can nevertheless be. Our estimates of average yields per acre, or of the essential outgoings of

---

Society, v, 1891, Bishops of Worcester, *The Red Book of Worcester*, Worcs. Record Society; Berkeley Estates, 1299/1300, MSS. Berkeley Castle.

† Some of the manors in each estate have been omitted mainly because the size of the virgate is uncertain or because the absence of names makes it difficult to eliminate multiple holders. In general, differences in the sizes of virgates have been allowed for by adjusting the holdings to a standard virgate of 30 acres. As the adjustment is of necessity very approximate, the figures in the table are also approximate, and are more reliable in the aggregate than in relation to any individual estate. The manors comprised in the table are as follows:

St Paul's: Beauchamp, Caddington, Barling, Barnet, Drayton, Nastock, Sutton, Kensworth, Ardeley, 'Adulfsnase', Sandon, Runwell, Chingford, Luffenhall, Heybridge (Tidwoltington).

Bishops of Winchester: Bitterne, Waltham, Droxford, Twyford, Stoke, Alresford, Beauworth, Cheriton, Sutton, North Waltham, Crawley, Mardon, Ecchingswell, Brightwell, and Harwell.

St Peter's, Gloucester: Churcham, Abbot's Barton, Brookthorp, Ridge, Abload, Cubberley, Buckholt, Ampney, Coln Roger, Coln St Aldwyn's, Aldsworth, Eastleach, Maisemore, Leadon, Highnam and Boxwell.

Glastonbury Abbey: Butleigh, Street, the Zoy manors, South Brent, East Brent, Berrow, Lympsham, Ashbury, Badbury, Winterbourne, Ham, Idmiston, Baltonsborough, Marksbury, Grittlington, Nettlington, Wrington, Sturminster Newton, Buriton, Buckland, Damerham (without Martin), Ditcheat, East Pennard, Doulting, Deverell, Shapwick, Ashcott, Moorlinch, Walton, Mells, Meare, Pilton.

St Swithin's Priory: Houghton Priors, Chilbolton, Chamberlain's Chilbolton, Michelmarsh.

Bishops of Worcester: Cleeve, Blockley, Tredington, Withington, Henbury-in-the-Saltmarsh, Paxford and Bibury, Berkeley, Wotton, Symondshill.

a peasant farm, or of the material needs of an average peasant family, may all be variable and uncertain; they are nevertheless sufficient to establish a rough relation between subsistence incomes defined as here and holdings of a certain size. In most thirteenth-century villages holdings of that size would be found within the range of averages we have allocated to our middling group. The correspondence is of course no more than approximate and would in some cases be found nearer the bottom, and in others nearer the top, of our range of middle-sized holdings, so that men with holdings of half a virgate would in some places fall short while in others might exceed the standard of life of a typical peasant. But whether they did so or did not would of course depend on the quality of land and on other local conditions affecting their net incomes from village lands.

Of the various variables entering into computations of peasant incomes, the weight of compulsory outgoings was probably the most important. All our computations have been based on the assumption that a very large part, perhaps more than half, of the gross produce of customary land had to be earmarked for various manorial payments. If so, in places where manorial payments were not heavy, i.e. where tenants held for money rent, and especially where that rent had been anciently fixed, e.g. on the Lincolnshire estates of Peterborough Abbey or about half the estates of the bishops of Durham, a holding might yield correspondingly larger net incomes than it would in the hands of villeins subject to full labour dues. It is thus possible that in regions like the Danelaw or Kent, where free tenures were numerous and payments for land relatively low, our middling group would in the thirteenth century be largely composed of holders of quarter virgates or of cotlands that would rank as mere smallholdings elsewhere.

Similar allowances have to be made for the predominantly pastoral areas where villagers derived the bulk of their income from sheep and cattle and where consequently the size of arable holdings does not provide a true measure of the economic resources of families. The same holds good of industrial and trading villages in which a large proportion of the population engaged in non-agricultural employments—the fishing and seafaring villages all along the East and the South coasts, the coalmining or iron working villages in the West Riding, the Forest of Dean, the Northumberland coastal area and the Weald of Sussex, or the salt-making villages of Norfolk or Cheshire, or the cloth-working villages which in some parts of England were to be found even in the thirteenth century.

Yet none of these allowances invalidate our initial generalization about the middle group and its half-virgate holdings. Free tenants may have been more numerous in English villages of the thirteenth century than the founders of economic history knew, but in the anciently settled core of medieval England taken as a whole they were no more than a sizeable minority; the predominantly pastoral areas were smaller in the thirteenth century than the topography and the geology of England or the later history of its land utilization might lead us to expect; industrial villages were few and far between. In general England's population in the thirteenth century was predominantly agricultural, her agriculture was in the main arable, her arable villages were in the main composed of customary tenants. The social group characteristic of the customary population of arable England in the thirteenth century would therefore be roughly representative of English rural society viewed as a whole.

E. *The village labourer*

Below this middling group lay the great mass of smallholders, i.e. men whose holdings were as a rule too small for true subsistence farming. At the bottom of the group were to be found the all-but-landless villagers possessing little more than the cottages in which they lived. Some of the men in the nethermost stratum were servants who may not even have possessed any cottages but resided under their masters' roofs. On the other hand the top of the group comprised men whom the documents might describe as 'ferlingers', i.e. holders of quarter virgates of customary land, who need not have fallen much short of the 'middling' villagers in output and in standard of life. But, then, we have already agreed that our lines of demarcation were faint as well as arbitrary, and that the groups marked off by them were bound to merge at the frontiers.

Taken as a whole, the smallholding population of thirteenth-century villages was very numerous, frequently more numerous than the middling group and sometimes more numerous than the rest of the village taken together. In the random sample of some 104 manors tabulated above tenants with ten acres and less formed more than one-half of the population on all estates except those of St Peter's, Gloucester, where manorial sources conceal from our view large numbers of tenants' sub-tenants. What this means in human terms is that about one-half of the peasant population had holdings insufficient to maintain their families at the bare minimum of subsistence.

This also means that in order to subsist an average smallholder had to supplement his income in other ways. We have seen that industrial and trading activities might sustain entire villages of smallholders in areas especially suited to such pursuits. Nuclei of petty traders and artisans with smallholdings could also be found in ordinary agricultural villages. There were smiths, carpenters, tilers, millers' assistants, and even hucksters and chapmen, everywhere; most villages also contained spinners, or rather spinsters, and some might harbour a few fullers and weavers. In addition, smallholders could find employment as communal employees, i.e. village shepherds, herdsmen, or swineherds. Some families eked out an income by what their womenfolk could earn by brewing ale. Judging by the fine paid for the breaking of assize of ale, alewives were numerous in most villages.

Most of the opportunities for employment must, however, have lain in agriculture. In the thirteenth-century villages containing or adjoining manorial demesnes, numbers of villagers were employed as full-time labourers, or *famuli*. On demesnes as large as that of the bishop of Winchester's manor of Downtown, the numbers of full-time staff, manorial officials and *famuli*, could approach 30. The number might be smaller elsewhere but never so small as not to employ a sizeable proportion of village smallholders. In addition the demesne might occupy considerable numbers in seasonal tasks. On most of the manorial demesnes in the thirteenth century grain was threshed and winnowed, wholly or in part, by the labour of hired men, and men were also hired to build and to roof the lord's farm buildings.

Substantial villagers would also employ hired labour. How important this employment was in any given place is often difficult to say, but there is little doubt that in almost all the villages some villagers worked for others. Manorial surveys now and again refer to the villeins' servants, and so do other documents. In the assessments for the Poll Taxes of 1379 and 1381 the names of the more substantial villagers are frequently followed by those of persons described as their *servientes*, presumably their resident labourers; and there is no reason for thinking that resident servants were to be found only in the fourteenth century or that the employment of labourers either in the fourteenth or in the earlier centuries was confined to resident servants. Judging from more modern examples, those of eighteenth- and nineteenth-century England, eighteenth-century Prussia or nineteenth-century Russia, the cultivation of holdings as large as a medieval virgate of 30 acres might very frequently require the help of hired labour. Bishop Latimer's father, a prosperous fifteenth-century villager farming the equivalent of two to four virgates, gave employment to six men. In addition, compulsory labour services from customary holdings as large as a whole virgate could be so heavy and so regular—e.g. from three to five days of manual labour per week—that they could not possibly have been discharged without recourse to hired men. Manorial and village by-laws recorded in court rolls abound with injunctions designed to safeguard the lord's supply of hired labour in harvest time against the competing claims of peasant employers. It is therefore obvious that a certain number of smallholders must have earned or supplemented their income by working for peasant masters.

Yet, in spite of the many and various openings for employment in a thirteenth-century village, the main body of smallholders must frequently have been under-employed. Modern commentators take it now for granted that some under-employment is an inescapable penalty of peasant existence. In the over-populated thirteenth-century countryside it must have been more inescapable than at other times and other places. Even the roughest of computations would be sufficient to demonstrate that in many a village where the numbers of smallholders was no more than average, e.g. on the abbot of Peterborough's manor of Kettering with its 40 to 50 smallholders, employment available on the 300 acres of demesne or on its few holdings in excess of one virgate would be insufficient to absorb all its idle hands. It certainly could not absorb them all through the year. It is not therefore surprising that such populous places as the abbot of Glastonbury's villages of Brent and Zoy should have sent out every year hundreds of 'garciones', i.e., unmarried young men, in search of employment elsewhere. The older men burdened with families and perhaps tied down by their smallholdings had to depend on such seasonal or occasional employment as these purely agricultural (in fact mainly cattle-rearing) villages could provide.

The failure to realize how incomplete and discontinuous the employment of village labourers was vitiates some recent statistical attempts to compute the income of the medieval village labourer by multiplying his daily wage by 250 or some other figure representing the total number of working days in the year. The calendar as well as the nature of agricultural operations were bound to make most rural employments intermittent and often no better than casual. If so, the supplementary income for wages would not wholly compensate smallholders for the acres they lacked. The descending order of acreages in our lists of smallholders might therefore be accepted as a true economic scale—a scale beginning with men who just managed to maintain themselves at a standard of life not far below that of the average peasant and ending with the indigent and presumably starving *pauperes*.

F. *The village rich*

There remains to consider the topmost layer of the thirteenth-century village, which by definition would be composed of men holding the equivalent of a virgate or more. This layer, as the two lower ones, is marked off by frontiers so arbitrary and so widely spaced as to admit great variations in acreages and in incomes. But in general the bulk of the holdings of this group will be found bunched at its bottom so that both the statistical average and the statistical mode would be at or near the holding of a single virgate. What this means in more homely language is that whereas the group as a whole might be fairly large (in many villages it approached and in some exceeded 25 per cent of the total), the numbers of truly wealthy peasants with more than one virgate would be very small. In the sample represented by our table they were barely 3 per cent of the total. Yet although in thirteenth-century villages the truly wealthy formed a small minority, the others also could, by comparison with villagers of lower rank, be regarded as well-to-do. If in the arable regions of England and on land of average quality a customary holding of half a virgate would be just sufficient to support a self-subsistent peasant, a holding twice that size should have left a substantial surplus over and above the family's essential needs.

Many households in this group could thus indulge in economic activities and afford economic outlays beyond the means of a typical peasant. We do not, of course, know how far the wealthier peasants indulged in the consumption of luxuries or semi-luxuries. In contemporary Germany satirical poets would be found ridiculing and castigating the wealthy peasants, the Meyer Helmbrechts of the famous poem, for apeing the habits and accoutrements of gentlemen. We have no literary evidence of similar ostentation in England; in fact the only major piece of literature devoted to peasant life occupied itself with the poverty-stricken Piers Plowman. But the absence of evidence is no evidence to the contrary, and unless and until such evidence is brought forward we must not exclude the possibility that in some parts of thirteenth-century England there were to be found peasants able and willing to buy for themselves the amenities of a gentler and more lavish life.

Even then too much importance must not be attached to this possibility. What we can guess about the preferences of peasant society and what we know of the activity of the village land market suggests that additional land made the first call on the free resources of substantial peasants. Not all the buyers of land were rich villagers, for we have seen that by acquiring additional acres smallholders were sometimes able to lift themselves out of the lowest rank. But where the evidence of villagers' transactions—mostly in court rolls—is sufficiently detailed to reveal the social condition of the parties, it invariably suggests that the wealthier villagers bought more than others. Similarly the few surviving pedigrees of peasant families invariably depict not only the rise of families from small beginnings but also continuous purchase of land at times when the buyers' prosperity was at its highest.

And this is as it should be. To a wealthy peasant as much as to a

40

poor one, the possession of land was an object to be pursued in all circumstances and at all costs. To him land was not only a 'factor of production', i.e. the means towards higher output and income, but also a 'good' worth possessing for its own sake, and enjoyed as a measure of social status, a foundation of family fortunes, and a fulfilment and extension of the owner's personality.

This, however, raises a yet further problem. How did the wealthier peasants employ their property: was it invariably run as a 'home farm' to augment the household's supply of food? Our guess must be that some of the holdings in this group were undoubtedly thus managed and differed from semi-virgates only in their somewhat larger scale of operation. It was on holdings thus managed that the poorer villagers would presumably be employed as servants and labourers; and it is from these holdings that a large part of marketable agricultural supplies must have come.

Yet this cannot be the whole answer. Our sources make it quite clear that in the thirteenth century the more substantial villagers sometimes sub-let portions of their holdings. Needless to say some of the sub-letting was done by villagers of more modest substance who found themselves unable to cultivate their land—widows, invalids, old folk. But there is little doubt that many of the lessors were wealthy peasants with more acres than they themselves could or wished to cultivate. Where we find a large peasant holding made up of widely separated blocks of land, sometimes in different villages, or containing numerous habitable houses with several identifiable cotlands (*vide* the holding of Herbert le Bute, a customary tenant of St Peter's, Gloucester, who in addition to his virgate of 48 acres in Abload held land in other places), the presumption is that the land could not have been exploited otherwise than by sub-letting. But there must have been some sub-letting on holdings which appear in surveys as single tenancies. For even where the documents record no, or very few, composite holdings, they may yet imply the existence of 'under-settlers', i.e. tenants' tenants. In the surveys the under-settlers occur very infrequently for the simple reason that manorial surveys concerned themselves only with the lord's direct tenants; but now and again, as in the estates of St Peter's of Gloucester or the bishops of Ely, the surveys, in defining the tenants' obligations, lay claim on the services (especially harvest services) of the sub-tenants, thus revealing their existence. Similar revelations, however fleeting and indirect, will be found in other documents of the period: the bailiffs' accounts, court rolls and assessments to taxes.

It is thus possible to regard some of the larger village holdings as petty peasant sub-manors of which portions would be directly cultivated by the principal owners, while the rest would bring in rents and possibly some services. Sub-manors of this type were most likely to be found on the very large holdings of three, four or more virgates in the possession of freemen or *francolani*. These men formed the layer sandwiched between the peasantry and the class above, and could on occasion approach the worth of petty squires and poorer knights. The existence of this class is assumed in legislation imposing the status of belted knighthood on freeholders with a certain minimum worth of land. The fact that this obligation had to be imposed by royal decree suggests that many a freeman of this or even greater competence might well be above the other villagers in substance yet still remain on the nether side of England's great social divide.

However, the wealthier peasants in the thirteenth century did not apparently confine the use of their surpluses and savings to purchases of land on their own account, but may also have helped to finance the land transactions of other men. Our evidence makes it obvious that in the thirteenth century the disposable money resources of average villagers must have been too small to provide the purchase price of holdings they were frequently buying. It is also difficult to understand how some of the villagers were able to find, without much apparent delay, the large sums of money which thirteenth-century landlords required as entry fines. Abroad the problem was frequently solved, if solved be the right term, by loans advanced by village money-lenders. But the curious and unique feature of the English village in the thirteenth century is the rarity of the professional money-lender, comparable to the *Wucher* or the *usurier* of the German and French villages. The Jews, before their expulsion in 1290, and the Italians, both before and after that date, do not appear to have operated in villages or to have sought or found many peasant customers. It is possible to argue that what kept them away from the villages was the difficulty of using the villein land as a security for loans. But why should they have not been lending money to smaller peasant freeholders?

An answer to this question, albeit a speculative one, is that the villagers in need of money drew upon the resources of the wealthier neighbours. That money was borrowed left and right is evidenced by numerous pleas of debt on the manorial court rolls. Yet except for some parsons dabbling in a little money-lending it is as a rule impossible to single out among the creditors any professional usurers. Most of the substantial villagers will be found among the creditors: the function of money-lending thus appears disseminated all through the upper ranks of the village society.

Further evidence of disseminated money-lending can also be descried among the names of men cited as pledges and guarantors for various land transactions. Most of the names can be identified as those of *probi homines*, the substantial villagers. This they had to be, since it was their job not only to vouch for the buyer's ability to pay but also to make the payment should the buyer fail to do so. But in that case why could not they have been called upon to find the money in the first instance, at the time of purchase. In fact judicial records contain several cases in which men acting as pledges claimed to have advanced the purchase money to the buyers. Only a few such cases are recorded in the surviving documents, but there is nothing in the record to suggest that in the thirteenth-century village they were in any way exceptional.

How this rural financing was organized, if organized it was, or how it was remunerated, if remunerated it had to be, remains a mystery. But however organized and remunerated, these financial operations must have created yet another position of power for the men who, as we have seen, could also operate as employers of their neighbours' labour and the lessors of their neighbours' land. Men so placed might still remain members of the village community and peasants in outlook and social behaviour, but judged by purely material tests, by their standard of life, their economic activities and resources, they stood at the furthest possible remove from the ideal type of medieval peasant.

G. *Stability and change*

The lines of demarcation that we have so far drawn across the village society of the thirteenth century should also enable us to trace the economic differences both before and after our chosen period. On the whole, the general configuration of rural society probably remained very nearly the same. At no time in medieval history was the village free from the economic differences which we find in the thirteenth-century sources. There were always large number of smallholders, a small group of village *kulaks* and an intermediate mass of middling peasants.

These persistent economic differentials are clearly visible in the Domesday Book. Even the most superficial interpretation of the Domesday Book will reveal the existence in the eleventh century of large numbers of smallholders, to say nothing of slaves. For what else were the *cottarii*, *cotsetti* and *servi* who formed at least 10 per cent of peasants listed in the Domesday Book! And it is quite possible that the *bordarii* (another 20 per cent) were also smallholders of one sort or another. Yet even these figures may underestimate the actual differences in individual holdings in 1086. Within each of the main Domesday categories, and especially in that of *villani*, i.e. full-fledged customary tenants, the holdings might at first sight appear to be very uniform in size, for as a rule the villeins are listed as if they held one virgate each, though in a few places the Domesday lists villeins who may have held half virgates. This equality and regularity may however be wholly fictitious. In the county of Middlesex, for which the Domesday Book happens to provide somewhat more detailed information of villeins, holdings, villeins are shown to be in possession of entire virgates, half virgates and multiples of virgates. True enough, within each of these three categories holdings seem to be all of the same size, but this regularity may also turn out to have been nothing more than an accounting device of the Domesday clerks. Mr Lennard has shown that in some manors, which happen to have been described more fully in the Domesday of the lands of the bishops of Ely, the distribution of holdings was less regular than it appears in the corresponding entries of the main, The Exchequer, Domesday. In early twelfth-century surveys available to us, such as those of Peterborough or Shaftesbury, the distribution of holdings is also less regular, and the inequalities are more clearly pronounced than in the Domesday Book. We may therefore suspect that, had the compilers of the Domesday Book been interested in the actual holders of land and not in the units of landholding, they might have recorded inequalities in the actual occupation of land which the uniform formulae of the Inquest conceal from our view.

However, no matter how we interpret the Domesday evidence for the eleventh century, there should be little doubt about the evidence of the twelfth century. All the records of that period reveal the existence of the same differences which we have noted in the later period—a large body of smallholders, a small number of wealthy villagers, and a mass of men of middle substance holding the economic equivalent of more than a quarter but rather less than a whole of a virgate of land of average quality.

At the same time the distribution of holdings and the relative numbers in each of our three groups may have differed somewhat from period to period. Thus the comparison of the Glastonbury surveys of the late thirteenth century with those of the late twelfth, or of the accounts of Peterborough estates of the beginning of the fourteenth century with a few surviving accounts and surveys of mid-thirteenth century, or of the abbey of Ramsey evidence at several points of time in the twelfth and thirteenth centuries, suggests that a proportion of smallholdings increased very considerably in the intervening period. Some of the increase reflected in surveys may have been fictitious, since a number of newly recorded smallholdings were probably held by men already listed among holders of other tenements. Nevertheless, most surveys contain residues of additional smallholdings which could not be explained in this way and which certainly denote net accretions to the main body of village smallholders.

Is this to be wondered at? At the time when population was growing faster than the supplies of land, the average size of holdings was bound to decline and additional population was bound to crowd into the bottom of the social scale.

The changes at the other pole of the social scale are more difficult to establish. Wealthy villagers with two and more virgates were to be found everywhere, but whether their numbers grew or declined is difficult to say. What we already know about the land market in the thirteenth century suggests that the main source of land which the persistent land-buyers of this period—the greater landowners and the humbler peasants—acquired were the lands of petty landowners or of the most substantial peasant freeholders. This might predispose us to expect that the numbers of such freeholders would decline in the thirteenth century. Yet there were some such men to be found on most manors in the thirteenth century, and the evidence is insufficient to tell us whether these numbers were any lower than they had been in the twelfth century.

At first sight the evidence about this and the other ranks of village society appears to be much more communicative in the closing centuries of the Middle Ages—late fourteenth and fifteenth. The old disequilibrium of land and men was being redressed; land was becoming more abundant; rents and entry fines lower. Yet it is obvious that the new dispensation could not benefit all the sections of peasantry in equal measure. The section of rural population to profit most was probably the lowest—the smallholders and the landless men. They profited as landholders from the greater abundance of land and from its cheapness. They declined in numbers by promotion into the groups above them, while those who remained in the ranks of wage earners profited from higher wages accompanied by stable or falling food prices.

The balance of benefits and losses at the other end of the social scale is much more difficult to draw. A very substantial villager with the equivalent of several virgates on his hands would, like all other villagers, benefit from greater opportunities for acquiring land and thus rounding off or enclosing his holdings but, like all other landowners, he would suffer from higher wages and—if he sub-let his land—from lower rents. So on *a priori* grounds a single generalized verdict applicable to all the wealthy villagers would not be possible. Those who did not sub-let too many acres and did not employ too many men—a substantial villager specializing in sheep farming would meet these requirements best—might derive from the new situation the maximum benefits with the minimum of losses. For the others the precise balance of advantages would depend on the proportions in which they combined the different sources of agricultural income. A village 'kulak' who derived most of his income from rents (probably an uncommon figure) might find himself on the losing side.

In this respect the great mass of villagers in the middling ranks shared the fortunes of wealthier peasants. For they too could benefit from lower land values and suffer from higher wages and somewhat lower food prices. Many more of them were now able to 'thrive' into the condition of 'kulaks' by enlarging their holdings, but whether their economic well-being and their income was thereby greatly enhanced, or enhanced at all, would also depend on the extent to which they were involved in sheep farming, cereal growing, employed labour or let their land.

Thus, except for the village smallholders, the difficulty of arriving at the clear balance of the gains and losses is very great, and this perhaps explains why historians in general are inclined to sidestep the issue and to confine their assessments solely to changes in the sizes of holdings and in the relative numbers of holders of tenancies of different sizes. Inquiries thus restricted are capable of being conducted in statistical terms, even though the results may appear more definite than they really are. They all agree in suggesting that the numbers of men with large or very large holdings, i.e. the equivalents of two virgates and more, became much larger in the fifteenth century. On the estates so far studied there were more men with very large holdings, and the total area of land in their hands was greater than before. From this it is easy to conclude that the English village in the fifteenth century suffered—or would 'benefited' be the right word?—from the same economic 'differentiation' which Lenin discerned in the Russian village of the late nineteenth century. As seen by Lenin the Russian village was at his time undergoing a 'capitalist' or 'pre-capitalist' transformation; its old equality of land-holdings and the middling rank of peasants representing the older equality were breaking up, while the class of petty capitalists grew at the top and a mass of proletarized agricultural labourers were accumulating at the bottom.

This scheme will not fit the history of English villages in the later Middle Ages. Whereas the increase in the English 'kulak' class is unmistakable, the decline in the numbers of the labouring poor is equally unmistakable. In most villages they were less numerous in the fifteenth century than they had been in the thirteenth, for the simple reason that their numbers were depleted twice over—as the result of the general decline in population and as the result of their promotion into higher ranks by acquisition of land.

Indeed social promotion may sometimes provide a truer and more convenient description of fifteenth century changes than 'stratification' or 'polarization'. In most fifteenth-century villages average holdings of all villagers grew, and as a result the largest holdings became larger and the smallest holdings became fewer. As for holdings of middling size, they would appear to increase or decline according to the positions of demarcation lines. If the lines were so drawn as to mark off the group holding the same number of acres per household as that we assigned to the middling group in the thirteenth century, i.e. more than a quarter virgate and less than a half virgate, the proportions of men in the group would appear to increase in some of the villages so far studied. In these villages the middling mass of villagers thus defined gained more recruits by promotion from below than it lost by promotion into the 'kulak' class above it. If, on the other hand, our demarcation lines were so re-drawn as to increase the size of the 'middling' holdings in the same proportion in which average holdings in villages increased, the relative numbers in this or indeed in any other group would not appear to be significantly different from similar proportions in the thirteenth century. Graphs fitted to the distribution of holdings in the same villages in the thirteenth and the fifteenth centuries would be very similar in shape, even though the fifteenth-century graph would run higher than the thirteenth-century one. In other words, an historian looking for statistical evidence of social differentiation might find it as clearly in the thirteenth century as in the fifteenth. The progress of social differentiation in the fifteenth century would often appear great or small according to the statistical method chosen to measure it.

Medieval Agrarian Society in its Prime

§ 8. Scandinavia

I. *The Scandinavian states, their geography*

Shortly after the middle of the eleventh century the political map of Scandinavia took the form it retained in the main during the whole of the medieval period. Sweden owned the Baltic coast from a point at the present boundary between the provinces of Blekinge and Smaaland right up into the great forests of northern Norrland, the provinces of Vaesterbotten and Norrbotten, for long but sparsely inhabited. Finland also belonged to the Swedish sphere of interest, but here, as in Norrland, Swedish penetration was not accomplished until the final decades of the period now under review. The political centre of the Swedish kingdom was the country round the Maelare, west of Stockholm, but agriculturally the large, interior plains of Oestergoetland and Vaestergoetland were most important. Only at a single point, the mouth of the river Goeta, did Sweden send a narrow wedge down to the West Coast.[1]

Sweden faced the Baltic; Norway the Skagerrak, the North Sea and the Atlantic. The Norwegian settlements stretched from the river Goeta in the south via Troendelag round Trondheim up to Haalogaland on the Arctic Circle. They were usually of rather small extent, but particularly in Troendelag, round the Oslo Fiord and in certain river valleys they stretched far up-country. Nevertheless, the interior of Norway was for the most part unsuitable for permanent settlement, though there were settlements that did not link up with the coast, such as Jaemtland, which, whether it originally belonged to Sweden or not, was included in Norway during our period.

Conditions for agriculture were far more favourable in the third Scandinavian kingdom, Denmark, than in Sweden or Norway. Denmark included the present-day Danish territory and also the most southerly part of the Scandinavian peninsula, the provinces of Skaane, Halland and Blekinge, that is to say all the districts in Scandinavia where soil and climate made really flourishing agriculture possible. Denmark was the only Scandinavian kingdom whose area was to a considerable extent arable.

---

[1] In this section the following transcriptions are used in all Scandinavian place and personal names, all untranslated Scandinavian expressions, and all book-titles: the Swedish and Norwegian letter å is written aa, the Swedish letter ä is written ae, the Swedish letter ö and the Danish and Norwegian ø are written oe.

Shortly after the political map of Scandinavia had been stabilized, i.e. after 1050, the North German chronicler Master Adam of Bremen gives us a description of the scenery, civilization and economy of the northern kingdoms. Of Denmark he says that Jutland is a sterile wilderness, but the Danish islands and Skaane are fertile, and he especially mentions the abundance of their harvests. Of Sweden he says the earth is rich in harvests and honey, and he adds that it is pre-eminent in its yield of livestock. Adam's description of Norway runs otherwise: the country is the most unfertile of all districts, and can be used only for livestock. As with the Arabs, the cattle are kept right out in the wilderness. Master Adam stresses the great part stock-raising plays in Norway in speaking of the provision of the Norwegian with food and clothing; and he indicates its importance in Sweden too in remarking that in both countries even the best-born men lived like their ancestors as herdsmen, supporting themselves by the work of their hands. An account of the journey of a German delegation to Lund in Skaane (1127) shows that stock-raising was important in Denmark, as in Norway and Sweden; the inhabitants fished, hunted and raised stock, and acquired all their wealth by these means; there was little tillage.

How fundamentally different agrarian—especially stock-raising—conditions were in different parts of Scandinavia may be illustrated by positive statements: on leaving Lund our German delegation were presented with a hoy laden with butter, obviously the chief product of the South Scandinavian pasturage. There is a sharply contrasting record that describes the stock-raising of Northern Scandinavia: about the year 900 the patrician farmer Ottar, settled in Haalogaland, had the following stock—20 cows, 20 swine, 20 sheep, some horses and 600 reindeer.

Master Adam's description gives a strikingly correct picture of the essentially different conditions in which the agrarian population of the three kingdoms of Scandinavia lived during the eleventh century. In Denmark, particularly on the islands and in Skaane, there was more arable land than in the other Scandinavian countries; it is clear that the proportion of tillage to pasturage seemed more normal here to a North German observer. In Sweden too, and especially on its plains, tillage had real economic significance, but for the agrarian population of the country as a whole stock-raising was more important. It was still more important in Norway, where according to Master Adam it was universal, and was carried on, according to him and other sources, in a special manner. Master Adam even goes as far as to deny the existence of tillage in Norway.

His description suffers not only from this type of exaggeration. It is highly schematic and insufficiently differentiated: it treats the three Scandinavian countries too much as economic units, and gives summaries for each. It is true that these bring out the essential differences resulting from natural conditions varying from country to country; but the actual differentiation by no means followed the frontiers: differences within the same country from province to province, or within the same province from district to district, were considerable. And there was not only the direct factor of dissimilar natural conditions, but also the political division of Scandinavia into three kingdoms, and the lack of coherence within each kingdom. This lack may be clearly seen in the fact that the law-books in which legal rules were summarized during the central Middle Ages were originally—and for a long time— valid only for a single province or region of the kingdom. These factors formed and developed agrarian classes and general agrarian conditions along rather different lines in the several districts.

It is therefore difficult to give a coherent account of the agrarian community in Scandinavia at the height of the Middle Ages. There is a further difficulty in the dispersed and sometimes extremely deficient character of the material, which varies in type from district to district. And this occasions a third difficulty: in the Scandinavian countries research has often been directed to different problems of agrarian history, and reached different stages. It is sometimes hard to reconcile the results.

For these reasons we must try to give on the one hand a general description of those aspects of the form and development of the agrarian community that are common to the whole of the Scandinavian area, on the other hand a specific description of conditions within a certain district that may be considered typical of the Scandinavian agrarian community at the height of its development. It is more or less obvious that in doing so we should choose the region of greatest agrarian importance, the Danish, giving but brief notice to a region where natural conditions brought about a unique development, as they did in the homeland of the patrician farmer Ottar, in Northern Norway, where reindeer were the chief source of wealth.

II. *Village and farm settlement*

A fundamental problem in the agrarian history of Scandinavia is the type of the original settlements and the age of the medieval type. There are two opposing theories. One takes the view that village settlement was primary in Denmark and on the Swedish plains, whereas scattered farm settlement, which occurs mostly in those parts of Scandinavia least suited for tillage, came later, and might even be secondary to village settlement in some parts. And village settlement, it is argued, goes back to ancient, prehistoric times.[1] Most scholars now hold quite the opposite opinion. According to them the medieval system of settlement does not date back farther than the Iron Age. During the earlier part of this Age farm settlement was still the rule: not until the Roman Iron Age and the Period of Migration, i.e. the former half of the first thousand years of our era, did the oldest villages come into being.[2] In time village settlement dominated in great parts of Scandinavia, especially in the districts best suited for agriculture, while in peripheral areas, or areas peripheral from the agrarian point of view, farm settlement remained predominant.

Village settlement was particularly regular during the central Middle Ages in Denmark, though not everywhere in Jutland, and not on the island of Bornholm. On this island farm settlement was the rule: each farm had large, contiguous stretches of ploughland, while the ownership and use of other ground was divided up irregularly among the farms.

In Sweden conditions varied: village settlement predominated in the tillage districts in the southern and central parts of the kingdom. Farm settlement was common in the provinces bordering on Norway, in the greater part of Norrland, on the island of Gotland, and everywhere in the forest districts. Yet in many places village-like communities developed, but relatively late. The so-called family village, which may be considered to have come about through the dividing up of a single farm, is of particular interest. Its characteristics are that the dwelling-houses lie together in one group, certain outhouses together in another, certain other buildings in a third, and so on.

In Norway, Meitzen, and many others with and after him, have thought that village settlement was primary. But this opinion is no longer generally current among scholars: no traces of a completely developed village organization can be observed anywhere in Norway. In parts, however, big-family farms have grown out of the separate farms —as in Sweden also—and there are other things reminiscent of condi-

---

[1] Our account ignores those authors who assume that the villages date back to a relatively recent period when the previously half-nomadic Scandinavians first settled down. Their assumption conflicts too much with the unanimous opinion of prehistoric scholars.

[2] The principal argument in favour of this is that Scandinavian Place-name scholars, rejecting an older, diametrically opposed view, are now certain that no place names are older than the Iron Age. The fields of the pre-Roman Iron Age, which are similar to the so-called Celtic fields in England, and many of which have been found in Jutland by G. Hatt ('Prehistoric fields in Jylland', *Acta Archaeologica*, II, 1931, pp. 117 ff.; *Landbrug i Danmarks Oldtid*, 1937, pp. 76 ff.), and medieval fields, which are similar to the *Hochaecker* of Germany, and some of which have recently been discovered east of Lund by G. Nordholm ('Kungsaengen Raeften eller Kungsmarken', *Skaanegillet i Stockholm Aarsskrift*, 1936, pp. 35ff.), indicate considerable differences between the agrarian conditions of the two periods. On the other hand recent excavations conducted by G. Hatt show that village-like settlements existed early in Denmark.

tions in a more highly developed village community, such as settlement in 'farm-clusters', a kind of strip system, and so on. But these phenomena are now held to be secondary, and to date back only in part to the centuries here discussed.

Just as there were certain tendencies towards the formation of village communities in the areas where definitely organized village communities had not originally existed, so settlements of a different kind occurred in those parts of Scandinavia where completely developed village communities were regular. We know from a more recent time, when conditions seem not to have differed much from those of the central Middle Ages, that detached farms formed 9·2 per cent of all settlements in Denmark west of the Sound. On Zealand and the small islands they formed only 3·1 per cent but in Jutland 15·3 per cent. In parts of Jutland right in the north and west they formed between 30 and 75 per cent. In all places where the soil is best suited for tillage, village settlement had spread most, whereas in sparser districts detached farms were more numerous. In these circumstances it is natural that in South-Western Skaane, which was extremely well suited for tillage, there were hardly any detached farms.[1] For Sweden we are able to distinguish the position in certain parts of Upland during the beginning of the fourteenth century: villages are predominant on the plain proper, but detached farms, younger than the villages, may be observed in the forest districts.[2] This distribution should be a pretty general rule.

The origin of the oldest Danish villages is much debated, but the debate lies outside the scope of this section. In the central Middle Ages we can see villages developing in various ways.

Legal regulations from that era clearly show that it was possible for new villages to be founded by moving out of the older ones and dividing up their ground. The older village was called *hoegby* ('high' or 'mound' village) or odal village, the village newly founded by the act of moving was called a thorp village. The foundation of a thorp village was often a co-operative undertaking, of course; from its very beginning it was a complete village-community. On the other hand, in Norway and certain districts of Sweden we can observe a development, partly post-medieval, that produces from a detached farm a community reminiscent in various ways of a South Scandinavian village. So we have the possibility that in a similar way the medieval Danish and Swedish

---

[1] Survey maps in the archives of the Swedish Land-Measurement Board, collected by G. Nordholm and in part published by him in 'Skaanes geometriska kartlaeggning foere storskiftena', *Svensk geografisk aarsbok*, 1929, bil. 2.

[2] Conditions in Upland may be inferred by comparing certain taxation rolls from the beginning of the fourteenth century, published in *Svenskt Diplomatarium*, III, 1842, pp. 86 ff., with various documents about and lists of the property of Upsala Cathedral.

villages developed from detached farms, and, as a result of the considerably more favourable conditions for agriculture in their regions, attained a higher stage of development at an earlier period.

And for a small part of the Danish agricultural area, the island of Falster, we can follow the growth of the villages during the early Middle Ages more closely. For we are acquainted with certain conditions on this island both at a point that may be assigned to the eleventh century and at about 1200. At the former time there were on Falster between 50 and 60 settlements to each of which belonged ground equivalent to at least two large farms. These settlements are usually of great age, and may be regarded as villages. The number of settlements which at this time owned land equivalent to one large farm, together with the detached farms founded up to about 1200, was not less than about 40. Of these about 30 had by the year 1200 grown so much that they were equivalent to at least two large farms, and many are known to be villages at a later period. In the eleventh century the older villages still included at least nine-tenths of the cultivated land: about 1200 they included only about four-fifths. Thus the share of the land on Falster owned by the villages that had recently developed out of farms increased considerably between these two points in time.[1] It is clear, therefore, that in the only part of the Danish agricultural area about which we have detailed knowledge, a considerable proportion of the villages developed from detached farms so recently as the early Middle Ages. There are many reasons to think that in other places also a large number of the new villages may have arisen during this period. For example, to judge from the place names, 700 of the Oestergoetland villages were founded during the Viking Period at the latest (i.e. before about 1060), but twice as many during the Middle Ages proper, chiefly no doubt during the early and central Middle Ages.

The details we have about Falster also help to determine the date when the distribution of settlements was completed in the tillage areas of Scandinavia, at least in the most important area, the Danish. For this area they indicate that the foundation of villages was at an end by about 1200: and whereas about a quarter of the villages existing on Falster at that time have since disappeared—mainly those of less extent and rather late foundation—since 1200 only a few villages have come into existence. We can see that conditions were rather similar in other districts favourable for agriculture, far from Falster, from the fact that the foundation of villages seems to have been completed on the Upland

[1] This is apparent from the so-called Falster list in *Liber Census Daniae* (ed. O. Nielsen, 1873, pp. 64 ff.), which for every village on Falster mentions the number of *bol* and the *terra in censu* (cf. below, p. 645). Cf. most recently on this S. Bolin, *Ledung och fraelse*, 1934, p. 22, footnote 1.

plain by the fourteenth century, when we have some possibility of surveying conditions there.

The actual area cultivated seems to have been considerable during the central Middle Ages. Attempts have been made to determine this extent on Falster for about the year 1200; but they have led to rather uncertain results. Some say that the area under cultivation then was twice as great as in the middle of the seventeenth century, others that it was only two-thirds of the area cultivated at the end of that century.[1] But whichever view be taken, it was important.

And the agricultural population was numerous accordingly. Halland provides safe material for comparison: in the thirteenth century there were about 9250 farmers in Halland, whereas in the seventeenth century the number of farms there was only 4000. For Sweden an area of four contiguous parishes in Upland provides a direct comparison: at a general levy at the beginning of the fourteenth century the number of taxpayers was nearly 350; at a similar levy in 1571 there were only 244.[2] These and many other reasons go to show that the agrarian population in the central Middle Ages was larger than during the first centuries of the post-medieval period.

The decline, in agriculture and in population, which is traceable in various ways, can be assigned for all the three Scandinavian states to the fourteenth century. It was formerly assumed that the Black Death was the direct and only cause of the decline; and there are still those who hold this opinion. Others think the Black Death played a much smaller part; that it is an element in a larger process. According to this new conception the cultivated area diminished and the population curve began to decline from the 1330's onwards, perhaps even from the 1320's, as is suggested by the fall in the price of land, the decline in renders and in taxes paid to the Papal Chair, and the more frequent mention of deserted farms. It would seem that the process took place later in Sweden than in Denmark. On the other hand, the beginning of effective Swedish colonization in Finland and of permanent Swedish settlement in larger and larger districts of the Norrland provinces is also placed in the fourteenth century. Whether the opening-up of the vast open spaces in the north and east attracted inhabitants from Southern and Western Scandinavia and thus contributed to the decline there, is a question that has never been asked, and that only future research can answer.

[1] K. Erslev (*Valdemarernes Storhedstid*, 1898, pp. 117 ff.) holds the former opinion, P. Lauridsen ('Om Skyldjord eller *terra in censu*', *Aarboeger för Nordisk Oldkyndighed*, 1903, pp. 58 ff.) the latter.
[2] The figures for the beginning of the fourteenth century are taken from the documents cited above, p. 471, note 2. It is certain that a larger percentage of the population was included in 1571 than at the beginning of the fourteenth century.

III. *Village forms*

The types of Scandinavian villages can be studied in the very many, very detailed surviving cadastres and land-survey maps, though these do not go back farther than the middle of the seventeenth century. In this work the Dane P. Lauridsen was the pioneer. He distinguished three essentially different fundamental types: the nucleus-village, where the farms lay around a rectangular or oval village green, and from which the cluster-village later developed; the long village, where the farms lay in two parallel rows opposite one another along a rather narrow village street; and finally the 'topographical' village, consisting of one long row of farms facing perhaps a stream, a lake, or a stretch of meadowland. Nordholm and Aakjaer, a Swede and a Dane, have however been able to show that villages of Lauridsen's three pure types are rather rare, but villages of transitional form between the types extremely common. According to Nordholm the fundamental and original type of Scandinavian village is a 'green-village, where the farms lie along or round a village street that was made by the traffic between tillage and pasture'. Where there were no physico-geographical hindrances, the village street was pretty broad and became a village green. But minor differences of topography and soil might stretch the village out long and narrow. And major physico-geographical variations might cause the farms of the village to lie in a single row along the actual division between tillage and pasture, or irregularly in the pasture itself.

The actual implications of this theory are best realized by considering the development of the village from its oldest farms. These were regularly situated on the boundary between the ground that was most suitable for tillage and ground that could conveniently be used as pasture during the oldest period, when the land under plough was not extensive. Tillage and pasture were marked off from one another by fences from the start. As the population grew the tillage grew. If, on account of the kind of soil, the fields were extended in only one direction—i.e. from the back of the buildings in the direction of the oldest cultivated fields—the village would take the form of a single row of houses along the old, still existent boundary between tillage and pasture, or of a cluster of houses on that part of the pasture that lay closest to the ploughland. In the former case we have a village of the type that Lauridsen called a 'topographical' village, in the latter case a cluster-village. But in other places it was possible to cultivate the soil in various directions. Then the village lost immediate contact with the pasture, and was by degrees completely surrounded by ploughland. Now the houses had to be placed in two rows opposite one another

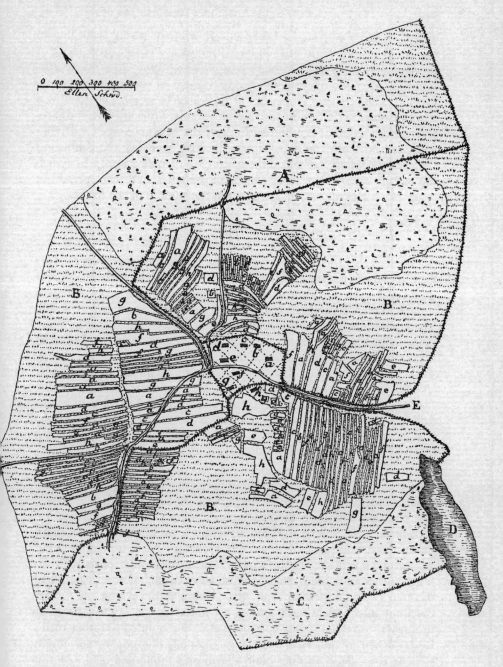

FIG. 9. Swedish open-field village, developed form (seventeenth century): Otterstorpaby, Vaestergoetland. A and C, wood; B, pasture; *a*, *b*, *c*, etc., farms and their lands.

along a narrow or round a broad village street or green, according to the geographical conditions. In the former case a village arose more or less corresponding to Lauridsen's long village, in the latter one resembling his so-called nucleus-village. In villages of this kind the village green had an important function for the villagers' stock. The green was naturally enclosed from the surrounding arable. Through this, and carefully fenced from it, went the cattle-drive that was necessary for driving stock to and from the stall. The cattle-drive was thus the connexion between the village green and the pasture. It formed a wedge by which the pasture reached the village through the fields, and then spread out again like a sack in the village green in the middle of the farms.

IV. *The village community*

The view that the Scandinavian village community sprang from some primitive communism is still current; but most modern scholars do not doubt that before the time of the fully developed community there was a period when the farmers had even greater liberty in tilling their soil. The conditions prevalent during this older period still existed in many places when the laws were codified in the thirteenth and fourteenth centuries, and may even be studied on the partition-maps of later times. Thus the provisions of the oldest Swedish provincial law, the older Vaestgoeta law, which is placed in the first half of the thirteenth century, show that the organization of the village community was by no means fully developed. It is true that the pasture was in the common ownership of the villagers: like the forest it could for certain purposes be used by all who owned a certain minimal amount of village land. And it was presumed that when new ground came under cultivation there might be a certain amount of co-operation between the villagers: the new ploughland was divided up amongst them on certain principles typical for the organization of the village community. But the consideration each farmer was bound to show his fellows was limited to a necessary minimum, being primarily the duty of fencing. There is no question of any farmer's bringing about a modification of existing property relations, as there is in most other Swedish and Danish laws. A peasant had the free right of moving from the village, transforming his former dwelling into a field, and setting up house on one of his fields or meadows, provided it was not completely surrounded by other men's land. When an inheritance was partitioned, one coparcener might settle in the village, another build a farm on an inherited field. All this presumes that the various fields and meadows of each farmer were far more extensive than was usual where the village community had been organized systematically. And indeed, in certain post-medieval land-surveying maps of Vaestgoetic villages we find a distribution of land very different from that typical for village-community organization: each farm in the village of Vartofta, for example, owned large contiguous parcels, not small strips distributed over the whole ploughland.[1] We may assume with fair certainty that this type of distribution of ownership is that of a village in *fornskifte* and *hambri*. These were the terms in the rather later Swedish laws from about and after 1300 for a village that had preserved an old-fashioned structure, and had not been subjected to the re-arrangement which by that time the laws encouraged.[2]

In Skaane too, and in other parts of Denmark also, there are traces of a type of distribution earlier than that stipulated as normal in the provincial codes of the first half of the thirteenth century. The oldest Scanian distribution that can be observed differs from the oldest distribution in Vaestergoetland. It is true that tillage and hay-meadow were divided up into a large number of small strips but their distribution to the farms of the village was quite unsystematic. The farmer's right of ownership over such separate strips must originally have been complete and unlimited; he must have been considered the owner of just those strips, not, as later, of a certain share of the village and its ground.[3]

Thus, in certain cases the provincial codes reflect conditions from the time before the complete development of the village community in Scandinavia; otherwise the community dominates the provisions of the codes altogether. Ownership of a share in the village meant possession of a *tomt* (Swedish) or toft (Danish). This was the ground in the village where the farm buildings were situated, and to which a parcel of field might be attached. The latter is a general rule in Denmark, where a toft might include as much as a hectare. When a new farm was built in a village, it received a toft, usually contiguous with the other tofts: its standard breadth is given in the Oestgoeta Law as 20 ells, i.e., about 12 metres. Farms on these new, 'sworn' tofts had the same rights as farms on old tofts. But possession of a *holmstoft* (an isolated toft), an enclosed area used for living-quarters in the village pasture, did not carry with it membership of the commune.

Uninhabited parts of plough- and hay-meadowland might also fall outside the village ground. Everywhere in Denmark we find mention of *ornum*. This was divided from the village ground by ancient custom and special boundary-marks, and was not subject to the general

[1] Cf. the map of Vartofta published in A. Meitzen's *Siedelung und Agrarwesen der Westgermanen und Ostgermanen, der Kelten, Roemer, Finnen und Slawen*, III, Atlas 1895, Anlage 144.

[2] Below, p. 645.

[3] I cannot agree with those scholars who postulate a stage before the division of the ploughland into strips when it was redistributed annually; for medieval laws and other medieval sources contain no trace of this redistribution. When it occurs in later times it is probably a secondary development.

provisions for village ground—the duties and limitations of the right of use that the increasing strictness of organization in the village community imposed on its men. An *ornum* was usually of considerable size; and its possessors must as a rule have belonged to the old farming aristocracy. Thus an *ornum* was an area that belonged entirely to one person, and was called his *enemaerke*. But even a whole village and its ground could belong to a single person or institution as *enemaerke*, although it might be tilled by several villagers, provided that the person or institution was sole owner of the whole village, that is, of all its tenures.

In Sweden *ornum* was called *urfjaell* in the provinces round the Maelare, and *hump* in Oestergoetland. The standard size of an *urfjaell*, too, seems often to have been considerable.

Included in the village lands were also cultivated areas of quite another kind than those just mentioned, but also different from the village land owned in common. These areas were parts of the village pasture that had been recently brought under cultivation. For certain Swedish laws allowed private members of the commune to make such clearings and to keep them for many years, or even for ever if there was other ground available for tillage for the rest of the villagers. In Denmark too there is mention of newly cultivated stretches, called *rud* (OE *rod*, and the place-name termination -*royd*), distinct from the commonly owned land.

'Village measures' were of great importance for the activity of the village community. In Scandinavia as elsewhere they varied greatly from district to district. Only those of the principal districts can be referred to here. The original Swedish village measure was everywhere the *attung* (*octonarius*), probably the eighth part of the village. After the middle of the thirteenth century, in the provinces round the Maelare, the *octonarius* was displaced—as we may infer from an assessment—by the *markland* (*marca terrae*), which was divided up into 8 *oeresland* (*orae terrae*), 24 *oertugland* (*solidi terrae*), and 360 *peningland* (*denarii terrae*).[1] According to the law an ordinary country church should have 4 *orae terrae*, so this should be about equivalent to a large standard farm. In Oestergoetland the *octanarius* remained the village measure, but in time lost its old meaning, for a village there might include far more than 8 *octonarii*.

In Denmark the *bol* (*mansus*), corresponding to a large farm, was originally the current unit. It certainly goes back to the eleventh century, when, in connexion with the military organization, the

---

[1] The common statement that the *marca terrae* was 192 *denarii terrae* is quite wrong for the early Middle Ages, as is shown by a large number of printed and unprinted sources—documents and cadastres.

Danish villages were ascribed a certain *bol* figure, corresponding to the number of standard farms they included. In the same way the separate farms of the village were allotted a certain *bol* figure, corresponding to the fraction of a standard farm, or the number of standard farms, they included. In Skaane the *bol* was the only land measure during the twelfth and thirteenth centuries, but in the rest of Denmark during those centuries new units were created. In Jutland and on Fünen the unit was the gold mark (*terra unius marcae auri*); in Zealand, probably somewhat later, in the very beginning of the thirteenth century, the unit was the *skyld* mark (*terra in censu unius marcae*). The Jutland valuation probably indicates the value of the farms, but the Zealand unit most likely has to do with a fresh state assessment, and indicates the tax to the state in silver.[1] Both the Zealand and the Jutland units, of which the former (*terra in censu unius marcae*) seems to be about three times as great as the latter (*terra unius marcae auri*), were divided in the same way as the Danish mark.

When new land was brought under cultivation by the community— and the Swedish and Danish laws tried to facilitate this in various ways —it was natural that each farm should receive a share of the newly acquired tillage in proportion to its size, that is, its share of the 'village measure'. The same principle was applied in the total partitions mentioned in Swedish and Danish laws. For these contained strict provisions that in certain circumstances the irregularities brought about by the earlier natural development should be abolished, so that a village in *hambri* should be re-partitioned, put into *laga laege* (lawful condition) as the phrase went. In doing so the principles of *solskifte*,[2] which came from the Continent, should be followed, in the Maelare provinces and Oestergoetland, as in Jutland and on the Danish islands. But in Skaane another arrangement was made, the so-called *bolskifte*. This meant that the various *aas*, groups of ridges, that together formed the arable should be divided into as many large parts as there were *bol* in the village. So every *bol* received one of these parts, and this was divided up in its turn among the farms constituting the *bol*, according to their *bol* figure.[3]

---

[1] But there are differing opinions about the character and date of the Zealand valuation.

[2] *Solskifte* means that the strips in a ridge-group were distributed according to the position of the farms in the village. For example, in a village totally under *solskifte*, a farm that lay east of another farm had in every ridge-group strips situated east of that other farm's strips. Thus the *solskiften* was made according to the course of the sun (Swedish *sol*=sun).

[3] A number of villages in *bolskifte* have been found in Skaane and also in Jutland and Zealand, where it was usual before *solskifte* was decreed. A village in *bolskifte* can easily be seen on the land-survey maps, as the strips of certain farms always lie side by side in the separate ridge-groups; the farms whose strips thus lie contiguous together form a *bol*. The strips allotted them in the same ridge-group always have a total area identical with the area there allotted to other farms which by themselves or together form a *bol*.

It is at present impossible to say how far such re-arrangements changed the conditions of ownership of the village ploughland. There are restrictions even in the laws themselves: at times adjustments are recommended instead of total re-partition; it is stipulated that in order to be able to claim partition a farmer must own a certain amount of land; in some cases unanimity is required for re-partition. In Skaane, when there were disputes between farms belonging to the same *bol*, only the strips of that *bol* were to be re-partitioned, not the whole ploughland of the village. We find similar provisions elsewhere.

Some villages were completely re-arranged according to the laws. But both in Sweden and Denmark there are villages that retained more primitive conditions of ownership than those stipulated, until the post-medieval period. It may well be possible one day to give statistics for large districts: an investigation has shown that conditions on Falster were just the opposite of those on Laaland—on the former island re-arrangements are numerous, on the latter few.

The tightening-up of the organization of the village community that these and other provisions in the laws indicate must have meant much for the farmers' right of ownership and use of their land. The tendency in the conditions of ownership must have been that the toft and the separate strips that were distributed over the ridges were soldered together into a really fixed unit, whose components were not and might not be taken from one another. It could not but be so, partly because according to general rule the area of the strips had to follow that of the toft, partly because in places all the taxes to the state were distributed among the tofts. The difficulties this occasioned are plain from a section of the Skaane law that reappears in Zealand law. Here the laws make no decree but are content to relate two contrary opinions. We may summarize them as follows. On the one hand, says the law, there are men who want to forbid the selling of strips from toft, for this would cause unfairness in the payment of tax, and make it impossible to divide up the arable according to the size of the tofts. But on the other hand, the law goes on, there are men who say that every farmer may freely sell his strips, since otherwise, if he becomes poor, he will be compelled to sell the whole farm and become a tenant. On Jutland, however, the right of the villagers to sell separate strips was not questioned. If strips were thus taken from the toft, they had in some respects a special position and were called *stuf*.

In Scandinavia as elsewhere it was natural that the spread and development of the village community system should make the farmers co-operate more and more. There are numerous legal provisions that regulate everybody's duties and rights in detail: they carefully fix the farmers' duty to fence arable and hay-meadows; they make rules for preventing a farmer from allowing his stock on to other villagers' ploughland; they give exact prescriptions about everybody's right to utilize the common forest and pasture. Together with later sources they make it possible for us to see the various systems of crop-rotation used in different regions of Scandinavia. In the main agricultural area, the Danish islands and Skaane, the three-field system was already the rule about 1200: each of the three fields was called a 'wong'. But every farmer was not bound to follow the regular rotation and to sow the strips lying in the same 'wong' one year with barley, the second year with rye, and in the third year let them lie fallow. The farmer had the full right to sow his strips in the fallow 'wong', provided he fenced them himself.[1] The three-field system was not the only one in Skaane and on the Danish islands. In the thirteenth century and much later there were two-field villages. There were also villages with only one 'wong', which was sown during a series of years, while the stock was confined to the pasture-land. This is called the 'all-corn system'. From eastern Denmark the three-field system spread in various directions, and came to Sweden, where it was later used in some places in Vaestergoetland. But in Sweden the two-field and all-corn systems were commoner: it is typical that the Oestergoetland Law decrees that when there is disagreement about the system, that party in the village shall prevail that wants to let half the land lie fallow. In Jutland the three-field system was usual in the more fertile, eastern districts; in other parts, the two-field and the all-corn systems.

All four cereals were cultivated in Denmark, but chiefly rye and barley. Both autumn and spring rye were used, the former mostly in Skaane and the Danish islands, no doubt. To judge from the almost leading position that oats take as a taxation item in a list of the incomes of the crown in 1231, the cultivation of oats must have been considerable in Denmark during the central Middle Ages. They were sown in the outlying edges of the 'wongs', in land situated farthest from the village. There are only very sporadic statements about the cultivation of wheat in Denmark during the central Middle Ages: it is thought that this cereal was usually cultivated on the field that formed part of the farm toft. In specially fenced patches flax, hemp, hops, turnips and cabbage were grown. During the fifteenth century Swedish laws lay it down that the tenants are liable to cultivate and maintain patches of hops. Of fruit trees, the apple was the most common. Gardening seems to have been encouraged by the religious houses that were numerous from the twelfth century onwards.

[1] The word for fencing one's own strip in this way is *brunngaerda*, i.e. fence as one would a well. 'Wong' is used here for the Swedish *vaang*, Danish *vang*. In medieval English, wong indicated furlong or shott, not field.

Norway and Sweden raised much the same crops as Denmark. But apparently in these countries barley was rather more important than rye. It has been both stated and denied that in Western Norway oats, and not barley, were the cereal most cultivated during the Middle Ages.

Agricultural conditions in the regions where the village community did not develop are best known from Norway. Here too, it is thought, settlement spread and a large number of new farms were founded during the years from about 1100 to the thirteenth century. There were no fully organized village communities in Norway, but as a result of partition at inheritance and land-buying there arose so-called neighbour-communities. In some respects conditions in them resembled those of the village community: there was a kind of strip system, the clustering of farms in village-like groups, and the farmer's duty to put up certain fences. These tendencies were particularly strong in the Westland, the Atlantic coast, but less noticeable in the Eastland, the country round Oslo Fiord and a little to the west, where detached farms were pre-dominant. We have some idea of the method of tillage from a provision that a tenant should leave a quarter of his land in fallow every year.

But in Norway stock-raising was far more important than tillage, and therefore the hay-crop was of greater economic significance for the farmers than the grain-crop. It is typical that in the Norwegian laws the size of the farms is sometimes indicated by the head of stock. The saeter system still current in Northern Scandinavia was the rule during the central Middle Ages in both Norway and Northern Sweden. The characteristic of this system was that during the summer the stock was let out far from the settlements on pastures in the forest districts; there they grazed at will, and for the herdspeople shielings were built.

No doubt the saeter system was used quite far to the south during the central Middle Ages, and must have been common in Southern Sweden also. But there is no reason to suppose that it touched Denmark. Master Adam's account of Norwegian stock-raising in the 1070's, that in Arab fashion the cattle were kept right out in the wilderness, is obvious proof that the saeter system was widespread in Norway at the very beginning of this period. But as it is described as characteristic of Norwegian stock-raising and is not mentioned in Sweden, we should be right in assuming that it was dominant in Norway but not in Sweden.

V. *Stock-raising and subsidiary branches of agriculture*

Our knowledge of stock-raising during these centuries in the Swedish and Danish agricultural areas is rather scanty. Unlike ploughland and hay-meadow, pasture was not usually private during the Middle Ages. The untilled and in certain cases untillable land immediately surrounding a village and its fields became village common. Large areas of this kind might belong to the province (province commons) or its subdivisions, the lowest administrative areas, called *haerad* in Southern Sweden and Denmark, and *hundred* in the provinces round the Maelare (*haerad* and *hundred* commons). At an early period the crown claimed part- or complete ownership of the uninhabited districts, and in several places succeeded in taking them. Thus the Swedish king owned a third of all the *haerad* commons in the southern provinces of Sweden (Goetaland). In Denmark from 1100 onwards the farmers had the right to use the forests, but the king owned them. This state of affairs received striking expression in the 1241 law for Jutland: the king owns the ground, the farmers the forest. Beside these commons belonging to village, *haerad* or hundred, province and crown, there were also forests in private ownership.

The common, the 'wong' under fallow, and the village street and green were the grazing places for the cattle, which were watched by herdsmen in either communal or private service. The swine were pastured in the mast-woods; the horses were often kept in a half-wild state in large droves in specially enclosed wooded pasture. As appears from the laws, a private member of the commune had the right to tether his stock in the 'wongs' on the hay strips that belonged to him.

In weighing up the relative importance of tillage and stock-raising in Sweden and Denmark during the central Middle Ages, we lack material that can be utilized statistically. We have no means of observing changes from one time to another. But various circumstances permit us to draw the conclusion that, compared with tillage, stock-raising was far more important in the economy of these two countries than was usual in the Europe of the central Middle Ages or later in Scandinavia. The German delegation that visited Lund, the centre of one of the best agricultural districts in Scandinavia, in the 1120's, found little tillage but much stock-raising. Next to the herring caught in the Sound, a product of international importance, the most important Danish exports during the Middle Ages were dairy-products and stock. Danish horses were much appreciated in Western Europe at an early period, and they were exported in large numbers from Ribe. We have certain facts from about the middle of the fourteenth century concerning the value of the exports to Lübeck, Denmark's chief customer: the value of the exported herring was, of course, highest: next came butter and horses. The stock-products exported from Skaane to Lübeck were worth ten times as much as the grain exported by the same route. And towards the end of the Middle Ages there was a new important export from Denmark—oxen.

Conditions were similar in Sweden. The great importance of stock-raising here is emphasized by Master Adam, as has already been mentioned. Crown taxes in kind were largely paid in butter. In the middle of the fourteenth century butter was Sweden's most important export to Lübeck, which was the chief customer of that country. Of the total known export-value from Sweden to Lübeck, butter represented a quarter.

We need say little about the subsidiary branches of agriculture and other country industries. There was certainly a great deal of bee-keeping, for there are numerous legal provisions about the disputes over swarms and the hunting of wild bees.

The farmers might freely fetch fuel and timber in the forests, from which, of course, various products of importance for home consumption were extracted. But forestry was of real significance for the economy only in Norway, and not there until towards the end of the Middle Ages, when the timber exports to Western Europe became rather considerable.

Hunting was more important. In Denmark it was restricted to land-owners: as the crown had the right of ownership to the untilled forest regions, and minor woods must mostly have been privately owned by nobles, hunting cannot have meant very much for the farmers proper. It was otherwise in Sweden, where the commons were wholly or partly in the possession of the communes, and the enormous forests of Norrland provided inexhaustible preserves. But in Sweden the hunting of certain animals was reserved for the king, and during the fifteenth century prohibitions of hunting for the peasantry were promulgated. During the central Middle Ages, however, they had the right to hunt during certain seasons, different in different parts of the country, and for different kinds of animal. The hunting of fur-bearing animals was particularly important—sable, marten, ermine, otter, beaver and so on. This is brought out by the fact that in certain provinces the farmers paid some of their taxes in furs, and that there was a not inconsiderable export from Sweden.

Fishing too was of great importance for the agrarian population. From the thirteenth century onwards the Norwegian fisheries at Lofoten developed into a national industry. From the very beginning of the twelfth century the herring fishery in the Sound seems to have been very productive: buyers came from various European countries, and farmers from all over Denmark took part in the fishing. In the Baltic, too, an important fishery is mentioned, round Oeland. There was abundance of salmon in the rivers, and salmon are among the articles in which the population paid their taxes to the Scandinavian crowns during the Middle Ages.

We should mention the extraction of metals in connexion with the agrarian occupations for two reasons. Partly because in the mining provinces proper—Vaestmanland, Dalecarlia and Upland in Middle Sweden—the mining yeomen and miners also carried on subsidiary agriculture. Partly because during the early Middle Ages a number of small ore deposits all over Scandinavia were exploited; for instance in the beginning of the thirteenth century an iron-works in Halland is mentioned. And the extraction of bog-ore was widespread at this time everywhere in Scandinavia, and must have been mainly carried on by farmers. In some parts of Smaaland this occupation was so important that iron was one of the taxation items to the crown. And therefore the extraction of ore can be counted as an occupation by which the peasantry profited even outside the mining area proper.

Little is known of the crafts that may have been carried on in the country. There is sporadic mention of tanners and cobblers living in villages. We get an idea of the social position of these men from a decree of the year 1474, which states that tailors, tanners and cobblers, like others living in with the farmers and tenants, shall pay a half-tax to the crown. Smiths are quite often mentioned in the documents. In some districts they may have been especially occupied in the iron-industry proper, but they must also have worked for the needs of the agricultural population. The smiths had the same social position as the free farmers and tenants, together with whom they sometimes sat on the boards and juries functioning at the *ting*.[1]

Among woven products plain-cloth linen and wadmal are particularly to be noticed. It was mostly the women who were occupied with these textiles. They were so important in the national economy that in some parts the laws mention them as legal tender. And they were included in the taxes paid to the crown: this was so of wadmal in Northern Halland (Denmark) and of plain-cloth linen in Haelsingland (Northern Sweden).

Finally, we cannot pass over trade when describing the occupations of the agrarian population during the central Middle Ages in Scandinavia. It is true that in Scandinavia, as in other places, it was usually the duty of the farmers to take their wares to the nearest town and offer them for sale there. But from the Viking Period onwards the inhabitants of the coastal districts were in the habit of carrying on long-distance trade themselves. And their claims to retain this right were maintained and

[1] The extent to which crafts were carried on in the Scandinavian countryside has not been investigated at all. The above is based on documents from 1300 to 1347 in Sweden, Finland, and Denmark east of the Sound.

respected, at least here and there. Thus the farmers on the island of Oeland succeeded in preserving a certain right to trade with Danzig in their own produce. In Norway as late as the thirteenth century the agrarian population seems still to have been extensively occupied in trade and intercourse even with foreign countries; but later provisions endeavour to limit farmers' trading, and to forbid them to carry on foreign trade.

VI. *The agrarian classes and the ownership of land*

There remains the important question of the class divisions in the agrarian community. In the early Middle Ages slavery still flourished in Scandinavia. During the Viking Period the Scandinavians seem to have carried on systematic slave-hunting and -trading, and in the 1070's Master Adam says that slavery is a usual thing. In a Norwegian law three slaves are reckoned as belonging to a standard farm with twelve cows and three horses. The position of these thralls is also regulated by Swedish and Danish laws from the thirteenth century and the first decades of the fourteenth. But apart from this in both Denmark and Norway there is no trace of slaves after 1200, whereas in Sweden they are mentioned in documents still later. During the thirteenth century slavery was certainly rare, and subject to various limitations. By a Vaestergoetland statute of 1335 it was established that the child of a Christian bondwoman should in future be free. And this really meant the end of bondage.

Above the thralls was the class of freemen, obviously divided in many ways during the earlier centuries. Norwegian laws have the following divisions, whose members had differently graded wergelds: *jarl* (dux), *lenderman, hold* (member of a family that had owned a farm for four generations), *bonde* (peasant), *reksthegn* (farm-labourer), *lejsing* (freedman). In Denmark an aristocracy of *principes, majores* and *nobiles* is mentioned. In Sweden, over and above the farmers, are distinguished the *jarl* and the lord, who had a groom, a cook, and forty retainers.

But an important development of the twelfth and thirteenth centuries was that the old aristocracy of peasants either disappeared or changed, fused with other groups and was linked up with the royal power as a nobility of military service with the privilege of immunity from taxation. Fresh social appellations, imported from abroad, appeared all over Scandinavia and took the place of the previous ones. Barons, knights and squires were the three highest divisions of the new nobility, though the first mentioned soon vanished. In Sweden and Denmark there were only knights and squires and ordinary tax-free patricians (Swedish *fraelseman* and Danish *herreman*). On the whole these groups were not an aristocracy in the same sense as the old one. Only the highest of them came in part from the old patrician peasantry, attaining increased power as lords of the crown fiefs, and of course acquiring great allodial possessions. But the lowest divisions of the class contained men who were more or less ordinary peasants, or served for pay. In Sweden the transition between peasant and tax-free patrician (*fraelseman*) was free right into the fourteenth century.

The development of this new nobility of military service was one aspect of a process of which the other aspect concerned the peasants. They were freed from their previous liability to go into *ledung*, i.e. to do their service in person. Instead they undertook to pay certain permanent taxes to the crown. This process cannot be said to be completed in the Scandinavian kingdoms until the period from the last decades of the twelfth century to the end of the thirteenth. It is illuminating for the development in Sweden that about 1300 the peasants were liable to own shield and spear, sword and iron hat, whereas on various occasions in the fifteenth century they were forbidden to bear these weapons, among others.

It is clear that the distinction that thus arose between a tax-free nobility and a tax-paying peasantry was detrimental for the latter, and led to an increase in the lands of the former, just as it did on the Continent. There are various Danish and Swedish legal provisions that attempt to prevent feigned transfers of land from tax-paying peasants to tax-free nobles.

From the end of the eleventh century in Denmark, from the twelfth century in Norway, and from the first part of the thirteenth century in Sweden, the tax-free lands of the Church increased very much. But it should be noted that in the provinces round Lake Maelare the Church is not really important as a landowner until after 1250. Everywhere the peasantry and the lay aristocracy fought the accumulation of lands in the hands of the Church, as is apparent, for example, from the legal provisions about the right of bequest. And the various measures giving relatives pre-emption of inherited land should not be considered as evidence of an original state of affairs when the family was owner of the land, but of the crisis at the time when the laws came into being, when the Church in particular tried to get control of as large estates as possible, mostly perhaps by purchase.[1]

The accumulation of land in the hands of the nobility and the Church

[1] The price that the Upland Law fixes for purchase by relatives seems to be more, and not—as has been thought—less, than the normal one in the province at that time; and this speaks against the former alternative above. Not until the increase of land values continuing in Sweden until about 1350 did the standard price for purchase by relatives fall below the ordinary price for land.

led to only a slight increase in this manorial system. The farms, called in Denmark principal farms (*curiae principales*), that were run for the nobility and the prelates were not usually very large during the Middle Ages. The land that was apparently cultivated in 1344 on a farm run for the Swedish archbishop seems on the average to have corresponded to four large or eight standard peasant farms. In these circumstances the increase of the land of the nobility and the Church meant an increase in the number of land-tillers but not land-owners among the free agrarian population. The disappearance of the slave class by emancipation had the same effect. In this respect as in others the development in Scandinavia is later than, but in the main the same as, that in the rest of Europe.

We may distinguish several groups in the free, landless agrarian population. But it is not always possible to keep them apart, as the terms used seem ambiguous and were subject to sense-change during the central Middle Ages. The lowest division of this landless population is that of the labourers. Most is known about them from Sweden and Norway. It is clear that they came from the old serf class, and in part carried out the functions of the serfs. They received money wages and food for their work. Cultivation extended very rapidly during this period, and it seems to have been hard to get labour of this kind. We certainly find both Swedish and Norwegian legal provisions intended to facilitate the supply of labourers for the farmers. This can already be seen in a Norwegian law of the thirteenth century. In the laws for the Swedish provinces round Lake Maelare—which were codified from about 1300 onwards—all men and women without fixed abode are required to take service, if it is offered. Just before 1350 this liability had been extended to cover the poorer elements all over the country. After the Black Death, when the lack of labour was naturally felt more strongly, the Norwegian legislation was made more severe; in Norway too at this time work was compulsory.

Above the group of wage labourers we should place those who received for their own use a house and a plot in exchange for liability to do certain work for the landowner. In Denmark, where the cadastres of the fourteenth century contain the best information about their situation, a member of this class was called *gaardsaede* (*inquilinus*). They too must largely have come from the serf class. Their position varied greatly. Sometimes their land was only a few small patches, situated outside the common village land, but sometimes it comprised a small part of this. In a list of the estates and sources of income of the bishop of Roskilde about 1370, the highest figure for the ploughland of an *inquilinus* is 1/8 *marca in censu*, i.e. hardly as large as a peasant farm of minimum size. In a list of the lands of Aarhus Church from the beginning of the fourteenth century, i.e. before the agrarian decline, the ploughland of the *inquilini*—where it existed at all—was considerably less. Their liability to perform day-labour on the landowners' farms varies very much from case to case at both these times; some worked daily, others did two to four days a week according to the time of year. In another respect too the conditions of the *inquilini* differed, both during the beginning of the fourteenth century and about 1370; some paid a fixed fee to the landowner, others did not.

Above the *inquilinus* came the *landbo* (*colonus*, tenant), or—as he was called in Norway—the *leilending*. In the fourteenth century, which is the earliest time when we can determine the position of the *inquilini*, the boundary between them and the tenants is rather vague, as the *inquilini* sometimes paid fees to the landowners, and the tenants sometimes were liable for day-labour. But it is apparent that the tenants had a different position from the *inquilini*, a position exactly determined in law. The tenant system is certainly old in Scandinavia, older than the central Middle Ages, and is already completely developed in the oldest Scandinavian documents. In the Scandinavian laws of the central Middle Ages the tenants are free in all respects. They were equal to the landowning peasants in everything except that they did not own the land they tilled. Like the landowning peasants they were liable for military service, and when this national military organization was replaced by taxes to the crown, they became taxpayers too. The tenants held land that might equally well belong to farmers, nobles, priests, Church organizations, or the crown. On the other hand, at an early period, as appears from certain legal regulations, a noble or a peasant could till land leased from someone else besides his own; he then had a relation to this person corresponding roughly to that of a tenant. The landowner was called the tenant's land-*drott*. He received from the tenant earnest money, called *staedja* or *gipt*, at the beginning of the lease, and an annual fee called *landgille* or *avrad*. This was sometimes paid only in money, sometimes in kind—mostly corn—and money, sometimes only in kind. Conditions in this respect varied from village to village. In the Oestgoeta Law a certain standard annual render was stipulated for an *octonarius*: this included two days' labour to the landowner.[1] The length of the lease differed in various parts of Scandinavia. In Denmark it was for only one year, in Norway usually for three. In the Maelare provinces it was eight years, in Oestergoetland it seems to have been six. But in spite of this—at least in some parts of Scandinavia—under certain conditions the tenant might be given notice by the landowner before the lease expired; and there may be traces of a tenant's having the preference to a renewed contract when the lease expired. In Norway the *leilending* was early able to obtain a lifetime lease to a farm. In

[1] Cf., for *octonarius* above, p. 644.

another respect too, according to the laws, the situation of the tenants varied in various parts of Scandinavia: while in Denmark they owned the farm buildings themselves, in Norway and Sweden these belonged wholly or in part to the landlords, and the tenants were liable to keep them up. In practice, however, the Swedish-Norwegian system seems to have been accepted in Denmark also as early as the thirteenth century. And in Denmark too it became the rule that for certain sums the land-lords placed stock at the disposal of the tenants (*estimatio*).

It has already been said that the actual development blurred the boundary between *inquilinus* and tenant to a certain extent. In the same way the boundary became less definite between the tenant and the *bryte* (*villicus*). The *villici* were the highest class of the landless tillers. They were often quite simply bailiffs of large farms, ecclesiastical or royal perhaps. But there was also another kind of *villicus*: he held of some landowner, farmer or privileged person a farm with its appurtenant land, concluding with his landlord an agreement about the chattels belonging to the farm; the ownership of these was determined by a fixed quota; the landlord owned a certain part, the *villicus* another.[1] A Swedish document shows that in one case the landowner and the *villicus* each owned half the farm chattels. Unlike the tenant, the *villicus* did not have to pay a certain sum to his landlord, fixed for at least the period of the lease. He had to deliver up a certain part of the harvest, usually a third. But the common ownership of the chattels that was established between the landlord and the *villicus* seems to have been discontinued fairly soon. It is still clear after 1300, however, that the *villici* continue to deliver up a certain part of the harvest to the land-lords, while the tenants pay a fixed fee. But during the fourteenth century this distinction disappeared: whereas the *villici* of the bishop of Roskilde in Zealand often paid a fixed yearly fee during the 1370's, during the same period Uppsala Cathedral had on many of its farms tenants who did not pay a fixed fee, but delivered up a third of the harvest instead. Yet the *villici* were certainly still the highest class of the landless cultivators. This is obvious from the fact that the largest farms are regularly distributed to them. As stewards of these lands they often received the work, produce and money for which the *inquilini* were liable.

Besides these principal classes in agrarian society there appear others —in Sweden, for instance, *allmaenningskarl* (tiller of common land), *torpare* (*oppidarius*) and so on. These all seem to be pioneers who have started farming in the woods in common or private ownership.

It is obviously of great significance how far and in what direction the agricultural crisis of the fourteenth century affected the agrarian popula-

---

[1] Cf. above, p. 308.

tion. The development can be studied continuously only in certain areas: about the middle of the fourteenth century there must have been a decline in the population, for the price of tenures drops considerably during the century. And from Church cadastres after the middle of the century we are able to see that a number of smallholdings are waste: the lack of labour is obvious. In Zealand the fees from the tenants' farms of the Church dropped considerably up till the 1370's. In Upland in Sweden, according to a cadastre of the same period, several of the Church lands were newly cultivated. They had been taken into use again. Very often the tillers of these lands handed over a third of the harvest but paid no fixed fee. It would seem as if at this time the tenures included more land than before, even on the average more than was considered proper for a normal-sized peasant's farm about 1300. At the beginning of the fifteenth century, when we can once more have some idea of conditions in Upland, the render had been lowered in many places, though not consistently.[1]

These circumstances, which may be observed in various places in Scandinavia, along with other, parallel phenomena, must mean that the situation of the non-landowning agrarian classes had improved. And no doubt this was so in many respects. But on the other hand, at the same period we come across things that imply a different tendency. The tenants' right freely to give notice of the contract they have made with the landowners was limited in Denmark as early as the fourteenth century: to be freed from the land they have tilled they have to pay an extra fee, called *forlov*. And during the same century there are indications that on the Danish islands the tenants had no right to change their dwelling freely. Here, from the early fifteenth century onwards, there prevailed *vornedskab*, a kind of serfdom, under which the agrarian population was liable to remain in their native places and take over unoccupied farms at need. And this in its turn brought about a state of affairs very reminiscent of pure serfdom, e.g. actual trade in tenants. In Sweden at the beginning of the fifteenth century we can observe a slight tendency in this direction: some provisions of 1414 lay it down that a tenant may not leave his farm until the lease of six years has expired. And in Sweden too we can see that if the tenants' fees in money and kind diminished, on the other hand the work done had increased: according to the above-mentioned regulations a tenant was now liable to do eight days' work a year for his landlord, and one long-distance carting.

The position of the landowning peasants also changed in course of time: the dividing line between them and the tenants became less

---

[1] For conditions in Upland cf. primarily the cadastres of Upsala Cathedral from 1376 and 1471, both unpublished and in the Svenska Riksarkivet, Stockholm.

marked than it had been at an earlier date. As long as the tenants still paid their render to the landowners and tax to the crown, as they did in Denmark in the 1240's, the boundary between owners and non-owners was clear. But already before the end of the thirteenth century, in both Sweden and Denmark, the nobles had also been guaranteed immunity from tax for those farms that were run by tenants—a privilege that the Church too had, or got. The result was that the tenants' former fees to the crown fused with the renders to the landowners. From now on the difference between the tenant and the peasant was that the former paid the landlord, the latter the king. It is true that the peasant had an hereditary right to his land, but when a fixed fee to the crown was attached to it, his position was not really very different from that of the tenant. And it is obvious that in these circumstances the landowning peasant reaped an economic advantage from selling his land to a tax-free noble and afterwards cultivating it as a tenant. It was to check such transactions that the legislation already referred to was introduced.[1]

In other ways also the crown tried to prevent the lands of the tax-free class from increasing too much. For this increase would have caused the income of the crown to decline, and the taxes would have lain especially heavy on those peasants who still owned their land. On various occasions the crown succeeded in enacting that certain lands that had fallen by different means to tax-free institutions and persons should be taken from them and restored to their old owners, the peasants, who of course again became taxpayers. A Swedish instance of this policy, from 1396, is particularly famous: by it farms that had been transferred from tax-paying to tax-free owners after 1363 were restored to the former. From documents that have been preserved we see that the number of farms that had passed into the hands of the privileged classes since 1363 was very large. In 1396 they were made liable to tax under the crown, and thereby restored to landowning peasants.[2]

In spite of the precautions that the crown took in its own economic interests to maintain the tax-paying peasants in their ownership, the fundamental development was that the tax-paying peasantry's share of the land steadily decreased. Unfortunately this development has not been systematically investigated.

It is thought that in Denmark during the first half of the thirteenth century, half or even two-thirds of the land was held by landowning peasants. But when about the middle of the seventeenth century conditions can be properly surveyed, only 10 per cent of the land was in the

[1] Cf. above, p. 645.
[2] For the Swedish restoration of 1396 cf. G. G. Styffe, *Bidrag till Skandinaviens historia*, II, 1864, pp. lx ff. His estimate that in Upland, where there were between 8000 and 10,000 farms and thorps in the sixteenth century, about 1200 were returned to landowning farmers after 1396 (*loc. cit.* p. lxvi) is probably too high.

possession of the peasantry. In considering this last statement, however, it must be kept in mind that the land owned by the peasantry must have diminished very much during the sixteenth and the first part of the seventeenth centuries, the period called the Age of the Nobles in Danish history. In any case, at the end of the Middle Ages the Church was the greatest landowner in Skaane: about a third of the land in the province was in its possession.

It has been said of Norway in the first half of the fourteenth century that the crown owned about 20 per cent of the land, the Church about 25 per cent, the nobility about 15 per cent and the peasantry about 40 per cent. But very many of the peasants' farms must have been tilled by tenants. By 1625 the peasantry's share of the land is said to have decreased to 25 per cent.

No attempt has been made to elucidate the distribution of the land in Sweden. The reasons are simple: there is no material suitable for generalization; and extremely detailed investigation of the available records is required before it can be said whether results for even extremely limited areas are obtainable. But in Sweden too it is usually considered that the landowning peasantry was more numerous during the early Middle Ages than during the first period of modern times. The sources that have several times been cited to illustrate conditions in Upland during the fourteenth century do not conflict with this. It is possible to get a clear survey of the distribution of ownership in Sweden about the middle of the sixteenth century. At this time over 60 per cent of the agrarian population owned its own land. But this proportion, so favourable for the landowning peasantry, is largely due to conditions in Finland and Norrland, which was colonized late. For in both these areas almost all the land was owned by the peasantry. In Dalecarlia too the landowning farmers were in the great majority. But in the rest of the country they were hardly more than a third of the agricultural population. It is typical for the general situation that in the finest agricultural district of Sweden, Oestergoetland, only a seventh of the peasantry owned their land. The Swedish land that was not in the hands of the peasantry was divided fairly equally between the Church and the nobility.

This was the result of the development that took place in Scandinavia during the central and late Middle Ages. In many respects the actual starting-point of the development is uncertain, the development itself is frequently obscure, and frequently only vague outlines can be distinguished. Future research alone can throw light on conditions here, as on many other problems of agrarian history in Scandinavia during the Middle Ages.

CHAPTER VIII

Crisis: From the Middle Ages to Modern Times

I. *Introduction*

CRISIS is the word which comes immediately to the historian's mind when he thinks of the fourteenth and fifteenth centuries. That is, not necessarily a crisis as the word is commonly understood: not regression, absence of creative thought, lack of initiative and audacity, but essentially a break in equilibrium. The end of the Middle Ages was not only a time of decadence but was also one of preparation, of search for new solutions to enduring problems.

This is true in all fields and especially in the economic one, whether it is a question of industry, commerce or agriculture. Needless to say, studies devoted to the economic field during this age of transition (especially on the Continent) are neither numerous nor yet very satisfactory; this is perhaps why this essay offers fewer answers and certainties than questions and hypotheses. But the more the latter unfold, the greater becomes the conviction that from 1300 or 1350 until about 1450 or 1500 the countryside throughout most of the West underwent a difficult time. Its own evolution and the pressure of outside events—not to mention the possible transformation of the climate, which grew both colder and more unstable—forced important and brutal changes upon the two factors of rural life, labour and capital. Consequently, modes in which the two factors combined in earlier periods lost some of their virtue. Did they perhaps also harbour within themselves imperfections which were revealed only gradually, or did they suffer the onset of sclerosis after centuries of wear? They had, nonetheless, to be refashioned, superficially or profoundly, temporarily or permanently, in the light of circumstances, and this could be done only gropingly and at the cost of much friction.

In these conditions, it seems best to describe and explain these 150 years of our village past first by analysing the changes and then by establishing their effects. As we are not able to say much about the changes in the quality of labour, we shall in the first place examine changes in its quantity; in other words, we shall study demographic evolution—its speed, motive power and results. We shall then turn to capital, and as here the most potent influences came from political troubles of every kind, we shall recall the convulsions of the expiring

Middle Ages and unravel their complex economic effects. After quickly touching on political, intellectual and religious life and its principal tendencies, we shall be able to pause to consider repercussions of these different phenomena on the life of the countryside and, since all history is the men who make it, on its inhabitants, be they exploiting proprietors and lords or peasants.

II. *The labour factor: demographic evolution*

In the actual state of our knowledge—or rather of our conjectures—the phenomenon which probably weighed most heavily on agriculture and its fortunes in the fourteenth and fifteenth centuries was a more or less pronounced decline in population. Unfortunately it remains something of a mystery. Although the reality of the decline, except in certain regions, seems incontestable, its details are still hardly understood, its causes debatable and its consequences insufficiently established.

A. *The phenomenon and its variations*

That the declining Middle Ages lived through a reversal of the demographic trend is not now in any doubt. This may not be revealed unequivocally by any general and certain returns. But it is suggested by more restricted documentary sources and numerous indirect manifestations, even if their meaning happens to depend on rather refined interpretations.

The most important of the sources is the hearth-tax. Now it is far from clear what exactly the hearth was, or, on the assumption that it corresponded to a habitation, how many heads it normally comprised, three, four or five. Further, it is not certain from the different lists of taxpayers whether the territorial areas are comparable, the categories of taxpayers identical, or the composition of households constant. What is certain, however, is that the latter changed during periods of political or economic instability, precisely such as those that are considered here. But, allowing for all these uncertainties, it can at least be stated that from one enumeration to another the figures fell more often than not.

Indirect evidence corroborates this statement and the conclusion which it invites. The pressure of expansion which carried peasants from the Latin and Germanic world into the Slavonic lands and its merchants into the heart of Russia and to the shores of the Black Sea slowed down around 1300 or at least 1350; henceforth the horizon was hardly to be extended on land or sea. From the principality of Kiev where the *pustoshi*, the empty lands, disfigured the fourteenth-century countryside, to Aragon or Castile, where at the same moment the landlords unceasingly complained that *se les yerman las terras*, the recession was general. Everywhere the good times of the 'new towns' founded out of nothing on some virgin soil were over. On the contrary many a once-flourishing village presented a picture of desolation: the leprosy of *Dorfwüstungen* gnawed into huge stretches of Central and Northern Europe and attacked, although with less virulence, the more highly developed regions to the east of the Continent and the Atlantic

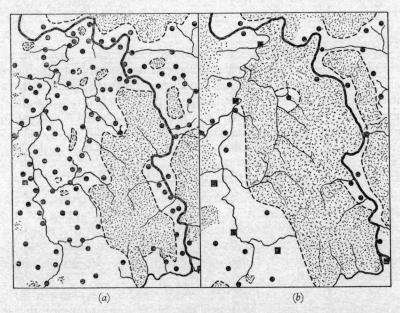

(a)   (b)

FIG. 10. The extension of woodlands in certain regions of Germany in the late Middle Ages: an example in the valleys of the Weser and the Diemel (a) 1290, (b) 1430. ● = villages, ■ = urban centres. (Note that although in 1430 the number of villages has decreased, the urban centres have increased from two to six.)

and Mediterranean countries. Even where all lights were not extinguished, the area of fields shrank. Where for two or three hundred years the question was of nothing but assarts, now appeared references to lands *vagues ou croissent épines et buissons* or *in silvas versae*. After climbing from height to height, life abandoned the far mountains and sank back to the plain: in the Eastern and Western Alps, as in the Massif Central and the Pyrenees, the labourer abandoned his latest and most hardly won conquests. Here early, there later, prices of land and wheat, instead of following a secular rise, contracted. At the same time wages rose, or tended to rise, to the point where in many instances, from Spain to Norway, kings, parliaments and municipal bodies occupied themselves in regulating them, and, sure sign of a labour crisis, the disparity between wage rates diminished. On the estates of the bishop of Winchester the tiler who, in the last decades of the thirteenth century, was paid three times as much as the agricultural day-labourer, in the first half of the fifteenth century earned barely a third more. It would be possible if space allowed to quote other facts, notably the shrinking numbers of small agricultural units or the introduction and spread of clauses in contracts which stipulated as an essential condition that a house of a certain value should be constructed on the holding, and laid down heavy fines for abandoning it.

Are not all these phenomena signs of a demographic retreat? Not necessarily. Other causes can be imagined and in fact have been assigned to all or at least to some of them. A lowering of the temperature or an increase in rainfall could force the least favoured lands out of cultivation, or at any rate make it impossible to sow wheat on them. Improvements in technique, such as a passage from extensive systems of cultivation to regular cereal production under a three-field rotation, could lead to a reorganization of inhabited and cultivated ground at the expense of elevated, sandy, wet, or distant lands, and to a concentration of effort on the richer or more accessible soils, and a regrouping of the population in larger centres. Economic developments (more precisely greater specialization, spread of commerce and mobility of labour and goods) and a crisis in feudal administration resulting from them, could stimulate or favour larger units to the detriment of smallholdings and predispose their occupants to move to the towns. The cupidity of landlords and larger farmers, avid to profit from the high prices of wool, meat and leather, could encourage the enlargement of herds of cattle and, above all, flocks of sheep at the expense of simple peasants and their rights of usage on the common land and could force many of them to give up their customary activities.

These possibilities are not lacking in relevance. They may explain the disappearance of villages and arable fields, *Dorf-* and *Flurwüstungen*, in the less advanced areas or those where the weather was harder. A climatic deterioration probably exercised an effect in Scandinavia, and so may also have done the improvement in cultural methods in Eastern and certain parts of North-Western Germany, the transformation of the economic structure and the urbanization in the Slavonic principalities on the eastern fringe of the Empire and in the Magyar kingdom, and the activities of the rich in Dauphiné. But all these influences had only a limited application. Agricultural technique (and we shall come back to this) improved little in the West during the later Middle Ages. Most centres of population of any importance declined.

Far from pushing out their walls and extending further their suburbs, the towns could barely occupy their existing limits. Toulouse, to take but one instance which has been recently studied, numbered 30,000 inhabitants in 1335, fell to 26,000 in 1385, 20,700 in 1398, 19,000 in 1405 and 8000 in 1430. The small townships (*bourgades*), which for long had been increasing in number, similarly reached their peak. If in Catalonia they maintained and even enlarged their position, elsewhere, in Germany and Brabant, they suffered from competition with the great cities and no more were founded. It has been reckoned that of 79 centres of population of an urban type mentioned in Russian documents of the fourteenth century, only four were new; of 51 places of the same kind enumerated for Mecklenburg in 1900, 35 already existed in 1300 and 46 in 1370. In England wages rose at the same rate in town and country, which is hard to reconcile with a flight from one to the other. The formation of large agricultural units and the extension of pasture was often belated, in the Gâtine as well as in Leicestershire, and seemed to be less the cause of the economic trend than its consequence. What we know of similar and parallel situations elsewhere, such as the economic progress in underdeveloped countries or the difficulties of feudal estates in other places, would not tell us why a certain village in Hungary at the end of the fifteenth century should count 18 peasants in possession of tenancies, 5 landless *inquilini* and 72 deserted holdings, or why between 1346 and 1440–70 the population of the Île de France should have melted away by half.

Thus, despite the theories which have here been rapidly sketched out and commented on, the demographic retreat appears incontestable. But it was not general. Certain countries and places escaped it. Here and there, epidemics, famines or wars struck with less savagery; mining or weaving provided a full-time occupation or at least supplementary earnings; colonization happened to have been belated and the soil still offered possibilities of further reclamation; grazing and industrial cultivation prospered; the needs of local markets or the influx of capital amassed by townsmen permitted an intensification of agricultural production by planting of vines or by costly irrigation works; the law could be specially favourable. All this encouraged births, put a brake on deaths, prevented departures and attracted strangers. While the *Ostsiedlung* slowed up and eventually stopped in the countries where it had first taken place, it continued beyond the Vistula, in Masovia and in Lithuania. If we can rely on an enumeration of rural owners of goods in 1312 and on a return of hearths in 1427, the number of inhabitants of the Tyrol increased in these 115 years by as much as 50 per cent. To judge from sources unluckily not to be accepted without caution, the density of human occupation appears to have risen in the north of Brabant between 1374 and 1437 from 6 to 32 per cent, while —and whatever the exact value of the documents, this divergence between neighbouring regions needs to be underlined—it slightly decreased or barely increased in the south. The same is true of Overyssel, at any rate in the fifteenth century, where some districts—specially pastoral ones—fell back, others progressed, and taken as a whole, population increased continuously so long as the region remained undisturbed (Table 2). In a general way, the countryside of Northern

Table 2. *Index of population movements of Salland (Overyssel)*
Base: 1397 = 100

Year	Total	Without poor families
1429	105·6	105·6
1433	107	109·6
1445	103·9*	110·2
1457	119·5	122·2
1474	122·2	126·1
1490	108·1†	122·6
1520	—	115·4
1601	106·8	117·1

* Some poor families not included in the census.
† Poor families not included in the census.

and Central Italy appears to have filled up steadily, so that gaps in the ranks of the peasantry left by earlier calamities were more than made good and the traces of pestilence of 1347–8 effaced before the turn of 1400. The scrutiny of two surveys drawn up in the middle of the fourteenth century and in 1403 and relating to the *mansi feudales* of the bishop of Pavia in the Appenines, not far from Bobbio, reveals that none of them were at that time abandoned, and gives the impression that between the two dates the number of tenants had actually increased. Other documents confirm this opinion: e.g. lists of soldiers called up in 1386 and 1405 from villages in the country around Bologna: figures in the second list are markedly higher than in the first: 80 instead of 30, 50 instead of 40, etc. Building of farms, deforestation, improvement of the irrigation system, all such works which at that time took place in the basin of the Po, amongst other regions, would, given the medieval technique, be difficult to reconcile with demographic recession. Finally, south of the Pyrenees, while the *repoblacion* of the kingdom of Valencia, the colonization of the Balearics and the conquest of Naples and the Two Sicilies drained Catalonia of many of her nationals (mostly townsmen, it is true), and the civil war of 1462–72 killed others, the number of households in Aragon rose from 42,683 in 1429 to 50,391 in 1496. It is thus possible to discern large areas where, apart from occasional troughs, population at least maintained itself in the later Middle Ages: the easternmost marches of Europe, the extreme north-west of the European plain, Lombardy and part of Christian Spain; all of these areas which were either newer, more dynamic, more peaceful, more urbanized, richer, or more hardworking than others. And in the rest of the West, too, small parts of the country-side resisted the recession to the end or succumbed only for a time. In several English counties, like Sussex, and perhaps in a few corners of Haut-Dauphiné, by the fifteenth century the axe of the settler began again to penetrate the forests, if indeed it had ever been completely idle. In 355 localities of Hainault, in which it is possible to compare the numbers of households in 1365 and 1469, 224 localities lost inhabitants while 115 gained some. Exceptions were thus not lacking of differing importance, permanent or temporary, national, regional or local.

It is precisely the number and variety of the exceptions, combined with the rarity of useful monographs, which renders the outlines of the phenomenon, its onset, intensity and subsidence, uncertain and blurred. For long it has been associated with the Black Death and this position still appears justified for some regions like Basse-Provence, Catalonia, Sweden and Scotland, where the figures for households increase or remain steady and assarts continue right up to 1348. But in most cases the first manifestations are more ancient. The abandoning of marginal lands, falling rents, and rising wages slowly build up towards 1340 in Maurienne and Haut-Dauphiné, 20 or 30 years earlier in Haute-Provence, the Massif Central, the Île de France and England, and before the fourteenth century in Normandy. West of the Vistula the *Drang nach Osten* lost much of its force and petered out probably by 1330. Even where, as in South-Western France, special and notably political considerations prolonged its existence, the movement to create new towns, the so-called *bastides*, practically ceased at this date. The demo-graphic decline thus began in general with the first decades of the fourteenth century.

At first its manifestations were weak. But by 1350, plague and war spread and hastened them. Soon after 1400 it reached its maximum, a maximum which varied of course from one country to another. On the low clay plains of Hainault described by a contemporary as *une terre à blé…fort peuplée*, the total of rural households in 1406 was only 20 per cent, and in 1469 only 5 per cent, less than in 1365. During the same lapse of time in the neighbouring Normandy, ravaged by maurauding soldiers, it collapsed to 60 per cent, and in the wild Massif de l'Oisans its fall accelerated to 46 per cent between 1339 and 1428, then to 26 per cent between 1429 and 1447 and lastly to 21·7 per cent in the three years 1448–50. At this latter date, abandoned villages and fields were too numerous to count in Hesse, Saxony and Brunswick. But to the east and west of these principalities, around Munster, or in Niederlausitz for example, the countryside was entirely free of them. Many factors explain these differences; chemical composition of the soil, scarcity or abundance of rain, rigour of climate, ease of communications or isolation, presence or absence, progress or retreat of agricultural industries and commerce, legal status of the peasantry, the lords' powers of coercion, and many others.

In the second quarter of the new century a revival got under way here and there, for example on the Côte d'Azur. A generation or two later it probably reached Russia, and certainly Saxony, the Erzgebirge, Hainault, Île de France, Poitou, Provence and England. By 1500 it was widespread. The modern world opened with a demographic increase.

B. *Causes: births and deaths, famine, plague and war*

Our uncertainty about the details and early phases of the demographic crisis makes it hard to pinpoint its causes and to answer the central problem: was the fall in the population due to a drop in the birth rate and a rise in the death rate taken together, or solely the consequence of the rise in the death rate?

It is possible, and indeed even probable, that the number of births fell, but it cannot be demonstrated beyond question. In order to prove it unanswerably we should have to draw up genealogical tables of families typical of their class and situation, such as was done some time ago in the famous case of the Rohrbach family of Frankfurt-am-Main; or to re-construct, within a narrow geographical limit, the composition of all families described in documents of all kinds, to classify the results chronologically and then to count the changes in the numbers of infants born before and after 1300 and between 1300 and 1500. Or else we should at least have to establish beyond doubt that the first symptoms of the recession made themselves felt earlier than the other factors which could have influenced the demographic change, particularly the various calamities which increased the death rate, such as the great famine of 1309–18. In the absence of definite knowledge of this kind all we can do today is to put forward the modest theory that such an earlier appearance seems plausible, and to assume that the average figure for the children or for individuals who constituted the household in the fourteenth and fifteenth century, which can be deduced from a few census-like enumerations (specially for a population of an Asiatic type with a high death rate), was lower than the one which would be needed to maintain the population at a constant level. In Freiburg im

Uechtland there was in 1450 1·74 offspring for the old city families, 2·97 for families recently settled in the town and 2·56 for the surrounding country; or 2·43 per household in Toulouse between 1350 and 1450; 3·3, 3·7 and 4·3 in Ypres in 1412, 1437 and 1492, respectively; 3·33 and 3·64 in Basle in 1446 and 1454; 3·61 at Dresden in 1453; 4·14 at Freiburg im Breisgau in 1444. The birth rate could well have been one of the decisive factors.

Table 3. *Population around Neufbourg in the Eure in 1310 and 1954*

Place	Number of households in the parish	Population* in 1310	Population in 1954 in villages†	total
Amfreville	50	175–200	182	429
Barquet	65	227–260	85	327
Epégard	80	280–320	24	236
Feuguerolles	76	266–304	138	138
Graveron-Sémerville	30	105–120	62	193
Iville	47	164–188	331	336
Les Authieux	40	140–150	116	134
Le Thuit-Signol	60	210–240	252	503
Le Troncq	85	297–340	131	131
La Neuville-du-Bosc	66	231–264	159	315
S. Nicolas-du-Bosc	40	140–160	93	161
S. Opportune-Bosc	72	262–288	87	149
Vitot	80	280–320	166	295
Vitotel	7	24–28	—	—
Totals	798	2801–3192	1826	3347

* The household is estimated at 3·5–4 persons.
† The reference is to the *Chef-lieu*, i.e. the principal site of the village, and not to its outlying parts.

But this only poses the problem in another way. If we agree that people had fewer children, we would still like to know why. The explanation which seems most acceptable at the present time is that it was because there was a relative scarcity of land. It is very hard to calculate or even to estimate the total population of the later Middle Ages; even with the help of that unique document, the Return of parishes and households in France of 1328, historians give such widely differing estimates for the population of France as 15, 22 or even 35 millions. All we can say is that the total population of Western Europe was very much smaller than it is today. In 1365, when it is true the demographic decline had already begun, the density of population in

Hainault was 28 persons to the square kilometre as against 263 today. But men and property were very unevenly distributed. Men conglomerated on the good soils; they did not wish to move to less populated places or to the towns, or perhaps, being prisoners of the feudal system, they were not able to do so. At any rate where they congregated they were thick on the ground. In France, the most populated country at that period, many districts supported as many, or very nearly as many, inhabitants as at the beginning of the twentieth century. Such districts were the region of Laon, the neighbourhood of Neufbourg (Table 3) and Beaumont le Roger, the hillsides around Bordeaux and the heights of Comminges; even in the Oisans region there were, in 1339, 2828 households, or about 13,000 people, compared with 13,805 people living there in 1911.

This was also the case in many places in England. Around Elloe, in the Fenland, settlement was almost as dense in 1260 as in 1951. Other parts were not so overcrowded, but most peasants had no more than a hovel, a garden and a small patch of a field. In spite of three centuries of clearing the waste, the average area of holdings was no larger; the process could barely keep abreast of the rising human tide. The village

Table 4. *Extent of holdings in three localities in the region of Namur in* 1289

Number of tenures

Area in *bonniers*★	Total figures			Percentage of total		
	Flavion	Haltinne	Viesville	Flavion	Haltinne	Viesville
20+	6	4	1	10·9	4·8	1·1
15+	4	—	2	7	—	2·1
14	—	—	—	—	—	—
13	1	1	1	1·8	1·2	1·1
12	—	4	2	—	4·8	2·1
11	2	2	—	3·6	2·4	—
10	—	3	1	—	3·6	1·1
9	3	3	—	5	3·6	—
8	4	2	1	7	2·4	1·1
7	5	2	1	9	2·4	1·1
6	3	9	4	5·5	10·8	4·3
5	3	3	6	5·5	3·6	6·6
4	3	5	6	5·5	6·1	6·6
3	8	11	8	14·6	13·2	8·7
2	3	7	10	5·5	8·4	10·9
1	5	13	25	9	15·7	27·1
less than 1	5	14	24	9	16·9	26·1

★ 1 *bonnier* equals 94 ares.

of Haltinne near Namur possessed in 1289 as many *terres de sartes* as *terres mansales*, but smallholdings there were as numerous as in Flavion which had none but *terres mansales*. Table 4 gives details of holdings on these two places together with the small commercial and administrative town of Viesville, and these agree with the results of researches in Flemish and French Flanders, in England and in Scotland.

Could a man live on as little as 1, 2 or even 3 hectares? No, not even if he worked the soil by hand and extracted from it a greater return than the lords did from their demesnes. Could he wrest new tillage from the forest? Hardly, for the forests that remained were essential to the poor and, besides, their organized exploitation was bringing an increasing return and diversity in industrial districts and even elsewhere. In 1297, well-grown woodlands feeding the metallurgical 'factories' in the south of the county of Namur were let out at 5 *sous* a year per *bonnier* (more or less one hectare), while fields in the same area fetched no more than 3 *sous* in rent. In 1350, in the agricultural region around Tournai, the annual income from the woods of Breuze and the farm of Wissempierre was 75 *livres* plus *lingne* for heating from 72 *bonniers*, and 93 *livres* from 90 *bonniers*, respectively. At the same time, in the north-west of Germany lords were attempting to suppress the rights of usage in forests or to restrict them to certain parts of the woodland and to free the rest from peasant rights, so as to be able to regulate cutting or to graze flocks in them. So there could be no question of new clearings, and indeed assarting was often expressly forbidden. The arable area could consequently not be extended and, worse still, the bad lands which had been taken into cultivation under demographic pressure became exhausted. In the Harz mountains, Thuringia and Westphalia, many place names ending in -*rode*, -*hagen*, -*hain*, -*feld*, -*hausen*, -*heim*, vanished from documents. Other lands, formerly fertile, were impoverished for lack of fallow periods, or manure, or a well-thought-out rotation of crops. Others again fell victim to soil erosion and dessication, the natural consequences of large-scale deforestation. All these lands were lost to cultivation. How, in such conditions, could new mouths be fed, or more married couples be provided for?

Could they have been fed and provided for by intensifying cultivation and making use of technical improvements, as had sometimes been done in the thirteenth century? But the very mention of more intensive cultivation suggests an alternative answer to our problem—an answer which takes a stage further one aspect of the solutions already expounded: the fall of population in the last analysis was no more than the fruit of a vicious economic system in which properties and income were maldistributed, and which encouraged people to consume and not to invest. Left to itself, agriculture forms little new capital which proprietors can employ in improvements which are often very costly. And such was the medieval social system that the little that was saved from consumption was deflected by the clergy and nobility into unproductive expenditure. The abbeys maintained at their principal seats and on their farms excessively large *familia*, and the monks themselves not infrequently lived in great style. The 46 monks at the abbey of Saint Martin de Tournai in 1289 kept 40 servants and 57 horses. The lay lords were even more prodigal and ostentatious. The more the English barons extracted from their estates, the more they enlarged their castles and expanded their personal households. In 1420-1 Richard Beauchamp, Earl of Warwick, consumed £800 of his income of £3000 in building work, while in the same year the Duke of Bedford took with him on his journey his chancellor, his treasurer, 24 esquires and 42 other persons; from 1446 to 1453 the Percys obtained £132 annually from their Sussex estates which they expended on 39 'ordinary' and 66 'extraordinary' payments to retainers. Thus little or no investment could be expected from the lords: in 1364 the Hospitallers of Poët in Provence devoted to it only 1 per cent of the gross profit of their *commanderie*. None could be expected from the peasants who had no surplus income available. For holdings were small, returns insufficient, the possibility of stock-raising reduced by clearings in the forest, charges heavy and often, where the law was ill-defined as in England, increased with the ability of the sitting tenant to pay more. At the beginning of the fourteenth century, entry fines—called *lods et ventes* on the Continent—rose at Taunton on the estates of the bishops of Winchester to £10 and sometimes £20 per virgate, which after deducting rent and other debts produced an income of £3, or even £2, sterling. Theoretically it would have been in the peasants' interest to sow seed more densely. They would have harvested proportionately more. But where could they have found the extra seed corn? The opportunities for increasing production in any direction were very slim.

Other factors could have played a part in reversing the demographic trend. One such factor, which would have set in motion a chain reaction of others, would have been the shortage of bullion, the existence and causes which will be discussed further. From this shortage would have followed a fall in prices, a more than proportionate reduction in profits, a slackening of the spirit of enterprise, the abandoning of unprofitable soils, and a shrinking of the means of subsistence. Another factor was the succession of bad harvests during the second decade of the fourteenth century: this might have administered a psychological shock and convinced the peasants of the advantage, indeed the absolute necessity, of reducing the number of their offspring, although, it is true, there is no evidence of 'birth control' in the later

Middle Ages, except maybe by the leading families of the nobility or urban patriciate, who produced markedly fewer children during the period. A reduction in the marriage rate might also have had an effect: we know how few marriages there were in the Rohrbach family which was referred to above, and how legislation in Italian towns, like Lucca and Siena, assumed that the number of marriages was falling. Eventually, matrimonial habits perhaps changed, as when Aeneas Silvius Piccolimini noticed the growing difference in the ages of spouses in Vienna in 1440.

Theories to account for a falling birth rate—scarcity of arable land, failure to invest, scarcity of money, new social habits—abound, and how satisfactory it would be if we could know which one to embrace, or which of the factors was the first to appear and to give impetus to the movement. But for this purpose we should have to date each factor, and it is unlikely that this could ever be done. This failure, however, is not wholly unmitigated, for none of these tendencies could have worked in isolation, but were probably complementary to each other. From the very moment when one phenomenon released the demographic regression, all the others came into play and their action and mutual reaction combined to give yet further impetus to the tendency. Thereafter, all the forces concerned had a common denominator, and moved in the same direction, which is clearly seen in the West in every field of activity from the end of the thirteenth century, and was aggravated in the following century by the great catastrophes. Everywhere the life force ebbed, the spirit of invention atrophied, the desire to undertake responsibility and risk flagged and complaisance and love of routine took their place. In this climate, which one scholar has compared to that of the later Roman Empire, how could the birth rate be kept up, or natural barriers to the growth of population be surmounted?

The importance of the fall in the birth rate must not of course be exaggerated. The later centuries of the Middle Ages suffered a heavier rise in mortality. Litanies still recited today in Christian countries recall Death's executioners: *fama, pestis, et bellum*. Famine, Pestilence and War were indeed adversaries to be dreaded by a world so near the margin of existence.

Famines were inevitable. Monoculture of corn was practised widely and alternative foodstuffs were lacking if corn should fail. Town authorities were afraid of incurring financial loss and lacked granaries and capital, and thus stored too little grain, especially at the beginning of our period. Medium- and long-distance trade was not unknown; Lübeck possessed 35 to 40 *Kornhäuser* in the early years of the fourteenth century, and in the course of the century Baltic corn sometimes penetrated up the valley of the Lys. Froissart records in 1359 that *il faisait si chier temps parmi le royaulme de France et si grant famine y couroit ... que, se blés et avainnes ne leur venissent de Haynaut et de Cambresis, les gens morussent de faim en Artois, en Vermandois et en l'evesquiet de Laon et de Rains.* But this traffic was not sufficiently developed to make good at reasonable prices a grain deficit of some importance. Moreover, it was slow and could not be quickly set in motion. A whole year of frightful scarcity elapsed before the magistrates of Flemish towns decided in the spring of 1317 to buy wheat which had been available in Mediterranean countries since July 1316. Above all, speculation and hoarding upset the balance of supply and demand. The historian Hocsem, who lived through those terrible years in Brabant, recalls that new cemetries were consecrated because there was no longer space in the old ones, and adds that corn was not entirely lacking, but that merchants preferred to send it to the coast where they obtained a better price. In August 1473, in Carpentras an enquiry conducted after a harvest failure found—and the evidence of those concerned was evidently near the truth—that half the Christian households had flour for four months while two-thirds of Jewish households had flour for nine. In such conditions one bad harvest was a serious matter, but two or three consecutive bad harvests were catastrophic for urban communities and also for the *manouvriers* or cottagers, the bulk of the peasantry, who possessed but a small plot of arable land and could only survive if the return from it was good.

After 1300, the bad seasons seemed to multiply. Whether this was due to a worsening of the climate and an increase in rainfall or not, the famines followed each other with increasing frequency. The first gripped the north of Europe during the second decade of the fourteenth century. Starting in various countries between 1309 and 1315 it lasted from three to five years. An Alsatian chronicler asserts that it reached such frightful proportions that corpses were cut down from the gibbet and eaten. Reality may have been less nightmarish, but it remained terrifying. 10 per cent of the population of Ypres, a workers' town, and 5·5 per cent of that of Bruges, died of starvation. Other times of scarcity, general or local, followed, whose duration and intensity varied according to whether they were due to two, three or four cold, wet or dry years. From the wealth of material one example can be quoted: in Languedoc, whose soil is not less, and if anything more, productive than that of the rest of the country taken as a whole, there were no less than eleven periods of scarcity in the course of 200 years. Seven of the eleven crises occurred in the fourteenth century and four in the fifteenth. In time famines appeared less frequently in southern France and in the rest of western Europe. The factors which contributed to this amelioration were the fall in population, a more far-sighted policy on the part of urban authorities who built large grain repositories, progress in navigation and specially the increasing use of vessels of large tonnage, like the Hanseatic *Kogge*. But scarcities never completely disappeared. Right up to the end of the Middle Ages food shortages exercised a potent influence on population trends. Deaths from starvation were the direct result, but a defective food supply which undermined public health and thus prepared the way for epidemics was equally to blame. In the region of Toulouse, as well as in the valleys of the Rhine and the Arno, the years before the first great outbreak of pestilence were years of bread shortage.

The middle of the fourteenth century marked the most violent explosion of plague. Before then outbreaks of infectious disease had occurred here and there, but the Black Death, a combination of bubonic and pneumonic plagues, was much more terrible. It first took a hold in Italy in 1347 and within two years, attended by torrential rains and supported by famine, it swept across almost the whole of Christian Europe. Either by good luck or because the population was better fed and thus more resistant, some regions, such as the greater part of the Low Countries, the surroundings of Metz, considerable areas of Franconia, Pomerania, Prussia, Bohemia, Silesia, and perhaps other places yet to be revealed by research, escaped. And even in regions where it was most triumphant, it struck irregularly and passed over certain localities. In the spring of 1349, it carried away 74 people in Horwood, while in next-door Shipton and Greenborough only five died in the former and eight in the latter. But its total effect was devastating in the towns. In Florence where, by chance, evidence of the fate of three merchant families has come down to us, one lost seven out of 14 children, the second five out of nine, and the third five out of 12; in Bordeaux 12 of the 20 canons of Saint-Seurin succumbed; in Hamburg 18 out of 40 butchers, 12 out of 34 master bakers, 27 out of 56 municipal officials, and 16 out of 21 members of the council fell victim to the disease. The countryside suffered equally: 615 out of 1800 inhabitants of Givry in Burgundy disappeared in four months; 35 out of 50 tenants of Crowland Abbey in the Cambridgeshire village of Oakington perished, 20 out of 42 in Dry Drayton, 33 out of 58 in Cottenham; the mortality in the Hundred of Farnham, Surrey, was fifteen times normal in 1348–9 and ten times normal in 1349–50; two-thirds of the inhabitants of Witney in Oxfordshire and Downton in Hampshire died, and one-third of Brightwell in Berkshire; in the mountains to the south of Salzburg, around Pongau, 24 per cent of the holdings relapsed to the waste between 1340 and 1392, 16 per cent were joined to neighbouring holdings and 26 per cent changed hands. In short, when the plague subsided, the population was reduced by 50 or 60, or even 70 per cent in some places, by 15 to 20 per cent in others, and on the average by 30 per cent. Modern historians agree with Froissart on this latter figure, for his saying *la maladie qui courut dont bien la tierce partie du monde mourut* is well known.

A reaction followed according to Levasseur's Law. Other chroniclers tell us that the survivors hurried to get married and that women became astonishingly fecund, frequently giving birth to triplets. In fact the Curé of Givry blessed 42 couples between 14 January and 24 February 1349, whereas in the previous year between 6 January and 31 December he had not conducted a single marriage service. In this way the gaps would before long have been made good, but, since many children had also perished, a generation later there was another falling off of births. The plague itself, of course, was by no means extinguished, and on several occasions its ravages were renewed. One such outbreak was unloosed in England in 1361–2, and writers of the time described it as the 'second plague' or *la mortalité des enfauntz*, which confirms what has just been said of the effects of the Black Death. Then again in 1368–9, in which year 13·4 per cent of the incumbents of the Diocese of York, 11 per cent of those of the archdeaconries of Lincoln and Stowe, and 23·5 per cent of those of Leicester and North-ampton, died instead of the usual 3·4 or 4 per cent. It struck again in 1374. Then followed a period in which it was less conspicuous, when it attacked only small areas, mostly towns. But there were violent outbreaks, as in Florence in 1400 and in Bruges in 1438, when 20 per cent of the population was decimated, and in Pavia in 1485, when 5000 out of 12,000 were killed. And in some places it was recurrent—London had twenty in the course of the fifteenth century, Frankfurt eighteen, and Hamburg ten. It made its influence felt also in the countryside by swelling the numbers of immigrants to the towns. Thus, it was ever-present in people's minds, who for instance in drawing up property contracts provided for the possibility that the plague would drive them out of the country. In 1459 the owner of a butcher's shop in Caylus made provision for such an eventuality, and in 1471 the proprietor of a dyeworks in Saint-Antonin, another town in Quercy, did the same. The Middle Ages lived out its time in the 'shadow of the epidemic', as one scholar puts it.

Nor was fourteenth-century Europe spared war, and this scourge was also a killer. But it killed many fewer than the plague. The battles of the time put relatively small forces in the field and the looting and violence was less murderous than contagious disease. Study of the effects of the *Drang nach Osten* has, however, revealed that on the eastern marches of Europe, at least in Ukermark and Prussia, the fall in population was set in motion by the breakdown of peace. And recent research on some estates in older parts of Europe, like the estate of Ouges in Burgundy, has confirmed the close correlation between demographic swings and military campaigns. The reason for this

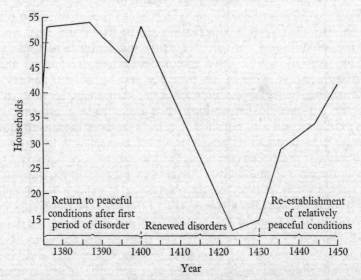

FIG. 11. Military operations and numbers of households in Ouges, Burgundy. (During the three first quarters of the fourteenth century epidemics and wars had reduced the population of Ouges by 30 per cent.)

connexion is simple. Warlike activities did not affect the size of the population solely through actual deaths. A document of 1469 clearly states that there were other, more serious, consequences. On that date, the Receiver of Subsidies of Hainault explains that the number of households in the county had fallen *tant par riches gens qui se sont boutté à sceureté es bonnes villes comme par autres qui se sont rendus fugitif parce qu'ilz ont esté mengiez et ne ont peu fournir les paiemens qu'ilz devoient à leurs maistres*. The troops put peasants to flight, and thus the regions into which they moved and which their presence threatened became depopulated. They also ruined and laid waste the occupied places. These last consequences were similar to those of other disasters like floods and the collapse of dams; they were as crushing as those of famines and epidemics, but they mainly concern capital and are more relevant to the section which follows.

All things considered, the fall in population was probably triggered off by a fall in the birth rate. But this fall did not reach a dangerous level until scarcities and, above all, the ensuing epidemics raised the death rate. It is also probable that it was accompanied by a 'structural' change in population. The catastrophes chiefly removed the least resistant and least productive elements, that is, children and old people. The figures for the municipal council of Hamburg already quoted are in this respect eloquent. This change moderated some of the consequences of the fall but aggravated others. And, unhappily for the rustic population, it was these aggravating consequences which concerned them most.

c. *Consequences: volume of production, wheat and commodity prices, wage levels, land values*

Some of the consequences of a falling population can be assumed *a priori*: a reduction in the area sown for corn, a fall in its price, a rise in wages, a drop in the value of arable land, and others, e.g. an increase in the cost of non-agricultural products, become evident only through the study of documents.

When total population began to sag, one would normally expect the area of fields to contract. This is in fact what happened in the fourteenth century, but to a somewhat limited and insufficient degree. Land was abandoned, the more so because under the pressure of increasing density of population less favourable soils had been brought into cultivation. Entire settlements were given up. Little can be said in this connexion about France, for it is hard to distinguish the effects of population changes from those of war, but the story of the German countryside at the end of the Middle Ages is full of the *Wüstungen* to which reference has been made earlier in this chapter. In the localities which were completely deserted, some of the fields might be partly annexed by the neighbouring holdings, but more often they returned to pasture and scrub. And in most of the settlements that survived, smokeless hearths and tenantless holdings were common. Studies which have been directed to this problem have produced impressive figures. Two alone will suffice to demonstrate the principle. The first is a concrete example: in 1419, 6561 *manses* of the Teutonic Order out of 31,525 were unoccupied, let us say 21 per cent. Less than twenty years later, this proportion had risen to 40 per cent in some commanderies, and to 50 or even 80 per cent in others. Our second figure gives an overall view. The two last centuries of the Middle Ages witnessed the extinction of one-quarter of the places which had been inhabited in 1300 within the actual confines of Germany. Other detailed researches have produced similar results for many regions in Scandinavia. So far as we can judge at the present moment, in other countries the phenomenon was not so spectacular, probably because it was less violent. It entailed the disappearance of villages and hamlets in marginal areas, such as in the Alps, in the heart of Spain, in various parts of England, but it revealed itself mostly in the rapid increase in vacant lands. Even in the Low Countries which had been spared by the great plague of 1348 there were now frequent references to fields *en tries et vaukes*.

But this retreat in the arable area did not follow directly that of population, and, more important, even in those places where it was most pronounced it was still less than proportionate to the fall in population. We shall see later that the price of corn was fairly buoyant in most countries up to about 1370. Logically, the cultivated area itself was also maintained until that date. Further, during the rest of the fourteenth and in the course of the fifteenth centuries, these prices did not lose their absolute and relative value permanently: deficient harvests often pushed them up for one or more years. These intermittent periods of dear grain were not the only influences which prevented the fall in corn sowings. Country dwellers always had to assure themselves of cash balances with which to pay rents and taxes. They were also afraid to find themselves short of bread if the harvest failed, and this spectre of famine also haunted town dwellers. These two factors worked together to prevent arable acreages from falling. But the most powerful brake of all was undoubtedly the traditional obstinacy of the countryman, buttressed by the precarious condition of many peasants between 1300 and 1325, and by the ambitions of others. No one who knows peasants could doubt that, given a free choice, their response to a fall in prices would inevitably be to increase rather than reduce the size of their fields. They earned less and therefore they attempted to sell more, and in order to do so they took over at least some of the lands freed by the fall in the numbers of their fellow-cultivators. Besides, many had only a few acres to begin with, and some indeed no more than a cottage. Here was a chance for the former to enlarge their holdings and the latter to acquire one. How could they fail to make the most of this opportunity and to become settlers on this or that vacant holding providing they had the livestock and equipment and could lay their hands on it under reasonable conditions? At the other end of the scale there were the larger farmers whose forebears had been gradually rising since the thirteenth century and who tilled 40 or 50 acres, or more. They, too, took the opportunity to extend their lands. Such men were those 'free tenants' of the bishop of Durham, whom the Halmote Courts accused of provoking and aiding the flight of serfs in order to gain their lands for themselves. Indeed, if they were not put off by the rise in agricultural wages, they seized their opportunities even more avidly than their poorer fellows.

Everywhere—and we shall return later to this point—the demographic recession was accompanied by an increase in the average extent of holdings and in the number of the larger ones. In this way the disequilibrium between supply and demand for corn, and the tendency of the latter's price to fall, was re-inforced. But what could simple rustics know about supply and demand and economic trends? Furthermore, was this trend so easy to perceive? Was it not to a large extent masked by the disordered movement of prices?

Indeed, the movement of prices during this period shows two marked characteristics: on the one hand, instability, on the other hand, a tendency, both absolute and relative, to decline which manifested itself more or less clearly in different markets. Even today corn is a commodity whose demand is most inelastic. It was much more so in the fourteenth and fifteenth centuries when foodstuffs were less varied and substitutes hardly existed. Some regions regularly produced or imported several different bread grains which its inhabitants appreciated: these grains did not always behave similarly in the same climatic conditions, and because of this they were able to a certain extent to compensate for each other. This is doubtless the explanation of the inverse correlation of prices of wheat and rye exhibited at Strasbourg at the beginning of the fifteenth century. From a high level—an average of 4·92 gold francs per hectolitre—between 1391 and 1400, the price of wheat fell to 4·00 between 1401–10 and then to 3·76 from 1411 to 1420; the price of rye on the other hand, low at the beginning— 2·65—rose during the same period to 2·72 and 3·11. But possibilities of this kind were limited so that price levels were sensitive to small changes in supply. At the end of the Middle Ages, from 1441 to 1450, years unscarred by any great disasters in the region, corn was sold at Albi successively (if one adopts as the base of 100 the average figure for 1431–40), at 20, –, 111, 37, –, 19, 21, 11, 24, 20 and at Frankfurt-am-Main at 80, 67, 72, 63, 75, 87, 73, 63, 67, 58. The amplitude of fluctuations from 11 to 111, and even from 58 to 87, cannot be described as small. And one can imagine what it could become when climatic conditions were unfavourable or when war and pestilence interrupted agricultural activity. Prices would suddenly rise, only to fall precipitously a few months later.

These repeated changes were cut across by a fundamental phenomenon which to a certain extent they conceal from view and the full effect of which they damp down: the collapse of the price of corn in money and of its value in terms of other commodities. Several factors helped to draw it down. To begin with there was a superabundance of supply. Population decreased and, what was worse, the proportion of consumers shrank in relation to the producers of agricultural products.

General disasters removed, and continued to choose as victims, the least resistant individuals, old people, children, the sick, in short all those who did not work or whose output was small. Moreover, the country-side was less affected than the towns, and as a result—and we shall return to this question later—the towns probably drew more heavily upon the population of the countryside. Those, however, who were attracted to the towns were most probably artisans, day labourers, or *bordiers* toiling away on their poor patches of ground, rather than the better-provided peasants. A substantial reduction in arable area was therefore necessary. People resigned themselves to it half-heartedly, and, as we have just shown, the reduction was slow and insufficient. Normal harvests were therefore able to produce an over-abundance. Hence prices had to fall and, in accordance with King's law, or rather with its reciprocal calculated by Jevons and Bouniatian, because of the inelastic demand they fell more than proportionately to the excess of grain, i.e. very heavily indeed. They did so all the more because another economic law intervened: the law of diminishing returns. Wherever a choice was possible, less favourable ground was given up. It can be said of course that this tendency should have expressed itself in increased yield per seed, and that not much of any such increase can be found in documents. The argument is, however, hardly relevant, mainly because surviving documents relate to the yields of manorial demesnes which contained very few fields of inferior quality. The marginal costs of production thus fell, which caused or at least helped prices to fall. A third factor worked in the same direction: as has been shown for Forncett, the holdings most heavily burdened with charges were the first to be deserted. On this estate in Norfolk the landlord was forced between 1358 and 1378 to take back 18 of 25 holdings subject to 'week work', and of which the annual rent was a minimum of 24d. against an average of 10·75d. for the rest. Lastly, in so far as it operated and was not compensated by devaluations, the scarcity of money, which will be discussed together with wars, helped to push prices down.

A fall in prices: so far so good. It is not, however, enough to arrive at this *a priori* conclusion by deduction alone. It is essential to find documentary proof and to build up a clear picture of its original date, its duration, phases and extent. To do this we must dispose of three sorts of evidence. First, we need series of statistics which are at once homogeneous, complete and numerous. They should each be derived from a single type of text so as not to confuse, for instance, purchase prices with selling prices, or a free price with an imposed or customary price. They should be extracted from documents abundant enough for the averages to be truly significant. They should cover the whole period in question and every year, or at any rate most of the years, in it, because when only some years are given those particular years may turn out to be years of crisis. They should include many markets and preferably those attended by the mass of producers rather than the ones in large towns supplied by merchants, for the grain trade was not sufficiently developed to level out price movements at different places and to impose everywhere prices current in the more important markets. In 1338 in the Southern Alps of France, where, it is true, the mountains favoured an enclosed and traditional way of life, the same quantity of grain was worth 25 *sous* in one place, but 36, 48, 56, 60 and even 80 *sous* in other places. Secondly we need precise knowledge of the duration and intensity of what one of the fathers of economic history has called 'elementary occurrences' (*Elementare Ereignisse*), those non-economic factors which were capable of affecting prices. This information would allow us to eliminate from our statistical tables all traces of such variables. And lastly, we need indices of the cost of living to which we can relate our statistical series so as to establish the changes not only in grain prices but in the purchasing power of grain in terms of other commodities.

The reality is very wide of this mark. On the one hand we have a few tables, some satisfactory, some less so, relating almost exclusively to large centres or estates, not purged—could they ever be?—of the various *pointes erratiques*. The most we are able to do is to convert the data into equivalent weights of silver, not into purchasing power. On the other hand we have some fragmentary information of little use except to confirm what we know already from other sources. This is all we possess; but little as it is, it may be sufficient to establish that in the later Middle Ages most of the West experienced a fall in the value of grain and to enable us to discover more or less clearly the essential features of the fall.

We know least about the beginnings. This is because many of the statistical collections available up till now do not go back to the first half of the fourteenth century. Only Rogers's and Beveridge's researches provide fairly reliable information for this period. As is shown in Table 5, which is based on them, the price of corn began to decline in England from the third decade. Other original evidence, not reproduced here for lack of space, permits us to fix the precise date at 1325. The trend was perhaps—thanks to recent investigations for the Île de France, we dare to say, probably—the same, at least at some points, on the other side of the Channel. But in any case if there was, and where there was, a fall it did not continue beyond 1348.

From 1348, for the next 20 to 25 years, prices remained at a high level. Figures relating to England or worked out for Frankfurt-am-Main clearly show this. The averages calculated by d'Avenel for the

Table 5. *Price of a quarter of wheat in England in the fourteenth century*

Period	s.	d.	Grains of pure silver
1301–1310	5	7¼	1387
1311–1320	7	10¼	1945
1321–1330	6	11⅝	1726
1331–1340	4	8¾	1170
1341–1350	5	3⅜	1303
1351–1360	6	10⅝	1705
1361–1370	7	3¼	1779
1371–1380	6	1¼	1511
1381–1390	5	2	1279
1391–1400	5	3	1300

Table 6. *Price of a hectolitre of rye at Frankfurt from* 1350 *to* 1400
(adjusted to the denier current in 1360)

Period	Deniers
1351–1360	147
1361–1370	213
1371–1380	146
1381–1390	111
1391–1400	129

whole of France express a similar situation. Admittedly they have been obtained by a questionable method, but they are corroborated on this point by two royal ordinances fixing the weight of bread. In the first, John the Good laid down that in his reign the price of a *setier* of wheat, the Paris measure, could vary between 24 and 40 *sous*. In the second, in 1372, Charles V reduced these limits to 8 and 24 *sous* and added: *de présent le blé est L bon marché et pourra être L aussi bon et meilleur dans les temps a venir*. At Genoa, too, whose position was a special one, prices, as far as one can rely on some scattered facts, held up as elsewhere, until 1370–5.

Several circumstances explain this state of affairs. Some were general, namely, plagues and inclement weather, recurrent and un-relenting during this quarter of a century, a rise in wages which carried up with it costs of production and the purchasing power of artisans and day labourers, and a similar trend in industrial prices.

With the later of these dates the fall began again everywhere, and except for recoveries whose length and intensity varied from region to region, it continued for at least a century. There were exceptions, Normandy amongst other places, where prices were stimulated until

1450 by the occupation, and collapsed after the departure of the English (Table 7). But these were exceptions to the general rule.

Table 7. *Price, in sous, of a setier of wheat at Neufbourg from 1395 to 1455*

1397	20	1450	30
1405	27	1452	15
1437	60	1454	12
1445	40		

Nevertheless the force of the movement and its outward form differed in different countries. In most the fall was absolute and steep, in others it was relative and apparently less serious.

Figures demonstrate better than words the speed and the phases—the same speed but different phases—of the movement in the countries where the fall was steep. The two columns on the left of Table 8 continue those of Tables 5 and 6; the next two are based on the researches of Hanauer and Usher; the last one derives from the rates of conversion fixed yearly by the count of Flanders's officials to permit payment in silver for rents in kind; rates which it is probable equate at least crudely with the fluctuations of the markets of Bruges, Ghent, Courtrai, Alost and Rupelmonde.

Table 8. *Prices of wheat and rye in the fifteenth century as a percentage of the average price of 1401 to 1410*
(in units of silver weight)

Period	England (wheat)	Frankfurt (rye)	Strasbourg (wheat)	Albi (wheat)	Flanders (wheat)
1391–1400	90	96	—	—	—
1401–1410	100	100	100	100	100
1411–1420	81	83	89	318	75
1421–1430	80	74	94	389	92
1431–1440	102	112	66	240	106
1441–1450	77	78	94	145	74
1451–1460	81	100	95	64	77
1461–1470	74	53	66	42	56
1471–1480	59	50	56	55	65
1481–1490	70	92	103	74	100
1491–1500	57	78	88	48	71

To these facts taken from the very heart of the medieval West could be added others relevant to its peripheral areas, such as Norway or Poland.

As the preceding statistical tables show, a recovery took place everywhere between 1481 and 1490. It persisted in certain places, in Poitou, for instance, where a hectolitre of wheat sold for 0·40 *franc-or* from 1461 to 1472, rose to 0·70 from 1473 to 1486, then to 0·75 from 1487 to 1514. In this province, and probably in others in France, the long-term tendency was thus reversed before 1500. But elsewhere the upturn registered from 1481 to 1490 was not maintained, and the decline did not definitively give way to a rising trend until the first or second decade of the sixteenth century, as in Antwerp, or even indeed until the fourth or fifth decade, as at Frankfurt.

It should now be unnecessary to underline the extent of the movement in this first group of countries and regions. The figures given above give a good enough idea of the movement. They make it possible, for instance, to calculate that in Frankfurt the ten-year average price of rye fell from 100 between 1351 and 1400, to 81 between 1401 and 1450, and to 68 between 1451 and 1500. These figures agree with others, especially those which Grund has established for Lower Austria, and according to which the price of wheat fell in that country from the fourteenth century to the fifteenth century by 35 per cent.

In a second group of markets, after the end of the fourteenth century, prices behaved differently. At Toulouse, apart from two feverish outbursts, they oscillated around the same level. At Namur (see Fig. 12), in Paris, in Milan, at Dubrovnik (Ragusa), in Bohemia, they did not change either. But in some of these places like Paris, prices remained stable but low. In most of them, they kept their nominal level, but declined in relative value and in purchasing power: for while grain prices remained relatively constant, other prices, particularly those of wages and industrial goods, rose. The term 'price scissors' is the graphic image created in our own time to describe this phenomenon, and we shall use it again later.

However, even if the winter grains, wheat, rye and spelt, were of fundamental importance, other crops also mattered. On demesnes as on small holdings, landlords and peasants sowed spring cereals, fodder, leguminous and industrial crops, tended vines, kept farmyard animals and raised cattle. We ought to know the values of all these products and how they fluctuated between 1300 and 1500, but scarcity of evidence and shortage of space obliges us to keep to brief generalities. The curves traced by corn and other products of arable farming broadly defined and those traced by animal products sometimes diverge from each other. This, as we have already noticed in the case of winter wheat, was due to different reactions to the same climatic conditions, and to the temporary substitution of one commodity for another which had become too costly. But taken all together there was a positive correlation between winter wheat on the one hand, and oats, peas and beans on the other, which the graph in Fig. 13 demonstrates and such monographs on the subject as are available confirm: at Crawley in England, wheat was sold at an average price of 7s. 7d. a quarter from 1315 to 1383, then at 5s. 7¾d. from 1384–1448, while oats fell between the first and second periods from 2s. 10½d. to 2s. 2¾d.; at

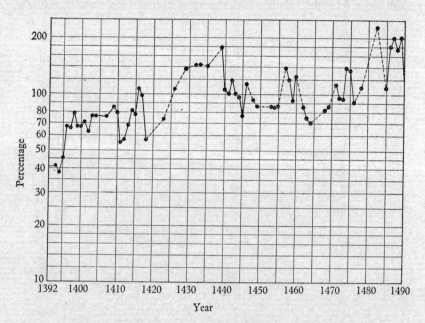

FIG. 12. Price of the basic cereal, spelt, at Namur from 1392 to 1490 as a percentage of average price, 1450–74 (logarithmic scale). (The line is continuous when data are available at yearly intervals; when figures for one or more intermediate years are missing the line is dotted.)

Göttingen in Germany the price of leguminous crops declined in the course of the fifteenth century even more than that of wheat.

It could have been otherwise with animal products. As they occupied a less essential place in the range of foodstuffs, demand for them was more a function of the volume of the supply and of the resources of consumers, and consequently prices tended to be more stable. Let us take the case of meat as an example. The statutes of one hospital in Strasbourg as well as German ordinances regulating payments in silver and in kind to workers of all grades show that at the end of the fourteenth and during the fifteenth centuries, consumption of meat was considerable in all ranks of society. Was it so 100 or 200 years earlier? Apparently not. We may assume that it increased after 1350 or 1400 with the help of higher wages, lower bread prices and a relative increase in production and that it counteracted the fall in prices that this increase would normally have brought about. This hypothesis is supported by the tables which follow: the first is compiled from Rogers's figures, the second constructed by Abel out of various elements assembled by d'Avenel and Hanauer, and the third borrowed

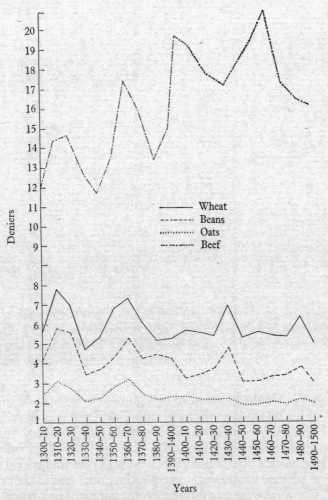

FIG. 13. Prices of some farm products in England, 1300–1500, in deniers. (Prices have not, as was done before, been converted into a common unit of money or an equivalent weight of silver; the fall in agricultural goods is thus in reality heavier than it appears in the graph.)

from the works of Pelc, whose documentary base is unfortunately rather meagre.

Table 9. *Comparative change in prices of wheat and beef in England in the fourteenth and fifteenth centuries*

	In *deniers*		In percentage	
	wheat (quarter)	beef (piece)	wheat (quarter)	beef (piece)
1301–1350	73	157	100	100
1351–1400	74	180	101	115
1401–1450	70	219	96	140
1451–1500	66	213	90	136

Table 10. *Comparative change in prices of corn and livestock products in France and Alsace from 1350 to 1525*

	France		Alsace	
	corn	livestock	corn	livestock
1351–1375	100	100	100	100
1376–1400	48	76	71	81
1401–1425	55	84	64	87
1426–1450	74	100	74	78
1451–1475	33	49	49	—
1476–1500	40	53	59	67
1501–1525	52	77	50	63

Table 11. *Comparative change in prices of wheat, wages, livestock products and industrial products (building materials and metals) at Cracow from 1360 to 1500*

Period	Wheat	Livestock	Wages	Industrial products
1361–1400	100	100	100	100
1401–1450	84	160	128	180
1451–1500	59	100	100	96

What is true of meat is also true of butter, the price of which in the later Middle Ages rose in all centres of production except, perhaps, Holland.

And equally new outlets could open up to the producers of a third group of goods: luxuries, like wine, the demand for which is also more elastic than that of corn, and raw materials destined for various industries on the spot or in distant places reached by trade. In the Île de France at the beginning of the fourteenth century grain depreciated while wine became dearer. The same change later took place in the Tyrol according to Stolz: from 1300 to 1450 the price of wheat did not alter, but that of wine climbed from 48 to 64 Kr. per hectolitre.

Thus, prices of different farm products did not all react to the fall in population in the same way. Some went up or remained steady while corn sagged. This was an open invitation to both lord and peasant to reduce their losses by changing their farming methods, and we shall return to this later.

We have just described losses, for losses they indeed were. A fall in the price of cereals as expressed in money or silver weight might be of little significance in itself. It became serious only when other prices did not fall at the same rate. Unfortunately for the rural world of the later Middle Ages this is exactly what happened. Wages rose considerably and so very likely did the price of industrial goods in agricultural use.

Although this has been denied, the demographic recession did cause a rise in wages of all kinds. This document of Namur of 1453, for instance, selected from a hundred others, is proof of it. It deplores *la grande diminution de peuple qui est en nostre dit comté pour cause des mortalitez qui ont régné ou pays, par quoy à grant peinne on puet recouvrer mesnies et labouriers, si non à despenser plus grande la moittié que l'on ne faisoit paravant.* Why should this be thought surprising? After all labourers suffered more than other classes from the calamities of the time simply because they were poorer; the survivors were therefore better able to stand up to their employers and demand a reduction in the length of their tasks, and more often a rise in their wages. Some of them, having taken over vacant lands, became tenants or enlarged their meagre holdings and thus did not hire themselves out any more, or at most hired themselves part-time. In many regions other factors, such as the development of rural industry in England or the growth of towns in Eastern Europe, further aggravated the shortage of agricultural labour and made piece-workers and wage-earners more demanding.

This tendency did not everywhere appear in an identical guise. It did not develop at the same time in all countries. Sometimes it did not begin till the fifteenth century, as in Bordeaux. In many other places, notably the Île de France, it was already over by then. Elsewhere again, e.g. in Austria, and probably also at Strasbourg, it ceased about 1450. Its incidence was not uniformly intense at all times and places. Most frequently it slowed down sharply after 1400. In Flanders it was probably less striking than in neighbouring areas. The decline of the cloth industry there and its replacement by industries employing few journeymen, as well as the rationalization of certain manufacturing processes, had deprived many town workers of their livelihood. As a consequence the town drew fewer men from the countryside, which in its turn had more hands to offer as agricultural production switched to stockraising. Lastly, all occupations were not equally affected. Comparison of data relating to the estates of Winchester and Westminster, made by Beveridge, illustrate the differences in timing, intensity and occupations.

Table 12. *Wages from 1300 to 1450 on the ecclesiastical estates oj Winchester and Westminster*
(price in pence of threshing and winnowing of 3 qtrs.)

Date	Winchester	Westminster	Westminster as Percentage of Winchester
1300–1309	3·83	6·51	170
1310–1319	4·05	8·01	198
1320–1329	4·62	6·68	145
1330–1339	4·92	7·35	149
1340–1349	5·03	7·41	147
1350–1359	5·18	13·02	251
1360–1369	6·10	12·76	209
1370–1379	7·00	12·33	175
1380–1389	7·22	10·82	150
1390–1399	7·23	10·44	144
1400–1409	7·31	11·00	150
1410–1419	7·25	12·40	179
1420–1429	7·23	10·00	138
1430–1439	7·23	13·00	179
1440–1449	7·25	13·00	179

Table 13. *Changes in wages according to occupation on the Westminster estates*
(in pence per day)

Date	Carpenter	Labourer	Thatcher and mate	Tiler and mate
1330–1339	4·56	2·18	4·04	6·34
1340–1349	4·26	2·03	4·75	6·44
1350–1359	5·90	4·00*	6·00	8·40
1360–1369	6·09*	3·96	8·36	11·25*
1370–1379	5·93	4·79	9·58*	9·67
1380–1389	5·89	3·53	7·61	8·75
1390–1399	5·00	3·50	8·00	—

* Asterisks denote the peak of each series.

But, although date, duration and scale might vary, the rise was general and usually well marked. The following tables show this, as well as the figures given above for Cracow and below for the English estates of Tavistock and Oakington. The first one covers all occupations, and a rudimentary cost of living index has enabled Hamilton to convert these figures into nominal and real wages; the second, taken from Postan and based on facts collected by Beveridge, concerns agricultural occupations; the third, based on Pribram's researches, concerns one only of these occupations: the digging of ditches in vineyards in the summer.

Table 14. *Wages in Navarre between* 1300 *and* 1450
(base: average of 1421–1430 = 100)

	Nominal	Real
1308	16·2	
1309	17	
1310	16·8	
1346–1350	17·5	
1351–1355	22·1	55·7
1356–1360	26·6	61·6
1361–1365	25·4	65·6
1366–1370	—	—
1371–1375	45·6	72·4
1376–1380	50·4	72·5
1381–1385	58·6	79·2
1386–1390	59·4	75·3
1391–1395	73·1	86·6
1396–1400	82	97·5
1401–1405	96	116·9
1406–1410	95·9	105·3
1411–1415	104·4	107·6
1416–1420	104·1	103·5
1421–1425	100·1	104·9
1426–1430	100·6	95·2
1431–1435	111·5	92·2
1436–1440	104·5	94·4
1441–1445	106·3	93·8
1446–1450	105·8	

The prices of industrial produce essential to the peasant, whether produced by large-scale industries or small-scale ones, appear to have followed a similar course. If this course cannot be demonstrated in black and white it is because the relevant information is specially exiguous: chroniclers' complaints about the dearness of life, odd facts

Table 15. *Wheat and wages on the estates of the bishop of Winchester between 1300 and 1480*
(base: average 1300–1319 = 100)*

	Corn (in deniers)	Corn (in silver)	Wages (in silver)	Wages as percentage of corn
1320–1339	89	90	124	140
1340–1359	90	79	133	148
1360–1379	106	89	169	154
1380–1399	80	65	188	235
1400–1419	90	68	189	210
1420–1439	93	64	189	200
1440–1459	80	53	189 .	236
1460–1479	86	47	188	220

* As the price level of corn was exceptionally high during the famine of 1315–16, B. Slicher van Bath has calculated the same series taking the average of 1328–39 as the base (100). Though more accurate in relation to grain this method risks being less useful in relation to wages, as it eliminates all trace of a possible rise in wages before the period in question, that is before 1330.

Table 16. *Wheat by 'Landmetzen' and day-rates at Klosterneuburg between 1410 and 1530*
(base: average 1410–1420 = 100)

	In grammes of silver		As percentage of base	
	Wheat	Wages	Wheat	Wages
1410–1420	9·26	2·32	100	100
1420–1430	9·92	1·76	107	76
1430–1440	16·57	2·17	179	94
1440–1450	8·37	2·22	90	96
1450–1460	5·98	2	65	86
1460–1470	—	1·99	—	86
1470–1480	5·17	1·87	56	81
1480–1490	6·93	3·60	75	155
1490–1500	7·33	2·70	79	116
1500–1510	6·01	2·79	65	120
1510–1520	7·05	2·82	76	121
1520–1530	7·81	2·75	84	119
1530–1540	8·71	2·72	94	117

which cannot be combined, rare series of figures which include too few articles, and do not as a rule go back beyond 1350 or even 1400, and, on top of all else, sometimes contradict each other. Such a documentation cannot provide more than very halting conclusions. If we refer again to Thorold Rogers, the 'price scissors', so dear to W. Abel, began early, about 1317-20, on the English side of the channel at least. On the morrow of the Black Death it became more general and pronounced, as is evident from the table below. Lastly, it was, if not

Table 17. *Corn and industrial products in England in the fourteenth and fifteenth centuries* (in deniers)

	Corn (qtrs.)	Iron (108 lb.)	Horse-shoes (100)	Wheels	Laths (1000)	Tiles (1000)	Hurdles (100)	2nd qlty. cloth (24 yds.)
1261–1350	69	49	53·75	23	53·75	33·25	109	398·75
1351–1400	73	103	117·25	56·75	86·25	55·75	218	558·50
1401–1450	69	74			84	61·50		468
1451–1500	66	67·5			77	69		544

actually aggravated, as at Cracow in the first half of the fifteenth century, at least perpetuated, as in England until the last decades of the century.

It is even less easy to explain the growing disparity between the prices of grain and industrial goods than it is to affirm and measure it. Demand for the latter could have grown while, as we have seen, demand for the former remained slack or even fell back. Goods which were absolutely essential, especially bread, cost less; people could therefore spend a larger part of their income on manufactured produce: the opposite, in effect, of the phenomenon experienced in many regions in modern times, i.e. a rise in agricultural prices and a correlated fall of industrial prices. Wages went up, calamities, scarcities and epidemics carried away people, but left intact buildings and property to such an extent that the wealth of the survivors increased. At Albi the 686 heads of houses enumerated in 1357 disposed of as much capital (but did they make equally productive use of it?) as 1623 men in 1343, and 82 per cent of them as against 69 per cent fifteen years earlier possessed more than £10. Finally, as is always the way in troublous times, people were seized with a craving for pleasure; *après la peste*, wrote a Norman chronicler, *vint un nouvel monde qui delaissèrent la gregnieur partie de la prudomie et des vesteures anciennes.*

Supply could equally have changed in the opposite direction. Supply of grain was not sufficiently reduced for reasons which we know: fluctuations of price, fear of scarcity, the need to earn money with which to pay obligations and taxes, the propensity of peasants to extend their tillage rather than reduce it. Add to these the fact that trade in corn had probably progressed during the fifteenth century relatively more than the older and better-developed trade in manufactured goods, whereas the trade in industrial goods may have diminished. One reason for this was that industrial goods always adapt themselves more readily than foodstuffs to the changes in the market and contract more easily when it is necessary to preserve the price level. Another reason was perhaps that the number of artisans had fallen. Before coming to a conclusion on this point we must first supply the answer to a problem which can only be touched on here: that of likely changes in the respective importance of town and country populations, or to use an Italian expression, of *inorbamento*, in the later Middle Ages. In normal times medieval towns did not produce enough men to maintain the number of their inhabitants; moreover, they suffered more than villages from famine and pestilence. The question is, did they succeed in replacing 'extraordinary losses' amongst their members quickly, completely and adequately, and thus in maintaining the numerical relationship between peasant and artisan? Several factors played a part, and sometimes a contradictory part, in this matter. Country folk willingly took refuge in towns to escape war and hunger, and some of them put down permanent roots there, but wealthy bourgeois and their servants fled from towns to get away from the plague. The town administration as a rule encouraged immigration, but gilds discouraged it. Wages were often higher in towns, but the cost of living was dearer, mostly because taxes became more and more burdensome: thus in 1447 they formed 25 per cent and in 1500 76 per cent of the revenues of Munich. In general a survey of the registers of the bourgeoisie—Table 18 condenses the data for Lübeck and Lüneburg—and the results of some researches into urban surnames—at Albi in 1357 49 per cent of the surnames were unknown in 1343—leads one to believe that this immigration was swollen after great catastrophes, but that it was composed of a large majority—74 per cent at Göttingen— of men without professional qualifications. If so the relative number of artisans and the volume of their production were reduced, at any rate during the second half of the fourteenth century, a period in which,

Table 18. *Influence of the plague on accession of new bourgeois**

	Lübeck	Lüneburg
Average 1317–1349	175	29
January–July 1350	75	} 36
August–September 1350	196	
1351	422	95
1352	255	86
1353	210	82
1354	236	52
1355	205	73

* The rise in immigration was perhaps greater than tables of this kind show. The poorest arrivals doubtless were not able to buy the right, often costly, to bourgeoisie.

for example, ordinances intended to moderate the rise in wages multiplied in Cologne.

Other factors too, besides changes in the volume of supply and demand, could have contributed to the effect of the 'price scissors'. Industrial products are less subject to the law of diminishing returns and its effects than are agricultural goods. They embody a larger share of paid manual labour and are more sensitive to the effects of a rise in wages.

One last consequence of the new demographic trend follows from those which have already been discussed. Agricultural land lost some of its value. Its abundance, the abandonment of the least fertile soils and the decline in the real price of corn exercised an irresistible pressure on land values, which sooner or later were bound to give way. In Denmark the price of land fell from 100 in 1334-9 to 60 in 1340-5, 65·7 in 1350-69, 37·1 in 1370-89 and 77·1 in 1380-99. In the region of Lübeck 7 *manses* were sold for 161 marks in 1323 and 80 in 1370. At Forncett in Norfolk the rent per acre fell from 10·75*d.* in 1370 to 8*d.* in the first and 7*d.* in the second half of the fifteenth century. Even in the region of Namur, which had been spared by the first great outbreak of pestilence, the successive farm rents of the same land, instead of regularly rising as in the past, all began to go down after about 1360. One could add to these many examples relating to France, but of course in the case of France there was another overriding factor to which we must now turn, namely, war.

III. *Capital: disorder and destruction*

Diruptus, devolutus, heremus, ruynosus carensque fere pagesiis hominibus et tenanciariis, diu et per longa tempora inhabitabilis propter guerras, mortalitates, afflictiones et tribulationes predictas. In this preamble to the act of assessment for rent (*accensement*) of Mouillac in Quercy of 1476, as in countless documents of the same kind, wars took pride of place in the catalogue of scourges which afflicted the later Middle Ages. Philippe de Commynes confirmed this when he wrote in his *Chronique* that in 1465 the subjects of the house of Burgundy were rich *a cause de la longue paix qu'ilz avoient eue.* Thus a few pages must be devoted to military operations, less to establish the facts which are known and do not directly concern us, than to set out their consequences for the countryside.

The facts. In this connexion all that needs to be stressed is how frequent and profound were the disturbances. In eastern Europe, from 1228 to Ivan III's accession to the throne in 1462, the princes of the

Russian plain let loose no less than 90 conflicts. Central and western Europe were no better off. There was above all the Hundred Years War which, throughout nearly two centuries, pressed heavily on the fortunes of the two great monarchies of the West, and after 1356 piled ruin upon ruin over the land of one of them. But even if it far surpassed in its scale and effects all the other conflagrations of the period, it was not alone in sowing wreckage and desolation. If a priest of Cahors could declare that he 'had seen in his lifetime nothing but war in his diocese', the commander of the Teutonic Order in Westphalia could state with equal force in 1411 that in his *baillie* 'all is in ruins and is daily ruined through pillage and burning because the land is never free from war'. The quarrels of the houses of Orleans and Burgundy were matched by those of York and Lancaster. The struggles of Gaston Phoebus and Jean d'Armagnac in 1359-60 were not more disastrous for the region of Toulouse than were the contentions of the bishop of Liège and the count of Namur in 1430 for their lands and subjects. The *écorcheurs, retondeurs, brigands* and *routiers* were no better, or worse, than the *compagnie di ventura*; or the risings of subjects against their lords, of peasants against the nobility or the state; or the *vendette, fehden* and *guerres d'amis*; or the exactions of the impoverished notables, rapacious knights, roman barons, Junkers of Mecklenburgh and Western Pomerania and English law-breakers. The conclusion is inescapable: disorder always brought strangulation to medieval Europe, but never was the stranglehold more deadly and certainly never were its consequences more disastrous than in the final phase of the period.

Such consequences as affect population have already been discussed here: loss of human life and abandonment, temporary or permanent, partial or total, of disputed or occupied regions. It is true that not more than a few thousand combatants opposed each other on the field of battle: only six to eight thousand for instance fought on the French side at Crécy and Agincourt. But even so the upper classes paid heavily with their lives. As for the masses, they paid their tribute in the intervals of the struggle. Between encounters regular troops, garrisons and disbanded soldiers consigned the people to the horrors of individual assassination or collective massacre. Many sought refuge in other parts of the country and specially in the towns; and some left never to return. In 1412, on the morrow of the first war against Poland, the Prussian nobility demanded for the first time that no city should receive a peasant without the consent of his lord. And a contemporary German poem shows us the peasants who

> Ettlich sind och so cluoger sinner
> Das si ir herren tuond endrinnen
> Und werdend burger in stetten.

But disorder had certain other effects which demand more careful attention. To begin with, unlike plague and famine, it encompassed goods as well as, and perhaps more than, persons. At times cold-blooded strategy, at other times passion, led to the burning and destruction. Villages laid waste, churches knocked down, castles torn apart, cottages flattened, brambles in the fields and scrub in the woodland clearings: a Jacques Callot working in the fourteenth and fifteenth centuries would not have lacked subjects for his engravings. He could also have recorded on copper the depredations of the men at arms *qui riffloient tout*, as Commynes put it, and the requisitions of goods, corn, cattle and wool at prices so arbitrarily low as to become no more than legalized pillage.

Yokel and lord alike were victim of these *misères de la guerre. Per omnes generaliter fines nostros*, wrote three clerics of Liège in 1351, *guerre durissime viguerunt quarum certe pretextu nunc incendiis, nunc rapinis contigit infinitos agrorum depauperari cultores.* Some documents are more specific and provide figures. We hear from one such document that the 25 taxable inhabitants of a village in French Flanders lost in one year at the end of the fifteenth century 1100 *livres*, that is 55 per cent of their possessions. Is this an exaggeration born of a desire to defraud the Exchequer? It could be. But exaggeration has its limits, and the fact remains that on the rolls of the royal *taille* of France the proportion of insolvent householders, *miserabiles*, grew with each revision. There was another side to this too: disorder allowed men to escape payment of their rent and, if it went on for long, to be rid of rents for good, to free themselves from servitude, to appropriate land. In this respect it is typical that the Statutes of Parma of 1255 suspended the arbitrary assumption of liberty during time of war. These advantages to the peasant were of course slight, and, except perhaps for some poor souls, were not sufficient to balance the material damage.

The lords suffered still more. They lost farms in the disturbances, important buildings, as well as livestock and farm equipment. During the quarrels of 1302–3 the King of France and his Flemish adversaries burnt at least 14 and perhaps as many as 22 of the 40 farms, and at least 5 of the 20 mills, of Saint-Martin de Tournai. By 1340 the opening of the Hundred Years War had inflicted on the same abbey losses of some 1500 *livres*, that is, the equivalent of two to two-and-a-half years' revenue.

To re-erect ruined walls and replace equipment and stock required capital resources which the victims often did not possess. And, indeed, where could they have obtained them? Not from their lands. We have just pointed out that at the first hint of war rents dwindled away and sometimes fell entirely into desuetude. The lord of Neufbourg experienced this: with the arrival of the English in the region his rents, as shown in Table 19, decreased drastically, and his pannage, collected

Table 19. *War and rent in the seigneurie of Neufbourg*

Remission granted on the yields of the fieffes
(total due: 781 *livres*)

1397	50		1445	466
1405	42		1446	429
1428	173		1447	394
1436	352	*English*	1448	357
1437	356	*occupation*	1449	303
1444	517		1450	304
			1454	268
			1457	235
			1461	181
			1487	103

on pigs pasturing in the woods, tumbled from 23*l*. 7*s*. in 1397 to 4*l*. 19*s*. in 1434 and 3*l*. 12*s*. in 1444. The powerful canons of Notre-Dame de Paris and the humble knight of Sologne, Jean de Givernay, suffered likewise: from the outbreak of military operations around Suçy the canons could not collect the *taille* and, when 40 years later they again demanded its payment, they were forced to conduct interminable lawsuits against their men. At the same time Jean de Givernay declared that *il me soloit estre payé au jour Saint Berthomier dix sols parisis de menus cens par plusiers personnes et sur plusiers héritages, avec autres rentes de blé et d'avoine, mais je ne puis rien avoir ne recouvrer nulle cognoissance, car chacun dit qu'il ne me doit rien.* Could they draw finance from the disorders themselves, i.e. from Froisssart's *grans proufis*, from booty, ransoms, looting conducted under the protection of the prince, or at the head of a *grande compagnie*? Equipping the latter was an even greater expense; absence at war resulted in neglect of the estate; and the profession of arms was not always a lucky one. Far from enriching himself, the Burgundian Jehan Ryolet ruined himself in the wars. Brigandage was repugnant to most gentlemen, so they frequently found themselves unable to clear away the rubble from the ruins or to fill the empty stalls in their stables, much less to help their tenants repair their tumbledown dwellings and re-stock their outbuildings. But others may have disposed of sufficient means: nobles, often of recent or modest extraction, who were not repelled by a bandit's life; men who exploited the hostilities more cunningly than others by supplying the opponents with men and goods; individuals enriched by public service, industry, commerce; even enterprising peasants. The destruction thus paved the way for new masters.

The more important conflagrations had also another consequence which did not necessarily follow from the other afflictions of the time: they had to be paid for, and the payment required either new impositions or devaluations; and while impositions burdened the peasant, the devaluations hit the great majority of landowners, most of whom had by now become mere recipients of land rents. From the first phase of the Hundred Years War the English budget climbed from between £40,000 and £70,000 to £200,000. Borrowing or raising of revenue by extraordinary means such as the sale of franchises, or requisitioning goods for re-sale at an advantageous price, could help to meet this swollen expenditure. Such measures were, however, no more than palliatives. Taxation was indispensable. This could be indirect taxation, as on English wool, the producers of which already burdened with requisitions were additionally hit by export duties rising sometimes to 35 or 50 per cent of its value. Or it could be direct taxation, notably, as in France, feudal aid and the royal *taille*. In 1433 the inhabitants of Saint-Cloud had to provide an extraordinary contribution of 15 Paris *sous* per *arpent*, which was three times the amount of the rent; in the mid-fifteenth century the inhabitants of some barren villages in the Nord had to find each year the equivalent of 2 or 2·25 per cent, or after 1449, of 0·85 per cent of their fortune. These new charges were in themselves excessive and as dangerous socially as economically. Circumstances and methods of raising the taxes made them even more disastrous. The collecting agents used to embezzle them, and the aristocracy, clergy and burghers of certain towns were granted exemption from them. Ennoblements, emigration to free districts, and the acquisition of landed property by privileged individuals constantly aggravated the burden; in the end, at Wavrin, one of the localities in the Nord just referred to, those exempted from tax possessed 400 *bonniers* and those subjected to it, 60; the peasants were, in fact, like in a German fable of the late Middle Ages, the donkey bowed down beneath the baggage of the other classes. Finally economic conditions made the levies even more crushing. The rise of prices had deeply eaten into, and continued to eat into, profit margins in the countryside. It is significant that every prince in the fifteenth century wishing to repopulate a devastated area, no matter whether his name was Charles VII, Philippe le Bon or René d'Anjou, offered the future colonists exemption from taxes for five, ten or twenty years as the first bait.

The State has at all times found in monetary manipulation a way out of financial difficulties: it reduces debts (though it does the same to fixed revenues, which is what the bulk of the revenues of royal domains was), and thereby assures substantial profits. In the Low Countries, France, the Empire, Italy, almost everywhere, such manipulations multiplied in the fourteenth and fifteenth centuries at the precise moment when governments were most hard pressed. The silver content of the Viennese *denier*, for instance, fell from 778 milligrammes in the third quarter of the thirteenth century to 127 in 1497, and that of the Genoese *lire* from 56 grammes to no more than 13 in 1493.

That manipulations of this kind were born of the necessity to balance budgets in disequilibrium may seem an inescapable conclusion. But it is less so than it seems. The debasements of the period could have also been provoked by a scarcity of the means of payment as, for instance, in England. Trade was developing, the use of money was clearly spreading through the countryside, yet stocks of silver were not increasing; in the fourteenth century the mining of silver in Western Europe slowed down or ceased altogether; the most easily reached strata were worked out; others were not successfully exploited until about 1450 when the problems of drainage and the removal of copper were solved. Public disorder, as well as the raising of the official value of bullion, encouraged hoarding of precious metals and discouraged their delivery to the mint. Imports continued to exceed exports. Governments, lacking the power to expand credit, were forced to reduce the intrinsic value of the coins in circulation, or, as Henry V of England put it in 1411, to lighten them 'because of the lack of money'. This is not the place to discuss these notions. We must confine ourselves to the comment that some good reasons have been found for them, but before we can accept them we ought to be better informed about the relevant data: amongst other things the state of western Europe's balance of trade, the development of its mining production, the exact timing of economic movements, notably those of prices, the relative increase in the volumes of transactions, the changes in the velocity of circulation, the habits of hoarding, and the use of non-metallic money.

A third theory can also be imagined. Could the measures in question have been inspired not so much by vulgar financial needs as by a true economic policy, e.g. that of a purposeful lowering of exchange rates, or the even more sophisticated policy of a 'floating money standard'? These policies would have aimed at arresting deflation, combating hoarders, facilitating exports and, by all these means, re-animating business.

Whichever happens to be the explanation we accept—and the others should not thereby be rejected—it is in any case agreed that the devaluations of the later Middle Ages were very largely inflationary. They directly affected prices and reduced in this way the real value of fixed revenues. Most land rents at that time were typical of this kind of income. A celebrated passage in the *Quadriloge invectif* draws this conclusion: 'the people have this advantage, that their purse is like the water butt which collected and still collects rain from the gutters of all the riches of the kingdom . . . because the weakness of money has diminished the payments they must make and the rents which they owe to us.'

But the taxations and revaluations called forth by rising expenditure were not solely due to the disorders of the time. The constant progress of the State was equally responsible. It is this political evolution as well as changing intellectual and religious ideas which we need now to consider for a brief moment in order to put the last touches to the picture in which the lords and peasants of the late Middle Ages lived. This will allow us to complete the balance sheet of the forces which animated and orientated their actions.

IV. *The political and social background*

The disturbances which have just been described did not bring with them everywhere the same political consequences. Where the State still lacked firm structure and doctrinal justification they merely provoked fragmentation. This is how events turned out in Russia and most other countries in Eastern Europe. Civil wars and foreign attacks had so weakened the princes that they were constrained to cede much of their power to the nobles on whose support they depended. In doing so they helped to consolidate the economic position of the nobles by increasing their revenues and providing them with a weapon against the depopulation of their estates. For the lords were now able to remit to their tenants or to immigrants all or part of the public revenues which had now passed into their possession. Conversely, they could make use of the authority which they henceforth possessed to demand more from their dependants, or to tie them even closer to the soil.

In the West the development was precisely opposite: by revealing the evil effects of a breakdown of authority the troubled times established the case for centralization. 'Sovereign' power in its different forms became concentrated more and more in the hands of a few physical and moral persons, incarnations of the 'State', and of their representatives. For the mass of the population, the most obvious result was to aggravate the burden which weighed on the country folk. Officials, judges, mercenaries, were bound to be expensive, and thus to lead to taxation. And the weight of this fell almost entirely on the people, especially those who lived in the country. Around 1250 Danish peasants possessed half, or perhaps as much as two-thirds, of the land;

around 1650, after four centuries of subjection to contributions from which the nobility and clergy were exempt, they held no more than one-tenth.

The progress of the State pressed down on the villagers in other ways too, especially in the Empire. The local and traditional tribunals were more and more replaced by superior courts run by *doctores* who were not known and whose integrity (not without reason) was suspect, and who practised a new, the Roman, law, rather than the ancient customary one. The State now advanced a claim, mainly under cover of this *jus*, to the entire ownership of waste, forest and water, and to their exclusive use, or at any rate to the right to regulate arbitrarily their utilization. The villages also had to submit to orders from above and from distant places, and to officials sent from outside, and sometimes to new demands of military services. These were grievances which the history of the Swiss Confederation, or the *Bauernkrieg*, reveal as of fundamental importance.

The nobles found that for them the consequences of these developments were even more serious: from the moment when the prince possessed himself of his own agents and soldiers, they had no further social function, no reason for existing. They also lost part of their income: the State could not build itself up nor strengthen itself except at the expense of their seignorial rights, such as their right to dispense justice, which up to that time had always brought them considerable revenue. On the other hand they could henceforth seek careers in the army or administration or wangle pensions. But the chance of doing this fell only to certain individuals and anyway required attendance at court and neglect of their own property.

The ecclesiastical lords were also penalized by the progress of the civil power. To quote only one case, the Franconian monastery of Langheim poured out, in vain, a fortune in the attempt to obtain *Unmittelbarkeit*, i.e. their direct subordination to the Empire, and thereby to escape from the temporal authority of the bishop of Bamberg. But the clerics too were forced to shoulder the financial burden of Roman centralization. Added to the incompetence of the abbots, pontifical taxes were to be the source of the tribulations against which Saint-Martin de Tournai was to struggle throughout the first half of the fourteenth century.

At the same time there were ideas abroad calculated to drive simple minds to rebellion. Of course they were ancient, as ancient as Christianity itself. They distilled its very essence. Did they not proclaim that all men were descended from Adam and bought by the blood of Christ, that all men were equal and freedom was their natural state, that God knew the wicked and desired their punishment, that riches existed not only for those that possessed them, but ought to be used for the greater good of the next world, that 'where there is property, there are singular existences, and wherever there are singular existences there are private corners, and where there are private corners, there is mire and rust'? Had not these ideas been clearly formulated in the Gospels and expounded by the Fathers of the Church?

Moreover, they were not really so very revolutionary. In the course of time, under the influence of ancient works or of medieval forgeries, they had undergone some distortion especially so far as private property was concerned. Following Gratian himself, writers had come to declare that the latter had been unknown before the Fall and was one of its penalties, an *ordo poenalis post peccatum*. But between this and an invitation to men to rise and do away with inequalities, abolish servitude, punish injustice, or collectivize the land, there was a far cry.

Yet such as they were, these sentiments were not without danger to the established order, above all when they happened to reach the humble folk, little used to subtleties and distinctions. And this is what in fact happened in the late Middle Ages. From the thirteenth century onwards they were spoken so frequently and so loudly that in the end they spread beyond intellectual circles. In isolated documents like the famous Florentine Act of 6 August 1289, or in treatises like the three German customaries compiled at this period, jurists, following their master Irnerius, vied with each other in insisting on the freedom and equality of mankind. Writers in the vulgar tongues, like a Van Maerlant or a Boendaele in the Low Countries, denounced the dangers of wealth and attacked social inequalities vehemently. The most orthodox of preachers, like Thomas Brinton, bishop of Rochester, exalted the state of poverty and castigated the vices and machinations of the great. True enough, all this took place, was said and written in the cities, but quite a few peasants came to town, and the town also came to them in the shape of wandering preachers, like John Ball. They soon picked up these ideas and, in their simplicity, soon carried them to excess. In the *Bauernkrieg*, the German preachers would appeal to divine law.

The growing preponderance of the town finally corrupted the atmosphere of the country. A world dominated by a commercial bourgeoisie could not but despise the peasants, Jacques Bonhomme for France, or donkeys for the Empire. The landlords who gave way to the temptations of city life and who swopped 'manor' for 'mansion' lost contact with their people and were unlikely to remain the close, friendly, understanding, humane masters who, German literature of the period declared, were more desired by the rustic than a board groaning with food and drink.

V. The lot of the masters—difficulties, reactions, results

The consequences of the phenomena analysed in the preceding pages varied in extreme. Should one, in order to examine them faithfully, try to sub-divide the rural population into a large number of categories to be then passed under review? This method, however, breeds confusion and, what is worse, betrays reality. Even if those concerned were divided into ten, fifteen or more classes, we could still not eliminate the borderline or difficult case, or lay down clear boundaries. So the best way remains to distinguish quite simply between lords, landowners and wealthy people, on the one hand, and peasants, tenants and humble people on the other. But it must never be forgotten that this distinction is an artificial one, and that the terms, 'lord', 'landowner' and 'rich man' are no more synonymous than are their opposites.

In whatever way the members of the first group exploited their possessions they were bound to be touched by the events described above. But they did not all find themselves in the same situation, nor were they equally affected, not did they all react in an identical manner, nor arrive at similar results.

A. The difficulties

Whatever his situation or behaviour no lord could escape the impact of change, be it demographic, economic, political or social. Did he cultivate his own demesne? The value of the corn which he harvested was likely to depreciate absolutely or relatively to other commodities, and, unless he had at his disposal sufficient numbers of tenants subjected to labour services or of working lay-brethren enabling him to dispense with paid labour (and this was becoming more and more unusual) it cost him more to produce. Did he adopt hereditary leases at rents in kind, mostly in grain? Then as a result of the 'price scissors', the rents in kind lost their purchasing power. Or did he receive money rents? Then, unless he stipulated payment in units of account not linked to real money and equivalent to a fixed weight of precious metal, devaluation ate into these. Did he let out his lands on farm? Then the stagnation in the prices of agricultural products and the growing scarcity of tenants constrained him to reduce the farm at each renewal. Should he refuse to moderate his demands, he would sometimes provoke prolonged vacancies on a large part of his lands. On every supposition he drew less from his fields. The same was true of his woods and grasslands where fewer livestock pastured. And if he possessed rights over his men, the latter were fewer and were often impoverished by events. His tolls on trade were often smaller and their collection disorganized. The bursar of Durham, who had stored away in his coffers £3741 in 1292, and £4526 in 1308, gathered in only £1752 in 1335, £2004 in 1373, £1144 in 1446 and £1399 in 1499. During the first half of the fifteenth century, the Percys recorded a fall of one-third in the revenues produced from their estates in Sussex.

Regular clerics and magnates were prepared better than other landlords to weather the crisis. Constricted, but at the same time stimulated, by the bounds of custom and canon law, the former had applied and went on applying themselves successfully and energetically to the defence of what they had; in particular they gave way less to the desires of their tenants for emancipation, and, amongst other things, protected their right to forced labour and thereby found an easier way to check the rise in wages. Living, moreover, in a closed economy they depended less on markets, price levels and general economic conditions. Better educated, they made use earlier and more widely of the written record, the best guarantee against negligence, forgetfulness and rule of thumb. The great laymen also were able to cope with changing conditions. Vaster, more compact and consequently richer in labour services, their estates were, as a rule, because of these advantages, better and more economically run. And their hold over justice permitted them to preserve intact, nay, indeed, even to increase if necessary, the burden of charges due from their people.

Many other factors apart from these we have just mentioned could aggravate or attenuate the damage suffered by the landlords. Some were geographic, such as the fertility of the soil, presence or absence, abundance or scarcity, of fertile or marginal lands. Some were technical, such as improved methods of farming, especially those of manuring, rotation of crops, or combining arable with animal husbandry. Some were economic, like the proximity of an important town or the existence of agricultural industries within the region. Some were legal, such as manorial law, which in some places laid down the precise total of services due, and in others left a greater or smaller margin for arbitrary actions, the village code, which admitted, forbade or hindered the abandonment of land, the rules of succession of freeholds and fiefs which either favoured one of the heirs or imposed an equal division: this last a less dangerous reef than previously because of the dwindling population, yet one upon which a large family risked foundering. Some again were political, such as the strength or weakness of the central power, able or powerless to protect the masses against the nobles who may have been tempted to raise personal dues to compensate for falling incomes from land. Some were psychological, such as conservatism of the milieu or the class, or an environment friendly to adaptation, transformation and progress. Some were individual, such as skill, inefficiency or negligence in management, ability to make both ends meet, or prodigality. And finally some were accidental, such as the extent of the gaps in population made by public disasters and the ravages caused by troubles of all kinds. It is easy to understand why landlords should have been affected in very unequal measure.

B. *The reactions*

It is also easy to understand why they reacted differently. All sought to maintain their income at as high a level as possible. But they did not all pursue this objective in the same way.

To fight against the absolute or relative decline in grain prices, especially in countries where it was pronounced and lasted into the fifteenth century, would have been an excellent defence against the changes, but sudden jumps in prices caused by the epidemics and the failures of harvests for a long time obscured the utility of such a policy from the eyes of the majority. Besides, the towns, a redoubtable power, were altogether hostile to it. Their hostility was disarmed only after the fall in prices was very marked and appeared to be definitive. It was not until 1394 that the English Commons showed any liking for the export of grain. In fact this is all that was done once the necessity for action was recognized and opposition to it overcome; and this was all that could be done: to authorize and encourage its export and hinder or prevent its import. Now, with the tendency to overproduction being all but general, tariff dues were somewhat ineffective.

The growing scarcity of population and the growing demand for labour presented more pressing problems for an economy so un-rationalized, so unmechanized and so wasteful of man-hours. A man threshed 72 litres of corn in the thirteenth century, 120 at Harwell in 1613, and from 500 to 900 in France just before the Revolution. But at least these problems appeared easier to solve and the landlords set themselves with conviction to their solution.

To begin with, most of them thought only to impose a solution by force. On the morrow of the plagues, the pressing need was to cultivate the abandoned holdings. To meet this need the landlords went back, or sought to go back, on the freedom to abandon holdings granted or tolerated during the period of demographic and economic expansion; forbade tenants to leave the estate during a stated period or without permission; made arrangements with each other to facilitate the search for and restitution of fugitives; obliged relations or neighbours to take up the deserted plots or to pay the dues thereon; wrote into new contracts clauses, up to that time unknown or rare, designed to tie the

tenants to the soil or to impose an obligation to build a house. Their
own demesnes were also crying out for regular labourers and harvest
workers at reasonable cost. The lords sought therefore to extort the
maximum work for the least wage from their tenants and in a more
general way from their *homines,* the individuals subjected to what
would have been called at the height of the Middle Ages *bannum et
justitia.* They demanded of them the effective performance of every
ancient *corvée,* even those which had previously been converted into
money payments; the difference between the conventional value of
commuted services and the market value of a day's labour at the end of
the fourteenth century was that of 1*d.* to 2½*d.*; the savings realized
in this way were by no means small. In certain cases the lords even
imposed new services. They also set about the day labourers. A
prohibition was placed on their moving from one employer to another
without permission of the former, on their refusing to work, and above
all, on their demanding a wage higher than the legal rate. For, mostly
at the instance of the small landowners and employers, and to curb the
*Gebreste und Schade, der in unserm Land aufgestanden ist von Bauleuten
und Arbeitern dasz jedermann immer warter will der grozen Löhne und will
sich keines Baues unterwinden, davon unser Land ungebauen leit,* the
enactments of fixed maximum rates multiplied after 1348–50. From
Spain to Norway, princes, parliaments and city magistrates vied with
each other to regulate wages. At times they were content merely to
fix an upper limit and to punish by fine or prison sentence any offer
or demand for more. At other times they went further; in 1438 the
town of Colmar, for instance, decreed that from then onwards the
vineyard workers should no longer hire themselves out in advance,
but should be taken on each day exclusively in the cemetery, to which
only masters seeking workmen and workmen who accepted the local
rates should be admitted, and that those workers who refused the
tariff and took an engagement elsewhere should be banished for a
month and could only return to the city with the permission of the
senate.

More often than not these measures of coercion had only a limited
effect and were abandoned after a time. Some came up against the
opposition of peasants who formed communities powerful enough to
defend their customs or were in a position to carry their complaints to
the tribunal of a prince disposed to support them against the exactions
of their lords. These very same lords indeed frequently violated the
regulations. In order to lay hands on much-needed labour they did not
fail, as soon as they possessed the financial means, to pay more than the
legal reward either indirectly or in a roundabout way. So measures of
this kind were for the most part transitory. Here and there public

bodies continued to 'tax' wages, if not always in the hope of preventing their rise, then at least in that of controlling or moderating it or of spreading it over a number of years. But most of them renounced a policy of restraint.

This policy was pursued mainly on the eastern frontiers of Christianity; in the rest of the West it was pursued with but a variable intensity in some parts only. Some Italian towns more or less strictly refused to allow the *contadini* to settle within their walls, and this forced them to remain at the mercy of the landowners, large and small, who were of course burgesses of the towns. Some lords in France and the Low Countries succeeded in transforming serfdom, which frequently entailed purely personal obligations, into a 'real' condition, i.e. one attached to the land and weighing upon all the inhabitants of a locality; such measures were all indirect and relatively light.

In certain areas in the South of Europe, the nobles reacted more drastically. Not in Bavaria where they lived on their rents from land and thus suffered less than others from a shortage of labour; they limited themselves to increasing or trying to increase rents and entry fines. Nor in the Tyrol where they had to deal with a prince who took care to protect all his subjects against arbitrary acts. But along the Middle and Upper Rhine where in many cases the landlords were themselves the princes, and where the difficulty of finding other forms of income drove them to extract the utmost from their demesnes and from their holdings, they forbade their tenants to leave without their consent and at the same time imposed upon them additional charges to the profit of the demesne—above all the compulsion to serve as a labourer (*Gesindezwangdienst*). They could do the same in the Austrian Alps where they possessed rights of public jurisdiction over their estates and created thus a screen or barrier between the prince and their dependants; they extended their demesnes by incorporating peasant holdings or by appropriating common lands; they consequently demanded extra labour services, for instance, twenty days a year instead of six as previously. In Bohemia, too, in the second half of the fourteenth century the burden of obligations increased; in the course of the fifteenth century successive legal measures obliged tenants to provide a replacement before leaving their fields, farm servants who had left their lords' service without taking up land to return to their masters, town dwellers to deliver up husbandmen who had sought refuge there, and country people who had been settled less than a certain period in cities to return to their villages.

In Muscovite and Kievan Russia, the landlords, during the first period, concentrated their attention on easily saleable natural products, such as wax, honey, furs and salt, and gave up cultivating themselves estates needing labour which was hard to find and producing corn which was hard to sell. They set themselves instead to attract settlers by means of loans, temporary exemptions from dues and promises of protection against public disorder. Then in the fifteenth century, progressively as the economy began to move forward, they changed their attitude to a policy of force and reduced gradually the peasants' freedom of movement. The *Sudebnik* of Ivan III in 1497 no longer permitted the abandonment of holdings except during two weeks in the autumn and on payment of a substantial sum.

But it was in Schleswig, in Denmark, and above all in the newly 'colonized' countries beyond the Elbe, that measures of this kind were most numerous and most rigorously applied. In the last mentioned region, the reversal of the demographic trend had placed the landowning class in a particularly delicate position. Population was less dense than formerly, and tenants, no matter why or in what way they had dwindled, could only be replaced with difficulty. Their lands, however, could not lie fallow, for rents and other dues from them formed the larger part of the smaller lords' income. They were thus forced to take up and cultivate the land themselves. In this they were helped by political struggles and the progress of trade. The former ruined their princely antagonists, and left them masters of the situation. They now demanded or seized sovereign rights as the price of their services; they dominated the Diets; they imposed their will on the towns. In this way they succeeded in progressively transforming the public *corvées*, such as that of cartage for the army, into labour services and in forcing new tasks on those whom they had subjected to their powers of jurisdiction and turned into *Gerichtuntertanen*. They also strangled attempts at emigration, demanded replacements or fines from peasants who sought permission to leave their holdings, agreed among themselves not to engage those who had left without consent, and obliged urban magistrates to hand over those who had surreptitiously taken shelter behind their walls; in Prussia they finally obtained from the Diet, by a decree of 1494, the right to hang fugitives without trial. Thus, not without trouble, they acquired the labour they needed. Outlets they found more easily, especially if they were not too far removed from the sea coast and could escape heavy transport costs. Merchants from the West, and in particular from Holland, had discovered Baltic grain. They demanded it in the fifteenth century in ever-growing quantities, until a point was reached by 1500 when in order to satisfy their demands the Junkers found it profitable to expel their tenants so as to extend their demesnes. Thus forcibly and in a manner well adapted to the agricultural depression there arose the *Gutsherrschaft*, the system which came to full maturity with the economic recovery of the sixteenth century, but which at the same time prepared the final rupture between Eastern and Western Europe.

For in the West most landowners, after a period of rigidity, adapted themselves. Rather than use force, they sought to resolve the problem of labour sometimes by modifying the details, at other times by transforming profoundly the whole system of exploiting their demesnes. Detailed modification aimed at preventing tenants leaving, or at offsetting departures by the arrival of strangers who were offered attractive conditions of rents, lengthy contracts and privileged personal status.

As to rent, the total amount could be changed. In fact it was lowered almost everywhere to a substantial extent. Examples for England and the Empire have been given above. Here are some others for France, where the Hundred Years War entailed particularly heavy sacrifices by landowners. In the Graves district of Bordeaux, the same vines were leased in 1391 for a third of the crop, in 1394 for a quarter, in 1416 for a sixth and finally for an insignificant sum of money. Further north, on the lands of Saint-Germain-des-Prés, the average rent per *arpent* tumbled, in spite of devaluations, from 84 *deniers* around 1350 to 55 around 1450 and 30 around 1470–80. In areas specially ravaged and in need of re-population, settlers were granted reductions more striking still, even sometimes total exemptions from rent for periods which varied with the difficulties. The abbey of Solignac in Limousin lengthened it without a break throughout the first half of the fifteenth century from one or two, to 15, 18, 19, or even 31, years, only to shorten it again after 1450. Sometimes this reduction affected equally or even solely the other seignorial rights, like the French *lods et ventes* or the English 'entry fines'. On some estates of the abbey of Glastonbury the latter climbed from £1 or less on an average per virgate about 1250 to £12 and more about 1345, then fell to a purely nominal figure by 1450.

The form of the rent was also often changed to meet the peasants' wishes. Where it was still in kind—a much commoner occurrence than is ordinarily believed—it was in some cases converted into money. But this happened only in some cases. The money economy had probably not achieved in the fourteenth and fifteenth centuries the progress of which so many authors write. If it was increasing, it was in another manner, or rather in two other manners: the most burdensome and odious labour services, like the English 'week work', when not actually abolished became commutable, and share-cropping gave way very largely to money payments even in its most favoured stronghold, the vineyard. In Sury-le-Comtal, in Forez, 43 per cent of the rented lands held from the Priory of Saint-Romain-le-Puy were given in *champart* in 1350 and only 13 in 1400. This type of payment to which the grower had always been hostile hardly survived except in a particular form which fitted into certain precise needs. Some peasants were too poor or too impoverished to be capable of taking up, keeping or extending their holdings without loans of livestock, equipment, or seed, or all three. Some landlords hoped to increase or at least to maintain the earning capacity of their lands by dividing them into plots of a certain size, but the only way in which they could induce people to take them was by offering substantial advances. Some townsmen who had made money and had bought property as an investment and in order to supply themselves with victuals in time of scarcity were ready to sink capital, for irrigation or other uses, on condition that they participated in its profits. Share-cropping under contracts of *métayage* solved these difficulties and met these require-ments, and was very popular in the Mediterranean countries. In Italy, where great merchants and other citizens of lesser rank owned much of the available land, and where the *contadini* were probably economi-cally and politically weaker, *métayage* became well established from the thirteenth century onwards: of the 15,000 properties listed in the survey of Siena in 1316, 6500 were leased and 5000 of these were in *mezzadria*. South of the Alps *métayage* easily established itself and was even extended, except perhaps around Padua and Verona. North of the Alps it took root in Provence before 1300; after that date it gained ground everywhere: in Béarn, in the region of Albi and Toulouse, in Bas-Quercy, in Limousin. In Central France it profited from the merging of holdings operated by prudent landlords, such as those of the Gâtine in Poitou, who began towards the end of the Middle Ages to regroup the little holdings of the *manouvriers* into farms better suited to the demands of rational technique and the needs of large families. It gained more ground—as we shall see in a moment—as lords gave up direct exploitation of their lands. But farther north it was employed only in heavily devastated regions and then only in an incomplete form: in Sologne and the Île de France, the Hundred Years War once over, demesnes were given up in favour of a method which combined the time lease (*bail à ferme*) for the fields with the *bail à cheptel* for the live-stock. Elsewhere proprietors granted loans to settlers fairly regularly on plots of a certain size, but did not demand or obtain a share of its fruits.

Another method of retaining or attracting peasants was to increase the duration of the tenancies. Peasants had never cared to take up land on an uncertain title or for a very brief term. The abbot of Pontigny, as well as many others, drew attention to this when, in 1336, he begged permission from the chapter general of Cîteaux to grant leases for more than five years contrary to the rules of the Order; it was impossible to find any longer, he said, settlers willing to enter into such short leases. Besides, the desire for rational management favoured a policy of letting out for periods which were not excessively short. Maximilian of Austria seemed to have realized this in the Act of 1502 in which he ordered the substitution on his estates in the Tyrol of hereditary grants in place of revokable leases which encouraged the farmer to exhaust the soil. But on the other hand, in a world which was constantly changing, landlords clung to their right to preserve or to recover from time to time the disposal of their property. Between these contradictory tendencies one or the other predominated according to the pressure exerted by the parties, the importance which they attributed to the matter, the density of the population and other relevant circumstances. The numbers of 'tenants at will' diminished in certain parts of England, but in other parts the number of copyholds, 'tenements *ad placitum*', increased, at least in the fifteenth century. These uncertainties lead us to ask whether we should not pay as much attention to periods as we do to regions. In Italy lettings on short term increased on the estates and land of the townsmen. In several districts in southern Germany the free lease (*Freistift*), which the donor could revoke each year, caused the *Baumannsrecht*, or three-year lease, and here and there the *Erbrecht*, to lose ground as well. In other parts, in the Tyrol, a large part of Bavaria, the neighbourhood of Salzburg, or Berchtesgaden, as well as in Franconia, the opposite happened, and *Leibrecht* and *Erbrecht*—i.e. servile and hereditary tenures—gained ground markedly after 1350, specially under pressure from the territorial princes. In France the difficulties of the time halted the spread of the *bail à ferme*, except on the ancient demesnes. People preferred hereditary leasing and renting on long lease, or new types of lease like the leases for three lives (*baillée à trois têtes*); where it was employed, as in Bas Quercy, for example, a renewal clause was sometimes added to the contract of lease, which gave it some appearance of perpetuity.

When the landlords owned not only land, but also the men who worked it and the very air they breathed, they held another trump card against depopulation of their estates: the improvement of personal status of those under their jurisdiction. That this was effective was shown in 1433 when the duke of Brunswick-Wolfenbüttel suggested to his prelates and vassals that they should lighten servile dues in order to arrest the abandonment of holdings by peasants. The measure could also have significant political effects, of importance in these times of perpetual disorders; so significant that certain concessions aimed at nothing more. It was to reward the town and territory of Bregenz for their trustworthy behaviour and to confirm them in this attitude that the count de Montfort granted them privileges in 1409, and it is to the Scottish struggles for independence that the rapid disappearance of villeinage in that country can be attributed. Carefully handled, such a transformation could prove to be not too bad a bargain. Did not the King of France and the landlords of north-western Germany in the process of liberating their serfs or *Laten*, in the thirteenth and early fourteenth centuries pocket tidy sums of money, save themselves enormous administrative expense and recover the disposal of lands let out on hereditary leases? It is true that at the very same moment the grandees of Northern Spain were acting quite differently; they imagined that they could put a stop to the losses of men and also the losses of money which resulted or might result from the resettlement (*repoblacion*) of the south by resurrecting forgotten rights, by creating new exactions and by a whole series of measures designed to bind their tenants to the soil. Landlords of the fourteenth and fifteenth century could be tempted to do likewise and to seek, at the risk of depopulating their lands or causing a revolution, to compensate themselves for the fall in real income by an increase in personal obligations. Thus two possible paths were open, leading in opposite directions. Which of them was followed was a matter of temperament, skill or daring, and, more than anything, of the possibilities and circumstances at any one time.

Some lords chose to aggravate the condition of their men, although with varying success. In the *trecento* the Roman barons held their people up to ransom and turned their lands into a desert, or at least a semi-desert. The rich landowners of Christian Spain followed the policies of their ancestors. According to a declaration of Juan I to the Cortes at Valladolid in 1385, the Castilians overwhelmed the occupiers of their lands with *grandes pedidos*, with *fuercas* and *muchos males*, and put many of them to flight. Their Catalonian neighbours added what the masses called *malos usos*, and what Queen Maria de Luna, in a letter to Benedict XIII, branded as *malas, detestables, pestiferas, execrables, abominables servidumbres y contumbres ... contra Dios y la justicia*; they fed the discontent which exploded in the fifteenth century and overcame them and their pretensions. Not a few landlords of the Empire behaved in a similar way, as we have seen above in connexion with forced labour, *Gesindezwangdienst*, and attachment to the soil. They too had to face uprisings at the end of the Middle Ages, but they conceded nothing to the insurgents. In Hungary the great landlords did what they could to hinder those who departed for the towns, the population of which did not cease growing, and increased the weight of the *census* and *taxae*. Finally we must recall what has already been said about the advances—smaller than is sometimes alleged, but nevertheless incontestable—made during this period by territorialized serfdom (*servage réel*), more properly described as 'serfdom of the air'.

On the other hand, in other countries and lands the status of countryfolk improved. The practice of collective enfranchisement still existed. Sometimes it was the crowning event of an ancient movement, as in Dauphiné where Humbert II abolished in 1341 the arbitrary *taille*, the hearth tax and other extraordinary impositions, and then in 1349 the mortmain, and where the regime became in that way as liberal as in neighbouring Provence. Sometimes it was stimulated by the wish to prevent emigration. Thus even before the Black Death serfdom began to disappear in Franconia, where the peasants were open to the attractions of the new towns, and, more pressing still, the Slavonic East. More often it followed the passing of troops: at Cessey in Burgundy, which then numbered only two households where 30 or 40 were previously, mortmain was suppressed in 1442; in 1431, on the morrow of hostilities which had, literally, '*tout mix à ruyne*', the count of Namur renounced this right throughout his principality. The rhythm of concessions was nevertheless infinitely more leisurely than in the twelfth and thirteenth centuries—it could in any case not have maintained a pace as rapid as in earlier times. Even in Gascony and Guienne, where the Hundred Years War had raged, almost all the charters of franchise date from before 1321. The importance of the privileges granted was equally restricted; one obligation only of the *homines* and *servi* commonly disappeared—mortmain; others remained, notably the *taille*. Thus if the events of the later Middle Ages favoured rural emancipation, they did so not by encouraging the landlords to bestow collective charters of manumission. The more usual effect was to make escape for the villeins easier; to offer them the possibility of winning or buying enfranchisement individually; to push the authorities towards the abolition or reduction of forced labour and of the types of tenure which were appropriate to forced labour and separated men subject to it from freemen; and finally to provide the stronger communities with the possibility for demanding and obtaining a gradual transformation of local customs.

Qualitative or quantitative changes of rent, the lengthening of the duration of concessions, improvement of the legal position of the inhabitants; these methods achieved their objective, particularly in France where, because of war, they were applied more generally than elsewhere. They allowed more far-sighted landowners to keep their tenants, or to attract new ones. This they did slowly when the lords had to rely on the local population. Half a century after the return of peace, the seigneur of Neufbourg still had fewer men than before the outbreak of military operations. They did this more speedily when they succeeded in stimulating currents of immigration. From 1470 to 1480, for instance, 200 families from western and west-central France settled on the lands of the Bordeaux abbey of Sauve-Majeure, while Bretons and people from Touraine and Limousin were established on the estates of Sénonais, and Italians on those of Outre-Siagne.

But to avert desertions by tenants or to recruit new ones was to meet only one of the problems presented by the decline of population and by the rise in the cost of labour. There was also another question to which the measures just discussed brought but a partial solution; and that was the exploitation of the demesne. This task could not be carried out solely by forced labour; servants and day labourers were absolutely essential. But wages of these people had risen steeply; and this difficulty could in most cases be resolved only by modifying not merely the details but the fundamental structure of the landed estate, i.e. by abandoning its direct exploitation.

To give it up meant to reduce responsibility for its conduct, to be assured of steady revenues, to be free to take up other occupations, to leave the manor for the town, and many other benefits which landlords at the close of the Middle Ages greatly appreciated. But more often, in fact above all else, it was an act of prudent management. If vigilantly conducted, a directly cultivated estate could still sometimes be more profitable: the domain of Pessac in the Gironde was leased out for three pipes of wine in 1356, but after being taken over by its owner, it brought in $9\frac{1}{2}$ in 1361 and six in 1367. But usually it would have been nonsense to expect a profit. Bailiffs were expensive and lacking in zeal; servants and day workers put up ever-increasing demands; forced labourers performed their tasks grudgingly, and their work was often worth less than the meals which custom obliged the lords to serve. Consequently, receipts barely exceeded expenses, if indeed they exceeded them at all. It was much better to dismiss the overseers, dissolve the *familia*, convert labour services into money payments or suppress them, and let out the lands. To become a *rentier du sol* was usually to increase one's income or to stabilize it. In regions where personal services had remained heavy, it was also a way of solving at least partially the problem of holdings and tenants; with the demesne alienated, labour services which were heaviest could be abolished. Those from whom they had been exacted could then devote more of their time to their own lands and extend the latter by whatever vacant plots were available.

These reasons were not all new and had been acted on earlier. In the hope of profiting from the rise in the price of corn, some landowners had in the thirteenth century kept the demesnes. Or after having let them out, took them over again and indeed enlarged them as some English landlords, like the monks of Canterbury, had done. But others, already before 1300, had rented out their demesnes, the outlying and smaller ones to begin with, the more extensive and better situated ones later. Demesnes thus rented out probably formed no more than a minority on the English side of the Channel, but a substantial minority nonetheless, since, to take an example, in North Warwickshire 32, and in South Warwickshire 47, estates consisted at that time solely of rented holdings, against 50 and 49 typical manors provided with demesnes. At that time, estates thus transformed already constituted a majority in the north-west of Germany, the Low Countries, France and Italy.

With the fourteenth century and its crises, especially its labour crisis, the numbers of these estates grew everywhere. Wages became ruinous, even for the Cistercian abbeys which were no longer able to recruit the hordes of *conversi barbati* who had up to that time provided them with staff and workmen who were both reliable and cheap. The number of lay brethren fell at Meaux, for instance, from forty in 1249 to seven in 1349, three in 1380 and none in 1393, or at Bordesley from ten in 1332 to one in 1380. Hired labour had to be employed instead, and on the Cistercian estate of Ouges in Burgundy in 1381 payments of wages absorbed in this way more than 60 per cent of all receipts, including those of seignorial rights. Swollen expenses, such as these, swept away

Table 20. *Receipts and wages at Ouges in* 1381

Description	Receipts	Wages
Silver, in francs	173	100
Wheat, in *émines*	131	86
Oats, in *émines*	79	3

the last hesitations and resistances, the forces of inertia, the attachment to things and people present and past, to homesteads and servants, to tradition. The most prudent or recalcitrant contented themselves for a time with renting or leasing small portions of their demesne. Then they also proceeded to let out the greater part. First they granted it in entirety and for relatively short terms. Eventually, for lack of tenants for the whole, they divided it into plots of a size that one family could cultivate without the help of strangers. The plots were generally let out on a sharecropping lease (*métayage*) in Southern Europe, on 'land-and-stock leases' or *à ferme* in the North and in England, on hereditary leases (*Erbrecht*) in the East. At length the only lands remaining under the management of the owners were of smaller landlords possessing only one or two estates or farms; those which adjoined the residence of the great lords and which directly supplied their household daily supplies; and occasionally those whose profitability was safeguarded or restored by energetic re-conversion. At the dawn of the modern era a certain number of poor Saxon knights themselves superintended the cultivation of the lands, while Tyrolean nobles administered two large *Meierhöfe*, one near their castle and the other in the neighbourhood of their palaces at Innsbruck, and the monks of Durham managed directly the granges where they had specialized in stock raising.

We have just referred to lands whose profitability was restored by energetic reconversion. To continue old activities on changed levels of wages and prices, or to transform more or less fundamentally the structure of the manor were not indeed the only methods of meeting changing economic conditions. In a great number of cases technical adaptation was also possible. Theoretically there were two objectives to aim at: to increase the yield of the existing cultivation of winter and spring grains, or to turn to more remunerative crops.

The first alternative was not generally pursued very far. To do so would have meant investing capital and labour in improved management of water supplies, or into deeper ploughing, or into more thorough cultivation. But there was a general reluctance to devote money and manpower which were scarce to the production of corn which had become relatively abundant and cheap. It seemed more rewarding to attempt a reduction of costs. The rotation of crops was sometimes modified: as when some districts in lower Alsace considered a good harvest every other year with less labour was more worthwhile than two mediocre harvests in three years, and hence gave up the three-year rotation for a two-year one; or when landlords of western Germany appropriated the forests, forcibly regrouped cornfields in more compact parcels on the richer lands, and passed in this way from *Feldwaldwirtschaft* to the three-field system; or when newer countries, like Hungary, which had up till then been untouched by the latter system, or had at any rate hardly used it, now adopted it as a common practice. Elsewhere, one cereal giving higher yields, utility or market value, was substituted for another. On numerous spring-sown lands barley gained at the expense of oats; it gave a return of six instead of two to one, could be more thickly sown, was superior in nutritional value, could be used to feed livestock and to brew beer and could be sold for more money. Buckwheat, undemanding in cultivation and useful as fodder, established itself in less favourable parts, specially in North-Western Germany and France. Occasionally methods of working were improved by irrigation, as in Northern Spain under the influence of the *huertas* of Valencia and Murcia. Or tools could be bettered. Bohemia and Poland, where the 'price scissors' were probably less in evidence than in other regions, increasingly adopted instruments made of iron after the fashion of the West. Flanders perfected a light plough which required one man instead of two or three, and one or two horses instead of four to six draught animals. The same principality, and other countries, replaced the sickle with the long- or short-handled scythe, which had the double advantage of economizing labour and harvesting the straw for use as litter. The list may appear long, but must not mislead us: the measures enumerated were of secondary importance and limited application. In this connexion it is significant that the fourteenth and fifteenth centuries neither produced treatises of rural economy nor brought those of the immediately preceding generation up to date. It did not even exhibit a sustained interest in the latter: of 51 medieval manuscripts of *Anonymous Husbandry* of Walter of Henley and of the *Seneschaucy*, 33 date from before 1330, eleven date variously between 1330 and 1400 and only seven date after 1400.

More important were the changes made in another direction: reduction of the areas sown with bread grains and replacement of the latter with roots, leguminous and fodder plants, with industrial crops, with plantations such as the vine, with pasture and forest.

Peas, beans and vetches were highly valued. They were the main ingredient of the potage which was, with bread and broth, the basis of contemporary diet. They nourished cattle in the winter and helped to develop livestock rearing which was more profitable than cultivation. They provided the soil with nitrogen. In England, and doubtless on the Continent too—although lack of detailed study prevents us from knowing for certain—the cultivation of legumes increased. At Waterham it occupied 0·6 per cent of the area sown in 1297–1302, and 10 per cent in 1345–50; in Leicestershire in the fifteenth century it covered a third and sometimes a half of the area sown.

Table 21. *Wheat, barley and leguminous crops in receipts of 25 estates of Leicester Abbey in the fourteenth and fifteenth centuries*
(as percentage of total receipts)

Date	Wheat	Barley	Peas
1363	21·5	57	17
1399	14	45	?
1401	?	?	32·5
1470	14·5	42·5	30

Some landlords and rural communities were not content to extend leguminous plants only at the expense of summer corn. To obtain more, they interfered with the rotation of crops. A few, in the lower valley of the Rhine and in Flanders, sowed the fallow, and 'stole' a harvest from it. But contrary to what is often written, this remained an exceptional and temporary practice. Others, like the monks of Ramsey, created empirically new rotational systems.

Table 22. *Rotation of crops on the estate of Ramsey Abbey at Holywell*

Field	1400	1401	1402	1403	1404	1405
Bradeway	2b	2c	1		2b	2c
Northrup	2b	2c	2b		2b	2c
Crowholdale	2b	2c	2b		2b	2c
Hogfurlong	2c	1 and 2b	3		1 and 2c	1
Sevonacre	2c	1	3		2c	1
Whaddon	2c	1 and 2a	3		2c	1
Thyneacre	?	2b	2c		3	2b
Schepingfurlong	?	2b	2c		3	1
Eastlong	?	2c	2b		2b	2c
Subcroft	?	2b	3		2a	2a
Prestlade	?	3	2b		1	3
Wodebroke	?	2b	2c		3	2b
Batedele	?	2b	2c		3	2b
Mareway	?	3	1		1	3
Redholmacre	?	3	1		1	3
Brerecroft	?	3	2		3	

(1 = wheat; 2a = oats; 2b = barley; 2c = peas; 3 = fallow)

Roots, especially turnips, which, like peas, were suitable for human and animal consumption, and plants of the clover family suitable mainly for fodder, were also probably sown in larger quantities, sometimes even with winter corn, to give, according to the Flemish expression, *dubbelvruchten* or *navruchten*, a 'second' or a 'belated' harvest.

Industrial crops could equally share the fields with grain, but they demanded a fertile soil, abundant labour and repeated manuring. Production, therefore, increased only gradually and in specially favoured areas, such as the northern Low Countries. There, in a region spared by the plagues, rich in coastal pastures and, as a consequence, liberally bestowed with manure of large flocks and herds, and served by easy communications with corn-growing areas, rape was cultivated. In the valley of the Moselle flax was re-instated in the place which it occupied in an earlier period before the rise in the price of corn. The countryside around Erfurt and Speier specialized in woad and madder. These are but a few examples.

Alongside these annual crops, and fitted into old and new cycles, permanent cultivations, e.g. plantations, made their appearance. But their spread was limited for two reasons. Wherever open fields, fixed rotations or common land prevailed, plantations were practicable only on plots cleared from the waste or created by consolidating several and then withdrawn from the common pasture. They also needed large outlays of capital and labour. To make tillage suitable for the vine, for example, plants had not only to be bought but to have constant attention lavished on them. While townsmen possessed the money and peasants could provide labour, the average landlord could lay his hands on neither. Plantations, therefore, throve in regions where townsmen and peasants could pool their resources. In this connexion one example is revealing: while the vine retreated in the fourteenth century in many parts of France, such as around Toulouse, due to the rise in wages, it spread in other parts, notably in some districts of Dauphiné where many of the inhabitants of Grenoble acquired property. Now nowhere else was urban capital and rural labour so closely associated as in Italy, a result of early purchases of land by small burgesses and the widespread practice of *mezzadria*. Plantations therefore developed particularly in Italy. Somewhat less than they might have done, because money available in the towns was often swallowed up in unproductive expenditure like the building of villas, but to a greater extent than elsewhere. They took the form of rice, mulberry trees, vines, olive trees, vegetables, fruit trees and saffron. To point to one particular case, saffron, already grown in Tuscany, was introduced in the fourteenth century to the Marches of Romagna, the Abruzzi and Lombardy, and in the fifteenth to the neighbourhood of Padua, Brescia, Montferrat and in the *Mezzogiorno*. Under the inducement of prices more favourable than those of corn, plantations developed in importance in other regions, more perhaps on peasant holdings than on demesnes; the vine, profiting from an increase in consumption of wine by all classes, was grown over a wide area stretching from Spain through Southern Germany and Austria as far as the Harz mountains; fruit in Normandy and Auvergne; hops, used for brewing, also in the Harz, in Holland and through the southern part of the Low Countries.

But the best means of increasing the profitability of an enterprise was to give greater place to livestock rearing. Animals are a highly perishable form of possession, especially sheep which are very sensitive to climatic conditions—on the damp lands of Ramsey Abbey for every ten ewes only seven lambs were born, and deaths numbered 25 per cent —and were frequently decimated by murrain. But they needed few hands to tend them, and provided many products—meat, butter, cheese, leather, wool—whose price level was steadier than that of grain. The problem was winter and even summer feed; for, apart from exceptional areas favoured by relief and water supplies and sometimes by history (as when the lack of hands after the Christian re-conquest had forced Castile to dedicate itself to pastoral husbandry), meadows were rather few; often an average of between three and ten acres for every 100 of arable. We already know one of the solutions reached by landowners—an extension of the cultivation of leguminous crops. A second was elaborated in fourteenth-century Flanders: a system of improved *Feldgraswirtschaft*, which allowed for the alternation of winter corn, summer corn, fallow and three to six years of pasture. The third was the one to which most recourse was had, and it consisted in converting fields into pasture after having regrouped them and if possible withdrawn them from common use. It could be adopted most easily, indeed almost of necessity, in areas badly affected by the demographic decline, by the *Wüstungen* of which there was mention earlier in the chapter, particularly in Germany and the Roman *campagna*. It was introduced by compulsion and cunning in other parts, especially in England at the end of the fifteenth century. Attracted by the rise in the price of wool brought about by the growth of the native cloth industry, monks, nobles, but more than any the gentry, provoked the departure of their tenants and 'enclosed' their holdings; in the words of a contemporary—'thei leave no grounde for tillage, thei inclose al into pastures, thei throw doune houses, thei plucke downe towns and leave nothing standyng but only the churche to be made a shepehowse'. To achieve their ends, these 'ambitious grazier-landlords' laid unworthy hands on communal lands. The lords acted in the same way in Haute Provence. Some appropriated areas of woods and *landes*, and arrogated to themselves the more important rights and uses on them. Others in a countryside of pronounced and contrasting relief, organized alpine pastures and transhumance. Others again, improved pastures by irrigation or manuring.

Thanks to such measures, stock-raising was intensified everywhere. Cattle raising developed particularly on the periphery of the West—Norway, Denmark, Poland, Hungary, Tyrol, Styria and in some older countries, such as Holland, which according to a survey of 1494 lived *metter koe, met vogelen ende visschen*, probably also Flanders (where the true churn was invented in the fourteenth century), in the Alps and finally in areas, like those around Aurillac and Metz, where burgesses turned landowners sought with greater tenacity or farsightedness than others to increase the returns from their farms. As for sheep, numbers went on growing on the largest estates, particularly in Castile where the association of the flockmasters, the *Mesta*, officially founded in 1273, never ceased increasing its business dealings, but even more on the holdings of peasants. In 1384 around Courtrai, rural holdings of from one to six *bonniers* possessed 20, 50 or 70 wool-bearing animals; in 1417 eight parishes near Vence possessed 25,000 head between them.

The last possible adaptation, especially in depopulated or devastated parts, was to dig fish ponds and, where trees sold well or horses, cows and, of course, pigs could be pastured, to manage the woodlands on a large scale. The great German forests of Mosigkauerheide near Dessau and the Letzingerheide date from the later Middle Ages.

c. *The results*

Just as the possibilities were infinitely diverse, so were also the results and final consequences. These varied considerably from one seignorial estate to another, and within the same seignorial estate from one manor to its neighbour, and on the same manor from one period to another. At Lullington, in Sussex, the receipts of St Albans rose sharply from 1327 to 1350; at Woolstone in Berkshire they fell from 1308 to 1325, rose from 1325 to 1332, then fell steadily except for a short break, until 1354. At this date the budget of the archbishopric of Bordeaux, if reduced to seignorial revenues alone, would have been in deficit, but from 1361 to 1367 the product of the demesnes and seignorial dues together would have sufficed to cover the expenses of the prelate and his household. From these examples the difficulties and dangers of drawing general conclusions are obvious. One manor would be affected as early as 1320, another would not be badly touched until 20, 30 or even 50 years later. On some, like those of Tavistock Abbey in Devonshire, the position was soon adjusted; on others profits fell to a lasting and often considerable degree: at Wilburton from £40 to £60 a year in 1320 to £25 in 1460, or at Forncett from an average of £93 a year between 1275 and 1304 to £74 in 1376–7 and even lower to £51 in 1377–8.

This fall was all the more dangerous because, from what we know of medieval budgets and their movements, it coincided with mounting expenses and also sometimes with destruction of capital. Arms became more complicated; fortifications expanded; so-called 'aid' to princes appeared necessary; the taste for luxury grew, even on the humblest manors: one petty Saxon knight of the fifteenth century devoted 27 per cent of his income to wearing apparel of which more than half was for his own personal use. Public and private warfare was prolonged and created havoc. All these things could have the direst consequences.

Most large landlords escaped them. They were better prepared to face an agricultural crisis, and they accordingly suffered less than their smaller counterparts. They also found compensations more easily. If they possessed sovereign powers, they could use taxes as a remedy; in 1500 no more than 10 per cent of the revenues of the count in the Tyrol were drawn from land, as against 50 per cent in 1300. If they could not levy taxes, they could impose higher personal charges on their dependent tenants, or extend them to all who breathed the air of their *districtus*. They could obtain royal lands, charges and pensions. Finally, their social position led them to devise, and their wealth enabled them to pursue, a ruthless policy of family aggrandizement: to find eligible matches for their children, and to pass the bulk of their fortune to only one of their descendants, even despite customary practice, and to be prepared to cast the others into the already swollen ranks of impecunious petty nobility.

In this way the great titled families, or at least their elder branches, were often able to maintain themselves. Even more, many combined or were absorbed by inter-marriage. Amongst others, the Nevilles in England absorbed several families and their estates. In Castile at the end of the Middle Ages the grandees were often lords of whole provinces. The most obvious exceptions to this were the religious communities of Northern Italy. Victims of the policies of the *signorie*, of papal finance, of appropriation by absentee heads, of the weakness of their leaders, they lost in the fourteenth and fifteenth centuries a large part of their possessions. Under the pressure of the *potentes* or in order to favour relations and friends, or because they were in low waters, they leased their lands out at derisory rents: for 25 florins where they could have obtained 180; and afterwards they were compelled to make these temporary concessions perpetual and finally to surrender their entire rights over them.

The small landowners could not extricate themselves so easily from such a situation. They suffered more from the fall in receipts from the land since these formed the largest part, if not all, of their income. And compensations were harder for them to find. No rich heiresses for them in their walk of life; no fat pensions; no possibility, lacking as they did control of justice, of replacing the lowered value of their rents with heavier personal dues. What then? To hurl themselves recklessly into warfare? This was a two-edged weapon: men could win at it, as Froissart and the story of Bascot de Mauléon show, but men could also lose, and at any event to engage in war entailed neglecting one's property. To become a *malandrino* in Italy, a *routier* in France, a *hidalgo handido* or a *corsaris* in Spain hardly conformed to ideals of chivalry. In the last resort there were but three honest and reasonably certain paths to survival. First, a man could place himself, if an occasion should arise, in the shadow of a prince or magnate: by this means he could at least maintain and sometimes even improve his position. This is proved by the fate of the aristocracy of the Île de France who, living, as they did, close to the court and its followers, rode out the storm more successfully than their equals in any Capetian province; or the lords of

Hohenems who, relying on the strength of the Hapsburgs, created in the fourteenth and fifteenth centuries around their fortress a true *territorium*. Secondly, at the risk of scandalizing supporters of the feudal tradition like the Pseudo Puigpardines of Catalonia who could not understand 'how the knighthood could be reduced to such an extremity', he could settle down on his estate with the deliberate intention of becoming a country gentleman, if not actually a farmer. He would then superintend on the spot his *métayers*, or conduct personally the management of the property, take up more land for rent to complement his own, dispose on the market the product of his own animal husbandry and reduce such unproductive expenditure as warlike arms and 'status symbols'. Or thirdly, a man could turn towards activities characteristic of the bourgeoisie—industry, e.g. iron manufacture, trade, finance; activities which many of the nobility in Northern and Central Italy adopted with little hesitation, but which fewer of their brothers on the other side of the Alps chose to follow. Barcelona had at the end of the Middle Ages no more than 25 knights out of a population of 35,000.

Not to choose one of these paths or, having chosen it, not to follow it energetically, was to condemn oneself, as A. Sapori says, *alla morte o a una vita di miserie materiali e morali*. Life could be lived for a while from hand to mouth and funds could be borrowed from the money-lenders in the neighbouring town—the practice was indeed so common in certain countries like Bohemia, that the public authorities there occasionally declared a moratorium on debts for knights. Now and again a tithe would have to be sold, a lease, a field, a second one, then another. Finally the unhappy landowner would vanish from the scene. He might well remain a nobleman, but socially he would be no more than what was called in the region around Namur a *povre gentilhomme*, or in Provence a *nobilis mendicans*. He had given up his place to the more fortunate buyer.

The agricultural crisis had thus the ultimate result of accelerating the rhythm of this perpetual movement towards renewal of the land-owning and governing classes. At a rate faster in some parts of the country than in others, real property passed from the nobility, sometimes to the peasantry, often to officials, but most frequently to the middle classes. Sometimes the latter obtained land by means of loans which the debtors could not repay. Sometimes they bought it directly so as to remove some of their capital from the risks inherent in the conduct of business; or in order to acquire access to credit accorded more willingly to the owners of landed property than to the owners of merchandise or money wealth; or in order to lay hands on some verdure for the summer, foodstuffs in case of scarcity, a refuge beyond the reach of epidemics; or in order to provide for wife and children in case of premature death; or in order to sacrifice to fashionable behaviour; or in order to climb another rung in the social scale. This transfer of property had been both early and active in Italy and had worked to the benefit of the smaller bourgeois families and of the *popolo grasso*. It continued after 1300. In the parts of France affected by the Hundred Years War the trend was intensified at the same date. From 1380 to 1460 the family of Perrote, nourished by the proceeds of trade, built up in Normandy a considerable inheritance of landed property at the expense of the victims of hostilities. In the fifteenth century the family of Etampes, nobodies enriched by service with the king and ennobled in 1404, became great lords of Sologne. Developments like these reached the point where at last in big towns and even in whole provinces the rules prohibiting the handing over of fiefs to commoners were lifted. A century earlier, in 1329 and 1350, in the Empire the bourgeois of Thuringia and the ancient March of Meiszen received similar liberties to acquire *Rittergüter*. An *Informacie* in Holland in 1514 revealed that at that time the best lands of the province belonged to townsmen. In England this process was less widespread: war profiteers, like a William of Montague in the fourteenth century or a John Fastolf in the fifteenth, built up immense fortunes in a very short time, but to judge from the city of London in 1436, merchants there invested less in land than their peers in other countries; or rather they had not developed this habit by the last third of the fifteenth century.

In Tuscany or in Catalonia some of these newly rich men adopted a mentality and a way of life which they assumed was more suited to their station; they settled down on their estates and sank into idleness. Others spent no more than a small part of their capital on them. But most thought more of output and economy than of consumption. They surveyed their lands, made improvements, such as irrigation in Italy or drainage in the Low Countries, re-erected in due course farm buildings and filled them with equipment and livestock, and, when the occasion presented itself, bought back *cens* and other seignorial rights. At the moment when the Middle Ages were giving way to the modern era they injected both large- and medium-sized properties with new vigour. Thus in the hands either of their old masters or their new ones, at the price of certain changes, these estates were able to survive the crisis.

However, these changes could for the peasants be sometimes favourable and sometimes troublesome, and their varying fortunes must now be depicted before we complete the last panel of the many-sided picture of rural life in the fourteenth and fifteenth century.

VI. *The peasants: individuals and classes; troubles in the countryside*

The complex and varied evolution of the peasantry in Western Europe in the later Middle Ages was dominated by two tendencies which were in some parts of long standing, in others comparatively recent, but which everywhere became more marked in our period. There was on the one hand the lessening of the economic and legal contrasts between different social groups set in motion by the declining condition of the most favoured and the advancing condition of the humbler folk, as a result of which both fused into a relatively homogeneous class. On the other hand there was a growing disparity between those enjoying the advantages of greater wealth—the more substantial cultivators of the land, who approximate to our modern farmers—and those subject to restrictions of personal status—the serfs. To illustrate these apparently contradictory tendencies, the condition of the upper peasantry and the mass of the country people and serfs must be briefly examined. To complete the picture a few pages will also have to be devoted to a brief story of rural communities and popular peasant rebellions.

A. *Economic and legal classes*

Before the beginning of the fourteenth century some peasants cultivated on their own behalf a considerable area. Some significant figures given above for the region of Namur are typical of the Continent (Table 4). And, despite the obstacles put in the way of division and transfer of property by landlords and manorial custom, the position in England was similar: in 1327 ten of the 120 families of Wigston in the Midlands paid 70 per cent of the taxes levied in the district. Sometimes those concerned owned the freehold of the land, but more often they held it as tenants from one or more landlords. But the distinction already undermined by economic and legal transformations was becoming less and less significant and the time was not far off when French jurists would identify *proprietas* with *dominium utile*. What counted most and continued to count to an ever greater degree was the extent of the area to be cultivated.

In most cases these 'sanguine men, high-coloured and benign', held on tenaciously to their position and even improved it. True enough, they suffered from the agricultural crisis, from the fall in the price of wheat and the rise of wages: they were, after all, enthusiastic supporters of official regulation of the latter. But they were probably less affected by the crisis than landlords and particularly the lesser landlords. For unlike them they did not have to bear any costs of administration and to submit to expenses which were irreducible because determined by the social code, and they could more easily replace the labour of hired workmen by their own and that of their families. No doubt some fell by the wayside. But others resisted and even improved their position, while newcomers filled the gaps. For the crisis was not exclusively damaging to the peasant. It provided the wealthier, the more skilled and the more daring among them with greater opportunities. Cultivators might succumb to epidemics, owners or tenants might be ruined by war and be forced to sell their rights, landlords might lease their demesnes and divide or alienate their ancient *mansus* or fractions, 'quarters' or 'virgates': all such happenings threw land on the market and provided occasion for the survivors to enlarge their existing holdings. Landlords' agents often seized these opportunities and so did the more substantial tenants, usually descendants of men settled on the soil for generations, who had little by little managed to consolidate their position. This process is clearly revealed in statistical series like those for Weedon Beck, which unfortunately cover only one-third of our period (Table 23). It also emerges from the history of rural families. In

Table 23. *Rents paid by tenants at Weedon Beck*

Rents paid	Total Numbers			Percentage of total		
	± 1248	± 1300	1365	± 1248	± 1300	1365
+ £1	—	—	2	—	—	2·7
15s.–£1	—	—	1	—	—	1.4
10s.–15s.	3	4	7	3·7	3·6	9·6
5s.–10s.	46	33	26	56·8	30	35·6
2·5s.–5s.	15	26	8	18·5	23·6	10·95
1s.–2·5s.	7	18	8	8·6	16·4	10·95
— 1s.	1	19	18	1·2	17·3	24·65
Works only	9	7	3	11·1	6·4	4·1
Hens	—	3	—	—	2·7	—

Wigston, where it is true the large proportion of free lands favoured such activities, the Randolff family accumulated between 1200 and 1450, by small purchases and by inheritance, 150 acres, two or three farms, numerous rents, and emerged as gentlemen. It must be admitted that they and those who imitated them promptly abandoned agriculture for trade or industry. 'Richard Randolff gentelman', as he was called in a deed of 1432, became a grocer in Leicester four miles away from the village of his forefathers.

For the mass of rural dwellers the agricultural crisis had consequences harder to disentangle. The crisis affected both their material condition and their legal status, and it affected differently those who had sufficient land to provide a subsistence for their families and the *undermanni* or *famuli* who lived chiefly by hiring out their labour.

In certain respects the situation was favourable to the former at least in regions where the demographic retreat was serious. Rents were lightened, labour services became less onerous, the property market was well supplied. At Weedon Beck in the fourteenth century, as has just been shown, only a few peasants profited from the last circumstance, but elsewhere larger numbers were able to exploit it, as in Neufbourg in the fifteenth century. Similarly the same occurred in Soughton in

Table 24. *Average area of holdings ('mouvances') at Neufbourg in the fourteenth and fifteenth centuries*

	Total figures		Percentage of total	
Area	1397–8	1496–7	'mouvances'	
20 acres or more	15	12	3·2	2·9
10 to 20	21	31	4·5	7·6
5 to 10	61	67	13·1	16·4
4 to 5	10	24	4·1	5·9
3 to 4	37	25	7·9	6·1
2 to 3	49	42	10·5	10·3
1 to 2	86	73	18·5	17·8
less than 1	177	135	38·9	33

Leicestershire. In 1341, of nineteen tenants on free lands, two shared between them more than 120 acres and the seventeen others less than 40; and of 51 tenants on villein lands, two possessed slightly more than a virgate of 24 acres, 21 a virgate, three half a virgate, and 25 a simple cottage. In 1477 there were four tenants on free lands, one of whom cultivated 170 acres and three others between them cultivated 60; while on villein lands, out of 20 tenants seven had 2 to 3 virgates, three had 1 to 2, three half a virgate, four less than half, and only three a cottage. The average size of a holding had thus grown between the two dates. It is true that it fell in other countries during the same period, specially in the south and south-west of Germany, but this could be something of an illusion created by the abandonment of the ancient system of *Hufen*, or the substitution of individual holdings for family enterprises, in other words by the relaxation of administrative constraints and of communal practices, or by the introduction of partible inheritance of land.

On the other hand certain tendencies, such as the growing disparity between agricultural and industrial prices, and the introduction or aggravation of public dues, inevitably worked against the small and medium-sized farmer. The price disparity affected them by virtue of their dependence, unavoidable even though limited, upon the market. No matter what variety of crops they sowed, or planted in their gardens, their enclosures and summer fields, or what animals they housed in their byres, whether a cow, a few sheep, pigs and poultry, or what forest resources were at their disposal, they could never be totally self-sufficient. Certain commodities, such as pitch for the animals or iron for plough and hoe, had to be bought, and certain services, such as the weaving of their flax and hemp and the making of shoes from their leather, had to be paid for. They had also to meet their obligations to their landlords and to pay their taxes to the State, of which the former were often, and the latter always, due in the form of money. They therefore had to sell some of what they produced and were bound to suffer consequently from the distortions of the price level. Many tried to escape by reducing their purchases and by adapting their production. They substituted wood for iron in their tools, devoted a larger area to more profitable crops, such as the vine or the hop, and increased their livestock, especially sheep. But the arrangement of the fields and customary rules prevented them from going very far in this direction. While it may sometimes have been possible to withdraw, as in Devon, some small pieces of the 'infield', or some *devèses*, as in Bas Quercy, from customary routine and from collective constraint, this could not become a general practice, except for more important individuals capable of standing up to the community. And it was precisely the activities of these men, enclosing large parts of their land and, even worse, appropriating all or part of the woodlands and waste, which obliged the peasants of many regions to reduce instead of to increase the number of sheep and pigs. As for the dues imposed by the State renascent in the midst of ruins, or levied by those who disputed its power, their weight and their menace have already been emphasized; in the counterpoise of favourable and unfavourable factors they frequently tipped the balance for the worse.

All in all the economic condition of what we might call the middle-class peasant more often worsened than improved, and this tendency was intensified as the later Middle Ages advanced. Many of the small landowners of 1300, especially in Italy, Spain, the north of the Low Countries and the 'black land' of Russia, lost their foothold during the fourteenth and fifteenth centuries, through their inability to repair the damage caused by war, to undertake essential improvements and to satisfy the demands of the kings and the nobles. Many tenants also became enmeshed in circumstances beyond their control.

In Italy they borrowed to set themselves up on a *métairie*, found themselves unable to repay the money and had to leave in search of new proprietors who would lend more money to pay off the debt to the old one. Five tenants followed each other in seven years on one small farm belonging to Bernard Macchiavel in Sant' Andrea in Percussina near Florence; the same number in less than ten years on another farm. In Spain, peasants were overwhelmed by the burden of *malos usos*. In Dauphiné in the fourteenth century and in English villages in the late fifteenth century, they suffered from the contraction of the common lands. Elsewhere too they were forced to mortgage their possessions. If only we had detailed studies, period by period, of rent changes, their distribution and the purpose for which they were instituted, how much light it would throw on our problems!

The condition of the economically weakest, who comprised the largest group, was different. In 1289 in the relatively fertile village of Haltinne in the region of Namur 41 per cent of the inhabitants possessed less than three hectares; in the foothills of the Provençal Alps 16 of the 28 households subject to the Hospitallers at La Roque-Esclapon had no draught animals, and out of 20 at Chamonsac one only possessed an ox and another a donkey. These *malnutriti* (to use an expressive Italian phrase), were they *lavoratori rurali* or *famuli*, found their situation eased in various ways.

At the beginning of the fourteenth century the *lavoratori* might possess a hovel with a croft, a scrap of ground, no more than an acre or two, or five at most. Today this would not be sufficient to support a household, even though its members might go without all but the barest necessities. How much worse it would be in the Middle Ages when the productivity of the soil was so low, when the fields lay fallow half the time, when seed was sown less thickly, and when a grain of corn sown often brought no more than four or five in return. In order to live these people hired themselves out as day labourers or harvesters, or went from place to place threshing grain, or became carpenters' mates or builders' labourers. In the later Middle Ages they got the opportunity to extend their holdings by taking up vacant lands. We have already seen how at Soughton the group of 'cottagers' had dwindled from 25 in 1341 to no more than three in 1477. And this was certainly not an isolated case. A study covering 150 English 'manors' reveals that the figures for holdings above and below 5 acres shrank by 10 per cent and 35 per cent respectively. At Ouges in Burgundy, tenants in 1409 disposed on an average of four to five 'day works' (*journaux*); in 1445, fewer in number, they had ten to twenty. Methodical research through continental *censiers* and rentals on the size of peasant holdings from 1300 to 1500 would probably reveal an increase in the average area of these, and a shrinkage in the number of the smallest holdings. It is true that in some cases this double tendency could have arisen at least partly from the reduction in the extent of the common lands which has been noted in the last paragraph, a reduction which might have driven the least favoured individuals to leave in search of less rapacious lords or of localities legally and economically more advanced. In the second place wages, and particularly agricultural wages, began to rise in the first decades of the fourteenth century, and, allowing for variations according to time and place, to the amount of labour service available and to the existence or absence of rural industry, they continued to rise steadily until some time in the fifteenth century. Convincing evidence on this point has already been quoted.

The *famuli*, servants dwelling on the farm, also benefited from the action of these factors, specially from the rise in wages. While their wages remained lower, and often considerably lower, than those of day labourers, they nevertheless rose noticeably, as the following tables show. In interpreting Table 26 it should be remembered that the domestic servants of Crowland Abbey received, as well as their wages in cash, a reward in kind which amounted at the beginning of the period to a quarter of maslin every 10·6 weeks; this was reduced to a quarter for every twelve weeks between 1360 and 1377 and raised to a quarter for every ten weeks after 1379.

The normal remuneration of labourers in the countryside around

Table 25. *Wages of* famuli *at Tavistock in pence per week*

Year	Ploughman	Shepherd
1298	$3\frac{1}{2}$	3
1334	4	—
1358	—	4
1373	6	6
1380	7	—
1385	8	—
1387	—	7 to 8

Table 26. *Wages of* famuli *at Oakington in shillings per year*

Period	Driver	Holder	Shepherd	Maid
1258–1322	4	5	4	2
1361–1370	5	7	7	7
1371–1380	6·9	7·11	6·6	6·10
1381–1390	6·9	8·5	5·8	7
1391–1400	7·7	9·1	6·1	5·7
1401–1410	7·8	10	8·2	7·8

1400 thus reached a decent level which was maintained for the remainder of the period. German peasants in these groups were subject from this period onwards to the same taxes as other cultivators, and produced a substantial part, sometimes as much as a quarter or more, of the total yield of the tax. The average wage of a first-rate agricultural labourer, such as a man who drove the plough or the cart, together with the earnings of his wife and son, has been reckoned, in England, as equal to the income obtainable from cultivating 20 acres. The difficulties of computations of this kind and the dangers of drawing conclusions from them are obvious, but it seems incontestable that the differences between the situation of many small wage earners in 1300, 1350 and 1400 and the middle class peasant were much reduced. Of many, but not all. There remained the destitute 15 or 20 per cent, a proportion which seems unacceptably large to our modern eyes. At the end of the Middle Ages not the whole but the greater part of the rural population shared approximately the same economic standard of life.

In spite of countless local variations and contrasts, similar rearrangements occurred in the groupings and classifications of personal and legal status. The status of most peasants changed between 1300 and 1500, and, as we have already seen, it changed in different directions. In some cases it improved. Whole villages would obtain the reduction or suppression of some obligations, most usually those of heriot. Serfs were in various ways able to break the ties which bound them to their masters. Some were enfranchised collectively or individually. Others were allowed to leave the estates, and aided by careless administration, often ceased after a time to pay *capitagium*. Others profited by the troubles of the times, such as the Black Death, and fled, and their lords either could not trace them, or were unable to prove their rights over them. On the other hand the status of some peasants worsened. Sometimes it did so indirectly, as in Italy. In that country from early times the towns had fought for political, economic and even intellectual reasons for the freedom of the *adscriptitii* and the *servi*. Right up to the fifteenth century they endeavoured to make freedom theoretically more widespread and complete, but at the same time they in fact narrowly restricted it to the greater advantage of their inhabitants, many of whom were landowners, both large and small. For example, they circumscribed the rights of bourgeoisie or even denied them altogether to the *contadini*, thus virtually forcing them to remain on the land. Or else, as happened in Bologna in 1376, any other form of lease than the *mezzadria*, which was far more advantageous to the lessor than the *affito*, was forbidden. The condition of the countryman worsened far more directly in the eastern Empire as well as in some parts of the West. Many lords increased the burden of their dues or extended them to all who 'rose up in the morning or laid themselves down to sleep' on their lands, or in the fifteenth and more especially in the sixteenth centuries introduced new obligations. Now, amidst these movements, and often because of them, men's legal status tended to level out. This was also due to a transformation of many personal obligations into money payments incumbent on property, to the greater frequency of property transactions which transferred free lands into the hands of the unfree (or vice versa), and to the subjection of all individuals to the same courts. In each region an ever-growing proportion of the population shared the same legal status. Thus, as the Middle Ages drew to a close the great majority of peasants were, as in England and in the Tyrol, virtually free; or, as in the greater part of France, the south-west and centre of Germany, they were villeins subject to charges often identical in name but variable in incidence (mostly heriot); or, particularly in other parts of the Empire, they were *Grundhörige*, men who held serf land, but whose present status was not necessarily that of serfdom.

As for the true serfs, the men 'servile in body' (*serfs de corps*), a few were still to be found everywhere at the close of the Middle Ages, but their number diminished considerably during the period while their social position deteriorated. The Count of Hainault's *hommes de maisnie* who died numbered 53 in 1317, 13 in 1350, an average of seven from 1400 to 1410, and only four in the following years. At Forncett there were 19 villein families in the English sense of the term in 1400, but in 1500 there were no more than eight, in 1525 only five, in 1550 three and none at all in 1556. This reduction in numbers was bound to affect the position of the group. The serfs were not juridically affected, for their obligations moved in the same direction as those of the rest of the population and did not differ greatly from them; light *chevage*, moderate *formariage*, nothing else. Nor were they economically touched, for they could round off their holdings or take leases from the demesne and cultivate on their own account up to 100 acres and more, just as easily as other peasants. But they suffered socially. Serfdom appeared more and more as a personal blemish, and those who bore the taint were loaded with further disabilities. Not only were they prohibited from taking holy orders, from being knighted, from exercising public duties or from acting as witnesses, but they were also forbidden to enter corporations of craftsmen. In 1387 for the first time a city law in London enacted that no one could be accepted as an apprentice unless he had first sworn that he was not a bondsman, and that he was 'a free man born and fremannes sone'. Under such conditions, it was harder for serfs to find marriage partners outside their own class. They were, and felt themselves to be, more and more isolated at the bottom of the social ladder. Where slaves existed, as they did in Russia, they experienced a similar evolution. From being servants, many became tenants of land and improved their position, but they kept their status.

The lessening of the material and legal contrasts was probably not the only factor in this extensive regrouping of peasants into a relatively coherent class. Without doubt the position and policy of the towns in many parts of the continent contributed to this result. Ever since their foundation the towns had grown in power and they reached the point where they could dream of extending their economic and political domination over the countryside. By the thirteenth century many ot them had at least partly achieved this ambition and had more or less effectively imposed their will on the surrounding regions. In the fourteenth century they tightened their hold, and their citizens considered themselves superior to those who lived in the country. The scorn they felt for the latter was openly expressed in much of the German and Italian literature of the later Middle Ages. This made countrymen feel more acutely that they formed a distinct class, and shared a common status, that of *rustici*.

B. *The rural communities*

The existence of this 'rural bloc' strengthened the village community. Other phenomena also worked towards the same end; first of all changes in the position of the lords. Where, as in some parts, the landowners had become nothing more than *rentiers du sol*, limiting themselves to the collection of their various dues, they left to the villagers the business of settling their own problems. The assemblies which dealt with these problems were more often than not presided over by the landlords' officers, but often these men acted more as leaders of the tenants than as agents of the proprietors. In other parts the lords attempted to compensate themselves for the drop in their income from land by manipulating customary law, such as increasing personal obligations, and there they unwittingly compelled the villagers to join together to resist these actions. Elsewhere they surrendered their lands to the new rich, to townsmen, to businessmen determined to extract the maximum from their property; and this also provoked a reflex reaction from their tenants. Again the intervention of the growing State could re-inforce the rural community; it raised taxes, the assessment of which was sometimes entrusted to those liable to the taxes or to their proxies. War or other calamity could also necessitate or permit a re-arrangement of the settlement to improve defence (the *Schansen* of Germany owed their existence to this), or to reorganize or rationalize cultivation. Eventually the general tendency, as always in difficult times, was towards control and co-operation. In the towns a corporate economy was developing: in the country associations of the kind described as *communautés taisibles* (informal communities) took on new vigour: friends and close relations would join together to take over waste lands and above all to bring back into cultivation deserted fields. The wind of change was towards unity.

It is true that some factors retarded this movement. Population was unstable: of 49 *chefs d'ostel* who in 1463 made up Antoing, a small place in Hainault, 21 had names unknown eight years earlier. The steady rise of the most enterprising peasants deprived the class of its natural leaders: the rise of the Randolffs of Wigston into the ranks of the gentry and their consequent departure from the native village has been described above. Occasionally too, as happened in Provence, instead of promoting concentration, the re-population which followed calamities took the form of isolated houses which encouraged individualism. Although the strengthening of the landlords' rule demonstrated to the *rustici* the advantages of joint resistance, it could sometimes take away their opportunities for doing so.

In general the forces of fusion triumphed over those of fission. They did not do so in eastern Europe, where the *volosts*, which for a long time had freely administered large areas of Russia, collapsed before the power of the landlords and their agents. But nearly everywhere in the West the village community, the *Dorfgemeinschaft*—a useful German expression—played an increasingly important part. Sometimes it acted unofficially. It coped with its lord. It saw to it that he respected custom; and if he did not, it proceeded against him to restrain his contraventions. It bargained with him and bought or extracted from him many a concession. In Friuli it boycotted any individual who agreed to pay a rent higher than normal and re-possessed the land of a tenant who was unjustly evicted. It also played an official part in replacing the lord in many ways. In economic matters it decided such questions as how many animals were to be allowed to graze on the common pasture. Occasionally it dealt with legal questions. But very rarely it intervened in political ones. Thanks to their geographical situation, the wealth of their animal husbandry and transit trade, and the weakness of their overlords, the alpine communities, from the *Urkantone* of central Switzerland to the villages of the regions of Briançon, Hauestein, Hotzenwald, Appenzell, Bregenz and Vorarlberg, by unifying themselves into *Einigungen* and *Eidgenossenschaften*, succeeded in obtaining real independence.

c. *Popular revolts*

If we recall the events which have been discussed in these pages we can easily understand why the later Middle Ages suffered severe social upheavals. Economic problems and frictions, political innovation, intellectual and religious fermentation, all conspired to set alight and to fan the spirit of rebellion, even in country communities traditionally slow to be roused.

Doubtless there had been earlier outbursts amongst the peasantry. Marc Bloch asserts that revolts were inseparable from a feudal regime. But never before had they assumed such grave proportions as in the fourteenth and fifteenth centuries, because never before had the causes of discontent been so numerous or so clearly recognized.

There were to begin with the usual discontents: the obligation of the *aratores*, as the theorists of medieval society called them, to feed the other classes, the clergy, the townsmen, the lords. Many were convinced that the priests squandered the product of the tithes and offerings. John Hus accused the clerics of 'maintaining a host of menials of no practical use to the sacred ministry, likewise of buying superfluous vases, silver platters, fine drinking vessels, spoons, cushions, sumptuous beds, of constructing splendid mansions, of pulling down those that were still habitable in order to build new ones, of keeping magnificent riding horses and decking them out in costly harness'. Circumstances also required ever-larger numbers of peasants to seek the help of the urban bourgeoisie and more especially city capitalists and money-lenders, buyers of rents and lenders on short term. Above all there were the lords, whom a Czech poem of the fourteenth century likened to drones and threatened with a similar fate. Whether the obligations with which they burdened the land and the air remained the same, were increased or were lightened, they still provoked complaint. Where they remained unchanged they weighed more heavily than of yore, both materially, because economic progress whittled away the income of debtors and increased their needs—for clothing for instance —and psychologically, because they appeared to all men less and less justified, because they were contrasted with the new-found prosperity of some and restricted their activities, or because they happened to have been reduced on neighbouring estates or regions. Where they were lightened the progress already gained made people more exigent: both rural and city dwellers, newly enfranchised and secure in their position, were amongst the leading supporters of the uprisings in Bohemia and the Tyrol. Where the obligations increased under pressure from nobles trying to stave off ruin or from the bourgeoisie determined to get a return on their investment, the masses revolted against such *novelletés* and demanded the restoration of the *altes Recht*. Most of the time they had an erroneous idea of what the 'old rights' were. They denounced as new and improper dues which a careless administration had simply omitted for a time to levy, as well as dues which had always been collected within the memory of man, but which, to believe the outcry, had not existed in ancient times, 'in the time of Henry I' as the English peasants of 1377 put it. Thus while avowing conservative intentions, popular opposition turned more and more into a reforming force and was pushed in that direction by some of the leaders and by the concept of *naturalis justicia*. In this way they came in certain places and at certain moments to regard the seignorial regime in its entirety as an innovation and demanded its suppression. The plotters on the *Bundschuh* of Lehen in 1513 declared expressly *dasz sie furterhin keinen herren me wolten haben und gehorsam sin dan allein den Keiser und den Babst*.

No other overlord but emperor and pope indeed, but it behoved emperor, king, territorial prince or their agents not to go too far. Men willingly sought princely protection against the encroachments of the lords, but they were not so tolerant of its intervention in their affairs. Grievances peculiar to the fourteenth and fifteenth centuries were, so to speak, added to the traditional peasant grievances and were concerned with the very activities of the State. Firstly, the creation of heavy direct and indirect taxation and abuse in its collection; then the institution of superior courts where men were judged neither by their peers nor according to ancient custom, but by *doctores* spouting roman law; the introduction under cover of this law of strict limitation of the usages of the waste and woodland, and hunting and fishing rights therein; the transformation of the political and administrative structure which subjected men to orders from above applied by officials nominated by the central powers; increases in military obligations, either in the form of service or forced labour, such as the enlargement of fortifications: these were the innovations, the true innovations, against which men could legitimately invoke the *altes Recht*.

These grievances did not exist everywhere, and where they did they were not equally acute. Here the lords tenaciously defended their post, there they resigned themselves without too great a struggle to the necessity of drawing less from their lands and their men. In one region the peasants had hitherto enjoyed considerable liberty and thus were less inclined to suffer the meddling of the State; in another they had been bitted and bridled for so long that they had lost all thought of kicking over the traces. Besides, apart from the economic and political situation of the countryside, neither atmosphere nor circumstances were equally favourable at all times and places to the use of violence. At one time, for instance, religion could be an element of order; at another it could be transformed into a formidable revolutionary force. At one period a leader would appear who would precipitate the floating discontent and would attract the masses; at another, equally propitious, there was nobody to risk launching a movement of revolt. So the incidence of peasant agitation varied in period, length and intensity. Some few countries, like Scotland, escaped it altogether. In others it never went beyond a passive or individual resistance, isolated acts of disobedience, occasional burnings or aggression, as in Poland where in the fifteenth century the nobles had no need to do more than forbid the carrying of arms by country people. In others again, namely in France and in Flanders, the grievances exploded prematurely in uprisings which were soon crushed. But in some countries—England, Spain, Bohemia, northern Italy and specially in the Empire—trouble broke out later and with much greater force.

The scene of the first real revolt was the seaboard of Flanders in the second decade of the fourteenth century. In it farmers and other tillers of the soil, many of whom were far from needy, ranged themselves against the prince, his agents and his taxes, but also against those who drew their income from the soil, the nobility and the clergy. The revolt was crushed after five years of bitter conflict and bargaining, and the punishment was merciless. For this reason, or because of the predominant position of the towns, or the prosperity of the countryside, there was never again to be a true peasant rebellion in Flanders.

The French Jacquerie of May and June 1358 was quite a different affair. It was an outburst of rage on the part of country folk, who felt themselves unfairly hit by the war and its aftermath and by the fall in the price of corn. Pushed beyond the limits of endurance they suddenly turned against those who held them in subjection the arms that many of them had learnt to use to defend themselves from the disbanded soldiers. It was quickly over. And it remained a unique phenomenon. The lords of the Capetian kingdom were to face their men again in other armed risings, but none had more than a local background, such as some villages in the Nivernais, and almost all were settled peacefully by agreement and judicial verdict.

Troubles of the same kind in England paved the way for the great uprising of 1381. The same, but more frequent, because of the change in demesne policy in the thirteenth century. The popularity of direct exploitation of the demesne aggravated and hardened the attitude of seignorial management, especially towards forced labour. Peasants in England, more often than their fellows on the Continent, had refused service unless forced by legal action, or had assumed free status and attempted to prove it before the *curia regis*. At Ogbourne in Wiltshire, for instance, there were no less than five cases of this sort between 1300 and 1345. An atmosphere of insubordination spread abroad. The plague came, and with it regulation of wages by Parliament. This measure, and the way in which the royal courts pursued those who transgressed it, increased the discontent, or more accurately enlarged it and changed its nature. The blame was cast henceforth on the State and its agents, as much as, if not more than, on the lords, and in this way, because the State's writ ran everywhere, all discontents were fused into one, in the North as in the South, in the East as in the West. An excuse to spark off the revolt was provided by the government's difficulties and the Poll Tax, and Wat Tyler and his fellows were there to fan the flames. We know how the revolt failed, although at one point it reached the very threshold of victory. But the reverse did not altogether discourage the peasants. Others rose again in the fifteenth century; Kentish men, for instance, rebelled in 1450 under Jack Cade.

At the end of the fourteenth century Christian Spain experienced its first great revolt. Other risings followed in the fifteenth century in all the States except Castile. In Catalonia, where the rebels had the support of the monarchy, they were more successful than in any other country. Arbitrating between the *remensas* and their lords, the King abolished the *malos usos* by the edict of 1486, and authorized enfranchisement for the price of a small sum.

Not long before 1400 signs of unrest were also evident in Bohemia. Religious questioning soon joined social discontent: according to the Chronicle of Laurent de Brezova, those affected by the new ideas held that *quod in supradicto regno hominum vivancium usque ad resureccionem generalem duraturo longe ante cessabit omnis exactor et quiescet tributum et omnis principatus et secularis dominacio cessabit.* Added to this was nationalistic fervour. And in 1419 a struggle was unleashed which raged for twenty years. Its example spread to Transylvania where, in 1437, the peasants formed themselves into an army and fought for a whole year.

While Wat Tyler was leading his English revolt, a movement of unrest was shaking fourteenth-century Italy. It ranged the Ticinese against the feudal lords of Piedmont and the bankers who held many of the manors in debt. But this rising, and others which agitated the countryside around Ravenna in 1430 and around Piacenza in 1460, were less violent than the social struggles Italy had known before 1300. Only in Friuli in 1511, and in the Trentino in 1525, did the tide-race of revolution boil and surge as it had done in an earlier century.

The drama of the highest point and the ultimate failure of the peasant movements of revolt—the *Bauernkrieg*—was played out in the lands encircling the Alps at the beginning of the sixteenth century. Even more than the English and Bohemian revolts, this Peasant's War was a long time brewing. Riots continued throughout the fifteenth century beyond the Rhine, especially in the South-West where the small size of the territorial principalities made the burden of the rising State harder to bear, and where the example of the neighbouring Swiss whetted men's desire for freedom. Between one uprising and the next the spirit of resistance was strengthened, and under the influence of its leaders and their politico-religious theories it became more and more radical. Finally, it outgrew its local field to inflame an ever-widening area. Local and informal groups merged into the larger conspiracy of the *Bundschuh* and from there into open war. The flame was kindled in the South-West in June 1524 and spread swiftly northwards to the Palatinate, Hesse, Brunswick, Franconia, Saxony, and encompassed the whole of the South as far as Carinthia and Carniola, with the exception of Bavaria. But the conflagration produced nothing but a heap of ashes.

Thus, outside Catalonia, the peasants had nothing to show for their sufferings but failure, and for good reason. They lacked everything: political judgment, sense of proportion, intelligent leaders, financial means, organization. How with these handicaps could they have hoped to impose their demands on the State, or to overthrow the rule of the lords which had already survived plague, famine and total war?

VII. *Conclusion: development and preparation*

These pages have been penned between the contradictory pressures of an unusually wide canvas and an extremely brief exposition, and they have multiplied the distinctions without exhausting the diversities of the material. But the main conclusion is inescapable. While the countryside of Europe in the fourteenth and fifteenth centuries, and particularly between 1350 and 1450, suffered many dark days, specially in the regions in which more corn than other goods was produced, and in those—often the same ones—clouded by epidemics of disease and the birth pangs of our modern society, the foundation stone of its economy, the manorial system, survived. It was forced to adapt itself, but it survived.

Different areas produced their own solutions to the problem of adaptation. In this respect the contrast between the countries East and West of the Elbe immediately springs to mind. In the countries to the East the manorial system became entrenched and in the West the system lost much of its significance and vitality.

In the East the problems of agriculture and the opportunities open to enterprising men were favourable to the *Gutsherrschaft*, which provided a framework for the renewal of direct exploitation, the extension of the demesne, the intensification of labour services and the tightening of the lords' power.

In the West a transformation similar in certain respects took place in a few areas. Personal services were made heavier in the Austrian Alps, in Aragon and Castile and in some parts of Germany and France where real serfdom put down deeper roots. Demesnes were again enlarged at the end of the fifteenth century in Central Europe. But, unlike the East, there was no relation between the two phenomena. The *novae allodiationes* of Hungary, for instance, were cultivated with the assistance of servants and day labourers. The surviving demesnes in England were transformed into stock-raising enterprises and their enlargement did not require extra services from the tenants. Thus on this side of the Elbe the bond between demesne and forced labour was decisively broken.

In the remainder of the West as well, the great landlords moved further away from the classical type of estate organization. To forestall the desertion of their tenants and to encourage immigration they granted new 'liberties', both individual and collective, and modified duration, price and details of land leases. Rather than pay ruinously high wages they let off most of their farms. In these ways the country folk improved the conditions of their lives and many of the richer amongst them seized the opportunities thus offered to increase their holdings at the expense of the demesne.

This giving up of traditional methods and the economic and political upheavals of the time undermined the personal basis of the manorial system and consequently weakened it. Landowners changed frequently and often had no time to put down roots. Many lived in towns and had no contact with their men except from time to time through their agents. Their estates were no longer for them familiar fields and woods but merely figures in an account book, or at most names. Peasants were equally mobile and their holdings changed hands ceaselessly. Especially in areas devastated by war or depopulation, they were tempted to abandon their familiar parish, their church and cemetery, for a less ravaged or more fertile spot, or another community whose lord offered them easier terms. The holdings, even where they had until then preserved their ancient manorial entities, were carved up; the old firm framework of the *mansus* and its successors was fragmented and passed from one hand to another with astonishing speed. One holding in the region of Namur had four occupants in fifteen years, and another near Bordeaux had twelve in less than three generations. In such conditions the fields which cost their cultivators so much toil were looked at in a new way. They were no longer a patrimony to be handed on from father to son and to be ordered by immemorial custom, but anonymous possessions to be exploited for a period limited by a contract. A climate of opinion was thus created, and in many places accepted, in which law replaced tradition and profit and loss transformed the ancient way of life.

With its framework undermined and its spirit weakened the manorial system also retreated before hostile forces. These forces were the State with its taxes, courts and officials; the towns with their middle classes; and the rural communities, where the 'village' was henceforth of greater significance than the 'manor', the *Dorfgemeinschaft* than the *Hofgemeinschaft*.

But all the forces at work in the later Middle Ages were not prejudicial to the manorial system. Its leaders were regenerated, its techniques rationalized, purged, consolidated. Of the old landlords, only those who were strong enough, astute enough or hard working enough overcame their problems, and the new landlords were rich, active and energetic. Neither of them was likely to stand idly by. On the contrary they were determined to extract as much as possible from their lands, and their experience in the conduct of affairs and the capital they could dispose of enabled them to do so.

The pressure of events caused methods of exploiting the land to adapt. These changes, already noticeable in some places in the twelfth century, quickened in pace and became more widespread, particularly in regions where cities, industries and rural areas lived in symbiosis. Infertile soils were allowed to return to scrub and tillage was re-arranged in compact plots. Leguminous plants, industrial crops, plantations, pasture, even forest, took the place of corn which had become over-abundant and under-valued. Occasionally to facilitate these improvements crop rotations were re-arranged. Some regions specialized in certain commodities, such as milk, butter and cheese, in areas either damp like Holland, assured of easy outlets like Norway, or mountainous like the Alpine cantons; vines in many parts of Southern Germany, Lower Austria or in the neighbourhood of towns; fruit in Normandy and Auvergne; mulberry trees in the South; flax, hops and many other things. A wealth of experience and many lessons for the modern age to draw upon.

In the rural field, as well as in other sectors of social life, the modern world has inherited many important features from the Middle Ages: the framework of manor and village community, a regenerated and invigorated governing class, a respect for the law and an awareness of technique, new ideas on farming methods. In country life there was no complete break between the fourteenth and fifteenth and the sixteenth centuries, but a large measure of continuity, re-alignment and evolution.

Bibliographies

EDITOR'S NOTE (First Edition)

At an early stage the editors abandoned the notion of compiling a general bibliography. If made complete, this would be little less than a bibliography of medieval history, which would be superfluous. Further, contributors had drawn up their bibliographies on divergent lines; had often inserted valuable notes explaining the methods adopted; and sometimes had thrown the bibliography almost into narrative form. It was therefore decided to leave each bibliography as it stood, with merely editorial correction. The great difficulties of communication since August 1939, which have robbed us of one bibliography entirely, confirmed us in this policy. One result of it is that certain books recur in several lists. We have left them in all, because they both register the contributor's debt and, in a rough way, the greatness, or at least the utility, of the recurring books.

EDITOR'S NOTE (Second Edition)

All the bibliographies in the second edition have been revised and brought up to date, some by the authors of the new and revised chapters, others by historians specially commissioned to do so. Needless to say the principles on which the new or revised bibliographies have been compiled remain the same as in the first edition, with the result that the new bibliographies differ from each other as much as the old ones in the principle of selection and in the manner of presentation. The arguments in favour of this policy have been set out in Professor Clapham's note to the bibliographies in the first edition.

Abbreviations

The following abbreviations are used for the journals most often quoted:

AHES.   *Annales d'histoire économique et sociale.*
AHR.   *American Historical Review.*
ASI.   *Archivio Storico Italiano.*
AVS.   *Archivio Vittorio Scialoja.*
EHR.   *English Historical Review*
EcHR.   *Economic History Review*
EJ.   *Economic Journal; EJ.* (Ec. Hist.), Historical supplement to *EJ.*
EC.   *Economia e Storia.*
ESAR.   *An Economic Survey of Ancient Rome* (ed. Terrey Frank)
HJ.   *Historisches Jahrbuch.*
HZ.   *Historische Zeitschrift.*
JRS.   *Journal of Roman Studies.*
MIA.   *Materialy i issledovaniya po arkheologii SSSR.*
(N)AV.   *(Nuovo) Archivio Veneto.*
RB.   *Revue Belge de Philologie et d'Histoire.*
RH.   *Revue historique*
TRHS.   *Transactions of the Royal Historical Society.*
VSWG.   *Vierteljahrschrift für Sozial– und Wirtschaftsgeschichte.*
ZAA.   *Zeitschrift für Agrargeschichte und Agrarsoziologie.*
ZSS.   *Zeitschrift der Savigny-Stiftung für Rechtsgeschichte.*

CHAPTER I

The Settlement and Colonization of Europe

A Revision of the Bibliography of the First Edition, by ECKART SCHREMMER

I. COUNTRIES AND PEOPLES

ABEL, W. *Geschichte der deutschen Landwirtschaft.* Stuttgart, 1962.

A Historical Geography of England before A.D. 1800. Ed. by H. C. Darby. Cambridge, 1936.

ARNOLD, W. *Ansiedlungen und Wanderungen deutscher Stämme. Zumeist nach hessischen Ortsnamen.* Marburg, 1875.

BACH, A. *Die Siedlungsnamen des Taunusgebiets in ihrer Bedeutung für die Besiedlungsgeschichte.* Bonn, 1927.

BLOCH, MARC. *Les caractères originaux de l'histoire rurale française.* Oslo and Paris, 1931.

—— 'Régions naturelles et groupes sociaux', in *AHES.* I, 1932; 'Champs et villages', in *ibid.* VI, 1934.

BOELES, P. C. J. A. *Friesland tot de elfde eeuw.* The Hague, 1927.

CAGGESE, R. *Classi e comuni rurali nel medio evo italiano,* I. Florence, 1907.

DEMANGEON, A. 'La géographie de l'habitat rural', in *Ann. de Géographie,* XXXVI, 1927.

Deutsche Siedlungsforschungen, R. Kötzschke zum 60. Geburtstage dargebracht. Ed. W. Uhlemann. Leipzig, 1927.

DION, ROGER. *Essai sur la formation du paysage rural français.* Tours, 1934.

DOPSCH, A. *Die ältere Wirtschafts- und Sozialgeschichte der Bauern in den Alpenländern Österreichs.* Leipzig and Oslo, 1930.

EKWALL, E. *Studies in English place-names.* Stockholm, 1936.

ENGEL, F. 'Die ländlichen Siedlungen und ihre Geschichte. Der Landkreis Schaumburg Lippe', in *Die deutschen Landkreise.* Niedersachsen D 12, 1955.

EVERS, W. 'Ortsnamen und Siedlungsgang im mittleren Ostfalen', in *Berichte zur deutschen Landeskunde,* 9, 1951.

FOX, CYRIL. *The Archeology of the Cambridge Region.* Cambridge, 1923.

GALLOIS, J. *Régions naturelles et noms de pays.* Paris, 1908.

Geschichte Schlesiens. Ed. H. Aubin. Breslau, 1938. [see also H. v. Loesch, *Verfassungsgeschichte bis* 1526, and H. Aubin, *Wirtschaftsgeschichte.*]

GRADMANN, R. 'Das mitteleuropäische Landschaftsbild nach seiner geschichtlichen Entwicklung', in *Geogr. Zeitschr.* VII, 1901.

—— *Das ländliche Siedlungswesen des Königreichs Württemberg.* Stuttgart, 1913.

GRAND, R. and DELATOUCHE, R. *L'Agriculture au Moyen Age: De la Fin de l'Empire Romain au XVIᵉ Siecle.* Paris, 1950.

GRAY, H. L. *English field-systems.* (Harvard Hist. Studies, XXII.] Cambridge, Mass. 1915.

GRUND, A. *Die Veränderungen der Topographie im Wiener und Wiener Becken.* Leipzig, 1901.

GUTTENBERG, E. VON. *Land- und Stadtkreis Kulmbach.* 1952.

HAFF, K. *Die dänischen Gemeinderechte.* Leipzig, 1909.

Handbuch der deutschen Geschichte. Ed. O. Brandt, A. O. Meyer, etc. Potsdam, 1936 ff. [Special paragraphs on the history of settlement, by K. Steinacker, F. Steinbach H. Heimpel.]

HANSSEN, G. *Agrarhistorische Abhandlungen.* 2 volumes. Leipzig, 1880.

HARTMANN. L, M, *Geschichte Italiens im Mittelalter.* 3 vols. Gotha, 1897–1911 (Vol. 2nd ed. 1923).

HAUCK, A. *Kirchengeschichte Deutschlands.* 5 vols. 3rd and 4th ed. Leipzig, 1904–20.

HELBOK, A. *Grundlagen der Volksgeschichte Deutschlands und Frankreichs.* Berlin, 1935–8.

HÖMBERG, A. K. *Grundfragen der deutschen Siedlungsforschung.* Berlin, 1938.

Introduction to the Survey of English place-names, Part 1. Ed. A. Mawer and F. M. Stenton. Cambridge, 1929.

Jahresberichte für deutsche Geschichte. Ed. A. Brackmann and Fritz Hartung. Leipzig, 1927 ff. [For the years 1925 ff. each volume contains in part 1A a review of recent literature on 'Historische Geographie und Siedlungsgeschichte', in part 2D, E regional surveys, including neighbouring countries.]

KÖTZSCHKE, R. *Die siedlungsgeschichtliche Forschung auf deutschem Boden. Vergangenheit und Gegenwart* 32, 1942.

KRISCHE, PAUL. *Mensch und Scholle.* Berlin, 1936. (Maps.)

—— *Kartenwerk zur Geschichte und Geographie des Kulturbodens.* Berlin, 1936.

LAMPRECHT, K. *Deutsches Wirtschaftsleben im Mittelalter. Untersuchungen über die Entwicklung der materiellen Kultur des platten Landes auf Grund der Quellen zunächst des Mosellandes*, I–III. Leipzig, 1886.

LIPPERT, J. *Sozialgeschichte Böhmens in vorhussitischer Zeit.* 2 vols. Vienna, 1896–8.

LONGNON, A. *Les noms de lieu de la France.* Ed. by P. Marichal and L. Mirot. Paris, 1922.

LÜTGE, F. *Deutsche Sozial- und Wirtschaftsgeschichte*, 2nd edition. Berlin-Göttingen-Heidelberg, 1960.

MAGER, F. *Entwicklungsgeschichte der Kulturlandschaft des Herzogtums Schleswig in historischer Zeit*, 1. Breslau, 1930.

MAURER, G. L. VON. *Geschichte der Fronhöfe, der Bauernhöfe und der Hofverfassung in Deutschland.* 4 volumes. Erlangen, 1862, 1863.

—— *Einleitung zur Geschichte der Mark-, Hof-, Dorf- und Stadt-verfassung und der öffentlichen Gewalt.* 2nd edition. Vienna, 1896.

—— *Geschichte der Markenverfassung in Deutschland.* Erlangen, 1856.

MAWER, A. *Problems of place-name study.* Cambridge, 1929.

MEITZEN, A. *Siedlungen und Agrarwesen der Westergermanen und Ostgermanen, der Kelten, Römer, Finnen und Slaven.* 3 volumes. Berlin, 1896.

MITTEIS, H. *Der Staat des hohen Mittelalters.* 4th edition. Weimar, 1953.

PETERKA, O. *Rechtsgeschichte der böhmischen Länder*, 1. Reichenberg, 1923. [Bibl.]

PIRENNE, H. *Histoire de Belgique*, 1. 5th ed. Brussels, 1929.

PLANITZ, H. *Die deutsche Stadt im Mittelalter. Von der Römerzeit bis zu den Zunftkämpfen.* Graz-Cologne, 1954.

—— 'Frühgeschichte der deutschen Stadt', in *ZSS.* Germanic section, 63, 1964.

SCHIER, B. *Hauslandschaften und Kulturbewegungen im östlichen Mitteleuropa.* (Beiträge zur Sudetendeutschen Volkskunde, XXI.] Reichenberg, 1932.

SCHLESIGNER, W. *Mitteldeutsche Beiträge zur deutschen Verfassungsgeschichte des Mittelalters.* Göttingen, 1961.

SCHLÜTER, O. 'Deutsches Siedlungswesen', in *Reallexikon der germanischen Altertumskunde*, ed. S. Hoops, 1, 1911–13.

SCHMID, H. F. 'Die slavische Altertumskunde und die Erforschung der Germanisation des deutschen Nordostens', in *Zeitschr f. slav. Philologie*, I and II, 1925. [Bibl.]

—— 'Die sozialgeschichtliche Auswertung der westslavischen Ortsnamen in ihrer Bedeutung für die Geschichte des nordostdeutschen Koloniallandes', in *Deutsche Siedlungsforschungen*, Leipzig, 1927. [Bibl.]

SCHUMACHER, K. *Siedlungs- und Kulturgeschichte der Rheinlande von der Urzeit bis in das Mittelalter.* II and III. Mainz, 1923.

SCHNEIDER, FEDOR. *Die Entstehung von Burg und Landgemeinde in Italien.* Berlin, 1924.

SCHWARZ, ERNST. *Die Ortsnamen der Sudetenländer als Geschichtsquelle.* Munich, 1931.

STEINBACH, F. *Ursprung und Wesen der Landgemeinde nach rheinischen Quellen.* Cologne-Opladen, 1960.

—— 'Geschichtliche Siedlungsformen in der Rheinprovinz' in *Zeitschrift des Rheinischen Vereins für Denkmalspflege und Heimatschutz*, 30, Number 2, 1937.

—— *Studien zur westdeutschen Stammes- und Volksgeschichte.* Jena, 1926.

STEPHENSON, C. *Borough and Farm. A Study of Urban Origins in England.* Cambridge, Massachusetts, 1953.

THOMPSON, J. W. *Economic and social History of the Middle Ages (300–1300).* 2nd edition. New York 1969.

VINOGRADOFF, P. *The growth of the Manor*. 3rd ed. London, 1920.
WARTBURG, W. VON. 'Ein neuer Erklärungsversuch für die mit court und gebildeten Ortsnamen', *Rheinisch Vierteljahrsblatt* 17, Number 1, 1952,
WATTENBACH-LEVISON, *Deutschlands Geschichtsquellen im Mittelalter. Vorzeit und Karolinger*. Number 1: *Die Vorzeit von den Anfängen bis zur Herrschaft der Karolinger*; Supplement: *Die Rechtsquellen*, Weimar 1952/53.
WELLER, K. *Besiedelungsgeschichte Württembergs vom 3. bis 13. Jahrhundert*. Stuttgart, 1938.
WOPFNER, H. 'Urkunden zur deutschen Agrargeschichte', in *Ausgewählte Urkunden zur deutschen Verfassungs- und Wirtschaftsgeschichte*, III, Stuttgart, 1928.
Zeitschrift für Ortsnamenforschung. Munich, 1925 ff.

II. PARTICULAR PERIODS AND TOPICS

i. *The Ancient World*

AUBIN, H. 'Die wirtschaftliche Entwicklung des römischen Deutschlands', in *HZ*. CXLI, 1930.
BRANDT, K. H. 'Zur Besiedlung des Werderlandes in Urgeschichtlicher Zeit', in *Das alte Büren*, edited by R. Stein, Bremen, 1957.
CAPELLE, W. *Das alte Germanien*. Jena, 1929.
COLLINGWOOD, R. G. and MYRES, J. N. L. 'Roman Britain and the English settlements', in *Oxford History of England*, 1936. [Bibl.]
DANNENBAUER, H. 'Adel, Burg und Herrschaft bei den Germanen', in *H.J.*, Volume 61, 1941.
DÖLLING, H. *Haus und Hof in Westgermanischen Volksrechten*. Münster, Westphalia, 1958.
DOPSCH, A. *Wirtschaftliche und soziale Grundlagen der europäischen Kulturentwicklung aus der Zeit von Cäsar bis auf Karl den Grossen*. 2 vols. 2nd ed. Vienna, 1923–4. [English (abridged) translation, *The Economic and Social Foundations of European Civilisation*, London, 1937.]
FLEISCHMANN, W. *Caesar, Tacitus, Karl der Gross und die deutsche Landwirtschaft*. Berlin, 1911.
—— *Altgermanische und altrömische Agrarverhältnisse in ihrer Beziehung und Gegensatz*. Leipzig, 1906.
GRADMANN, R. 'Die altgermanischen Siedlungsformen in Skandinavien und in Süddeutschland', in *Forschung und Fortschritt*, 1938.
GROSSER, M. *Die Herkunft der französischen Gewannfluren*. Berlin, 1932.
HAARNAGEL, W. 'Zur Grabung auf der Feddersen Wierde, 1935–1958' in *Germania*, 1961 and in *ZAA.*, 10, 1962.
HAFF, K. 'Zur Geschichte des germanischen Grundeigentums', in *ZSS.*, Germanic section, 49, 1929.
—— 'Zu den Problemen der Agrargeschichte des germanischen Nordens', in *HZ*. CLV, 1936.
HALLER, J. *Der Eintritt der Germanen in die Geschichte*. Berlin, 1939.
HAVERFIELD, F. and MACDONALD, G. *The Roman Occupation of Britain*. 1924.
HEITLAND, W. E. *Agricola. A study of Agriculture and Rustic Life in the Greco-Roman World*. Cambridge, 1921.
HÖMBERG, A. *Die Entstehung der westdeutschen Flurformen: Blockgemengflur, Streifenflur, Gewannflur*. Berlin, 1935.
HOOPS, J. *Waldbäume und Kulturpflanzen im germanischen Altertum*. Strassburg, 1905.
HOPFNER, TH. *Griechisch-lateinisches Quellenbuch zur Siedlung und Geschichte der Germanen im Böhmisch-Mährischen, Schlesischen und Karpathenraume*. Stuttgart-Prag 1943.
JANKUHN, H. 'Vorgeschichtliche Landwirtschaft in Schleswig-Holstein', in *ZAA*. 9, 1961.
JULLIAN, C. *Histoire de la Gaule*, V–VIII. Paris, 1920–6.
—— 'L'Analyse des terroirs ruraux', in *Revue des études anciennes* [Fac. de lettres de Bordeaux], XXVIII, 1926.

KIRBIS, W. *Siedlungs- und Flurformen germanischer Länder.* Göttingen, 1952.

KROESCHELL, K. 'Die Sippe im germanischen Recht', in *ZSS.*, Germanic section, Volume 77, 1960.

MARTINY, R. *Hof und Dorf in Alt-Westfalen.* Stuttgart, 1926.

MUCH, R. *Die Germanen des Tacitus.* Heidelberg, 1937.

NORDEN, E. *Die germanische Urgeschichte in Tacitus Germania.* Leipzig, 1920.

OELMANN, F. *Gallo-Römische Strassensiedlungen und Kleinhausbauten,* Bonner Jahrbücher, 128, 1923.

OSTERMANN, K. *Die Besiedlung der mittleren oldenburgischen Geest.* Stuttgart, 1931.

REINERTH, H. (Editor). *Vorgeschichte der deutschen Stämme,* 3 volumes. Leipzig–Berlin, 1940.

RHAMM, K. *Urzeitliche Bauernhöfe in Germanisch-Slawischem Waldgebiet,* Braunschweig, 1908.

—— *Die Grosshufen der Nordgermanen,* Braunschweig, 1905.

ROSS, D. W. *The Early History of Landholding among the Germans,* London, 1883.

ROSTOVTZEFF, M. *The Social and Economic History of the Roman Empire.* Oxford, 1926. [German edition (enlarged), *Gesellschaft und Wirtschaft im römischen Kaiserreich,* 2 vols. Leipzig, 1931.]

ROTHART, H. 'Das Eschdorf', in *Festgabe für Friedrich Philippi,* 1923.

SCHLÜTER, 'Die Siedlungsräume Mitteleuropas in Frühgeschichtlicher Zeit', in *Forschungen zur deutschen Landeskunde,* 63, 1952.

—— 'Die frühgeschichtlichen Siedlungsflächen Mitteldeutschlands', in *Festschrift zum 23. deutschen Geographentage in Magdeburg,* Braunschweig, Berlin and Hamburg, 1929.

SCHMIDT, L. *Geschichte der germanischen Stämme. Die Ostgermanen,* 2nd edition. Munich, 1941.

SCHNEIDER, H. *Germanische Altertumskunde.* Munich, 1938.

STEINBACH, F. 'Gewanndorf und Einzelhof', in *Historische Aufsätze Aloys Schulte zum 70. Geburtstage,* Düsseldorf, 1927.

STEINBACH, F. and BECKER, E. 'Geschichtliche Grundlagen der kommunalen Selbstverwaltung in Deutschland', in *Rheinisches Archiv,* XX, Bonn, 1932.

TACITUS. *Germania.* Ed. W. Reeb and H. Klenk [with essays by A. Dopsch, H. Reis and K. Schumacher]. Leipzig, 1930.

WAHLE, E. *Deutsche Vorzeit,* 3rd edition. Tübingen, 1953.

WALSER, E. and PEKÁRY, T. *Die Krise des römischen Reiches. Berichte über die Forschungen zur Geschichte des 3. Jahrhunderts '193–284 n.Chr.) von 1939 bis 1959,* Berlin, 1962.

WÜHRER, K. *Beiträge zur ältesten Agrargeschichte des germanischen Nordens.* Jena, 1935.

ii. *The Transition to the Middle Ages*

AUBIN, H. 'Zum Übergang von der Römerzeit zum Mittelalter auf deutschem Boden. Siedlungsgeschichtliche Erörterungen über das Städteproblem', in *Festschrift für A. Schulte.* Düsseldorf, 1927.

BARGER, E. 'The problem of Roman survivals in Germany', in *EHR.* L, 1935.

BERGENGRUEN, A. *Adel und Grundherrschaft im Merowingerreich.* Wiesbaden, 1958.

BURY, J. B. *A History of the later Roman Empire from the death of Theodosius I to the death of Justinian.* 2 vols. London, 1923.

CHECCHINI, A. 'I fondi romano-bizantini considerati in relazione con l'arimannia', in *Arch. Giurid. Ital.* LXXVIII, 1902.

CURWEN, E. CECIL. *Air Photography and the Evolution of the Corn-Field.* (Econ. Hist. Soc. Bibliographies and Pamphlets, No. 2, 2nd ed. [1938].)

DES MAREZ, G. *Le problème de la colonisation franque et du régime agraire en Belgique.* Brussels, 1926.

DHONDT, H., de LAET, S. J., and HOMBERT, P. 'Quelques considérations sur la fin de la domination romaine et des débuts de la colonisations franque en Belgique', in *Antiqué Classique,* XVIII, 1948.

EKWALL, E. *English place-names in -ing.* Lund, 1923.

ERNST, V. 'Zur Besiedlung Oberschwabens', *Festschrift zum 70. Geburtstag von D. Schäfer*. Jena, 1915.

ERNST, W. *Mittelfreie*. Stuttgart, 1920.

GAMILLSCHEGG, E. *Germanische Siedlungen in Belgien und Nordfrankreich. Abhaundlungen der Akademie Berlin*, 1937.

—— *Romania Germanica*. 3 vols. Berlin, 1934–5.

GOESSLER, P. 'Die Alamannen und ihr Siedlungsgebiet', in *Deutsches Archiv für Landes- und Volksforschung*, 7, 1943.

GROEBEL, M. 'Beiträge zur Siedlungsgeschichte der Wied'. Dissertation, Bonn, 1911.

HAFF, K. 'Geschlechtshöfe und freie Marken in Skandinavien und Deutschland', in *VSWG*, XXVIII, 1935.

HEGEL, K. *Städte und Gilden der germanischen Völker im Mittelalter*. 2 volumes. Leipzig, 1891.

HOFBAUER, S. *Die Ausbildung der grossen Grundherrschaften im Reiche der Merowinger*. Baden–Brünn–Leipzig–Vienna, 1927.

KORNEMANN, E. Articles 'Bauernstand' and 'Domänen', in PW. Suppl. IV.

DE LAET, S. J., DHONDT, J., NENQUIN, J. 'Les Laiti du Namurois et l'origine de la Civilisation Mérovingienne', in *Etudes d'Historie et d'Archéologie Namuroises*, Volume I. Namur, 1952.

LEEDS, E. T. 'A Saxon village near Sutton Courtenay', in *Archaeologia*, LXXIII, LXXVI, 1923, 1927.

LESNE, E. *La propriété ecclésiastique en France aux époques romaine et mérovingienne*. Paris, 1910.

LOT, F. *La fin du monde antique et les débuts du Moyen-âge*. Paris, 1927.

—— 'La conquête du pays d'entre Seine et Loire les Francs', in *RH*. CLXV, 1930.

—— 'Du régime de l'hospitalité', in *RB*. VII, 1928.

DES MAREZ, G. *Le Probleme de la colonisation franque et du regime agaire en Basse-Belgique*. Brussels, 1926.

MAVER, G. Article, 'Slavi', in *Enciclopedia Italiana*.

MAYER, ERNST, 'Dorf- und Geschlechtsverband', in *ZSS*. XLI, 1920.

MÜLLER-WILLE, W. 'Siedlungs-, Wirtschafts- und Bevölkerungsräume im westlichen Mitteleuropa um 500 n. Chr.', in *Westfälische Forschungen*, 9, 1956.

—— *Germanisches Volkserbe in Wallonien und Nordfrankreich*. 2 vols. Bonn, 1937.

PETRI, F. *Zum Stand der Diskussion über die fränkische Landnahme und die Entstehung der germanisch-romanischen Sprachgrenze*. Darmstadt, 1954.

PHILIPPI, D. *Die Erbexen*. Breslau, 1920.

RÜBEL, K. *Die Franken, ihr Eroberungs- und Siedlungssystem im deutschen Volkslande*. Bielefeld–Leipzig, 1904.

SCHIBES, A. *Die fränkischen und alemannischen Siedlungen in Gallien, besonders im Elass und Lothringen*. Strasbourg, 1894.

SCHMIDT, LUDWIG. *Geschichte der deutschen Stämme bis zum Ausgang der Völkerwanderung. Die Ostgermanen*. 2nd ed. Munich, 1934.

SCHÖNFELD. Article 'Laeti', in P.W. XXIII.

SEECK, O. *Geschichte des Untergangs der antiken Welt*. 6 vols. Berlin, 1895–1920.

STÖBE, H. 'Die Unterwerfung Norddeutschlands durch die Merowinger und die Lehre von der sächsischen Eroberung', in *Wissenschaftliche Zeitschrift der Friedrich Schiller Universität Jena*. No. 6, 1956–57, Social and Philological File.

STOLL, H. 'Alamannische Siedlungsgeschichte, archäologisch behandelt', in *Zeitschrift für Württembergische Landesgeschichte*, VI, 1942.

VEECK, W. *Die Alemannen in Württemberg*, I. Berlin, 1931.

VILMINOT, L. *L'Installation des Barbares dans le Department des Vosges, Revue archéologique*, 1938.

VINOGRADOFF, P. 'Social and economic conditions of the Roman Empire in the fourth century', in *The Cambridge Medieval History*, I, 1911.

WAGNER, H. *Die Frage des Grundeigentums, der Markgenossenschaft und der Grundherrschaft bei den westgermanischen Völkerschaften beziehungsweise Stämmern von Caesar bis auf Clodwig*. Dissertation, Heidelberg–Würzburg–Aumühle, 1940.

WARTBURG, W. VON. *Umfang und Bedeutung der germanischen Siedlungen in Nortdgallien im Spiegel der Sprache und der Ortsnamen. Vorträge und Schriften der Deutschen Akademie der Wissenschaften zu Berlin.* Book 36, 1950.
WERNER, J. *Das alamannische Graberfeld von Bülach.* Basle, 1953.

iii. *The Early Middle Ages*

ABEL, H. 'Die Besiedlung von Geest und Marsch am rechten Weserufer bei Bremen', in *Deutsche Geographische Blätter*, Volume 41, Number 1–2, Bremen, 1933.
BAAKEN, G. *Königtum, Burgen und Königsfreie.* Constance-Stuttgart, 1961.
BALDAUG, O. *Das karolingische Reichsgut in Unterrätien.* Innsbruck, 1930.
BETHGE, O. 'Über "Bifänge"', in *VSWG.*, Volume XX, 1927.
BITTERAUF, TH. *Die Traditionen des Hochstifts Freising.* 2 vols. Berlin, 1905–9.
CARO, E. 'Die Landgüter in den fränkischen Formelsammlungen', in *Historische Viertel-jahrsschrift*, VI, 1903.
—— 'Studien zu den älteren St. Galler Urkunden', in *Jahrb. f. Schweizer Gesch.* XXVI, XXVII, 1901–2.
DANNENBAUER, H. *Die Entstehung Europas.* Stuttgart. Volume 1, 1959, Volume 2, 1962.
—— 'Bevölkerung und Besiedlung Alemanniens in der frankischen Zeit', in *Grundlagen der mittelalterlichen Welt.* Stuttgart, 1958.
DOPSCH, A. *Die Wirtschafts-Entwicklung der Karolingerzeit, vornehmlich in Deutschland.* 2 vols., 2nd ed. Weimar, 1920–1.
DÜMMLER, E. *Geschichte des ostfränkischen Reiches.* 2nd edition, 1887.
DUMAS, A. 'Quelques observations sur la grande et la petite propriété à l'époque carolingienne', in *Revue Historique de droit français et étranger*, 1926.
EGGERS, A. *Der königliche Grundbesitz im 10. und beginnenden 11. Jahrhundert.* Weimar, 1909.
ENGEL, F. *Das Rodungsrecht der Hagen-Siedlungen.* Hildesheim, 1949.
ENNEN, E. *Frühgeschichte der Europäischen Stadt.* Bonn, 1953.
—— *Die Bedeutung der Kirche für den Wiederaufbau der in der Völkerwanderungszeit zerstörten Städte; Kölner Untersuchungen*, 1950.
ERNST, V. 'Zur Besiedlung Oberschwabens', in *Festschrift für Dietrich Schäfer*, Jena, 1915.
FLACH, J. *Les origines de l'ancienne France* (X^e et XIe siècles]. 4 vols. Paris, 1886–1917. [Many sources.]
FROMMHOLD, G. 'Der altfränkische Erbhof, ein Beitrag zur Erklärung des Begriffes der terra salica', in *Untersuchungen zur deutschen Staats- und Rechtsgeschichte.* Number 148. Breslau, 1938.
GLADIES, D. VON. 'Die Schenkungen der deutschen Könige zu privatem Eigen nach ihrem wirtschaftlichen Inhalt', in *VSWG.* XXX, 1937.
GOETZ, W. *Die Entstehung der italienischen Kommunen im frühen Mittelalter. Sitzungs-berichte die Akademie der Wissenschaft*, 1944.
GUÉRARD, P. *Polyptique de l'abbé Irminon.* Ed. A. Longnon. 2 vols. Paris, 1886–95.
GUTTENBRUNNER, S., JANKUHN, H. and LAR, W. *Völker und Stämme in Süd-Ost-Schleswig im frühen Mittelalter*, 1952.
HALPHEN, L. *Études critiques sur l'histoire de Charlemagne* (Part 2, c. III: 'L'agriculture et la propriété rurale'). Paris, 1921.
HARTMANN, L. M. *Zur Wirtschaftsgeschichte Italiens im frühen Mittelalter. Analekten.* Gotha, 1904.
HAUPTMANN, L. 'Hufengrössen im bayrischen Stammes- und Kolonialgebiet', in *VSWG.* XXI, 1928.
HOCHHOLZER, H. 'Sicilien als Beispiel der mittelmeerischen Kulturschichtung', in *HZ.* CLV, 1936.
HOEDERATH, H. TH. 'Hufe, Manse und Mark in der Quellen der Grossgrundherrschaft Werden am Ausgang der Karolingerzeit', in *ZSS.*, Germanic section, 68, 1951.
HOMANS, G. C. 'Terroirs ordonnés et champs orientés. Une hypothèse sur le village anglais', in *AHES.* VIII, 1936.

ILGEN, TH. 'Die mittelalterliche Wirtschaftsverfassung am Niederrhein', in *Westdeutsche Zeitschr.* XXXII, 1913.

JORET, CH. *Les noms de lieu d'origine non-romaine et la colonisation germanique et scandinave en Normandie.* Paris, 1914.

KÄMMEL, O. *Die Besiedlung des deutschen Südostens vom Anfang des* 10. *bis zum Ende des* 11. *Jahrh.* Leipzig, 1909.

KLEBEL, E. 'Herzogtümer und Marken bis 900', in *Entstehung des Deutschen Reiches.* Published by H. Kaempf, 1956.

KOEBNER, R. 'Das Problem der slawischen Burgsiedlung und die Oppelner Ausgrabungen', in *Zeitschr. d. Vereins f. Gesch. Schlesiens,* LXV, 1931.

KÖTZSCHKE, R. 'Thüringen in der deutschen Siedlungsgeschichte', in *Festschrift für A. Tille,* 1930.

—— 'Hufe und Hufenordnung in mitteldeutschen Fluranlagen', in *Festschrift für A. Dopsch.* Baden–Vienna–Leipzig, 1938.

—— 'Salhof und Siedelhof im älteren deutschen Agrarwesen'. Edited by H. Helbig. *Berichte über die Verhandlungen der sächsischen Akademie der Wissenschaften zu Leipzig.* Philosophical–Historical Class, 100, Number 5. Berlin, 1953.

KURTH, G. *Etudes franques.* 2 volumes. Paris, 1919.

LÉVI-PROVENÇAL, É. *L'Espagne Musulmane au Xme, siècle. Institutions et vie sociale.* Paris, 1932.

LOESCH, H. VON. 'Zur Grösse der deutschen Königshufen', in *VSWG.* XXII, 1929.

LOT, F. 'De l'origine et de la signification historique et linguistique des noms de lieu en -*ville* et en -*court*', in *Romania,* LXI, 1933.

LÜTGE, F. 'Die Hufe in der thüringisch-hessischen Agrarverfassung der Karolingerzeit', in *Schmollers Jahrbuch,* LXI, 1937.

—— 'Hufe und Mansus', in *VSWG.* XXX, 1937.

—— *Die Agrarverfassung des frühen Mittelalters im mitteldeutschen Raum vornehmlich in der Karolingerzeit.* Jena, 1937.

MARTINY, R. *Hof und Dorf in Altwestfalen. Das Westfälische Streusiedlungsproblem.* Stuttgart, 1926.

MORTENSEN, H. 'Zur Entstehung der deutschen Dorfformen inbesondere des Waldhufendorfs', in *Nachrichten der Akademie der Wissenschaften in Göttingen,* Philosophical–Historical Class, 1946–47.

NEUNDÖRFER, D. *Studien zur ältesten Geschichte des Klosters Lorsch.* Berlin, 1920.

PFAFFEN, K. 'Natur- und Kulturlandschaft am deutschen Niederrhein', in *Berichte zur deutschen Landeskunde,* 20, 1958.

PROU, M. 'La Forêt en Angleterre et en France', in *Journal des Savants,* 1915.

RANZI, F. *Königsgut und Königsforst im Zeitalter der Merowinger und Ludolfinger und ihre Bedeutung für den Landesausbau,* Halle-Saale, 1939.

RIETSCHEL, S. *Die Civitas auf deutschen Boden bis zum Ausgang Karolingerzeit.* Leipzig, 1894.

ROTTHOFF, G. *Studien zur Geschichte des Reichsgutes in Niederlothringen und Friesland während der sächsich-salischen Kaiserzeit.* Rhenish Archives, 44, 1953.

SCHILLINGER, E. *Die Siedlungsgeschichte des Breisgaues bis zum Ende der Karolingerzeit unter besonderer Berücksichtigung der Ortsnamen,* Dissertation, Freiburg-im-Breisgau, 1944.

SCHMID, H. F. 'Die Burgbezirksverfassung bei den slavischen Völkern in ihrer Bedeutung für die Geschichte ihrer Siedlung und ihrer staatlichen Organisation', in *Jahrb. f. Kultur und Geschichte der Slawen,* N.S. II, 2, 1926.

SCHRÖDER-LEMBKE, G. 'Zur Flurform der Karolingerzeit', in *ZAA.* 176, 1953.

SCHÜNEMANN, K. 'Zue Geschichte des deutschen Landesausbaues im Mittelalter', *Südostdeutsche Forschungen,* 1, 1935.

—— 'Vorstufen des deutschen Städtewesen', in *Vergangenheit und Gegenwart,* 27, 1937.

—— *Die Entstehung des Städtewesens in Südost-Europa.* Breslau, 1928.

SPERLING, W. 'Die Entstehung der Fluren um Trebur', in *Archiv für hessische Geschichte und Altertumskunde,* Series, 26, 1961.

STEFFENS, H.-G. 'Die Siedlungskontinuität im mittelalterlichen Gau Stormarn', in *Archäol. Geogr.* 7, 1958.

STEINBACH, F. 'Rheinische Anfänge des deutschen Städtewesens', in *Jahrbücher des Kölner Geschichtsvereins*, 25, 1950.

STENTON, F. M. *Documents illustrative of the Social and Economic History of the Danelaw.* London, 1920.

—— *The free peasantry of the Northern Danelaw.* Lund, 1926.

—— 'Types of manorial structure in the Northern Danelaw', in Vinogradoff, P., *Oxford Studies in Social and Legal History*, II, 1910.

THIMME, H. 'Forestis', in *Arch. f. Urkundenforschung*, II, 1990.

THOMPSON, J. W. *The dissolution of the Carolingian fisc in the ninth century.* University of Carolina Publications in History, 23. Berkeley and London, 1953.

TIMM, A. *Studien zur Siedlungs- und Agrargeschichte Mitteldeutschlands.* Cologne–Graz, 1956.

TOUR, IMBART DE LA. 'Les colonies agricoles et l'occupation des terres désertes à l'époque carolingienne', in *Mélanges Paul Fabre*, 1902.

VERLINDEN, C. 'L'histoire urbaine dans la péninsule ibérique', in *RB*. XV, 1936.

WAMPACH, C. *Geschichte der Grundherrschaft Echternach im Frümittelalter.* Volume 1: Textband, Volume 2: Quellenband. Luxembourg, 1929–30.

WELLNER, M. *Zur Entstehungsgeschichte der Markgenossenschaften: Die Vierdörferwald bei Emmendingen.* Breisgaü, 1938.

iv. *The Eleventh, Twelfth and Thirteenth Centuries*

ABEL, W. 'Verdorfung und Gutsbildung in Deutschland zu Beginn der Neuzeit'. in *ZAA*, 9, Number 1, 1961.

AUBIN, H. 'Wirtschaftsgeschichtliche Bemerkungen zur ostdeutschen Kolonisation', in *Gedächtnisschrift f. G. v. Below*, Stuttgart, 1928.

BADER, K. S. *Das mittelalterliche Dorf als Friedens- und Rechtsbereich.* Weimar, 1957.

BARLOW, F. *The feudal kingdom of England.* London–New York–Toronto, 1955.

BISHOP, T. A. M. 'Assarting and the growth of the open fields', in *EcHR*. VI, 1935.

BLOCH, MARC. 'Défrichements, peuplement et franchises rurales. XIIᵉ–XIIIᵉ siècles', in *Bulletin de la Faculté des Lettres de l'Université de Strasbourg*, 1927. [Selected sources.]

BOEREN, P. C. *Étude sur les tributaires d'église dans la comté de Flandre du XIIᵉ au XVᵉ siècle.* Amsterdam, 1936.

BONVALOT, E. T. *Le tiers état d'après la coutume de Beaumont.* 1883.

BOSAU, HELMOLD VON. *Chronica Slavorum.* Ed. B. Schmeidler (Script. rer. Germ.), Hanover, 1909; English translation, ed. F. J. Tschan, Columbia University Press, 1935. [Bibl.]

BÖTTGER, H. *Siedlungsgeschichte des Siegerlandes.* Siegen, 1951.

DE BORCHGRAVE, EMIL. *Histoire des colonies belges, qui s'établirent en Allemagne pendant de XIIᵉ et le XIII siècle.* Brussels, 1865.

BORN, M. *Siedlungsentwicklung am Osthang des Westerwaldes.* Marburg, 1957.

—— *Wandlung und Beharrung ländlicher Siedlung und bäuerlicher Wirtschaft. Untersuchungen zur frühneuzeitlichen Kulturlandschaftsgenese im Schwalmgebiet.* Marburg, 1961.

BRUNS-WÜSTENFELD, K. *Beiträge zur Geschichte der Kolonisation und Germanisierung der Uckermark.* Dissertation, Kiel, 1914.

BRUTAILS, J. A. *Étude sur la condition des populations rurales du Roussillon.* Paris, 1891.

BÜTTNER, H. *Staufer und Zähringer im politischen Kräftespiel zwischen Bodensee und Genfersee während des 12. Jahrhunderts.* Zürich, 1961.

CARO, G. *Neue Beiträge zur deutschen Wirtschafts- und Sozialgeschichte. Gesammelte Aufsätze.* Leipzig, 1911.

—— *Beiträge zur älteren deutschen Wirtschafts- und Verfassungsgeschichte. Gesammelte Aufsätze.* Leipzig, 1905.

CHALENDON, F. *Histoire de la Domination normande en Italie et en Sicile.* 2 volumes. Paris, 1901.

CONRAD, H. *Die mittelalterliche Besiedlung des deutschen Ostens und das deutsche Recht.* Cologne–Opladen, 1955.

CURIE-SEIMBRES, A. *Essai sur les villes fondées dans le sud-ouest de la France aux* 13ᵉ *et* 14ᵉ *siècles sous le nom générique de bastides*. Toulouse, 1880.

DEIKE, L. *Die Entstehung der Grundherrschaft in den Hollerkolonien an der Niederweser*. Bremen, 1959.

DELISLE, L. *Études sur la condition de la classe agricole et l'état de l'agriculture en Normandie au Moyen âge*. Paris, 1903.

Deutsche Ostforschung edited by H. Aubin, O. Brunner *et al*. Leipzig, 1942.

DUBY, G. *L'économie rurale et al vie des campagnes dans l'Occident mediéval (France, Angleterre, Empire IXe–XVe siècles)*. 2 volumes. Paris, 1962.

DUVIVIER, CH. 'Hospites. Défrichements en Europe et spécialement dans nos contrées aux XIᵉ, XIIᵉ et XIIIᵉ siècles', in *Revue de l'histoire et d'Archéologie*, I, Brussels, 1859.

EBERT, W. *Ländliche Siedelformen im deutschen Osten*. Berlin, 1937.

EMMERICH, W. 'Siedlungsforschung in Oberfranken' in *Archiv für Geschichte von Oberfranken* 39, 1959.

FISCHER, H. *Die Siedlungsverlegung im Zeitalter der Stadtbildung unter besonderer Berücksichtigung des österreichischen Raumes*. Vienna, 1952.

FOLKERS, J. U. 'Die mittelalterlichen Ansiedlungen fremder Kolonisten in Nordwestdeutschland (800–1000)', in *Volk und Rasse*. Number 2 and 3. Munich, 1927 and 1928.

GISLEBERT. *Chronicon Hamoniense*. Ed. W. Arndt (Script. rer. Germ.), Hanover, 1869; ed. L. Vanderkindere (Recueil de textes pour servir à l'étude de l'hist. de Belgique), Brussels, 1904.

GOTHEIN, E. 'Die Hofverfassung auf dem Schwarzwald', in *Zeitschr. f. d. Gesch. des Oberrheins*, N.S. I, 1886.

VON GUTTENBERG, E. *Grundzüge der Territorialbildung am Obermain*. Würzburg, 1925.

HAMM, E. *Die Städtegründungen der Herzöge von Zähringen in Südwestdeutschland*. Freiburg-im-Breisgau, 1932.

HAMPE, K. *Der Zug nach dem Osten*. 2nd ed. Leipzig, 1935.

—— *Das Hochmittelalter*. Berlin, 1949.

HELBIG, H. *Deutsche Siedlungsforschung im Bereich der mittelalterlichen Ostkolonisation*, Jahrbuch für Geschichte Mittel- und Ostdeutschlands II, 1954.

HELBIG, K. *Das Hochmittelalter*. Berlin, 1949.

HELLMANN, M. *Das Lettenland im Mittelalter*. Münster–Cologne, 1954.

HESSLER, W. *Mitteldeutsche Gaue des frühen und hohen Mittelalters*. Berlin, 1957.

HEWITT, H. J. *Mediaeval Cheshire*. Manchester, 1929.

HOFFMANN, E. 'Die Entwicklung der Wirtschaftsprinzipien im Cisterzienser-Orden', in *Historisches Jahrbuch der Görres-Gesellschaft*, XXXI, 1910.

HOMBITZER, A. *Beiträge zur Siedlungskunde und Wirtschaftsgeographie des Siebengebirges und seiner Umgebung*. Dissertation, Bonn, 1913.

HUIZINGA, J. *Burg en kerspel en Walcheren*. Amsterdam, 1935.

ILGEN, TH. 'Zum Siedlungswesen im Klevischen', in *Westdeutsche Zeitschr*. XXIX, 1910.

JANKUHN, H., SCHLESINGER, W. and SCHWARZ, E. *Siedlung und Verfassung der Slawen zwischen Elbe, Saale und Oder*. Edited by H. Ludat, Giessen, 1960.

VON INAMA-STERNEGG, K. TH. *Sallandstudien*. Tübingen, 1889.

JAGER, H. *Entwicklungsperioden agrarer Siedlungsgebiete im Mitteleren Westdeutschland seit dem frühen 13. Jahrhundert*. Würzburg, 1958.

JEGOROV, D. N. *Die Kolonisation Mecklenburgs*. 2 vols. [See H. Witte, *Jegorovs Kolonisation Mecklenburgs. Ein kritisches Nachwort*, Breslau, 1930–2.]

KLEBEL, E. *Siedlungsgeschichte des deutschen Ostens, Veröffentlichungen des Südosteuropainstituts*. Munich, 14, 1940.

KOEBNER, R. 'Deutsches Recht und deutsche Kolonisation in den Piastenländern', in *VSWG*. XXV, 1932.

KÖTZSCHKE, R. *Quellen zur Geschichte der ostdeutschen Kolonisation im 12. bis 14. Jahrh*. 2nd ed. Leipzig, 1931.

—— 'Die Anfänge des deutschen Rechts in der Siedlungsgeschichte des Ostens. Jus Teutonicum'. *Berichte über die Verhandlungen der Sächsischen Akademie der Wissenschaften*, 93, 2, 1941.

KÖTZSCHKE, R. *Ländliche Siedlung und Agrarwesen in Sachsen*. Remagen, 1953.

KÖTZSCHKE, R. and EBERT, W. *Geschichte der ostdeutschen Kolonisation*. Leipzig, 1937. [Bibl.]

KOSSMANN, E. O. *Die deutschrechtliche Siedlung in Polen dargestellt am Lodzer Raum*. Leipzig, 1937.

KRENZLIN, A. 'Die mittelalterlich-frühneuzeitlichen Siedlungsformen im Raume von Gross-Berlin. Ein Beitrag zur Frage der ostdeutschen Plangewannfluren', in *Die Erde*, 90, 1959.

—— *Historische und wirtschaftliche Züge im Siedlungsformenbild des westlichen Ostdeutschland unter besonderer Berücksichtigung von Mecklenburg-Vorpommern und Sachsen*. Frankfurt-am-Main, 1955.

KROESCHELL, K. *Weichbild. Untersuchungen zur Struktur und Entstehung der mittelalterlichen Stadtgemeinde in Westfalen*. Cologne–Graz, 1960.

—— 'Waldrecht und Landsiedelrecht im Kasseler Raum', in *Hessisches Jahrbuch für Landesgeschichte*, 4, 1954.

—— *Stadtbildung und Weichbildrecht in Westfalen*. Münster, Westphalia, 1960.

KUHN, W. *Geschichte der deutschen Ostsiedlung in der Neuzeit*. 2 vols. and 1 vol. maps. 1955–57.

LAPPE, J. 'Die Bauerschaften und Huden der Stadt Salzkotten', in *Deutschrechtliche Beiträge*, VII, 4, 1912.

LATOUCHE, R. 'Un aspect de la vie rurale dans le Maine au XIe et au XIIe siècle. L'établissement des bourgs', in *Le Moyen Âge*, 1937.

LEIPOLDT, J. *Die Geschichte der ostdeutschen Kolonisation im Vogtland auf Grundlage der Siedlungs-Formen-Forschung*. Leipzig, 1927.

LENNHARD, R. *Rural England 1086–1135*. Oxford, 1959.

LESTOCQUOY, J. *Les Villes de Flandre et d'Italie sous le gouvernement des patriciens (11–15 centuries)*. Paris, 1952.

Liber fundationis claustri s. Mariae virginis in Heinrichow. Ed. G. A. Stenzel, Breslau, 1854; German translation, ed. P. Bretschneider, Breslau, 1927.

LUDAT, H. *Vorstufen und Entstehung des Städtewesens in Osteuropa*. Cologne–Braunsfeld, 1955.

MAYER, TH. 'Aufgaben der Siedlungsgeschichte in den Sudetenländern', in *Deutsche Hefte für Volks- und Kulturbodenforschung*, 1, Number 3, no date.

—— 'Die Entstehung des "modernen" Staates im Mittelalter und die freien Bauern', in *ZSS.* LVII, 1937.

—— 'Die Besiedlung und politische Erfassung des Schwarzwaldes im Hochmittelalter' in *Zeitschrift für Geschichte des Oberrheins*, Series 52, 1938.

MOLITOR, E. *Die Pfleghaften des Sachsenspiegels und das Siedlungsrecht im sächsischen Stammesgebiet*. Weimar, 1941.

MORTENSEN, H. 'Fragen der nordwestdeutschen Siedlungs- und Flurforschung', *Nachrichten der Akademie der Wissenschaften in Göttingen*. Philosophical-Historical Class, 1946–47.

—— 'Probleme der mittelalterlichen deutschen Kulturlandschaft', in *Berichte zur deutschen Landeskunde* 20, 1958.

MUGGENTHALER, H. *Kolonisatorische und wirtschaftliche Tätigkeit eines deutschen Zisterzienserklosters im XII. und XIII. Jahrhundert*. Munich, 1924.

—— *Die Besiedlung des Böhmerwaldes*. Passau, 1929.

PFITZNER, J. *Die Besiedlung der Sudeten bis zum Ausgang des Mittelalters. Deutsche Hefte für Volks- und Kulturbodenforschung*. 1930–1.

'Pipevallensis Abbatiae fundationis historia et de boscorum destructione.' Dugdale, *Monasticon*, pp. 434 ff.

PIRENNE, H. *Les Villes du Moyen Age*, Brussels, 1927.

PLESNER, J. *L'émigration de la campagne à la ville libre de Florence au 13e siècle*. Copenhagen, 1934.

POHLENDT, H. *Die Verbreitung der mittelalterlichen Wüstungen in Deutschland*. Göttingen, 1950.

POSTAN, M. M. 'The Famulus; The estate labourer in the XIIth and XIIIth Centuries.' *The Economic History Revue supplements*, 2. London–New York, 1953.

POWER, E. E. 'Peasant life and rural conditions *c.* 110 to *c.* 1500'. in *The Cambridge Medieval History*, VII, 1932. [Bibl.]

PROU, M. 'Les coutumes de Lorris', in *Nouv. Revue d'hist. de droit franç.* VIII, 1884.

QUIRIN, K. *Die deutsche Ostsiedlung im Mittelalter*. Göttingen–Frankfurt–Berlin, 1954.

ROBERT, G. 'La Loi de Beaumont dans les domaines de St. Remi de Reims', in *Travaux de l'Académie nationale de Reims*, CXXXIV, 1914.

—— 'La Ville neuve de Florent', in *ibid.* CXLIII, 1930.

SCHMID, H. F. 'Die sozialgeschichtliche Erforschung der mittelalterlichen deutschrecht-lichen Siedlung auf polnischem Boden', in *VSWG.* XX, 1927. [Bibl.]

SCHMIDT, H. *Lippische Siedlungs- und Woldgeschichte*, 1940.

SCHULZE, E. O. *Die Kolonisierung und Germanisierung zwischen Saale und Elbe*. Leipzig, 1896.

STEINMANN, P. *Bauer und Ritter in Mecklenburg. Wandlungen der gutsherrlich-bäuerlichen Verhältnisse vom 12./13. Jahrhundert bis zur Bodenreform 1945*. Schwerin, 1960.

STENTON, F. M. *The first century of English feudalism*. Oxford, 1932.

STOLZ, O. 'Beiträge zur Geschichte der alpinen Schwaighöfe', in *VSWG.* XXV, 1932.

THIELE, P. AUGUSTINUS. *Echternach und Himmerod. Beispiele benediktinisches und zister-ziensischer Wirtschaftsführung im 12. und 13. Jahrhundest*. Stuttgart, 1964.

TIMM, A. *Die Waldnutzung in Nordwestdeutschland im Spiegel der Weistümer. Einleitende Untersuchungen über die Umgestaltung des Stadt-Land-Verhältnisses im Spätmittelalter*. Cologne–Graz, 1960.

TIMMERMANN, O. F. 'Zur Frage der Landnahme in den deutschen Alpen', in *Berichte zur deutschen Landeskunde*, 18, 1957.

TUMLER, P. M. *Der deutsche Orden im Werden, Wachsen und Wirken bis 1400, mit einem Abriss der Geschichte des Ordens von 1400 bis zur neusten Zeit*. Vienna, 1955.

TURNER, C. J. *Select pleas of the Forest*. (Selden Society.) 1901.

TYC, T. *Die Anfänge der dörflichen Siedlung zu deutschem Recht in Grosspolen*. (German translation.) Breslau, 1930.

TZSCHOPPE, A. G. and STENZEL, G. A. *Urkundensammlung zur Geschichte des Ursprungs der Städte und der Einführung und Verbreitung deutscher Kolonisten und Rechte in Schlesien und der Oberlausitz*. Hamburg, 1832.

VERRIEST, L. *Le régime seigneurial dans le comté de Hainault du XIᵉ siècle à la révolution*. Louvain, 1916–17.

WANDSLEB, A. *Die deutsche Kolonisation des Orlagaues. 7. bis 13. Jahrhundert*. Jena, 1911.

WEISS, R. 'Über die grossen Kolonistendörfer des 12. und 13. Jahrhunderts zwischen Leine und Weser, Hagendörfer', in *Zeitschr. d. hist. Vereins für Niedersachsen*, 1908.

WOSTRY, W. 'Das Kolonisationsproblem', in *Mitteilungen des Vereins für Geschichte der Deutschen in Böhmen*, LX, 1922.

ZAHNBRECHER, F. X. *Die Kolonisationstätigkeit des Hochstifts Freising in den Ostalpen-ländern*. Dissertation, Munich, 1907.

CHAPTER II

Agricultural and Rural Life in the Later Roman Empire

A revision of the bibliography of the First Edition, by J. R. MORRIS.

The following is a selective bibliography, which inevitably, like agriculture, touches upon other social and economic institutions. Reference may still be usefully made to the appropriate articles in encyclopedias, such as Daremberg, C. and Saglio, E. *Diction-naire des antiquités grecques et romaines*, and Pauly-Wissowa *et al. Realencyclopä die*. *L'année philologique* also provides a comprehensive bibliography of classical scholarship. Russian works have not been included, but most may be found in *Vyestnik Dryevnyei Istorii*.

Specially recommended books are starred *; those with extensive and useful biblio-graphies are marked (B).

I. General Works Upon the History of the Later Roman Empire

Bury, J. B. *History of the Later Roman Empire.* 2 vols. London, 1923.
—— *Cambridge Medieval History*, vol. I. Cambridge, 1911.
Dill, S. *Roman Society in the Last Century of the Western Empire.* 2nd ed. London, 1925.
Dopsch, A. *Grundlagen der Europäischen Kulturentwicklung.* 2 vols. Vienna, 1923–4. (English translation, M. E. Beard and N. Marshall, *Economic and Social Foundations of European Civilization*, London, 1937.)
Gibbon, E. *Decline and Fall of the Roman Empire.* Ed. J. B. Bury, I–IV. 2nd ed. London, 1909–10.
Heichelheim, F. *Wirtschaftsgeschichte des Altertums.* 1st ed. Leiden, 1938. (English edition in progress.)
*Jones, A. H. M. *The Later Roman Empire.* 3 vols. Oxford, 1964.
Latouche, R. *The Birth of the Western Economy. Economical Aspects of the Dark Ages.* Translated from the French by F. M. Wilkinson. New York, 1961.
Lot, F. *La Fin du monde antique et les débuts du Moyen-Age.* Paris, 1927. (English translation, P. and M. Leon, *The End of the Ancient World and the Beginnings of the Middle Ages*, London, 1931.)
Macmullen, R. *Soldier and Civilian in the Later Roman Empire.* Harvard, 1963.
Ostrogorsky, G. *History of the Byzantine State.* Translated by J. Hussey. Oxford, 1956.
Rostovtzeff, M. *Social and Economic History of the Roman Empire.* 2nd ed. by P. M. Fraser. Oxford, 1957.
Russell, J. C. 'Late Ancient and Mediaeval Population'. *Transactions of the American Philosophical Society*, 1958.
Seeck, O. *Geschichte des Untergangs der antiken Welt.* 6 vols. I, 4th ed., II–VI, 2nd ed. Stuttgart, 1920–2.
Stein, E. *Histoire du Bas-Empire.* (French edition by J-R. Palanque). 2 vols. Bruges, 1949–59.

II. Agriculture

i. Ancient

(a) Original Authorities

Theophrastus (372–287 B.C.). *Historia Plantarum* and *De Causis Plantarum.* Ed. Wimmer. Paris, 1866. (English translation of *Historia Plantarum*, Hart, Loeb Library, 2 vols. London, 1916.)
M. Porcius Cato (234–149 B.C.). *De Agri Cultura.* Ed. Goetz. Leipzig, 1922. (English translation, Hooper and Ash, Loeb Library, London, 1934.)
M. Terentius Varro (116–28 B.C.). *Res Rusticae.* Ed. Goetz. Leipzig, 1929. (English translation, Hooper and Ash, with Cato, *above*.)
P. Vergilius Maro (70–19 B.C.). *Georgica.* Ed. Hirtzel. Oxford Classical Texts. Oxford, 1900. (English translation, Fairclough, Loeb Library, London, 1916.)
L. Junius Moderatus Columella (c. 65 A.D.). *De Re Rustica* and *De Arboribus.* Ed. Lundström. Upsala, de *Arboribus*, 1897; de *Re Rustica*, I and II, 1917; X, 1902; XI, 1907. Other books, ed. T. G. Schneider, Leipzig, 1794. (English translation, Anon., *Of Husbandry in Twelve Books and his Book concerning Trees*, London, 1745.)
C. Plinius Secundus (A.D. 23/4–79). *Naturalis Historia*, book XVIII. Ed. Mayhoff, Teubner Texts, vol. III. Leipzig, 1892. (English translation, Bostock and Riley, IV, London, 1856.)
Rutilius Tauris Aemilianus Palladius (c. A.D. 450). *De Agricultura.* Ed. Schmitt. Leipzig, 1898. (With French translation, ed. Nisard, Paris, 1877.)
Geoponica (compiled in the eleventh century A.D. from earlier material). Ed. Beckh. Leipzig, 1895. (English translation, Owen, London, 1805.)

b) Climate and Geography

BROOKS, C. E. P. *Climate Through the Ages.* London, 1949.
CARY, M. *The Geographic Background to Greek and Roman History.* Oxford, 1949.
ROMANI, M. *La distribuzioni geografica dei fenomeni economici nell' impero romano.* Milan 1941.
SEMPLEX, E. *Geography of the Mediterranean Region.* London, 1932.

(c) Modern Works on Ancient Agriculture

ABERG, E. A. 'The Early Plough in Europe', *Gwerin* I (1956–7), 171.
BEHLEN, H. *Der Pflug und das Pflügen bei den Römern und in Mitteleuropa in Vorgeschichtlicher Zeit.* Dillenburg, 1904.
BILLIARD, R. *L'agriculture dans l'antiquité d'apprès les Géorgiques de Virgile.* Paris, 1928.
—— *Culture de la vigne dans l'antiquité d'après les Géorgiques de Virgile.* Lyons, 1913.
BURFORD, A. 'Heavy Transport in Classical Antiquity'. *Ec. H.R.* XIII (1960), 1–18.
CAMPS-FABRER, H. *L'olivier et l'huile dans l'Afrique romaine.* Algiers, 1953.
DE ROBERTIS, F. M. 'La produzione agricola in Italia dalla crisi del III secolo all'eta dei Carolingi'. *Ann. della Fac. di Ec. e Comm. della Univ. di Bari*, n.s. VIII (1948), 67–271.
DICKSON, A. *Husbandry of the Ancients.* 2 vols. London, 1788.
DION, R. *Histoire de la vigne et du vin en France des origines au XIXe siècle.* Paris, 1959.
*DRACHMAN, A. G. *Ancient Oil Mills and Presses.* Copenhagen, 1932.
FORBES, R. J. *Studies in Ancient Technology.* Leiden, 1955– .
GEORLETTE, R. *L'agriculture dans l'antiquite d'apres les vieux auteurs latins.* Brussels, 1960.
GRADMANN, R. *Der Getreidebau im deutschen und römischen Altertum.* Jena, 1909.
GRAND, R. & DELATOUCHE, R. *L'agriculture au Moyen Age, de la fin de l'empire romain au XVIe siècle.* Paris, 1950.
HEHN, V. *Kulturpflanzen und Haustiere.* 8th ed. Berlin, 1911.
*HEITLAND, W. E. *Agricola.* Cambridge, 1921.
JASNY, N. *The Wheats of Classical Antiquity.* Baltimore, 1944.
KOLENDO, J. 'Techniques rurales'. *Annales*, XV, 1960, 1099–1114.
LEICHT, P. S. *Operai, artigiani e agricoltori in Italia dal secolo VI al XVI.* Milan, 1946.
LESER, P. *Entstehung und Verbreitung des Pfluges.* Münster, 1931.
*MICKWITZ, G. 'Economic Rationalism in Graeco-Roman Agriculture'. *EHR.* LII (1937), 577–89.
MORITZ, L. A. *Grain-Mills and Flour in Classical Antiquity.* Oxford, 1958.
NETOLITZKY, F. *Unser Wissen von den alten Kulturpflanzen Mitteleuropas*, in 20. *Bericht Röm.-Germ. Kommission.* Frankfurt a.M., 1931.
PETER, H. 'Il diritto agrario nel tardo impero romano'. *Riv. di dir. agr.* 1954, 421–36.
RASI, P. *Le corporazioni fra gli agricoltori.* Milan, 1940.
RAU, K. H. *Geschichte des Pfluges.* Heidelberg, 1845.
REICHTER, W. *Der Weinbau im römischen Altertum.* Schaffhausen, 1932.
RENARD, M. 'Technique et agriculture en pays trevire et remois'. *Latomus* XVIII (1959), 77–109 and 307–33.
ROUILLARD, G. *La vie rurale dans l'empire byzantine.* Paris, 1953.
RUGGINI, L. *Economia e societa nell' Italia Annonaria.* Giuffre, Milan, 1961. (B)
SEGRE, A. 'Note sulla storia dei cereali nell'antichita'. *Aegyptus* XXX (1950) 161–97.
SINGER, C. (ed.) *A History of Technology.* 2 vols. Oxford, 1954–6.
SLICHER VAN BATH, B. H. *The Agrarian History of Western Europe A.D. 500–1850.* Translated from the Dutch. London, 1963.
*WEBER, M. 'Agrarverhältnisse im Altertum. *Gesammelte Ausätze zur Sozial- und Wirtschaftsgeschichte.* Tübingen, 1924, pp. 1–277.
WHITE, L. *Mediaeval Technique and Social Change.* Oxford, 1962.

ii. *Agriculture in the post-Roman Mediterranean Lands (a Selection)*

GUYOT, J. *Culture de la Vigne.* Paris, 1931.
MOHAMMED-BEN-MOHAMMED AL IDRÎSI. *Description de l'Afrique et de l'Espagne.* (French translation, R. Dozy and M. J. de Goeje, Leyden, 1866.)

MORGAN, O. S. (ed.). *Agricultural Systems of Middle Europe.* New York, 1933.
SERRES, O. DE. *Le Théâtre d'Agriculture et Mesnage des Champs.* Paris, 1600.
TOWNSEND, J. *A Journey through Spain in the years 1786 and 1787.* 2nd ed. London, 1791.
WILLCOCKS, W. and CRAIG, J. *Egyptian Irrigation.* 2 vols. London, 1913.
YOUNG, A. *Travels in France, 1787, 1788, 1789.* Ed. C. Maxwell. Cambridge, 1929.

iii. *Agriculture in Northern Europe*

BLOCH, M. *Les caractères originaux de l'histoire rurale française.* Oslo and Paris, 1931.
CURWEN, E. C. 'Prehistoric Agriculture in Britain', in *Antiquity*, I, 261, 1927.
GRAY, H. L. *English Field Systems.* Cambridge, Mass. 1915.
MEITZEN, A. *Siedelung und Agrarwesen der Westgermanen und Ostgermanen, der Kelten, Römer, Finnen, und Slawen.* 3 vols. Berlin, 1895.
PASSMORE, J. B. *The English Plough.* London, 1930.
PROTHERO, R. E. (Lord Ernle). *English Farming, Past and Present.* 5th ed. London, 1936.
VINOGRADOFF, P. *The Growth of the Manor.* 3rd ed. London, 1921.

III. INSTITUTIONS

(a) *Original Authorities*

Codex Theodosianus. Ed. T. Mommsen and P. M. Meyer. 3 vols. Berlin, 1905. Ed. with Commentary, P. Gothofredus. 2nd ed. with notes by J. D. Ritter. 6 vols. Leipzig, 1736–45.
Corpus Juris Civilis. Ed. T. Mommsen and P. Kruger. 3 vols. Berlin, 1928–9.
Papyri Diplomati. Ed. Marini. Rome, 1805.

(b) *Taxation*

BOTH, H. *Die Grundzüge der Diokletianischen Steuerverfassung.* Darmstadt, 1928.
CASTAGNOLI, F. *Le ricerche sui resi della centuriazione.* Rome, 1958.
DELEAGE, A. *La capitation du Bas-Empire.* Mâcon, 1945.
JONES, A. H. M. 'Overtaxation and the Decline of the Roman Empire'. *Antiquity*, XXXIII (1959), 39–43.
KARAYANNOPULOS, J. *Das Finanzwesen des frühbyzantinischen Staates.* Munich, 1958.
LOT, F. *Nouvelles recherches sur l'impot foncier et la capitation personelle sous le bas-Empire.* Paris, 1955.
LOT, F. *L'impot foncier et la capitation sous le bas-empire et à l'époque franque.* Paris, 1928.

(c) *The Colonate*

BRISSAND, J. *Le régime de la terre dans la société étatiste du Bas-Empire.* Paris, 1927.
*CLAUSING, R. *The Roman Colonate: the Theories of its Origin.* New York, 1925.
COLLINET, P. 'Le colonat dans l'empire romain et "le servage".' *Récueils de la société Jean Bodin*, 2, 1937.
COULANGES, FUSTEL DE. 'Le Colonat romain', in *Recherches sur quelques Problèmes d'Histoire.* Paris, 1885.
GANSHOF, F. L. *Antiquité Classique*, XIV (1945) 261–77.
JONES, A. H. M. *Past and Present*, XIII (1958) 1–13.
PALASSE, M. *Orient et Occident à propos du colonat romain au bas empire.* Paris, 1950.
ROSTOWTZEW, M. *Studien zur Geschichte des Römischen Kolonates.* Leipzig, 1910.
SAUMAGNE, C. *Byzantion*, XII (1937) 487–581.
SEGRE, A. *Traditio*, V (1947) 103–33.

(d) *Land Tenure and Management*

AYMARD, J. 'Les capitalistes romains et la viticulture italienne'. *Annales*, 3 (1947), 257–65.
BEANDOUIN, E. *Les grandes domaines dans l'Empire romain.* Paris, 1909.
*BOAK, A. E. R. and YOUTIE, H. C. eds. *The Archive of Aurelius Isodorus.* Ann Arbor, 1960.

GUMMERUS, H. *Der Römische Gutsbetrieb als wirtschaftlicher Organismus.* Leipzig, 1906.
—— *Die Fronden der Kolonen.* Helsingfors, 1907.
HARMAND, L. *Le patronat.* Paris, 1957.
MITTEIS, H. L. *Zur Geschichte der Erbpacht im Altertum.* Leipzig, 1901.
—— *Reichsrecht und Volkrecht in den östlichen Provinzen des Römischen Kaiserreichs.* Leipzig, 1935.
SCHULTEN, A. *Die Römischen Grundherrschaften.* Weimar, 1896.
WEBER, M. *Römische Agrargeschichte.* Berlin, 1891.
ZULUETA, F. DE. 'De Patroniis Vicorum', in *Oxford Studies in Social and Legal History*, I. Oxford, 1909.

IV. REGIONAL STUDIES

The most useful guide to date of the economic aspects of the Roman provinces is *An Economic Survey of Ancient Roma*, edited by Tenney Frank, published in 1933-8, in Baltimore by the Johns Hopkins Press. It covers the period of Roman rule up to approximately the middle of the fourth century A.D. In each of the following regional biographies, the author responsible for the relevant section of the survey will be quoted, with the standard abbreviation of the title of the survey: ESAR.

(a) Eastern Provinces

BOUCHER, E. S. *Syria as a Roman Province.* Blackwell, Oxford, 1916.
BROUGHTON, T. R. S. 'Roman Asia', *ESAR.*
CALDER, W. M. & KEIL, J. (eds.). *Anatolian Studies presented to William Hepburn Bucker.* Manchester, 1939.
CHAPOT, V. *La province romaine d'Asie.* Paris, 1904.
COLEMAN-NORTON, P. R. (ed.). *Studies in Roman economic and social history presented to Allan Chester Johnson.* Princeton, 1951.
DOWNEY, G. *A history of Antioch in Syria from Seleucus to the Arab conquest.* Princeton, 1961.
HEICHELHEIM, F. 'Roman Syria', *ESAR.*
JONES, A. H. M. *Cities of the Eastern Roman Provinces.* Oxford, 1937.
—— *The Greek city from Alexander to Justinian.* Oxford, 1940.
LARSEN, J. A. O. 'Roman Greece', *ESAR.*
MAGIE, D. *Roman rule in Asia minor.* Princeton, .
PETIT, P. *Libanus et la vie municipal E Antioche au IV siècle après J.C.* Paris, 1955.
SHAMAN, L., TADMOR, N. & EVENARI, M. The Ancient Desert Agriculture of the Negev. *Ketavim*, 9, (1958), 1–2.
TCHALENKO, G. *Villages antiques de la Syrie du nord.* I–III. Paris, 1953.
VOGELSTEIN, H. *Die Landwirtschaft in Palästina zur Zeit der Mischna.* I. Berlin, 1894.

(b) Egypt

BELL, H. J. 'An epoch in the agrarian history of Egypt, in *Récueil Champollion*'. Paris, 1922.
GELZER, M. *Studien zur Byzantinischen Verwaltung Aegyptens.* Leipzig, 1909.
HARDY, E. T. *The large estates of Byzantine Egypt.* New York, 1931.
HOHLWEIN, N. 'Le blé d'Egypte' in *Etudes de Papyrologie.*
JOHNSON, A. C. 'Roman Egypt', *E.S.A.R.* II, Baltimore, 1936.
—— *Egypt and the Roman Empire.* Ann Arbor, University of Michigan Press, 1951. (Jerome Lectures, 2nd series.)
JOHNSON, A. C. & WEST, L. C. 'Byzantine Egypt', *ESAR.*
—— 'Byzantine Egypt', *Economic Studies.* Princeton, 1949.
JONGUET, P. *La vie municipale dans l'Egypte romaine.* Paris, 1911.
LEWIS, N. *L'industrie du Papyrus.* Paris, 1934.
MILNE, J. G. *A history of Egypt under Roman Rule.* 3rd ed., London, 1934.

MITTEIS, L. & WILCKEN, U. *Grundzuge und Chrisomathie der Papyruskund.* 4 vols., Leipzig, 1912.
ROUILLARD, G. L. *L'administation civile de L'Egypte byzantine.* Paris, 1923.
SCHNEBEL, M. *Die Landwirtschaft in Hellenistischen Agypten.* Munich, 1925.
TAUBENSCHLAG, R. *The law of Greco-Roman Egypt in the light of the Papyir* (332 B.C.–640 A.D.). Warsaw, 1955.
WALLACE, S. *Taxation in Roman Egypt. From Augustus to Diocletian.* Princeton, 1938.
WILLCOCKS, W. & CRAIG, J. *Egyptian irrigation.* 2 vols., London, 1913.

(c) Africa

ALBERITNI, E. *L'Afrique Romaine.* Paris, 1932.
BARADEZ, J. *Fossatum Africae.* Paris, 1949.
BERNARD, A. *Afrique septentrimale et occidentale.* Paris, 1937–9.
CHARLES-PICKARD, G. *La civilisation de L'Afrique romaine.* Paris, 1959.
COURTOIS, C. *Les vandales et l'Afrique.* Paris, 1955.
GAUCKLER, P. *Enquête sur les installations hydrauliques romaines eu Tunisie.* 3 vols., Tunis, 1897–1900.
HAYWOOD, R. M. 'Roman Africa', *ESAR.*
JULIEN, C. H. ANDRE. *Histoire del'Afrique du Nord, Tunisie —— Algerie —— Maroc, Des origines a la conquete Arabe (647).* Paris, 1956.
NORSA, G. & VITELLI, M. *Testi e Studi,* 53: Papiro Vaticano Greco II, 1931. (A late 2nd century A.D. survey of part of Marmarica): Ministère des Travaux Publiques. *Atlas des Centuriations romaines de Tunisie.* Paris, 1954.
ROMANELLI, P. *Storia delle province Romane dell' Africa.* Rome, 1959.
WARMINGTON, B. H. *The North African Provinces from Diocletian to the Vandal conquest.* Cambridge, 1954.

(d) Italy, Sicily, Sardinia

FRANK, TENNEY. 'Rome and Italy of the Empire', *ESAR.*
HANNESTAD, K. *Le évolution des resources agricoles de l'Italie du IV au VI siècle de notre ère.* Copenhagen, 1962.
LUZATTO, J. *An Economic History of Italy from the fall of the Roman Empire to the beginning of the sixteenth century.* Translated by P. Jones, New York, 1961.
MARESCALCHI, A. & DALMASSO, G. *Storia del vite del vino in Italia,* I & II. Milan, 1931–3.
MELONI, P. *L'amministrazione della Sardegna da Augusto all' invasione Vandalica.* Rome, 1958.
NISSEN, H. *Italienische Laudeskunde.* 2 vols., Berlin, 1883–1902.
ROBERTIS, F. M. DE. 'La produzione agricola in Italia dalla crisi del III secolo all' eta dei Carolingi'. *Ann. della Fac. di Ec. e Comm. della Universita di Bari,* n.s. VIII (1948).
RUGGINI, L. (B) *Economia e Societa nell' Italia 'Annonaria'.* Milan, 1961.
SCRAMUZZA, V. M. 'Roman Sicily', *ESAR.*
SEXENI, E. *Communita rurali rell' Italia antica.* Rome, 1955.

(e) Danubian Regions

GEROV, B. *Untersuchungen uber die west Thrakischen Lander in Romischer Zeit.* (In Russian with German synopsis.) Sophia, 1961.
GREN, E. *Kleinasien und der Ostbalken in der wirtschaftlichen Entwicklung der römischen Kaiserzeit.* Uppsala, 1941.
KAPHAN, F. *Zwischen Antike und Mittelalter das Donau-Alpenland im Zeitalter St Severins.* Munich, 1946.
MOCKSY, A. *Die Bevölkerung von Pannonien bis zu den Markomannen-Kriegen.* Budapest, 1959.
PARVAN, V. *Dacia.* Cambridge, 1928.
VOIT, L. *Raetia Latina. Quellen zur Geschichte der Romischer Donan-provinzen.* Dusseldorff, 1959.

(f) Spain

BOUCHIER, E. S. *Spain under the Roman Empire*. Blackwell, Oxford, 1914.
MOHAMMED-BEN-MOHAMMED, AL IDRÎSI. *Description de l'Afrique et de l'Espagne*. French translation R. Dozy and M. J. de Goeje, Leyden, 1866.
PIDAL, M. (*ed.*). *Historia de Espana*, II. Madrid, 1936.
TOWNSEND, J. *A Journey through Spain in the years 1786 and 1687*. 2nd ed. London, 1791.
VAN NOSTRAND, J. J. 'Roman Spain', *ESAR*.

(g) Gaul

BLOCH, M. *Les caractères originaux de l'histoire rurale française*. Paris, 1955; with commentary by R. Dauvergne, Paris, 1956.
BROGAN, O. *Roman Gaul*. London, 1953.
DILL, Sir SAMUEL. *Roman Society in Gaul in the Merovingian Age*. London, 1926.
DUVAL, P-M. *La vie quotidienne en Gaule pendant la paix Romaine*. Paris, 1959.
GRENIER, A. *Manuel d'archéologie gallo-Romaine*. Paris, 1931.
—— 'La Gaule Romaine', *ESAR*.
HATT, J. J. *Histoire de la Gaule Romaine (120 B.C.–451 A.D.)*. Paris, 1959.
JULLIAN, C. *Histoire de la Gaule*, VII and VIII. Paris, 1926.
YOUNG, A. *Travels in France 1787, 1788, 1789*. ed. C. Maxwell, Cambridge, 1929.

(h) Germany

MEITZEN, A. *Siedelung und Agrarwesen der West-Germanen und Ostgermanen der Kelten, Romer, Finnen und Skaren*. 3 vols., Berlin, 1895.
SCHUMACHER, K. *Der Ackerbau in vorrömische u. römische Zeit*. 1922.

(i) Britain

Ordnance Survey Map of Roman Britain, 3rd edn.
APPLEBAUM, S. Agriculture in Roman Britain. *Agric. Hist. Rev.*, VII (1958) 66 sqq.
'The Pattern of Settlement in Roman Britain'. *Agric. Hist. Rev.*, XI (1963) 1 sqq.
BONSER, W. *Romano-British Bibliography 55 B.C.–A.D. 449*. Oxford, Blackwell, 1964.
COLLINGWOOD, R. G. & MYRES, J. L. N. *Roman Britain and the English Settlements*.
CURWEN, E. 'Prehistoric Agriculture in Britain', *Antiquity* (1927), 261.
GRAY, H. L. *English Field Systems*. Cambridge Mass., 1915.
HELBAEK, H. 'Early Crops in South Britain'. *Proc. Prehist. Soc.* XVIII (1952) 194.
MANNING, W. H. 'The plough in Roman Britain', *JRS*. 54 (1964), 54.
PROTHERO, R. E. (Lord Ernle). *English Farming Past and Present*. 6th ed., London, 1962.
RICHMOND, I. A. *Roman Britain*. Penguin Books, London, 1955.
—— (ed.): *Roman and Native in North Britain*. London, 1958.
RIVET, A. L. F. *Town and Country in Roman Britain*. London, 1958.
VINOGRADOFF, P. *The Growth of the Manor*. 3rd ed., London, 1921.

CHAPTER III

The Evolution of Agricultural Technique

I. TREATISES ON AGRONOMY

i. *The Latin Agronomists*

Cato the censor, Varro, Virgil, Pliny, Columella, Palladius.

ii. *The Early Middle Ages*

The Capitulare de Villis. See Guérard, 'Explication du capitulaire "de Villis"', in *Acad. des Inscriptions et Belles-Lettres, Mémoires*, XXI, 1857. On commentators see W. von Wartburg, 'The localization of the *Capitulare de Villis*,' in *Speculum*, XV, 1940 and F. L. Ganshof, 'Observations sur la localisation du "Capitulare de Villis"', in *Le Moyen-Age*, 1949.

WANDELBERT OF PRÜM. 'De mensium XII nominibus', in *Mon. Germ. Poet. Lat.* II.
   For the plants cultivated the following may be added: Anthimus, *De observatione ciborum, epistula ad Theudericum regem Francorum,* ed. V. Rose, Lipsiae, 1877.

iii. *Mediterranean Europe*

Geoponica, sive Cassiani Bassi scholastici De re rustica eclogae. Ed. H. Beckh. Lipsiae, 1895. [First half of tenth century.]
IBN AL AWAM. *Le livre de l'agriculture (Kitab al Felahah, XIIe siècle).* Traduit de l'arabe par J. J. Clément Mullet. Paris, 1864–7. See L. Olson and H. L. Eddy, 'Ibn al Awan, a soil scientist of moorish Spain', in *Geog. Review,* 1943.
PIETRO DEI CRESCENZI. *Liber cultus ruris.* 1471. The composition of this work was finished in 1304. It was translated into French in 1373 by order of Charles V. Editors and translators have given it various titles—*Opus ruralium commodorum, Libro dell' Agricoltura, Libro delle villerecce Utilità, La livre des prouffits champestres et ruraux.* See L. Savastano, *Contributo allo studio critico degli scrittori agrari italici: Pietro dei Crescenzi,* Acireale, 1922 and L. Olson, 'Pietro dei Crescenzi: the founder of modern agronomy', in *Agricultural History Review,* 1944.

iv. *England*

Thirteenth century: WALTER OF HENLEY, *La Dite de Hosebondrie* and an anonymous *Hosebondrie.* Edited with two other treatises in *Walter of Henley's Husbandry. Together with an anonymous Husbandry, Seneschaucie and Robert Grossetestes Rule's.* Ed. E. Lamond. (Royal Hist. Soc. 1890.)
Fleta. Ed. J. Selden. 1647. [Of little original value.]
Fifteenth century: MAYSTER JON GARDENER. *The Feate of Gardeninge.* Ed. A. Amherst (Mrs E. Cecil). *Archaeologia,* LIV, 1895.
Sixteenth century: JOHN FITZHERBERT, *The Boke of Husbandrye,* 1523. Ed. W. W. Skeat. (English Dialect Soc. 1882.)
See HARVEY, W. 'Walter of Henley and the old Farming', in *Agriculture,* 59, 1952–3.
MACDONALD, D. *Agricultural Writers from Sir Walter Henley to A. Young,* 1200–1800, London, 1908, and Eileen Power, 'On the need for a new edition of Walter of Henley', in *TRHS.* 4th series, XVII, 1934.
OSCHINSKY, D. 'Medieval Treatises on estate Management', in *EcHR.* 2nd ser. VIII, 1956.
RICHARDSON, H. G. and SAYLES, G. O. *Fleta,* vol. II, 1956. (Selden Society Publications, vol. 72).

v. *France*

BRIE, JEHAN DE. *Le bon berger ou le vray régime et gouvernement des bergers et bergères.* Ed. Paul Lacroix. Paris, 1879. [This treatise, which was written in 1379 by order of Charles V. is known to us only in an abridged version printed in the first half of the sixteenth century.]
CROHORY, J. *Devis sur la vigne, vin et vendanges.* Paris, 1550.
ESTIENNE, CH. *Praedium rusticum.* Lutetiae, 1554.
—— *L'agriculture et la Maison Rustique.* Paris, 1564.
Le Ménagier de Paris. Traité de Morale et d'Economie Domestique, composé vers 1393 par un Bourgeois Parisien. Ed. J. Pichon. (Soc. des Bibliophiles français. Paris, 1846.) English translation (abridged, with introd. and notes) by Eileen Power, *The Goodman of Paris,* London, 1928.
SERRES, OLIVIER DE. *Théâtre d'agriculture et Mesnage des Champs.* Paris, 1600.

vi. *Germany*

HERESBACHIUS (Conrad Hertzbach). *Rei rusticae libri quatuor, universam rusticam disciplinam complectentes.* Cologne, 1571.

II. PICTORIAL REPRESENTATIONS

References will be found conveniently in:

MILLAR, E. G. *English Illuminated Manuscripts of the Twelfth to Thirteenth Centuries*, Paris, 1926, and *English Illuminated Manuscripts of the Fourteenth and Fifteenth Centuries*, Paris, 1928.

See also

LE SÉNÉCAL, J. 'Les occupations des mois dans l'iconographie du Moyen-Age', in *Bulletin de la Société des Antiquaires de Normandie*, XXXV, 1924.

The Luttrell Psalter. With introduction by E. G. Millar. 1932.

WEBSTER, J. C. 'The Labors of the Months in antique and mediaeval Art to the End of the Twelfth Century', *Princeton Monographs in Art and Archaeology*, 1938.

STERN, H. 'Représentations gallo-romaines des mois', in *Gallia*, IX, 1951.

—— 'Poésies et représentations carolingiennes et byzantines des mois', in *Revue Archéologique*, XLV, 1955.

III. GENERAL WORKS

It is impossible to list all the general works pertinent to this subject and to do so would involve a repetition of the bibliographies of other chapters. But the following works will more particularly be useful:

BELÉNYESY, M. 'Der Ackerbau und seine Produkte in Ungarn im XIV. Jahrhundert', in *Acta Ethnogr. Ac. Sc. Hung.*, VI, 1957.

CURWEN, E. C. *Plough and Pasture*. London, 1946.

FORBES, R. J. *Studies in ancient technology*. Leyde, 6 vols., 1955–8.

GRAND, R. and DELATOUCHE, R. *L'agriculture au Moyen Age de la fin de l'Empire romain au XVIᵉ siècle*. Paris, 1950.

Historia Agriculturae, annual bibliography, from 1953, Dutch Institute for agricultural History, Groningen and Agricultural University at Wageningen.

KRZYMOWSKI, R. G. *Geschichte der deutschen Landwirtschaft*. 2 Auf., 1951.

LINDEMANS, P. *Geschiedenis van de landbow in België*. Antwerp, 1952.

SLICHER VAN BATH, B. H. 'The rise of intensive husbandry in the Low Countries, in Britain and in the Netherlands', Papers delivered to the Oxford–Netherlands historical conference 1959, ed. by J. S. Bromley and E. H. Kossmann, London, 1960.

—— *De agrarische geschiedenis van West-Europa*, (500–1850). 2nd ed. Utrecht, 1962.

STEENSBERG, A. 'Modern Research of agrarian History in Denmark', in *Laos*, Uppsala, 1951.

IV. MONOGRAPHS

Among the most recent or least-known works the following are particularly worthy of note:

A

BRUNO, M. G. *Il lessico agricolo latino e le sue continuazioni romanze*, Instituto Lombardo di Scienze e Lettere, Milan, 1958.

—— *Apporti dalle glosse alla conoscenza del lessico agricolo latino*, Inst. Lomb. di Sc. e Let., Milan, 1959.

COLIN, G. S. 'La noria marocaine et les machines hydrauliques dans le monde arabe', in *Hespéris*, XIV, 1932.

DRACHMANN, A. G. *Ancient Oil Mills and Presses*, Copenhagen, 1932.

DUBY, G. 'Techniques et rendements agricoles dans les Alpes du Sud en 1338', in *Annales du Midi*, 1958.

JASNY, N. *The Wheats of classical Antiquity*, Johns Hopkins University Studies in historical and political Science, Baltimore, 1944.

KOLENDO, J. 'Z problematyki rozwoju rolnictwa w Galii rzymskiej', in *Przeglad Historyczny*, t. 51, translated with abridged footnotes: 'Techniques rurales. La moissonneuse antique en Gaule romaine', in *Annales E.S.C.* 1960).

LUQUET, G. H. and RIVET, P. 'Sur le tribulum', in *Mélanges Jorga*, 1933.

PARAIN, CH. 'Das Problem der tatsächlichen Verbreitung der technischen Fortschritte in der römischen Landwirtschaft', in *Zeitschrift für Geschichtswissenschaft*, 1960.

SCHEUERMEIER, P. *Bauernwerk in Italien, der italienischen und rätoromanischen Schweiz*, 2 vols., Zürich, 1943 and 1956.

SCLAFERT, TH. 'Usages agraires dans les régions provençales avant le XVIIIᵉ siècle. Les assolements', in *Revue de Géographie alpine*, 1941.

—— 'Cultures en Haute Provence. Déboisements et pâturages au Moyen age', *Les hommes et la terre*, IV, Paris, 1959.

SERENI, E. *Storia del paesaggio agrario italiano*. Bari, 1961.

SICARD, G. 'Les techniques rurales en pays toulousain aux XIVᵉ et XVᵉ siècles d'apres les contrats de métayage' in *Annales du Midi*, 1959.

SERGUEENKO, M. E. 'Sur l'économie rurale de l'Italie antique' (en russe) in *Vestnik Drevnej Istorii*, 1953, 3.

WIELOWIEJSKI, J. 'Development of agriculture in polish territories at the period of contacts with the Celtic and Roman culture', in *Ergon*, vol. II, 1960.

B

BELÉNYESY, M. 'La culture permanente et l'évolution du système biennal et triennal en Hongrie médiévale', in *Ergon*, vol. II, 1960.

BISHOP, T. A. M. 'The rotation of crops at Westerham, 1297–1350', in *EcHR*. 2nd ser., 9, 1958–9.

JUILLARD, E., MEYNIER, A., DE PLANHOL, X., and SAUTTER, G. 'Structures agraires et paysages ruraux. Un quart de siècle de recherches françaises', *Annales de l'Est*, publiées par la Faculté des Lettres de l'Université de Nancy, Mémoire no. 17, 1957.

RODERICK, A. J. 'Openfield Agriculture in Herefordshire in the Middle Ages', in *Trans. Woolhope Nat. Field Club*, 33, 1949.

SCHRÖDER-LEMBKE, G. 'Enstehung und Verbreitung der Mehrfeldwirtschaft in Nordöst Deutschland', in *ZAA*. 1954.

VERHULST, A. 'Bijdragen tot de studie van de agrarische structuur in het Vlaamse land. Het probleem van de verdwijning van de braak in de Vlaamse landbouw (XIIᵉ–XVIIᵉ eeuw)', in *Naturwetenschappelijk tijdschrift*, 1956.

—— 'Probleme der mittelalterlichen Agrarlandschaft in Flandern', in *ZAA*. 1961.

C

Agrarethnographie, Institut für deutsche Volkskunde, Berlin, 1957.

FINBERG, H. P. R. 'The Domesday plough-team', in *EHR*. 1951.

HAUDRICOURT, A. G. and JEAN-BRUNHES DELAMARRE, M. *L'homme et la charrue*. Paris, 1955.

LEE, N. E. *Harvests and Harvesting through the ages*. Cambridge, 1959.

LENNARD, R. 'The composition of demesme plough-teams in XIIth century England', in *EHR*. 1959.

PARAIN, CH. 'Les anciennes techniques agricoles', in *Revue de Synthèse*, 1957.

PAYNE, F. G. 'The British plough: some stages in its development', in *The agricultural History Review*, 1957.

PODWIŃSKA, Z. 'Origines et propagation de la charrue sur les territoires polonais', in *Ergon*, vol. II, 1960.

SACH, F. '*Rádlo*' et '*pluh*' en pays tchécoslovaque. I. *Les plus vieux outils* (*en tchèque*). Prague, 1961.

SLICHER VAN BATH, B. H. 'The influence of economic conditions on the development of agricultural tools and machines in history', in *Studies in industrial economics*, vol. II: Mechanization in agriculture, 1960.

STEENSBERG, A. *Ancient harvesting Implements*. Copenhagen, 1943.

TIMM, A. 'Zur Geschichte der Erntegeräte', in *ZAA*. 1956.

VAN DER POEL, J. M. G. 'Middeleeuwse ploegen in de Nederlanden', in *Handelingen van het XXIVᵉ Vlaams Filologencongres*, Louvain, 1961.

D

BASSERMANN-JORDAN, F. *Geschichte des Weinbaues.* Frankfurt-am-Main, 1907.
CHEVALIER, A. 'Histoire et amélioration des pommiers et spécialement des pommiers à cidre', in *Revue de Botanique appliquée,* 1921.
DION, R. *Histoire de la vigne et du vin en France des origines au XIXᵉ siècle.* Paris, 1959.
GIBAULT, G. *Histoire des légumes.* Paris, 1912.
HAUDRICOURT, A. G. and HÉDIN, L. *L'homme et les plantes cultivées,* Paris, 1943.
PARAIN CH. 'Vorindustrielle Pressen und Keltern und ihre Verbreitung in Westeuropa', in *Deutches Jahrbuch für Volkskunde,* II, 1962.
SANGERS, W. J. *De ontwikkeling van de Nederlandse tuinbouw (tot het jaar 1930).* 1952.

E

DEVÈZE, M. 'LA vie de la forêt française au XVIᵉ siècle', *Les hommes et la terre,* VI, 2 vols. Paris, 1961.
FOURNIER, G. 'La vie pastorale au Moyen Age dans les Monts Dore', in *Mélanges Philippe Arbos,* Clermont-Ferrand, 1953.
HUNGER, V. *Un haras royal en Normandie* (1338). Paris, 1927.
JACOBEIT, W. 'Schafhaltung und Schäfer in Zentraleuropa bis zum Beginn des 20. Jahrhunderts', *Veröffentlichungen des Instituts für deutsche Volkskunde, Bd.* 25, Berlin, 1961.
LENNARD, R. 'Statistics of sheep in medieval England', in *Agricultural History Review,* 1959.
STOLZ, O. 'Beiträge zur Geschichte der alpinen Schwaighöfe', in *VSWG.* 1932.
TROW-SMITH, R. *A history of British livestock husbandry to 1700.* London, 1957.

CHAPTER IV

Agrarian Institutions of the Germanic Kingdoms from the Fifth to the Ninth Century

A revision of the bibliography of the First Edition, by ECKART SCHREMMER

I. GENERAL

ABEL, W. *Geschichte der deutschen Landwirtschaft.* Stuttgart, 1962.
Adel und Bauern im deutschen Staat des Mittelalters. MAYER, TH. (Editor). Leipzig, 1943.
AUBIN, H. *Vom Altertum zum Mittelalter.* Munich, 1949.
BAAKEN, G. *Königtum, Burgen, Königsfreie.* Constance–Stuttgart, 1961.
BADER, K. S. 'Staat und Bauerntum im deutschen Mittelalter', in *Adel und Bauern im deutschen Staat des Mittelalters,* edited by Th. Mayer. Leipzig, 1943.
BECKER-DILLINGEN, J. *Quellen und Urkunden zur Geschichte des deutschen Bauern, Urzeit bis Ende der Karolingerzeit.* Berlin, 1935.
VON BELOW, G. 'Die Haupttatsachen der älteren deutschen Agrargeschichte', in *Probleme der Wirtschaftsgeschichte,* 2nd edition. Tübingen, 1926.
—— *Geschichte der deutschen Landwirtschaft des Mittelalters in ihren Grundzügen, aus dem Nachlass,* edited by F. Lütge, 1937.
BÖCKENFÖRDE, E. W. *Die deutsche verfassungsgeschichtliche Forschung im 19. Jahrhundert.* Berlin, 1961.
BOSCH-INEICHEN. 'Die Königsfreien von Emmen/Luzern', in *Aus Verfassungs- und Landesgeschichte,* Festschrift für Th. Mayer. Lindau–Constance, 1954.
BOG, I. *Dorgemeinde, Freiheit und Unfreiheit in Franken.* Stuttgart, 1956.
BOSL, K. 'Freiheit und Unfreiheit; zur Entwicklung der Unterschichten in Deutschland und Frankreich während des Mittelalters', in *VSWG.* 144, 1957.
—— 'Staat, Gesellschaft, Wirtschaft im deutschen Mittelalter' in Gebhardt *Handbuch der deutschen Geschichte,* 8th edition. Stuttgart, 1954.
—— *Die Frühformen der Gesellschaft im mittelalterlichen Europa.* München, 1964.

VON BRUNN, U. A. 'Frühe soziale Schichtungen im nordischen Kreis und bei den Germanen', in *Festschrift Mainz*, 1952.

BRUNNER, O. 'Die Freiheitsrechte in der altständischen Gesellschaft', in *Aus Verfassungs- und Landesgeschichte*, Festschrift für Th. Mayer. Lindau–Constance, 1954.

—— *Land und Herrschaft*, 4th edition. Vienna–Wiesbaden, 1959.

—— 'Moderner Verfassungsbegriff und mittelalterlicher Verfassungsbegriff und mittelalterliche Verfassungsgeschichte', in *Mitteilungen des Österreichlisch Instituts für mittelalterliche Verfassungsgeschichte*, 14, Supplement Volume.

CARO, G. *Beiträge zur älteren deutschen Wirtschafts- und Sozialgeschichte, Gesammelte Aufsätze*. Leipzig, 1905.

CIPOLLA, C. 'Della supposta Fusione degli Italiani coi Germani', in *Rendiconti della Reale Accad. dei Lincei*, Series 5, IX, Rome, 1900.

DAHN, F. *Die Könige der Germanen*. 12 vols. Munich, 1861–1911.

DANNENBAUER, H. 'Adel, Burg und Herrschaft bei den Germanen', in *HJ*. 61, 1941.

—— 'Die Freien im Karolingischen Heer' in *Aus Verfassungs- und Landesgeschichte*, Festschrift für Th. Mayer. Lindau–Constance, 1954.

DIEHL, A. 'Die Freien auf der Leutkircher Heide', in *Zeitschrift für Württembergische Landesgeschichte*, Volume 4, 1940.

DOPSCH, A. *Herrschaft und Bauer in der deutschen Kaiserzeit*. Jena, 1939.

FLEISCHMANN, W. *Caesar, Tacitus, Karl der Grosse und die deutsche Landwirtschaft*. Berlin, 1911.

—— *Altgermanische und altrömische Agrarverhältnisse in ihren Beziehungen und Gegensätzen*. Leipzig, 1906.

GRAND, R. and DELATOUCHE, R. *L'Agriculture au Moyen Age de la Fin de l'Empire Romain au XVIᵉ Siècle*. Paris, 1950.

GRÖSCH, G. *Markgenossenschaft und Grossgrundherrschaft im frühen Mittelalter*, 1911.

HAFF, J. 'Zur Geschichte des germanischen Grundeigentums', in *ZSS.*, Germanic Section, 1929.

HANSSEN, G. *Agrarhistorische Abhandlungen*, 2 volumes. Leipzig, 1880.

HAUPTMANN, L. 'Colonus, Barschalk und Freimann' in *Wirtschaft und Kultur*, Festschrift für A. Dopsch. Baden–Leipzig, 1938.

HODGKIN, T. *Italy and her Invaders*. 8 vols. Oxford, 1880–99.

HÖMBERG, A. K. *Die Entstehung der Westfälischen Freigrafschaften als Problem der mittelalterlichen Verfassungsgeschichte*. Münster, 1953.

JANDA, A. 'Die Barschalken', in *Veröffentlichungen des Seminars für Wirtschafts- und Kulturgeschichte an der Universität Wien*. Vienna–Budapest, 1926.

JANKUHN, H. *Gemeinschaffstform und Herrschaftsbildung in frühermanischer Zeit*. Neumünster, 1939.

KÖTZSCHKE, R. *Allgemeine Wirtschaftsgeschichte des Mittelalters*. Jena, 1924.

KOLLNIG, K. R. 'Freiheit und freie Bauern in Elsässischen Weistümern', in *Elsass-Lothringisches Jahrbuch*, Volume 19, 1941.

LÜTGE, F. 'Das Problem der Freiheit in der frühen deutschen Agrarverfassung', in *Festschrift für A. Fanfani*. Florence, 1962.

—— 'Die Unfreiheit in der ältesten deutschen Agrarverfassung Thüringens', in *Jahrbücher für Nationalökonomie und Statistik*, 144, 1936.

—— *Die Agrarverfassung des frühen Mittelalters im mitteldeutschen Raum, vornehmlich in der Karolingerzeit*. Jena, 1937.

—— *Geschichte der deutschen Agrarverfassung vom frühen Mittelalter bis zum 19. Jahrhundert*. Stuttgart, 1963.

—— *Deutsche Sozial- und Wirtschaftsgeschichte*. 2nd edition. Berlin–Göttingen–Heidelberg, 1960.

—— *Studien zur Sozial- und Wirtschaftsgeschichte. Gesammelte Aufsätze*. Stuttgart, 1963.

VON MAURER, G. L. *Geschichte der Markenverfassung in Deutschland*. Erlangen, 1856.

—— *Einleitung zur Geschichte der Mark-, Hof-, Dorf- und Stadtverfassung und der öffentlichen Gewalt*. 2nd edition. Vienna, 1896.

—— *Geschichte der Fronhöfe, der Bauernhöfe und der Hofverfassung in Deutschland*. 4 volumes. Erlangen, 1862–63.

MAYER, TH. *Adel und Bauern im deutschen Staat des Mittelalters.* Leipzig, 1943.

—— 'Königtum und Gemeinfreiheit im frühen Mittelalter', in *Deutsches Archiv für die Erforschung des Mittelalters*, 1943. Reprinted in *Mittelalterliche Studien*, Volume 1, 1959.

—— 'Baar und Barschalken', in *Mitteilungen des oberösterreichischen Landesarchivs*, Volume 3, 1954.

—— 'Die Königsfreien und der Staat des frühen Mittelalters', in *Das Problem der Freiheit in der deutschen und schweizerischen Geschichte*. Mainau-Vorträge, Lindau–Constance, 1953, 1955.

—— *Mittelalterliche Studien, Gesammelte Aufsätze.* Lindau–Constance, 1958.

—— *Fürsten und Staat. Studien zur Verfassungsgeschichte des Mittelalters.* Weimar, 1950.

MEITZEN, A. *Siedlungen und Agrarwesen der Westgermanen und Ostgermanen, der Kelten, Römer, Finnen und Slawen.* 3 volumes. Berlin, 1895.

METZ, W. 'Waldrecht, Hägerrecht und Medem', in *ZAA.* 1953–4.

—— *Staufische Güterverzeichnisse. Untersuchungen zur Verfassungs- und wirtschaftsgeschichte des 12. und 13. Jhs.* Berlin, 1964.

MITTEIS, H. *Der Staat des hohen Mittelalters.* 4th edition. Weimar, 1953.

—— 'Formen der Adelsherrschaft im Mittelalter', in *Festschrift für Fritz Schulz.* Weimar, 1951.

—— *Lehnrecht und Staatsgewalt.* 2nd edition, 1958.

MOMMSEN, T. 'Ostgothische Studien', in *Neues Archiv der Gesellschaft für ältere deutsche Geschichtskunde*, XIV, part 2, Hanover, 1888–9.

NJEUSSYCHIN, A. J. *Die Entstehung der abhängigen Bauernschaft als Klasse der frühfeudalen Gesellschaft in Westeuropa vom 6.–8. Jahrhundert.* Berlin, 1961.

NOTTARP, H. *Die Bistumserrichtung in Deutschland im 8. Jahrhundert.* Stuttgart, 1920.

OTTO, E. F. *Adel und Freiheit im deutschen Staat des frühen Mittelalters, Studien über nobiles und Ministerialen. Neue Deutsche Forschungen. Abetilung mittelalterliche Geschichte*, Volume 2. Berlin, 1937.

REIPRICH, B. *Zur Geschichte des ostgothischen Reiches in Italien.* Gross-Strehlitz, 1885.

SCHLESINGER, W. *Mitteldeutsche Beiträge zur deutschen Verfassungsgeschichte des Mittelalters* (complete treatises), 1961.

—— *Die Entstehung der Landesherrschaft vorwiegend nach mitteldeutschen Quellen.* Dresden, 1941.

—— 'Herrschaft und Gefolgschaft in der germanisch-deutschen Verfassungsgeschichte', in *HZ.*, 176, 1953.

SCHMIDT, L. *Geschichte der deutschen Stämme bis zum Ausgange der Völkerwanderung*, I. Berlin, 1910.

STEINBACH, F. 'Ständeproblem des frühen Mittelalters', in *Rheinische Vierteljahrsblätter.* Volume 7, 1937.

SUNDWALL, J. *Abhandlungen zur Geschichte des ausgehenden Römertums.* Fordhandlingar LXI. Ofversigt af Finska Vetenskaps-Societetens.) Helsingfors, 1919.

TELLENBACH, G. *Königtum und Stände in der Werdezeit des Deutschen Reiches.* Weimar, 1939.

THOMPSON, J. W. *Economic and Social History of the Middle Ages (300–1300).* 2nd edition. New York, 1959.

WAAS, A. *Die alte deutsche Freiheit; ihr Wesen und ihre Geschichte.* Munich–Berlin, 1939.

WAGNER, H. *Die Agrarverfassung bei den westgermanischen Völkerschaften in der Zeit von Caesar bis auf Chlodwig.* Würzburg, 1940.

WATTENBACH-LEVISON, *Deutschlands Geschichtsquellen im Mittelalter, Vorzeit und Karolinger*, Number 1: *Die Vorzeit von den Anfängen bis zur Herrschaft der Karolinger*, Supplement: *Die Rechtsquellen.* Weimar 1952–53.

WELLER, K. 'Die freien Bauern in Schwaben', in *ZSS.*, Germanic Section, Volume 57, 1937.

WENSKUS, R. 'Amt und Adel in der Merowingerzeit', in *Mitteilungsblatt des Marburger Universitäsbunds für 1959*.

WITTICH, W. *Die Grundherrschaft in Nordwestdeutschland*. Leipzig, 1896.
—— 'Die Frage der Freibauern' in *ZSS*. Germanic Section, Volume 22, 1901.
—— 'Epochen der deutschen Agrargeschichte', in *Grundriss der Sozialökonomik*, Section
VII. Tübingen, 1914.
WOPFNER, H. *Urkunden zur deutschen Agrargeschichte*. Stuttgart, 1928.
ZEISS, H. 'Die Barschalken und ihre Standesgenossen', in *Zeitschrift für Bayerische
Landesgeschichte*, 1. Munich, 1928.

II. ITALY

CIPOLLA, C. 'Della supposta Fusione degli Italiani coi Germani', in *Rendiconti della Reale
Accad. dei Lincei*, Series 5, IX, Rome, 1900.
DAHN, F. *Die Könige der Germanen*. 12 vols. Munich, 1861–1911.
HARTMANN, L. M. *Zur Wirtschaftsgeschichte Italiens im frühen Mittelalter*. Gotha, 1904.
HLAWITSCHKA, E. *Franken, Alemannen, Bayern und Burgunder in Oberitalien 774–962*.
Freiburg-im-Breisgau, 1960.
HODGKIN, T. *Italy and her Invaders*. 8 vols. Oxford, 1880–99.
MOMMSEN, T. 'Ostgothische Studien', in *Neues Archiv der Gesellschaft für ältere deutsche
Geschichtskunde*, XIV, part 2, Hanover, 1888–9.
REIPRICH, B. *Zur Geschichte des ostgothischen Reiches in* Italien. Gross-Strehlitz, 1885.
SCHMIDT, L. *Geschichte der deutschen Stämme bis zum Ausgange der Völkerwanderung*,
i. Berlin, 1910.
SUNDWALL, J. *Abhandlungen zur Geschichte des ausgehenden Römertums*. (Fordhandlingar
LXI. Ofversigt af Finska Vetenskaps-Societetens.) Helsingfors, 1919.

III. THE LOMBARDS

BOGNETTI, G. P. *Sulle origini dei Comuni rurali del medio evo*. Pavia, 1927.
BUTLER, W. F. *The Lombard Communes. A History of the Republics of North Italy*. London,
1906.
CHECCHINI, A. 'Comuni rurali Padovani', in *Nuovo Archivio Veneto*, LXXV (New Series,
XXXV), Venice, 1909.
JANKUHN, H. *Gemeinschaftsform und Herrschaftsbidlung in frühgermanischer Zeit*. Neu-
münster, 1939.
LEICHT, P. S. *Studi sulla proprietà fondiaria nel medio evo*. Verona and Padua, 1907.
SALVIOLI, G. 'Sullo stato e la popolazione d'Italia prima e dopo le invasioni barbariche',
in *Atti della Reale Accademia di Palermo*, Series 3, V, Palermo, 1900.
—— *Città e campagne prima e dopo il mille: contributo alla storia economica d' Italia nel medio
evo*. Palermo, 1901.
—— *Studi sulla storia della proprietà fondiaria in Italia: la proprietà fondiaria nell' agro
modenese durante il medio evo*. Modena, 1917.
—— *Storia economica d' Italia nell' alto medio evo*. Naples, 1913.
SCHNEIDER, F. *Die Reichsverwaltung in Toscana*, I. (Bibl. des königlichen preussischen
historischen Instituts in Rom, XI.) Rome, 1914.
—— *Die Entstehung von Burg und Landgemeinde in Italien*. Berlin-Grünewald, 1934.
SCHUPFER, F. 'Delle ordini sociali e del possesso fondiario appo i Langobardi', in
Sitzungsberichte der Kaiserlichen Akademie, XXXV, Vienna, 1861.
—— *Delle instituzioni politiche longobardiche*. Florence, 1863.
—— 'Aldi, liti e romani', in *Enciclopedia Giuridica Italiana*, I, Milan, 1892.
SELLA, P. *La Vicinio come elemento costitutivo del Comune*. Milan, 1898.
SEREGNI, G. 'La Popolazione agricola della Lombardia nell' età barbarica', in *Archivio
storico Lombardo*, Series 3, pp. 5–77, Milan, 1895.
TAMASSIA, N. 'Le Associazioni in Italia nel periodo precomunale', in *Archivio Giuridico*,
LXI, Modena, 1898.
VILLARI, P. *Le Invasioni Barbariche in Italia*. Milan, 1901. [Translation, L. Villari, 2 vols.
London, 1902.]
VINOGRADOFF, P. G. 'The Origin of Feudal Relations in Lombard Italy', in *Journal of
the Russian Ministry of Education*, St Petersburg, 1880. [In Russian.]

IV. Spain

CÁRDENES, F. DE. *Ensayo sobre la historia de la propriedad territorial en España.* 2 vols. Madrid, 1873–5.

PÉREZ PUJOL, E. *Historia de las Instituciones sociales de la España Goda.* 4 vols. Valencia, 1896.

STACH, W. 'Die geschichtliche Bedeutung der westgotischen Reichsgründung', in *Historische Vierteljahrsschrift,* XXX, Dresden, 1936.

TORRES, M. 'El Estado Visigotico', in *Anuario de historia del Derecho Español,* III, Madrid, 1926.

—— *Lecciones de Historia del Derecho Español.* 2 vols. 2nd ed. Salamanca, 1933–4.

—— *Historia de Espana.* Ed. R. Menéndez Pidal, III. Madrid, 1936.

V. The Burgundians

BAETHGEN, F. 'Das Königreich Burgund in der Deutschen Kaiserzeit', in *Jahrbuch der Stadt Freiburg-im-Breisgau,* 5, 1942.

BINDING, C. *Das burgundisch-romanische Königreich.* Leipzig, 1868.

CAILLEMER, E. 'L'établissement des Burgondes dans le Lyonnais', in *Mém. de l'acad. de Lyon,* XVIII, Paris-Lyon, 1878–9.

FEBVRE, L. *Histoire de la Franche Comté.* 7th edition. Paris, 1922.

GAMILLEFSCHEG, E. *Romania Germanica.* 3 volumes. Leipzig–Berlin, 1936.

GAUPP, E. T. *Die Germanischen Ansiedlungen und Landteilungen in den Provinzen des Römischen Westreiches.* Breslau, 1844.

Gesetze der Burgunder, edited by F. Beyerle, in *Germanenrechte,* 10, 1936.

HAVET, J. 'Du Partage des Terres entre les Romains et les Barbares chez les Burgondes et les Visigoths', in *RH.* VI, Paris, 1878.

HOFMEISTER, A. *Deutschland und Burgund im frühen Mittelalter.* Leipzig, 1914.

JAHN, A. *Die Geschichte der Burgundionen und Burgundiens.* 2 vols. Halle, 1874.

POUPARDIN, R. *Le royaume de Bourgogne,* 1907.

SALEILLES. 'De l'établissement des Burgundes sur les domaines des Gallo-Romains', in *Revue Bourguignonne,* Dijon, 1891.

VI. The Franks

Algemene Geschiedenis der Nederlanden. Edited by J. A. van Houtte, 12 volumes. Utrecht, 1949–1958.

BERGENGRUEN, A. *Adel und Grundherrschaft im Merowingerreich.* Wiesbaden, 1958.

BLOCH, M. 'Observations sur la conquête de la Gaule Romaine par les Rois Francs', in *RH.* CLIV, Paris, 1927.

BLOCK, P. J. *Geschichte der Niederlande.* 6 volumes. Gotha, 1902–1918.

BOSL, K., *Franken um 800. Strukturanalyse einer fränkischen Königsprovinz.* München, 1959.

DOPSCH, A. *Wirtschaftliche und soziale Grundlagen der Europäischen Kulturentwicklung.* 2 vols. Vienna, 1918–24. [Translation, M. G. Beard and N. Marshall, *The Economic and Social Foundations of European Civilization,* London, 1937.]

DÜMMLER, E. *Geschichte des ostfränkischen Reiches.* 2nd edition. 1887.

EWIG, E. 'Die fränkischen Teilungen und Teilreiche (511–613)', in *Akademie der Wissenschaften und der Literatur, Abhandlung der geistes- und sozialwissenschaftlichn Klasse.* Mainz, 1952, Number 9.

—— *Die fränkischen Teilreiche im 7. Jahrhundert (613–714).* Trier, 1954.

—— 'Civitas, Gau und Territorium in den Trierschen Mosellanden', in *Rheinische Vierteljahrsblätter* 17, 1952, Number 1.

FOUSTEL DE COULANGES, N. D. *Histoire des institutions politiques de l'ancienne France.* 7 volumes. 2nd edition. 1907–1914.

Geschiedenis van Nederland, edited by H. Brugmans. 8 volumes. 1935–38.

VON GUTTENBERG, E. *Grundzüge der Territorialbildung am Obermain.* Würzburg, 1925.

HOFBAUER, S. *Die Ausbildung der grossen Grundherrschaften im Reiche der Merowinger.* Brünn, 1927.

HOLWERDA, J. H. 'De Franken in Nederland', in *Oudheidkundige Mededeelingen uit 's Rijksmuseum van Oudheiden te Leiden,* New Series II and V, Leiden, 1920 and 1924,
—— 'Aus Holland', in *Deutsches Archäologisches Institut. Römish-Germanische Kommission.* 16th Report, Frankfort-on-Main, 1927.

KURTH, G. *Etudes franques.* 2 volumes, Paris, 1919.

LAET, S. J., DHONDT, J., NENQUIN, J. 'Les Laiti du Namurois et l'origine de la civilisation mérovingienne', in *Etudes d'Histoire et d'Archaeologie Namuroises,* Volume I. Namur, 1952.

LEVISON, W. *Aus rheinischer und fränkischer Vorzeit. Ausgewählte Aufsätze.* Edited by W. Holtzmann. Düsseldorf, 1948.

LOT, F. 'La conquête du pays d'entre Seine-et-Loire par les Francs', in *RH.* CLXV, 1930.

MAREZ, G. *Le Problème de la colonisation franque et du régime agraire en Basse-Belgique.* Brussels, 1926.

MAYER, TH. 'Rheinfranken in der deutschen Geschichte' in *Korrespondenzblatt des Gesellschaftsvereins,* 82, 1934.

METZ, W. *Das Karolingische Reichsgut.* Berlin, 1960.

PETRI, F. *Germanisches Volkserbe in Wallonien und Nord-Frankreich.* 2 volumes. 1937.

PIRENNE, H. *Histoire de Belgique.* 7 volumes. 1900–1932.

REESE, W. *Die Niederlande und das Deutsche Reich.* Berlin, 1941.

SCHMEIDLER, B. *Franken und das Deutsche Reich im Mittelalter.* Erlangen, 1930.

STEINBACH, F. and PETRI, F. *Zur Grundlegung der europäischen Einheit durch die Franken.* Leipzig, 1939.

STEINBACH, F. 'Das Frankenreich', in *Handbuch der deutschen Geschichte.* Constance, 1934.

THIELE, P. AUGUSTINUS. *Echternach und Himmerod. Beipiele benediktinischer und zisterziensischer Wirtschaftsführung im 12. und 13. Jh.* Stuttgart, 1964.

WAAS, A. 'Das Kernland des alten Deutschen Reichs am Rhein und Main', in *Deutsches Archiv für Geschichte des Mittelalters,* 7, 1944.

WAMPACH, C. *Geschichte der Grundherrschaft Echternach im Frühmittelalter,* Volume I: Textband; Volume 2: Quellenband. Luxembourg, 1929–30.

VII. THE SAXONS

BEMMANN, R. and JATZWANCK, J. *Bibliothek der sächsischen Geschichte,* Volume 1–3. Leipzig, 1910–32.

BRANDI, K. 'Karls des Grossen Sachsenkriege', in *Niedersächsisches Jahrbuch für Landesgeschichte,* X, Hildesheim, 1933.

DOPSCH, A. *See above under* The Franks.

KÖTZSCHKE, R. and KRETZSCHMAR, H. *Sächsische Geschichte.* 2 volumes. 1935.

LINTZEL, M. 'Die Unterwerfung Sachsens durch Karl den Grossen und der sächsische Adel', in *Sachsen und Anhalt,* Volume 10. 1934.
—— 'Der sächsische Stammesstaat und seine Eroberung durch die Franken', in *Historische Studien,* ed. E. Ebering, CCXXVII, 1933.
—— Articles on 'Sachsen und Anhalt', in *Jahrbuch der Hist. Kom. für die Provinz Sachsen und für Anhalt,* I–VII, Magdeburg, 1925–31.
—— *Die Stände der deutschen Volksrechte hauptsächlich des Lex Saxorum.* Halle, 1933.

MARTINY, R. *Hof und Dorf in Altwestfalen.* Stuttgart, 1926.

MUCH, R. 'Sachsen', in Hoops, *Reallexicon der germanischen Altertumskunde,* IV, Strasburg, 1918–19.

ROTTHOFF, G. 'Studien zur Geschichte des Reichsgutes in Niederlothringen und Friesland während der sächsisch-salischen Kaiserzeit', in *Rheinisches Archiv,* 44, 1953.

RACHFAHL, F. 'Schleswig-Holstein in der deutschen Agrargeschichte', in *Jahrbücher für Nationalökonomie und Statistik,* CXIII (Series 3, XXXVIII), Jena, 1909.

Neues Archiv für Sächsische Geschichte, Volume 1–63, 1880–1942.

SCHMIDT, L. 'Zur Entstehungsgeschichte des sächsischen Stammes', in *Zeitschrift der Gesellschaft für Schleswig-Holsteinische Geschichte*, LXIV, Kiel, 1936.
SERING, M. *Erbrecht und Agrarverfassung in Schleswig-Holstein auf geschichtlicher Grundlage*. Berlin, 1908.

VIII. THE FRISIANS

CARSTEN, R. H. *Chauken, Friesen und Sachsen zwischen Elbe und Vlie*. Hamburg, 1941.
DÜMMLER, E. 'Geschichte des Ostfränkischen Reichs', in *Jahrbücher der deutschen Geschichte*. 3 volumes. 1887–88.
Die Friesen, edited by C. Borchling and R. Muuss. Breslau, 1931.
GIERKE, J. 'Die Geschichte des deutschen Reichrechts', in *Untersuchungen zur Deutschen Staats- und Rechtsgeschichte*, ed. O. Gierke, Parts 63 and 128, Breslau, 1901–17.
HAARNAGEL, W. 'Zur Grabung auf des Feddersen Wierde 1955–1959', in *Germania*, 39, 1957.
HECK, P. *Die altfriesische Gerichtsverfassung*. Weimar, 1894.
ILGEN, TH. 'Die Grundlagen der mittelalterlichen Wirtschaftsverfassung am Niederrhein', in *Westdeutsche Zeitschrift*, Volume 32, 1913.
KLINGENBORG, M. *Ansicht der friesischen Geschichte im Mittelalter*, 120, 1909.
MOLLWO, H. *Die Friesen und das Reich*, Dissertation, Hamburg, 1942.
MUCH, R. 'Friesen', in Hoops, *Reallexicon*, II, Strasburg, 1913–15.
SUNDERMANN, H. F. *Friesische und niedersächsische Bestandteile in den Ortsnamen Ostfrieslands*. Emden, 1901.
SWART, F. 'Zur friesischen Agrargeschichte', in *Staats- und sozialwissenschaftliche Forschungen*, ed. G. Schmoller and M. Sering, Part 145, Leipzig, 1910.
WAAS, A. 'Das Kernland des alten Deutschen Reichs an Rhein und Main', in *Deutsches Archiv für Geschichte des Mittelalters*, 7, 1944.
ZIEHEN, E. 'Rheinfranken und das Reich 843–961', in *Archiv für Hessische Geschichte*, Series 22, 1942.

IX. THE ANGLO-SAXONS

CHADWICK, H. M. *Studies in Anglo-Saxon Institutions*. Cambridge, 1805.
—— *The Origin of the English Nation*. Cambridge, 1907.
COLLINGWOOD, R. G. and MYRES, J. N. L. *Roman Britain and the English Settlements*. 2nd ed. Oxford, 1937.
HAVERFIELD, F. G. *The Romanization of Roman Britain*. 2nd ed. Oxford, 1912.
HODGKIN, R. H. *A History of the Anglo-Saxons*. 2 volumes. 2nd edition. 1939.
KEMBLE, J. M. *History of the Saxons in England*. 2 vols. London, 1848.
LENNARD, R. 'Englisches Siedelungswesen', in Hoops, *Reallexicon*, I, Strasburg, 1911–13.
—— 'From Roman Britain to Anglo-Saxon England', in *Wirtschaft und Kultur. Festschrift zum 70. Geburtstag von Alfons Dopsch*, Baden near Vienna, Leipzig, 1938.
LEVISON, W. *England and the Continent in the 8th century*. 2nd edition. 1950.
LIEBERMANN, F. *Die Gesetze der Angelsachsen*. 3 vols. Halle, 1903–16.
MAITLAND, F. W. *Domesday Book and Beyond*. Cambridge, 1897.
—— 'The Survival of Archaic Communities', in *Law Quarterly Review*, IX, London, 1893. [Reprinted in *Collected Papers*, II, Cambridge, 1911.]
NASSE, E. *Ueber die mittelalterliche Feldgemeinschaft und die Einhegungen des sechzehnten Jahrhunderts in England*. Bonn, 1869.
POGATSCHER, A. *Zur Lautlehre der griechischen, lateinischen und romanischen Lehnworte im Altenglischen*. (Quellen und Forschungen zur Sprach- und Kulturgeschichte der germanischen Völker, part 64.) Strasburg, 1888.
SCHWARZ, E. *Goten, Nordgermanen, Angelsachsen*. Berne–Munich, 1951.
SEEBOHM, F. *The English Community*. London, 1883.
—— *Tribal Custom in Anglo-Saxon Law*. London, 1902.
VINOGRADOFF, P. *The Growth of the Manor*. London, 1905.

X. THE THURINGIANS

DEVRIENT, E. 'Angeln und Warnen', in *Neue Jahrbücher für das Klassische Altertums Geschichte*, VII, Leipzig, 1901.

DOBENECKER, O. *Regesta diplomatica necnon epistularia Thuringiae.* 4 volumes till 1288. Jena, 1896–1919.

FLACH, W. 'Stamm und Landschaft Thüringens im Wandel der Geschichte', in *Blätter für deutsche Landesgeschichte*, 84, 1938.

GERBING, L. 'Die frühere Ausdehnung des Waldes in Südwest Thüringen', in *Mitteilungen der geographischen Gesellschaft für Thüringen*, xxv, Jena, 1907.

GÖTZE, HÖFER P. and ZSCHIESCHE, P. (eds.). *Die vor- und frühgeschichtlichen Altertümer Thüringens.* Würzburg, 1909.

GRÖSSLER, H. 'Die Besiedlung der Gaue Friesenfeld und Hassegau', in *Zeitschrift des Harz-Vereins für Geschichte und Altertumskunde*, VIII, Wernigerode, 1875.

HÖFER, P. 'Die Frankenherrschaft in den Harzlandschaften', in *Ibid.* XL, Wernigerode, 1907.

—— 'Die sächsische Legende zum thüringisch-fränkischen Kriege', in *Zeitschrift des Vereins für Thüringische Geschichte und Altertumskunde*, xxv, Jena, 1906–7.

KÖTZSCHKE, R. 'Thüringen in der deutschen Siedlungsgeschichte', in *Festschrift A. Tille*, 1930.

LÜTGE, F. 'Die Hufe in der thüringisch-hessischen Agrarverfassung der Karolingerzeit', in *Schmollers Jahrbuch* 61, 1937.

MASCHKE, E. 'Thüringen in der Reichsgeschichte', in *Zeitschrift des Vereins für thüringische Geschichte und Altertumskunde*, Series 32, 1937.

MENTZ, G. *Ein Jahrhundert Thüringische Geschichtsforschung, Bibliographie.* Jena, 1937.

ROTTSTADT, V. 'Besiedlung und Wirtschaftsverfassung des Thüringer Waldes', in *Staats- und sozialwissenschaftliche Forschungen*, part 179, ed. G. Schmoller and M. Sering, Munich and Leipzig, 1914.

SCHATTE, W. *Die thüringischen Siedlungsnamen in ihre Bedeutung für die altdeutsche Landes- und Volkskunde.* (Thesis.) Halle, 1903.

SCHLUETER, O. *Die Siedelungen in nordöstlichem Thüringen.* Berlin, 1903.

SCHNEIDER, F. and TILLE, A. *Einführung in die Thüringische Geschichte.* Jena, 1931.

SCHRÖDER, E. 'Über Ortsnamenforschung', in *Zeitschrift des Harz-Vereins für Geschichte und Altertumskunde*, XL, Wernigerode, 1907.

WERNEBURG, A. 'Die Namen der Ortschaften und Wüstungen Thüringens', in *Jahrbücher der Königlichen Akademie gemeinnütziger Wissenschaften zu Erfurt*, New Series, XII, Erfurt, 1884.

WÜTSCHKE, J. *Beiträge zur Siedlungskunde des nördlichen subharzynischen Hügellandes.* (Thesis.) Halle, 1907.

XI. THE ALLEMANNI

BAUER, A. *Gau und Gesellschaft der Alemannen. Ein Beitrag zur Verfassungsgeschichte der Alemannen.* Stuttgart, 1927.

ERNST, V. *Die Entstehung des deutschen Grundeigentums.* Stuttgart, 1926.

HELBOK, A. 'Die deutschen Weiler-Orte', in *Mitteilungen des Österreichischen Instituts für Geschichtsforschung*, XI, Innsbruck, 1929.

—— 'Zur früheren Wirtschafts- und Kulturgeschichte des alemannischen Raumes', in *Zeitschrift für die Geschichte des Ober-Rheins*, New Series, XLV, Carlsruhe, 1931.

—— 'Sippensiedlung und Grundherrschaft', in *Deutsche Hefte für Volks- und Kulturbodenforschung*, II, Breslau, 1932.

—— 'Zur Frage der germanischen Wirtschaftskultur', in *VSWG.* XXII, 1929.

KLUGE, F. 'Sippen-Siedlungen und Sippennamen', in *VSWG.* VI, 1908.

MAURER, F. *Oberrheiner, Schwaben, Südalemannen. Räume und Kräfte im geschichtlichen Aufbau des deutschen Südwestens*, 1942.

STEINBACH, F. *Studien zur westdeutschen Stammes- und Volksgeschichte.* Jena, 1926.

VEECK, W. *Die Alamannen in Württemberg. Germanische Denkmäler der Völkerwanderungszeit*, I. Stuttgart, 1921.

—— 'Die Reihengräberfriedhöfe des frühen Mittelalters und die historische Forschung', in *Römish-Germanische Kommission*, 16th Report, Frankfort-on-Main, 1927.

WAIG, G. J. *Die Alamannen in ihrer Auseinandersetzung mit der römischen Welt*, Volume I. 2nd edition. 1943.

WELLER, K. *Geschichte des schwäbischen Stammes bis zum Untergang der Staufer*. Munich–Berlin, 1944.

XII. THE BAVARIANS

BARGER, E. 'The Problem of Roman Survivals in Germany', in *EHR*. I, London, 1935.

BOSL, K. *Geschichte Bayerns*, Volume I. *Vorzeit und Mittelalter*. Munich, 1952.

DACHS, H. 'Sippensiedlung oder Grundherrschaft', in *Korrespondenzblatt des Gesamtvereins der deutschen Geschichts- und Altertumsvereine*, LXXVIII, Berlin, 1930.

—— 'Römisch-germanische Zusammenhänge in der Besiedlung und den Verkehrswegen Altbayerns', in *Die Ostbairischen Grenzmarken* (Verein für Ostbairische Heimatforschung), Passau, 1924.

DOEBERL, M. *Entwicklungsgeschichte Bayerns*. 3 volumes. Munich, 1916–28–31.

DOLLINGER, P. *L'Evolution des classes rurales en Bavière*. Paris, 1949.

ETTMAYER, K. VON. 'Die Geschichtlichen Grundlagen der Sprachenverteilung in Tirol', in *Mitteilungen des Instituts für Österreichische Geschichtsforschung*, IX, Innsbruck, 1913–15.

FASTLINGER, M. *Die wirtschaftliche Bedeutung der bayerischen Klöster in der Zeit der Agilolfinger*. Freiburg-im-Breisgau, 1903.

GUTMANN, F. *Soziale Gliederung der Bayern zur Zeit des Volksrechtes*. Strasbourg, 1906.

RIETZLER, S. *Geschichte Bayerns*. 8 volumes. Gotha, 1887–1914. Volume I and 2. 2nd edition, 1927; Register, 1932.

RIEZLER, S. 'Die Landnahme der Baiuwaren', in *Sitzungsberichte der Bayerischen Akademie*, XVI, Munich, 1921.

SCHIFFMANN, C. *Das Land ob der Enns*. Munich and Berlin, 1922.

WEBER, F. 'Beiträge zur Anthropologie und Urgeschichte Bayerns', in *Münchener Gesellschaft für Anthropologie, Ethnologie und Urgeschichte*, XIV, 1901–2.

XIII. THE CAROLINGIAN EMPIRE

ARBMAN, H. *Schweden und das Karolingische Reich*. Stockholm, 1937.

BAIST, G. 'Zur Interpretation der Brevium Exempla und des Capitulare de Villis', in *VSWG*. XII, 1914.

BALDAUF, O. *Das karolingische Reichsgut in Unterrätien*. Innsbruck, 1930.

BLOCH, M. 'L'origine et la date du capitulare de Villis', in *RH*. CXLIII, Paris, 1923.

BOSL, K. *Franken um 800*. Munich, 1959.

DANNENBAUER, J. 'Politik und Wirtschaft in der altdeutschen Kaiserzeit' in *Festschrift für J. Haller*, 1940.

DOPSCH, A. *Die Wirtschaftsentwicklung der Karolingerzeit*. 2 parts. 2nd ed. Wiemar, 1921–2.

—— 'Carlomagno y el "Capitulare de Villis",' in *Anuario de Historia del derecho español*, II, Madrid, 1925.

—— *Naturalwirtschaft und Geldwirtschaft in der Weltgeschichte*. Vienna, 1930.

—— 'Freilassung und Wirtschaft im frühen Mittelalter', in *Festskrift til Halvdan Koht*, Oslo, 1933.

DUMAS, A. 'Quelques observations sur la grande et la petite propriété à l'époque carolingienne', in *Revue Historique de droit français et étrangers*, 1926.

ELSNER, W. *Zur Entstehung des Capitulare de Villis*. (Thesis.) Kiel, 1929.

GAREIS, K. *Die Landgüterordnung Karls des Grossen*. Berlin, 1895.

KÖTZSCHKE, R. 'Karl der Grosse als Agrarpolitiker', in *Festschrift für E. Stengel*. Münster–Cologne, 1952.

HAUPTMANN, L. 'Hufengrössen im bayrischen Stammes- und Kolonialgebiete', in *VSWG*. XXI, 1928.

LOT, F. 'La grandeur des fiscs à l'époque carolingienne', in *RB*. III, 1924.

LÜTGE, F. *Die Agrarverfassung des frühen Mittelalters im mitteldeutschen Raum vornehmlich in der Karolingerzeit*. Jena, 1937.

—— 'Hufe und Mansus in den mitteldeutschen Quellen der Karolingerzeit', in *VSWG*. 30, 1937.

MAYER, T. 'Zur Entstehung des Capitulare de Villis', in *VSWG*. XVII, 1924.
—— 'Hufe und Mansus in den mitteldeutschen Quellen der Karolingerzeit', in *VSWG*., 30, 1937.
METZ, W. 'Reichsadel und Krongutsverwaltung in Karolingischer Zeit', in *Blätter für deutsche Landesgeschichte*, 94, 1958.
—— *Das Karolingische Reichsgut*. Berlin, 1960.
PATZELT, E. 'Die karolingische Renaissance', in *Deutsche Kultur*. Historische Reihe, I, ed. W. Brecht and A. Dopsch, Vienna, 1924.
—— *Die fränkische Kultur und der Islam*. (Veröffentlichungen des Seminars für Wirtschafts- und Kulturgeschichte an der Universität Wien. Ed. A. Dopsch, IV.) Vienna, 1932.
PIRENNE, H. *Mahomet et Charlemagne*. Paris and Brussels, 1937. [Translation, Bernard Miall, London, 1939.]
RANZI, F. *Königsgut und Königsforst im Zeitalter der Karolinger und Ludolfinger und ihre Bedeutung für Landesausbau*. Halle/Saale, 1939.
STEINITZ, B. 'Die Organisation und Gruppierung der Krongüter unter Karl dem Grossen, *VSWG*., 9, 1913.
TELLENBACH, G. 'Vom Karolingischen Reichsadel zum deutschen Reichsfürstenstand', in *Adel und Bauern im deutschen Staat des Mittelalters*, edited by Th. Mayer. Leipzig, 1943.
THOMPSON, J. W. *The dissolution of the Carolingian Fisc in the ninth century*. University of California Publications in History 23, Berkeley and London, 1935.
VERHEIN, K. 'Studien zu den Quellen zum Reichsgut der Karolingerzeit', in *Deutsches Archiv für Erforschung des Mittelalters* 10, 1953–54.
VOGEL, W. *Die Normannen und das fränkische Reich bis zur Gründung der Normandie (799–911)*. Heidelberg, 1906.

CHAPTER V

Agrarian Conditions in the Byzantine Empire in the Middle Ages

I. SOURCES

Akty russkogo na sv. Afone monastyrja sv. velikomučenika i celitelja Pantelejmona [Documents of the Russian monastery of the holy martyr and healer Panteleimon on Mt Athos]. Kiev, 1873.
ASHBURNER, W. 'The Farmer's Law', in *Journal of Hellenic Studies*, XXX (1910), 85–108; XXXII (1912), 68–95.
—— 'A Byzantine Treatise of Taxation', in *ibid*. XXXV (1915), 76–84. New edition: Dölger, F. *Beiträge zur Geschichte der byzantinischen Finanzverwaltung* (1927), 113–23.
BEES, N. A. Σερβικὰ καὶ βυζαντιακὰ γράμματα Μετεώρου [Serbian and Byzantine documents from the Monastery of Meteora], in Βυζαντίς II (1911–2), 1–100.
BOMPAIRE, J. *Actes de Xéropotamore*. Paris, 1964.
CHONIATES, MICHAEL. 'Hypomnestikon', in Migne, *P.G.* CXL, 377–82. New edition: Stadtmüller, G. Michael Chomiates (1934), 283–6.
Chronicle of Morea, ed. John Schmitt. London, 1904.
DÖLGER, F. *Aus den Schatzkammern des Heiligen Berges*. Munich, 1948.
—— 'Sechs byzantinische Praktika des 14. Jahrhunderts für das Athoskloster Iberon', in *Abh. d. Bayer. Akad. d. Wiss., Philos-hist. Klasse*, N.F. 28. Munich, 1949.
FLORINSKIJ, T. *Afonskie akty* [Documents from Athos]. St Petersburg, 1880.
FOURMY, M. H. and LEROY, M. 'La vie de Philarète', in *Byzantion*, IX (1934), 85–170.
GOUDAS, M. Βυζαντιακὰ ἔγγραφα τῆς ἐν Ἄθῳ ἱερᾶς μονῆς τοῦ Βατοπεδίου [Byzantine documents from the monastery of Vatopedi on Athos], in Ἐπετηρὶς Ἑταιρείας Βυζαντινῶν Σπουδῶν [Annual of the Society of Byzantine Studies], IV (1927), 211–48.
GUILLOU, A. *Les archives de Saint-Jean-Prodrome sur le mont Ménécée*. Paris, 1955.

KEKAUMENOS. *Strategikon*, ed. V. Vasiljevskij and V. Jernstedt. St Petersburg, 1896.
KTENAS, CHR. Χρυσόβουλλοι λόγοι τῆς ἐν Ἄθῳ ἱερᾶς μονῆς τοῦ Δοχειαρίου [Golden Bulls from the monastery of Dochiariou], in Ἐπετηοὶς Ἑταιρείας Βυζαντινῶν Σπουδῶν, IV (1927), 285–311.
LASKARIS, M. *Vatopedskata gramota na car Ivan Asenja II* [The Vatopedi document of the Tsar Ivan Asen II]. Sofia, 1930.
—— *Actes serbes de Vatopédi*. Prague, 1935.
LAURIOTES, ALEXANDROS. Ἀθωῖτις Στοά [Documents from Athos], in *Vizantijskij Vremennik*, V (1898), 483–93.
MEYER, PH. *Haupturkunden für die Geschichte der Athosklöster*. Leipzig, 1894.
MIKLOSICH, F. and MÜLLER, J. *Acta et diplomata graeca medii aevi*, I–VI, Vienna, 1860–90.
MOŠIN, V. 'Akti iz svetogorskih arhiva' [Documents from the archives of Mt Athos], in *Spomenik of the Serbian Academy of Sciences*, XCI, 1939.
MOŠIN, V. and SOVRE, A. *Supplementa ad acta graeca Chilandarii*. Ljubljana, 1948.
Νόμος γεωργικός, see Ashburner, W. 'The Farmer's Law'.
Novels of the Byzantine Emperors, see Zachariae a Lingenthal, C. E. *Jus Graeco-Romanum*, III.
PEIRA, 'Practica ex actis Eustathii Romani', see *ibid.* I.
PETIT, L. 'Actes de Pantocrator', in *Vizantijskij Vremennik*, X (1903).
—— 'Actes de Xénophon', in *ibid.*
—— 'Typicon de Grégoire Pacourianos', in *ibid.* XI (1904).
PETIT, L. and KORABLEV, B. 'Actes de Chilandar', in *ibid.* XVII (1911); XIX (1912).
PETIT, L. and REGEL, W. 'Actes d'Esphigménou', in *ibid.* XII (1906).
REGEL, W., KURTZ, E., and KORABLEV, B. 'Actes de Zographou', in *ibid.* XIII (1907).
—— 'Actes de Philothée', in *ibid.* XX (1913).
REGEL, W. Χρυσόβουλλα καὶ γράμματα τῆς ἐν τῷ Ἁγίῳ Ὄρει Ἄθῳ ἱερᾶς καὶ σεβασμίας μονῆς του Βατοπεδίου [Golden Bulls and documents from the monastery of Vatopedi on Mt Athos]. St Petersburg, 1898.
ROUILLARD, G. and COLLOMP, P. *Actes de Lavra*, I. Paris, 1937.
SATHAS, K. *Bibliotheca graeca medii aevi*, I–VII. Venice–Paris, 1862–94.
SOLOVJEV, A. and MOŠIN, V. *Grčke povelje srpskih vladara* [Greek documents of the Serbian rulers]. Belgrade, 1936.
SVORONOS, N. G. *Recherches sur le cadastre byzantin et la fiscalité aux XIᵉ et XIIᵉ siècles: le cadastre de Thèbes*. Athens–Paris, 1959.
TAFEL, G. L. F. and THOMAS, G. M. *Urkunden zur älteren Handels- und Staatsgeschichte der Republik Venedig*, I–III. Vienna, 1856–7.
THEOPHYLACTUS OF OCHRIDA. Epistolae, in Migne, *P.G.* CXXVI, 307–557.
USPENSKIJ, P. *Vostok christianskij. Istorija Afona* [The Christian East. A history of Athos]. I–III. Kiev, 1871.
USPENSKIJ, F. I. 'Vizantijskie zemlemery' [Byzantine surveyors], in *Trudy VI archeol. s'ezda v Odesse 1884 g.*, II (1888), 274–341.
—— 'Akt otvoda zemli monastyrju Bogorodicy Milostivoj' [A document of assignement of land for the monastery of Eleusa], in *Izvestija of the Russian Archaeological Institute in Constantinople*, I (1896), 1–34.
USPENSKIJ, F. I. and BENEŠEVIČ, V. *Actes de Vazélon*. Leningrad, 1927.
ZACHARIAE A LINGENTHAL, C. E. *Jus Graeco-Romanum*, I, III. Lipsiae, 1856, 1857= Zepos, J. and P. *Jus graecoromanum*, IV, I. Athens, 1931.

II. MODERN WORKS

ABRAMSON, M. L. 'Krest' janstvo v vizantijskich oblastjach Južnoj Italii (IX–XI vv.)' [Peasantry in Byzantine regions of Southern Italy (9th–11th centuries)], in *Viz. Vremennik*, VII (1953), 161–93.
—— 'Votčina v Južnoj Italii IX–XI vv.' [Patrimonial property in Southern Italy from the 9th to the 11th century], in *Vizantijskie očerki* (Moscow–Leningrad, 1961), 137–73.
ANDREADES, A. M. Ἱστορία τῆς ἑλληνικῆς δημοσίας οἰκονομίας [History of the Greek public economy]. Athens, 1918.

ANDREADES, A. M. 'Deux livres récents sur les finances byzantines', in *Byz. Zeitschrift*, XXVIII (1928), 287–323.

—— 'The Economic Life of the Byzantine Empire', in *Byzantium*, ed. by N. H. Baynes and H. St L. B. Moss, Oxford, 1949, 51–70.

ANGELOV, D. 'Feodalizmŭt vŭv Vizantija' [The feudalism in Byzantium], in *Istoričeski pregled*, III, 2 (1946–7), 217–33.

—— 'Prinos kŭm narodnostnite i pozemleni otnošenija v Makedonija (Epirskija despotat) prez pŭrvata četvŭrt na XIII vek' [A contribution to the ethnical and agrarian conditions in Macedonia (the Despotate of Epirus) during the first quarter of the 13th century], in *Izvestija na Kamarata na narodnata kultura*, IV, 3 (1947), 1–46.

—— *Agrarnite otnošenija v severna i sredna Makedonija prez XIV vek* [Agrarian conditions in North and Middle Macedonia in the 14th century]. Sofia, 1958.

BACH, E. *Les Lois agraires byzantines du Xe siècle*, in *Classica et Mediaevalia*, V (1942), 70–91.

BAYNES, N. H. *The Byzantine Empire*. Chap. VI, pp. 99–113: Land-holding and Taxation. London, 1925, revised 1943.

BELL, H. I. 'The Byzantine Servile State in Egypt', in *Journal of Egyptian Archaeology*, IV (1917), 86–106.

—— 'An Epoch in the Agrarian History of Egypt', in *Recueil d'études égyptologiques dédiées à la mémoire de I. Fr. Champollion* (Bibl. de l'École des Hautes Études, fasc 234, 1922), 261–71.

BEZOBRAZOV, P. V. 'Patmosskaja piscovaja kniga' [The terrier of Patmos], in *Viz. Vremennik*, VII (1900), 68–106.

—— 'Afonskie dokumenty' [Documents from Athos], in *Viz. Obozrenie*, I (1915), 53–76.

BINON, ST. *Les origines légendaires et l'histoire de Xéropotamou et de St Paul de l'Athos*. Louvain, 1942.

BRATIANU, G. I. *Études byzantines d'histoire économique et sociale*. Paris, 1938.

BRÉHIER, L. 'Les populations rurales au IXe siècle d'après l'hagiographie byzantine', in *Byzantion*, I (1924), 177–90.

BRENTANO, L. 'Die byzantinische Volkswirtschaft', in *Schmollers Jahrb.*, XLI (1917), 1–50.

CHARANIS, P. 'On the Social Structure of the Later Roman Empire, in *Byzantion*, XVII (1944–5), 39–58.

—— 'The Monastic Properties and the State in the Byzantine Empire', in *Dumbarton Oaks Papers*, IV (1948), 53–118.

—— 'On the Social Structure and Economic Organization of the Byzantine Empire in the Thirteenth Century and Later', in *Byzantinoslavica*, XII (1951), 94–153.

CONSTANTINESCU, N. A. 'Question agraire dans l'Empire byzantin', in *Revue hist. du sud-est europ.* I (1924), 233–50.

—— 'Réforme social ou réforme fiscale? Une hypothèse pour expliquer la disparition du servage de la glèbe dans l'Empire byzantin', in *Bull. de la Section Hist. de l'Acad. Roumaine*, XI (1924), 94–109.

—— 'La communauté de village byzantin et ses rapports avec le petit Traité fiscal byzantin', in *ibid.*, XIII (1927), 160–74.

DIEHL, CH. *Etudes sur l'administration byzantine dans l'exarchat de Ravenne*. Paris, 1888.

—— *L'Afrique byzantine*. Paris, 1896.

—— *Byzantium: Greatness and Decline* (with Introduction and Bibliography by P. Charanis). Rutgers University Press, 1957.

DANSTURP, G. 'The State and Landed Property in Byzantium to 1250', in *Classica et Mediaevalia*, VIII (1946), 221–67.

DÖLGER, F. *Regesten der Kaiserurkunden des oströmischen Reiches*, I–IV. Munich–Berlin, 1924, 1925, 1932, 1960.

—— *Beiträge zur Geschichte der byzantinischen Finanzverwaltung, besonders des 10. und 11. Jahrhunderts*. Leipzig–Berlin, 1927.

—— 'Die Frage des Grundeigentums in Byzanz', in *Bull. of the Intern. Committee of Hist. Sciences*, V (1933), 5–15; reprinted in *Byzanz und die europäische Staatenwelt*, Ettal, 1953, 217–32.

—— *Byzantinische Diplomatik. 20 Aufsätze zum Urkundenwesen der Byzantiner*. Ettal, 1956.

DÖLGER, F. *Παρασπορά*. 30 *Aufsätze zur Geschichte, Kultur und Sprache des byzantinischen Reiches*. Ettal, 1961.

FERRADOU, A. *Des biens des monastères à Byzance*. Bordeaux, 1896.

FREJDENBERG, M. M. 'Razvitie feodal'nych otnošenij v vizantijskoj derevne v XI–XII vv.' [Development of feudal relations in the Byzantine village in the 11th and 12th centuries], in *Učenye zapiski Velikolukskogo gos. ped. inst.* I (1956), 105–34.

—— 'Ekskussija v Vizantii XI–XII vv.' [Immunity in Byzantium in the 11th and 12th centuries], in *ibid.* III (1958), 339–65.

GELZER, M. *Studien zur byzantinischen Verwaltung Ägyptens*. Leipzig, 1909.

GLYKATZI-AHRWEILER, H. 'La politique agraire des empereurs de Nicée', in *Byzantion*, XXVIII (1958), 51–66, 135–6.

—— 'La concession des droits, incorporels. Donations conditionneles, in *Actes du XII* Congrès Intern. des Études byzantines*, Ochride 1961, vol. II, Belgrade 1964, 103–14.

GORJANOV, B. T. 'Vizantijskoe krest'janstvo pri Paleologach' [The Byzantine peasantry under the Palaeologi], in *Viz. Vremennik*, III (1950), 19–50.

—— 'Pozdnevizantijskij immunitet' [The late Byzantine immunity], in *ibid.* XI (1956), 177–99; XII (1957), 97–116.

—— *Pozdnevizantijskij feodalizm* [The late Byzantine feudalism]. Moscow, 1962.

HARDY, E. R. *The Large Estates of Byzantine Egypt*. New York, 1931.

HARTMANN, L. M. *Untersuchungen zur Gesichte der byzantinischen Verwaltung in Italien*. Leipzig, 1889.

JAKOVENKO, P. *K istorii immuniteta v Vizantii* [Contribution to the history of immunity in Byzantium]. Jur'ev, 1908.

—— *Gramoty Novogo Monastyrja na ostrove Chiose* [Documents from Nea Mone in Chios]. Jur'ev, 1917.

KARAYANNOPULOS, J. *Das Finanzwesen des frühbyzaotinischen Staates*. Munich, 1958.

KAŽDAN. A. P. 'Vizantijskoe sel'skoe poselenie' [Byzantine rural settlement], in *Viz. Vremennik*, II (1949), 215–44.

—— *Agrarnye otnošenija v Vizantii XIII–XIV vv.* [Agrarian conditions in Byzantium in the 13th and 14th centuries]. Moscow, 1952.

—— 'K voprosu ob osobennostjach feodal'noj sobstvennosti v Vizantii VIII–X vv.' [On the particularities of the feudal property in Byzantium from the 8th to the 10th century], in *Viz. Vremennik*, X (1956), 48–65.

—— *Derevnja i gorod v Vizantii IX–X vv.* [City and village in Byzantium in the 9th and 10th centuries]. Moscow, 1960.

—— 'Ekskussija i ekskussaty v Vizantii X–XII vv.' [Immunity and immunists in Byzantium from the 10th to the 12th century], in *Viz. očerki* (Moscow, 1961), 186–216.

LEFEBURE DES NOËTTES, CT. 'Le systeme d'attelage du cheval et du boeuf à Byzance et les conséquences de son emploi', in *Mélanges Diehl*, I (Paris, 1930), 183–90.

LEMERLE, P. 'Esquisse pour une histoire agraire de Byzance: les sources et les problèmes, in *RH*. CCXIX, I (1958), 32–74, 254–84; CCXIX, 2 (1958), 43–94.

LEVČENKO, M. V. 'Materialy dlja vnutrennej istorii Vostočno-Rimskoj imperii V–VI vv.' [Materials for the inner history of the Eastern Roman Empire in the 5th and 6th centuries], in *Viz. Sbornik* (Moscow–Leningrad, 1945), 12–95.

—— 'Cerkovnye imuščestva v Vostočno-Rimskoj imperii V–VII vv.' [Church property in the Eastern Roman Empire from the 5th to the 7th century], in *Viz. Vremennik*, II (1949), 11–59.

LIPŠIC, E. E. 'Vizantijskoe krest'janstvo i slavjanskaja kolonizacija' [The Byzantine peasantry and the Slav colonization], in *Viz. Sbornik* (1945), 95–143.

—— 'O putjach formirovanija feodal'noj sobstvennosti i feodal'noj zavisimosti v balkanskich i maloazijskich provincijach Vizantii' [On the ways of formation of feudal property and feudal dependence in the Byzantine provinces on the Balkans and in Asia Minor], in *Viz. Vremnnik*, XIII (1958), 28–59.

—— *Očerki istorii vizantijskogo obščestva i kul'tury, VIII–pervaja polovina IX veka* [Essays on history of the Byzantine society and civilisation in the 8th and the first half of the 9th century]. Moscow–Leningrad, 1961.

LITAVRIN, G. G. *Bolgarija i Vizantija v XI–XII vv.* [Bulgaria and Byzantium in the 11th and 12th centuries]. Moscow, 1960.

MALAFOSSE, J. 'Les lois agraires à l'époque byzantine. Tradition et exégèse', in *Recueil de l'Acad. de Législation*, XIX. Toulouse, 1949.

MONNIER, H. 'Études de droit byzantin. L'épibolé', in *Nouv. revue hist. de droit français et étranger*, XVI (1892), 125–64, 497–542, 637–72; XVIII (1894), 433–86; XIX (1895), 59–103.

MUTAFČIEV, P. 'Vojniški zemi i vojnici v Vizantija prez XIII–XIV v.' [Military estates and soldiers in Byzantium in the 13th and 14th centuries], in *Spisanie of the Bulgarian Academy of Sciences*, XXVIII (1923), 1–113.

NOVAKOVIĆ, St. 'Pronijari i baštinci' [Pronoiars and patrimonial proprietors], in *Glas of the Serbian Academy*, I (1887), 1–102.

OSIPOVA, K. A. 'Razvitie feodal'noj sobstvennosti na zemlju i zakrepoščenie krest'janstva v Vizantii x v.' [Development of the feudal landed property and peasant servility in Byzantium in the 10th century], in *Viz. Vremennik*, X (1956), 66–80.

OSTROGORSKY, G. 'Die ländliche Steuergemeinde des byzantinischen Reiches im 10. Jahrhundert', in *VSWG*. XX (1927), 1–108.

—— 'Das Steuersystem im byzantinischen Altertum und Mittelalter', in *Byzantion*, VI (1931), 229–40.

—— 'Le grand domaine dans l'Empire byzantin', in *Recueils de la Société Jean Bodin*, IV (1949), 35–50.

—— *Pour l'histoire de la féodalité byzantine*. Brussels, 1954.

—— *Quelques problèmes d'histoire de la paysannerie byzantine*. Brussels, 1956.

—— 'Das byzantinische Kaiserreich in seiner inneren Struktur', in *Historia Mundi*, VI (1958), 445–73.

—— 'K istorii immuniteta v Vizantii', in *Viz. Vremennik*, XIII (1958), 55–106; French translation: 'Pour l'histoire de l'immunité à Byzance', in *Byzantion*, XXVIII (1958), 165–254.

—— 'Vizantijska seoska opština', in *Glas of the Servian Academy of Sciences and Arts*, CCL (1961), 141–160; French translation: 'La commune rurale byzantine,' in *Byzantion*, XXXII (1962) 139–66.

PANČENKO, B. A. 'Krest'janskaja sobstvennost' v Vizantii' [The peasant property in Byzantium], in *Izvestija of the Russian Archaeological Institute in Constantinople*, IX (1904), 1–234.

PIGULEVSKAJA, N. V., LIPSIC, E. E., SJUZJUMOV, M. JA., and KAŽDAN, A. P. 'Gorod i derevnja v Vizantii v IV–XII vv.' [City and village in Byzantium from the 4th to the 12th century], in *Actes du XIIᵉ Congrès Intern. des Études byzantines*, Ochride 1961, vol. I, Belgrade, 1963, 1–44.

ROSTOVTZEFF, M. *The Social and Economic History of the Roman Empire*. Oxford, 1926.

ROUILLARD, G. *L'administration civile de l'Egypte byzantine*. 2nd ed. Paris, 1928.

—— 'Les archives de Lavra', in *Byzantion*, III (1926), 253–64.

—— 'Recensement de terre sous les premiers Paléologues', in *ibid.* XII (1937), 105–18.

—— 'L'épibolé au temps d'Alexis Iᵉʳ Comnène', in *ibid.* X (1935), 81–9.

—— *La vie rurale dans l'Empire byzantin*. Paris, 1953.

SETTON, K. M. 'On the Importance of Land Tenure and Agrarian Taxation in the Byzantine Empire, from the Fourth Century to the Fourth Crusade, in *American Journal of Philology*', LXXVI (1953), 225–359.

RUDAKOV, A. P. *Očerki vizantijskoj kul'tury po dannym grečeskoj agiografii* [Sketches of Byzantine civilisation based upon Greek hagiography]. Moscow, 1917.

SJUZJUMOV, M. JA. 'O charaktere i suščnosti vizantijskoj obščiny po Zemledel'českomu zakonu' [On the character and the essence of the Byzantine community according to the Farmer's Law], in *Viz. Vremennik*, X (1956), 27–47.

—— 'Bor'ba za puti razvitija feodal'nych otnošenij v Vizantii' [Struggle for the ways of the development of feudal relations in Byzantium], in *Viz. očerki* (1961), 34–63.

SOKOLOV, I. 'Krupnye i melkie vlasteli v Fessalii' [The greater and lesser nobles of Thessaly], in *Viz. Vremennik*, XXIV (1923), 35–44.

SOKOLOV, I. 'Materialy po zemel'no-chozjajstvennomu bytu Vizantii' [Materials for the agrarian conditions of Byzantium], in *Izvestija Akad. Nauk. SSSR*, (1931), No. 6, 683–712.

SOLOV'EV, A. V. 'Fessalijskie archonty v XIV v.' [The archons of Thessaly in the 14th century], in *Byzantinoslavica*, IV (1932), 159–74.

STADTMÜLLER, G. 'Michael Choniates, Metropolit von Athen', in *Orientalia Christiana*, XXX, 2 (1934), 122–324.

—— 'Landesverteidigung und Siedlungspolitik im oströmischen Reich', in *Bull. de l'Inst. archéol. bulgare*, IX (1935), 392–9.

STEIN, E. *Studien zur Geschichte des byzantinischen Reiches*. Stuttgart, 1919.

—— 'Untersuchungen zur spätbyzantinischen Verfassungs- und Wirtschaftsgeschichte', in *Mitteilungen zur Osmanischen Geschichte*, II (1923–5), 1–62.

—— 'Vom Altertum im Mittelalter. Zur Geschichte der byzantinischen Finanzverwaltung', in *VSWG*. XXI (1928), 158–70.

—— 'Paysannerie et grands domaines dans l'Empire byzantin', in *Recueil de la Société Jean Bodin*, Brussels, 1937, 123–33.

UDAL'COVA, Z. V. *Italija i Vizantija v VI veke* [Italy and Byzantium in the 6th century]. Moscow, 1959.

USPENSKIJ, K. N. 'Ekskussija-immunitet v vizantijskoj imperii' [Immunity in the Byzantine Empire], in *Viz. Vremennik*, XXIII (1917–22), 74–117.

USPENSKIJ, F. I. 'Značenie vizantijskoj i južnoslavjanskoj pronii' [The significance of Byzantine and Southern-Slav pronoia], in *Sbornik V.N. Lamanskomu*. St Petersbrug, 1883, 1–32.

—— 'K istorii krest'janskogo zemlevladenija v Vizantii' [Contribution to the history of peasant landownership in Byzantium], in *Žurnal Min. Nar. Prosv*. CCXXV (1883), 30–87, 301–60.

—— 'Sledy piscovych knig v Vizantii' [Traces of terriers in Byzantium], in *ibid*. XXCCV (1883), 187–201; CCXXXI (1884), 1–46, 289–335; CCXL (1885), 1–52.

—— 'Mnenija i postanovlenija konstantinopol'skich pomestnych saborov XI i XII v. o razdače cerkovnych imuščestv' [Judgements and decrees of the Byzantine local synods of the 11th and 12th centuries touching the bestowal of church property], in *Izvestija of the Russian Archaeological Institute in Constantinople*, V (1900), 1–48.

—— 'Social'naja evoljucija i feodalizacija Vizantii' [Social evolution and feudalization of Byzantium], in *Annaly*, II (1923), 95–114.

VASILIEV, A. A. 'On the Question of Byzantine Feudalism', in *Byzantion*, VIII (1933), 584–604.

VASIL'EVSKIJ, V. G. 'Materialy k vnutrennej istorii vizantijskogo gosudarstva' [Materials for the inner history of the Byzantine state], in *Žurnal Min. Nar. Prosv*. CCII (1879), 160–232, 368–438; CCX (1880), 98–170, 355–440.

VERNADSKIJ, G. V. 'Zametki o krest'janskoj obščine v Vizantii' [Observations on the peasant community in Byzantium], in *Učenye zapiski russk. učebn. kolleg. v Prage*, I, 2 (1924), 81–97.

—— 'Sur l'origine de la Loi agraire', in *Byzantion*, II (1925), 169–80.

VIŠNJAKOVA, A. 'Chozjajstvennaja organizacija mon. Lemviotissy' [The economic organization of the monastery of Lemviotissa], in *Viz. Vremennik*, XXV (1927), 33–52.

XANALATOS, D. A. *Beiträge zur Wirtschafts- und Sozialgeschichte Makedoniens im Mittelalter, hauptsächlich auf Grund der Briefe des Erzbischofs Theophylaktos von Achrida*. Munich, 1937.

ZACHARIÄ VON LINGENTHAL, K. E. *Geschichte des griechisch-römischen Rechts*. 3. Aufl. Berlin, 1892; reprinted: Aalen in Württemberg, 1955.

ZAKYTHINOS, D. A. 'Processus de féodalité', in *L'Hellénisme contemporain*, II, 2 (1948). 499–534.

CHAPTER VI

The Rise of Dependent Cultivation and Seignorial Institutions

Compiled by MME. E. CARPENTIER

I. THE SEIGNORIAL SYSTEM IN GENERAL AND ITS ORIGINS

BLOCH, M. *Seigneurie française et manoir anglais* (Cahiers des Annales, 16). Paris, 1960.
BOUTRUCHE, R. 'Histoire des institutions. Moyen-Age', in *IXᵉ Congrès intern. des Sciences historiques*, I, Rapports. Paris, 1950.
—— *Seigneurie et féodalité*, vol. I: *Le premier âge des liens d'homme à homme*. Paris, 1959.
DOPSCH, A. *Wirtschaftliche und soziale Grundlagen der Europaïschen Kulturenwicklung aus der Zeit von Cäsar bis auf Karl den Grossen*. 2 vols. 2nd ed. Vienna, 1924.
DUBY, G. *L'économie rurale et la vie des campagnes dans l'Occident médiéval*. 2 vols. Paris, 1962.
KOTZSCHKE, R. 'Manorial system', in *Encyclopedia of the Social Sciences*, X, 1933.
LACOMBE, P. *L'Appropriation du Sol*. Paris, 1923.
LATOUCHE, R. *Les origines de l'économie occidentale* (L'Evolution de l'Humanité, 43). Paris, 1956.
PERRIN, CH-E. *La Seigneurie rurale en France et en Allemagne du début du IXᵉ à la fin du XIIᵉ siècle*. 3 fasc. Paris, les Cours de Sorbonne, 1951–5.
—— *Recueils de la Société Jean Bodin*, vol. III, *la Tenure*. Brussels, 1938.
—— *Recueils de la Société Jean Bodin*, vol. IV, *le Domaine*. Brussels, 1949.
SAINT-JACOB, P. DE. 'Recherches sur la structure terrienne de la seigneurie', in *Annales de l'Est, mémoire no. 21*. Nancy, 1959.
VINOGRADOFF, P. *Outlines of Historical Jurisprudence*, I. Oxford, 1920.

II. RURAL CONDITIONS IN THE ROMAN EMPIRE

1. *General Works*

BEAUDOIN, E. 'Les grands domaines dans l'Empire romain', in *Nouvelle Revue historique de droit français et étranger*, 1897 and 1898.
BOGNETTI, G. P. 'La proprietà della terra nel passaggio dal mondo antico al Medio Evo occidentale', in *Atti del Conv. Naz. di Dir. Agrario*. Florence, 1958.
CHEVALLIER, R. 'La centuriation et les problèmes de la colonisation romaine', in *Etudes rurales*, no. 3, 1961.
GUMMERUS, H. *Der römische Gutsbetrieb als wirtschaftlicher Organismus nach den Werken der Cato, Varro und Columella* (Beiträge zur alten Geschichte, V). Leipzig, 1906.
KORNEMANN. 'Bauernstand und Domänen', in Pauly, *Realencyc.* Supplement IV, 1924.
MITTEIS, L. 'Zur Geschichte der Erbpacht im Altertum', in *Abhandlungen der phil.-histor. Kl. der K. sächsischen Gesellschaft der Wissenschaften*, XX, 1891.
PIGANIOL, A. 'La crise sociale du Bas-Empire', in *Journal des Savants*, 1955.
ROSTOVTZEFF, M. *The Social and Economic History of the Roman Empire*. 2nd ed. revised by P. M. Fraser. 2 vols. Oxford, 1957.
SCHULTEN, A. *Die römischen Grundherrschaften*. Weimar, 1896.

2. *Egypt*

HARDY, E. R. *The large estates of Byzantine Egypt*. New York, 1931.
JOHNSON, A. C. *An economic survey of ancient Rome*: vol. II, *Roman Egypt to the reign of Diocletian*. Baltimore, 1938.
ROSTOVTZEFF, M. *A large estate in Egypt in the third century B.C.* (University of Wisconsin Studies in the Social Sciences and History, VI) Michigan, 1922.
SCHWARTZ, J. *Les archives de Sarapion et de ses fils. Une exploitation agricole aux environs d'Hermoupolis Magna (de 90 à 133 P.C.)* (Inst. fr. d'Archéol. orientale, Bibl. d'étude, vol. XXIX) Cairo, 1961.

3. Italy

SALVIOLI, G. 'Sulla distribuzione della proprieta fondaria in Italia al tempo dell' impero romano', in *Archivio giuridico*, LXII, 1899.
SERENI, E. *Communità rurali nell'Italia antica.* Rome, 1955.

4. Africa

CARCOPINO, J. 'L'inscription d'Aïn-el-Djemala', in *Mélanges d'archéologie et d'histoire*, XXVI, 1906.
—— 'Encore l'inscription d'Aïn-el-Djemala', in *Klio*, VIII, 1908.
—— 'Les Tablettes Albertini', in *Journal des Savants*, 1952.
COURTOIS, C., LESCHI, L., PERRAT, CH., and SAUMAGNE, CH. *Tablettes Albertini, actes privés de l'époque vandale.* Paris, 1952.
LAMBERT, J. 'Les Tablettes Albertini', in *Revue africaine*, XCVII, 1953.
PALLASSE, M. 'Les Tablettes Albertini intéressent-elles le colonat romain du Bas-Empire?', in *Rev. hist. de droit français et étranger*, 4th ser. XXXIII, 1955.
PERNOT, M. 'L'inscription d'Henchir Mettich', in *Mélanges d'archéologie et d'histoire*, XXI, 1901.
PEZZANA, A. 'Osservazioni sulle Tablettes Albertini', in *Arch. Giurid. Filippo Serafini*, 6th ser. XIII, 1953.
SCHULTEN, A. 'Die lex Manciana', in *Abhandlungen der k. Gesellschaft zu Göttingen, phil.-hist. Kl.*, N.F., II, no. 3, 1897.
—— 'Die "lex Hadriana de rudibus agris"', in *Klio*, VII, 1907.
TOUTAIN, J. 'L'inscription d'Henchir Mettich', in *Mémoires présentés par divers savants à l'Académie des Inscriptions*, 1st ser. XI, I, 1897.

5. Gaul

BROGAN, O. *Roman Gaul.* London, 1953.
GRENIER, A. *Manuel d'archéologie gallo-romaine:* vol. II, part II, Navigation-Occupation du Sol. Paris, 1934.

6. Britain

COLLINGWOOD, R. G. and MYRES, J. N. L. *Roman Britain and the English Settlement.* (Oxford History of England). 1936.
FINBERG, H. P. R. *Roman and Saxon Withington.* Leicester, 1955.
HAFEMANN, D. *Beitrage zur Siedlungs-geographie des römischen Britannien.* I. Teil: *Die militärischen Siedlungen.* (Abhandlungen der Mainzer Akademie der Wissenschaften und der Literatur, Matematisch-naturwissenschaftliche Klasse, 3) Wiesbaden, 1956.

7. The Colonate

BOLKESTEIN, H. *De colonatu romano eiusque origine.* Amsterdam, 1906.
FUSTEL DE COULANGES. 'Le Colonat romain', in *Recherches sur quelques problèmes d'histoire*, Paris, 1885.
GANSHOF, F. L. 'Le Statut personnel du colon au Bas-Empire', in *L'Antiquité classique*, 1945.
GUMMERUS, H. 'Die Fronden der Kolonen', in *Ofuersigt af Finska Vetenskapssocietetens Förhandlijer*, IV, no. 3, 1905-7.
JONES, A. H. M. 'The Roman Colonate', in *Past and Present*, XIII, 1958.
KUBLER, B. 'Sklaven und Kolonen in der römischen Kaiserzeit', in *Festschrift J. Vahlen*, Berlin, 1900.
PALLASSE, M. *Orient et Occident à propos du colonat romain au Bas-Empire.* Paris, 1950.
ROSTOVTZEFF, M. *Studien zur Geschichte des römischen Kolonats* (supplement 1, *Archiv für Papyrusforschung*). Leipzig, 1910.
SEGRÈ, A. 'The Byzantine Colonate', in *Traditio*, V, 1947.
SEGRÈ, G. 'Studio sulla origine e lo sviluppo storico del colonato romano', in *Archivio giuridico*, XLII–XLVI, 1889-91.

8. *The 'patrocinia vicorum*

DILIGHENSKI, G. G. 'The problem of agrarian patronage in later Roman Empire' (in Russian), in *Vestnik Drevnii Istorii*, 1955.

DIOSDI, G. 'Zur Frage der Entwicklung des Patrociniums in Acgypten', in *JJP*. XIV, 1962.

GELZER, M. *Studien zur byzantinischen Verwaltung Aegyptens* (Leipziger Histor. Abhandlungen, 13). Leipzig, 1909.

HAHN, I. 'A kesei csázarkori patrocinium viszonyok kialakulásanak kérdeschéz', in *Antik Tanulmányok*, II, Budapest, 1955.

HARMAND, L. *Libanius. Discours sur les patronages*. Paris, 1955.

—— *Un aspect social et politique du monde romain. Le patronat sur les collectivités publiques, des origines au Bas-Empire*. Paris, 1957.

MARTROYE, F. 'Les patronages d'agriculteurs et de vici aux IV ème et V ème siècles', in *RH*. 1928.

THIBAULT, F. 'Les patrocinia vicorum', in *VSWG*. II, 1904.

ZULUETA. 'De patrocinia vicorum', in *Oxford Studies in Legal and Social History*, I, 1909.

III. THE MEDIEVAL MANOR AND ITS PEASANTRY

1. *Frankish States* (in general)

BALON, J. 'La structure du domaine', in *Tijdschrift vor Rechtsgeschiedenis*, 1958.

—— *Jus medii aevi*. I, *La structure et la gestion du domaine de l'Eglise au Moyen Age dans l'Europe des Francs*. Namur, 1959.

—— *Jus medii aevi*. II, *Lex juridictio. Recherches sur les assemblées judiciaires et législatives, sur les droits et sur les obligations communautaires dans l'Europe des Francs*. Namur, 1960.

BLOCH, M. 'Les invasions: (A) deux structures économiques; (B) occupation du sol et peuplement', in *Annales d'Histoire sociale*, 1945.

CONSTABLE, G. 'Nona et decima. An aspect of carolingian economy', in *Speculum*, 1960.

DOPSCH, A. *Die Wirtschaftsentwicklung der Karolingerzeit vornehmlich in Deutschland*. 2 vols. 2nd ed. Weimar, 1922.

DUBLED, H. '*Allodium* dans les textes latins du Moyan-Age', in *Le Moyen Age*, 1951.

—— 'Quelques observations sur le sens du mot *villa*', in *Le Moyen Age*, 1953.

DUMAS, A. 'Observations sur la grande et la petite propriété à l'époque carolingienne', in *RH*. 1926.

FUSTEL DE COULANGES. *L'alleu et le domaine rural pendant l'époque mérovingienne*. Paris, 1889.

GRATZIANSKI, N. P. 'Zur Auslegung des terminus villa in der Lex Salica', in *ZSS*. Germanic Section, LXVI, 1948.

GUERARD, B. *Polyptyque de l'abbé Irminon*, I (*Prolègomènes*). Paris, 1844. [Abbreviated edition, with some supplementary notes, in A. Longnon, *Polyptyque de l'abbaye de Saint-Germain-des-Prés*, I, 1885 (Publications de la Soc. de l'histoire de Paris)].

HERLIHY, D. 'Church property on the European Continent, 701–1208', in *Speculum*, 1961.

METZ, W. *Das Karolingische Reichsgut. Eine Verfassungs -und Verwaltungsgeschichtliche Untersuchung*. Berlin, 1960.

PERRIN, CH-E. *Recherches sur la seigneurie rurale en Lorraine d'après les plus anciens censiers* (*IXe–XIIe siècles*). Strasbourg, 1935.

SALIN, E. *La civilisation mérovingienne d'après les sépultures, les textes et le laboratoire*. 4 vols. Paris, 1949–59.

VERHEIN, K. 'Studien zu den Quellen zum Reichsgut der Karolingerzeit', in *Deutsches Archiv für Erforschung des Mittelalters*, 1953–5.

2. *Italy*

BOGNETTI, G. P. *Sulle origini dei comuni rurali del medio evo, con speciali osservazioni pei territori milanese e comasco*. (*Pubblicazioni della R. Universita di Pavia, Studi nelle scienze giuridiche e morali*, XXX.) Pavia, 1927.

CALISSE, C. 'Le condizioni della proprietà territoriale studiate sui documenti della provincia romana dei secoli VIII, IX e X', in *Archivio storico della R. Società romana di storia patria*, VII (1884) and VIII (1885).

CIPOLLA, C. M. 'Questioni aperte sul sistema economico dell'alto medio evo', in *Rivista storica italiana*, 1951.

HERLIHY, D. 'The agrarian revolution in Southern France and Italy. 801-1150', in *Speculum*, 1958.

—— 'The history of the rural seigneury in Italy, 751-1200', in *Agricultural History*, XXXIII, 1959.

JONES, P. J. 'An italian estate, 900-1200', in *EcHR*. 2nd ser. VII, 1956.

LEICHT, P. S. *Operai, artigiani, agricoltori in Italia dal secolo VI al XVI*. Milan, 1946.

LEICHT, S. *Studi sulla proprietà fundaria nel medio evo*. 2 vols. Verona, 1903-7.

LUZZATTO, G. *I servi nelle grandi proprietà ecclesiastiche italiane nei sec. IX e X*. Senigallia, 1909.

—— 'Mutamenti nell'economia agraria italiana dalla caduta dei carolingi al principio del secolo XI' in *Settimane di studio sull'alto medio evo*, II, Spoleta, 1955.

—— *Breve storia economica d'Italia dalla caduta dell' Impero romano al principio del cinquecento*. Turin, 1958.

PIVANO, S. *I contratti agrari in Italia nell'alto medio evo*. Turin, 1904.

SALVIOLI, G. *Le nostre origini: studi sulle condizioni fisiche, economiche e sociali d'Italia nel medio evo prima del mille*. Naples, 1913.

SERRA, G. *Contributo toponomastico alla teoria della continuità nel medio evo delle communità rurali romane e preromane dell'Italia superiore*. Cluj, 1931.

UDALTSOVA, Z. V. 'La popolazione dipendente delle campagne nell'Italia del VI secolo' (in Russian), in *Vestnik Drevnii Istorii*, 1955.

UDALTSOVA, Z. V. 'The dependent population of rural Italy in the sixth century' (in Russian), in *Vestnik Drevnii Istorii*, 1955.

3. France

BLOCH, M. *Les caractères originaux de l'histoire rurale française*. I, 2nd ed., Paris 1952; II (supplement established by R. Dauvergne), Paris, 1956.

BOUTRUCHE, R. *Une société provinciale en lutte contre le régime féodal: l'alleu en Bordelais et en Bazadais du XIᵉ au XVIIIᵉ siècle*. (Publ. de la Fac. des Lettres de l'Univ. de Strasbourg, vol. 100) Rodez, 1943.

CARABIE, R. *La propriété foncière dans le très ancien droit normand* (XIᵉ-XIIIᵉ s.). vol. I: *La propriété domaniale*. (Bibl. d'hist. du droit normand, 2nd ser. Etudes, vol. V, thèse de droit) Caen, 1943.

CHAUME, M. *Les origines du duché de Bourgogne*. Seconde partie: *Géographie historique*, fascicule 2. Dijon, 1932.

DAVID, M. *Le patrimoine foncier de l'église de Lyon de 984 à 1267* (Contribution à l'étude de la féodalité dans le Lyonnais). Lyon, 1942.

DÉLÉAGE, A. *La vie rurale en Bourgogne jusqu'au début du XIᵉ siècle*. 2 vols. Mâcon, 1941.

DION, R. 'La part de la géographie et celle de l'histoire dans l'explication de l'habitat rural du Bassin parisien', in *Publ. de la Soc. de Géo. de Lille*, 1946.

DUBLED, H. 'Administration et exploitation des terres dans la seigneurie rurale en Alsace aux XIᵉ et XIIᵉ siècles', in *VSWG*. 1960.

DUBY, G. *La Société aux XI. et XII. siècles dans la région mâconnaise*. (Bibl. générale de l'Ecole des Hautes Etudes, VIᵉ section) Paris, 1953.

—— 'Un inventaire des profits de la seigneurie clunisienne à la mort de Pierre le Vénérable', in *Studia Anselmiana*, vol. 40: *Petrus venerabilis*, 1956.

DUPONT, A. 'Quelques aspects de la vie rurale en Septimanie carolingienne (fin VIIIᵉ-IXᵉ siècles)', in *Annales de l'Institut d'Etudes occitanes*, 1954.

—— 'Considérations sur la colonisation et la vie rurale dans le Roussillon et la Marche d'Espagne au IXᵉ siècle', in *Annales du Midi*, 1955.

FLACH, J. *Les origines de l'ancienne France*, I and II. Paris, 1886-93.

FOREVILLE, R. and MOLLAT, M. 'Bibliographie pour servir à l'histoire de la société féodale et du régime seigneurial en France du IXᵉ au XIIIᵉ siècle', in *Revue d'hist. de*

la philosophie et d'histoire générale de la civilisation (publ. de la Fac. des Lettres de
Lille), 1946.

FOURNIER, G. 'La seigneurie en Basse Auvergne aux XIe et XIIe siècles, d'après les censiers
du cartulaire de Sauxillanges', in *Mélanges d'histoire du Moyen Age Louis Halphen*,
Paris, 1951.

—— 'La propriété foncière en Basse Auvergne aux époques mérovingienne et carolingienne', in *Bull. hist. et scient. de l'Auvergne*, 1957.

—— 'Les transformations du parcellaire en Basse Auvergne au cours du haut moyen-âge',
in *Annales de l'Est*, mémoire no. 21, Nancy, 1959.

—— 'Le Peuplement rural en Basse Auvergne durant le haut moyen-âge (Publ. de la
Fac. des Lettres et Sciences humaines de Clermont-Ferrand, fasc. XII), 1962.

GANSHOF, F. L. 'Les avatars d'un domaine de l'église de Marseille à la fin du VIIe et au
VIIIe siècle', in *Studi in onore di Gino Luzzatto*. Milan, 1949.

GRATZIANSKII, N. P. *Bourgoundskaia derevna v X–XII ctoletniakh*. Moscow, 1935.

HIGOUNET, CH. 'Observations sur la seigneurie rurale et l'habitat en Rouergue du IXe
au XIVe siècle', in *Annales du Midi*, 1950.

KONOKOTIN, A. V. *Očerki po agrarnoj istorii Severnoj Francii v IX–XIV vekakh* (Uč. Zap.
Ivanov. ped. inst. XVI), Ivanovo, 1958.

MUSSET, L. 'Notes pour servir d'introduction à l'histoire foncière de la Normandie.
Les grands domaines de l'époque franque et les destinées du régime domanial du
IXe au XIe siècle', in *Bull. de la Soc. des Antiq. de Normandie*, XLIX, 1942–5.

—— 'Un type de tenure rurale d'origine scandinave en Normandie. Le Mansloth', in
Mémoires de l'Acad. des Sciences, Arts et Belles-Lettres de Caen, 1952.

NAVEL, H. 'Recherches sur les institutions féodales en Normandie (région de Caen).
chap. VII: Recherches sur les anciens fiscs et domaines de la région de Caen', in
Bull. de la Soc. des Antiq. de Normandie, L, 1948–51.

PERRIN, CH-E. *Les classes paysannes et le régime seigneurial en France du début du IXe à la
fin du XIIe siècle*. Paris, les Cours de Sorbonne, 1953.

—— 'A propos d'une redevance en fossoirs inscrite au polyptyque d'Irminon', in *Etudes
d'histoire du droit privé offertes à Pierre Petot*, Paris, 1959.

SAINT-JACOB, P. DE. 'Etudes sur l'ancienne communauté rurale en Bourgogne', in
Annales de Bourgogne, 1941, 1943, 1946 and 1953.

SEE, H. *Les classes rurales et le régime domanial en France au moyen âge*. Paris, 1901.

TOCHIKAWA, I. 'Kita Furansu Kiten Shôen no Kiso-kôzô [the 'villications' in northern
France in the ninth century], in *Jinbun Gakuhô*, XVII, 1958.
shihai ni tsurte no Ichi Kôsatsu' [Village and manor in Souabe in the Early Middle
Ages], in *Keizai Kenkyû*, XXX, 1959.

4. *Germany*

BADER, K. S. 'Herrschaft und Staat im deutschen Mittelalter', in *HJ*. 1949.

BRUNNER, O. *Land und Herrschaft, Grundfragen der territorialen Verfassungsgeschichte
Österreichs in Mittelalter*. New edition, Vienna, 1959.

CARO, G. *Beiträge zur älteren deutschen Wirtschafts- und Verfassungsgeschichte*. Leipzig,
1905.

—— *Neue Beiträge zur deutschen Wirtschafts- und Verfassungsgeschichte*. Leipzig, 1912.

DANILOV, A. I. 'Niemetzkaia derevnia vtoroi poloviny VIII-natchala IX v. basseine
nijnego tetchenia Nekkara', in *Srednie Veka*, VIII, 1956.

DOLLINGER, PH. *L'évolution des classes rurales en Bavière depuis la fin de l'époque carolingienne jusqu'au milieu du XIIIe siècle*. Strasbourg, 1949.

DOPSCH, A. *Die freien Marken in Deutschland*. Baden bei Wien, 1933.

ERNST, V. *Die Entstehung des deutschen Grundeigentums*. Stuttgart, 1926.

HARSIN, P. 'Contribution à l'étude de la condition des personnes en Germanie dans le
haut moyen âge', in *RB*. VI, 1927.

INAMA-STERNEGG, K. TH. V. *Deutsche Wirtschaftsgeschichte*, I. 2nd ed. Leipzig, 1909;
II and III, 1901.

KLEIN, H. 'Hof, Hube, Viertelacker', in *Mitteilungen des österreichischen Instituts*, 1941.

LÜTGE, F. *Deutsche Sozial und Wirtschafts-Geschichte*. 2nd ed. Berlin, 1960.

MARTINI, F. 'Das Bauerntum im deutschen Schriftum von des Anfängen bis zum 16. Jahrhundert', in *Vierteljahrschrift für Litteraturwissenschaft und Geisteigeschichte*, 1944.

MASUDA, S. 'Chûsei Shoki Shuwâben no Kisoku-shihai-Sonraku Dantai to Kisoku-shihai ni tsurte no Ichi Kôsatsu' [Village and manor in Souabe in the Early Middle Ages], in *Keizai Kenkyû*, XXX, 1959.

MAYER, TH. *Adel und Bauern im Deutschen Staat des Mittelalters.* Leipzig, 1943.

PERRIN, CH. E. 'Une étape de la seigneurie: l'exploitation de la réserve à Prüm au IXe siècle', in *AHES.* VI, 1934.

RICHTERING, H. W. *Bäuerliche Leistungen im mittelalterlichen Westfalen mit besonderer Berücksichtigung der Naturalabgaben und ihrer Verbreitung.* Münster, 1949.

SCHLESINGER, W. *Die Entstehung der Landesherrschaft.* Dresden, 1941.

WITTICH, W. 'Die Frage der Freibauern', in *ZSS.* 1901.

5. England

ANDREWS, C. M. *The old English Manor.* Baltimore, 1892.

ASTON, T. H. 'The English Manor', in *Past and Present*, 1956.

—— 'The origins of the manor in England', in *TRHS.* 5th series, VIII, 1958.

AULT, W. O. *The Self-Directing Activities of Village Communities in Medieval England.* Boston, 1952.

—— 'Village By-Laws by Common Consent', in *Speculum*, XXIX, 1954.

DARBY, H. C. *The Domesday Geography of Eastern England.* Cambridge, 1952.

—— *The Domesday Geography of Midland England.* Cambridge, 1954.

FINBERG, H. P. R. *Tavistock Abbey. A Study in Social and Economic History of Devon.* Cambridge, 1951.

FUSIWARA, H. 'Chusei England no Riôshuteki Shihai to Mura' [The seignorial régime and the village community in mediaeval England], in *Shigaku Zasshi*, LXVI, 1957.

GRIFFITHS, W. A. 'Some notes of the Earlier Records of the Manor of Deythur', in *Montgomeryshire Collecs.* LI, 1949.

GUREVIC, A. JA. 'Melkie votčinniki v Anglii rannego srednevekov'ja', in *Izv. Akad. Nauk.*, Seri. ist. i Filos. vol. VIII, vol. 6, 1951.

—— 'Angliiskoie Krestianstvo v x-natchaha XI v', in *Srednie Veka*, IX, 1957.

HILTON, R. H. *The Economic Development of some Leicestershire estates.* 1947.

—— 'Peasant Movements in England before 1381', in *EcHR.* 2nd ser. II, 1949.

—— 'Life in the Medieval Manor (with a glossary of Manorial Terms)', in *Amateur Historian*, I, 1952–3.

—— 'The Content and Sources of English Agrarian History before 1500', in *Agric. Hist. Rev.* III, 1955.

HOMANS, G. C. 'The rural sociology of medieval England', in *Past and Present*, 1953.

HOYT, R. S. *The royal demesne in English constitutional history: 1066–1272.* Ithaca, 1950.

—— 'The nature and origins of the ancient demesne', in *EHR.* 1950.

—— 'Farm of the Manor and Community of the Vill in Domesday Book', in *Speculum*, XXX, 1955.

JOHN, E. *Land tenure in Early England.* Leicester, 1960.

KOSMINSKY, E. A. 'The evolution of feudal rent in England from the XIth to the XVth centuries', in *Past and Present*, 1955.

LENNARD, R. 'The economic position of the Domesday Villeins', in *EJ.* LVI, 1946 and LVII, 1947.

—— 'The economic position of bordars and cottars of Domesday Book', in *EJ.* LXI, 1951.

—— 'The Hidation of "demesne" in some Domesday entries', in *EcHR.* 2nd ser. VII, 1954.

—— 'The Demesne of Glastonbury Abbey in the XIth and XIIth centuries', in *EcHR.* 2nd ser. VIII, 1955.

—— *Rural England. 1086–1135. A Study of social and agrarian Conditions.* Oxford, 1959.

LIPSON, E. *The Economic History of England, I. The middle ages.* 11th ed. London, 1956.

MAITLAND, F. W. *Domesday Book and Beyond.* Cambridge, 1897.

MILLER, E. *The Abbey and Bishopric of Ely. The Social History of an Ecclesiastical Estate from the 10th century to the early 14th century.* Cambridge, 1951.

MORGAN, M. *The English Lands of the Abbey of Bec.* (Oxford historical Studies) London, 1946.

OSCHINSKY, D. 'Quellen zur Verwaltungs-und Wirschftsgeschichte der englischen Gutsherrschaft im Mittelalter', in *Mitteilungen des österreichischen Institut für Geschichtsforschung,* Bd 58, 1959.

POSTAN, M. *The 'Famulus', the Estate Labourer in the XIIth and XIIIth centuries.* (The Econ. Hist. Rev. Supplement, no. 2) Cambridge, 1954.

RAFTIS, J. A. *The Estates of Ramsey Abbey. A study in economic growth and organization.* (Pontifical Institute of Mediaeval Studies. Studies and Texts 3) Toronto, 1957.

SAWYER, P. H. 'The "Original Returns" and Domesday Book', in *EHR.* LXX, 1955.

SEEBOHM, F. *The English Village Community,* 4th ed. Cambridge, 1890.

STEPHENSON, C. 'Commendation and related problems in Domesday', in *EHR.* LIX, 1944.

VINOGRADOFF, P. *English Society in the eleventh century.* Oxford, 1908.

—— *The Growth of the Manor.* 2nd ed. London and New York, 1951.

6. Spain and Portugal

FERNANDEZ-MARTIN, P. 'El 'ultimo señor de las behetrias en Campos', in *Hispania,* XIX, 1959.

GARCIA GALLO, P. *Las instituciones sociales en Espana en la alta edad media* (Siglos VIII–XII). Madrid, 1945.

GUGLIELMI, N. 'El "Dominus Villae" en Castilla y Leon', in *Cuadernos de Historia de Espana,* LV, 1953.

HINOJOSA, E. DE. *El regimen senorial y la cuestion agraria en Cataluña durante la edad media.* Madrid, 1905.

MANS-PUIJERNAU, J. M. *Las clases serviles bajo la monarquia visigoda y en los estados cristinos de la reconquista española.* Barcelona, 1928.

PRIETO BANCES, R. *La explotacion rural del dominio de San Vicente de Oviedo en los siglos X al XIII.* Coïmbra, 1940.

REDONNET, L. 'EP Latifundia y su formacion en la España medieval', in *Estudios de Historia Social,* 1949.

SANCHEZ-ALBOANOZ, GL. 'Las behetrias', in *Anuario de historia del derecho español,* I, 1924.

—— 'Muchas páginas más sobre las behetrias', in *ibid.* IV, 1927.

7. Belgium, Low Countries

GANSHOF, F. L. 'Le domaine gantois de l'abbaye de St Pierre au Mont-Blandin à l'époque carolingienne', in *RB.* XXVI, 1948.

—— 'Manorial organization in the Low Countries in the 7th, 8th and 9th centuries', in *TRHS.,* 4th ser. XXXI, 1949.

—— 'Grondbezit en Gronduitbating tinjdens de vroege Middeleeuwen', in *Brabants Heem,* 1954.

—— *La Belgique carolingienne.* Brussels, 1958.

GENICOT, L. *L'économie rurale namuroise au bas moyen âge* (1199–1429). vol. I, *La Seigneurie foncière,* Namur, 1943. vol. II. *Les hommes; la noblesse,* Louvain, 1960.

STIENNON, J. *Etude sur le chartrier et le domaine de l'abbaye de St Jacques de Liège, 1015–1209.* (Bibl. de la Fac. de philos. et lettres de l'Univ. de Liège, fasc. 124) Paris, 1951.

VERHULST, A. E. 'En Basse et Moyenne Belgique pendant le haut moyen âge. Différents types de structure domaniale et agraire', in *Annales ESC.* 1956.

—— 'Types de structure agraire et domaniale en Belgique', in *Annales ESC.* 1958.

—— *De sint-Baafs-abdij te Gent en haar grondbezit.* Brussels, 1958.

VERRIEST, L. *Institutions médiévales,* I. Mons and Frameries, 1946.

IV. SLAVERY AND SERFDOM

AMIA, A. D. *Schiavitù romana e servitù medievale; contributo di studi e documenti.*

BLOCH, M. 'Liberté et servitude personnelles au moyen âge, particulièrement en France', in *Anuario de historia del derecho espanol*, 1933.

—— 'Les "inventions" médiévales', in *AHES.* VII, 1935.

—— 'Comment et pourquoi finit l'esclabage antique', in *Annales d'histoire sociale*, 1947.

BOUSSARD, J. 'Serfs et colliberti' (XIᵉ–XIIᵉ s.), in *Bibl. de l'Ecole des Chartes*, CVII, 1947–8.

—— 'Les Colliberti du cartulaire de Vierzon', in *Rev. hist. dr. fr. et étr.*, 1362.

CICOTTI, E. *Il tramonto della schiavitù nel mondo antico.* Turin, 1899. [French translation: *Le déclin de l'esclavage antique*, Paris, 1910].

DÉLÉAGE, A. *La capitation du Bas-Empire.* Paris, 1945.

DEVAILLY, G. 'Du nouveau sur les Colliberti. Le temoignage du cartulaire de Vierzon', in *Le Moyen Age*, 1961.

DIDIER, N. 'Les plus anciens textes sur le servage dans la région dauphinoise', in *Etudes d'histoire du droit privé offertes à Pierre Petot.* Paris, 1959.

DMITREV, A. D. *Der Aufstand der Westgoten an der Donau und die Revolution der Sklaven.* Berlin, 1952.

DUBLED, H. 'Mancipium', in *Revue du Moyen Age latin*, V, 1949.

DUBY, G. 'Géographie ou chronologie du servage? Note sur les servi en Forez et en Mâconnais du Xᵉ au XIIᵉ siècle', in *Mélanges Lucien Febvre*, I, 1953.

FOURNIER, G. 'L'esclavage en Basse Auvergne aux époques mérovingienne et carolingienne', in *Cahiers d'histoire*, 1962.

GSELL, ST. 'Esclaves ruraux dans l'Afrique romaine', in *Mélanges Gustave Glotz*, I, 1922.

JONES, A. H. M. 'Capitatio and Iugatio', in *Journ. of Roman Studies*, XLVII, 1957.

KAŽDAN, A. P. 'O nekotorych spornych voprosach istorii stanovlenija feodal' nych otnošenii v Rimskoj imperii', in *Vestnik Drevnii Istorii*, fasc. 4, 1953.

KONOKOTIN, A. V. 'Elements of slavery in merovingian and carolingian France' (in Russian), in *Uc. Ivanovo ped. inst.* IX, 1957.

KORSOUNSKY, A. R. 'La situation des esclaves, des affranchis et des colons dans les provinces occidentales de l'Empire romain aux IVᵉ–Vᵉ siècles', in *Documents du Centre culturel et économique de France—URSS*, série Histoire, no. 6, 1955.

LAUFFER, S. 'L'esclavage dans le monde gréco-romain', in *IXᵉ Congrès intern. des Sciences historiques. Rapports*, III, Gothenburg–Stockholm–Uppsala, 1960.

LIVI, R. *La schiavitù domestic nei tempi di mezzo e nei moderni.* Padua, 1928.

LUZZATTO, G. 'La servitù in Italia nell' età feudale in confronto ai paesi d'oltralpo', in *Xᵒ Congresso Intern. di Scienze storiche, Relazioni*, VII. Rome–Florence, 1955.

MIL'SKAJA, L. T. *Svetskaja votčina v Germanii VIII–IX w i ee rol' v zakrepoščenii krest'-janstva* (po materialam istočnikov južnov i jugo Zapadnoj Germanii). Moscow, 1957.

NEVSYKHIN, A. I. *Vozniknovenie zavisimogo Krest'janstva kak Klassa rannefeodal'nogo obščestva v Zapadnoj Europe VI–VIII w.* Moscow, 1956.

OURLIAC, P. 'Le servage dans la région toulousaine', in *Xᵒ Congresso intern. di Scienze storiche, Relazioni*, VII. Rome–Florence, 1955.

PALLASSE, M. 'La capitation et le problème du Bas-Empire', in *Rev. hist. de droit français et étranger*, 4th ser. XXXI, 1958.

PERRIN, CH. and VERNADSKY, G. 'Le servage en France, en Allemagne et en Russie au Moyen-Age', in *Xᵒ Congresso intern. di Scienze storiche, Relazioni*, III. Rome–Florence, 1955.

PETOT, P. 'L'origine de la mainmorte servile', in *Rev. hist. de droit français et étranger*, 1940–1.

—— 'Les fluctuations numériques de la classe servile en France du XIᵉ au XIVᵉ siècles', in *Xᵒ Congresso intern. di Scienze storiche, Relazioni*, VII. Rome–Florence, 1955.

Recueils de la Société Jean Bodin, vol. II: le Servage. 2nd ed. Brussels, 1959.

STAERMAN, M. *Krisis rabovladel'ceskogo straja v zapadnykh provincijakh Rimskoj imperii.* Moscow, 1957.

STEPHENSON, C. 'The problem of the common man in early medieval Europe', in *AHR*. 1946.

STOJČEVIĆ, D. 'De l'esclave romain au colon', in *XIe Congrès intern. des Sciences historiques, Résumé des communications*. Gothenburg–Stockholm–Uppsala, 1960.

VERLINDEN, CH. 'L'esclavage dans le monde ibérique médiéval', in *Anuario de historia del derecho espanol*, XI and XII, 1934–5. (With an introduction on the literature of medieval slavery and on 'l'esclavage pendant les derniers siècles de l'empire romain'.)

—— 'L'Esclavage dans l'Europe médiévale vol. I.: *Péninsule ibérique, France*. Bruges, 1955.

VERRIEST, L. 'Le servage en Flandre, particulièrement au pays d'Alost', in *Rev. hist. de droit français et étranger*, XXIII, 1950.

VITTINGHOFF, F. 'Die Bedeutung der Sklaven für den Uebergang von der Antike in das abendländische Mittelalter', in *XIe Congrès intern. des Sciences historiques, Résumé des communications*. Gothenburg–Stockholm–Uppsala, 1960.

WESTERMAN, W. L. 'Sklaverei', in Pauly, *Realency*. Supplement IV, 1924.

V. THE JUDICIAL POWERS OF THE LORD

AULT, W. O. *Private jurisdiction in England*. New Haven, Conn. 1923.

BADER, K. S. *Studien zur Rechtsgeschichte des mittelalterlichen Dorfes*. I. Teil: *Das mittelalterliche Dorf als Friedens-und Rechtsbereich*. Weimar, 1957.

KROELL, M. *L'immunité franque*. Paris, 1910.

LEMARIGNIER, J. F. 'La dislocation du *pagus* et le problème des *consuetudines* x^e–xie siècles', in *Mélanges d'histoire du Moyen Age Louis Halphen*. Paris, 1951.

Recueils de la Société Jean Bodin, vol. I: *les liens de vassalité et les immunités*. 2nd ed. Brussels, 1958.

RIETSCHEL, S. 'Landleihen, Hofrecht und Immunität', in *Mitteilungen des Instituts für österreichische Geschichtsforschung*, XXVII.

SALVIOLI, G. 'L'immunità e le giutizie delle chiese in Italia', in *Atti e memorie della R. Deputazione di Storia patria per le prov. Modenesi*, 3rd Series, V and VI, 1888–9.

SEELIGER, G. 'Die soziale und politische Bedeutung der Grundherrschaft im früheren Mittelalter', in *Abhandlungen der K. sächsischen Gesellschaft der Wissenschaften*, XXI, I, 1903.

—— 'Forschungen zur Geschichte der Grundherrschaft im früheren Mittelalter', in *Histor. Vierteljahrschrift*, VIII, 1905 and X, 1907.

—— 'The state and seignorial authority in early German history', in *AHR*. XIV.

SICKEL, W. 'Die Privatherrschaften im fränkischen Reiche', in *West deutsche Zeitschrift*, XV and XVI, 1896–7.

STENGEL, E. 'Grundherrschaft und Immunität', in *ZSS*. Germanic Section, XXV, 1904.

—— *Die Immunität in Deutschland bis zum Ende des 11. Jahrhunderts*, I. Innsbruck, 1910.

WIESSNER, H. *Zwing und Bann: eine Studie über Herkunft, Wesen und Wandlung der Zwing-und Bannrechte*. Baden bei Wien, 1935.

VI. THE 'MANSUS', 'HUFE' and 'HIDE'

CARO, G. 'Die Hufe', in *Deutsche Geschichtsblätter*, IV.

—— 'Schupphose und mansus servilis', in *VSWG*. VII, 1909.

DUBLED, H. 'Encore la question du manse', in *Revue du Moyen Age latin*, 1949.

—— 'La notion de propriété en Alsace du VIIIe au Xe siècle', in *Le Moyen Age*, 1959.

GANSHOF, F. L. 'Observations sur le manse à l'époque mérovingienne', in *Revue hist. de droit français et étranger*, XXVIII, 1955.

GRAND, R. 'Note d'économie agraire médiévale: mansus vestitus et mansus absus', in *Etudes d'histoire du droit privé offertes à Pierre Petot*. Paris, 1959.

HAFF, K. *Die dänische Gemeinderechte*. 2 vols. Leipzig, 1909.

—— 'Bosae, Bo und Hufe in den deutschdänische Grenzbezirken', in *Festschrift Ernst v. Mayer*. Weimar, 1932.

HERLIHY, D. 'The carolingian mansus', in *EcHR*. 2nd ser. XIII, 1960.

JOLLIPPE, J. E. A. 'A survey of fiscal tenements', in *EcHR*. VI, 1936.

LATOUCHE, R. 'Quelques aperçus sur le manse en Provence au Xᵉ et au XIᵉ siècles', in *Recueil de travaux offert à Clovis Brunel*, vol. II. Paris, 1955.

LOT, F. 'L'origine des manses de l'époque franque', in *Nouvelles recherches sur l'impôt foncier et la capitation personnelle sous le Bas-Empire*. Paris, 1935.

LÜTGE, F. 'Die Hufe in der thuringisch-hessischen Agrarverfassung der Karolingerzeit', in *Schmollers Jahrbuch für Gesetzgebung*, LXI, 1932.

—— 'Hufe und Mansus in den mitteldeutschen Quellen der Karolingerzeit im besonderen in dem Breviarium Lulli', in *VSWG*. XXX, 1937.

PERRIN, CH. E. 'Observations sur le manse dans la région parisienne au début du IXᵉ siècle', in *Annales d'histoire sociale*, 1945.

—— 'Le manse dans le polyptyque de l'abbaye de Prüm à la fin du IXᵉ siècle', in *Etudes historiques à la mémoire de Noël Didier*. Paris, 1960.

REICHEL, J. *Die Hufenverfassung der Karolingerzeit*. Leipzig, 1907. (Diss. Leipzig).

RHAMM, K. *Die Grosshufen der Nord-Germanen*. Brunswick, 1905.

SEARLE, E. 'Hides, virgates and Tenant Settlement at Battle Abbey', in *EcHR*. 2nd ser. XVI, 1963.

TULIPPE, O. 'Le manse à l'époque carolingienne', in *Annales de la Société scientifique de Bruxelles*, Série D, Sciences économiques, LVI, 1936.

VII. UNSEIGNORIALIZED COUNTRIES

GROSSES, J. A. 'Die friesche Hoofdeling', in *Mededeelingen der k. Akademie van Wetenschappen*, Afd. Letterkunde, 1933. (See also the review by R. His in *ZSS*. Germanic Section, 1934.)

MARTEN, GEORG and MÄCKELMAN, KARL. *Dithmarschen: Geschichte und Landeskunde Dithmarschens*. Heide i. Holstein, 1927.

SIEBS, B. *Grundlagen und Aufbau der altfriesichen Verfarsung*. Breslau, 1933 (Untersuchungen zur Deutschen Staats-und Rechtsgeschichte, CXLIV).

SWART, F. *Zur friesischen Agrargeschichte*. (Staats- und sozialwissenschaftliche Forschungen, CXLV.) Leipzig, 1910.

VAN BUIJTENEN, M. P. *De Grondslag van de Friese vrijheid*. Assen, 1953.

VIII. SOME SOURCES OF COMPARISONS

BERQUE, J. 'Sur un coin de terre marocaine: seigneur terrien et paysans', in *AHES*. VIII, 1937.

BLUM, J. *Lord and Peasant in Russia from the ninth to the nineteenth century*. London, 1961.

CAHEN, CL. 'L'évolution de l'iqtâ du IXᵉ au XIIIᵉ siècle. Contribution à une histoire comparée des sociétés médiévales', in *Annales ESC*. 1953.

DOMANOVSKY, S. 'La formation de la classe nobiliaire en Hongrie', in *Résumé des communications présentées au Congrès de Varsovie*, II, 1933.

JOUON DES LONGRAIS, F. *L'Est et l'Ouest. Institutions du Japon et de l'Occident comparées* (six études de sociologie juridique). Tokyo–Paris, 1958.

KAŽDAN, A. P. 'Formirovanie féodal' nogo pomest' ja v Vizantii x v', in *Visant. Vrem.* XI, 1956.

LEMERLE, P. 'Esquisse pour une histoire agraire de Cyzance', in *RH*. CCXIX, 1958.

LLOYD, J. E. *History of Wales*. 1911, 2nd ed. 1940.

MACBRIDE, G. M. *The land system of Mexico*. 1923.

—— *Chile: Land and Society*. New York, 1936.

OSTROGORSKY, G. *Quesques problèmes d'histoire de la paysannerie byzantine*. (Corpus Bruxellense Historiae Byzantinae, subsidia II) Brussels, 1956.

ROUILLARD, G. *La vie rurale dans l'Empire byzantin*. Paris, 1953.

THURNEYSSEN, R. 'Das keltische Recht', in *ZSS*. Germanic Section, 1935.

CHAPTER VII

Medieval Agrarian Society in its Prime

§ 1. FRANCE, THE LOW COUNTRIES AND WESTERN GERMANY

The aim of the following bibliography is merely to enable readers who desire to extend their knowledge of the subject to find their way about. Thus the sources for the history of the great estate in Western Europe from the eleventh to the fourteenth centuries are not listed and only secondary authorities are given, since the latter contain all the necessary information as to sources. To this rule four exceptions have been made: the *Polyptyque de l'abbé Irminon*, with the famous prolegomena to its edition by Benjamin Guérard, which are essential even for the period covered by this chapter; the *Livre de l'abbé Guillaume de Rijckel*, with a notable introduction to its edition by Henri Pirenne; the *'Veil Rentier' de messire Jehan de Pamele-Audenarde*, edited with an introduction by L. Verriest; and the work of Suger, abbot of Saint-Denis, *Liber de rebus in administratione sua gestis*, which has been referred to several times. This procedure appears to conform to the spirit governing the present volume.

I. GENERAL WORKS

A. *Europe in General*

DUBY, G. *L'économie rurale et la vie des campagnes dans l'Occident médiéval.* 2 vols. Paris, 1962.

Géographie et Histoire agraires. Actes du colloque international de Nancy. Nancy, 1959.

GRAND, R. and DELATOUCHE, R. *L'agriculture au moyen âge, de la fin de l'empire romain au XVIᵉ siècle.* Paris, 1950.

KÖTZSCHKE, R. *Wirtschaftsgeschichte des Mittelalters.* Jena, 1924.

KULISCHER, J. *Allgemeine Wirtschaftsgeschichte des Mittelalters u. der Neuzeit*, I. Munich and Berlin, 1928.

LATOUCHE, R. *Les origines de l'économie occidentale, IVᵉ–XIᵉ siècles.* Paris, 1956.

SLICHER VAN BATH, B. H. *De agrarische geschiedenis van West-Europa (500–1850).* Utrecht–Antwerp, 1960.

B. *Germany*

ABEL, W. *Geschichte der deutschen Landwirtschaft vom frühen Mittelalter bis zum 19. Jahrhundert.* Stuttgart, 1962.

LÜTGE, F. *Geschichte der deutschen Agrarverfassung vom frühen Mittelalter bis zum 12. Jahrhundert.* Stuttgart, 1963.

VON BELOW, G. 'Agrargeschichte', in Elster, Weber, Wiesen, *Handwörterbuch der Staatswissenschaften*, 4, I, Jena, 1923.

—— *Geschichte der deutschen Landwirtschaft des Mittelalters in ihren Grundzügen*, ed. F. Lütge. Jena, 1937. [A posthumous work.]

VON INAMA STERNEGG, K. T. *Deutsche Wirtschaftsgeschichte*, II and III, I. Leipzig, 1897–9.

WITTICH, W. 'Epochen der deutschen Agrargeschichte', in *Grundriss der Sozialökonomik*, VII, Tübingen, 1922.

C. *France*

BLOCH, M. *Les caractères originaux de l'histoire rurale française*, 2nd ed. vol. I, Paris, 1952. vol. II (Supplément établi par R. Dauvergne, d'après les travaux de l'auteur). Paris, 1956.

GUÉRARD, B. *Polyptyque de l'abbé Irminon ou Dénombrement des manses, des serfs et des revenus de l'abbaye de Saint-Germain-des-Prés sous le règne de Charlemagne, publié avec des Prolégomènes*, I. Paris, 1844.

JUILLARD, E. and MEYNIER, A. *Structures agraires et paysages ruraux. Un quart de siècle de recherches françaises.* Nancy, 1957.

LIZERAND, G. *Le régime rural de l'ancienne France.* Paris, 1942.

SÉE, H. *Les classes rurales et le régime domanial en France au moyen âge.* Paris, 1901.

D. *Holland*

NIERMEYER, J. F. *De wording van onze volkshuishouding. Hoofdlijnen uit de economische geschiedenis der noordelijke Nederlanden in de Middeleeuwen.* The Hague, 1946.

II. WORKS ON SPECIAL REGIONS

A. *Germany*

DÖBERL, M. *Die Grundherrschaft in Bayern vom 10. bis 13. Jahrhundert.* (Forschungen zur Geschichte Bayerns, XII, 1904.)

DOLLINGER, PH. *L'évolution des classes rurales en Bavière depuis la fin de l'époque carolingienne jusqu'au milieu du XIIIe siècle.* Strasbourg, 1949. Cp. Perrin, Ch.-E., 'Les classes rurales en Bavière au moyen âge', (*RH.* 1952).

DOPSCH, A. *Herrschaft und Bauer in der deutschen Kaiserzeit.* Jena, 1939.

LAMPRECHT, K. *Deutsches Wirtschaftsleben im Mittelalter.* 4 vols. Leipzig, 1886. [Deals particularly with the Mosel region.]

TIMM, A. *Studien zur Siedlungs- und Agrargeschichte Mitteldeutschlands.* Cologne–Graz, 1956.

WITTICH, W. *Die Grundherrschaft in Nordwestdeutschland.* Leipzig, 1896.

B. *Belgium*

GENICOT, L. *L'économie rurale namuroise au bas moyen âge (1199–1429).* I. *La seigneurie foncière.* Namur, 1943. II. *Les hommes. La noblesse.* Louvain, 1960.

LINDEMANS, P. *Geschiedenis van de landbouw in België.* 2 vols. Antwerp, 1952. [Deals with agricultural technique.]

MAREZ, G. DES. *Le problème de la colonisation franque et du régime agraire en Belgique.* Brussels, 1926. [The second part of the volume relates to our subject, dealing with Flanders and Brabant.]

VERHULST, A. 'En basse et moyenne Belgique pendant le haut moyen âge: différents types de structure domaniale et agraire', in *Annales ESC.* 1956.

—— 'Probleme der mittelalterlichen Agrarlandschaft in Flandern', in *Zeitschrift für Agrargeschichte,* 1961.

—— 'L'évolution géographique de la plaine maritime flamande au moyen âge', in *Revue de l'Université de Bruxelles,* 1–2, 1962–3.

VERRIEST, L. *Le régime seigneurial dans le comté de Hainaut du IXe siècle à la Révolution.* Louvain, 1916–7. [Very well documented.]

C. *France*

BEECH, G. T. *Rural Society in Medieval France. The Gâtine of Poiton in the eleventh and twelfth centuries,* Baltimore, 1964.

BOUTRUCHE, R. *Une société provinciale en lutte contre le régime féodal. L'alleu en Bordelais et en Bazadais, du XIe au XVIIIe siècle.* Rodez, 1947.

BRUTAILS, J. A. *Etude sur la condition des populations rurales du Roussillon au moyen âge.* Paris, 1891.

CARABIE, R. *La propriété foncière dans le très ancien droit normand (XIe–XIIIe siècles),* I: *La propriété domaniale.* Caen, 1943.

DÉLÉAGE, A. *La vie rurale en Bourgogne jusqu'au début du XIe siècle.* 3 vols. Mâcon, 1941.

DELISLE, L. *Etudes sur la condition de la classe agricole et l'état de l'agriculture en Normandie au moyen âge.* Evreux, 1851.

DUBLED, H. 'Administration et exploitation des terres de la seigneurie rurale en Alsace aux XIe et XIIe siècles', in *VSWG.* 1960.

DUBY, G. *La société aux XIe et XIIe siècles dans la région mâconnaise*. Paris, 1959.

FEUCHÈRE, P. 'Le défrichement des forêts en Artois du IXe au XIIIe siècle', in *Bull. Soc. Antiquaires de la Morinie*, XVIII, 1952.

FOURNIER, G. *Le peuplement rural en Basse Auvergne durant le haut moyen âge*. Paris, 1962.

—— 'Notes sur l'histoire du Brivadois. Le peuplement de la région de Lamothe durant le haut moyen âge', in *Almanach de Brioude*, 1964.

HIGOUNET, C. 'Observations sur la seigneurie rurale et l'habitat en Rouergne du IXe au XIVe siècle', in *Annales du Midi*, 1950.

LATOUCHE, R. 'Agrarzustände im westlichen Frankreich während des Hochmittelalters', in *VSWG*. XXIX, 1936.

—— 'Un aspect de la vie rurale dans le Maine au XIe et au XIIe siècle. L'établissement des bourgs', in *Le Moyen Age*, 1937.

—— 'Défrichement et peuplement rural dans le Maine du IXe au XIIe siècle', in *Le Moyen Age*, 1948.

MUSSET, L. 'Note pour servir d'introduction à l'histoire foncière de la Normandie. Les domaines de l'époque franque et les destinées du régime domanial du IXe au XIe siècle', in *Bulletin de la Société des Antiquaires de Normandie*, XLIX, 1942–5.

NEWMAN, W. M. *Le domaine royal sous les premiers Capétiens, 978–1180*. Paris, 1937.

PERRIN, C. E. *Recherches sur la seigneurie rurale en Lorraine d'après les plus anciens censiers*. Paris, 1935. [Of capital importance.] Cp. M. Bloch, 'La seigneurie lorraine. Critique des témoignages et problèmes d'évolution', in *AHES*. VII, 1935.

—— 'Esquisse d'une histoire de la tenure rurale en Lorraine au moyen âge', in *Recueils de la Société Jean Bodin*, III, 1938.

SCLAFERT, T. *Le Haut-Dauphiné au moyen âge*. Paris, 1926. Cp. R. Latouche, under the same title, in *Annales de l'Université de Grenoble*, V, 1928, and H. Nabholz, 'Eine Eidgenossenschaft in der Dauphiné', in *Festgabe für Bundesarchivar Heinrich Türler*, Berne, 1931.

—— *Cultures en Haute-Provence. Déboisements et pâturages au moyen âge*. Paris, 1959.

STRAYER, J. REESE. *The royal domain in the bailliage of Rouen*. Princeton, 1936.

TULIPPE, O. *L'habitat rural en Seine-et-Oise. Essai de géographie du peuplement*. Liège, 1934. Cp. M. Bloch, 'Les paysages agraires. Essai de mise au point', in *AHES*. VIII, 1936.

III. MONOGRAPHS

A. *Germany*

BEYERLE, K. 'Die Grundherrschaft der Reichenau', in *Die Kultur der Reichenau*, I, Munich, 1925.

GOTHEIN, E. 'Die Hofverfassung auf dem Schwarzwald dargestellt von der Geschichte des Gebietes von Sankt Peter', in *Zeitschrift für Geschichte des Oberrheines*, 1886.

KALLEN, G. 'Altenberg als Zisterzienserkloster in seiner Stellung zur Kirche u. zum Reich', in *Jahrbuch des Kölnischen Geschichtsvereins*, XVIII, 1936. [Only a few passages deal with economic history.]

KÖTZSCHKE, R. *Studien zur Verwaltungsgeschichte der Grossgrundherrschaft Werden an der Ruhr*. Leipzig, 1901.

B. *Belgium*

BONENFANT, P. 'La notice de donation du domaine de Leeuw à l'église de Cologne et le problème de la colonisation saxonne en Brabant', in *RB*. XIV, 1935.

D'HAENENS, A. *L'abbaye de Saint-Martin de Tournai de 1290 à 1350*. Louvain, 1961.

DUBY, G. 'La structure d'une grande seigneurie flamande à la fin du XIIIe siècle', in *Bibl. Ecole des Chartes*, 1956.

GANSHOF, F. L. 'Une étape de la décomposition de l'organisation domaniale classique à l'abbaye de Saint-Trond', in *Fédération archéologique et historique de Belgique*. Congrès de Liège, 1932; Annales, fasc. 4, 1934.

HANSAY, A. *Etude sur la formation et l'organisation économique du domaine de Saint-Trond depuis les origines jusqu'à la fin du XIIIe siècle*. Ghent, 1899.

HOEBANX, J. J. *L'abbaye de Nivelles des origines au XIVe siècle.* Brussels, 1952.
—— 'Documents relatifs aux "Corseries" de l'abbaye de Nivelles. Contribution à l'étude des réserves domaniales' in *Bulletin de la Commission Royale d'Histoire* (Brussels), CXXIX, 1963.
LAMY, H. *L'abbaye de Tongerloo depuis sa fondation jusqu'en 1263.* Louvain, 1914.
MILIS, L. 'De abdÿ ran Ename in de Middeleeuwen', *Handelingen der Maatschappÿ voor Geschiedemis en Oudheidkunde te Gent,* 1961.
MOREAU, E. DE, S. J. *L'abbaye de Villers en Brabant aux XIIe et XIIIe siècles.* Brussels, 1909.
PIRENNE, H. *Le livre de l'abbé Guillaume de Rijckel (1249–1272). Polyptyque et comptes de l'abbaye de Saint-Trond au milieu du XIIIe siècle.* Ghent, 1896.
SIMENON, G. *L'organisation économique de l'abbaye de Saint-Trond depuis la fin du XIIIe siècle jusqu'au courant du XVIIe.* Brussels, 1912.
SOENS, E. 'Het domein der Praemonstratenzer abdij van Ninove', in *Analecta Praemonstratensia,* 1928.
VANDERVEEGHDE, D. *Le domaine du Val Saint-Lambert de 1202 à 1387.* Paris, 1955.
VERHULST, A. E. *De Sint-Baafsabdij te Gent en haar grondbezit. (VIIe–XIVe eeuw).* Brussels, 1958. [With a résumé in French.]
VERRIEST, L. *Le polyptyque illustré dit 'Veil Rentier' de messire Jehan de Pamele-Audenarde (vers 1275).* Brussels, 1950 [with a notable introduction].
WARICHEZ, J. *L'abbaye de Lobbes depuis les origines jusqu'en 1200.* Louvain, 1928.

C. France

BRUHAT, L. *De administratione terrarum Sanctonensis abbatiae, 1047–1220.* La Rochelle, 1901.
COOPLAND, C. W. *The abbey of Saint-Bertin and its neighbourhood, 900–1350.* Oxford, 1914.
DAVID, M. *Le patrimoine foncier de l'église de Lyon de 984 à 1267.* Lyon, 1942.
DIDIER, N. *Etude sur le patrimoine de l'église cathédrale de Grenoble du Xe au milieu du XIIe siècle.* Grenoble, 1936.
DOM DU BOURG. *L'abbaye de Saint-Germain-des-Prés au XIVe siècle.* (Mém. de la Soc. d'hist. de Paris, 1900.)
DUBY, G. 'Economie domaniale et économie monétaire. Le budget de l'abbaye de Cluny entre 1080 et 1155', in *Annales, ESC.* 1952.
—— 'Un inventaire des profits de la seigneurie clunisienne à la mort de Pierre le Vénérable', in *Studia Anselmiana,* 40, 1956.
FAVIER, J. 'Un terroir cauchois au début du XIVe siècle. Le domaine de Longueil', in *Annales de Normandie,* XIII, 1963.
HIGOUNET, C. *La grange de Vaulerent.* Paris, 1965.
LASTEYRIE, C. DE. *L'abbaye de Saint-Martial de Limoges.* Paris, 1901.
LEBEL, G. *Histoire administrative, économique et financière de l'abbaye de Saint-Denis, étudiée spécialement dans la province ecclésiastique de Sens.* Paris, 1935.
LOT, F. *Etudes critiques sur l'abbaye de Saint-Wandrille.* Paris, 1913.
PERRIN, C. E. *Essai sur la fortune immobilière de l'abbaye alsacienne de Marmoutier aux X et XIe siècles.* Strasbourg, 1935.
PETER, J. *L'abbaye de Liessies en Hainaut depuis ses origines jusqu'après la réforme de Louis de Blois, 764–1566.* Lille, 1912.
PLATELLE, H. *Le temporel de l'abbaye de Saint-Armand, Des origines à 1340,* Paris, 1962.
SUGER, *Liber de rebus in administratione sua gestis,* ed. A. Lecoy de la Marche. Paris, 1867.
TISSET, P. *L'abbaye de Gellone au diocèse de Lodève. Des origines au XIIIe siècle.* Paris, 1933.
VALOUS, G. DE. 'Le domaine de l'abbaye de Cluny aux xe et xie siècles', in *Annales de l'Académie de Mâcon,* 3rd ser. XXXI, 1923.

D. Luxemburg

WAMPACH, C. *Geschichte der Grundherrschaft Echternach im Frühmittelalter.* 2 vols. Luxemburg, 1929–30.

E. *Holland*

MULLER, S. 'Een huishouden zonder geld', in *Tweemaandelijksch Tijdschrift*, V, 1899. [Deals with the domains of the cathedral of Utrecht.]

F. *Switzerland*

CARO, G. 'Zur Verfassungs- u. Wirtschaftsgeschichte des Klosters Sankt Gallen vornehmlich vom 10. bis 13. Jahrhundert', in *Neue Beiträge zur deutschen Wirtschafts-u. Verfassungsgeschichte*, Leipzig, 1911.

IV. PARTICULAR QUESTIONS

A. *Germany*

VON GLADISS, D. 'Die Schenkungen der deutschen Könige zu privatem Eigen nach ihrem wirtschaftlichen Inhalt', in *VSWG*. XXX, 1936.

HOFFMANN, E. 'Die Entwicklung der Wirtschaftsprinzipien im Zisterzienserorden während des 12. und 13. Jahrhunderts', in *HJ*. XXXI, 1910.

MAYER, T. 'Die Entstehung des "modernen" Staates im Mittelalter und die freien Bauern', in *ZSS. GA.* 1937.

RÖRIG, F. 'Luft macht Eigen', in *Festgabe Gerhard Seeliger zum 60. Geburtstag*. Leipzig, 1920.

SEELIGER, G. *Die soziale u. politische Bedeutung der Grundherrschaft im früheren Mittelalter.* Leipzig, 1903.

STUTZ, U. 'Zur Herkunft von Zwing u. Bann', in *ZSS. GA.* 1937.

WIESSNER, H. *Sachinhalt u. wirtschaftliche Bedeutung der Weistümer im deutschen Kulturgebiet.* Baden–Vienna, 1934.

—— *Zwing u. Bann.* Baden–Vienna, 1935.

WITTICH, W. 'Die Entstehung des Meierrechts u. die Auflösung der Villikationen in Niedersachsen u. Westfalen', in *VSWG*. II, 1894.

B. *Belgium*

DES MAREZ, G. 'Note sur le manse brabançon au moyen âge', in *Mélanges d'histoire offerts à Henri Pirenne*, I, Brussels, 1926.

DRAYE, H. *Landelijke cultuurvormen en kolonisatiegeschiedenis.* Louvain, 1941.

ERRERA, P. *Les masuirs.* 2 vols. Brussels, 1891.

—— 'Les waréchaix', in *Annales de la Soc. d'Archéologie de Bruxelles*, VIII, 1894.

GENICOT, L. 'L'évolution des dons aux abbayes dans le comté de Namur du Xᵉ au XIVᵉ siècle', in *Annales du XXXᵉ Congrès de la Fédération Arch. et Hist. de Belgique*, Brussels, 1935 and 1936.

—— 'Le servage dans les chartes-lois de Guillaume II, comte de Namur (1391-1418)', in *RB.* XXIV, 1945.

VERRIEST, L. *Le servage dans le comté de Hainaut. Les sainteurs. Le meilleur catel.* Brussels, 1910.

—— 'Etude d'un contrat privé de droit médiéval: le bail à cheptel vif à Tournai (1297–1334)', in *Revue du Nord*, 1946.

—— *Institutions médiévales.* Mons-Frameries, 1946.

—— 'Le servage en Flandre, particulièrement au pays d'Alost', in *Rev. hist. de droit français et étranger*, 1950.

VAN WERVEKE, H. 'Le mort-gage et son rôle économique en Flandre et en Lotharingie', in *RB.* VIII, 1929.

—— 'Comment les établissements religieux belges se procuraient-ils du vin au haut moyen âge', in *RB.* II, 1923.

WALRAET, M. 'Les chartes-lois de Prisches (1158) et de Beaumont-en-Argonne (1182). Contribution à l'étude de l'affranchissement des classes rurales au XIIᵉ siècle', in *RB.* XXIII, 1944.

C. France

AUBIGNAT, P. *L'amodiation dans l'ancienne Auvergne.* Dijon, 1910–11.

BLOCH, M. *Rois et serfs.* Paris, 1920.

—— 'Village et seigneurie', in *AHES.* IX, 1937.

DION, R. *Histoire de la vigne et du vin en France, des origines au XIXe siècle.* Paris, 1959.

GÉNESTAL, R. *Le rôle des monastères comme établissements de crédit étudié en Normandie du XIe à la fin du XIIIe siècle.* Paris, 1901.

GRAND, R. *Contribution à l'histoire du régime des terres. Le contrat de complant depuis les origines jusqu'à nos jours.* Paris, 1931.

JANNIAUX, G. *Essai sur l'amodiation dans l'ancienne Bourgogne.* Dijon, 1906.

MAHN, J. B. *L'ordre cistercien et son gouvernement des origines au milieu du XIIIe siècle, 1098–1265.* Paris, 1945.

PERRIN, C. E. 'De la condition des terres dites "ancingae"', in *Mélanges d'histoire du moyen âge offerts à M.F. Lot.* Paris, 1925.

—— 'Chartes de franchise et rapports de droit en Lorraine', in *Le Moyen Age*, 1946.

—— 'Le servage en France et en Allemagne', in *X^o Congresso Internazionale di Scienze storiche*, Rome, 1955. *Relazioni*, III.

D. Holland

ENKLAAR, D. T. 'Problemen van middeleeuwsch Gooiland', in *Tijdschrift voor Rechtsgeschiedenis*, XIV, 1936.

JANSEN, H. P. *Landbouwpacht in Brabant in de veertiende en vijftiende eeuw.* Assen, 1955.

SLICHER VAN BATH, B. H. *Mensch en land in de Middeleeuwen. Bijdrage tot een geschiedenis der nederzettingen in oostelijk Nederland.* 2 vols. Assen, 1944.

Thanks are also due to certain authors who have kindly permitted the first-mentioned of the writers to make use of a number of unpublished works. (1) Two studies by M. F. Vercauteren, entitled 'Note sur la valeur et l'importance économique des donations faites par les comtes de Flandre aux XIe et XIIe siècles' (summarized in *RB.* XVI, 1937, pp. 938–9) and 'Note sur l'extension de l'organisation domaniale en Belgique au haut moyen âge' (summarized in *Fédération archéologique et historique de Belgique*, XXXIe Session, Congrès de Namur, 1938, Annales, fasc. 1, pp. 48–49). (2) An important yet unpublished work by M. L. Voet, on the domains of the counts of Flanders (summarized as 'De graven van Vlaanderen en hun domein' in *Wetenschappelÿke Tÿdingen*, 1942 and 'Het vorstelÿk domein', in *Flandria Nostra*, V, Antwerp, 1960, pp. 70–98). (3) The researches of Mme Swolfs-Polfliet on the abbey of Affligem and of MM. Jamees and Vanderpoorten on the abbeys of Zonnebeke and Sint-Pieter of Ghent respectively. Finally the late F. Lot was good enough to place at the disposal of the first-mentioned writer a large number of notes which he has made on the subject of the agrarian régime in various parts of France.

§ 2. ITALY

The agrarian history of medieval Italy is regrettably poor in general works and surveys. What follows, therefore, is mainly a list of local studies, classified very roughly according to the arrangement of the chapter. The list is merely a selection, chosen as far as possible from recent secondary works; primary sources, on which the text of the chapter is principally based, have been almost entirely excluded. For a fuller bibliography, more particularly of social history, reference may be made to the *Bibliografia del Diritto Agrario Intermedio, I. Gli Studi*, ed. P. Fiorelli, M. Bandini, P. Grossi (Milan, 1962) and to the 'Bibliografia italiana di storia del diritto medioevale e moderno' published by R. Abbondanza in *Annali di Storia del Diritto*, vol. II *seq.*, 1958 *seq.*

I. GENERAL WORKS

A. *The natural background*

FISCHER, T. *La penisola italiana.* Turin, 1902.

MERLINI, G. *Le regioni agrarie in Italia.* Bologna, 1948.

MILONE, F. *L'Italia nell'economia delle sue regioni*. Turin, 1955.

MONTERIN, U. *Il clima sulle Alpi ha mutato in epoca storica?* Bologna, 1937.

PORENA, F. 'Sul deperimento fisico della regione italiana', in *Boll. Soc. Geog. It.* 1886.

B. The economic background

ALIANELLI, N. *Delle consuetudini e degli statuti municipali nelle provincie napoletane.* Naples, 1873.

BARBADORO, B. 'Finanza e demografia nei ruoli fiorentini d'imposta del 1352–5', in *Atti Cong. Internat. p. gli studi sulla popolazione.* Rome, 1932.

BELOCH, K. J. *Bevölkerungsgeschichte Italiens.* 3 vols. Berlin, Leipsig, 1937–61.

BESTA, E. *La Sardegna medioevale.* 2 vols. Palermo, 1908.

BIANCHINI, L. *Storia delle finanze del regno di Napoli.* 3 vols. Naples, 1859.

CAGGESE, R. *Roberto d'Angiò e i suoi tempi.* 2 vols. Florence, 1922, 1930.

CALASSO, C. *La legislazione statutaria dell'Italia meridionale.* Rome, 1929.

CARLI, F. *Storia del commercio italiano.* 2 vols. Padua, 1934, 1936.

CASINI, B. 'Contribuenti pisani alle taglie del 1402 e 1412', in *Boll. Stor. Pisano*, 1959–60.

CHALANDON F. *Histoire de la domination normande en Italie et Sicile.* 2 vols. Paris, 1907 (reprinted: New York, 1960).

CIPOLLA, C. M. 'Revisions in economic history: the trends in Italian economic history in the later Middle Ages', in *EcHR.* 1949.

—— 'Questioni aperte sul sistema economico dell'alto medio evo', in *Riv. Stor. It.* 1951.

—— 'I precedenti storici', in *Storia di Milano*, vol. VIII. Milan, 1957.

—— Introduction to *Storia dell'economia italiana*, Turin, 1959.

COGNASSO, F. 'Per la storia economica di Chieri nel sec. XIII', in *Boll. Stor.-Bibliogr. Subalpino*, 1911.

COLINI-BALDESCHI, L. 'Vita pubblica e privata maceratese nel Duecento e Trecento', in *Atti e Mem., Dep. Stor. Pat. p. le Marche*, 1903.

CRISTIANI, E. *Nobiltà e popolo nel comune di Pisa.* Naples, 1962.

DAVISO DI CHARVENSOD, M. C. 'I catasti di un comune agricolo piemontese del XIII secolo', in *Boll. Stor.-Bibliogr. Subalpino*, 1956.

DONNA, G. 'Aspetti della proprietà fondiaria nel comune di Chieri durante il XIII secolo', in *Accademia di Agricoltura di Torino, Annali*, 1941–2.

DOREN, A. *Italienische Wirtschaftsgeschichte*, Jena, 1934. (Italian translation, with notes, by G. Luzzatto. Padua, 1936.)

DOWD, D. F. 'The economic expansion of Lombardy, 1300–1500', in *Journal of Economic History*, 1961.

FALCO, G. 'I comuni della Campagna e della Marittima', in *Arch. Soc. Rom. Stor. Pat.* 1919–26.

FIUMI, E. 'Fioritura e decadenza dell'economia fiorentina', in *ASI.* 1957–9.

—— *Storia economica e sociale di San Gimignano.* Florence, 1961.

FOGLIETTI, R. *Il catasto di Macerata dell'anno, 1268.* Macerata, 1881.

GALASSO, G. 'Le città campane nell'alto medioevo', in *Arch. Stor. p. le prov. Napoletane*, 1958–60.

GENUARDI, L. *Il comune nel Medioevo in Sicilia.* Palermo, 1921.

GLÉNISSON, J. 'Documenti dell'archivio vaticano relativi alla collettoria di Sicilia', in *Riv. di Stor. della Chiesa in Italia*, 1948.

HEERS, J. *Gênes au XVe siècle.* Paris, 1961.

HERLIHY, D. 'Treasure hoards in the Italian economy, 960–1139', in *EcHR.* 1957.

—— *Pisa in the early Renaissance.* New Haven, 1958.

JONES, P. J. 'Florentine families and Florentine diaries in the fourteenth century', in *Papers of the Brit. School at Rome*, 1956.

LARSIMONT PERGAMENI, E. 'Censimenti milanesi dell'età di Carlo V', in *Arch. Stor. Lombardo*, 1948–9.

LOPEZ, R. S. 'Aux origines du capitalisme génois', in *AHES.* 1937.

—— 'The economic depression of the Renaissance', in *EcHR:* 1962.

—— 'The trade of medieval Europe, the South', in *Cambridge Ec. Hist. of Europe*, II. Cambridge, 1952.

LUZZATTO, G. 'La popolazione del territorio padovano nel 1281', in (N)AV. 1902.
—— 'Le finanze di un castello nel sec. XIII', in VSWG. 1913.
—— 'Les activités économiques du patriciat vénétien', in AHES. 1937.
—— 'L'inurbamento delle popolazioni rurali in Italia nei sec. XII e XIII', in Studi di storia e di diritto in onore di E. Besta, II. Milan, 1939.
—— Storia economica d'Italia, I. L'Antichità e il Medio Evo. Rome, 1949.
—— Storia economica dell'età moderna e contemporanea. Parte prima: L'età moderna. Padua, 1955.
MIRA, G. Aspetti dell'economia comasca all'inizio dell'età moderna. Como, 1939.
—— 'L'estimo di Perugia dell'anno 1285', in Annali della Fac. di Sc. Pol. ed Ec. e Comm. (Univ. di Perugia), 1955–6.
PARDI, G. 'Il catasto d'Orvieto del 1292', in Boll. Soc. Umb. Stor. Pat., 1896.
PERI, I. 'Città e campagne in Sicilia. Parte I: Dominazione normanna', in Atti Acc. Sc. Lett. Arti Palermo, 4th ser. XIII, 1952–3.
PLESNER, J. L'émigration de la campagne à la ville libre de Florence au XIII⁶ siècle. Copenhagen, 1934.
ROGNONI, N. P. 'Sulla popolazione e la distribuzione della proprietà in Vigevano', in Boll. Stor. Pavese, 1952.
RUSSELL, J. C. Late ancient and medieval population. Philadelphia, 1958.
SALVIOLI, G. Storia economica d'Italia nell'alto Medioevo. Naples, 1913.
SANTINI, U. Bologna alla fine del Quattrocento. Bologna, 1901.
SAPORI, A. Studi de storia economica medioevale. Florence, 1955.
TRASSELLI, C. 'Ricerche sulla popolazione di Sicilia nel sec. XV', in Atti Acc. Sc. Lett. Arti Palermo, 1954–5.
VARESE, P. 'Condizioni economiche e demografiche di Arezzo nel sec. XV', in Annuario del R. Ist. Magistrale 'V. Colonna', Arezzo. II, 1924–5.
VIOLANTE, C. La società milanese nell'età precomunale. Bari, 1953.
—— 'Storia ed economia dell'Italia medioevale', in Riv. Stor. It. 1961.
VITALE, V. 'Vita e commercio nei notai genovesi dei sec. XII e XIII', in Atti Soc. Ligure di Stor. Pat. 1949.
VOLPE, G. Studi sulle istituzioni comunali a Pisa. Pisa, 1902.
ZENO, R. I municipi di Calabria nel periodo aragonese. Rome, 1914.

II. AGRARIAN CONDITIONS

A. General Works

ARIAS, G. Il sistema della costituzione economica e sociale nell'età dei comuni. Turin, Rome, 1905.
CIPOLLA, C. M. 'La storia rurale italiana del medioevo nella Cambridge Economic History', in Riv. Stor. It. 1949.
FIUMI, E. 'Sui rapporti tra città e contado nell'età comunale', in ASI. 1956.
LEICHT, P. S. Operai, artigiani e agricoltori in Italia dal sec. VI al XVI. Milan, 1946.
ROSSI, B. 'La politica agraria dei comuni dominanti negli statuti della Bassa Lombardia', in Scritti giuridici in memoria di A. Arcangeli, II. Padua, 1939.

B. The Rural Economy

(i) Rural demography, colonization and reclamation
ALMAGIÀ, R. 'Saggio di carta antropogeografica dell'alta Val Venosta', in Boll. Soc. Geog. It. 1930.
BARATTA, M. 'Leonardo da Vinci negli studi per la navigazione dell'Arno', in Boll. Soc. Geog. It. 1905.
—— 'Sopra un'antica carta del territorio bresciano', in Boll. Soc. Geog. It. 1913.
—— 'Leonardo da Vinci e la Val di Chiana', in La Geografia, 1927.
BISCARO, G. 'La compagnia della Braida di Monte Volpe nell'antico suburbio milanese', in Arch. Stor. Lombardo, 1902.
BIZZARRI, D. 'Tentativi di bonifiche nel contado senese nei sec. XIII–XIV', in Bull. Senese di Stor. Pat. 1917.

BONASERA, F. *Fano, Studio di geografia urbana.* Fano, 1951.

CANESTRELLI, G. 'Il padule d'Orgia nel Medioevo', in *Riv. Geog. It.* 1914.

CASANOVA, E. *Precedenti storici, giuridici ed economici della legge per la bonifica integrale.* Milan, 1929.

CECCHINI, G. 'Saturnia e l'opera di colonizzazione senese nel sec. xv', in *Studi in onore di A. Fanfani*, II. Milan, 1962.

CIASCA, R. *Storia delle bonifiche del regno di Napoli.* Bari, 1928.

CIPOLLA, C. 'Le popolazioni dei XIII comuni veronesi', in *Misc. Dep. Veneta Stor. Pat.* 1882.

CIPOLLA, C. M. 'Per la storia delle terre della "bassa" Lombarda', in *Studi in onore di A. Sapori*, I, Milan, 1957.

DI BERENGER, A. *Dell'antica storia e legislazione forestale in Italia.* 2 vols. Treviso, Venice, 1859–63.

DONNA, G. *Lo sviluppo storico delle bonifiche e dell'irrigazione in Piemonte.* Turin, 1939.

ERRERA, C. 'La bonifica estense nel basso Ferrarese', *Riv. Geog. It.* 1934.

FERRARI, C. *La campagna di Verona all'epoca veneziana.* Venice, 1930.

FERRARI, G. 'La campagna di Verona dal sec. XII alla venuta dei Veneziani', in *Atti 1st. Veneto*, 1914.

—— 'La legislazione veneziana sui beni comunali', in *(N)AV.* 1918.

FIASCHI, R. *Le magistrature pisane delle acque.* Pisa, 1938.

FRASSOLDATI, C. *Le partecipanze agrarie emiliane.* Padua, 1936.

FUMAGALLI, A. 'Memoria storica ed economica sull'irrigazione dei prati nel Milanese', in *Atti Soc. Patriottica di Milano*, II, pt. 2, 1792.

GARUFI, C. A. 'Patti agrari e comuni feudali di nuova fondazione in Sicilia dallo scorcio del sec. XI agli albori del Settecento', in *Arch. Stor. Siciliano*, 1946.

GLORIA, A. *Il territorio padovano illustrato.* Padua, 1862.

GOLTARA, L. *L'irrigazione della provincia di Bergamo.* Rome, 1910.

HERLIHY, D. 'The agrarian revolution in southern France and Italy, 801–1150', in *Speculum*, 1958.

HIGOUNET, C. 'Les "Terre nuove" florentines du XIVe siècle', in *Studi in onore di A. Fanfani*, III, Milan, 1962.

IMBERCIADORI, I. 'Il problema del pane nella storia della bonifica maremmana', in *Atti Acc. dei Georgofili*, 1938.

KOVALEVSKY, M. 'Die wirtschaftlichen Folgen d. schwarzen Tod in Italien', in *VSWG.* 1895.

LECCE, M. 'Una bonifica in territorio veronese alla fine del XII sec.', in *ES.* 1954.

LODDO CANEPA, F. 'Lo spopolamento della Sardegna durante le dominazioni aragonese e spagnuola', in *Atti Cong. Internat. p. gli studi sulla popolazione*, I, Rome, 1932.

LOMBARDINI, E. in C. Cattaneo, *Notizie naturali e civili su la Lombardia.* Milan, 1844.

—— *Della condizione idraulica della pianura subappenina fra l'Enza ed il Panaro.* Milan, 1865.

—— 'Studi idrologici e storici sopra il grande estuario adriatico', in *Mem. 1st. Lomb. Classe Sc. Matematiche e Naturali*, 1870.

LUZIO, L. 'Sui centri scomparsi del Lazio', in *Atti XV Cong. Geog. It.* 1950.

MIGLIORINI, E. 'Per uno studio geografico delle localita abbandonate dall'uomo in Italia', in *Atti XV Cong. Geog. It.* 1950.

MOZZI, U. *I magistrati veneti alle acque ed alle bonifiche.* Bologna, 1927.

NICE, B. 'I centri abitati della Toscana con pianta regolare', in *L'Universo*, 1947.

ORTOLANI, M., ALFIERI, N. 'Deviazioni di fiumi piceni in epoca storica', in *Riv. Geog. It.* 1947.

PADERI, E. 'Variazioni fisiografiche del bacino di Bientina e della pianura lucchese durante i periodi storici', in *Mem. Soc. Geog. It.* 1932.

PARDI, G. 'A proposito di un articolo di M. Kovalevsky sulle conseguenze economiche della peste in Italia', in *Boll. Umb. di Stor. Pat.* 1896.

—— 'La popolazione del contado fiorentino nel 1401', in *Annuario statistico del comune di Firenze*, 1917–8.

—— 'La popolazione del distretto di Roma nel sec. xv', in *Arch. Soc. Rom. di Stor. Pat.* 1926.

PEDRESCHI, L. 'Pisa. Ricerche di geografia urbana', in *Riv. Geog. It.* 1951.

PERI, I. 'Censuazioni in Sicilia nel sec. XIII', in *ES*. 1957.

PLESNER, J. *Una rivoluzione stradale nel Dugento (Acta Jutlandica,* I). Aarhus, 1938.

SALVIOLI, G. 'La colonizzazione in Sicilia nei sec. XVI e XVII', in *VSWG*. 1903.

SENECA, F. 'Problemi economici e demografici del Trentino nei sec. XIII e XIV', in *Studi e ricerche storiche sulla regione trentina,* I, Padua, 1953.

SERENI, E. 'Note per una storia del paesaggio agrario emiliano', in *Le campagne emiliane nell'epoca moderna. Studi e ricerche storiche.* Milan, 1955.

—— *Storia del paesaggio agrario italiano.* Bari, 1961.

SORBELLI, A. 'Il senato bolognese e i boschi dell'Appennino alla fine del sec. XV', in *Atti Cong. Forest. It.* (Bologna, 1909), II, Bologna, 1910.

STOLZ, O. *Die Schwaighöfe in Tirol.* 1930.

TOMASSETTI, G. 'Della Campagna Romana nel medio evo', in *Arch. Soc. Rom. Stor. Pat.* 1878–1907.

TONIOLO, A. R. 'Le grandi bonifiche del Ravennate e del Ferrarese', in *L'Universo,* 1927.

—— 'Le variazioni storiche del litorale toscano tra l'Arno e la Magra', in *Atti X Cong. Geog. It.* I, Milan, 1927.

TRIFONE, R. *Storia del diritto forestale in Italia.* Florence, 1957.

ZIMOLI, G. C. 'Canali e navigazione interna dalle origini al 1500', in *Storia di Milano,* VIII, Milan, 1957.

(ii) *Agricultural organisation, production and technique*

ALEMANNI, L. *La coltivazione.* Florence, 1546.

BONAFEDE, P. *Il Tesoro dei Rustici* (1360), ed. in O. Mazzoni Toselli, *Origine della lingua italiana,* I, Bologna, 1831.

BURGUNDIO PISANO, *Liber vindemie de greco in latinum translatus,* ed. F. Buonamici, *Annali delle Università Toscane,* 1908.

CRESCENZI, PIER DEI. *Liber cultus ruris* (1304): various editions in various languages, 1471 seq.

FALCONE, G. *La nuova vaga, et dilettevole Villa.* Brescia, 1577.

GALLO, A. *Le venti giornate della vera agricultura.* Venice, 1567.

TANAGLIA, M. *De Agricultura,* ed. A. Roncaglia. Bologna, 1953.

TARELLO, C. *Ricordo di agricultura.* Venice, 1567.

TATTI, G. *Della Agricultura.* Venice, 1560.

VETTORI, P. *Coltivazione degli ulivi,* ed. Florence, 1621.

ACERBO, G. *L'economia dei cereali nell'Italia e nel mondo.* Milan, 1934.

ANDRICH, L. 'Gli statuti bellunesi e trevigiani dei danni dati e le wizae', *ASI*. 1904.

—— 'Note sui comuni rurali bellunesi' in *L'Ateneo Veneto,* 1903–5.

BERTAGNOLLI, C. *Delle. vicende dell'agricultura in Italia.* Florence, 1881.

BISCARO, G. 'La polizia campestre negli statuti del comune di Treviso', in *Riv. It. p. le Sc. Giur.* 1902.

BOYER, P. 'Le "Ruralium commodorum opus" de Pierre de Crescent', in *École nationale des chartes, Positions des thèses,* 1943.

CAFAGNA, L. 'La rivoluzione agraria in Lombardia', in *Annali,* II, 1959.

CAGGESE, R. 'Una cronaca economica del sec. XIV', in *Riv. delle Biblioteche e degli Archivi,* 1902.

CAROCCI, G. 'Problemi agrari del Lazio nel 1500', in *Studi Storici,* I, 1959–60.

CARUSO, A. 'Fonti per la storia della provincia di Salerno. L'archivio della *Dohana menae pecudum*', in *Rassegna storica salernitana,* 1952.

CASSANDRO, G. I. *Storia delle terre comuni e degli usi civici nell'Italia meridionale.* Bari, 1943.

CASTAGNOLI, F. *Le ricerche sui resti della centurazione.* Rome, 1958.

CHERCHI PABA, F. 'Lineamenti storici dell'agricoltura sarda nel sec. XIII', in *Studi storici in onore di F. Loddo Canepa,* II. Florence, 1959.

CHIUPPANI, G. 'L'antica legislazione agraria dei Bassanesi e il codice del 1444', in *Boll. Museo Civico di Bassano,* 1904–5.

CIPOLLA, C. 'Carta statutaria lombarda del sec. XIII risguardante i campari', in *Atti Acc. Sc. Torino*. 1898–9.

—— 'Documenti statutari veronesi dei sec. XIII e XIV risguardanti la saltaria', in *Acc. dei Lincei, Classe Sc. Mor. Rendiconti*. 1899.

CIPOLLA, C. M. 'Ripartizione delle colture nel pavese secondo le "misure territoriali" della metà del '500', in *Studi di economia e statistica* (Univ. di Catania, Fac. di Ec. e Comm.), 1950–1.

CONIGLIO, G. 'Agricoltura ed artigianato mantovano nel sec. XVI', in *Studi in onore di A. Fanfani*, IV, Milan, 1962.

CURIS, G. *Usi civici, proprietà collettive e latifondi nell'Italia Centrale e nell'Emilia*. Naples, 1917.

D'ANCONA, A. 'I dodici mesi dell'anno nella tradizione popolare', in *Arch. p. lo studio delle tradizioni popolari*, 1883.

DANIELLI, V. *Dominii collettivi ed usi civici della provincia di Pesaro ed Urbino*. Senigallia, 1908.

DE CUPIS, R. *Vicende dell'agricoltura e della pastorizia nell'Agro Romano*. Rome, 1911.

EVOLI, F. 'L'economia agraria delle provincie meridionali durante la feudalità', in *Arch. Stor. p. la Calabria e la Lucania*, 1931.

FILANGIERI, A. 'La "Dogana delle pecore" di Puglia e la struttura economico agraria del Tavoliere', in *Riv. di Ec. Agraria*, 1950.

FIUMI, E. 'Economia e vita privata dei fiorentini nelle rilevazioni statistiche di G. Villani', in *ASI*. 1953.

FLORIDIA, S. *Gli agrumi. Parte prima: Storia degli agrumi dal VI sec. avanti Cristo ai nostri giorni*. Catania, 1933.

GABOTTO, F. *L'agricoltura nella regione saluzzese dal sec. XI al XV*. Pinerolo, 1902.

GENNARI, G. *L'aratro*. Rome, 1944.

GENUARDI, L. *Terre comuni ed usi civici in Sicilia*. Palermo, 1911.

GLORIA, A. *Dell'agricoltura nel Padovano*. 2 vols. Padua, 1855.

GRIBAUDI, P. 'Olive e zafferano sulle colline di Torino', in *Boll. Stor.-Bibliog. Subalpino*, 1898.

HAUDRICOURT, A. G. and DELAMARE, J. B. *L'homme et la charrue*. Paris, 1955.

HOENIGER, T. 'La storia della vite e del vino in Alto Adige', in *Atti Acc. It. della Vite*, 1953.

IMBERCIADORI, I. 'Il primo statuto della dogana dei paschi maremmani (1419)', in *AVS*. 1938.

JASNY, N. *The wheats of classical antiquity*. Baltimore, 1944.

LATTES, A. 'Parole e simboli: wifa, brandon e wiza', in *Rendiconti Ist. Lomb.* 1900.

LECCE, M. 'Le condizioni zootecniche-agricole del territorio veronese nella prima metà del '500', in *ES*. 1958.

LOMBARDI, L. *Delle origini e delle vicende degli usi civici nelle provincie napoletane*. Naples, 1885.

MARANI, C. 'Camillo Tarello e gli inizi della scienza agronomica moderna', in *Riv. Stor. Ec.* 1941.

MARESCALCHI, A. and DALMASSO, G. *Storia della vite e del vino in Italia*. 3 vols. Milan, 1931–9.

MESSEDAGLIA, L. *Il mais e la vita rurale italiana*. Piacenza, 1927.

—— *Per la storia dell'agricoltura e dell'alimentazione*. Piacenza, 1932.

MOR, C. G. 'La vicinia di Crevole Sesia', in *Boll. Stor. prov. Novara*, 1924.

—— 'Sul commento di Girolamo Olives, giureconsulto sardo del sec. XVI, alla Carta de logu di Eleonora d'Arborea', in *Testi e documenti p. la storia del dirrito agraria in Sardegna*. Sassari, 1938.

—— 'L'Universitas Vallis Vedasche', in *Scritti storici e giuridici in memoria di A. Visconti*. Milan, 1955.

MOTTA, E. 'Per la storia della coltura del riso in Lombardia', in *Arch. Stor. Lombardo*, 1905.

NICCOLI, V. *Saggio storico a bibliografico dell'agricoltura italiana dalle origini al 1900*. Turin, 1902.

OLSON, L. 'Pietro de Crescenzi: the founder of modern agronomy', in *Agricultural History Review*, 1944.

PALMIERI, A. 'Dell'ufficio della Saltaria, specialmente nel periodo precomunale', in *Atti e Mem. Dep. Stor. Pat. p. la Romagna*, 1904.

Pier de' Crescanzi. Studi e documenti. Bologna (Soc. Agr.), 1933.

PUPILLO BARRESI, A. *Gli usi civici in Sicilia.* Catania, 1903.

RICCI, G. 'La "nobilis universitas bobacteriorum Urbis"', in *Arch. Soc. Rom. Stor. Pat.* 1893.

ROGNONI, C. *Saggio storico sull'antica agricoltura parmense.* Parma, 1897.

SAVASTANO, L. 'Contributo allo studio critico degli scrittori agrari italici, II. Pietro de' Crescenzi', in *Annali Stazione Sperimentale di Agrumicultura e Frutticultura di Acireale*, 1919–21.

—— 'Contributo 'etc.' III. Giovanni Joviano Pontano agrumicultore, Antonino Venuto e Gregorio dei Corno', in *ibid.* 1922.

SCHUPFER, F. 'Degli usi civici a altri diritti del comune di Apricena', in *Atti Acc. Lincei*, 4th ser. *Classe Sc. Mor.* II pt. I (*Memorie*), 1886.

SERENI, E. 'Il sistema agricolo del debbio nella Liguria antica', in *Mem. Acc. Lunigianese*, G. Cappellini, 1953.

—— 'Spunti della rivoluzione agronomica europea nella scuola bresciana cinquecentesca di Agostino Gallo e di Camillo Tarello', in *Misc. in onore di R. Cessi*, II, Rome, 1958.

SINGER, C., HOLMYARD, E. J., HALL, A. R., and WILLIAMS, T. I. *A history of technology*, II. *The Mediterranean civilisation and the Middle Ages.* Oxford, 1956.

SOLMI, A. 'Ademprivia. Studi sulla proprietà fondiaria in Sardegna', in *Arch. Giuridico*, 1904.

TARGIONI-TOZZETTI, A. *Cenni storici sulla introduzione di varie piante nell'agricoltura ed orticultura toscana.* Revised ed., E. Baroni. Florence, 1896.

TONIOLO, A. R. 'La distribuzione dell'oliva nel Veneto occidentale', in *Riv. Geog. It.* 1914.

TORRISI, N. 'Aspetti della crisi granaria siciliana nel sec. XVI', in *Arch. Stor. Sicilia Orientale*, 1957.

TROTTER, A. 'Il più antico documento relativo alla bachicultura in Italia', in *Riv. Stor. del Sannio*, 1919.

VITALI, G. 'L'evoluzione dell'aratro nell'agricoltura italiana', *Atti Acc. Georgofili*, 1942.

WEBSTER, J. C. *The labours of the months.* Evanston, Chicago, 1938.

WHITE, L. *Medieval technology and social change.* Oxford, 1962.

(iii) *Trade and the branches of agriculture*

Information on this must be drawn from scattered sources, in particular works on medieval commerce and economic policy, for which see the bibliographies in vols. II and III. Special mention may be made of the following:

BORLANDI, F. 'Note per la storia della produzione e del commercio di una materia prima. Il guado nel Medio Evo', in *Studi in onore di G. Luzzatto*, I, Milan, 1949.

—— '"Futainiers" et futaines dans l'Italie du Moyen Age', in *Hommage à Lucien Febvre*, II, Paris, 1953.

CARTA RASPI, R. *L'economia della Sardegna medievale. Scambi e prezzi.* Cagliari, 1940.

CIANO, C. 'Il porto di Lerici e la Lunigiana nel XIII secolo', in *ES.* 1960.

CIASCA, R. 'Per la storia dei rapporti tra Firenze a la regione del Vulture nel sec. XIV', in *ASI.* 1928.

CIPOLLA, C. M. 'In tema di trasporti medioevali', in *Boll. Stor. Pavese*, 1944.

DAY, J. 'Prix agricoles en Méditerrannée a la fin du XIVe siècle (1382)', in *Annales*, 1961.

DE BOÜARD, M. 'Problèmes de subsistance dans un état médiéval: le marché et les prix des céréales au royaume angevin de Sicile (1266–1282)', in *Annales*, 1938.

DELUMEAU, J. *Vie économique et sociale de Rome dans la seconde moitié du XVIe siècle.* 2 vols. Paris, 1957–9.

GLÉNISSON, J. 'Une administration médiévale aux prises avec la disette. La question des blés dans les provinces italiennes de l'Etat pontifical en 1374–5', in *Le Moyen Age*, 1951.

GUALAZZINI, U. 'Aspetti giuridici della politica frumentaria dei comuni nel Medio Evo', *Riv. di Stor. del Diritto It.* 1956.

HEERS, J. 'Il commercio nel Mediterraneo alla fine del sec. XIV e nei primi anni del sec. XV', in *ASI.* 1955.

LUZZATTO, G. 'Studi sulle relazioni commerciali tra Venezia e la Puglia', in (*N*)*AV.* 1904, pt. I.

MIRA, G. *Le fiere lombarde nei sec. XIV–XVI.* Como, 1955.

—— 'Il fabbisogno dei cereali in Perugia nei sec. XIII–XIV', in *Studi in onore di A. Sapori*, I. Milan, 1957.

—— 'Prime indagini sulle fiere umbre nel Medioevo', in *Studi in onore di E. Corbino*, II, Milan, 1961.

—— 'Taluni aspetti dell'economia medioevale perugina secondo una tariffa daziaria del sec. XIV', *Studi in onore di A. Fanfani*, III, Milan, 1962.

MENCHETTI, A. *Su l'obbligo della coltivazione del suolo nei comuni medioevali marchigiani.* Fermo, 1924 (reprinted *AVS.* 1935).

PETINO, A. *Lo zafferano nell'economia del medioevo.* Catania, 1950–1.

—— *Aspetti e momenti di politica granaria a Catania ed in Sicilia nel Quattrocento.* Catania, 1951–2.

—— 'Per la storia delle relazioni della Sicilia nei traffici internazionali del Medioevo', in *Studi Economici*, VIII, Naples, 1953.

PEYER, H. *Zur Getreidepolitik oberitalienischer Städte im 13 Jahrhundert.* Vienna, 1950.

POPOVIC-RADENKOVIC, M. 'Ragusa e la Puglia nel periodo angioino (1266–1442)', in *Arch. Stor. p. le prov. Napol.* 1958.

ROMANO, R. 'A propos du commerce du blé dans la Méditerranée des XIVe et XVe siècles', in *Hommages à L. Febvre*, II, Paris, 1954.

SILVESTRI, A. *Il commercio a Salerno nella seconda metà del Quattrocento.* Salerno, 1952.

SPOSATO, P. 'Aspetti della vita economica e commerciale calabrese sotto gli aragonesi', in *Calabria nobilissima*, 1952, 1953.

—— 'Partecipazione della nobiltà calabrese alla vita economica e commerciale della regione nella seconda metà del Quattrocento', in *Arch. Stor. p. la Calabria e la Lucania*, 1958.

TRASSELLI, C. 'Frumento e panni inglesi nella Sicilia del XV sec.', in *Annali della Fac. di Ec. e Comm.* Univ. di Palermo, 1955.

—— 'Produzione e commercio dello zucchero in Sicilia dal XIII al XIX sec.', in *ES.* 1955.

—— 'Sull'esportazione dei cereali dalla Sicilia nel 1407–8', in *Atti Acc. Sc. Lett. Arti*, Palermo, 1955.

YVER, G. *Le commerce et les marchands dans l'Italie méridionale au XIIIe et au XIVe siècle.* Paris, 1903.

(iv) *Settlement* (*Cf.* II B. i. *supra.*)

On this subject, even more than the food trade, details are scattered in unrelated works. Something may be learned from studies of modern settlement and rural architecture (for which see the book of F. Milone, *supra* I.A., and, for recent work, the *Bibliographie Géographique Internationale*). For medieval settlement the following may be consulted:

CIPOLLA, C. M. 'Popolazione e proprietari delle campagne attraverso un ruolo di contribuenti del sec. XII', in *Boll. Stor. Pavese*, 1946.

COLELLA, G. *Toponomastica pugliese dalle origini alla fine del Medioevo.* Trani, 1941.

GAMBI, L. 'Il censimento del Cardinale Anglic in Romagna nell'anno 1371', in *Riv. Geog. It.* 1947.

—— *L'insediamento umano nella regione della bonifica romagnola.* Rome, 1950.

—— *Le Rationes Decimarum: volumi e carte, e il loro valore per la storia dell'insediamento umano in Italia.* Imola, 1952.

GRIBAUDI, D. 'Sulle origini dei centri rurali di sommità', in *Riv. Geog. It.* 1951.

LACQUANTINI, L. 'Morfologia ed evoluzione dei centri abitati della Calabria', in *Boll. Soc. Geog. It.* 1946.

MORI, A. 'Ricerche sui centri della Valle del Metauro', in *Boll. Soc. Geog. It.* 1946.

ORTOLANI, M. 'Ricerche sul popolamento della pianura ferrarese', in *Boll. Soc. Geog. It.* 1950.

RIGOBON, M. 'Per la storia delle sedi umane nel Valdarno inferiore', in *Atti Ist. Veneto*, 1904.

WARD-PERKINS, J. 'Etruscan towns, Roman roads, and medieval villages: the historical geography of southern Etruria', in *The Geographical Journal*, 1962.

C. Rural Society

(i) General works

LEICHER, R. 'Historische Grundlagen d. landwirtschaftlichen Besitz-und Betrieb-sverhältnisse in Italien', in *VSWG.* 1960.

LEICHT, P. S., introd. to *Testi e documenti per la storia del diritto agrario in Italia. Secoli VIII–XVIII.* Milan, 1954.

PERTILE, A. *Storia del diritto italiano.* 2nd ed. 6 vols. Turin, 1896–1903.

SALVIOLI, G. *Manuale di storia del diritto italiano.* 9th ed. Turin, 1930.

SAPORI, G. 'Le condizioni giuridiche e sociali in cui si è sviluppata l'agricoltura italiana', in *La distribuzione della proprietà fondiaria in Italia. Relazione generale.* Ed. G. Medici. Rome, 1956.

SCHUPFER, F. *Il diritto privato dei popoli germanici con speciale riguardo all'Italia.* 3 vols. Città di Castello, Rome, 1913–5.

—— *Il diritto delle obbligazioni in Italia nell'età del Risorgimento.* 3 vols. Turin, 1921.

(ii) The Manor in Italy

BERNAREGGI, E. *Il sistema economico e la monetazione dei Longobardi nell'Italia superiore.* Milan, 1960.

BOGNETTI, G. P. *Sulle origini dei comuni rurali nel Medioevo.* Pavia, 1927.

BUZZI, G. 'La curia arcivescovile e la curia cittadina di Ravenna dall'850 al 1118', in *Bull. 1st Stor. It.* 1915.

CALISSE, C. 'Le condizioni della proprietà territoriale studiate sui documenti della provincia romana dei sec. VIII, IX e X', in *Arch. Soc. Rom. Stor. Pat.* 1884–5.

CESSI, R. 'Aspetti del regime agrario nell'antico ducato veneziano (sec. IX–XII)', in *Atti Ist Veneto*, 1957–8.

CICCAGLIONE, F. *Le istituzioni politiche e sociali dei ducati napolitani.* Naples, 1892.

CUSIN, F. 'Per la storia del castello medioevale', in *Riv. Stor. It.* 1939.

DARMSTÄDTER, P. *Das Reichsgut in d. Lombardei u. Piedmont (568–1250)*, Strasbourg, 1896.

DEL TREPPO, M. 'La vita economica e sociale in una grande abbazia del Mezzogiorno: San Vincenzo al Volturno nell'alto medioevo', in *Arch. Stor. p. le prov. Napoletane*, 1955.

ENDRES, R. 'Das Kirchengut im Bistum Lucca vom 8 bis 10 Jahrhundert', in *VSWG.* 1916–8.

ERCOLE, F. 'Il "villanatico" e la servitu della gleba in alcuni documenti piacentini dei sec. XII e XIII', in *Boll. Stor. Piacentino*, 1909–10.

EWALD, U. 'Arbeit schafft Eigentum', in *VSWG.* 1952.

FABIANI, L. *La Terra di S. Benedetto. Studio storico-giuridico sull'Abbazia di Montecassino dall'VIII al XIII secolo.* Montecassino, 1950.

FAINELLI, V. 'Intorno alle origini dei comuni rurali veronesi', in *(N)AV.* 1913.

FASOLI, G. 'L'abbazia di Nonantola fra l'VIII e l'XI sec. nelle ricerche storiche', in *Studi e documenti* (Dep. Stor. Pat. Modena), II, 1943.

FORMENTINI, U. 'La tenuta curtense degli antichi marchesi della Tuscia in Val di Magra e Val di Taro', in *Arch. Stor. p. le Prov. Parmensi*, 1928.

HERLIHY, D. 'The history of the rural seigneury in Italy, 751–1200', in *Agricultural History*, 1959.

—— 'Church property on the European continent, 701–1200', in *Speculum*, 1961.

JONES, P. J. 'An Italian estate, 900–1200', in *EcHR.* 1954.

LEICHT, P. S. *Studi sulla proprietà fondiaria nel medio evo*. Verona, Padua, 1903–7.
—— *Il diritto privato preirneriano*. Bologna, 1933.
—— 'Livellario nomine', in *Studi senesi*, 1905 (reprinted in *Scritti vari* II, 2, Milan, 1949).
—— 'L'organisation des grands domaines dans l'Italie du Nord pendant les xe–xiie siècles', in *Receuils de la Société Jean Bodin*, IV. *Le domaine*. Brussels, 1949.
—— 'Un contratto agrario dei paesi latini mediterranei', in *Studi in onore di A. Sapori*, I, Milan, 1957.
LIZIER, A. *L'economia rurale dell'età prenormanna nell'Italia meridionale*. Palermo, 1907.
LUZZATTO, G. *I servi nelle grandi proprietà ecclesiastiche dei sec. IX e X*. Pisa, 1910.
—— 'Mutamenti nell'economia agraria italiana dalla caduta dei carolingi al principio del sec. XI', in *Settimane di studio sull'alto medio evo*, II, Spoleto, 1955.
—— 'Vicinie e comuni', in *Riv. It. di Sociologia*, 1909.
PARADISI, B. *Massaricium ius*. Bologna, 1937.
PIVANO, S. *I contratti agrari nell'alto Medio Evo*. Turin, 1904.
—— 'Sistema curtense', in *Boll. 1st Stor. It.* 1909.
SALVIOLI, G. 'Massari e manenti nell'economia italiana medievale', *Gedächtnisschrift f. G. v. Below*. Stuttgart, 1928.
SCHNEIDER, F. *Die Entstehung v. Burg u. Landgemeinde in Italien*. Berlin, 1924.
SEREGNI, G. 'La popolazione agricola della Lombardia nell'età barbarica', in *Arch. Stor. Lombardo*, 1895.
SERRA, G. *Contributo toponomastico alla teoria della continuità nel medioevo delle comunità rurali romane e preromane dell'Italia superiore*. Cluj, 1931.
VACCARI, P. *La territorialità come base dell'ordinamento giuridico del contado*. Pavia, 1921.
VIOLANTE, C. 'Per lo studio dei prestiti dissimulati in territorio milanese (sec. x–xi)', in *Studi in onore di A. Fanfani*, I, Milan, 1962.
ZUCCHETTI, G. 'Il "Liber largitorius vel notarius monasterii Pharphensis"', in *Boll. 1st Stor. It.* 1927.

(iii) *The decline of the Manor*

BASSANELLI, E. *La colonia perpetua. Saggio storico-giuridico*. Rome, 1933.
BATTAGLIA, G. *L'ordinamento della proprietà fondiaria nell'Italia meridionale sotto i Normanni e gli Svevi*. Palermo, 1896.
BATTISTELLA, A. 'La servitù di masnada in Friuli', in *(N)AV*. 1906–8.
CAGGESE, R. 'La repubblica di Siena e il suo contado nel sec. xiii', in *Bull. Senese di Stor. Pat.* 1906.
—— *Classi e comuni rurali nel Medioevo italiano*. 2 vols. Florence, 1907–9.
CARABELLESE, F. 'Sopravvivenze di comuni rurali nel regno di Puglia sotto Federigo II di Hohenstaufen ed i suoi successori', in *Raccolta di scritti storici in onore del prof. G. Romano*. Pavia, 1907.
CARO, G. 'Zur Geschichte d. Grundherrschaft in Oberitalien', in *Jahrbücher f. National-ökonomie u. Statistik*, 1908.
CARTA RASPI, R. *Le classi sociali nella Sardegna medioevale, I. I servi*. Cagliari, 1938.
CENCETTI, G. 'Il contratto di enfiteusi nella dottrina dei glossatori e dei commentatori', in *Annali della Soc. Agrar. Bologna*, 1938–9.
CHECCHINI, A. 'Comuni rurali padovani', in *(N)AV*. 1909.
CIPOLLA, C. M. 'Per la storia della crisi del sistema curtense in Italia', in *Bull. 1st Stor. It.* 1950.
DE VERGOTTINI, G. *Origini e sviluppo della comitatinanza*. Siena, 1929.
DIAMARE, L. 'L'organizzazione interna del monastero cassinese nel sec. xiii', in *Arch. Soc. Rom. Stor. Pat.* 1945.
DI TUCCI, R. *La proprietà fondiaria in Sardegna dall'alto Medioevo ai nostri giorno*. Cagliari, 1928.
DIVIZIANI, A. 'Roviano e il suo statuto del sec. xiii', *Arch. Soc. Rom. Stor. Pat.* 1928.
DONNA, G. 'I borghi franchi nella politica e nella economia agraria della repubblica Vercellese', in *Annali Acc. Agr. Torino*, 1942–3.
FASOLI, G. 'Un comune veneto nel Duecento: Bassano', in *AV*. 1934.
—— 'Ricerche sui borghi franchi dell'alta Italia', in *Riv. Stor. Dir. It.* 1942.

FASOLI, G. 'La feudalità siciliana nell'età di Federico II', in *Riv. Stor. Dir. It.* 1951.

FICI LI BASSI, G. 'Contributo alla storia dei contratti agrari in Sicilia sotto i Normanni e gli Svevi', in *Riv. Legis. Comparata*, 1906.

GARUFI, C. A. 'Censimento e catasto della popolazione servile', in *Arch. Stor. Siciliano*, 1928.

GATTOLA, E. *Historia abbatiae Cassinensis per saeculorum seriem distributa.* Venice, 1733.

GOSSO, F. *Vita economica delle abbazie piemontesi (sec. X–XIV).* Rome, 1940.

GREGORIO, R. *Considerazioni sopra la storia di Sicilia.* Palermo, 1931.

LATTES, A. *Il diritto consuetudinario delle città lombarde.* Milan, 1899.

—— 'Le ingrossazioni nei documenti parmensi', in *Arch. Stor. p. le prov. Parm.* 1914.

LEICHT, P. S. 'Note sull'economia friulana al principio del sec. XIII', in *Festschrift zum 70 Geburtstag v. A. Dopsch.* Leipsig, 1938 (reprinted in *Scritti vari cit.*).

—— 'La formola d'affrancazione dei coloni nel periodo bolognese e i suoi antecedenti', in *Scritti in onore di V. Federici.* Florence, 1945 (reprinted in *Scritti vari*, II, 2, Milan, 1949).

LUZZATTO, G. 'Le sottomissioni dei feudatari e le classi sociali in alcuni comuni marchigiani', in *Le Marche*, 1906.

MARINELLI, O. 'L'affrancazione degli "homines" di Casalina nel territorio perugino (1270)', in *Boll. Umb. Stor. Pat.* 1954.

MEYER, K. *Blenio u. Leventina von Barabarossa bis Heinrich VII.* Lucerne, 1911.

MICHELI, G. *I livellari vescovili nelle terre di Berceto.* Parma, 1935.

MOCHI ONORY, S. *Origini storiche dei diritti essenziali della persona.* Bologna, 1927.

MOLTENI, G. 'Il contratto di masseria in alcuni fondi milanesi durante il sec. XIII', in *Studi Storici*, XXII, 1914.

NASALLI ROCCA, E. 'Giurisdizioni e diritti enfiteutici del vescovo di Piacenza in Firenzuola (sec. XIII)', in *Arch. Stor. p. le prov. Parm.* 1929.

—— 'Note sulle "ingrossazioni" nell'Emilia occidentale', in *Riv. Stor. Dir. It.* 1953–4.

PALMIERI, A. *La montagna bolognese del medio evo.* Bologna, 1929.

PASCUCCI, G. B. *Contratti agrari nel diritto statutario bolognese del sec. XIII.* Bologna, Parma, 1960.

ROMEO, R. 'La signoria dell'abate si S. Ambrogio di Milano sul comune rurale di Origgio nel sec. XIII', in *Riv. Stor. It.* 1957.

ROSSI, G. 'La valle di Diano e i suoi statuti antichi', in *Misc. Stor. It.* 1902.

SALVEMINI, G. 'Un comune rurale nel sec. XIII: Tintinnano', in his *Studi Storici.* Florence, 1901.

SANTOLI, Q. 'Il distretto pistoiese nei sec. XII e XIII', in *Bull. Stor. Pistoiese*, 1903.

SARDI, C. *Le contrattazioni agrarie del Medio Evo studiate nei documenti lucchesi.* Lucca, 1914.

SCHAEFER, P. *Das Sottoceneri im Mittelalter.* Aarau, 1931.

SEREGNI, G. 'Del luogo di Arosio e de' suoi statuti nei sec. XII–XIII', in *Misc. Stor. It.* 1902.

SIMEONI, L. 'Il comune rurale nel territorio veronese', in *(N)AV.* 1921.

——'La liberazione dei servi a Bologna nel 1256–7', in *ASI.* 1951.

STELLA, A. *Politica ed economia nel territorio trentino-tirolese dal XIII al XVIII secolo.* Padua, 1958.

STOLZ, O. *Rechtsgeschichte des Bauernstandes u. der Landwirtschaft in Tirol u. Vorarlberg.* Bolzano, 1949.

TORELLI, P. *Un comune cittadino in territorio ad economia agricola.* 2 vols. Mantua, 1930–52.

TRIFONE, R. *La legislazione angioina.* Naples, 1921.

VACCARI, P. *L'affrancazione dei servi della gleba nell'Emilia e nella Toscana.* Bologna, 1926.

WEBER, S. 'La manomissione dei servi nel Trentino', in *Studi Trentini*, 1923–4.

ZORSI, E. *Il territorio padovano nel periodo di trapasso da comitato a comune (Misc. Stor. Veneta,* ser. 4, III), 1930.

(iv) *The reorganisation of estates*

ALEATI, G. 'Tre secoli all'interno di una *possessio* ecclesiastico (Portalbera sec. XVI–XVIII)', in *Boll. Stor. Pavese*, 1948.

BARBIERI, G. 'Notizie sui beni ecclesiastici in Puglia fra il XIII e XIV sec.', in *ES*. 1954.

BESTA, E. *Il contratto do soccida nel suo svolgimento storico*. Palermo, 1908.

BOZZOLA, A. 'Appunti sulla vita economica del Monferrato nei sec. XIV–XV', in *Boll. Stor.-Bib. Subalp.* 1923.

CAFFARO, A. 'Un documento di mezzadria del sec. XV', in *Annali Acc. Ag. Torino*, 1892.

CATUREGLI, N. 'Le condizioni della chiesa di Pisa nella seconda metà del sec. XV', in *Boll. Stor. Pisano*, 1950.

CIPOLLA, C. 'Nuove considerazioni sopra un contratto di mezzadria del sec. XV', in *Atti Mem. Acc. Ag. Sc. Lett. Verona*, 1891.

CIPOLLA, C. M. 'Une crise ignorée. Comment s'est perdue la propriété dans l'Italie du Nord entre le XIe et le XVIe siècle', in *Annales*, 1947.

DAVISO DI CHARVENSOD, M. C. 'Coltivazione e reddito della vigna a Rivoli nel sec. XIV', in *Boll. Stor.-Bib. Subalp.* 1950.

DIETZEL, H. 'Ueber Wesen u. Bedeutung des Theilbaus in Italien', in *Zeitschrift f. die gesamte Staatswissenschaft*, 1884–5.

DI TUCCI, R. 'Storia del contratto agrario in Sardegna', in *AVS*. 1936.

FERRARIS, L. 'Evoluzione della società mezzadrile', in *N. Antologia*, July–Aug. 1939.

FRANCIA, V. 'Il contratto di soccida nel Bolognese nei sec. XIII e XIV', in *Arch. Giuridico*, 1922.

IMBERCIADORI, I. 'Il catasto senese del 1316', in *AVS*. 1939.

—— *Mezzadria classica toscana con documentazione inedita dal IX al XIV sec.* Florence, 1951.

—— 'I due poderi di B. Machiavelli ovvero mezzadria poderale nel '400', in *Studi in onore di A. Sapora*, II, Milan, 1957.

—— 'Proprietà terriera di Fr. Datini e parziaria mezzadrile nel '400', in *ES*. 1958.

JONES, P. J. 'A Tuscan monastic lordship in the later Middle Ages: Camaldoli', in *J. Eccl. Hist*. 1954.

—— 'Le finanze della badia cistercense di Settimo nel XIV sec.', in *Riv. Stor. Chiesa in It.* 1956.

LAZZARINI, V. 'Beni carraresi e proprietari veneziani', in *Studi in onore di G. Luzzatto*, I, Milan, 1950.

LECCE, M. *I beni terrieri del mon. di S. Michele in Campagna*. Verona, 1953.

—— 'I beni terrieri di un antico Istituto ospitaliero Veronese (sec. XII–XVIII)', in *Studi in onore di A. Fanfani*, III, Milan, 1962.

LECCISOTTI, T. *Le colonie cassinesi in Capitanata*. 3 vols. Montecassino, 1937–40.

LI GOTTI, A. 'Note sulla chiesa di S. Niccolò', in *Arch. Stor. Siciliano*, 1956.

LUZZATTO, M. 'Contributo alla storia della mezzadria nel medio evo', in *N. Riv. Stor*. 1948.

MARTINELLI, A. 'Origini e sviluppo della mezzadria in provincia di Reggio Emilia', in *Riv. di Ec. Agrar*. 1957.

NASALLI ROCCA, E. 'Soccide e contratti medioevali su bestiame nella regione piacentina', in *AVS*. 1939.

—— 'Per la storia del diritto agrario nel territorio piacentino. Un contratto duecentesco di colonia parziaria', in *Boll. Stor. Piacentino*, 1943.

PERUSINI, G. *I contratti agrari nel Friuli durante il dominio veneto*. Rome, 1939.

—— 'Consuetudini agrarie friulane del sec. XV', in *Lares*, 1942.

—— 'Il contratto di soccida in Friuli', in *AVS*. 1943.

RICCARDI, A. 'Le località e territori di S. Colombano', in *Arch. Stor. Lodigiano*, VII, VIII.

RICCI, A. *Storia di un comune rurale dell'Umbria (Baschi)*, (*Annali Scuola Normale di Pisa*, XXV), 1915.

RIDOLFI, L. 'Di alcune prime forme della mezzeria toscana in relazione alle sincrone pratiche culturali', in *Agric. Ital*. 1893.

ROSSI, B. 'Sopra un contratto cremonese di mezzadria del XV sec.', in *Boll. Stor. Cremonese*, 1931.

—— *Il fattore di campagna*. Rome, 1934.

SALVIOLI, G. 'La proprietà fondiaria nell'agro modenese durante l'alto medio evo', in *Atti Mem. Dep. Moden. Stor. Pat.* 1918.

STELLA, A. 'La proprietà ecclesiastica nella repubblica di Venezia dal sec. XV al XVII', in *N. Riv. Stor.* 1958.

TICCIATI, L. 'Sulle condizioni dell'agricoltura del contado cortonese nel sec. XIII', in *ASI.* 1892.

WERNER, E. 'Der florentiner Frühkapitalismus in marxistischer Sicht', in *Studi medievali*, I, 1960.

(v) *The peasantry in the later Middle Ages*

BOTTEA, T. V. 'La sollevazione dei rustici nelle valli di Non e di Sole 1525', in *Arch. Trentino*, 1882.

—— 'Le rivoluzioni delle valli del Nosio negli anni 1407 e 1477', *ibid.* 1883.

FIUMI, E. 'L'attivitá usuraria dei mercanti sangimignanesi nell'età comunale', in *ASI.* 1961.

GIULIANI, M. 'Lo scioglimento del comune di Pontremoli e la sollevazione dei villani', in *Arch. Stor. p. le prov. Parmensi*, 1952.

LEICHT, P. S. 'Un movimento agrario nel Cinquecento', in *Riv. It. Sociologia*, 1908 (reprinted in *Scritti vari*, I, Milan, 1943.

—— 'I rurali ed i parlamenti', in *Riv. Stor. Dir. It.* 1951.

MENCHETTI, A. *Storia di un comune rurale della Marca Anconitana (Montalboddo oggi Ostra)*. 2 vols., in various parts. Iesi, Macerata, Fermo, Senigallia, 1908–37.

MERLINI, D. *Saggio di ricerche sulla satira contro il villano*. Turin, 1894.

NASALI ROCCA, E. 'Prestazioni e oneri delle classi rurali nel Piacentino', in *Boll. Stor. Piacentino*, 1931–2.

—— 'I decreti signorili viscontei e sforzeschi e il diritto agrario', in *AVS.* 1937.

PALMIERI, A. 'I lavoratori del contado bolognese durante le signorie', in *Atti Mem. Dep. Stor. Pat. Romagna*, 1909–10.

—— 'Lotte agrarie bolognesi', *ibid.* 1923.

PAPALEONI, G. 'Un comune trentino al principio dell'età moderna', in *(N)AV.* 1920.

RASI, P. *Le corporazioni fra gli agricoltori*. Milan, 1940.

SALZANO, A. *Il 'Monte dei denari' e il 'Monte del grano' a Spoleto nella seconda metà del Quattrocento*. Spoleto, 1940.

SIMEONI, L. 'L'amministrazione del distretto veronese sotto gli Scaligeri', in *Atti Mem. Acc. Ag. Sc. Lett. Verona*, 1904–5.

SORBELLI, A. *Il comune rurale dell'Appennino emiliano nei sec. XIV e XV*, Bologna, 1910.

TOUBERT, P. 'Les statuts communaux et l'histoire des campagnes lombardes au XIV.[e] siècle', in *Mélanges d'archéologie et d'histoire*, 1960.

§ 3. SPAIN

I. BIBLIOGRAPHIES

AGUADO BLEYE, P. *Manual de historia de España*. 7th ed. 3 vols. Madrid, 1954.

BOISSONNADE, P. *Les études relatives a l'histoire économique de l'Espagne et leurs résultats*. Paris, 1913. (First published in *Revue de synthèse historique*, XXII (1911), 79–105, 198–227, and XXIII (1912), 75–97, 331–52.

Centro de Estudios Internacionales, Universidad de Barcelona, *Indice histórico español*. Barcelona, 1953——. A quarterly.

SÁNCHEZ ALONSO, B. *Fuentes de la historia española e hispano-americana*. 3 vols. Madrid, 1952.

II. GENERAL ECONOMIC HISTORIES

DE ASSO, IGNACIO, *Historia de la economía política de Aragón*. Saragossa, 1798; reprinted, 1947.

BARCELÓ, J. L. *Historia económica de Espana*. Madrid, 1952.

COLMEIRO, M. *Historia de la economía política en España*. 2 vols. Madrid, 1863.

VICENS VIVES, J. *Historia social y económica de España y América*. 5 vols. Barcelona, 1957–9.

The following works in English may also be consulted:

BOISSONNADE, P. *Life and Work in Medieval Europe.* London, 1927.

Cambridge Medieval History, VI (1936), chap. 12, and VII (1949), chap. 20. (Articles by Rafael de Altamira).

MERRIMAN, R. B. *The Rise of the Spanish Empire*, I (New York, 1918).

PIRENNE, H. *Economic and Social History of Medieval Europe.* London, 1936.

THOMPSON, J. W. *An Economic and Social History of the Middle Ages*, 300–1300. London, 1928.

——— *Economic and Social History of Europe in the Later Middle Ages*, 1300–1530. London, 1931.

III. SEIGNORIAL REGIMES

BENEYTO, J. *Del feudo a la economía nacional.* Madrid, 1953.

Comunicaciones del IV Congreso de Historia de la Corona de Aragón, I (Palma de Mallorca, 1959).

DE LA ESCOSURA Y HEVIA, ANTONIO. *Juicio crítico del feudalismo en España.* Madrid, 1856.

ESCUELA DE ESTUDIOS MEDIEVALES. *La reconquista española y la repoblación del país.* Saragossa, 1951.

FONT RIUS, J. M. *Instituciones medievales españolas.* Madrid, 1949.

——— 'La comarca de Tortosa a raíz de la reconquista cristiana', in *Cuadernos de historia de España*, XIX (1953), 104–126.

GARCÍA DE VALDEAVELLANO, L. 'El prestimonio: contribución al estudio de las manifestaciones del feudalismo en los reinos de León y Castilla durante la edad media', in *Anuario de historia del derecho español*, XXV (1955), 5–122.

GARCÍA RIVES, A. 'Clases sociales en León y Castilla', in *Revista de archivos, bibliotecas y museos*, XLI (1920), 233–52, 372–93, and XLII (1921), 19–36, 157–67.

DE HINOJOSA Y NAVEROS, EDUARDO. *El régimen señorial y la cüestión agraria en Cataluña durante la edad media.* Madrid, 1905. (Republished with other medieval studies in Hinojosa's *Obras*. 2 vols. Madrid, 1948 and 1955).

MAYER, E. *Historia de las instituciones sociales y políticas de España y Portugal durante los siglos V a XIV.* 2 vols. Madrid, 1925–6.

PUYOL Y ALONSO, J. *El abadengo de Sahagún: contribución al estudio del feudalismo en España.* Madrid, 1915.

SÁNCHEZ ALBORNOZ, C. 'Estudios de alta edad media: la potestad real y los señoríos en Asturias, León y Castilla', in *Revista de archivos, bibliotecas y museos*, XXXI (1914), 263–90.

——— 'Las behetrías: la encomendación en Asturias, León y Castilla', in *Anuario de historia del derecho español*, I (1924), 158–336.

——— 'Muchas páginas más sobre las behetrías', in *Anuario de historia del derecho español*, IV (1927), 5–157.

——— *En torno a los orígenes del feudalismo.* 3 vols. Mendoza, Argentina, 1942.

VERLINDEN, C. 'La grande peste de 1348 en Espagne', in *Revue belge de philologie et d'histoire*, XVII (1938), 103–46.

——— *L'esclavage dans l'Europe médiávale*, I: *Péninsule Ibérique-France.* Bruges, 1955.

VILAR, P. 'La déclin catalan du Bas Moyen-Age', in *Estudios de Historia Moderna*, VI (Barcelona, 1961), 1–68.

VICENS VIVES, J. *Historia de los remensas en el siglo XV.* Barcelona, 1945.

——— *El gran sindicato remensa*, 1488–1508. Madrid, 1954.

IV. COLLECTIONS OF DOCUMENTS

Boletín de la Real Academia de Historia. Madrid, 1877———.

Colección de documentos inéditos del Archivo General de la Corona de Aragón, VIII (Barcelona, 1847).

Cortes de los antiguos reinos de Aragón y de Valencia y Principado de Cataluña. 26 vols. Madrid, 1896–1922.

Cortes de los antiguos reinos de León y Castilla. 5 vols. Madrid, 1861–1903.

España sagrada, I (Madrid, 1866).

DE FLORANES, R. 'Apuntamientos curiosos sobre behetrías, su condición y privilegios y modo de hacer en ellas las filiaciones', in *Colección de documentos inéditos para la historia de España*, XX (Madrid, 1852), 407–502.

V. AGRICULTURE AND GRAZING

HERRERA, G. A. *Agricultura general.* 4 vols. Madrid, 1818–19. (First published in 1513).

BALARI Y JOVANY, J. *Orígenes históricos de Cataluña.* Barcelona, 1899.

CAVANILLES, A. J. *Observaciones sobre la historia natural, geografía, agricultura, población y frutos del Reyno de Valencia.* 2 vols. Madrid, 1795–7.

HAMILTON, EARL J. *Money, Prices, and Wages in Valencia, Aragon and Navarre, 1351–1500.* Cambridge, Mass. 1936.

KLEIN, JULIUS. *The Mesta.* Cambridge, Mass. 1920.

LAPORTA, F. L. *Historia de la agricultura española.* Madrid, 1798.

VICENS VIVES, J. *Historia social y ecónomica de España*, esp. II, 223–284.

ZACARIA, ABU. *Libro de agricultura.* 2 vols. Madrid, 1802 (A twelfth-century work translated by J. A. Banqueri).

§4. THE LANDS EAST OF THE ELBE AND GERMAN COLONIZATION EASTWARDS

A revision of the bibliography of the First Edition, by ERNST BIRKE.

APPELT, HEINRICH. 'Die Leubuser Gründungsurkunde und die Anfänge des mittelalterlichen Deutschtums in Schlesien', in *Schlesien, Jg.* 1/1956, 251–7.

AUBIN, GUSTAV. 'Die historische Entwicklung der ostdeutschen Agrarverfassung und ihre Beziehung zum Nationalitätenproblem der Gegenwart', in *Der ostdeutsche Volksboden. Aufsätze zu den Fragen des Ostens*, ed. W. Volz, enlarged edition, Breslau, 1926, 340–74.

—— *Zur Geschichte des gutsherrlich-bäuerlichen Verhältnisses in Ostpreussen von der Gründung des Ordensstaates bis zur Steinschen Reform.* Leipzig, 1910.

—— 'Das Werden der ostdeutschen Wirtschaft', in *Der deutsche Osten. Seine Geschichte, sein Wessen und seine Aufgabe*, ed. K. C. Thalheim and A. Hillen Ziegfeld, Berlin, 1936, 425–43.

AUBIN, HERMANN. 'Wirtschaftsgeschichtliche Bemerkungen zur ostdeutschen Kolonisation', in *Sozial- und Wirtschaftsgeschichte, Gedächtnisschrift für G. v. Below*, Stuttgart, 1929: *Von Raum und Grenzen des deutschen Volkes, Studien zur Volksgeschichte*, Breslauer Historische Forschungen, VI, Breslau, 1938.

—— 'Die Wirtschaft im Mittelalter', in *Geschichte Schlesiens*, I, 1938.

—— 'Zur Erforschung der deutschen Ostbewegung', in *Deutsche Schriften zur Landes- und Volksforschung*, II, Leipzig, 1939.

BENDIXEN, JENS ANDREAS. 'Verlagerung und Strukturwandel ländlicher Siedlungen. Ein Beitrag zur Siedlungsgeographie ausgehend von Untersuchungen in der südlichen Priegnitz', in *Schriften des Geographischen Instituts der Universität Kiel*, ed. O. Schmieder, H. Wenzel and H. Wilhelmy, VII, Kiel, 1937.

BERNARD, WALTER. *Das Waldhufendorf in Schlesien.* 1931.

BOSSE, HEINRICH. 'Der livländische Bauer am Ausgang der Ordenszeit', in *Mitteilg. für livländische Geschichte*, XXIV, 1933, 281 ff.

BRAND, H. *Die Übertragung altdeutscher Siedlungsformen in das ostholsteinische Kolonisationsgebiet. Im Rahmen einer Entwicklungsgeschichte ländlicher Siedlungen des oldenburgischen Landesteiles Lübeck.* Kiel, 1933.

BROSCH, FRANZ. 'Siedlungsgeschichte des Waxenbergischen Amtes Leonfelden.' Mit einem Anhang: Das Leonfeldener Urbar. Hgb. v. Erich Trinks. In *Jahrbuch des oberösterreichischen Musealvereines*, LXXXIV, Linz, 1939.

BRÜSKE, WOLFGANG. *Untersuchungen zur Geschichte des Lutizenbundes. Deutschwendische Beziehungen des 10.-12. Jahrhunderts.* Münster-Cologne, 1955. (Mitteldeutsche Forschungen, Bd. 3.)

BUJAK, FRANCISZEK. 'Stuya nad osadnictwem Malapolski', in *Rozprawy i Sprawozdania P.A.U.*, W. h.-f. XII, vol. XLVII, 176–428, Cracow, 1905.

DAME, CAI. 'Die Entwicklung des ländlichen Wirtschaftslebens in der Dresden-Meissner Elbtalgegend von der Sorbenzeit bis zum Beginn des 19. Jahrhunderts', in *Bibliothek der Sächsischen Geschichte und Landeskunde*, III, Leipzig, 1911.

'Deutschbalten und baltische Lande', in *Handwörterbuch des Grenz- und Auslanddeutschtums*, II, 1936, 104–241.

DOUBEK, F. A. and SCHMID, H. F. 'Das Schöffenbuch der Dorfgemeinde Krzemienica aus den Jahren 1451–1482. Herausgegeben, eingeleitet und bearbeitet von...', in *Quellen zur Geschichte der Rezeption*, II, Leipzig, 1931.

EBERT, WOLFGANG. *Ländliche Siedelformen im deutschen Osten.* Im Auftrag der landesgeschichtlichen Institute hrbg. v. Rudolf Kötzsche, mit 35 Kartenbildern auf 23 Tafeln. Leipzig, 1937.

ENGEL, FRANZ. 'Deutsche und slawische Einflüsse in der Dobbertiner Kulturlandschaft', in *Schriften des geographischen Institutes der Universität Kiel*, II, 3, 1934, 54 ff.

—— 'Erläuterungen zur historischen Siedlungsformenkarte Mecklenburgs und Pommerns', in *Zeitschrift für Ostforschung*, 2/1953, 208 ff.

FUCHS, C. J. 'Zur Geschichte des gutsherrlich-bäuerlichen Verhältnisses in der Mark Brandenburg', in *ZSS.*, Germanic Section, XI, 1891, 17 ff.

GAUSE, FRITZ. 'Die Gründung der Stadt Königsberg im Zusammenhang der Politik des Ordens und der Stadt Lübeck', in *Zeitschrift für Ostforschung* III, 1954, 517–36.

Geschichte Schlesiens. Herausgegeben von der Historischen Kommission für Schlesien unter Leitung von Hermann Aubin. 1, Von der Urzeit bis zum Jahre 1526. Breslau, 1938. 3. Aufl. Stuttgart, 1961. See von Loesch, Heinrich, 'Die Verfassung im Mittelalter', 242–321; Aubin, Hermann, 'Die Wirtschaft im Mittelalter', 322–87.

GLEY, WERNER. 'Die Besiedlung der Mittelmark von der slawischen Einwanderung bis 1624', in *Forschungen zum Deutschtum der Ostmarken*, II, 1, 1926.

GUTTMANN, BERNHARD. 'Die Germanisierung der Slawen in der Mark', in *Forschungen zur brandenburgischen und preussischen Geschichte*, IX, 395 ff.

HAMPE, KARL. 'Der Zug nach dem Osten', in *Natur und Geisteswelt*, DCCXXXI, 4th ed. Leipzig, 1939.

HEILSBERG, F. 'Geschichte der Kolonisation des Waldviertels', in *Jahrbuch für Landeskunde Niederösterreichs*, 1907.

HELLMANN, MANFRED. 'Herrschaftliche und genossenschaftliche Elemente in der mittelalterlichen Verfassungsgeschichte der Slawen', in *Zeitschrift für Ostforschung*, VII, 1958, 321–38.

HTADYLOWICZ, KONSTANTY JERZY. Zmiany krajobrazu i rozwój osadnictwa w Wielkopolsce od XIV do XIX wieku. Przedm. napisat Franciszek Bujak. (With synopsis in French.) In *Badania z dziejów spolecznich i gospodarczych*, XII, Lwów, 1932.

JOHANSEN, PAUL. 'Siedlung und Agrarwesen der Esten im Mittelalter', in *Verhandlungen der Gelehrten Estnischen Gesellschaft*, XXIII, Leipzig, 1925.

JORDAN, KARL. *Die Bistumsgründingen Heinrichs des Löwen.* Leipzig, 1939.

KAINDL, RAIMUND FRIEDRICH. *Geschichte der Deutschen in den Karpathenländern.* 3 vols. (Deutsche Landesgeschichten, VIII.) Gotha, 1907–11.

KASER, HANS. 'Der Volks- und Kulturboden des Slowakeideutschtums. Beiträge zur Siedlungsgeographie', in *Schriften des Osteuropa-Institutes in Breslau*, New Series, II, 1934.

KAPRAS, JAN. 'Velkostatky a fideikomisy v českém státě', in *Zvl. otisek z Právních Rozhledů*, Prague, 1918.

KASISKE, KARL. 'Die Siedlungstätigkeit des deutschen Ordens im östlichen Preussen bis zum Jahr 1410', in *Einzelschriften der Historischen Kommission für ost- und westpreussische Landesforschungen*, I, 1934.

—— 'Das Deutsche Siedelwerk des Mittelalters in Pomerellen', in *ibid.* VI, 1939.

KLAAR, ADALBERT. 'Die Siedlungstypen Niederösterreichs', in *Jahrbücher für Landeskunde Niederösterreichs*, New Series, XXIII, Vienna, 1930.

—— 'Die Siedlungsformen des oberösterreichischen Mühlviertels und des böhmischen Grenzgebietes', in *Deutsches Archiv für Landes- und Volksforschung*, XI, 1937, 131 ff.

KNAPP, GEORG FRIEDRICH. *Die Bauernbefreiung und der Ursprung der Landarbeiter in den älteren Teilen Preussens.* 2 vols. Leipzig, 1887.

—— *Grundherrschaft und Rittergut.* Leipzig, 1897.

KOEBNER, RICHARD. 'Deutsches Recht und deutsche Kolonisation in den Piastenländern', in *VSWG.* XXV, 1932, 313 ff.

—— 'Lokativ. Zur Begriffssprache der deutschen Kolonisation.' Offprint from *Zeitschrift des Vereins für Geschichte Schlesiens,* LXIII, Görlitz, 1929.

KÖTZSCHKE, PAUL RICHARD. *Das Unternehmertum in der ostdeutschen Kolonisation des Mittelalters.* Leipzig, 1894.

KÖTZSCHKE, RUDOLF and EBERT, WOLFGANG. *Geschichte der ostdeutschen Kolonisation.* Leipzig, 1937.

KÖTZSCHKE, RUDOLF. *Quellen zur Geschichte der ostdeutschen Kolonisation im 12. bis 14. Jahrhundert.* (Quellensammlung zur Deutschen Geschichte.) 1931, 159, 5th ed. 1935.

KRENZLIN, ANNELIESE. *Dorf, Feld und Wirtschaft im Gebiete der grossen Täler und Platten östlich der Elbe.* Remagen, 1952. (Forschungen zur deutschen Landeskunde, Bd. 70.)

KROFTA, KAMIL. *Prehled deějin selského stavu v Čechach a na Moravě.* Prague, 1912.

KUHN, WALTER. 'Das Spätmittelalter als technisches Zeitalter', in *Ostdeutsche Wissenschaft, Jahrbuch des ostdeutschen Kulturrates,* I, Munich, 1954, 69–93.

—— *Siedlungsgeschichte Oberschlesiens,* Würzburg, 1954. (Veröffentlichungen der Oberschlesischen Studienhilfe 4.)

—— 'Die Entstehung des mittelalterlichen schlesischen Kraftfeldes', in *Schlesien,* I/1956, 158–67.

—— 'Die deutsche Ostsiedlung vom Mittelalter bis zum 18. Jh.', in *Das östliche Deutschland, ein Handbuch hrsg. vom Göttinger Arbeitskreis.* Würzburg, 1959, 165–238.

LATZKE, WALTER. 'Die Besiedlung des Oppalandes im 12. und 13. Jahrhundert', in *Zeitschrift des Vereins für Geschichte Schlesiens* (1938), LXXVII, 44 ff.

LEHMANN, RUDOLF. 'Geschichte des Wendentums in der Niederlausitz bis 1815 im Rahmen der Landesgeschichte', in *Die Wenden. Forschungen zu Geschichte und Volkstum der Wenden,* II, 1930.

LEIPOLDT, JOHANNES. *Die Geschichte der ostdeutschen Kolonisation im Vogtland auf der Grundlage der Siedlungsformenforschung.* Plauen, 1927.

VON LOESCH, HEINRICH. 'Die Verfassung im Mittelalter', in *Geschichte Schlesiens,* I, 1938, 3, 1961.

LUDAT, HERBERT. 'Der Ursprung der ostdeutschen Wieken', in *VSWG.* XXIX, 1936, 114 ff.

—— 'Die ältesten geschichtlichen Grundlagen für deutsch-slawische Verhältnisse', in *Das östliche Deutschland,* Würzburg, 1959, 127–64.

—— *Vorstufen und Entstehung des Städtewesens in Osteuropa.* Cologne, 1955. (Osteuropa und der deutsche Osten, H. 3.)

—— 'Die Bezeichnung für "Stadt" im Slawischen', in *Syntagma Friburgense. Historische Studien, Hermann Aubin dargebracht zum 70. Geburtstag.* Lindau, 1956, 107–23.

LÜCK, KURT. 'Deutsche Aufbaukräfte in der Entwicklung Polens', in *Ostdeutsche Forschungen,* IV, 1934.

LÜTGE, FRIEDRICH. *Die Agrarverfassung des frühen Mittelalters im mitteldeutschen Raum, vornehmlich in der Karolingerzeit.* Jena, 1937.

MAAS, WALTHER. 'Über deutsche Dorfformen in Posen und die deutsche Sprachgrenze daselbst', in *Zeitschrift des Vereins für Volkskunde,* XXXIX, New Series, I, 1930, 274 ff.

MALECZINSKI, KAROL. 'Najstarsze targi w Polsce i stosunek ich do miast przed kolonizacyą na prawie niemieckiem', in *Studya nad historyą prawa polskiego,* 10, I, Lvov, 1926. Also in German: *Die ältesten Märkte in Polen und ihr Verhältnis zu den Städten vor der Kolonisierung nach deutschem Recht*; and appended: Zygmunt Wojciechowski, 'Die ältesten Märkte in Polen, kritisch-polemische Bemerkungen'; with reply by Maleczinski, Breslau, 1930.

VON MAYDELL, KURT. 'Forschungen zur Siedlungsgeschichte und zu den Siedlungsformen der Sudetenländer', in *Deutsches Archiv für Landes- und Volksforschung*, II,
1938, 212 ff.

MEITZEN, AUGUST. *Siedlung und Agrarwesen der West- und Ostgermanen, der Kelten,
Römer, Finnen und Slawen.* 3 vols. and Atlas. Berlin, 1893–6.

—— 'Urkunden schlesischer Dörfer. Zur Geschichte der ländlichen Verhältnisse und
der Flureinteilung insbesondere', in *Codex diplomaticus Silesiae*, IV, Breslau, 1863.

MORTENSEN, HANS and GERTRIUD. 'Die Besiedlung des nordöstlichen Ostpreussen bis
zum Beginn des 17. Jahrhunderts.' 1st and 2nd Parts. In *Deutschland und der Osten*,
VII–VIII, Leipzig, 1937–8.

NIEDERLE, LUBOR. *Manuel de l'antiquité slave*, I, II. (Collection de manuels publiées par
l'Institut d'études slaves, I, I; I, 2.) Paris, 1923, 1926.

VON NIESSEN, PAUL. *Geschichte der Neumark im Zeitalter ihrer Entstehung und Besiedlung von
den ältesten Zeiten bis zum Aussterben der Askanier.* 1905.

PETERKA, OTTO. *Rechtsgeschichte der böhmischen Länder.* 2 vols. 1923–8.

PFITZNER, JOSEF. *Besiedlungs- Verfassungs- und Verwaltungsgeschichte des Breslauer Bistums-
landes.* 1926.

—— 'Zur deutsch-slawischen Siedlungsgeschichte Meckelenburgs und Ostholsteins im
Mittelalter', in *Jahrbücher für Kultur und Geschichte der Slawen*, New Series, IX, 1933,
185 ff.

PLEHN, HANS. 'Die Besiedlung des Ordenslandes Preussen', in *Deutsche Erde*, II, 1903,
99 ff.

POTKAŃSKI, K. 'O pochodzeniu wsi polskiej', in *Ognisko*, 1903, No. 10.

RIEL, KLAUS. 'Die Siedlungstätigkeit des Deutschen Ordens in Preussen in der Zeit von
1410–66', in *Altpreussische Forschungen*, XIV (1937), 224–67.

RHODE, GOTTHOLD HRSG. *Die Ostgebiete des Deutschen Reiches.* 4., verb. Auflage,
Würzburg, 1957. (XVI, 336 S., 19 Karten, zahlreiche Tabellen.)

SCHILLING, FRIEDRICH. *Ursprung und Frühzeit des Deutschtums in Schlesien und im Land
Leubus.* Leipzig, 1938. (Ostdeutsche Forschungen, IV–V, 524.)

SCHIER, BRUNO. 'Hauslandschaften und Kulturbewegungen im östlichen Mitteleuropa'
in *Beiträge zur sudetendeutschen Volkskunde*, XXI, 1932.

SCHLEINITZ, HELLMUT. *Besiedlung und Bevölkerung der südlichen Grenzmark.* (Sonderheft
der Grenzmärkischen Heimatblätter.) 1936.

SCHLENGER, HERBERT. 'Formen ländlicher Siedlungen in Schlesien.' (Beiträge zur
Morphologie der schlesischen Kulturlandschaft.) In *Veröffentlichungen der Schlesischen
Gesellschaft f. Erdkunde u. d. Geographischen Instituts der Universität Breslau*, X,
Breslau, 1930.

SCHLESINGER, WALTER. 'Die deutsche Kirche im Sorbenland und die Kirchenverfassung
auf westslawischem Boden', in *Zeitschrift für Ostforschung*, I, 1952, 345–71.

—— 'Der Osten', in *Bruno Gebhardt: Handbuch der deutschen Geschichte*. Bd. 2: Von der
Reformation bis zum Ende des Absolutismus, 16. bis. 18. Jh. hrsg. v. Herbert
Grundmann, Stuttgart, 1955.

—— 'Die geschichtliche Stellung der mittelalterlichen deutschen Ostbewegung', in
HZ. 183/1957, 517–42.

SCHMID, HEINRICH FELIX. 'Die sozialgeschichtliche Erforschung der mittelalterlichen
deutschrechtlichen Siedlung auf polnischem Boden', in *VSWG*. XX, 1927, 310 ff.

SCHÜNEMANN, KONRAD. 'Zur Geschichte des deutschen Landesausbaus im Mittelalter',
in *Südostdeutsche Forschungen*, I. Jg., Munich, 1938, 30–46.

SCHULTZE, JOHANNES. 'Das Landregister der Herrschaft Sorau von 1381', in *Veröffentlichungen der historischen Kommission für die Provinz Brandenburg und die Hauptstadt
Berlin*, VIII, I. Brandenburgische Landbücher, I, Berlin, 1936.

SCHULZE, E. O. 'Die Kolonisierung und Germanisierung der Gebiete zwischen Saale und
Elbe', in *Preisschriften der fürstl. Jablonowskischen Gesellschaft*, XXXIII, 1896.

SEHRING, MAX. *Erbrecht und Agrarverfassung in Schleswig-Holstein auf geschichtlicher
Grundlage. Mit Beiträgen von R. Lerch, P. Petersen und O. Büchner.* 1908. (Die
Vererbung des ländlichen Grundbesitzes, VII.)

SELLKE. 'Die Besiedlung der Danziger Niederung im Mittelalter', in *Zeitschrift des westpreussischen Geschichtsvereins*, 1932.

SOMMERFELD, W. VON. *Geschichte der Germanisierung des Herzogtums Pommern oder Slawien bis zum Ablauf des 13. Jhs.* 1896.

TZSCHOPPE, GUSTAV-ADOLF and STENZEL, GUSTAV-ADOLF. *Urkundensammlung zur Geschichte des Ursprunges der Städte und der Einführung und Verbreitung Deutscher Kolonisten und Rechte in Schlesien und der Oberlausitz.* 1832.

TYC, THEODOR. *Początki kolonizacji wieskiej na prawie niemeckiem w Wielkopolsce.* Poznán, 1924. Also in German: *Die Anfänge der dörflichen Siedlung zu deutschem Recht in Grosspolen* (1200–1333). Breslau, 1930.

WEIZSÄCKER, WILHELM. 'Das deutsche Recht der bäuerlichen Kolonisten Böhmens und Mährens', in *Mitteilungen des Vereins für die Geschichte der Deutschen in Böhmen*, LI, 1912, 476 ff.—With bibliography. See *ibid.* LXVI, 1928, 3 ff.

WEBER, L. *Preussen vor 500 Jahren.* Danzig, 1878.

WOSTRY, WILHELM. 'Das Kolonisationsproblem', in *Mitteilungen des Vereins für die Geschichte der Deutschen in Böhmen*, LX, 1922, 1 ff. Also separately published, Prague, 1922.

ZABORSKI, BOGDAN. *O kształtach wsi w Polsce i ich rozmieszczeniu.* (With synopsis in French.) (Prace komisji etnogr. P.A.U., 1.) Cracow, 1926 (1927). Also in German: *Über Dorfformen in Polen und ihre Verbreitung.* Breslau, 1930.

ZORN, WOLFGANG. 'Deutsche und Undeutsche in der städtischen Rechtsordnung des Mittelalters in Ost-Mitteleuropa', in *Zeitschrift für Ostforschung*, I, 1952, 182–94.

§ 5. POLAND, LITHUANIA AND HUNGARY

Compiled by ALEKSANDER GIEYSZTOR.

I. POLISH TREATISES

ARNOLD, S. 'Władztwo biskupie na grodzie wolborskim w. XIII w.' [Episcopal power in the Wolborz castle in the thirteenth century], in *Rozprawy historyczne Towarzystwa Naukowego Warszawskiego*, I, Warsaw, 1921.

BALZER, O. 'Niemcy w Polsce' [The Germans in Poland], in *Kwartalnik historyczny*, XXV, Lwów, 1911.

—— *Narzaz w systemie danin ksiązęcych pierwotnej Polski* ['Narzaz' 'incisio' (a tax) in the ducal tax system in early Poland]. Lwów, 1928.

BUCZEK, K. 'W sprawie interpretacji dokumentu trzebnickiego z r. 1204' [On the interpretation of the Trzebnica document of 1204], in *Przegląd Historyczny*, XLVIII, Warsaw, 1957, 38–77.

—— *Ksiązęca ludność służebna w Polsce wczesnofeudalnej* [Duke's servants—'ministeriales' in early feudal Poland]. Wrocław, 1958.

BUJAK, F. 'Studia nad osadnictwem Małopolski' [Studies in Settlements in Małopolska —Little Poland], in *Rozprawy Akademii Umiejetności, Wydział Historyczno-filozoficzny*, XLVII, Cracow, 1905.

BURSZTA, J. *Od osady słowiańskiej do wsi współczesnej. O tworzeniu się krajobrazu osadniczego ziem polskich i rozplanowań wsi* [From the Slav settlement to the today's village. Formation of the settlement landscape and of the village forms]. Wrocław, 1958.

CHMIELEWSKI, S. 'Gospodarka rolna i hodowlana w Polsce w XIV i XV w. Technika i rozmiary produkcji' [The economy of agriculture and animal breeding in Poland in the XIVth and XVth centuries (English summary, pp. 153–8)], in *Studia z dziejów gospodarstwa wiejskiego*, vol. 2, Warsaw, 1962.

DABROWSKI, H. 'Rozwøj gospodarki rolnej w Polsce od XII do połowy XIV wieku' [Development of agricultural economy in Poland from the twelfth to the middle of the fourteenth century (English summary, pp. 131–36)], in *Studia z dziejów gospodarstwa wiejskiego*, vol. 2, Warsaw, 1962.

DEMBINSKA, M. *Konsumcja zywnościowa w Polsce średniowiecznej* [Food consumption in mediaeval Poland]. Wrocław, 1963.

DOBROWOLSKA, M. *Przemiany środowiska geograficznego Polski do XV w.* [Transformations of the geographical Polands environment to the 15th century]. Warsaw, 1961.

GĄSIOROWSKI, A. 'Ze studiów nad szerzeniem się tzw. prawa niemieckiego we wsiach ziemi krakowkiej i sandomierskiej do r. 1333' [The extension of the Teutonic law in the villages of the Cracow and Sandomierz lands until 1333], in *Roczniki Historyczne*, XXVI, Posen, 1960, 123–70.

GIEYSZTOR, A. 'W sprawie początków trójpolówki w Polsce i w krajach sasiednich' [On the beginnings of three fields system in Poland and the neighbour lands], in *Prace z dziejów Polski feudalnej ofiarowane Romanowi Grodeckie mu w 70 rocznicę urodzin*, Warsaw, 1960, 71–9.

GRODECKI, R. 'Książęca włość trzebnicka na tle majątków książęcych w Polsce XII w. [The Duke's estate at Trzebnica in the organization of Duke's estates in Poland in the Twelfth century], in *Kwartalnik historyczny*, XXVI–XXVII, Lwów, 1912–13.

—— *Początki immunitetu w Polsce* [The beginnings of immunity in Poland]. Lwów, 1930.

KACZMARCZYK, K. 'Ciężary ludności wiejskiej i miejskiej na prawie niolmieckim w Pesce XIII i XIV w.' [The taxation of the rural and urban population under German law in thirteenth and fourteenth century Poland], in *Przegląd historyczny*, XI, Warsaw, 1911.

KAINDI, R. F. *Geschichte der Deutschen in Galizien bis 1772*. Gotha, 1907.

KORTA, W. 'Rozwój terytorialny wielkiej świeckiej własności feudalnej w Polsce do połowy XIII wieku' [Territorial development of the great lay estates in Poland to the middle of the XIII century], in *Sobótka*, XVI, Wrocław, 1961, 528–66.

LADOGÓRSKI, T. *Studia nad zaludnieniem Polski XIV w.* [Studies on population of Poland in the 14th century]. Breslau, 1958.

LOWMIANSKI, H. *Podstawy gospodarcze formowania się państw słowiańskich* [The economic basis of early Slav States]. Warsaw, 1953.

—— 'Zagadnienie niewolnictwa u Slowian we wczesnym średniowieczu' [Problems of slavery among Slavs in the early middle ages], in *Pamietnik VIII powszechnego zjazdu historyków polskich*, I, Warsaw, 1958, 36–69.

—— 'Economic Problems of the Early Feudal Polish State', in *Acta Poloniae Historica*, III, Wrocław–Warsaw, 1960, 7–32.

LUDAT, H. *Bistum Lebus, Studien zur Gründungsfrage und zur Entstehung und Wirtschaftsgeschichte seiner schlesisch-polnischer Besitzungen*. Weimar, 1942.

MASŁOWSKI, J. 'Kolonizacja wiejska na prawie niemieckim w wojewodztwach sieradzkim, łęczyckim, na Kujawach i w ziemi dobrzynskiej do r. 1370' [Rural colonisation under German law in the voivodeships of Sieradz and Łęczyca in Kujawy and the Dobrzyn district up to 1370], in *Roczniki historyczne*, XIII, Posen, 1937.

MATUSZEWSKI, J. *Immunitet ekonomiczny w dobrach kościoła w Polsce do roku 1381* [Economic immunity in church lands in Poland to the year 1381]. Posen, 1936.

MODZELEWSKI, K. 'Z badań nad organizacją służebna w Polsce wczesnofeudalnej' [On the organisation of 'ministeriales' in the early feudal Poland], in *Kwartalnik historii kultury materialnej*, IX Warsaw, 1961, 703–42.

PODWIŃSKA, Z. *Technika uprawy roli w Polsce średniowiecznej* [Technique of soil cultivation in mediaeval Poland (English summary, pp. 362–71)]. Breslau–Warsaw, 1962.

POPPE, D. 'Ludność dziesiętnicza w Polsce wczesnosredniowiecznej' [The 'decimi' in early mediaeval Poland], in *Kwartalnik Historyczny*, LXIV, Warsaw, 1957, no. 1, 3–31.

RUTKOWSKI, J. *Histoire économique de la Pologne avant les partages*. Paris, 1927.

—— *Historia gospodarcza Polski (do 1864)* [Economic history of Poland to 1864]. Warsaw, 1953.

RUTKOWSKA-PŁACHCIŃSKA, A. 'W sprawie charakteru rezerwy pańskiej w okresie gospodarki czynszowej' [On the manorial reserve in the censive economy], in *Przeglad Historyczny*, XLVIII, 1957, 412–35.

—— *Sadeczyzna w XIII i XIV wieku. Przemiany gospodarcze i społeczne* [The land of Sącz in the thirteenth and fourteenth centuries. Economic and social transformations (German summary, pp. 185–187)]. Wrocław–Warasw, 1961.

SCHMID, H. F. 'Die Sozialgeschichtliche Erforschung der mittelalterlichen deutschrecht-lichen Siedlungen auf polnischen Boden', in *VSWG.* xx, 1927.

SCZANIECKI, M. *Nadania ziemi na rzecz rycerzy w Polsce do końca XIII w.* [Grants of land to 'milites' in Poland up to the 13th century]. Posen, 1938.

SEMKOWICZ, W. 'Włodycy polscy na tle porównawczym słowianskim' [Polish lower gentry against the comparative Slavonic background], in *Kwartalnik historyczny,* xxII, Lwow, 1908.

STRZEMSKI, M. 'Przemiany środowiska geograficznego Polski jako tła przyrodniczego rozwoju rolnictwa na ziemiach polskich od połowy trzeciego tysiaclecia p.n. do naszych czasów' [Changes in the Polish geographical environment as a natural background of the development of agriculture in Poland, since the middle of the third millenium B.C. up to now], in *Kwartalnik historii kultury material nej,* ix, Warsaw, 1961, 331–57.

SZELAGOWSKI, A. *Chłopi dziedzice we wsiach na prawie polskim do końka XIII w.* [Peasant haeredes in the villages under Polish law to the end of the thirteenth century]. Lwów, 1900.

TRAWKOWSKI, S. *Gospodarka wielkiej własności cysterskiej na dolnym Slasku w XIII wieku* [The economy of Cistercian estates in the Lower Silesia (French Summary, pp. 183–90)]. Warsaw, 1959.

TYC, T. *Die Anfänge der dörflichen Siedlung zu deutschem Recht in Grosspolen* (1200–1333). Breslau, 1930.

TYMIENIECKI, K. 'Majętność książęca w Zagościu' [Ducal estate in Zagość], in *Rozprawy Akademii Umiejętności Wydział Historyczno-filozoficzny,* LV, Cracow, 1912.

—— *Procesy twórcze formowania się społeczeństwa polskiego w. wiekach średnich* [Creative processes in the formation of Polish society in the Middle Ages]. Warsaw, 1921.

—— 'Z dziejów zaniku drobnej własności na Slasku w xiii w.' [On the history of the disappearance of the small estate in Silesia in the thirteenth century], in *Księga pamiątkowa ku czci Balzera,* II, Lwów, 1925.

—— *Z dziejów rozwoju wielkiej własności na Śląsku w XIII w.* [On the history of the development of the large estate in Silesia in the thirteenth century]. Posen, 1926.

—— *Pisma wybrane* [Selected studies]. Warsaw, 1956.

TYMIENIECKI, K. *Smardowie polscy* [The Polish 'smard']. Posen, 1959.

WOJCIECHOWSKI, Z. 'La condition des nobles et le problème de la féodalité en Pologne au moyen-âge', in *Revue historique du droit français et étranger,* xv–xvi, Paris, 1936–7.

WOLFARTH, W. *Ascripticii w Polsce* ['Ascripticii' in Poland (French summary, pp. 248–53)]. Wrocław-Cracow, 1959.

II. SOURCES

Codex diplomaticus catedralis ad S. Venceslaum 1166–1423, (Monumenta medii aevi historica res gestas Poloniae illustrantia edit. Coll. hist. Acad. lit. cracoviensis I, vIII.), ed. F. Piekosiński. Cracow, 1879, 1882.

Codex diplomaticus et commemorationum Masoviae generalis I (ad 1247), ed. J. Kochanowski. Warsaw, 1919.

Codex diplomaticus Majoris Poloniae ad a. 1136, *usque ad a.* 1597, ed. E. Raczyński. Posen, 1840.

Codex diplamaticus nec non epistolaris Silessae, U–II, 961–1220, ed. K. Maleczyriski, Wrocław, 1956–9.

Codex diplomaticus Majoris Poloniae (984–1444). ed. I. Zakrewski, F. Piekosiński. 5 vols. Posen, 1877–1908.

Codex diplomaticus monasterii Tinecensis 1105–1506, ed. W. Ketrzyński and S. Smolka. Lwów, 1875.

Codex diplomaticus Poloniae Minoris 1178–1450, (Mon. med. aevi III, ix, x, xvII.) ed. F. Piekosiński, 4 vols. Cracow, 1876–1905.

Codex diplomaticus prussicus (1148–1404), ed. J. Voigt, 6 vols. Königsberg, 1836–61.

Codex diplomaticus Silesiae, vols. 1, 2, 4, 6, 10, 14. Breslau, 1827 *seq.*

Codex diplomaticus Warmiensis. (Monumenta hist. Warmien. I, II, v, ix.) Braunsberg, 1860–1906.

Diplomata monasterii Clarae Tumbae, ed. E. Janota. Cracow, 1865.

Kodeks dyplomatyczny Księstwa Mazowieckiego (1196–1506) [Diplomatic codex of the Duchy of Mazovia, 1196–1506], ed. J. T. Lubomirski. Warsaw, 1862.

KOZTOWSKA-BUDKOWA, Z. *Repertorium polskich dokumentów doby piastowskiej* [Repertory of Polish documents of the Piast era]. Cracow, 1937.

Księga Henrykowska, ed. R. Grodecki. Posen–Wrocław, 1949.

Liber fundationis claustri S. Mariae Virginis in Heinrichow (1259–1310), ed. G. S. Stenzel. Breslau, 1854.

Monumenta Poloniae Historica, I–VI, ed. anast. Warsaw, 1960–1.

Najstarszy zwód prawa polskiego [The oldest Polish common law] ed. J. Matuszewski. Warsaw, 1959.

Pomerellisches Urkunkenbuch, ed. M. Perlbach, 2 vols. Danzig, 1881–2.

Urkundensammlung zur Geschichte des Fürstentums Öls (1149–1493), ed. W. Häusler. Breslau, 1883.

Zbiór dokumentów małopolskich [Collection of the Little Poland charters], I, 1257–1420, II, 1421–1441, ed. S. Kuraś, Cracow, 1962–3.

III. LITHUANIA, TREATISES

AVIZONIS, K. *Die Entstehung und Entwicklung des litauischen Adels bis zur litauisch-polnischen Union* 1385. Berlin, 1932.

CONZE, W. *Agrarverfassung und Bevölkerung in Litauen und Weissrussland*. Leipzig, 1940.

DUNDULIENE, P. 'Zemledelie v Litve v epokhu feodalizma' [Agriculture in the feudal Lithuania], in *Trudy Instituta Etnografii*, XXXII, Moscow, 1956, 3–47.

IVINSKIS, Z. *Geschichte des Bauernstandes in Litauen von den ältesten Zeiten bis zum Anfang des 16 Jahrh.* Berlin, 1933.

JURGINIS, J. 'Zemledelie i technika selskogo: :khoziaistva Litvy' [Agriculture and her technique in Lithuania], in *Lietuvos TSR Mokslu Akademijos Darbai*, A 1, Vilnius, 1955, 99–132.

KAMIENIECKI, W. 'Rozwój własności na Litwie w dobie przed pierwszym statutem' [The development of property in Lituania in the period before the first statute], in *Rozprawy Akademii Umiejetności. Wydzial Historyczno-filozoficzny*, LVII, Cracow, 1914.

—— *Społeczeństwo litewskie w XV wieku* [The Lithuanian society in the 15th century]. Warsaw, 1947.

KUTRZEBA, S. *Historia ustroju Polski w zarysie*, I, II, Litwa [A history of the Polish constitution in outline, vol. II, Lituania]. Lwów, 1921.

ŁOWMIAŃSKI, H. *Studia nad początkami społeczeństwa i państwa litewskiego* [A Study of the beginnings of Lituanian society and nobility], I–II, Wilno, 1931–2.

—— 'Z zagadnień spornych społeczeństwa litewskiego wieków średnich' [Some controvertible problems of the Lithuanian mediaeval society], in *Przeglad Historyczny*, XL, Warsaw, 1950, 96–127.

OCHMANSKI, J. 'Rolnictwo na Litwie feudalnej w świetle nowszych badań' [Agriculture in the feudal Lithuania in the light of the new research], in *Kwartalnik historii kultury materialnej*, IX, Warsaw, 1961, 819–26.

PASHUTO, V. T. *Obrazovanie litovskogo gosudarstva* [The Origins of the Lithuanian State]. Moscow, 1959.

IV. LITHUANIA, SOURCES

Akty Litovskoj Metriki [Lithuanian Chancery papers], I, 1/1413–98, ed. F. I. Leontovitch. Warsaw, 1896.

Akty otnosiachtchiesie k istorii Iuzhnoi i Zapadnoi Rosii [South and West Russia Papers], I, 1361–1506, ed. N. Kostomarov. St Petersburg, 1863.

Akty otnosiashtchiesia k istorii Zapadnoi Rossii [West Russia papers], I, 1340–1506, ed. I. Gregorovitch. St Petersburg, 1846.

Archiwum książąt Lubartowiczów-Sanguszków w Slawucie [Archives of the princes, Lubartowicz-Sanguszko in Slawucie], I–III. Lwów, 1887–90.

Arkheograficeskii sbornik dokumentov otnosiachtchikhsia k istorii Severozapadnoi Rusi [Archaeo-graphical collection of North-West Russia papers]. I, Wilno, 1867.
Codex diplomaticus ecclesiae necnon dioceseos vilnensis, vol. I, fasc. I, (1387–1468), ed. J. Fijałek and W. Semkowicz. Cracow, 1932–50.
Codex diplomaticus Lithuaniae, ed. E. Raczyński. 1845.
Codex epistolaris Vitoldi, 1376–1430. (Mon. med. aevi. VI), ed. A. Prochaska. Cracow, 1882.
Skarbiec dyplomatów do dziejów Litwy, Rusi Litewskiej [The diplomats' treasure-house of the history of Lithuania, and Lithuanian Russia], ed. I. Danilowicz, 2 vols. Wilno, 1861–2.

V. HUNGARY, TREATISES

BELITZKY, J. *A magyar gabonakivitel története ioóś-ig* [History of the Hungarian export of cereals down to 1860]. Budapest, 1932.
DOMANOVSKY, A. *Geschichte Ungarns.* München, 1923.
—— *Zur Geschichte der Gutsherrschaft in Ungarn* (Festschrift Dopsch.). Vienna, 1938.
ERDÉLY, L. *Egy házi fördesur és szolgái a kózékorban* [Church property and serfs in the Middle Ages]. Budapest, 1907.
ERDUJHELYI, M. *A Kolostorok és káptalok befolyása Magayrorszég mezögazdasági fejlödésére a mohácsi vész elött* [The influence of monasteries and chapters on the agrarian evolution of Hungary before the battle of Mohács]. Budapest, 1903.
—— *Szerzeteseink mezögazdasági tevékenysége 1526 elött* [The agrarian activity of the clergy before 1526]. Budapest, 1906.
HERMANN, O. *A magyarok nagy ösfog lalkozása* [The principal primitive occupation of the Hungarians]. Budapest, 1909.
JEKELIUS, E. *Wirtschaftsgeschichte Burgenlandes.* 1909.
KAINDI, R. F. *Geschichte der Deutschen in Ungarn und Siebenbürgen bis 1763.* Gotha, 1907.
KALÁSZ, E. *A szentgotthárdi apátság birto kviszonvaiiés a cisterci rend gazdálkodása a középkorbna* [The domains of the abbey of Szentgotthard and the economic activity of the Cistercians in the Middle Ages]. Budapest, 1932.
SINKOVICS, I. *A magyar nagy birtok élete a XV század elején* [Life on great estates early in the fifteenth century]. Budapest, 1933.
SZEKFÜ, G. *Serviensek és familiarisok* [The *servientes* and the *familiares*]. Budapest, 1913.
TAGÁNY, K. 'A földközösseg története Magyarországon' [The history of communal use of land in Hungary], in the review *Magy. Gazdaságtört, Szemle*, 1894.
—— *A soltészségek történetéröl* [On the history of *scolteties*]. 1914.

Note. The above-mentioned works in Magyar were not accessible to the author. He wishes to express his thanks to Prof. Domanovsky of Budapest for information without which the composition of the Hungarian sections of this chapter would have been impossible.

ACSADY, I. *A Magyar jöbágyság története* [History of the Hungarian dependent peasants]. Budapest, 1950. Russian translation: *Istoria vengerskogo krepostnogo krestianstva*, Moscow, 1956.
LEDERER, E. 'La structure de la société hongroise du début du moyen-âge', in *Etudes historiques publiées par la Commission nationale des historines hongrois*, I, Budapest, 1960, 195–218.
GYÖRFFY, GY. 'Einwohnerzahl und Bevölkerungsdichte in Ungarn bis zum Anfang des XIV Jahrhunderts', in *Etudes historiques*, o.c., 163–95.
PACH, ZS. P. 'Das Entwicklungsniveau der feudalen Agrarverhältnisse in Ungarn in der zweiten Hälfte des XV. Jahrhundertes', in *Etudes historiques*, o.c., 387–436.

§ 6. RUSSIA

SOURCES AND LITERATURE

I. BIBLIOGRAPHIES AND OTHER GUIDES

A complete bibliography of works (including items in periodical publications) in
Russian on historical matters published in the U.S.S.R. from the Revolution of October,
1917 to 1952 is available:

Istoriya SSSR, ukazatel' sovetskoi literatury za 1917–52 *gg.*, 1 [History of the U.S.S.R., an
   index of Soviet Literature, 1917–52]. Moscow, 1956. The Appendix, with the same
   title and issued in the same year, gives details of the classification used and indexes
   of authors, commentators, editors, reviewers, and title entries, as well as personal,
   geographic and ethnic names.

A useful guide to some earlier materials of interest to economic historians, although
not primarily concerned with history, is:

ZELENIN, D. K. *Bibliograficheskii ukazatel'* [Bibliographic index] (*Zapiski po otdeleniyu
   etnografii*, 40, *vyp.* 1), Moscow, 1913.

Further guidance on published materials may be obtained from works such as:

Istochnikovedenie istorii SSSR [On sources for the history of the U.S.S.R.]. Moscow,
   1940, vol. 1 by M. N. Tikhomirov deals with the period to the end of the eighteenth
   century, and vol. 2 by S. A. Nikitin the period nineteenth century to the early
   1890's; this work is now in process of being superseded by another of the same title;
   vyp. 1, by M. N. Tikhomirov was published, Moscow, 1962.
*Istoriografiya istorii SSSR s drevneishikh vremen do Velikoi oktyabr'skoi sotsialisticheskoi
   revolyutsii* [The historiography of the history of the U.S.S.R. from ancient times to
   the Great October Socialist Revolution], Moscow, 1961.
RUBINSHTEIN, N. L. *Russkaya istoriografiya* [Russian historiography], Moscow, 1941.

Guides to major collections of archival materials include:

Arkhiv Akademii nauk SSSR, Obozrenie arkhivnykh materialov [U.S.S.R. Academy of
   Sciences Archives, Survey of archival materials], vols. 1–3, (*Trudy Arkhiva*, vyp. 1,
   5 i 9), Moscow–Leningrad, 1933–50.
Arkhivy SSSR, Leningradskoe otdelenie Tsentral'nogo istoricheskogo arkhiva [Archives of
   the U.S.S.R., Leningrad Section of the Central Historical Archives]. Leningrad,
   1933.
CHEREPNIN, L. V. *Russkie feodal'nye arkhivy XIV–XV vekov* [Russian 14th–15th cent.
   feudal archives]. 2 vols., Moscow–Leningrad, 1948–51.
Kratkii ukazatel' arkhivnykh fondov Otdela rukopisei [Brief index of the archival resources
   of the Department of Manuscripts (of the Lenin Library)]. Moscow, 1948.
KUDRYUMOV, M. G. *Opisanie aktov, khranyashchikhsya v arkhive Arkheograficheskoi
   komissii* [Description of deeds preserved in the Archeographic Commission's
   archives] (in *Letopis' zanyatii Arkheograficheskoi komissii za* 1918 *god*, vyp. 31),
   Petrograd, 1923.
Opisanie Rukopisnogo otdeleniya Biblioteki Akademii nauk SSSR [Description of the
   Manuscript Section, U.S.S.R. Academy of Sciences Library], 1, *Rukopisi*, 3,
   vyp. 1 (6 Istoriya), Leningrad, 1930.
Putevoditel' po arkhivu Leningradskogo otdeleniya Instituta istorii [Guide to the archives of
   the Leningrad Section of the Institute of History]. Moscow–Leningrad, 1958.

A useful index to the location of particular terms is:

KOCHIN, G. E. *Materialy dlya terminologicheskogo slovarya drevnei Rossii* [Materials for a
   terminological dictionary of ancient Russia]. Moscow–Leningrad, 1937.

II. CHRONICLES

Russian Chronicles are for the most part collected, and in part critically edited, in the series entitled *Polnoe sobranie russkikh letopisei* [Complete Collection of Russian Chronicles] formerly published by the Archeographic Commission founded in 1835. Since 1917 the series has been in part re-edited and publication continued by the Russian, later U.S.S.R., Academy of Sciences. English translations of two of the most important chronicles are:

CROSS, S. H. and SHERBOWITZ-WETZOR, O. P. *The Russian Primary Chronicle.* (Harvard Studies and Notes in Philology and Literature), Cambridge, Mass., 1953.

MITCHELL, R. and FORBES, N. *The Chronicle of Novgorod 1016–1471.* (Camden Third Series, xxv), London, 1914.

III. LEGAL DOCUMENTS

Acts of public law have been collected in the monumental series published by the Russian Government on the initiative of Count N. P. Rumyantsov:

Sobranie gosudarstvennykh gramot i dogovorov [Collection of State Papers and Treaties]. Four parts, 1813–28.

Acts of public and private law are to be found in the following collections published by the Archeographic Commission:

Akty arkheograficheskoi ekspeditsii [Acts of the Archeographical Expedition]. 4 vols. St Petersburg, 1836.

Akty istoricheskie [Historical Acts], 5 vols. and 12 vols. of addenda, St Petersburg, 1841–72.

Akty yuridicheskie [Legal Acts]. 1838.

Akty otnosyashchiesya do yuridicheskago byta drevnei Rossii [Acts relating to the legal life of ancient Russia]. 3 vols. 1857–84.

D'YAKONOV, M. A. *Akty, otnosyashchiesya k istorii tyaglago naseleniya* [Deeds relating to the history of the tax-paying population]. Yur'ev, 1897.

Akty Moskovskogo gosudarstva [Acts of the Moscow State]. Published by the Academy of Sciences, 3 vols. 1890–1901.

Other collections include:

Feodal'naya derevnya Moskovskogo gosudarstva XIV–XVI vv. [The feudal village of the Moscow State, 14th–16th cents., a collection of documents]. Moscow–Leningrad, 1935.

GORCHAKOV, M. *O zemel'nykh vladeniyakh vserossiiskikh mitropolitov, patriarkhov i Sv. Sinoda, 988–1738 gg.* [On the landholdings of the All-Russian Metropolitans, Patriarchs and the Holy Synod, 988–1738]. St Petersburg, 1871.

Pamyatniki istorii Velikogo Novgoroda i Pskova [Monuments relating to the history of Novgorod the Great and of Pskov]. Leningrad–Moscow, 1935.

Pamyatniki sotsial'no-ekonomicheskoi istorii Moskovskogo gosudarstva XIV–XVII vv. [Monuments relating to the social and economic history of the Moscow State, 14th–17th cents.]. vol. 1, Moscow, 1929.

Sbornik gramot Kollegii ekonomii [Collection of Papers of the Economic Collegium]. 2 vols., Moscow, 1922.

In 1949, the Institute of History, U.S.S.R. Academy of Sciences, commenced publication of series intended to include all deeds, already published or not, up to the early sixteenth century. The volumes are:

Gramoty Velikogo Novgoroda i Pskova [Papers of Novgorod the Great and of Pskov]· Moscow–Leningrad, 1949.

Dukhovnye i dogovornye gramoty velikikh i udel'nykh knyazei XIV–XVI vv. [Wills and contracts of the Grand and Apanage Princes, 14th–16th cents.], Moscow–Leningrad, 1950.

Akty feodal'nogo zemlevladeniya i khozyaistva XIV–XVI vekov [Deeds relating to feudal landowning and economy, 14th–16th cents.]. parts 1–3, Moscow, 1951–61.
Akty sotsial'no-ekonomicheskoi istorii Severo-vostochnoi Rusi kontsa XIV–nachala XVI v. [Deeds relating to the social and economic history of North-East Rus', end 14th–early 16th cents.]. 3 vols. Moscow, 1952–64.

A recent critical edition of Russian legal materials for the period to the mid-seventeenth century is to be found in fascicules 1–6 of: *Pamyatniki russkogo prava*, Moscow, 1952–7. These include the early treaties between Rus' and Byzantium, charters ascribed to Vladimir and Yaroslav, treaties of Novgorod, Pskov and Smolensk with the Germans, ecclesiastical and lay statutes, as well as the early laws known as *Russkaya Pravda* (available in a translation by G. Vernadsky found in his: *Medieval Russian Laws* (Records of civilization, Sources and Studies, XLI), New York, 1947) and the law codes of 1497, 1589 and 1649. One local statute which is included in Vernadsky's translation is available in another English version:

DEWEY, H. W. 'The White Lake Charter', in *Speculum*, XXXII, 1957, 79–83.

IV. CADASTRAL SURVEYS, ACCOUNT BOOKS

Of first-rate importance and of great value as a source of economic history are the cadastral records (the so-called *pistsoviya knigi*) which represent a combination of agricultural surveys, i.e. records of properties and economies, with population censuses of a sort. The cadastral records of Novgorod (*Novgorodskiya pistsoviya knigi*, 3 vols. 1859–86; also Maikov, V. V., *Kniga pistsovaya po Novgorodu Velikomu kontsa XVI v.* [A late 16th cent. cadastral survey for Novgorod the Great], St Petersburg, 1911, are of particular value because they reflect the social revolution involved by the subjection of Novgorod to Muscovite dominion: see also the cadastral records of the Moscow State, *Pistsoviya knigi moskovskogo gosudarstva* (XVI veka), 3 vols. Moscow, 1872–95.

A number of other survey and account books relating to the sixteenth and seventeenth centuries have been published, e.g.:

Kniga klyuchei i dolgovaya kniga Iosifo-Volokolamskogo monastyrya XVI v. [The book of keys and debt book of the Joseph of Volotsk monastery of the 16th cent.]. Moscow–Leningrad, 1948.
Lavochnye knigi Novgoroda Velikogo 1583 g. [The books of stalls of Novgorod the Great, 1583]. Moscow, 1930.
Tamozhennye knigi Velikogo Ustyuga, Tot'my i Sol'vychegodska XVII v. [Customs books of 17th cent. Velikii Ustyug, Tot'ma and Sol'vychegodsk]. Moscow, 1950.
Tamozhennye knigi Moskovskogo gosudarstva XVII v. [Customs books of the 17th cent. Moscow state]. 3 vols. Moscow, 1950–1.

V. ARCHAEOLOGICAL MATERIALS

Archaeological research has produced a mass of new material relevant to Russian medieval economic history. Unfortunately, most of it is scattered in various serial publications such as:

Izvestiya GAIMK; *Kratkie soobshcheniya IIMK*; *Sovetskaya arkheologiya*; or in the partly monographic series: *Materialy i issledovaniya po arkheologii SSSR* (here abbreviated as *MIA*).

A new monographic series, *Arkheologiya SSSR, Svod arkheologicheskikh istochnikov* [Archaeology of the U.S.S.R., Summary of archaeological sources], recently started, promises to be a most useful guide.

A few items of particular relevance to various aspects of agrarian history are:

ARTSIKHOVSKII, A. V. *Drevnerusskie miniatyury kak istoricheskii istochnik* [Ancient Russian miniatures as a historical source]. Moscow, 1944.

KIR'YANOV, A. V. 'Istoriya zemledeliya Novgorodskoi zemli, X-XV vv.' [The history of tillage in the Novgorod territory, 10th–15th cents.]. in *MIA*. no. 65, Izd-vo AN SSSR, Moscow, 1959.

KUKHARENKO, YU. V. 'Srednevekovye pamyatniki Poles'ya' [Medieval remains in Polesye], *Arkheologiya SSSR, Svod arkheologicheskikh istochnikov*, El-57 (,) Moscow, 1961.

LYAPUSHKIN, I. I. 'Gorodishche Novotroitse' [The fortified settlement of Novotroitse] *MIA*. no. 74 (,) Moscow–Leningrad, 1958.

MONGAIT, A. L. *Archaeology in the U.S.S.R.* Moscow, 1959.

RYBAKOV, B. A. *Remeslo drevnei Rusi* [Handicrafts of ancient Rus']. Moscow, 1948.

SEDOV, V. V. 'Sel'skie poseleniya tsentral'nykh raionov Smolenskoi zemli' [Village settlements of the central districts of the Smolensk territory], *MIA*. no. 92 (,) Izd-vo AN SSSR, Moscow, 1960.

TARAKANOVA, S. A. 'Ob arkheologicheskom izuchenii sel'skikh feodal'nykh poselenii v pyatinakh Velikogo Novgoroda' [On the archaeological study of rural feudal settlements in the districts of the territory of Novgorod the Great], in *Trudy GIM*, vyp. *XI*, Moscow, 1940.

TSALKIN, V. I. 'Materialy dlya istorii skotovodstva i okhoty v Drevnei Rusi' [Materials for a history of livestock farming and hunting in Ancient Rus'], *MIA*. no. 51 (,) Izd-vo AN SSSR, Moscow, 1956.

Of great interest and importance are the birch bark letters found during the excavations at Novgorod:

ARTSIKHOVSKII, A. V. *Novgorodskie gramoty na bereste* [Novgorod birch bark letters]. Moscow, 1953 (with M. N. Tikhomirov), letters 1–10; 1954, letters 11–83; 1958 (with V. I. Borkovskii), letters 84–136; 1958 (with V. I. Borkovskii), letters 137–194 1963 (with V. I. Borkovskii), letters 195–318, 1963, letters 319–405.

VI. SECONDARY SOURCES

Of general studies on the history of Russian economics it is necessary to mention:

DOVNAR-ZAPOL'SKII, M. V. *Istoriya russkago narodnago khozyaistva* [History of Russian Economy], vols. 1–2, Moscow, 1925.

KULISHER, I. M. *Istiriya russkogo narodnogo Khozyaistra* [History of Russian National National Economy]. vol. 1, 1911.

LYASHCHENKO, P. I. History of the National Economy of Russia to the 1917 Revolution, N.Y. 1949; a translation of the one-volume 1939 edition of: *Istoriya narodnogo khozyaistva SSSR* [History of the National Economy of the U.S.S.R.]. 3 vols., Gospolitizdat, Moscow, 1950–6.

Information U.S.S.R. (basically a translation of vol. 50 of the Great Soviet Encyclopaedia, contains an historical outline). Oxford, 1962.

Two important series of papers on agrarian history are:

Ezhegodnik po agrarnoi istorii vostochnoi Evropy [Yearbook on the agrarian history of Eastern Europe]. 1958, Tallin, 1959; 1959 Moscow, 1961; 1960, Moscow, 1962; 1961, Riga, 1963.

Materialy po istorii zemledeliya SSSR [Materials on the history of agriculture in the U.S.S.R.], 1–2, Moscow–Leningrad, 1952–6; with the third issue, Moscow, 1959, the title of this series became: *Materialy po istorii sel'skogo khozyaistva i krest'yanstva SSSR* [Materials on the history of farming and the peasantry of the U.S.S.R.].

The following lists some of the most important items relevant to medieval Russian agrarian history. Many of the works listed themselves contain extensive bibliographies.

Atlas istorii srednikh vekov [Atlas of medieval history]. GUGK, Moscow, 1952.

Atlas istorii SSSR, chast' 1 [Atlas of the history of the U.S.S.R., part 1]. Moscow, 1949.

BAKHRUSHIN, S. V. *Knyazheskoe khozyaistvo XV i pervoi poloviny XVI veka* [The princely economy of the 15th and first half of the 16th cent.], reprinted in Bakhrushin, S. V., *Nauchnye trudy*, II, Izd-vo AN SSSR, Moscow, 1954.

BERNADSKII, V. N. *Novgorod i Novgorodskaya zemlya v XV veke* [Novgorod and the Novgorod territory in the 15th cent.]. Izd-vo AN SSSR, Moscow–Leningrad, 1961.

BLUM, J. *Lord and peasant in Russia from the 9th to the 19th century*, Princeton, 1961.

BUCHINSKII, I. E. *O klimate proshlogo russkoi ravniny* [On the climate of the past in the Russian plain]. Gidrometeoizdat, Leningrad, 1957.

CHEREPNIN, L. V. *Obrazovanie russkogo tsentralizovannogo gosudarstva v XIV–XV vekakh*, Izd-vo. Sots.-ek. lit. Moscow, 1960.

DANILOVA, L. V. *Ocherki po istorii zemlevladeniya i khozyaistva v Novgorodskoi zemle v XIV–XV vv*. [Sketches on the history of landholding and economy in the 14th–15th cent. Novgorod territory]. Izd-vo AN SSSR, Moscow, 1955.

ECK, A. *Le moyen âge russe*. Paris, 1933.

EL'YASHEVICH, V. B. *Istoriya prava pozemel'noi sobstvennosti v Rossii* [A history of the law of landed property in Russia]. 2 vols. Paris, 1948–51.

GNEVUSHEV, A. M. *Ocherki ekonomicheskoi i sotsial'noi zhizni sel'skago naseleniya Novgorodskoi oblasti* [Studies in the economic and social life of the rural population of the Novgorod region]. vol. I, 1915.

GORSKII, A. D. *Ocherki ekonomicheskogo polozheniya krest'yan Severo-vostochnoi Rusi XIV–XV vv*. [Essays on the economic situation of the peasants in North-East Rus' in the 14th–15th cents.]. Izd-vo Moskovskogo universiteta, Moscow, 1960.

GREKOV, B. D. *Krest'yane na Rusi s drevneishikh vremen do 17 v.* [The peasants in Rus' from the earliest times to the 17th cent.]. Izd-vo AN SSSR, Moscow–Leningrad, 1946.

—— 'Ocherki po istorii feodalizma v Rossii' [Outlines of the history of feudalism in Russia, *Izvestiya GAIMK*, 72 (,) Moscow–Leningrad, 1934.

—— 'Rabstvo i feodalizm v Kievskoi Rusi' [Slavery and feudalism in Kiev Rus'], *Izvestiya GAIMK*, 86 (,) Moscow–Leningrad, 1934.

GROMOV, G. G. 'Podsechno-ognevaya sistema zemledeliya krest'yan Novgorodskoi oblasti v XIX–XX vv.' [The slash and burn or fire system of tillage of Novgorod oblast peasants in the 19th–20th cents.], in *Vestnik Moskovskogo universiteta, Istoriko-filologicheskaya seriya*, no. 4, 1958.

KASHIN, V. N. 'Krest'yanskaya zhelezodelatel'naya promyshlennost' na poberezh'e Finskogo zaliva po pistsovym knigam 1500–5 gg.' [Peasant iron-making on the shores of the Gulf of Finland according to the cadastral surveys of 1500–5], in *Problemy istorii dokapitalisticheskogo obshchestva*, no. 4, 1934.

KOPANEV, A. I. *Zemlevladenie Belozerskogo kraya XV–XVI vv*. [Landownership of the Belozero krai in the 15th–16th cents.]. Moscow–Leningrad, 1951.

LAPPO-DANILEVSKII, A. S. *Ocherk istorii obrazovaniya glavneishikh razryadov krest'-yanskago naseleniya* [An outline of history of the formation of the main categories of peasant population]. St Petersburg, 1905.

MILYUKOV, P. N. *Spornye voprosy finansovoi istorii moskovskago gosudarstva* [Debatable questions of the financial history of the Moscow State]. St Petersburg, 1892.

Ocherki istorii SSSR [Outlines of the history of the U.S.S.R.], *Period feodalizma IX–XV vv*. [Feudal period, 9th–15th cents.], 2 vols., Izd-vo AN SSSR, Moscow, 1953; *Konets XV v.-nachalo XVII v*. [End 15th–early 17th cents.], Moscow, 1955.

Ocherki po istorii russkoi derevni X–XIII vv. [Sketches on the history of the Russian 10th–13th cent. village], *Trudy GIM*, vyp. 32 i 33, Goskul'tprosvetizdat, Moscow, 1956, 1959.

PAVLOV-SIL'VANSKII, N. P. *Feodalizm v drevnei Rusi* [Feudalism in ancient Russia]. St Petersburg, 1907.

—— *Feodalizm v udel'noi Rusi* [Feudalism in Russia of the apanage period], St Petersburg, 1910.

Pochvenno-geograficheskoe raionirovanie SSSR [The division of the U.S.S.R. into soil and geographic districts]. Izd-vo AN SSSR, Moscow, 1962.

PRONSHTEIN, A. P. *Velikii Novgorod v XVI veke*. Kharkov, 1957.

ROZHKOV, N. A. *Gorod i derevnya v russkoi istorii* [Town and village in Russian history]. Petrograd, 1923.

—— *Sel'skoe khozyaistvo Moskovskoi Rusi v XVI veke* [Agriculture of Moscow Rus' in the 16th cent.]. Moscow, 1899.

SAKHAROV, A. M. *Goroda severo-vostochnoi Rusi XIV–XV vv.* [The towns of north-east Rus' in the 14th–15th cents.]. Moscow, 1959.

SAVICH, A. A. 'Glavneishie momenty monastyrskoi kolonizatsii russkogo severa XIV–XVII vv.' [Major aspects of monastic colonisation of the Russian north in the 14th–17th cents.], in *Sbornik Obshchestva istoricheskikh, filosofskikh i sotsial'nykh nauk pri Permskom un-te.*, vyp. 3, Perm', 1929; translated as: Savich, A., *Die Agrarwirtschaft der Klostergüter des russichen Nordens im 14.–17. Jahrhundert*, Zeitschrift für osteuropische Geschichte, V (1931), VI (1932).

—— *Solovetskaya votchina XV–XVII v.* [The Solovki estate in the 15th–17th cents.]. Perm', 1927.

SMIRNOV, P. P. 'Obrazovanie Russkogo tsentralizovannogo gosudarstva v XIV–XV vv.' [The formation of the Russian centralised state in the 14th–15th cents.], in *Voprosy istorii*, no. 2–3, no. 4, 1946.

—— *Posadskie lyudi i ikh klassovaya bor'ba do serediny XVII veka* [The people of the artisan and trading quarter and their class struggles prior to the mid-17th cent.]. 2 vols. Moscow–Leningrad, 1947–8.

SMITH, R. E. F. *The Origins of Farming in Russia*. Paris, The Hague, 1959.

SZEFTEL, M. 'Aspects of feudalism in Russian history', in *Feudalism in history*, ed. by R. Coulborn, Princeton, 1956.

TIKHOMIROV, M. N. *Drevnerusskie goroda* [Ancient Russian towns]. 2nd ed. Gospolitizdat, Moscow, 1956; translated as: *The towns of ancient Rus*, Moscow, 1959.

—— *Srednevekovaya Moskva v XIV–XV vekakh* [Medieval Moscow in the 14th–15th cents.]. Izd-vo Moskovskogo universiteta, Moscow, 1957.

TRET'YAKOV, P. N. 'Drevlyanskie "grady"' [The Drevlyane 'towns'], in *Akademiku B. D. Grekovu ko dnyu semidesyatiletiya*, Izd-vo AN SSSR, Moscow, 1952.

—— 'Podsechnoe zemledelie v Vostochnoi Evrope' [Slash and burn tillage in Eastern Europe], in *Izvestiya GAIMK*, 14, vyp. 1, Moscow, 1932.

URLANIS, B. Ts. *Rost naseleniya v Evrope* [The growth of population in Europe]. Moscow, 1941.

VASIL'EV, K. G. and SEGAL, A. E. *Istoriya epidemii v Rossii* [A history of epidemics in Russia]. Medgiz, Moscow, 1960.

VESELOVSKII, S. B. *K voprosy o proiskhozhdenii votchinnago rezhima* [On the problem of the origin of the heritable tenure regime]. Moscow, 1927.

—— *Selo i derevnya v severo-vostochnoi Rusi XIV–XVI vv.* [Village and hamlet in 14th–16th cent. North-Eastern Rus']. Moscow–Leningrad, 1936.

—— *Feodal'noe zemlevladenie v severo-vostochnoi Rusi* [Feudal landholding in North-Eastern Rus']. vol. I, Izd-vo AN SSSR, Moscow–Leningrad, 1947.

YANIN, V. L. *Denezhno-vesovye sistemy russkogo srednevekov'ya, domongol'skii period* [Monetary and weight systems of the Russian middle ages, pre-Mongol period]. Izd-vo Moskovskogo universiteta, Moscow, 1956.

ZELENIN, D. K. *Russkaya sokha, eya istoriya i vidy* [The Russian *sokha*, its history and forms]. Vyatka, 1907.

§7. ENGLAND

I. BIBLIOGRAPHIES

DAVENPORT, F. G. *A Classified list of Printed Original Materials for English Manorial and Agrarian History during the Middle Ages*. Boston, 1824.

GROSS, C. *The Sources and Literature of English History from the earliest times to about 1485*. 2nd ed. London, 1915.

MOORE, M. L. *A Select Bibliography of English Medieval Economic History*. London, 1914.

—— *Two Select Bibliographies of Medieval Historical Study*. London, 1912.

II. Sources

Public Record Office: *Calendar of Close Rolls. Patent Rolls. Cleria Regis Rolls. Inquisitions. Post Mortem.* H.M. Stationery Office. *In progress.*

AULT, W. O. (ed.). *Court Rolls of the Abbey of Ramsey and of the Honor of Clare.* New Haven, 1928.

BERESFORD, M. W. and ST. JOSEPH, J. K. S. *Medieval England: an aerial survey.* Cambridge, 1958.

BLAND, A. E., BROWN, B. A., and TAWNEY, R. H. (eds.). *English Economic History: Select Documents.* London, 1914.

BRACTON, —. *De Legibus et Consuetudines Angliae.* Ed. T. Twiss (6 vols.) [Rolls Ser.]. London, 1878–83. Ed. G. E. Woodbine. Vols I and II. New Haven, 1915. (In progress.

——*Note Book.* Ed. F. W. Maitland. 3 vols. London, 1887.

BRIDGEMAN, C. G. O. (ed.). *The Burton Abbey 12th Century Surveys.* Wm. Salt Arch. Soc., 1916.

BROOKE, C. N. L. and POSTAN, M. M. (eds.). *Carte Nativorum: A Peterborough Abbey Cartulary of the Fourteenth Century* (Northants. Rec. Soc.), xx. 1950.

BROWN, R. J. (ed.). *Chester County Court Rolls* (Chetham Soc.), LXXXIV. Manchester, 1925.

BROWNELL, J. (ed.). *The Ledger Book of Vale Royal Abbey* (Lancs. and Cheshire Rec. Soc.), LXVIII. Manchester, 1914.

CHAUCER, GEOFFREY. *Works.* Ed. W. W. Skeat. 7 vols. Oxford, 1894–7.

CHIBNALL, M. (MORGAN, MISS M.) (Ed.) *Selected Documents of the English Lands of the Abbey of Bec* (Camden Soc.) 3rd Ser, LXXVII.

DALE, M. E. (ed.). *The Court Rolls of Chalgrove Manor, 1278–1313* (Beds. Hist. Rec. Soc.), XXVIII.

DAVIS, R. H. C. *The Kalendar of Abbot Samson of Bury St. Edmunds* (Camden Soc., 3rd Series), LXXXIV.

DOUGLAS, D. C. (ed.). *Feudal Documents from the Abbey of Bury St. Edmunds* (Brit. Acad.), VIII. London, 1932.

DOUGLAS, D. C. and others. *English Historical Documents, vols. II and III.*

DUGDALE, W. (ed) *Monasticon Anglicanum* (new ed.), 6 vols. London, 1817–30.

ELTON, C. I. (ed.). *Rentalia et Custumaria Michaelis de Ambresbury* (Somerset Rec. Soc.). London, 1891.

FARR, M. W. (ed.). *Accounts and Surveys of the Wiltshire Lands of Adam of Stratton* (Wilts. Arch. and Nat. Hist. Soc.), XIV. 1959.

FARRER, W. (ed.). *Court Rolls of the Honor of Clitheroe in the County of Lancashire.* 3 vols. Manchester, 1897–1913.

—— *Early Yorkshire Charters.* 3 vols. Edinburgh, 1914–16.

FISHER, F. N. (ed.). 'Eggington Court Rolls 1306–7, 1311–12', in *Trans. Derbys. Arch. & Nat. Hist. Soc.,* LXXV, 1956.

GLANVIL, RANULF DE. *Tractatus de Legibus et Consuetudinibus Regni Anglie.* Ed. G. E. Woodbine. New Haven, 1887.

GREENWELL, W. (ed.). *Bishop Hatfield's Survey* (Surtees Soc.), XXXII. Durham and London, 1857.

——*Boldon Buke.* Surtees Soc., XXV, 1852.

HALE, W. H. (ed.). *The Domesday of St. Pauls* (Camden Soc.), London, 1858.

—— *Registrum . . . Prioratus Beatae Mariae Wigornitusis* (Camden Soc.). London, 1865.

HALL, H. (ed.). *Pipe Roll of the Bishopric of Winchester, 1208–9.* London, 1903.

HART, W. H. (ed.). *Historia et Cartularium Monasterii Sancti Petri Gloucestriae* (Rolls Ser.). 3 vols. London, 1863–7.

HART, W. H. and LYONS, P. A. (eds.). *Cartularium Monasterii de Rameseia* (Rolls Ser.). 3 vols. London, 1884–93.

HARVEY, B. F. (ed.). *Custumal and Bye-Laws of the Manor of Islip* (Oxen. Rec. Soc.). 40.

HILTON, R. H. (ed.). *Ministers' Accounts of the Warwickshire Estates of the Duke of Clarence.*

—— (ed.). *The Stoneleigh Ledger Book* (Dugdale Soc.), XXIV. 1960.

HOLLINGS, M. (ed.). *The Red Book of Worcester.* Parts I–IV. (Worcester His. Soc.). 1937–51.

ILLINGWORTH, W. *Placita de Quo Warranto* (Rec. Com.). London, 1818.

—— *Rotuli Hundredorum.* 2 vols. (Rec. Com.). London, 1812–18.

LAMOND, E. (ed.). *Walter of Henley's Husbandry, together with an anonymous Husbandry, Seneschancie and Robert Grosseteste's Rules*, Introd. by W. Cunningham. London, 1890.

LANDOR, W. N. (ed.). *The Altewas Court Rolls,* 1259–61 (William Salt Archaeol. Soc., New Ser. x). London, 1907–10.

LANGLAND, W. *The Vision of William concerning Piers the Plowman.* Ed. W. W. Skeat. 2 vols. Oxford, 1886.

LARKING, L. B. (ed.). *The Knights Hospitallers in England* (Camden Soc.). London, 1857.

LEES, B. (ed.). *Records of the Templars in England in the Twelfth Century* (Brit. Acad. IX). London, 1935.

LONGSTAFFE, W. H. D. and BOOTH, J. *Halmota Prioratus Dunelmensis* (Surtees Soc.), LXXXII. Durham and London, 1889.

MAITLAND, F. W. (ed.). *Select Pleas in Manorial Courts,* I (Selden Soc. II). London, 1889.

—— *Pleas of the Crown for the County of Gloucester in* A.D. 1221. London, 1884.

MAITLAND, F. W. and BOULDON, N. P. (eds.). *The Court Baron* (Selden Soc. IV). London.

MIDGELEY, L. M. (ed.). *Ministers' Accounts of the Earldom of Cornwall* 1296–1297. Vol. I and II. Camden 3rd Series, LXVI and LXVII. 1942 and 1945.

MUHLFELD, N. E. (ed.). *Survey of the Manor of Wye.* New York, 1933.

NEILSON, N. (ed.). *Cartulary and Terrier of the Priory of Bilsington* (Brit. Acad.), VII. London, 1928.

—— *A Terrier of the Fleet* (Brit. Acad.). London, 1920.

PAGE, F. M. (ed.). *Wellingborough Manorial Accounts* (Northants. Rec. Soc.). Kettering, 1936.

Pipe Roll Society, Publications of the. *Passim.*

POWELL, E. *A Suffolk Hundred in the Year* 1283. Cambridge, 1910.

REDWOOD, B. C. and WILSON, A. E. (eds.). *Custumals of the Sussex Manors of the Archbishop of Canterbury* (Sussex. Rec. Soc.), LVII. 1958.

ROSE, G. and ILLINGWORTH, W. (eds.). *Placitorum Abbreviato* (Rec. Com.). London, 1811.

ROYCE, D. *Landboc sive Registrum monasterii Winchelcumba.* 2 vols. Exeter, 1892–1903.

SALTER, H. E. (ed.). *Eynsham Cartulary.* 2 vols. (Oxford Hist. Soc.). Oxford, 1907–8.

SAYLES, G. O. (ed.). *The Court of King's Bench under Edward I.* (Selden. Soc). London, 1936.

SCARGILL-BIRD, S. R. (ed.). *Custumals of Battle Abbey* (Camden Soc.). London, 1887.

SELDEN, J. (ed.). *Fleta.* 2nd ed. London, 1685.

STAPLETON, T. (ed.). *Chronicon Petroburgense* (Camden Soc.). London, 1849.

Statutes of the Realm. 11 vols. (Rec. Com.). London, 1810–11.

STENTON, F. M. (ed.). *Documents illustrative of the Social and Economic History of the Danelaw* (Brit. Acad.) London, 1920.

—— *Transcriptions of Charters relating to Gilbertine Houses* (Lin. Rec. Soc.). Lincoln, 1922.

—— *Gilbertine Charters* (Linc. Rec. Soc.). Lincoln, 1926.

—— 'The Free Peasantry of the Northern Danelaw', in *Bull. de la Soc. Royale de Lettres de Lund.* Lund and London, 1926.

STITT, F. B. (ed.). *Lenton Priory Estate Accounts* 1296 *to* 1298 (Thornton Soc.). Nottingham, 1959.

STUBBS, W. *Select Charters and other Illustrations of English Constitutional History.* 9th ed. Revised by H. W. C. Davis. Oxford, 1929.

TAIT, J. (ed.). *The Chartulary or Register of the Abbey of St. Werburgh, Chester.* 2 vols. (Chetham Soc.), new ser. LXXIX. 1920–3.

THORPE, J. (The Younger) (ed.). *Custumale Roffense.* London, 1788.

TOMS, E. (ed.). *Chertsey Abbey Court Roll Abstract, Parts* 1 *and* 2 (Surrey Rec. Soc.). XLVI–XLVIII.

TURNER, G. J. *Select Pleas of the Forest* (Selden Soc.). London, 1901.
—— *A Calendar of the Feet of Fines relating to the County of Huntingdon*. Cambridge, 1913.
TURNER, G. J. and SALTER, E. H. *The Black Book of St. Augustine*. 2 vols. (Brit. Acad. 1). London, 1915–24.
TURTON, R. B. *The Manor and Forest of Pickering* (N. Riding Rec. Soc.), New ser. I–IV. 1897.
WATKIN, A. DOM. (ed.). *The Great Chartulary of Glastonbury, Vols. I–III.* (Somerset Rec. Soc.), LIX and LXIV.
WILLIS, D. (ed.). *The Estate Book of Henry de Bray of Herleston* (Camden Soc.). London, 1916.
WIGRAM, S. R. (ed.). *The Cartulary of the Monastery of St. Frideswide at Oxford*. 2 vols. (Oxford Hist. Soc). Oxford, 1895–6.
WILSON, A. E. (ed.). *Custumals of the Manors of Loughton, Willingdon and Goring*. (Sussex Rec. Soc.), LX. 1961.

III. MODERN WORKS

ANDREWS, C. M. *The Old English Manor*. Baltimore, 1892.
ASHLEY, W. J. *Introduction to English Economic History and Theory*. 2 vols. London, 1888–1894.
—— *The Bread of our Forefathers*. Oxford, 1928.
ASTON, T. H. 'The English Manor'. *Past and Present*, x. 1956.
AULT, W. O. *Private Jurisdiction in England*. New Haven, 1923.
—— 'Some Early English By-Laws', in *EHR*. XLV, 1930.
—— 'By-Laws of Gleaning and the Problems of Harvest', *EcHR*. 2nd ser. XIV, 1961.
—— 'Village By-Laws by Common Consent', *Speculum*, XXIX.
BANNISTER, A. T. *Manorial Custom on the Hereford Bishopric Estates, EHR.* XLIII, 1928.
BAKER, A. R. H. 'Open Fields and Partible Inheritance on a Kent Manor', *EcHR*. 2nd ser, XVII, 1964.
BAZELY, M. L. 'The Forest of Dean', *Bristol and Glouc. Arch. Soc.* XXIII, 1910.
—— 'The Extent of the English Forests in the Thirteenth Century', *TRHS*. 4th ser. IV, 1921.
BEAN, I. M. W. *The Estates of the Percy Family, 1416–1537*. Oxford, 1958.
—— 'Plague, Population and Economic Decline in the later Middle Ages', *EcHR*. 2nd ser. XV, 1963.
BENNETT, H. S. 'The Reeve and the Manor in the Fourteenth Century', *EHR*. XLI, 1926.
—— *Life on the English Manor 1150–1400*. Cambridge, 1937.
BEVERIDGE, W. H. 'The Yield and the Price of Corn in the Middle Ages', *EJ*. (Ec. Hist.), 1929.
—— 'Westminster Wages in the Manorial Era', *EcHR*. 2nd ser. VIII, 1955.
BERESFORD, M. W. *The Lost Villages of England*. Lutterworth, 1954.
—— 'Lot Acres', *EcHR*, XIII, 1943.
BISHOP, T. A. M. 'The Distribution of Manorial Demesne in the Vale of Yorkshire', *EHR*. XLIX, 1934.
—— 'Assarting and the Growth of the open fields', *EcHR*, VI, 1935.
—— 'Monastic Demesne and the Statute of Mortmain', *EHR*. XLIX, 1934.
—— 'Monastic Granges in Yorkshire', *EHR*. LI, 1936.
BLOCH, M. 'Champs et villages', *AHES*. VI, 1934.
—— 'Les Paysages agraires' [essai ae mise au point], *AHES*. VIII, 1936.
—— *Feudal Society*, London, 1961.
BLOUNT, T. *Tenures of Land and Customs of some Manors* with supplement. London, 1909.
BOWEN, E. G. 'The Monastic Economy of the Cistercians in Straton, Florida', *Trans. Cardigan Antiq. Soc.* I.
BUTLIN, R. A. 'Northumberland Field Systems', *Agric. Hist. R.*, XII, 1964.
CAM, H. M. 'Studies in the Hundred Rolls', *Oxford Studies in Soc. and Legal Hist.* ed. P. Vinogradoff, XI. Oxford, 1921.

CAM, H. M. 'Manerium cum Hundredo', *EHR*. XLVII, 1932.
—— 'Early Groups of Hundreds', *Historical Essays in Honour of James Tait*, Manchester, 1933.
CARUS-WILSON, E. M. 'Evidence of Industrial Growth on some Fifteenth-Century Manors', *EcHR*. 2nd ser. XII, 1959.
CHIBNALL, M. (MORGAN, MRS., M.). *The English Lands of the Abbey of Bec*. Oxford, 1946.
CLAPHAM, J. H. 'A Thirteenth Century Market Town', *Cambridge Hist. Journ*. IV, 1932–4.
CLARK, A. 'Serfdom on an Essex Manor', *EHR*. XX, 1905.
—— 'Copyhold Tenure at Felsted, Essex', *EHR*. XXVII, 1912.
COULTON, G. G. *The Medieval Village*. Cambridge, 1925.
COX, J. C. *The Royal Forests of England*. London, 1905.
CRAWFORD, J. S. *Air Survey and Archaeology*. London, 1924.
DARBY, H. C. (ed.). *An Historical Geography of England Before 1800*. Cambridge, 1936.
—— *The Drainage of the Fens*. Cambridge, 1940.
—— *The Medieval Fenland*. Cambridge, 1940.
—— 'Clearing of the English Woodland', *Geography*, XXXVI.
DARBY, H. C., TERRETT, L. B. and others. *The Domesday Geography*, I–IV. Cambridge, 1952–62.
DAVENPORT, F. J. 'The Decay of Villeinage in East Anglia', *TRHS*., new ser. XIV, 1900.
—— *The Economic Development of a Norfolk Manor*. Cambridge, 1906.
DENHOLM-YOUNG, N. *Seignorial Administration in England*, London, 1937.
DICKINSON, P. and FISCHER, W. B. *The Medieval Land Surveys of County Durham*, Research Pap., No. 2, Dept. of Geography, Durham University, 1959.
DONKIN, R. A. 'Cistercian sheep-farming and wool-sales in the thirteenth century', *Agric. Hist. Rev*. VI, 1958.
DONNELLY, J. S. 'Changes in the Grange Economy of English and Welsh Cistercian Abbeys, 1300–1540', *Traditio* X.
DOUGLAS, D. L. 'The Social Structure of Medieval East Anglia', *Oxford Studies in Soc. and Legal History*, ed. P. Vinogradoff, IX. Oxford, 1927.
DREW, J. S. 'Manorial Accounts of St. Swithun's Priory (Winchester)', *EHR*. LXII, 242.
DRUMMOND, T. C. and WILBRAHAM, A. *The Englishman's Food, a History of Five Centuries of English Diet*. 1939–40.
DUBY, G. *L'économie rurale et la vie des campagnes dans l'occident médiéval*, vols. I–II. Paris, 1962.
EDWARDS, J. G., GALBRAITH, V. H. and JACOB, E. F. (Eds.). *Historical Essays in Honour of J. Tait*, 1933.
EKWALL, E. 'Names of Trades in English Place-Names', *Historical Essays in Honour of James Tait*. Manchester, 1933.
FARMER, D. L. 'Some Price Fluctuations in Angevin England', *EcHR*. 2nd ser. IX, 1956.
FEILING, K. G. 'An Essex Manor in the Fourteenth Century', *EHR*. XXVI, 1911.
FINBERG, H. P. R. *Tavistock Abbey. A Study in the Social and Economic History of Devon*. Cambridge, 1951.
—— (ed.). *Gloucestershire Studies*. Leicester, 1957.
FISHER, W. R. *The Forest of Essex*. London, 1887.
GRANT, I. F. *The Social and Economic Development of Scotland before 1603*. London, 1930.
GRAS, N. S. B. *The Evolution of the English Corn Market*. Cambridge, Mass. 1915.
—— *The History of Agriculture in Europe and America*. New York, 1925.
GRAS, N. S. B. and C. C. *The Economic and Social History of an English Village*. Cambridge, Mass. 1930.
GRAY, H. L. 'The Commutation of Villein Services before the Black Death', *EHR*. XXIX, 1914.
—— *The English Field Systems*. Cambridge, Mass. 1915.

HALCROW, E. M. 'The Decline of Demesne Farming on the Estates of Durham Cathedral Priory', *EcHR.* 2nd ser. VII, 1955.

HALL, H. and NICHOLAS, F. 'Manorial Accounts of the Priory of Canterbury 1260–1420', *Bull. of the Inst. of Hist. Research*, VIII.

HALLAM, H. E. *The New Lands of Elloe: a Study of Early Reclamation in Lincolnshire.* Leicester, 1954.

—— 'Some Thirteenth-Century Censuses', *EcHR.* 2nd ser. X, 1958.

—— 'Population Density in Medieval Fenland', *EcHR.* 2nd ser. XIV, 1961.

HARLEY, J. B. 'Population Trends and Agricultural Developments from the Warwickshire Hundred Rolls of 1279', *EcHR.* 2nd ser. XI, 1958.

HELLEINER, K. F. 'Population Movement and Agrarian Depression in the Later Middle Ages', *Canad. Journ. Econ. and Pol. Sci.* XV, 1950.

HENDERSON, C. *Essays in Cornish History.* Oxford, 1935.

HEWITT, H. J. *Mediaeval Cheshire.* Manchester, 1925.

HILTON, R. H. *The Economic Development of some Leicestershire Estates in the Fourteenth and Fifteenth Centuries.* Oxford, 1947.

—— 'Peasant Movements in England before 1381', *EcHR.* 2nd ser. II. 1949.

—— 'Winchcombe Abbey and the Manor of Sherborne', *Univ. Birm. Hist. Journ.* II, 1950.

—— *The Victoria County History of Leicester*, II. Oxford, 1954.

—— *The Social Structure of Rural Warwickshire in the Middle Ages* (Dugdale Soc. Occasional Papers). IX.

HOLDSWORTH, W. *History of English Law.* 9 vols. London, 1921–5. With tables and index by S. Potton. London, 1932.

HOLMES, G. A. *The Estates of Higher Nobility in Fourteenth-Century England.* Cambridge, 1957.

HOMANS, G. C. 'Men and Land in the Middle Ages', *Speculum*, XI, 1936.

—— 'Terroirs ordonnés et champs orientés; une hypothèse sur le village anglais', *AHES.* VIII, 1936.

—— *English Villages of the Thirteenth Century.* Boston, 1941.

—— 'The Frisians in East Anglia', *EcHR.* 2nd ser. X, 2, 1957.

HONE, N. *The Manor and Manorial Records.* London, 1926.

HOSKINS, W. G. (ed.). *Studies in Leicestershire Agrarian History.* 1949.

—— *The Midland Peasant: the Economic and Social History of a Leicestershire Village.* 1957.

HOSKINS, W. G. and FINBERG, H. P. R. *Devonshire Studies.* 1952.

HOYT, R. S. *The Royal Demesne in English Constitutional History: 1066–1272.* 1951.

—— 'Farm of the Manor and Community of the Vill in Domesday Book', *Speculum*, XXX, 1955.

JOHNSTONE, H. 'Everyday Life in some Medieval Records', *History*, XI, 1927.

JOLIFFE, J. E. A. 'Northumbrian Institutions', in *EHR.* XLI, 1926.

—— *Pre-Feudal England; the Jutes.* Oxford, 1933.

—— 'A Survey of Fiscal Tenements', *EcHR.* VI, 1936.

KENNETT, W. *Parochial Antiquities.* 2 vols. Oxford, 1818.

KNOOP, D. and JONES, G. P. *The Medieval Mason.* Manchester, 1934.

KOSMINSKY, E. A. 'Services and Money Rents in the Thirteenth Century', *EcHR.* V, 1935.

—— 'The Small Estate in Medieval England' (Russian), *Izvestia Acad. Nauk.* Seria Istorii i filosofii, 4, 1944.

—— 'Labour on English Manorial Estates', *Voprosi Istorii*, I, 1946.

—— *Studies in the Agrarian History of England in the Thirteenth Century.* Oxford, 1956.

KRAUSE, J. T. 'The Medieval Household large or small?', *EcHR.* 2nd ser. IX, 1957.

LAPSLEY, G. T. *The County Palatine of Durham.* London, 1900.

LENNARD, R. V. 'What is a Manorial Extent?', *EHR.*, XLIV, 1929.

—— 'An Unidentified Twelfth Century Custumal of Lawshall, Suffolk', *EHR.* LI, 1936.

—— 'Manorial Traffic and Agricultural Trade in Medieval England', *Journ. of Proceedings of the Agric. Economics Soc.* V, 1938.

—— 'The Destruction of Woodland in the Eastern Counties under William the Conqueror', *EcHR*. xv, 1945.

—— 'The Economic Position of Bordars and Cottars of Domesday Book', *EJ*. LXI.

—— 'The Economic Position of Domesday Sokemen', *EJ*. LVII.

—— *Rural England*, 1086–1135. Oxford, 1959.

LEVETT, A. E. 'The Black Death on the Estates of the Bishopric of Winchester', *Oxford Studies in Soc. and Legal Hist.* Ed. P. Vinogradoff. Oxford, 1916.

—— 'The Courts and Court Rolls of St. Alban's Abbey', *TRHS*. 4th ser. VII 1924.

—— 'Baronial Councils and their Relations to Manorial Courts' *Mélange d'Inst. du Moyen Âge offerts à M. Ferdinand Lot.* Paris, 1926.

—— 'The Financial Organization of the Manor', *EcHR*. I, 1927.

—— 'Notes on the Statute of Labourers', *EcHR*. IV, 1932.

—— *Studies in Manorial History.* Oxford, 1938.

LEWIS, G. R. *The Staunaries.* Cambridge, Mass., 1908.

LIPSON, E. *Economic History of England. I, The Middle Ages.* London, 1915. 7th revised ed. London, 1937.

McFARLANE, K. B. 'Bastard Feudalism', *Bull. Inst. Hist. Res.* xx, 1943–5.

—— 'The Investment of Sir John Fastolf's profits of War', *TRHS*. VII, 1957.

MAITLAND, F. W. *Domesday Book and Beyond.* Cambridge, 1897.

—— 'History of a Cambridgeshire Manor', *Collected Papers*, II. Cambridge, 1911.

MALDEN, H. E. 'Villeinage in the Weald of Surrey', *Surrey Archaeol. Collections*, xx, 1907.

MAWER, A. 'A study of Place Names in relation to Craft Names', *Historical Essays in Honour of James Tait.* Manchester, 1933.

MILLER, E. *The Abbey and Bishopric of Ely. The Social History of an Ecclesiastical Estate from the tenth century to the early fourteenth century.* Cambridge, 1951.

MOORE, S. A. 'Right of Common upon the Forest of Dartmoor', *Dartmoor Preservation Assoc. Publications*, I, Plymouth, 1890.

MORRIS, W. A. *The Frankpledge System.* New York, 1910.

NIELSON, N. 'Customary Rents', *Oxford Studies in Soc. and Legal Hist.*, ed. P. Vinogradoff. II, Oxford, 1910.

—— 'Custom and Common Law in Kent', *Harvard Law Review*, 1925.

—— *Economic Conditions on the Manors of Ramsey Abbey.* Philadelphia, 1898.

—— 'English Manorial Farms', *AHR*. xxxiv, 1929.

NICHOLS, J. F. 'An Early Fourteenth Century petition from the Tenants of Bocking to their Manorial Lord', *EcHR*. II, 1930.

OSCHINSKY, D. 'Medieval Treatises on Estate Accounting', *EcHR*. xvII, 1947.

—— 'Quellen zur Verwaltungs- und Wirtschaftsgeschichte der englischen Gutsherrschaft in Mittelalter', *Mitteilungen d. Instituts für Österreich. Geschichtsforschung*, LVIII.

—— 'Medieval Treatises on Estate Management', *EcHR*. 2nd ser. VIII, 1950.

PAGE, F. M. '"Bidentes Hoylandie"; a Medieval Sheep Farm', *EJ*. (Ec. Hist.), 1929

—— 'The Customary Poor Law of three Cambridgeshire Manors', *Cambridge Hist. Journ.* III, 1929–31.

—— *The Estates of Crowland Abbey.* Cambridge, 1934.

PAINTER, S. *Medieval Society.* Ithaca, 1951.

PALMER, A. N. and OWENS, E. *History of Ancient Tenures of Land in the Marches of North Wales.* 2nd ed. Wrexham, 1910.

PARKER, J. H. and TURNER, T. H. *Some Account of Domestic Architecture in England.* 3 vols. Oxford, 1877.

PELHAM, R. A. 'Some Aspects of the East Kent Wool Trade in the Thirteenth Century', *Archaeologia Cautiana*, XLIV, 1932.

—— 'Further Evidence on the Distribution of Sheep in Medieval Sussex', *Sussex Notes and Queries*, v, 1935.

PETIT DUTAILLIS, C. *Studies and Notes Supplementary to Stubb's Constitutional History.* 3 vols. Manchester, 1908–29.

PHELPS-BROWN, E. H. and HOPKINS, S. V. 'Seven Centuries of Wages and Prices: Some earlier estimates', *Economica*, XXVIII, 1961.

PITKINS, D. S. 'Partible Inheritance and the Open Fields', *Agric. Hist.* XXXV, 1961.

Place Names Society Publications. [In progress.]

POLLOCK, F. and MAITLAND, F. W. *History of English Law before the Time of Edward I*, 2nd ed. Cambridge, 1898.

PONSONBY, C. *Wootton: the History of an Oxfordshire Parish*. Oxford, 1947.

POOLE, A. L. *Obligations of Society in the XII and XIII Centuries*, (Foul Lectures, 1944). Oxford, 1947.

POSTAN, M. M. 'The Chronology of Labour Services', *TRHS* 4th ser. XX, 1937.

—— 'Some Social Consequences of the Hundred Years' War', *EcHR.* XII, 1942.

—— 'The Rise of a Money Economy', *EcHR.* XIV, 1944.

—— 'Some Economic Evidence of Declining Population in the later Middle Ages', *EcHR.* 2nd ser. II, 1950.

—— 'The Manor in the Hundred Rolls', *EcHR.* 2nd ser. III, 1950.

—— 'Glastonbury Estates in the Twelfth Century', *EcHR.* 2nd ser. V, 1953.

—— 'Die wirtschaftlichen Grundlagen d. mittelalterlichen Gesellschaft'. *Jahrb. Nationalök. u. Statistik*, 1954.

—— *The Famulus: the Estate Labourer in the Twelfth and the Thirteenth Centuries*, (Supplement No. 2 to *EcHR.*) Cambridge, 1954.

—— 'Village Livestock in the Thirteenth Century', *EcHR.* 2nd ser. XV, 1962.

—— 'The Costs of the Hundred Years' War', *Past and Present*, 27, 1964.

POSTAN, M. M. and TITOW, J. Z. 'Heriots and Prices on Winchester Manors', *EcHR*, 2nd ser. XI, 1959.

POWER, E. 'The Position of Women', *Legacy of the Middle Ages*. ed. C. Crump and E. Jacob. Oxford, 1926.

—— *The Wool Trade in English Medieval History*. Oxford, 1941.

PUTNAM, B. H. *The Enforcement of the Statute of Labourers*. New York, 1908.

RAFTIS, J. A. *The Estates of Ramsey Abbey*. Toronto, 1957.

REES, W. *South Wales and the March, 1284–1415*. Oxford, 1924.

RICHARDSON, H. G. 'The Parish clergy of the Thirteenth and Fourteenth Century', *TRHS.* 3rd ser. VI, 1912.

ROGERS, J. E. T. *History of Agriculture and Prices in England*, I–II. Oxford, 1866–92.

ROSS, C. D. *The Estates and Finances of Richard Beauchamp, Earl of Warwick* (Dugdale Soc. Occasional Paper). Stratford-on-Avon, 1950.

ROSS, C. D. and PUGH, T. B. 'Materials for the Study of Baronial Incomes in Fifteenth Century England', *EcHR.* 2nd ser. VI, 1953.

ROUND, J. H. *Feudal England*. London, 1905.

RUSSELL, J. C. *British Medieval Population*. Albuquerque, 1948.

SALZMAN, L. F. (ed.). *Ministers' Accounts of the Manor of Petworth*, 1347–53 (Sussex Rec. Soc.) LV. 1955.

SALZMAN, L. F. *English Industries of the Middle Ages*. Oxford, 1923.

—— *English Life in the Middle Ages*. Oxford, 1926.

—— 'The Legal Status of Markets', *Cambridge Hist. Journ.* II.

SCHREINER, J. 'Wages and Prices in England in the Later Middle Ages', *Scand. Econ. Hist. Rev.* II.

SEEBOHM, F. *The English Village Community*. 4th ed. London, 1890.

SEEBOHM, M. E. *The Evolution of the English Farm*. London, 1927.

SELDEN, J. *The History of Tithes*. London, 1618, 1726.

SLATER, G. *The English Peasantry and the Enclosure of Common Fields*. London, 1907.

SMITH, R. A. L. *Canterbury Cathedral Priory; A Study in Monastic Administration*. Cambridge, 1943.

SOMERVILLE, R. *History of the Duchy of Lancaster*, I. London, 1953.

STENTON, Sir F. M. *The First Century of English Feudalism*. 2nd ed. Oxford, 1961.

—— 'Types of Manorial Structure in the Northern Danelaw', *Oxford Studies in Soc. and Legal Hist.*, ed. P. Vinogradoff, II. Oxford, 1910.

—— 'Sokeman and the Village Waste', *EHR*, XXXIII, 1918.

—— 'The Road System in Medieval England', *EcHR*. VII, 1936.

STEPHEN, J. T. *A History of the Criminal Law of England*. 3 vols. London, 1883.

STRAKER, S. E. *Wealden Glass*. Hove, 1933.

STUBBS, W. *Constitutional History of England*. 3 vols. Oxford, 1874–8. [With later editions.]

THIRSK, J. 'The Common Fields', *Past and Present*, 29, 1964.

TITOW, J. 'Evidence of Weather in the Account Rolls of the Bishopric of Winchester, 1209–1350', *EcHR*. 2nd ser. XII, 1960.

—— 'Some Evidence of the Thirteenth Century Population Increase', *EcHR*. 2nd ser. XIV, 1961.

TREHEARNE, R. F. 'The Knights in the Period of Reform and Rebellion, 1258–67: a critical phase in the rise of a new class', *Bull. Inst. Hist. Res.* XXI, 1946–8.

TUPLING, G. H. *Economic History of Rossendalt*. Manchester, 1927.

—— 'Markets and Fairs in Medieval Lancashire', *Historical Essays in Honour of James Tait*, Manchester, 1933.

UTTERSTRÖM, G. 'Climatic Fluctuations and Population Problems in early Modern History', *Scand. Ec. Hist. Rev.* III.

Victoria History of the Counties of England, ed. W. Page, L. F. Salzman and R. B. Pugh. [In progress.]

VINCENT, J. M. 'The Battle Abbey Records in the Huntingdon Library', *AHR*. XXXVII, 1932.

VINOGRADOFF, P. *Villeinage in England*. Oxford, 1892.

—— 'An Illustration of the Continuity of the Open Field System', *Quarterly Journ. of Economics*, XXII, 1908.

—— *English Society in the Eleventh Century*. Oxford, 1908.

WAKE, J. 'Communitas Villae', *EHR*. XXXVII, 1922.

WILLARD, J. F. 'Inland Transportation in England during the Fourteenth Century', *Speculum*, I, 1926.

—— 'The Use of Carts in the Fourteenth Century', *History*, XVII, 1933.

—— *Parliamentary Taxes on Personal Property*, 1290–1334. Cambridge, Mass., 1934.

WRIGHT, E. C. 'Common Law in the Thirteenth Century Royal Forest', *Speculum*, III, 1928.

§ 8. SCANDINAVIA

Compiled by ARTHUR PEETRE

The following selected bibliography, which originally included printed works used by the late author in the preparation of this section, has been supplemented with works printed up to date. Manuscript sources are not listed.

I. SOURCES

AAKJAER, S. (ed.). *Kong Valdemars Jordebog*, vols. I–III. Copenhagen, 1926–45.

ALMQUIST, J. A. (ed.). 'Arvid Trolles jordebok 1489', in *Historiska Handlingar*, 31, Stockholm, 1938.

BEAUCHE, L. (ed.). *Loi de Vestgothie*. Paris, 1894.

BERGELIN, A. (ed.). *The Law of the Westgoths*, III. Rock Island, 1906.

BRAHE, P. *Gamble grefwe Peer Brahes...oeconomia eller huuezholdz-book*. Stockholm, 1920.

BRINCHMANN, CHR. and AGERHOLT, J. (eds.). *Olav Engelbrektssoens jordebog*. Oslo, 1926.

CHRISTENSEN, C. A. (ed.). 'Roskildekirkens Jordeboeger og Regnskaber', in *Danske Middelalderlige Regnskaber*, 3 Raekke, 1 Bind, Copenhagen, 1956.

——(ed.). 'Liber Capituli Arusiensis', in *Corpus Codicum Danicorum*, vol. II, Copenhagen, 1960.

COLLIN, H. S. and SCHLYTER, C. J. (eds.). *Corpus iuris Sueo-Gotorum antiqui*. vol. I–13, Stockholm, 1827–77.

HANSEN, R. and JESSEN, W. (eds.). 'Liber censualis episcopi Sleswicensis', in *Quellensamlung der Gesellschaft für Schleswig-Holsteinische Geschichte*, IV, Kiel, 1904.

HEISE, A. (ed.). 'Brudstykker af Viborg Bispestols Jordebog i de sidste katholske Tider', in *Diplomatarium Vibergense*, Copenhagen, 1879.

HOLMBÄCK, A. and WESSÉN, E. (eds.). *Svenska landskapslagar tolkade och förklarade för nutidens svenskar*. ser. 1-6, Stockholm, 1933-63.

HUITFELDT, H. J. (ed.). *Biskop Eysteins Jordebok*. Christiania, 1879.

JOHNSEN, O. A., KOLSRUD, O. and TARANGER, A. (eds.). *Norges gamle Love* 1388-1604. Christiania-Oslo, 1912-34.

KEYSER, R., MUNCH, P. A., STORM, G., and HERTSBER, E. (eds.). *Norges gamle Love indtill* 1387. vols. 1-5. Christiania, 1846-95.

KJAER, A. (ed.). 'Fortegnelse over Hartvig Krummediges norske Jordegods', in *Sproglige og historiske Afhandlinger viede Sophus Bugges Minde*, Christiania, 1908.

KLEMMING, G. (ed.). 'Sumlen', in *Nyare bidrag till kännedom om de svenska landsmålen och folkliv*. Bihang I, Stockholm, 1886.

LUNDHOLM, K.-G. (ed.). 'Jordeboken C 39 i Riksarkivet', in *Yearbook of the New Society of Letters at Lund* 1954, Lund, 1955.

MATTHIESEN, C. M. A. (ed.). 'Procurationes sacerdotum jn archidiaconatu riipensi', in *Nya Kirkehistoriske Samlinger*, I, Copenhagen, 1857-9.

MEISSNER, R. (ed.). 'Norwegisches Recht. Das Rechtsbuch des Gulatings', in *Schriften der Akademie für Deutsches Recht. Germanenrechte*, Bd. 6, Weimar, 1935.

—— (ed.). 'Norwegisches Recht. Das Rechtsbuch des Frostathings', in *Schriften der Akademie für Deutsches Recht. Germanenrechte*, Bd. 4, Weimar, 1938.

—— (ed.). 'Landrecht des Königs Magnus Hakonarson', in *Schriften des Deutschrechtlichen Instituts. Germanenrechte*, Neue Folge, Weimar, 1941.

—— (ed.). 'Bruchstücke der Rechtsbücher des Borgarthings und des Eidsivathings', in *Schriften des Deutschrechtlichen Instituts. Germanenrechte*, Neue Folge, Weimar, 1942.

MUNCH, P. A. (ed.). 'Registrum praediorum et Redituum ad Ecclesias Dioecesis Bergensis saeculo P.C. XIV((, vulgo distum Bergens kalvskin', Christiania, 1843.

—— (ed.). 'Registrum praediorum munkalivensium', in *Codex Diplomatarius Monasterii Sancti Michaelis, Bergensis Dioecesis, vulgo Munkalif dicti*, Christiania, 1845.

—— (ed.). *Aslak Bolts Jordebog*. Christiania, 1852.

NIELSEN, O. (ed.). 'Dalum klosters jordebog 1533', in *Samlinger til Fyens Historie og Topographie*, IV, Odense, 1867.

—— (ed.). 'Samling af Adkomstakter, Indtaegtsangivelser og kirkelige Vedtaegter for Ribe Domkapittel, nedskrevet 1290-1518, kaldet "Oldemoder" (Avia Ripensis)', Copenhagen, 1869.

—— (ed.). *Liber Census Daniae*, Copenhagen, 1873.

—— (ed.). 'Annales pensiones omnium bonorum monasterii Esromensis anno domini MCDXC septimo', in *Codex Esromensis*, Copenhagen, 1880-1.

OSSIANNILSSON (DOVRING), F. (ed.). 'Fogdö klosters jordebok', in *Yearbook of the New Society of Letters at Lund*, Lund, 1945.

PEETRE, A. (ed.). 'Skoklosters medeltida jordeböcker', in *Publications of the New Society of Letters at Lund*, 42, Lund, 1953.

PONTOPPIDAN, E. (ed.). 'Registrum capituli Schlesvicensis', in *Annales ecclesiae Danicae*, II, Copenhagen, 1744.

RIETZ, J. E. and HERRSTROM, B. (eds.). *Praediorum monasterii Vadstenensis index*. Lund, 1850.

SCHWERIN, C. VON (ed.). 'Schwedische Rechte. Älteres Westgötalag, Uplandslag', in *Schriften der Akademie für Deutsches Recht. Germanenrechte*, Bd. 7, Weimar, 1935.

SILFVERSTOLPE, C. (ed.). 'Vadstena klosters jordebok', in *Historiska Handlingar*, 16:1, Stockholm, 1898.

STYFFE, C. G. (ed.). 'Computatio domini Rauonis de Barnekow super advocacia Nicopinghe', in *Bidrag till Skandinaviens historia*, I, Stockholm, 1859.

WELANDER, S. (ed.). 'Herr Aage Axelssons (Thott) "jordebok"', in *Yearbook of the New Society of Letters at Lund*, Lund, 1957.

WESSÉN, E. (ed.). *Corpus codicum suecicorum medii aevi*. vols. 1, 4, 5, 6, 8, 9, 12. Stockholm, 1943-50.

II. LITERATURE

AAKJAER, S. 'Villages, cadastres et plans parcellaires au Danemark', in *AHES*. Paris, 1929.
—— 'Bosaettelse og bebyggelseformer i Danmark', in *Bidrag till bondesamfundets historie, utg. Instituttet for sammenlignende kulturforskning,* I–II, Oslo, 1933.
—— 'Maal, Vaegt og Taxter i Danmark', in *Nordisk Kultur,* XXX, Stockholm, 1936.
—— 'Land Measurement and Land Valuation in Medieval Denmark', in *The Scandinavian Economic History Review,* vol. VII:2, Stockholm, 1959.
—— 'Maal, Vaegt og Taxter i Danmark', in *Nordisk Kultur,* XXX, Stockholm, 1936.
BJOERKVIK, H. 'Det norske kronogodset i mellomalderen', in *Historisk Tidsskrift,* vol. 40, Oslo, 1961.
BOLIN, S. *Ledung och fraelse,* Lund, 1934.
BULL, E. 'Byene i Norge i Middelalderen', in *Nordisk Kultur,* XVIII, Stockholm, 1933.
CHRISTENSEN, A. E. 'Danmarks befolkning og bebyggelse i middelalderen', in *Nordisk Kultur,* II, Stockholm, 1938.
DOVRING, F. *Attung och markland.* Lund, 1947.
ERIKSSON, M. 'Jordbruket under medeltiden', in *Svenska folket genom tiderna,* red. av E. Wrangel, vol. II, Stockholm, 1938.
ERIXON, S. 'Byar och samfaelligheter', in *Svensk Lantmaeteritidskrift,* Stockholm, 1955.
ERSLEV, K. *Valdemarernas Storhedstid.* Copenhagen, 1898.
HAFSTRÖM, G. *Ledung och marklandsindelning.* Uppsala, 1949.
—— 'Hammarskipt', in *Skrifter utg. av Institutet fö rättshistorisk forskning,* II:I, Stockholm, 1951.
HAGEN, A. 'Korndyrkningi i Noreg i eldre tid', in *Instituttet for sammenlignende kulturforskning,* Ser. A. XIV, Oslo, 1933.
—— 'Studier i Jernalderens gaardssamfund', in *Universitetets Oldsakssamlings Skrifter,* IV, Oslo, 1953.
HALD, K. *Vore stednavne.* Copenhagen, 1950.
HANNERBERG, A. 'Jordbrukets yttre rationalisering från det medeltida solskiftet till 1947 års jordbruksreform', in *Svensk Geografisk Årsbok,* 26, Stockholm, 1950.
HANNERBERG, A. 'Die Älteren skandinavischen Ackermasse', in *Lund Studies in Geography,* Ser. B, no. 12, Lund, 1955.
—— 'Byamål och tomtreglering i Mellansverige före solskiftet', in *Meddelanden från Geografiska Institutionen vid Stockholms Högskola,* no. 119. Stockholm, 1959.
HASUND, S. 'Korndyrkinga i Norge', in *Bidrag til Bondesamfundets Historie, utg. Instituttet for sammanlignende kulturforskning,* I–II, Oslo, 1933.
—— Or *Norges bondesoge.* vol. I–II. Oslo, 1942–4.
HATT, G. 'Praehistoric fields in Jylland', in *Acta archaeologica,* II, Copenhagen, 1931.
—— *Landbrug i Danmarks Oldtid.* Copenhagen, 1937.
—— 'The ownership of Cultivated Land', in *Det kgl. danske Videnskabernes Selskabs Skrifter, hist.-filol. medd.* XXVI, 6, Copenhagen, 1939.
JESSEN, K. 'Oldtidens korndyrkning i Danmark', in *Viking, tidsskrift for norrön arkeologi,* Oslo, 1951.
JOHNSEN, O. A. 'Norges folk i middelalderen', in *Nordisk Kultur,* II, Stockholm, 1938.
JUTIKKALA, E. 'Besittningen av åkerjord i Finland före tegskiftets införande', in Rig, vol. 29, Stockholm, 1946.
LAURIDSEN, P. 'Om Skyldjord eller terra in censu', in *Aarboeger for Nordisk Oldkyndighed,* II Raekke, 18 Bind, Copenhagen, 1903.
LUNDHOLM, K.-G. *Sten Sture d. ä. och stormännen.* Lund, 1956.
MEINICH OLSEN, K. *Norsk almenningsrett.* Oslo, 1928.
MEITZEN, A. *Siedlungen und Agrarwesen der Westgermanen und Ostgermanen, der Kelten, Römer, Finnen und Slaven,* vol. III. Berlin, 1895.
MEYER, P. *Danske bylag.* Copenhagen, 1949.
NORBORG, L.-A. *Storföretaget Vadstena kloster.* Lund, 1958.
NORDHOLM, G. 'Kungasängen Räften eller kungsmarken', in *Skånegillets i Stockholm Åsskrift,* Stockholm, 1936.

NORDHOLM, G. 'Skånes geometriska kartläggning fröre storskiftena', in *Svensk geografisk Årsbok*, Stockholm, 1929.

RISE HANSEN, C. and STEENSBERG, A. *Jordfordelning og Udskiftning*. Copenhagen, 1951.

ROSÉN, J. *Kronoavsöndringar under äldre medeltid*. Lund, 1949.

SCHUECK, A. 'Ur Sveriges medeltida befolkningshistoria', in *Nordisk Kultur*, II, Stockholm, 1938.

STEENSBERG, A. 'Jorddyrkning i middelalderen', in *Fra nationalmuseets Arbejdsmark*, Copenhagen, 1957.

STEINNES, A. *Jordetal og marketal*. Oslo, 1929.

—— 'Maal, vekt og verderegning i Noreg i millomalderen og ei tid etter', in *Nordisk Kultur*, XXX, Stockholm, 1936.

WEIBULL, C. G. *Skånska jordbrukets historia intill 1800-talets början*. Lund, 1923.

WIDDING, O. *Markfaellensskap og Landskifte*. Copenhagen, 1949.

VISTED, KR. and STIGUM, H. *Vaar gamle bondekultur*, I. Oslo, 1951.

WUEHRER, K. *Beitraege zur ältesten Agrargeschichte des germanischen Nordens*. Jena, 1935.

CHAPTER VIII

Crisis: From the Middle Ages to the Modern Times

Listed below are both works of general interest and some more special contributions the data of which have been used to illustrate the author's account by concrete instances.

I. GENERAL SURVEYS OF THE ECONOMIC SITUATIONS, FOURTEENTH AND FIFTEENTH CENTURIES

ABEL, W. *Agrarkrisen und Agrarkonjunktur in Mitteleuropa vom 13 bis zum 19 Jahrhundert*. Berlin, 1935.

DELATOUCHE, R. 'Agriculture médiévale et population', in *Les Etudes Sociales*, 1955, n. 28, 13–23.

—— 'La crise du XIV siècle en Europe occidentale', in *Les Etudes Sociales*, 1959, n. 2–3, 1–19.

DOBB, M. *Studies in the Development of Capitalism*. London, 1946.

DUBY, G. *L'économie rurale et la vie des campagnes dans l'Occident médiéval (France, Angleterre, Empire, IX–XV siècles)*. Paris, 1962.

GRAUS, F. 'Die erste Krise des Feudalismus', in *Zeitschrift für Geschichtswissenschaft*, III, 1955, 552–92.

HILTON, R. H. 'Y eut-il une crise générale de la féodalité?', in *Annales ESC.*, VI, 1951, 23–30.

KOETZSCHKE, R. *Allgemeine Wirtschaftsgeschichte des Mittelalters (Handbuch der Wirtschaftsgeschichte*, ed. G. Brodnitz). Jena, 1924.

KOSMINSKY, A. E. 'The Evolution of Feudal Rent in England from the XIth to the XVth Centuries', in *Past and Present*, no. 7, April 1955, 12–36.

—— 'Peut-on considérer le XIV et XV siècles comme époque de la décadence de l'économie européenne?', in *Studi in onore di Armando Sapori*, Milan, 1957, I, 553–69.

KOWALEWSKY, M. *Die ökonomische Entwicklung Europas bis zum Beginn der Kapitalistischen Wrtschaftsform (Bibliothek der Volkswirtschaftslehre und Gesellschaftswissenschaft)*, III–V. Berlin, 1905–11.

KULISCHER, J. *Allgemeine Wirtschaftsgeschichte des Mittelalters und der Neuzeit (Handbuch der mittelalterlichen und neueren Geschichte*, ed. von Below and Meinecke), vol I. Munich and Berlin, 1927; revised ed. 1954.

LEWIS, A. R. 'The Closing of the Medieval Frontier', in *Speculum*, XXXIII, 1958, 475–83.

LUETGE, F. 'Das 14–15 Jahrhundert in der Sozial- und Wirtschaftsgeschichte', in *Jahrbücher für Nationalökonomie und Statistik*, CLXII, 1950, 161–213.

PERROY, E. 'A l'origine d'une économie contractée. Les crises du XIV siècle', in *Annales. ESC.*, IV, 1949, 167-82.

POSTAN, M. M. 'The Fifteenth Century', in *EcHR.* vol. IX, no. 2, 1939, 160-7.

—— 'Die wirtschaftlichen Grundlagen der mittelalterlichen Gesellschaft', in *Jahrbücher für Nationalökonomie und Statistik*, CLXVI, 1954, 180-205.

SLICHER VAN BATH, B. H. *De agrarische geschiedenis van West Europa (500-1850)*. Utrecht-Antwerp, 1960.

II. MAIN NATIONAL, REGIONAL OR LOCAL STUDIES OF RURAL LIFE

DOPSCH, A. *Die ältere Wirtschafts- und Sozialgeschichte der Bauern in den Alpenländern Oesterreichs (Instituttet for Sammenlignende Kulturforskning, Serie A: Forelesninger IX)*. Oslo, 1930.

STOLZ, O. *Rechtsgeschichte des Bauernstandes und der Landwirtschaft in Tirol und Vorarlberg.* Bozen, 1949.

D'HAENENS, A. *L'abbaye Saint-Martin de Tournai de 1290 à 1350. Origines, évolution et dénouement d'une crise.* Louvain, 1961.

GENICOT, L. *L'économie rurale namuroise au bas moyen âge. 1199-1430. I, La seigneurie foncière. II, Les hommes. La noblesse.* Louvain, 1943 and 1960.

SABBE, E. 'Grondbezit en Landbouw, economische en sociale toestanden in de kastelenij Kortrijk op het einde der XIV eeuw', in *Handelingen van de Koninklijke Geschieden–Oudheidkundige Kring van Kortrijk*, Nieuwe reeks, XV, 1936, 394-452.

VAN UYTVEN, R. 'La Flandre et le Brabant "terres de promission" sous les ducs de Bourgogne', in *Revue du Nord*, XLIII, 1961, 281-318.

VERRIEST, L. *Le régime seigneurial en Hainaut du XI siècle à la Révolution.* Louvain, 1917.

GRAUS, F. *Dějiny venkovské ho lidu v Čechách v době předhusitské. II. Dějiny venkovského lidu od poloviny 13. stol. do roku 1419 [History of rural populations in Bohemia during the pre-Hussite period. II. History of rural populations from the mid thirteenth century until 1411.]* Prague, 1957.

ALLIX, A. *L'Oisans au moyen âge. Étude de géographie historique en haute montagne, d'après des documents inédits.* 2nd ed. Paris, 1929.

BÉZARD, Y. *La vie rurale dans le sud de la région parisienne de 1450 à 1560.* Paris, 1929.

BLOCH, M. *Les caractères originaux de l'histoire rurale française.* new ed. Paris, 1952.

BOUTRUCHE, R. *La crise d'une société. Seigneurs et paysans du Bordelais pendant la Guerre de Cent ans* (Publications de la Faculté des Lettres de l'Université de Strasbourg, fasc. 110). Paris, 1947.

BOUYSSOU, L. 'Étude sur la vie rurale dans la région d'Aurillac au XV siècle', in *Positions des thèses de l'École des Chartes*, 1941.

DE RIBBE, C. *La société provençale à la fin du moyen âge d'après des documents inédits.* Paris, 1898.

DUBY, C. 'Le grand domaine de la fin du moyen âge en France, in *Première conférence internationale d'histoire économique. Stockholm 1960.*

FOURQUIN, G. *Les campagnes de la région parisienne à la fin du moyen âge.* Paris, 1964.

FOSSIER, R. and L. 'Aspects de la crise frumentarie du XIV siècle en Artois et en Flandre gallicantes, in *Recueil de travaux offert à M. Clovis Brunel*, I, Paris, 1955, 436-47.

GRAND, R. (with the collaboration of R. Delatouche,). *L'agriculture au moyen âge, de la fin de l'empire romain au XVI siècle (L'agriculture à travers les âges*, III). Paris, 1950.

GUÉRIN, I. *La vie rurale en Sologne aux XIV et XV siècles.* Paris, 1960.

LATOUCHE, R. *La vie en Bas-Quercy du quatorzième au dix-huitième siècle (Bibliothèque Méridionale publiée sous les auspices de la Faculté des Lettres de Toulouse*, 2nd ser., XIX). Toulouse, 1923.

—— 'L'exploitation agricole dans le Maine du XIII au XVI siècle', in *Annales de Bretagne*, LI, 1944, 218-29.

LUC, P. *Vie rurale et pratique juridique en Béarn aux XIV et XV siècles.* Toulouse, 1943.

PERROY, E. 'La crise économique du XIV siècle d'après les terriers foréziens', in *Bulletin de la Diana*, XXIX. 1944, 67–80.

RAVEAU, P. *L'agriculture et les classes paysannes dans le Haut-Poitou au XVI siècle* (Bibliothèque d'histoire économique). Paris, 1926.

SCLAFERT, T. *Le Haut-Dauphiné au Moyen Age* (Faculté des Lettres de l'Université de Paris. Thèse pour le doctorat ès lettres). Paris, 1926.

—— *Cultures en Haute-Provence. Déboisements et pâturages au Moyen Age.* Paris, 1959.

TULIPPE, O. *L'habitat rural en Seine-et-Oise. Essai de de géographie du peuplement* (*Cercle des Géographes liégeois*, fasc. 22, et *Travaux du Séminaire de géographie de l'Université de Liège*, fasc. XLII). Liège, 1934.

ABEL, A. *Die Wüstungen des ausgehenden Mittelalters. Ein Beitrag zur Siedlungs—und Agrargeschichte Deutschlands* (*Quellen und Forschungen zur Agrargeschichte*, vol. I.) 2nd ed., Stuttgart, 1955.

Deutsche Agrargeschichte, ed. by G. FRANZ, vol. II. W. ABEL, *Geschichte der deutschen Landwirtschaft von frühen Mittelalter bis zum 19 Jahrhundert*, 1962; vol. III. F. LÜTGE, *Geschichte der deutschen Agrarverfassung vom . . .*, 1963; vol. IV, G. FRANZ, *Geschichte des Bauernstandes vom . . .*, 1963.

HUPPERTZ, B. *Räume und Schichten bauerlicher Kulturformen in Deutschland.* Bonn, 1939.

KELTER, E. 'Das deutsche Wirtschaftsleben des 14 und 15 Jahrhunderts im Schatten der Pestepidemien', in *Jahrbücher für Nationalökonomie und Statistik*, CLXV, 1953, 161–208.

LAMPRECHT, K. *Deutsches Wirtschaftsleben im Mittelalter, besonders am Moselland*, 3 vols. Leipzig, 1886–8.

LÜTGE, F. *Die bayerische Grundherrschaft, Untersuchungen über die Agrarverfassung Altbayerns im 16–18 Jahrhundert.* Stuttgart, 1949.

—— *Die mitteldeutsche Grundherrschaft und ihre Auflösung.* 2nd ed. Stuttgart, 1957.

MAYER, T. *Adel und Bauern im deutschen Staat des Mittelalters.* Leipzig, 1943.

MORTENSEN, H. 'Die mittelalterliche deutsche Kulturlandschaft und ihr Verhältnis zur Gegenwart', in *VSWG*. XLV, 1958, 17–36.

von zur MUEHLEN, H. 'Kolonisation und Gutsherrschaft in Ostdeutschland', in *Geschichtliche Landeskunde und Universalgeschichte. Festgabe für H. Aubin zum 23. Dezember 1950*, 83–95.

MÜLLER-WILLE, W. *Der Landkreis Münster.* Münster-Cologne, 1955.

PERRIN, C. E. *La société allemande à la fin du moyen âge* (Stencylé). Paris, 1947.

TIMM, A. *Studien zur Siedlungs-und Agrargeschichte Mitteldeutschlands.* Cologne-Graz, 1956.

PACH, Z. P. 'Das Entwickungsniveau der feudalen Agrarverhältnisse in Ungarn in der zweiten Hälfte des XV Jahrhunderts', in *Etudes Historiques publiées par la Commission nationale des historiens hongrois*, I. Budapest, 1960, 387–435.

CIPOLLA, C. M. 'L'economia milanese. I movimenti economici generali (1350–1500)', in *Storia di Milano*, VIII, 347–373.

DE CUPIS, C. *Le vicende dell'agricoltura e della pastorizia nell'agro romano.* Roma, 1911.

DOREN, A. *Italienische Wirtschaftsgeschichte. Erster Band* (*Handbuch der Wirtschaftsgeschichte*, ed. G. Brodnitz). Jena, 1934.

LUZZATTO, G. *Storia economica d'Italia*, I. Rome, 1949.

—— 'Per la storia dell'economia rurale in Italia nel secolo XIV', in *Eventail de l'histoire vivante. Hommage à Lucien Fèbure*, II. Paris, 1953, 105–113.

PALMIERI, A. *La montagna bolognese del medio evo.* Bologna, 1929.

SAPORI, G. 'Le condizioni giuridiche e social in cui si è sviluppata l'agricoltura italiana', in *La distribuzione della proprietà fondiaria in Italia. I, Relazione generale.* Rome, 1956.

NIERMEYER, J. F. *De wording van onze volkshuishouding* (Servire's Encyclopaedie). The Hague, 1946.

TYMIENIECKI, K. 'Quelques parallèles de l'histoire agraire du moyen âge', in *Acta Poloniae Historica*, I, 1958, 9–32.

CARSTEN, F. L. *The origins of Prussia*. Oxford, 1954.

BLUM, J. *Lord and Peasant in Russia from the Ninth to the Nineteenth Century*. London and Princeton, 1961.

Historia social y economica de España y América, ed. J. Vicens Vivès. II. *Patriciado urbano* by S. SOBREQUÉS VIDAL. Barcelona, 1957.

BEAN, J. M. W. *The Estates of the Percy Family, 1416–1537*. Oxford, 1958.
DAVENPORT, F. G. *The Economic Development of a Norfolk Manor, 1086–1565*. Cambridge, 1906.
FINBERG, H. P. R. *Tavistock Abbey. A Study in the Social and Economic History of Devon*. Cambridge, 1951.
FRANKLIN, T. B. *A History of Scottish Farming* (Nelson's Agricultural Serie). Edinburgh, 1952.
GRASS, N. S. B. *The Economic and Social History of an English Village* (Harvard Economic Studies, XXXIV). Cambridge, Mass., 1930.
HILTON, R. H. *The Economic Development of some Leicestershire Estates in the 14th and 15th Centuries*. Oxford, 1947.
—— 'Medieval Agrarian History', in *The Victoria History of the Counties of England. Leicestershire*, II, London, 1954, 181–98.
JACOB, E. F. *The Fifteenth Century (1399–1485)* (*The Oxford History of England*, 6). Oxford, 1961.
KNOWLES, D. *The Religious Orders in England. II. The End of the Middle Ages*. Cambridge, 1955.
LEVETT, A. E. *Studies in Manorial History*. Oxford, 1938.
LIPSON, E. *The Economic History of England*. vol. I. 10th ed. London, 1949.
MAITLAND, F. W. 'The History of a Cambridgeshire Manor', in *EHR*. IX, 1894, 417–39 or *Collected Papers*, II, 366–402. Cambridge, 1911.
MORGAN, M. *The English Lands of the Abbey of Bec*. Oxford, 1946.
MUHLFELD, H. E. *A Survey of the Manor of Wye. (Studies in History, Economics and Public Law edited by the Faculty of Political Science of Columbia University, 331)*. New York, 1933.
NEILSON, N. *Economic conditions on the Manors of Ramsay Abbey*. Philadelphia, 1898.
PAGE, F. M. *The Estates of Crowland Abbey: A Study in Manorial Organisation (Cambridge Studies in Economic History)*. Cambridge, 1934.
RAFTIS, J. A. *The Estates of Ramsey Abbey. A Study in Economic Growth and Organization*. Toronto, 1957.
ROBO, E. *Medieval Farnham*. Farnham, 1935.
SMITH, R. A. L. *Canterbury Cathedral Priory: A Study in Monastic Administration (Cambridge Studies in Economic History)*. Cambridge, 1943.

III. DEMOGRAPHIC TRENDS AND THEIR FACTORS

ABEL, W. 'Wachstumsschwankungen mitteleuropäischer Völker seit dem Mittelalter', in *Jahrbücher für Nationalökonomie und Statistik*, CXLII, 1935, 670–92.
ARNOULD, M. A. *Les dénombrements de foyers dans le comté de Hainaut (XIV–XVI siècle)* (Académie royale de Belgique. Commission royale d'histoire, Publications in 4to). Brussels, 1956.
BARATIER, E. *La Démographie provençale du XIII au XVI siècle*. Paris, 1961.
BAUTIER, R. 'Feux, population et structure sociale au milieu du XV siècle. L'exemple de Carpentras', in *Annales ESC*. XIV, 1959, 255–68.
BELOCH, K. J. *Bevölkerungsgeschichte Italiens*. 3 vol. Berlin-Leipzig, 1937, 1939, 1961.
BENNET, M. K. *The World's Food*. Stanford, 1954.

BERESFORD, M. *The Lost Villages of England.* London, 1954.

BOENISCH, F. 'Der Stand der Wüstungsforschung in der Niederlausitz', in *Abhandlungen und Berichte des Naturkundemuseums Görlitz*, 36, 1960, 9–51.

BOOS, H. *Geschichte der rheinischen Städte-Kultur*, 2nd ed. vol. III. Berlin, 1899.

BRAURE, M. 'Étude économique sur les châtellenies de Lille, Douai et Orchies d'après des enquêtes fiscales des XV et XVI siècles', in *Revue du Nord*, XIV, 1928, 85–116 and 165–200.

BUOMBERGER, F. *Bevölkrungs-und Vermögensstatistik in der Stadt und Landschaft Freiburg (im Uechtland) um die Mitte des 15 Jahrhunderts.* Bern, 1900 (also published in *Zeitschrift für schweizerische Statistik*, XXXVI, 1900.)

CIPOLLA, C. M. 'Per la storia della crisi del sistema curtense in Italia. Lo sfaldamento del manso nell'Appenino bobbiese', in *Bullettino dell'Istituto storico italiano per il Medio Evo e Archivio Muratoriano*, no. 62, 1950, 283–304.

CIPOLLA, C., DHONDT, J., POSTAN, M. M., and WOLFF, P. 'Anthropologie et démographie. Moyen âge', in *IX Congrès international des sciences historiques. I, Rapports*, 55–80; *II, Actes*, 31–44. Paris, 1950 and 1951.

CUVELIER, J. *Les dénombrements de foyers en Brabant (XIV–XVI siècle)* (Académie royale de Belgique. Commission royale d'histoire. Publications in 4to). Brussels, 1912.

An Historical Geography of England. Ed. by H. DARBY. Cambridge, 1936.

DELATTE, I. 'La Hesbaye liégeoise à la fin du XIII siècle', in *Bulletin de la Société royale Le Vieux Liège*, no. 104–5, 1954, 290–7.

DE ROBILLARD DE BEAUREPAIRE, C. *Recherches sur la population de la généralité et du diocèse de Rouen avant 1789 (Mémoires de la Société des Antiquaires de Normandie, XXVIII).* Évreux, 1872.

GANSHOF, F. L. *Over stadsontwikkeling tusschen Loire en Rijn gedurende de Middeleeuwen.* 2nd ed. Brussels, 1944.

GENICOT, L. 'L'étendue des exploitations agricoles dans le comté de Namur à la fin du XIII siècle', in *Études rurales*, 5, 1962, 5–31.

GLÉNISSON, J. 'Essai de recensement et d'interprétation des sources de l'histoire démographique en France au XIV siècle', in *XI Congrès international des sciences historiques. Stockholm, 1960. Résumé des communications.* 44–46.

GORISSEN, F. *Stede-Atlas van Nijmegen.* Arnhem, 1956.

GRUND, A. *Die Veränderungen der Topographie im Wiener Walde und Wiener Becken (Geographische Abhandlungen, ed. A. Penck, VIII).* Leipzig, 1901.

GYÖRFFY, Gij. 'Einwohnerzahl und Bevölkerungsdichte in Ungarn bis zum Anfang des XIV Jh.' in *Études historiques publiées par la Commission nationale des historiens hongrois.* Budapest, 1960, 163–93.

HALLAM, H. E. 'Population Density in Medieval Finland', in *EcHR.* 2nd ser. XIV, 1961–2, 71–81.

HELLEINER, K. 'Europas Bevölkerung und Wirtschaft im späteren Mittelalter', in *Mitteilungen des Instituts für Oesterreichische Geschichtsforschung*, LXII, 1954, 254–69.

—— 'Population Movement and Agrarian Depression in the Later Middle Ages', in *Canadian Journal of Economics and Political Science*, XV, 1949, 368–77.

HIGOUNET, C. 'Cisterciens et bastides', in *Le Moyen Âge*, LVI, 1950, 69–84. (With references to other contributions relating to that subject.)

JAEGER, H. 'Die Ausdehnung der Wälder in Mitteleuropa über offenes Siedlungsland, in *Géographie et histoire agraire. Annales de l'Est, Mémoires*, no. 21. Nancy, 1959, 300–12.

JIMENEZ DE GREGORIO, F. 'La poblacion de la Jara toledana', in *Estudios Geograficos*, XI–XVI, 1950–5.

—— 'Repoblacion y pobliamento del campo murciano', in *Anales de la Universidad de Murcia. Filosofia y Letras.* XV, 1956–1957, 85–143.

KEYSER, E. *Bevölkerungsgeschichte Deutschlands*, 2nd ed. Leipzig, 1941.

KNUELL, B. *Historische Geographie Deutschlands im Mittelalter.* Breslau, 1903.

KRENZLIN, A. 'Das Wüstungsproblem im Lichte ostdeutscher Siedlungsforschung', in *ZAA.* VII, 1959, 153–69.

KUHN, W. *Geschichte der deutschen Ostsiedlung in der Neuzeit*, 2 vols. Cologne-Graz, 1955-7.

LLOBET, S. 'Evolucion del pobliamento y poblacion de la comarca del Vallés, in *Estudios Geograficos*, III, 1942, 751-832.

LOT, F. 'L'état des paroisses et des feux de 1328', in *Bibliothèque de l'École des Chartes*, XC, 1929, 51-107.

—— *Recherches sur la population et la superficie des cités remontant à la période gallo-romaine* (*Bibliothèque de l'École des Hautes Études. Sciences historiques et philologiques*, vols. 287 and 296). Paris, 1945 and 1950.

MARTIN-LORBER, O. 'Une communauté d'habitants dans une seigneurie de Cîteaux aux XIII et XIV siècles', in *Annales de Bourgogne*, 30, 1958, 7-36.

MOLS, R. *Introduction à la démographie historique des villes d'Europe, du XIV au XVIII siècle*, 3 vols. Louvain, 1955.

MORTENSEN, H. 'Neue Beobachtungen über Wüstungsbandfluren und ihre Bedeutung für die mittelalterliche deutsche Kulturlandschaft', in *Berichte zur deutschen Landeskunde*, X, 1952, 341-61.

NORBORG, L. A. *Storförelaget Vadstena Kloster*. Lund, 1958. (With a German summary).

NORTIER, M. 'Aperçus sur la population de la vicomté de Coutances vers 1365-1368 d'après deux comptes de fouage', in *Notices, mémoires et documents publiés par la Société d'Archéologie et d'Histoire Naturelle du Département de la Manche*, LXV, 1957, 7-13.

POHLENDT, H. *Die Verbreitung der mittelalterlichen Wüstungen in Deutschland*. (*Göttingen geographische Abhandlungen*, ed. H. Mortensen, no. 3). Göttingen, 1953.

PORTAL, C. 'Essai d'étude démographique sur Cordes (Tarn)', in *Bibliothèque de l'École des Chartes*, LV, 1894, 133-42.

POSTAN, M. M. 'Some Economic Evidence of Declining Population in the Later Middle Ages', in *EcHR*. 2nd ser. vol. II, no. 3, 1950, 221-46.

POSTAN, M. M. and TITOW, J. 'Heriots and prices on Winchester Manors', in *EcHR*. 2nd ser. vol. XI, 1958-9, 392-411.

Quellen zur Steuer-, Bevölkerungs- und Sippengeschichte des Landes Tirol im 13, 14 und 15 Jahrhundert. Festgabe zum 80 Lebensjahre O. Redlichs (Schlern-Schriften, H. 44). Innsbrück, 1939.

REINCKE, H. 'Bevölkerungsprobleme der Hansestädte', in *Hansische Geschichtsblätter*, LXX, 1951, 1-33.

—— 'Bevölkerungsverluste der Hansestädte durch den Schwarzen Tod 1349/1350', in *Hansische Geschichtsblätter*, LXXII, 1954, 88-90.

ROCA TRAVER, Fr. A. 'Cuestiones de demografia medieval', in *Hispania. Revista española de Historia*, XIII, 1953, 3-36.

RUSIŃSKI, W. 'Wüstungen. Ein Agrarproblem des feudalen Europas', in *Acta Poloniae Historica*, V, 1962, 48-78.

RUSSELL, J. C. *British Medieval Population*. Albuquerque, 1948.

SCHARLAU, K. 'Neue Probleme der Wüstungsforschung', in *Berichte zur deutschen Landeskunde*, XVII, 1956, 266-75.

SCHNYDER, W. 'Die Bevölkerung der Stadt und Landschaft Zürich von 14. bis 17. Jahrhundert', Zürich, 1925.

SCHULTZ, A. *Deutsches Leben im 14 und 15 Jahrhundert*. Revised ed. Leipzig, 1892.

SLICHER VAN BATH, B. A. *Een samenleving onder spanning. Geschicdenis van het platteland in Overijssel*. Assen, 1957.

SZABÓ, I. 'La répartition de la population en Hongrie entre les bourgades et les villages, dans les années 1449-1526', in *Études historiques publiées par la Commission nationale des historiens hongrois*, I. Budapest, 1960, 359-85.

TITOW, J. Z. 'Some Evidence of the Thirteenth Century Population Increase', in *EcHR*. 2nd ser. XIV, 1961-2, 218-23.

TRABUT-CUSSAC, J. P. 'Bastides ou forteresses. Les bastides de l'Aquitaine anglaise et les intentions de leurs fondateurs', in *Le Moyen Âge*, LX. 1954, 81-135.

VIVIER, R. 'Une crise économique au milieu du 14 siècle', in *Revue d'histoire économique et sociale*, VIII. 1920, 199-230.

WEBER, D. *Die Wüstungen in Württemberg. Ein Beitrag zur historischen Siedlungs- und Wirtschaftgeographie von Württemberg (Stuttgarter geographische Studien, no. 4/5).* Stuttgart, 1927.
WOLFF, P. *Commerce et marchands de Toulouse (vers 1350–vers 1450).* Paris, s. d. [1954].
—— 'Trois études de démographie médiévale en France méridionale', in *Studi in onore di Armando Sapori*, Milan, 1957, 495–503.

BRITTON, C. E. *A Meteorological Chronology to A.D. 1450 (Meteorological Office, Geophysical Memoirs*, LXX). London, 1937.
FLOHN, H. 'Klimatschwankungen im Mittelalter und ihre historisch-geographische Bedeutung', in *Berichte zur deutschen Landeskunde.* Stuttgart, 1949–50, 347–57.
—— 'Klimatschwankungen der letzten 1000 Jahre', in *Verhandlungen des deutschen Geographentages*, XXXI, 1957, 201–14.
LE ROY LADURIE, E. 'Histoire et climat', in *Annales. ESC.* XIV, 1959, 3–34.
STEENSBERG, A. 'Archaeological dating of the climate change in North Europe about A.D. 1300', in *Nature*, CLXVIII, 1951, 672–674.
UTTERSTRÖM, G. 'Climatic Fluctuations and Population Problems in Early Modern History', in *The Scandinavian Economic History Review*, III, 1955, 3–4.
WEIKINN, C. *Quellenkunde zur Witterungsgeschichte Europas von der Zeitwende bis zum Jahre 1850.*

CAPRA, P. J. 'Au sujet des famines en Aquitaine au XIV siècle', in *Revue historique de Bordeaux et du département de la Gironde*, IV, (1955) 1–32.
LARENAUDIE, M. J. 'Les famines en Languedoc aux XIV et XV siècles', in *Annales du Midi*, LXIV, 1952, 27–39.
LUCAS, H. S. 'The great European famine of 1315, 1316 and 1317', in *Speculum*, V, 1930, 343–77.
VAN WERVEKE, H. 'La famine de l'an 1316 en Flandre et dans les régions voisines', in *Revue du Nord*, XLI, 1959, 5–14.

BALLARD, A. *The Black Death on the Manors of Witney, Brightwell, and Downton (Oxford Studies in Social and Legal History*, V, 181–216). Oxford, 1916.
BOUDET, M. and GRAND, R. *Étude historique sur les épidémies de peste en Haute-Auvergne (XIV–XVIII siècle).* Paris, 1902.
CARPENTIER, E. *Une ville devant la peste. Orvieto et la peste noire de 1348.* Paris, 1962.
COVILLE, A. 'Écrits contemporains sur la peste de 1348 à 1350', in *Histoire littéraire de la France*, XXXVII, 1938, 325–90.
CREIGHTON, C. *A History of Epidemics in Britain from A.D. 664 to the Extinction of Plague.* Cambridge, 1891.
GASQUET, F. A. *The Great Pestilence (A.D. 1348–9) now commonly known as the Black Death.* London, 1893; reprinted 1908.
GRAS, P. 'Le registre paroissial de Givry (1334–1357) et la peste noire en Bourgogne', in *Bibliothèque de l'École des Chartes*, C, 1939, 295–308.
HOENIGER, R. *Der Schwarze Tod in Deutschland.* Berlin, 1882.
KLEIN, H. 'Das Grosse Sterben von 1348/49 und seine Auswirkung auf die Besiedlung der Ostalpenländer', in *Mitteilungen der Gesellschaft für Salzburger Landeskunde*, C, 1960, 91–170.
LEVETT, A. E. *The Black Death on the Estates of the See of Winchester (Oxford Studies in Social and Legal History*, V, 7–180), Oxford, 1916.
PRAT, C. 'La peste noire à Albi', in *Annales du Midi*, LXIV, 1952, 15–25.
SALTMARSH, J. 'Plague and Economic Decline in England in the Later Middle Ages', in *The Cambridge Historical Journal*, VII, 1941–3, 23–41.
SCHREINER, J. *Pest og Prisfall i Senmiddelalderen. Et Problem i Norsk Historie(Avhandlinger utgitt av det Norske Videnskaps—Akademi i Oslo, II. Hist.—Filos. Klasse*, 1948, no. I). Oslo, 1948.

THOMPSON, A. H. 'Registers of John Gynewell, Bishop of Lincoln, for the Years 1347–1350', in *Archaeological Journal*, LXVIII, 1911, 301–360.

—— 'The Pestilences of the Fourteenth Century in the diocese of York', in *Archaeological Journal*, LXXI, 1914, 97–154.

VAN WERVEKE, H. *De zwarte dood in de Zuidelijke Nederlanden (1349–51) (Mededelingen van de Koninklijke Vlaamse Academie voor Wetenschappen, Letteren en Schone Kunsten van België. Kl. der Letteren*, Jg. XII, no. 3). Brussels, 1950.

VERLINDEN, C. 'La grande peste de 1348 en Espagne. Contribution à l'étude de ses conséquences économiques et sociales', in *RB*. XVII, 1938, 103–146.

IV. PRICES AND WAGES

ABEL, W. 'Wüstungen und Preisfall im spätmittelalterlichen Europa', in *Jahrbücher für Nationalökonomie und Statistik*, CLXV, 1953, 380–427.

BEVERIDGE, W. 'Wages in the Winchester Manors', in *EcHR*. III, 1, Nov. 1936, 22–43.

BEVERIDGE, E. 'Westminster Wages in the Manorial Era', in *EcHR*. 2nd ser. VIII, 1955–1956, 18–35.

D'AVENEL, G. *Histoire économique de la propriété, des salaires, des denrées et de tous les prix en général depuis l'an 1200 jusqu'en l'an 1800*. 6 vols., 2nd ed. Paris, 1913–19.

DELVAUX, B. '*L'évolution des prix et des salaires à Namur aux XIV et XV siècles*. Louvain (unpublished dissertation), 1960.

Documents pour servir à l'histoire des prix et des salaires en Flandre et en Brabant (XV–XVIII siècles), general editor, C. VERLINDEN (*Rijksuniversiteit te Gent. Werken uitgegeven door de Faculteit van de Letteren en Wijsbegeerte*, 125 Afl.). Bruges, 1959.

ELSAS, J. *Umriss einer Geschichte der Preise und Löhne in Deutschland vom ausgehenden Mittelalter bis zum Beginn des neunzehnten Jahrhunderts*. 2 vols. Leide, 1936 and 1940.

HAMILTON, E. J. *Money, Prices and Wages in Valencia, Aragon and Navarre, 1351–1500 (Harvard Economic Studies*, LI). Cambridge, Mass., 1936.

HANAUER, A. *Études économiques sur l'Alsace ancienne et moderne. II. Denrées et salaires*. Paris and Strasbourg, 1878.

KELTER, E. *Geschichte der obrigkeitlichen Preisregelung. I. Die obrigkeitliche Preisregelung in der Zeit der mittelalterlichen Stadtwirtschaft (Bonner Staatswissenschaftliche Untersuchungen*, ed. H. von Beckerath, A. Spiethaff and W. Vleugels, no. 21). Jena, 1935.

MESTAYER, M. 'Prix du blé et de l'avoine de 1329 à 1793' [à Douai], in *Revue du Nord*, XLV, 1963, 157–178.

MEUVRET, J. 'Les prix des grains à Paris au XV siècle et les origines de la mercuriale', in *Paris et Île-de-France. Mémoires publiés par la Fédération des Sociétés historiques et archéologiques de Paris et de l'Île-de-France*, XI, 1960, 283–311.

PELC, J. *Ceny w Krakowie w latach 1369–1600. Les prix à Cracovie de 1369 à 1600 (Badania z dziejów społecznych i gospodarczych pod redakcja Prof. Fr. Bruyaka*, no. 14). Lwow, 1935.

PERROY, E. 'Wage labour in France in the later middle ages', in *EcHR*., 2nd ser. VIII, 1955–1956, 232–9.

PLATZER, H. *Geschichte der ländlichen Arbeitsverhältnisse in Bayern (Altbayerische Forschungen*, II–III). Munich, 1904.

PRIBRAM, A. F. *Materialen zur Geschichte der Preise und Löhne in Oesterreich*, I. Vienna, 1938.

RAVEAU, P. 'La crise des prix en Poitou au XVI siècle', in *RH*. CLXII, 1929, 1–44 and 268–93.

—— *Essai sur la situation économique et l'état social en Poitou au XVI siècle (Bibliothèque d'histoire économique)*. Paris, 1931.

ROGERS, J. E. T. *A History of Agriculture and Prices in England*. vols. I–IV. Oxford, 1866–82.

ROSSI, E. and ARCARI, P. M. 'I prezzi a Genova dal XII al XV secolo', in *La vita economica italiana*, VIII, 1933, 53–87.

SCHOLLIERS, E. *Loonarbeid en Honger. De levensstandaard in de XV en XVI eeuw te Antwerpen*. Antwerp, 1960.

SCHREINER, J. *Pest og prisfall i Senmiddelalderen, Et problem i Norsk Historie.* Oslo 1948.
—— 'Wages and prices in England in the later Middle Ages', in *The Scandinavian Economic History Review*, II, 1954, 61–73.
SILLEM, M. J. A. *Tabellen van marktprijzen van granen te Utrecht in de jaren 1393 tot 1644 (Verhandelingen der Koninklijke Akademie van Wetenschappen te Amsterdam. Afdeeling Letterkunde.* N. R. Part III, 4). Utrecht, 1901.
STRAYER, J. R. 'Economic conditions in the county of Beaumont le Roger, *1261–1313*', in *Speculum*, XXVI, 1951, 277–87.
TADIĆ, J. 'Les archives économiques de Raguse', in *Annales. ESC.* XVI, 1961, 1168–75.
USHER, A. P. 'The General Course of Wheat Prices in France: 1350–1788', in *The Review of Economic Statistics*, XII, 1930, 159–169.
—— 'Prices of Wheat and Commodity Price Indexes for England, 1259–1930', in *The Review of Economic Statistics*, XIII, 1931, 103–113.
VAN DER WEE, H. *The Growth of the Antwerp Market and the European economy. Vol. I. History of prices and wages in Brabant (fourteenth–sixteenth centuries).* Louvain, 1963.
VAN HOUTTE, H. *Documents pour servir à l'histoire des prix de 1381 à 1794* (Académie royale de Belgique, Commission royale d'histoire, Publications in 4to). Brussels, 1902.

BLOCH, M. *Esquisse d'une histoire monétaire de l'Europe* (Cahiers des Annales, no. 9). Paris, 1954.
CIPOLLA, C. M. *Studi di storia della moneta. I. I movimenti dei cambi in Italia dal secolo XIII al XV (Pubblicazioni della Università di Pavia. Studi nelle scienze giuridiche e sociali,* 101). Pavia, 1948.
KOVACEVIC, D. 'Dans la Serbie et la Bosnie médiévales: les mines d'or et d'argent', in *Annales ESC.* XV, 1960, 248–258.
LAURENT, H. *La loi de Gresham au moyen âge. Essai sur la circulation monétaire entre la Flandre et le Brabant à la fin du XIV siècle.* Brussels, 1933.
NEF, J. 'Mining and Metallurgy in Medieval Civilisation', in *Cambridge Economic History*, II, 430–494.
REY, M. 'Les émissions d'écus à la couronne à l'Hôtel des Monnaies de Paris vers la fin du XIV siècle et dans les premières années du XV (1385–1413)', in *Mélanges d'histoire du moyen âge dédiés à la mémoire de Louis Halplen*, 595–603, Paris, 1951.
VAN WERVEKE, H. 'Currency Manipulation in the Middle Ages: the Case of Louis de Male, count of Flanders', in *TRHS.* 4th ser. vol. XXXI, 1949, 115–27.

CARUS-WILSON, E. M. and COLEMAN, D. *England's Export Trade, 1275–1547.* Oxford, 1963.
FRANZ, G., ABEL, W. and CASCORBI, G. *Der deutsche Land-Warenhandel.* Hanover, 1960.
GRASS, N. S. B. *The evolution of the English Corn Market from the Twelfth to the Eighteenth Century* (Harvard Economic Studies, XIII). Cambridge, Mass., 1915, repr. 1926.
HENNINGS, H. H. 'Die Lübecker Kornhaüser zu Beginn des 14 Jahrhunderts', in *Städtewesen und Bürgertum als geschichtliche Kräfte, Gedächtnisschrift für F. Rörig*, Lübeck, 1953.
KERLING, N. J. M. *Commercial relations of Holland and Zeland with England from the late 13th century to the close of the middle ages.* Leiden, 1954.
NAUDÉ, W. *Die Getreidehandelspolitik der europäischen Staaten vom 13 bis zum 18 Jahrhundert, als Einstellung in die preussische Getreidehandelspolitik (Acta Borussica).* Berlin, 1896.
PETINO, A. *Aspetti e momenti di politica granaria a Catania ed in Sicilia nel quattrocento.* Catania, 1951–2.
RUNDSTEDT, H. G. von. *Die Regelung des Getreidehandels in den Städten Südwestdeutschlands und der deutschen Schweiz im späteren Mittelalter und im Beginn der Neuzeit (Beiheft 19 zur Vierteljahrsschrift für Sozial–und Wirtschaftsgeschichte).* Stuttgart, 1930.
SERRAO, J. 'Le blé des Iles Atlantiques', in *Annales. ESC.* IX, 1954, 337–41.
USHER, A. P. *History of the grain trade in France, 1400–1710* (Harvard Economic Studies, IX). Cambridge, Mass. 1913.

ZIENTARA, B. 'Einige Bemerkungen über die Bedeutung des Pommerschen Exports im Rahmen des Ostsee-Getreidenhandels im 13. und 14. Jahrhundert', in *Hansische Studien. Heinrich Sproemberg zum 70. Geburtstag*, Berlin, 1961, 422-431.

V. WARS AND THEIR CONSEQUENCES

BOUTRUCHE, R. 'La dévastation des campagnes pendant la Guerre de Cent Ans et la reconstruction agricole de la France', in *Publications de la Faculté des Lettres de l'Université de Strasbourg*, fasc. 106, *Mélanges 1945, III, Études historiques*, 127-63.

DENIFLE, P. *La désolation des églises, monastères et hôpitaux en France pendant la Guerre de Cent ans.* 2 vols. Paris, 1897-9.

LESORT, A. 'La reconstitution des églises après le guerre de Cent Ans', in *Revue d'Histoire de l'Église de France*, XX, 1934, 177-215.

McFARLANE, K. B. 'The Investment of Sir John Fastolf's Profits of War', in *TRHS*. 5th ser. VIII, 1957, 91-116.

PERROY, E. *La Guerre de Cent Ans.* 4th ed. Paris, 1944.

POSTAN, M. M. 'Some Social Consequences of the Hundred Years War', in *EcHR.*, XII, 1942, 1-12.

TUCOO-CHALA, P. *Gaston Fébus et la vicomté de Béarn (1343-1391).* Bordeaux, 1960.

WADDINGTON, C. H. 'Note sur la dépopulation des campagnes gâtinaises pendant la Guerre de Cent Ans et leur reconstitution économique', in *Annales de la Société historique et archéologique du Gâtinais*, XXXIX, 1930, 164-178.

VI. THE POLITICAL AND INTELLECTUAL MILLIEU

AUBIN, C. Der Einflusz der Rezeption des römischen Rechtes auf den deutschen Bauernstand', in *Jahrbücher für Nationalökonomie und Statistik*, 16, 1912, 721-42.

GRUNDMANN, H. 'Freiheit als religiöses, politisches und persönliches Postulat im Mittelalter', in *HZ*. 183, 1957, 23-53.

VOLTELINI, H. von. 'Der Gedanke der allgemeinen Freiheit in den deutschen Rechtsbüchern', in *ZSS*. Germanic Section, LVII, 1937, 182-209.

BRACK, H. 'Werner Rovelincks Bauernspiegel', in *HJ*. LXXIV, 1955, 139-149.

DE LAGARDE, G. *La naissance de l'esprit laïque au déclin du moyen âge. III. Secteur social de la scolastique.* Paris, 1942.

DEVLIN, M. A. *The Sermons of Thomas Brinton, Bishop of Rochester, (1373-1389) (Camden Society*, 3rd ser., LXXXV-LXXXVI). London, 1954.

HUEGLI, H. *Der deutsche Bauer im Mittelalter, dargestellt nach den deutschen literarischen Quellen vom 11-15 Jh.* Berne, 1928.

OWST, G. R. *Literature and Pulpit in Medieval England*, 2nd ed. Cambridge, 1961.

SERRARENS, Ed. A. 'Kommunisme in de Middelnederlandsche Letterkunde', in *Tijdchrift voor Taal en Letteren*, XVI, 1928, 1-32 and 77-127.

VII. THE LORDS

A. *Their action and achievements*

AUBIN, G. *Zur Geschichte des gutsherrlichbäuerlichen Verhältnisses in Ostpreuszen von der Gründung des Ordenstaates bis zur Steinschen Reform.* Leipzig, 1910.

CARUS WILSON, E. M. 'Evidence of Industrial Growth on some Fifteenth-Century Manors', in *EcHR.*, 2nd ser. XII, 1959-60, 197-205.

CIPOLLA, C. M. 'Une crise ignorée. Comment s'est perdue la propriété ecclésiastique dans l'Italie du Nord entre le XI et le XVI siècle', in *Annales. ESC.* III, 1947, 317-27.

DELATOUCHE, R. 'Le droit familial de quelques grandes maisons féodales de l'Ouest de la France, du 13 au 16 siècle', in *École nationale des Chartes. Positions des Thèses*, 1934, 49-50.

DE VAISSIÈRE, P. *Gentilshommes campagnards de l'ancienne France.* 3rd ed. Paris, 1904.

DEBIEN, G. *En Haut Poitou. Défricheurs au travail. XV–XVIII siècles.* Paris, 1952.

DONNELLY, J. S. 'Changes in the Grange Economy of English and Welsh Cistercian Abbeys, 1300–1450', in *Traditio*, x, 1954, 399–458.

DUBY, G. 'La seigneurie et l'économie paysanne. Alpes du Sud, 1338', in *Études rurales*, 2, 1961, 5–36.

FOURNIER, C. 'La création de la grange de Gergovie par les Prémontrés de Saint-André et sa transformation en seigneurie (XII–XVI siècles)', in *Le Moyen Âge*, LVI, 1950, 307–55.

HALCROW, E. M. 'The Decline of Demesne Farming on the Estates of Durham Cathedral Priory', in *EcHR.*, 2nd ser. 1954–55, 345–56.

HILTON, R. H. *Social structure of rural Warwickshire in the Middle Ages (Dugdale Society occasional papers* no. 9). Oxford, 1950.

HILTON, R. H. 'Kibworth Harcourt: A Merton College Manor in the Thirteenth and Fourteenth Centuries', in *Studies in Leicestershire Agrarian Society edited by W. G. Hoskins. Transactions of the Leicestershire Archaeological Society.* 1948.

HOLMES, G. A. *The Estates of the Higher Nobility in Fourteenth Century England.* Cambridge, 1957.

IMBERCIADORI, I. *Mezzadria classica toscana con documentazione inedita dal IX al XIV sec. (Pubblicazioni della Academia economico-agraria dei Georgofili).* Florence, 1951.

JANSEN, H. P. H. *Landbouwpacht in Brabant in de 14 en 15 eeuw.* Assen, 1955.

JEANCARD, R. *Les Seigneuries d'Outre-Siagne de la reine Jeanne à François I.* Cannes, 1952.

KOPPE, W. 'Rodung und Wüstung auf den Bungsbergen', in *Zeitschrift der Gesellschaft für schleswig-holsteinerische Geschichte,* LXXX, 1956, 29–72 and LXXXI, 1957, 31–62.

MAGER, F. *Geschichte des Bauerntums und der Bodenkultur im Lande Mecklenburg.* Berlin, 1955.

LESNIKOV, M. P. 'Beiträge zur Baltisch-Niederländischen Handelsgeschichte am Ausgang des 14 und zu Beginn des 15 Jahrhunderts', in *Wissenschaftliche Zeitschrift der Karl Marx Universität, Leipzig,* VII, 1957–8, *Gesellschafts–und Sprachwissenschaftliche Reihe,* no. 5.

MALOWIST, M. 'The Economic and Social Development of the Baltic Countries from the Fifteenth to the Seventeenth Centuries', in *EcHR.*, 2nd ser. vol. II, no. 2, 1959, 177–89.

—— 'Über die Frage der Handelspolitik des Adels in den Ostseeländern im 15 und 16 Jahrhundert', in *Hansische Geschichtblätter,* 75, 1957, 29–47.

MARTIN-LORBER, O. 'L'exploitation d'une grange cistercienne à la fin du XIV et au début du XV siècle', in *Annales de Bourgogne,* 29, 1957, 161–80.

MERLE, L. *La métairie et l'évolution agraire de la Gâtine poitevine, de la fin du Moyen Âge à la Révolution.* Paris, 1958.

PAINTER, S. *Studies in the History of the English Feudal Barony,* Baltimore, 1943.

PETIT, A. 'La métairie perpetuelle en Limousin au XV siècle', in *Nouvelle Revue historique de Droit français et étranger,* XLIII, 1919, 365–418.

POSTAN, M. M. 'Chronology of Labour Services', in *TRHS.* 4th ser. XX, 1937, 169–93.

RICHARD, J. 'Les états de service d'un noble bourguignon au temps de Philippe le Bon', in *Annales de Bourgogne,* XXIX, 1957, 113–24.

RODOLICO, N. 'Il ritorno alla terra degli Italiani', in *Atti della R. Accademia dei Georgofili,* 1933.

ROSKELL, J. S. 'The Social Composition of the Commons in a Fifteenth Century Parliament', in *Bulletin of the Institute of Historical Research,* XXIV, 1951, 152–72.

SALTMARSH, J. 'A College Home-Farm in the 15th Century', in *EJ (Ec. Hist.)* III, no. 11, February 1936, 155–72.

SAPORI, A. *Studi di storia economica medievale (Biblioteca storica Sansoni.* New ser., v) 2nd ed. Florence, n.d. [1946].

—— 'Problemi di storia economica e sociale. Rendita fondiaria e origine del capitalismo e la funzione della nobiltà', in *Nuova Rivista Storica,* XLII, 1958, 114–31.

SCHNEIDER, J. *La ville de Metz aux XIII et XIV siècles.* Nancy, 1950.

SICARD, G. *Le métayage dans le Midi toulousain à la fin du Moyen Âge.* Toulouse, 1957.

STARK, W. *Ursprung und Aufstieg des landwirtschaftlichen Grossbetriebs in den böhmischen Ländern (Rechts- und staatswissenschaftliche Abhandlungen . . . der deutschen Universität in Prag.* no. 7). Brünn, Prague, Leipzig, Vienna, 1934.
THRUPP, S. L. *The merchant class of medieval London.* Chicago, 1948.
WEISS, H. *Die Zisterzienerabtei Ebrach.* Stuttgart, 1962.
WELTI, L. *Geschichte der Reichsgrafschaft Hohenems und des Reichhofes Lustenau (Forschungen zur Geschichte Vorarlbergs und Lichtensteins,* vol. 4). Innsbrück, 1930.

B. *Technical aspects*

ABEL, W. 'Wandlungen des Fleischverbrauchs und der Fleischversorgung in Deutschland seit dem ausgehenden Mittelalter', in *Berichte über Landwirtschaft,* new ser. XXII, 1938, 411–52.
ASHLEY, W. *The Bread of our Forefathers.* Oxford, 1928.
BELÉNYESY, M. 'Angaben über die Verbreitung der Zwei- und Dreifelderwirtschaft im mittelalterlichen Ungarn', in *Acta Ethnographica,* V, 1956, 183–8.
BENNET, M. K. 'British Wheat Yield per Acre for Seven Centuries', in *EJ (Ec. Hist.),* III, No. 10, February 1935, 12–29.
BERESFORD, M. 'The Deserted Villages of Warwickshire', in *Birmingham Archaeological Society. Transactions and Proceedings,* LXVI, 1945–46, 49–106.
BEVERIDGE, W. 'The Yield and Price of Corn in the Middle Ages', in *EJ (Ec. Hist.),* I, 2 May 1927, 155–67.
BISHOP, T. A. M. 'The rotation of crops at Westerham, 1297–1350', in *EcHR.,* IX, 1, November 1938, 38–44.
DAVISO DI CHARVENSOD, M. 'Coltivazione e reddito dell vigna a Rivoli nel secolo XIV', in *Bolletino storico-bibliografico subalpino,* XLIII, 1950, 1–13.
DIECK, A. 'Über das Alter des Buchweizenanbaues in Nordwestdeutschland', in *Zeitschrift für Agrargeschichte und Agrarsoziologie,* II, 1954, 26–29.
DOORMAN, G. *De Middeleeuwse Brouwerij en de Gruit.* The Hague, 1955.
DUBY, G. 'Techniques et rendements agricoles dans les Alpes du Sud en 1338', in *Annales du Midi,* LXX, 1958, 403–414.
JAEGER, H. *Die Entwicklung der Kulturlandschaft im Kreise Hofgeismar.* Göttingen, 1951.
——'Zur Entstehung der heutigen grossen Forsten in Deutschland', in *Berichte zur deutschen Landeskunde,* XIII, 1954, 156–171.
LENNARD, R. 'Statistics of Corn Yields in Mediaeval England: Some Critical Questions', in *EJ (Ec. Hist.),* III, nos. 11 and 12 February 1936 and 1937, 173–92 and 325–49.
LINDEMANS, P. *Geschiedenis van de landbouw in België.* 2 vols., Antwerp, 1952.
OSCHINSKY, D. 'Medieval Treatises on Estate Managements', in *EcHR,* 2nd ser., VIII, 1955–6, 296–309.
PAGE, F. M. '"Bidentes Hoylandie". A Mediaeval Sheep-Farm', in *EJ (Ec. Hist.),* I, no. 4, January 1929, 602–13.
PETINO, A. *Lo zofferano nell'economia del medio evo.* Catania, 1951–1952.
SABBE, E. *De belgische vlasnijverheid. I, De zuidnederlandsche vlasnijverheid tot het verdrag van Utrecht* (1713) *(Rijksuniversiteit te Gent. Werken uitgegeven door de Faculteit van de Wijsbegeerte en Letteren.* 95 afl.) Bruges, 1943.
SLICHER VAN BATH, B. A. 'De invloed van de economische omstandigheden op de technische ontwikkeling van de landbouw in het verleden', in *Landbouwkundig Tijdschrift,* 74, 1962, 159–79. See also 'The influence of economic conditions on the development of agricultural tools and machines in history', in J. L. Mey, *Mechanization in agriculture,* 1960, 1–36.
——'The Rise of Intensive Husbandry in the Low Countries', in *Britain and the Netherlands,* Oxford, 1960, 130–53.
TIMM, A. *Die Waldnützung in Nordwestdeutschland im Spiegel der Weistümer.* Cologne-Graz. 1960.
VERHULST, A. 'Bijdragen tot de Studie van de agrarische Struktuur in het Vlaamse Land. 2, Het Problem van de Verdwijning van de Braak in de Vlaamse Landbouw (XIII–XVII eeuw)', in *Naturwetenschappelijk Tijdschrift,* XXXVIII, 1956, 213–219.

VIII. The Peasantry

a. Individuals and communities

AULT, W. O. 'Village assemblies in Medieval England', in *Album H. M. Cam*. Paris and Louvain, 1960.

BADER, K. 'Bauernrecht und Bauernfreiheit im späteren Mittelalter', in *HJ*, LXI, 1941, 51–87.

——*Dorfgenossenschaft und Dorfgemeinde*. Cologne-Graz, 1962.

BALTL, H. 'Die österreichischen Weistümer. Studien zur Weistumgeschichte', in *Mitteillungen des Instituts für österreichische Geschichtsforschung*, LIX, 1951, 365–410 and LXI, 1953, 38–78.

BLOCH, M. 'Les transformations du servage', in *Mélanges d'histoire du moyen âge offerts à M. F. Lot*. Paris, 1925.

BOG, I. *Dorfgemeinde, Freiheit und Unfreiheit in Franken*. Stuttgart, 1956.

BLUM, J. 'The Rise of Serfdom in Eastern Europe', in *AHR*, LXII, 1956–7, 807–36.

BOSSUAT, A. 'Le servage en Nivernais au XV siècle d'après les registres du Parlement', in *Bibliothèque de l'École des Chartes*, CXVII, 1959, 89–134.

GENICOT, L. 'Formorture et mortemain dans le comté de Namur après 1431', in *Études d'histoire et d'archéologie namuroises dédiées à F. Courtoy*, 499–517, Namur, 1952.

GOURON, M. *Les chartes de franchises de Guyenne et Gascogne (Société d'histoire du droit. Catalogue des chartes de franchise de la France*, IX). Paris, 1935.

GRAUS, F. 'Au bas moyen âge: Pauvres des villes et pauvres des campagnes', in *Annales. Économies. Sociétés. Civilisations*, XVI, 1961, 1053–65.

HARMJANZ, H. *Ostpreussische Bauern*. 3rd ed. Königsberg, 1939.

HOSKINS, W. G. *The Midland Peasant. The Economic and Social History of a Leicestershire Village*. London, 1957.

IMBERCIADORI, I. 'I due poderi di Bernardo Machiavelli ovvero mezzadria poderale nel '400', in *Studi in onore di Armando Sapori*, Milan, 1957, 833–46.

LEICHT, P. S. *Operai, Artigiani, Agricoltori in Italia dal Secolo VI al XVI*. Milan, 1946.

PALMIERI, A. 'I lavoratori del contado bolognese durante le Signorie', in *Atti e memorie della R. Deputazione di storia patria per le provincie di Romagna*, ser. III, vol. XXVIII, 1910, 18–78.

PERRIN, C. E. 'Chartes de franchise et rapports de droit en Lorraine', in *Le Moyen Âge*, XLII, 1946, 11–42.

QUIRIN, K. H. *Herrschaft und Gemeinde nach mitteldeutschen Quellen des 12.–18. Jahrhunderts* (*Göttinger Bausteine zur Geschichtswissenschaft*, no. 2). Göttingen, 1952.

ROERIG, F. 'Luft macht eigen', in *Festgabe für G. Seeliger*, 51–78, Leipzig, 1920.

Le servage. Communications présentées à la Société Jean Bodin. 2nd ed. Brussels, 1959. See especially P. Petot, C. Verlinden and F. Joüon de Longrais's contributions on French, Spanish and English villainage.

SLICHER VAN BATH, B. H. *Boerenvrijheid*. Groningen, 1948.

TOUBERT, P. 'Les statuts communaux et l'histoire des campagnes lombardes au XIV siècle', in *Mélanges d'archéologie et d'histoire publiés par l'École française de Rome*, LXXII, 1960, 397–508.

VACCARI, P. *L'affrancazione dei servi della gleba nell'Emilia et nella Toscana (R. Accademia dei Lincei. Commissione per gli atti delle Assemblee costituzionali italiane dal medio evo al 1831. Appendice. L'affrancazione dei servi della gleba nei comuni italiani*). Bologna, 1962.

VAILLANT, P. *Les libertés des communautés dauphinoises des origines au 5 Janvier 1355*. Paris, 1951. On this book, see an important recension by V. Chomel in *Annales. Économie. Sociétés. Civilisations*, XI, 1956, 347–60.

VERRIEST, L. *Le servage dans le comté de Hainaut. Les sainteurs. Le meilleur catel* (*Mémoires publiés par l'Académie royale de Belgique. Classe des Lettres*, 2nd ser., VI). Brussels, 1910.

——'Le servage en Flandre, particulièrement dans le pays d'Alost', in *Revue historique de droit français et étranger*, 1950, 35–66.

B. *Social movements at the end of the period*

FEHR, H. 'Der Ursprung der Eidgenossenschaft', in *Zeitschrift für schweizerisches Recht*, new ser. LXI, 1942, 169–202.

FRANZ, G. *Die agrarischen Unruhen des ausgehenden Mittelalters. Ein Beitrag zur Vorgeschichte des Bauernkrieges*. Marburg, 1930.

——*Der deutsche Bauernkrieg*. 4th ed. Darmstadt, 1956.

HILTON, R. H. 'Peasant movements in England before 1381', in *EcHR.*, 2nd ser., vol. II, no. 2, 1949, 117–136.

HILTON, R. H. and FAGAN, H. *The English Rising of* 1381. London, 1950.

MACEK, J. *Die hussitische revolutionäre Bewegung*. Berlin, 1958. Or *Le mouvement hussite en Bohême*, 2nd ed. Prague, 1958.

——*Tyrolská selská válka a Michal Gaismair*. Prague, 1960.

MAYER, T. 'Die Entstehung der schweizer Eidgenossenschaft und die deutsche Geschichte', in *Deutsches Archiv für Geschichte des Mittelalters*, VI, 1943, 150–87.

MAUGIS, E. 'La journée de huit heures et les vignerons de Sens et d'Auxerre devant le Parlement en 1383–1393', in *RH*, CLXV, 1924, 203–218.

MEYER, K. 'Der Ursprung der Eidgenossenschaft', in *Zeitschrift für schweizerische Geschichte*, XXI, 1941, 335–97.

OBENAUS, H. *Recht und Verfassung der Gesellschaften mit St. Jörgenschild in Schwaben*. Göttingen, 1961.

PALMIERI, A. 'Lotte agrarie bolognesi nei secoli XIII e XIV (Rustici e borghesi contro la nobilità)', in *Atti e memorie della R. Deputazione di storia patria per le provincie di Romagna* 4th ser., vol. XIII, 1923, 7–63.

PETIT-DUTAILLIS, C. and LEFÈBVRE, G. *Studies and Notes supplementary to Stubbs' Constitutional History* (*Publications of the University of Manchester, Historical Series*, LIV). Manchester, 1930.

RÉVILLE, A. and PETIT-DUTAILLIS, C. *Le soulèvement des travailleurs d'Angleterre en 1381* (*Mémoires et Documents publiés par la Société de l'École des Chartes*, II). Paris, 1898.

ROSENTHAL, H. W. *Die bäuerlichen Manifeste als Mittelpunkt einer historisch-soziologischen Untersuchung der vorreformatorischen Bauernbewegung*. Mainz, 1931.

INDEX

Individual monasteries and abbeys are
grouped together under 'monasteries'.

Aakjaer, 640
Aarhus Church, Denmark, 654
Abdar-Rahman I, 54, 441
Abel, W., 556 n., 686, 692
Aben, Albaithar, 441
Abu, Zacaria, 441–2, 445–6
Adalard, 161
Adam of Bremen, 634, 648, 650, 652
Adolf of Schauenburg, 84
Aelius, 187
Africa
    agriculture, 129; irrigation, 103, 105;
        tree crops, 101
    circumcelliones, 124
    fortifications, 113
    Imperial authority, 30
    land tenure, 111, 114, 117–18, 259
    Romano-German states, 181
    taxation, 114–5
        see also Algeria, Egypt, Libya
Agilolfings of Bavaria, 46, 196
Agricola, 8
agriculture
    arable land, cereals, 104, 108, 125, 126,
        127, 137, 140, 149, 151–3, 155–8,
        159–64, 179, 371, 372, 384–5, 450,
        459, 480, 524–8, 548–9, 553–4, 556,
        557, 558, 583–4, 600–2, 647, 648, 678,
        680, 716; bad harvests, 671; growth
        in arable land, 68, 297; decline in
        arable land, 663; monoculture of
        corn, 672
    bees, bee-keeping, 210, 483, 493, 497,
        530
    common field, communal farming, 42,
        109, 189, 193, 357, 446, 451; *see also*
        land tenure, common land, com-
        munes
    dairy and poultry, 177–9, 445
    demesne farming, 411–12, 601, 607,
        680
    grassland, 137
    hops, 165, 647, 719
    horses, 94, 130, 139, 142–4, 171, 172,
        173, 175, 192, 297, 315, 445, 446, 451,
        528–9; imperial stud farms, 94;
        saddle horses, 176, 445; breeding in
        Spain, 445; breeding in England,
        555; Danish stock, 649
    implements, 98, 99, 125, 128–31, 142–58,
        376, 445–6, 716–17; harness, 144, 231,

agriculture (*cont.*)
    297, 315; harrow and hoe, 129, 153,
        154, 527; ploughs, 18, 61, 98, 107–8,
        125, 128, 149–51, 373–4, 451, 479,
        522–4, 717; sickles and scythes, 98,
        129–30, 155–6, 376, 528; vehicles, 145
    industrial crops, 717, 718
    irrigation, 102–5, 146–8, 174, 440, 716,
        724
    mules, 143, 176, 445
    open-field system, 19, 37, 41–2, 49, 558,
        641
    oxen: Danish exports of, 649; used for
        threshing and draught, 130, 138, 139,
        142–4, 157, 297, 451, 528–9
    plantation system, 49, 718–19
    prices of products, *see* prices
    rotation systems, 49, 62, 108, 125, 127,
        134–42, 166, 179, 243, 276, 296–7, 368,
        373, 375, 446, 479, 524, 526, 663, 716,
        718, 741
    soils, 93, 100, 106, 107, 127, 549, 559,
        741
    stock-raising, 94–5, 108, 131–3, 135, 141,
        171–6, 298, 356, 379–83, 411, 491,
        492, 493, 553–6, 642, 648–50, 689,
        717, 719–20, 740; breeding, 94, 172,
        175–6, 177, 383; cattle, 17, 94, 108,
        131–2, 135, 171–6, 210–11, 230, 480,
        485, 528–9, 555, 720; goats, 93, 173,
        174, 177, 529; pigs, 131, 172, 173,
        178, 445, 449, 480, 529, 649; sheep,
        81, 108, 126, 132, 135, 171–5 *passim*,
        177, 297, 380–2, 411, 438–9, 445, 446,
        485, 529, 554, 583, 591, 596, 719, 720;
        transhumance, 94, 132–3, 380, 439,
        445; *see also* horses, mules, oxen
    strip fields, 79, 109, 111
    techniques, 663; burning, 97, 136, 146,
        524–6, 527, 530; fencing and ditch-
        ing, 158–9, 642; fertilizing, 95, 97,
        103, 133, 134, 137, 145, 146, 377–8,
        446; dry-farming, 97, 100, 101, 102,
        104–5, 373; harrowing, 154, 527;
        harvesting, 99, 129–31, 138; in
        northern lands, 106–9; marling, 145–6,
        288; ploughing and ridging, 96–8,
        107–8, 133, 138, 151–3, 155–6, 367,
        373–4, *see also* implements, ploughs;
        weeding, 155; transhumance, *see*
        stock-raising

agriculture (*cont.*)
tree crops, 100–1, 108, 131, 147, 164, 167–9, 230, 719, 741
tropical crops, rice, 54, 147, 370, 719
vegetables and fodder crops, 99, 131, 135, 141, 164–7, 210, 525, 528, 583–4, 717, 718, 741
vines, viticulture, 54, 68, 94, 100, 101, 108, 129, 131, 169–70, 210, 230, 297, 357, 371, 372–3, 442, 480, 717, 719, 741; rent of vineyards, 229, 411, 412, 709
Arabs and, 54–5, 93, 160, 166, 177, 440–3; irrigation, 146–8, 440
Belgium, 147, 149, 158, 171, 178; irrigation, 147
Britain, 179, 548–59; Anglo-Saxons and, 192; arable, cereals, 108, 162, 548–9, 553–4, 556, 557, 558, 583, 600–2, 717, 718; communal regulation, 572–4; crop rotation, 107, 108, 136, 138, 140, 571–3, 583–4; depression, 595; deterioration of land, 556–9; fertilizers, 145; field systems, 111, 193, 558, 571–3; fruit, 108; Highland zone farming, 106; hops, 165; horses, 555; implements and methods, 146 (Devonshiring), 149, 150, 151, 155, 156; innovations, 590; marginal land, 551, 591, 601; peasant husbandry, 600–4; soils, 106, 127, 549, 559; stock-raising, livestock, sheep, 171, 177, 553–6, 583, 591, 596, 740; vegetables and fodder crops, 164, 583–4, 717
Byzantine, 210, 230
Carolingian, 45, 139–40, 158, 170, 174, 192
Denmark, 161, 171, 633–4, 647–9, 720
Flanders 141, 143, 150–1, 156, 166, 172, 175, 179, 297, 298, 717, 720
France, 108, 127–9, 296–7, 717, 720; vines, 297, 719; *see also* Normandy
Gaul, cereals, 162; crop rotation, 136, 139; development under Romans, 107, 127, 171; implements and methods, 107, 130, 149, 156; stock breeding, 172
Germany, arable, cereals, 149, 162, 163, 556; cropping systems, 136, 137, 140, 152, 716; development in Rhineland, 179; hops, 165; horses, 143; irrigation, 147, 148; implements and methods, 140, 150, 151, 155, 156, 158; pigs, 178; vegetables, 164, 165; vines, 170, 741
Ireland, 171
Italy, 92, 136, 141, 342, 343–4, 353, 371,

agriculture (*cont.*)
418; cereals, 94–5, 104, 105, 162, 163, 371, 384–5; commercial farming, 388–9, 391; communal farming, 357, 368, 369, 425; controls, 390–1, 422; crop rotation, 127, 136, 368, 373, 375; fertilization, 377–8; hiring of stock and equipment, 425; horticulture, 179, 370; implements and methods, 96, 367, 373–7; irrigation, 147, 148, 355, 357, 359, 361, 363, 383; milling, 376; monsoon crops, rice, 147, 370, 719; open-field system, 375; soils, 127; stock-raising, sheep, transhumance, 132–3, 356, 367, 379–83, 386, 389, 392, 394, 411; tree crops, 369, 372, 390, 719; vegetables and fruit, 164, 166, 361, 372
Low Countries, 137, 192 (Frisia); hops, 719; *see also* Belgium, Flanders
Normandy: arable, cereals, 152–3, 155–6; crop rotation, 297; fencing, 159; fertilizing, 146; fruit, 168–9, 719, 741; horses, 173, 176; implements, 145; pigs, 173
Poland, 60, 125, 491, 716, 720
Russia, 512, 518, 519, 546; cereals and arable, 524–8; crop rotation, 524, 526, 546; implements, 522–4, 527, 528; livestock, 528–9; slash-and-burn system, 524–6, 527, 530; vegetables, 525, 528
Slavonic lands, 61, 163, 449, 450, 451, 459, 479–80, 484–5; bee-keeping, 483; vineyards, 480
Scotland, 137, 150, 162, 171
Spain, 54–5, 438–47; cereals, 443, 444; communal effort, 446–7; controls, 436; crop rotation, 446; fertilizers, 95, 134, 146, 446; horticulture, 54, 179, 441–2; implements, 445; irrigation, 54–5, 147–8, 441–2, 716; livestock, transhumance, 55, 132–3, 143, 172, 177, 438–9, 445, 446, 720; vegetables and fruit, 166, 441–2; vineyards, 131, 442
Visigoths and, 184
Switzerland, 163
see also horticulture, market gardening
Al Mulei, 147
Alans, 28, 32
Albemarle, Countess of, 555
Albericus Cornu, bishop of Chartres, 79–80
Albert the Bear, of Brandenburg, 85
Albigensian Wars, 91
Alboin, 31

Alemanni, agricultural writer, 377
Alemanni, 22, 23–4, 28, 29, 32, 35, 36, 37, 40, 51, 181, 194–6
  conquered by Franks, 30, 37, 187, 194, 196
  forest worship, 21
  genealogiae of, 37, 38
  laws, 172, 195, 288
Algeria, 102, 111, 177, 237
Alfonso IX of Spain, 132
Alfonso X of Spain, 132
Alfonso XI of Spain, 132
Alfonso the Wise, 444
Alfred the Great, 193
allelengyon system of taxation, 213–14, 220–1
Almohades, 441
allodia, 451, 460, 474–6, 478
Almoravides, 441
Alphonse of Poitiers, 298
Alsace-Lorraine, Alsace, 29, 195, 299, 306, 333
altaria, 330–1
Ambresbury, Michael, abbot of Glastonbury, 582
Ambrose, St, 253
Ammianus Marcellinus, 24
Andalusia, 433 n.
Angevin dynasty, 360
Angles, 29, 194, 576
  trade with Britain, 192
Anjou, René d', 698
Anglo-Saxons, 32, 35, 37, 39, 52, 163, 270, 592
  founding of kingdoms of, 192–3
Anthimus, 165
Antonine empire, 259
Antonio de Beatis, 167
Apollo Smintheus, 101
Apulia, 57, 116, 132
Aquitaine, Duke of, 70
Arabs, 66, 198
  agriculture of, 54–5, 93, 160, 166, 177, 440–3; *see also* Moors
  and irrigation, 146–8, 440
  in Spain, 2, 34–5, 53, 54–5, 433, 436, 439, 440–3
  invasion of Byzantine empire, 207, 208
Arianism, 188, 197
Armagnac, Jean d', 695
Armenia, 166
Armorica, 274, 277, 283
Arpad, house of, 58
Arrieta, Juan de Valverde, 448 n.
Asia: land tenure, 116–17
Asia Minor, 123, 208, 219, 227
ass, the 176, 445

Asso, I. de, 440 n., 443 n.
Athaulf, King, 184
Athos, 231
Attila, 29
Augustine, St, 44, 264
Augustinians, 88
Augustus, 113
Aurelianus, 22, 23, 26
Aurelius Victor, 114
Austin Canons, 300, 331
Austria, 453
  population, 664
Authari, the, 183
Avars, 30, 31, 50, 194
Avenel, d', 682, 686

Babenberg, Margraves, 67
Baccio, Andrea, 371
Baden, 195
Baist, G., 149 n.
Baldwin V, of Flanders, 75, 301
Balbo, 104
Balearic Islands, 250, 665
Ball, John, 610, 702
Ball family, 594
Ballesteros, A., 442 n.
Baltic lands, 58, 62, 452, 463, 466, 476, 481
  paganry of, 249
  trade, 485; *see also* Estonia, Livonia
Bamberg, Bishopric of, 68, 701
Beaufort, Cardinal, 597
ban, bannum, the right of punishment, 262, 276, 289, 315, 333, 334, 701, 706
Barbo, Archbishop, 170
Barcelona, Count of, 445
Bardi family, 350
barley, varieties of, 161; *see also* agriculture, arable land and cereals
barrow burials, 513, 517
Basil II, 220, 221
Batavians, 186
Baudouin, abbot of Sint-Bavo, 73, 320
Baudouin, 73
Bavaria, Bavarians, 30, 32, 35, 46, 67, 195–6, 199
  forest clearance, 291
  Frankish control in, 30, 196, 198
  land tenure, 43, 65, 707, 711
  law, 43, 288
  peasant unrest, 739
Bayeux tapestry, 154
Beauchamp family, 579
Beauchamp, Richard, Earl of Warwick, 671
Beaumont, Charter of, 78
Bede, the Venerable, 41, 279, 280

Bedford, Duke of (1420), 671
beer, 165
bees, bee-keeping, 178, 210, 530, 650, *see also* honey
Bela IV, King of Hungary, 491
Belgium
   agriculture, 149, 158, 171, 178; irrigation, 147
   German settlements in, 36, 43
   place names, 36
   Roman villas in, 9
Belgrade, 54
Belyaev, I. D., 517
Benedict of Nursia, St, 44
Benedict XIII, Pope, 712
Benedictine order, 44, 291, 300, 302-3, 315, 474, 490, 577, 580, 583, 587, 593, 597
Bennett, H. S., 557, 614 n.
Benno II, bishop of Osnabruck, 68
Bentivoglio family, 418
Berbers, 54, 55
Berkeley Estates, 619-21
Bernard of Clairvaux, 76
Berry, duc de, 157
Beveridge, 557, 681, 689, 690
Beyerle, F., 34 n.
birth rate; *see* population
Bishop, T. A. M., 19 n.
Black Death, the, *see* plague
Black Prince, the, 599
Bloch, M., 19 n., 735
Boendale, 702
Bogolyubskii, Andrei, 535
Bohemia, 29, 31, 58, 59, 60, 67, 68, 87, 89, 449, 452, 453, 455, 456, 459, 461, 463, 466, 473, 480, 483, 484, 707, 716, 723, 735, 737
Boii, the, 29
Boissonnade, P., 441 n., 443 n.
Bonafede, Paganino, 367
Boniface (Winfrid), St, 45
Bonhomme, Jacques, 702
Botero, 352
Bottigelli family, 387
Bouniatian, 680
bourgeoisie, landed wealth of, 304-5
bourgs, *see* villages
Bouviers, Gilles, de, 394
Bracciolini, Poggio, 389
Brandenburg, 7, 84, 89, 90, 163, 175, 454, 455, 460, 461, 463, 466, 473, 475, 476, 477, 483, 485
Bray cartularies, 595
Braybrokes, Henry, 595
Braybrokes, Robert, 595
Bremen, archbishop of (1106), 75

Brennos, 284
Breslau, 475, 476
Breughel, Pieter, the elder, 147, 156
Bridbury, A., 568 n.
Brie, John de, 176, 177
Brienne, Count of (1056), 144
brigands, 124, 292, 430
Brinton, Thomas, bishop of Rochester, 702
Britain
   agriculture, 179, 548-59; Anglo-Saxon, 192; arable, cereals, 108, 162, 548-9, 553-4, 556, 557, 558, 583, 600-2, 717, 718; communal regulation, 572-4; crop-rotation, 107, 108, 136, 138, 140, 571-3, 583-4; depression, 595; deterioration of land, 556-9; fertilizers, 145; field systems, 111, 193, 558, 571-3; fruit, 108; Highland Zone farming, 106; hops, 165; horses, 555; implements and methods, 146 (Devonshiring), 149, 150, 151, 155, 156; innovations, 590; marginal land, 551, 591, 601; peasant husbandry, 600-4; soils, 106, 127, 549, 559; stock-raising, livestock, sheep, 171, 177, 553-6, 583, 591, 596, 740; *see also* horses; vegetables and fodder crops, 164, 583-4, 717
   Anglo-Saxon occupation of, 29, 37, 192-3
   cloth industry, 568, 597, 621
   corn exports, 705
   famine, 565
   feudalism, 579, 596, 597
   forest clearance, 10, 52, 70-1, 77, 80-1, 666
   forest laws, 81, 551
   fortifications, 63
   fourth-century conditions, 27
   German colonization, 2, 181
   labour supply, 566-9, 570; labour commuted to rent, 603, 605-8, 610, 615-16
   land hunger, 80, 552-6, 563-5, 608
   land reclamation, 52, 70, 80-1, 175, 548-52, 559, 560, 566; *see also* forest clearance
   land tenure: common land, 171, 729; ecclesiastical estates, 550, 553, 557, 559, 577-8, 580, 582, 583, 584, 586, 587, 588-9, 594, 602, 619-21; *see also* individual monasteries and bishoprics, esp. Winchester; enclosures, 553, 590, 591; hereditary system, 613; the lord's monopoly, 601; magnates

Britain (cont.)
and gentry, 592–600; under Roman rule, 111, 118; under Wessex laws, 193; peasants' holdings, 80, 193, 558, 563, 566, 567, 600–32 passim, 725–6; smallholders, 662–4, 628–32; see also manorial system
land values, 552, 554, 557, 593, 596, 597, 614
manorial (seignorial) system, 80, 192–3, 235, 236, 238, 255, 261, 262, 266, 267, 270–1, 554, 558, 563, 566, 571–91, 597, 600–4, 611, 618, 715; the demesne, 566, 575–6, 578–91 passim, 596, 601, 603–7, 737, 740; the hide, 277, 278, 280; leases and rents, 575–6, 589, 601, 603–7 passim, 611, 615–16, 626, 726–7
money scarcity, 699
Norman conquest, 65, 70, 237, 549, 592, 605
parliamentary petitions, 569, 609
peasants: dues and services, 589, 600–11, 615–16; freedom, 613–14, 732; Romano-British, 123; Scandinavian immigrants, 65, 80; status, 39, 91, 601, 604–28, 732; three levels, 618–28; unrest, 608–10, 736–9
place names, 37, 52, 57, 118, 192, 548
plague, Black Death, 562, 569–70, 588, 590, 608, 609, 674, 675, 738
population, 560–70, 582, 630, 669; decolonization, 559; see also Scotland
price of corn and meat, 682–3, 685–7, 691–2
Roman influence, 10, 11, 12
rural financing, 627–8
rural industry, 688; see also cloth-working
slaves, 628
taxation and fines, 280, 561, 562, 573–4, 588, 623, 698; church scot, 603; entry fines, 553, 563, 566, 589, 630, 709; death duties, 565; marriage fines, 603; poll tax, 623, 738; royal taxes, 600, 603; tallage, 563, 589, 603
towns, 8–9, 64, 118
Viking settlements, 55, 56, 57, 65
villages, 37, 40, 80, 111, 123, 563, 566, 571, 574, 576, 621–2, 631–2
wages, 566–7, 588, 608–9, 664, 688–92, 730–1, 738
war profiteers, 724
Britons transported to Germany, 180
Brittany, 56, 187, 304, 305, 306
Brunner, H., 33 n.
Brunswick, 667, 739

Brunswick-Wolfenbüttel, Duke of, 711
Brutails, J.-A., 440 n.
buffaloes, 381
Bulgarians, 31
butter, 177–8
Burgundian settlements, 31, 34, 185
Burgundy
Frankish control, 30
land tenure, 32, 43, 185–6, 255, 267, 284, 292, 304, 325, 326, 329, 333, 729
mortmain, 713
Burkhard, bishop of Worms, 69
Byzantine Empire, 31, 55
agriculture, 210, 230
famine and plague, 217
feudalism, 216–21, 226–30; pronoia system, 226–8
labour supply, 205, 214, 231
land values, 230–1
land tenure, 206, 210–34 passim; ecclesiastical estates, 220, 223–5, 231; exempt property, 214; lay landlords, 182, 215–34 passim; military estates, 51, 183, 216, 218, 219, 222, 226; neighbours' rights, 216; state property, 223–4
military strength, 226
Peasants' Law, 209, 211
peasants' militia, 208, 219
peasants' rights, 206, 208, 210–34 passim
population movements, 232–3
primitive economic technique, 231
social system, 215, 219, 226
taxation, 205, 206, 211–14, 219–21 passim, 227; 231–2; allelengyon system, 213–14, 220–1; exemptions, 223, 225
village communities, 207–15, 230

Cade, Jack, 738
Caesar, Julius, 12, 16, 17, 92, 94, 119, 172, 181, 273
Callot, Jacques, 696
canals, 147–8
Cantelow, William, 554 n.
Capetian dynasty, 298
capital, 461
Capitulare de villis, 49, 165, 175, 179, 198, 200, 203, 250
Carolingian era, Carolingian Empire, 152, 190, 247, 260, 288
agriculture in, 45, 139–40, 158, 174, 192; vineyards, 170
economy of, 197–8, 203, 204
forest clearance, 43
land tenure, 188–9, 198–9, 203
seignorial system, 45, 237, 239–43
the villa, 305, 332–3

Carraresi family, 416
Carthage, 117
Carthusians, 157
Casimir the Great, 467
Carinthia, 739
Cassius, Dio, 153, 171
Castile, *see* Spain
Catalonia, *see* Spain
Cato, M. Porcius, 14–15, 98, 129, 131, 132,
    133, 134, 135, 158, 389
Cattaneo, 353
cattle, *see* agriculture: stock-raising
Celts, 9, 12, 29, 31, 37, 52–3, 118, 171,
    272; traces in Auvergne, 185;
    Celto-Romans, 193
cereals, *see* agriculture, arable land
Certaldo, Paolo da, 387
Cesarius of Arles, St, 263
Chamavi, 187
Champagne, Count of, 80
charitable institutions in Byzantium, 224
Charlemagne, 46, 48–50, 55, 68, 161, 196,
    199, 200, 237, 260, 303
    agricultural price edicts, 204
    his *Capitulare de villis*, 49, 165, 175, 179,
    198, 200, 203, 250; plan for Rhine–
    Danube canal, 198; *see also* Carol-
    ingian Empire
Charles V of France, 176
Charles VII of France, 698
Charles VIII of France, 166
Charles IX of France, 168
Charles Martel, 197
Charles of Anjou, 382
Charles the Bald, 279, 288
Charter of Beaumont, 78
Charter of Lorris, 74, 78
Charter of the Forest (1217), 81
Charter of the Franchise of Bruges, 175
Chattuarii, the, 187
Chauci, the, 19
cheese, 177–8, 385
Cherepnin, 539, 543
Chilperic, 188
Christianity
    adopted by Clovis, 188
    Anglo-Saxons and, 192
    in Hungary, 494
    in Russia, 507, 513
    spread under Charlemagne, 198
Chrysostom, St, 123
Church, the
    and agriculture, 44, 61; *see also* monas-
    teries
    and the Franks, 45, 197
    and peasants, 70, 71
    as colonizing agent, 46

Church, the (*cont.*)
    attitude to slavery, 248–9, 434
    disintegration of parochial system, 355
    ecclesiastical estates, 4, 44–5, 48, 49, 50,
    51, 66, 70, 72–4, 78, 119, 122, 199,
    200–1, 215, 285, 299–303, 306–18
    passim, 331–3, 395–6, 408, 409, 411,
    476, 488, 499, 577–8, 587, 602,
    619–21, 653–4, 656, 657, 659, 722;
    administration of, 319–26, 357, 400,
    409, 410, 411, 474, 539, 582–3, 584,
    586, 588, 704, 715; in Byzantium,
    220, 223–5, 231; *curiae, grangiae*, 474;
    labour on, 315; secularization of, 203;
    and seignorial system, 261, 415; *see
    also* monasteries
    ecclesiastical ostentation, 671, 735
    ecclesiastical revenues; tithes and altaria,
    48, 61, 302, 330–1, 467, 498–9, 504,
    577, 721
    growing power in sixth century, 185
    in Prussia, 460
    moral and material decay, 417
Church, Slavonic, 451
church-scot, 603
Cicero, 16, 104, 251, 377
cider, 169
circumcelliones, 124
Cistercians, 71, 76–7, 81, 84, 291, 292,
    296, 298, 300, 301, 331, 332, 359, 411,
    460, 461, 715
    in Britain, 578
    in E. Europe, 88, 453, 474, 492, 501, 502
Claudius II, 22, 112
climate, 92, 135, 170–1, 663, 667, 673, 684
    rainfall, 96, 97, 673
    of Russia, 511
Clotaire I, 171
cloth-making
    in Britain, 568, 597, 621
    in Flanders, 688
    in Scandinavia, 651
Clovis, 30, 35, 187
    adopts Catholicism, 188
Coeur, Jacques, 167
Collingwood, R. G., 18 n.
Colmeiro, M., 440 n.
coloni, *see* peasants
Columba, St, 44
Columella, L. Junius Moderatus, 95, 96,
    100, 104, 105, 128, 129, 130, 133, 134,
    135, 138, 144, 162, 250, 377
Comans, the, 275
Commodus, 22
commons, common land, *see* land tenure
communes, communal regulation, *see* land
    tenure

Commynes, Philippe de, 375, 694, 696
Comnenian dynasty, 222, 225, 226
Conrad II, emperor, 401
Constantine the Great, 23, 25–6, 27, 122, 252, 259, 260
    Law of A.D. 332, 115, 119
Constantine VII, 214 n., 217, 218
Constantius Chlorus, 187
Cordova, 54, 66
corn mills, 99, 125, 211, 376, 471
corn, price of, 677–88, 691–2
Cornwall, Duchy of, 555
Cornwall, Earl of, 579
Corsica, 136, 348
Cosmas of Prague, 53
Council of Chalcedon, 225
Council of Gangra, 248
Council of Ver, 203
Courland, 457
Crescenzi, Pietro dei, 136, 367, 374, 375, 378, 382, 383, 394, 419
Crete, 385
Croats, 31
Crusades, 71
Cugerni, the, 187
Cyprian, St, bishop of Carthage, 92, 97
Czechs, 2, 53, 58, 59, 483

Dacia, 11, 12, 22–3, 24
Dagobert, 194
Dagworth family, 599
Dalecarlia, 659
Dalmatia, 104
Damiani, Peter, 354
Dammartin, Countess of, 320
Danelaw, 65, 574, 576, 580, 605, 612, 613, 621
Danes, 29, 38
Dante, 340, 418
Dardanus, 112
Dauphiné, 339
Decapolis, the, 123
de Clare, Richard, 594 n.
de Courson, A., 274 n.
de Fraxino, Thomas, 579
de Havile, Thomas, 604
de Huntingfield, Roger, 554 n.
de Lacy family, 550, 555, 579
de Lacy, Henry, 582
de la Rivière, Monseigneur, 166
De la Ruelle, 163
demesne, the, see seignorial system
de Montfort, Simon, 595
Denmark
    agriculture: arable, cereals, 161, 633–4, 647; buildings, 171; crop rotation, 647; stock-raising, 648–9, 720

Denmark (cont.)
    cloth-making, 651
    fishing, 649, 650
    forests, 52, 649
    hamlets, 111
    horses and oxen as exports, 649
    hunting, 650
    land tenure: the bol, 139, 277, 278, 280, 644–6; communes, 645; common land, 649; ecclesiastical estates, 653–4, 656, 657, 659; fornskifte, 139; leases, 655–6; ornum, 38, 643–4; ; peasant holdings, 658, 700; solskifte, 52, 139, 645; see also seignorial system
    peasant status, 652–9
    seignorial system, 238, 654
    taxation, 653, 658
    village and farm settlements, 635–8, 654
de Vere, Hugh, 554 n.
Diocletian, 22, 25, 27, 28, 113, 205
    price edict of, 122, 161, 162, 163, 205
Dithmarschen, 39 n., 190, 239, 266, 282
Domesday Book, 65, 70, 175, 190 n., 285, 548, 549, 561, 562, 578, 586, 628, 629
Domitian, 11
Dopsch, A., 32 n.
Drusus, 191
Durham, estates of bishops of, 621, 678, 704

ecclesiastical estates, see Church, the
ecclesiastical revenues, see Church, the
Edward I of England, 595
Edward II of England, 581
Edward III of England, 588, 596
Egerland, 87, 88
Egidius, 187
Egypt
    agriculture, 102–3, 116
    land tenure, 116, 117, 121, 122, 206, 207
    taxation, 113, 199–20
Eleanor, Queen, 595
Ellwangen, abbot of, 81
Ely, estates of bishop of, 586, 607
emphyteusis, see land tenure
enclosures, 158–9, 244, 296, 368–9, 590, 591, 728
England see Britain
Ermland, 457, 471
Erslev, K., 639 n.
Este family, 409, 411
Estienne, Ch., 153, 154, 155, 157, 158, 166, 167
Etampes family, 724

fairs, 387
Falcone, Giuseppi, 376, 379

Falster, island of, 638–9
family ties, influence on settlement, 17, 38
famine, 672–4, 678, 691
Fastolf, Sir John, 597, 598, 724
Ferrante, King, 430
fertilizers, see agriculture
Festus, 129
feudalism
    origins of, 39, 265–6
    and social unrest, 735
    in Britain, 579, 596, 597
    in Byzantine Empire, 215, 219, 226–30
    in France, 57, 74
    in Frankish territory, 39
    in Italy, 394, 399, 401, 404, 405, 408,
        409, 421, 429
    in Roman Empire, 122
    in Spain, 433, 435
    in Western Europe, 65, 69, 71
Finland, 249, 639, 659
Firmus, 105
fishing
    in Russia, 529–30
    in Scandinavia, 649, 650
Fitz Hammes family, 579
Fitzherbert, John, 146, 150, 154
FitzStephen, William, 64
Flanders, counts of, 321, 337, 683
Flanders, 71, 74
    agriculture, 141, 143, 150–1, 156, 166,
        172, 175, 179, 297, 298, 717, 720
    cloth industry, 688
    land tenure: ecclesiastical estates,
        299–301, 331; landed bourgeoisie,
        305; princely estates, 303–4; the
        villa, 305; leaseholds, 327
    peasant unrest, 737
flax, 164, 718
Flemings, 86, 87, 461, 464, 472, 473, 502
Florence, 362, 381, 384, 386, 393, 402, 403,
    418, 423, 425
Folgore da Sangimignano, 410
Florentine Act of 6 August 1289, 702
Ford, Roger, abbot of Glastonbury, 582
forest clearance, 10, 12, 19–21, 43–5, 46–9,
    68, 69–70, 71 n., 72, 77–84, 88, 89,
    93, 136, 186, 194, 290–1, 293–6
    passim, 356, 366, 439, 452, 453, 455,
    458, 509, 512, 542, 666
    erosion caused by, 105, 670
    see also under individual countries
forest laws, 49, 69, 70–1, 81, 172, 179, 186,
    551
forest villages, see villages
forests
    divinity of, 21, 45, 52
    Frankish conception of ownership, 42

forests (cont.)
    importance in animal husbandry, 135,
        172–4
    rights of usage, 670
    in Scandinavia, 21, 52, 647, 650
Forncett estate, Norfolk, 680, 694, 721,
    732
fortifications
    castles, 112–3
    expansion in fourteenth to fifteenth
        century, 621, 736
    fortified villas, 25, 112–13
    fortress system in the East, 58, 59–60, 62
    fortresses of the West, 63, 64, 65
    in Italy, 64, 349, 356, 393, 394, 395, 401
    Russia, 508, 515, 516, 517, 520
    Saxony, 190
France
    agriculture, 108, 127–9, 296–7, 716,
        720; vines, 297, 719; see also Nor-
        mandy
    Capetian dynasty, 69
    export of wine, 385
    feudal organization, 57; anarchy, 69
    forest clearance, 46, 77–80, 136, 294,
        295
    formation of, 51
    fortifications, 63
    German colonization, 5, 181, 184
    land reclamation, 290–6 passim; see also
        forest clearance
    land tenure: common land, 174, 313,
        729; ecclesiastical estates, 49, 70, 73–4,
        78, 285, 299, 301, 306–16 passim;
        grants à champart, 312; peasant
        proprietors, 49, 57, 304; royal estates,
        298; transfer of property, 724; the
        villa, 305–6, 308; see also seignorial
        system
    land utilization, 69–70, 71
    land values, 694
    peasant unrest, jacqueries, 288, 737
    population, 664, 666, 668–9
    Saracen attacks, 55
    seignorial system, 266, 276, 322–37,
        passim, 709–10; leases and rents, 327,
        329, 709, 710–11, 713
    serfdom and enfranchisement, 335–7,
        707, 712, 732, 740
    taxation, 334, 698
    town growth, 64
    Viking settlements, 56
    villages, 40, 73–4
    see also Burgundy, Gaul, Normandy
Franchise of Bruges (1515), 175
franchise, charters of, 74, 267, 401, 404,
    406, 407, 698, 713

franchise, charters of (*cont.*)
  of Beaumont, 78
  of Bruges, 175
  of Lorris, 74, 78
Francis I of France, 167
Franconia, 30, 68, 87, 89, 170, 306, 316,
  711, 713, 739
Frankish Empire
  and the Roman Church, 45, 197
  in Greek lands, 227
  land tenure, 45, 188–9, 198–203, 278,
    280, 284
  royal ownership of forests, 42
  Salic Law, 17, 33, 35, 41, 142, 168, 186–8
  slavery in, 247
  taxation, 202
  vassals in, 274
Franks
  Chamavic Franks, 38
  conquest and settlement by, 2, 22, 28,
    30, 32, 34–40 *passim*, 43, 111, 186–8
  first among German tribes, 196
  intermarriage with Romans, 187
  Ripuarian Franks, 38
  'Salian' Franks, 28
Frederick II, 132, 412
Frederick, archbishop of Bremen (1106),
  292
Frescobaldi family, 350, 387, 388
Frings, T., 150
Frisia (Friesland), Frisians, 12, 38, 186, 194,
  198, 239
  agriculture, 137, 192
  land tenure, 190–1, 265, 266, 282, 304
  new dynasties, 285–6
  under Frankish rule, 196
Froissart, Jean, 176, 673, 675, 697, 722
fruit-growing
  fruits, 100, 101, 108, 131, 147, 164,
    167–9, 192
  wild fruits, 168, 173; *see also* vines
Fuero of Leon, 66
Fulk the Good, Count, 65

Gaetani family, 411
Gallienus, 22
Gallo, Agostino, 365, 368, 376, 377, 378,
  383, 418
'gardeners', 478
Garlande, Jean de, 142, 150
Gascony, 599
Gaul
  agriculture; cereals, 162; crop rotation,
    136, 139; development under
    Romans, 107, 127, 171; implements
    and methods, 107, 130, 149, 156;
    stock-breeding, 172

Gaul (*cont.*)
  artistocracy in, 273
  brigands in, 124
  British in, 29
  Clovis in, 30
  country life, 27
  forest clearance, 10
  German settlements in, 2, 34–6, 186–8,
    197
  land tenure, 31, 40, 118; under
    seignorial system, 237, 238, 239–45,
    277
  population decrease, 107
  Romans in 31; Romano-German states,
    181
  taxation, 121
  town growth, 8, 118
  village chiefdoms, 283
  villas, 113
  see also France
Geisa, King of Hungary, 89
German colonization, 12–13, 18–19, 21,
  28–39, 67–8, 83–6, 89–90, 91
  in Britain and N. Gaul, 181
  eastwards, 2–3, 5, 449–86, 661, 666, 675
  settlements 'under German law', 457–9,
    468, 469, 481, 500–6
  see also under individual tribes
Germany, German states
  agriculture: arable, cereals, 149, 162,
    163, 556; cropping systems, 136, 137,
    140, 152, 716; development in Rhine-
    land, 179; hops, 165; horses, 143;
    irrigation, 147, 148; implements and
    methods, 140, 150, 151, 155, 156,
    158; pastureland, 297; pigs, 178; vege-
    tables, 164, 165; vines, 170, 719, 741
  assaults on Roman Empire, 21–4, 28–30
  Christianity in, 45
  extent of Empire, 58
  feudalism, 69
  forests and forest clearance, 10, 12, 19,
    21, 43–4, 45, 46–9, 68, 70, 77, 81–2,
    84, 174, 291, 299, 662, 670, 716, 721
  formation of, 51
  fortifications, 63
  land hunger, 19–20, 21, 69, 82, 89
  land reclamation, 83, 291, 295, 312; *see
    also* forest clearance
  land tenure, 14–18, 20, 21, 35–7;
    ecclesiastical estates, 45, 51, 199,
    200–1, 299, 300–1, 303, 306–12
    passim, 316, 317–18, 460; *Hufen*, 41,
    88, 90, 189, 191, 201, 202–3, 277;
    peasant proprietors, 304; princely
    estates, *principes*, 273, 303–4; royal
    estates, 299; under Charlemagne, 48;

Germany, German States (cont.)
  the villa, 299, 306; see also Prussia, seignorial system
  laws, 194, 204
  origin of 'marks', 42, 312
  Ostmark, 198
  peasants: bound to the soil, 27, 707, 708; status and dues, 69, 83, 708, 711, 732; unrest, 737
  place names, 40, 48, 68, 76, 195, 196, 272–3, 670
  population, 664, 667, 668, 677
  Roman settlements in, 10, 11, 12, 13
  seignorial system, 236, 237, 238, 245, 322–34 passim, 460; leaseholds, 327, 329, 711
  serfdom, 338
  Slav conquest, 31
  slaves in, 251
  tribal leagues, 26
  village chiefdoms, 283
  villages, 19–20, 190, 191; Angerdorf, 464; Dorfgemeinschaft, 734; Gewanndorf, 19–20, 465; Waldhufendorf, 46–7, 68, 75, 78, 82, 83, 194, 296, 455, 458; see also Prussia
Gibbon, E., 220
Gilbert of Clare, 554 n.
Gildo, 105
Gimip family, 594
Giraldus Cambrensis, 77
Gislebert of Le Mons, 82
Givernay, Jean de, 697
Givry, the Curé of, 675
goats; see agriculture, stock-raising
Godfrey, abbot of Peterborough, 582
Godomar, 34
Golden Bull (Hungary), 499
Gonzaga family, 417
Gonzaga, Federico, 419
Gothic tribes, movements of, 13, 23; see also Visigoths
Gratian, 702
Gray, A. L., 571
Greece
  agriculture, 92, 127, 129
  Christianity in, 249
  Frankish rule in, 227
  land tenure in classical Greece, 109
  trade, 197
Greek civilization, 9
Gregorian ideals, 300
Gregory of Tours, 33, 151, 247
Gregory I, the Great, 199, 247, 250
Grekov, B. D., 510, 539, 543
Grimm, 18 n.
Grund, 684

Gryvet family, 594
Guérard, 288 n.
Guicciardini, Francesco, 350, 364, 416
Guillaume aux Blanche Mains, 336
Guntramm, 268–9

Hadrian, 8
Hadrian's Wall, 12, 99
Hainault, Count of, 732
Hallam, 612
Hamilton, E. J., 445 n.
Hanauer, 683, 686
Hapsburg dynasty, 723
Hatt, G., 636 n.
Haudricourt, M. A., 144 n.
Hawkwood family, 599
Helbok, A., 7
Helmold, chronicler, 84, 85, 86
Henry II, Emperor, 67, 68
Henry III, Emperor, 401
Henry IV, Emperor, 299
Henry I of England, 586, 736
Henry II of England, 80, 581, 587
Henry III of England, 581
Henry V of England, 699
Henry III of France, 133
Henry, abbot of Sint-Bavo, 320
Henry I, Duke, 473
Henry of Eastry, 582
Henry the Lion of Saxony, 85, 87
Heraclius, 51, 207, 208, 216
Herbert le Bute, 626
herbs, 165–6
Heresbach, Conrad, 144, 151, 154, 156
Herodotus, 102
Hermunduri, 194
Herrad of Landsberg, 144
Hessians, 194
Hiero of Syracuse, 116
Hierocles, 117
Hildesheim, bishop of, 76
Hinojosa, E. de, 436 n.
Hocsem, 673
Hohenstaufen dynasty, 299, 360
Holland
  agriculture, 741
  Iron age hutments, 111
  land tenure, 305, 724
  organized settlement, 71, 75–6
Hollanders, 86, 87
Holstein, 163, 190, 467, 480, 482
Holwerda, 186
Homans, 576
Homberg, 13 n.
Homer, 109
honey, 169, 451; see also bees
Honorius, 29, 187

hops, *see* agriculture
horses, *see* agriculture
horticulture, 165–7, 179, 647
Hospitallers, Knights, 578, 671
hospites, 49–50, 60, 71 n., 72–4, 78, 80, 181, 183, 184, 185
Hufen, see land tenure
Hugues, Varin, abbot of Liessies, 320
Humbert II, 713
Hundred Rolls of 1279, 575, 579, 606, 618
Hundred Years War, 320, 598–600, 695, 696, 698, 709, 710, 713, 724
Hungary
   agriculture, 137, 163, 486, 495, 716, 720
   the Comans, 275
   conversion to Christianity, 494
   expansion into Russian territory, 508
   forest clearance, 89
   German colonization, 2, 83, 454, 455, 456, 459; 'under German law', 505–6
   land tenure, 59, 490–1, 494–5
   Magyars, 58, 62
   peasant status, 495
   population decline, 664
   relations with Poland, 487
   Slav and Mongol invasions, 31, 505
   slaves, 494
   taxation and peasants' dues, 62, 496, 499, 500, 505–6, 712
   towns, 499
   trade, 386
   villages, 465
   viticulture, 495
Hungerford family, 589
Huns, 23, 28
Huntingfield, Roger de, 554 n.
Hus, John, 735

Ibn al Awam, 153, 154, 166
Ibn Khaldun, 441
Ibn Loyon, 441
Iberian Peninsula, 29, 66; *see also* Spain
Iceland, 56
Igor, Prince (945), 531, 534
Illyria, 9, 22, 30
Imola, Benvenuto da, 340, 349, 393
Ine of Wessex, 37, 41, 43, 193
Inquisitions Post Mortem, 579, 594 n., 604 n.
Investiture Quarrel (Germany), 299, 300
Ireland, 13
   agriculture, 171
   land tenure, 53, 159
   monks in, 44
   serfdom, 118
   Viking settlements, 55, 56
Irminon, abbot of St Germain-des-Prés, 49, 72, 142, 158, 161, 162, 303, 308

iron, 125
irrigation, 102–3, 104–5, 146–8, 174, 355, 357, 359, 361, 363, 440, 716
Isidore of Seville, 134, 146
Islam, *see* Moslems
Isle of Man, 56
Italy
   agriculture, 92, 136, 141, 342, 343–4, 353, 371, 418; cereals, 94–5, 104, 105, 162, 163, 371, 384–5; commercial farming, 388–9, 391; communal farming, 357, 368, 369, 425; controls 390–1, 422; crop rotation, 127, 136, 368, 373, 375; demesne farming, 411; fertilization, 377–8; hiring of stock and equipment, 425; horticulture, 179, 370; implements and methods, 96, 367, 373–7; irrigation, 147, 148, 355, 357, 359, 361, 363, 383, 724; milling, 376; monsoon crops, rice, 147, 370, 719; open-field system, 375; soils, 127; stock-raising, sheep, transhumance, 132–3, 356, 367, 379–83, 386, 389, 392, 394, 411; tree crops, 369, 372, 390, 719; vegetables and fruit, 164, 166, 361, 372
   Arab and Magyar invasions, 393
   brigands, 430
   climate, 340–1, 361, 371–2
   communes, 401–6 *passim,* 421–2, 427, 429
   derelict land (395), 119
   estate management, 9, 10
   fairs and markets, 387
   feudalism, 348, 394, 399, 401, 404, 405, 408, 409, 421, 429
   forms of rural settlement, 393–5
   fortifications, *castra, castella,* 63, 349, 356, 393, 394, 395, 401
   German conquests and settlements, 2, 30, 181–4, 355
   land enclosure, 368–9, 392
   land reclamation, 344, 353–68 *passim* 402, 409, 417; forest clearance, 356–7, 366
   land values, 353, 355, 402
   land tenure, 9–10, 54, 115–16, 122, 350–1; centuriation, 109–10; common land, 356, 368–9; ecclesiastical estates, 395–6, 408–11 *passim,* 417, 722; *latifundia,* 116, 340, 396, 397, 408, 418; *métayage,* 710; *principes castellorum,* 273; transfer of property, 724; *see also* seignorial system
   Lombard conquest, 34, 182
   money economy, 409
   peasants, 401, 406, 419–31, 728–9, 731;

Italy (*cont.*)
community at Villafranca, 357; serfs, 402–4, 406, 429; as tenants, 9–10, 417–18, 423–6; *trecento* treatment, 712; unrest, 737, 738
place names, 355, 356
population, 182, 345, 347, 354, 361–2, 394, 665
rural debts, 428
rustic nobles, 352
Saracen attacks, 55
seignorial system, 236, 237, 238, 240, 245, 246, 356, 358, 376, 393–419 *passim*, 427; the demesne, 400, 406, 410–12, 415; fragmentation, 354; tenancy and leases, 358, 376, 396–400 *passim*, 402, 407, 412–18 *passim*, 426–7, 711
slavery, 247, 395–7, 399
taxation, 287, 403, 405, 419, 425, 428–31
towns and urban policy, 64, 345–53 *passim*, 402–4; *see also* Florence, Venice
trade, 346–7, 349, 350, 351, 353, 383–92
transport, 389
urban capital and rural labour, 719
villa building, 418
vines, vineyards, 357, 371, 372–3, 391–2, 411, 412
Ivan I, Kalita, grand duke of Moscow, 521
Ivan III, the Great, grand duke of Moscow, 508, 545, 694, 708
Izyaslav Mstislavich, 518

James the Conqueror (Spain), 440
Jerome, St, 113, 157
Jevons, 680
Jews, 450, 595, 627, 673
John the Good, 682
John, King of England, 81, 166
John Chrysostom, St, 288
John Tzimisces, 220
Joliffe, J. E. A., 576
Juan I of Spain, 712
Julian, Emperor, 28, 167, 187
Jullian, 10 n.
Justinian I, 30, 94, 103, 115, 121, 182, 207, 209, 259, 263
Justinian II, 209
Jüterbock, 473
Jutes, 29, 576
Jutland, 52, 636, 637, 645, 647, 649

Kemble, 192
Klein, J., 439 n.
Knapp, G. F., 478 n.

Koloman, King, 62
Kosminsky, E. A., 575, 605, 618
Kulm, Law of, 90
Kulmer Handfeste, 1233, 460
Kulmerland, 89

labour supply, 33, 122, 314–16, 328–9, 688, 693, 705
and seignorial tenancies, 240–1, 293
wage-labourers, 203, 425–6, 434, 438, 654, 709
Britain, 566–9, 570, 688
Byzantine Empire, 205, 214
Lactantius, 25
Lancaster, Duchy of, 565, 579, 589, 591, 596, 597
Lancaster, Edmund Duke of, 582
land reclamation, 125, 290
labour for, 292–5
in Britain, 52, 70, 80–1, 175, 548–52, 559, 560, 566
in France, 167, 290–6 *passim*
in Germany, 83, 291, 295, 312
in Italy, 344, 353–68 *passim*, 402, 409, 417
in the Low Countries, 75–6, 175, 282, 290, 291, 292, 724
in Slavonic lands, 453
see also forest clearance
land tenure
allodia, 451, 460, 474–6, 478
centuriation, 109–11
clan system, 53
commons, common land, 41, 81, 109, 174, 235, 276, 278, 281–3, 313, 330, 344, 356, 446, 649, 729, 730; State claim on, 701; *see also*, agriculture, commonfield system
communes, communal regulation, 15, 42, 190, 191, 276, 357, 368–9, 446–7, 485, 518–19, 520, 532, 538–9, 546, 642, 650, 733–4
Constantine's Law (A.D. 332), 115, 119
demesne, the, *see* seignorial system
ecclesiastical estates, 4, 44–5, 48, 49, 50, 51, 66, 70, 72–4, 78, 119, 122, 199, 200–1, 215, 285, 299–303, 306–18 *passim*, 331–3, 395–6, 408, 409, 411, 476, 488, 499, 577–8, 587, 602, 619–21, 653–4, 656, 657, 659, 704, 715, 722; administration of, 319–26, 357, 400, 409, 410, 411, 474, 539, 582–3, 584, 586, 588; in Byzantium, 220, 223–5, 231; labour on, 315; secularization of, 203; and seignorial system, 261, 415; *see also* monasteries
effect of population decline, 678–9, 703

land tenure (*cont.*)

emphyteusis, 26–8, 228, 397, 400, 409

hereditary rights and duties, 16–17, 26–7, 28, 198, 210, 227, 228, 245, 246, 256–7, 407, 408, 466, 478, 488, 534, 547, 613, 658, 711

hospites, 49–50, 72–4, 293

Hufen, 41, 88, 90, 189, 191, 201, 202–3, 277, 314, 317, 318, 464–7, 470, 471, 475–6, 482, 727

imperial estates, 10, 94, 117, 118, 119, 121

latifundia, 116, 117, 132, 247, 249, 251, 252, 255, 287, 340, 396, 397, 408, 418, 433

métayage, mezzadria, share-cropping, 143, 198, 199, 211, 324–6, 414, 710, 715, 719

military estates, 28, 51, 59, 183, 188, 216, 218, 219 222, 226

neighbours' rights, 17, 38, 188, 216

peasants holdings, 9–10, 25–8, 34, 39, 41, 48, 49–50, 51, 61, 63–76 passim, 81, 83, 86, 88, 115, 206–34 passim, 304–5, 417–18, 423–6, 434–6, 451, 466–7, 474, 476–8, 488, 489, 492, 493, 521, 558, 563, 566, 567, 600–32 passim 657–9, 700; in Britain, 193, 558, 563, 566, 567, 600–11 passim; see also under peasants, seignorial system

princes and lay lords, 48, 202, 215, 273, 303–4, 321, 460, 601, 704; in Byzantine Empire, 225–6

pronoia system, 226–8, 229

restrictions on movements, 705–6

rights of usage, 313

Tablettes Albertini, 111

transfer of property, 723–4

villae, 9, 10, 110–13, 122, 192, 305–19

see also seignorial system

Africa, 111, 114–15, 117–18, 124, 259

Asia, 116–17

Bavaria, 43, 65, 195–6

Britain: ecclesiastical estates, 550, 553, 557, 559, 577–8, 580, 583, 584, 586, 587, 588–9, 594, 602, 619–21; see also individual monasteries, bishoprics; enclosures, 553, 590, 591; hereditary system, 613; lord's monopoly, 601; magnates and gentry, 592–600; peasants' holdings, 80, 193, 558, 563, 566, 567, 600–32 passim, 725–6; smallholders, 622–4, 628–32; under Roman rule, 111, 118; under Wessex laws, 193

Burgundian, 32, 43, 185–6

land tenure (*cont.*)

Byzantine Empire, 206, 210–34; ecclesiastical, 220, 223–5, 231; exempt property, 214; lay landlords, 182, 215–34 passim; military estates, 51, 183, 207–8, 216, 218, 219, 222, 226; neighbours' rights, 216; state property, 223–4

Carolingian Empire, 188–9, 198–9

Egypt, 116, 117, 121, 122, 206, 207

France: common land, 174, 313, 729; ecclesiastical estates, 49, 73–4, 78, 285, 299, 301, 306–16 passim; grants à champart, 312; peasant proprietors, 49, 57, 304; royal estates, 298; transfer of property, 724; villa, 305, 308

Frankish Empire, 45, 188–9, 198–203

Gaul, 31, 40, 118

Germany, 14–18, 20, 21, 35–7; ecclesiastical estates, 45, 51, 199, 200–1, 299, 300–1, 303, 306–12 passim, 316, 317–18, 460; Hufen, 41, 88, 90, 189, 191, 201, 202–3, 277; origin of 'marks', 42, 312; peasant proprietors, 304; princely estates, principes, 273, 303–4; royal estates, 299; under Charlemagne, 48; villa, 299, 306

Greece, 109

Ireland, 53, 159

Italy, 9–10, 54, 115–16, 122, 350–1; centuriation, 109–10; common land, 356, 368–9; ecclesiastical estates, 395–6, 408–11 passim, 417, 722; latifundia, 116, 340, 396, 397, 408, 418; métayage, 710; principes castellorum, 273; transfer of property, 724

Lombardy, 51, 183, 253, 284, 397, 410, 417

Low Countries; Flanders, 299–301, 303–4, 305; Frisia, 191; Holland, villae, 305

Poland, 452, 467, 487–9, 491; cmethones and hortulani, 502–3, 505; ecclesiastical estates, 488; latifundia, 488; peasants' holdings, 488, 492

Prussia, 476, 482, 483

Roman Empire, 25–8, 115–24 passim; see also Byzantine Empire

Russia, 227, 518–21, 534–47; communes, 518–19, 532, 546; ecclesiastical estates, 518, 520, 539, 542; manorial system, 532; peasants' holdings, 521; rents, 540–1, 542; opposition to monastic tenure, 545

Scandinavia, 38, 139, 277, 278, 652–9

Slavonic lands, 61, 88–9, 451–2, 460–1; ecclesiastical estates, 449, 460, 474–5;

land tenure (*cont.*)
>hospites, 452; *Hufen*, 482; peasants' holdings, 466-7, 474, 476; Teutonic knights' claims, 460-1
>Spain, 66-7, 722; common land, 446; perpetual tenants, 436; seignorial system, 434-7, 446

land use
>litigation, 356
>peak of, 77

land values, 662, 677, 694
>Byzantine, 230-1
>in Britain, 552, 554, 557, 593, 596, 597, 614
>in Italy, 353, 355, 402
>in Sweden, 653

language, 23

latifundia, *see* land tenure

Latimer, Bishop, 623

Laurence I, bishop of Breslau, 473

Laurent de Brezova, chronicle of, 738

Lauridzen, P., 639 n., 640, 642

Lausitz, Margravate of, 58

Lennard, R. V., 18 n., 150 n., 548, 585, 629

Law of Kulm, 90

Law of Yaroslav, 513, 518, 519, 531-4

Le Bouvier, Gilles, 142, 143, 167, 172, 178

Lechfeld, battle of, 56

Leitmeritz, Collegiate Church of, 60

Lemnos, 231

Leo VI, 216

Leonardo da Vinci, 363

Leontius, bishop of Bordeaux, 44

Leovigild, 185

Lesort, A., 268 n.

Levison, W., 88 n.

Lewis, the Great, King of Hungary, 491, 500

Lex Salica, *see* Salic law

Libanius, 265

Liberius, 181

Libya, Libyans, 55

Lidya, 96, 121

Liège, bishop of 695

Lithuania, 482, 486, 489, 493, 498, 505, 508, 536, 664
>Union with Poland, 487, 490, 499

Liudger, abbot, 45

Liutprand, laws of, 183

Livonia, 457

Livy, 273

Lluch, R. Gayano, 440 n.

locators, 86, 462-3, 471-2
>in Poland, 501-2, 503

location, charters of, 461

Lombards, 197
>conquest of Italy, 31, 34, 182-4

Lombards (*cont.*)
>fall of, 198
>intermarriage with Romans, 183, 184-5

Lombardy, 54
>agriculture, 369, 370, 375, 376, 377, 379, 383, 386, 387, 389, 394, 411; irrigation, 147, 355
>land reclamation, 358-9, 363, 364, 366
>land tenure, 51, 183, 253, 284, 397, 410, 417, 423
>land values, 353, 355
>population, 354

London, 64

Longobards, 13

Lopez, R. S., 439 n.

Lorraine, 35

Lorris, Charter of, 74, 78, 336

Lot, F., 31 n.

Lotharingia, 291, 299-300, 303, 309, 318

Louis VI of France, 73-4, 298, 336

Louis VII of France, 74, 78

Louis IX (St Louis) of France, 174, 291

Louis XII, of France, 166

Louis XIII, of France, 165

Louis the German, 253

Louis the Pious, 48, 200

Louis, son of Charlemagne, 198

Low Countries
>agriculture, 137; hops, 719
>famine, 673
>land reclamation, 75-6, 290-6 *passim*, 724
>leasehold system, 326
>peasant status, 728
>population, 665, 669-70
>prices and wages, 683, 685, 688
>serfdom and enfranchisement, 337, 707
>vacant lands, 678
>*see also* Flanders, Frisia, Holland

Lucterius the Cadurcian, 273

Lucullus, 167

Lûll, Blessed Raimon, 289

Luni, bishop of (1212), 414

Luni, bishop of (1230), 410

Lusatia, 291, 453, 455, 466, 473, 476, 483

Luther, Martin, 367

Luxemburg, 336

Macchiavel, Bernard, 729

Machiavelli, 351

Macrobius, 100

MacFarlane, 596

Magdeburg, 84, 87

Mager, F., 21 n.

Magyars, 55, 56, 58, 62

Mahaut, Countess, 169

Maitland, F. W., 549, 605

maize, 370
Majorian, 259
malaria, 361, 364, 365
Malaspina family, 416
Malatesta family, 388, 409, 411
manses, see seignorial system
Marcomanni, the, 12, 29, 181, 196
Marcomannic Wars, 21–2, 180
Marcus Aurelius, 12, 22, 95, 119, 181
'Mardelles', 112
Maria de Luna, Queen of Spain, 712
Marienburg, 479
market gardening, 167, 441
Marlborough, Thomas, of Evesham, 582
marriage fines, 603
Martini, Francesco di Giorgio, 363
Martiny, R., 19 n.
Masovia, 664
Masovia, Duke of, 460
Matilda, Empress, 585
matrimonial habits, 672, 675
Mattiaci, the, 12
Maximian, 187
Maximilian of Austria, 711
Mecklenburg, 7, 84, 85, 86, 87, 88, 89, 90,
    163, 453, 455, 457, 463, 466, 477, 482,
    664, 695
Medici family, 381, 389, 416
Meinhard, abbot of Marmoutier, 320, 321
Meinwerk, bishop of Paderborn, 68
Meillet, Antoine, 273
Meissen, margrave of, 85, 87, 88
Meissen, 58, 453, 463, 472, 477, 479, 480,
    483
Meitzen, A., 19 n., 185, 190, 191, 635
Melania, 122
Merovingian Empire, 39, 42, 43, 196–7,
    247
Merriman, R. B., 437 n., 447 n.
Mesopotamia, 102, 207
mezzadria, 414, 719
Miguel Antonio de Texada, 445
Miklosich-Müller, 227, 228 n., 229 n.,
    230 n., 231 n., 232 n.
mills, *see* corn mills
Mirandola family, 416
Misica (Mieszko), 58
Moesia, 28
molmen, mollands, 606, 615
monasteries and abbeys
    Aankt Gallen in Swabia, 309
    Affligem, abbey of, 315
    Altenburg, 291
    Altenkamp, 291
    and agriculture, 133, 331, 332
    and land reclamation, 43, 81, 291–3,
        331, 332

monasteries and abbeys (*cont.*)
    and military duties, 251
    Arrovaise in Artois, 78
    as credit institutions, 299–300
    Beaune-la-Rolande, 320
    Bonvante, 157
    Bordesley, 715
    Brauweiler, 69
    Bury St Edmunds abbey, 555, 612
    Camaldoli, 407, 416
    Chiaravalle, near Milan, 359, 411
    Christ Church Priory, Canterbury, 582,
        583
    Christ Church Priory, Romney Marsh,
        555
    Cîteaux, 313
    Cluny, 297
    Crowland abbey, 552, 602, 607, 674,
        730–1
    De Duinen (Flanders), 301
    Disibodenberg, 68
    Durham, 716 (*see also* Durham, estates
        of bishops)
    Eberbach, 170
    Echternach, in Luxemburg, 331
    Einsiedeln, 82
    Evesham, 606
    Fulda, 45, 46
    Glastonbury abbey, 550, 553, 555, 558,
        564, 566, 569, 582, 584, 586, 591, 613,
        614, 617, 619–20, 624, 629, 709
    Goldenkron, 461
    Guillerval, near Etampes, 320
    Heinrichau, 89, 90
    Hohenfurth, 461
    Illsenburg, 167
    Langheim, 701
    Leicester abbey, 717
    Léoncel, 133
    Leubus, abbey of, 460, 474
    Liessies in Artois, 307, 320
    Lorsch, abbey of, 45, 308
    Kremsmunster, 46
    Marmoutier (Alsace), 306, 315, 316,
        317, 318, 320, 321
    Meaux, 715
    monastic *seigneuries*, 243
    monastic settlements, 43, 44–5, 51, 70,
        71–2, 88, 545; *see also* ecclesiastical
        estates
    Mont-Saint-Michel, 323
    Muri (Switzerland), 268
    Ninove, in Flanders, 331
    Nonantola, 358
    Norwich Cathedral Priory, 582
    on Athos, 231
    Ouges, in Burgundy, 715

monasteries and abbeys (*cont.*)
Paderborn in Westphalia, 309
Pannonholm abbey, 490
Panteleimon, Novgorod, 518
Pegau on the White Elster, 76
Peterborough abbey, 560, 580, 607, 614, 621, 624, 629
Pontigny, abbey of, 710
Prémontré, 313
Prüm, 152, 318
Ramsey abbey, 555, 584, 586, 590, 629, 718, 719
Reichenau (Swabia,) 307, 309
Remiremont, 293
S. Ambrogio at Origgio, 356, 416
S. Caterina, 411
S. Giulia of Brescia, 396, 406
S. Giustina of Padua, 416
S. Maria della Caita, Venice, 414
Saint-Amand, 303, 307, 310
Saint-Bertin, 307, 313, 315, 318
Saint-Lambert of Liège, 323
Saint-Martin of Tournai, 323
Saint-Romain-le-Puy, 709
Saint-Seurin, 674
Saint-Vaast of Arras, 315, 328
Saint-Vincent of Le Mans, 293
Saintes, abbey of, 307
San Pedro de Cardena (Burgos), 435
Shaftesbury abbey, 619
Siegburg, 88
Sint-Bavo, 303, 307, 310, 311, 318, 320, 323
Sint-Peter of Ghent, 310, 322, 323
Sint-Truiden, 309, 310, 311, 312, 316, 317, 320, 321, 323, 324, 325, 326
Solignac, 709
St Albans, 582
St Avit of Orleans, 295
St Denis, 70, 74, 293, 307, 309, 312, 314, 320, 321, 322
St Dié, 293
St Emmeram of Regensburg, 308
St Gall, abbey of, 268
St Gallen, 45
St Gemme, 70
St Germain-des-Prés, 174, 240, 241, 243, 279, 285, 303, 308, 313, 315, 709
St Jean d'Angely, 70
St Martin-de-Tournai, 671, 696, 701
St Mary of Roncevaux, 133
St Mihiel, 268
St Peter in the Black Forest, 76
St Peter's, Gloucester, 583, 619, 622, 626
St Vincent at Metz, 152
St Swithin's Priory, Winchester, 553, 558, 560, 602, 616, 619–20

monasteries and abbeys (*cont.*)
Tavistock, 602, 721
Trebnitz in Silesia, 472
Villers, in Brabant, 301, 332
Wallingwells, Nottingham, 80
Werden on the Ruhr, abbey of, 45, 306, 307, 310, 312, 316, 317, 318, 321, 329
Westminster, 566, 567, 689
money economy, 211, 229, 438, 709, 741
accounting system, 582–3
bullion shortage, 671, 680
burgess capitalists, 461
devaluation, 698–700
in Britain, 588, 699; rural financing, 627–8
in Italy, 409
in Slavonic lands, 469, 472, 499
in Spain, 437–8, 444–5
see also wages
money-lending, 428
Mongols, 31, 163, 505, 512, 527, 535, 536, 537, 544, 545–6
Mongolian Bulgars, 28, 30
Monomakh, Vladimir, 547
Montecassino, charter of, 401
Montfort, Count de, 712
Montfort, Simon de, 595
Montierender survey, 242, 274
Moors (Arabs), Moslems, in Spain, 2, 34–5, 53, 54–5, 433, 436, 439, 440–3
Moravia, 89, 449, 452–9 *passim*, 460, 461, 466, 473, 483, 484
Morigny Chronicle, the, 73
Morocco, 147
mortmain, 713
Möser, Justus, 190
Moslems, Islam, 124, 197, 249, 512; *see also* Moors
Mouillac in Quercy, 694
Mstislavich, Izyaslav, 518
Mstislavich, Rostislav, 519
mules, 143, 176, 381, 445
multure, 600
Myres, J. N. L., 18 n.

Namur, count of (1430), 695, 713
Naples, Kingdom of, 364, 366, 388
Naristi, 196
nationalities, development of, 2, 51
Nero, 118, 192
Nervii, the, 187
Netherlands, *see* Low Countries
Neufbourg, seigneurie of, 697, 713, 727
Neville family, 722
Nicephorus Phocas, 219–20
Nielsen, O., 638 n.
Norbert, St., 291

Norbertians, *see* Praemonstratensians
Norden, 16 n.
Nordholm, G., 636, 637 n., 640
Normandy
    agriculture: arable, cereals, 152–3,
        155–6; crop rotation, 297; fencing,
        159; fertilizers, 146; fruit, 168–9, 719,
        741; horses, 173, 176; implements,
        145; pigs, 173
    annexation by France, 298
    extension and settlement, 56, 78
    feudal organization, 57
    forest clearance (thirteenth century), 78,
        290–1
    forest laws, 173
    land reclamation, 175
    land tenure: ecclesiastical estates in,
        299; the *ferme muable*, 325; the *villa* in,
        305, 306
    serfs, 336
Norrland, 639, 656
Northmen, Vikings, 52, 55, 56–8, 450, 519
Norway
    agriculture, 741; stock-raising, 172,
        634, 720
    forests, 52; timber exports, 650
    land tenure, 239, 266, 655–6; ecclesias-
        tical estates, 653, 659; *Odal* estates, 38
    peasant status, 652–9
    taxation, 653
    trade, 652
    village and farm settlements, 633, 636
Notre Dame de Paris, 78, 697
Novilius, 119

Odin, 52
Odo, bishop, 84
Odoacer, 181
Oestergoetland, 644, 645, 647, 655, 659
Okhotsk, founding of, 546
olives, 100–1, 114, 131, 164, 230, 371, 372
Olga, Princess (tenth century Russia), 519,
    520, 531
open-field system, *see* agriculture
oranges, 147
Orosius, 185
Orsini family, 411
Ostermann, 18 n.
Ostrogoths, 34, 181–2
Ottar, Norwegian farmer, 634, 635
Otto of Freising, 62
Otto II, Emperor, 401
Otto III, 299
Otto the Great, 58
Ottoman Empire, 94
oxen, *see* agriculture
Oxford Parliament, 1258, 595

Pacello, Don, 166
Palatinate, the, 29
Paleologi, 229
Palestine, 207
Palissy, Bernard, 146
pariage, 72
parliamentary petitions, 569, 609
Parma, Statues of, 696
Paston, Robert, of Castor, 594
Pavia, estates of bishop of, 665
peasants
    bound to the soil, 27, 707, 708
    coloni, 10, 26, 27, 196, 241, 256–60,
        264–5, 288, 398
    dues, duties, 26, 33, 39, 59–62, 64, 66,
        88, 188, 230, 233, 314–16, 450, 451,
        466–8, 472, 481–2, 494, 496–500,
        503–6, 530–47 *passim*, 654, 704–8,
        711–14, 728, 731–2, 740; as cause
        of revolts, 735–6; under seignorial
        system, 235, 239, 240–1, 273–4, 288,
        328–9, 333–4, 338, 339, 395, 396,
        398–9, 434–7, 496, 589, 600–11 *passim*;
        labour commuted to rent, 603, 605–8,
        610, 615–16; mortmain, 713
    free status, 39, 54, 80, 189–90, 254,
        467–8, 495, 604–14 *passim*, 655, 657,
        713, 732; in Byzantine Empire, 204,
        208–13, 221, 229, 231; community at
        Villafranca, 357
    in Britain, 39, 65, 70; land holdings, 80,
        193, 558, 563, 566, 567, 600–32
        passim, 725–6; as smallholders, 622–4,
        628–32; unrest, 608–10, 736–9
    in Denmark: landholdings, 658, 700
    in France: landholdings, 49, 57, 304;
        as serfs, 335–7, 707, 712, 732, 740;
        unrest, 288, 737
    in Germany: landholders, 304; status,
        and dues, 27, 69, 83, 338, 707, 708,
        711, 732; unrest, 737
    in Italy, 401, 406, 419–31, 728–9, 731;
        community at Villafranca, 357; serfs,
        402, 406, 429; as tenants, 9–10, 417–18,
        423–6; *trecento* treatment, 712; un-
        rest, 737, 738
    in Russia: land holdings, 521, 534; status,
        509, 518, 530–47 *passim*, 707–8, 728
    in Scandinavia, 652–9
    in Slavonic lands; dues and taxes,
        469–70, 481–2, 483
    in Spain: status and obligations, 434–8,
        712, 728, 729; subjection to *malos
        usos*, 436–7; unrest, 737
    in Sweden, 652–9
    in town populations, 65, 91, 203, 315;
        peasant-burgesses, 91

peasants (cont.)
land holdings, 9–10, 25–8, 34, 38, 39,
41, 48, 49–50, 51, 61, 63–76 passim,
81, 83, 86, 88, 115, 193, 206–34
passim, 304–5, 417–18, 423–6, 434–6,
466–7, 474, 476–8, 488, 489, 492, 493,
521, 558, 563, 566, 567, 600–32
passim, 657–9, 700, 725–30; see also
seignorial system
paroikoi, 229–33 passim
relations with Church, 71–2
transference from Roman to German
lords, 204
unrest, 608–10, 702, 712, 735–9
see also serfs
Peasant-noblemen in Prussia, 476
Peasants' Revolt, 608–10
Peasants' War, the, 738–9
Pegolotti, 385
Pelc, 687
Pelham family, 560, 579, 589
Pepin the Short, 171, 260
Percy family, 597, 671, 704
Perrote family, 724
Perruzzi family, 387
perry, 169
Persia, Persians, 31, 207, 263
Pertinax, 10
Peter of Lille, St, 301
Petrarch, 418, 419
Petronius, 116
Petrushevsky, 509
Peverell family, 594
Philip I of France, 298
Philip VI of France, 176
Philip Augustus, 74, 178, 298
Philippe le Bel, 176
Philippe le Bon, 698
Phoebus, Gaston, 695
Phoenicians, 9, 177
Piast dynasty, 58
Piccolimini, Aeneas Silvius, 672
Pictet, 104
Piers Plowman, 625
pigs, see agriculture, stock-raising
Piove di Sacco, 401
Pipewell abbey, Chronicle of, 81
Pippin, 194, 197
Pirenne, H., 34 n., 197
Pirmin, abbot, 21
place names
as index of rural chiefdoms, 272
Anglo-Saxon, 192
Belgium, 36
Burgundian, 284
England, 37, 52, 57, 118, 190 n., 548
Eastern Europe, 452, 456, 458, 483–4

place names (cont.)
France, 40, 48, 57, 82, 118, 272–3, 291
Frankish empire, 188, 190, 191, 284
Germany, 40, 48, 68, 76, 195, 196,
272–3, 670
Italy, 272–3, 355, 356
Lombardy, 183, 284
Low Countries, 291
Scandinavia, 636 n.
plague, 119, 217, 569–70, 666, 674–5, 738
Black Death, 346, 350, 362, 426, 427,
437, 448, 562, 569, 588, 590, 608, 609,
639, 654, 666, 674, 675, 692, 713,
731
influence on bourgeois accession, 693
plantation system, 54
Pliny, the Elder, 96, 98, 107, 116, 129, 130,
145–6, 149, 162, 163, 164, 165, 167,
177, 373, 374
Pliny, the Younger, 112, 133
ploughs, types of, see agriculture, implements
Podolia, 486
Poland
agriculture and land use, 60, 61, 125,
491, 716, 720
expansion into Russia, 508
forest conservation, 455
and Galicia, 536
German colonization, 2, 5, 89, 455–9
passim, 466; 'under German law',
457, 500–4
land reclamation, 453
land tenure, 58, 59, 449, 452, 467,
487–9, 491; cmethones and hortulani,
502–3, 505; ecclesiastical estates, 488;
latifundia, 488; peasants' holdings,
488, 492; see also seignorial system
peasants' dues, 59, 60, 496, 503–4
peasants' status, 485, 489, 737
place names, 458, 484
prices and wages, 687
seignorial system, 491–2, 504
taxation, 60, 496, 499
town and country planning, 473
villages, 492, 501–2, 504–5
war with Prussia, 695
Polish Statute, 1347, 467
Pomerania, 7, 89, 90, 451, 453, 457, 466,
467, 472, 480, 695
Pontine Marshes, 102, 127
Pope, Alexander (1296), 616
population
birth rate, 667–8, 672, 676–7
consequences of decline, 677–94
effects of war, 675–6
fluctuations in, 661–77, 734

population (*cont.*)
  Britain, 559, 560–70, 582, 630, 666, 669
  Germany, 664, 667, 668, 677
  Italy, 182, 345, 347, 354, 361–2, 394, 665
  Russia, 517, 527
  Scandinavia, 639, 657, 666, 677
  Slavonic lands, 485
Postan, 690
poultry, 178–9
Praemonstratensians, 88, 291, 300, 331, 332, 460
  missions in E. Europe, 453
Premyslids, house of, 58
Pribram, 690
price edicts of Charlemagne, 204
prices
  agricultural/industrial disparity, 728
  manipulation of, 391, 444
  of corn, 677–88, 691–2, 715, 737, 741
  of meat, 685–88
  of wool, 589
Primasius of Hadrumetum, 248
Probus, 22, 103, 181
Procopius, 115
Prosper Aquitanus, 32
Provisions of Westminster, 1259, 595
Prussia, 2, 58, 452–5 *passim*, 458
  the Church in, 460
  land tenure, 476, 482, 483
  peasant dues, 467, 471
  seignorial system, 459
  serfdom, 483
  Teutonic knights in, 89, 425, 459, 461
  town and country planning, 473
  villages, 466, 469, 485
  war against Poland, 695

Quadi, the, 12, 13, 196

rabbits, 175, 179
racial amalgamation, intermarriage, 183, 184–5
rainfall, *see* climate
Randolff family of Wigston, 734
ransoms, 598–9
Rashin, A. G., 563 n.
Ravenna, archbishops of, 358
Recared I, 185
Reeb, 15 n.
Reid, Clement, 108
reindeer, 634, 635
René of Anjou, 168
Retinger, J. H., 447 n.
rice, 147, 370, 443, 719
Richard of London, abbot of Peterborough, 582

Richard Ruffus, 586
Rhaetia, 11
Rittergut, 477
rituals, 275
road-making, 12
Robert II of France, 298
Robert, abbot of Peterborough, 582
Roger, abbot of St Albans, 582
Rogers, Thorold, 681, 686, 692
Rohrbach family, 667, 672
Rollo, 56, 65
Roman Empire
  agriculture, 92–124 *passim*, 126–36, 149, 155, 162, 167, 172, 343, 368; irrigation, 147, 344
  colonization, settlements, 1, 3, 8–13, 120
  decline in the West, 22, 24, 28–30, 124, 180–1, 192
  feudal conditions in, 122
  land tenure, 25–8, 115–24 *passim*, 289; *coloni*, colonates, 10, 26, 27, 256–60, 264–5, 287; rights on provincial soil, 106
  local government institutions, 109
  taxation, 95, 113–14, 120–1
  see also Byzantine Empire
Romano-German sgates, 181
Romanus I Lecapenus, 216, 217, 218, 220
Romanus II, 218
Romny-Borshevo culture, 516
Romulus, 109
Roskilde, estates of bishop of, 654, 656
Rostovtseff, M., 8 n., 10 n.
Rothamsted experimental station, 105, 558
Rothar, King of Lombards
Rothert, H., 19 n.
Rotuli de Domanibus, 587
Roumania, Roumanians, 23, 500
Round, Horace, 592
Rurik, 519
Rurik dynasty, 534, 547
Russell, 561
Russia
  agriculture, 512, 518, 519, 546; cereals and arable, 524–8; crop rotation, 524, 526, 546; implements, 522–4, 527, 528; livestock, 528–9; slash-and-burn system, 524–6, 527, 530; vegetables, 525, 528
  barrow burials, 513, 517
  bees and honey, 530
  centralized state, 541, 544, 545
  Christianity in, 507, 513
  climate, 511
  forest lands, 513–14, 516, 520, 529–30; clearance, 509, 512, 542

Russia (*cont.*)
  fortifications, fortified castles, 508, 515, 516, 517, 520
  German colonization, 83, 455
  hunting and fishing, 529–30
  land tenure, 518–21, 534–47, 734; communes, 518–19, 532, 536, 538–9, 546; ecclesiastical estates, 518, 520, 539, 542; hereditary rights, 227, 534; manorial system, 532; opposition to monastic tenure, 545; peasant holdings, 521, 534; rents, 540–1, 542
  Law Code of 1497 (*Subednik*), 545, 546
  Law of Yaroslav, 513, 518, 519, 531–4
  Mongol invasions, 512, 514, 527, 536, 545–6
  paganism, 520
  peasant status, serfdom, 509, 518, 530–47 *passim*, 707–8, 728
  population, 517, 527
  power of the nobles, 700
  Slav settlements, 510, 518, 535
  slaves, 531, 533–4, 537, 540–1, 543, 733
  trade, 536
  Vikings in, 56, 59, 519
  villages and towns, 209, 512–17, 520
  wealth of the court, 530
Rutilius Namatianus, 112
Ryolet, Jehan, 697

St Germain-des-Prés
  see monasteries
St John, Knights of, 460
Saint Maur-des-Fossés, *polyptyque* of, 242, 288
St Paul's, estates of canons of, 606, 619–20
Salian Franks, *see* Franks
Salic law, 17, 33, 35, 41, 142, 168, 186–8
Salimbeni family, 351
Salvian, 123, 185
Salzburg, 196, 198
Samson, abbot, of Bury St Edmunds, 582
Santa Giulia of Brescia, 266–7
Sapori, A., 723
Saracens, 50, 55, 56, 176
Sardinia, 254, 340, 341, 347, 348, 364, 368, 369
Sarmatians, 13, 23, 26, 31
Sathas, 228 n.
Saxons, 21, 22, 29, 30, 38, 171, 196, 576
  absorption by Frankish Empire, 197, 198
  growth of tribal state, 189–90
  trade with Britain, 192
  see also Anglo-Saxons
Saxony, 7, 163
  fortifications, 190
  land reclamation, 291

Saxony (*cont.*)
  land tenure, 38, 266, 299, 304, 306, 327, 329, 338, 716
  peasants' dues and services, 316, 338
  peasant unrest, 739
  villages abandoned, 667
Scandinavia
  agrarian conditions, 633–5
  climate, 663
  common land, 647
  forests, 647; divinity of, 21, 52
  German settlements, 38
  peasant status, 652–9
  place names, 636 n.
  population, 639, 657, 666, 677
  raiders from, 2; *see also* Northmen
  religious houses in, 647
  slave-trading, 652, 654
  taxation, 645, 653, 658
  trade, 651–2
  village and farm settlements, 52, 635–48
  see also individual countries
Schleswig, Schleswig-Holstein, 190, 193, 480, 708
Schlüter, O., 13 n.
Schmiedl, L., 190 n.
Schneider, 31 n.
Schulze, see Slavonic villages
Scotland, 12, 53, 737
  agriculture, 137, 150, 162, 171
  population, 666
  struggle for independence, 712
  Viking settlements, 56
Seebohm, 192, 605, 606, 607
seed trade, 167
seignorial (seigneurial, manorial) system, 72, 235–89, 721
  alleux, 266–7, 282
  and labour for reclamation, 293
  break-up of, 307, 314, 317–19, 402–10 *passim*, 723–4, 740, 741
  coloni, colonates, 10, 26, 256–60, 264–5, 288, 398
  decline of slavery under, 246–55, 396, 399
  demand for suppression, 736
  the demesne, 239, 240, 242, 243, 255, 257, 270, 279, 280, 282, 283, 301, 307, 308–14, 319, 320, 328, 329, 395, 400, 406, 410, 411, 412, 415, 435, 460, 474–5, 566, 575–6, 578–91 *passim*, 714–15, 737, 740
  franchises, 267, 401, 404, 406, 407
  free and servile manses, 41, 241–5, 246, 252–5, 277–81, 285, 289, 397
  hôtises, 278
  incomes, 88, 721–2

seignorial system (*cont.*)
  leases and rents, 88, 240–1, 322–7, 395–400 *passim*, 402, 407–8, 410, 412–18, 601, 603–7 *passim*, 611, 615–16, 655–6, 709–11, 713, 715, 726–7
  monopolies, 334
  origins, 289, 332–4
  peasants' duties under, 235, 239–41, 266–8, 273–4, 288, 328–9, 333–4, 338, 339, 395, 396, 398–9, 434–7
  reductions in rights, 701, 709
  reorganisation in eleventh to twelfth century, 319–32
  State and, 701
  survival of, 739
  Britain (manorial), 80, 192–3, 235, 236, 238, 255, 261, 262, 266, 267, 270–1, 554, 558, 563, 566, 571–91, 597, 600–4, 611, 618, 715; the demesne 566, 575–6, 578–91 *passim*, 596, 601, 603–7, 737, 740; the hide, 277, 278, 280; leases and rents, 575–6, 589, 601, 603–7 *passim*, 611, 615–16, 626, 726–7
  Denmark, 139, 238, 654
  Eastern Europe, 456, 459, 491–5 *passim*, 504
  France, 266, 276, 322–37 *passim*, 709–10; leases and rents, 327, 329, 709, 710–11, 713
  Gaul, 237, 238, 239–45, 277
  Germany, 236, 237, 238, 245, 322–34 *passim*, 406; leaseholds, 327, 329, 711
  Italy, 236, 237, 238, 240, 245, 246, 356, 358, 376, 393–419 *passim*, 427; the demesne, 400, 406, 410–12, 415; fragmentation, 354; tenancy and leases, 358, 376, 396–400 *passim*, 402, 407, 412–18 *passim*, 426–7, 467, 558, 711
  Poland, 491–2, 504
  Russia, 532
  Slavonic lands, 459; demesnes, *Vorwerk*, 456, 460, 474–80
  Spain, 434–7, 446
Semnones, the, 21
Seneca, 94, 116
Septimania, 50, 51
Serbia, 227, 231
Serbo-Croatia, 54
serfs, serfdom, 253–4, 316, 335–8, 402, 403, 404, 406, 434, 435, 438, 483, 509, 533–5, 543,545, 546, 605–10, 654, 707, 713, 725, 731–3, 740
  see also feudalism, slaves
Sernander, R., 21 n.

Serres, Olivier de, 128, 134, 144, 146, 153, 154, 157, 166
Servius, 128 n.
Severi, the, 22
Severus, Alexander, 117, 181
Sforza family, 363, 370
Sforza, Ludovico, 382
share-cropping, *see* land tenure, *métayage*
sheep, sheep-farming, *see* agriculture
shepherd's crook, 177
Sicily, 181, 250, 342, 345, 347, 350, 364, 388, 389, 392
  agriculture, 104, 132, 340, 361, 368, 371, 374, 376, 379, 380, 381, 384, 385, 391, 411
  Arab invasions, 360
  land tenure, 115, 122, 397, 413, 417, 418, 423
  'the granary of Italy', 384
  Saracen settlements, 55, 56, 360
  wage-labourers, 425
Sidonius Apollinaris, 112
Siedelmann family, 462
Siegfried, archbishop of Mainz, 68–9
Sigambrians, 186
Sigebert the Merovingian, 194
Sigismund, King of Hungary, 491
Silesia, 7, 58, 60, 89, 90, 163, 452, 455, 457, 466, 467, 468, 471, 472, 473, 475, 478–81 *passim*, 483, 484, 485
Silius Italicus, 95
silk production, in Spain, 443
Simon of Felstead, 586
Sismondi, C. J. L. S. de, 353
Sixtus IV, Pope, 392
Sjöbeck, 21 n.
Skaane, 645, 646, 647, 659
slaves, slave-trading, 17, 53, 105, 116, 125, 180, 211, 228, 230, 239–40, 272–3, 286–7
  as seignorial tenants, 9, 241, 250, 251–2, 279, 396, 399, 733
  caravan routes, 249
  decline of, 10, 33, 246–55, 287, 654
  in Britain, 270, 628
  in E. Europe, 449–50, 451, 493, 494–5
  in Russia, 531, 533–4, 537, 540–1, 543
  in Scandinavia, 652, 654
  in Spain, 434
Slavonic lands
  agriculture, 61, 163, 449, 450, 451, 459, 479–80, 484–5; bee-keeping, 483; vineyards, 480
  boundary with Franks, 46
  the Church in, 88, 451
  see also land tenure, ecclesiastical

Slavonic lands (cont.)
  German colonization, 2, 58, 85, 89–91,
    449–86; colonization 'under German
    law', 457–9, 468, 469, 481
  land reclamation and forest clearance,
    65, 453, 454, 458
  land tenure, 61, 88–9, 451–2, 460–1;
    ecclesiastical estates, 449, 460, 474–5;
    hospites, 452; Hufen, 482; peasants'
    holdings, 466–7, 474, 476; Teutonic
    knights' claims, 460–1; see also
    seignorial system
  money economy in, 469, 472; burgess
    capitalists, 461
  paganry, 249
  peasant dues, taxation, 469–70, 481–2,
    483
  place names, 452, 456, 458, 483–4
  population growth, 485
  Rittergut, 477
  Scandinavian conquests, 57–8
  seignorial system, 459; demesnes,
    Vorwerk, 456, 460, 474–80
  Slav settlements, 2, 28, 30–1, 68, 194,
    208, 535
  slavery, 449–50, 451
  social organization, 52–3, 449–50
  taxation, 469–70, 483
  town and country planning, 473–4
  towns, 453, 481
  trade, 451, 485–6; market rights, 472
  villages, 86, 455, 458, 461, 463–73, 481
  see also individual countries
Slovakia, 484
Slovenes, 31, 46
Slicher van Bath, B., 691
Small, 107
socage, 262
soil, see agriculture
Solov'ev, 512
solskifte, 52, 645
Southorp family, 594
Spain
  agriculture, 54–5, 438–47; cereals, 443,
    444; communal effort, 446–7; con-
    trols, 436; crop rotation, 446;
    fertilizers, 95, 134, 146, 446; horticul-
    ture, 54, 179, 441–2; implements,
    445; irrigation, 54–5, 147–8, 441–2,
    716; livestock, transhumance, 55,
    132–3, 143, 172, 177, 438–9, 445, 446,
    720; vegetables and fruit, 166, 441–2;
    see also vineyards
  climate, 432, 439
  Corona de Aragón, 447
  feudalism, 433, 435
  forest clearance, 439

Spain (cont.)
  fortresses, 66
  German colonization, 30, 34, 50, 51,
    184; see also Iberian peninsula
  land tenure, 66–7, 722; common land,
    446; perpetual tenants, 436; see also
    seignorial system
  Moors, Moslems, in, 433–4, 436, 439,
    440–3
  the new rich, 724
  oligarchic society, 433
  peasant status and obligations, 434–8,
    712, 728, 729; subjection to malos
    usos, 436–7; unrest, 737
  population, 448, 665–6
  'Reconquest', 447
  Romano-German states, 181
  seignorial system, 271 (Castile), 434–7,
    446
  silk production, 443
  slaves, 434
  Spanish Mark established, 198
  towns, 64, 66, 67, 437, 439, 444, 664
  trade, 437, 439, 444, 447; price-fixing,
    444
  vineyards, 131, 442, 719
Spitignev, Duke, 60
Stafford, earls of, 590, 597
state, power of, 700–1
Statute of Labourers, 608
Statue of Merton, 81
Statutes of Parma, 696
Steinbach, F., 7, 14 n., 18 n., 19 n.
Stenton, F. M., 575
Stephen, King of England, 63, 585
Stephen I, St, King of Hungary, 58, 490–1
Stephen, Robert, 617
Stilicho, 187
stock-raising, see agriculture
Stolz, 688
Strabo, 104, 135, 158
Strozzi, Palla, 389
Stubbs, W., 593
Stutz, U., 33 n.
Styffe, G. G., 658 n.
Suevi, the, 22, 28, 196
sugar, production in Spain, 442
Suger, abbot of St Denis, 70, 74, 293, 309,
    314, 320
Sutton Courtenay, 40 n.
Swabia, Swabians, 13, 29, 81, 83, 170, 194,
    299
Sweden, 239, 633
  agriculture, 634; arable, cereals, 634,
    647, 648; bees, honey, 634, 650;
    hops, 647; open-field system, 641;
    saeter system, 648; stock-raising,

Sweden (cont.)
  634, 648–9, 650; two-field system, 647
  cloth-making, 651
  forests, 52, 650
  hunting, 650
  land tenure, 643–4, 646, 656–9 passim; common land, 649; communes, 645, 650; ecclesiastical estates, 653, 657, 659
  land values, 653
  mining, 651
  peasant status, 652–9
  population, 639
  taxation, 650, 653, 658
  Vaestgota law, 642, 643, 652
  village and farm settlements, 645–7
Switzerland, 29, 142, 195, 701
  agriculture, 163
  free comunities, 338–9, 734, 739
  trade, 386, 734
Svyatoslav, 531, 534
Sylvester, Pope, 122
Symonds, 104
Synod of Quierzy, 253
Syria, 113, 207

Tabace, 101
Tablettes Albertini, 111, 114, 115
Tacitus, 12–18, 21, 33, 35, 42, 192, 193, 251, 273, 281, 342
Taifali, the, 181
Tassilo, Duke, 46
Tanaglia, Michelangelo, 368
Tasso, 389
Taunton, Vale of, 550, 553
taxation
  as cause of revolts, 736
  grazing tax, 95, 232
  hearth tax, 232, 279, 661
  land-tax, 113–14, 120, 205, 232
  poll-tax, 113–5, 208, 267
  tallage, 334, 405, 603
  Britain, 280, 561, 562, 573–4, 588, 623, 698; church scot, 603; entry fines, 553, 563, 566, 589, 630, 709; death duties, 565; marriage fines, 603; poll tax, 623, 738; poll tax on sheep, 132; royal taxes, 600, 603; tallage, 563, 589, 603
  Byzantine Empire, 205, 206, 211–14, 219–23 passim, 227, 231–2, 258, 280; allelengyon system, 213–14, 220–1; exemptions, 223, 225
  France, 334, 698
  Frankish Empire, 202
  Italy, 287, 403, 405, 419, 425, 428–31

taxation (cont.)
  Poland, 60, 496, 498
  Roman Empire, 95, 113–14, 120–1; see also Byzantine Empire
  Scandinavia, 650, 653, 658
  Slavonic lands, 469–70, 483
Templars, 460, 461, 502, 578, 580
Teutonic Order, 89, 90, 175, 453, 455, 456, 457, 459, 460, 461, 463, 464, 467–8, 476, 489, 508, 677, 695
Teutons, 21
textiles, 164
Texada, Miguel Antonio de, 445
Theodoric the Ostrogoth, 30, 102, 181, 182, 184, 204, 252
Theodosius II, 113
Theophrastus, 93
Theorodius I, 114
Theudebert, 196
Thierry, son of Clovis, 165
Thierry d'Hireçon, bishop of Arras, 126
Thompson, J. W., 441 n.
Thuringia, Thuringians, 29, 30, 68, 82, 84, 170, 193–4, 196, 304, 670, 724
Tiberius Gracchus, 116
Tikhomirov, 527
tithes, 48, 61, 302, 330–1, 451, 454, 467, 468, 472, 500, 538, 603, 735
Titow, J. Z., 557
Titus, 186
Tokhtamysh khan, 508
Torello, 136
Tot family, 594
Totila, 182, 204
towns
  effect of population decline, 664, 680, 693
  growth of, 8–11 passim, 64–7 passim, 71, 89–91, 116–19 passim
  in Britain, 8–9, 64, 118
  in Eastern Empire, 205
  in Italy, 64, 345–53 passim, 402–4
  in Slavonic lands, 453, 472–3, 481, 688
  in Spain, 437, 439, 444, 664
  town and country planning in E. Europe, 473–4
  and trade, 203, 298, 304–5, 353
  villes neuves, 74, 78, 80, 86, 292, 296, 336
townsmen, relation to land, 90, 710
trade, 197, 203, 298, 304, 321
  in corn, 443, 672–3, 692, 705, 708; see also prices
  Italy, 346–7, 349, 350, 351, 353, 383–92
  Russia, 536
  Scandinavia, 651–2
  Slavonic lands, 89, 450, 451, 485–6; market rights, 472
  Spain, 437, 439, 443, 444

Trajan, 8, 11, 12, 180
transhumance
   see agriculture
transport, 145, 389
Transylvania, 23, 163, 500, 505, 738
Trehearne, 593 n.
Treveri, the, 187
Tunisia, 111
Turks, as landlords in Yugoslavia, 280
Tuscany, 183, 340, 353, 357, 359, 363, 366,
   369, 370, 371, 372, 375, 380, 381, 394,
   410, 413, 414, 415, 417, 418, 423, 426,
   431, 724
Tyler, Wat, 738
Tyrol, the, 410, 424, 429, 430, 664, 688,
   707, 711, 716, 720, 721, 732, 735

Uppsala cathedral, 656
Urlanis, 517
Usher, 683
Uspensky, 229 n.

Vaestgota law, 642, 643
Valencia, 665
Valens, 96
Valentinian I, 114
Vandals, 28, 32; in Africa, 114
Vandelbert of Prüm, 152
Van Maerlant, 702
Varangians, 58
Varro, M. Terentius, 104, 105, 129, 131,
   132, 133, 134, 158, 247, 251
Varini, 194
Vasil'evich, Vasilii, 521
vassals, 251, 284, 429
vegetables, see agriculture
Venantius Fortunatus, 33, 44
Vendôme, Count of, 69
Venice
   Venetian republic, 227, 350, 351–2, 358,
      363, 366, 381, 382, 384, 386, 388, 415,
      416, 418
Vercauteren, 34 n.
verjuice, 169
Vernadskij, 209 n.
Veselovskii, S. B., 510
Vespasian, 11
Vézelay, abbot of, 126
Vicelin, provost of Neumünster, 84
Vikings, see Northmen
villae, 9, 10, 110–13, 122, 314
   as origin of Anglo-Saxon manors, 192
   decomposition of, 305–19, 328, 332
Villafranca, 357
villages
   Angerdorf, 464
   bourgs, 73, 78, 306, 315

villages (cont.)
   community life under seigneuries, 276
   deserted, wasted, 69, 662, 663, 664, 667,
      677, 678
   ecclesiastical ownership, 201
   forest villages (Waldhufendorf), 46–7, 68,
      75, 78, 83, 194, 296, 455, 458, 465–6,
      469
   Gewanndorf, 19–20, 465
   growth and development of, 40, 42, 52,
      72, 86, 113, 295–6
   nucleated, 108, 194, 209, 242, 295, 393,
      576
   Ordensland, 464
   submission to lords, 269–70
   villes neuves, 74, 78, 80, 86, 292, 296,
      336
   Waldhufendorf, see forest villages
   see also land tenure, communes
   Britain, 37, 40, 80, 111, 123, 563, 566,
      571, 574, 576, 621–2, 631–2
   Byzantine communities, 207–15, 230
   Celtic hamlets, 37
   France, 113, 244
   Frankish empire, 188
   German states, 19–20, 35, 190, 191;
      Angerdorf, 464; Dorfgemeinschaft, 734;
      Gewanndorf, 19–20, 465; Waldhufen-
      dorf, 46–7, 68, 75, 78, 82, 83, 194, 296,
      455, 458
   Italy, 393
   Poland, 492, 501–2, 504–5
   Prussia, 485
   Russia, 512–17, 520
   Scandinavia, 52, 635–42
   Slavonic lands, 86, 455, 458, 461, 463–73,
      481, 485; the Schulze (head-man),
      468–9, 471
   Visigothic, 185
Villages, Jean de, 167
Villani, Matteo, 362
Villeneuve-le-Roi, charter of, 74
Villeneuve Saint-Georges, 281
Vinci, see Leonardo da
Vinogradoff, P., 509, 585, 605
Virgil, 96, 98, 128, 162
vines, vineyards, 54, 68, 94, 100, 101, 108,
   129, 131, 169–70, 210, 230, 297, 357,
   371, 372–3, 442, 480, 717, 719, 741;
   rent of, 229, 411, 412, 709
Visconti family, 363, 409, 417
Visigoths, 23, 28, 30, 31, 32, 34, 43
   agriculture, 184
   conquered by Franks, 187
   settlements in Gaul and Italy, 184–5
viticulture, see vines
Vives, J. Vicens, 433 n., 437 n., 442

Volhynia, 486, 536
Vorwerk, see land tenure
Vyatichi, the, 531

wages
  rise in, 608–9, 662–3, 664, 677, 678, 688–94, 715, 730–1
  regulation of, 706
Waldhufendorf, see villages
Walburg-Wolfegg, Prince, 151 n.
Walcheren, Island of, 75
Wales, 53, 145
  agriculture, 171, 555
  free land, 193
  Kings of the *cantrefs*, 274, 283
  serfdom, 118
  Welsh border, 37
Walia, Visigothic king, 184
Walter, abbot of Peterborough, 582
Walter of Henley, 583, 717
war, toll of, 675–6, 694–8, 721, 728
War of the Roses, 588, 596, 695
Warwick, earl of, *see* Beauchamp, Richard
water conservation, 101
water-mills, 99, 125, 211
Weedon Beck, 726
'welsh' as unfree, 31
Wends, Wendish lands, 2, 58, 62, 449–50, 451, 454, 457, 475, 481, 482, 483
Wessex, *see* Ine of Wessex
Westphalia, 85, 91, 190, 338, 670
wheat, varieties of, 160–1, 372
  see also agriculture, cereals
wheelbarrows, 145
Wichmann, archbishop of Magdeburg, 85, 87, 472, 473
Wilfred of Barcelona, 66

Willem van Rijckel, abbot of Sint-Truiden, 320, 321, 323, 325
William of Woodford, 582
  abbot of Peterborough
William of Wykeham, 588
William of Montague, 724
William the Conqueror, 65, 70, 237, 249, 592, 594
Willigis, bishop of Mainz, 68
willow plantations, 170
Winchester, estates of bishop of, 125, 553, 557, 559, 560, 563, 564, 566, 567, 582, 584, 588–9, 590, 591, 597, 602, 613, 614, 619, 623, 663, 671, 689, 691
Winfrid, *see* Boniface
windmills, 211
Wiprecht of Groitzsch, Count, 84, 461
Witigonen family, 461
Wojciechowski, Z., 59 n.
wool, wool prices, 588, 589
Wool Staple in Calais, 588
Worcester, estates of bishops of, 582, 601, 602, 606, 607, 619–20
Wührer, K., 21 n.
Würtemberg, 195
Würzburg, 198

Yakovlev, A. I., 517
Yaroslav
  see Russia, Law of Yaroslav
Young, Arthur, 144, 156, 353, 373
Yugoslavia, 280

Zatochnik, Daniil, 514
Zealand, 637, 646, 656
Zosimus, 124